LINKING THINKING

JUNIOR CYCLE MATHEMATICS 1

James Trimble, Aisling Quirke, Audrey Byrne

CONSULTANT AUTHOR: **Louise Boylan**

Gill Education
Hume Avenue
Park West
Dublin 12
www.gilleducation.ie

Gill Education is an imprint of M.H. Gill & Co.

© James Trimble, Aisling Quirke, Audrey Byrne and Louise Boylan 2021

ISBN: 978-0-7171-90140

All rights reserved. No part of this publication may be copied, reproduced or transmitted in any form or by any means without written permission of the publishers or else under the terms of any licence permitting limited copying issued by the Irish Copyright Licensing Agency.

Design: EMC Design Ltd

Illustrations: EMC Design Ltd, Derry Dillon and Andriy Yankovskyy

At the time of going to press, all web addresses were active and contained information relevant to the topics in this book. Gill Education does not, however, accept responsibility for the content or views contained on these websites. Content, views and addresses may change beyond the publisher or author's control. Students should always be supervised when reviewing websites.

For permission to reproduce photographs, the authors and publisher gratefully acknowledge the following:

© Alamy: 84, 164C 180, 220TL, 245TL, 262C, 381, 399, 403C, 403B, 516; © Bord Gáis Energy: 197; © Code This Lab S.r.l: 486; © Dublin Airport Authority: 182R; © Explorium National Sport & Science Centre, Dublin, explorium.ie: 319; © Getty Images: 485; © Google Maps/iStock: 245BR; © iStock/Getty Premium: 3, 21, 42, 49, 54, 56, 79, 83, 90, 92, 94, 96, 99, 100, 101, 106, 108TR, 108BL, 108BR, 110, 113, 121, 123, 126, 132, 135, 153, 156, 159, 160, 165, 167C, 168T, 169B, 172, 182L, 186, 190, 191, 194, 199, 201, 208, 209, 220CL, 220CR, 230, 237, 238, 251, 254, 255, 256, 257, 260, 262T, 262B, 262R, 265, 268, 269, 272, 273, 276T, 276B, 279L, 279BR, 280T, 280B, 281, 282, 283, 290, 303, 304, 305, 311, 316, 318, 331, 336, 348L, 354, 361L, 366, 369, 377, 378, 389, 390, 393, 394, 395, 400, 403T, 405, 406, 407, 408T, 408B, 410, 415, 417, 419, 424, 425, 427, 428, 429, 436, 437L, 438, 442, 442, 438, 444B, 444C, 447, 448L, 450, 452, 453B, 454L, 454R, 456, 467, 505, 507, 518, 531, 534, 538C, 539, 541, 545, 546, 550, 552, 553, 558, 559, 560, 561, 562; © James Trimble: 538B; © Shutterstock: 23, 72, 107, 108BC, 134, 163, 164CL, 164CB, 167T, 221, 279TR, 324, 329, 348R, 382, 409, 444T, 445, 448R, 453T, 510; © Trish Steel: 437R; © Tucker Simmons/VelvetRopes.com: 168C.

The authors and publisher have made every effort to trace all copyright holders. If, however, any have been inadvertently overlooked, we would be pleased to make the necessary arrangement at the first opportunity.

The authors would like to express their gratitude to Emily Lynch and Hannah McAdams for all of their help and advice throughout this project.

James would like to thank family and friends for all their support, especially Patsy Trimble and Emily Barnes, two people who love to think. James would like to dedicate his work on the series to his sister Ann Margaret Trimble.

Aisling would like to thank friends and family, particularly Ann and Seamie Quirke for their encouragement and support throughout the project and always.

Audrey would like to thank her friends and family, especially Liam, Patricia and Lynn. Even though they never really understood what she was doing, they always supported her 100%. She couldn't have done it without them.

Louise would like to thank friends and family, particularly Joe, Danny and Josh Heron, and Mairead and Christy Boylan for their continued support.

Contents

Introduction ix
Learning Outcomes x

Section A Introducing concepts and building skills

1 Number, coordinate plane and symmetry — 2

1·1	Introducing natural numbers, integers and the number line	2
1·2	Introducing the coordinate (Cartesian) plane	6
1·3	Introducing area and perimeter of basic shapes on the Cartesian plane	9
1·4	Axis of symmetry	13
1·5	Reflecting shapes on the coordinate plane	15
	Revision questions	17

2 Sets, number and chance — 22

2·1	Sets and set notation	22
2·2	Number sets	27
2·3	Venn diagrams	31
2·4	Chance	35
	Revision questions	38

3 Points, lines and angles — 40

3·1	Points, lines, line segments and rays	40
3·2	Parallel and perpendicular lines	45
3·3	Angles	50
	Revision questions	55

4 Working with numbers — 57

4·1	Working with integers	57
4·2	Order of operations	61
4·3	Properties of numbers	64
4·4	Index form	68
	Revision questions	70

5 Fractions, decimals and percentages — 72

5·1	Fractions	72
5·2	Working with fractions	75
5·3	Working with decimals	82
5·4	Working with percentages	86
5·5	Percentages in context	89
	Revision questions	91

6 Probability 1 — 94

6·1	Introduction to probability	94
6·2	Calculate the probability of a single event	97
6·3	The fundamental principle of counting	100
	Revision questions	104

7 Patterns — 108

7·1	Introduction to patterns	108
7·2	Representing patterns	111
7·3	Examining the rate of change of a pattern	114
7·4	Identifying a pattern as linear or non-linear	118
	Revision questions	120

8 Working with variables — 123

8·1	Working with variables	123
8·2	Multiplying terms	127
8·3	Dividing terms	130
	Revision questions	133

9 Solving linear relations — 135

9·1	Linear patterns in context	135
9·2	Solving basic linear equations	139
9·3	Solving more complicated linear equations	142
9·4	Creating and solving linear equations	143
9·5	Introduction to functions	146
9·6	Linear functions	151
9·7	Solving linear relations using multiple representations	154
	Revision questions	157

10 Ratio, proportion and scaling — 160

10·1	Ratio and proportion	160
10·2	Scaling	163
	Revision questions	167

11 Angles — 169

11·1	Vertically opposite angles	170
11·2	Alternate angles	173
11·3	Corresponding angles	177
	Revision questions	180

12 Linking Thinking revision material — 184

Linking Thinking questions — 184
Mathematical investigations — 190

Section B Moving forward

13 Money matters 1 — 194

- 13·1 Earning an income — 194
- 13·2 Calculating VAT (value added tax) — 197
- 13·3 Household bills — 199
- 13·4 Profit and loss — 201
- 13·5 Simple and compound interest — 204
- 13·6 Currency exchanges — 208
- **Revision questions** — 211

14 Maths in motion — 214

- 14·1 Measuring distance and time — 214
- 14·2 Speed — 218
- 14·3 Rate of change graphs — 221
- **Revision questions** — 227

15 Polygons — 231

- 15·1 Introduction — 231
- 15·2 Introduction to triangles — 235
- 15·3 Constructing triangles using angles and sides — 238
- 15·4 Types of triangles and area of triangles — 240
- 15·5 Right-angled triangles — 246
- 15·6 Interior and exterior angles in triangles — 248
- **Revision questions** — 252

16 Circles 1 — 254

- 16·1 Introduction to circle terms — 254
- 16·2 Area and perimeter of a disc — 257
- 16·3 Compound shapes involving circles — 261
- **Revision questions** — 263

17 Area, volume and surface area — 265

- 17·1 Perimeter and area of shapes — 265
- 17·2 Nets and surface area of rectangular solids — 269
- 17·3 Volume of rectangular solids — 273
- 17·4 Volume of a cylinder — 276
- **Revision questions** — 280

18 Collecting and representing data — 283

- 18·1 Types of data — 283
- 18·2 Gathering data — 286
- 18·3 Representing data — 290
- 18·4 Representing continuous data — 295
- 18·5 Introduction to statistical investigations — 298
- **Revision questions** — 300

19 Indices — 302

19·1	Index (scientific) notation	302
19·2	Multiplying variables with powers	304
19·3	Dividing variables with powers	306
19·4	A power on a power	307
19·5	Square root of a number	309
	Revision questions	310

20 Working with expressions — 312

20·1	Expressions	312
20·2	Evaluating expressions	317
20·3	Multiplying an expression by a term	319
20·4	Multiplying expressions	322
20·5	Factorising using a factor common to all terms in an expression	324
20·6	Factorising using common factors from a group of terms	327
	Revision questions	329

21 Linear relationships — 332

21·1	Solving linear equations	332
21·2	Solving linear equations with two unknowns by graphing	338
21·3	Solving linear equations with two unknowns by trial and improvement and by elimination	343
21·4	Creating and solving simultaneous equations	346
21·5	Graphing linear functions	349
	Revision questions	353

22 Triangles — 355

22·1	Theorem terms	355
22·2	Congruent triangles	358
22·3	Pythagoras's theorem	363
	Revision questions	367

23 Quadrilaterals and transformations — 370

23·1	Rectangles and squares	370
23·2	Compound shapes	372
23·3	Parallelograms: angles and sides	375
23·4	Parallelograms: diagonals bisecting	379
23·5	Transformations of objects	382
	Revision questions	387

24 Further sets — 389

24·1	Revision of sets	389
24·2	Word problems involving two sets	392
24·3	Further operations used with set notation	394
	Revision questions	398

25 Linking Thinking revision material — 402

Linking Thinking questions — 402
Mathematical investigations — 411

Section C Applying our skills

26 Analysing data — 414

26·1 Review of data collection — 414
26·2 Representing data — 416
26·3 Measures of central tendency and spread — 422
26·4 Drawing conclusions and making inferences — 428
26·5 Misuses of statistics — 432
Revision questions — 434

27 Probability 2 — 436

27·1 Revision of basic probability and fundamental principle of counting — 436
27·2 Experimental probability and relative frequency — 438
Revision questions — 443

28 Money matters 2 — 446

28·1 Revision of *Money matters 1* — 446
28·2 Percentage increase or decrease — 449
28·3 Income tax and other deductions on earnings — 451
Revision questions — 454

29 Circles 2 — 458

29·1 Revision of *Circles 1* — 458
29·2 Angles in a semicircle — 461
29·3 Cyclic quadrilaterals — 465
Revision questions — 466

30 Further geometry — 468

30·1 Constructions revision — 468
30·2 Further constructions — 471
30·3 Theorems revision — 473
30·4 Similar triangles — 477
Revision questions — 482

31 Working with the coordinate plane — 486

31·1	Midpoint of a line segment	486
31·2	Length of a line segment (distance between two points)	491
31·3	Slope of a line	494
31·4	Equation of a line	497
31·5	Working with the equation of a line	499
31·6	Graphing lines when given the equation of the line	502
31·7	Point of intersection of two lines (simultaneous equations)	505
	Revision questions	507

32 Inequalities — 510

32·1	Graphing inequalities on the number line	510
32·2	Solving linear inequalities	515
	Revision questions	516

33 Non-linear relationships — 518

33·1	Non-linear patterns	518
33·2	Quadratic functions	522
33·3	Multiplying linear expressions revision	524
33·4	Factorising – Difference of two squares (quadratic expression)	527
33·5	Factorising – Quadratic trinomial expressions 1 (positive constant)	529
33·6	Factorising – Quadratic trinomial expressions 2 (negative constant)	531
33·7	Dividing expressions	533
33·8	Solving quadratic equations	534
	Revision questions	537

34 Trigonometry — 539

34·1	Pythagoras revision	539
34·2	Trigonometric ratios	542
34·3	Using your calculator to work with trigonometric ratios	546
34·4	Finding missing sides and angles	547
34·5	Trigonometry in the real world	550
	Revision questions	554

35 Linking Thinking revision material — 557

Linking Thinking questions	557
Mathematical and statistical investigations	563

Answer key — 565

Introduction

Linking Thinking 1 covers the entire Ordinary Level course and can be used by all students at both Higher and Ordinary Levels, in First and Second Year, to help establish the building blocks. After completing Sections A and B, we recommend that **Higher Level students move on to *Linking Thinking 2* during Second Year**, to complete the Higher Level material. This recommendation is to allow the course to be covered as efficiently as possible. Meanwhile, Ordinary Level students finish out section C in *Linking Thinking 1*.

The *Linking Thinking* series places student thinking and understanding at the centre of the educational experience. The series views the four contextual strands: Number; Geometry and trigonometry; Algebra and functions; and Statistics and probability, **through the lens of the Unifying strand**.

A **spiral learning approach** has been embedded throughout the books, where underlying concepts are reinforced at every opportunity to maximise conceptual understanding of Mathematics. The spiral learning approach also promotes student's ability to see mathematics as sensible, useful, and worthwhile, and instils a belief in diligence, perseverance and one's own efficacy. Units, questions and examples have been scaffolded to **address learner diversity**. Examples and questions which require students to take the Mathematics further have been included throughout the books in different forms, notably in the **Taking it further** questions.

The practice questions have been carefully formulated to ensure that students maximise their conceptual understanding of a mathematical situation in a variety of different ways. Initial **Practice questions** promote understanding and help students recall the concepts that underpin the unit. They also help students carry out the procedures accurately, effectively, and appropriately. The **Step-by-step strategies** and **Worked examples** act as a template of how to carry out procedures in this way.

The Unifying strand is embedded through the spiral approach and notably through the Something to think about, Discuss and discover and Linking Thinking features. The context-based questions, starting with the engaging **Something to think about** challenges, help students improve their ability to formulate, represent, and solve mathematical problems. The context-based questions also help students make **connections within and between strands**, as well as connections between mathematics and the real world. **Discuss and discover** tasks have been developed to promote student's capacity for logical thought, reflection, explanation, justification, generalisation and **ability to communicate** Mathematics effectively in verbal and written form. These features are designed not only to enhance mathematical skills but also to promote the key skills that underpin the new Junior Cycle.

The **revision questions** have been carefully assembled to address the main aspects of each Unit, from the mathematical core skills to the more abstract thinking in the **Taking it further** section of the revision exercises.

Linking Thinking revision units appear at precise points in the books to promote student understanding of building blocks and to help students make connections within, and between, the contextual strands. The Linking Thinking revision units also help students investigate patterns, formulate conjectures, and engage in tasks in which the solution is not immediately obvious, to prepare them for whatever challenge the final exam presents.

The Linking Thinking Units also provide ideas and strategies for the completion of Mathematical and Statistical Investigations, in preparation for **Classroom-Based Assessments** (CBAs).

James Trimble, Aisling Quirke, Audrey Byrne and Louise Boylan

> Teachers and schools may choose to cover Section C in *Linking Thinking 1* with Higher Level students, depending on their students and context. The inclusion of the Learning Outcomes at the start of each unit allows for flexibility when planning.

Unifying strand

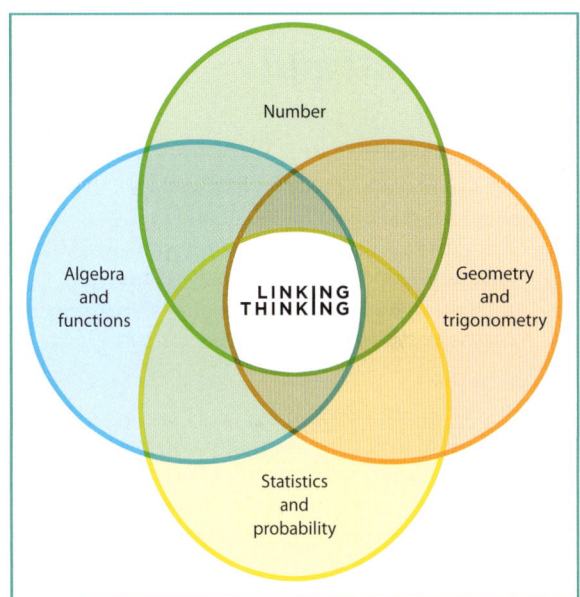

The key skills symbol appears throughout the textbook. The colours used relate to this diagram and highlight which skills have been activated in a particular activity.

Learning Outcomes

Learning Outcomes are statements that describe what knowledge, understanding, skills and values students should be able to demonstrate having studied mathematics in Junior Cycle. Junior Cycle Mathematics is offered at Ordinary and Higher Level. The majority of the Learning Outcomes set out in the following tables apply to all students. Additional Learning Outcomes for those students who take the Higher Level Mathematics examination are highlighted in bold. As set out here the learning outcomes represent outcomes for students at the end of their three years of study.

All Learning Outcomes are stated in full here to assist planning.

Unifying strand

Building blocks
Students should be able to:
- **U.1** recall and demonstrate understanding of the fundamental concepts and procedures that underpin each strand
- **U.2** apply the procedures associated with each strand accurately, effectively, and appropriately
- **U.3** recognise that equality is a relationship in which two mathematical expressions have the same value

Representation
Students should be able to:
- **U.4** represent a mathematical situation in a variety of different ways, including: numerically, algebraically, graphically, physically, in words; and to interpret, analyse, and compare such representations

Connections
Students should be able to:
- **U.5** make connections within and between strands
- **U.6** make connections between mathematics and the real world

Problem solving
Students should be able to:
- **U.7** make sense of a given problem, and if necessary mathematise a situation
- **U.8** apply their knowledge and skills to solve a problem, including decomposing it into manageable parts and/or simplifying it using appropriate assumptions
- **U.9** interpret their solution to a problem in terms of the original question
- **U.10** evaluate different possible solutions to a problem, including evaluating the reasonableness of the solutions, and exploring possible improvements and/or limitations of the solutions (if any)

Generalisation and proof
Students should be able to:
- **U.11** generate general mathematical statements or conjectures based on specific instances
- **U.12** generate and evaluate mathematical arguments and proofs

Communication
Students should be able to:
- **U.13** communicate mathematics effectively: justify their reasoning, interpret their results, explain their conclusions, and use the language and notation of mathematics to express mathematical ideas precisely

Number strand

Students should be able to:

- **N.1** investigate the representation of numbers and arithmetic operations so that they can:
  - **a.** represent the operations of addition, subtraction, multiplication, and division in $\mathbb{N}$, $\mathbb{Z}$ and $\mathbb{Q}$ using models including the number line, decomposition, and accumulating groups of equal size
  - **b.** perform the operations of addition, subtraction, multiplication, and division and understand the relationship between these operations and the properties: commutative, associative and distributive in $\mathbb{N}$, $\mathbb{Z}$ and $\mathbb{Q}$ **and in $\mathbb{R}\backslash\mathbb{Q}$, including operating on surds**
  - **c.** explore numbers written as a^b (in index form) so that they can:
    - **I.** flexibly translate between whole numbers and index representation of numbers
    - **II.** use and apply generalisations such as $a^p a^q = a^{p+q}$; $\frac{(a^p)}{(a^q)} = a^{p-q}$; $(a^p)^q = a^{pq}$; and $n^{\frac{1}{2}} = \sqrt{n}$, for $a \in \mathbb{Z}$, and $p, q, p-q, \sqrt{n} \in \mathbb{N}$ and for $a, b, \sqrt{n} \in \mathbb{R}$, and $p, q \in \mathbb{Q}$
    - **III.** use and apply generalisations such as $a^0 = 1$; $a^{\frac{p}{q}} = \sqrt[q]{a^p} = \left(\sqrt[q]{a}\right)^p$; $a^{-r} = \frac{1}{(a^r)}$; $(ab)^r = a^r b^r$; and $\left(\frac{a}{b}\right)^r = \frac{(a^r)}{(b^r)}$, for $a, b \in \mathbb{R}$; $p, q \in \mathbb{Z}$; **and $r \in \mathbb{Q}$**
    - **IV.** generalise numerical relationships involving operations involving numbers written in index form
    - **V.** correctly use the order of arithmetic and index operations including the use of brackets
  - **d.** calculate and interpret factors (including the highest common factor), multiples (including the lowest common multiple), and prime numbers
  - **e.** present numerical answers to the degree of accuracy specified, for example, correct to the nearest hundred, to two decimal places, or to three significant figures
  - **f.** convert the number p in decimal form to the form $a \times 10^n$, where $1 \leq a < 10, n \in \mathbb{Z}, p \in \mathbb{Q}$, and $p \geq 1$ and $0 < p < 1$

- **N.2** investigate equivalent representations of rational numbers so that they can:
  - **a.** flexibly convert between fractions, decimals, and percentages
  - **b.** use and understand ratio and proportion
  - **c.** solve money-related problems including those involving bills, VAT, profit or loss, % profit or loss (on the cost price), cost price, selling price, compound interest for not more than 3 years, income tax (standard rate only), net pay (including other deductions of specified amounts), value for money calculations and judgements, mark up (profit as a % of cost price), **margin (profit as a % of selling price), compound interest, income tax and net pay (including other deductions)**

N.3 investigate situations involving proportionality so that they can:
  a. use absolute and relative comparison where appropriate
  b. solve problems involving proportionality including those involving currency conversion and those involving average speed, distance, and time

N.4 analyse numerical patterns in different ways, including making out tables and graphs, and continue such patterns

N.5 explore the concept of a set so that they can:
  a. understand the concept of a set as a well-defined collection of elements, and that set equality is a relationship where two sets have the same elements
  b. define sets by listing their elements, if finite (including in a 2-set or **3-set** Venn diagram), or by generating rules that define them
  c. use and understand suitable set notation and terminology, including null set, ∅, subset, ⊂ complement, element, ∈, universal set, cardinal number, #, intersection, ∩, union, ∪, set difference, \, ℕ, ℤ, ℚ, ℝ and ℝ\ℚ
  d. perform the operations of intersection and union on 2 sets **and on 3 sets**, set difference, and complement, including the use of brackets to define the order of operations
  e. investigate whether the set operations of intersection, union, and difference are commutative and/or associative

Geometry and trigonometry strand

Students should be able to:

GT.1 calculate, interpret, and apply units of measure and time

GT.2 investigate 2D shapes and 3D solids so that they can:
  a. draw and interpret scaled diagrams
  b. draw and interpret nets of rectangular solids, **prisms (polygonal bases), cylinders**
  c. find the perimeter and area of plane figures made from combinations of discs, triangles, and rectangles, including relevant operations involving pi
  d. find the volume of rectangular solids, cylinders, **triangular-based prisms, spheres**, and combinations of these, including relevant operations involving pi
  e. find the surface area and **curved surface area (as appropriate)** of rectangular solids, **cylinders, triangular-based prisms, spheres,** and combinations of these

GT.3 investigate the concept of proof through their engagement with geometry so that they can:
  a. perform constructions 1 to 15 in *Geometry for Post-Primary School Mathematics* (**constructions 3 and 7 at HL only**)
  b. recall and use the concepts, axioms, theorems, corollaries and converses, specified in *Geometry for Post-Primary School Mathematics* (section 9 for OL **and section 10 for HL**)
     I. axioms 1, 2, 3, 4 and 5
     II. theorems 1, 2, 3, 4, 5, 6, 9, 10, 13, 14, 15 **and 11, 12, 19**, and appropriate converses, including relevant operations involving square roots
     III. corollaries 3, 4 **and 1, 2, 5** and appropriate converses
  c. use and **explain** the terms: theorem, proof, axiom, corollary, converse, and implies
  d. create and evaluate proofs of geometrical propositions
  e. display understanding of the proofs of theorems 1, 2, 3, 4, 5, 6, 9, 10, 14, 15, **and 13, 19**; and of corollaries 3, 4, **and 1, 2, 5** (full formal proofs are not examinable)

GT.4 evaluate and use trigonometric ratios (sin, cos, and tan, defined in terms of right-angled triangles) and their inverses, involving angles between 0° and 90° at integer values and **in decimal form**

GT.5 investigate properties of points, lines and line segments in the co-ordinate plane so that they can:
  a. find and interpret: distance, midpoint, slope, point of intersection, and slopes of parallel **and perpendicular** lines
  b. draw graphs of line segments and interpret such graphs in context, including discussing the rate of change (slope) and the y intercept
  c. find and interpret the equation of a line in the form $y = mx + c$; $y - y_1 = m(x - x_1)$; **and** $ax + by + c = 0$ (for $a, b, c, m, x_1, y_1 \in \mathbb{Q}$); including finding the slope, the y-intercept, and other points on the line

GT.6 investigate transformations of simple objects so that they can:
  a. recognise and draw the image of points and objects under translation, central symmetry, axial symmetry, and rotation
  b. draw the axes of symmetry in shapes

Algebra and functions strand

Students should be able to:

AF.1 investigate patterns and relationships (linear, quadratic, doubling and tripling) in number, spatial patterns and real-world phenomena involving change so that they can:
  a. represent these patterns and relationships in tables and graphs
  b. generate a generalised expression for linear **(and quadratic)** patterns in words and algebraic expressions and fluently convert between each representation
  c. categorise patterns as linear, non-linear, **quadratic, and exponential (doubling and tripling)** using their defining characteristics as they appear in the different representations

AF.2 investigate situations in which letters stand for quantities that are variable so that they can:
  a. generate and interpret expressions in which letters stand for numbers
  b. find the value of expressions given the value of the variables
  c. use the concept of equality to generate and interpret equations

AF.3 apply the properties of arithmetic operations and factorisation to generate equivalent expressions so that they can develop and use appropriate strategies to:
  a. add, subtract and simplify
     I. linear expressions in one or more variables with coefficients in $\mathbb{Q}$
     II. quadratic expressions in one variable with coefficients in $\mathbb{Z}$
     III. expressions of the form $\frac{a}{(bx+c)}$, where $a, b, c \in \mathbb{Z}$
  b. multiply expressions of the form
     IV. $a(bx + cy + d); a(bx^2 + cx + d);$ and $ax(bx^2 + cx + d)$, where $a, b, c, d \in \mathbb{Z}$
     V. $(ax + b)(cx + d)$ **and** $(ax + b)(cx^2 + dx + e)$, where $a, b, c, d, e \in \mathbb{Z}$
  c. divide quadratic and **cubic expressions** by linear expressions, where all coefficients are integers and there is no remainder
  d. flexibly convert between the factorised and expanded forms of algebraic expressions of the form:
     I. axy, where $a \in \mathbb{Z}$
     II. $axy + byz$, where $a, b \in \mathbb{Z}$
     III. $sx - ty + tx - sy$, where $s, t \in \mathbb{Z}$
     IV. $dx^2 + bx; x^2 + bx + c;$ **and** $ax^2 + bx + c$, where $b, c, d \in \mathbb{Z}$ and $a \in \mathbb{N}$
     $x^2 - a^2$ **and** $a^2x^2 - b^2y^2$, where $a, b \in \mathbb{Z}$

AF.4 select and use suitable strategies (graphic, numeric, algebraic, trial and improvement, working backwards) for finding solutions to:
  a. linear equations in one variable with coefficients in $\mathbb{Q}$ and solutions in $\mathbb{Z}$ **or in** $\mathbb{Q}$
  b. quadratic equations in one variable with coefficients and solutions in $\mathbb{Z}$ or **coefficients in $\mathbb{Q}$ and solutions in $\mathbb{R}$**
  c. simultaneous linear equations in two variables with coefficients and solutions in $\mathbb{Z}$ **or in** $\mathbb{Q}$
  d. linear inequalities in one variable of the form $g(x) < k$, and graph the solution sets on the number line for $x \in \mathbb{N}, \mathbb{Z},$ and $\mathbb{R}$

AF.5 generate quadratic equations given integer roots

AF.6 apply the relationship between operations and an understanding of the order of operations including brackets and exponents to change the subject of a formula

AF.7 investigate functions so that they can:
  a. demonstrate understanding of the concept of a function
  b. represent and interpret functions in different ways—graphically (for $x \in \mathbb{N}, \mathbb{Z},$ and $\mathbb{R}$, [continuous functions only], as appropriate), diagrammatically, in words, and algebraically—using the language and notation of functions (domain, range, co-domain, $f(x) =, f:x \mapsto,$ and $y =$) (drawing the graph of a function given its algebraic expression is limited to linear and quadratic functions at OL)
  c. use graphical methods to find and interpret approximate solutions of equations such as $f(x) = g(x)$ and approximate solution sets of inequalities such as $f(x) < g(x)$
  d. make connections between the shape of a graph and the story of a phenomenon, including identifying and interpreting maximum and minimum points

Statistics and probability strand

Students should be able to:

SP.1 investigate the outcomes of experiments so that they can:
  a. generate a sample space for an experiment in a systematic way, including tree diagrams for successive events and two-way tables for independent events
  b. use the fundamental principle of counting to solve authentic problems

SP.2 investigate random events so that they can:
  a. demonstrate understanding that probability is a measure on a scale of 0–1 of how likely an event (including an everyday event) is to occur
  b. use the principle that, in the case of equally likely outcomes, the probability of an event is given by the number of outcomes of interest divided by the total number of outcomes
  c. use relative frequency as an estimate of the probability of an event, given experimental data, and recognise that increasing the number of times an experiment is repeated generally leads to progressively better estimates of its theoretical probability

SP.3 carry out a statistical investigation which includes the ability to:
  a. generate a statistical question
  b. plan and implement a method to generate and/or source unbiased, representative data, and present this data in a frequency table
  c. classify data (categorical, numerical)
  d. select, draw and interpret appropriate graphical displays of univariate data, including pie charts, bar charts, line plots, histograms (equal intervals), ordered stem and leaf plots, and **ordered back-to-back stem and leaf plots**
  e. select, calculate and interpret appropriate summary statistics to describe aspects of univariate data. Central tendency: mean (**including of a grouped frequency distribution**), median, mode. Variability: range
  f. evaluate the effectiveness of different graphical displays in representing data
  g. discuss misconceptions and misuses of statistics
  h. discuss the assumptions and limitations of conclusions drawn from sample data or graphical/numerical summaries of data

Section A
Introducing concepts and building skills

1. Number, coordinate plane and symmetry — 2
2. Sets, number and chance — 22
3. Points, lines and angles — 40
4. Working with numbers — 57
5. Fractions, decimals and percentages — 72
6. Probability 1 — 94
7. Patterns — 108
8. Working with variables — 123
9. Solving linear relations — 135
10. Ratio, proportion and scaling — 160
11. Angles — 169
12. Linking Thinking revision material — 184

Unit 1

Number, coordinate plane and symmetry

Topics covered within this unit:

1·1 Introducing natural numbers, integers and the number line

1·2 Creating the coordinate (Cartesian) plane

1·3 Introducing area and perimeter of basic shapes on the coordinate (Cartesian) plane

1·4 Axis of symmetry

1·5 Reflecting shapes on the coordinate plane

The Learning Outcomes covered in this unit are contained in sections:
N.1a GT.5 GT.6

Key words
Natural number
Integer
Coordinate (Cartesian) plane
Origin
Area
Perimeter
Axis of symmetry
Axial symmetry

Something to think about ...

The famous mathematician and philosopher René Descartes was ill in bed. He noticed a fly on the ceiling.

He started to think, 'How could I explain where exactly this fly is on the ceiling? It's near the middle, but a little bit to the right, and down towards the door.'

'This will not do,' he thought.

Can you figure out a better, more precise way to describe exactly where the fly is on the ceiling?

You can use the **problem-solving toolkit** to help with this type of problem:

1. What are you trying to find out, and what do you already know?
2. Will a diagram (picture) help you?
3. Can you come up with a strategy to solve the problem?
4. Solve the problem.

1·1 Introducing natural numbers, integers and the number line

By the end of this section, you should be able to:
- explain what a natural number is
- explain what an integer is
- construct (draw) a number line
- add and subtract natural numbers and integers using the number line

Natural numbers

Natural numbers were one of the first number systems ever created in Mathematics. They were used by people in the Stone Age for counting things like property and enemies.

They are positive **whole numbers** (no fractions or decimals) that start at 1 and continue to infinity ∞ (forever). The lowest natural number is the number 1, but there is no 'highest' natural number.

> **Natural numbers** are whole positive counting numbers. They have a special symbol, which is ℕ.
> ℕ = {1, 2, 3, 4, … ∞}

Think of natural numbers like candles on a birthday cake. You could have 1 candle for your 1st birthday, 18 candles for your 18th birthday, but you will never have a birthday cake to celebrate your 14·375th birthday or your $25\frac{2}{5}$th birthday. Likewise, on the day you were born, you did not receive a birthday cake with 'zero' candles to congratulate you for being 0 years old.

We can represent natural numbers (ℕ) in a variety of ways, such as writing them out 1, 2, 3, and so on. We can also draw them on a number line.

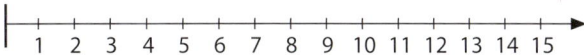

You will notice zero is **not** included in the set of natural numbers. ℕ starts at the number 1.

We can use a number line to **add** or subtract natural numbers. To add, we move to the **right** and to **subtract**, we move to the **left**, as shown below.

Addition
2 + 7 = 9

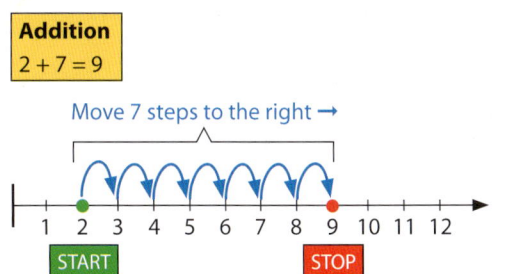

Subtraction
7 − 4 = 3

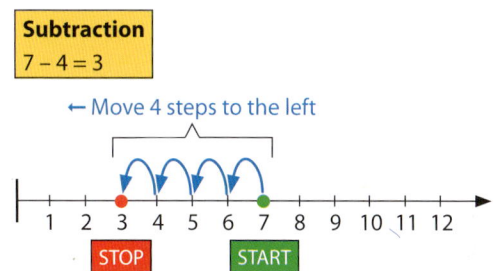

Integers

Positive integers are written the same way as natural numbers, e.g. 1, 2, 3 … to infinity.

Negative integers, however, are written with a 'minus' or 'negative' sign in front of them, e.g. −1, −2, −3 … to infinity.

Integers are represented by the letter ℤ (from the German word *Zahlen*, which means numbers).

To the right are some examples of where you might see negative integers in everyday life.

> **Integers** are the collection of whole positive and negative numbers, including zero.
> Integers (ℤ) = {− ∞ … −4, −3, −2, −1, 0, 1, 2, 3, 4, … ∞}

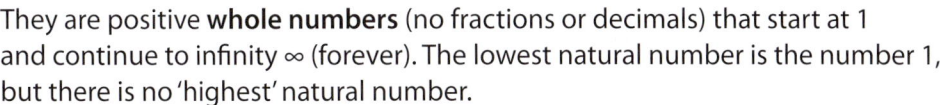

Temperature

Golf scores

Buttons in a lift

Section A Introducing concepts and building skills

Drawing the number line to include integers

Zero is included on the **integer** number line. The positive numbers are to the right of zero and the negative numbers are to the left of zero. The number zero itself is neither positive nor negative.

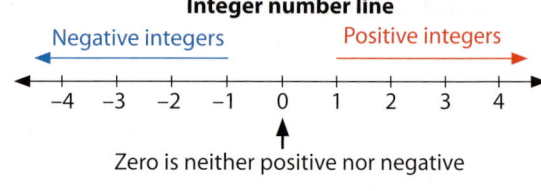

The first number on the left side of zero is –1, then –2, –3 and so on as you move further away from 0. This is because the numbers are **decreasing** in size. For example, –5 is less than –1.

A real-life example of this can be seen in multi-storey car parks. The floor on –3 is **lower** than the floor on –1. Furthermore, a temperature a reading of –20°C is **lower** than a temperature of –10°C.

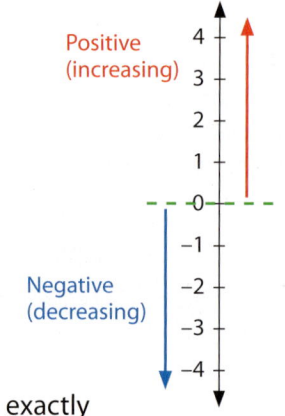

Number lines do not have to be horizontal, they can also be vertical. In this case, we move up for positive (increasing) and down for negative (decreasing).

Adding and subtracting integers ($\mathbb{Z}$) on the number line

Adding and subtracting integers ($\mathbb{Z}$) on the number line is done exactly the same way as adding or subtracting natural numbers ($\mathbb{N}$) on the number line.

Addition
–3 + 5 = 2

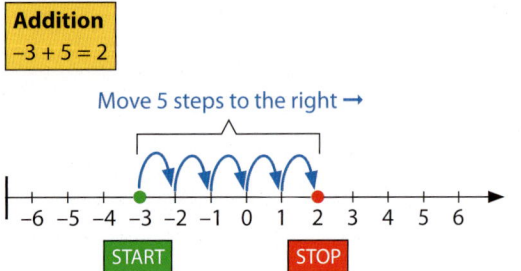

Subtraction
–2 – 4 = –6

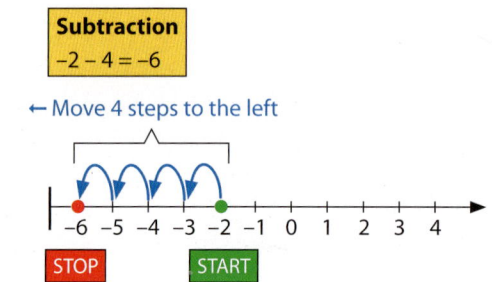

Natural numbers vs integers

This table will help you to understand the differences and similarities between natural numbers and integers.

Natural numbers	Integers
Whole numbers	Whole numbers
Positive	Positive and negative
Does NOT include zero	DOES include zero
Symbol $\mathbb{N}$	Symbol $\mathbb{Z}$

How to draw a number line

1. Use a ruler to draw a straight line.

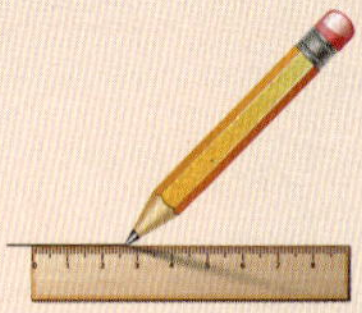

2. Divide the line into **equal** sections.

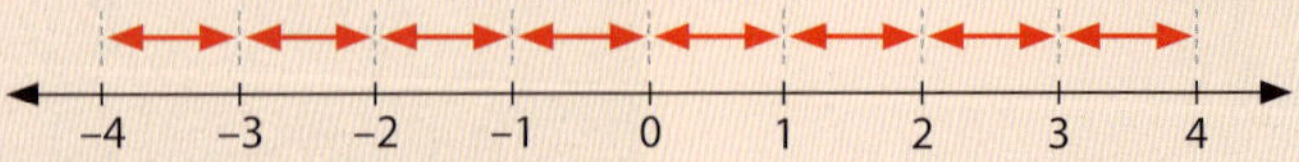

3. Insert the numbers. Numbers moving to the right are positive and increasing, numbers moving to the left are negative and decreasing.

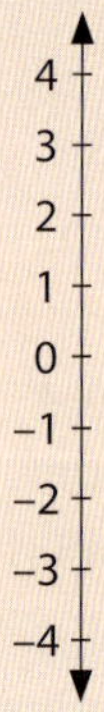

You can also draw a vertical number line using the same method.

Practice questions 1·1

Complete this set of questions without the use of a calculator.

1. Use the number line provided to answer the following questions. You may draw a vertical number line to help find the answers, if you prefer.

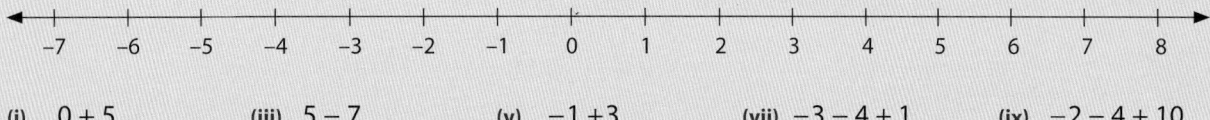

   (i) $0 + 5$
   (ii) $8 - 8$
   (iii) $5 - 7$
   (iv) $-5 + 3$
   (v) $-1 + 3$
   (vi) $3 + 2 - 6$
   (vii) $-3 - 4 + 1$
   (viii) $8 - 12 + 3$
   (ix) $-2 - 4 + 10$
   (x) $-6 + 7 + 4 - 11$

2. For each of the questions below, draw a separate number line into your copy and show the solution on your number line.

   (i) $1 + 4$
   (ii) $3 + 6$
   (iii) $7 - 3$
   (iv) $13 - 9$
   (v) $3 - 4$
   (vi) $5 - 2$
   (vii) $3 - 6$
   (viii) $0 - 4$
   (ix) $-1 - 4$
   (x) $-2 - 3$
   (xi) $5 - 0 + 3$
   (xii) $-2 + 4 - 6$

3. (i) Write three integers bigger than -7
   (ii) Write three integers smaller than 1

4. Explain in your own words what a natural number is. Give three examples of where you would see natural numbers in everyday life.

5. Explain in your own words what an integer is. Give three examples of where you would see integer numbers in everyday life.

6. Kevin is in a hotel and staying on floor 2. His car is parked on floor -3 in the underground car park. How many flights of stairs must Kevin travel to reach his car?

7. The current temperature outside is 5°C. If the temperature decreases by 9°C, what is the new temperature?

8. A hotel lift is on floor 4. It travels down 7 floors and then up 5 floors. What floor is the lift on now?

9. On Monday, the price of petrol decreased by 6 cents. On Tuesday, it increased by 9 cents. What was the overall decrease or increase of the price of petrol by the end of the day on Tuesday?

10. Write down any three integers which, when added or subtracted from each other, will give a total of -11. Show your working.

11. Copy the table below and put a tick (✓) in the correct box in each row to show whether each statement is always true, sometimes true, or never true. The first one has been completed for you.

	Statement	Always true	Sometimes true	Never true
(i)	If you add two natural numbers, the result will be a natural number.	✓		
(ii)	If you add a negative integer to a positive integer, the sum is zero or less.		✓	
(iii)	If you add an integer to a natural number, the result will be an integer.	✓		
(iv)	The answer to $-5 + 5$ is a natural number.			✓
(v)	If you add two integers, the sum is zero.			✓
(vi)	$-2·57$ is an integer.			✓

Section A Introducing concepts and building skills

1·2 Introducing the coordinate (Cartesian) plane

By the end of this section you should be able to:
- draw a coordinate (Cartesian) plane
- plot points on a coordinate (Cartesian) plane

Let's return to Rene Descartes. How could he describe the exact position of the fly on the ceiling?

What if he used two number lines, and placed a square grid on them like this:

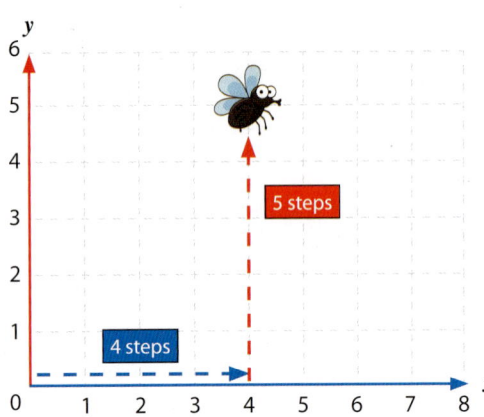

If we look at the blue line we can see it is a horizontal number line, and if we look at the red line we can see it is a vertical number line (in this case, we are only dealing with positive numbers).

If you were to describe the position of the fly, how could you do it?

When René Descartes discovered this type of grid, he made five very important rules.

1. Both lines should start at zero. Descartes named this very special point the 'origin' as it is the point where we must always start counting from. It is also referred to as (0, 0).

2. There should be exactly the same distance between each number on a number line. Always use graph paper.

3. Always move across (horizontal) first, then move up (vertical).

4. The **horizontal** line is called the *x*-axis, and the **vertical line** is called the *y*-axis.

5. To write the exact position (or coordinates) of the fly, combine the horizontal value and the vertical value in brackets; (4, 5)

    x-axis value is **1st**   *y*-axis value is **2nd**

This type of grid is called **the coordinate plane** (also known as the Cartesian plane, in Descartes's honour).

> The **coordinate plane** is sometimes referred to as the **Cartesian plane** or the *x*–*y* **plane** and is used to plot (*x*, *y*) pairs on a two-line graph.

How to plot (draw) a point on the coordinate plane
Let's plot the point (2, 3) on the coordinate plane.

1. Start at the 0 (the origin) on the *x*-axis and move across 2 units in the positive direction of the *x*-axis.

2. Once you are at the *x*-axis coordinate, move up 3 units in the positive direction of the *y*-axis.

3. Stop when you have moved up three units. Now draw a small dot at that point.

4. Label this point using the *x* and *y* coordinates. You have now plotted (drawn) the point (2, 3).

Linking Thinking 1

Practice questions 1·2·1

1. Using the Cartesian plane shown, write down the coordinates of each object.

   Use the middle of the object as its location. The first answer has been completed for you.
   - (i) Flower (3, 2)
   - (ii) Bee (,)
   - (iii) Car (,)
   - (iv) Duck (,)
   - (v) Rabbit (,)
   - (vi) Spider (,)
   - (vii) Tree (,)
   - (viii) Emoji (,)
   - (ix) Dog (,)
   - (x) Turtle (,)

   Remember to count **across** first (x-axis), then count **up** (y-axis).

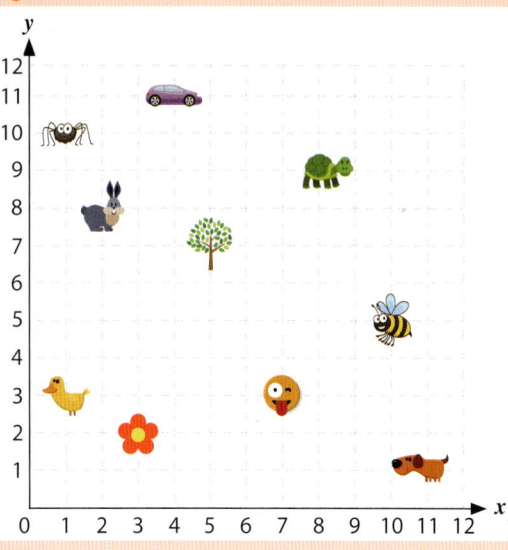

2. Copy the coordinate plane shown and plot (draw) the points (coordinates) given. The first one has been completed for you.
   - (i) $A = (1, 4)$
   - (ii) $B = (5, 8)$
   - (iii) $C = (8, 10)$
   - (iv) $D = (9, 1)$
   - (v) $E = (1, 10)$
   - (vi) $F = (6, 3)$
   - (vii) $G = (10, 10)$
   - (viii) $H = (4, 0)$
   - (ix) $I = (0, 8)$
   - (x) $J = (0, 0)$

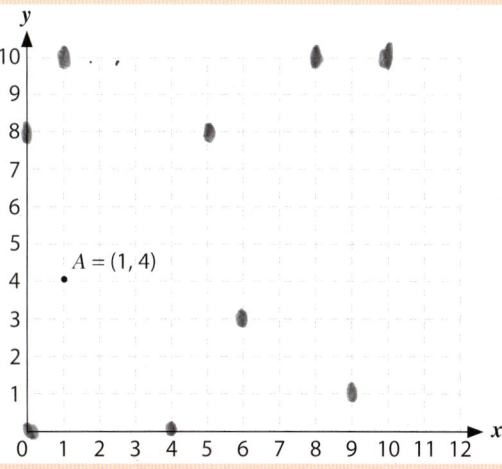

3. Copy the Cartesian plane provided for each section of this question.
   - (a) (i) Plot and label the following four points.
     $A = (1, 4)$ $B = (5, 4)$ $C = (5, 1)$ $D = (1, 1)$
     (ii) Join the points in the following order:
     A to B, B to C, C to D and finally D to A.
     What shape have you created?
   - (b) (i) Plot and label the following three points.
     $A = (1, 3)$ $B = (4, 1)$ $C = (0, 0)$
     (ii) Join the points in the following order:
     A to B, B to C, C to A.
     What shape have you created?
   - (c) (i) Plot and label the following four points.
     $A = (1, 3)$ $B = (5, 3)$ $C = (4, 1)$ $D = (0, 1)$
     (ii) Join the points in the following order:
     A to B, B to C, C to D and finally D to A.
     What shape have you created?
     (iii) If you were to create two triangles, which points could you join together? Show this on your diagram.

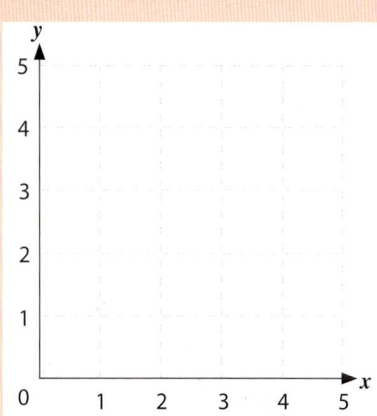

Section A Introducing concepts and building skills

Expanding the Cartesian plane

> The **origin** is the point (0, 0) where the two number lines on a Cartesian (coordinate) plane meet.

So far, we have looked at just the positive sides of the Cartesian plane. Let's extend it to look at the **positive** and **negative** sides of the Cartesian plane. This is where we will use the integer number lines. The positive and negative number lines will meet at zero, also known as the origin.

We draw (or plot) points on this coordinate plane exactly the same way as we did in previous examples.

Move across (left or right on the *x*-axis) first, then move up or down on the *y*-axis).

In this example, the points are:

$A = (-4, 6)$ $B = (-8, -6)$
$C = (7, 4)$ $D = (6, -4)$

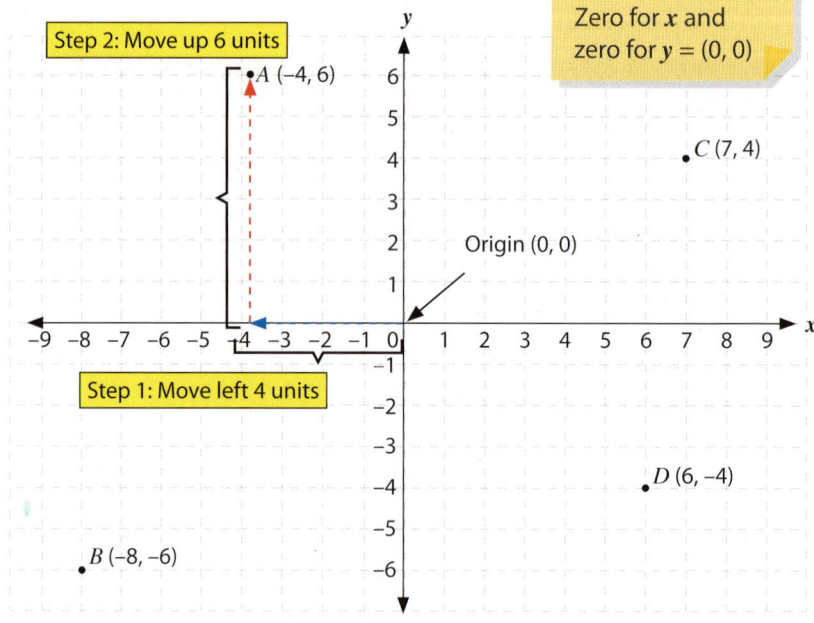

Practice questions 1·2·2

1. Using the Cartesian plane on the right, write down the coordinates of the following objects. Use the middle of the object as its location.

   The first answer has been completed for you.

   (i) Flower (−5, −3)   (vi) Emoji (,)
   (ii) Bee   (,)   (vii) Mouse (,)
   (iii) Car   (,)   (viii) Dog (,)
   (iv) Spider (,)   (ix) Rabbit (,)
   (v) Tree   (,)   (x) Turtle (,)

   Remember: you must go across (*x*-axis) first, then move up or down (*y*-axis).

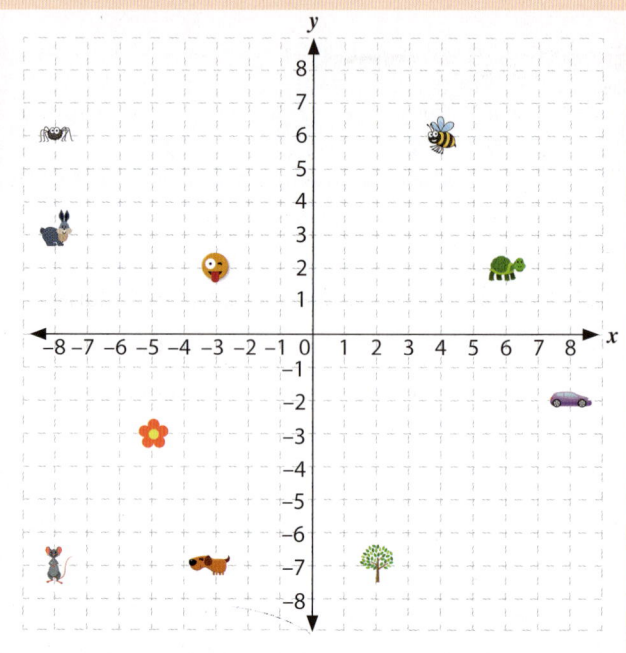

8   Linking Thinking 1

2. Copy the Cartesian plane opposite into your copybook, and plot (draw) points using the coordinates listed below. Label your points with the letters given. The first one has been completed for you.

(i) $A = (4, 2)$ (v) $E = (-6, 0)$
(ii) $B = (2, -4)$ (vi) $F = (0, -8)$
(iii) $C = (-6, 6)$ (vii) $G = (0, 0)$
(iv) $D = (-7, -4)$ (viii) $H = (-3, -7)$

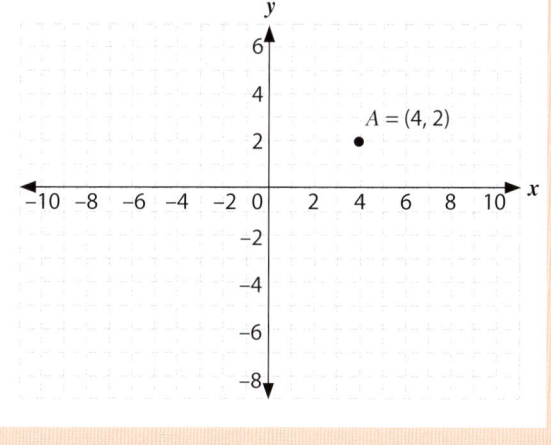

1.3 Introducing area and perimeter of basic shapes on the Cartesian plane

By the end of this section you should be able to:
- find the area of a regular shape
- find the perimeter of a regular shape
- break up combined shapes into simpler shapes, and find the total area and perimeter of these shapes

Area of a shape

> The **area** of a flat or plane figure (shape) is the number of unit squares that can be contained within it.

The unit square is usually a standard unit, e.g. square units, a square metre, a square centimetre.

How to find the area of a regular shape using the coordinate plane

Worked example 1

Find the area of the rectangle made by the following points on the Cartesian plane.
$A = (2, 5)$ $B = (7, 5)$ $C = (7, 2)$ $D = (2, 2)$

Solution

Step 1 Plot the points on the Cartesian plane.
Step 2 Join up the points to form a rectangle.
Step 3 Count the number of 'squares' contained within the rectangle.

Area = 15 square units

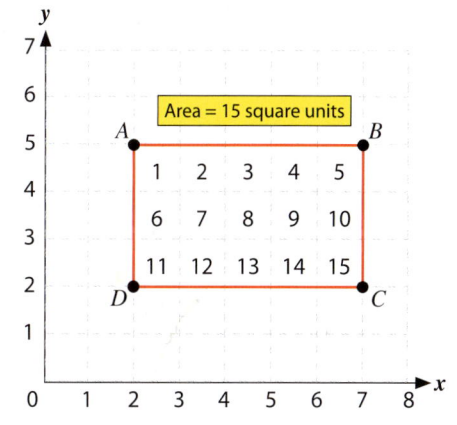

Section A Introducing concepts and building skills

Perimeter of a shape

The **perimeter** of a shape can be found by adding together the lengths of all of the edges (sides).

Worked example 2

Find the perimeter of the shapes in the diagram below.

Solution

Step 1 Count how many units there are along each side of the shape.

Step 2 Add together the measurements for each side to find the total perimeter.

Perimeter of $A = 6 + 4 + 6 + 4 = 20$ units

Perimeter of $B = 3 + 5 + 3 + 5 = 16$ units

Perimeter of $C =$
$2 + 1 + 2 + 1 + 2 + 1 + 2 + 3 = 14$ units

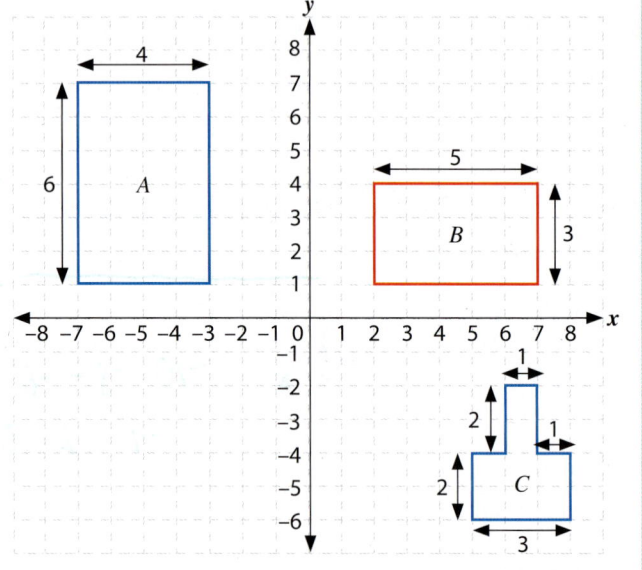

Practice questions 1·3·1

1. Find the area and perimeter of the shapes in the diagram on the right.

2. Draw a coordinate plane on graph or squared paper and plot the following points. Join them up in alphabetical order to form a square or a rectangle, then find the area and perimeter of each shape you have drawn.

   (i) $A = (2, 3)$ $B = (6, 3)$
         $C = (6, 1)$ $D = (2, 1)$

   (ii) $P = (-3, 1)$ $Q = (-3, 5)$
         $R = (3, 5)$ $S = (3, 1)$

   (iii) $L = (2, 6)$ $M = (4, 6)$
         $N = (4, 0)$ $O = (2, 0)$

   (iv) $W = (1, 1)$ $X = (5, 1)$
         $Y = (5, -5)$ $Z = (1, -5)$

   (v) $E = (-2, -1)$ $F = (-4, -1)$
         $G = (-4, -6)$ $H = (-2, -6)$

   (vi) $C = (0, 0)$ $D = (-4, 0)$
         $E = (-4, 5)$ $F = (0, 5)$

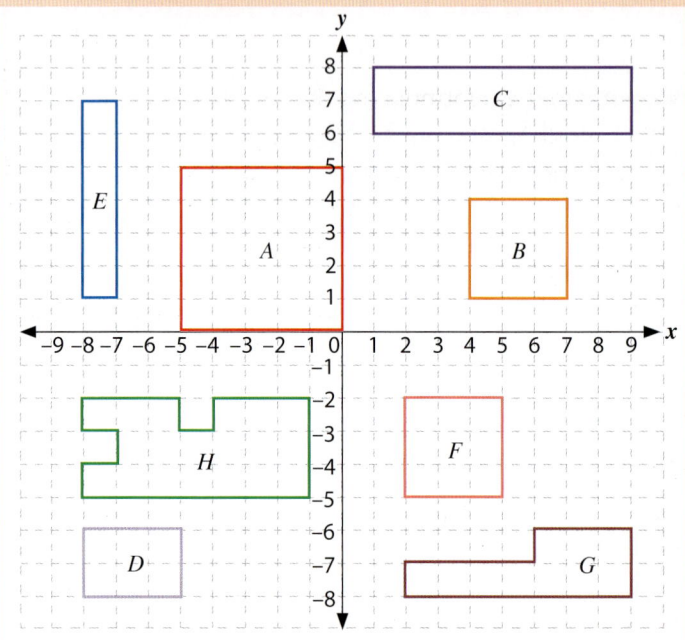

10   Linking Thinking 1

Using a formula to find the area of rectangles and squares

Sometimes it is easier to find the area of a rectangle or square if we use a formula. In the diagram on the right, we can count up the number of squares to find the length, similarly we can count across the number of squares to find the width.

> Area of a rectangle = length × width

By multiplying the length by the width, we can find the area.

In this case: area = 6 × 4 = 24 square units

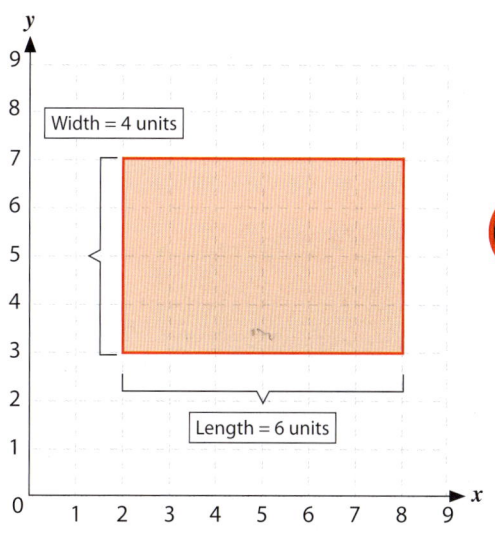

Worked example 1

Find the area of the following shapes.

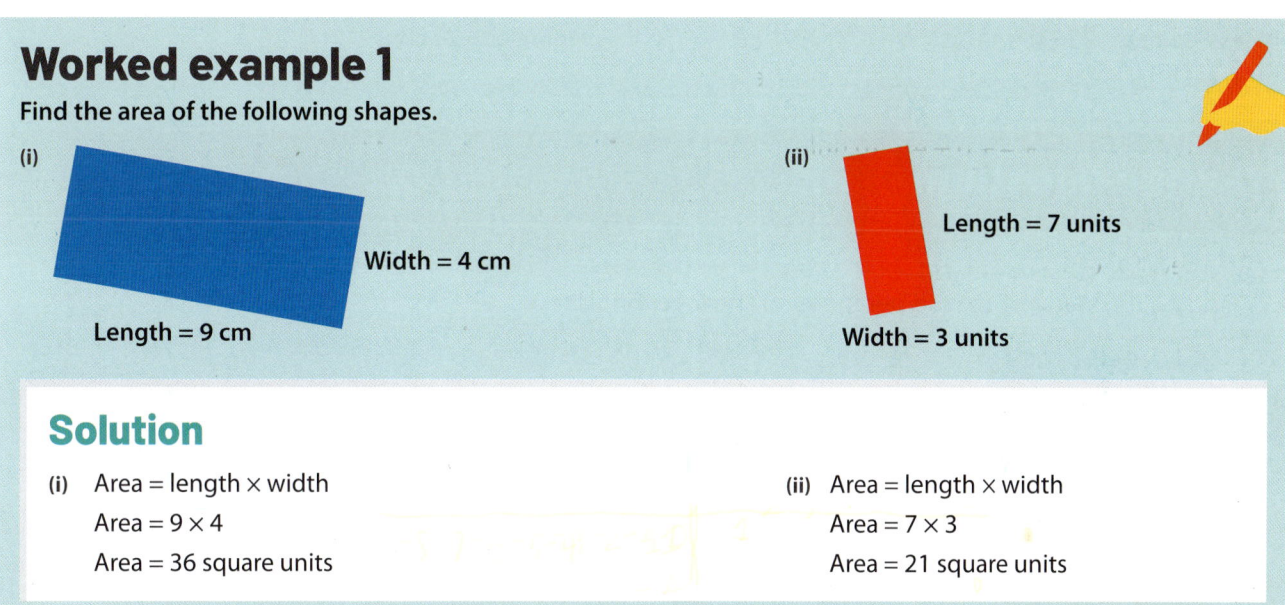

Solution

(i) Area = length × width
Area = 9 × 4
Area = 36 square units

(ii) Area = length × width
Area = 7 × 3
Area = 21 square units

Perimeter of a rectangle

We can also use a formula to find the perimeter of a rectangle or square. In the diagram on the right, we can count the number of squares to find the width, and we can count the number of squares across to find the length.

> Perimeter of a rectangle = length + width + length + width

By adding the lengths to the widths, we can find the perimeter.

In this case:

Perimeter = 6 + 4 + 6 + 4 = 20 units

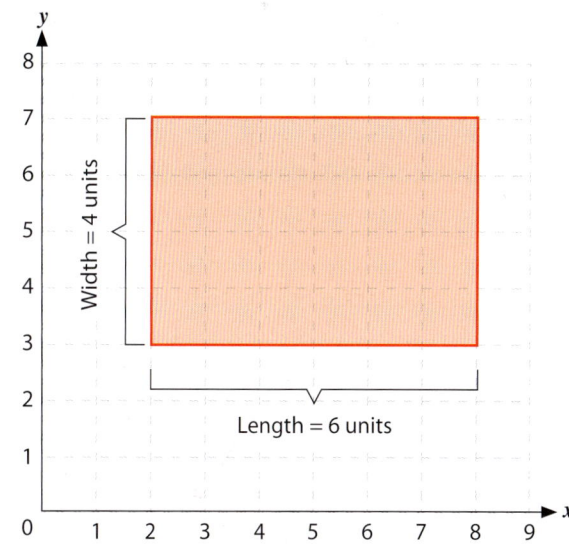

Section A Introducing concepts and building skills

Worked example 2

Find the perimeter of the following shapes.

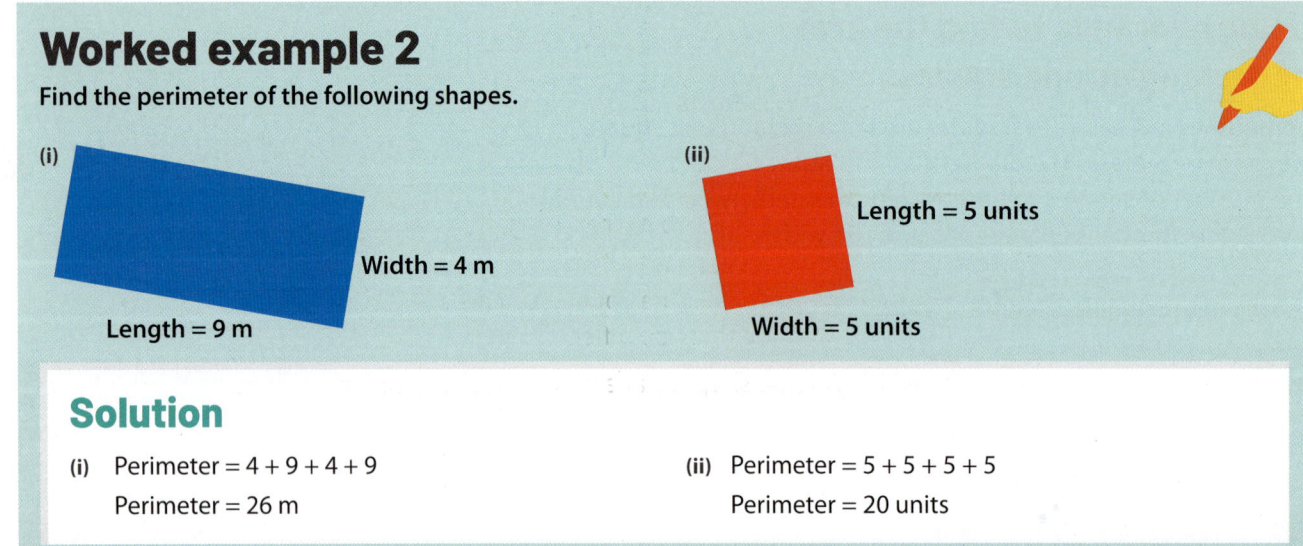

Solution

(i) Perimeter = 4 + 9 + 4 + 9
   Perimeter = 26 m

(ii) Perimeter = 5 + 5 + 5 + 5
   Perimeter = 20 units

Practice questions 1·3·2

1. Find **(a)** the area and **(b)** the perimeter of the following shapes.

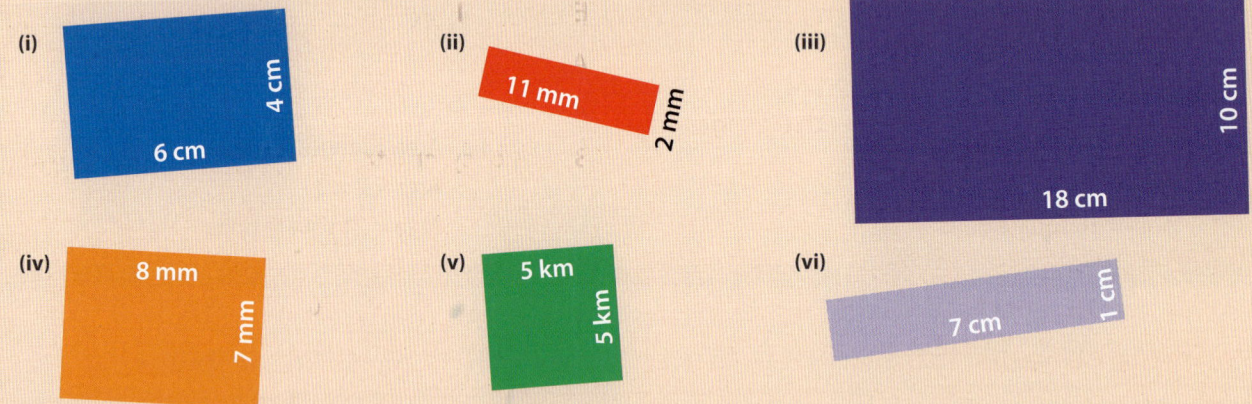

2. Seán wants new carpeting for his bedroom. His bedroom is in the shape of a rectangle, with a width of 3 metres and a length of 5 metres.

   What is the minimum amount of carpet he needs to purchase to cover his entire bedroom floor?

3. A square-shaped room measures 4 metres on one side.
   (i) What is the area of this room?
   (ii) What is the perimeter of this room?

4. The coordinate plane opposite shows a character called Steve. Find:
   (i) the area of Steve
   (ii) the perimeter of Steve.

   It might be helpful to break Steve into separate squares and rectangles.

5. Ciaran wants new tiles for his dining room. His dining room measures 7·2 metres by 4·5 metres in a rectangle shape. He has bought 33 m² (metres squared) of tiles. How much wastage (area of tiles left over) will there be after laying the tiles on the dining room floor?

1.4 Axis of symmetry

By the end of this section you should:
- understand how to draw the axis of symmetry of a given shape

> An **axis (line) of symmetry** divides a figure into two mirror image halves.

If you can reflect (or flip) a figure over a **line** and the figure appears unchanged, then the figure has reflection **symmetry** or an **axis (line) of symmetry**. The **line** that you reflect through is called the **axis of symmetry**.

Some shapes have one line of symmetry, some shapes have many lines of symmetry and some shapes have no lines of symmetry.

Here are some examples.

Rectangles

If you try to fold this rectangle along the dotted line, the two halves don't match up.

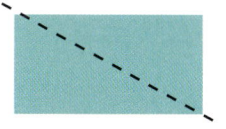 

So this is **not** a line of symmetry.

If you fold it along the dotted line below, the folded parts sit perfectly together, with all edges matching.

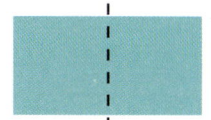 

This **is** a line of symmetry.

Triangles

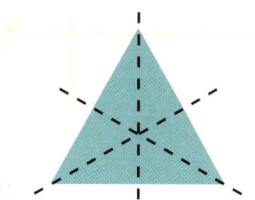

Equilateral triangle
All sides equal
All angles equal
3 lines of symmetry

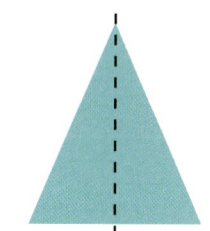

Isosceles triangle
2 sides equal
2 angles equal
1 lines of symmetry

Scalene triangle
0 sides equal
0 angles equal
0 lines of symmetry

Discuss and discover

Write your name in block capital letters and discover how many (if any) axes of symmetry each letter has.

Are there any letters which do not have an axis of symmetry?

Practice questions 1·4

1. Copy the shapes below and draw their line or lines of symmetry with dotted lines. Note some shapes may have no lines of symmetry.

   (i)  (ii)  (iii)  (iv) 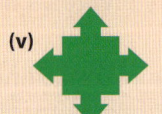 (v)  (vi)

2. Each of the images below are symmetrical. One half of each shape has been completed.

   Copy the diagrams, and draw the other half of the symmetrical shape.

   (i) (ii)  (iii)  (iv)  (v)

3. For each of the questions below,
   (a) copy the coordinate plane provided
   (b) plot the points given
   (c) join points in alphabetical order
   (d) draw in the line or lines of symmetry of the resulting shape.

   (i) $E = (1, 2), F = (3, 2), G = (3, 1), H = (1, 1)$
   (ii) $I = (-3, 3), J = (-4, 1), K = (-2, 1)$
   (iii) $A = (-3, -1), B = (-4, -2), C = (-3, -3), D = (-2, -2)$
   (iv) $L = (0, 0), M = (2, -2), N = (0, -2)$
   (v) $Q = (0, 2), R = (-2, 0), S = (0, -2), T = (2, 0)$

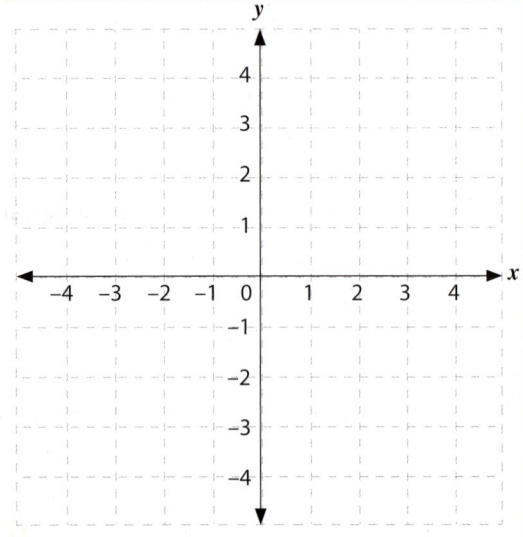

Linking Thinking 1

1·5 Reflecting shapes on the coordinate plane

By the end of this section you should be able to:
- reflect shapes through the x-axis and the y-axis

Sometimes we want to 'reflect' or get a mirror image of a shape on the Cartesian plane.

> Finding the image of an object under **axial symmetry** means to find the reflection of the object in a line.

Worked example

(i) Reflect the blue shape in the y-axis.
(ii) Reflect the red shape in the x-axis.

Solution

(i)

Step 1 Choose a point on each vertex (corner) of the **object** (shape).

Step 2 Draw a straight line from point A, parallel to the x-axis and count how many squares it is to the y-axis.

Step 3 Extend this line beyond (through) the y-axis, the same number of squares. Stop, and mark that point as A' (called 'A prime').

Step 4 Apply steps 2 and 3 to all other points on the shape.

Step 5 Join up all points on opposite side of the y-axis to create the **image**.

(ii) Repeat all steps from part (i) to reflect the red shape in the x-axis.

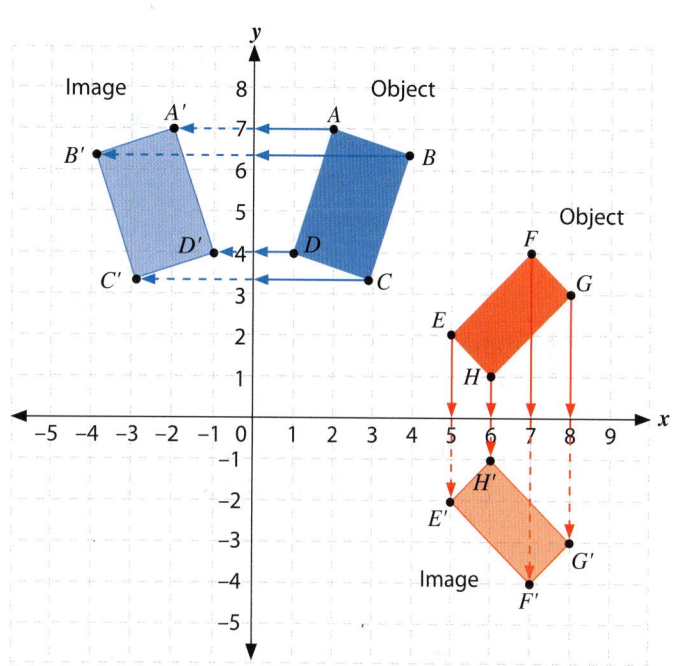

Practice questions 1·5

1. Copy the Cartesian planes shown into your copybook.

   Draw the objects, and then draw the images under axial symmetry through the y-axis (the vertical axis).

(i)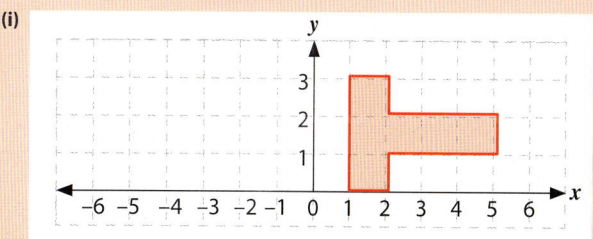

(ii)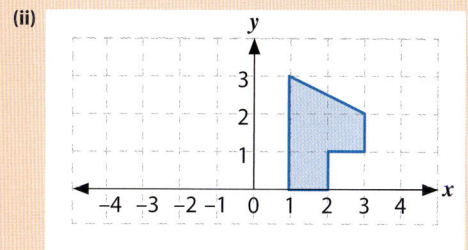

(iii)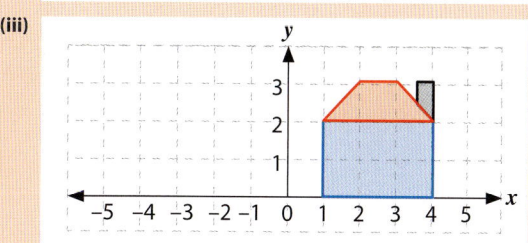

Section A Introducing concepts and building skills

2. Copy the coordinate planes below into your copybook.
   Draw the objects shown, and then draw the images under axial symmetry through the x-axis (the horizontal axis).

(i)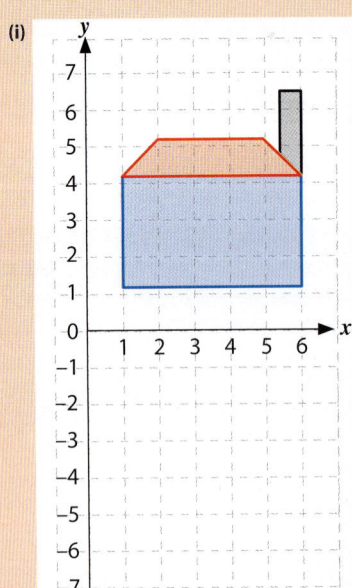
(ii)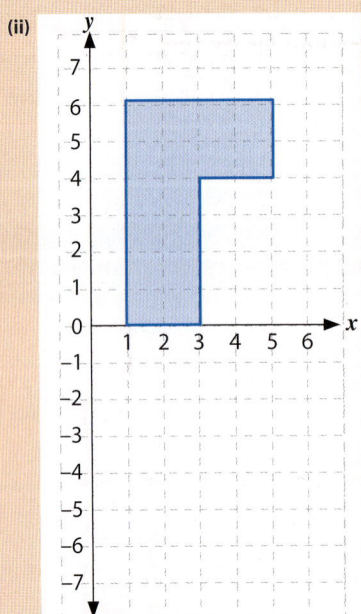
(iii)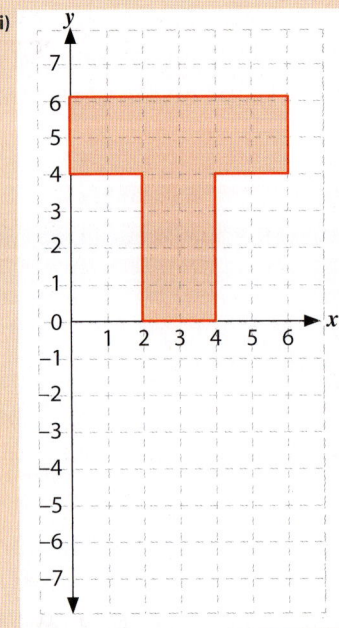

3. Copy the coordinate plane opposite into your copybook.
   (i) Draw the image of the squares under axial symmetry through the x-axis.
   (ii) Draw the image of the squares under axial symmetry through the y-axis.

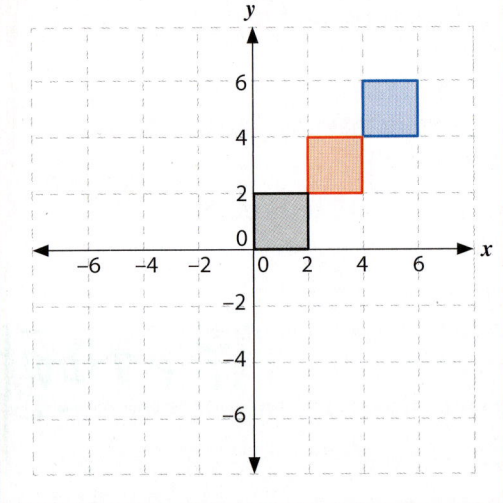

4. Copy the pictures below and reflect the figure through the line of symmetry provided.

(i)

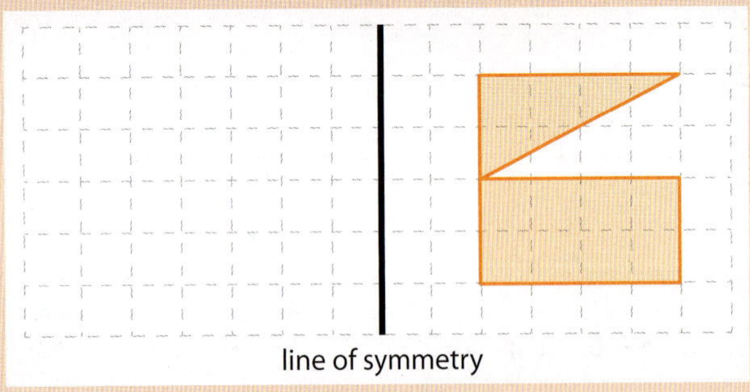

line of symmetry

(ii)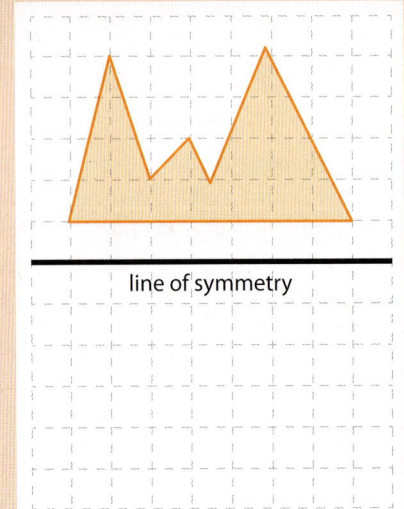

line of symmetry

Linking Thinking 1

5. The diagram shows a coordinate plane, with three points A, B and C, plotted.

   (i) Copy the diagram and use the given points and any additional necessary ones to create a figure that is symmetric about the line l (the line l is its axis of symmetry).

   (ii) What are the coordinates of the additional points?

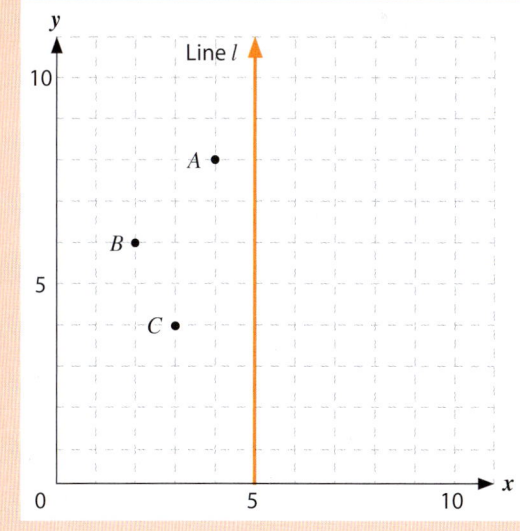

6. (i) Given the following lines of symmetry, a, b, c and d, construct a symmetric figure through each one in the plane and record its coordinates.

   (ii) Explain how you know the figures are symmetrical.

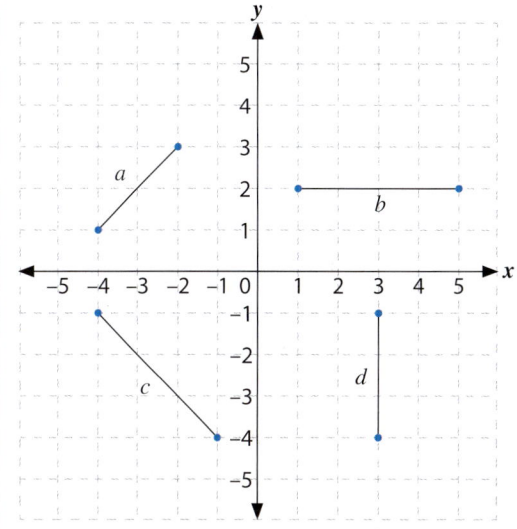

Revision questions

1A Core skills

1. Use the number line below to solve the following.

   (i) $1 + 8$ (ii) $3 + 4$ (iii) $7 + 5$ (iv) $17 - 9$ (v) $13 - 8$ (vi) $18 - 7$ (vii) $14 - 8$ (viii) $15 - 8$

2. Use the number line below to solve the following.

   (i) $1 + 4$ (ii) $4 - 6$ (iii) $0 - 5$ (iv) $-1 - 3$ (v) $5 - 6$ (vi) $3 - 7$ (vii) $5 - 9$ (viii) $0 - 0$

Section A Introducing concepts and building skills

3. Copy the Cartesian plane shown here.
   Draw and label the following points.

   A = (2, 5)
   B = (−3, 2)
   C = (4, −2)
   D = (−2, 2)
   E = (0, 0)
   F = (6, −1)
   G = (4, 0)
   H = (0, −5)
   I = (−4, −5)

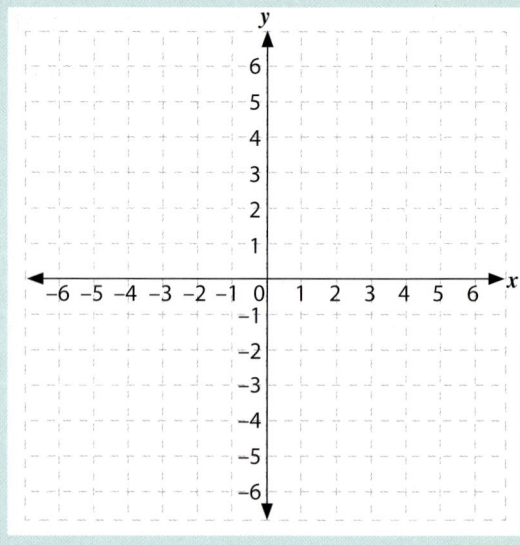

4. Find (i) the area and (ii) the perimeter of the shapes A, B and C below.

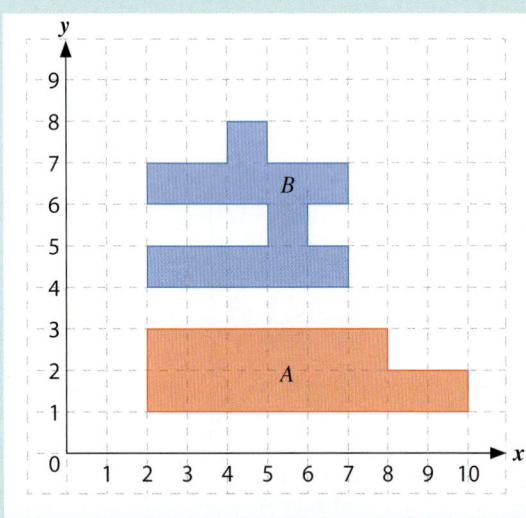
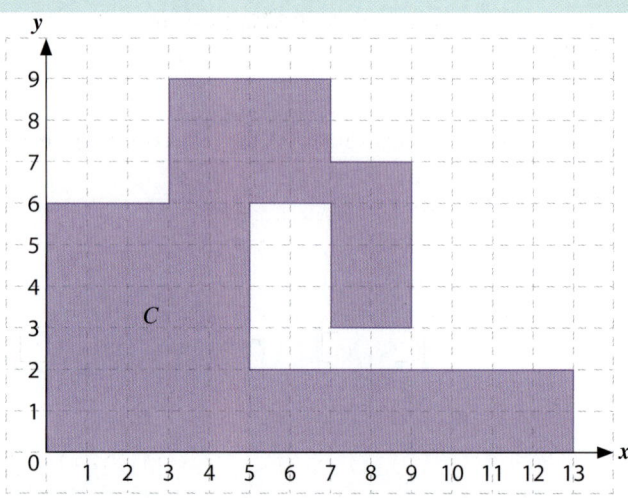

5. Copy the shapes below and draw in the axis (or axes) of symmetry. If you think there are no axes of symmetry for a particular shape, write 'none' below it.

   (i)   (ii)   (iii)   (iv)   (v)   (vi)

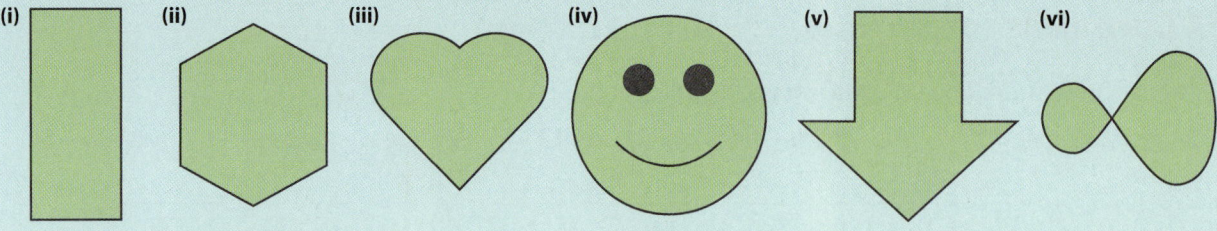

6. Write any word in capital letters and draw all the lines of symmetry of each letter.

18   Linking Thinking 1

7. Draw the diagrams below and reflect through the axis stated.

(i) Reflect shapes (a) and (b) through the *x*-axis.   (ii) Reflect shapes (c) and (d) through the *y*-axis.

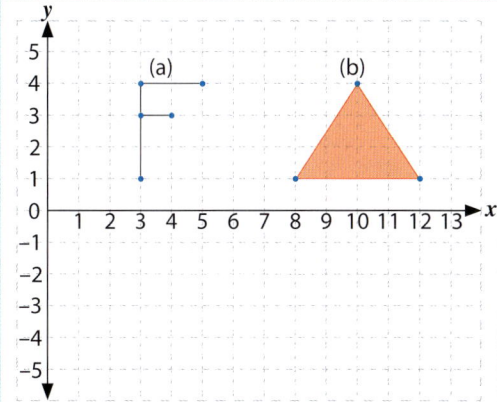 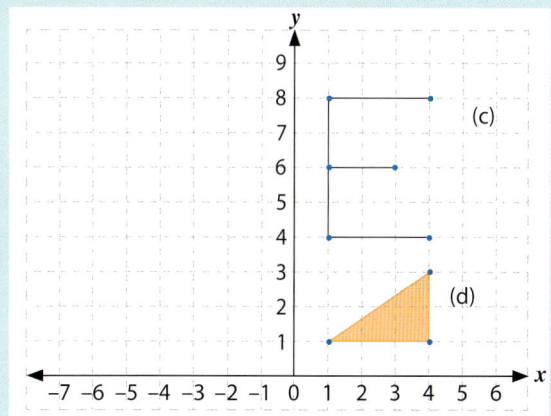

1B Taking it FURTHER

1. Write the missing numbers for each number line below. Then, explain how you worked out the missing values.

(i)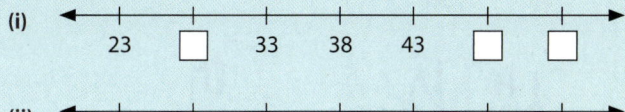

(ii)

2. Plot the following points on a coordinate plane.

$A = (-4, 1)$ $B = (-2, -2)$ $C = (2, -2)$ $D = (4, 1)$ $E = (0, 6)$ $F = (0, 7)$

(i) Using a ruler, join the points together in alphabetical order.

(ii) Draw a straight line to join point F to point A, and another to join point A to point D.

(iii) Is AD a line of symmetry for the shape $ABCDEF$? Give a reason for your answer.

3. Copy the diagram opposite.

(i) Reflect the object through the *x*-axis.

(ii) Reflect the object through the *y*-axis.

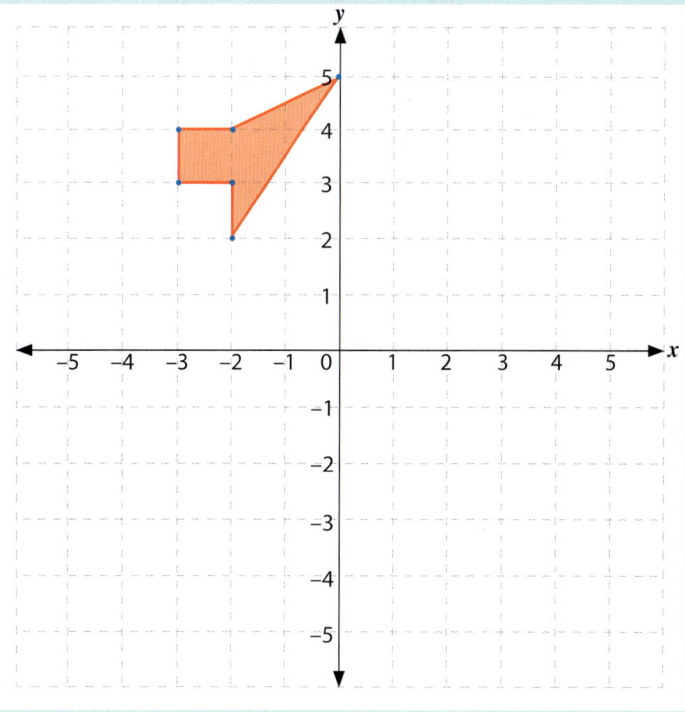

Section A Introducing concepts and building skills

4. Complete the following in your copybook.

(i)

Draw a picture of a symmetrical snowman. Draw the line of symmetry with a dotted line.

(ii)

Draw a picture of a symmetrical space alien. Draw the line of symmetry with a dotted line.

(iii)

Draw a picture of a symmetrical sailboat. Draw the line of symmetry with a dotted line.

(iv)

Draw a symmetrical picture of a friend. Draw the line of symmetry with a dotted line.

5. (i) Draw a picture of a square and a rectangle.
   (ii) Draw all the lines of symmetry that each shape has.
   (iii) Explain why a square has more lines of symmetry than a rectangle.

6. Draw a separate coordinate plane for each set of points provided.
   (i) Join the points in alphabetical order and name the shape created.
   (ii) Draw the line or lines of symmetry though each shape. Note that some shapes may have more than one line of symmetry, or may not have any at all.
   (a) $A = (2, 2)$ $B = (2, 4)$ $C = (4, 2)$ $D = (4, 4)$
   (b) $Q = (1, 1)$ $R = (2, 3)$ $S = (3, 1)$
   (c) $E = (3, 1)$ $F = (5, 1)$ $G = (6, 3)$ $H = (4, 4)$ $I = (2, 3)$
   (d) $J = (0, 0)$ $K = (2, 0)$ $L = (0, 3)$ $M = (2, 3)$

7. Copy the table below and put a tick (✓) in the correct box in each row to show whether each statement is always true, sometimes true, or never true.

Statement		Tick **one** box only for each statement		
		Always true	Sometimes true	Never true
(i)	The area of a rectangle or square is the length × width.			
(ii)	If a rectangle has an area of 24 cm², its width must be 3 cm and its length must be 8 cm.			
(iii)	If a rectangle has an area of 36 m², the perimeter must be 4 metres times 9 metres.			
(iv)	If you increase the perimeter of a square, the area will stay the same.			
(v)	If you increase the area of a rectangle, the perimeter will decrease.			

Linking Thinking 1

8. A square field has a side length of 4 units.
   (i) What is its area?
   (ii) What is its perimeter?
   (iii) If the field can be rectangular, is it possible to keep the value of the area you have found above, but change the total size of the perimeter?
   If possible, give an example.
   (iv) Draw a diagram of the 'new' field and explain your answer. (Note: total area must still equal 16 square units.)
   (v) If the area of the field must remain at 16 square units, how many different values of the perimeter are there? Justify your answers using diagrams.
   (Note: you may only use natural numbers for length and width.)
   (a) What is the largest perimeter?
   (b) What is the smallest perimeter?
   (vi) Is the following statement true or false?
   'If the area of a rectangular shape remains unchanged, you cannot change the length of the perimeter.'
   Give a reason for (justify) your answer.

Now that you have completed the unit, revisit the

 **Something to think about ...**

question posed at the start of this unit.

Unit 2
Sets, number and chance

Topics covered within this unit:
2·1 Sets and set notation
2·2 Number sets
2·3 Venn diagrams
2·4 Chance

The Learning Outcomes covered in this unit are contained in the following sections:
N.1d N.2a N.5a N.5b N.5c
N.5d SP.2b

Key words
Set
Element
Cardinal number
Subset
Null set
Factor
Prime number
Highest common factor
Lowest common multiple
Rational numbers
Universal set
Union
Intersection

Something to think about ...

Last November, there were 15 windy days, 17 rainy days, and 5 days that were both windy and rainy. How can this be true, since November contains only 30 days? Were there any days where it was neither windy nor rainy?

You can use the **problem-solving toolkit** to help with this type of problem:

1. What are you trying to find out, and what do you already know?
2. Will a diagram (picture) help you?
3. Can you some up with a strategy to solve the problem?
4. Solve the problem.

2·1 Sets and set notation

By the end of this section you should be able to:
- define the terms: set, element, cardinal number, subset and null set
- recognise the symbols for element, cardinal number, subset and null set
- describe a set in three different ways
- understand what it means if sets are equal

> A **set** is a collection of objects that have some characteristics in common.

We usually use capital letters to represent sets.

We call the objects in a set the **elements** of that set.

> An **element** is an object in a set.

Sets can contain any type of element: numbers, letters, objects, people, etc.

Notation

- ∈ means 'is an element of'
- ∉ means 'is not an element of'
- When listing the elements of a set, we use curly brackets { }
- Each element contained within a set is listed inside these curly brackets separated by a comma

Let's think of a set of letters. For this example, we can use the five vowels in the alphabet: a, e, i, o and u. We need to give this set a name, so we'll call it 'V' (for 'vowels'):

$$V = \{a, e, i, o, u\}$$

We can say that **a** ∈ **V**, because the letter 'a' is included in the set.

We can also say that **s** ∉ **V**, because the letter 's' is not included in the set.

Now let's try another set of letters. This time, we can use the letters in the word 'banana'. We can call the set 'B'. We write the set as follows:

$$B = \{a, b, n\}$$

We can say that **a** ∈ **B** and **c** ∉ **B**, because the letter 'a' is in the set, and the letter 'c' is not in the set.

> Even if an element is present in a set more than once, it only appears once in the list of elements for that set.

Defining a set

Discuss and discover

Working with a classmate, decide if each of the following is a set.

Explain your reasoning in each case.

(i) All the capitals of European countries
(ii) All the easy questions in your Maths book
(iii) The last six letters in the alphabet
(iv) All the beautiful flowers in the park
(v) Sports played by students in the class
(vi) The colours of the rainbow

What new information did you discover during this task?

Having completed the task above, you can see that **a set must be well defined**. This means that our description of the elements of a set is clear. For example, {tall people} is not a set, because people could disagree about what 'tall' means.

> A **set** is a well-defined collection of objects that have something in common.

Describing a set

A set can be described by writing a description of its elements, by listing all of its elements, or by writing a rule for the set.

Consider the following set, F, based on the Carlow flag.

Description in words: F is the set of colours on the Carlow flag
Listing elements: F = {red, yellow, green}
Writing a rule: F = { f | f is a colour on the Carlow flag}

The rule F = { f | f is a colour on the Carlow flag} is read as 'F is the set of elements **such that** all elements of F are colours on the Carlow flag.'

> The capital F is the name of the set. As explained above, sets are usually named with capital letters. The small f refers to the elements of the set.

Section A Introducing concepts and building skills

The picture on the right shows the set of the days of the week (W).

We can describe this set in the following ways:

Description in words: W is the set of days of the week

Listing elements: W = {Monday, Tuesday, Wednesday, Thursday, Friday, Saturday, Sunday}

Writing a rule: W = {w | w is a day of the week}

Sets can be drawn in circles. You can practice by drawing out the following sets in your copybook:

Set G
G is the set of letters in the word 'game'
G = {g, a, m, e}
G = {g | g is a letter in the word 'game'}

Set C
C is the set of colours in the rainbow
C = {red, orange, yellow, green, blue, indigo, violet}

Set J
J = {j | j is a month beginning with 'J'}
J = {January, June, July}

Cardinal number

Consider the set of the days of the week (W) described above. There are 7 elements in this set.

The number of elements in a set is called the **cardinal number**. The symbol for cardinal number is #.

In the example above, #W = 7.

> The **cardinal number (#)** of a set is the number of elements in the set.

Subsets

Consider again the set W.

This set contains some smaller sets inside it, as shown.

Circled in red are the days of the week beginning with 'T'. Let's call this set T.

Circled in blue are the days of the weekend.

These smaller sets are called **subsets** of the larger set.

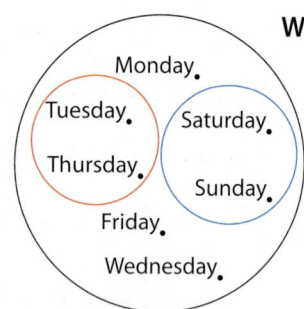

> Set A is called a **subset** (⊂) of another set B if every element of A is also an element of set B.

The symbol for a subset is ⊂. Using the example above, we can see that set T is a subset of set W. Mathematically, this would be written as T ⊂ W.

> Every set is a subset of itself.

> Have you noticed that the subsets for days beginning with 'S' and weekend days are the same? When two sets or subsets are the same, we say they are equal.

Null set

Let's look at the set A, which is the set days of the week beginning with 'A'. When we try to list the elements of this set, we can see that there aren't any.

If a set contains no elements, it is called the **null set**. The symbol for the null set is ∅ or an empty pair of curly brackets { }.

> The **null set**, ∅ or { }, is a set that contains no elements.

> The null set is a subset of every set, including the null set itself.

Linking Thinking 1

Equal sets

As we saw when looking at the days of the week, if two sets have the exact same elements, they are said to be **equal sets**.

For example, set A = {3, 2, 1} and set B = {2, 1, 3}. They both contain the elements 1, 2 and 3, so A = B.

Discuss and discover

Consider the people in your school community.

Work with the person beside you to answer the following questions.

(i) Is your school community a set? Justify your answer using your knowledge of the definition of a set.
(ii) Could you write a rule to describe this set?
(iii) Could you name an element of the set? How would you write this?
(iv) Can you name a subset of this set?
(v) How would you find the cardinal number of one subset of the set?

Worked example

Consider the set A = {M, A, T, H, S}.

(i) Describe set A in two different ways.
(ii) Find #A.
(iii) List five subsets of A with three elements.
(iv) Write down four sets that are equal to A.

Solution

(i) A = {letters of the word MATHS}; A = $\{x \mid x$ is a letter in the word MATHS$\}$
(ii) #A = 5
(iii) {M, A, T}; {M, A, H}; {M, A, S}; {A, T, S}; {S, H, T}; etc.
(iv) {A, T, H, S, M}; {T, H, S, M, A}; {H, S, M, A, T}; {S, M, A, T, H}; etc.

Practice questions 2·1

1. List the elements of each of the following sets.
   (i) First five letters of the English alphabet
   (ii) Colours of the rainbow
   (iii) Letters in the word APPLE
   (iv) Vowels used in the word MONDAY
   (v) Numbers from 1 to 10 (inclusive)
   (vi) The last four months of the year

2. Write a description in words for each of the following sets.
   (i) X = {April, August}
   (ii) P = {thumb, index, middle, ring, little}
   (iii) A = {Tuesday, Thursday}
   (iv) G = {Mercury, Venus, Earth, Mars}

3. Copy the table below and match each symbol with its meaning:

Symbol			Meaning
1.	∅	A.	Is an element of
2.	∈	B.	The number of elements in a set
3.	#	C.	Empty set
4.	⊂	D.	Is not an element of
5.	⊄	E.	Is a subset of

4. Rewrite each of the following statements using set notation.
   (i) 2 is an element of set Q
   (ii) May is not a day of the week
   (iii) The number of elements in set D is 8
   (iv) The set {1, 2} is in the set S
   (v) J is the null set
   (vi) 2 is not a letter in the alphabet

5. For the following pairs of sets, investigate if A and B are equal. Give reasons to support your answer.
   (i) A = the letters in the word SEAT
   B = {b | b is a letter in the word TASTE}
   (ii) A = {2, 6, 10, 14}
   B = {6, 2, 14, 16}
   (iii) A = {1, 3, 5, 7, 9}
   B = all natural numbers less than 10
   (iv) A = {1, 2, 3}
   B = {a, b, c}

6. Which of the following are sets? Justify your answer using your knowledge of the definition of a set.
   (i) {hearts, diamonds, clubs, spades}
   (ii) The sporty students in the class
   (iii) {January, February, March, April, May}
   (iv) The students in the class older than 16

7. Let A = {2, 3, 4, 5, 6, 7}, B = {2, 4, 7, 8} and C = {2, 4}.
   Use ⊂ or ⊄ to make the following statements true.
   (i) B __ A
   (ii) C __ A
   (iii) B __ C
   (iv) C __ C
   (v) ∅ __ B
   (vi) C __ B

8. Describe the following sets in as many ways as possible.
   (i) The set of the first five counting numbers.
   (ii) The set of the letters in the word MATHEMATICS
   (iii) P = {p | 2 ≤ p ≤ 7}

9. Copy the table below and put a tick (✓) in the correct box to show whether each statement is always true, sometimes true, or never true.

	Statement	Always true	Sometimes true	Never true
(i)	The null set is a subset of all sets.	✓		
(ii)	An element can be a member of two sets at once.			
(iii)	The cardinal number of equal sets is the same.			
(iv)	If an element is present in a set more than once, you must list it more than once.			

10. Two sets P and Q are given as follows:
    P = {3, 5, 7, 9, 11, 13} and Q = {8, 10, 12, 14, 16, 18}
    State, giving reasons, which of the following are true.
    (i) 13 ∈ P, 9 ∈ P but 13 + 9 ∉ P
    (ii) 5 ∈ P, 7 ∈ P and 5 + 7 ∈ Q
    (iii) 3 ∈ P, 13 ∈ P but 13 − 3 ∉ Q
    (iv) 7 ∉ Q, 9 ∉ Q but 7 + 9 ∈ Q

2·2 Number sets

By the end of this section you should:
- be able to recall natural numbers and integers
- be able to calculate the HCF and LCM
- be able to define and give examples of prime numbers
- understand the rational numbers set
- recognise the symbols for the rational numbers set

Natural numbers

In Unit 1, we learned about natural numbers. We can now see that natural numbers are a set. **Natural numbers** are the set of positive whole numbers starting at 1 and continuing to infinity. This set is represented by $\mathbb{N}$.

$\mathbb{N} = \{1, 2, 3, 4, 5, 6, \ldots \infty\}$

Factors

> A **factor** is a number that will divide evenly (with no remainder) into another number.

1 is a factor of all numbers.

Each number is a factor of itself.

For example, the set of the factors of 12 are {1, 2, 3, 4, 6, 12} because all of these numbers divide exactly into 12.

Odd and even numbers

A natural number is even if it can be divided evenly by 2. This means that 2 is a factor of all even numbers.

A natural number is odd if it cannot be divided evenly by 2. This means that 2 is never a factor of an odd number.

Prime numbers

> A **prime number** is a positive number that has exactly **two** different whole number factors, which are 1 and the number itself.
> P = {2, 3, 5, 7, 11, 13, 17 ...}

The factor(s) of 1 are just 1 itself i.e. $1 \times 1 = 1$. This means that 1 only has one factor and, since a prime number must have 2 factors, 1 cannot be a prime number.

The factors of 2 are 2 and 1. It has exactly two different factors, so it is a prime number. 2 is the only even prime number, because all other even numbers can be divided by 2.

The number 1 is not prime. The number 2 is prime.

Prime factors

We can 'break apart' numbers into prime factors. When we do this, we find out which prime numbers multiply together to make the original number. For example, 20 can be broken down as $2 \times 2 \times 5$

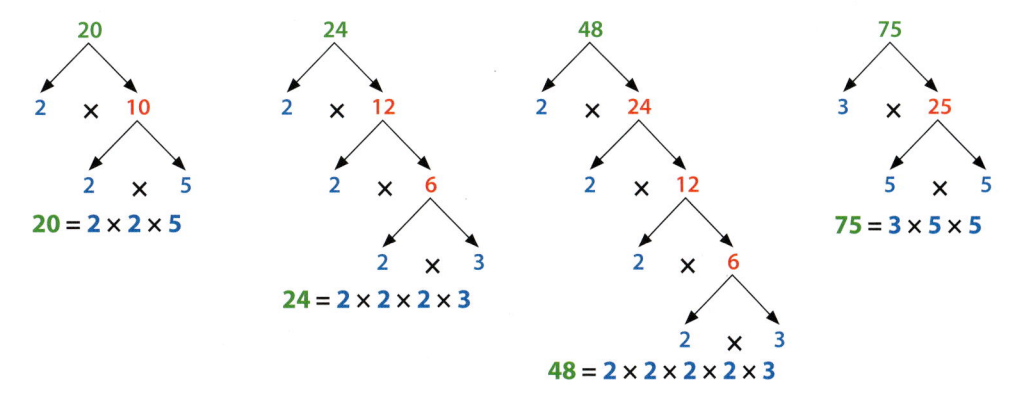

```
       20                  24                    48                      75
      /  \                /  \                  /  \                    /  \
     2    10             2    12               2    24                 3    25
          / \                 / \                   / \                     / \
         2   5               2   6                 2   12                  5   5
    20 = 2 × 2 × 5              / \                   / \            75 = 3 × 5 × 5
                               2   3                 2   6
                        24 = 2 × 2 × 2 × 3               / \
                                                        2   3
                                                48 = 2 × 2 × 2 × 2 × 3
```

To find prime factors of a number, we continuously divide by the lowest prime that will go into it, until we cannot divide it any further. The prime factors are the list of primes that divided in without any remainder.

Section A Introducing concepts and building skills

Highest common factors (HCF)

> The **highest common factor (HCF)** is the largest number that is a factor of two (or more) other numbers.

Worked example 1
Find the highest common factor (HCF) of 18, 24 and 36.

Solution

Method 1

Step 1 List the sets of the factors of 18, 24 and 36.
- 18: {1, 2, 3, 6, 9, 18}
- 24: {1, 2, 3, 4, 6, 8, 12, 24}
- 36: {1, 2, 3, 4, 6, 9, 12, 18, 36}

Step 2 Circle the common factors in the sets.
- 18: {①, ②, ③, ⑥, 9, 18}
- 24: {①, ②, ③, 4, ⑥, 8, 12, 24}
- 36: {①, ②, ③, 4, ⑥, 9, 12, 18, 36}

Step 3 Pick the highest circled number.
HCF = 6

Method 2

Alternatively, we can use the prime factors.

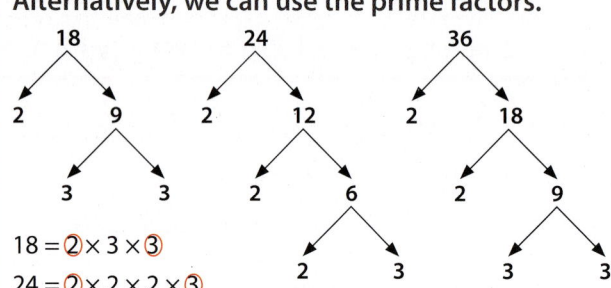

(factor trees for 18, 24, 36)

$18 = ② \times 3 \times ③$
$24 = ② \times 2 \times 2 \times ③$
$36 = ② \times 2 \times ③ \times 3$

The prime factors have one 2 and one 3 in common.
HCF = 2 × 3 = 6

Multiples

A **multiple** of a number is the number multiplied by another whole number. For example, multiples of 3 are 3, 6, 9, 12, 15, 18 …

> The **lowest common multiple (LCM)** is the lowest number that is a multiple of two or more numbers.

Worked example 2
Find the lowest common multiple of 4, 6 and 8.

Solution

Method 1

Step 1 List the sets of the multiples of 4, 6 and 8.
- Multiples of 4: {4, 8, 12, 16, 20, 24, 28, 32, …}
- Multiples of 6: {6, 12, 18, 24, 30, 36, 42, 48, …}
- Multiples of 8: {8, 16, 24, 32, 40, 48, 56, 64, …}

Step 2 Circle the common multiples.
- Multiples of 4: {4, 8, 12, 16, 20, ㉔, 28, 32, 36, 40, ㊽, …}
- Multiples of 6: {6, 12, 18, ㉔, 30, 36, 42, ㊽, …}
- Multiples of 8: {8, 16, ㉔, 32, 40, ㊽, 56, 64, …}

Step 1 Pick the lowest circled number.
LCM = 24

Method 2

List the prime factors.

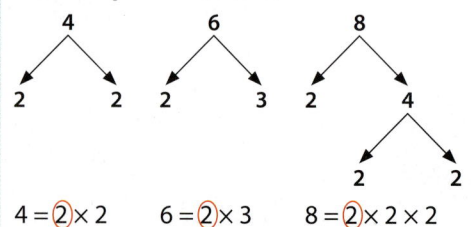

(factor trees for 4, 6, 8)

$4 = ② \times 2 \qquad 6 = ② \times 3 \qquad 8 = ② \times 2 \times 2$

These factors have prime factor 2 in common.

All the factors of each term need to be used to find the LCM (use the common factor(s) only once).

LCM = ② × 2 × 2 × 3
LCM = 24

Practice questions 2·2·1

1. List all the elements of the set of factors of the following numbers.
   (i) 6   (ii) 15   (iii) 27   (iv) 40   (v) 64

2. List the first five elements of the set of multiples of the following numbers.
   (i) 2   (ii) 3   (iii) 5   (iv) 6   (v) 8

3. List all the prime numbers between the following pairs of numbers.
   (i) 1 and 10   (ii) 15 and 25   (iii) 100 and 110

4. Find the prime factors of each of the following numbers.
   (i) 18   (ii) 32   (iii) 40   (iv) 45   (v) 72   (vi) 144

5. Find the highest common factor (HCF) of the following numbers.
   (i) 16 and 18   (iii) 36 and 42   (v) 30 and 48   (vii) 15, 45 and 60
   (ii) 27 and 45   (iv) 12, 24 and 88   (vi) 12, 16 and 20   (viii) 18, 48 and 56

6. Find the lowest common multiple (LCM) of the following numbers.
   (i) 4 and 5   (iii) 6 and 9   (v) 3 and 8   (vii) 5, 10 and 15
   (ii) 6 and 8   (iv) 2, 3 and 5   (vi) 2, 6 and 4   (viii) 3, 8 and 6

7. (a) Express the following numbers as products of their prime factors (i) 60 and (ii) 96.
   (b) Using the answer to (a), find the highest common factor of 60 and 96.
   (c) Using the answer to (a), find the lowest common multiple of 60 and 96.

8. Tom is a carpenter. He was given some free planks of wood. Some of them are 16 m long and some are 24 m long.

   He wants to cut them up so that he has equal size planks to make using them easier.

   What is the longest length Tom can cut the planks into, to avoid wasting any wood?

9. Nassim is training for a triathlon. As part of her training she swims every 3 days, runs every 4 days and cycles every 5 days.

   If she did all three activities today, in how many days will she do all three activities again on the same day?

10. Sadiq has 15 apples, 9 bananas and 18 oranges. He wants to put all of the fruit into baskets with each basket having the same number of pieces of fruit in it.

    Without mixing the fruit, what is the greatest number of pieces of fruit Sadiq can put in each basket?

Taking it FURTHER

11. (i) Is the lowest common multiple of an even number and an odd number even or odd? Give an example to support your answer.
    (ii) If one number is a factor of a second number, what is the highest common factor and the lowest common multiple? Give an example to support each answer.
    (iii) If two numbers do not have any common factor, what is the highest common factor and the lowest common multiple? Support each answer with an example.

Section A Introducing concepts and building skills

Integers

We looked at integers in Unit 1. They are a clearly defined group of numbers, so that means they are also a set.

> **Integers** are the set of positive and negative whole numbers, including zero.
> This set is represented by the letter $\mathbb{Z}$.
> $\mathbb{Z} = \{-\infty, \ldots, -4, -3, -2, -1, 0, 1, 2, 3, 4, \ldots, \infty\}$

Rational numbers

When we divide natural numbers and integers, we do not always end up with whole numbers.

For example, if you divide 3 bars of chocolate between 6 people, each person would get $\frac{1}{2}$ a bar of chocolate.

The number $\frac{1}{2}$ is not part of $\mathbb{N}$ or $\mathbb{Z}$, as it is not a whole number. It is part of the rational numbers.

> **Rational numbers** can be expressed as a fraction where both the numerator (top) and the denominator (bottom) are whole numbers. However, the denominator can never be equal to zero. The rational numbers set is represented by $\mathbb{Q}$.

The notation $\mathbb{Q}$ comes from the German word *quotient*, meaning **ratio**, hence the term **ratio**nal. This is because the numerator and denominator are in ratio to each other.

The set $\mathbb{Q}$ includes positive and negative whole numbers and fractions, which means that all natural numbers and integers are rational numbers. It also includes zero.

$\mathbb{N}$ and $\mathbb{Z}$ are subsets of $\mathbb{Q}$.

We will learn how to work with rational numbers in Unit 5.

> **Invisible Maths!**
> Any whole number can be written as a fraction by placing it over 1. For example, 5 is the same as $\frac{5}{1}$.

Practice questions 2·2·2

1. Answer 'true' or 'false' to each of the following statements. Justify your answer in each case, using your knowledge of the definitions of the different sets of numbers.
   (i) Every integer is a natural number.
   (ii) Every natural number is a rational number.
   (iii) Every rational number is an integer.
   (iv) Every integer is a rational number.
   (v) Every natural number in an integer.
   (vi) Every rational number is a natural number.
   (vii) Rational numbers are a subset of integers.
   (viii) Natural numbers are a subset of integers.

2. List the elements of the following sets.
   (i) {natural numbers less than 6}
   (ii) {prime numbers between 10 and 20}
   (iii) {odd integers between −10 and 6}
   (iv) {even numbers between 25 and 35}
   (v) {multiples of 3 less than 30}
   (vi) {factors of 32}

3. (a) (i) In your own words, explain what natural numbers are.
       (ii) What letter is used to represent natural numbers?
   (b) (i) In your own words, explain what integers are.
       (ii) What letter is used to represent integers?
   (c) (i) In your own words, explain what rational numbers are.
       (ii) What letter is used to represent rational numbers?

4. Write the answers to each of the following as a rational number.
   (i) 3 Swiss rolls divided between 9 people
   (ii) 4 bars of chocolate divided between 8 people
   (iii) 5 pizzas divided between 20 people
   (iv) 6 cakes divided between 30 people

Linking Thinking 1

5. Copy the table below and put a tick (✓) in the correct box in each row to show whether each statement is always true, sometimes true, or never true.

	Statement	Always true	Sometimes true	Never true
(i)	Every number has an even number of factors			
(ii)	All prime numbers are odd			
(iii)	An integer is a whole number			
(iv)	Negative numbers are natural numbers			
(v)	Adding natural numbers gives a natural number answer			

2.3 Venn diagrams

By the end of this section you should:
- understand the universal set
- be able to draw a Venn diagram
- understand and be able to list the elements of the union and intersection of sets
- be able to represent the natural numbers, integers and rational numbers on a Venn diagram

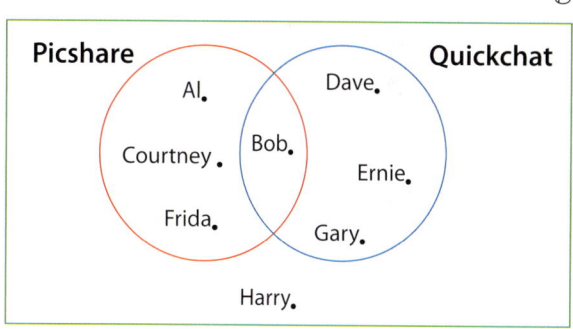

The **universal set** is the set of all the elements relevant to a given question. It is represented by $\mathbb{U}$.

Venn diagrams were introduced in 1880 by an English mathematician called John Venn.

A Venn diagram is a way of representing sets and the relationships between different sets.

The diagram consists of a rectangle representing the universal set and a number of circles (for your course, two circles) representing the sets involved.

For example: eight students were interviewed about their social media accounts and the findings are shown in the Venn diagram.

From this Venn diagram, we can identify the following sets:

- $\mathbb{U}$ = {Al, Bob, Courtney, Dave, Ernie, Frida, Gary, Harry}
  The rectangle contains all the students who were interviewed. This is known as the universal set (i.e. $\mathbb{U}$).

- P = {Al, Bob, Courtney, Frida}
  These are all the students in the PicShare circle (i.e. the students who have a PicShare account).

- Q = {Bob, Dave, Gary, Ernie}
  These are all the students in the Quickchat circle (i.e. the students who have a Quickchat account).

- Bob has both social media accounts, so he goes in the overlap between the two circles.

- Harry has neither social media account, so he goes outside of both circles.

When dealing with sets, a dot is placed into the diagram beside each element. No element can appear in the diagram more than once.

Let's have a look at some Venn diagrams.

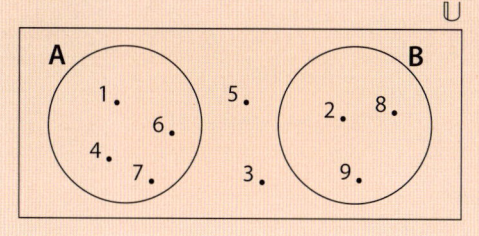

$\mathbb{U}$ = {1, 2, 3, 4, 5, 6, 7, 8, 9}. This is all the elements in the universal set (represented by the rectangle).

A = {1, 4, 6, 7}. These are all the elements in the set A.

B = {2, 8, 9}. These are all the elements in the set B.

Note that set A and set B have no elements in common.

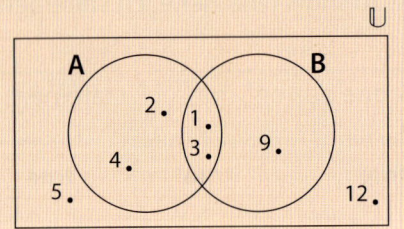

𝕌 = {1, 2, 3, 4, 5, 9, 12}
A = {1, 2, 3, 4}
B = {1, 3, 9}

If set A and set B have some elements in common, we draw two overlapping circles to represent them.

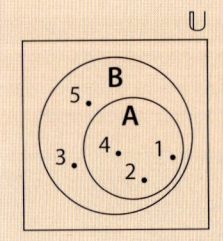

Note that 1 and 3 are common to both sets. They are in A and in B. The set {1, 3} is a subset of both A and B.

𝕌 = {1, 2, 3, 4, 5}
A = {1, 2, 4}
B = {1, 2, 3, 4, 5}

If set A is a subset of set B, then the circle representing set A is drawn inside the circle representing set B.

Note that set A is a subset of B.

Intersection and union of sets

The union of two sets A and B is the set of all elements in A or B, or both. The union of A and B is written as A∪B.

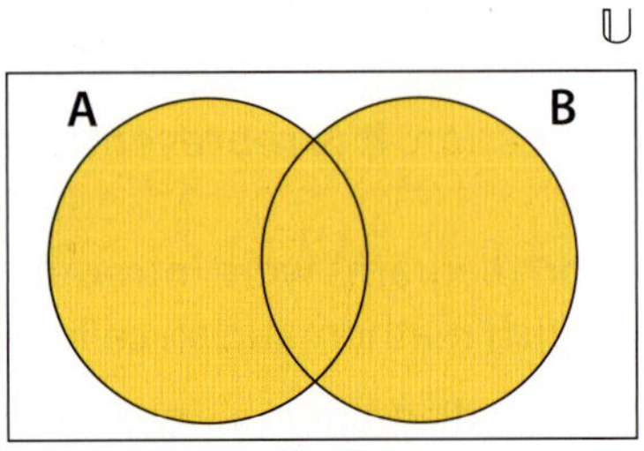

If set A = {a, b, c} and B = {2, 4, 6}, then A∪B = {a, b, c, 2, 4, 6}.

In the Venn diagram on the right, the area shaded in yellow represents the union of A and B. Every element inside both circles is in A∪B.

Be careful – the union symbol ∪ and the universal symbol 𝕌 look very similar.

The intersection of two sets A and B is the set of elements that are in common between the set A and the set B. The intersection of A and B is written A∩B.

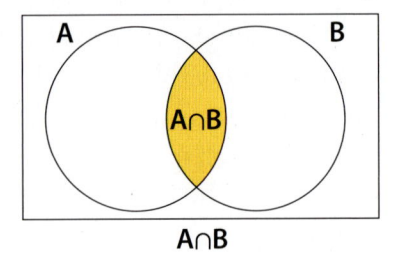

If A = {1, 2, 3, 4, 5, 6} and B = {2, 3, 5, 7, 9} then A∩B = {2, 3, 5}.

The elements 2, 3 and 5 are in common between A and B.

In the Venn diagram on the right, the area shaded in yellow represents the intersection of A and B.

Every element inside the overlapping area of A and B is a member of the set A∩B.

Worked example 1

If 𝕌 = {1, 2, 3, 4, 5, 6, 7, 8, 10}, X = {2, 3, 5, 8} and Y = {1, 2, 4, 5, 6, 10}

(i) Draw a Venn diagram to represent these sets.
(ii) List the elements of X∪Y.
(iii) List the elements of X∩Y.
(iv) Find #X∪Y and #X∩Y.
(v) Describe in words the elements outside the circles.

Solution

(i) [Venn diagram with X containing 3, 7, 8; intersection containing 2, 5; Y containing 1, 4, 6, 10; outside: 9]

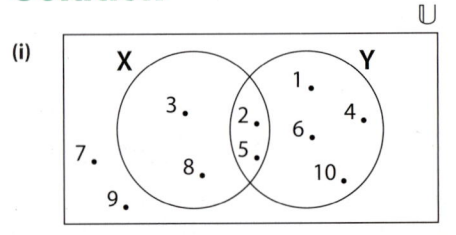

(ii) X∪Y = {1, 2, 3, 4, 5, 6, 8, 10}
(iii) X∩Y = {2, 5}
(iv) #X∪Y = 8   #X∩Y = 2
(v) The elements that are in the universal set, 𝕌, but not in X or Y.

Remember
 # = the number of elements in the set.

Linking Thinking 1

Number sets on a Venn diagram

Earlier in this book, we discussed three different sets of numbers. We are going to look at them again here now.

Rational numbers ($\mathbb{Q}$) are numbers that can be expressed as a fraction.

Integers ($\mathbb{Z}$) are whole positive and negative numbers, **including** zero. Since all whole numbers can be expressed as a fraction, integers are part of the rational numbers set.

Integers are a subset of rational numbers. In mathematical language, we say $\mathbb{Z} \subset \mathbb{Q}$.

Natural numbers ($\mathbb{N}$) are whole positive numbers, **excluding** zero.

Since integers are whole positive and negative numbers, natural numbers are part of the integer numbers set.

Since integers are part of the rational numbers set, natural numbers are also part of the rational numbers set.

Natural numbers are a subset of both integers and rational numbers. In mathematical language, we say $\mathbb{N} \subset \mathbb{Z}$ and $\mathbb{N} \subset \mathbb{Q}$.

If we put this all together, we get $\mathbb{N} \subset \mathbb{Z} \subset \mathbb{Q}$. This can be represented on a Venn diagram, as shown.

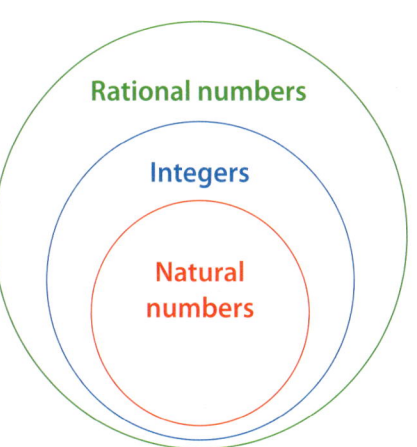

Worked example 2

Copy the Venn diagram shown.

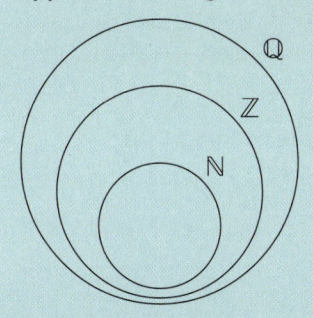

Put the numbers below in the correct position on the Venn diagram.
$4, \ 0, \ \frac{3}{4}, \ -7, -\frac{2}{3}, \ 9, \ -1$

Solution

Natural numbers: $\{4, 9\}$
positive whole numbers

Integers: $\{0, -7, -1, 4, 9\}$
negative and positive whole numbers

Rational numbers:
$\{\frac{3}{4}, -\frac{2}{3}, 0, -7, -1, 4, 9\}$
fractions, negative and positive whole numbers

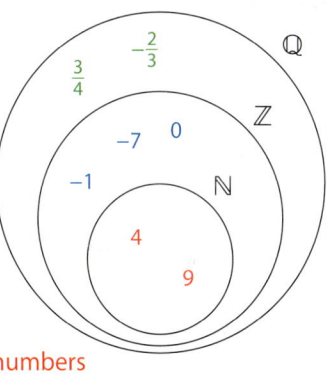

Practice questions 2·3

1. Copy the Venn diagram shown below four times and shade the following regions.
   (i) A
   (ii) B
   (iii) A∪B
   (iv) A∩B

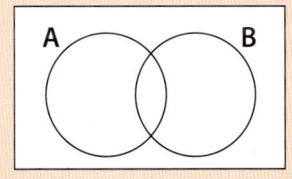

2. Use the Venn diagram shown to list the elements of the following sets.
   (i) A
   (ii) B
   (iii) A∩B
   (iv) A∪B
   (v) 𝕌

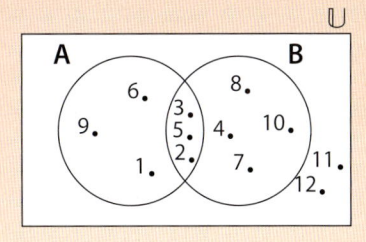

3. Use the Venn diagram shown to answer the following questions.

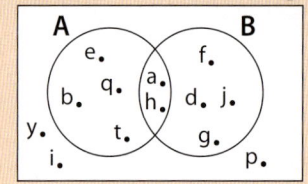

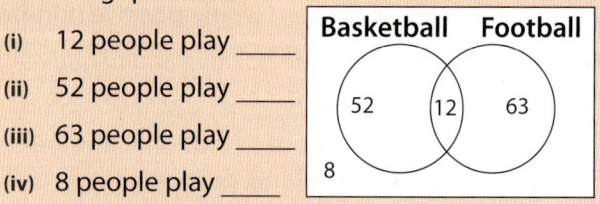

   (a) List the elements of the following sets.

   (i) A (ii) B (iii) U

   (b) Find:

   (i) #(A∪B) (ii) #(A∩B)

4. Copy the Venn diagrams given and put the people shown in the table in the correct position on the Venn diagram.

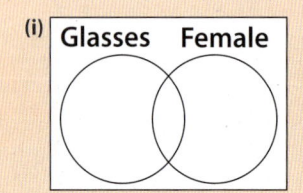

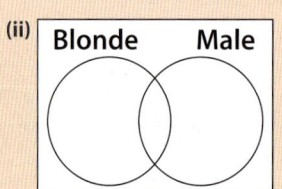

   | Jack | Katie | Sarah | Peter | Liz | Dean |

   (i) Glasses / Female

   (ii) Blonde / Male

5. Put the numbers shown below into the correct position on the Venn diagrams given.

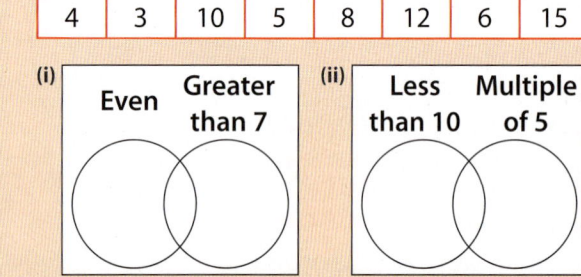

   | 4 | 3 | 10 | 5 | 8 | 12 | 6 | 15 |

   (i) Even / Greater than 7

   (ii) Less than 10 / Multiple of 5

6. Draw a Venn diagram to represent each of the following sets.

   (i) U = {1, 2, 3, 4, 5, 6}, A = {2, 4, 6}, B = {2, 3, 6}
   (ii) U = {1, 3, 5, 7, 9, 11}, A = {1, 5, 11}, B = {3, 9}
   (iii) U = {1, 2, 3, 4, 5, 6, 7}, A = {2, 3, 7}, B = {1, 2, 3, 4}
   (iv) U = {2, 4, 6, 8, 10, 12}, A = {8, 12}, B = {2, 6, 8, 10, 12}

7. A group of students were asked if they played basketball or football. The numbers shown in these sets represent the cardinal number (#) of the set.

   Sometimes, instead of showing every element in a set, we can just use the cardinal number (#) of the set.

   Use the Venn diagram shown to answer the following questions.

   (i) 12 people play _____
   (ii) 52 people play _____
   (iii) 63 people play _____
   (iv) 8 people play _____
   (v) How many people play only one of the two sports?
   (vi) How many students in total were asked?

8. The Venn diagram shows information about a group of children. The numbers shown in these sets represent the cardinal number (#) of the set.

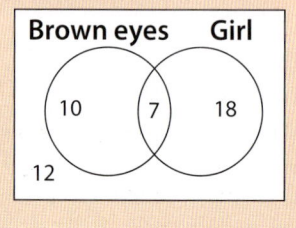

   (i) How many girls are in the group?
   (ii) How many brown eyed girls are in the group?
   (iii) How many boys are in the group?
   (iv) How many people are in the group?

9. Given A = {factors of 48} and B = {factors of 20}

   (i) List the elements of set A and set B.
   (ii) Draw a Venn diagram to represent A and B.
   (iii) Explain in words what the overlapping region means in this question.
   (iv) Use your Venn diagram to find the HCF of 20 and 48.

10. (a) Describe using set notation the shaded region shown in each of the Venn diagrams below.
    (b) Describe in words what the shaded region represents in each of the Venn diagrams below.

    (i) H, N (ii) H, N (iii) H, N

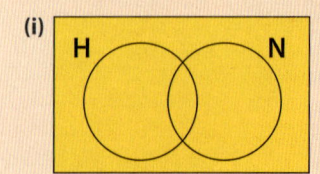

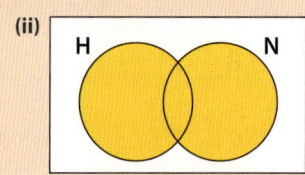

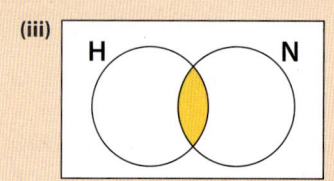

Linking Thinking 1

11. Given $\mathbb{U}$ = {natural numbers from 1 to 20},
    P = {odd numbers less than 20} and
    Q = {multiples of 3 less than 20}:

    (a) List the elements of:

    (i) P (ii) Q (iii) P∪Q (iv) P∩Q

    (b) Find:

    (i) #P (ii) #Q (iii) #P∪Q (iv) #P∩Q

    (c) Draw a Venn diagram to represent these sets.

12. Given $\mathbb{U}$ = {natural numbers less than 10},
    A = {prime numbers less than 10} and
    B = {even numbers less than 10}:

    (i) List the elements of set A.

    (ii) List the elements of set B.

    (iii) Draw a Venn diagram to represent these sets.

    (iv) List the elements of A∪B.

    (v) Find #(A∩B).

    (vi) Fiona says that A∩B is a subset of A. Do you agree with Fiona? Justify your answer.

13. Copy the Venn diagram shown.

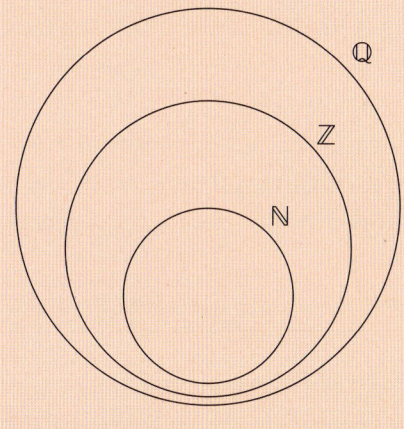

    Put the numbers in the list below in the correct position in the Venn diagram.

    $6, 0, \frac{3}{8}, -9, -\frac{4}{5}, 7, -3$

2·4 Chance

By the end of this section you should be able to:
- calculate the chance of something happening

In Maths, we often want to work out the chance (probability) that something happens.

Consider the set of musical instruments shown on the right.

If a musical instrument is chosen at random from this set, what is the chance that it will have strings?

There are eight instruments in the set. Four of the instruments have strings.

We can say that the chance of picking a stringed instrument is 4 out of 8.

We usually write the chance of something happening as a fraction, a decimal or a percentage.

So, the chance of picking a stringed instrument is $\frac{4}{8}$, which is $\frac{1}{2}$ as a fraction, 0·5 as a decimal or 50% as a percentage.

In the above example, we worked out the chance of picking a stringed instrument by dividing the number of times we could pick a stringed instrument (what we want) by the number of instruments (total number of options).

The formula to find the chance of something happening is:

Chance of something happening = $\dfrac{\text{number of times we get what we want}}{\text{total number of possible options}}$

The chance of something happening is always between 0% and 100%, or 0 and 1.

Converting from fractions to decimals and percentages

The chance of something happening is usually worked out as a fraction using the formula above. Some questions will also ask you to give your answer as a decimal or a percentage.

A percentage is 'out of 100', e.g. 17% = 17 out of 100, or $\frac{17}{100}$, or 0·17

Section A Introducing concepts and building skills   35

To convert a fraction to a decimal

A fraction is made up of one number over another number, e.g. $\frac{3}{4}$. You can say this as 'three-quarters' or 'three over four' or even '3 divided by 4'.

When one number is over another number, this means we must divide the top number by the bottom number.

In mathematical language, we must divide the numerator by the denominator.

> Does the shape of a fraction look familiar? It's the same as the symbol for division, ÷. The top dot stands in for the numerator, and the bottom dot stands in for the denominator.

Numerator
The top half of the fraction
The number of parts you have

A line separates the numerator and the denominator

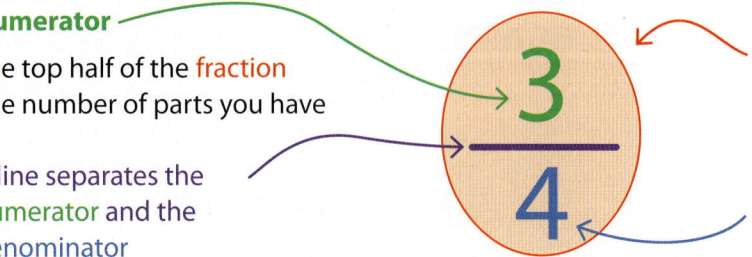

Fraction
The whole thing

Denominator
The bottom half of the fraction
The number of parts in a whole

$$\frac{3}{4}$$

To convert a fraction to a percentage

The easiest way to convert a fraction to a percentage is to multiply the fraction by 100%.

> Converting between fractions, decimals and percentages will be revisited in Unit 5.

Worked example 1

Convert the following fractions to (i) a decimal and (ii) a percentage.

(a) $\frac{2}{5}$ (b) $\frac{3}{4}$

Solution

(a) (i) $\frac{2}{5} = 2 \div 5 = 0\cdot 4$

   (ii) $\frac{2}{5} \times 100\%$
$= \frac{200}{5}$
$= 40\%$

(b) (i) $\frac{3}{4} = 3 \div 4 = 0\cdot 75$

   (ii) $\frac{3}{4} \times 100\%$
$= \frac{300}{4}$
$= 75\%$

Worked example 2

There are 24 students in a class: 18 boys and 6 girls. If a student is picked at random, find the chance that the student picked is:

(i)   a boy   (ii)   a girl

Give your answer as a fraction, a decimal and a percentage.

Solution

(i) Chance of picking a boy = $\frac{\text{number of times we get a boy}}{\text{total number of students in the class}}$
$= \frac{18}{24}$
$= \frac{3}{4}$
$= 0\cdot 75$ as a decimal
$= 75\%$ as a percentage

(ii) Chance of picking a girl = $\frac{\text{number of times we get a girl}}{\text{total number of students in the class}}$
$= \frac{6}{24}$
$= \frac{1}{4}$
$= 0\cdot 25$ as a decimal
$= 25\%$ as a percentage

Linking Thinking 1

Practice questions 2·4

1. If a letter is picked at random from the Venn diagram shown, what is the chance that it will be an element of …?

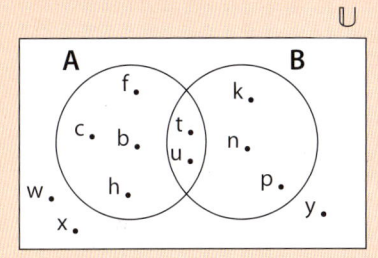

   (i)   set A
   (ii) set B only
   (iii) neither set A or set B
   (iv) A∪B
   (v)   A∩B

   Give all your answers as a fraction, a decimal and a percentage.

2. If a number is picked at random from the Venn diagram shown, what is the chance it will be …?

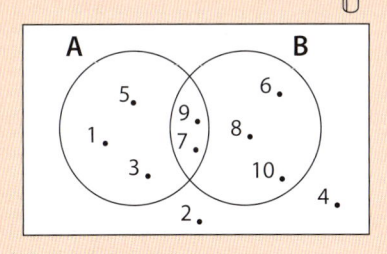

   (i)   an odd number
   (ii) an even number
   (iii) a prime number
   (iv) in either set A or set B
   (v)   greater than 7
   (vi) less than 4

   Give all your answers as a fraction, a decimal and a percentage.

3. If a number is picked at random from the Venn diagram shown, what is the chance is will be …?

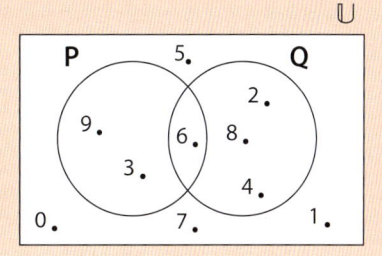

   (i)   a multiple of 2
   (ii) a multiple of 3
   (iii) a factor of 6
   (iv) not a natural number
   (v)   a prime number greater than 5
   (vi) evenly divisible by 2

   Give all your answers as a fraction, a decimal and a percentage.

4. $\mathbb{U}$ = {numbers between 1 and 20 inclusive},
   X = {prime numbers less than 20} and
   Y = {even numbers less than or equal to 20}

   (a) Draw a Venn diagram to represent the sets above.
   (b) If a number is picked at random from the Venn diagram, what is the chance it will be …?

   (i)   even
   (ii) odd
   (iii) even and prime
   (iv) odd and prime
   (v)   a multiple of 5
   (vi) divisible by 3

   Give all your answers as a fraction, a decimal and a percentage.

5. A = {letters is the word EXAMINATION} and
   B = {letters in the word MATHEMATICS}

   (a) Draw a Venn diagram to represent the sets above.
   (b) If a letter is picked at random, what is the chance it will be …?

   (i)   a vowel
   (ii) a consonant
   (iii) in the word MATHS
   (iv) in the word EXAMS

Revision questions

2A Core skills

1. Explain the following terms in your own words.
   - (i) Factor
   - (ii) Multiple
   - (iii) Prime number
   - (iv) Natural number
   - (v) Integer
   - (vi) Rational number

2. | 27 | 13 | 9 | 10 | 48 | 8 |

   From the list of numbers above, find:
   - (i) an odd number
   - (ii) an even number
   - (iii) a factor of 52
   - (iv) a multiple of 4
   - (v) a prime number
   - (vi) two numbers whose sum is prime

3. Find the prime factors of each of the following numbers.
   - (i) 30
   - (ii) 56
   - (iii) 81

4. Find (a) the highest common factor (HCF) and (b) the lowest common multiple (LCM) of each of the following pairs of numbers.
   - (i) 20 and 24
   - (ii) 54 and 90

5. A = {1, 2, 3, 5, 8} and B = {2, 4, 5, 7}
   - (i) List the elements of A∪B.
   - (ii) List the elements of A∩B.
   - (iii) What is #(A∪B)?

6. Copy the Venn diagrams below and shade the specified region in each.
   - (i) A∪B 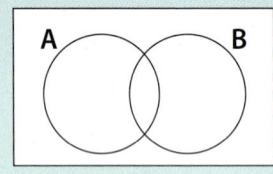
   - (ii) A∩B

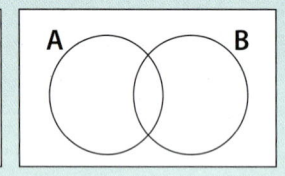

7. Use the Venn diagram shown to list the elements of the following.
   - (i) $\mathbb{U}$ 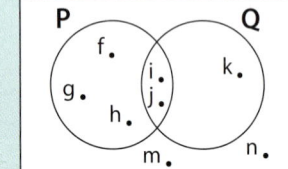
   - (ii) P
   - (iii) Q
   - (iv) P∪Q
   - (v) P∩Q

8. $\mathbb{U}$ = {1, 3, 5, 7, 9, 11, 13, 15, 17, 19}
   A = {1, 3, 5, 7, 13} and B = {1, 3, 9, 11, 15}
   - (a) Draw a Venn diagram to represent these sets.
   - (b) Use your Venn diagram to find the following.
     - (i) #(A∪B)
     - (ii) #(A∩B)
     - (iii) #B
     - (iv) #A

9. The Venn diagram shows the number of students who play rugby (R) or tennis (T). 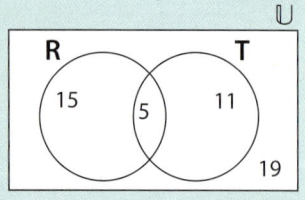
   Use the information on the diagram to answer the questions.
   - (a) How many students were questioned?
   - (b) A student was picked at random. What is the chance that the student played …?
     - (i) both tennis and rugby
     - (ii) rugby only
     - (iii) neither tennis nor rugby

   Give your answers as a fraction, a decimal and a percentage.

2B Taking it FURTHER

1. $\mathbb{U}$ = {positive integers from 1 to 20},
   P = {multiples of 2 less than 20} and
   Q = {multiples of 4 less than 20}
   - (a) List the elements of
     - (i) P and Q
     - (ii) P∪Q
     - (iii) P∩Q
   - (b) Draw a Venn diagram to represent these sets.
   - (c) Is P⊂Q? Justify your answer.
   - (d) Investigate whether
     #(P∪Q) = #(P) + #(Q) − #(P∩Q)
   - (e) If a number is selected at random from these sets, what is the chance it is a prime number?

38 Linking Thinking 1

2. Copy the table below and put a tick (✓) in the correct box in each row to show whether each statement is always true, sometimes true, or never true.

Statement		Tick **one** box only for each statement		
		Always true	Sometimes true	Never true
(i)	If A∪B = ∅, then A = ∅ and B = ∅			
(ii)	If A∩B = ∅, then A = ∅ or B = ∅ or both A and B are empty sets			
(iii)	A∩∅ = A			
(iv)	A rational number is also an integer			

3. (i) Set A = {m, p} has two elements. Given that it has four subsets, list these subsets.

(ii) Set B = {k, j, n}. How many subsets does set B have? List these subsets.

4. Copy the table below and put a tick (✓) in the correct box in each row to show whether each statement is always true, sometimes true, or never true.

Statement		Tick **one** box only, for each statement		
		Always true	Sometimes true	Never true
(i)	The intersection and union of two sets contain the same elements.			
(ii)	If something is in set A and B then it is also in A∩B.			
(iii)	If set A contains five elements, #A = 8.			
(iv)	If something is in set A it is also in A∪B.			

5. Copy the Venn diagram shown opposite.

(a) Put the numbers below in the correct position in the Venn diagram.

$-3, 8, 0, \frac{3}{4}, -11, 6, \frac{-7}{9}, 9, -2, 0.25$

(b) If a number is picked at random from this Venn diagram, what is the chance it will be …?

(i) a natural number

(ii) an integer

(iii) a rational number

6. A green light flashes every 3 seconds. A blue light flashes every 8 seconds. A yellow light flashes every 11 seconds. They all start flashing at the same time.

After how many seconds will they next all flash at the same time?

7. Sarah sells bags of different kinds of homemade chocolates. She made €27 selling bags of milk chocolates, €18 selling white chocolates, and €45 selling dark chocolates. Each bag of chocolates costs the same.

What is the most money that Sarah could have charged for each bag of chocolates?

8. Hannah thinks of two numbers.

The highest common factor (HCF) is 6.

The lowest common multiple (LCM) is a multiple of 24.

Write down two possibilities for Hannah's numbers.

9. Here are some facts about a number.
- It is a common factor of 288 and 360
- It is a common multiple of 4 and 6
- It is larger than 25

Find the two possible numbers that it could be.

Now that you have completed the unit, revisit the

Something to think about …

question posed at the start of this unit.

Unit 3

Points, lines and angles

Topics covered within this unit:

3·1 Points, lines, line segments and rays

3·2 Parallel and perpendicular lines

3·3 Angles

The Learning Outcomes covered in this unit are contained in the following sections:
GT.3a GT.3b

Key words
Plane
Point
Ray
Line segment
Midpoint
Construction
Arc
Intersect
Parallel
Perpendicular
Right angle
Bisector
Angle
Supplementary angles

Something to think about ...

KEY SKILLS

The selection of 360 as the number of degrees in a circle was probably based on the fact that 360 is approximately the number of days in a year. Its use is often said to originate from the methods of the ancient Babylonians.

The Babylonians used the bones on four fingers of one hand to count to 12, and then the five fingers on the other hand to count to $12 \times 5 = 60$

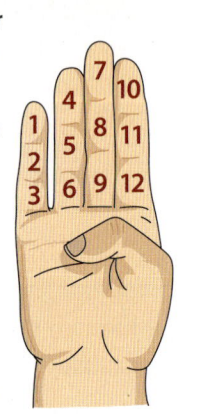

From this, we derive the modern-day usage of 60 seconds in a minute, 60 minutes in an hour, and 360 degrees in a circle.

A degree, usually denoted by ° (the degree symbol), is a measurement of plane angle, representing $\frac{1}{360}$ of a full rotation.

Another motivation for choosing the number 360 is that it is easily divisible: 360 has 24 divisors (including 1 and 360), including every number from 1 to 10 (except 7).

What number could have been used which is divisible by every number between 1 and 10?

3·1 Points, lines, line segments and rays

By the end of this section you should:

- understand what a plane, point, line, line segment, ray, midpoint and length of a line are
- understand what a construction is in Mathematics
- be familiar with the instruments used in constructions in Mathematics
- be able to construct a line segment of a given length

A 'plane' (e.g. the Cartesian plane) is a flat surface like the top of the desk, or the teacher's board, except that it goes on and on forever in every direction.
A word we use for 'going on forever' is infinity, and the symbol for infinity is ∞.

> A **plane** is a flat surface that goes on forever in every direction.

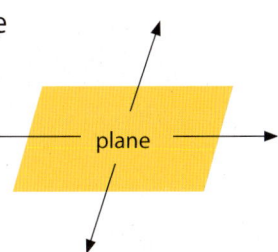

Discuss and discover

KEY SKILLS

(i) Make a list of what you already know about lines.
(ii) Working in pairs, find the minimum number of points you would need if you want to construct (draw) a line.
(iii) How did you solve this problem?
(iv) How can you be sure you have found the minimum number of points?

Line

> A **point** is an exact location in a space or on a plane. A point is represented by an italic uppercase letter.

There is exactly one straight line through any two points.

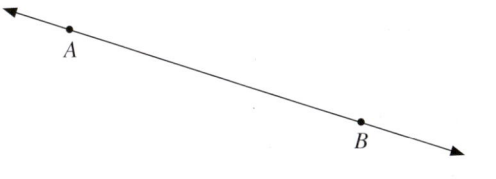

We denote (represent) a line as AB or BA.

The arrows indicate that the line extends to infinity (∞) in both directions.

Ray

> **A ray** is a line that starts at one point and continues to infinity in one direction.

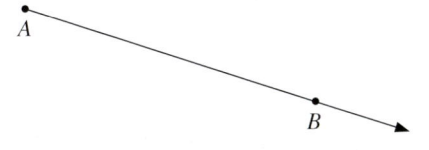

The image above shows a ray that starts at A and goes through point B and extends to infinity (∞). This ray is denoted by $[AB$. The square bracket shows there is one endpoint and it extends to infinity in the opposite direction.

The arrow at the end shows that the ray continues to infinity in that direction.

Line segment

> A **line segment** is a part of a line. It has two end points.

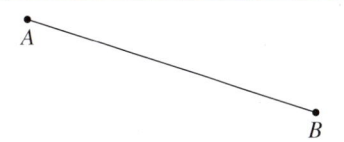

A line segment is denoted by $[AB]$ or $[BA]$. The square brackets show there are two endpoints.

A line segment is the shortest distance between two points. It has a fixed length, so there are no arrows at the ends.

A line segment is always a straight line.

Length of a line segment

The length of a line segment is the distance between the two end points of a line segment.

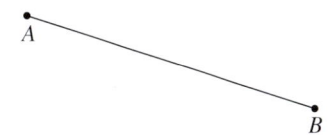

The distance from A to B is equal to the distance from B to A.

The notation used to describe the distance between points A and B is $|AB|$ or $|BA|$.

If point C lies on the line segment between point A and point B, then $|AB| = |AC| + |CB|$

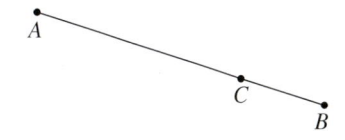

Section A Introducing concepts and building skills

Midpoint of a line segment

> The **midpoint** of a line segment is the point that divides it into two parts of the same length.

$|AC| = |CB|$

The midpoint is therefore equal to $\frac{|AB|}{2}$

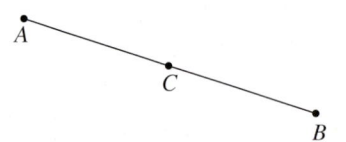

Constructions

> A **construction** is the drawing of various shapes, lines and angles using a compass, straight edge, ruler, protractor and set square.

When you're drawing a construction:
- Always use a sharp pencil
- Always leave all lines or marks you make during the construction. **Do not** erase these construction marks and lines.

Construction tools

Straight edge

Compass

A straight edge is simply a guide for the pencil when drawing straight lines. In most cases, you will use a ruler for this, since it is the most likely to be available.

A compass is a drawing instrument used for drawing circles and curves.

It has two legs – one with a point and the other with a pencil.

Using a compass

1. Hold the compass firmly at the top and place the pointed end of the compass on the paper.
2. Slowly rotate the compass around so that the pencil begins drawing the circle or curve. Do not apply any pressure to the pencil or the width of your circle will change.
3. When the drawing is complete, lift the compass from the paper. Set the compass aside in a safe place, taking care not to touch the sharp point.

Protractor

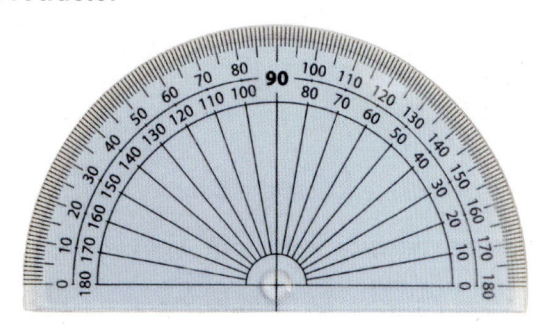

Set square

Protractors are used to measure angles.

Protractors usually have two sets of numbers going in opposite directions.

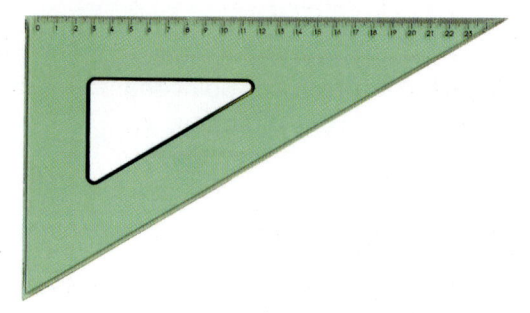

A set square is used to provide a straight edge at a right angle (90° angle), 60°, 45° or 30° to an existing line.

Constructing a line segment

In Maths, we often need to construct a line segment of a specified length.
In this example, we are constructing a line segment that is 10 cm long.

1 Draw a line of any length. Mark a point at the end of the line and label it A. This is the starting point of the line.

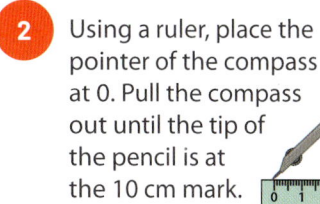

A

2 Using a ruler, place the pointer of the compass at 0. Pull the compass out until the tip of the pencil is at the 10 cm mark.

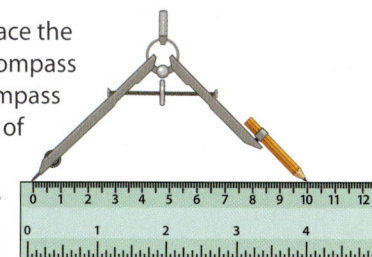

3 Place the pointer of the compass at A and mark an arc on the line with the pencil point. Mark the point where the arc and the line intersect as B.

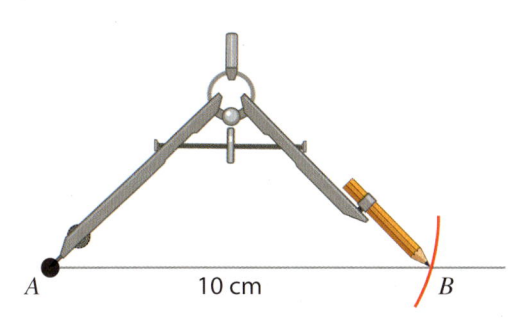

4 $[AB]$ is the required line segment of length 10 cm.

A   10 cm   B

An **arc** is any smooth curve joining two points.

If lines or arcs **intersect**, this means they cross over at a point.

Worked example 1

Indicate whether each of the coloured items below are line segments, rays or lines.
Give a reason for your answer and show how the construction is written in mathematical notation.

Solution

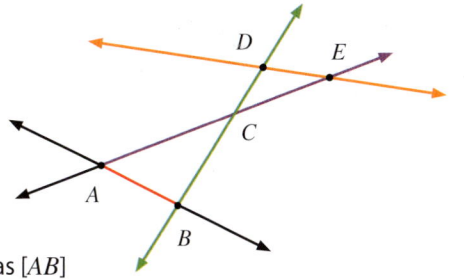

Green is a line, as it extends to infinity (∞) in both directions, indicated by the arrows at the ends, written as BD

Orange is a line, as it extends to infinity (∞) in both directions, indicated by the arrows at the ends, written as DE

Purple is a ray. It starts at point A and extends to infinity (∞) in the direction of E. It is written as $[AE$

Red is a line segment, as it ends at point A and point B. It is written as $[AB]$

Black are three rays. They all start at a point and extend to infinity (∞). They are written as $[A, [A, [B$

Worked example 2

Name (using symbols and letters) three line segments using the diagram on the right.

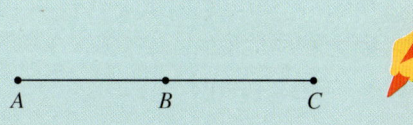

A   B   C

Solution

A line segment is a line that starts at a point and ends at a second point. In this case, three line segments within this diagram are:

Line segment $[AB]$ or $[BA]$ Line segment $[AC]$ or $[CA]$ Line segment $[BC]$ or $[CB]$

Section A Introducing concepts and building skills

Worked example 3

(a) Construct a line segment [XY] that has a length of 80 mm.

1 cm = 10 mm

(b) Using only a ruler, find the midpoint of the line segment [XY] and mark it T.

(c) Find (using a ruler):

　(i)　|XT|　　　　(ii)　|TY|　　　　(iii)　|TY| + |XT|

Solution

(a) Using a straight edge and compass, construct the line segment [XY] as outlined in Construction 8.

(b) Using a ruler, measure a distance 40 mm from the point X and mark this point as T. This is the midpoint of the line segment [XY].

(c) (i)　|XT| = 40 mm

　　(ii)　|TY| = 40 mm

　　(iii)　|TY| + |XT| = 40 mm + 40 mm

　　　　|TY| + |XT| = 80 mm

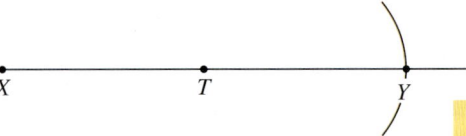

The diagram here is not to scale.

Not to scale means the diagram is **not full size**. It's scaled down.

Practice questions 3·1

1. How many points are necessary to draw a straight line?

2. Label each of the following drawings as a point, line, ray, line segment or none of these.

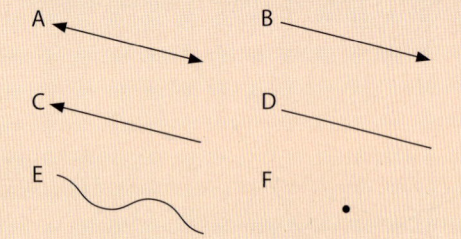

   A　　B　　C　　D　　E　　F

3. (i) What is the word for a straight path that goes to ∞ (infinity) in both directions?

   (ii) What is the word for a part of a line with two endpoints?

   (iii) What is the word for a part of a line that has one endpoint and goes to infinity in one direction?

   (iv) What is a point?

4. What word is used to describe the orange parts in this diagram?

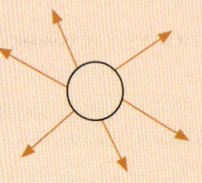

5. Using the diagram below:

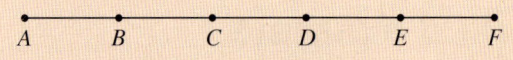

   A　　B　　C　　D　　E　　F

   (i) List all the points marked.

   (ii) Using letters and symbols, list ten line segments contained in the diagram.

6. Sketch a drawing of the following using a ruler and pencil only (diagrams should not exceed 6 cm).

   (i) [AB]　　(iii) [EF　　(v) [TU]

   (ii) AB　　(iv) Z

7. (i) Construct a line segment [AB] of 8 cm.

   (ii) Using only a ruler, find the midpoint of [AB] and mark it M.

8. (i) Construct a line segment [XZ] of 12 cm.

   (ii) Using only a ruler, find the midpoint of [XZ] and mark it T.

9. (i) Construct [XY] if |XY| = 100 mm

   (ii) Using only a ruler, find the midpoint of [XY] and mark it M.

Linking Thinking 1

10. (i) Construct [MN] if |MN| = 88 mm.

(ii) Using only a ruler, find the midpoint of [MN] and mark it T.

11. (i) Construct [PQ] if |PQ| = 10·2 cm.

(ii) Using only a ruler, find the midpoint of [PQ] and mark it M.

12. A torch is shown below.

In your opinion, which of the following is the best description of the light produced by this torch?

(a) A line

(b) A line segment

(c) A ray

Give a reason for your answer.

3·2 Parallel and perpendicular lines

By the end of this section you should:
- understand what is meant by parallel and perpendicular lines, and perpendicular bisectors
- be able to construct parallel and perpendicular lines, and perpendicular bisectors
- be able to identify situations where parallel and perpendicular lines appear in the world around us.

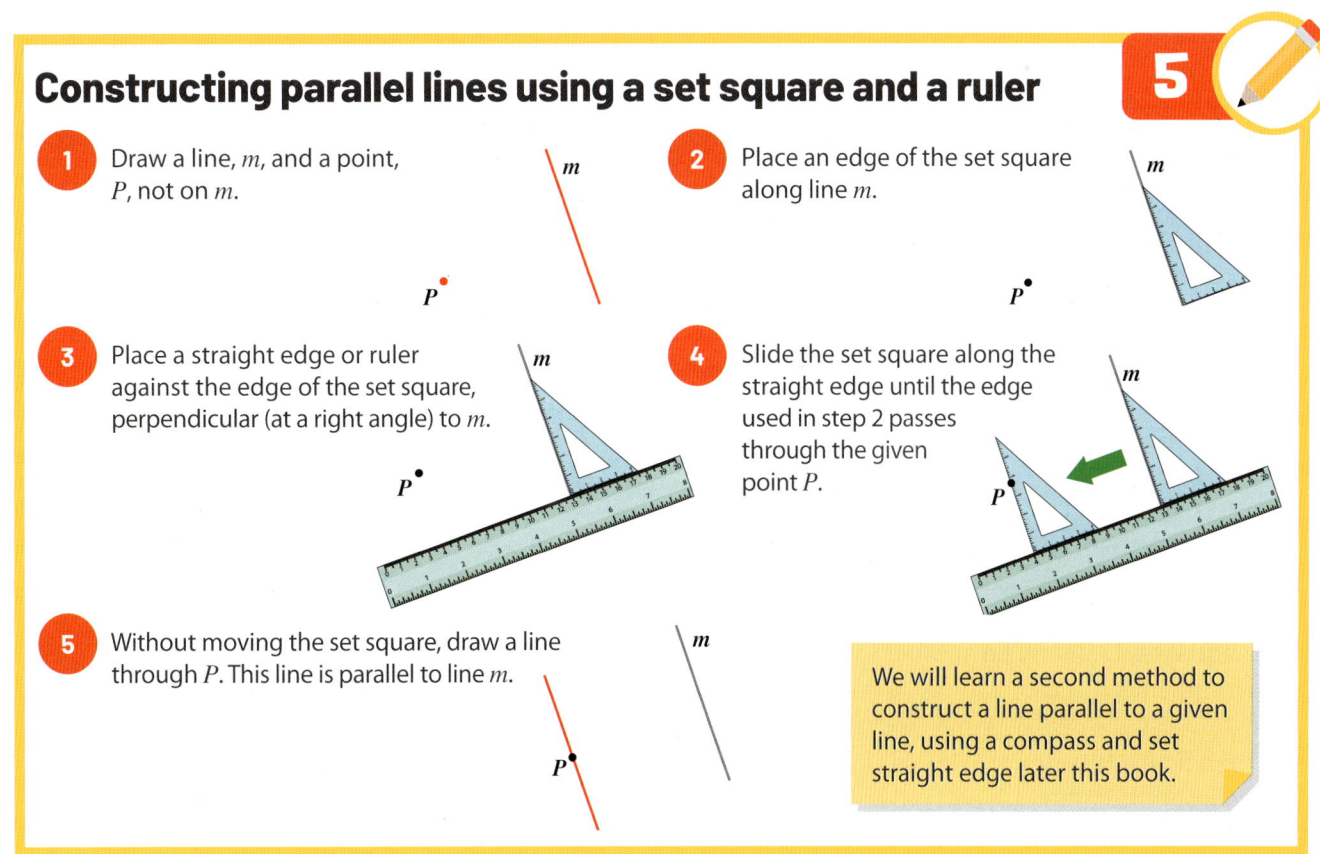

Parallel lines

> Lines are **parallel** if they are always the same distance apart, and will never meet.

To show that two lines are **parallel**, we can use points on each of the lines and the **symbol** ∥

For example, to show the two lines are parallel, AB ∥ CD

Or, on a diagram, arrows can be used (in red below).

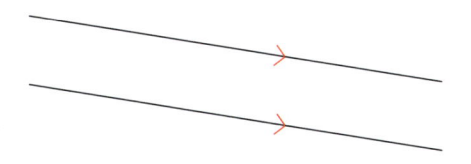

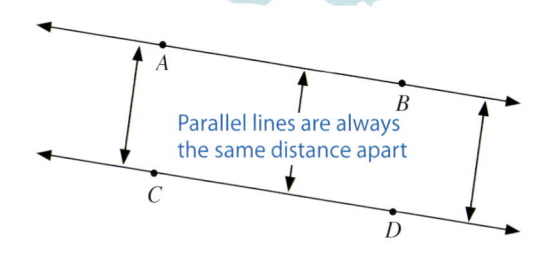

Parallel lines are always the same distance apart

Constructing parallel lines using a set square and a ruler

1 Draw a line, m, and a point, P, not on m.

2 Place an edge of the set square along line m.

3 Place a straight edge or ruler against the edge of the set square, perpendicular (at a right angle) to m.

4 Slide the set square along the straight edge until the edge used in step 2 passes through the given point P.

5 Without moving the set square, draw a line through P. This line is parallel to line m.

We will learn a second method to construct a line parallel to a given line, using a compass and set straight edge later this book.

Section A Introducing concepts and building skills

Perpendicular lines

Two lines are **perpendicular** if they intersect like a perfect T or cross. This is also known as a **right angle**.

A **right angle** is an angle of 90°, as in a corner of a square.

To show that two lines are perpendicular we can use points on each of the lines and the symbol ⊥

So, to show the two given lines are perpendicular, we say $AB \perp CD$

Symbols used to show a right angle (90°) are ∟ or □

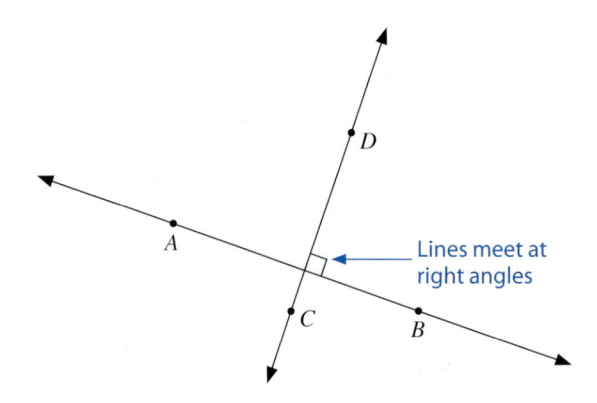

Lines meet at right angles

Constructing perpendicular lines using a compass and a ruler

1 Draw a line, l, and mark a point P on l.

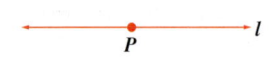

2 Place your compass point on P. Keeping the compass width fixed, draw two arcs on l either side of P.

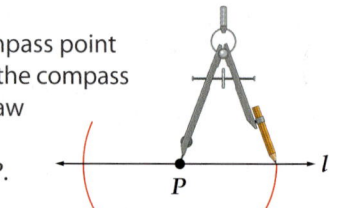

3 Increase the width of the compass a little bit. Place the compass point where the arc crossed the line on the right side and make a small arc above the line l.

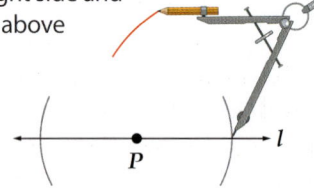

4 Without changing the width of the compass, place the compass point where the arc crossed the line on the left side of P. Draw another arc such that the two arcs intersect.

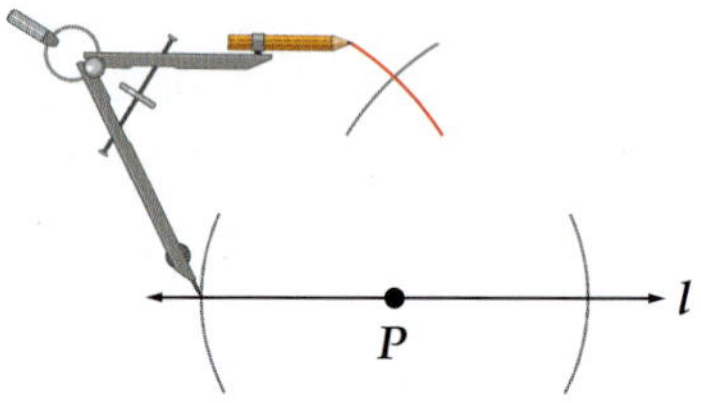

5 With your straight edge, connect the intersection of the two small arcs to point P. This new line is perpendicular to the given line and passes through the point P.

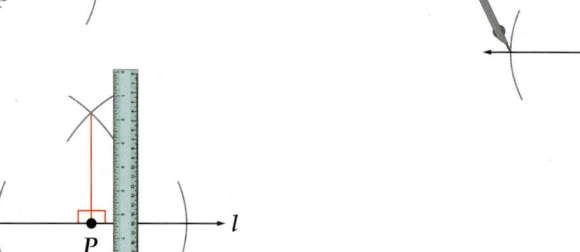

Perpendicular bisector of a line segment

A bisector is something that cuts an object into two equal parts. It can be applied to angles and line segments.

A perpendicular bisector of a line segment $[AB]$ is a line perpendicular to $[AB]$ and passing through the midpoint of $[AB]$.

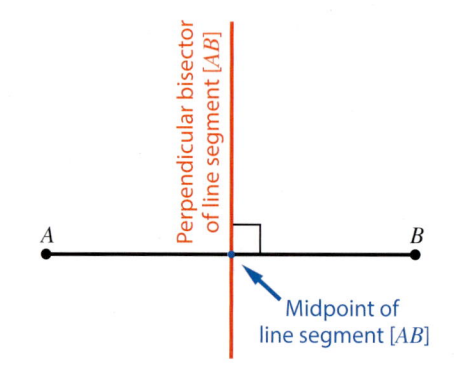

Perpendicular bisector of line segment $[AB]$

Midpoint of line segment $[AB]$

Linking Thinking 1

Constructing a perpendicular bisector using a compass and a ruler

1. Draw a line segment [AB]. Place the compass point at A. Use a compass setting that is greater than half of the length of [AB]. Draw an arc.

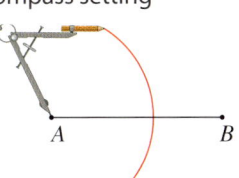

2. Keep the same compass setting. Place the compass point at B. Draw an arc such that it intersects the first arc at two points.

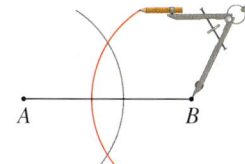

3. Draw a line through the two points of intersection.

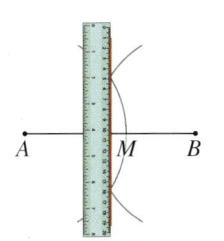

4. Mark the right angle on the diagram. This line is the perpendicular bisector of [AB]. It passes through M, the midpoint of [AB]. Therefore, |AM| = |MB|

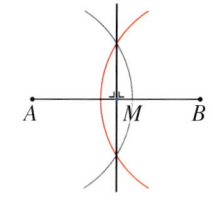

Worked example 4

State whether the following lines are parallel, perpendicular or neither. Give a reason for your answer and indicate how it is written in mathematical language (where possible).

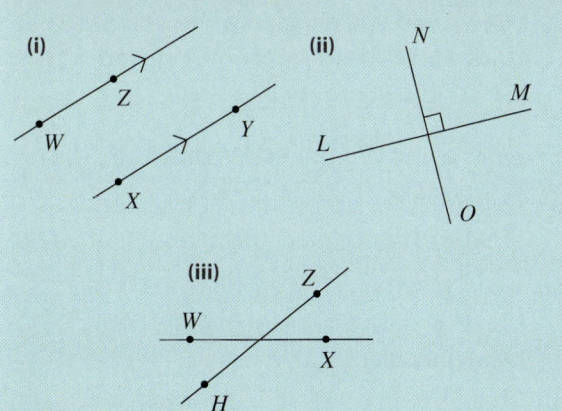

(i) (ii) (iii)

Solution

(i) Parallel – the lines are equal distance apart along their entire length. This is written as $WZ \parallel XY$ in mathematical language.

(ii) Perpendicular lines – they meet at a 90° angle (at a right angle). This is written as $NO \perp LM$ in mathematical language.

(iii) The lines WX and HZ are neither perpendicular nor parallel.

Worked example 5

Using the map opposite, find:
(i) one street that is perpendicular to Hope Street
(ii) one street that is parallel to Hope Street.

In each case, give a reason for your answer.

Solution

(i) Hope Street is perpendicular to Wallace Street because they meet at a right angle (90°). I verified this using a set square.

(ii) Hope Street is parallel to Whitby Street, as they are an equal distance apart along their length. I verified this using a ruler.

Note: There are several correct answers for both parts (i) and (ii).

Section A Introducing concepts and building skills   47

Practice questions 3.2

1. State whether the following lines are parallel, perpendicular, or neither. Give a reason for each answer, and express the relationship between the lines in mathematical language, using symbols and numbers where possible.

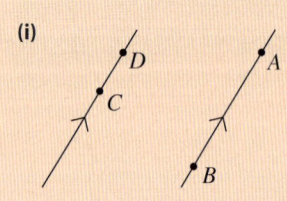

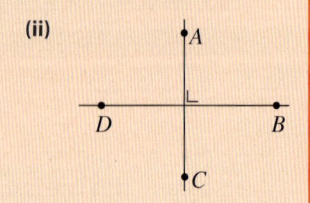

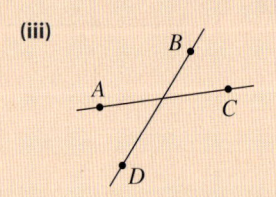

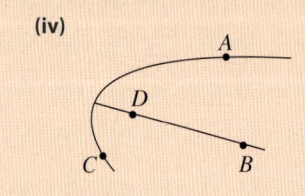

   (i), (ii), (iii), (iv)

2. (i) Draw a line segment [MN] of length 10 cm. Mark a point 5 cm anywhere directly above this line, and label it Q.

   (ii) Construct a line parallel to MN which passes through Q.

   (iii) How could you confirm the line you have drawn is parallel to [MN]?

3. (i) Draw a line segment [XY] of length 120 mm using only a ruler. Mark a point 70 mm anywhere directly above this line, and label it W.

   (ii) Construct a line parallel to [XY] which passes through W.

   (iii) How could you confirm the line you have drawn is parallel to [XY]?

4. (i) Draw a line segment [AB] of length 9 cm using only a ruler. Mark a point 4.5 cm from one end of this line, and label it Q.

   (ii) Construct a line perpendicular to [AB] at point Q.

   (iii) How could you confirm the line you have drawn is perpendicular to [AB]? *(Hint: use a set square)*

5. (i) Draw a line segment [XY] of length 100 mm. Mark a point 5.5 cm from one end of this line, and label this point N.

   (ii) Construct a line perpendicular to [XY] at point N.

   (iii) How could you confirm the line you have drawn is perpendicular to [XY]?

6. (i) Draw a line segment [PQ] of length 85 mm. Mark a point 4.7 cm anywhere directly above this line, and label it A.

   (ii) Construct a line parallel to PQ which passes through A.

   (iii) How could you confirm the line you have drawn is parallel to [PQ]?

7. (i) Draw a line segment [PQ] of length 9 cm.

   (ii) Construct the perpendicular bisector of [PQ] and hence mark the midpoint of [PQ].

   (iii) How could you check the line you have drawn is both a bisector of [PQ] and perpendicular to [PQ]?

8. (i) Draw a line segment [MN] of length 10 cm.

   (ii) Construct the perpendicular bisector of [MN] and hence mark the midpoint of [MN].

   (iii) How could you check the line you have drawn is both a bisector of [MN] and perpendicular to [MN]?

9. (i) Construct [AB] if |AB| = 11 cm.

   (ii) Construct the perpendicular bisector of [AB] and hence mark the midpoint of [AB].

   (iii) How could your check the line you have drawn is both a bisector of [AB] and perpendicular to [AB]?

10. The blue line in the circle below is the radius of the circle and the red line touches the circle once and only once. Are the lines perpendicular?

11. The map below is of Chelsea, which is a part of Manhattan in New York, USA.

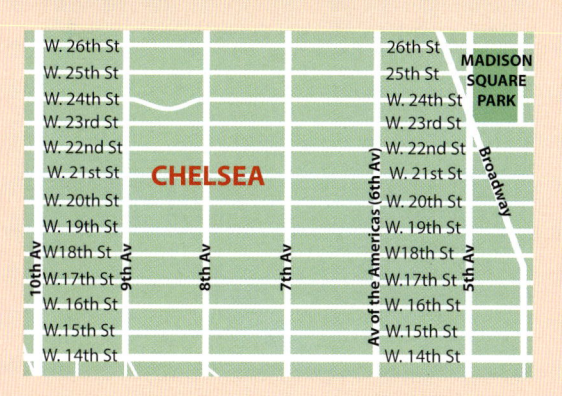

    (i) List three pairs of streets that are parallel.
    (ii) List three pairs of streets that are perpendicular to each other.
    (iii) List one pair of streets which are neither parallel nor perpendicular to each other.

12. The photo below shows the lines on an airport runway.

    (i) Are the rows of white lines parallel, perpendicular, or neither?
    (ii) When a plane is rolling on this runway, does it normally roll parallel or perpendicular to the white lines shown on this image?

13. The photo below shows steel train tracks fixed to wooden planks known as 'sleepers'.

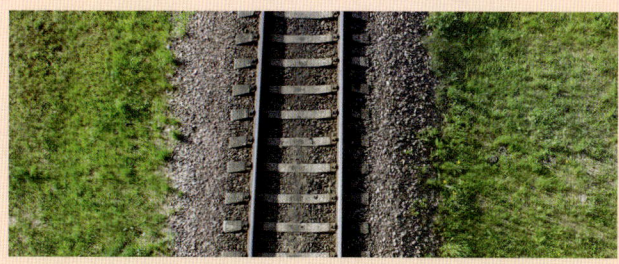

    (i) Are the sleepers parallel or perpendicular to the train tracks?
    (ii) Are the sleepers parallel or perpendicular to each other?

14. Opposite is an image from behind the goal posts on a GAA pitch. The two vertical posts are referred to as the uprights and the horizontal bar is referred to as the cross bar.

    (i) Are the two uprights parallel or perpendicular to each other?
    (ii) Is the crossbar parallel or perpendicular to the uprights?

15. Below is a diagram which gives the various markings on a pitch used for hurling and Gaelic football.

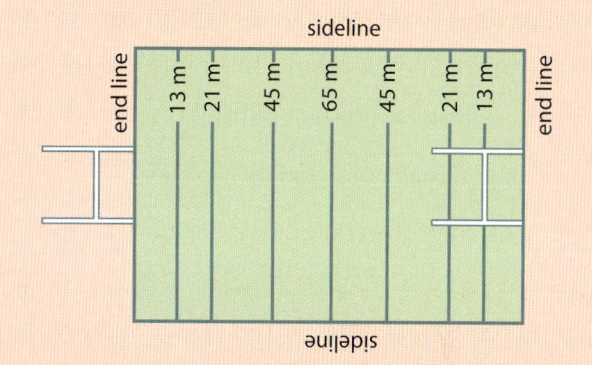

    (i) Which vertical line in this diagram represents the midpoint of the side lines? Give a reason for your answer.
    (ii) Are the side lines parallel or perpendicular to the end lines?
    (iii) What is the total length of the pitch from end line to end line?

16. Examine the photo opposite, which shows Liberty Hall in Dublin.

    (i) There is a lift inside this building that travels vertically up through the building. As the lift rises up through the building, is its path parallel or perpendicular to the street below?
    (ii) Give three examples of things that are parallel which you might see in everyday life.
    (iii) Give three examples of things that are perpendicular which you might see in everyday life.

Section A Introducing concepts and building skills

3.3 Angles

By the end of this section you should:
- understand what is meant by angle and how it is measured
- be able to name the parts of an angle and label angles using letters
- be able to use a protractor
- be able to construct an angle of given degrees
- be able to construct an angle bisector and understand what it does to an angle

An angle is the figure formed by two rays, called the arms of the angle, sharing a common endpoint, called the vertex of the angle.

The symbol used for an angle is ∠

Parts of an angle

- The two straight sides are called the **arms**.
- The point where the arms meet is called the **vertex**.
- The angle is the amount of rotation (turn) between the arms.

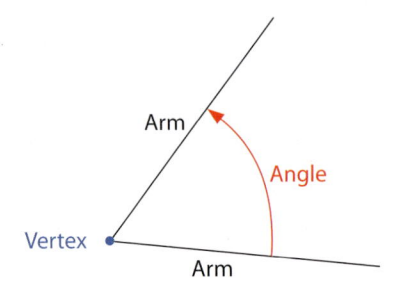

There are two main ways to label angles.

1. You can give the angle a name, usually a capital letter like A or B, or a Greek letter like α (alpha) or θ (theta).

2. You can use the three letters on the shape that define the angle, with the **middle letter** being the vertex (the angle itself).

For example, in the given diagram, the angle θ could also be called ∠ACB or ∠BCA.

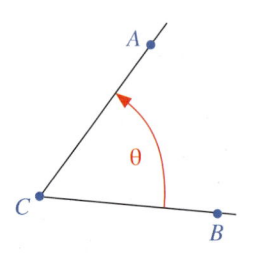

Degrees

Angles are measured in degrees. The symbol for degrees is a little circle °.

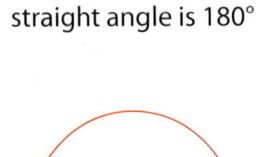

| A quarter circle or a right angle is 90° | A half circle or a straight angle is 180° | Three quarters of a circle is 270° | The full circle is 360° |

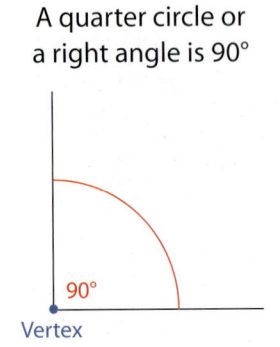

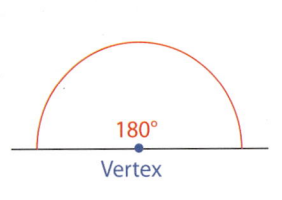

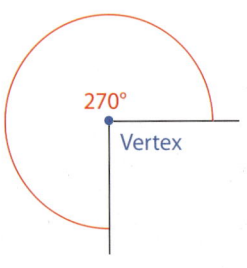

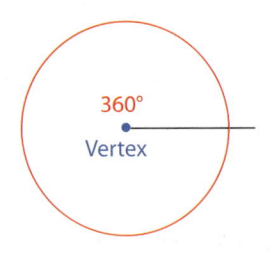

Types of angles

Null angle 0°

Ordinary angles – less than 180°

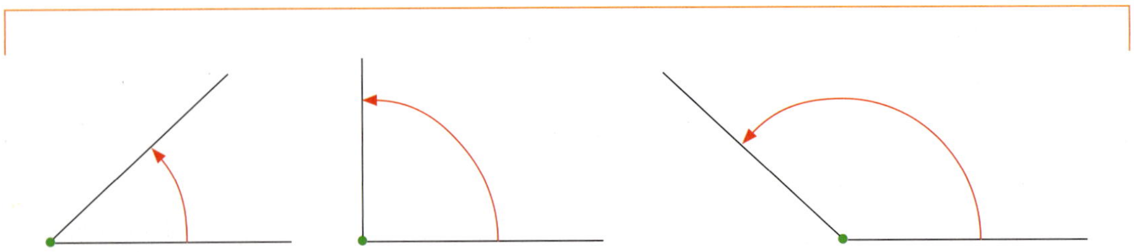

Acute angle is less than 90°   Right angle is 90° angle   Obtuse angle is between 90° and 180°

50 Linking Thinking 1

Reflex angles – between 180° and 360°

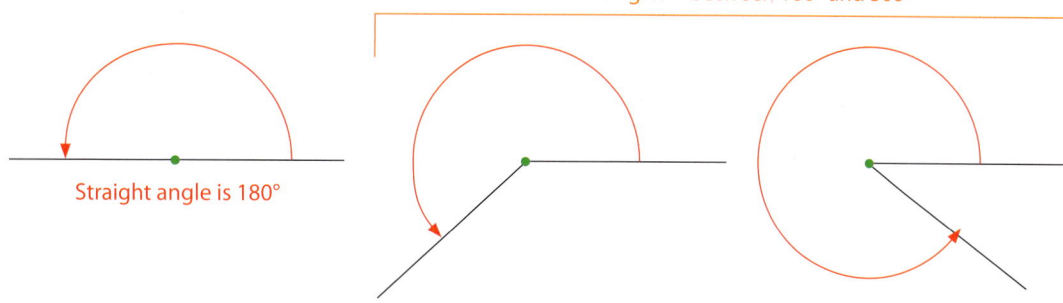

Straight angle is 180°

Supplementary angles add together (sum) to make 180°.

Supplementary angles

65°

115°

$|\angle BDC| + |\angle ADC| = 180°$

Supplementary angles do not have to be beside each other.

Measuring an angle with a protractor

1. Place the midpoint of the protractor on the **vertex** of the angle.

2. Line up one arm of the angle with the zero line of the protractor (where you see 0).

3. Read the degrees where the arm crosses the number scale.

In this example, one arm of the angle lines up with the 0 on the **lower** set of numbers, so we need to read the **lower** set of numbers.

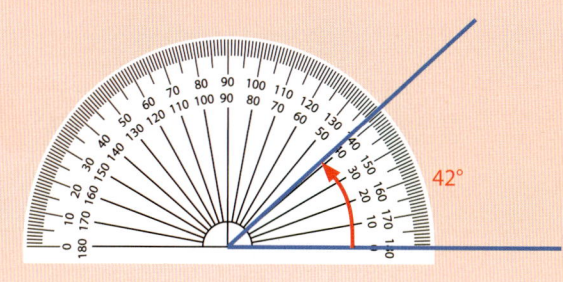

In this example, one arm of the angle lines up with the 0 on of the **upper** set of numbers, so we need to read the **upper** set of numbers.

A protractor has two sets of numbers. One set goes from 0° to 180°, the other set from 180° to 0°. Place it so that one side of the angle lines up with one of the zeros, and read that set of numbers.

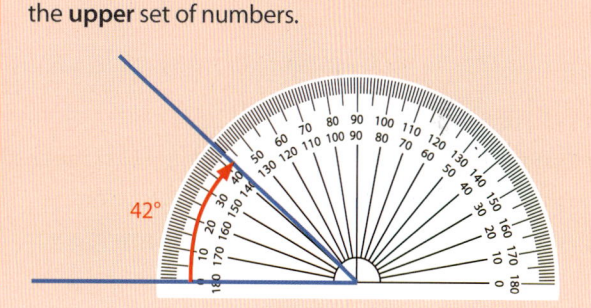

42°

42°

Constructing an angle using a protractor

We will construct an angle of 55° on the given ray [AB.

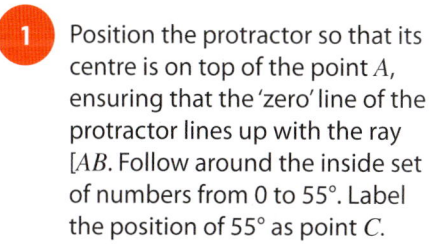

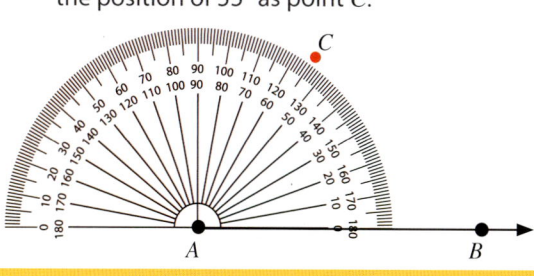

1. Position the protractor so that its centre is on top of the point A, ensuring that the 'zero' line of the protractor lines up with the ray [AB. Follow around the inside set of numbers from 0 to 55°. Label the position of 55° as point C.

2. Use a straight edge to draw a straight line from point A (which will be the vertex of the angle), to point C.

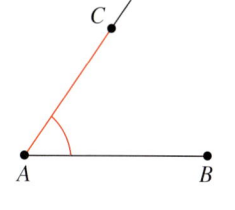

3. Mark in the measure of the required angle $|\angle CAB| = 55°$

55°

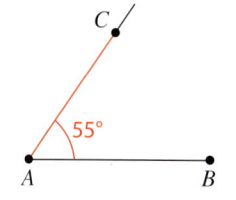

$|\angle CAB|$ is the size of the angle. Point C is on one arm, A is the vertex and point B is on the other arm.

Section A Introducing concepts and building skills

Bisector of an angle

An angle bisector is a line or ray that divides an angle into two equal angles.

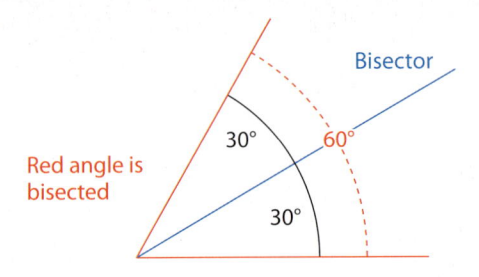

Red angle is bisected

Constructing a bisector of a given angle using a compass and a straight edge

1. Draw ∠A, as shown. Place the compass at A. Draw an arc that intersects both arms of the angle. Label the intersections B and C.

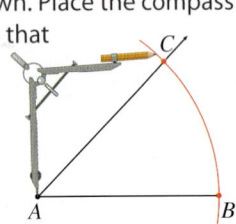

2. Reduce the width of the compass slightly and place the compass at C. Draw an arc.

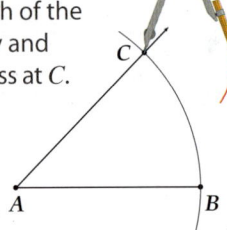

3. Keep the same compass setting. Place the compass at B. Draw an arc such that it intersects the arc drawn in Step 2. Label the intersection of the two arcs G.

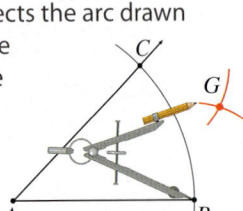

4. Use a straight edge to draw a line through A and G.

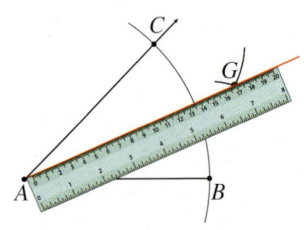

[AG] bisects ∠A. Therefore |∠GAC| is equal to |∠GAB|

Worked example

(i) Estimate and draw a sketch of an angle that measures 40°.
(ii) Draw the angle accurately using a protractor.
(iii) Name the type of angle that you have just drawn.

Solution

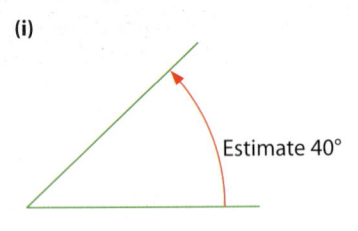

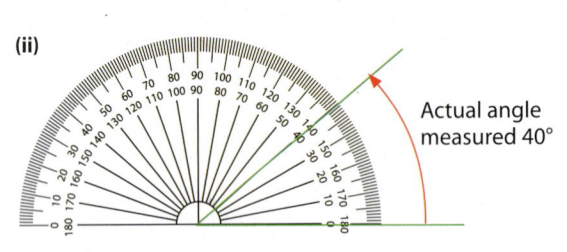

(i) Estimate 40°

(ii) Actual angle measured 40°

(iii) Since the measure of the angle is less than 90°, it is an acute angle.

Practice questions 3.3

1. Reading the measurements from the protractor below, find the measure of the
   (i) blue angle and (ii) red angle.

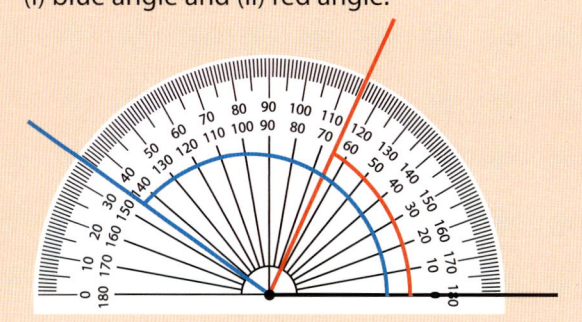

2. (i) Estimate and draw a sketch of a 60° angle.
   (ii) Using a protractor, construct a 60° angle.
   (iii) Name the type of angle you have just drawn.

3. (i) Estimate and draw a sketch of a 90° angle.
   (ii) Using a protractor, construct a 90° angle.
   (iii) Name the type of angle you have just drawn.

4. (i) Estimate and draw a sketch of a 120° angle.
   (ii) Using a protractor, construct a 120° angle.
   (iii) Name the type of angle you have just drawn.

5. (i) Using a protractor, construct a 180° angle.
   (ii) Name the type of angle you have just drawn.

6. (i) Using a protractor, construct a 200° angle.
   (ii) Name the type of angle you have just drawn.

7. (i) Using a protractor, construct a 300° angle.
   (ii) Name the type of angle you have just drawn.

8. Using the letters on the arms of the angles and at the vertex, name each of the following angles (i) to (vii).

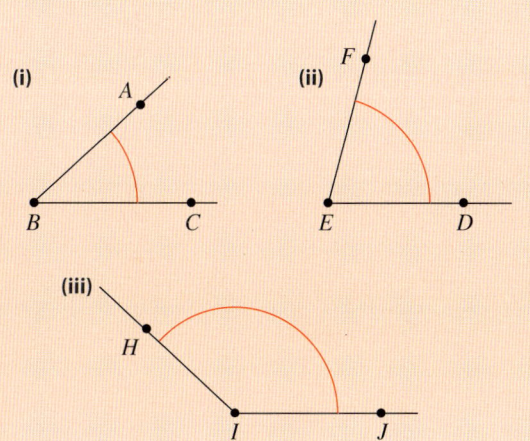

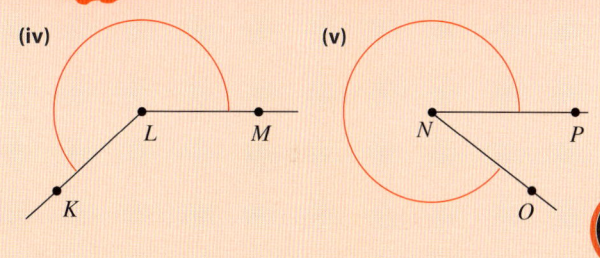

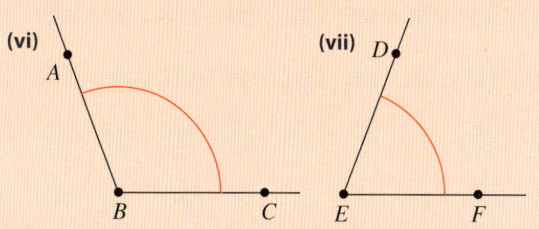

9. (i) Draw a line segment [AB] of length 10 cm.
   (ii) Using [AB], construct an angle of 70°.
   (iii) Label the angle you have just drawn.

10. (i) Draw a line segment [XY] of length 9 cm.
    (ii) Using [XY], construct an angle of 50°.
    (iii) Label the angle you have just drawn.

11. (i) Draw a line segment [XY] of length 85 mm.
    (ii) Using [XY], construct an angle of 80°.
    (iii) Construct the bisector of this angle.
    (iv) Use a protractor to confirm that the bisector has divided the angle in half.

12. (i) Draw a line segment [MN] of length 7.5 cm.
    (ii) Using [MN], construct an angle of 65°.
    (iii) Construct the bisector of this angle.
    (iv) Use a protractor to confirm that the bisector has divided the angle in half.

13. (i) Draw a line segment [PQ] of length 8 cm.
    (ii) Using [PQ], construct an angle of 75°.
    (iii) Construct the bisector of this angle.
    (iv) Use a protractor to confirm that the bisector has divided the angle in half.

Section A Introducing concepts and building skills

14. A starfish is pictured below.

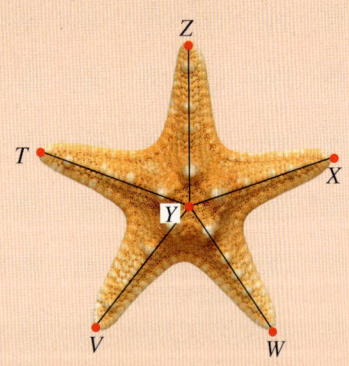

Using the lines and a protractor, find:

(i) |∠ZYX| (iii) |∠WYV| (v) |∠TYZ|
(ii) |∠XYW| (iv) |∠VYT|

15. Below is a picture of Áras an Uachtaráin, Dublin.

(i) How many right angles can you find in the above picture?
(ii) How many acute angles can you find?
(iii) How many obtuse angles can you find?

16. Find the size of |∠ABC|.

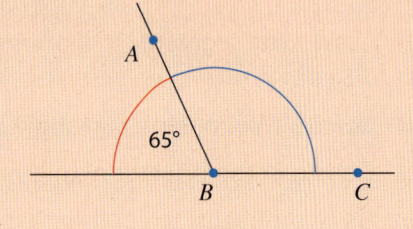

17. The two angles below are supplementary angles. Find the size of |∠DEF|.

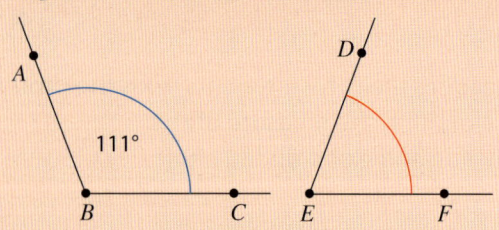

18. Below is a diagram that represents a basketball court.

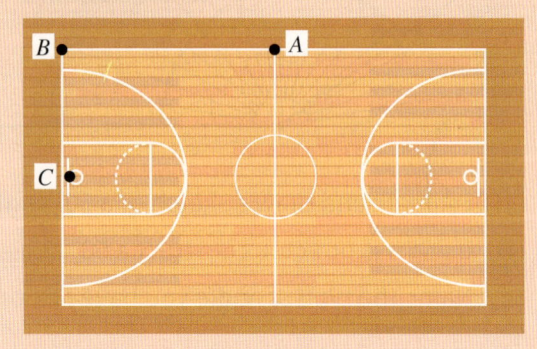

Using a protractor, find the following angles.

(i) |∠ABC| (ii) |∠BCA| (iii) |∠BAC|

19. (i) Find |∠XZY| in the diagram below.

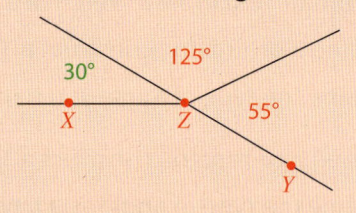

(ii) What term is used to describe an angle like 55° or 30°?

(iii) What term is used to describe an angle like 125° or |∠XZY|?

(iv) What term is used to describe the sum of 125° and 55° or the sum of |∠XZY| and 30°?

> The sum of a set of numbers is what you get if you add the numbers together.

54 **Linking Thinking 1**

Revision questions

3A Core skills

1. (i) What is the word for a straight path that is infinite (goes on and on) in both directions?
   (ii) What is the word for a part of a line with two endpoints?
   (iii) What is the word for a part of a line that has one endpoint and goes on for infinity in one direction?
   (iv) What is a 'point' in geometry?

2. (i) Construct $[AB]$ if $|AB| = 9.5$ cm.
   (ii) Using only a ruler, find the midpoint of $[AB]$ and label it M.

3. (i) Construct a line segment $[XY]$ of length 90 mm. Mark a point 65 mm directly above this line and label it Q.
   (ii) Construct a line parallel to XY that passes through Q.
   (iii) How could you confirm the line you have drawn is parallel to $[XY]$?

4. (i) Construct $[MN]$ if $|MN|$ 10.5 cm. Mark a point 5 cm above one end of this line and label this point T.
   (ii) Construct a line perpendicular to $[MN]$ at point T.
   (iii) How could you confirm the line you have drawn is perpendicular to $[MN]$?

5. (i) Construct $[PQ]$ if $|PQ| = 11$ cm.
   (ii) Construct the perpendicular bisector of $[PQ]$ and hence mark the midpoint of $[PQ]$.
   (iii) How could you check the line you have drawn is both a bisector or $[PQ]$ and perpendicular to $[PQ]$?

6. Label each of the following angles in red as one of the following: null angle, acute angle, right angle, obtuse angle, straight angle, reflex angle or full angle.

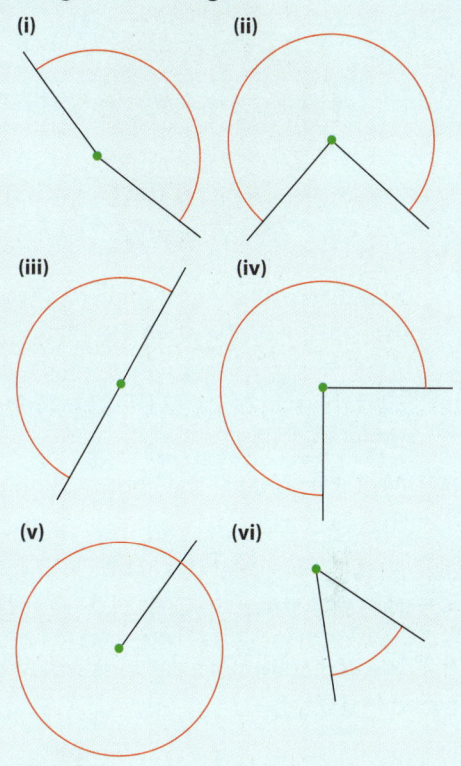

   (i)   (ii)
   (iii) (iv)
   (v)   (vi)

7. (i) Construct a ray $[AB$ of any length.
   (ii) Using ray $[AB$, construct an angle of 75°.
   (iii) Label the angle.

8. (i) Construct $[MN$ of any length.
   (ii) Using $[MN$, construct an angle of 65°.
   (iii) Construct the bisector of this angle.

9. State whether the following pairs of angles are supplementary or not.

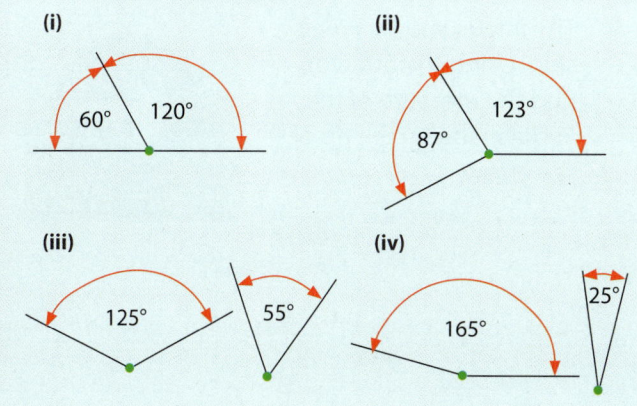

   (i) 60°, 120°
   (ii) 87°, 123°
   (iii) 125°, 55°
   (iv) 165°, 25°

Section A Introducing concepts and building skills

3B Taking it FURTHER

1. An orange is made up of 10 identical segments.

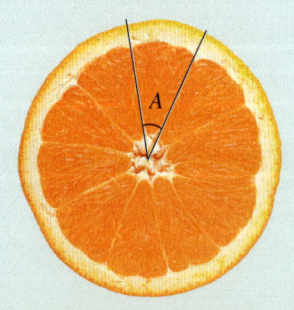

   A **sector** is part of a circle formed by two radii and the arc that connects them.

   (i) Find the size of ∠A at the centre for one of these sectors.
   (ii) Find the angle at the centre using three of these sectors.
   (iii) Find the angle at the centre using five of these sectors.

2. Below is a diagram of a cat looking up at a bird in a tree.

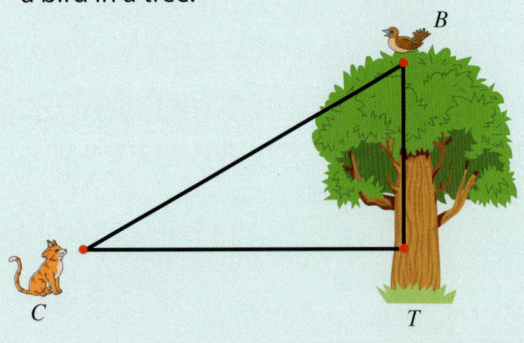

   Using a protractor, find the following angles.
   (i) |∠BCT| (ii) |∠CTB| (iii) |∠TBC|

3. The image shows a road sign. Using a protractor, find the measure of the angle made by the tip of the arrow.

4. Below is a builder's sketch for a roof.

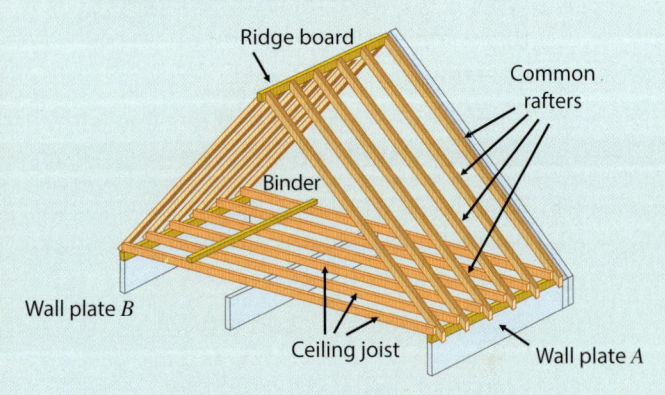

   (i) Are the common rafters parallel or perpendicular to each other?
   (ii) Is the ridge board perpendicular or parallel to the rafters?
   (iii) Are the ceiling joists parallel or perpendicular to each other?
   (iv) Are the ceiling joists parallel or perpendicular to the wall plate A?
   (v) Is wall plate A parallel or perpendicular to wall plate B?

5. John has a plank of wood that is 8 metres long.
   (i) Construct a line segment to represent the plank, with 1 m in real life represented as 1 cm on the diagram.
   (ii) John wishes to bisect the plank. Use a construction to bisect the line segment from part (i).

6. (i) Construct an angle of 88°.
   (ii) Bisect this angle using a construction.
   (iii) Bisect the two angles formed in part (ii) using a construction.

Now that you have completed the unit, revisit the

Something to think about ...

question posed at the start of this unit.

Unit 4

Working with numbers

Topics covered within this unit:
- 4·1 Working with integers
- 4·2 Order of operations
- 4·3 Properties of numbers
- 4·4 Index form

The Learning Outcomes covered in this unit are contained in the following sections:

N.1a N.1b N.1c.I N.1c.IV N.1c.V

Key words
- Operations
- Commutative property
- Associative property
- Distributive property
- Index
- Power
- Exponent

Something to think about ...

KEY SKILLS

A school uses a phone tree method to get a message to the parents of its students.

Using this method, the school rings 3 parents and gives them the message.

Each of these parents then ring 3 more parents, who also ring 3 more and so on.

How many parents will get the message by the fifth round of calls?

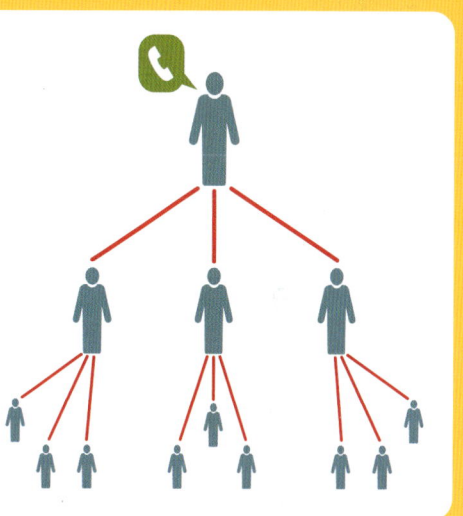

4·1 Working with integers

By the end of this section, you should be able to:
- use the array model to multiply integers
- multiply and divide integers

In Unit 1, we learned how to add and subtract integers using number lines. In this section, we will deal with multiplying and dividing integers.

Section A Introducing concepts and building skills

Multiplication using number lines

- **Consider 4 × 2**

Starting at 0 on the number line. Moving in the positive direction, as both numbers are positive, we do four jumps of two.

So 4 × 2 = 8

- **Now consider (−3) × 2**

Again, we start at 0 on the number line but this time we will move in the negative direction. This is because one of the numbers is negative. We do three jumps of two.

So (−3) × 2 = −6

- **Finally, let's consider (−4) × (−2)**

Again, we start at 0, facing the negative side. This time, however, we will jump backwards, as the second number is also negative. We do four jumps of two.

So (−4) × (−2) = +8

From the above examples, we can see:

- a **positive** number multiplied by a **positive** number gives a **positive** answer.
- a **negative** number multiplied by a **positive** number gives a **negative** answer.
- a **negative** number multiplied by a **negative** number gives a **positive** answer.

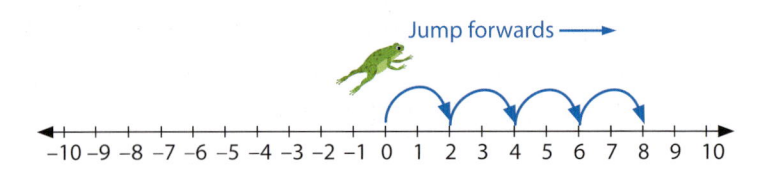

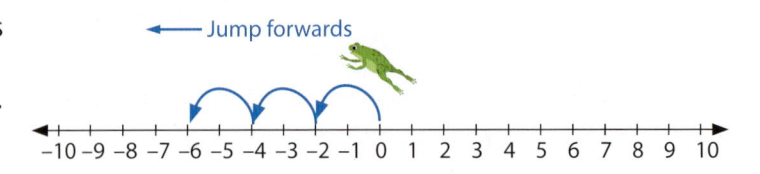

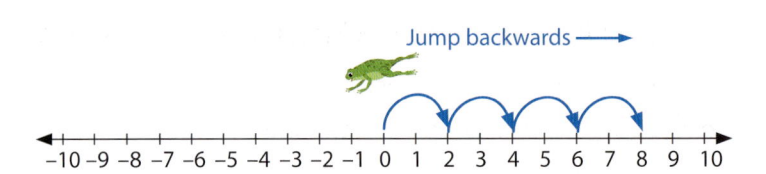

> \+ is the positive sign.
> − is the negative sign.
> When a number has no sign, it means that it is positive. (Zero has no sign because it is neither positive nor negative)

Discuss and discover

(i) Work with the person beside you to copy and complete the table below. The first line is done for you.

		Result
(−3) × 3	(−3) + (−3) + (−3)	−9
(−3) × 2		
(−3) × 1		

(ii) Look at the Result column of your table.
Do you notice a pattern in these numbers?

(iii) Use the pattern observed above to copy and complete the table below.

	Result
(−3) × (−1)	
(−3) × (−2)	
(−3) × (−3)	

(iv) Copy the following sentences and fill in the blanks.
When you multiply a positive integer by a negative integer the result is _____ .
When you multiply a negative integer by a negative integer the result is _____ .

> We often put brackets around negative numbers to avoid confusion between the sign of the number and the operation being done (add, subtract, multiply, divide, etc.).

Using the array model for multiplication

An **array model** is a rectangular diagram or model that can be used for multiplication.

We can break up the rectangle into smaller boxes to make the calculation easier.

Then we find the area of each of the boxes and add these up, to get the area of the whole, which is the product of the original terms.

For example, to multiply 27 × 12, we can break 27 into 20 + 7 and 12 into 10 + 2. Then we arrange these figures along the sides of the rectangle, as shown.

We then find the area of each smaller box by multiplying the length by the width.

Finally, we add the areas of each smaller box to find the total.

   200 + 70 + 40 + 14 = 324

This means that 27 × 12 = 324

	20	7
10	200	70
2	40	14

What about multiplication with negative numbers?

Earlier we learned: (−3) × 3 = −9

We can see that a **negative** number multiplied by a **positive** number gives a **negative** answer.

Let's go back to 27 × 12, but this time break the 27 into 30 − 3.

Using the array model, we can see 300 − 30 + 60 − 6 = 324

	30	−3
10	300	−30
2	60	−6

How would we handle the multiplication of two negative numbers?

Let's now represent 27 × 12 as (30 − 3) × (15 − 3)

Using the array model and our previous answers, we know

   450 − 45 − 90 + ? = 324

   315 + ? = 324

   315 + 9 = 324   Therefore, −3 × −3 = 9

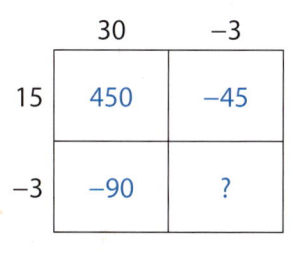

	30	−3
15	450	−45
−3	−90	?

So, we can see that a **negative** number multiplied by a **negative** number gives a **positive** answer.

We learned in Unit 2 that integers are whole positive and whole negative numbers.

When multiplying or dividing integers, we may be asked to multiply or divide:

- two positive integers
- two negative integers
- a negative integer and a positive integer (in either order).

Rule of signs

Two like (same) signs multiply or divide to give a **positive** sign.

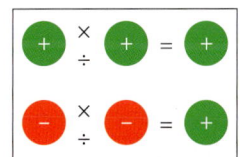

Two unlike (different) signs multiply or divide to give a **negative** sign.

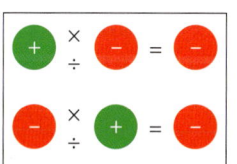

Multiplying and dividing integers

1. Use the rules of signs to decide whether the answer is positive or negative.
2. Multiply or divide the numbers as normal.

Section A Introducing concepts and building skills

Worked example

Find the value of each of the following.

(i) $6 \times (-4)$ (ii) $(-2) \times (-10)$ (iii) $(-48) \div (-6)$ (iv) $(-6) \times (-7) \times (-2)$

Solution

(i) $6 \times (-4)$
$(+) \times (-) = -$ (unlike signs)
$6 \times 4 = 24$
Answer is -24

(ii) $(-2) \times (-10)$
$(-) \times (-) = +$ (like signs)
$2 \times 10 = 20$
Answer is 20

(iii) $(-48) \div (-6)$
$(-) \div (-) = (+)$ (like signs)
$48 \div 6 = 8$
Answer is 8

(iv) $(-6) \times (-7) \times (-2)$
Multiply two at a time
$(-) \times (-) = (+)$ (like signs)
$6 \times 7 = 42$
$(+) \times (-) = (-)$ (unlike signs)
$42 \times 2 = 84$
Answer is -84

Practice questions 4.1

1. Use a number line to multiply each of these.

(i) 3×4 (ii) 6×2 (iii) $8 \times (-2)$
(iv) $(-2) \times 5$ (v) $(-3) \times 4$ (vi) $(-2) \times (-3)$

2. Use the array model to find the total area of each large rectangle.

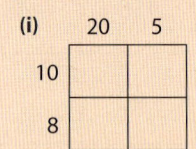

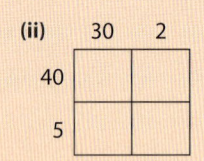

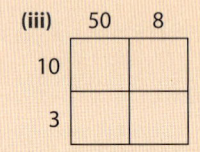

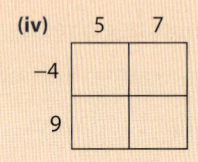

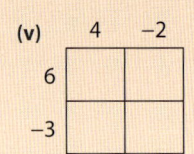

(i) 20, 5 / 10, 8
(ii) 30, 2 / 40, 5
(iii) 50, 8 / 10, 3
(iv) 5, 7 / −4, 9
(v) 4, −2 / 6, −3
(vi) 5, −3 / −6, 8

3. Use the array model to multiply each of the following, using at least one negative number.

(i) 23×19 (iii) 78×65 (v) 35×64
(ii) 16×27 (iv) 42×56 (vi) 83×45

4. Will the result of each of the following be positive or negative? Justify your answers.

(i) $(-14) \times (-9)$ (iv) $8 \div (-1) \div 2$
(ii) $(-28) \div (-7)$ (v) $5 \times (-3) \times 4 \times (-2)$
(iii) $(-7) \times (-8) \times 1$ (vi) $(-6) \times (-4) \times (-9) \times 1$

5. Find the value of each of the following.

(i) $(-3) \times 9$ (iv) $(-12) \div (-4)$
(ii) $(-45) \div 5$ (v) $(-5) \times (-3) \times 2$
(iii) $0 \times (-10)$ (vi) $(-1) \times (-4) \times (-2) \times 3$

6. Copy and complete these calculations.

(i) $\square \times 5 = -20$ (iv) $40 \div \square = -8$
(ii) $(-80) \div \square = 4$ (v) $100 \div \square = -25$
(iii) $16 \times \square = -32$ (vi) $15 \times \square = -60$

7. Find the value of each of the following.

(i) $\dfrac{(-3) \times (-4)}{(-2)}$ (iv) $\dfrac{(-7) \times (-5) \times (-2)}{5}$

(ii) $\dfrac{5 \times (-6)}{(-2)}$ (v) $\dfrac{8 \times (-9) \times (6)}{(-2) \times (6)}$

(iii) $\dfrac{(-6) \times (-4)}{2}$ (vi) $\dfrac{(-4) \times (-7) \times 3}{(-12)}$

Linking Thinking 1

8. Copy the table below and put a tick (✓) in the correct box in each row to show whether each statement is always true, sometimes true, or never true.

Statement		Tick **one** box only for each statement		
		Always true	Sometimes true	Never true
(i)	Multiplying two negative numbers together will give a positive answer.			
(ii)	Multiplying a negative number by itself will give a negative answer.			
(iii)	Dividing a negative number by a positive number will give a positive answer.			
(iv)	A number must be either positive or negative.			
(v)	Multiplying/dividing like signs gives a positive result.			

4.2 Order of operations

By the end of this section you should:
- understand what an operation is
- understand the order in which operations are performed
- perform calculations using order of operations

Operations are things we do to numbers, like adding, subtracting, multiplying, dividing, squaring, etc.

Discuss and discover

KEY SKILLS

Working with a classmate, answer the following questions.

(i) Find two different values for the following: $3 + 2 \times 4$
(ii) Which answer do you think is correct?
(iii) Think about this problem in a real-life situation.
 If you bought one pen that cost €3 and 4 pencils costing €2 each, what is your total bill?
(iv) The order we carry out operations matters.
 A number of problems are shown in the table below, along with the correct answer.
 Copy and complete the table and fill out which operation was done first, second, etc.

Problem	Correct answer	1st operation	2nd operation	3rd operation
$14 - 3 \times 2$	8			
$24 + 16 \div 4$	28			
$2 \times (9 + 5) - 2$	26			
$(7 - 4)^2 \times 5$	45			
$8 + 4(2 + 1)^2 \div 3$	20			

(v) Copy and complete the following sentences based on the table above.
 Multiplication comes _____ *before/after* addition and subtraction.
 Division comes _____ *before/after* addition and subtraction.
 Brackets must be solved _____ *first/last*.

(vi) Put the following operations in the order they should be done.

| Addition/Subtraction | Multiplication/Division | Indices/Exponents/Powers | Brackets |

Section A Introducing concepts and building skills

A number sentence will often be made up of numbers and operations. A number sentence can also be called an 'equation' if it contains an equal sign, or an 'expression' if it has no equal sign.

When performing operations, there can be only one correct answer. We need a set of rules in order to avoid this kind of confusion.

Order of operations

The following order of operations is based on the idea of doing the "most powerful operations" first and working your way to the least powerful operations.

1. Do things in BRACKETS first.
2. Next, do the EXPONENTS or INDICES (powers) e.g. 5^2, 2^3, 3^4, etc.
3. Next, MULTIPLY or DIVIDE (these operations are equal in strength so do them from left to right as you see them)
4. Finally, ADD or SUBTRACT (again these operations are equal in strength so do them in the order they appear)

You can use the word BEMDAS or BIMDAS to help you remember the order of operations.

BEMDAS and BIMDAS are the same thing. It depends on whether you use the word exponent or index.

1. **B**rackets   ( ) { } [ ]
2. **E**xponents/**I**ndices n^2
3. **M**ultiplication and **D**ivision   × and ÷ (from left to right)
4. **A**ddition and **S**ubtraction   + and − (from left to right)

Alternatively, you could use the word GEMS to remember the order of operations

1. **G**roupings   ( ) { } [ ]
2. **E**xponents n^2
3. **M**ultiplication and division   × and ÷ (from left to right)
4. **S**ubtraction and addition   − and + (from left to right)

Worked example

Use the order of operations rules to find the value of

(i) $9 \div 3 + 4$ (ii) $8 + (6 \div 3) \times (-4)$ (iii) $35 - 10 \div 2 \times 5 + 3$ (iv) $2 \times (3 \times 6 - 4) + 7$

> Multiplication and division are of equal importance in terms of their position in the order of operations, so we do them as they appear from left to right.

Solution

(i) $9 \div 3 + 4$
    Step 1 $= 3 + 4$ (division first)
    Step 2 $= 7$ (addition last)

(ii) $8 + (6 \div 3) \times (-4)$
    Step 1 $= 8 + 2 \times (-4)$ (brackets first)
    Step 2 $= 8 - 8$ (multiplication next)
    Step 3 $= 0$ (subtraction last)

(iii) $35 - 10 \div 2 \times 5 + 3$
    Step 1 $= 35 - 5 \times 5 + 3$ (division first)
    Step 2 $= 35 - 25 + 3$ (multiplication next)
    Step 3 $= 10 + 3$ (subtraction next)
    Step 4 $= 13$ (addition last)

(iv) $2 \times (3 \times 6 - 4) + 7$
    Step 1 $= 2 \times (18 - 4) + 7$ (brackets, multiply)
    Step 2 $= 2 \times 14 + 7$ (complete brackets)
    Step 3 $= 28 + 7$ (multiplication next)
    Step 4 $= 35$ (addition last)

Practice questions 4.2

1. Evaluate the following, showing all your workings.
   - (i) $7 + 8 \times 3$
   - (ii) $20 - 4 \times 2$
   - (iii) $17 + 3 \times 6$
   - (iv) $7 \times 3 - 2 \times 4$
   - (v) $8 + 3 \times 2 - 4$
   - (vi) $14 \div 2 - 10 \div 5$

2. Evaluate the following, showing all your workings.
   - (i) $(3 + 2) \times 4$
   - (ii) $3 \times (2 + 6)$
   - (iii) $12 \div (9 - 6)$
   - (iv) $(5 + 7) \div (-3)$
   - (v) $(10 - 6) \times 4$
   - (vi) $(3 - 2) \times 5$

3. Evaluate the following, showing all your workings.
   - (i) $6 \times 8 - 18 \div (2 - 4)$
   - (ii) $5 + (2 \times 10 - 5) - 6$
   - (iii) $(5 + 3) \times 2 + 10 \div (8 - 3)$
   - (iv) $(10 \times 3 - 20) + 3 \times (9 \div 3 + 2)$

4. Using the numbers 2, 3 and 4 once only and any operations or brackets, write an expression that equals each number below. Try to do this in more than one way.
   - (i) 9
   - (ii) 10
   - (iii) 14
   - (iv) 20
   - (v) 6

5. How many different answers can you get by inserting one pair of brackets in the following sum?
   $10 + 20 - 12 \div 2 \times 3$
   Write each sum, then find the value of it.

6. Use each of the numbers 2, 3, 7 and 8, brackets ( ) and the signs +, −, ×, ÷ to make each of the numbers from 30 to 40. You can use each number just once in each calculation.

Taking it FURTHER

7. Copy each number sentence. Use brackets to make each number sentence true.
   - (i) $36 \div 4 \times 3 = 3$
   - (ii) $20 \div 5 \times 2 + 3 = 5$
   - (iii) $10 - 4 \div 2 - 1 = 6$
   - (iv) $6 \times 2 + 8 \div 4 = 15$

8. Jane works out $8 + 3 \times 6$ and gets 66. Mark works out $8 + 3 \times 6$ and gets 26.
   - (i) Explain what each person did to get their answer?
   - (ii) Which answer is correct? Justify your answer using your knowledge of the order of operations rules.

9. Big Trucks Ltd rents trucks for €275 per hour and charges a 2-hour minimum per day. One customer rents a truck on Monday for 1 hour, Tuesday for 3 hours and Wednesday for 2 hours. Write a number sentence (also called an 'expression') to represent this situation, then find how much the customer pays.

10. In a certain game, Brian scores 35 points, Lucy scores 15 points less than Brian, and Cara scores half as many points as Lucy.
    - (i) Write this information as a number sentence.
    - (ii) Evaluate the sentence from part (i) to find how many points Cara scores.

Taking it FURTHER

11. Using all four numbers 3, 4, 6 and 8 only once, there are over 30 different ways of getting the answer 24 by adding, subtracting, multiplying and dividing. Can you find 10 ways?

4.3 Properties of numbers

By the end of this section you should understand and be able to use:
- the commutative property of numbers
- the associative property of numbers
- the distributive property of numbers

Commutative property

Consider the two rectangles shown.

The area of rectangle A = length × width
$$= 7 \times 4$$
$$= 28$$

The area of rectangle B = length × width
$$= 4 \times 7$$
$$= 28$$

Therefore, we can say $7 \times 4 = 4 \times 7$

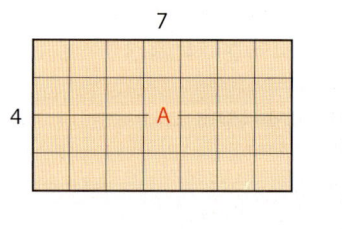

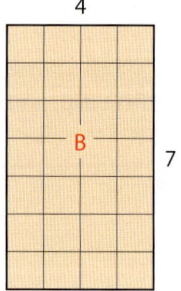

In general, we say that when we are multiplying, the order we multiply the numbers in does not change the answer. This is known as the **commutative property** of multiplication.

Will this work for the perimeter of these rectangles?

Starting in the bottom left corner of each rectangle,

Perimeter of A = 4 + 7 + 4 + 7   Perimeter of B = 7 + 4 + 7 + 4
$$\qquad = 22 \qquad\qquad\qquad\qquad\qquad = 22$$

Therefore, we can say $4 + 7 = 7 + 4$

In general, we say that when we are adding, the order we add the numbers in doesn't matter. This is known as the **commutative property** of addition.

> The **commutative property** states that the order in which we carry out operations of multiplication and addition does not matter.

> The word 'commutative' comes from 'commute', which means 'to move around'. So, the commutative property is the one that refers to moving numbers around.

Discuss and discover

KEY SKILLS

Working with the person beside you, pick any three numbers and investigate if the commutative property works for:

(i) addition   (ii) subtraction   (iii) division   (iv) multiplication

Associative property

Evie and Ruairí are counting some coloured sweets.
Evie groups the purple and blue sweets together as shown.
She then adds the yellow sweets to get a total of 13 sweets.

Ruairí groups the purple and yellow sweets as shown.
He then adds the blue sweets to get a total of 13 sweets.

Therefore, we can say $(6 + 3) + 4 = (3 + 4) + 6$

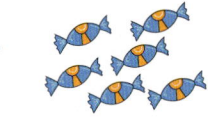

Linking Thinking 1

In general, we say that when we are adding, it doesn't matter what way we group the numbers before we add them.

This is known as the **associative property** of addition.

This also works with multiplication, as shown.

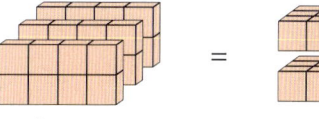

$(2 \times 4) \times 3$
$= 8 \times 3$
$= 24$

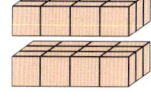

$2 \times (4 \times 3)$
$= 2 \times 12$
$= 24$

> The word 'associative' comes from 'associate', which means 'to group together'. So, the associative property is the rule that refers to grouping.

> The **associative property** states that how we group numbers (put them into brackets) does not matter.

Discuss and discover

Working with the person beside you, pick any three numbers and investigate if the associative property works for

(i) addition (ii) subtraction (iii) division (iv) multiplication

Distributive property

Consider how we can calculate the following: $3 \times (2 + 4)$

Using the array model:

$3 \times (2 + 4) = 18$

	2	4
3	6	12

Using the order of operations rule the solution to this question works out as follows.

$\quad 3 \times (2 + 4)$ (brackets first)
$= 3 \times (6)$ (then multiplication)
$= 18$

Now consider what would happen if we did the multiplication first and then the addition.

$\quad 3 \times (2 + 4)$
$= (3 \times 2) + (3 \times 4)$
$= 6 + 12$
$= 18$

	3
2	6
4	12

From this example, we can see that $3 \times (2 + 4) = (3 \times 2) + (3 \times 4)$. This is called the **distributive property** of multiplication.

3 groups of (2 + 4) is the same as 3 groups of 2 plus 3 groups of 4

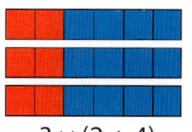

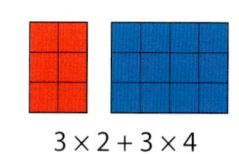

> The **distributive property** states that multiplying a number by a group of numbers added together is the same as doing each multiplication separately and then adding the results.

$3 \times (2 + 4)$ = $3 \times 2 + 3 \times 4$

> Distributive comes from the word 'distribute', which means 'to spread out'.

Discuss and discover

Working with the person beside you and using any three numbers of your own choosing, investigate whether the distributive property works for subtraction.

Section A Introducing concepts and building skills

Worked example

Use the numbers and the property to create an equation and verify that the property is true for each of the following:

(i) Numbers: 8 and 3   Property: commutative property of multiplication
(ii) Numbers: 6, 5 and 12   Property: associative property of addition
(iii) Numbers: 2, 3 and 11   Property: distributive property of addition

Solution

(i) Is $8 \times 3 = 3 \times 8$?
Verify:
Left side:
$8 \times 3 = 24$
Right side:
$3 \times 8 = 24$
Compare answers:
$24 = 24$

(ii) Is $6 + (5 + 12) = (6 + 5) + 12$?
Verify:
Left side:
$6 + (5 + 12) = 6 + 17$
$= 23$
Right side:
$(6 + 5) + 12 = 11 + 12$
$= 23$
Compare answers:
$23 = 23$

(iii) Is $2 \times (3 + 11) = (2 \times 3) + (2 \times 11)$?
Verify:
Left side:
$2 \times (3 + 11) = 2 \times 14$
$= 28$
Right side:
$(2 \times 3) + (2 \times 11) = 6 + 22$
$= 28$
Compare answers:
$28 = 28$

Practice questions 4.3

1. Rewrite the following problems in two different ways using the commutative property. Find the answer for each one.

    (i) $6 \times 2 \times 5 =$
    (ii) $3 \times 1 \times 8 =$
    (iii) $7 \times 9 \times 4 =$
    (iv) $2 \times 10 \times 5 =$
    (v) $6 \times 3 \times 7 =$
    (vi) $2 \times 9 \times 8 =$

2. Rewrite the following problems in two different ways using the commutative property. Find the answer for each one.

    (i) $6 + 4 + 2 =$
    (ii) $9 + 2 - 7 =$
    (iii) $12 + 4 + 3 =$
    (iv) $7 + 6 + 8 =$
    (v) $(-3) + 9 + 11 =$
    (vi) $5 - 4 + 7 =$

3. Rewrite the following problems using the associative property and find the answer.

    (i) $3 + (2 - 4)$
    (ii) $5 + (10 + 8)$
    (iii) $(9 - 4) + 7$
    (iv) $(7 + 6) + 2$
    (v) $(3 + 12) - 9$
    (vi) $(8 + 6) + 8$

4. Rewrite the following problems using the associative property and find the answer.

    (i) $(4 \times 3) \times 2$
    (ii) $2 \times (3 \times 5)$
    (iii) $8 \times (3 \times 1)$
    (iv) $6 \times (7 \times 5)$
    (v) $(10 \times 3) \times 2$
    (vi) $(9 \times 5) \times 2$

5. Use the distributive property to solve the following.

    (i) $4 \times (5 + 5)$
    (ii) $2 \times (7 - 4)$
    (iii) $6 \times (5 + 3)$
    (iv) $2 \times (7 - 9)$
    (v) $(-2) \times (6 + 2)$
    (vi) $5 \times (5 + 7)$
    (vii) $3 \times (6 + 9)$
    (viii) $4 \times (6 - 3)$
    (ix) $(-2) \times (9 - 6)$

6. Identify the property being described in each of the following statements:
   (i) This property means the *numbers can be moved around*.
   (ii) This property deals with *grouping of numbers*.
   (iii) This property multiplies *the value outside the brackets with each of the terms in the brackets*.
   (iv) This property says that *changing the grouping of numbers that are either being added or multiplied does not change the value of it*.
   (v) This property says *the brackets can be moved*.

7. For each equation below, identify the property used. Justify your answer in each case.
   (i) $(5 + 9) + 6 = 6 + (5 + 9)$
   (ii) $3 \times (7 + 4) = (3 \times 7) + (3 \times 4)$
   (iii) $10 \times (9 \times 3) = (10 \times 9) \times 3$
   (iv) $14 \times (2 \times 7) = (2 \times 7) \times 14$
   (v) $(8 - 3) \times 6 = (8 \times 6) - (3 \times 6)$
   (vi) $(4 \times 18) \times 10 = 4 \times (18 \times 10)$

8. Use the numbers and the given property to create an equation and check that your equation is true.
   (i) 4, 6 and 9
       Associative property of addition
   (ii) 9 and 12
        Commutative property of multiplication
   (iii) 10, 7 and 5
         Associative property of multiplication
   (iv) 2, 3 and 5
        Distributive property of addition

9. (i) John and David are each building a wall. John's wall will be 3 bricks across and 8 bricks high. David's wall will be 8 bricks across and 3 bricks high. Which of them needs the most bricks? Justify your answer.

   (ii) A rectangle has a width of 4 cm and a length of 10 cm.

   The rectangle is folded, so that it creates a rectangle with a width of 4 cm and a length of 5 cm and another rectangle with a width of 4 cm and a length of 5 cm.

   Does the area of the original rectangle change? Justify your answer with mathematical calculations.

   (iii) Alex, Ben and Charlie are the selling tickets to raise money for their sports clubs. There is a prize for selling the most tickets.

   Alex sold 42 the first week, 59 the second week and 78 the third week.

   Ben sold 59 the first week, and 78 the second week but only 42 in the third week.

   The first week, Charlie sold 78, the second week he sold 59, and the third week he also sold 42.

   Who wins the prize? Justify your answer with mathematical calculations.

10. Copy the table below and put a tick (✓) in the correct box in each row to show whether each statement is true or false.

	Statement	True	False
(i)	The associative property works for subtraction.		
(ii)	The distributive property works for addition.		
(iii)	The commutative property works with division.		
(iv)	The associative property works for multiplication.		
(v)	The distributive property works for subtraction.		

4.4 Index form

By the end of this section you should:
- understand that indices (powers) represent repeated multiplication
- be able to convert between expanded and index form
- be able to find the value of numbers expressed in index form

We use indices to simplify multiplication problems that use the same number more than once.

> When the index is a natural number, the **index** indicates how many times to multiply the number by itself.

Consider the calculation $2 \times 2 \times 2 \times 2 \times 2$

We are simply multiplying 2 by itself 5 times. A more convenient way to write this is 2^5, which is said as '2 to the power of 5'.

The notation 2^5 is **index form**. The $2 \times 2 \times 2 \times 2 \times 2$ is known as expanded form.

To convert from expanded form to index form:

1. Write the number that is repeated down first. This number is called the base.
2. Count the number of times the base number appears
3. Write the number of times the base appears as a small number to the upper right of the base number. This number is called the index number.

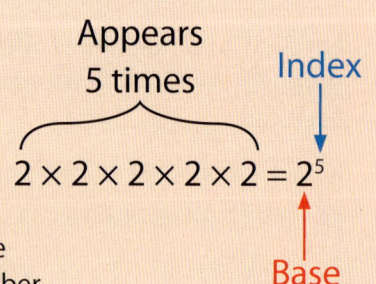

$$\underbrace{2 \times 2 \times 2 \times 2 \times 2}_{\text{Appears 5 times}} = 2^5$$

Index ↓ / Base ↑

> The index number can also be called the **power** or **exponent**.

The index number tells you how many times the base number should be multiplied by itself.

When the index number is two, the base number has been **squared**.

When the index number is three, the base number has been **cubed**.

When the index number is greater than three we say that it has been multiplied **to the power of the index**: 2^7 is read as '2 to the power of 7'.

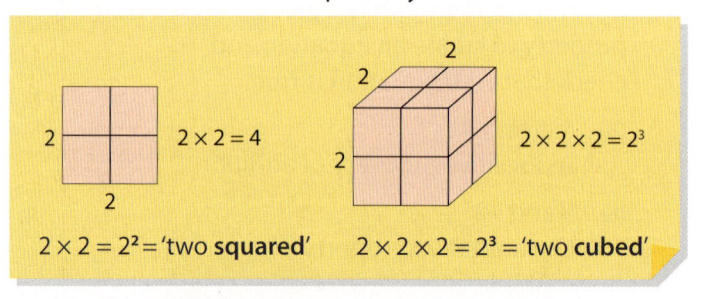

$2 \times 2 = 4$
$2 \times 2 = 2^2 =$ 'two **squared**'

$2 \times 2 \times 2 = 2^3$
$2 \times 2 \times 2 = 2^3 =$ 'two **cubed**'

Scientific calculators have a 'power' button. This button may be labelled x^y or y^x or $x^\blacksquare$.

To work out 4^{10} on a scientific calculator:

1. Enter **4**
2. Press the index button x^y or y^x or $x^\blacksquare$
3. Enter **1** **0**
4. Press **=**

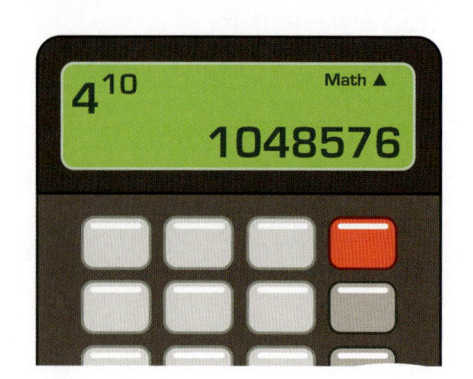

4^{10}
1048576

You should get the answer 1 048 576.

> Any number to the power of 1 will always be the number itself.
>
> For example, $5^1 = 5$ and $326^1 = 326$

68 Linking Thinking 1

Worked example

(i) Rewrite $3 \times 3 \times 3 \times 3 \times 3 \times 3 \times 3 \times 3 \times 3$ in index form.

(ii) Rewrite 5^6 in expanded form.

(iii) Evaluate $3^3 + 2^4$

(iv) Evaluate $7^2 + (15 - 12)$

Solution

(i) There are nine 3s, so $= 3^9$

(ii) The exponent is six, so there should be six 5s
$5 \times 5 \times 5 \times 5 \times 5 \times 5$

(iii) $3^3 + 2^4 = 27 + 16$
$= 43$

(iv) $7^2 + (15 - 12)$
$= 7^2 + 3$ (brackets first)
$= 49 + 3$ (then indices)
$= 52$ (then addition)

Remember: indices come second in the order of operations.

Practice questions 4.4

1. Identify the base and the index in each of the following.

    (i) 2^5 (iii) 6^8 (v) 4^3

    (ii) 3^6 (iv) 9^7 (vi) 5^4

2. Rewrite the following in index form.

    (i) $4 \times 4 \times 4 \times 4 \times 4 \times 4$

    (ii) $22 \times 22 \times 22 \times 22 \times 22$

    (iii) $9 \times 9 \times 9 \times 9$

    (iv) $17 \times 17 \times 17$

    (v) $10 \times 10 \times 10 \times 10 \times 10 \times 10$

    (vi) $8 \times 8 \times 8 \times 8 \times 8 \times 8 \times 8 \times 8 \times 8 \times 8$

3. Rewrite the following in expanded form and evaluate, using your calculator.

    (i) 5^7 (iii) 1^8 (v) 7^2

    (ii) 2^6 (iv) 8^9 (vi) 4^3

4. Without using your calculator, find the value of the following.

    (i) 2^4 (iii) 12^1 (v) 3^3

    (ii) 8^2 (iv) 9^2 (vi) 1^9

5. Copy the table below and fill in the blanks.

	Expanded form	Index form	We say	Value
(i)	12×12			144
(ii)			2 cubed	
(iii)		1^6		
(iv)				25
(v)			0 to the power of 6	

6. Evaluate each of the following.

    (i) $(11 - 9)^3 + 3^2$ (iii) $(3^2 + 11) \times 2 - 25$

    (ii) $6 \times 10^2 \div 30$ (iv) $10 - 15 \div 5 + 2^3 \times 5$

7. Simplify the following, leaving your answer in index form.

    (i) $5 \times 5 \times 6 \times 6$

    (ii) $3 \times 5 \times 3 \times 5$

    (iii) $7 \times 4 \times 7 \times 4 \times 7 \times 4 \times 7$

    (iv) $9 \times 9 \times 3 \times 9 \times 3$

    (v) $2 \times 5 \times 6 \times 6 \times 2 \times 6 \times 2 \times 5$

    (vi) $8 \times 5 \times 8 \times 8 \times 5 \times 8 \times 4$

Section A Introducing concepts and building skills

Taking it FURTHER

8. (i) Rewrite 2^5 in expanded form.
   (ii) Rewrite 2^3 in expanded form.
   (iii) Using your answers above or otherwise, rewrite $2^5 \times 2^3$ in expanded form.
   (iv) Convert the answer to part (iii) into index form.
   (v) Complete the following equation: $2^5 \times 2^3 = 2^{\square}$
   Do you notice anything?

9. (i) Rewrite 3^7 in expanded form.
   (ii) Rewrite 3^4 in expanded form.
   (iii) Using your answers above or otherwise, rewrite $3^7 \times 3^4$ in expanded form.
   (iv) Convert the answer to part (iii) into index form.
   (v) Complete the following equation: $3^7 \times 3^4 = 3^{\square}$
   Do you notice anything?

Revision questions

4A Core skills

1. Use the array model to multiply each of the following.
   (i) 12×15
   (ii) 24×13
   (iii) 42×35
   (iv) 62×43
   (v) 78×54
   (vi) 22×98

2. Find the value of each of the following.
   (i) -3×4
   (ii) $-2 \times -6 \times -3$
   (iii) $9 \times (5 - 7)$
   (iv) $\frac{(-4) \times (-9)}{(-6)}$
   (v) $\frac{8 \times (-8)}{12 - 16}$
   (vi) $\frac{(-2)^2 \times (-5)}{(-8) + 10}$

3. Find the value of each of the following. Show all the steps used.
   (i) $2^2 \times 8 + 1$
   (ii) $(11 + 9) \times 3^2$
   (iii) $(6 - 3)^2 - 2 \times 4$
   (iv) $2^2 - 3 \times (10 - 6)$
   (v) $((7 - 11) + 15) \times 4^2$
   (vi) $((2 \times 6) + 60) \div 6^2$

4. Copy and fill in the blanks using the given numbers in each problem. You cannot use a number more than once.
   (i) (_____)^2 + _____ × _____ = 19
   Use 2, 3 and 5
   (ii) _____ + _____ × _____ − _____ = 32
   Use 3, 5 and 6
   (iii) (_____ + _____) × _____ = 64
   Use 3, 5 and 8
   (iv) _____ + (_____ ÷ _____)^2 − _____ = 30
   Use 8, 12, 7 and 40

5. Identify the property being shown in each equation below. Justify your answer in each case.
   (i) $(2 + 3) + 12 = 2 + (3 + 12)$
   (ii) $5 \times 6 = 6 \times 5$
   (iii) $3 \times (4 \times 6) = (3 \times 4) \times 6$
   (iv) $4 \times 23 = 4 \times (20 + 3)$
   (v) $(2 + 3) + 5 = (3 + 2) + 5$
   (vi) $8 \times 74 = 8 \times (70 + 4)$

6. Rewrite the following in index form.
   (i) $2 \times 2 \times 2 \times 2 \times 2 \times 2 \times 2$
   (ii) $10 \times 10 \times 10 \times 10 \times 10 \times 10$
   (iii) $3 \times 3 \times 3 \times 3 \times 3 \times 3$
   (iv) $4 \times 4 \times 4 \times 4$
   (v) $6 \times 6 \times 6 \times 6 \times 6 \times 6 \times 6 \times 6$
   (vi) $8 \times 8 \times 8 \times 8 \times 8$

7. Rewrite each of the following in expanded form.
   (i) 12^7
   (ii) 3^6
   (iii) 10^5
   (iv) 2^8
   (v) 4^5
   (vi) 7^4

8. Simplify each of the following, leaving your answer in index form.
   (i) $7 \times 7 \times 7 \times 3 \times 3 \times 3 \times 3$
   (ii) $19 \times 19 \times 19 \times 19 \times 2 \times 2$
   (iii) $13 \times 13 \times 4 \times 4 \times 4 \times 4$
   (iv) $2 \times 2 \times 4 \times 4 \times 4 \times 4$
   (v) $3 \times 3 \times 3 \times 5 \times 5 \times 5 \times 5$
   (vi) $8 \times 8 \times 2 \times 2 \times 2 \times 6 \times 6$

4B Taking it FURTHER

1. Using any combination of operations (×, +, −) and the numbers 3, 5 and 6, make the largest possible number and the smallest possible number. Each number and operation can only be used once.

2. Using each of the numbers 1, 2, 3, 4 and 5 once only and the operations × and ÷ once only, what is the smallest whole number you can make?

3. On a calculator, find as many ways as possible to make the number 15 by using the number 2 and any of the operations +, −, × and ÷. You can use the number 2 and any of the operations as many times as you like.

4. Philip withdraws €1 000 from his bank account. He spends €500 fixing his car, then he divides the remaining money into 5 equal parts. He gives away 4 parts and keeps 1 part for himself. Finally, he goes to a restaurant with his girlfriend and spends €60 on meals. Write a numerical expression to represent this situation, and then find how much money Philip has left from the €1 000 he withdrew.

5. Two rectangular gardens have the same width of 10 metres. However, the length of one is 20 metres while the other is 30 metres. Write a numerical expression for the area of the two gardens combined and find this area.

6. Aaron, Belinda and Charlie each have a box.
   Aaron's box is 12 cm long, 8 cm wide and 5 cm high.
   Belinda's box is 8 cm long, but it is 12 cm wide, and 5 cm high.
   Charlie's box is only 5 cm wide, but it is 8 centimetres long, and it is the tallest box, 12 cm high.
   They are arguing about which box will hold the most. Which box do you think will hold the most?
   Justify your answer using what you know about the properties of numbers.

   Remember: volume = length × width × height

Now that you have completed the unit, revisit the

Something to think about ...

question posed at the start of this unit.

Unit 5

Fractions, decimals and percentages

Topics covered within this unit:
5·1 Fractions
5·2 Working with fractions
5·3 Working with decimals
5·4 Working with percentages
5·5 Percentages in context

The Learning Outcomes covered in this unit are contained in the following sections:
N.1e N.2a N.2c

Key words
Fraction
Proper fraction
Improper fraction
Mixed fraction
Reciprocal
Decimal
Terminating decimal
Recurring decimal
Percentage
Cost price
Selling price
Profit
Loss

The way we represent fractions today probably came from the ancient Hindus.

Around 630 CE, Brahmagupta, an Indian mathematician, would write the fraction two-quarters without the bar in the middle as $\genfrac{}{}{0pt}{}{2}{4}$

The Arabians came up with the bar in the middle (called the *vinculum*).

Something to think about ...

KEY SKILLS

My mother baked a cake and left it in the fridge.

My dad woke during the night and ate half of the cake. Then my sister woke and ate one-third of what remained. Later, I woke up and ate one-quarter of the rest. Finally, my mother woke and ate one-fifth of the remaining cake.

What fraction of the original cake was left in the morning?

5·1 Fractions

By the end of this section, you should:
- understand fractions
- be able to convert between equivalent fractions

A **fraction** is a number written in the form of one number divided by another number.

A fraction represents part of a whole. When something is broken up into a number of equal parts, the fraction shows how many of those parts you have.

There are two main parts of a fraction: the numerator and the denominator.

The numerator is how many parts you have. The denominator is how many parts the whole was divided into. Fractions are written with the numerator over the denominator and a line in between them.

$\dfrac{3}{4}$ ← **Numerator**
    ← **Denominator**

72   Linking Thinking 1

Types of fraction

There are three different types of fraction.

1. **Proper fractions**

   > A **proper fraction** is one where the numerator is less than the denominator.

   $$\frac{1}{2} \quad \frac{5}{8} \quad \frac{13}{21}$$ The numerator is less than the denominator

   Note that a proper fraction is always less than one.

2. **Improper fractions**

   > An **improper fraction** is one where the numerator is greater than the denominator.

   $$\frac{3}{2} \quad \frac{7}{5} \quad \frac{14}{9}$$ The numerator is greater than the denominator

   Note that an improper fraction is always greater than one. They are sometimes called 'top-heavy' fractions.

3. **Mixed fractions**

   > A **mixed fraction** has both a whole number part and a fraction part.

   $$1\frac{1}{2} \quad 3\frac{3}{4} \quad 2\frac{1}{4}$$ Whole number part / Fraction part

Converting an improper fraction to a mixed fraction

1. Divide the numerator by the denominator.
2. Write down the whole number answer.
3. Write down any remainder above the denominator.

For example:

Convert $\frac{17}{3}$ to a mixed fraction

1. $17 \div 3 = 5$ remainder 2
2. Whole number = 5, remainder 2
3. $\frac{17}{3} = 5\frac{2}{3}$ as a mixed fraction

Converting a mixed fraction to an improper fraction

1. Multiply the whole number part by the fraction's denominator.
2. Add that to the numerator.
3. Write the result on top of the denominator.

For example:

Convert $3\frac{5}{6}$ to an improper fraction

1. $3 \times 6 = 18$
2. $18 + 5 = 23$
3. $3\frac{5}{6} = \frac{23}{6}$ as an improper fraction

Equivalent fractions

Sometimes fractions may look different and have different numbers, but are actually the same value. We call these equivalent fractions.

> **Equivalent fractions** are fractions with different numerators and denominators that represent the same value.

The following are equivalent fractions:

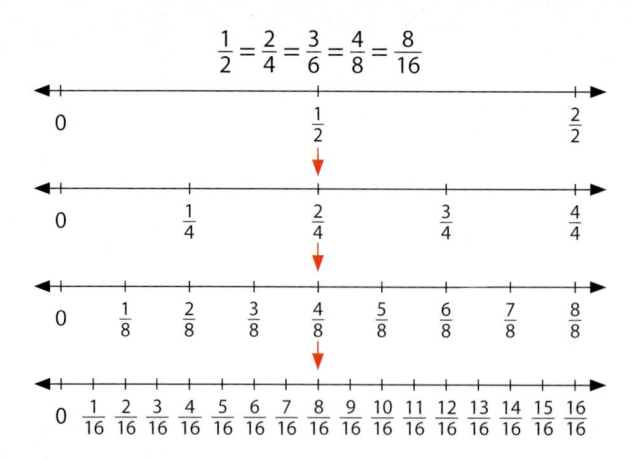

$$\frac{1}{2} = \frac{2}{4} = \frac{3}{6} = \frac{4}{8} = \frac{8}{16}$$

Equivalent fractions can be found by multiplying or dividing both the numerator and the denominator by the same number.

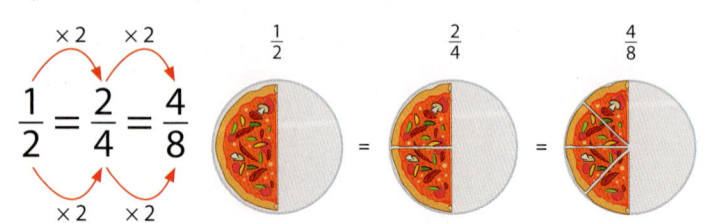

$$\frac{1}{2} = \frac{2}{4} = \frac{4}{8}$$
(×2, ×2 on top; ×2, ×2 on bottom)

Here are some more equivalent fractions, this time by dividing:

We choose the number we divide by carefully so that the results (both top and bottom) stay whole numbers.

If we keep dividing until we can't go any further, then we have simplified the fraction (made it into its simplest form).

$$\frac{18}{36} = \frac{6}{12} = \frac{1}{2}$$
(÷3, ÷6)

Worked example

Examine the following fractions.

(i) $\frac{3}{5}$ (ii) $2\frac{1}{3}$ (iii) $\frac{14}{4}$

(a) Name the type of fraction shown in each case. Justify your answers.

(b) Convert any improper fraction to a mixed fraction.

(c) Convert any mixed fractions to improper fractions.

(d) Write down two equivalent fractions for each of the fractions given.

Solution

(a) (i) $\frac{3}{5}$ is a proper fraction because the numerator is less than the denominator.

  (ii) $2\frac{1}{3}$ is a mixed fraction because it has a whole number part and a fraction part.

  (iii) $\frac{14}{4}$ is an improper fraction because the numerator is greater than the denominator.

(b) The only improper fraction is (iii) $\frac{14}{4}$

  $14 \div 4 = 3$ remainder 2
  $\frac{14}{4} = 3\frac{2}{4}$
  $= 3\frac{1}{2}$

(c) The only mixed fraction is (ii) $2\frac{1}{3}$

  $2\frac{1}{3} = \frac{1}{3} + \frac{1}{3} + \frac{1}{3} + \frac{1}{3} + \frac{1}{3} + \frac{1}{3} + \frac{1}{3} = \frac{7}{3}$

  Alternatively, $(2 \times 3) + 1 = 6 + 1$
  $2\frac{1}{3} = \frac{7}{3}$

(d) To find equivalent fractions, multiply (or divide) both the numerator and the denominator by the same number. For example,

  (i) $\frac{3}{5} \times \frac{2}{2} = \frac{6}{10}$ and $\frac{3}{5} \times \frac{3}{3} = \frac{9}{15}$

  (ii) $2\frac{1}{3} = \frac{7}{3}$ $\frac{7}{3} \times \frac{3}{3} = \frac{21}{9}$ and $\frac{7}{3} \times \frac{5}{5} = \frac{35}{15}$

  (iii) $\frac{14}{4} \times \frac{2}{2} = \frac{28}{8}$ and $\frac{14}{4} \div \frac{2}{2} = \frac{7}{2}$

Practice questions 5·1

1. What fraction of each of the following is shaded?
   (i)   (ii)   (iii)
   (iv)   (v)   (vi)

2. Name the type of fraction shown. Justify your answer in each case.
   (i) $\frac{3}{2}$ (iii) $6\frac{4}{5}$ (v) $3\frac{1}{3}$
   (ii) $\frac{5}{7}$ (iv) $\frac{2}{9}$ (vi) $\frac{11}{8}$

3. Write the following improper fractions as mixed fractions.
   (i) $\frac{7}{2}$ (iii) $\frac{25}{7}$ (v) $\frac{19}{4}$
   (ii) $\frac{14}{5}$ (iv) $\frac{40}{6}$ (vi) $\frac{33}{8}$

4. Write the following mixed fractions as improper fractions.
   (i) $3\frac{2}{5}$ (iii) $1\frac{5}{9}$ (v) $5\frac{2}{3}$
   (ii) $4\frac{1}{6}$ (iv) $2\frac{3}{8}$ (vi) $9\frac{1}{2}$

5. Decide whether the following pairs of images represent equivalent fractions. Justify your answer in each case.
   (i)   (iii)   (v)
   (ii)   (iv)   (vi)

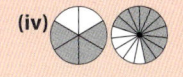

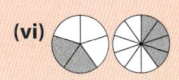

6. Copy and fill in the missing numbers to find equivalent fractions.
   (i) $\frac{2}{5} = \frac{\Box}{10} = \frac{12}{\Box} = \frac{\Box}{40}$ (iv) $\frac{80}{100} = \frac{\Box}{50} = \frac{20}{\Box} = \frac{\Box}{5}$
   (ii) $\frac{3}{4} = \frac{\Box}{16} = \frac{18}{\Box} = \frac{\Box}{44}$ (v) $\frac{3}{8} = \frac{\Box}{24} = \frac{15}{\Box} = \frac{\Box}{56}$
   (iii) $\frac{5}{3} = \frac{\Box}{15} = \frac{30}{\Box} = \frac{\Box}{36}$ (vi) $\frac{8}{40} = \frac{\Box}{20} = \frac{2}{\Box} = \frac{\Box}{5}$

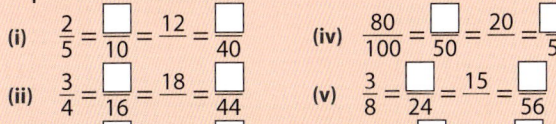

7. A bag contains 60 marbles. 24 of them are yellow, 15 are red and the rest are green.
   Rebecca removes one marble at random from the bag. What is the chance the marble is …?
   (i) yellow   (ii) red   (iii) green
   Express your answers as a rational number in its simplest form.

8. Use the Venn diagram shown to work out what portion (fraction) of the numbers are …
   (i) natural numbers
   (ii) integers
   (iii) prime numbers
   (iv) mixed fractions
   (v) negative numbers

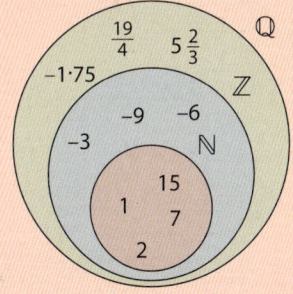

5·2 Working with fractions

By the end of this section you should be able to:
- add and subtract fractions
- multiply and divide fractions

Adding and subtracting fractions

There are three simple steps to add or subtract fractions

1. Check whether the denominators are the same, because we can easily add or subtract fractions when the denominators are the same.

2. If the denominators are not the same, find the lowest common multiple (LCM) of the denominators and convert each fraction into an equivalent fraction with the LCM as the denominator.

3. Add or subtract the numerators. Put the answer over the same denominator. If necessary, you can then simplify the fraction.

Section A Introducing concepts and building skills

Worked example 1

Express the following as a single fraction.

$\frac{3}{4} + \frac{2}{3}$

Solution

LCM of 4 and 3 = 12

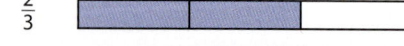

$\frac{3}{4} = \frac{9}{12}$

$\frac{2}{3} = \frac{8}{12}$

$\frac{9}{12} + \frac{8}{12} = \frac{17}{12} = 1\frac{5}{12}$

Worked example 2

Express the following as a single fraction.

(i) $3\frac{1}{2} + 1\frac{4}{5}$

(ii) $\frac{5}{6} - \frac{7}{10}$

Solution

(i) $3\frac{1}{2} + 1\frac{4}{5}$

Convert into improper fractions

$3\frac{1}{2} = \frac{7}{2}$ $1\frac{4}{5} = \frac{9}{5}$

$= \frac{7}{2} + \frac{9}{5}$

LCM of 2 and 5 = 10

$\frac{7}{2} = \frac{35}{10}$ $\frac{9}{5} = \frac{18}{10}$

$3\frac{1}{2} + 1\frac{4}{5} = \frac{35}{10} + \frac{18}{10}$

$= \frac{53}{10}$

$= 5\frac{3}{10}$

(ii) $\frac{5}{6} - \frac{7}{10}$

LCM of 6 and 10 = 30

$\frac{5}{6} = \frac{25}{30}$ $\frac{7}{10} = \frac{21}{30}$

$\frac{5}{6} - \frac{7}{10} = \frac{25}{30} - \frac{21}{30}$

$= \frac{4}{30}$

$= \frac{2}{15}$

Practice questions 5·2·1

1. Represent each of the following as a single fraction.

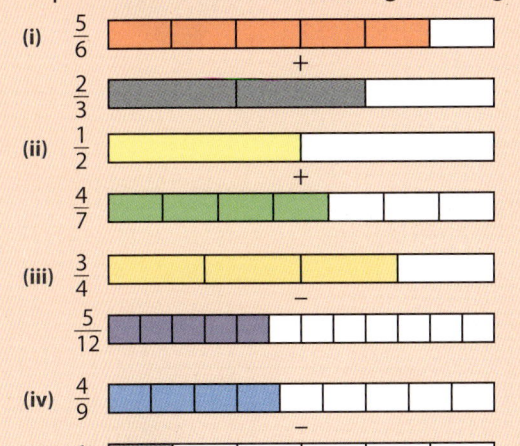

   (i) $\frac{5}{6}$ + $\frac{2}{3}$

   (ii) $\frac{1}{2}$ + $\frac{4}{7}$

   (iii) $\frac{3}{4}$ − $\frac{5}{12}$

   (iv) $\frac{4}{9}$ − $\frac{1}{6}$

2. Find the value of each of the following.

   (i) $\frac{3}{4} + \frac{1}{2}$ (iii) $\frac{1}{4} + \frac{3}{10}$ (v) $\frac{1}{2} + \frac{2}{3} + \frac{4}{5}$

   (ii) $\frac{2}{5} + \frac{3}{7}$ (iv) $\frac{5}{9} + \frac{3}{8}$ (vi) $\frac{8}{9} + \frac{2}{3} + \frac{5}{6}$

3. Find the value of each of the following.

   (i) $\frac{7}{4} - \frac{8}{5}$ (iii) $\frac{3}{5} - \frac{1}{2}$ (v) $\frac{1}{2} + \frac{13}{8} - \frac{11}{12}$

   (ii) $\frac{3}{2} - \frac{9}{7}$ (iv) $\frac{5}{9} - \frac{2}{5}$ (vi) $\frac{13}{2} - \left(\frac{7}{4} - \frac{1}{10}\right)$

4. Find the value of each of the following.

   (i) $3\frac{1}{2} + 1\frac{3}{8}$ (iii) $2\frac{4}{5} - 1\frac{1}{3}$ (v) $3\frac{3}{10} + 4\frac{3}{5} + \frac{9}{2}$

   (ii) $5\frac{2}{7} + 2\frac{3}{5}$ (iv) $4\frac{2}{3} - 1\frac{1}{8}$ (vi) $1\frac{2}{3} + \frac{23}{9} - 2\frac{1}{2}$

5. Adam's family ordered a large pie for their dinner. The pie was cut into 8 equal pieces.

   Adam ate 1 piece, his brother ate 2 pieces, and his mother ate 3 pieces.

   (i) What fraction of the pie did each person eat?

   (ii) What fraction of the pie was eaten altogether?

   (iii) What fraction was left?

6. A jug holds 2 cups of liquid. A recipe for punch is $\frac{1}{2}$ cup of orange juice, $\frac{1}{4}$ cup of strawberry juice, $\frac{3}{8}$ cup of grapefruit juice and $\frac{1}{6}$ cup of lemonade.

   Is the jug big enough for the punch? Explain.

7. A cookie recipe uses $\frac{3}{4}$ cup of chocolate chips. Sarah has $\frac{2}{3}$ cup. Does she have enough?

   If your answer is yes, explain why it is enough.

   If your answer is no, how much more does Sarah need?

8. At a pizza party, Lee and his friends ate $3\frac{1}{4}$ cheese pizzas and $2\frac{3}{8}$ pepperoni pizzas. How much pizza did they eat in total?

9. A rectangular garden is $8\frac{2}{5}$ metres long and $6\frac{3}{4}$ metres wide. The owner wants to put a path around the whole garden. What is the total length of the path?

10. Stephanie went jogging three days this week. She jogged $3\frac{2}{3}$ km on Monday, $4\frac{1}{5}$ km on Wednesday, and $2\frac{2}{9}$ km on Friday. How many km did she jog this week?

Multiplying fractions

Multiplying fractions using the array method

Consider $\frac{2}{3} \times \frac{3}{4}$

We decide which fraction to show vertically: if we choose $\frac{2}{3}$, we divide the rectangle vertically in 3, and shade 2 of the 3 parts in green, as shown.

We then divide the rectangle horizontally in 4, and shade 3 of the parts in red, as shown.

We then count the number of boxes where the green and red shading overlap and express them as a fraction over the total number of boxes.

So $\frac{2}{3} \times \frac{3}{4} = \frac{6}{12}$ or, in its simplest form, $\frac{1}{2}$

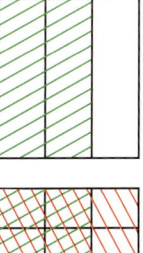

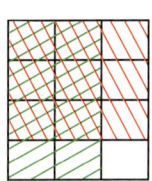

Section A Introducing concepts and building skills

Discuss and discover

Use the array model to multiply the following fractions.
(i) $\frac{1}{2} \times \frac{3}{4}$ (ii) $\frac{4}{5} \times \frac{2}{3}$ (iii) $\frac{1}{4} \times \frac{5}{6}$ (iv) $\frac{2}{3} \times \frac{4}{7}$ (v) $\frac{3}{8} \times \frac{2}{3}$ (vi) $\frac{9}{6} \times \frac{3}{4}$

KEY SKILLS

Multiplying fractions using fraction strips

A fraction strip is a rectangular piece of paper or plastic that can be used to represent different parts of the same whole. Fraction strips can be used to perform operations on fractions.

The fraction strip shown has $\frac{4}{9}$ shaded:

$2 \times \frac{4}{9} = \frac{8}{9}$

$1.5 \times \frac{4}{9} = \frac{6}{9}$

$1 \times \frac{4}{9} = \frac{4}{9}$

$\frac{1}{2} \times \frac{4}{9} = \frac{2}{9}$

$\frac{1}{4} \times \frac{4}{9} = \frac{1}{9}$

$\frac{3}{4} \times \frac{4}{9} = \frac{3}{9}$

Discuss and discover

The fraction strip shown represents $\frac{2}{5}$

Working with the person beside you, represent the following on separate fraction strips.
(i) $2 \times \frac{2}{5}$ (ii) $4 \times \frac{2}{5}$ (iii) $\frac{1}{2} \times \frac{2}{5}$ (iv) $\frac{1}{4} \times \frac{2}{5}$ (v) $\frac{1}{8} \times \frac{2}{5}$

KEY SKILLS

Multiplication

Multiplication using fraction strips can be very time consuming. It is easier to multiply fractions using the following steps:

Multipying fractions

1. Multiply the numerators by each other. The result is the numerator of the answer.
2. Multiply the denominators by each other. The result is the denominator of the answer.
3. Simplify the fraction if necessary.

Worked example

Express the following as a single fraction.
(i) $\frac{2}{7} \times \frac{3}{5}$ (ii) $2\frac{3}{4} \times \frac{5}{6}$

Solution

(i) $\frac{2}{7} \times \frac{3}{5}$

$= \frac{2 \times 3}{7 \times 5}$

$= \frac{6}{35}$

(ii) $2\frac{3}{4} \times \frac{5}{6}$

Convert $2\frac{3}{4}$ into an improper fraction: $\frac{11}{4}$

$2\frac{3}{4} \times \frac{5}{6} = \frac{11}{4} \times \frac{5}{6}$

$= \frac{55}{24}$

$= 2\frac{7}{24}$

Linking Thinking 1

Practice questions 5·2·2

1. Use the array method to multiply the following fractions.
   - (i) $\frac{1}{2} \times \frac{1}{4}$
   - (ii) $\frac{1}{2} \times \frac{1}{3}$
   - (iii) $\frac{1}{5} \times \frac{2}{3}$
   - (iv) $\frac{3}{4} \times \frac{2}{3}$
   - (v) $\frac{3}{5} \times \frac{2}{3}$
   - (vi) $\frac{5}{6} \times \frac{3}{4}$

2. Use fraction strips to multiply $\frac{4}{5}$ by each of the following.
   - (i) 2
   - (ii) 3
   - (iii) $\frac{1}{2}$
   - (iv) $1\frac{1}{2}$
   - (v) $\frac{1}{4}$
   - (vi) $\frac{3}{4}$

3. Find the value of each of the following.
   - (i) $\frac{1}{8} \times \frac{3}{4}$
   - (ii) $\frac{2}{7} \times \frac{4}{5}$
   - (iii) $\frac{5}{6} \times \frac{2}{9}$
   - (iv) $2\frac{2}{5} \times 1\frac{3}{4}$
   - (v) $3\frac{4}{7} \times 2\frac{5}{8}$
   - (vi) $3\frac{2}{3} \times 4\frac{11}{12}$

4. Find the value of each of the following.
   - (i) $\frac{1}{2} \times \frac{1}{5} \times \frac{1}{4}$
   - (ii) $\frac{1}{6} \times \frac{2}{3} \times \frac{4}{7}$
   - (iii) $\frac{2}{9} \times \frac{4}{5} \times \frac{3}{4}$

5. A large chocolate shake takes $\frac{8}{9}$ of a litre of milk to make. If an extra-small shake takes $\frac{1}{7}$ the amount of milk needed for a large shake, how much milk does the extra-small shake take?

6. Jacob is baking chocolate chip muffins. The recipe uses $\frac{3}{4}$ cup of sugar for 12 muffins. Jacob wants to make 9 muffins. How many cups of sugar does he need?

7. There was $\frac{5}{8}$ of a cake left in the fridge. Daniel ate $\frac{1}{4}$ of the leftover cake.
   - (i) How much of the cake did Daniel have?
   - (ii) How much cake was left after Daniel was finished?

8. At a particular movie, $\frac{1}{8}$ of the seats in the cinema were empty.

   $\frac{2}{7}$ of the seats that were full were filled with teenagers.

   What fraction of the cinema was filled with teenagers?

9. $\frac{2}{5}$ of the t-shirts Jack owns are a plain colour and of these $\frac{3}{7}$ are green. What fraction of all of his t-shirts are green?

10. Gillian's bedroom is rectangular and measures $2\frac{3}{8}$ metres wide and $3\frac{5}{6}$ metres long.
    What is the area of her bedroom?

11. There are 30 students in a class. $\frac{1}{3}$ of the students get a bus, $\frac{1}{5}$ cycle, $\frac{1}{6}$ are driven, and the rest walk to school.
    - (i) What fraction of the students in the class walk to school?
    - (ii) How many of the students in the class walk to school?

Division of fractions

Dividing fractions using fraction strips

$3\frac{1}{2} \div \frac{1}{2}$

$3\frac{1}{2}$ divided by $\frac{1}{2}$ means we have to find out how many times $\frac{1}{2}$ of a unit fits into $3\frac{1}{2}$ units.

From the fraction strips on the right we can see that there are seven $\frac{1}{2}$ within $3\frac{1}{2}$

So $3\frac{1}{2}$ divided by $\frac{1}{2}$ = 7

$\frac{1}{2} \div \frac{1}{6}$

$\frac{1}{2}$ divided by $\frac{1}{6}$ means that we have to find how many times $\frac{1}{6}$ of a unit fits into one $\frac{1}{2}$ of a unit.

From the fraction strips on the right we can see that there are three $\frac{1}{6}$ within $\frac{1}{2}$

So $\frac{1}{2}$ divided by $\frac{1}{6}$ = 3

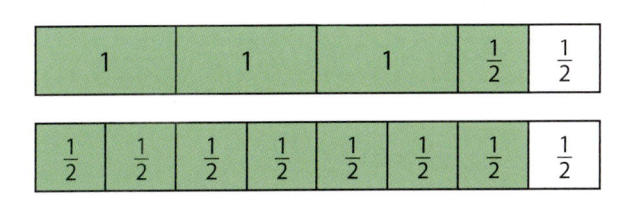

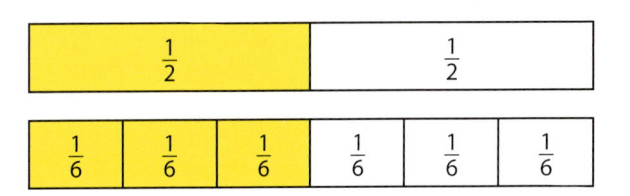

Section A Introducing concepts and building skills

Discuss and discover

KEY SKILLS

Working with the person beside you, represent the following on separate fraction strips.

(i) $2 \div \frac{1}{3}$ (ii) $3.5 \div \frac{1}{4}$ (iii) $\frac{1}{4} \div \frac{1}{2}$

The **reciprocal** of a fraction is the fraction turned upside-down (inverted). For example, $\frac{5}{2}$ is the reciprocal of $\frac{2}{5}$.

Dividing fractions by multiplying reciprocals

It may not always be practical to draw fraction strips each time we are dividing fractions, so we can use the steps shown for $\frac{1}{2} \div \frac{3}{4}$.

1 Leave the first fraction as it is.
$$\frac{1}{2} \div \frac{3}{4} = ?$$

2 Change the division sign to a multiplication sign and find the reciprocal of the second fraction, by turning it upside-down.
$$\frac{1}{2} \times \frac{4}{3} = ?$$

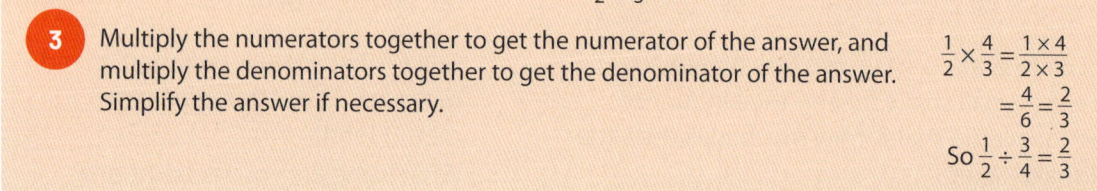

3 Multiply the numerators together to get the numerator of the answer, and multiply the denominators together to get the denominator of the answer. Simplify the answer if necessary.

$$\frac{1}{2} \times \frac{4}{3} = \frac{1 \times 4}{2 \times 3}$$
$$= \frac{4}{6} = \frac{2}{3}$$
So $\frac{1}{2} \div \frac{3}{4} = \frac{2}{3}$

Worked example

Express the following as a single fraction.

(i) $\frac{4}{9} \div \frac{3}{10}$ (ii) $4\frac{5}{6} \div 2\frac{3}{8}$

Solution

(i) $\frac{4}{9} \div \frac{3}{10}$

Reciprocal of $\frac{3}{10}$ is $\frac{10}{3}$

$= \frac{4}{9} \times \frac{10}{3}$

Multiply the numerators by each other and the denominators by each other:

$= \frac{40}{27}$

(ii) $4\frac{5}{6} \div 2\frac{3}{8}$

Convert into improper fractions

$4\frac{5}{6} = \frac{29}{6}$ $2\frac{3}{8} = \frac{19}{8}$

So the question becomes:

$= \frac{29}{6} \div \frac{19}{8}$ (reciprocal of $\frac{19}{8}$ is $\frac{8}{19}$)

$= \frac{29}{6} \times \frac{8}{19}$ (multiply the fractions)

$= \frac{232}{114}$ (divide top and bottom by 2, to simply)

$= \frac{116}{57}$

Linking Thinking 1

Practice questions 5·2·3

1. Use fraction strips to calculate of the following.
   - (i) $3 \div \frac{1}{5}$
   - (ii) $2 \div \frac{2}{3}$
   - (iii) $4\frac{1}{2} \div \frac{1}{4}$
   - (iv) $\frac{1}{2} \div \frac{1}{8}$
   - (v) $\frac{1}{5} \div \frac{1}{10}$
   - (vi) $\frac{3}{4} \div \frac{1}{8}$

2. Find the value of each of the following.
   - (i) $\frac{5}{12} \div \frac{1}{4}$
   - (ii) $\frac{5}{9} \div \frac{2}{3}$
   - (iii) $\frac{3}{8} \div \frac{4}{5}$
   - (iv) $1\frac{2}{3} \div \frac{5}{6}$
   - (v) $2\frac{1}{2} \div 3\frac{3}{4}$
   - (vi) $2\frac{1}{5} \div 4\frac{2}{7}$

3. Three-fifths of a bar of chocolate is divided among four friends. What fraction of the bar did each person get?

4. Fiona has a plank of wood that is $7\frac{1}{2}$ m long. She wants to cut the plank into pieces measuring $\frac{5}{12}$ m. How many pieces will she have?

5. A plumber has a piece of pipe that is $4\frac{3}{8}$ cm long. She divides the pipe into pieces that are $1\frac{2}{3}$ cm long. How many full pieces does she have?

6. Suppose you have $\frac{11}{12}$ of a cheesecake. How many servings can you make of each of the following sizes?
   - (i) $\frac{1}{4}$ of the cheesecake
   - (ii) $\frac{1}{3}$ of the cheesecake
   - (iii) $\frac{1}{6}$ of the cheesecake

7. David and Ryan mow lawns to earn money during the summer holidays. On a particular day, David is mowing for $2\frac{3}{4}$ hours and mows 8 lawns. Ryan mows for $1\frac{1}{3}$ times as long as David.
   - (i) How long did David spend mowing each lawn?
   - (ii) How many hours did Ryan spend mowing?

   What assumptions do you make?

8. Copy the table below and put a tick (✓) in the correct box in each row to show whether each statement is always true, sometimes true, or never true.

	Statement	Always true	Sometimes true	Never true
(i)	An improper fraction is greater than 1.			
(ii)	Finding a fraction of something makes it smaller.			
(iii)	A fraction is between zero and one.			
(iv)	When you multiply a proper fraction by another proper fraction the answer must always be less than one.			
(v)	Dividing by a fraction makes a number smaller.			
(vi)	Dividing the top and bottom of a fraction by the same number makes the fraction smaller in value.			

   Tick **one** box only for each statement

Taking it FURTHER

9. Find the value of each of the following.
   - (i) $\left(\frac{7}{4} - \frac{2}{5}\right) \times 2\frac{3}{8}$
   - (ii) $\frac{1}{2}\left(\frac{4}{9} + \frac{5}{12}\right)$
   - (iii) $\dfrac{2\frac{1}{3}\left(\frac{3}{4} + \frac{5}{3}\right)}{\frac{1}{4}}$

10. Place one of the numbers 1, 2, 3, or 4 into each space to try to make (a) the largest possible number and (b) the smallest possible answer. Use each number once only.
    - (i) $\frac{\square}{\square} + \frac{\square}{\square}$
    - (ii) $\frac{\square}{\square} - \frac{\square}{\square}$
    - (iii) $\frac{\square}{\square} \times \frac{\square}{\square}$
    - (iv) $\frac{\square}{\square} \div \frac{\square}{\square}$

5.3 Working with decimals

By the end of this section you should:
- understand what a decimal is and the different types of decimals
- be able to round decimals to a given number of decimal places
- be able to round numbers to a given number of significant figures

Decimals are numbers that use a decimal point followed by digits that show a value smaller than one.

The decimal point helps in separating the whole number place from the decimal place.

When you move right in this place value system, every number is divided by 10.

Decimals are used in cases that require more accuracy than can be provided by whole numbers.

One of the best examples of this is money.

If we have one €1 coin, two 20-cent coins and a 5-cent coin, we write this as €1·45.

Any number can be written in decimal form.

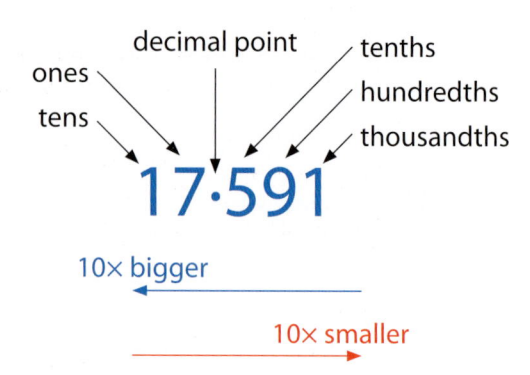

ones, tens, decimal point, tenths, hundredths, thousandths

17·591

10× bigger
10× smaller

Types of decimal number

There are three different types of decimal numbers.

1. **Terminating decimals**

   A **terminating decimal** is one that does not go on forever, so you can write down all its digits.

   Hasta la vista, baby

   A 'terminating' decimal!

   Examples of terminating decimals include 0·15, 0·02, 2·345 and so on.

2. **Recurring decimals**

   A **recurring decimal** is a decimal number which goes on to infinity, but where some of the digits are repeated over and over again.

   Examples of recurring decimals include:

   $\frac{1}{3} = 0·333…$ (the '3' repeats forever)

   $\frac{1}{7} = 0·142857142857…$ (the '142857' repeats forever)

   The part that repeats is usually shown by placing dots over the first and last digits of the repeating pattern. For example, $\frac{1}{3} = 0·\dot{3}$ and $\frac{1}{7} = 0·\dot{1}4285\dot{7}$.

3. **Decimals that go on forever but don't have digits that repeat**

   For example, pi (π) = 3·14159265358979323846 2643…

   In 2015, Rajveer Meena (India) recited π to 70 000 decimal places. He wore a blindfold while doing so, and it took him nearly 10 hours.

Rounding

Since some decimals go on forever, we are often asked to 'round' them to a certain number of decimal places.

Rules for rounding

If, for example, we are asked to round a decimal correct to two decimal places, we need to look at the number in the third decimal place.

If the number in the third decimal place is **less than 5**, leave the first two decimal numbers unchanged.

If the number in the third decimal place is **5 or more**, increase the second decimal number by one.

'Zero to four, just ignore;
Five to nine, one to climb'

Worked example 1

(i) Round 3·27 to one decimal place.

(ii) Round 5·1284 to three decimal places.

Solution

(i) **Step 1** 3·27 has 2 in the first decimal place. Since we are rounding to one place, we need to look at the *second* decimal place.

Step 2 Since 7 is in the second decimal place and is 5 or more, we increase the number in the first decimal place by 1

Step 3 So, 3·27 rounds to 3·3

(ii) **Step 1** 5·1284 has 8 in the third decimal place. Since we are rounding to three places, we need to look at the *fourth* decimal place.

Step 2 Since 4 is in the fourth decimal place and is less than 5, we leave the number in the third decimal place as it is.

Step 3 So, 5·1284 rounds to 5·128

Significant figures

Another method of giving an approximate answer is to round using significant figures.

For example, if we want to know how many people attended a football match, a figure of 32 000 would be acceptable even if the exact number was 31 964.

To round to a number of significant figures, count the numbers from left to right, and then round off from there using the rules of rounding.

When there are leading zeros (such as 0·**006**), don't count them because they are only there to show how small the number is.

For example:

- 2·339 rounded to 3 significant figures is 2·34
- 125·7 rounded to 1 significant figure is 100
- 0·0168 rounded to 2 significant figures is 0·017

Worked example 2

(i) Round 456 327 to three significant figures. (ii) Round 638·29 to two significant figures.

Solution

(i) **Step 1** 456 327 has 6 as its third significant figure. Since we are rounding to three significant figures, we need to look at the *fourth* significant figure, which is 3

Step 2 Since 3 is less than 5, we do not change the third figure. Let all remaining values be zero

Step 3 So, 456 327 rounds to 456 000

(ii) **Step 1** 638·29 has 3 as its second significant figure. Since we are rounding to two significant figures, we need to look at the *third* significant figure, which is 8

Step 2 Since 8 is greater than 5, we increase the second significant figure by 1. Make all remaining values zero.

Step 3 So, 638·29 rounds to 640

Converting fractions to decimals

As discussed in 5·1, a fraction is a number written in the form of one number divided by another number.

To convert a fraction to a decimal, we divide the numerator (top) by the denominator (bottom). Your calculator will display this answer in what is known as standard form, i.e. as a fraction. To convert from standard form to decimal form we can use the standard to decimal button.

Converting decimals to fractions

1. Put the decimal over 1.

2. Multiply the numerator and the denominator by 10 for every number after the decimal point.

3. Express the fraction in its simplest form.

For example, $0.17 = \frac{0.17}{1} = \frac{0.17 \times 10 \times 10}{1 \times 10 \times 10} = \frac{17}{100}$

Worked example 3

(i) Convert $\frac{2}{5}$ into a decimal. (ii) Convert 0·375 into a fraction.

Solution

(i) $\frac{2}{5}$

Divide 2 by 5 to give an answer of 0·4

$\frac{2}{5} = 0.4$

(ii) **Step 1** Put decimal over 1 $\frac{0.375}{1}$

Step 2 3 places after the decimal $\frac{0.375}{1} \times \frac{10 \times 10 \times 10}{10 \times 10 \times 10}$

Step 3 Simplify (÷25) $= \frac{375}{1\,000}$

$= \frac{3}{8}$

Practice questions 5·3

1. State whether each of the following decimals are terminating, recurring or neither. Justify your answer in each case.

   (i) $0.5\dot{7} = 0.5777777...$

   (ii) 0.34

   (iii) $e = 2.7182818284590...$

   (iv) 0.7426

   (v) $0.\dot{3}1\dot{2} = 0.312312312...$

   (vi) $1.4142135623730950...$

Linking Thinking 1

2. Copy and complete the table by rounding the original number to:
   (a) 2 decimal places
   (b) 1 decimal place
   (c) a whole number

	Original number	2 decimal places	1 decimal place	Whole number
(i)	12·419			
(ii)	84·3524			
(iii)	0·765			
(iv)	104·936			
(v)	8·442			

3. Copy and complete the table by rounding the original number to:
   (a) 3 significant figures
   (b) 2 significant figures
   (c) 1 significant figure

	Original number	3 significant figures	2 significant figures	1 significant figure
(i)	217·8			
(ii)	3·092			
(iii)	73·285			
(iv)	0·60828			
(v)	0·003826			

4. Copy and complete the table by converting the fraction to a decimal and then rounding.

	Fraction	Decimal	Rounded to one decimal place		Fraction	Decimal	Rounded to one decimal place
(i)	$\frac{1}{2}$			(iv)	$\frac{2}{3}$		
(ii)	$\frac{1}{4}$			(v)	$\frac{1}{8}$		
(iii)	$\frac{7}{20}$			(vi)	$\frac{3}{4}$		

5. Convert the following decimals to fractions. Simplify where necessary.
   (i) 0·7
   (ii) 0·13
   (iii) 0·55
   (iv) 0·025
   (v) 0·08
   (vi) 0·6
   (vii) 0·305
   (viii) 0·625
   (ix) 0·36
   (x) 0·005

6. (i) Convert 0·6 into a fraction and hence find $\frac{3}{4} \times 0.6$
   (ii) Convert $\frac{3}{4}$ into a decimal and hence find $\frac{3}{4} \times 0.6$

7. Copy the table below and put a tick (✓) in the correct box in each row to show whether each statement is always true, sometimes true, or never true.

	Statement	Always true	Sometimes true	Never true
(i)	Adding two decimals gives a whole number.			
(ii)	Decimals are less than 1.			
(iii)	Converting a fraction to a decimal changes its value.			
(iv)	A number with two decimal places is bigger than a number with one decimal place.			
(v)	Dividing a decimal by a whole number reduces its value.			

Section A Introducing concepts and building skills

5.4 Working with percentages

By the end of this section you should be able to:
- find a percentage of a number
- express one number as a percentage of another
- use percentages to solve problems in context

A **percentage** is a number expressed as a fraction of 100. It is denoted using the percent sign, %.

When the number is complete or whole then you have 100%. If there are 30 students in your class and everyone is in school, then we have 100% attendance. If you score 64% on a test, then you have scored 64 out of 100.

Expressing a number as a percentage of another number

To express one number as a percentage of another, for example €30 out of €400, follow these steps:

> Both quantities must be in the same units.

1. Write the numbers as a fraction of each other €30 out of €400 = $\frac{30}{400}$
2. Multiply by 100 $\frac{30}{400} \times 100 = 7.5$
3. Add the % symbol $= 7.5\%$

So €30 is 7.5% of €400

Finding a percentage of a number

To determine the percentage of a number, for example 15% of 200, follow these steps:

1. Convert the percentage to a fraction $15\% = \frac{15}{100}$
2. Multiply the fraction by the number $\frac{15}{100} \times 200$

$\frac{15}{100} \times 200 = \frac{3\,000}{100} = 30$

So 15% of 200 is 30

Finding a number, when given a percentage of it

To determine the entire number when given a percentage of it, for example 12% of a number is 72, follow these steps:

1. Find 1% of the number by dividing both sides by the given percentage 12% = 72
   1% = 6
2. Multiply both sides by 100 to find the entire number 100% = 600

Worked example 1

(i) Which is larger, 23% of 150 or 22% of 159?

(ii) What percent is 100 millimetres of 4 metres?

(iii) In a car park, 60% of all the cars are blue. If there are 240 blue cars, how many cars in total are in the car park?

Solution

(i) 23% of 150   22% of 159

$= \frac{23}{100} \times 150$ $= \frac{22}{100} \times 159$

$= 34 \cdot 5$ $= 34 \cdot 98$

34·98 is larger than 34·5

Therefore, 22% of 159 is larger than 23% of 150

(ii) To express 100 mm as a percentage of 4 m we must first convert them both to the same unit.

1 cm = 10 mm

1 m = 100 cm

1 m = 1 000 mm

4 m = 4 × 1 000 = 4 000 mm

$\frac{100}{4\,000} \times 100 = 2 \cdot 5\,\%$

(iii) 60% = 240

Find 1% first: $\frac{240}{60} = 1\%$

Then find 100% (total): $\frac{240}{60} \times 100 = 400$ cars

Converting between fractions, decimals and percentages

Fractions, decimals, and percentages are three ways to describe parts of one whole.

- A fraction can be written as a decimal or a percentage.
- A decimal can be written as a fraction or a percentage.
- A percentage can be written as a fraction or a decimal.

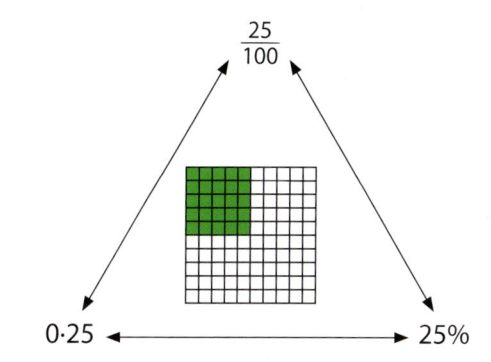

$\frac{25}{100}$ 0·25   25%

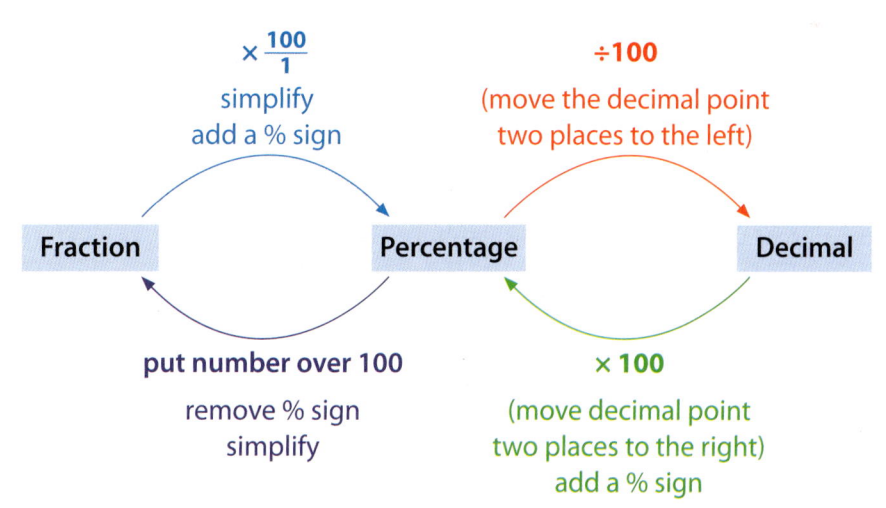

Fraction → **Percentage**: $\times \frac{100}{1}$, simplify, add a % sign

Percentage → **Fraction**: put number over 100, remove % sign, simplify

Percentage → **Decimal**: ÷100 (move the decimal point two places to the left)

Decimal → **Percentage**: × 100 (move decimal point two places to the right) add a % sign

Section A Introducing concepts and building skills

Worked example 2

Write each of the following as a fraction, a decimal and a percentage.

(i) 35%   (ii) 0·425   (iii) $\frac{3}{8}$

Solution

(i) $35\% = \frac{35}{100}$
 $= 0.35$ as a decimal
 $35\% = \frac{35}{100}$ (simplify: ÷ 5)
 $= \frac{35 \div 5}{100 \div 5}$
 $= \frac{7}{20}$ as a fraction

(ii) 0.425
 $= 0.425 \times 100$
 $= 42.5\%$ as a percentage
 0.425
 $= \frac{425}{1\,000}$ (simplify: ÷ by 25)
 $= \frac{425 \div 25}{1\,000 \div 25}$
 $= \frac{17}{40}$ as a fraction

(iii) $\frac{3}{8}$
 $= 3 \div 8$
 $= 0.375$ as a decimal
 $\frac{3}{8} = 0.375$
 $= 0.375 \times 100$
 $= 37.5\%$ as a percentage

Practice questions 5·4

1. Convert the following fractions to decimals and percentages.
   (i) $\frac{3}{4}$ (ii) $\frac{3}{5}$ (iii) $\frac{7}{20}$ (iv) $\frac{1}{20}$ (v) $\frac{8}{25}$ (vi) $\frac{1}{8}$

2. Convert the following decimals to fractions and percentages.
   (i) 0·4   (ii) 0·17   (iii) 0·74   (iv) 0·05   (v) 0·375   (vi) 0·225

3. Convert the following percentages to decimals and fractions.
   (i) 36%   (ii) 55%   (iii) 8%   (iv) 3%   (v) 24·5%   (vi) 68·5%

4. Copy the table below and fill in the missing values.

	Fraction	Decimal	Percentage		Fraction	Decimal	Percentage
(i)		0·8		(vi)			5%
(ii)			24%	(vii)	$\frac{2}{5}$		
(iii)	$\frac{7}{8}$			(viii)		0·02	
(iv)			45%	(ix)			60%
(v)		0·14		(x)	$\frac{1}{4}$		

5. Find the value of each of the following.
   (i) 75% of 396   (ii) 15% of 20   (iii) 32% of 325   (iv) 25% of 530   (v) 8% of 83   (vi) 74% of 44

6. Express each quantity as a percentage. Round your answers to two decimal places where needed.
   (i) Score of 36 marks out of 60   (iii) 5 kg out of 60 kg   (v) 6 hours out of 24 hours
   (ii) 80 ml glass out of 400 ml   (iv) 150 cm out of 500 cm   (vi) 72 g out of 90 g

7. Express each quantity as a percentage. Round your answers to two decimal places where needed.
   (i) 60 cm cut out of 5 m rope
   (ii) 12 hours out of 3 days
   (iii) 75 cents out of €15
   (iv) 60 g out of 1·5 kg
   (v) 180 seconds out of 3 minutes
   (vi) 200 ml out of 3 litres

> 1 kilogram = 1 000 grams
> 1 litre = 1 000 millilitres

Taking it FURTHER

8. In each case below, decide which option you would prefer to be given. Justify your answer with mathematical calculations.

(i) 10% of €4   or $\frac{3}{4}$ of 80 cents

(ii) $\frac{3}{5}$ of 2 pizzas   or   28% of 5 pizzas

(iii) 15% of 60 sweets   or $\frac{1}{8}$ of 72 sweets

5·5 Percentages in context

By the end of this section you should be able to:
- use percentages in everyday situations including percentage profit/loss and VAT

Some of the most common percentages in context questions involve money. Areas include percentage profit/loss and value added tax (VAT).

Percentage profit/loss

When calculating the percentage profit/loss we need to know some information: the cost price and the selling price.

> The **cost price (CP)** is the amount for which an article is bought.
> The **selling price (SP)** is the amount for which an article is sold.

For example, if a person buys an item for €15 and sells it for €20, the cost price is €15, and the selling price is €20.

If the selling price is greater than the cost price, then there is a gain, or profit.

> **Profit** = selling price − cost price

If the selling price is less than the cost price, then there is a loss.

> **Loss** = cost price − selling price

The formula to calculate the percentage profit/loss is:

$$\text{Percentage profit/loss} = \frac{\text{profit/loss}}{\text{cost price}} \times 100$$

Worked example 1

Paul bought a bike for €200. The following year, he sold it for €160.
(i) Did Paul make a profit or a loss?
(ii) How much did Paul make/lose?
(iii) Calculate Paul's percentage profit/loss.

Solution

(i) Since Paul sold his bike for less than he bought it for, he made a loss.

(ii) Cost price = €200
Selling price = €160
Loss = cost price − selling price
= 200 − 160
= €40

(iii) Percentage loss = $\frac{\text{loss}}{\text{cost price}} \times 100$
= $\frac{40}{200} \times 100$
= 20%

Section A Introducing concepts and building skills

VAT

Value added tax (VAT) is charged on most of the goods and services you buy.
It is a tax added on to the cost of the item or service.

> **Calculating the cost including VAT**
> 1. Multiply the cost by the VAT rate to find the VAT.
> 2. Add the VAT to the cost.

Worked example 2

A mobile phone costs €450 before VAT, and VAT is charged at the rate of 23%.
How much does the customer have to pay?

Solution

Method 1

23% of €450 = $\frac{23}{100} \times 450$

VAT = 103·50

Cost including VAT = 103·50 + 450
 = €553·50

Method 2

100% + 23% = 123%   (price including VAT)

= $\frac{123}{100} \times 450$
= €553·50

Practice questions 5·5

1. A new healthy snack bar is being sold in the shops.

   Each bar weighs 40 g and contains 2 g of protein, 3 g of fat and 35 g of carbohydrate.

   What percentage of protein, fat and carbohydrate does each bar contain?

2. A toy manufacturing company released a toy car that measured 20 cm in length. They reduced the length of the model by 30% to produce a miniature version of the same car. How long is the miniature car?

3. A student got 74% on a Maths test that had 20 questions. How many questions did the student answer correctly on this test? Round your answer to the nearest whole number.

4. In a sale, shirts were reduced by 20% and sold for €15 each. What was the original price of the shirts before the sale?

5. Find the percentage profit or loss in each of the following. Give your answer to two decimal places where necessary.

   (i) Cost price = €350
       Selling price = €400
   (ii) Cost price = €250
        Selling price = €235
   (iii) Cost price = €300
         Profit = €75
   (iv) Cost price = €720
        Loss = €63
   (v) Selling price = €1 518
       Loss = €132
   (vi) Selling price = €540
        Profit = €60

6. Mr. Smith gets his gas bill. The amount to be paid is €87·89 excluding VAT. The VAT on a gas bill is 13·5%. Calculate, rounded to the nearest cent:

   (i) the amount of VAT to be paid on the bill
   (ii) the total cost of the bill, including VAT

7. A man gets his car serviced. The cost of the parts is €95·00 excluding VAT. The cost of the labour is €80·00 excluding VAT. The VAT on the parts is paid at 23%; the VAT on labour is at 13·5%. Calculate to the nearest cent:

   (i) the amount of VAT to be paid on the parts
   (ii) the total cost of the parts including VAT
   (iii) the amount of VAT to be paid on the labour
   (iv) the total cost of the labour including VAT
   (v) the final bill the man has to pay

8. Mary scored 13 out of 20 in her Maths exam and 27 out of 40 in her English exam.

   By converting both of her results to a percentage, determine which subject she did better in.

9. The price of an item changed from €120 to €100. Then later the price decreased again from €100 to €80.

   Which of the two decreases was larger in percentage terms?

Taking it FURTHER

10. Alan bought 120 pens at a cost of €2 per pen. He sold 72 of them for €2·50 per pen and the remaining at the price of €2 per pen. Find his percentage profit or loss.

Revision questions

5A Core skills

1. Which amount in each of the following pairs is smaller? Justify your answer.
   - (i) 40% or $\frac{1}{4}$
   - (ii) 0·4 or $\frac{5}{8}$
   - (iii) 0·5 or 5%

2. Write the following amounts in descending (largest to smallest) order.

   $$12\% \quad \frac{3}{8} \quad 0·0123 \quad 42\% \quad \frac{1}{5} \quad 0·45$$

3. Write the following amounts in ascending order, i.e. smallest to largest. Where necessary, round to two decimal places.

   $$30\% \quad \frac{1}{3}, \quad 0·35 \quad \frac{3}{7} \quad 45\% \quad 0·04$$

4. Change each of the following into percentages. Give your answers to three significant figures.
   - (i) 43 out of 250
   - (ii) 37 out of 40
   - (iii) 69 out of 320
   - (iv) 38 out of 72
   - (v) 45 out of 120
   - (vi) 78 out of 356

5. Which amount in each of the following pairs is bigger?
   - (i) 75% of 65 or 70% of 93
   - (ii) 85% of 17 or 10% of 649
   - (iii) 65% of 180 or 34% of 712

6. Find the value of each of the following.
   - (i) $\frac{1}{2} \times \frac{3}{5} + \frac{1}{4}$
   - (ii) $\frac{5}{6} - \frac{1}{5} \times \frac{5}{8} + \frac{2}{3}$
   - (iii) $\left(\frac{1}{4} + \frac{5}{6} - \frac{1}{3}\right) \times \frac{8}{5}$
   - (iv) $\frac{14}{15} \div 4\frac{2}{3} \times \frac{5}{8} + 2\frac{3}{4}$

7. A short necklace has 32 gold beads and 8 black beads. A long necklace has a total of 60 beads. Both necklaces have the same fraction of gold beads and black beads. How many black beads are on the long necklace?

8. Copy the table below and put a tick (✓) in the correct box in each row to show whether each statement is always true, sometimes true, or never true.

	Statement	Tick **one** box only for each statement		
		Always true	Sometimes true	Never true
(i)	Three is less than four, so one-third of a chocolate bar must be smaller than one-quarter of the same chocolate bar.			
(ii)	$\frac{2}{3} + \frac{3}{5} = \frac{5}{8}$			
(iii)	A natural number can be written as a fraction.			
(iv)	3% is the same as 0·3			
(v)	Percentages are between 0% and 100%.			
(vi)	$\frac{1}{2}$ of $\frac{1}{3}$ is $\frac{1}{6}$			
(vii)	Half of a Hawaiian pizza is the same as half of a pepperoni pizza.			

Linking Thinking 1

5B Taking it FURTHER

1. The three blind mice stole a piece of cheese. The first mouse ate $\frac{1}{3}$ of the cheese. Later, the second mouse ate $\frac{1}{3}$ of the remaining cheese. Finally, the third mouse ate $\frac{1}{3}$ of what was then left of the cheese.
   What fraction of the cheese is left?

2. At a school in Aytown, $\frac{7}{8}$ of the students study Science. In the neighbouring town, Beeville, 0·79 of the students study Science. Which town has the highest percentage of students studying Science?

3. By selling a table for €240, a carpenter makes a loss of 20%.
   (i) Find the cost price of the table.
   (ii) What would be his percentage profit or loss if he sold the table for €360?

4. A farmer sold two horses for €18 000 each.
   On one he gained 15%, and on the other he lost 15%.
   Find his overall percentage profit or loss. Give your answer to two decimal places.

5. A shopkeer bought 1 500 bananas at a rate of €20 per dozen. She sold 800 bananas at four for €5 and the remaining bananas at four for €3. Find her percentage profit or loss.

   A dozen = 12

6. VAT is increased from 12% to 21%. How much extra will someone have to pay for a television that costs €350 before VAT?

7. James says, 'The more something costs, the greater the amount of VAT that has to be paid on it.'
   Is James correct? Justify your answer.

8. Suppose 2 kg of sugar contains 9 000 000 sugar crystals. How many sugar crystals are there in …?
   (i) 5 kg of sugar
   (ii) 1·2 kg of sugar

Now that you have completed the unit, revisit the

Something to think about …

question posed at the start of this unit.

6

Probability 1

Topics covered within this unit:
- 6·1 Introduction to probability
- 6·2 Calculate the probability of a single event
- 6·3 The fundamental principle of counting

The Learning Outcomes covered in this unit are contained in the following sections:

SP.1a SP.1b SP.2a N.5a N.5b

Key words
Probability
Event
Experiment
Trial
Outcome
Fundamental principal of counting
Sample space
Two-way table
Tree diagram

Something to think about ...

KEY SKILLS

The Truly Scrumptious ice cream shop has a half-price sundae special. Customers can get one of 10 flavours, one of 4 syrups and one of 60 toppings on their ice cream sundae.

(i) How many possible sundae combinations can be made?

(ii) If it takes 6 minutes to create one ice cream sundae, how many minutes would it take to create all possible combinations?

(iii) Convert the total time taken in minutes to days.

6·1 Introduction to probability

By the end of this section you should:
- understand that probability is a measure on a scale of 0–1 of how likely an event is to occur
- be able to use the language of probability to discuss events

In Unit 2, we looked at how to calculate the chance of something happening. Complete the revision question below to remind yourself of the concept of chance.

Revision question

The Venn diagram shows the number of students who play rugby (R) or tennis (T). Use the information on the diagram to answer the questions.

A student was picked at random. What is the chance that the student played …?

(i) both tennis and rugby

(ii) rugby only

(iii) neither tennis nor rugby

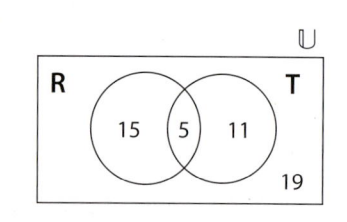

Give your answers as a fraction, a decimal and a percentage.

94   Linking Thinking 1

In Mathematics, the correct name for chance is 'probability'. Probability is the branch of Mathematics that allows us to calculate how likely (or unlikely) it is that an event will happen.

Probability is the chance (or likelihood) of something happening.

An **event** or outcome is a possible result in an experiment. The probability of an event is how likely it is that the event will occur.
Simple events are where one experiment happens at a time and it will have a single outcome.

Examples of events could be:
- getting 'tails' when tossing a coin
- rolling a '7' with two dice
- picking a number that is odd or even.

The probability of simple events is denoted by P(E) where E is the event. It is said as 'probability of an event'.

The probability of an event ocurring (or not occurring) will always lie between 0 and 1. For example, tossing a coin is an example of a simple probabilty experiment, the events (outcomes) of this experiment are heads or tails:

$$P(heads) = \frac{1}{2} \text{ and } P(tails) = \frac{1}{2}$$

Another example could be using a spinner.

The outcome of this experiment is the spinner landing on a particular colour.

If Chloe spins a spinner and it lands on green:
- the **experiment** is spinning the spinner
- the **event** (or outcome) is the colour the spinner lands on.

These can be said to be the events connected with the experiment.

So when the spinner lands on green, an event can be said to have occurred.

The mathematical language of probability

To understand probability, we must understand the language used to desribe the chances of something happening. For example:

What is the likelihood of rain today?

What's the probability my bus will arrive on time?

What are the chances our school will win the league cup this year?

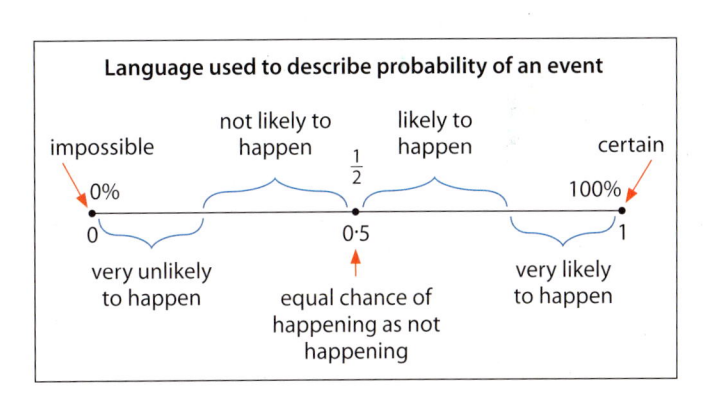

Language used to describe probability of an event

impossible | not likely to happen | $\frac{1}{2}$ | likely to happen | certain
0% | | | | 100%
0 | very unlikely to happen | 0·5 equal chance of happening as not happening | very likely to happen | 1

- If something is certain to happen, it has a probability of 1 (or 100%).
- If something is certain **not** to happen (impossible) it has a probability of 0 (or 0%).
- All other events have a probability between 0 and 1 (0% and 100%).

You cannot have a negative value for probability.

The probability of an event can be expressed as a fraction, decimal or percentage.

Section A Introducing concepts and building skills

Discuss and discover

Working with your classmates, list:
- 3 events that are certain to happen
- 3 events that will never happen (impossible)
- 3 events that might happen.

Assign a probabilty value to each of the 3 events you think might happen.

KEY SKILLS

Certain questions in probabilty involve dice, spinners, playing cards, etc. It is important you know about these objects.

Know your dice!

A die is a cube consisting of six faces. Each face has a number of dots from one to six.

Opposite faces of a die add up to seven.

Note: Die is singular for one cube; dice is plural for two or more cubes.

Know your cards!

There are a total of 52 cards in a deck, excluding two 'Joker' cards.

There are four suits: hearts, diamonds, spades and clubs.

There are 13 cards in each suit.

There are 26 red cards and 26 black cards.

There are four cards of each value.

The jacks, queens and kings are picture cards. Thus, there are a total of 12 picture cards in the deck.

A deck of cards has 13 cards in 4 suits

	A	2	3	4	5	6	7	8	9	10	J	Q	K
Hearts	Ace ♥	2 ♥	3 ♥	4 ♥	5 ♥	6 ♥	7 ♥	8 ♥	9 ♥	10 ♥	Jack ♥	Queen ♥	King ♥
Diamonds	Ace ♦	2 ♦	3 ♦	4 ♦	5 ♦	6 ♦	7 ♦	8 ♦	9 ♦	10 ♦	Jack ♦	Queen ♦	King ♦
Clubs	Ace ♣	2 ♣	3 ♣	4 ♣	5 ♣	6 ♣	7 ♣	8 ♣	9 ♣	10 ♣	Jack ♣	Queen ♣	King ♣
Spades	Ace ♠	2 ♠	3 ♠	4 ♠	5 ♠	6 ♠	7 ♠	8 ♠	9 ♠	10 ♠	Jack ♠	Queen ♠	King ♠

Practice questions 6.1

1. Copy and label the probability scale below. Place the following events where you think they should go. Justify your answer.

   0 ———————————— 0·5 ———————————— 1

   (i) The sun will rise tomorrow.
   (ii) If I toss a coin, it will land on heads.
   (iii) Christmas day will be in June.
   (iv) It will rain tomorrow.
   (v) I will win the lottery if I don't have a ticket.
   (vi) Humans will visit the planet Mars by the year 2050.

2. Which of the values below could represent the probability of an event occurring?

   (i) 2·1
   (ii) −3
   (iii) $\frac{2}{3}$
   (iv) $\frac{5}{4}$
   (v) $1\frac{1}{7}$
   (vi) 72·4%
   (vii) 0·001
   (viii) 99·999
   (ix) 110%
   (x) 0·999124

Linking Thinking 1

3. State the letter you think best represents the following events on the number line.
   (i) An event that is impossible
   (ii) An event that has an even chance of happening
   (iii) An event that is certain to happen
   (iv) An event that is very likely to happen
   (v) An event that is unlikely to happen
   (vi) An event that is likely to happen

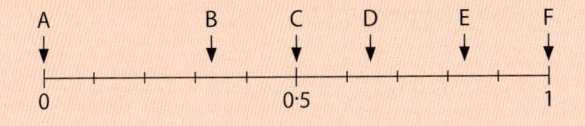

   A   B   C   D   E   F
   |---------|------|---|------|----|
   0   0·5   1

4. Assign a probability value to the following events. In each case, justify your answer.
   (i) The sun will rise in the north.
   (ii) Saint Patrick's Day will be in March.
   (iii) If I toss a coin, it will land on tails.
   (iv) If you roll two standard dice, you will obtain a score of zero.
   (v) A natural number chosen at random will be even.
   (vi) A person will have a birthday on the 32nd of June.

Taking it FURTHER

5. Think of an event that would have the following probability.
   (i) 0·5
   (ii) $\frac{2}{7}$
   (iii) 70%
   (iv) $\frac{5}{6}$

6·2 Calculate the probability of a single event

By the end of this section you should:
- be able to list all possible outcomes of an experiment
- understand how to calculate basic single event probabilities

In experiments involving chance, we must use the correct language to accurately describe what we are doing and the results obtained.

An **experiment** or **trial** is the event or action of doing something and recording results, e.g. tossing a coin, rolling a dice, choosing a marble from a bag, etc.

An **outcome** is a possible result of an experiment or trial.

Probability of an event happening

When there are multiple outcomes to a trial, the probability of an event occurring P(E) is

$$P(E) = \frac{\text{number of outcomes favourable to that event}}{\text{number of possible outcomes}}$$

Worked example 1

Calculate the probability of rolling the number 3 on a standard die.

Solution

$P(3) = \frac{1}{6}$

→ There is only one number 3 on a standard die, number of favourable outcomes = 1

→ There are six possible outcomes, which can occur when rolling a standard die {1, 2, 3, 4, 5, 6}
Number of possible outcomes = 6

This is known as a **theoretical probability**.

Section A Introducing concepts and building skills

> **Theoretical probability** predicts the outcome(s) we expect to happen in the long term.

If you toss a coin 10 times, theoretical probability states that you should get five heads and five tails. In real life, this is seldom the case. However, if you toss a coin 10 000 times, you will see results of 50% heads and 50% tails, as predicted by theoretical probability.

We usually just say 'probability' instead of 'theoretical probability'.

Probability of an event not happening

It is important to note that the sum of the probabilities of an event happening and an event not happening must equal 1. If E is an event, then we can write:

$$P(E \text{ happening}) + P(E \text{ not happening}) = 1$$
$$P(E \text{ happening}) = 1 - (E \text{ not happening})$$
or
$$P(E \text{ not happening}) = 1 - (E \text{ happening})$$

Worked example 2

In Worked example 1, we saw that the probability of rolling the number 3 on a standard die was $\frac{1}{6}$. Calculate the probability of not rolling a 3 on a standard die.

Solution

Method 1
There are five favourable outcomes {1, 2, 4, 5, 6}
There are six possible outcomes on a standard die {1, 2, 3, 4, 5, 6}
P(not rolling a 3) = $\frac{5}{6}$

Method 2
P(not rolling a 3) = 1 − P(rolling a 3)
P(not rolling a 3) = 1 − $\frac{1}{6}$
P(not rolling a 3) = $\frac{5}{6}$

Worked example 3

One card is randomly selected from a deck of 52 playing cards. Find the probability that the card selected was (i) an ace, (ii) a red card, (iii) not an ace.

Solution

(i) Number of favourable outcomes = 4   Total number of outcomes = 52
P(ace) = $\frac{4}{52} = \frac{1}{13}$

(ii) Number of favourable outcomes = 26   Total number of outcomes = 52
P(a red card) = $\frac{26}{52} = \frac{1}{2}$

(iii) There are 52 cards in the deck, of which 4 are aces. This means 48 cards are 'not an ace'
Number of favourable outcomes = 48   Total number of outcomes = 52
P(not an ace) = $\frac{48}{52} = \frac{12}{13}$ **OR**   P(not an ace) = 1 − P(ace)
P(not an ace) = 1 − $\frac{4}{52}$
P(not an ace) = $\frac{48}{52} = \frac{12}{13}$

Fractions should always be expressed in their simplest form.

Worked example 4

Karla spins the pointer on this spinner. All sections of the spinner are equal in size.
(i) List the possible outcomes.
(ii) Find the probability that the pointer lands on:
   (a) black   (b) red   (c) not yellow   (d) blue

Solution

(i) The possible outcomes are white, yellow, red and black

(ii) (a) No. of favourable outcomes = 1; no. of possible outcomes = 4
$$P(black) = \frac{1}{4}$$

(b) No. of favourable outcomes = 1; no. of possible outcomes = 4
$$P(red) = \frac{1}{4}$$

(c) No. of favourable outcomes = 3; no. of possible outcomes = 4
$$P(not\ yellow) = \frac{3}{4}$$

(d) No. of favourable outcomes = 0 (as there is no blue section); no. of possible outcomes = 4
$$P(blue) = \frac{0}{4} = 0$$

Practice questions 6·2

1. A paper bag contains 3 green tiles, 2 yellow tiles and 1 blue tile. Liz draws a single tile without looking.
   (i) List the possible outcomes.
   (ii) What is the probability that the tile is …?
      (a) green   (b) yellow
      (c) blue   (d) pink

2. Shauna rolls a standard die, numbered 1 to 6.
   (i) List the possible outcomes.
   (ii) What is the probability of each of the following outcomes?
      (a) 1   (d) A number less than 5
      (b) An even number   (e) A positive integer
      (c) A prime number

3. A jar contains 9 black, 22 red, 26 orange and 13 green marbles.

   A marble is picked at random and its colour is recorded.
   (i) List all the possible outcomes.
   (ii) What is the probability of choosing …?
      (a) a green marble
      (b) a black marble
      (c) a yellow marble
      (d) any colour marble except for red

4. This table shows the number of birthdays each month for a first-year class.

Month	January	February	March	April	May	June	July	August
Number of students	2	4	3	2	5	8	5	3

A student is picked at random. What is the probability of each of the following events?
(i) The student has a birthday in March
(ii) The student has a birthday in June
(iii) The student does not have a birthday in August

Section A Introducing concepts and building skills

5. A regular five-sided spinner has the numbers 1 to 5 marked on its sections. All sections are equal in size.
   After one spin, what is the probability of getting …?

   (i) an even number (ii) a prime number (iii) a factor of 6 (iv) a factor of 16

6. Two hundred and fifty tickets for a raffle were sold. One ticket, drawn at random, wins the prize.

   (i) Raul purchased 1 ticket. What is the probability Raul will win?

   (ii) Maria purchased 10 tickets. What is the probability Maria will win?

   (iii) Ivan purchased 25 tickets. What is the probability Ivan will **not** win?

7. A bag contains a number of jelly beans. Each jelly bean is red, green, blue or orange. Abraham takes a jelly bean at random from the bag. The table below shows the probability of each outcome.

Colour of jelly bean	Red	Green	Blue	Orange
Probability	0·20	0·05	0·15	x

   (i) What is the probability that Abraham chooses an orange jelly bean?

   (ii) What is the probability that Abraham does **not** choose a blue jelly bean? Express your answer as a percentage.

8. In a class of 40 students, 8 are in the drama club and 12 are in the art club. A student can only be in one club. If a student is selected at random, what is the probability that the selected student is …?

   (i) in the drama club (ii) in the art club (iii) not in any club

6·3 The fundamental principle of counting

By the end of this section you should:
- understand and be able to use the fundamental principle of counting to solve problems

You go to a restaurant to get some breakfast. The menu offers pancakes, waffles and fruit salad, with one of the following drinks: coffee, juice, hot chocolate or tea.
How many different choices of food and drink do you have?

We could start this question by listing all of the options available to us.

Pancakes and coffee	Waffles and coffee	Fruit salad and coffee
Pancakes and juice	Waffles and juice	Fruit salad and juice
Pancakes and hot chocolate	Waffles and hot chocolate	Fruit salad and hot chocolate
Pancakes and tea	Waffles and tea	Fruit salad and tea

Linking Thinking 1

Writing out all the possible combinations gives us a list of 12 options. This is known as systematic listing.

However, we could have worked out the total number of options much faster using the **fundamental principle of counting (FPoC)**.

The fundamental principle of counting is used to work out the total number of outcomes in a probability problem. You multiply the number of choices for each option together to get the total number of possible ways two or more options can be combined.

> The **fundamental principle of counting** (FPoC) is a rule that allows you to find the number of ways that a combination of events can occur.

As mentioned earlier in this unit, the result of a probability experiment is called an outcome or an event.

If we perform one operation and then another (as in the example above, choosing a meal and then a drink), we can mathematically calculate the total number of choices possible by using the FPoC.

Fundamental principle of counting (FPoC)

(first choice)   AND   (second choice)

m × n = number of possible outcomes

When there are m ways to do one thing and n ways to do another, then there are $m \times n$ ways of doing both.

The FPoC can be applied in this way, no matter how many options there are in a problem.

You will notice in the problem above that there were 12 different possible options for breakfast, including three types of meal and four types of drink. If we multiply 3 by 4, we get 12.

(pancakes, waffles, fruit salad) × (coffee, juice, hot chocolate, tea) = number of breakfast options
            3   ×   4   = 12

Sample space diagrams

When the number of choices increases, it can become difficult to list all combinations. To assist with this, we can use a sample space diagram. A sample space diagram makes sure we don't forget any outcomes.

> A **sample space** is the list or set of all possible outcomes.

There are two main types of sample space diagrams:
1. Two-way tables
2. Tree diagrams

1. Two-way tables

If there are a lot of possible outcomes involved, a two-way table is a convenient way to list them.

Here is a two-way table of all possible outcomes for tossing a coin and rolling a die simultaneously (at the same time).

		Possibilities for the die					
		1	2	3	4	5	6
Possibilities for the coin	Heads (H)	H1	H2	H3	H4	H5	H6
	Tails (T)	T1	T2	T3	T4	T5	T6

> A **two-way table** is a way of listing all possible outcomes when combining a number of choices within two categories.

Section A Introducing concepts and building skills

All of the choices for one of the categories are listed in the left vertical column.

The choices for the other category are listed along the top horizontal row. If we use our breakfast example from earlier, the two-way table would look like this:

		Drink			
		Coffee (C)	Juice (J)	Hot chocolate (H)	Tea (T)
Food	Pancakes (P)	PC	PJ	PH	PT
	Waffles (W)	WC	WJ	WH	WT
	Fruit salad (F)	FC	FJ	FH	FT

Worked example

Patrick has decided to purchase a new car. The colours the garage offer are silver, black and red. The types of car are five-door or three-door.

(i) How many different options of car are available to Patrick?
(ii) List all the possible combinations of car Patrick could purchase.

Solution

(i) Use the FPoC:

Number of colours available = 3
Number of types of car = 2
Total number of combinations = 3 × 2
Total number of combinations = 6

We can use $m \times n$ or 3 (colours) multiplied by 2 (door types)

(ii) Create a two-way table to show all the possible options.

	Silver car	Black car	Red car
Five-door car	Silver five-door car	Black five-door car	Red five-door car
Three-door car	Silver three-door car	Black three-door car	Red three-door car

2. Tree diagrams

> A **tree diagram** is a way of listing all possible outcomes when combining a number of choices within two or more categories.

A tree diagram is a way of seeing all the possible probability 'routes' for two (or more) events. Its name comes from the fact that, when complete, the diagram looks similar to the branches of a tree. Each branch of the tree represents a different outcome. When we follow the branches of the tree, we can see all of the possible outcomes.

Worked example 1

Draw a tree diagram to illustrate all the different outcomes when tossing a coin twice.

Solution

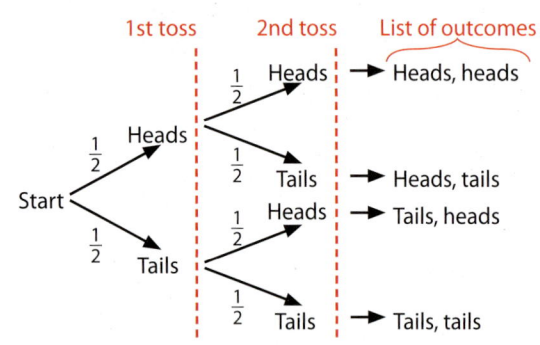

Notes on the tree diagram:
- Each of the four branches represents a different possible outcome in the sample space.
- The probabilities along each set of branches, coming from one point, must add up to 1.
- By following the branches, we can tell that the outcomes (sample space) are {(H,H), (H,T), (T,H), (T,T)}

Note: H = heads and T = tails

Linking Thinking 1

Worked example 2

On this spinner, the pointer is spun once and the colour is recorded.
The pointer is spun a second time and the colour is recorded.

(i) Draw a tree diagram to list the possible outcomes.
(ii) Find the probability of getting the same colour on both spins.
(iii) Find the probability of getting different colours on each spin.

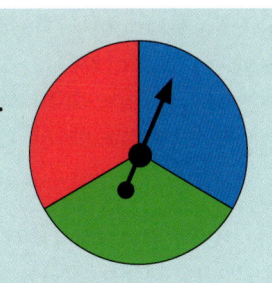

Solution

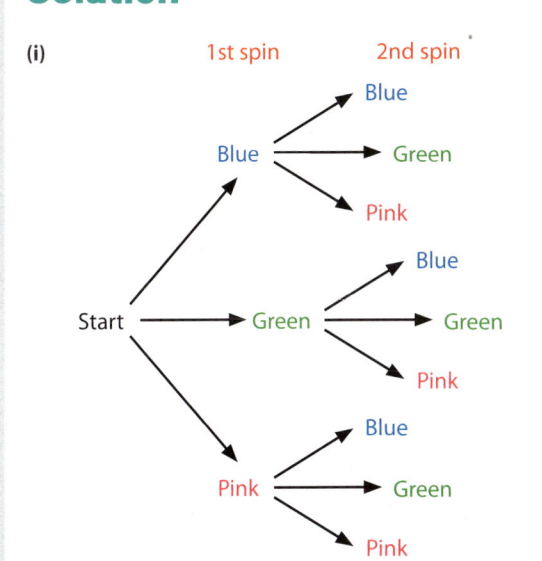

(i)

1st spin	2nd spin	Possible outcomes
Blue	Blue	Blue, blue
Blue	Green	Blue, green
Blue	Pink	Blue, pink
Green	Blue	Green, blue
Green	Green	Green, green
Green	Pink	Green, pink
Pink	Blue	Pink, blue
Pink	Green	Pink, green
Pink	Pink	Pink, pink

List of all possible outcomes, also known as a sample space

(ii) From the tree diagram, we know there are nine possible outcomes. Three outcomes have the same colours:

(blue, blue), (green, green), (pink, pink)

P(same colours) = $\frac{3}{9} = \frac{1}{3}$

(iii) There are a total of nine outcomes. Six outcomes have different colours:

(blue, green), (blue, pink), (green, blue), (green, pink), (pink, blue), (pink, green)

P(different colours) = $\frac{6}{9} = \frac{2}{3}$

Practice questions 6·3

1. You are getting ready to go out after school. In your wardrobe you have the following choices of what to wear: a red t-shirt, a blue t-shirt, or a white t-shirt; a pair of jeans or a pair of tracksuit bottoms.

   (i) How many different outfits could be made with these choices?

   (ii) List all the possible outcomes of what you could wear.

2. Jinny is buying a new mountain bike. She can choose from five paint colours – black, blue, red, silver or gold – and two seat colours – grey or black.

   (i) How many different combinations of paint and seat colours are possible?

   (ii) Draw a two-way table to display all the possible combinations of paint and seat colours.

   (iii) Suppose Jinny were to choose colours by pointing at the table without looking. What is the probability she would end up with a silver bike and grey seat?

3. A cinema sells three sizes of popcorn (small, medium, large) with three choices of toppings (sweet, salty, plain).

   (i) How many possible ways can a box of popcorn be purchased?

   (ii) Draw a table to display all the possible combinations of popcorn available.

Section A Introducing concepts and building skills

4. Clown Burger shop offers 4 types of burgers, 5 types of drinks, and 3 types of desserts. If a meal consists of one burger, one drink and one dessert, how many possible meals can be chosen?

5. A school considers choosing a Head Boy and a Head Girl from a group of three boys (Seán, Ruben and David) and five girls (Blessing, Anita, Katie, Rita and Gia).
   (i) How many different combinations are possible?
   (ii) List all possible combinations.

6. A bag contains four blue counters and four green counters. One counter is picked and then replaced. A second counter is then picked.
   (i) Copy the tree diagram and complete it based on the information above. 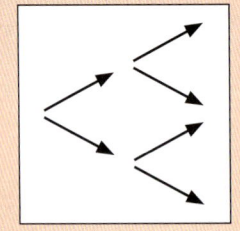
   (ii) List all the outcomes which are possible.
   (iii) What is the probability of choosing two blue counters?
   (iv) What is the probability of choosing two counters that are not the same colour?

7. A box of chocolates contains three dark chocolates and two white chocolates. A chocolate is picked and then replaced. A second chocolate is then picked. 
   (i) Draw a tree diagram to show all the possible outcomes.
   (ii) What is the probability that both chocolates picked will be the same colour?
   (iii) What is the probability that the chocolates will be different colours?

8. The Murphy family plan to take a trip in the autumn.
   - There are 15 destinations they could choose from.
   - They could travel by train, ship or plane.
   - They could take this trip either by themselves, or with a tour group.

   How many different ways can the Murphys organise their holiday?

9. A window comes in 5 different styles, 8 different sizes and with 3 different types of glass. How many possible different windows can be ordered?

10. Jo always dresses in a t-shirt, jeans, and runners. There are 72 different outfits she can make with them. If she has eight t-shirts and three pairs of jeans, then how many pairs of runners does she have?

Revision questions

6A Core skills

1. Copy the probability scale shown and label the following events on it.
   (i) The chance of getting an even number when rolling a die
   (ii) The chance of winning the National Lottery
   (iii) The chance of rain in March in Ireland
   (iv) The chance of getting no Maths homework today

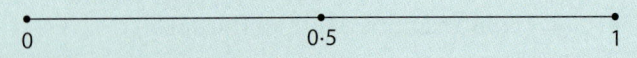

2. Describe an event that you think has a probability of:
   (i) 0·3
   (ii) 50%
   (iii) $\frac{9}{10}$
   (iv) 1
   (v) 0

3. Elaine is picking randomly from a bag containing tiles numbered 1 to 10. Write down the probability that the number she picks is:
   (i) 6
   (ii) 4 or less
   (iii) a multiple of 3
   (iv) odd
   (v) 21

4. The weather forecast says that there is a 30% chance of rain tomorrow. 
   (i) What is the probability it will not rain?
   (ii) Would you bring an umbrella to school tomorrow? Justify your answer.

5. If the letters of the word 'crocodile' are placed into a bag. One letter is drawn out a random. What is the probability of picking …?
   (i) the letter d
   (ii) the letter c
   (iii) a vowel
   (iv) a consonant
   (v) not the letter o
   (vi) the letter z
   (vii) the letter y

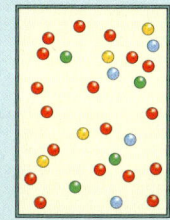

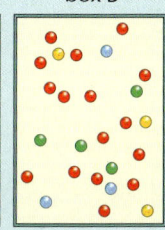

6. Two boxes, each containing a number of marbles, are shown.

   box A   box B

   Box A contains 30 marbles, 18 of which are red. Box B contains 26 marbles, 16 of which are red.

   Which box do you have a better chance of choosing a red marble from? Justify your answer.

7. A teacher wants to buy one fountain pen, one notebook and one pencil from a stationery shop. If there are 10 types of fountain pen, 12 types of notebook and 5 types of pencil, how many combinations of fountain pen, notebook and pencil could the teacher buy?

8. You are choosing curtains, paint, and carpet for your room. You have 12 choices of curtains, 8 choices of paint, and 20 choices of carpet. How many ways can you choose curtains, paint and carpet for your room?

9. A shop sells jackets that come in sizes small, medium or large, with a colour choice of red or grey.
   (i) Draw a tree diagram to illustrate all the possibilities of jacket you could buy.
   (ii) If you were to randomly pick up a jacket, what is the probability if would be a red jacket in size medium?

10. Harry is making a sandwich using bread, cheese and meat. He has two types of bread and three types of cheese. If he can make 30 different types of sandwich, how many different types of meat does he have to choose from?

11. Look at the following information and then answer the questions below.

    $\mathbb{U}$ = {1, 2, 3, 4, 5, 6, 7, 8, 9, 10, 11, 12, 13, 14, 15}

    A = {factors of 12}   B = {multiples of 3}

    (i) Draw a Venn diagram to represent this information
    (ii) If a number is selected at random, what is the probability that it will be …?
        (a) an even number
        (b) a prime number
        (c) a factor of 12 and a multiple of 3
        (d) neither a factor of 12 nor a multiple of 3

6B Taking it FURTHER

1. A class had a survey to find out how many students were left-handed and how many were right-handed. The results are presented in the table.

	Girls	Boys
Right-handed	13	14
Left-handed	2	1

   If a person is picked at random from this class, what is the probability that they are …?
   (i) a girl
   (ii) a left-handed person
   (iii) a right-handed boy

2. A spinner numbered 1 to 8 and a standard die are shown.

   The spinner is spun and the die rolled. The numbers that appear on each are added together to give a total score.

   (i) Copy the table below and list all the possible scores. Some scores have already been added.

		Number on the spinner							
		1	2	3	4	5	6	7	8
Number on die	1	1 + 1 = 2							
	2	2 + 1 = 3		2 + 3 = 5				2 + 7 = 11	
	3	3 + 1 = 4			3 + 4 = 7				
	4	4 + 1 = 5					4 + 6 = 10		
	5	5 + 1 = 6							5 + 8 = 13
	6	6 + 1 = 7				6 + 5 = 11			

(Note: numbers in **black** represent the score obtained)

   (ii) How many possible outcomes are there?
   (iii) What is the probability of scoring 8?
   (iv) What is the probability of scoring an even number?
   (v) What is the probability of scoring a multiple of 3?
   (vi) What is the probability of **not** scoring a prime number?

3. Neither Andrew nor David like to set the table for dinner. They each toss a coin to decide who will set the table.
   - If both coins show heads, David sets the table.
   - If both coins show tails, Andrew sets the table.
   - If the coins show a head and a tail, Andrew and David set the table together.

   (i) Calculate the probability the David will have to set the table on a particular day.
   (ii) What is the probability they both have to set the table on a particular day?

4. A coin is tossed three times. Each result is recorded.
   (i) Display all possible outcomes using a tree diagram.
   (ii) What is the probability of getting three heads?
   (iii) What is the probability of getting two tails and one head?
   (iv) What is the probability of getting heads, then tails, and finally heads?

5. Explain the fundamental principle of counting (FPoC) in your own words. Do you think it is an easier way of calculating the total number of outcomes than by using a tree diagram or two-way table? Justify your answer.

6. A restaurant offers starters, main courses and desserts. It has three kinds of starters, five kinds of main courses and four desserts.
   (i) How many choices are on offer if each customer gets one starter, one main course and one dessert?
   (ii) How many choices are on offer if each customer only gets one starter and one main course?

7. Samuel wants to know if he can go a whole month without wearing the exact same outfit twice.

   He has three pairs of tracksuit bottoms, six t-shirts and three pairs of runners. Can he make a unique outfit for each day of the month? Assume a month contains 30 days. Justify your answer.

8. A group of students were asked which after-school clubs they attended.

The Venn diagram below shows the answers given.

Photography: 6, Coding: 35, Both: 9, Neither: 52

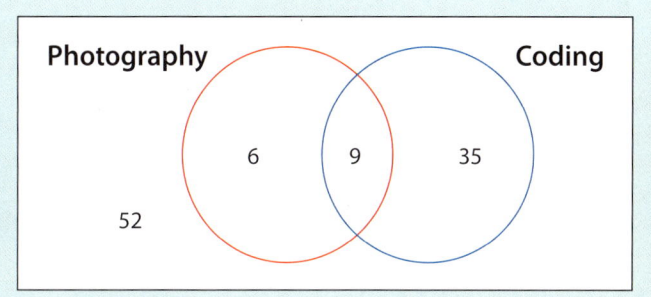

(i) How many students were asked which after-school clubs they attended?

(ii) A student is chosen at random from the group. Calculate the probability that:
- (a) the student goes to Photography club
- (b) the student goes to both clubs
- (c) the student doesn't go to Coding club
- (d) the student doesn't go to either club
- (e) the student goes only to Photography club **or** Coding club, not both

9. The Gardaí use photographs of various facial features to help witnesses identify suspects. One basic identification kit contains photos of 195 hairlines, 99 eyes/eyebrows, 89 noses, 105 mouths and 74 chins/cheeks.

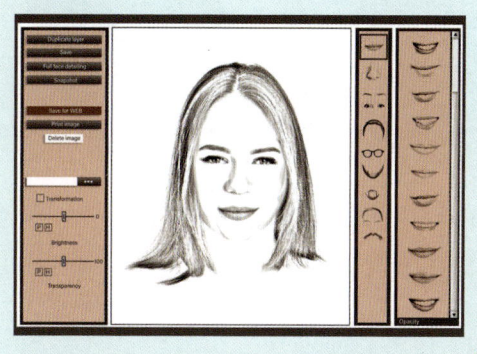

(i) Calculate how many different faces this identification kit can produce. Give your answer in the following forms:
- (a) The exact number
- (b) The number rounded to three significant figures
- (c) The number written in words

(ii) The developer of the identification kit claims that it can produce billions of different faces. Is he correct? Justify your answer.

Now that you have completed the unit, revisit the

Something to think about ...

question posed at the start of this unit.

Now try question 1 on page 185

7 Patterns

❓ Something to think about …

A high-speed train is moving between two posts along a straight track, a distance 3·78 km apart. It travels 60 metres in the first second. After 2 seconds, the total distance travelled is 120 metres. After 3 seconds, the train has travelled a total distance of 180 metres.

If the train continues to travel at this rate, how many seconds does it take to travel between the posts?

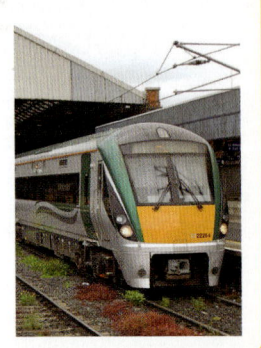

KEY SKILLS

Topics covered within this unit:
- 7·1 Introduction to patterns
- 7·2 Representing patterns
- 7·3 Examining the rate of change of a pattern
- 7·4 Identifying a pattern as linear or non-linear

The Learning Outcomes covered in this chapter are contained in the following sections:
AF.1a   AF.1c   AF.7d   N.4   GT.5b

Key words
Pattern
Stage
Variable
Linear graph
Slope (rate of change)

7·1 Introduction to patterns

By the end of this section you should:
- understand what a pattern is
- be able to find a given stage in a basic pattern

We see patterns every day – patterns on clothing, carpets, wallpaper, books and magazines, and more.

A **pattern** can be explained as a repeated design or recurring sequence. It is an ordered set of numbers, shapes, or other mathematical objects, arranged according to a rule.

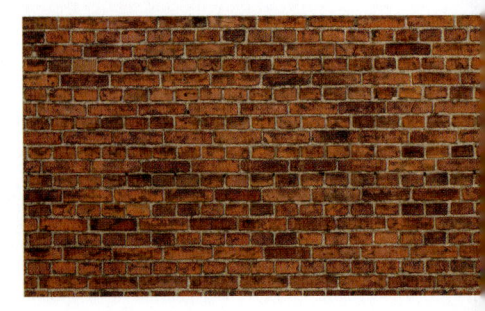

There are many different types of patterns. Some have pictures (graphics); others have numbers or letters. Here are some examples of basic patterns.

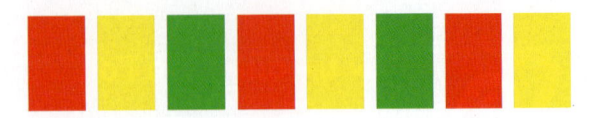

108   Linking Thinking 1

These are known as repeating patterns, meaning the pattern continually repeats itself.

We also have patterns which can increase or decrease in size. Here are some examples:

Example of a growing pattern (increasing in size)   Example of a reducing pattern (decreasing in size)

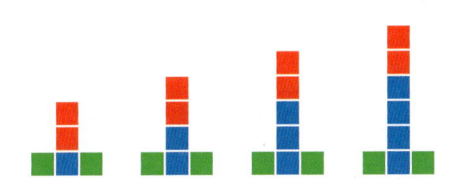

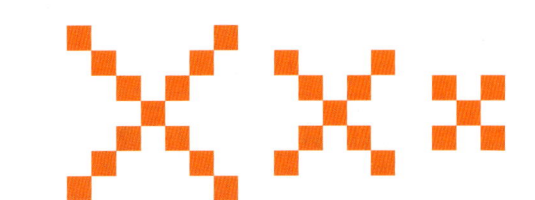

Not all patterns are made up of shapes. We can use numbers or letters.

Examples of increasing numerical patterns
- 2, 4, 6, 8, 10, …
- −4, −1, 2, 5, 8, 11, …

Examples of decreasing numerical patterns
- 21, 18, 15, 12, 9, …
- 5, 1, −3, −7, −11, −15, …

The one thing all patterns have in common is that they contain a key. The key to every pattern is that they follow a rule (or a formula). Once you understand what the key is, you can predict any stage in the pattern.

> The **stage** is the position of any particular object in a pattern. Every pattern has multiple stages e.g. the first stage, the second stage, the third stage and so on.

Worked example

Consider the following pattern: M, A, T, H, S, M, A, T, H, S, M, A, …

This is a repeating pattern where the first stage (in this case a letter) = M, the second stage = A and so on.

Using this pattern, find:

(i) the 7th stage   (ii) the 11th stage   (iii) the 157th stage

Solution

(i) By observation, we can see that the 7th letter in the pattern is A.
Therefore, 7th stage = A

(ii) By observation, we can see that the 11th letter in the pattern is M.
Therefore, 11th stage = M

Remember, all patterns must follow a basic rule or formula.

(iii) Find the 157th stage of this pattern.

You may have found the first two answers by simply writing out the repeating pattern in a line or a table. To find the 157th stage, however, we have to come up with a different strategy.

It would be very time consuming to write out this pattern to 157 letters, so we have to find a key to help us find the answer.

If we examine the pattern, we notice that the 5th stage is the letter 'S' and five stages later is also 'S'. This means that the 10th stage is also 'S', as is the 15th stage, and so on. Therefore we can say that any stage which is a multiple of 5 (or can be divided evenly by 5) will be an 'S'.

How can this help us to find stage 157?

The nearest number to 157 that is divisible by 5 is '155'. As a multiple of 5, 155 must be an 'S'. Since we know that the pattern repeats, there are two ways to find stage 157 in the M, A, T, H, S pattern:

- start at stage 155 and count forwards two stages through the pattern to stage 157; or
- start at stage 160 and count backwards three stages through the pattern to stage 157.

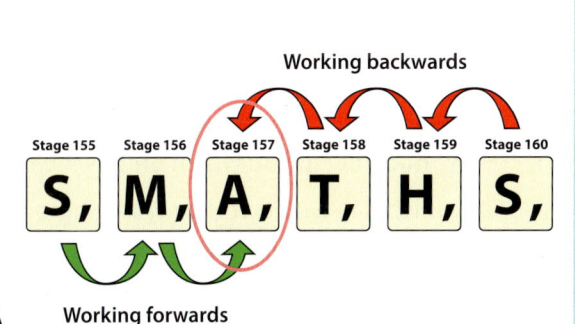

Both methods provide the same result.   Stage 157 = A

Section A Introducing concepts and building skills   109

Practice questions 7·1

1. Name the two animals missing in this pattern.

2. Copy the pattern provided and draw the next three stages.

3. Copy the patterns below and draw the next stage in each case.
   (i) 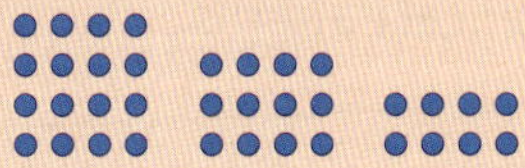
   (ii)

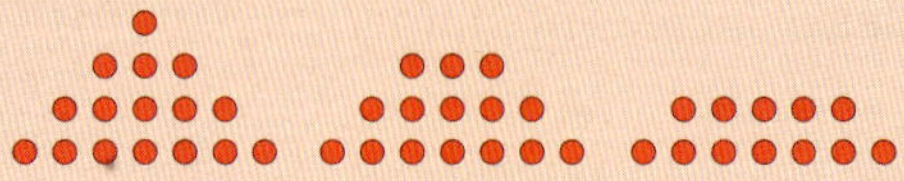

4. Copy the patterns below and draw the next two stages in each case.
   (i) 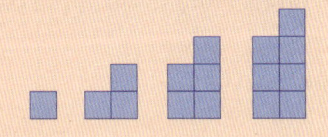
   (ii)

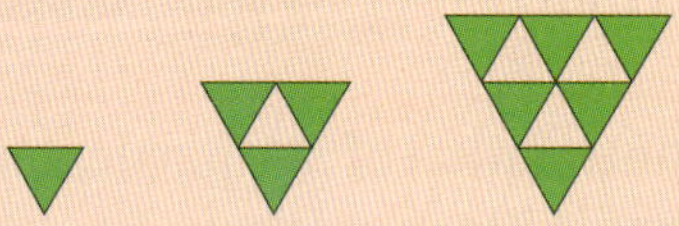

5. List the next three numbers for each of the patterns below.
   (i) 3, 5, 7, 9, 11, …
   (ii) −4, −1, 2, 5, …
   (iii) 5, 11, 17, 23, …
   (iv) 7, 2, −3, −8, −13, …
   (v) 77, 88, 99, …

6. Copy the patterns below and fill in the missing numbers in each case.
   (i) 2, 4, 6, ☐, 10, ☐, 14, ☐
   (ii) 7, 14, ☐, 28, 35, ☐, 49
   (iii) 98, 94, ☐, 86, 82, ☐
   (iv) 6, 3, ☐, −3, −6, ☐, −12
   (v) −15, ☐, −5, ☐, 5, 10, 15
   (vi) $\frac{1}{8}, \frac{1}{4}$, ☐, 1, 2, ☐, 8, ☐

7. Ronnie likes to eat his Smarties in a particular way. He eats three yellow Smarties first, then five blue Smarties, then seven orange Smarties. If he decides to eat the green Smarties next and wants this pattern to continue, how many green Smarties do you think Ronnie will eat?

8. Sarah got a new video game. She scored 7 points on the first level, 12 points on the second level, 17 points on the third level, 22 points on the fourth level, and 27 points on the fifth level. If this pattern continues, how many points will Sarah score on the sixth level?

9. You are visiting a theme park for a week. On Monday you go on 6 rides, on Tuesday you go on 10 rides and on Wednesday you go on 14 rides. 
   (i) On Friday, how many rides do you go on?
   (ii) How many rides do you go on in total over both Saturday and Sunday?

10. On the first day after buying a new big screen TV you watch 80 minutes of TV. Your mum tells you to halve the amount of time each day you spend watching. 
    (i) How much TV do you watch on the second day?
    (ii) On which day would you be watching only 5 minutes of TV?
    (iii) Will there eventually be a day where your TV viewing time = 0? Justify your answer.

11. These letters form a pattern, P, E, N, C, I, L, P, E, N, C, I, L, P, E, …
    (i) Write out the next three stages of the pattern.
    (ii) What letter will stage 303 be?

7·2 Representing patterns

By the end of this section you should:
- understand increasing and decreasing patterns
- be able to represent a pattern in a table
- be able to represent a pattern by drawing a graph

So far, we have looked at simple repeating patterns, and basic number patterns. Now we are going to investigate 'growing' (or 'increasing') and 'shrinking' (or 'decreasing') patterns.

These patterns always have values that are changing by a fixed certain amount.

A value that changes (or varies) is called a **variable**.

Worked example 1

You receive a savings box as a birthday present on Sunday. The savings box already has €5 in it. From Monday, you plan to save €2 per day.
(i) How much money will be in your savings box after 7 days?
(ii) Identify the variables in this situation.

Solution

(i) There are several ways we can figure this out.

Method 1
Write out the pattern for seven days:
€5, €7, €9, €11, €13, €15, €17, €19
Which amount is correct for day 7?
Remember you started with €5, then you saved €2 a day for 7 days.
You saved €14 over seven days ($2 \times 7 = 14$).
We can now add the €5 that was already in the savings box, which means that after 7 days, you have €14 + €5 = €19 in your savings box.

Method 2
Build a table:
After seven days, you would have €19 in your savings box.

Days	Amount
Start	€5
1	€7
2	€9
3	€11
4	€13
5	€15
6	€17
7	€19

(ii) In this situation the number of days and the amount in the savings box are changing (or 'varying'). So, the variables are the number of days and the amount in the savings box.

Drawing a graph of a pattern

Sometimes it is helpful to draw a graph of a pattern to help us understand what is happening.

Worked example 2

John sends two messages from his mobile phone every day. Draw a graph to show the total amount of messages John sends in five days.

Solution

It will help if we create a table showing the information. At the start (day 0), John has sent 0 text messages. On day 1, he has sent 2 messages, on day 2 he has sent 4 text messages, and so on.

Day	0	1	2	3	4	5
Number of texts sent	0	2	4	6	8	10

Section A Introducing concepts and building skills

Method

Step 1. Draw a horizontal and vertical axis.

Step 2. Label each axis – in this case, the number of days on the horizontal axis and the number of texts on the vertical axis.

Step 3. On day 1, John sends 2 texts. Move across to 1 on the x-axis (number of days), and move up 2 units on the y-axis (number of texts sent).

Step 4. Draw a point to represent this information.

Step 5. Repeat this procedure for day 2, when John had sent a total of 4 texts.

Step 6. Continue until you have plotted points for all 5 days.

Step 7. Finally, using a ruler, join up all the points to form a straight line.

From the graph, we can see that John sent a total of 10 text messages over 5 days.

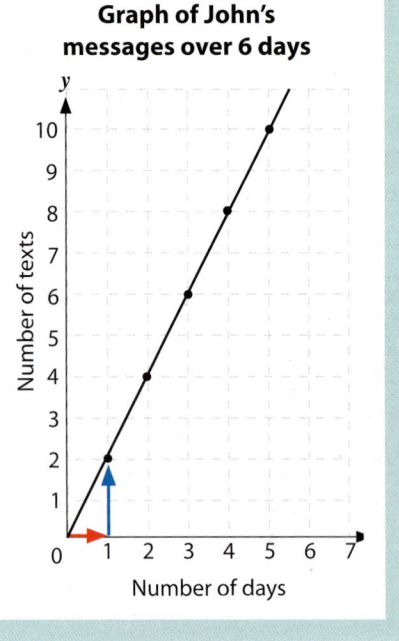

When we are working with graphs, it is important we pay close attention to the scale, axes, label and title – or **SALT**.

Scale: Choose horizontal and vertical scales that will accurately show the data.

Axes: On each axis, the scale is clearly shown and increments (values) evenly spaced.

Label: Label each axis identifying the data shown and the units used. For example, 'number of days' and 'number of messages sent'.

Title: The title should explain the purpose of the graph. For example, 'Graph of John's messages over 6 days'.

It is important to remember that graphs can go down as well as up. We read graphs from left to right. When a graph moves in a downward direction, it is representing a **decreasing pattern**. We draw this graph exactly the same way as an increasing pattern.

Worked example 3

Fiona has €18 on Sunday night. From Monday, she must spend €3 per day on lunch for five days.

(i) Create a table to show how Fiona's money is decreasing each day.

(ii) Draw a graph to show this information.

(iii) Will Fiona have enough money to buy lunch for 8 days? Explain your answer.

Solution

(i)

Day	Amount
0 (start)	18
1	15
2	12
3	9
4	6
5	3
6	0

(ii) Graph of Fiona's money (decreasing pattern)

(iii) We can see after 6 days, Fiona will not have any money left. So, she will not have enough money to buy lunch for 8 days.

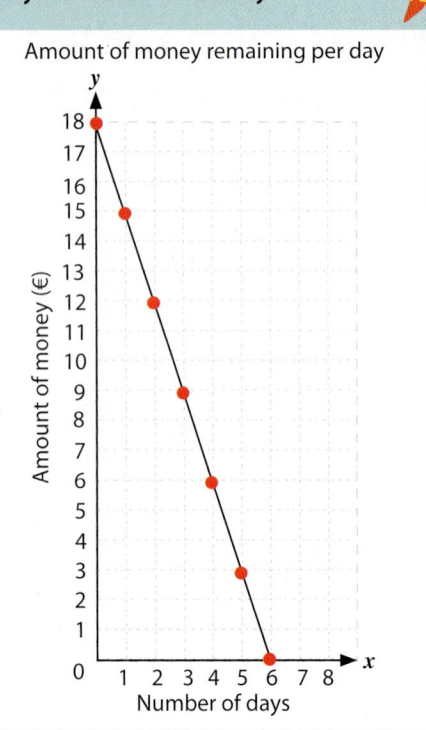

Discuss and discover

KEY SKILLS

Look at the two graphs provided. Which graph (A or B) do you think correctly displays the information?

For the incorrect graph, list the changes that would need to be made in order for it to correctly represent the data.

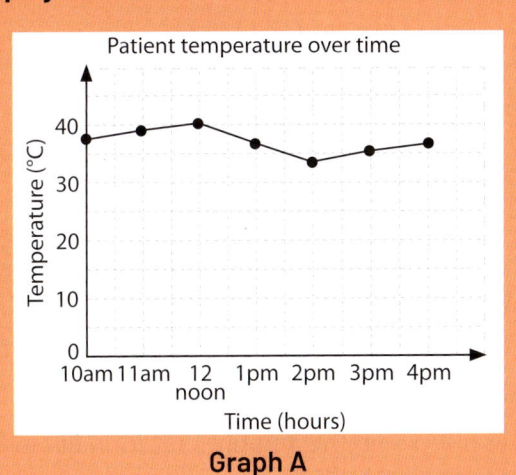

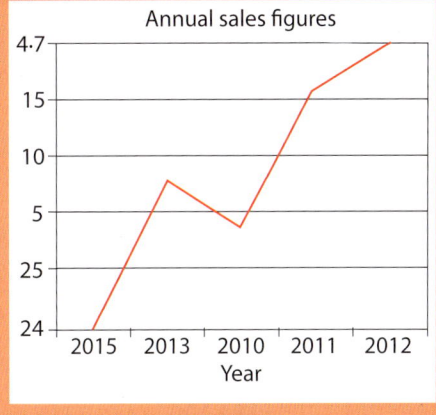

Graph A — Patient temperature over time

Graph B — Annual sales figures

Practice questions 7·2

1. Niamh saves €2 per day in her savings box for 6 days.
   (i) Create a table to show how much money Niamh has saved after 6 days.
   (ii) Draw a graph to show how much money Niamh has saved after 6 days.
   (iii) Identify the variables in this question.

2. When a flower is purchased, it is 2 cm tall. Each day, it grows 3 cm taller.
   (i) Create a table to show how tall the flower will be after 5 days.
   (ii) Draw a graph to show how tall the flower will be after 5 days.
   (iii) Identify the variables in this question.

3. An ice cube is at a temperature of −8°C. Every two minutes, the temperature increases by 1°C.
   (i) What will the temperature be in 8 minutes?
   (ii) Draw a graph to show this information.
   (iii) Identify the variables in this question.

4. A baker was putting cakes onto plates. He put 4 cakes on the first plate, 6 cakes on the second plate, 8 cakes on the third plate and 10 cakes on the fourth plate.
   (i) If this pattern continues, how many cakes will the baker put on the sixth plate?
   (ii) Draw a graph to show this information.
   (iii) Identify the variables in this question.

5. Raj was baking some gingerbread men. He used two jellies for the eyes and one jelly for the nose.
   (i) Create a table showing how many jellies Raj would need for 7 gingerbread men.
   (ii) Draw a graph showing the number of jellies Raj needed for 7 gingerbread men.
   (iii) How many complete gingerbread men could Raj make if he had 200 jellies?

Section A Introducing concepts and building skills

6. A ball starts at a height of 21 metres. It then falls at a constant rate of 3 metres per second.
   (i) After how many seconds will the ball hit the ground?
   (ii) Draw a graph to show this information.
   (iii) Identify the variables in this question.

7. A bus is carrying 24 people. At each stop, 4 people get off the bus. No one gets on the bus.
   (i) How many stops must the bus make so all the passengers have gotten off?
   (ii) Draw a graph to show this information.
   (iii) At which stop will the bus contain 8 passengers?

8. Mary and John each get a bank account. Mary starts by putting €10 into her account and then adds €2 per week. John doesn't put anything into his account at the start, but saves €4 into it every week.
   (i) Create a table showing Mary's savings and a table showing John's savings over the first 7 weeks.
   (ii) Draw a graph showing the amount that Mary has in her account each week for the first 7 weeks.
   (iii) Using the same axes and scale, draw a graph showing the amount that John has in his account each week, for the first 7 weeks.
   (iv) During which week will the amounts in their accounts be equal?

Taking it FURTHER

9. Two identical containers are being filled with water.
   Each container is 30 cm tall. Container A is empty at the start of the experiment. Once the experiment starts, the water level rises by 3 cm per minute.
   Container B already contains water at a height of 5 cm before the experiment begins. Once the experiment starts, the water level rises by 2 cm per minute.
   (i) Create a table showing how the water levels in each container change over 5 minutes.
   (ii) Draw a graph showing the height of the water in container A over 10 minutes.
   (iii) Using the same axes and scale, draw a graph showing the height of the water in container B over 10 minutes.
   (iv) Will the containers ever contain exactly the same level of water? Justify your answer.

7·3 Examining the rate of change of a pattern

By the end of this section you should:
- understand what the slope (rate of change) of a graph is
- be able to calculate the slope of a straight line graph
- understand how the rate of change in a pattern/graph is linked to its slope

There are many different types of pattern, but for now, we will be looking at patterns that have the same rate of change in each stage. These are called linear patterns.

> A **linear pattern** exists if the points that make it up form a straight line.
> A linear pattern has the same difference between stages.

Worked example 1

A snail is crawling along the path. Every 1 minute, the snail crawls 3 cm.
(i) Draw a table to show how far the snail has crawled in 6 minutes.
(ii) Draw a graph to show the snail's progress after 6 minutes.

Solution

(i)

Time taken (minutes)	Distance travelled (cm)
Start 0	0
1	3
2	6
3	9
4	12
5	15
6	18

(ii) Graph of snail's progress along the path

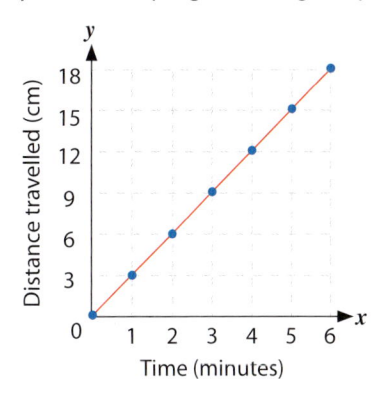

Using a graph to find the speed of an object

If we had been given the graph in the example above and we wanted to find the snail's average speed, we could use the speed formula:

$$\text{Average speed} = \frac{\text{distance travelled}}{\text{time taken}}$$

In this case, the snail travelled 18 cm in 6 minutes.

So, its average speed would be: Average speed = $\frac{18 \text{ cm}}{6 \text{ minutes}}$ = 3 cm per minute

Alternatively, we can find what is called the **rate of change** of the graph. The rate of change is how one thing changes compared to another.

There is a special name for this: **slope**. It is represented by the letter m.

Slope (m) = rate of change

$$\text{Slope } (m) = \frac{\text{rise}}{\text{run}}$$

Finding the slope of a straight line (linear) graph

1 Pick any two different points on the graph, e.g. A and B.

2 Using a ruler, draw a straight horizontal line from A so that the end this line is directly below point B (blue arrow).

3 Using a ruler, draw a straight line up from the end the horizontal line, so that it meets point B (green arrow).

We have now made a small triangle.

To find how fast the snail is going, we need to work out how much his distance is changing in a given time.

4 Using our triangle, we can see the distance (the **rise**) is cm, and the time (the **run**) is 2 minutes. To find the snail's speed which is the slope of the graph – we divide the rise by the run.

Slope (m) = $\frac{\text{rise}}{\text{run}}$

In this case, slope (m) = $\frac{6}{2}$ = 3

So the snail is travelling at 3 cm per minute.

Slope has no units, it is just a ratio.

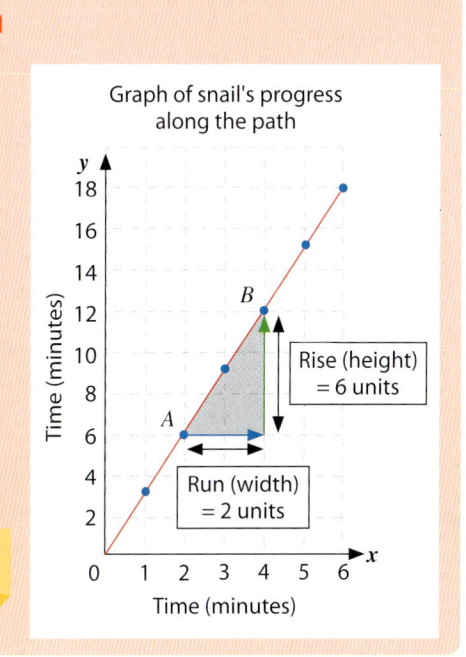

Graph of snail's progress along the path

Rise (height) = 6 units

Run (width) = 2 units

Section A Introducing concepts and building skills

> The slope is also known as the **rate of change**.
> The slope of a graph is the rate at which it changes.

It is important to remember that the slope of a graph can be a positive or negative number (including fractions). The next example shows a decreasing graph, which always has a negative slope.

Worked example 2

Jodie has a tin with 32 sweets in it. She eats four sweets a day.

(i) Create a table to show how many sweets will remain in the tin after five days.
(ii) Draw a graph to show how the number of sweets decrease each day.
(iii) Find the slope of this graph.

Solution

(i)

Number of days	Number of sweets Remaining in tin
Day 0 (start)	32
Day 1	28
Day 2	24
Day 3	20
Day 4	16
Day 5	12

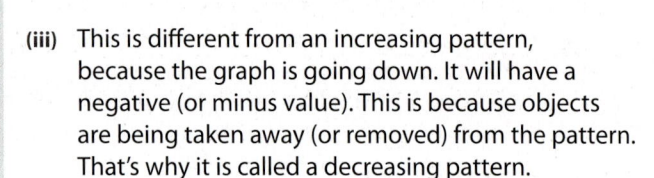

(ii) [Graph showing number of sweets in tin decreasing from 32 to 12 over 5 days]

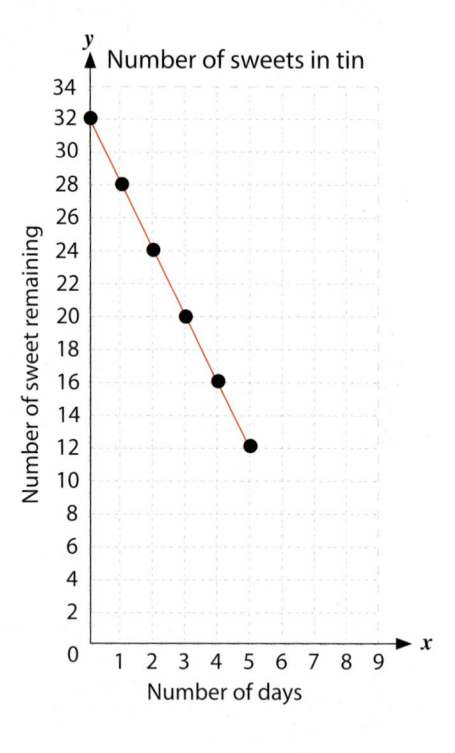

(iii) This is different from an increasing pattern, because the graph is going down. It will have a negative (or minus value). This is because objects are being taken away (or removed) from the pattern. That's why it is called a decreasing pattern.

We can still use the slope formula, but this time we use the **decrease** in height (the **fall**) divided by the width (**run**).

For a decreasing pattern

Slope = $\frac{rise}{run}$

but the rise will have a negative (−) value.

Using the formula :

Slope = $\frac{rise}{run} = \frac{-8}{2} = -4$

This is what we would expect, because Jodie was removing 4 sweets per day.

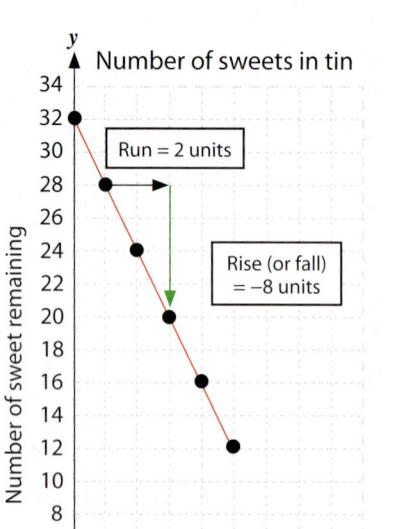

> A decreasing, or negative, slope can be thought of as $\frac{fall}{run}$

[Graph showing Run = 2 units and Rise (or fall) = −8 units]

Practice questions 7·3

1. Find the slopes of the following graphs.

   (i) [graph: line from (0,0) to approximately (6,10)]

   (ii) [graph: line from (0,0) to approximately (4,11)]

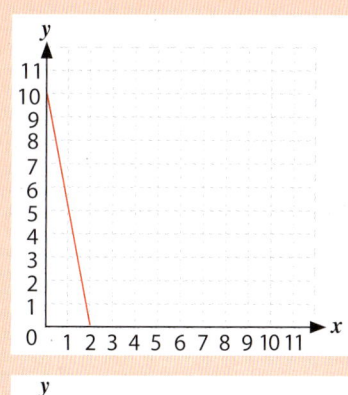

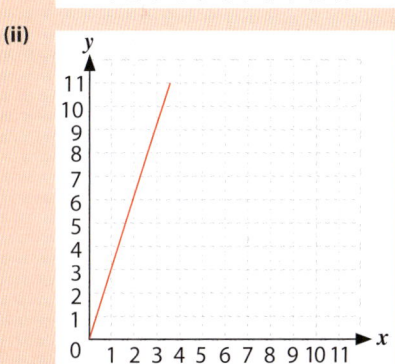

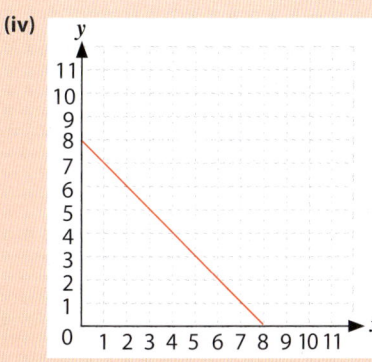

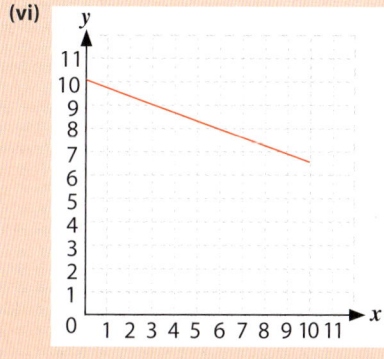

   (iii) [graph: line from (0,0) to approximately (10,5)]

   (iv) [graph: line from (0,8) to approximately (8,0)]

   (v) [graph: line from (0,10) to approximately (2,0)]

   (vi) [graph: line from (0,10) to approximately (10,7)]

2. It has been observed that a particular plant grows exactly 2·5 cm per week. It measured 2 cm when it arrived at the garden centre.

   (i) Create a table showing the growth of the plant over 6 weeks.

   (ii) Draw a graph to show the plant's growth over 6 weeks.

   (iii) Find the slope of this graph.

   (iv) What do you notice about the slope of the graph and the rate at which the plant is growing?

   (v) Do you think that this plant could continue growing at this rate forever? Give a reason for your answer.

3. A car has 10 litres of fuel. For every 8 kilometres it travels, it uses 1 litre of fuel.

   (i) Create a table showing how much fuel the car uses over 80 kilometres.

   (ii) Draw a graph to show how much fuel the car will use over 80 kilometres.

   (iii) Find the slope of this graph.

   (iv) What do you notice about the slope of the graph and the rate at which the car is using fuel?

   (v) How much fuel has the car used after travelling 48 kilometres?

4. Joe is beginning a new weight-lifting programme. He lifts 24 kg on his first visit to the gym. One week later, he progresses to lifting 28 kg. After two weeks, Joe is able to lift 32 kg. His progress continues in this way over a period of time.

   (i) Create a table showing the weights Joe can lift over his first eight weeks at the gym.

   (ii) Create a word formula to explain how the pattern of weights grows.

   (iii) After how many weeks will Joe be able to lift 124 kg?

   (iv) Will this pattern continue forever? Justify your answer.

Section A Introducing concepts and building skills

7.4 Identifying a pattern as linear or non-linear

So far, all the graphs we have looked at are known as linear graphs, this is because they consist of a straight line. If we draw a graph of a pattern and it forms a straight line, it is known as a linear pattern.

> Look at the first four letters of 'linear' – this will help you remember it forms a straight **line**.

Here are some examples of linear graphs:

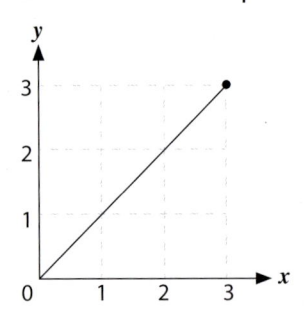

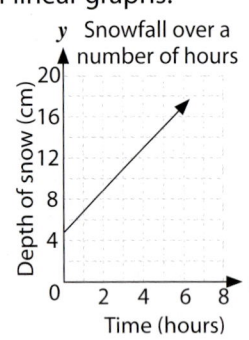

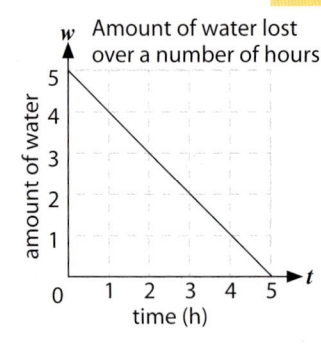

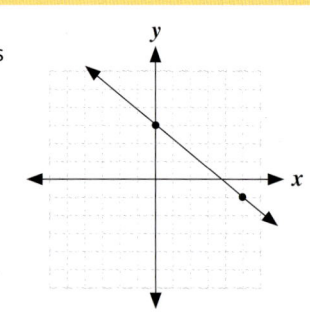

The patterns used to create these graphs are known as linear patterns. In each case, these graphs have a constant slope, or rate of change.

The first difference is the number that is added (or subtracted) to get from one value in the pattern to the next. To calculate the first difference, we do the following:

> **First difference = (any value) − (the value that came before it in the pattern)**

Increasing linear pattern	Decreasing linear pattern
5, 9, 13, 17, …	20, 17, 14, 11, …
First difference: +4 +4 +4	First difference: −3 −3 −3

Worked example 1

Students in a first-year class were raising money for charity. Some students had a 'bowl-a-thon'.
The table and the graph show the money that one student raised.

Graph of money raised

Time (hours)	Money raised (€)
1	8
2	16
3	24
4	32
5	40

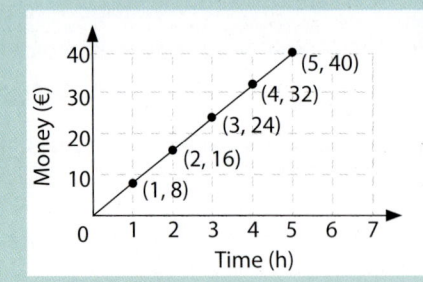

> If a pattern has a constant first difference, then that pattern will always be linear.
>
> The first difference is always the same as the slope of the graph, for a linear pattern.

Prove that this pattern is linear, without using the given graph.

Solution

In the table provided, we can investigate the change in the pattern. If this is the same value all of the time, we can say that the pattern is linear. A linear pattern forms a straight line when graphed.

The change (first difference in the pattern) is the same constant number. Therefore, we can say the pattern is linear.

Time (hours)	Money raised (€)	Change (first difference)
1	8	
		+8
2	16	
		+8
3	24	
		+8
4	32	
		+8
5	40	

Linking Thinking 1

Worked example 2

State whether the following patterns are linear, and give a reason for your answer.

(i) 12, 8, 4, 0, –4, –8
(ii) 1, 4, 9, 16, 25, 36

Solution

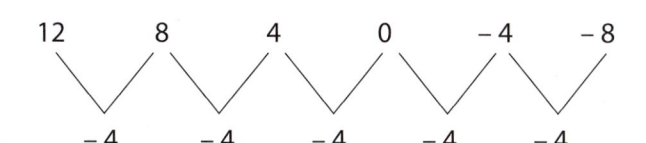

(i)

Pattern	12		8		4		0		–4		–8
First difference		–4		–4		–4		–4		–4	

The first difference is constant (the same each time), therefore the pattern is linear.

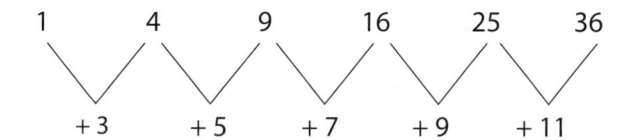

(ii)

Pattern	1		4		9		16		25		36
First difference		+3		+5		+7		+9		+11	

The first difference is not constant, therefore the pattern is not linear.

Practice questions 7·4

1. Investigate if the following patterns are linear. Justify your answer.
   (i) 5, 7, 9, 11, 13
   (ii) 4, 8, 16, 32, 64
   (iii) –7, –4, –1, 2, 5
   (iv) –3, –8, –12, –17, –22
   (v) 11, 14, 17, 20, 23
   (vi) 2, 1, 0, –1, –2
   (vii) 71, 50, 39, 18, –3
   (viii) 1, 1, 2, 3, 5, 8, 13

2. The diagram shows a pattern of matchsticks. 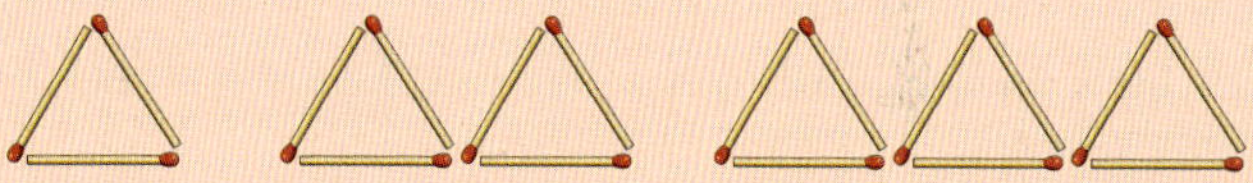
   (i) Draw the next two stages of the pattern.
   (ii) Create a table showing how many matchsticks would be needed to complete the first seven stages of this pattern.
   (iii) Is this pattern linear? Justify your answer.

3. (i) Create a table to show the number of squares in the first four stages of the pattern opposite. 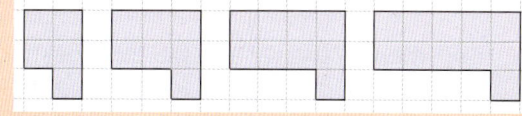
   (ii) Draw a graph to show how the number of squares increases with each stage of the pattern. Place the stage number on the horizontal axis, and the number of squares on the vertical axis.
   (iii) Find the slope of this graph.
   (iv) Is this a linear pattern? Justify your answer.
   (v) What do you notice about the value of the slope and the value of the first difference in this pattern?

4. Daisy lends her sister €20, with the agreement that if she pays the loan back within one week, she must pay €22. If it takes her two weeks to pay the loan back, she must pay €24. If it takes her three weeks to pay back the loan, she will have to pay €26, and so on.
   (i) Create a table to show how much Daisy's sister would have to pay back if it took her six weeks to repay the loan.
   (ii) Is this pattern linear? Justify your answer.

Section A Introducing concepts and building skills

(iii) Draw a graph based on the table from part (i) of this question

(iv) Find the slope of this graph.

(v) What do you notice about the slope and the first difference in the table in part (i)?

5. Investigate if the following patterns are linear. Justify your answer in each case.
   (i) $\frac{1}{6}, \frac{3}{6}, \frac{5}{6}, \frac{7}{6}, \frac{9}{6}$ (ii) 0·3, 0·7, 1·1, 1·5, 1·9   (iii) $-\frac{5}{4}, -\frac{7}{4}, -\frac{9}{4}, -\frac{11}{4}$ (iv) $\frac{1}{2}, \frac{1}{3}, \frac{1}{4}, \frac{1}{5}, \frac{1}{6}$

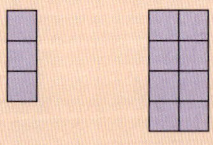

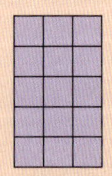

6. The diagram on the right shows a growing pattern.
   (i) Draw the next two stages of the pattern.
   (ii) Create a table showing how many squares would be needed to complete each of the first five stages of this pattern.
   (iii) Draw a graph to show how the number of squares increases with each stage of the pattern. Place the stage number on the horizontal axis, and the number of squares on the vertical axis.
   (iv) Is this pattern linear? Justify your answer by two methods.

Revision questions

7A Core skills

1. Fill in the next three stages of each of the patterns below.
   (i) 3, 6, 9, 12, …
   (ii) 7, 14, 21, 28, …
   (iii) 0, −4, −8, −12, …
   (iv) −8, −6, −4, −2, …
   (v) 66, 77, 88, 99, …
   (vi) 11, 8, 5, 2, …
   (vii) 31, 23, 15, 7, …
   (viii) $\frac{1}{2}, \frac{1}{4}, \frac{1}{8}, \frac{1}{16}, …$

2. State if each of the patterns below is linear or non-linear. Justify your answer.
   (i) 4, 8, 12, 16, 20
   (ii) 6, 2, −2, −6, −10
   (iii) 0, 5, 9, 15, 19, 22
   (iv) 18, 26, 38, 44, 70
   (v) 2, 8, 13, 21, 29
   (vi) 1·7, 1·4, 1·1, 0·8, 0·5
   (vii) $\frac{1}{4}, \frac{1}{2}, \frac{3}{4}, 1$
   (viii) $1, \frac{4}{5}, 0·6, \frac{4}{10}$

3. The diagram shows a staircase built from blocks. This staircase goes up three steps. 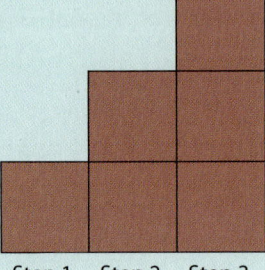
   (i) Draw the next two steps in the pattern.
   (ii) How many blocks are needed to make step 6?
   (iii) Is this pattern linear? Justify your answer.
   (iv) Identify the variables in this question.

4. L, U, N, C, H, L, U, N, C, H, L, U … is a pattern that continues to infinity. 
   (i) What letter will the 258th stage be?
   (ii) What letter will 1 000th stage be?
   (iii) Explain how you found your answers.

5. Liam has a part-time job at which he earns €9·50 per hour.
   (i) Create a table showing how much Liam would earn in seven hours.
   (ii) Draw a graph showing how much Liam would earn in seven hours.
   (iii) How long would Liam have to work to earn €85·50?
   (iv) Do Liam's wages follow a linear pattern? Justify your answer.
   (v) Identify the variables in this question.

Linking Thinking 1

6. A taxi company charges €4 per trip, plus an additional €2 per kilometre driven.
   (i) Create a table showing how much a trip of 8 kilometres would cost.
   (ii) Draw a graph showing the cost of a 10 kilometre trip.
   (iii) Identify the variables in this question.
   (iv) Find the slope of this graph.
   (v) Does the taxi fare represent a linear pattern? Justify your answer.
   (vi) What do you notice about the value of the slope of the graph and the value of the first difference?
   (vii) How much would it cost to travel 8 kilometres?
   (viii) If your fare was €18, what distance have you travelled?

7B Taking it FURTHER

1. Brona is saving for a games console. She received a gift of €50 and plans to save €20 per week.
   (i) Create a table showing how much money Brona will actually have in her savings box after 5 weeks.
   (ii) Draw a graph showing how much money Brona will have after 8 weeks.
   (iii) Find the slope (rate of change) of the graph you have drawn.
   (iv) Is this a linear pattern? Justify your answer.
   (v) What do you notice about the value of the slope in part (iii) and the first difference of the pattern?

2. Jack builds a snowman using 1 kilogram of snow. The next day, the sun starts to shine, and the snow begins to melt at a rate of 125 grams per hour.

   1 kilogram = 1 000 grams

   (i) Construct a table showing how much snow is remaining after 5 hours.
   (ii) Draw a graph to show the rate at which the snow is melting. Put the number of hours on the x-axis of your graph.
   (iii) Find the slope of the graph you have drawn. What do you notice about the slope of the graph and the rate at which the snowman is melting per hour?
   (iv) Is this a linear pattern? Justify your answer.

3. Big Claw the crab challenged Flicker the turtle to a 60 cm race.

   Because Big Claw is faster than Flicker, he offered to give Flicker a 10 cm head start.

   Flicker agreed and the race began. After 5 seconds, Big Claw had crawled 6 cm, and Flicker had crawled 4 cm. If they continue at this rate, who do you predict will win the race?

   Show all your work (thinking) and use it to justify your answer is correct.

4. Rory and Marie both bought a hot chocolate. Rory bought a large hot chocolate that contained 300 ml, and Marie bought a medium hot chocolate that contained 180 ml.

   Rory drinks 8 ml every 5 seconds, and Marie drinks 4 ml every 5 seconds,
   (i) How long will it take each person to finish their hot chocolate? Give your answer in seconds. Show all your work (thinking), and use it justify your answer is correct.
   (ii) Is there any time when Rory and Marie have the same amount of hot chocolate in their cups? Justify your answer showing supporting work.

5. The picture shows a pattern made from triangles. At each stage, two triangles are added: stage 1 contains 4 triangles, stage 2 contains 6 triangles, stage 3 contains 8 triangles, and so on.

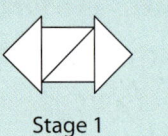

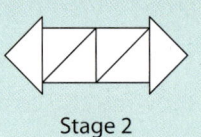

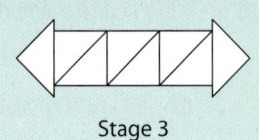

Stage 1   Stage 2   Stage 3

   (i)   Sketch the next two stages of the pattern.
   (ii) Draw a table showing the number of triangles needed to complete the first seven stages of the triangle.
   (iii) Draw a graph showing the first 10 stages of the pattern.
   (iv) Find the slope of the graph you have drawn.
   (v)   What do you notice about the slope of the graph, and the rate at which the number of triangles are increasing?
   (vi) Is this a linear pattern? Justify your answer.
   (vii) What do you notice about the value of the slope of the graph and the first difference in the table?

6. The diagram shows an arrangement of tables and chairs in a linear pattern.

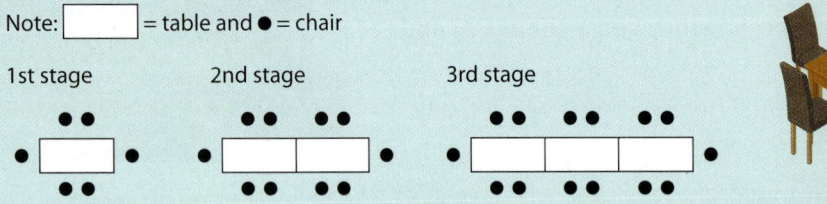

   Note: ▭ = table and ● = chair

   1st stage   2nd stage   3rd stage

   (i)   Draw the next stage of the pattern.
   (ii) Create a table to show the number of chairs in the first eight stages of the pattern.
   (iii) Draw a graph to show the relationship between the number of tables and chairs for the first eight stages of the pattern.
   (iv) Find the slope of your graph.
   (v)   What do you notice about the slope of the graph and the rate at which the number of chairs are increasing?

Now that you have completed the unit, revisit the

Something to think about ...

question posed at the start of this unit.

Now try question 3 on pages 186–7

Unit 8

Working with variables

Topics covered within this unit:
- 8·1 Working with variables
- 8·2 Multiplying terms
- 8·3 Dividing terms

The Learning Outcomes covered in this unit are contained in the following sections:
AF.2a   AF.2b

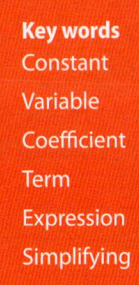

Key words
Constant
Variable
Coefficient
Term
Expression
Simplifying

? Something to think about ...

KEY SKILLS

The word 'algebra' comes from a Latin variant of Arabic word *al-jabr*. It came from the title of a book, *Hidab al- jabrwal- muqubala*, written by mathematician Arab-Mohammed ibn-Musa al-Khowarizmi in 825 CE. But the roots of this subject date back to 1900 BCE and it was actually found that the Babylonians came up with the concept of algebra.

A caretaker at a golf course has written down a term for the number of bags of fertiliser he can fit into his shed. If that term is $456ab$, find the term which describes the number of bags of fertiliser that can fit into one-quarter of his shed.

8·1 Working with variables

By the end of this section you should be able to:
- understand what constants, variables and coefficients are
- be able to add and subtract terms

> **A constant** is a fixed value, it is a number on its own.

Examples of constants include
$1, 2, -1, -20, 3\,000, 0{\cdot}022, -4{\cdot}67, \frac{7}{12}$

> **A variable** is a symbol that stands for a number (e.g. stage in a pattern, day of the week, price of an apple).

A variable:
- is usually a letter like x, y, a, b
- is a quantity that can change or vary, taking on different values

Section A Introducing concepts and building skills

> A **coefficient** is a number or symbol which is multiplied by a variable.

Term	Coefficient	Variable (s)	Meaning
$4x$	4	x	$4 \times x$
$-0.4a$	-0.4	a	$-0.4 \times a$
$\frac{3}{4}a$	$\frac{3}{4}$	a	$\frac{3}{4} \times a$
x	1	x	$1 \times x$
xy	1	x, y	$x \times y$

> A **term** is either a single number or variable, or numbers and variables multiplied together.

Invisible Maths

For a single value, for example x, the following are true:

- There is a coefficient of **1** to the left of every variable e.g. $x = 1x$
- Every number has an index of **1** e.g. $x = x^1$
- There is a denominator of **1** for every number e.g. $x = \frac{x}{1}$
- There is a **positive sign** to the left of every number e.g. $x = +x$

> **Invisible Maths!**
> In fact, x could be written as $\frac{+1x^1}{1}$, and still have the same value. However, this would not be practical, so the '1s' are usually invisible.

Terms are separated by mathematical operators ($+$, $-$, $\times$ or $\div$)

Like terms are terms that contain the same variables raised to the same power. Only the coefficients of like terms are different.

Like terms	Reason
$4x$, $3x$, $-5x$	All x are to the power of 1
$-2a^2$, $20a^2$	All a are to the power of 2
$2xy$, xy	All x are to the power of 1 All y are to the power of 1
$7x^3y^2$, $-4x^3y^2$	All x are to the power of 3 All y are to the power of 2

Unlike terms are terms that do not contain the same variables raised to the same power.

Unlike terms	Reason
$2x$, $3y$	No x value in second term
	No y value in first term
$7x^2y^3$, $-4x^3y^2$	x has power of 2 in 1st term and x has power of 3 in the 2nd term
	y has power of 3 in 1st term and y has power of 2 in the 2nd term

Simplifying expressions

> An **expression** is a mathematical sentence that can contain constants, variables (e.g. x or y) and operators (like $+$, $-$, $\times$, $\div$).

> **Simplifying** terms or writing an expression in its simplest form involves grouping and adding or subtracting like terms.

When adding (or subtracting) like terms, you add (or subtract) the coefficients and keep the variable(s).

> You can only add or subtract like terms.

Worked example

Simplify the following.

(i) $4x + 6y + x + 4y$
(ii) $2a^2 - b + 4a^2$
(iii) $2xy^2 - x^2y + 10xy^2 - 23x^2y$
(iv) $4a^2b^3 - 6a^3b^2 + 3a^2b^3 - 9a^3b^2 - 4a^2b^3$

Solution

(i) **Step 1** Identify like terms $\quad 4x + 6y + x + 4y$
Step 2 Group like terms $\quad 4x + x + 4y + 6y$
Step 3 Simplify $\quad 5x + 10y$

(ii) **Step 1** Identify like terms $\quad 2a^2 - b + 4a^2$
Step 2 Group like terms $\quad 2a^2 + 4a^2 - b$
Step 3 Simplify $\quad 6a^2 - b$

(iii) $2xy^2 - x^2y + 10xy^2 - 23x^2y$
$2xy^2 + 10xy^2 - 23x^2y - x^2y$
$12xy^2 - 24x^2y$

(iv) $4a^2b^3 - 6a^3b^2 + 3a^2b^3 - 9a^3b^2 - 4a^2b^3$
$4a^2b^3 + 3a^2b^3 - 4a^2b^3 - 9a^3b^2 - 6a^3b^2$
$3a^2b^3 - 15a^3b^2$

Practice questions 8.1

1. Copy and complete the following table, identifying the terms as being either like terms or unlike terms. Give a reason for your answer in each case.

Terms	Like terms/Unlike terms	Reason
$x, 2x, 4x$		
$3, a, -3a$		
$3x^2, 2x^2, -4x$		
$5x^3y^2, -3x^3y^2$		
$9a^2b^3, -8a^3b^2$		

2. Identify the coefficient, the variable, and the constant term of the following expressions.

   (i) $4x + 6$
   (ii) $10 - 4y$
   (iii) $12 + x$
   (iv) $0.5\alpha - 5$
   (v) $\frac{3}{4}x - 0.0006$
   (vi) $a + 0.78$

3. Identify all of the 'invisible' Maths in each of the following.

   (i) x
   (ii) $2x$
   (iii) $5x - y$

4. Simplify the following.

   (i) $a + a + a + a + a + a$
   (ii) $x + y + x + y + x$
   (iii) $4x + 2y + 6x + 10y$

5. Simplify the following.

   (i) $2 + 4x + 5 + 6x$
   (ii) $4x + 8 + 3 + 10$
   (iii) $3 + 6x + 11x + 7$
   (iv) $12m + 3n + 14m$
   (v) $4p + 3q + 5q - 6p$
   (vi) $2a - 8y + 4a - 10y$
   (vii) $5 - 6x + 10x - 7$
   (viii) $12 - 6b + 10b - 7$

6. Simplify the following.

   (i) $6a + 13b + 6a + b$
   (ii) $4\alpha + 5\beta - 23\alpha + 18\beta$
   (iii) $33m - 5n - 23n + 18m$

   > α and β are letters from the Greek alphabet.

7. Simplify the following.

(i) $x^2 + y + x^2 + y$

(ii) $8x^2 + 10y + 14x^2 + y$

(iii) $23ab + 13bc + 12bc + 16ab$

8. Simplify the following.

(i) $9db + 11dc + 7dc - 24db$

(ii) $4m^2 + 5n^2 - 23m^3 + 18n^2$

(iii) $m^2 - 45n^2 - 23n^2 + 18m^2$

Taking it FURTHER

9. Simplify the following.

(i) $3x + \frac{3}{4}y - \frac{5}{3}y + 9x$

(ii) $5x + \frac{3}{5}y - \frac{6}{5}y - x$

(iii) $\frac{11}{2}x + 15y + \frac{7}{3}y - 4x$

(iv) $12p - 5x - 4p + xb + xb - 6$

(v) $12 + 9m + \frac{5}{6} + \frac{3}{4}m$

10. Find an expression for the perimeter of each of the following rectangles.
(Hint: Perimeter = length + width + length + width)

(i) $4x$ by $5y$

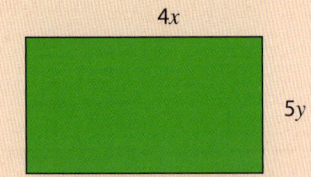

(ii) $15.5c$ by $4.5b$

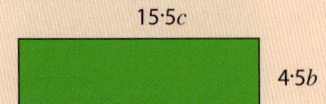

(iii) $7\frac{1}{4}d$ by $6\frac{1}{3}d$

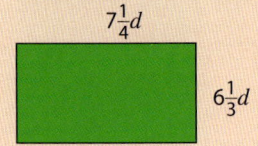

11. Orla has $4x$ pencils, Tom has $5y$ pencils, Joanne has $6x$ pencils and Mary has $12y$ pencils. Write down the total number of pencils that the group has in the simplest form in terms of x and y.

12. The number of trees in one park is $12n$, a second park has $14m$ trees, a third park has 23 trees and a fourth park has $56n$ trees. Find the total number trees in all four parks, in terms of n and m.

13. The total perimeter of a rectangle is $12d + 14c$. Find a term for the length and a term for the width of this rectangle.

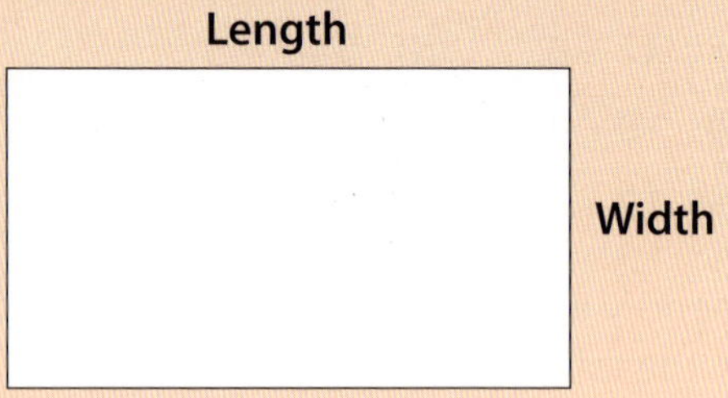

Length

Width

8·2 Multiplying terms

By the end of this section you should:
- understand how to multiply terms

Multiplying one term by another term

1. Sign × sign
2. Coefficient × coefficient
3. Variable × variable

Two brackets side by side ( )( ) with no + or − or ÷ between them, means multiply the contents of one bracket by the contents of the other bracket

Discuss and discover

KEY SKILLS

Working with a classmate, copy and complete the table below.

3 × 3	3^2
2 × 2 × 2	2^3
5 × 5 × 5 × 5	5^4
x × x	
y × y × y	
a × a × a × a	
b × b × b × b × b	

1. Can you find a pattern (using powers) to find the power of the answer in the table?
2. What have you learned about multiplying terms and powers from completing this table?

Multiplying variables with the same base

To multiply variables of same **base** we add the **indices/powers**:

Base → a^p ← Index/power

$a^p \times a^q = a^{p+q}$

Here are some examples:

$x \times x = (x^1)(x^1) = x^{1+1} = x^2$

$x^3 \times x^2 = (x^3)(x^2) = x^{3+2} = x^5$

$a \times a \times a = (a^1)(a^1)(a^1) = a^{1+1+1} = a^3$

$n \times n \times n \times n = (n^1)(n^1)(n^1)(n^1) = n^{1+1+1+1} = n^4$

This is a type of simplifying.

Worked example 1

Simplify the following.

(i) $3 \times 8x$ (ii) $(4x)(7x)$
(iii) $(a^2)(-2a^2)(a)$ (iv) $(-2y^2)(-y)$

$(+) \times (+) = +$
$(-) \times (-) = +$
$(-) \times (+) = -$
$(+) \times (-) = -$

Solution

(i) $3 \times 8x$
  $(+) \times (+) = +$ (sign × sign)
  $3 \times 8x = 24x$ (number × term)
  Simplified $24x$

(ii) $(4x)(7x)$
  $(+) \times (+) = (+)$ (sign × sign)
  $4 \times 7 = 28$ (coefficient × coefficient)
  $x \times x = x^2$ (variable × variable)
  Simplified $28x^2$

(iii) $(a^2)(-2a^2)(a)$
  $(+) \times (-) \times (+) = (-)$ (sign × sign × sign)
  $1 \times 2 \times 1 = 2$ (coefficient × coefficient × coefficient)
  $a^2 \times a^2 \times a^1 = a^5$ (variable × variable × variable)
  Simplified $-2a^5$

(iv) $(-2y^2)(-y)$
  $(-) \times (-) = (+)$ (sign × sign)
  $2 \times 1 = 2$ (coefficient × coefficient)
  $y^2 \times y = y^3$ (variable × variable)
  Simplified $2y^3$

Multiplying terms with different variables

$x \times y = (x)(y) = xy$
$a \times b^2 = (a)(b^2) = ab^2$
$m^2 \times n^2 = (m^2)(n^2) = m^2 n^2$

This is a type of simplifying.

Worked example 2

Simplify the following.

(i) $(8a)(-9b)$ (ii) $\left(-\frac{1}{4}n\right)\left(-\frac{2}{5}m\right)$ (iii) $(2m^2)(-3n)(mn)$ (iv) $4x^2 \times 4y^2 \times xy^2$

Solution

(i) $(8a)(-9b)$
  $(+) \times (-) = (-)$ (sign × sign)
  $8 \times 9 = 72$ (coefficient × coefficient)
  $a \times b = ab$ (variable × variable)
  Simplified $-72ab$

(ii) $\left(-\frac{1}{4}n\right)\left(-\frac{2}{5}m\right)$
  $(-) \times (-) = (+)$ (sign × sign)
  $\frac{1}{4} \times \frac{2}{5} = \frac{2}{20} = \frac{1}{10}$ (coefficient × coefficient)
  $n \times m = mn$ (variable × variable)
  Simplified $\frac{1}{10}mn$

(iii) $(2m^2)(-3n)(mn)$
  $(+) \times (-) \times (+) = (-)$
  $2 \times 3 \times 1 = 6$
  $m^2 \times n^1 \times m^1 n^1 = m^3 n^2$
  Simplified $-6m^3 n^2$

(iv) $4x^2 \times 4y^2 \times xy^2$
  $(+) \times (+) \times (+) = (+)$
  $4 \times 4 \times 1 = 16$
  $x^2 \times y^2 \times xy^2 = x^3 y^4$
  Simplified $16x^3 y^4$

Practice questions 8·2

1. Copy and complete the following table.

	Expression	Simplified expression
(i)	$(x)(x)(x)$	
(ii)	$(a)(b)(b)$	
(iii)	$(\ )(a^4)$	a^6
(iv)	$(2p)(\ )$	$6p^3$
(v)	$(3m^2)(-5m^4)$	
(vi)	$(4ab)(\ )$	$8a^2b^4$

2. Simplify the following.
   (i) $2 \times 5a$
   (ii) $7 \times 2x$
   (iii) $(3)(7a)$
   (iv) $(4)(7n)$
   (v) $(3)(6y)$
   (vi) $(3)(8m)$

3. Simplify the following.
   (i) $(3a)(4b)$
   (ii) $(5c)(2b)$
   (iii) $(2w)(2x)$
   (iv) $8t \times (-3d)$
   (v) $(-7s)(2y)$
   (vi) $-g \times 7k$

4. Simplify the following.
   (i) $(4g)(3g)$
   (ii) $(9h)(3h)$
   (iii) $(3t)(-4t)$
   (iv) $(-7d)(5d)$
   (v) $(-6h)(5e)$
   (vi) $(9n)(-3p)$

5. Simplify the following.
   (i) $(4w)\left(\frac{1}{2}\right)$
   (ii) $(9d)\left(\frac{1}{3}\right)$
   (iii) $(10x)\left(-\frac{1}{2}\right)$
   (iv) $\left(\frac{1}{3}y\right)\left(-\frac{1}{2}y\right)$
   (v) $\left(\frac{1}{2}m^2\right)\left(-\frac{2}{3}m\right)$
   (vi) $\left(\frac{1}{2}m^2\right)\left(-\frac{2}{5}m\right)$

6. Simplify the following.
   (i) $(4ab)(3a)$
   (ii) $(6p)(-2p^2)$
   (iii) $(8s)(2s^2)$
   (iv) $(5mn)(-3m^2n)$
   (v) $(4ab^2)(-5ab)$
   (vi) $\left(\frac{1}{2}x^2\right)\left(-\frac{2}{3}xy\right)$

7. Simplify the following.
   (i) $(4x^2)(-5xy)$
   (ii) $(5pq)(-2p^2q^2)$
   (iii) $(xy)(-x^2y^2)$
   (iv) $(mn)(-4n)$

8. Simplify the following.
   (i) $(x^2)(-2xy)(-4xy)$
   (ii) $(5xy)(x^2y^2)(-xy)$
   (iii) $(a)(b^2)(-a^2b^2)$
   (iv) $(mn)(-4n)$

9. The area of a rectangle is found by multiplying the length by the width. For the following rectangles find the area in terms of a and b.

Length	Width
$3a$	$4a$
$6ab$	$8ab$
$10ab$	$12ab$

10. The area of a triangle is found by multiplying half the base by the perpendicular height. For the following triangles, find the area in terms of a and b.

Base	Perpendicular height
$4a$	$4a$
$12ab$	$4·6ab^2$
ab	a

11. An egg carton is rectangular and is $7y$ cm long on one side and $6x$ cm along its width, as shown below.

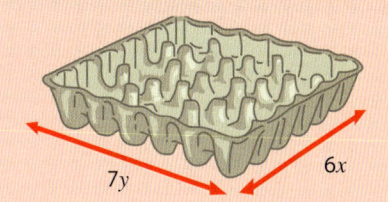

$7y$ $6x$

Find the total area of the base of the egg carton in terms of x and y.

8.3 Dividing terms

By the end of this section you should:
- understand how to divide terms

Discuss and discover

Copy and complete the table below.

Fraction	Method to simplify	Simplified result
$\dfrac{3}{3}$	Divide numerator and denominator by 3	1
$\dfrac{5 \times 5 \times 5}{5}$	Divide numerator and denominator by 5	5^2
$\dfrac{5 \times 5 \times 5 \times x}{5 \times 5}$	Divide numerator and denominator by 5×5	$5x$
$\dfrac{y \times y \times y}{y}$		
$\dfrac{a \times a \times a \times a}{a \times a}$		
$\dfrac{b \times b \times b \times b \times b}{b \times b \times b}$		
$\dfrac{27 \times n \times n \times n \times n \times m \times m}{12 \times n \times m \times m}$		

Compare your table with another student from your class and discuss if there is a pattern (using powers) to find the power of the simplified result in the table?

What have you learned about dividing terms from completing this table?

Dividing variables

Within any fraction, you can divide the numerator and denominator by the same number or variable to simplify the fraction.

$\dfrac{x}{y}$ means x divided by y

Dividing a term by another term

1. Divide the numerator and denominator by their highest common factor
2. Divide the numerator and denominator by all common variables
3. Sign ÷ sign

$\dfrac{\text{numerator}}{\text{denominator}}$

Here are some examples:

$x \div y = \dfrac{(x)}{(y)} = \dfrac{x}{y}$

$6a \div 2a^2 = \dfrac{(6a)}{(2a^2)} = \dfrac{6a}{2(a)(a)} = \dfrac{3}{a}$

$4n^2 \div 4n^2 = \dfrac{4n^2}{4n^2} = \dfrac{1}{1} = 1$

130 Linking Thinking 1

Worked example

Simplify the following.

(i) $8b \div 2$ (iii) $20ay \div 4a$ (v) $\dfrac{-44x^3y^2}{4x^3y^2}$

(ii) $6d \div 4d$ (iv) $\dfrac{24x^2}{8x}$ (vi) $\dfrac{-15ab}{20a^2b}$

Recall simplifying fractions:
$\dfrac{14}{8} = \dfrac{14 \div 2}{8 \div 2} = \dfrac{7}{4}$

Solution

(i) $8b \div 2$

$\dfrac{(8)(b)}{2}$

$\dfrac{4b}{1}$ (dividing numerator and denominator by 2)

Simplified $4b$

(ii) $6d \div 4d$

$\dfrac{(6)(d)}{(4)(d)}$

$\dfrac{(3)(d)}{(2)(d)}$ (dividing numerator and denominator by 2)

$\dfrac{(3)(1)}{(2)(1)}$ (dividing numerator and denominator by d)

Simplified $\dfrac{3}{2}$

(iii) $20ay \div 4a$

$\dfrac{20ay}{4a}$

$\dfrac{5(a)(y)}{1(a)}$ (dividing numerator and denominator by 4)

$\dfrac{(5)(1)(y)}{(1)(1)}$ (dividing numerator and denominator by a)

$\dfrac{(5)(y)}{1}$

Simplified $5y$

(iv) $\dfrac{24x^2}{8x}$

$\dfrac{24(x)(x)}{8(x)}$

$\dfrac{3(x)(x)}{1(x)}$ (dividing numerator and denominator by 8)

$\dfrac{(3)(1)(x)}{(1)(1)}$ (dividing numerator and denominator by x)

Simplified $3x$

(v) $\dfrac{-44x^3y^2}{4x^3y^2}$

$\dfrac{-11(x)(x)(x)(y)(y)}{1(x)(x)(x)(y)(y)}$ (dividing numerator and denominator by 4)

$\dfrac{-11(1)(1)(1)(y)(y)}{(1)(1)(1)(y)(y)}$ (dividing numerator and denominator by x^3)

$\dfrac{(-11)(1)(1)}{(1)(1)(1)}$ (dividing numerator and denominator by y^2)

Simplified -11

(vi) $\dfrac{-15ab}{20a^2b}$

$\dfrac{-3(a)(b)}{4(a)(a)(b)}$ (dividing numerator and denominator by 5)

$\dfrac{(-3)(1)(b)}{(4)(1)(a)(b)}$ (dividing numerator and denominator by a)

$\dfrac{(-3)(1)}{(4)(a)(1)}$ (dividing numerator and denominator by b)

Simplified $\dfrac{-3}{4a}$

$\dfrac{(+)}{(+)} = (+)$
$\dfrac{(-)}{(-)} = (+)$
$\dfrac{(-)}{(+)} = (-)$
$\dfrac{(+)}{(-)} = (-)$

Working with variables

Practice questions 8.3

1. Simplify the following.

(i) $8a \div 4$ (iv) $\dfrac{14n}{-7}$

(ii) $-12e \div 6$ (v) $\dfrac{6c}{-2}$

(iii) $9y \div 3$ (vi) $\dfrac{-8m}{-4}$

2. Simplify the following.

(i) $\dfrac{21m}{7}$ (iv) $\dfrac{12b}{-8}$

(ii) $\dfrac{-20p}{5}$ (v) $\dfrac{-6t}{18}$

(iii) $\dfrac{10d}{2}$ (vi) $\dfrac{18d}{4}$

Section A Introducing concepts and building skills

3. Simplify the following.
   (i) $\dfrac{8g}{4g}$
   (ii) $\dfrac{12a}{6a}$
   (iii) $\dfrac{-20b}{4b}$
   (iv) $\dfrac{30x}{-10x}$
   (v) $\dfrac{-24p}{6p}$
   (vi) $\dfrac{-100v}{50v}$

4. Simplify the following.
   (i) $12ay \div (-4a)$
   (ii) $-24tw \div (-6t)$
   (iii) $\dfrac{14x^2y}{7xy}$
   (iv) $\dfrac{18ab^2}{-6ab}$
   (v) $\dfrac{-14xy}{7xy}$
   (vi) $\dfrac{24ab}{-12ab}$

5. Simplify the following.
   (i) $-12ay \div (-4a)$
   (ii) $-18dg \div 4d$
   (iii) $\dfrac{-14de}{7e}$
   (iv) $\dfrac{-6tw}{24t}$
   (v) $\dfrac{15st}{-5st}$
   (vi) $\dfrac{-12a}{18ab}$

6. Simplify the following.
   (i) $-\dfrac{16a^3}{a^2}$
   (ii) $\dfrac{32x^4}{x^4}$
   (iii) $\dfrac{-21c^3d^2}{7cd}$
   (iv) $\dfrac{-27x^2y^3}{9xy}$
   (v) $\dfrac{24ab^2}{-8ab}$
   (vi) $\dfrac{-18a^2b}{-9a^2b}$

7. Oisín received $32x$ marbles as a gift for him and his three brothers. If Oisín has to share these marbles with three of his brothers, how many will each person get? Give your answer in terms of x.

8. The number of cows John has is $90y$. If John wants to divide his cows equally between 15 fields, how many cows go into each field? Give your answer in terms of y.

9. Jack has a rectangular floor with an area of $4x^2$, as shown.
   Find the area of one-quarter of this floor.

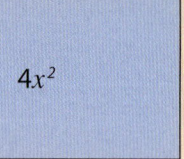

   $4x^2$

10. Bridget has a rectangular field with an area of $12ab^2$, as shown.
    Find the length if the width is $2ab$.

    $12ab^2$

11. Mary Ann saves money in a piggy bank. She records how much she saves in a notebook in code form, so she is the only one who knows the actual amount saved. If she records her total savings as $350xy$, write down a term which represents one fifth of her savings.

12. Harry recorded the total number of chairs to put in a hall for a concert as $450x^2y$. The number of rows of seats Harry arranged in the hall is $45xy$. How many seats are in one row of the hall?

13. Copy and complete the following table.

	Expression	Simplified expression
(i)	$\dfrac{6x}{3}$	
(ii)	$\dfrac{10a^2}{2a}$	
(iii)	$\dfrac{-8p^3q}{4pq}$	
(iv)	$\dfrac{\square}{3x}$	$5x^2$
(v)	$\dfrac{\square}{7a^2}$	$3a^2b^4$
(vi)	$\dfrac{-20x^5y^3}{\square}$	$4x^2y$

Revision questions

8A Core skills

1. Simplify the following.
   - (i) $5x + 6 + 2x$
   - (ii) $7 + 6x - 2x$
   - (iii) $4x + 6x + 3$
   - (iv) $2a^2 - 5 + 7a^2 + 7$
   - (v) $8 + 3a + 4a$
   - (vi) $5a - 2a + 4b$
   - (vii) $6a + 5b - 2a + 3b$
   - (viii) $8x^2 + 7 - 3x^4 + 3$

2. Simplify the following.
   - (i) $2x^2 + y + 3x^2 - 4y$
   - (ii) $3ab + 14ba - bc + 6ab$
   - (iii) $3x^2 + 10y^2 - 12x^2 + 2y$
   - (iv) $2ab + 3bc + 12cb + 16ba$

3. Expand each of the following, simplifying if necessary.
   - (i) $8s \times 2s$
   - (ii) $5mn \times (-3m^2n)$
   - (iii) $4x^2 \times 5x \times 2x$
   - (iv) $7pn \times (-4p^2n)$
   - (v) $(3e)(e^2)(2d)$
   - (vi) $(4ab)(-6a^2b)$
   - (vii) $(2a^2)(-3ay)(-5ab)$
   - (viii) $(mn)(-4nm)(-5mn)$

4. Expand each of the following, simplifying if necessary.
   - (i) $12x \div 3$
   - (ii) $21x^3 \div 3x^2$
   - (iii) $14d \div 7$
   - (iv) $8x^4 \div 4x^2$
   - (v) $\dfrac{14x^6}{2x^2}$
   - (vi) $\dfrac{8x^2}{4x}$
   - (vii) $\dfrac{-10a}{2a}$
   - (viii) $\dfrac{-6x}{-3}$
   - (ix) $\dfrac{32ab^2}{-4ab}$
   - (x) $\dfrac{-144d}{-6c^3d^2}$

5. Expand each of the following, simplifying if necessary.
   - (i) $\left(\dfrac{2}{3}w\right)\left(\dfrac{1}{2}\right)$
   - (ii) $\left(\dfrac{1}{3}x\right)\left(-\dfrac{2}{7}x\right)$
   - (iii) $(m^2)\left(-\dfrac{3}{5}m\right)$
   - (iv) $\left(\dfrac{9}{13}d\right)\left(\dfrac{1}{3}a\right)$
   - (v) $\left(\dfrac{2}{3}x\right)\left(-\dfrac{3}{8}y\right)$
   - (vi) $\left(\dfrac{3}{11}m^2\right)\left(-\dfrac{2}{3}n\right)$

8B Taking it FURTHER

1. The area of a rectangle is found by multiplying the length by the width.
   For the following rectangles, find a simplified expression for the area.

	Length	Width
(i)	$4x$	$4y$
(ii)	$10xy$	$8x$
(iii)	$6mn$	$5mn$

2. The perimeter of a rectangle is found by multiplying the length by 2 and adding the result to the width multiplied by 2.
   This can be expressed as:
   Perimeter $= (2l + 2w)$
   For the following rectangles, find a simplified expression for the perimeter.

	Length (l)	Width (w)
(i)	$3a$	$3a$
(ii)	$6m$	$4m^2$
(iii)	$4xy$	$10xy$

3. Shown is a rectangle, with width $2x$. The area of the rectangle is $8x^2$. Find the perimeter of the rectangle.

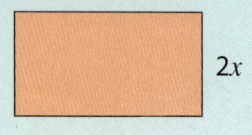

   $2x$

4. A rectangle has length $5x$ and width $2y$. Find a term for the area of the rectangle.

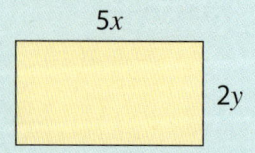

   $5x$

   $2y$

5. A rectangle and square have the same area. The rectangle has length $12x$ and width $3x$. Find the length of each side of the square.

6. The rule for a certain pattern is that, after the first two values, each value is found by multiplying the two previous values. The first two values are $2x$ and $3y$. Find the next three values.

7. The total number of seats on a train is represented by the term $565xy$. If there are $5xy$ seats in each row of seats on the train, find the term that describes the number of rows on the train.

8. A car park is rectangular in shape. If the car park can hold $896ab$ cars, find an expression that describes how many cars can fit into:

   (i) $\frac{1}{4}$ of the car park.

   (ii) $\frac{1}{a}$ of the car park.

Now that you have completed the unit, revisit the

? Something to think about ...

question posed at the start of this unit.

Unit 9
Solving linear relations

Topics covered within this unit:
- 9·1 Linear patterns in context
- 9·2 Solving basic linear equations
- 9·3 Solving more complicated linear equations
- 9·4 Creating and solving linear equations
- 9·5 Introduction to functions
- 9·6 Linear functions
- 9·7 Solving linear relations using multiple representations

The Learning Outcomes covered in this unit are contained in the following sections:

AF.1a AF.1b AF.1c AF.2a
AF.2b AF.2c AF.4a AF.7a

Key words
Equation
Equate
Linear equation
Function
Couple
Domain
Range
Codomain
Linear function

? Something to think about... KEY SKILLS

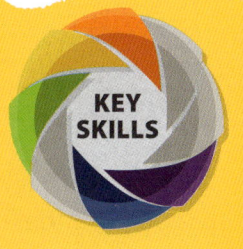

Sophie was given a money box by her dad for her birthday. She could choose the money box she wanted from the following three options:

Box 1 had no money in it but dad promised he would add €4 every day.

Box 2 had €10 in it and a promise from dad to put €3 in every day.

Box 3 had €20 in it and a promise from dad to put €2 in every day.

Which box should Sophie choose? Justify your choice with words, tables, expressions, equations or graphs.

9·1 Linear patterns in context

By the end of this section you should be able to:
- create a general formula for a linear pattern
- use an equation to solve for any term of a linear pattern

In Unit 7, we learned how to represent a linear pattern using a table or a graph. This is an essential skill, but sometimes it is easier to represent a pattern by developing a formula.

A formula is a rule or fact written with mathematical symbols. It usually has an equals sign (=) and special symbols (usually letters) to represent variables.

Let's consider the following situation.

Jim is starting a new fitness regime. He is planning on doing a particular exercise every day, starting with 5 minutes the first day and increasing the length of time spent at the exercise by 2 minutes each day.

Section A Introducing concepts and building skills

The table shows Jim's exercise times over the first 5 days:

Day	0	1	2	3	4	5
Exercise time (min)	5	7	9	11	13	15

A **word formula**, we could use to describe Jim's exercise time is:

Time spent each day = 5 minutes at the start of his regime + 2 minutes multiplied by the number of days

This can be written more simply as a **mathematical formula**:

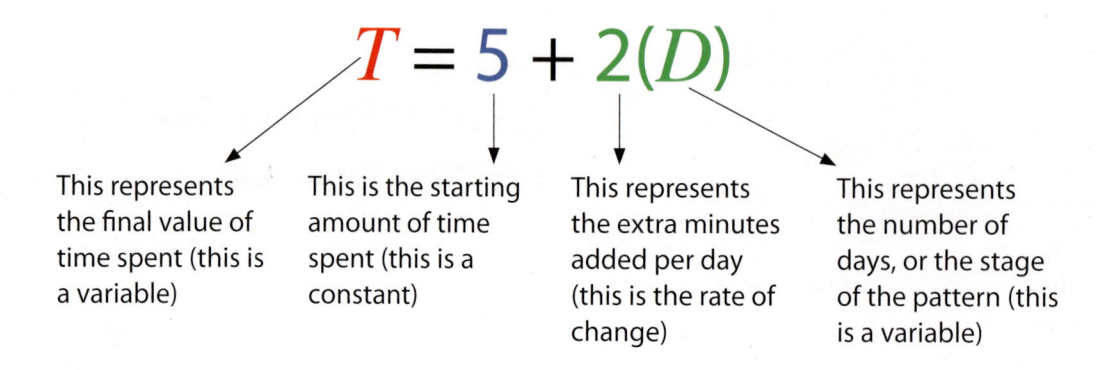

$$T = 5 + 2(D)$$

- T: This represents the final value of time spent (this is a variable)
- 5: This is the starting amount of time spent (this is a constant)
- 2: This represents the extra minutes added per day (this is the rate of change)
- D: This represents the number of days, or the stage of the pattern (this is a variable)

We can use this formula to quickly find how much time Jim spends exercising on any particular day.

For example, how many minutes did Jim spend exercising on day 12?

In this case, the number of days is 12, so we put '12' in as the D value.

$T = 5 + 2(D)$

$T = 5 + 2(12)$

$T = 5 + 24$

$T = 29$ minutes

In general, a formula for a linear pattern can be formed as:

> Value (total) = starting value + rate of change (stage number)

Worked example

Holly is saving for a new phone. She received a gift of €50 and plans to save €20 per week.

(i) Create a table showing how much money Holly will have in her savings after five weeks.

(ii) Describe the pattern in words:

Total amount in savings = _____

(iii) In the table, identify the variables and the constant.

(iv) Using the sentence you created in part (ii), create a formula for the pattern. Explain what each letter you have used stands for.

(v) Use your formula to find out how much money Holly will have after six weeks.

(vi) If the phone costs €210, use trial and improvement to find out how long it will take for Holly to save for the phone.

Solution

(i)

Week	Start	1	2	3	4	5
Amount (€)	50	70	90	110	130	150

(ii) Total amount in savings = the €50 she started with, plus €20 for each week that passes.

(iii) The variables (what is changing) are:
- the number of weeks
- the amount of money saved

The constants (what is staying the same) are:
- the €20 every week
- the €50 she started with

(iv) Amount = $s + 20(w)$
s = the starting amount of €50
w = how many weeks have passed

(v) After six weeks,
Amount = $s + 20(w)$
Amount = $50 + 20(6)$
Amount = $50 + 120$
Amount = 170
Holly has saved €170

(vi) If the phone costs €210, then we can use trial and improvement to solve for w.
We know from part (v) above that Holly has saved €170 after 6 weeks.
Amount = $s + 20(w)$

Let the number of weeks equal 7
Amount = $50 + 20(7)$
Amount = 190
€190 is not enough to purchase a new phone

Let the number of weeks equal 8
Amount = $50 + 20(8)$
Amount = 210
€210 is enough to purchase a new phone

Therefore, it will take Holly 8 weeks to save enough money for a new phone.

> Trial and improvement is where we guess what the answer could be and see if it works in the question. If it doesn't work, then we guess a different possible answer. We continue guessing and checking answers until we find the right one.

Practice questions 9·1

1. Identify the variables and the constants in each of the following:

(i) $a = 5 + 12c$
(ii) $t = b + 5$
(iii) $f = m - 4d$
(iv) $x = -7 + 11y$
(v) $k = 4g + 2$
(vi) $t = -4 - 10p$
(vii) $\theta = -24 + 9e$
(viii) $r = 5x - 7$
(ix) $\beta = 10y - 12$
(x) $d = -6 - 23n$

2. Using the information below, create a formula in each case, given:

Value (total) = starting value + (rate of change × stage number)

	Starting value	Rate of change	Stage number
(i)	4	6	a
(ii)	2	9	v
(iii)	7	−3	t
(iv)	−10	2	d
(v)	−50	−8	n
(vi)	−21	4	s
(vii)	117	−34	r
(viii)	1 024	−64	t
(ix)	−99	24	k
(x)	0	−59	x

3. Copy the table provided and identify the starting value, rate of change and stage number in the following formulae.

	Formula	Starting value	Rate of change	Stage number
(i)	$x = 7 + 24(y)$			
(ii)	$t = -4 + 13(s)$			
(iii)	$m = 31 - 76(n)$			
(iv)	$p = -17 - 3(q)$			
(v)	$y = 10 + 2(x)$			

Section A Introducing concepts and building skills

4. (i) A plant is 2 cm tall and grows 1 cm each month. Write a formula to calculate its height for any month.

   (ii) A baker has 5 cakes and bakes a further 3 every hour. Write a formula to calculate the number of cakes he will have at a given time.

   (iii) Gerry has read 50 pages of his book and he will read a further 8 pages every hour. Write a formula to calculate the number of pages he will have read in a given time.

   (iv) A pyramid has a base with 100 blocks (layer 0). For each new layer, 8 blocks are removed, i.e. layer 1 will contain 92 blocks, layer 2 will contain 84 blocks, etc. Write a formula to calculate the number of blocks in any given layer.

5. Tom's wages are calculated using the following formula:

   $$\text{wages} = 3 + 9.8(h)$$

   where h represents the number of hours worked. Calculate Tom's wages if he worked the following number of hours:

   (i) one hour
   (ii) five hours
   (iii) nine hours
   (iv) 38 hours (a week of work)

6. A taxi fare is calculated using the following rule:

   €4·00 pick-up fee and €1·10 per kilometre travelled.

   (i) Write a formula to represent this information, explaining the meaning of the letters you have used.

   (ii) Using your formula, calculate the total cost of a 10 km journey.

   (iii) Use trial and improvement – or any other valid mathematical method – to find how many kilometres you could travel if you had €27·10.

7. (i) Draw the next two stages of the pattern of blocks shown.

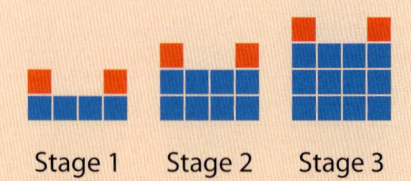

   Stage 1   Stage 2   Stage 3

   (ii) Copy the table below and complete it for the first six stages of the pattern.

Stage	Number of red blocks	Number of blue blocks	Total number of blocks
1	2	4	6
2	…	…	…

   (iii) Identify the variables in the table.

   (iv) Write a word formula to explain how to find the total number of blocks in any stage of the pattern.

   (v) Write a mathematical formula to find the total number of blocks in any stage of the pattern. Explain the meaning of any letters you use.

   (vii) (a) How many blocks in total are there in stage 100?
   (b) How many of those blocks are red?
   (c) How many of those blocks are blue?

8. (i) Draw the next stage of the pattern of dots shown.

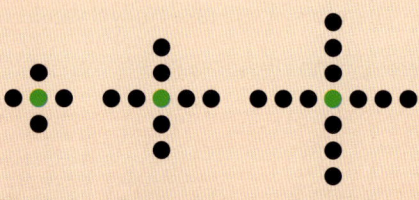

   Stage 1   Stage 2   Stage 3

   (ii) Copy the table below and complete it for the first six stages of the pattern.

Stage	Number of green dots	Number of black dots	Total number of dots
1	1	4	5
2	…	…	…

   (iii) Identify the variables in the table.

   (iv) Write a word formula to explain how to find the total number of dots in any stage of the pattern.

   (v) Write a mathematical formula to find the total number of dots in any stage of the pattern. Explain the meaning of any letters you use.

   (vi) (a) How many dots in total are there in stage 57?
   (b) How many of those dots are green?
   (c) How many of those dots are black?

   (vii) Use trial and improvement – or any other valid mathematical method – to find which stage of the pattern contains exactly 77 dots.

9.2 Solving basic linear equations

By the end of this section you should be able to:
- solve basic linear equations

> An **equation** is an expression that has an equals (=) sign.

Equations have three parts: the left side, the right side, and the equals sign.

For all equations, the left-hand side (LHS) is equal to the right-hand side (RHS).

When two things are equal, they create an equation.

For example, $12 = 7 + 5$

This equation states that 12 is equal to the sum of 7 and 5, which is true.

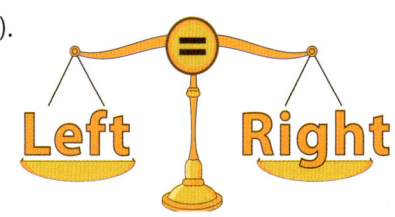

Using variables

The most common equations contain one or more variables. If we let x stand for an unknown number, we can write an equation like this one: $x = 12 + 5$

We know the left side and right side are equal, so we can see that x must be equal to $12 + 5$, thus it must be 17. This is the only value that x can have that makes the equation a true statement.

We say that $x = 17$ 'satisfies' the equation.

This process of finding the value of the unknowns is called **solving the equation**. We often say that we 'solve for x', meaning that we solve the equation to find the value of the unknown number, x.

The equals sign means that the left side and the right side have the same value.

For example, $x = 3$ could be shown as:	$2y = 8$ could be shown as:	However, if you try to balance $5 = 7$, the scale would look like this.
You can see this is true because the equation is balanced. $1x = 3$ $x = 3$	This is true, as the equation is balanced. $2y = 8$ $y = 4$	We can see this statement is not true, since 5 is less than 7. So, we know that $5 \neq 7$.

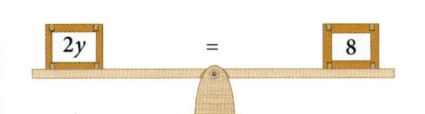

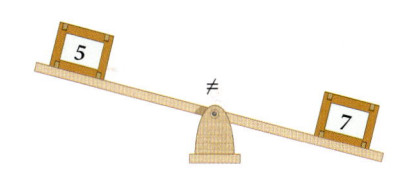

> $\neq$ means not equal to

Two equal expressions

In algebra, an equation is created by equating two expressions. An expression is a combination of numbers and symbols (usually letters). Expressions were covered in Unit 8.

When we equate the expressions, we create an equation: $2y + 4 = 10$

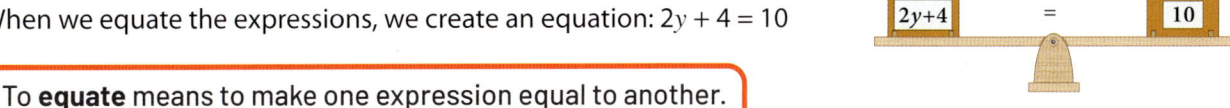

> To **equate** means to make one expression equal to another.

Solving an equation means finding the value for the variable that will make the original equation 'true'. To solve the equation, we must therefore find a number that can replace the variable (letter). At all stages in the process, both sides of the equation must be equal.

Section A Introducing concepts and building skills

Worked example 1

Study the following equations and find the value of a and b that would make each equation true.

(i) $a + 12 = 17$ (ii) $20 - b = 5$

Solution

(i) Check if $a = 4$, then
$4 + 12 = 17$,
but $16 \neq 17$ therefore a cannot $= 4$ ✗
If $a = 5$, then
$5 + 12 = 17$
$17 = 17$ ✓
Therefore, $a = 5$

(ii) Check if $b = 10$, then
$20 - 10 = 5$,
but $10 \neq 5$ therefore b cannot $= 10$ ✗
If $b = 15$, then
$20 - 15 = 5$
$5 = 5$ ✓
Therefore, $b = 15$

Worked example 2

The scales are balanced in each of the following diagrams. Find the unknown values and explain how you found your answer.

Solution

(i) 
1 box = 5
Answer: 1 box = 5 units

(ii) 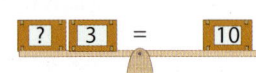
1 box + 3 = 10
$1b + 3 = 10$
To get b on its own (solve for b), we must subtract 3 from both sides.
$1b + 3 - 3 = 10 - 3$
$1b = 7$
Answer: 1 box = 7 units

(iii) 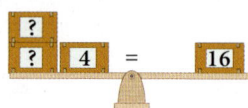
2 boxes + 4 = 16
$2b + 4 = 16$
$2b + 4 - 4 = 16 - 4$ (subtract 4 from both sides)
$2b = 12$
$\frac{2b}{2} = \frac{12}{2}$ (divide both sides by 2)
$b = 6$
Answer: 1 box = 6 units

Fundamental rule in Maths
Whatever operation you do (add, subtract, divide, multiply) to one side of an equation, you must also do to the other. This way, both sides of the equation remain equal.

Solving linear equations

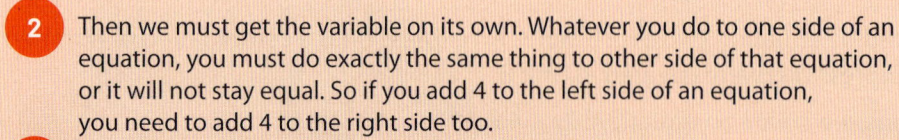

1. Identify the unknown variable (or the variable whose value needs to be found).
2. Then we must get the variable on its own. Whatever you do to one side of an equation, you must do exactly the same thing to other side of that equation, or it will not stay equal. So if you add 4 to the left side of an equation, you need to add 4 to the right side too.
3. Verify your answer by substituting it back into the equation.

Worked example 3

Solve the following equations.

(i) $3n + 4 = 19$
(ii) $5x - 6 + 2x = 29$

Solution

(i) $\quad 3n + 4 = 19$
$\quad 3n + 4 - 4 = 19 - 4 \quad$ (subtract 4)
$\quad\quad\quad 3n = 15 \quad$ (divide by 3)
$\quad\quad\quad \frac{3n}{3} = \frac{15}{3}$
$\quad\quad\quad n = 5$

$\quad 3(5) + 4 = 19 \quad$ (verify)
$\quad\quad 19 = 19 \checkmark$

(ii) $\quad 5x - 6 + 2x = 29$
$\quad\quad 7x - 6 = 29 \quad$ (combine like terms)
$\quad 7x - 6 + 6 = 29 + 6 \quad$ (add 6)
$\quad\quad 7x = 35$
$\quad\quad \frac{7x}{7} = \frac{35}{7} \quad$ (divide by 7)
$\quad\quad x = 5$

$\quad 5(5) - 6 + 2(5) = 29 \quad$ (verify)
$\quad\quad 25 - 6 + 10 = 29$
$\quad\quad\quad\quad 29 = 29 \checkmark$

Practice questions 9·2

1. For each of the following, find the value to be placed into the box, which makes the equation true.

    (i) $\square + 7 = 10$
    (ii) $\square + 9 = 21$
    (iii) $\square + 78 = 91$
    (iv) $\square - 10 = 43$
    (v) $\square - 3 = 17$
    (vi) $\square - 10 = -2$
    (vii) $\square - 11 = -8$
    (viii) $\square + 4·5 = 19$
    (ix) $\square - 0·5 = 3$
    (x) $\square - \frac{1}{3} = 1$
    (xi) $2 + \square = -4$
    (xii) $6 + \square = 2$

2. When $x = 5$, work out the values of the expressions below.

    (i) $2x + 13$
    (ii) $5x - 5$
    (iii) $3 + 6x$
    (iv) $11x - 29$

3. When $p = -2$, work out the values of the expressions below.

    (i) $3p + 10$
    (ii) $5p - 15$
    (iii) $-4p + 4$
    (iv) $-9p - 15$

4. Find the value inside each of the boxes below. Show all of your working.

    (i) $y + y = 22$
    (ii) $x + x + x = 54$
    (iii) $t + t + 11 = 37$
    (iv) $k + k + 11 = 43$
    (v) $n + n + n + n + 16 = 64$
    (vi) $z + z + z + 9 = 61 + 11$

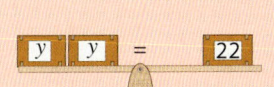

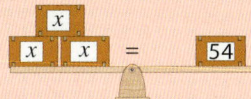

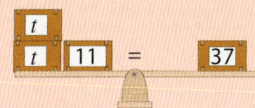

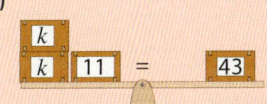

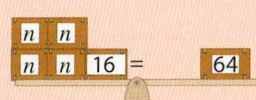

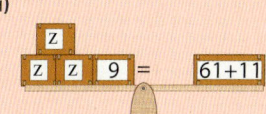

5. Solve the equations below, and verify your answer.

    (i) $10p = 50$
    (ii) $25h = 100$
    (iii) $2z + 6 = 18$
    (iv) $3k - 2 = 10$
    (v) $5r + 4 = 34$
    (vi) $5a - 3 = 7$
    (vii) $9t + 1 = 100$
    (viii) $3n - 5 = 25$

6. Solve the equations below, and verify your answer

    (i) $4p + 8 = 52$
    (ii) $5n + 3 = 38$
    (iii) $11j - 11 = 0$
    (iv) $2t + 4 + 3t = 49$

Section A Introducing concepts and building skills

7. Solve the equations below, and verify your answers.

(i) $6α + 5 − 4α = 13$

(ii) $2x − 5 + 4x + 6 = 25$

(iii) $−4w + 6 + 10w = 66$

(iv) $−4k − 11 + 3k + 8k = 24$

(v) $6z − 5 + 4z + 6 − 7z = 31 + 2 − 9 + 7$

(vi) $5β + 11 − 4 + 2β = 77 − 14$

(vii) $1·5h + 2 + 3·5h − 5 = 52$

9·3 Solving more complicated linear equations

By the end of this section you should be able to:
- solve linear equations that contain a variable on both sides

So far we have been working with equations that contain a variable on only **one** side of the equals sign, e.g. $3x + 5 = 32$. However, this is not always the case.

We must also be able to work with equations that contain a variable on **both** sides.

Worked example 1
Solve the equation: $2x + 6 = x + 11$

Solution

$2x + 6 = x + 11$
$2x + 6 − 6 = x + 11 − 6$ (subtract 6 from both sides)
$2x = x + 5$
$2x − x = x − x + 5$ (subtract x from both sides)
$x = 5$

Verify answer:
$2x + 6 = x + 11$
When $x = 5$
$2(5) + 6 = 5 + 11$
$10 + 6 = 16$
$16 = 16$ ✓

Worked example 2
Solve the equation: $\frac{10 + 2x}{3} = 6$

Solution

$\frac{10 + 2x}{3} = 6$

$3\left(\frac{10 + 2x}{3}\right) = 6(3)$ (multiply both sides by 3 to make the denominator on LHS equal to 1)

$\frac{10 + 2x}{1} = 6(3)$

$10 + 2x = 18$
$10 + 2x − 10 = 18 − 10$ (subtract 10 from both sides)
$2x = 8$
$\frac{2x}{2} = \frac{8}{2}$ (divide both sides by 2)
$x = 4$

Verify answer:
$\frac{10 + 2x}{3} = 6$
When $x = 4$
$\frac{10 + 2(4)}{3} = 6$
$\frac{18}{3} = 6$
$6 = 6$ ✓

Linking Thinking 1

Practice questions 9·3

1. Find the value of the variable in each of the following and verify your answer.
   - (i) $9x = 32 - 7x$
   - (ii) $4s + 3 = -21 - 8s$
   - (iii) $-18 + 2r = 6 - 2r$
   - (iv) $4f + 20 = 7f - 4$
   - (v) $21b + 58 = 26 + 5b$
   - (vi) $14 + 6z = -28z - 20$
   - (vii) $2x + 6 = x + 11$
   - (viii) $-2h + 29 = 5 + 2h - 24$

2. Find the value of the variable in each of the following and verify your answer.
   - (i) $3t + 4 = t + 12$
   - (ii) $9z + 3 = 5z - 13$
   - (iii) $7 + 5j = 8j + 1$
   - (iv) $10n + 7 = 4n + 25$
   - (v) $3z + 10 = 2z + 7$
   - (vi) $4x - 3 = 2x + 27$
   - (vii) $-3c + 4 = -4c + 3$
   - (viii) $4w + 2 = 2w + 28$

3. Find the value of the variable in each of the following and verify your answer.
   - (i) $2(x + 3) = 10$
   - (ii) $4(x - 1) = 12$
   - (iii) $2(5x - 3) = 14$
   - (iv) $5(n + 6) = 20$
   - (v) $2(p - 1) = -4$
   - (vi) $2(y + 3) = 14$
   - (vii) $3(2\alpha - 1) = 15$
   - (viii) $4(j - 2) = 32$

4. Find the value of the variable in each of the following and verify your answer.
   - (i) $2(r + 3) = r + 7$
   - (ii) $5(2q - 1) = 3q + 9$
   - (iii) $3(k - 1) = 2(k + 1)$
   - (iv) $5(x + 2) = 3(x + 4)$
   - (v) $2(f - 4) = 3(f + 2)$
   - (vi) $4(\alpha + 2) = 2(\alpha + 5)$
   - (vii) $3(n - 4) = 2(n + 1)$
   - (viii) $10(\beta + 37) = 40(\beta + 22)$

5. Find the value of the variable in each of the following and verify your answer.
   - (i) $\frac{y}{5} = 7$
   - (ii) $\frac{x}{2} = 8$
   - (iii) $\frac{t}{7} = 11$
   - (iv) $\frac{n}{14} = 9$
   - (v) $\frac{v + 6}{9} = 21$
   - (vi) $\frac{9 - c}{10} = 9$
   - (vii) $\frac{20 + y}{13} = 29$
   - (viii) $\frac{19 - z}{2} = 16$
   - (ix) $\frac{4p}{2} = 8$
   - (x) $\frac{10c}{5} = 8$

6. Find the value of the variable in each of the following and verify your answer.
   - (i) $\frac{12k}{3} = 20$
   - (ii) $\frac{9g}{4} = 18$
   - (iii) $\frac{4f + 4}{2} = 22$
   - (iv) $\frac{7d + 13}{5} = 11$
   - (v) $\frac{5t - 8}{9} = 8$
   - (vi) $\frac{2w + 10}{3} = 24$
   - (vii) $\frac{15 - h}{-16} = 8$
   - (viii) $\frac{6 + n}{-12} = -13$
   - (ix) $\frac{x - 22}{-24} = 17$
   - (x) $\frac{3 - b}{-12} = 29$

9·4 Creating and solving linear equations

By the end of this section you should be able to:
- generate and solve linear equations using variables

> A **linear equation** is an algebraic equation in which the highest power of the variables is 1. When graphed, a linear equation is represented by a straight line.

Many mathematical problems begin as word problems. To solve a mathematical word problem, the words must be analysed and turned into a mathematical expression. Once we have done this, it becomes much easier to work with.

There are many problems that involve relationships among known and unknown numbers (variables). These can be put in the form of equations. The equations are generally stated in words and it is for this reason we refer to these problems as 'word' problems.

This section will involve solving word equations.

> **Solving a word equation**
>
> 1. Read the problem carefully. Determine what is known and unknown and what question is being asked.
> 2. Represent the unknown quantities in terms of a variable, e.g. x, y.
> 3. Use diagrams where appropriate.
> 4. Find formulae or mathematical relationships between the known and unknown values.
> 5. Solve the equation for the unknown value.
> 6. Verify your answer.

Worked example 1

The sum of two numbers is 31. One of the numbers exceeds the other by 11. Find the numbers.

Solution

Let the unknown number be represented by x

Since the second number exceeds x by 11, we can write it as $x + 11$

We know the sum of the two numbers equals 31, so we can write $x + x + 11 = 31$

Exceeds means 'is bigger than'.

Now we have a linear equation, which we can solve:

$x + x + 11 = 31$
$2x + 11 = 31$ (combine like terms)
$2x + 11 - 11 = 31 - 11$ (subtract 11)
$2x = 20$
$x = 10$

We know the second number was $x + 11$
So, the second number must be $10 + 11 = 21$
Therefore, the two numbers are 10 and 21
Verify answer:
$10 + 21 = 31$ ✓

Worked example 2

The perimeter of a rectangular swimming pool is 152 m. Its length is 2 m more than its width. What are the length and the width of the pool?

Solution

Let the unknown be represented by w
The width is w and the length will be $w + 2$
Perimeter = length + width + length + width
Perimeter = $(w + 2) + (w) + (w + 2) + (w)$
Perimeter = $4w + 4$

$152 = 4w + 4$ (we know the perimeter total = 152 m from the question)
$152 - 4 = 4w + 4 - 4$ (subtract 4 from both sides)
$148 = 4w$
$\frac{148}{4} = w$ (divide both sides by 4)
$37 \text{ m} = w$

Therefore width = 37 m and length = 39 m

Drawing a diagram can be helpful when answering this type of question.

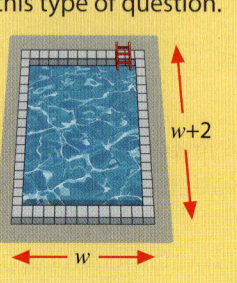

Worked example 3

The present age of Joe's sister is four times the present age of Joe. After 6 years, their ages will add to 32 years. Find their present ages.

Solution

Let Joe's age = x

	Joe	Sister	Sum
Present age	x	$4x$	
Age 6 years later	$x + 6$	$4x + 6$	$5x + 12$

Sum of their ages = 32 years

$$5x + 12 = 32$$
$$5x + 12 - 12 = 32 - 12 \quad \text{(subtract 12)}$$
$$5x = 20$$
$$\frac{5x}{5} = \frac{20}{5} \quad \text{(divide by 5)}$$
$$x = 4$$

Therefore, Joe is 4 years old and his sister is 16 years old.
In 6 years, Joe will be 10 years old and his sister will be 22 years old.

Practice questions 9.4

1. You bought a magazine for €4, and four video games. You spent a total of €28. How much did each video game cost?

2. José is four years older than Pedro. The sum of their ages is 36. Find each person's age.

3. In one day, Precious and Jan together potted 74 plants. If Precious potted 48, how many did Jan pot?

4. Henry solved a certain number of algebra problems in an hour. His older brother Frank solved four times as many. Together, they solved 80. How many were solved by each?

5. A car and a bicycle are worth €15 600 together. If the car is worth 12 times the value of the bicycle, find the value of each item.

6. The perimeter of a rectangle is 108 cm. It is twice as long as it is wide. Find (i) the length and (ii) the width of the rectangle.

7. The present age of Simon's mother is three times the present age of Simon. After 5 years, their ages will add to 66 years. Find their present ages.

8. A football team lost 4 more games than it won. If the team played 46 games:
    (i) how many did it lose?
    (ii) how many did it win? Verify your answer.

9. If it requires 180 m of fencing to enclose a rectangular field 30 m wide, how long is the field?

10. Jordan wants to build a pen for his rabbit. He wants it to be three times as long as it is wide, and he wants to use no more than half of his 240 metres of chicken wire. What are the maximum dimensions he can make his pen?

11. Two people were the only candidates in an election. Candidate A received 311 votes more than Candidate B. If the total number of votes counted was 13 689, how many votes did each person receive?

12. A rectangular playground measures x times $3x + 2$ metres.
    (i) Write an expression that describes the perimeter of the playground.
    (ii) The playground has a perimeter of 76 metres. Find the value of x.

13. In a triangle, the largest angle is three times the size of the smallest angle, and 30° larger than the third angle.

    There are 180° in a triangle.

    (i) Write an equation to show the sum of all three angles in terms of x.
    (ii) What is the value of the smallest angle?
    (iii) What is the value of the largest angle?

Section A Introducing concepts and building skills

9.5 Introduction to functions

By the end of this section you should:
- recognise when a relation (rule) describes a valid function
- be able to find the domain and range for a function

> A **function** is a relation (rule) between a set of inputs and a set of outputs with the property that each input maps (corresponds) to only one output.

A function can be thought of as a machine that is open on two ends. You put something into one end (input), it gets changed by a relation (rule) and then the result (output) pops out the other end.

> A **couple** is an input paired with its corresponding output, for example (5, 15).

Functions are typically named with a single letter, like f.

$f(x)$ is read 'f of x', and represents the output of the function f corresponding to an input x.

$p(t)$ would be read 'p of t', and represents the output of the function p corresponding to an input t.

The set of inputs is known as the domain, and the set of outputs is known as the range.

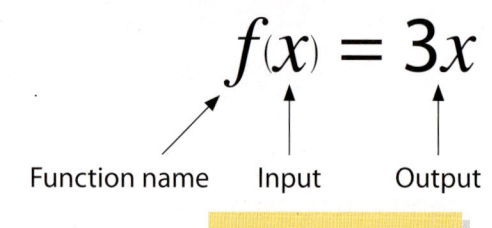

$$f(x) = 3x$$

Function name   Input   Output

This is read as 'f of x equals three x'

> The **domain** is the set of inputs or x-coordinates.
> The **range** is the set of outputs or y-coordinates.

Worked example 1

Look at the function machine opposite.

The rule states that any number put into the machine (the input) is multiplied by 5 to get the output.

For example, if 8 was the input, then $8 \times 5 = 40$, so 40 would be the output.

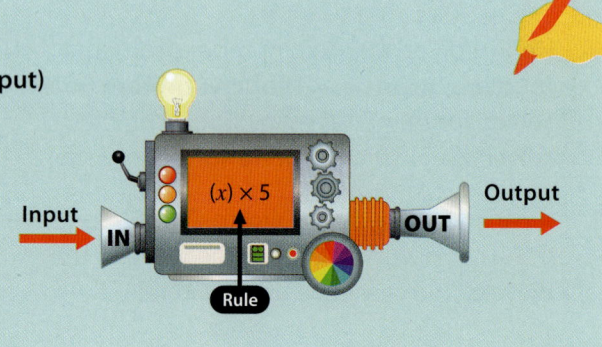

(i) What would be the output for the following numbers?
    (a) 1   (b) 2   (c) 3   (d) 4   (e) 5

(ii) List the domain and range in part (i).

(iii) List the couples in the function from part (i).

Solution

(i) Create a table of the input, rule and output.

Input (x)	Rule	Output (y)
1	$(x) \times 5$	5
2	$(x) \times 5$	10
3	$(x) \times 5$	15
4	$(x) \times 5$	20
5	$(x) \times 5$	25

(ii) The domain = {1, 2, 3, 4, 5}, as these are the input – or x – values.

The range = {5, 10, 15, 20, 25}, as these are the output – or y – values.

(iii) The couples are (1, 5), (2, 10), (3, 15), (4, 20), (5, 25)

Recall that the elements within a set are listed inside curly brackets.

The input is known as (x) and the output is known as (y).

Worked example 2

(i) Create an input-output table for the function $f(x) = x + 4$, when the input values are $\{-2, -1, 0, 1, 2, 3\}$
(ii) List the elements of the domain and range.
(iii) List the couples.

Solution

(i)

Input (x)	x + 4	Output (y)
−2	(−2) + 4	2
−1	(−1) + 4	3
0	(0) + 4	4
1	(1) + 4	5
2	(2) + 4	6
3	(3) + 4	7

(ii) The domain is a list of x values (input):
$\{-2, -1, 0, 1, 2, 3\}$
The range is a list of the y values (output): $\{2, 3, 4, 5, 6, 7\}$

(iii) The couples are (−2, 2), (−1, 3), (0, 4), (1, 5), (2, 6), (3, 7)

This is a function because each input has exactly one output.

In the above examples, we saw how to create an output from a given rule. However, if we have a list of the inputs and outputs, we can work backwards to find the rule.

Discover the pattern of the function by asking: **What happened to the input to get the output?**

Then we write the rule as an equation.

Worked example 3

Find a relation (rule) that created the input-output table shown.

Input (x)	Rule	Output (y)
5	?	9
10		14
15		19
20		24

Solution

Look at the output and see how it has changed compared to the input.

Input (x)	Rule	Output (y)	Rule
5	? + 5 = 9	9	4 + 5 = 9
10	? + 10 = 14	14	4 + 10 = 14
15	? + 15 = 19	19	4 + 15 = 19
20	? + 20 = 24	24	4 + 20 = 24

We can see from the table that the number 4 was added to the input each time.
So the rule for this function is 'input plus 4' or $f(x) = x + 4$

Mapping functions

Another way to present input-output values is by drawing a mapping diagram. We 'map' the input to the output using arrows.

A function must obey the following rule: **There is exactly one output for each input value.**

Section A Introducing concepts and building skills

When drawing a mapping diagram, there must be exactly one arrow leaving each input.

This is a function because each input has exactly one output.

Rule: Multiply by 5 ✓

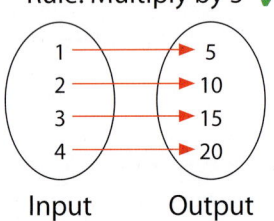

Input	Output
1	5
2	10
3	15
4	20

This is not a function because some inputs have more than one output, and also one input has no output.

Rule: Square root of input ✗

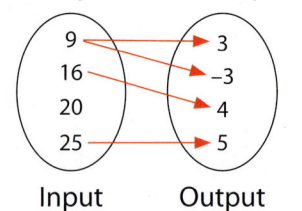

Input	Output
9	3
16	−3
20	4
25	5

This is a function because each input has exactly only one output.

Rule: Input squared ✓

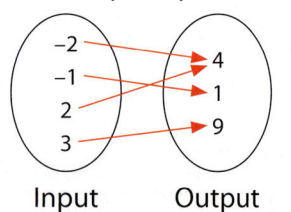

Input	Output
−2	4
−1	1
2	9
3	

> Two inputs can have the same output.

We have already discussed domain and range, but every function also contains a codomain.

> The **codomain** is the set of all the possible outputs to which a function could be mapped.

Worked example 4

(i) Copy and complete the function map provided, where $f(x) = 2x + 1$
(ii) List all the elements of the domain, range and codomain.

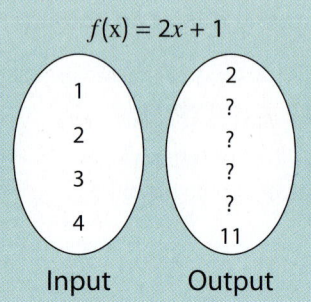

$f(x) = 2x + 1$

Input	Output
1	2
2	?
3	?
4	?
	?
	11

Solution

(i) $f(x) = 2x + 1$

Input	Output
1	2
2	3
3	5
4	7
	9
	11

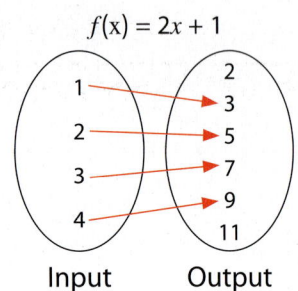

(ii) The domain = {1, 2, 3, 4}
The range = {3, 5, 7, 9}
The codomain = {2, 3, 5, 7, 9, 11}
Notice that the range is a subset of the codomain.

Linking Thinking 1

Practice questions 9.5

1. Copy and complete the input-output tables below.

(i)
Input (x)	Rule	Output (y)
	$4x$	
2		
4		
6		
8		
10		

(ii)
Input (x)	Rule	Output (y)
	$2x + 3$	
7		
9		
11		
13		
15		

(iii)
Input (x)	Rule	Output (y)
	$5x - 8$	
4		
8		
12		
16		
20		

(iv)
Input (x)	Rule	Output (y)
	$14 - 6x$	
1		
2		
3		
4		
5		

(v)
Input (x)	Rule	Output (y)
	$\frac{1}{2}x + 6$	
10		
20		
30		
40		
50		

(vi)
Input (x)	Rule	Output (y)
	$\frac{1}{3}x - 2$	
27		
30		
33		
36		
39		

2. Find the rule that satisfies each of the input-output tables below.

(i)
Input (x)	Rule	Output (y)
	$x + ?$	
1		8
2		9
3		10
4		11
5		12

(ii)
Input (x)	Rule	Output (y)
	?	
7		14
12		24
17		34
22		44
27		54

(iii)
Input (x)	Rule	Output (y)
	?	
5		12
7		16
9		20
11		24
13		28

(iv)
Input (x)	Rule	Output (y)
	?	
30		70
25		55
20		40
15		25
10		10

Section A Introducing concepts and building skills

(v)

Input (x)	Rule	Output (y)
	?	
10		15
12		16
14		17
16		18
18		19

(vi)

Input (x)	Rule	Output (y)
	?	
9		−22
18		−40
27		−58
36		−76
45		−94

3. State if each of the following mapping diagrams represents a function or not. Justify your answer.

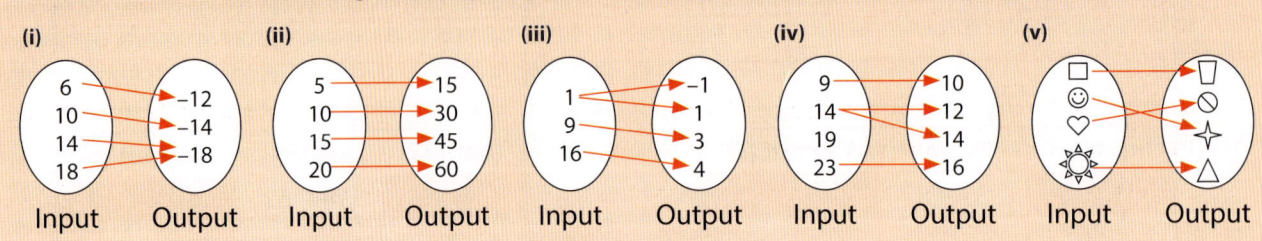

(i) Input: 6, 10, 14, 18 → Output: −12, −14, −18

(ii) Input: 5, 10, 15, 20 → Output: 15, 30, 45, 60

(iii) Input: 1, 9, 16 → Output: −1, 1, 3, 4

(iv) Input: 9, 14, 19, 23 → Output: 10, 12, 14, 16

(v) Input: square, smiley, heart, sun → Output: cup, prohibition, star, triangle

4. List the domain, range, codomain and couples for each of the functions below.

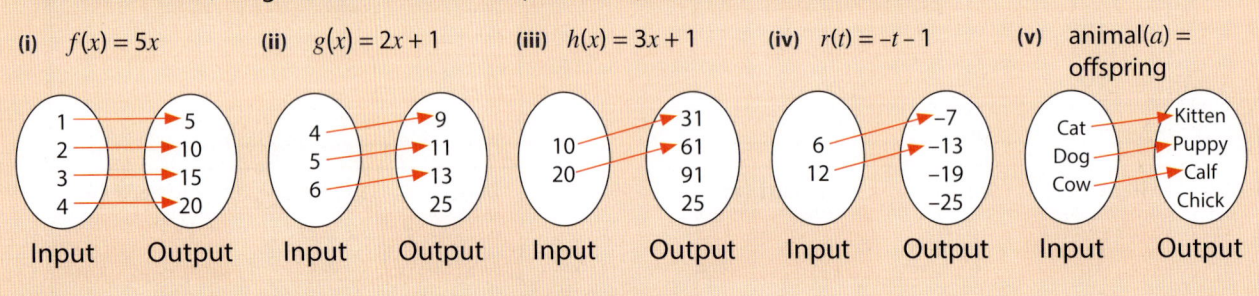

(i) $f(x) = 5x$

(ii) $g(x) = 2x + 1$

(iii) $h(x) = 3x + 1$

(iv) $r(t) = -t - 1$

(v) animal(a) = offspring

(i) Input: 1, 2, 3, 4 → Output: 5, 10, 15, 20

(ii) Input: 4, 5, 6 → Output: 9, 11, 13, 25

(iii) Input: 10, 20 → Output: 31, 61, 91, 25

(iv) Input: 6, 12 → Output: −7, −13, −19, −25

(v) Input: Cat, Dog, Cow → Output: Kitten, Puppy, Calf, Chick

5. (a) Copy and complete the mapping diagrams below.

(b) List the domain, range and couples of the relation in each case.

(i) Rule: Multiply by 5

(ii) Rule: Multiply by 5 and add 1

(iii) $f(x) = 4x - 2$

(iv) $f(x) = 7 - 2x$

(v) $f(x) = \frac{1}{2}x - 6$

(i) Input: 1, 2, 3, 4

(ii) Input: 1, 2, 3, 4

(iii) Input: 3, 6, 9, 12

(iv) Input: 9, 11, 13, 15

(v) Input: 18, 24, 30, 36

6. Using the function mapping diagrams below, find the relation (rule) in each case.

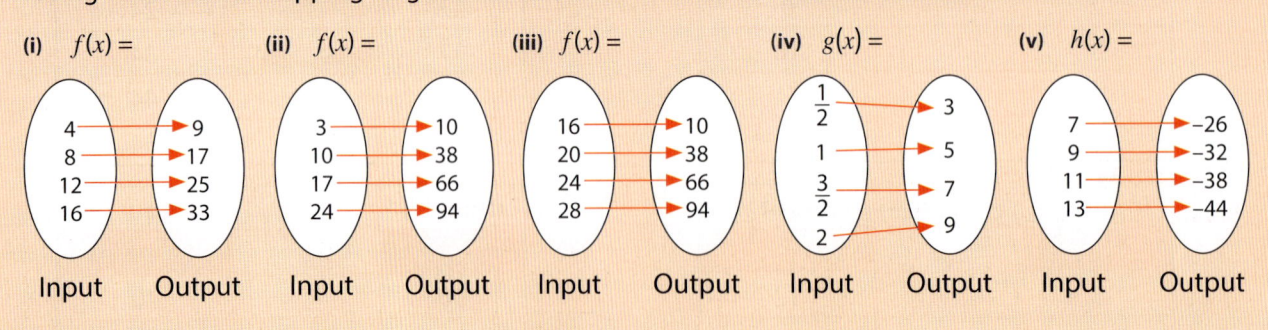

(i) $f(x) = $

(ii) $f(x) = $

(iii) $f(x) = $

(iv) $g(x) = $

(v) $h(x) = $

(i) Input: 4, 8, 12, 16 → Output: 9, 17, 25, 33

(ii) Input: 3, 10, 17, 24 → Output: 10, 38, 66, 94

(iii) Input: 16, 20, 24, 28 → Output: 10, 38, 66, 94

(iv) Input: $\frac{1}{2}$, 1, $\frac{3}{2}$, 2 → Output: 3, 5, 7, 9

(v) Input: 7, 9, 11, 13 → Output: −26, −32, −38, −44

150 Linking Thinking 1

9.6 Linear functions

By the end of this section you should:
- understand what a function is
- be able to work with functions and the formulae associated with them

When we were working with linear patterns in Unit 7, we saw that if we were to draw a graph of the pattern, it would always be a straight line. This is also known as a linear function.

We now have several ways to find the unknown value in a linear equation (also known as a linear function):
- Create a word equation, and substitute in values to solve for an answer
- Create a table and find the missing value
- Draw a graph and read information from the graph

> A **linear function** is a mathematical expression which, when graphed, will form a straight line.

Writing function relations for input-output tables

A linear function is very like a linear pattern. There is always a relation (rule). This relation can be written as an equation. Each stage of the function can be predicted by this relation.

When dealing with functions, we don't use the word 'stage'. It is more mathematically correct to use the words 'input' and 'output'.

Worked example 1

Recall the function machine from 9.5.

The relation states that any number that is put in (the input) is multiplied by 12, and the result is the output.

(i) What would be the output for the following numbers?
    (a) 1   (b) 2   (c) 3   (d) 4   (e) 5

(ii) Is this a linear function (pattern)?

Solution

(i) Create a table to show the input, relation and output.

Input (x)	Rule $12x$	Output (y)
1	12(1)	12
2	12(2)	24
3	12(3)	36
4	12(4)	48
5	12(5)	60

(ii) Examine the first difference.

Input (x)	Rule $12x$	Output (y)	First difference
1	12(1)	12	+12
2	12(2)	24	+12
3	12(3)	36	+12
4	12(4)	48	+12
5	12(5)	60	

The first difference is constant, so the function is linear.

Worked example 2

The function machine performs the following:

$$\text{output} = 4 \text{ times the input} + 2$$

Find the output value for each of the following inputs.

(i) Input = 5   (ii) Input = 6   (iii) Input = 8

Solution

Create a table, multiplying each input by 4 and then adding 2.

	Input (x)	Rule $4x + 2$	Output (y)
(i)	5	4(5) + 2	22
(ii)	6	4(6) + 2	26
(iii)	8	4(8) + 2	34

> Remember to use the correct order of operations.

Worked example 3

A tree measures 24 cm high. After one year it measures 35 cm high, in the second year it measures 46 cm high, in the third year it is 57 cm high, and so on.

(i) If the tree continues to grow at this rate, how tall will the tree be after 5 years?
(ii) How many years will it take for the tree to be 101 cm tall?

Solution

(i) **Method 1: Using an equation**

Create an equation to show how the height of the tree changes with time

Height = start amount plus 11cm each year
$$H = 24 + 11(x)$$

For five years, let $x = 5$
$H = 24 + 11(5)$
$H = 24 + 55$
$H = 79$

In five years, the tree will be 79 cm tall.

Method 2: Using a table

Create a table to show how the height of the tree changes with time.

Year (x)	Height of tree (cm)
Start (0)	24
1	35
2	46
3	57
4	68
5	79

(ii) **Method 1: Using an equation**

Using the equation above, we know the value of H and must find the unknown value of x:

$$H = 24 + 11(x)$$
$101 = 24 + 11x$
$101 - 24 = 11x$
$77 = 11x$
$\frac{77}{11} = x$
$7 = x$

In year 7, the tree will be 101 cm tall

Method 2: Using a table

If we continued the table above, we would see the tree will be 90 cm in year 6. It takes 7 years to reach 101 cm.

Year (x)	Height of tree (cm)
Start (0)	24
1	35
...	...
5	79
6	90
7	101

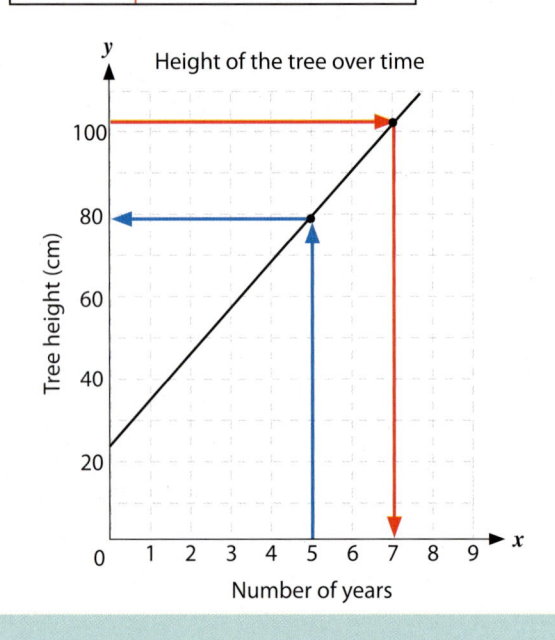

Method 3: Using a graph

From the graph, we see it takes 5 years for the tree to reach 79 cm. After 7 years, the tree will be 101 cm tall.

Practice questions 9·6

1. The initial height of a liquid in a glass cylinder is 5 cm. As liquid is added the height increases by 2 cm per minute.
   (i) Create an equation to show how the height of the liquid increases over time.
   (ii) What will be the height of the liquid after 4 minutes?
   (iii) After how many minutes will the height of the liquid be 17 cm?
   (iv) Draw a graph showing how the height of the liquid changes over 10 minutes.
   (v) Does your graph represent a linear function? Justify your answer.

2. Fiona's office has recycled 3 kg of paper so far this year. The new recycling plan aims to have the office recycling 2 kg of paper each week.
   (i) Create an equation to show how much paper will be recycled over time.
   (ii) What is the total amount of paper that the office will have recycled after 6 weeks?
   (iii) After how many weeks will the office have recycled 15 kg of paper?
   (iv) Draw a graph to show the total amount of paper the office has recycled in 10 weeks.
   (v) Does your graph represent a linear function? Justify your answer.

3. A puppy named Snowball was born weighing 500 g. He then gained 1 kg every month for a year.
   (i) Create an equation to show how much weight Snowball gains over time.
   (ii) What weight will Snowball be in kg after 7 months?
   (iii) Draw a graph to show how much weight in kg Snowball gains over 10 months.
   (iv) From your graph, estimate Snowball's weight in kg after 3·5 months.
   (v) Does your graph represent a linear function? Justify your answer.

4. A taxi company charges a €2 pick-up fee, plus an additional €3 per kilometre driven.
   (i) Create an equation to show how the cost of the taxi rises with the distance travelled.
   (ii) How much will it cost to travel 9 kilometres?
   (iii) How far will I have travelled if my bill is €17?
   (iv) How many kilometres is a taxi ride that costs €32?
   (v) Draw a graph to show how much a taxi would charge for a 23-kilometre journey.
   (vi) Does your graph represent a linear function? Justify your answer.

Taking it FURTHER

5. A bucket contains 1 litre of water. The bucket develops a small leak in the base and loses 150 ml (millilitres) of water every minute.
   (i) Create an equation to show the rate at which the volume (amount) of water is decreasing in the bucket.
   (ii) How many millilitres of water has the bucket lost after 4 minutes?
   (iii) Draw a graph showing the loss of water over 6 minutes.
   (iv) Is your graph linear? Justify your answer.
   (v) Using your graph, determine how many minutes will pass until the bucket is completely empty.
   (vi) Create and solve an equation to show how much time will pass until the bucket has 250 ml remaining.

9.7 Solving linear relations using multiple representations

By the end of this section you should be able to:
- solve a linear relation problem using a variety of ways

Throughout this unit, we have seen there are many ways to work with a mathematical pattern, equation or function. The following example shows how each method can be used.

> A pattern can be represented by an equation or function. Therefore, patterns, equations and functions are all interlinked.

Worked example

Gemma buys a new phone on Sunday. She receives 32 GB of free data on her phone. From Monday, she uses 4 GB of data per day, every day.

(i) Create a table to show how much data she has remaining after 5 days.
(ii) Draw a graph to show this information.
(iii) Find the slope (rate of change) of this graph.
(iv) Explain this pattern in words, stating the amount of data remaining after any number of days.
(v) Write a mathematical formula to find the amount of data Gemma has left on any particular day. Use your word sentence above to help.
(vi) Using either the table, graph or formula you have made, find out how many days it will take for Gemma to use up all of her free data.

Solution

(i)

Number of days	Number of GB of data remaining
Start (Day 0)	32
Day 1	28
Day 2	24
Day 3	20
Day 4	16
Day 5	12

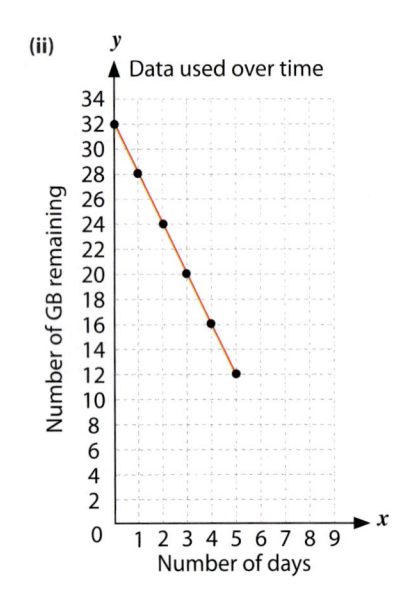

(ii) *Data used over time* — graph showing Number of GB remaining (y-axis) vs Number of days (x-axis), with points (0,32), (1,28), (2,24), (3,20), (4,16), (5,12).

(iii) Slope = $\frac{\text{rise}}{\text{run}} = \frac{-12}{3} = -4$

> You can choose different values to find the slope, and the answer should still be the same.

(iv) The amount of data Gemma has left on any particular day is the amount of data she started with minus 4 GB for each day that has passed.

(v) Amount left = Start amount − 4 (each day)

$A = S - 4(D)$

Where A = amount of data left, S = starting amount, D = number of days

Linking Thinking 1

Worked example (continued)

> This example shows that there are sometimes several different methods that we can use to find a solution.

Solution

(vi) Method 1: Using a table

Number of days	Amount of data remaining (GB)
Start (Day 0)	32
Day 1	28
Day 2	24
Day 3	20
Day 4	16
Day 5	12
Day 6	8
Day 7	4
Day 8	0

From the table, we can see by the end of day 8, Gemma will have 0 GB data remaining.

Method 2: Using the graph

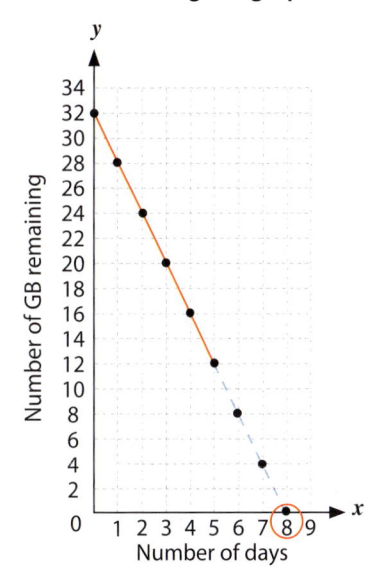

Method 3: Using the formula, with trial and improvement

$A = S - 4(D)$

We need to set the amount to 0 GB and we started with 32 GB. We then use trial and improvement, by filling in different numbers for the days.

$0 = 32 - 4(5)$ (five days)
$0 = 32 - 20$
$0 = 12$ Not true, so it must be more than five days

$0 = 32 - 4(10)$ (ten days)
$0 = 32 - 40$
$0 = -8$ Not true, so it must be less than 10 days

$0 = 32 - 4(8)$ (eight days)
$0 = 32 - 32$
$0 = 0$ ✓ so answer is 8 days

After 8 days, Gemma will have 0 GB data remaining.

Method 4: Solving the equation

$A = S - 4(D)$

We need to get D (the number of days) on its own, when $A = 0$

$A = S - 4(D)$
$0 = 32 - 4(D)$
$0 - 32 = 32 - 32 - 4(D)$ (subtract 32 from both sides)
$-32 = -4(D)$
$\frac{-32}{-4} = \frac{-4D}{-4}$ (divide both sides by −4)
$8 = D$

After 8 days, Gemma will have 0 GB data remaining.

Practice questions 9·7

1. Mobile phone companies often package their products to make them more attractive to potential users. If you average 356 minutes per month in talk time, which of the following packages is the best deal, for you? Justify your answer.

Package A		Package B	
Handset	Free	Handset	€10 per month
Monthly charge	€39·95	Monthly charge	€35·95
Free minutes per month	300	Free minutes per month	350
Price per minute outside of the plan	€0·12	Price per minute outside of the plan	€0·08

Section A Introducing concepts and building skills

2. Logs are stacked in a pile with 24 logs on the bottom row and 15 on the top row. There are 10 rows in all, with each row having one less log than the row below it, i.e. bottom row has 24 logs, the next row has 23 logs, and so on. How many logs are in the stack?

3. Daisy looks for her favourite type of stone on the beach every morning. The first day, she finds 3 stones. The next day, she finds 8 stones. On the third day, she finds 13 stones in a cave. On the fourth day, she finds 18 stones as she walks by the water. If Daisy keeps finding stones in this way, how many will she find on the eighth day? Explain how you got your answer and how you know your answer is correct.

4. Holly is saving money to buy a ticket to a concert. On Sunday, she has €5 in her savings box. Holly is going to feed and walk the neighbour's dog each day from Monday through Friday while they are away on holiday. She will earn €9 each day for taking care of the dog. The neighbours will pay her when they get home on Friday night.

    (i) How much money will Holly have in her savings box after the neighbours pay her on Friday night?

    (ii) The concert ticket is on sale for €55·00 on Saturday morning. Will Holly have enough money to buy the concert ticket? Justify your answer.

5. It's time for the annual St Patrick's Day parade. The First Year class decides to march in a special formation this year. Two people walk in the first row, four people walk in the second row and six people walk in the third row and so on. This pattern continues on.

    (i) If the all the students in First Year are marching in 10 full rows, how many students are in First Year?

    (ii) Use numbers, words, tables or pictures to explain how you know your answer is correct.

6. The tower clock known as Big Ben in London, England, chimes every hour, on the hour. At one o'clock it chimes once, at two o'clock it chimes twice, at three o'clock it chimes three times, and so on. How many times does it chime between 12:01 am and 12:01 pm?

7. A supermarket store wants to stack cans in a triangular display similar to the one in the picture. There are 100 cans to put on display.

    (i) How many rows high can the cans be stacked?

    (ii) Will there be any cans left over? Justify your answer.

Taking it FURTHER

8. The follow shows a growing pattern. It starts with two red tiles and nine blue tiles.

    Start   Stage 1   Stage 2

    (i) How many red tiles do we need for stage 4 of the pattern?

    (ii) How many red tiles will we need for …?
       (a) stage 10 of the pattern   (b) stage 100   (c) stage 1 298

    (iii) How many blue tiles do we need for …?
       (a) stage 4 of the pattern   (b) stage 10   (c) stage 157

    (iv) If there are 4 red tiles, how many blue tiles are there?

    (v) If there are 10 red tiles, how many blue tiles are there?

    (vi) If you have to use exactly 33 blue tiles in making the design, how many red tiles would you need?

    (vii) If you had exactly 35 tiles, which stage of the pattern could you make?

    (viii) Which of the following numbers of tiles can **never** be used to create any complete stage of this pattern: (a) 43, (b) 44, (c) 45? Justify your answer, showing all work done.

Revision questions

9A Core skills

1. Solve the following equations and verify your answers.
   - (i) $x + 2 = 7$
   - (ii) $a - 4 = 11$
   - (iii) $p - 6 = -9$
   - (iv) $3z + 4 = 10$
   - (v) $4t - 2 = 18$
   - (vi) $\frac{v}{5} = 20$
   - (vii) $\frac{2h}{3} = 4$
   - (viii) $\frac{2f}{6} = 7 - 4$

2. Solve the following equations and verify your answers.
   - (i) $3d - 7 = d + 11$
   - (ii) $-5r + 6 = 3r - 2$
   - (iii) $7a - 10 = 3a + 2$
   - (iv) $4w + 11 = w + 5$
   - (v) $7x - 25 = 2x + 15$
   - (vi) $2k + 7 = 12 - 3k$
   - (vii) $3\alpha - 5 = 4\alpha - 7$
   - (viii) $8 - 4\beta = 10 - 2\beta$

3. Simplify and solve the following:
   - (i) $5(2d - 3) = 15$
   - (ii) $18 = 3(2p - 4)$
   - (iii) $2(x + 6) = 22 - 3x$
   - (iv) $13 - 3n = 4n - 1$
   - (v) $f - 18 = 2(2f - 3)$
   - (vi) $3t - 27 = 4(2t - 3)$
   - (vii) $x(x + 5) = x^2 - 15$
   - (viii) $7\alpha + 2 = 5(\alpha - 2) + 2$

4. (a) Copy and complete the input-output tables shown below.
   (b) List the domain, range and couples for each table.

   (i)
Input (x)	Rule	Output (y)
	$2x - 1$	
3		
5		
7		
9		
11		

   (ii)
Input (x)	Rule	Output (y)
	$-3x - 3$	
14		
19		
24		
29		
34		

   (iii)
Input (x)	Rule	Output (y)
	$-0.5x - 1.5$	
-2		
-4		
-6		
-8		
-10		

5. Copy the input-output tables shown below.
   (a) Using the inputs and their corresponding outputs, write out what the rule is in each case. Your rule should be in terms of x.
   (b) Complete the tables.

   (i)
Input (x)	Rule	Output (y)
	?	
1		6
2		8
3		10
4		12
5		14

   (ii)
Input (x)	Rule	Output (y)
	?	
1		1
2		1.5
3		2
4		2.5
5		3

   (iii)
Input (x)	Rule	Output (y)
	?	
5		16
10		36
15		56
20		76
25		96

Section A Introducing concepts and building skills

6. Gia is x years old. Her mother is 4 times Gia's age. Gia's brother is 6 years younger than Gia.

   (i) Write two equations which describe the ages of Gia's mother and Gia's brother. Let x = Gia's age.

All three ages sum to 48.

   (ii) Write an equation to show this.

   (iii) Solve the equation from part **(ii)** to find Gia's age.

   (iv) How old was Gia's mother when Gia was born?

7. The width of a rectangle is x cm. Its length is 5 cm longer than its width.

   (i) Write down an expression (formula) for the perimeter of the rectangle, giving your answer in its simplest form.

   (ii) If the perimeter of the rectangle is 62 cm, work out the length of the rectangle.

8. The diagram shows the lengths of some of the sides of a sandpit in metres.

   (i) Find the value of x.

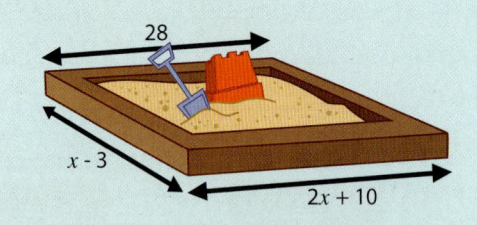

(sides shown: 28, $x-3$, $2x+10$)

   (ii) Find the perimeter of the sandpit.

9. State if the following represents a function or not. Justify your answer in each case.

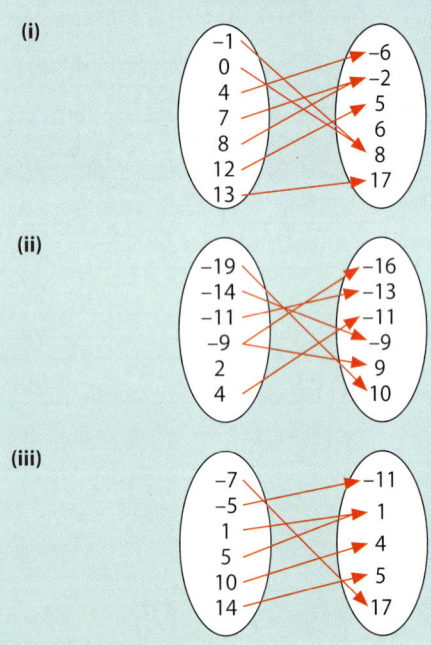

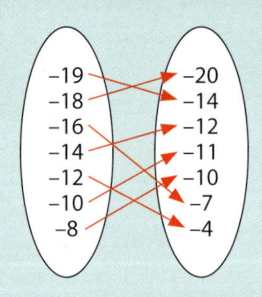

(i) mapping from {−1, 0, 4, 7, 8, 12, 13} to {−6, −2, 5, 6, 8, 17}

(ii) mapping from {−19, −14, −11, −9, 2, 4} to {−16, −13, −11, −9, 9, 10}

(iii) mapping from {−7, −5, 1, 5, 10, 14} to {−11, 1, 4, 5, 17}

(iv) mapping from {−19, −18, −16, −14, −12, −10, −8} to {−20, −14, −12, −11, −10, −7, −4}

10. (i) List the domain, range and codomain of the function represented in the mapping diagram below.

   (ii) List the ordered pairs (couples).

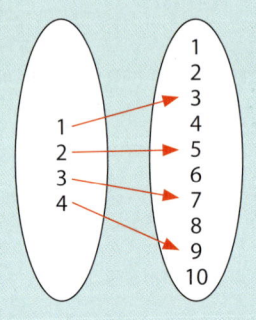

(mapping from {1, 2, 3, 4} to {1, 2, 3, 4, 5, 6, 7, 8, 9, 10})

11. Half of a herd of deer are grazing in the field. Three-quarters of the remaining deer are playing nearby. The rest, nine deer in total, are drinking water from the pond. Find the number of deer in the herd.

9B Taking it FURTHER

1. The triangle shown is known as an isosceles triangle (two of its sides are the same length). (sides: $2r+3$, $r+3$)

   (i) Using the information provided, write an equation for the perimeter of the triangle in terms of r, giving your answer in its simplest form.

   (ii) Calculate the value of r if the perimeter of the triangle is 49 cm.

2. A room can be hired for parties. There is a flat fee of €50 and a further fee of €10 per person.

   (i) Write an expression to show the cost of the room for any given number of people. Explain any letters you have used.

   (ii) If a party cost €400, how many people attended? Justify your answer, showing all workings (e.g. graph, table, formula).

Linking Thinking 1

3. Dustin is baking a Christmas cake. He has a choice of two ovens. A normal oven, or a fan assisted oven. The time it takes to bake the Christmas cake in each oven is given by the following formulae:

Normal oven: $t = 7.5w + 40$

Fan oven: $t = 3.25w + 30$

where w = mass in kilograms and t = time taken in minutes.

(i) How much quicker is it to cook a small 4 kilogram Christmas cake in a fan oven than in a normal oven?

(ii) How much slower would it be to cook a 6 kilogram Christmas cake in a normal oven than in a fan oven?

(iii) How many kilograms is the Christmas cake if it takes 4 hours and 55 minutes to fully cook in a normal oven?

4. Mike's grandfather is six times the present age of Mike. After 5 years, their ages will add to 87. Find their present ages.

5. (a) Complete the pattern in each of the mapping diagrams provided, and create a rule for each.

(b) Are all patterns linear? Justify your answer, showing all work.

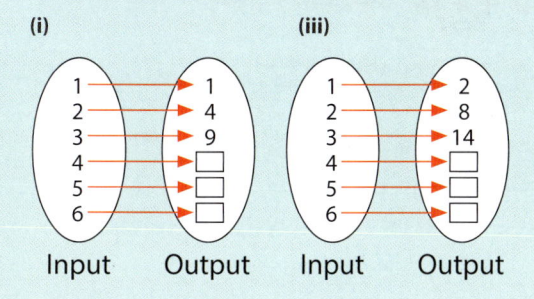

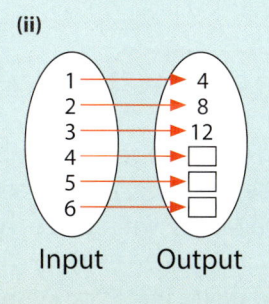

(i)

Input	Output
1	1
2	4
3	9
4	☐
5	☐
6	☐

(iii)

Input	Output
1	2
2	8
3	14
4	☐
5	☐
6	☐

(ii)

Input	Output
1	4
2	8
3	12
4	☐
5	☐
6	☐

6. Emma's courier service has a unique pricing structure. She charges €4·10 to pick up your parcel, and then a fixed charge of €1·03 per km she must travel to deliver your package.

(i) Write an expression to show how much Emma will charge for any distance travelled.

(ii) Umer wants a package collected and delivered to a location 5 km away. How much will it cost him?

(iii) Bruno has €20. He wants to have a package picked up and delivered to a location 17·5 km away. Does he have enough money? Justify your answer with supporting work.

(iv) Draw a graph showing how much money it would cost to pick up a parcel and deliver it to a location up to and including 15 km away.

(v) Is your graph linear? Justify your answer.

(vi) How much would it cost to have a parcel picked up and delivered a distance of 4·5 km? Use your graph from part **(iv)** or any other valid mathematical method to answer.

(vii) Emma wants to change her pricing policy, so that it now costs

$$c = 0.5 + 1.5d$$

where c = total cost and d = distance travelled.

Discuss, using any valid mathematical method, which pricing structure is better. Justify your answer.

Now that you have completed the unit, revisit the

Something to think about ...

question posed at the start of this unit.

Unit 10

Ratio, proportion and scaling

Topics covered within this unit:
10·1 Ratio and proportion
10·2 Scaling

The Learning Outcomes covered in this unit are contained in the following sections:
N.2b GT.2a

Key words
Ratio
Direct proportion
Scaling
Scale
Scale diagram

Something to think about ...

KEY SKILLS

Scale drawings are based on the geometric principle of similarity. Two figures are similar if they have the same shape, even though they may have different sizes.

You are asked to make a scale drawing of a campground. The picnic area is a rectangle and has a length of 44 metres and a width of 21 metres in real life.

Draw a scale diagram of this picnic area using a suitable scale.

10·1 Ratio and proportion

By the end of this section you should:
- understand what a ratio is
- be able to divide amounts in a given ratio
- understand direct proportion
- be able to solve problems using direct proportion

Ratio

A **ratio** is a relationship between two amounts.

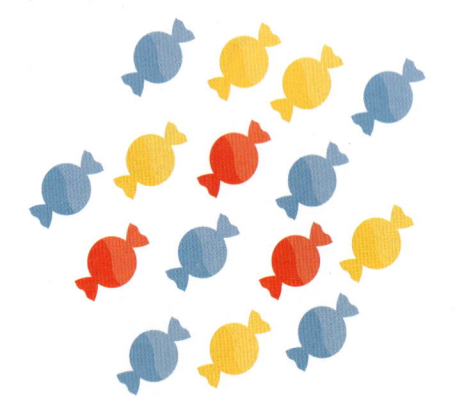

Ratios show how much of one thing there is compared to another. When we express ratios in words, we use the word 'to' – we say, 'the ratio of something to something else'. In Maths, we replace the word 'to' with a colon (:).

In the picture to the left:

The ratio of red sweets to yellow sweets is 3 : 5

The ratio of red sweets to blue sweets is 3 : 7

The ratio of blue sweets to yellow sweets is 7 : 5

Linking Thinking 1

Solving questions involving ratios:
How can we divide 35 blocks of chocolate in the ratio 4 : 3?

1. Add the parts to find the total number of parts.
   e.g. 4 : 3 = 4 + 3 total parts = 7

2. Divide, to find one part.
   e.g. 35 chocolate squares, one part = 35 ÷ 7 = 5

3. Multiply to find the required share.
   e.g. 4 × 5 = 20   3 × 5 = 15
                 20 : 15

Simplifying ratios

Consider the image shown.

The ratio of frogs to penguins is 9 : 6

However, we can see that for every 3 frogs there are 2 penguins, so the ratio can also be written as 3 : 2

Ratios are generally written in simplest form. **To simplify a ratio, find the highest common factor (HCF) of the numbers and divide both sides by the HCF.**

Sharing in a given ratio

A ratio in the form 3 : 2 means that a quantity is divided into 5 parts (3 + 2) and then shared in such a way that the first portion is $\frac{3}{5}$ of the total and the second share is $\frac{2}{5}$ of the total.

Worked example 1

(i) Write the ratio 24 : 36 in its simplest form.
(ii) Share €240 in the ratio 5 : 3.
(iii) Carol and Danielle shared some prize money in the ratio 2 : 3, respectively. Danielle got €360. How much did Carol get?

Solution

(i) 24 : 36
HCF of 24 and 36 = 12
Divide both sides by 12
24 ÷ 12 : 36 ÷ 12
2 : 3

(ii) **Step 1** Add together the ratio parts
5 + 3 = 8 parts

Step 2 Divide to get 1 part
240 ÷ 8 = 30

Step 3 Multiply to find the required share
30 × 5 = 150
30 × 3 = 90

€240 shared in the ratio 5 : 3 = €150 : €90

(iii) **Step 1** Add together the ratio parts
2 + 3 = 5 parts
Carol's share = $\frac{2}{5}$
Danielle's share = $\frac{3}{5}$
$\frac{3}{5}$ = 360

Step 2 Divide to get 1 part
360 ÷ 3 = 120

Step 3 Multiply to find the required share
120 × 2 = 240

Carol got €240

Section A Introducing concepts and building skills

Proportion

If two things are proportional, it means that they are related to each other in a specific way.

Direct proportion

> **Direct proportion** relates to two things, whereby as one increases the other increases.

For example, if a babysitter is paid an hourly rate, then the more hours he works, the more pay he will get. In this case, the time worked is directly proportional to the money earned.

Worked example 2

A football coach is buying new footballs for his team. If 8 balls cost €96, how much will 10 balls cost?

Solution

8 footballs   = €96
1 football   = € 96 ÷ 8 = €12   (divide by 8)
10 footballs = €12 × 10 = €120   (multiply by 10)
Therefore, 10 footballs cost €120

The cost of the footballs is directly proportional to the number bought.

Practice questions 10·1

1. Write the ratios shown in the images below. Give your answers in the simplest form.

   (i) Apples to pears

   (ii) Cats to dogs

   (iii) Spiders to ladybirds

   (iv) Chocolate bars to ice creams

   (v) Books to pens

   (vi) Pumpkins to cabbages

2. Simplify the following ratios.
   - (i) 6 : 3
   - (ii) 18 : 10
   - (iii) 16 : 36
   - (iv) 42 : 24
   - (v) 5 : 25
   - (vi) 48 : 60

3. Divide each of the following quantities in the given ratio.
   - (i) €50 in the ratio 2 : 3
   - (ii) 81 km in the ratio 5 : 4
   - (iii) 121 g in the ratio 9 : 2
   - (iv) 105 hrs in the ratio 8 : 7
   - (v) 169 cm in the ratio 8 : 5
   - (vi) 28 cents in the ratio 3 : 4

4. A company offers to give €50 to charity for every €200 raised by its employees. What is the ratio (in simplest form) of the money given by the company to the money given by the employees?

Linking Thinking 1

5. There are 24 students in a class. The ratio of boys to girls is 5 : 3.
   (i) How many boys are in the class?
   (ii) How many girls are in the class?

6. Jackie gave €100 to her daughter Kailey and asked her to spend 3 parts and save 2 parts of the total amount.
   (i) Write a ratio to represent the ratio of spending to saving.
   (ii) How much did Kailey spend?
   (iii) How much did she save?

7. Ronan and Jessica are candidates in an election. They receive votes in the ratio 7 : 9. If the successful candidate receives 1 080 votes, how many votes were cast in total?

8. A recipe uses a sugar to flour ratio of 10 : 3. If you used 70 g of sugar, how many grams of flour would you need to use?

9. The ratio of black cars to white cars in a car park is 5 : 3. If there were 40 black cars, how many white cars were in the car park?

10. On Mr Murphy's farm the ratio of cows to sheep is 9 : 2. If there were 72 cows on the farm, how many sheep were there?

11. The cost of a taxi is €40·50 for 15 km. Find the cost for 20 km.

12. Ramon has a part-time job in a supermarket. He earns €7 an hour during the week and €8·50 an hour at the weekend. Last week he worked 7 hours during the week and 4 hours over the weekend. How much did he earn last week?

Taking it FURTHER

13. I mixed up some diluted orange in two glasses.
    The first glass had 200 ml of orange concentrate and 300 ml of water.
    The second glass had 100 ml of orange concentrate and 200 ml of water.
    Which glass has the highest concentration of orange? Justify your answer.

10·2 Scaling

By the end of this section you should be able to:
- draw scale diagrams of 2D shapes
- interpret scale diagrams

An everyday use of proportion is **scaling**.

> **Scaling** is the process of showing a real object with its accurate sizes reduced or enlarged proportionately by a certain amount, called the scale.

Maps and scale drawings form a crucial part of everyday life. Scale drawings are useful in a variety of careers from surveyors, to town planning and architecture.

Scale diagrams (or drawings) are often used to represent a smaller or larger object, shape or image.

The scale used will depend on the reduction or enlargement of the object.

A **scale diagram** is a drawing that shows a real object with accurate sizes reduced or enlarged by a certain amount.

The scale is shown as:

Length on drawing : Actual length

Scale 1 : 20 000

On the left is a picture of the Donegal International Airport runway and a scale diagram of the runway.

1 cm on the scale diagram is equal to 20 000 cm in the actual runway

This means that the scale diagram is 20 000 times smaller than the actual runway.

Examples of scale ratios

A medium-sized wall map of the world

Scale: 1 : 30 000 000, which represents 1 cm to 30 000 000 cm, which is 1 cm to 300 km.

The 300 km is found by dividing 30 000 000 by 100 to convert to metres, then by 1 000 to convert to kilometres.

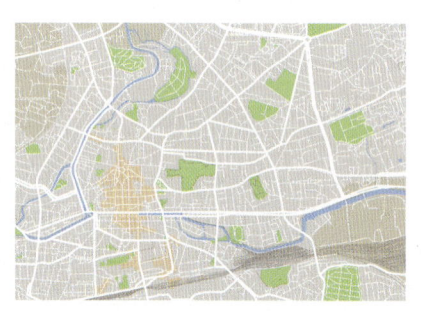

A map for walkers or hikers

Scale: 1 : 25 000, which represents 1 cm to 25 000 cm, which is 1 cm to 250 m.

The 250 m is found by dividing 25 000 by 100 to convert to metres.

An architect's drawing

Scale: 1 : 100, which represents 1 cm to 100 cm, which is 1 cm to 1 m.

The 1 m is found by dividing 100 cm by 100 to convert to metres.

Worked example 1

Using the scale diagram on the right, find the actual distance between A and E.

Solution

Step 1 Place a ruler up to the scale. You need to do this to work out how much distance (in cm) is equal to 200 m.

The ruler shows us it is 2 cm.

This tells us that the scale is

2 cm : 200m

or 1 cm : 100 m

Graphics not to scale

164   Linking Thinking 1

Step 2 Use the ruler to work out the distance between A and E in centimetres.

The ruler shows us it is 8 cm.

Step 3 Using the scale found in step 1:
Since 1 cm : 100 m   (multiply both sides by 8)
8 cm : 800 m

So, the distance between A and E is 800 m.

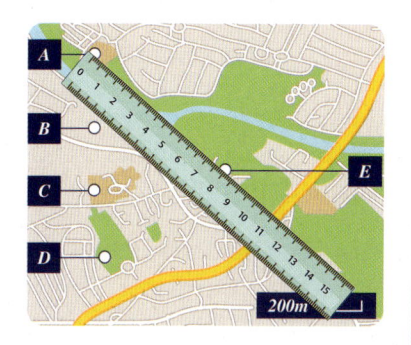

Graphics not to scale

Worked example 2

Declan is producing a scale drawing of a swimming pool he plans to build. The pool's dimensions are 2 m by 6 m. When he measures the drawing on his plan he sees that it is 8 cm by 24 cm. What scale should he include on his plan?

Solution

To answer this question, you should use the same units. The question uses metres and centimetres, so change everything to centimetres.

From the information presented, we can see that:
in Declan's drawing, 8 cm = 200 cm in real life.

We can divide 200 by 8 to see what 1 cm represents: $200 \div 8 = 25$ cm

The scale he should use is 1 cm : 25 cm, or simply 1 : 25.

Practice questions 10·2

1. Convert the following values into centimetres.

   (i) 3 m   (ii) 40 mm   (iii) 2 km   (iv) 3·5 km   (v) 10 000 mm   (vi) 0·5 m   (vii) 1·25 km

2. Copy and complete the following table.

	(i)	(ii)	(iii)	(iv)	(v)	(vi)	(vii)	(viii)
Scale	1 : 3	1 : 4		1 : 35	3 : 10		2 : 5	
Length on diagram	5 cm	12 cm	1·5 m		18 mm	8 cm		4·7 cm
Actual length	15 cm		9 m	21 m		2·4 km	30 m	70·5 m

3. Which of the following should every map show?

   (a) An ocean

   (b) A train station

   (c) A scale

4. What is the actual distance between A and B in metres, using this map, given the ruler is measuring centimetres?

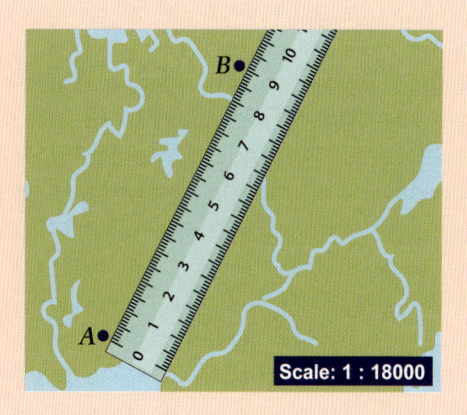

   Scale: 1 : 18000

Section A **Introducing concepts and building skills**

5. On a map, a scale is used where 1 cm on the map represents 50 m in reality.
   (i) What is the ratio that is equivalent to this?
   (ii) The distance between two shops on the map is 4·5 cm. What is the actual distance between the shops?

6. A scale on a map shows that 2·5 cm represents 15 km.
   What number of actual km are represented by 17·5 cm on the map?

7. The Ardmore Convention Centre is 4 cm away from the airport on a city map. The scale of the map is 1 cm = 11 km. In real life, what is the distance between the Ardmore Convention Centre and the airport?

8. A particular map shows a scale of 1 cm : 5 km. What would the map distance (in cm) be if the actual distance is 14 km?

9. Conor is using an internet tool to design his ideal skateboard park. The scale on the design is 1 : 150. Conor measures the drawing dimensions to be 10 cm by 13 cm. What size would his skateboard park be in real life? Give your answer in metres.

10. Mr O'Leary makes model cars. He wants to make a model of a car that is 3 m in length. He wants his model to be 15 cm long. What scale should he use to achieve this?

11. Eoin is considering working on his house. He has plans drawn up by an architect. The scale on the plans is 1 : 200. Eoin measures the length of the roof extension on the plan to be 2 cm, how long will it be in real life?

12. Emily is a civil engineer who designs tower blocks and residences. She needs to make a computer model to accompany her latest proposal. The actual tower blocks will measure 400 m high. She wants to use a scale of 1 : 2 000. How high will her model be in centimetres?

13. A map has a scale of 1 : 4 000. On the map, the distance between two houses is 9 cm. What is the actual distance between the houses? Give your answer in metres.

14. A rectangular swimming pool is 50 m long and 25 m wide. Draw a scale drawing of the base of swimming pool using a scale of 1 : 1 000.

15. The scale drawing of a tree is 1 : 500. If the height of the tree on paper is 20 cm, what is the height of the tree in real life?

16. Timmy drew a scale drawing of a house and its lot. The back patio, which is 10 m wide in real life, is 2 cm wide in the drawing. What scale did Timmy use?

17. Patsy drew a scale drawing of a school. In real life, the gym is 50 m wide. It is 10 cm wide in the drawing. What is the scale of the drawing?

18. The plan for a house is shown opposite. The measurements marked on the diagram are in metres and are dimensions of the actual rooms of the house. Draw a scale diagram of the actual plan for the house using an appropriate scale.

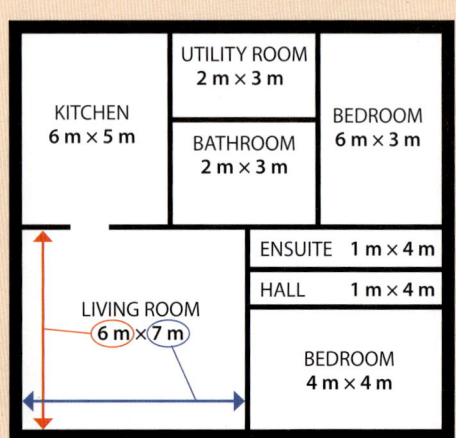

Revision questions

10A Core skills

1. Divide each of the following quantities in the given ratio.
   - (i) €70 in the ratio 7 : 3
   - (ii) 66 m in the ratio 3 : 5
   - (iii) 144 kg in the ratio 1 : 3
   - (iv) 78 hrs in the ratio 5 : 1
   - (v) 240 cm in the ratio 13 : 2
   - (vi) 225 cents in the ratio 7 : 2

2. Eight pens cost €24. Find the cost of six pens.

3. Maria drew a scale drawing of a house. The scale of the drawing was 1 cm : 3 m. The kitchen is 3 cm in the drawing. How long is the actual kitchen?

4. Angela measured a university and made a scale drawing. The scale of the drawing was 1 cm : 2 m. If the actual length of a building at the university is 62 m, how long is the building in the drawing?

5. Ozzie drew a scale drawing of a swimming pool. The diving board, which is 12 m long in real life, is 3 cm long in the drawing. What is the scale of the drawing?

6. Kevin measured a hotel and made a scale drawing. In real life, a room in the hotel is 20 m wide. It is 4 cm wide in the drawing. What scale did Kevin use?

7. Diane drew a scale drawing of her primary school. In real life, the school yard is 63 m wide. It is 9 cm wide in the drawing. What scale did Diane use for the drawing?

8. A particular map shows a scale of 1 : 5 000. What is the actual distance between town A and town B if the distance between them on the map is 8 cm?

9. The table shows the ingredients needed to make 36 mince pies.

Ingredient	Amount for 36 pies
Plain flour	330 g
Lard	75 g
Butter	75 g
Mincemeat	720 g

Calculate the amounts needed to make 48 mince pies.

Section A Introducing concepts and building skills

10B Taking it FURTHER

1. On Tom's farm, the ratio of hens to ducks is 19 : 4. If there are 304 hens on the farm, how many ducks are there?

2. Riona is collecting milk from dairy farms that will be taken and made into cheese. On a map, the distance from one farm to the next is 25 cm. In real life, this distance is 15 km. What is the map's scale?

3. A parade departs from City Hall and finishes at a park, 4 km away. On a map with a scale where 2 cm = 1 km, what is the distance between City Hall and the park?

4. Denise wants to check out a book from her local library, but it is not available. Denise decides to visit the library in Oak Grove, 52 km away, to see if that location has a copy of the book. On a map, the two libraries are 13 cm apart. What is the map's scale?

5. On a map that shows the location of film stars' houses, two Hollywood actors' houses are 4 cm apart. What is the actual distance between the actors' houses if the scale of the map is 2 cm = 1 km?

6. The boundary of a town is a perfect square. The length of one of the sides of the town boundary is 10 km long. Using an appropriate scale, draw a scale diagram of the town boundary.

7. There are 26 letters in the English alphabet and 24 in Korean. What is the ratio of letters in the Korean alphabet to letters in the English alphabet?

8. The Earth takes 24 hours to rotate around its own axis and the moon takes 27 days. What is the ratio of the time taken by the moon to the time taken by the Earth to rotate around their respective axes?

Now that you have completed the unit, revisit the

Something to think about ...

question posed at the start of this unit.

Now try questions 2, 5, 6, 7 and 8 on pages 185–90

Unit 11

Angles

Topics covered within this unit:
- 11·1 Vertically opposite angles
- 11·2 Alternate angles
- 11·3 Corresponding angles

The Learning Outcomes covered in this unit are contained in the following sections:

`GT.3b` `GT.3c` `GT.3d` `GT.3e`

Key words
- Axiom
- Vertically opposite angles
- Theorem
- Proof
- Transversal
- Alternate angles
- Converse
- Corresponding angles

Something to think about ...

Elements is the oldest surviving large-scale logical written work of Mathematics. *Elements* is a collection of 13 books attributed to the ancient Greek mathematician Euclid, who lived in Egypt in 300 BCE. It has proven to be very important in the development of logic and modern science.

Using only a pencil, ruler and compass, Euclid wrote 465 theorems, as well as definitions, postulates, propositions and mathematical proofs, all of which are contained in *Elements*.

The definition of parallel lines as a pair of straight lines in a plane that do not meet is Definition 23 in Book I of Euclid's *Elements*. What do you think definitions 1–22 could be?

Study the picture to the right. The sides of the Leaning Tower of Pisa are parallel to each other, and the lines marked p and q are also parallel.

Find the measure of the angles marked with the letters A, B, C, D, E, F and G, without using a protractor.

Section A Introducing concepts and building skills

11·1 Vertically opposite angles

By the end of this section you should:
- understand and define the terms axiom and theorem
- be able to find the measure of vertically opposite angles

An **axiom** is a statement that is taken to be true without being proven.

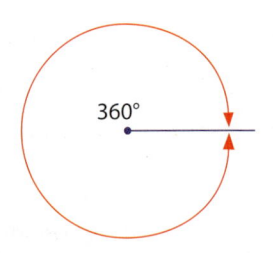

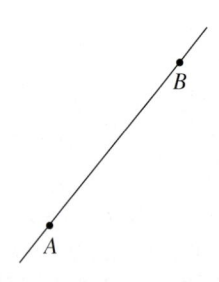

Axiom: A full angle is equal to 360°.

Axiom: A straight angle is equal to 180°, also called a straight line.

Axiom: There is only one straight line through two points.

Discuss and discover

KEY SKILLS

Working with a classmate, answer the following questions.

(i) What does $|\angle A| + |\angle B| = ?$
(ii) What does $|\angle A| + |\angle C| = ?$
(iii) What does this tell you about $|\angle B|$ and $|\angle C|$?
(iv) How would you use a protractor to verify that your ideas about $|\angle B|$ and $|\angle C|$ are correct?

What have you discovered about angles during this activity?

Vertically opposite angles are the angles opposite each other when two lines cross.

The word 'vertical' in this case means they share the same vertex (corner point), not the usual meaning of up-down.

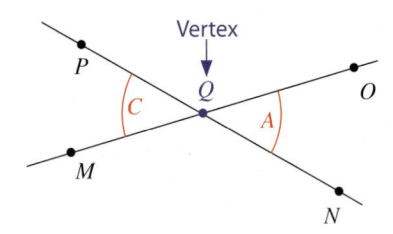

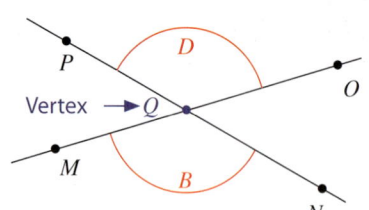

> For vertically opposite angles look for an 'X' shape.

∠A is vertically opposite to ∠C

Recall from naming angles:

∠OQN is another way of naming ∠A using points

In the diagram above:

$$|\angle A| = |\angle C|$$
or
$$|\angle OQN| = |\angle PQM|$$

∠B is vertically opposite to ∠D

∠PQM is another way of naming ∠C using points

In the diagram above:

$$|\angle B| = |\angle D|$$
or
$$|\angle MQN| = |\angle PQO|$$

Linking Thinking 1

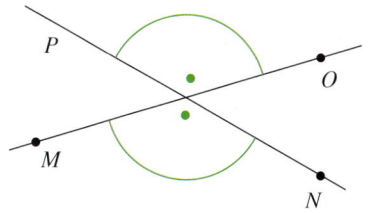

In Mathematics, equal angles are often shown by using the same mark in the angles (as shown below), usually single or double dashes, or dots.

A **theorem** is a statement that can be proven to be true in a series of logical steps using axioms and/or other theorems.

A **proof** contains a series of logical mathematical arguments (steps) used to show the truth of a theorem.

In a proof, we can use:
- axioms such as 'a straight angle is equal to 180°'
- existing theorems

The result of a proof is often called a theorem.

Theorem (1) Vertically opposite angles are equal in measure

Proof of the theorem: Vertically opposite angles are equal in measure

Supplementary angles (two angles that sum to 180°) are used in this proof.

Line 1 $|\angle A| + |\angle B| = 180°$ (straight angle)

Line 2 $|\angle D| + |\angle B| = 180°$ (straight angle)

$|\angle A| - |\angle D| = 0°$ (after subtracting line 2 from line 1)

$|\angle A| = |\angle D|$ (which are vertically opposite)

Similarly, it can be show that $|\angle B| = |\angle C|$

For Junior Cycle Mathematics, students should display an understanding of the proofs of theorems (full formal proofs are not examinable).

Worked example

Using the diagram on the right, and given that $|\angle C|$ is equal to 120°, find the value of the following and give the axiom or theorem used in each part.

(i) $|\angle A|$ (iii) $|\angle B|$

(ii) $|\angle D|$ (iv) $|\angle A| + |\angle B| + |\angle C| + |\angle D|$

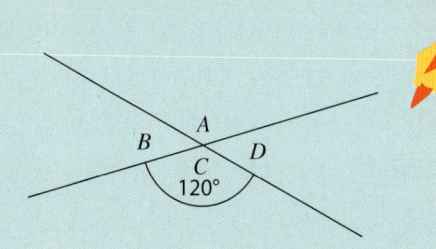

Solution

(i) $|\angle A| = 120°$ (vertically opposite to $|\angle C|$)

(ii) $|\angle D| + |\angle A| = 180°$ (straight angle)

     $|\angle D| + 120° = 180°$

           $|\angle D| = 180° - 120°$

           $|\angle D| = 60°$

(iii) $|\angle B| = 60°$ (vertically opposite to $|\angle D|$)

(iv) $|\angle A| + |\angle B| + |\angle C| + |\angle D|$

     $120° + 60° + 120° + 60°$ (all from previous parts of the question)

     $= 360°$ (a full angle and what would be expected given the diagram)

Section A Introducing concepts and building skills

Practice questions 11·1

1. Find the measure of the unknown angles shown in the following diagrams **and** give the axiom or theorem used in each part. (Diagrams not to scale)

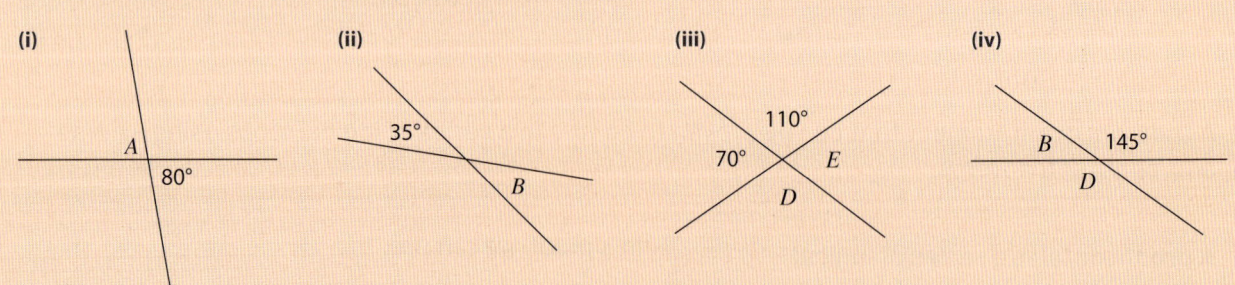

   (i) A, 80°

   (ii) 35°, B

   (iii) 110°, 70°, E, D

   (iv) B, 145°, D

2. Contrails left by aircraft in the sky are shown in the picture.

   Find the measure of the following angles shown in the picture **and** give the axiom or theorem used in each case.

   (i) $|\angle Z|$ (ii) $|\angle X|$ (iii) $|\angle Y|$

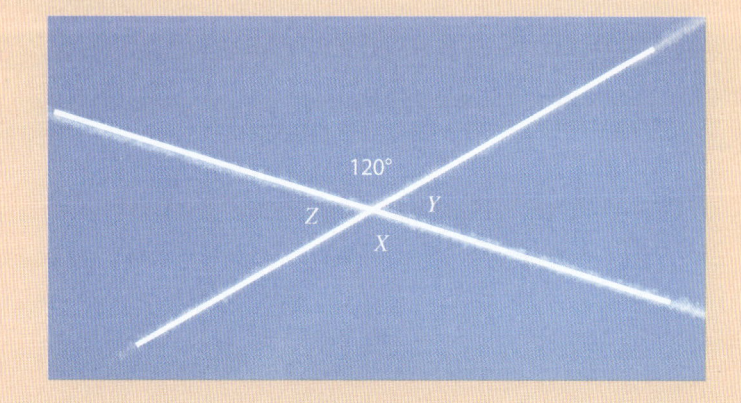

   (120°, Z, X, Y shown in picture)

3. Look at the image of a pair of scissors.

   (i) If the scissors are moved so that $|\angle A| = 30°$, find $|\angle B|$

   (ii) If the scissors are moved so that $|\angle A| = 100°$, find $|\angle C|$

   (iii) If the scissors are moved so that $|\angle A| = 10°$, find $|\angle B|$

   (iv) If the scissors are moved so that $|\angle B| = 10°$, find $|\angle D|$

4. (i) Use a ruler to draw two intersecting lines.

   (ii) Use a protractor to measure the four angles at the point where the lines intersect.

   (iii) What do you notice about the vertically opposite angles?

   (iv) Calculate the sum of the four angles.

   (v) Repeat parts (i) to (iv) two more times by drawing new lines.

5. Copy the table below and put a tick (✓) in the correct box in each row to show whether each statement is always true, sometimes true, or never true.

Statement		Tick **one** box only for each statement		
		Always true	Sometimes true	Never true
(i)	A theorem is always correct.			
(ii)	An axiom can be proven.			
(iii)	Vertically opposite angles are equal in measure.			
(iv)	A proof never has an end.			

11·2 Alternate angles

By the end of this section you should:
- understand and be able to define the terms transversal and alternate
- be able to find the measure of alternate angles

> A **transversal** is a line that crosses at least two other lines.

Transversal crossing two lines

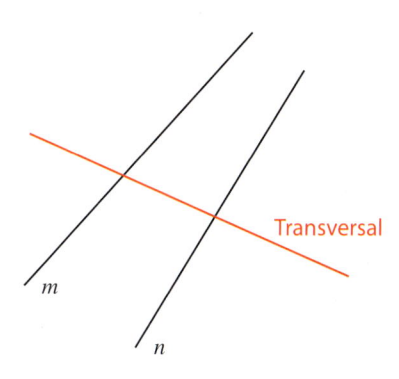

Transversal crossing two parallel lines ($n \parallel m$)

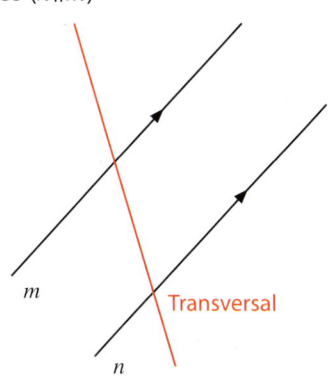

Transversal crossing three lines

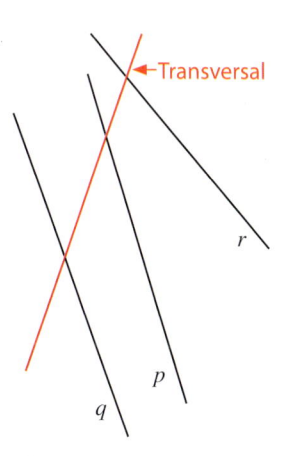

> **Alternate angles** are pairs of angles on the inner side or outer side of two lines but on opposite sides of a transversal.

Alternate interior angles are a pair of angles on the inner side of each of two parallel lines, but on opposite sides of the transversal.

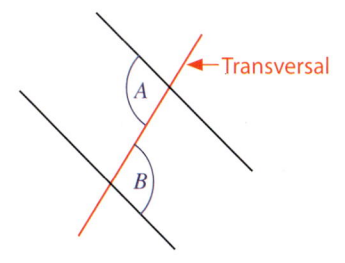

$\angle A$ and $\angle B$ are a pair of alternate interior angles

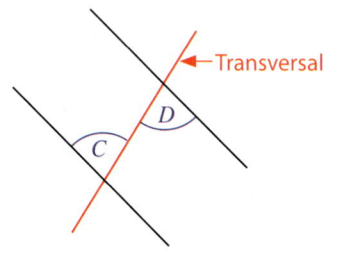

$\angle C$ and $\angle D$ are a pair of alternate interior angles

> Look for the 'Z' shape. The lines involved in alternate angles make a Z shape (it can also be back-to-front).

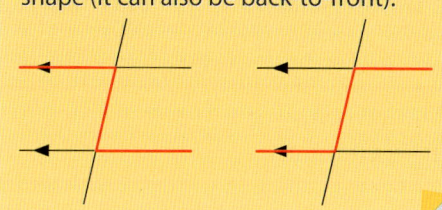

Alternate exterior angles are a pair of angles on the outer side of each of two parallel lines, but on opposite sides of the transversal.

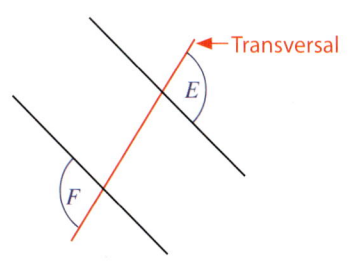

$\angle E$ and $\angle F$ are a pair of alternate exterior angles

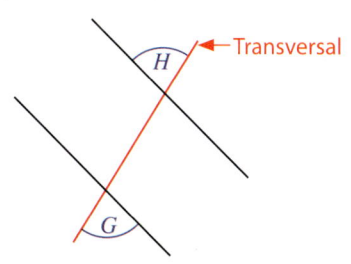

$\angle G$ and $\angle H$ are a pair of alternate exterior angles

Section A Introducing concepts and building skills

Discuss and discover

Working with a classmate:

Draw two lines that are an equal distance apart and parallel, as shown.

Draw a third line that cuts both lines at any angle as shown.

(i) Mark the angles A, B, C, D, as shown.
(ii) Using a protractor, measure $|\angle A|$ and $|\angle B|$
(iii) What have you discovered about $|\angle A|$ and $|\angle B|$?
(iv) Repeat parts (i) to (iii) for another pair of alternate angles.

What have you discovered about alternate angles?

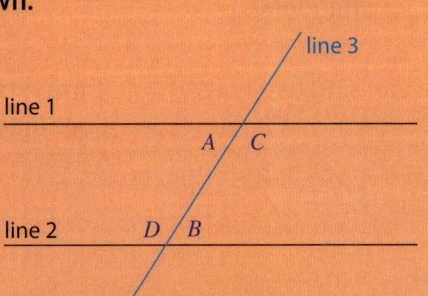

KEY SKILLS

Theorem (3) If a transversal makes equal alternate angles on two lines, then the lines are parallel

For example, in the diagram below, $|\angle A| = |\angle B|$ therefore $m \| n$ (line m is parallel to line n)

$|\angle A| = |\angle B|$

$|\angle C| = |\angle D|$

$|\angle E| = |\angle F|$

$|\angle H| = |\angle I|$

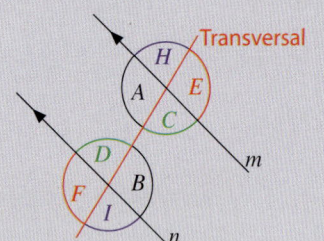

The two arrows on the lines m and n show that these lines are parallel.

> The **converse** of a theorem happens when the conclusion and the starting point of a theorem are switched.

For example, if you have a general theorem that says 'if this, then that', then the converse theorem would say 'if that, then this'.

e.g.

Theorem: If a shape is made up of exactly three straight lines and contains three angles, then it is a triangle.

Converse theorem: If a shape is a triangle, then it has exactly three straight lines and contains three angles.

Not all converses are true, even if the original statement is true. For example, the following statement is true all the time:

If it is cold, then my knee hurts.

However, the converse may not be true all the time:

If my knee hurts, then it is cold.

Your knee could hurt from other factors, but if you have a sensitivity to the cold, your knee will hurt whenever it is cold, so the converse is not always true.

Now that we have looked at Theorem 3, which stated that if a transversal makes equal alternate angles on two lines, then the lines are parallel, we can now state the converse of Theorem 3 as follows:

Converse theorem (3) If two lines are parallel, then any transversal will make equal alternate angles with them.

Worked example

Given that $|\angle BXY|$ in the diagram is equal to 70°, find each of the following angles and give the axiom or theorem used in each part to justify your answer.

(i) $|\angle XYG|$ (iv) $|\angle AXC|$
(ii) $|\angle XYE|$ (v) $|\angle EYF|$
(iii) $|\angle CXY|$ (vi) $|\angle GYF|$

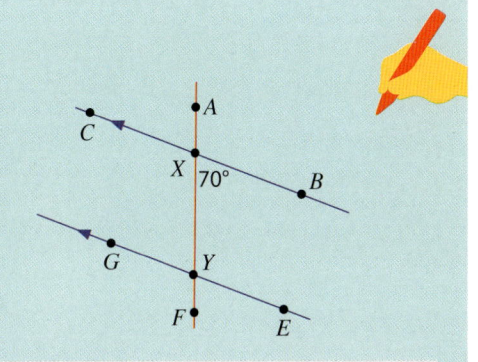

Solution

(i) $|\angle XYG| = 70°$ ($\angle XYG$ is alternate angle to $\angle BXY$)

(ii) $|\angle XYE| + |\angle XYG| = 180°$ (straight angle $|\angle EYG| = 180°$)
$|\angle XYE| + 70° = 180°$
$|\angle XYE| = 180° - 70°$
$|\angle XYE| = 110°$

(iii) $|\angle CXY| = 110°$ ($\angle CXY$ is alternate angle to $\angle XYE$)

(iv) $|\angle AXC| + |\angle CXY| = 180°$ (straight angle $|\angle AXY| = 180°$)
$|\angle AXC| + 110° = 180°$
$|\angle AXC| = 180° - 110°$
$|\angle AXC| = 70°$

(v) $|\angle EYF| = |\angle XYG|$ (vertically opposite angles)
$|\angle EYF| = 70°$

(vi) $|\angle GYF| + |\angle EYF| = 180°$ (straight angle $|\angle GYE| = 180°$)
$|\angle GYF| + 70° = 180°$
$|\angle GYF| = 180° - 70°$
$|\angle GYF| = 110°$

Practice questions 11·2

1. Copy the diagrams below of two parallel lines, and mark in two pairs of alternate angles and a transversal. Using your protractor verify that the alternate angles are equal in measure.

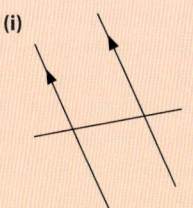

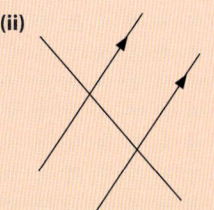

   (i)   (ii)

2. Using the diagram below, find each of the following angles and give the axiom or theorem used in each part to justify your answer.

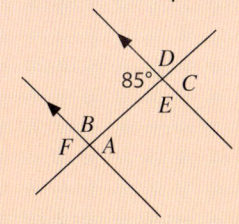

   (i) $|\angle A|$ (iv) $|\angle D|$
   (ii) $|\angle B|$ (v) $|\angle E|$
   (iii) $|\angle C|$ (vi) $|\angle F|$

Section A Introducing concepts and building skills   175

3. Using the diagram below, find each of the following angles and give the axiom or theorem used in each part to justify your answer.

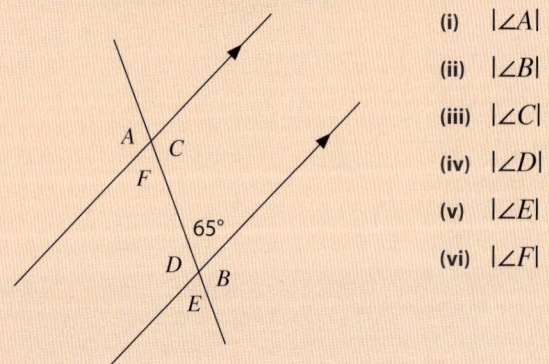

   (i) |∠A|
   (ii) |∠B|
   (iii) |∠C|
   (iv) |∠D|
   (v) |∠E|
   (vi) |∠F|

4. |∠UTR| in the diagram below is equal to 122°. Using the diagram, find each of the following angles and give the axiom or theorem used in each part to justify your answer.

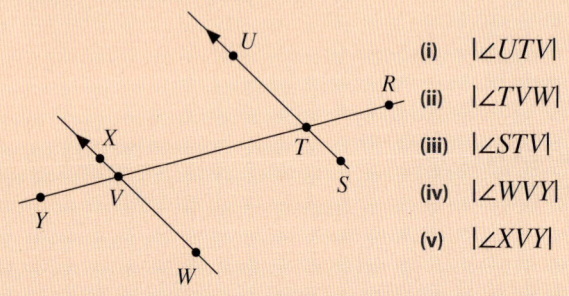

   (i) |∠UTV|
   (ii) |∠TVW|
   (iii) |∠STV|
   (iv) |∠WVY|
   (v) |∠XVY|

5. For each of the diagrams below, state whether each of the pairs of lines cut by the transversal are parallel or not, and give the axiom or theorem to justify your answer.

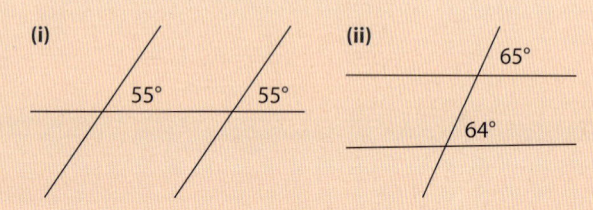

   (i)
   (ii)

6. |∠EFC| in the diagram below is equal to 78°

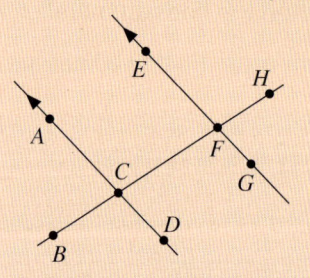

   Find each of the following angles and give the axiom or theorem used in each part to justify your answer.

   (i) |∠FCD| (iii) |∠ACF| (v) |∠BCD|
   (ii) |∠GFH| (iv) |∠ACB|

7. Using the diagram shown, find the measure of the following angles.

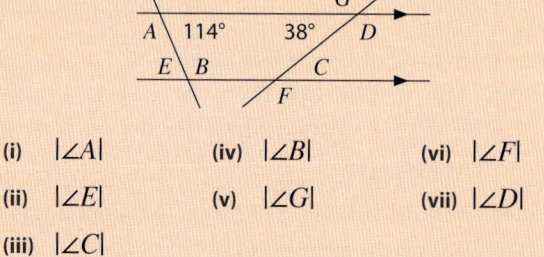

   (i) |∠A| (iv) |∠B| (vi) |∠F|
   (ii) |∠E| (v) |∠G| (vii) |∠D|
   (iii) |∠C|

8. The diagram below shows a cross-section through a set of stairs.

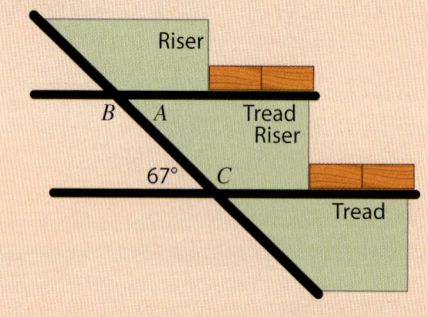

   Using the diagram, find the following angles.
   (i) |∠A| (ii) |∠B| (iii) |∠C|

9. Below is a map of a part of the city of Chicago, Illinois, USA. The angle between N Keeler Ave and W Grand Ave (marked as angle C in the map) is 68°. N Tripp Ave, N Keeler Ave, N Kedvale Ave are all parallel to each other.

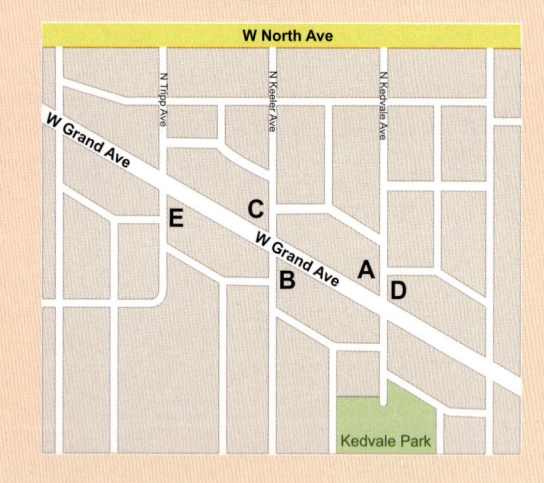

   Find the measure of the following angles.

   (i) |∠E| (iii) |∠A|
   (ii) |∠B| (iv) |∠D|

11·3 Corresponding angles

By the end of this section you should be able to:
- identify corresponding angles
- find the measure of corresponding angles in parallel lines

> **Corresponding angles** are the angles in matching corners, when any two lines are crossed by a transversal.

Four pairs of **corresponding angles** are shown below. Note: there are no parallel lines in these diagrams.

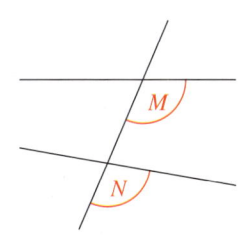

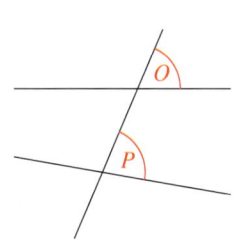

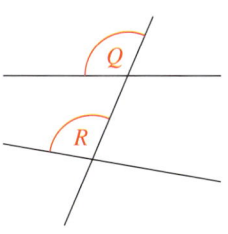

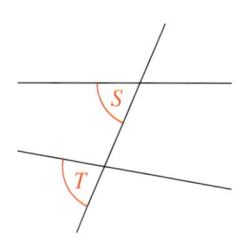

To find corresponding angles look for the 'F shape'. A pair of corresponding angles is made up of one angle inside the lines and one outside the lines.

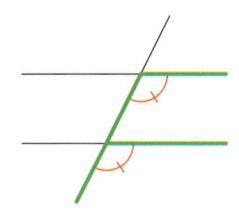

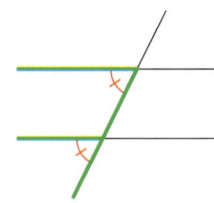

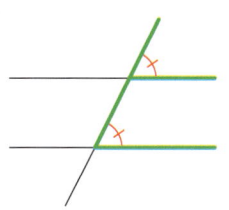

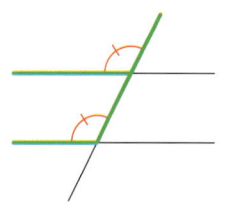

Discuss and discover

KEY SKILLS

Working with a partner, draw two lines (1 and 2) that are an equal distance apart and parallel, as shown.

Draw a third line that cuts both lines at any angle, as shown.

(i) Mark the angles X, Y, W, Z, M, N, O, P
(ii) Mark the corresponding angles $|\angle W|$ and $|\angle Z|$
(iii) Using a protractor, measure $|\angle W|$ and $|\angle Z|$
(iv) What can you conclude about $|\angle W|$ and $|\angle Z|$?
(v) Repeat parts (i) to (iv) for the other pairs of corresponding angles.

What have you discovered about the corresponding angles within parallel lines?

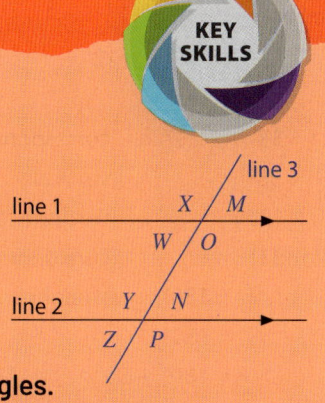

Section A Introducing concepts and building skills

Theorem (5) Two lines are parallel if and only if for any transversal, corresponding angles are equal

Converse Theorem (5) When the two lines being crossed by a transversal are **parallel**, the corresponding angles are equal.

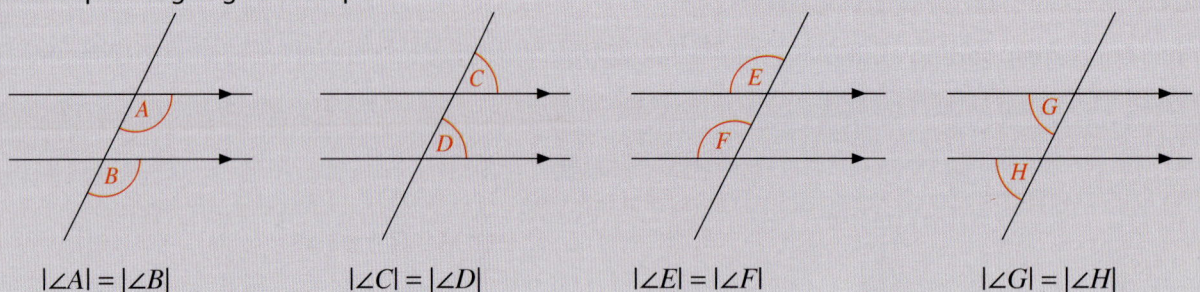

|∠A| = |∠B| |∠C| = |∠D| |∠E| = |∠F| |∠G| = |∠H|

Worked example

Using the diagram, find the measure of the following angles and give the theorem and/or axiom used to justify your answer (diagram not to scale).

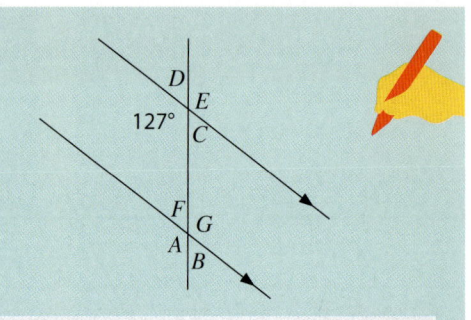

(i) |∠A| (iv) |∠D| (vii) |∠G|
(ii) |∠B| (v) |∠E|
(iii) |∠C| (vi) |∠F|

Solution

(i) |∠A| = 127°   (corresponding angles in parallel lines)
(ii) |∠A| + |∠B| = 180°   (straight angle is equal to 180°)
      127° + |∠B| = 180°
              |∠B| = 180° − 127°
              |∠B| = 53°
(iii) |∠C| = 53°   (corresponding angles in parallel lines)
(iv) |∠D| = 53°   (vertically opposite angles)
(v) |∠E| = 127°   (vertically opposite angles)
(vi) |∠F| = 53°   (corresponding angles in parallel lines)
(vii) |∠G| + |∠F| = 180°   (straight angle is equal to 180°)
      |∠G| + 53° = 180°
              |∠G| = 180° − 53°
              |∠G| = 127°

Linking Thinking 1

Practice questions 11·3

1. (i) Copy the diagrams of two parallel lines and a transversal.
   (ii) Mark in two pairs of corresponding angles
   (iii) Use a protractor to measure the corresponding angles.
   (iv) What do you notice about the corresponding angles?
   (v) Repeat parts (i) to (iv) two more times with other pairs of parallel lines and transversals. What do you notice?

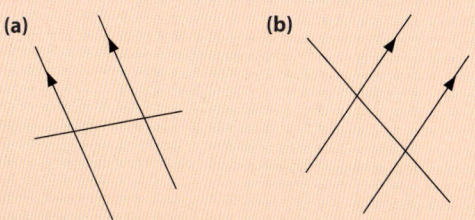

2. Using the diagram below, find the measure of the following angles and give the theorem and/or axiom used to find the angle in each case (diagram not to scale).

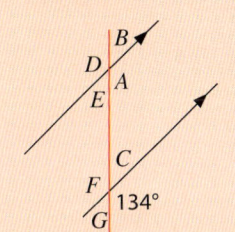

   (i) $|\angle A|$ (v) $|\angle E|$
   (ii) $|\angle B|$ (vi) $|\angle F|$
   (iii) $|\angle C|$ (vii) $|\angle G|$
   (iv) $|\angle D|$

3. Using the diagram below, find the measure of the following angles and give the theorem and/or axiom used to find the angle in each case (diagram not to scale).

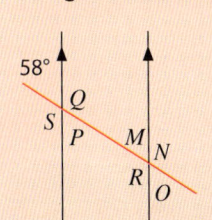

   (i) $|\angle M|$ (v) $|\angle Q|$
   (ii) $|\angle N|$ (vi) $|\angle R|$
   (iii) $|\angle O|$ (vii) $|\angle S|$
   (iv) $|\angle P|$

4. In each of the following diagrams, state whether each of the pairs of lines cut by the transversal are parallel or not, and give a reason for your answer.

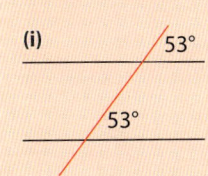

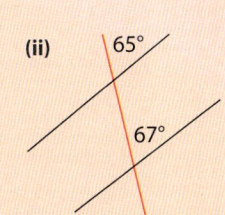

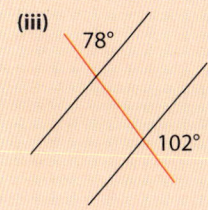

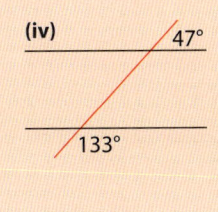

   (i) 53°, 53°
   (ii) 65°, 67°
   (iii) 78°, 102°
   (iv) 47°, 133°

5. Below is map of Dungloe, Co. Donegal. R259 is parallel to Chapel Rd, and Caravan Rd is a straight road.

   Find the following angles, and give the theorem and/or axiom used to justify your answer (diagram not to scale).

   (i) $|\angle A|$ (ii) $|\angle B|$ (iii) $|\angle C|$

6. Below is an aerial image of the runways at Logan international Airport, Boston, USA.

    Runways 22R and 22L are parallel runways. The acute angle between runways 15R and 22L is 78°, as indicated in the diagram.

    Find the following angles.
    (i) $|\angle A|$
    (ii) $|\angle B|$
    (iii) $|\angle C|$
    (iv) $|\angle D|$
    (v) $|\angle E|$

7. Below is a picture of road markings. Both pairs of lines are parallel and one angle of 64° is marked.

    Find the following angles.
    (i) $|\angle A|$
    (ii) $|\angle B|$
    (iii) $|\angle C|$

Revision questions

11A Core skills

1. Copy the diagrams of two parallel lines and a transversal.
    (i) Mark in two pairs of alternate angles.
    (ii) Use a protractor to measure the alternate angles.
    (iii) What do you notice about the alternate angles?

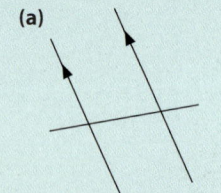

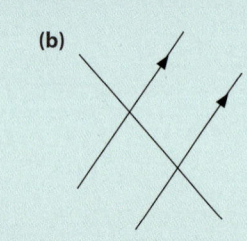

2. Study the diagram on the right.
   (i) Which angle is vertically opposite to ∠A?
   (ii) Which angle corresponds to ∠D?
   (iii) Which angle is alternate to ∠C?
   (iv) Which angle corresponds to ∠G?
   (v) Which angle is alternate to ∠G?
   (vi) Which angle corresponds to ∠F?
   (vii) Which angle is alternate to ∠D?
   (viii) Name a pair of angles that add up to 180°.

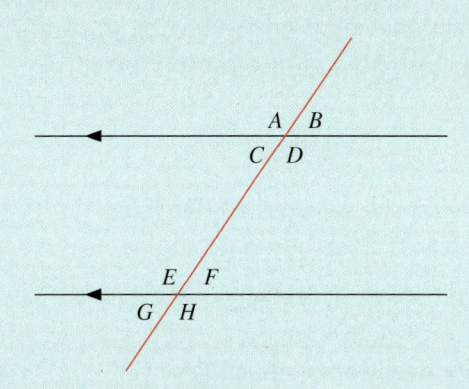

3. Write down whether each of the pairs of angles (A and B) in each of the following diagrams are vertically opposite, alternate or corresponding angles.

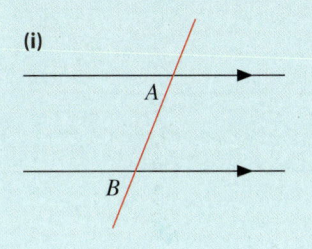

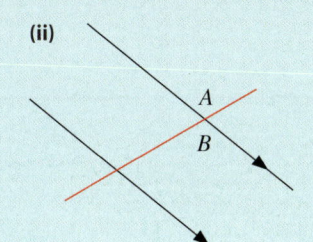

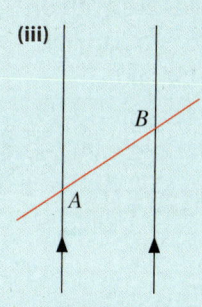

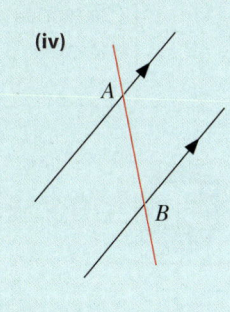

4. In each of the diagrams below, find the measure of angles X and Y and give the theorem and/or axiom used in each case (diagrams not to scale).

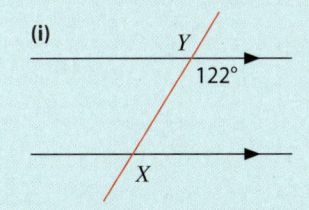

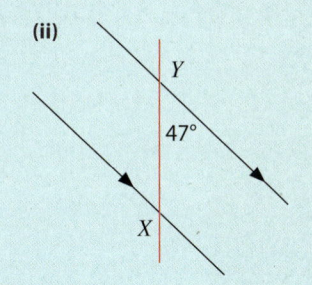

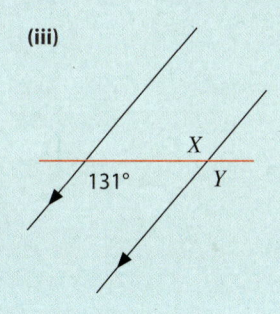

5. In each of the diagrams below, find the measure of the unknown angles (mark with letters A to U) and give the theorem and/or axiom used in each case (diagrams not to scale).

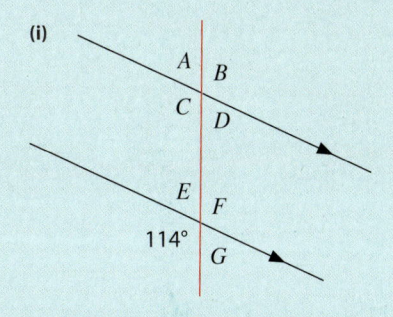

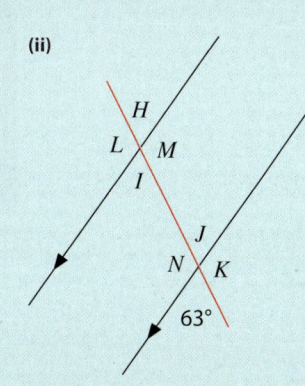

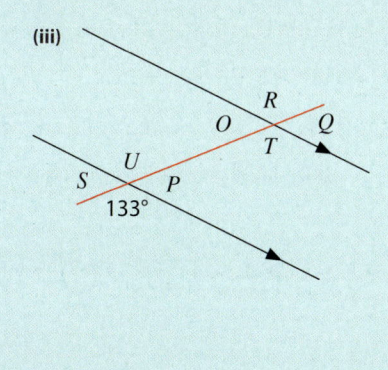

6. Copy the table below and put a tick (✓) in the correct box in each row to show whether each statement is always true, sometimes true, or never true.

	Statement	Tick **one** box only for each statement		
		Always true	Sometimes true	Never true
(i)	A transversal crossing two lines creates equal alternate angles.			
(ii)	Corresponding angles are always equal.			
(iii)	Vertically opposite angles are always equal.			
(iv)	The converse of a theorem must be true.			
(v)	Corresponding angles are both on the outer side of the two parallel lines to which they belong.			

↗ 11B Taking it FURTHER

1. Railway tracks crossing are shown in the diagram below. One angle (75°) is shown in the diagram.

   Find the following angles.

   (i) $|\angle A|$ (vi) $|\angle F|$

   (ii) $|\angle B|$ (vii) $|\angle G|$

   (iii) $|\angle C|$ (viii) $|\angle H|$

   (iv) $|\angle D|$ (ix) $|\angle I|$

   (v) $|\angle E|$ (x) $|\angle J|$

2. On the right is an aerial image of the parallel runways at Dublin Airport. One angle (77°) is shown in the diagram.

   Find the following angles.

   (i) $|\angle A|$

   (ii) $|\angle X|$

   (iii) $|\angle Y|$

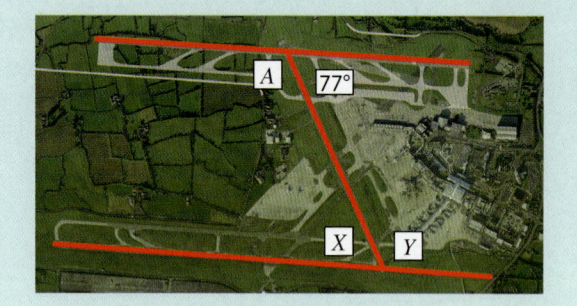

3. Below is an image of forest where two trees have fallen to form two parallel lines. One tree, still upright, acts as a transversal of these two felled trees. One angle between one of the trees and the transversal (56°) has been marked in on the diagram.

Find the following angles.

(i) |∠A|
(ii) |∠B|
(iii) |∠C|
(iv) |∠D|
(v) |∠E|
(vi) |∠F|
(vii) |∠G|

4. Three arrows where aimed and fired at a tree. The picture opposite shows how the arrows landed on the tree. Two of the arrows landed parallel to each other.

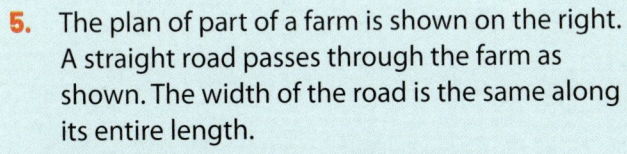

Find the following angles and give the axiom or theorem to justify your answer in each case.

(i) |∠A|
(ii) |∠B|
(iii) |∠C|
(iv) |∠D|
(v) |∠E|

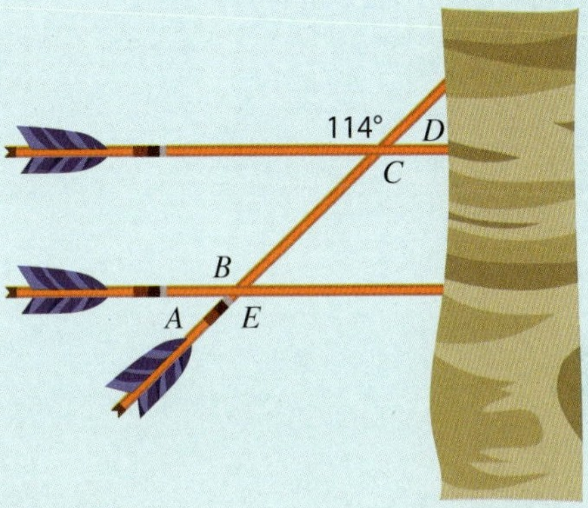

5. The plan of part of a farm is shown on the right. A straight road passes through the farm as shown. The width of the road is the same along its entire length.

Find the following angles and give the axiom or theorem to justify your answer in each case.

(i) |∠M|
(ii) |∠O|
(iii) |∠P|

Now that you have completed the unit, revisit the

Something to think about ...

question posed at the start of this unit.

Unit 12
Linking Thinking revision material

By the end of this unit you should be able to:

- make connections between concepts and the real world
- work on problems individually or with others; compare approaches and adapt your own strategy
- break up a problem into manageable parts
- make sense of a given problem and use Maths to solve it
- represent a mathematical problem in a variety of different ways
- interpret and evaluate how reasonable your solution is in the context of an original problem
- reflect on the strategy you used to solve a mathematical problem identify limitations and suggest improvements

Linking Thinking questions

Reference grid

Question number	Number, coordinate plane and symmetry (A.1)	Sets, number and chance (A.2)	Points, lines and angles (A.3)	Working with numbers (A.4)	Fractions, decimals, percentages (A.5)	Probability 1 (A.6)	Patterns (A.7)	Working with variables (A.8)	Solving linear relations (A.9)	Ratio, proportion and scaled diagrams (A.10)	Angles (A.11)
1		✓		✓		✓					
2					✓	✓		✓		✓	
3		✓			✓	✓	✓				
4		✓	✓								✓
5				✓	✓					✓	
6	✓						✓		✓	✓	
7	✓				✓					✓	
8	✓				✓			✓	✓	✓	

Questions

1. **(a)** Use the list of numbers shown below to answer the following questions.

   $$2 \quad \tfrac{1}{2} \quad 0 \quad 1 \quad 3 \quad \tfrac{2}{7} \quad -5 \quad 6 \quad -7 \quad 9$$

   (i) Identify as many natural numbers as possible from the list. Justify your answers using your knowledge of the definition of natural numbers.

   (ii) Identify as many integers as possible from the list. Justify your answers using your knowledge of the definition of integers.

   (iii) Identify as many rational numbers as possible from the list. Justify your answers, using your knowledge of the definition of rational numbers.

   (b) Taking the list of numbers given in part **(a)** as the universal set, draw a Venn diagram to represent the following sets:

   A = {prime numbers}   B = {factors of 12}

   Use the Venn diagram to answer the following questions.

   (i) List the elements of A∪B

   (ii) List the elements of a subset of B containing two elements.

   (iii) Find #(A∩B)

   > Negative numbers can't be prime.

   (c) Pick a number from the list given in part **(a)** above to answer each of the following questions.

   (i) What is the probability of getting a 7 when you throw a standard six-sided die?

   (ii) What is the probability of getting heads when you flip a fair coin?

   (iii) What is the probability of picking a day of the week beginning with S?

   (d) Use any combination of the numbers in the list given in part **(a)** above to demonstrate the following:

   (i) The associative property of addition

   (ii) The commutative property of multiplication

   (iii) The distributive property of multiplication

2. Pat is an avid hillwalker and he decides to walk from Bray seafront to Greystones Harbour, and back again. He wants to work out how long the round trip is going to take him.

   The route is a 6 km walk beginning at the seafront in Bray and ending at the harbour in Greystones.

   Pat would like to include a few breaks during his trip: a short break of 10 minutes for a snack on the way; 30 minutes in Greystones to take photos and have lunch; and another 10 minute break at some point on the way back.

   Pat knows that he can travel 5 km in one hour.

   (a) **(i)** How long does it take to cover 1 kilometre along the route?

   (ii) Taking breaks into account, how long would it take Pat to complete his round trip from Bray to Greystones and back to his starting point in Bray?

Section A Introducing concepts and building skills

(b) (i) What percentage of the total time does Pat spend taking a break for a snack on the way to Greystones? Give your answer correct to two decimal places.

(ii) What percentage of the time does Pat spend taking photos and having lunch in Greystones? Give your answer correct to two decimal places.

(iii) At one point during the walk, Pat receives a phone call. What is the probability that the call comes at a time when he was walking (i.e. not taking a break)? Give your answer correct to two decimal places.

(c) Pat has two companions on the hike, John and Cathal. They collected money for charity before the walk. The amount collected was €700. The amount collected by each Pat : John : Cathal was in the ratio 5 : 3 : 2. How much did each of them collect individually?

3. (a) In golf, the winner is the person who gets the lowest score. Each hole played has a designated number of shots it should take to 'putt' the ball. This is called par. For example, a par 3 hole should take 3 shots to putt the ball. Some common golf scoring terms and their scores are shown in the table below.

Term	Meaning	Score
Albatross	Three shots under par	−3
Eagle	Two shots under par	−2
Birdie	One shot under par	−1
Par	Correct number of shots for the hole	0
Bogey	One shot over par	+1
Double bogey	Two shots over par	+2

(i) Jakob and Larissa play 9 holes of golf together. The following are their scores for the 9 holes:

Jakob: par, bogey, albatross, birdie, double bogey, eagle, par, bogey, eagle

Larissa: bogey, eagle, par, albatross, double bogey, eagle, birdie, par, double bogey

Work out each person's score and determine the winner, given that the person with the lowest score at the end wins.

(ii) The scores from −3 to +2 form a pattern. Is this pattern linear or non-linear? Justify your answer.

(b) Scientists have engineered a new type of rubber ball. The scientists who developed the ball state that every time the ball hits the ground, it bounces back to reach 75% of its previous height. Assuming the scientists are correct, Imagine dropping this ball from the top of these well-known structures.

The Eiffel Tower, France — 324 m

The Statue of Liberty, USA — 93 m

The Burj Khalifa, UAE — 830 m

For each structure, calculate the following.

- (i) What height will the ball reach after its first bounce?
- (ii) What height will the ball reach after its second bounce?
- (iii) What is the least number of bounces that it will take for the ball to be at a height that is less than a quarter of its original height?

(c) A modern set of golf clubs typically consists of three woods, one hybrid, seven irons and one putter. The rules of golf allow you to carry fourteen clubs in your bag, so many golfers add a wedge and a specialty hybrid.

If a golfer, whose golf bag contains the fourteen clubs described above, removes a club at random, without looking in the bag, what is the chance he selects each of the following? Give your answer as (a) fraction (b) decimal (c) percentage. Give your answer to two decimal places, where necessary.

- (i) A wood
- (ii) An iron
- (iii) A putter
- (iv) A club that is not a hybrid

4. (a) (i) What is the measure of the angles marked on the following clocks?
   (ii) Classify each of the angles as either acute, obtuse, reflex or right-angled.

(b) The numbers on the face of a clock are as follows: {1, 2, 3, 4, 5, 6, 7, 8, 9, 10, 11, 12}
A is the set of even numbers on the face of a clock, and B is the set of odd numbers on the face of a clock.

- (i) Write the elements of the set A and the set B.
- (ii) Represent sets A and B in a Venn diagram.
- (iii) Find: (a) A∪B   (b) A∩B   (c) #A

(c) A clock company, Boyle and Sons, want to design clock faces that use the twelve numbers on the clock face in special ways.

- (i) They want to divide the clock face using one straight line, so that the numbers in each part of the clock face add up to the same total. Copy the picture of the clock and draw this line.
- (ii) They want to divide the clock face into three sections, using two lines (not intersecting), so the numbers in each section add up to the same total. Copy the picture of the clock and divide it into these three sections.
- (iii) They want to divide the clock face into six sections (using lines or curves) so that in each section there are exactly two numbers. The sum of the numbers in each section must be the same. Copy the picture of the clock and divide it into these six sections.

5. (a) Aisha is designing a rectangular garden that measures 15 m by 19·5 m. It has a fence around the outside and the following features:
- A patio at the front of the garden, 15 m × 4·5 m rectangle
- A lawn, 15 m × 12 m rectangle
- A path between lawn and vegetable patch, 15 m × 1·5 m rectangle
- A vegetable patch at the back of the garden, next to the fence, 15 m by 1·5 m rectangle

> Make a rough sketch first, before you try to draw the garden to scale. This will help you to visualise what the garden looks like.

Draw a plan of Aisha's garden using the scale 1 m = 1 cm.

(b) Aisha has the following two choices of paving stone for the 15 m by 4·5 m patio:

Size	Each pack covers	Cost per pack
Stones A	8·6 m²	€139·75
Stones B	7·4 m²	€128·50

Given that she can only buy full packs of stones, which stones should Aisha choose to get the lowest price? Justify your answer.

(c) (i) Calculate the area of the garden taken up by the vegetable patch and the lawn.

(ii) Express the answer to (i) as a percentage of the total area of the garden. Give your answer correct to two significant figures.

6. (a) Bob is a painter. He wants to mix white and black paint to make grey paint. He uses 6 litres of white paint and 4 litres of black paint to make 10 litres of grey paint.

(i) What is the ratio (in simplest form) of white to black paint in the grey paint?

(ii) How much black paint would he need to make 25 litres of grey paint?

(b) Bob needs to paint three rectangular walls using this grey colour. The dimensions of these walls are:
- Wall A: width 4·5 m and length 3·1 m
- Wall B: width 5·2 m and length 2·8 m
- Wall C: width 4·9 m and length 3·2 m

(i) If 1 litre of the grey mix covers 16 m² and he is going to paint 2 coats on each wall, how much paint will he need to paint the three walls? Give your answer to the nearest litre.

(ii) How much white and black paint will he need to make enough grey to paint the three walls?

(c) Bob charges a €100 flat fee plus €50 an hour for his painting service.

(i) Identify the variables and the constants in this situation. Explain the meaning of any letters you have used.

(ii) Form an equation to represent the cost of a painting job done by Bob, for any number of hours.

(iii) Copy and complete the following table:

Time (hours)	0	1	2	3	4	5	6	7	8
Cost (€)	100								

(iv) Draw a graph to represent the cost of a 10-hour job.

(v) Find the slope of the graph.

(vi) Use your graph to estimate the cost of a 5·5-hour job and verify your answer using the equation you formed in part (ii).

(vii) Use your graph to estimate how long Bob was working if he earned €275. Verify your answer using the equation you formed in part (ii).

7. **(a)** Each point on the graph shown represents a bag of muesli.
  (i) Which point shows the heaviest bag?
  (ii) Which point shows the cheapest bag?
  (iii) Which points show bags with the same mass?
  (iv) Which points show bags with the same price?
  (v) Which gives the best value for money, bag *F* or bag *C*? Justify your answer.

(b) Sam likes to eat muesli for breakfast. The table below shows the calories in his other favourite breakfast items.

Breakfast item	Calories
Muesli	219
One serving of yoghurt	50
Glass of apple juice	86
Cup of coffee	25

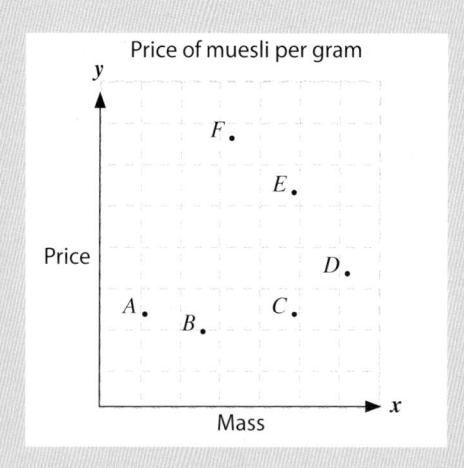

  (i) For a healthy diet, Sam aims to consume around 2 700 calories a day. He wants his breakfast to have between 15% and 20% of the 2 700 calories.

  What are the minimum and maximum number of calories he could have for breakfast?

  (ii) For breakfast, Sam has:

   • two servings of muesli
   • two servings of yoghurt
   • one glass of apple juice
   • one cup of coffee

   Calculate the total calories he consumes and work out what percentage, to the nearest whole number, of his daily intake it represents.

(c) Lara makes her own muesli. To make 500 g of muesli, she needs:

   • 325 g oats
   • 35 g nuts
   • 140 g mix of raisins, apricot, cranberries and sunflower seeds

  1 kg of oats costs €0·80; 100 g of nuts cost €1·40 and a 500 g bag of the fruit and seeds mix costs €0·96. A box of similar muesli from a shop costs €2·94 for 500 g.

  (i) How much does Lara save by making her own muesli?

  (ii) On a particular day, Lara wants to make 600 g of her own muesli. How much of each ingredient will she need?

(d) Olga also makes her own muesli from oats, fruit and seeds.

  By mass, she wants $\frac{3}{5}$ of the muesli to be oats and the remainder to be a mixture of fruit and seeds.

  (i) She is going to make the muesli using 900 g of oats. How many grams of the fruit and seeds mixture will Olga need?

  (ii) For the mixture, she wants there to be four times as much fruit as there are seeds. Find the ratio of fruit to seeds in the mixture.

  (iii) Calculate what weight of fruit Olga needs to make the muesli.

8. Sebastian is building a rectangular wall using rectangular bricks.
   He lays the bricks in rows of equal length to make the wall.
   (a) The wall will be 6 rows high. He allows a height of 12 cm for each brick.
      (i) Find the total height of the wall. Give your answer in cm.
      The wall will be 5·6 m long. He allows a length of 28 cm for each brick.
      (ii) Find the number of bricks he will need in each row.
      (iii) Find the total number of bricks that will be in the wall.
   (b) Sebastian buys 135 bricks in total, to allow for breakages.
       The bricks cost 60 cents each, excluding VAT.
       The VAT rate for the bricks is 13·5%.
       Find the total cost of the bricks, including VAT.
   (c) Sebastian builds the wall using red bricks and grey bricks.
       He buys twice as many red bricks as grey bricks.
       Find the number of red bricks he buys (remember that he bought 135 bricks in total).
   (d) The instructions for making the mortar for the wall are given as follows:
       For every 50 kg of cement, you will need 175 kg of sand.
       Sebastian is going to use 30 kg of cement. Find how many kilograms of sand he will need.

Mathematical investigations

Introduction to mathematical investigation

Maths can be used to investigate and solve problems in everyday life. In Junior Cycle Mathematics, you are required to carry out two classroom-based assessments (CBAs), which are investigations using your Maths skills.

In preparation for your CBAs, this section contains a list of investigations which you can do, to practice and develop your skills as a mathematical investigator.

> Sometimes it's hard to come up with an idea. It can be helpful, throughout this process, to discuss with classmates how you could develop your investigation.

When carrying out an investigation, consider the following strategy:

1 Define your problem
Why did you pick this problem? What are you trying to find out? Can you predict what the outcome will be?

2 Make assumptions where necessary
Are these assumptions reasonable? (e.g. all prices are in euros) Justify your assumptions.

3 Break up the problem into manageable parts
What are you going to do first? What will you do after that? etc.

4 **Translate the problem into Maths**
Identify any variables. Draw diagrams if helpful. Form an equation using mathematical notation, etc.

5 **Engage with the problem**
Research and record data where necessary
Work out any calculations needed (show your work clearly)
Can you identify any patterns?
Use tables, graphs, formulas, etc.
Can you find more than one way to work out the problem?

6 **Present your solution**
Can you present it in different ways? (As a statement, a graph, a diagram, etc.)

7 **Interpret any findings**
Comment on your solution, linking it to the original problem.
Is it reasonable? Does it make sense?
Is it what you predicted?
Were your assumptions justified?

8 **Reflect on your investigation**
What were the strengths and weaknesses of your strategy?
If you were to investigate this problem again, what would you do differently?
What have you learned by carrying out this investigation?

9 **Extend and generalise your findings**
How could the results of your investigation apply to other problems?

Mathematical investigation examples

1. You are given the task of painting your classroom. The goal of the task is to paint the classroom for the lowest possible price. You can use the internet as a means of finding the prices for paint, ladders etc.

   Refer back to the strategy given on the previous page and consider the following points when carrying out this investigation:

   - What is a reasonable budget?

   - Using a safe method, find the area to be painted in your classroom. Remember windows, doors, whiteboards, etc. won't need to be painted.

   - Using an appropriate scale, draw a scaled diagram of the surfaces that need to be painted in your classroom.

   - Research which shops and brands of paint would be most suitable. How many coats of paint will be needed?

   - Who will do the painting? Will there be a cost for that?
     Do they have equipment or will the cost of this need to be considered?

   - Could your strategy be applied to the painting of any room?

   This first investigation has been extended to provide some tips that might be useful.

2. Investigate how many ways you can make €2, using coins.

3. If everyone in your class introduced themselves by shaking hands just once, investigate how many hand shakes would take place.

4. You are on the Student Council at your school and you want to change your school uniform. Investigate the information you will need to bring to the principal to support the change.

5. Investigate and design a route for a 5 km fundraising walk or run in your locality.

6. You have been asked to bake cupcakes for your class fundraiser. You want to make as many cupcakes as possible for the cheapest price, while still making a good profit. Investigate the options.

7. If you have €100 in any denominations, investigate the maximum it could weigh and the maximum height it could reach if stacked.

8. Investigate whether taller people have bigger feet.

9. Investigate a pattern found in nature (e.g. petals on a flower, seashells).

10. In a sale, the store reduces all prices by 25% each week. Investigate how long, if ever, it will take for the prices to reach €0.

11. Investigate how many ways there are to walk up a flight of stairs. Consider the different patterns for how you could go up the steps: one step at a time, two steps at a time, etc.

12. Investigate what the chances are that a person in Ireland could be struck by lightening.

13. Investigate the relationship between attendance in a class and the day of the week.

14. Investigate the probability that you can score a point (goal/hit a target/basket, etc.) out of 100 attempts.

15. Investigate reaction time to an event.

16. Investigate how much pet food to have on hand when going on holidays for two weeks.

17. Based on a recipe for making 6 cupcakes, investigate the ratios involved in making a higher number of cakes (e.g. 12 cupcakes, 15 cupcakes, 20 cupcakes).

18. If you take a stick of normal, dry spaghetti and bend it until it breaks, it will sometimes break into more than two pieces. Investigate the probability that a stick of spaghetti will break into more than two pieces when bent.

Section B
Moving forward

13	Money matters 1	194
14	Maths in motion	214
15	Polygons	231
16	Circles 1	254
17	Area, volume and surface area	265
18	Collecting and representing data	283
19	Indices	302
20	Working with expressions	312
21	Linear relationships	332
22	Triangles	355
23	Quadrilaterals and transformations	370
24	Further sets	389
25	Linking Thinking revision material	402

Unit 13

Money matters 1

Something to think about ...

Shauna is opening a savings account with €900.

The bank pays 5% interest on the balance in her account at the end of each year, and charges €5 fees at the end of each year.

If she doesn't do anything else with her account, what will the final balance be at the end of three years?

Topics covered within this unit:
- 13·1 Earning an income
- 13·2 Calculating VAT (value added tax)
- 13·3 Household bills
- 13·4 Profit and loss
- 13·5 Interest
- 13·6 Currency exchanges

The Learning Outcomes covered in this unit are contained in the following sections:
N.1e N.2c N.3b AF.2

Key words
- VAT (value added tax)
- Kilowatt hour (kWh)
- Interest
- Principal
- Simple interest
- Compound interest
- Exchange rate

13·1 Earning an income

By the end of this section, you should:
- understand how to calculate rates of pay
- be able to convert pay to monthly, weekly, daily and hourly rates

There are many different ways in which people can earn money. Some people work for themselves (self-employed) and charge a fee for their services, or sell goods for a profit. However, most people work for a company or an organisation and are paid a weekly or monthly wage for their service.

The table below shows the main ways of earning an income from an employer.

	Earning an income
Salary	A pre-determined amount is paid for the year. The pay period could be weekly, every two weeks (fortnightly) or every month. *Examples: teachers, soldiers, civil servants (i.e. people who work for the government)*
Wages	Wages are based on an hourly rate of pay. *Examples: shop assistants, mechanics, waitresses*
Commission	People who do this type of work usually have a fixed wage or **salary**. However, they will receive a bonus – or **commission** – which is a percentage of the value of the goods sold. *Examples: estate agents, car salespeople, insurance agents*

Worked example 1

Convert an annual salary of €32 000 to (i) monthly (ii) fortnightly (iii) weekly (iv) hourly salary (assume a 40-hour week is worked).

Solution

(i) As there are 12 months in a year, monthly salary = $\frac{32000}{12}$ = 2 666·666 = €2 666·67

(ii) A fortnight is equal to 2 weeks. There are 52 weeks in the year.

If you are paid fortnightly you will receive 26 payment periods.

Fortnightly payment = $\frac{32\,000}{26}$ = 1230·7692 = €1 230·77

(iii) Weekly payment = $\frac{32\,000}{52}$ = 615·384 = €615·38

(iv) We have been told to assume a 40-hour week and there are 52 weeks in a year. The number of hours worked will be 52 × 40

Hourly payment = $\frac{32\,000}{52 \times 40}$ = $\frac{32\,000}{2\,080}$ = 15·384 = €15·38

When dealing with money, we generally round to two decimal places, unless told otherwise.

Worked example 2

Convert a monthly salary of €2 500 to (i) weekly and then (ii) hourly amounts. Assume it is a 40-hour week.

Solution

(i) When we are given a monthly salary, we must first multiply it by 12 to find the annual salary. Then divide this answer by 52 to find the weekly amount.

Weekly salary = $\frac{2\,500 \times 12}{52}$ = 576·923 = €576·92

(ii) We have been told that a 40-hour week is worked.

Hourly salary = $\frac{576 \cdot 92}{40}$ = 14·423 = €14·42

We cannot divide a monthly salary by four weeks, as some calendar months in the year might contain almost five weeks.

Worked example 3

Joan sells pastries and soft drinks to hotels. She is paid €1 200 per month plus a commission of 5% of her total sales. In May, Joan's sales totalled €18 500. Calculate her total pay for May.

Solution

Total pay for May = €1 200 + 5% of €18 500

5% of €18 500 = $\frac{5}{100} \times 18\,500$ = 925

Total pay for May = €1 200 + €925 = €2 125

In some types of employment, a person will receive a basic hourly rate. However, they may also receive a bonus for working longer than the normal specified hours (overtime), or for working on a weekend. The extra payment may be calculated as **'time-and-a-half'** or **'double time'**. Time-and-a-half is the hourly rate muliplied by 1·5 and double time is the hourly rate multiplied by 2.

Worked example 4

Sally works 40 hours a week. She is paid €11·30 per hour.

(i) Calculate Sally's weekly wage.
(ii) In a particular week, Sally worked 6 hours overtime for which she was paid time and a half. How much did Sally earn in that week?
(iii) At Christmas, Sally worked her 40-hour week, but also worked for 8 hours on a Sunday, for which she was paid double time. How much did Sally earn that week?

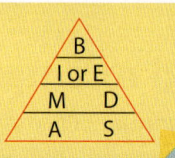

> Remember to use the correct order of operations (BIMDAS) when multiplying.
>
> B
> I or E
> M D
> A S

Solution

(i) Weekly wage = €11·30 × 40 hours = €452

(ii) Weekly wage plus 6 hours overtime at time and a half. Her hourly rate for this overtime was €11·30 × 1·5 = €16·95

Weekly wage = (€11·30 × 40 hours) + (€16·95 × 6 hours)
= €452 + €101·70
= €553·70

(iii) Sally worked an extra 8 hours on Sunday at double time. Her hourly rate for this day was €11·30 × 2 = €22·60

Weekly wage = (€11·30 × 40 hours) + (€22·60 × 8 hours)

Weekly wage = €452 + €180·80

Weekly wage = €632·80

Practice questions 13·1

1. Assuming a 40-hour week, convert the following annual salaries to:
   (a) monthly   (c) weekly
   (b) fortnightly (d) hourly amounts
   (i) €36 500   (iii) €19 750   (v) €105 000
   (ii) €48 700   (iv) €65 995

2. Assuming a 40-hour week, convert the following monthly salaries to:
   (a) fortnightly   (c) hourly amounts
   (b) weekly
   (i) €3 500   (iii) €6 012   (v) €2 667·50
   (ii) €4 475   (iv) €5 450

3. Simon works in the local florist shop and earns €9·40 per hour for a 40-hour week. Jane works in the hardware shop next door and earns €10·70 per hour for a 38-hour week.
   (i) Which person has the higher weekly wage?
   (ii) By how much?

4. Jill works in a garden centre. She is paid €9·75 per hour. Last week, she received wages that totalled €312. How many hours did Jill work? Assume no overtime was paid.

5. Ling has a part time job in a cinema. She works every Saturday and Sunday from 4 pm to 10 pm.
   (i) How many hours does Ling work per week?
   (ii) Ling earns €105 per week. How much does she earn per hour?

6. Bobby is paid €11·75 per hour. Last week he worked 24 hours at the normal rate and 5 hours at double time. On Friday he received his wages, which totalled €282. Bobby thinks he has been underpaid.
   (i) Is he correct? Justify your answer with supporting work.
   (ii) How much should Bobby have been paid last week?

7. Cindy has a part time job in the local supermarket. She is paid €9·20 per hour from Monday to Friday and €13·80 an hour on weekends. During a week of her school holidays, she worked from 3 pm to 6 pm Monday to Friday, and 8:30 am to 1:30 pm on Saturday and Sunday.
   Calculate her income for the week.

8. Nikita sells cars for a living. She is paid a basic salary of €1 000 per month plus 3% commission on any sales. In July she sold cars worth €95 200. Calculate her total pay for July.

9. Phillip is a real estate agent. He is paid a basic salary of €800 per month plus 0·5% commission on any houses he sells. Last month he sold four houses valued at €250 000, €384 000, €415 000 and €925 000 respectively.
   Find his total income for the month.

13.2 Calculating VAT (value added tax)

By the end of this section you should:
- understand to how to calculate the amount of VAT being charged on an item
- understand how to calculate the relevant rate of VAT, given the necessary values

Value added tax (VAT) is a tax charged on the sale of most goods and services in Ireland. VAT is charged at different rates for various goods and services.

Each year the Irish Government holds an annual budget in which VAT rates may increase or decrease.

> **Value added tax (VAT)** is a tax charged on the sale of most goods and services in Ireland.

We have already worked with VAT in Section A, Unit 5. In this unit, we will deal with more advanced problems involving VAT.

Worked example 1

John receives his electricity bill. The total bill, including VAT at 13·5%, is €215·65.

(i) How much was the bill before VAT had been added?
(ii) How much VAT had been added to the bill?

Solution

Let original bill = 100%
Original bill plus VAT at 13·5% = 100% + 13·5% = 113·5%

(i) 113·5% = €215·65
$1\% = \frac{215\cdot65}{113\cdot5}$
1% = 1·90
100% = 1·90 × 100
Original bill = €190

(ii) Total VAT added = €215·65 − €190
Total VAT added = €25·65

Worked example 2

A farmer is purchasing new animals for his farm. The total bill was €2 515·20. This included a charge of €115·20 for VAT.

(i) What was the bill for the animals before VAT was added?
(ii) At what percentage rate was VAT charged?

Solution

(i) Cost before VAT is added = final cost − VAT
= €2 515·20 − €115·20
= €2 400 was the cost before VAT was added.

(ii) Express the VAT as a percentage of the price before VAT.

Rate of VAT = $\frac{\text{VAT paid}}{\text{price before VAT was added}}$

Rate of VAT = $\frac{115\cdot20}{2\,400} \times \frac{100}{1}$

Rate of VAT = $0\cdot048 \times \frac{100}{1}$

Rate of VAT = 4·8%

> VAT is always charged on the cost (original price) of an item or service.

Section B Moving forward

Practice questions 13·2

1. A builder quotes a price of €700 to fix your roof. This quote includes VAT at 23%. What is the cost of the bill before VAT is added?

2. A camera costs €238 and this price includes VAT at 23%. Calculate the price before VAT.

3. Mia gets her car serviced. The cost of the parts is €211·15 excluding VAT at a rate of 23%. The cost of the labour (work done by the mechanic) is €110 excluding VAT at a rate of 13·5%. Calculate:
   (i) The amount of VAT to be paid on the parts
   (ii) The total cost of the parts including VAT
   (iii) The amount of VAT to be paid on the labour
   (iv) The total cost of the labour including VAT
   (v) The final bill Mia has to pay

4. Kyle visits a pet shop and purchases a new puppy, a dog bed and a lead. The total bill comes to €182·50, including VAT added at 23%.
   (i) What was the total of the bill before VAT was added? Give your answer to the nearest cent.
   (ii) How much VAT did he have to pay?

5. A family gets an extension to their house. The VAT rate on labour is 13·5% and the VAT rate on materials is 23%. If the labour costs €8 500 and €10 500 was spent on materials, how much will the family pay for the extension?

6. You want to buy a new drone. You can purchase one in Ireland for €249 plus 23% VAT, or you can buy the same model online from France for a total price €235 plus a €39·99 delivery fee.
   (i) How much does each option cost in total?
   (ii) Which option would you choose? Justify your answer.

7. Fionn is buying a new games console. The total cost of the console is €490·77. This includes a charge of €91·77 for VAT.
   (i) Calculate the cost of the games console before VAT was added.
   (ii) At what rate is the VAT charged?

Taking it FURTHER

8. The table below lists the prices of certain goods or services excluding VAT. Copy and complete the table. Give your answer to the nearest cent for money, and one decimal place for the VAT rate.

Goods/Services	Price excluding VAT	Rate of VAT	VAT payable	Total price including VAT
Two-course meal	€45·00	13·5%		
Hair colour and cut	€85·00		€29·75	
Debs dress	€189·99	23%		
Three cups of coffee	€8·85			€10·04
Five tickets to cinema		13·5%		€48·24

13.3 Household bills

By the end of this section you should:
- understand how to calculate household bills

In this section we will be dealing with various types of bills, including electricity charges, mobile phone tariffs, insurance, etc., as well as purchasing items through hire purchase.

Electricity and gas bills are the most common type of bill received by households in Ireland.

The usage is usually recorded by a meter. The reading from the meter is taken by companies to calculate the amount of electricity or gas used by the customer.

Electricity is sold in units. These units are called **kilowatt hours** (kWh). When you buy electricity, they charge you by the kilowatt hour. When you use 1000 watts for 1 hour, that's one kilowatt hour.

A **kilowatt hour** (kWh) is the basic unit of electricity.

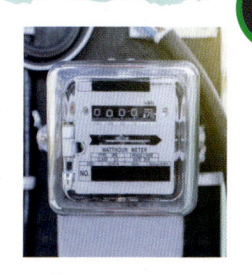

1 kWh is the amount of energy used by a 1kW (1000 watt) electric heater for 1 hour.

Worked example 1

Find the values of A, B, C, D, and E in the bill below.

Your electricity bill in more detail:

Abbreviations   a: actual reading   e: estimated reading   c: customer reading   P: price change   cr: credit

Your last bill

Your last bill	€200·00
Payments / Transactions	€200·00 cr
Balance brought forward	€0·00

Usage to date

meter number	current reading	previous reading	unit usage	unit price	unit type	Amount
XX	28047 e	27047 a	A	0·1672	General	B
Total electricity charges						€167·20

Standing charges and other items

Standing charge	61 days @	C	/ day		€23·68
PSO Levy Oct/Nov					€6·96
VAT	13·5% of €197·84				D

Payments / Other Transactions

Payment due	E

Terms you might see in a standard household bill:

Meter readings: Your present and previous meter readings are shown.

Standing charge: A fixed daily cost on your bill, no matter how much electricity you use in your home.

Public Service Obligation Levy (PSO) is mandated by the government. It is a charge that is used to support renewable energy.

Solution

A = present meter reading − previous meter reading
A = 28 047 − 27 047
A = 1 000 units

To find B, we multiply the number of units by the charge per unit, in this case 0·1672 (notice this value is in euros)
B = 1 000 × 0·1672 = 167·2
B = €167·20

To find C, we set up an equation.
$61 \times C = 23.68$
$\frac{61 \times C}{61} = \frac{23.68}{61}$ (dividing both sides by 61)
$C = \frac{23.68}{61}$
C = 0·388

D is 13·5% of €197·84
$D = 197.84 \times \frac{13.5}{100}$
D = 26·708
D = €26·71

E is the final total of the bill, so we must add up all the charges:
E = €167·20 + €23·68 + €6·96 + €26·71
E = €224·55

Practice questions 13.3

1. The table below shows an extract from an ESB bill.

   (i) Calculate the number of units used.

   (ii) Calculate the total charge due in euros and cents.

ESB Meter Readings	
Present	58 125
Previous	57 350
No. of units used	
Rates per unit	€0·15
Total charge	€

2. A phone company charges 6 cents per minute for calls and 15 cents per text. If Adam sent 30 texts and made voice calls totalling 45 minutes, calculate his bill in euros and cents.

3. Below is part of a gas bill. Find the values for A, B, C, D, E and F.

Meter readings		Units used and rate	Description	Amount
Present	Previous	A × €0·1265	General domestic	B
3 005	2367			
Standing charge		46 days × €0·38		C
PSO levy				€8·11
Total				D
VAT at 13·5%				E
Final amount due				F

4. The table below shows a sample of electricity used over a two-month period. Using the information in the table, find the missing values for each person.

	Name	Previous units reading	Present units reading	Number of units used	Cost per unit (in cents)	Total cost of units used (€)	Standing charge (€)	Total due before VAT (€)	VAT due at 13·5% (€)	Total amount due (€)
(i)	Leo	18 500	19 700		8·1		€10·50			
(ii)	Bart	23 261	23 821		4·9		€8·36			
(iii)	Mary	47 968	48 236		6·32		€5·50			
(iv)	Raj	59 820	60 450		5·6		€3·36			
(v)	Vicky	99 800	100 101		11·2		€7·49			

5. Mr Johnson works out the cost of the gas he used last year. At the start of the year, the gas meter reading was 8 569 units. At the end of the year, the reading was 9 872 units.
   Each unit of gas he used cost 8·3 cents. The PSO levy was €49·28, and the standing charge was €213·98

   (i) Calculate the total cost of the gas he used last year.

   (ii) If VAT at 13·5% is charged, what is his total bill for the year?

6. Alison travels by car to her meetings. Alison's company pays her 35 cents for each kilometre she travels. One day Alison writes down the distance readings from her car.

   - Start of the day: 2 430 kilometres
   - End of the day: 2 658 kilometres

   Work out how much the company pays Alison for her day's travel.

7. Fionn is buying a new mobile phone. He can choose one of the following monthly packages. Assume a month has 30 days.

Pay as you go	RED 15
No monthly charge	€15 monthly charge
For the first 2 minutes of calls each day: 10 cents per minute	For the first 3 minutes of calls each day: no charge
For the rest of that day: 5 cents per minute	For the rest of that day: 3 cents per minute
5 gigabytes of data per day	Unlimited data

Fionn reckons he spends 10 minutes on the phone each day. He uses 3 gigabytes of data each day.

(i) Which tariff should he choose? Justify your answer by showing all your work.

(ii) Fionn's mother also buys a phone. She knows she will definitely spend 80 minutes on the phone each day, but will not use any data. Which package should she choose? Justify your answer by showing all your work.

(iii) When is RED 15 the cheaper package? Justify your answer by showing all your work.

13.4 Profit and loss

By the end of this section you should be able to:
- calculate profit and loss using percentages

When you purchase an item and sell it for more money than you have paid, you have made a profit. However, if you purchase an item and sell it for less than you originally paid, you have made a loss. You have already met many of the terms associated with this topic in Section A, Unit 5.

Profit: if the selling price is greater than cost price

Profit or gain = selling price − cost price
(Note: profit will be a positive value)

If an article is sold at a profit of 10%, then the selling price = 110% of cost price.

$$\text{Percentage profit} = \frac{\text{profit}}{\text{cost price}} \times \frac{100}{1}$$

Loss: if the selling price is less than cost price

Loss = selling price − cost price
(Note: loss will be a negative value)

If an article is sold at a loss of 10%, then selling price = 90% of cost price.

$$\text{Percentage loss} = \frac{\text{loss}}{\text{cost price}} \times \frac{100}{1}$$

In general, we express profit or loss as a percentage of the cost price, unless instructed to do otherwise.

Worked example 1

Andy buys a car for €4 000. He then sells it for €5 500. Find the value of the following in euros:
(i) The cost price (ii) the selling price (iii) the profit or loss made (iv) the percentage profit or loss.

Solution

(i) The cost price is the amount of money Andy paid for the car = €4 000

(ii) The selling price is what Andy sold the car for = €5 500

(iii) The profit = selling price − cost price
= €5 500 − €4 000
= €1 500

(iv) The percentage profit
$$\text{Percentage profit} = \frac{\text{profit}}{\text{cost price}} \times \frac{100}{1}$$
$$= \frac{€1\ 500}{€4\ 000} \times \frac{100}{1}$$
$$= 37.5\%$$

Section B Moving forward

Worked example 2

Aaron bought a laptop for €420 and sold it at a profit of $12\frac{1}{2}$%.
Find (i) the profit he made in euros (ii) the sale price of the laptop.

Solution

(i) Profit = 12·5% of €420 = €52·50

(ii) Selling price = cost price + profit
 = €420 + €52·50
 = €472·50

Alternative solution to part (ii):
Cost price = 100%
Selling price = cost price + profit
Selling price = 100% + 12·5% = 112·5%
Selling price = 112·5% of €420
Selling price = €472·50

Worked example 3

Paul owns a game shop. He has bought too many copies of a particular game, so he decides to sell them at a loss of 40%. He is selling each game for €18. Find the value of the following:

(i) The cost price Paul paid for the game.
(ii) The loss in euros Paul makes on each game sold.

Solution

(i) Selling price = cost price − loss
Selling price = 100% − 40%
Selling price = 60%

This means that the selling price is 60% of the cost price.
To find the actual cost price we must find 100%

60% = €18
1% = $\frac{18}{60}$
1% = 0·3
100% = 0·3 × 100 = €30

(ii) Loss = Selling price − cost price
Loss = 18 − 30
Loss = −12
Paul is making a loss of €12 on each game sold.

> A negative sign in front of an answer indicates a loss is being made.

Practice questions 13·4

1. Calculate the percentage profit earned on the following items.
   Give your answer to two decimal places where necessary.

    (i)   A games console player that cost €119 and sold for €155.

    (ii) A house bought for €365 000 and sold for €518 000.

    (iii) A bicycle costing €74 and sold for €105.

2. Copy the table and fill in the missing information. The first line has been completed for you.

	Cost price	Selling price	Profit or loss	Percentage profit or loss of the selling price (give answer to one decimal place)
(i)	€350	€270	−€80	22·9% loss
(ii)		€100	€78	
(iii)	€2 500		−€1 800	
(iv)	€4 024		−€850	
(v)		€8 400	€1 200	
(vi)	€6 797		−€365	
(vii)		€11 000	€3 400	
(viii)	€100 200		−€1 500	
(ix)	€999 999		−€33 000	

3. The price of a jacket is €50. The price is reduced by 15% during a sale.
   Calculate the sale price of the jacket.

4. Karl bought a tablet for €200 and sold it for €280. Express the profit as a percentage of the cost price.

5. Find the cost price when:
   (i) Selling price = €795 and profit = 6%
   (ii) Selling price = €980 and loss = 12%
   (iii) Selling price = €216 and loss = 4%
   (iv) Selling price = €504 and profit = 12%

6. Find the selling price when:
   (i) Cost price = €875 and profit = 5%
   (ii) Cost price = €750 and loss = 15%
   (iii) Cost price = €480 and profit = $12\frac{1}{2}$%
   (iv) Cost price = €675 and loss = 92%
   (v) Cost price = €1 020 and loss = 10·7%
   (vi) Cost price = €10 000 and loss = 17·5%

7. A travel agent sells a package holiday for €810. She makes a profit of 8%.
   How much money did the travel agent make on the sale?

8. Jane purchased a house for €500 000. She spent €60 000 on renovations and €5 000 on landscaping the garden. If she sold the house for €610 000, find the percentage loss or gain in the transaction. Give your answer to the nearest whole number.

Taking it FURTHER

9. A man sells two wristwatches; one at a profit of 30% and another at a loss of 30%, but each at the same selling price of €200. Calculate the net profit or loss in euros.

10. A shopkeeper offers a 15% discount on all toys. He offers a further reduction of 4% on the reduced price to the customers who pay by cash.
    (i) If a customer pays by bank card, how much do they pay for a toy priced at €20?
    (ii) If a customer pays using cash, how much do they pay for a toy priced at €20?

11. A used-car dealer sold one car at a profit of 25% of the dealer's purchase price for that car, and sold another car at a loss of 20% of the dealer's purchase price for that car. If the dealer sold each car for €20 000, what was the dealer's total profit or loss, in euros, for the two transactions combined?

13·5 Simple and compound interest

By the end of this section you should be able to:
- understand simple and compound interest
- solve problems involving simple and compound interest

If you have a savings account with a bank and deposit some money, the bank will pay you extra money for saving with them. This is called **interest**. Similarly, if you need to borrow money from a bank, the bank will expect you to pay back more than you borrowed from them in the first place. How much extra money you pay them back depends on the **interest rate** set by the bank. Banks and other institutions make their money by charging more interest on their loans compared to the interest they give on their savings accounts.

The following key terms are important for this section:

P = Principal	The sum of money borrowed or invested over a period of time.
i = Interest rate	The rate at which interest is paid on a loan or savings. This value is usually represented as a percentage.
t = Time	The length of time for which the money is borrowed or invested. This value can be expressed in days, weeks, months or years.
F = Final amount	The final sum of money due, including interest at the end of the investment or borrowing period.

There are two types of interest rates available:
1. Simple interest
2. Compound interest

> **Interest** is the sum of money that you pay for borrowing or that is paid to you for investing.

Simple interest

Simple interest is calculated by multiplying the **principal** amount by the interest rate and the duration of a loan or investment. Generally, simple interest paid or received over a certain period is a fixed percentage of the principal amount that was borrowed or loaned.

> **Simple interest** is interest that is always calculated on the initial principal.

$$\text{Simple interest} = \text{principal} \times \text{rate} \times \text{time}$$

> When doing calculations, always use the decimal form for interest value.
> $i = \dfrac{\text{percentage rate}}{100}$

Worked example 1

A college student obtains a simple interest loan to purchase a car which costs €2 800.
The annual interest rate on her loan is 6%. She repaid the entire loan at the end of 3 years.
(i) Calculate the interest she paid over the 3 years of her loan.
(ii) What was the final amount of the loan?

Solution

(i) This is a simple interest loan where:
Principal = €2 800   Rate = 6% ($\dfrac{6}{100} = 0.06$)
Time = 3 years
  Interest = principal × rate × time
  Interest = 2 800 × 0·06 × 3
  Interest = €504

(ii) Final amount of the loan = principal + interest
  Final amount = €2 800 + €504
  Final amount = €3 304

Compound interest

Compound interest is the addition of interest to the principal sum of a loan or savings account. Basically, it is interest on interest.

> **Compound interest** is interest that is calculated not only on the initial principal, but also the accumulated interest of previous years.

Compound interest is calculated using the formula:

$$F = P(1 + i)^t$$

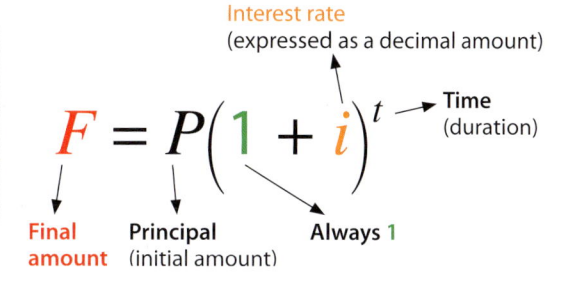

Remember to use the decimal form for interest rate.

You cannot use the formula if:
1) The interest rate, i, changes during the period.
2) Money is added or subtracted during the period.

$$F = P(1 + i)^t$$

- F = Final amount
- P = Principal (initial amount)
- 1 = Always 1
- i = Interest rate (expressed as a decimal amount)
- t = Time (duration)

This formula appears in the *formulae and tables* booklet.

Worked example 2

You invested €5 000 at an interest rate of 3% for 2 years. The bank pays you compound interest annually. What is your total return on this investment?

Solution

Principal = €5 000 i = 3% (0·03) t = 2 years

$F = P(1 + i)^t$

$F = 5\,000(1 + (0·03))^2$

$F = 5\,000(1·03)^2$

$F = 5\,000(1·0609)$

$F = 5\,304·5$

Final amount = €5 304·50

> Remember the BIMDAS order of operations. We must solve the power before we multiply.

Worked example 3

You borrowed €1 500 for 3 years at 7% interest that is compounded annually (once a year).
(i) The entire loan is due to be repaid at the end of the third year. What amount will you repay?
(ii) How much interest did you pay?

Solution

(i) Principal = €1 500 i = 7% (0·07) t = 3

$F = P(1 + i)^t$

$F = 1\,500(1 + 0·07)^3$

$F = 1\,500(1·07)^3$

$F = 1\,500(1·225)$

$F = 1\,837·56$

Final amount due = €1 837·56

(ii) Interest = amount repaid − amount borrowed

Interest = €1 837·56 − €1 500

Interest = €337·56

Worked example 3

€8 000 is invested at a rate of 4% per annum. At the beginning of the second year, an additional €800 is added to this amount. The interest rate for the second year increases to 5·3%.

(i) How much is this investment worth after 1 year?
(ii) What is the final amount in the account after 2 years?
(iii) How much interest was earned on the investment over a period of 2 years?

> 'Per annum' is a Latin term that means annually or each year.

Solution

(i) Find value of investment at the end of year 1:   (4% interest)

Principal = €8 000 $i = 4\%$ (0·04) $t = 1$
$F = P(1 + i)^t$
$F = 8\,000(1 + 0·04)^1$
$F = 8\,000(1·04)^1$
$F = 8\,320$
Final amount at the end of year 1 = €8 320

(ii) Value of investment at the end of year 2:
New principal = €8 320 + €800 = €9 120
$i = 5·3\%$ (0·053) $t = 1$
$F = P(1 + i)^t$
$F = 9\,120(1 + 0·053)^1$
$F = 9\,120(1·053)^1$
$F = 9\,603·36$
Final amount at the end of year 2 = €9 603·36

(iii) Amount of interest earned:
Total interest = final amount − initial amount − additional sum invested
Total interest = €9 603·36 − €8 000 − €800
Total interest = €803·36

Discuss and discover

You wish to take out a loan for €1 000 for a holiday and pay it back in full at the end of two years.

Using appropriate research methods, compare rate and overall cost in a:
- bank
- credit union
- short-term money lender

Which organisation will offer the best value for the loan? Explain your reasoning.

KEY SKILLS

Practice questions 13·5

1. (i) For the formula below, identify the terms as being either a variable or a constant.
   (ii) Explain what each variable represents.

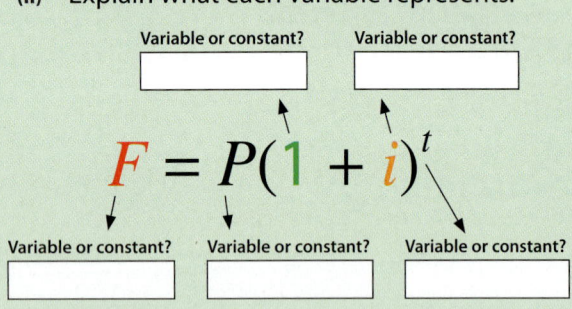

   $F = P(1 + i)^t$

   Variable or constant? (for each of F, P, 1, i, t)

2. €10 000 is invested for two years at a rate of 3%. Calculate the value of the investment at the end of two years using:
   (i) simple interest
   (ii) compound interest

206   Linking Thinking 1

3. Find the simple interest and compound interest earned on each of these amounts over the specified number of years.

	Principal	Rate (%)	Time (years)	Type of interest paid	Total amount	Total interest earned
(i)	€100	5	1	Simple		
(ii)	€700	3	1	Compound		
(iii)	€2 500	2·5	2	Simple		
(iv)	€4 350	6	3	Simple		
(v)	€10 000	1·5	2	Compound		
(vi)	€299	4·5	3	Compound		
(vii)	€250 000	1·5	3	Simple		
(viii)	€250 000	1·5	3	Compound		
(ix)	€23 550	11	2	Simple		
(x)	€3 000 000	0·5	3	Compound		

4. A savings account in a bank contains €495 and earns 3% interest compounded annually.
   (i) How much money will there be in the account after three years?
   (ii) How much interest has been earned?

5. A principal of €2 000 is placed in a savings account at 3% per annum compounded annually.
   How much is in the account after
   (i) one year
   (ii) two years
   (iii) three years?

6. Which of the following loans charges less interest?
   Loan A: A simple interest loan of €10 000 at a rate of 7% per annum for 3 years.
   Loan B: A compound interest loan of €10 000 at a rate of 6·5% per year for 3 years.

7. Find the difference between the simple interest and the compound interest on €6 000 for two years at 4·5% per annum.

8. Lin obtained a loan of €25 000 from the Syndicate Bank to renovate her house. If the rate of interest is 8% compounded annually, how much will she have to pay to the bank at the end of two years to clear her loan? Assume she makes no payments before this time.

9. Shelly took a loan of €11 000 from AB Finance to purchase a car. If the company charges compound interest at 12% per annum during the first year and $12\frac{1}{2}$% per annum during the second year, how much will she have to pay back at the end of the 2 years?

10. €1 200 is placed in an account at 4% compounded annually for 2 years. The final amount is then withdrawn and placed in another bank at the rate of 5% compounded annually for 3 years. What is the balance in the second account at the end of the third year?

Taking it FURTHER

11. Hannah borrowed €20 000 from a bank at 12% simple interest per annum. She loaned it to Andy at the same rate, but compounded annually.
    (i) Find the total profit she made at the end of two years.
    (ii) Express her profit as a percentage of the original sum of money.

13.6 Currency exchanges

By the end of this section you should:
- understand exchange rates
- be able to flexibly convert different currencies

An **exchange rate** is the rate at which one currency may be converted into another.

Discuss and discover

Research exchange rates from different financial institutions, for example, the bank, credit union and post office.

Selecting one of these providers, convert:
- €1 into US dollars
- €2 into US dollars
- €3 into US dollars
- €10 into US dollars
- €100 into US dollars

Can you explain how to convert euros to US dollars to your friend?
Can you find a way to work backwards converting dollars back to euros?

When people travel to foreign countries, they must change their money into foreign currencies.

A foreign **exchange rate** is the price of one country's currency in terms of another's. Like all prices, exchange rates rise and fall.

The currency of Ireland is the euro. When we refer to foreign currency, we mean the money that a different country uses, such as baht in Thailand or rupees in India.

Not all currencies have the same value. We use exchange rates to convert from one currency to another.

Currency exchange is an example of a directly proportional relationship.

Solving problems involving currency exchange

1. Write the given exchange rate such that the required currency is on the right-hand side.
2. Divide both sides by an appropriate value to get 1 on the left-hand side.
3. Multiply both sides to get the value required.

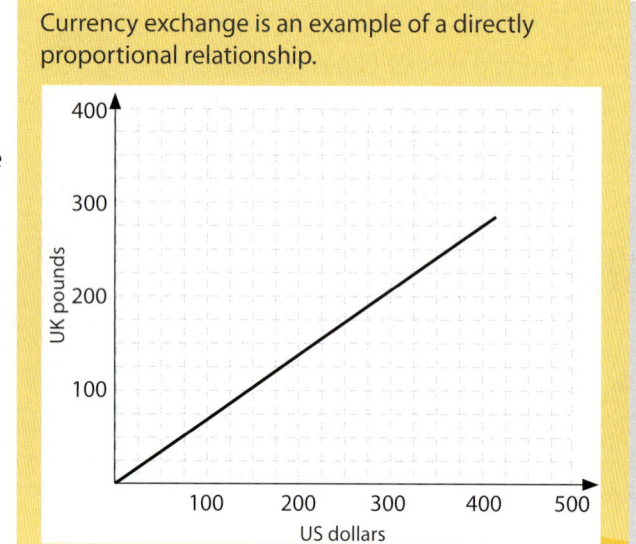

Worked example 1

Cathy is planning to visit America for a holiday. She needs to exchange €500 into dollars for her spending money. If the exchange rate offered is €1 = $1·12, how many dollars should she receive?

Solution

Step 1   €1 = $1·12   (we want dollars, so put dollars on the right-hand side)

Step 2   Not required since the left-hand side is already = 1

Step 3   €1 × 500 = $1·12 × 500   (multiply both sides by 500)
            €500 = $560

Worked example 2

Jacob is returning to Ireland from a trip to visit his friend in Poland. The unit of currency in Poland is called the zloty (zł). Jacob has 400 zloty (zł) and wants to convert them to euros. If the exchange rate is 4·17 zł = €1, how much, to the nearest euro, will he receive?

Solution

Step 1 $4·17 \text{ zł} = €1$ (we want euros, so put it on the right)

Step 2 $\frac{4·17 \text{ zł}}{4·17} = \frac{€1}{4·17}$ (divide both sides by 4·17)

Step 3 $1 \text{zł} \times 400 = \frac{€1}{4·17} \times 400$ (multiply both sides by 400)

$400 \text{ zł} = 0·24 \times 400$

$400 \text{ zł} = €96$ Therefore Jacob receives €96

In the retail currency exchange market, different buying and selling rates will be quoted by money dealers. Most trades are to or from the local currency. When going abroad, you need to change money to the currency of the country you are visiting. It is important to know the exchange rate and amount of commission charged to get the best possible deal.

If you want to change a different currency into euros, the institution will buy the foreign currency from you at the '**we buy**' rate.

If you want to change euros into a different currency, the institution will sell you this currency at the '**we sell**' rate. They will usually charge a commission as well. This is an extra charge for their service.

	We Buy	We Sell
USA	1·4280	1·2507
JAPAN	173·204	153·358
UK	0·7205	0·5620
SWITZERLAND	1·7160	1·5587
AUSTRALIA	1·7596	1·5681
CANADA	1·6028	1·4292
DENMARK	7·7532	7·1170
NORWAY	8·4145	7·7207

In general, the 'we buy' rate will be higher than the 'we sell' rate. Take care to use the correct rate when answering a question where you are given two rates.

Worked example 3

Kai wants to visit his parents in New Zealand. He needs to change €800 into New Zealand dollars (NZD). He visits his local bank and the exchange rate available is shown below.

	We sell	We buy
New Zealand dollars (NZD)	1·66	1·79

(i) How many New Zealand dollars will Kai get for €1 000?

(ii) If the bank charges a commission fee of 2·5% of the euro value, how much will Kai have to pay for the transaction?

(iii) When Kai returns to Ireland, he has $350 New Zealand dollars left. He wants to exchange these for euros. How much, to the nearest cent, will he receive?

Solution

(i) Firstly, Kai is buying dollars, so the bank is selling dollars. Therefore, we must use the 'sell rate' in our currency conversion.

$€1 = \$1·66$

$€1 \times 1\,000 = \$1·66 \times 1\,000$

$€1\,000 = \$1\,660$

Kai receives $1 660 (NZD)

(ii) The bank charges a 2·5% commission on the euro amount of the transaction.

Find 2·5% of €1 000

$1\,000 \times \frac{2·5}{100} = 25$

Kai must pay a commission of €25

(iii) On his return from New Zealand, Kai has $350 (NZD) that he wants to convert back to euros.

In this case, Kai is selling the dollars and the bank is buying them. Therefore, we use the 'we buy' rate $1·79 = €1

$\$1 = \frac{€1}{1·79}$

$\$1 \times 350 = \frac{€1}{1·79} \times 350$

$\$350 = €195·53$

Kai receives €195·53

Practice questions 13·6

Use the table below to answer questions 1 to 8.

Currency	Value of €1
UK pound sterling	0·92
US dollar	1·24
Turkish lira	6·51
New Zealand dollar	1·79
Polish zloty	4·25
Swiss franc	1·16

1. Jack lives in Dublin. His uncle lives in Poland. For his birthday, Jack received 200 zloty from his uncle. How much is this in euros?

2. (i) If you have €50, how much will you receive if you change it to UK pounds sterling (£)?

   (ii) If you have £90, how much will you receive if you convert it to euros (€)?

3. Niamh wants to buy a pair of runners from a UK website. The prices of the runners are £39·99.
   How much will she have to pay in euros?

4. (i) Imir is travelling to Turkey on holidays. He has €175 to spend. What is the value of this in Turkish lira?

   (ii) Imir arrives back in Ireland. He has 100 Turkish lira that he didn't spend. How many euros is this worth?

5. William has €15. The video game he wants to buy costs $25 US dollars. Does he have enough money to buy the game? If not, how many more euros does he need? Give your answer to the nearest cent.

6. An Irish family are on holiday in San Francisco (USA). At a café, they order 2 hot dogs, 1 hamburger, 2 pizzas and 1 chicken salad. They also order 5 soft drinks. Work out their total bill in euros (€).

Menu	
Hot dog	$5·25
Chicken salad	$6·15
Pizza	$4·80
Hamburger	$3·70
Any soft drink	$2·50

7. An American airline is offering return flights from Dublin to New York for $799. A UK airline is offering the same flights for £600. You will be paying the fare in euros.

   (i) Which company is offering the cheapest fare?

   (ii) What is the difference in price between the two air fares? Give your answer in euros.

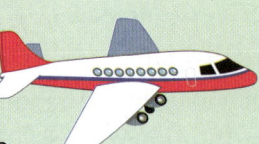

Taking it FURTHER

8. A combo burger meal costs $12 in New Zealand, £4·69 in London, $5·99 in the USA, 20 Turkish lira in Turkey, 6·50 Swiss francs (CHF) and 19 zloty in Poland. Find the cost of each meal in euros.

9. Below is the price of currency exchange rates from your local bank. Use the information provided in the table to answer the following questions. A commission of 1·5% is applied to all transactions.

Currency	We buy	We sell
UK pound sterling	0·92	0·87
US dollar	1·24	1·16
Turkish lira	6·51	6·30
New Zealand dollar	1·79	1·66
Polish zloty	4·25	4·09
Swiss franc	1·16	1·08

(i) Phillip has €300. He wants to convert this to US dollars.
   (a) How many dollars will he get? Give your answer to two decimal places.
   (b) How much commission does the bank receive in dollars on the transaction?

(ii) Mel has just returned from a trip to London. She has £105 and want to change it to euros.
   (a) How many euros will she get? Give your answer to two decimal places.
   (b) How much commission does the bank receive in pounds on the transaction?

(iii) Samantha travels to Switzerland for a conference. She converts €1 100 into Swiss francs (CHF).
   (a) How many Swiss francs will she get? Give your answer to two decimal places.
   (b) When Samantha returns home to Ireland, she has 500 Swiss francs which she did not spend. She wants to convert these back to euros. How many euros will she receive?
   (c) How much commission does the bank receive from the conversion of Swiss francs to euros? Give your answer in euros.

(iv) Victoria is travelling from Poland to Ireland. She has 5 000 zloty.
   (a) How many euros will she get? Give your answer to two decimal places.
   (b) How much commission does the bank receive on the transaction? Give your answer in euros.
   (c) On returning to Poland, Victoria has €72. She exchanges this for Polish zloty. How many zloty did she receive?
   (d) How much commission does the bank receive on the transaction? Give your answer in euros.
   (e) Overall, how much, did Victoria pay for both currency transactions? Give your answer in euros.

Revision questions

13A Core skills

1. Karl has a part time job. He is paid €11·20 per hour from Monday to Friday and €15·60 per hour on weekends. In a particular week he worked from 8 am to 6 pm each day from Monday to Friday, and 11:30 am to 5 pm on Saturday. Calculate his income for the week.

2. Juan works in an art gallery. He is paid a basic salary of €1 650 per month plus 12·5% commission on any sales. Last month Juan made sales amounting to €4 350. Calculate his total wage for the month.

3. A Silicon Valley entrepreneur earns €8 000 000 per year. Assuming there are 24 hours in a day, how much does she earn …?
   (i) each month
   (ii) each week
   (iii) each day
   (iv) each hour

4. Which of these two banks offers a better deal if you were converting €320 to US dollars? Justify your answer.
   - **Bank A** charges commission at €5·50 per transaction and offers an exchange rate of €1 = $1·15
   - **Bank B** charges no commission and offers an exchange rate of €1 = $1·10

5. A camera is for sale for €300 in Ireland and the same camera is for sale for $350 in the USA. The exchange rate is $1·00 = € 0·71. Is there a price difference between the two countries? If so, calculate the percentage difference, correct to one decimal place, between the price in euros and dollars.

6. Vincent receives the gas bill shown below. Find the values of A, B, C, D and E.

Blue Gas Suppliers					
Meter reading		Number of units used	Rate per unit	Description	Amount
Present	Previous	A	€0·11	Cost of units used	B
8 0893	8 0491			Standing charge	€26·47
				PSO levy	€6·10
				Total excluding VAT	C
				VAT @ 13·5%	D
				Total including VAT	E

7. Jade runs an online website selling replacement parts for computers. She sells some items for a profit and some at a loss. Copy the table below and fill in the missing information.

Item	Cost price	Selling price	Percentage profit or loss
Replacement screen for phone	€70	€91	
New battery for computer tablet		€50	15%
Phone charger	€30		−25%
Power supply for laptop		€90	35%
Wireless keyboard	€35	€56	
External memory drive	€15	€35	
Blue tooth mouse	€25		−40%

8. Kelly wants to open her own graphics design company. She borrows €15 000 for 3 years to pay for the start-up cost. The bank charges her interest at a rate of 3·5% per year, which is compounded annually. How much interest will Kelly have to pay on the loan?

9. Congratulations! You have won €500 000 in the lottery. You decide to invest €200 000 into a post office savings account for 3 years. The post office offers an interest rate of 3% which is compounded annually. At the end of the second year, you decide to withdraw €50 000.

   (i) Calculate how much money you have in your account at the end of 2 years. Be sure to subtract the €50 000 you have withdrawn.

   (ii) Calculate how much money you have in your account after 3 years.

   (iii) If you had not withdrawn any money, what would have been the final value in your account after 3 years?

13B Taking it FURTHER

1. (i) Martina works for an electrical firm and earns €23·60 per hour for a 36-hour week. For any additional hours that she works in a given week, she is paid time and a half. If Martina worked 45 hours in a given week, calculate her wage for that week.

   (ii) If Martina works on a Saturday or Sunday, she is paid double time. Last week Martina worked from 8 am to 5 pm from Monday to Friday. On Saturday she worked from 11 am to 2 pm and on Sunday she worked from 11:30 am to 2 pm. Calculate how much Martina has earned for the week.

2. A farmer sells beef to a wholesaler for €8 per kilogram. The wholesaler sells it to a butcher for a 60% profit. However, the butcher is forced to sell the beef at a 15% loss. How much is the butcher charging for 1 kilogram of beef?

3. You are buying a new car valued at €20 000. You pay €4 000 cash to the dealership and borrow the remaining amount. The bank charges you 9% interest, which is compounded annually.
   (i) You agree to pay the loan amount plus interest back at the end of the three years. What is the total amount you had to pay back to the bank?
   (ii) How much interest did you have to pay on the loan?
   (iii) If instead, you paid the loan plus interest back at the end of two years, how much less interest would you have paid?

4. There are two shops, PJ Sports and Live Style, which both stock the latest football jersey. The retail price of the jersey is €70.
   PJ Sports is offering 14% off the selling price and Live Style is offering $\frac{1}{6}$ off the selling price.
   Which shop would you buy the sports jersey in? Justify your answer.

CC BANK 5·8% for amounts of €100 or more

AWE BANK 5·9% for a minimum 2 year deposit

BETABANK 6·7% for a 1 year fixed-term deposit

5. Paula finds out the interest rates offered by three banks.
   She has €1 200 to invest.
   (i) Which bank offers the best rate?
   (ii) To get the best rate, how long should she leave her money in the bank?
   (iii) Which bank would you choose? Justify your answer.

6. Simon is ordering jewellery from the USA. Each item cost $23·17. The exchange rate is €1 = $1·12
   (i) What is the price in euros for each item?
   (ii) The total charge for Simon's order before VAT is added is €330. The VAT charged on the items was €75·90. Find the percentage of VAT charged on the items ordered.

7. Ciara wants to buy a new laptop. The usual price of the laptop is €440. The laptop is on special offer in three different shops.

Shop A offers 10% off the usual price.	Shop B offers $\frac{1}{5}$ off the usual price.	Shop C allows you to pay a €100 deposit and €30 per month for 12 months.

   (i) How much would the laptop cost in each of the shops A, B and C?
   (ii) Which shop do you think Ciara should buy her laptop from? Justify your answer.

8. Mia is comparing the cost of two electricity companies. She used 620 units of electricity last month.
   (i) Copy the tables into your copybook and fill in the missing information.

Clear Power	€
Standing charge	9·47
18·5 cents per unit	
Sub-total	
13·5% VAT	
Total	

Power One	€
No standing charge	
First 50 units free, then 25 cents per unit	
Sub-total	
13·5% VAT	
Total	

   (ii) What is the price difference between the two bills?
   (iii) Mia contacted the more expensive company. The company offered her a 7% discount off her total bill. Which company should Mia get her electricity from? Give a reason for your answer.

Now that you have completed the unit, revisit the

Something to think about ...

question posed at the start of this unit.

Unit 14

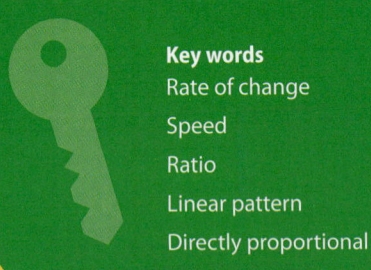

Maths in motion

Topics covered within this unit:
14·1 Measuring distance and time
14·2 Speed
14·3 Rate of change graphs

The Learning Outcomes covered in this unit are contained in the following sections:

GT.1 N.2b N.3a N.3b N.4
AF.1a AF.7d GT.5b

Key words
Rate of change
Speed
Ratio
Linear pattern
Directly proportional

Something to think about ...

KEY SKILLS

Five students took part in an unusual 100 m race, in which the runners start in different places and at different times.

Below is some information regarding the race:

- Amy starts running on the starting pistol. She runs the 100 metres in 12 seconds.
- Brandon starts running from the 20-metre mark. He reaches the finish line (at the 100-metre mark) in 16 seconds. 
- Charlie starts running two seconds after the starting pistol. He crosses the finish line at the same time as Amy.
- David runs the full 100 metres at 7 metres per second. He started running at the sound of the starting pistol.
- Emma started running at the starting pistol at 9 metres per second but gave up after 6 seconds.

Use the given information above to answer the following questions.

1. Which runner was the fastest?
2. Which runner won the race?
3. Represent each runner's race on a distance/time graph.

14·1 Measuring distance and time

By the end of this section, you should:
- understand the units of distance and time
- be able to convert between units of distance and time
- understand and be able to use the 24-hour clock
- be able to interpret and use timetables

Distance is a numerical description of how far apart two objects are. It is also called **length**.

214   Linking Thinking 1

Units of distance

Distance is measured in millimetres (mm), centimetres (cm), metres (m) and kilometres (km).

Converting between units of distance

- To convert distance (length) from a larger unit into a smaller unit, multiply by the relevant power of 10.
- To convert distance (length) from a smaller unit into a larger unit, divide by the relevant power of 10.

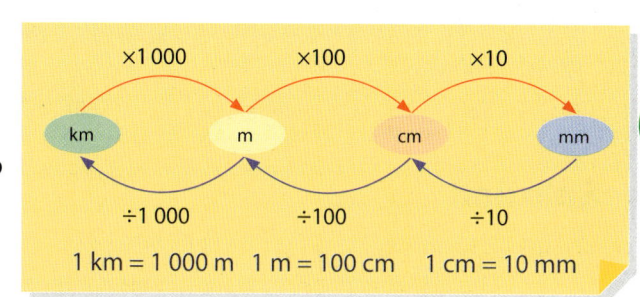

km ×1000→ m ×100→ cm ×10→ mm
km ÷1000← m ÷100← cm ÷10← mm
1 km = 1 000 m   1 m = 100 cm   1 cm = 10 mm

Time

Units of time

Time is measured in seconds (s), minutes (min) and hours (hr). These units of time are related as follows:

60 s = 1 min   60 min = 1 hr   24 hr = 1 day   7 days = 1 week

Converting between hours, minutes and seconds

- To convert time from a larger unit into a smaller unit, multiply by 60.
- To convert time from a smaller unit into a larger unit, divide by 60.

h ×60→ min ×60→ s
h ÷60← min ÷60← s
1 hr = 60 min   1 min = 60 s

24-hour clock

The 24-hour clock is a way of telling the time in which the day runs from midnight to midnight and is divided into 24 hours.
It does not use am or pm.

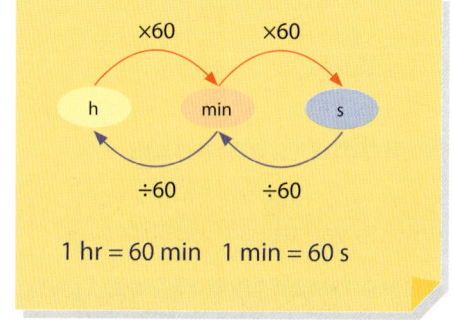

03:30
15:30

A time in the 24-hour clock is written in the form hours:minutes (for example, 01:23). Numbers under 10 usually have 0 in front, e.g. 09:07.

Converting from the 24-hour clock to the 12-hour clock

Times before noon: Add 'am' and remove the 0 at the start if present
                    e.g. 02:15 = 2:15 am; 06:45 = 6:45 am; 10:36 = 10:36 am

Times after noon: Subtract 12 from the hour and add 'pm'
                    e.g. 16:35 = 4:35 pm; 21:07 = 9:07 pm; 23:58 = 11:58 pm

For the 24-hour clock, midnight is generally taken as 00:00. But sometimes it can be written as 24:00. Both are acceptable.

Converting from the 12-hour to the 24-hour clock

Times before noon: Remove the 'am' and add a 0 at the start if the number is under 10
                    e.g. 7:30 am = 07:30; 11:25 am = 11:25

Times after noon: Remove the 'pm' and add 12 to the hour part
                    e.g. 3:42 pm = 15:42; 8:10 pm = 20:10

Worked example

(a) Convert the following times in the 12-hour clock to times in the 24-hour clock.
   (i)   2:12 am   (ii)   8:36 pm   (iii)   12:15 pm

(b) Convert the following times in the 24-hour clock to times in the 12-hour clock.
   (i)   14:36   (ii)   02:45   (iii)   23:56

> 12 midnight is the start of the day and so it is 00:00 hours. 12 noon is the middle of the day and so it is 12:00.

Solution

(a) (i)   2:12 am
This is before noon, so we remove the 'am' and add 0
2:12 am = 02:12

(ii)   8:36 pm
This is after noon, so we remove the 'pm' and add a 12 to the hour part
8:36 pm = 20:36

(iii)   12:15 pm
This is after noon, so we remove the 'pm'
12:15 pm = 12:15

(b) (i)   14:36
This is after noon, so we subtract 12 and add 'pm'
14:36 = 2:36 pm

(ii)   02:45
This is before noon, so we remove the 0 and add 'am'
02:45 = 2:45 am

(iii)   23:56
This is after noon, so we subtract 12 and add 'pm'
23:56 = 11:56 pm

Reading timetables

In everyday life, the 24-hour clock is commonly used in bus, train and plane timetables. Why do you think this is the case?

Discuss and discover

Below is a portion of the Dublin–Waterford train timetable.

		2 MON TO SAT	1 2 MON TO SAT	2 ★ MON TO SAT	2 ★ MON TO SAT	2 MON TO SAT	2 MON TO SAT	1 2 MON TO SAT	2 MON TO SAT
DUBLIN Heuston	Dep	07:25	10:15	13:15	15:10	16:40	17:35	18:35	20:15
Park West & Cherry Orchard	Dep	..	..	..	..	..	..	..	20:23
Clondalkin Fonthill	Dep	….	….	….	….	….	….	….	20:27
Adamstown	Dep	..	..	..	..	..	..	..	20:32
Hazelhatch & Celbridge	Dep	….	….	….	….	16:55	….	….	20:37
Sallins & Naas	Dep	..	..	..	..	17:04	17:53	..	20:46
Newbridge	Dep	07:47	….	….	15:33	….	….	18:58	20:54
Kildare	Dep	07:53	10:42	..	15:39	17:17	18:06	19:05	21:01
Athy	Dep	08:13	10:59	13:58	15:56	17:35	18:25	19:23	21:16
CARLOW	Dep	08:26	11:11	14:10	16:07	17:47	18:36	19:37	21:28
Muine Bheag (Bagenalstown)	Dep	08:43	11:22	14:24	16:19	17:58	18:48	19:49	..
Kilkenny MacDonagh	Arr	09:01	11:40	14:41	16:36	18:17	19:06	20:08	….
Kilkenny MacDonagh	Dep	09:05	11:45	11:46	16:40	18:21	19:10	20:13	
Thomastown	Dep	09:16	11:55	14:56	16:51	18:31	19:21	20:23	….
WATERFORD Plunkett	Dep	09:40	12:20	15:25	17:15	19:00	19:46	20:48	..

Work with the person beside you to answer the following questions:

(i)   How many trains leave Dublin for Waterford between 7 am and 9 pm daily?
(ii) How long does the 15:10 train stop for in Kilkenny MacDonagh?
(iii) What train(s) stops in Hazelhatch and Celbridge?
(iv) Which train travels from Dublin to Kildare fastest?
(v)   If Sean must be in Athy at 4:15 pm, what is the latest train he should take from Dublin Heuston?
(vi) Ann works in Newbridge on Saturday. She finishes work at 7:30 pm. If she lives in Carlow, can she take the train home after work? Justify your answer.

Practice questions 14·1

1. What is the most appropriate unit to measure each of the following?
   (i) The distance from Dublin to Cork
   (ii) The length of your fingernail
   (iii) The length of a table
   (iv) The time to cook a pizza
   (v) The length of the school day
   (vi) The time it takes to blink

2. Put these units of measure in order from smallest to largest on the line below:

   millimetres (mm)   metres (m)   kilometres (km)   centimetres (cm)

   smallest ←————————————————————————————————————→ largest

3. Convert the following units of distance and time into the unit shown in brackets beside the question.
   (i) 10 km (m)
   (ii) 500 cm (mm)
   (iii) 30 min (s)
   (iv) 3 600 s (hr)
   (v) 1 200 mm (m)
   (vi) 24 hr (min)

4. Convert the following times from hours and minutes to hours. Give your answers as decimals correct to two places.
   (i) 1 hour and 40 minutes
   (ii) 3 hours and 10 minutes
   (iii) 2 hours and 18 minutes
   (iv) 2 hours and 23 minutes

5. Convert these 12-hour times to 24-hour times.
   (i) 3:15 am
   (ii) 8:25 pm
   (iii) Midnight
   (iv) 2:55 pm
   (v) 1:27 am
   (vi) Noon

6. Convert these 24-hour times to 12-hour times.
   (i) 07:40
   (ii) 18:27
   (iii) 00:01
   (iv) 10:35
   (v) 19:54
   (vi) 05:56

7. Tracey caught the bus to work at 07:52 and arrived at her stop at 08:45. From there, it took her 11 minutes to walk to work.
   (i) How long was Tracey's bus journey?
   (ii) What time did Tracey arrive at work?

8. Part of the timetable for a bus from Cork to Shannon airport is shown. Study the timetable and answer the questions:

Station	Departure Time
Cork	07:35
Mallow	08:05
Charleville	08:30
Limerick	09:05
Shannon Airport	09:28

   (i) How long does it take to go from Cork to Mallow?
   (ii) How long does it take to go from Charleville to Limerick?
   (iii) How long does it take to go from Cork to Shannon airport?
   (iv) If the bus is delayed by 25 minutes and Ada has to check in for a flight 2 hours beforehand, will she make a flight at 11:30?

9. Study the train timetable shown and answer the following questions:

Athlone		08:55	10:55	13:55	15:55	17:55	19:55	21:55	23:55
Ballinasloe	07:00	09:22	11:22	14:22	16:22	18:22	20:22	22:22	00:22
Aughrim		09:35	11:35	14:35	16:35	18:35	20:35	22:35	00:35
Loughrea		09:50	11:50	14:50	16:50	18:50	20:50	22:50	00:50
Craughwell		10:05	12:05	15:05	17:05	19:05	21:05	23:05	01:05
Oranmore		10:15	12:15	15:15	17:15	19:15	21:15	23:15	01:15
Galway	07:45	10:25	12:25	15:25	17:25	19:25	21:25	23:25	01:25

   (i) You need to meet a friend for a coffee at Galway station at 1:45 pm. Which train from Athlone would you recommend taking? Justify your answer.
   (ii) What time should you leave Ballinasloe to get to Galway in the shortest possible time?
   (iii) If you arrive in Oranmore at 15:15 from Athlone, how long have you been travelling for?
   (iv) If you arrive in Galway at 19:25, what time did you leave Athlone?
   (v) You are delayed in Craughwell. If you arrive in Galway at 21:37 after a 23-minute train ride from Craughwell, how long was the delay in Craughwell?

Section B Moving forward

10. The table shows some of the flights leaving Dublin airport for London Heathrow on a particular day.

Departing		Arriving	
DUB	06:40	LHR	08:05
DUB	07:30	LHR	09:05
DUB	08:50	LHR	10:15
DUB	09:50	LHR	11:10
DUB	12:10	LHR	13:25
DUB	13:40	LHR	14:55
DUB	14:40	LHR	15:55
DUB	15:50	LHR	17:10

  (i) Stephen must be in London for a business meeting at 12:30 pm. The hotel where the meeting is being held is half an hour from Heathrow airport. What is the latest flight he can take from Dublin airport? Justify your answer with mathematical calculations.

  (ii) How long will Stephen's flight take?

  (iii) Stephen lives 45 minutes from Dublin airport. He would like to be at the airport 1 hour before his flight. What time will he have to leave his house to do this?

14·2 Speed

By the end of this section you should:
- understand that speed is a rate of change
- be able to use the speed formula to calculate speed, distance and time using correct units
- be able to use the ratio method to calculate speed, distance and time using correct units

A **rate of change** is a relationship between two quantities.

Speed is a rate of change, commonly used in everyday life. It is the rate of change of distance in relation to time.

Speed is the distance travelled per unit time.

$$\text{Average speed} = \frac{\text{distance travelled}}{\text{time taken}}$$

To calculate speed, we need to know the distance travelled and the time taken to travel this distance.

The units used to measure speed are a combination of the unit of distance and the unit of time.

If an object is travelling at 100 km/hr, this means that in 1 hour it would travel an average distance of 100 km, in 2 hours 200 km, and in half an hour 50 km.

We can be given any two of the three measurements: speed, distance or time, and asked to calculate the third measurement, so we need to remember three formulae to do this:

$$\text{Speed} = \frac{\text{distance}}{\text{time}} \qquad \text{Time} = \frac{\text{distance}}{\text{speed}} \qquad \text{Distance} = \text{speed} \times \text{time}$$

The most common units of speed are metres per second (m/s) and kilometres per hour (km/hr).

To help us remember these formulae we can use the **D**istance–**S**peed–**T**ime triangle.

Cover the measurement you are trying to find. For example, if we cover 'speed', we are left with distance over time. If we want to find a distance, we cover 'distance', we are left with speed × time.

Speed as a ratio

A **ratio** is a way of comparing numbers.

Speed can be written as the ratio of distance to time and is written as **distance : time**.

A speed of 80 km/hr can be written as a ratio in the form 80 : 1

Worked example 1

(i) Alex runs a 400 m race in a time of 50 seconds. What is his average speed?

(ii) Claire took part in a cross-country race and completed the course in 1 hour and 12 minutes. Her average speed for the race was 17·5 km per hour. What was the distance that she ran?

(iii) Jane runs at an average speed of 4 metres per second. How long will it take her to run a 3 000-metre race at this pace?

Solution

(i) Speed = $\frac{\text{distance}}{\text{time}} = \frac{400 \text{ m}}{50 \text{ s}} = 8$ m/s

(ii) Firstly, convert the minutes into hours:

$12 \div 60 = 0.2$ hours

Time = 1·2 hr   Speed = 17·5 km/hr

Distance = speed × time
= 17·5 × 1·2
= 21 km

(iii) Speed = 4 m/s and distance = 3 000 m

Time = $\frac{\text{distance}}{\text{speed}}$

Time = $\frac{3\,000}{4} = 750$ s

Convert 750 s into minutes and seconds

$750 \div 60 = 12.5$ minutes

= 12 minutes and 30 seconds

Worked example 2

Use the ratio method to calculate the speed of a journey of 45 km if it takes one and a half hours to complete.

Solution

Distance : Time

45 km : 1 hr 30 min

÷1·5 (45 km : 1·5 hours) ÷1·5
    (30 km : 1 hours)

Speed = 30 km/h

We want to find the distance travelled in 1 hour, so we divide both sides by 1·5.

We can also use the ratio method to find the time or distance.

Worked example 3

Find the time taken to complete a journey of 200 m at a speed of 40 m/s.

Solution

The speed is 40 m/s, which means that in 1 second the distance travelled is 40 m.

Distance : Time

×5 (40 m : 1 sec) ×5
   (200 m : 5 sec)

Time = 5 seconds

We are given a distance of 200 m, which is 5 times 40 m.

We must also multiply the time by 5, to find the time taken to cover 200 m.

Practice questions 14·2

1. John is travelling at a speed of 60 km/hr.
   (i) Explain in words what this means.
   (ii) If John continues to travel at this speed, how far will he travel in half an hour?
   (iii) John is 12 km away from his home. If he continues to travel at 60 km/hr, how long, in minutes, will it take him to reach his house?

2. Usain Bolt ran the 100 metre sprint in 9·58 seconds. Work out his average speed in metres per second. Give your answer correct to two decimal places.

3. A shark attacking a shoal of fish swims at a speed of 13 metres per second for half a minute. How far does the shark swim in this time?

4. Zach is late for class and is running down the corridor to the classroom at a speed of 2 m/s. The length of the corridor is 150 metres. How long will it take him to reach his classroom?

5. A truck leaves Dublin at 8:00 am and arrives in Belfast at 10:30 am. 
   If the distance is 140 km, what was the average speed of the truck?

6. Calculate the distance that you would travel if you drove for:
   (i) 6 hours and 15 minutes at 40 km/h
   (ii) 30 minutes at 33 km/h
   (iii) 45 minutes at 60 km/h
   (iv) 90 minutes at 45 km/h

7. How long do the following journeys take to complete?
   (i) 240 km at 60 km/h
   (ii) 60 km at 40 km/h
   (iii) 360 km at 30 km/h
   (iv) 253 km at 46 km/h

8. A lorry travels 320 km in four and a half hours. If it travels at a constant speed, how far, to the nearest kilometre, will it travel in …?
   (i) 1 hour
   (ii) 7 hours
   (iii) 5 hours and 13 minutes
   (iv) half an hour

9. Using the ratio method, calculate the speed of the following journeys.
   (i) 150 m in 20 s
   (ii) 48 km in 1 hr and a half
   (iii) 250 m in 15 s
   (iv) 60 km in 1 hr and 15 min
   (v) 1400 m in 1 min and 45 s
   (vi) 260 km in 2 hr and 30 min

10. Copy and complete the following table. Round your answers to two decimal places where necessary.

	Speed	Distance	Time
(i)	75 km/h	105 km	
(ii)	10 m/s		15 minutes
(iii)		36 km	20 minutes
(iv)	78 km/h		2 hours 10 minutes
(v)		800 m	3·5 minutes
(vi)	50 m/s	320 m	

11. A standard (or Olympic) triathlon race involves 1 500 m of swimming, followed by a 40 km cycle, and finally a 10 km run. If Áine took 20 minutes for the swim, 55 minutes for the cycle and 35 minutes for the run, what was her average speed, in km/hr, throughout the event? Give your answer to two decimal places.

12. Michael swims 10 lengths of a 50 m pool in 8 minutes. He rests for 10 minutes and then swims a further 15 lengths at 68 seconds per length. 
    What is his average speed, in m/s, correct to two decimal places, for …?
    (i) the first 10 lengths
    (ii) the last 15 lengths

13. A family are travelling in a car at a steady speed of 85 km/h, and have covered 120 km since they left home at 10:00 am. They plan to have lunch at the next town, which is 220 km from home.
    At what time, to the nearest minute, will they have lunch?

220 Linking Thinking 1

Taking it FURTHER

14. Dublin's port tunnel has a length of 4·5 km and runs from Dublin port to the M50 motorway. The speed limit inside the tunnel is 80 km/h.

    A traffic management system takes a photo of a vehicle when it enters the tunnel and when it leaves the tunnel. The time a driver takes to make it between the two points is used to determine if they have been speeding.

    The table below shows the entry and exit times for three vehicles. Did any of these vehicles break the speed limit?

Vehicle	Time of entry	Time of exit
A	08:22	08:26
B	13:48	13:51
C	18:05	18:08

14·3 Rate of change graphs

By the end of this section you should:
- be able to draw distance/time graphs and tables
- be able to use the distance/time graphs and tables to calculate speed
- understand that the relationship between distance and time is proportional for a constant speed
- understand that speed is a rate of change
- understand the steeper the line the greater the rate of change
- be able to tell the story of a distance/time graph
- understand and tell the story of other rate of change graphs

Distance/time graphs

Discuss and discover

Work with the person beside you to consider the table below. It shows the distance of an object from a start point over a period of time. Use it to answer the following questions:

Time (s)	0	1	2	3	4	5	6	7	8
Distance from start (m)	0	10	20	30	40	50	60	70	80

(i) Do you notice a pattern in the table?
(ii) What happens for every 1 second increase in time?
(iii) Is this constant across the 8 seconds?
(iv) How could you describe the speed of the object?
(v) Use the speed formula to calculate the speed of the object at 2, 4 and 6 seconds. What do you notice? What does this tell you about the speed of the object?
(vi) Draw a graph to represent the distance travelled by the object against time. What does the graph look like? What is the rate of change of the graph?
(vii) What is the slope of the graph? What do you notice about the rate of change, the slope of the graph and the speed of the object?

We were introduced to linear patterns, rate of change and slope in Section A, Unit 7.

Having completed the activity above, we can see that when the rate of change remains the same the graph will always be a straight line. This type of pattern is called a **linear pattern**.

> A **linear pattern** is one in which the rate of change remains constant.

When we calculated the speed for this data, we saw that it was 10 m/s. The rate of change is also 10.

Therefore, for a distance/time graph the **rate of change is equal to the speed**.

In addition, we can see that as the time spent travelling increases, the distance travelled will also increase.

This type of relationship is called a **directly proportional relationship**.

> A **directly proportional** relationship exists between two variables when they both begin at 0 and then as one measurement increases the other one also increases.

The **graph** of a **directly proportional relationship always goes through (0, 0)**.

This type of graph will always form a straight line because distance travelled is **directly proportional** to the time spent travelling. The more time you spend travelling the greater the distance you will travel.

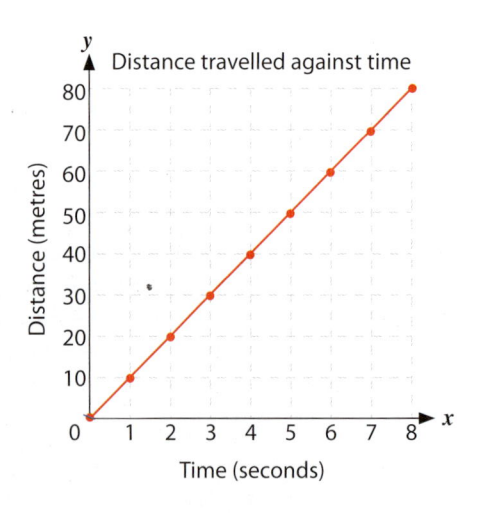

Discuss and discover

Can you think of any other proportional relationships?
(Hint: Numbers of hours worked is directly proportional to the money earned by a worker.)

Now consider measuring the distance of a second object over the same time. The results are shown in the table below.

Time (s)	0	1	2	3	4	5	6	7	8
Distance from start (m)	0	20	40	60	80	100	120	140	160

For every 1-second increase in time, there is a 20-metre increase in the distance travelled. This increase stays constant during the 8 seconds recorded. We can therefore say that the object is travelling at a constant speed of 20 m/s.

If we calculate the speed using the distance/time formula for this object: 80 ÷ 4 = 20 m/s

We see that this object is moving faster than the first one. It has covered the same distance in a shorter time.

Let's look at the graph for this object (shown in blue).

Notice that the graph is still a straight line.

The rate of change is 20. For every 1 unit across, the graph goes up 20.

The speed is 20 m/s.

We can also see the line is much steeper than the red graph above.

The steepness of the line is referred to as the **slope** of the line.

The slope of the line is determined by the rate of change.

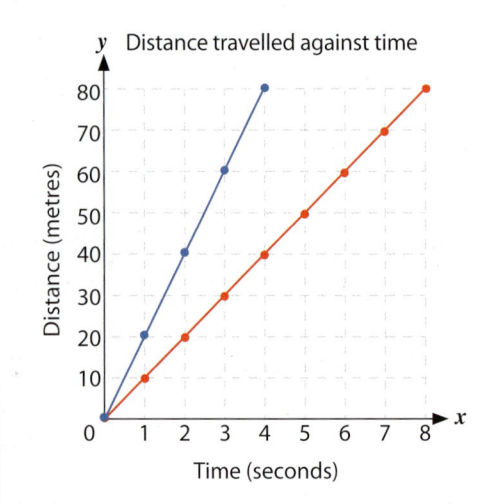

> **Slope = rate of change**
>
> The steeper the line, the greater the slope and hence the greater the rate of change.
>
> A horizontal line has a slope of zero and hence no rate of change.

222 Linking Thinking 1

For distance/time graphs, the rate of change or slope of the line is the speed.

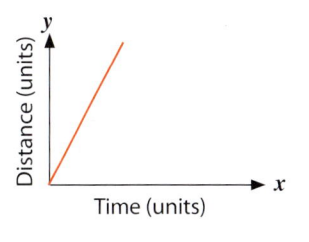

A steep line indicates a fast speed

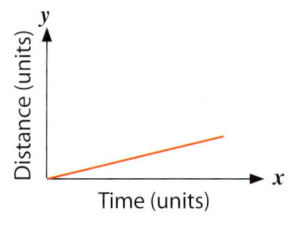

A shallow line indicates a slow speed

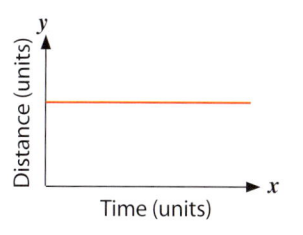

A flat line indicates zero speed; the object is stationary

Up to now, we have looked at objects travelling at a constant speed.
In reality, it is unlikely that an object will complete its entire journey at the same speed.
When driving a car, for example, there are different speed limits. The car might change speed if it is stuck in a traffic jam, going up a hill or if the driver stops at a shop.

Discuss and discover

Charlie goes for a cycle on a Saturday afternoon. The graph here tells the story of his journey. Working with the person beside you, use the graph to answer the questions:

(i) How far does Charlie cycle?
(ii) How long does it take Charlie to reach D?
(iii) Explain what is happening between B and C.
(iv) Does Charlie cycle faster from A to B or from C to D? Justify your answer.
(v) For how long is Charlie actually cycling?
(vi) At D Charlie decides to return home. After 15 minutes of cycling, he feels really tired and decides to take a break at point E. He is now 3 km from home. Mark point E on the graph.

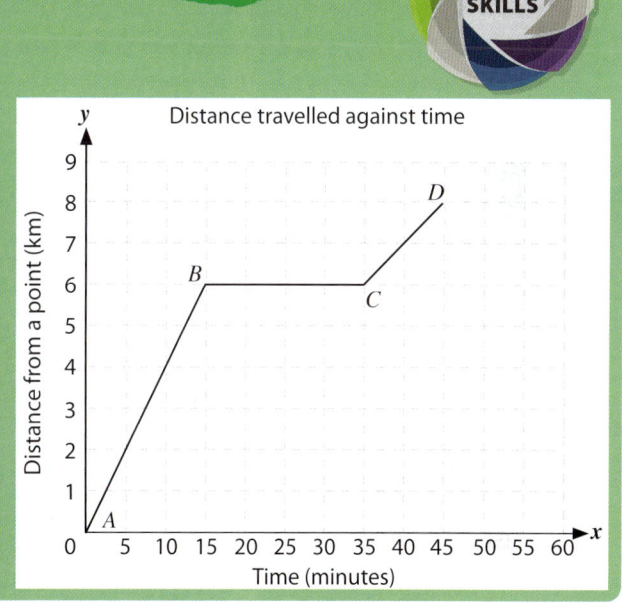

Main points to remember for distance/time graphs

- The vertical axis represents the distance travelled from the starting point.
- The higher up the point is the further it is from the starting point, and the lower it is the nearer to the starting point.
- The horizontal axis represents time.
- The closer to the left the point is, the less time has elapsed. The further right it is, the more time has elapsed.
- A straight slanted line represents a constant or steady speed.
- The steeper the line the faster the speed.
- A line sloping upwards is moving away from the starting point.
- A line sloping downwards is moving back towards the starting point.
- A straight horizontal line in the graph means the object is stopped (stationary).
- When the object is stationary, the speed is zero.

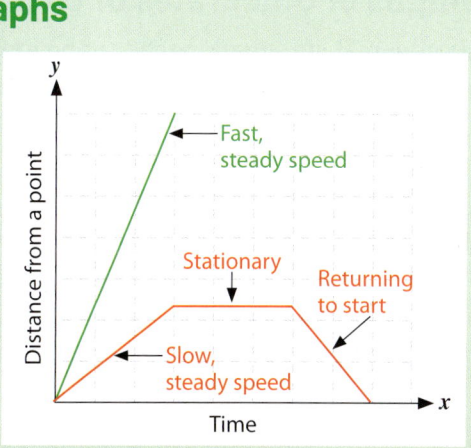

Section B Moving forward 223

Worked example 1

Match each distance/time graph with its correct description:

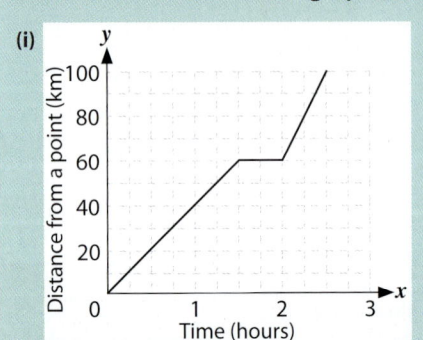

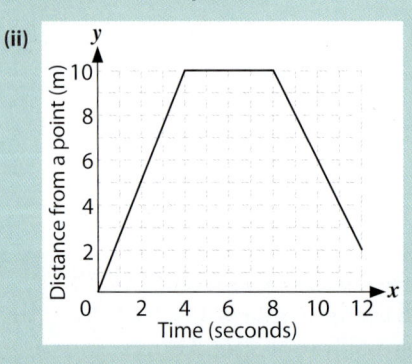

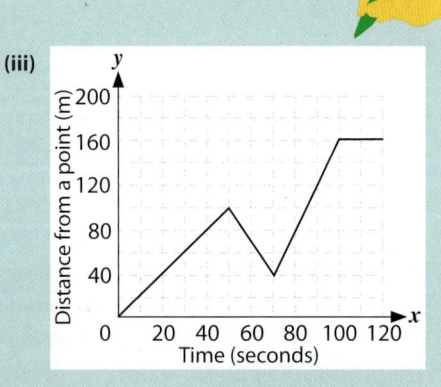

(i) [Graph: Distance from a point (km) vs Time (hours), showing line from 0 rising to 60 km at 1.5 hours, horizontal to 2 hours, then rising to 100 km at 3 hours]

(ii) [Graph: Distance from a point (m) vs Time (seconds), showing line rising from 0 to 10 m at about 4 seconds, horizontal to 8 seconds, then falling to 2 m at 12 seconds]

(iii) [Graph: Distance from a point (m) vs Time (seconds), showing line rising to about 100 m at 50 seconds, falling to 40 m, rising to 160 m at about 100 seconds, then horizontal to 120 seconds]

A   A small child cycles her bike 10 metres along the footpath. She stops for 4 seconds then turns around and cycles back towards her house. Two metres from home she falls off her bike.

B   John left home walking at a moderate speed. He realised that he forgot his phone and turned around to go home to get it. On the way back, he realised it was in his pocket, so he turned around to head back to his friend's house. He walked a bit faster to help make up some lost time. When he got to his friend's house, he stayed to watch a movie.

C   A bus leaves Kilkenny station at 9:00 am and reaches Wexford station at 10:30 am. It stops here for half an hour. It then continues for 30 minutes, reaching Gorey 40 km later.

Solution

(i) goes with description **C**

Reasons: the bus travels for one and a half hours; it stops (horizontal line) for half an hour; it travels a further 40 km in the next 30 minutes.

(ii) goes with description **A**

Reasons: the child travels 10 m; she turns and starts to head back to home; she stops 2 m from home.

(iii) goes with description **B**

Reasons: John is moving away from the starting position, but then after 50 seconds he heads back towards the starting position. Before getting back to the start, John turns back around and heads away at a greater pace than before. The graph ends with a straight line, showing that John was stopped in the one position for some time (watching a movie).

Graphs of other rates of change

Another real-life situation that can be modelled using rate of change graphs is filling (or emptying) a container with a liquid. In this case, we would plot the depth of the liquid against time.

Consider the container shown, which is being filled at a steady rate. After 2 seconds, the depth of the water is 1 cm, after 4 seconds the depth is 2 cm, etc. The graph shows what happens over 8 seconds.

Now consider what happens if the width of the container is changed.

If the width of the container is narrower, the depth of the water will increase faster. Since the line represents the rate of change (slope) of depth, it will be steeper.

If the width of the container is wider, the depth of the water will increase more slowly. Since the line represents the rate of change (slope) of depth, it will be less steep.

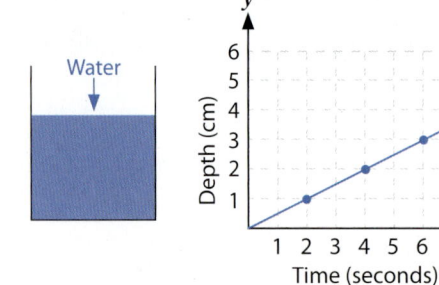

> The points lie in a straight line, as long as the flow of the liquid is steady.

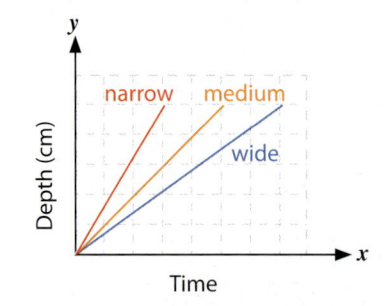

Linking Thinking 1

Worked example 2

Draw a depth/time graph to represent water filling the container shown at a steady rate.

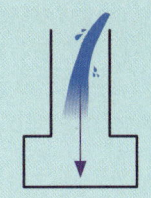

Solution

The container suddenly changes from wide to narrow. The water fills the wider part first. Since this part is wider the slope of the line will be less steep.

When the water reaches the narrower part the container fills up faster and the slope of the line is steeper. This produces a graph as shown.

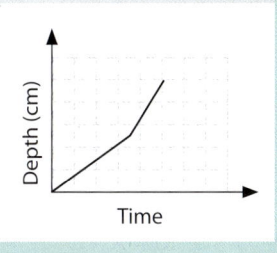

Practice questions 14.3

1. Explain each of the following terms in your own words.
   (i) rate of change
   (ii) linear pattern
   (iii) directly proportional
   (iv) slope of a line

2. A cruise ship is travelling at a constant speed of 30 km/hr. The graph shown represents the first four hours of its journey.
   Use the graph to answer the questions below.

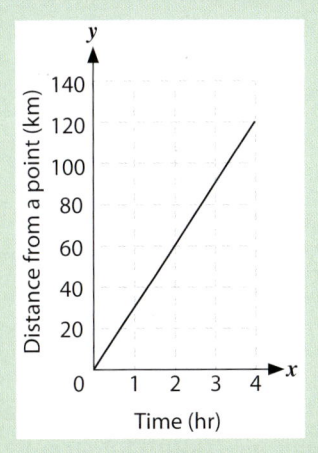

   (a) How far will the ship travel in ...?
      (i) 2 hours
      (ii) 3 and a half hours
   (b) How long would it take the ship to travel ...?
      (i) 90 km
      (ii) 45 km

3. Calculate the speed for each of the following graphs.
   (i)
   (ii)
   (iii) 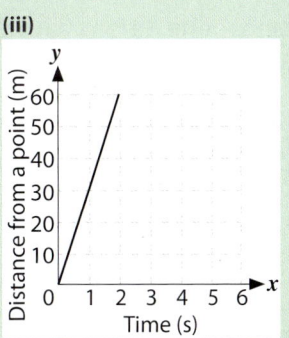
   (iv)

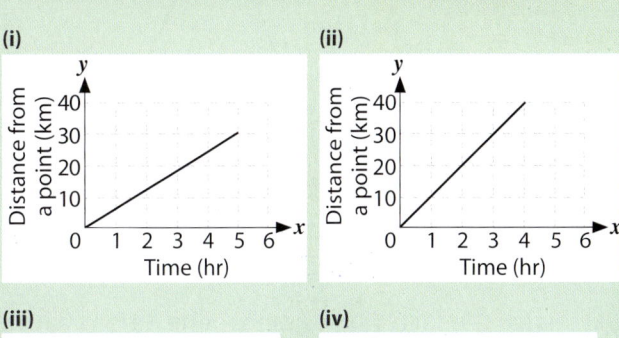

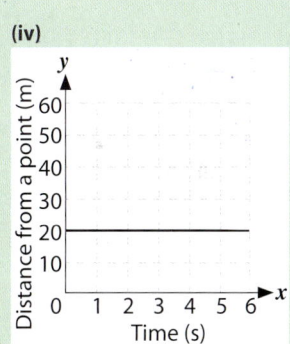

4. The graph on the right shows the distance travelled by objects A, B, C over a period of time. Rank the objects in order from fastest to slowest. Justify your answer.

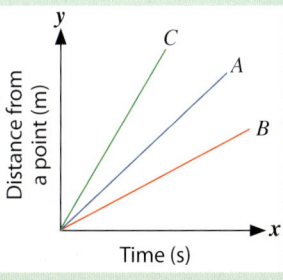

5. The graph shown represents a certain car journey. Study the graph and answer the questions.
   (i) Which part of the graph shows that the car is stopped at traffic lights? Given a reason for your answer.
   (ii) Which part of the graph represents the fastest speed? Explain your choice.

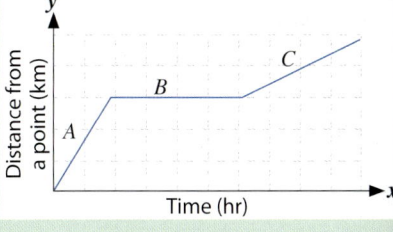

Section B Moving forward

6. Match the following distance/time graphs with their description.

   (i) [Graph: triangular peak — Distance from a point vs Time]

   (ii) [Graph: straight line increasing — Distance from a point vs Time]

   (iii) [Graph: horizontal line — Distance from a point vs Time]

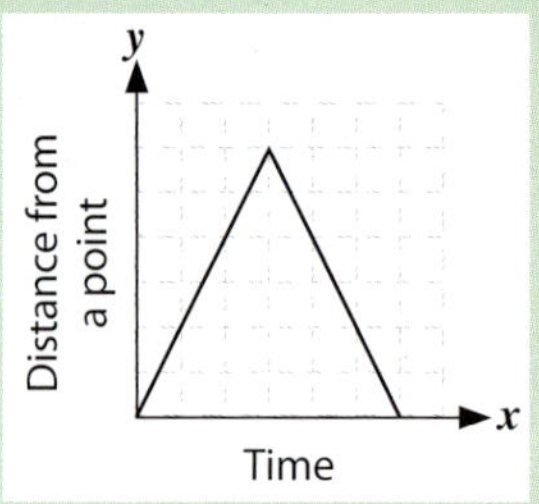

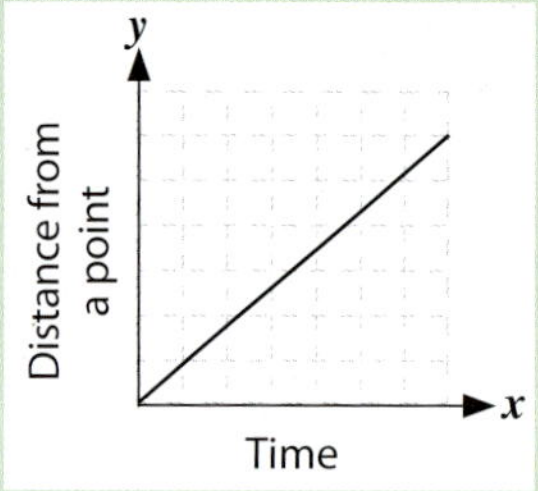

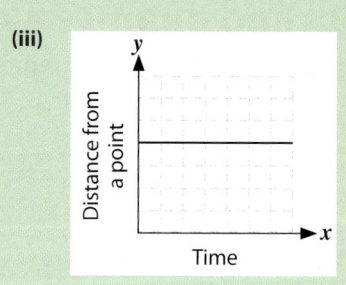

   A A car remains parked all day in a carpark.

   B An athlete sprints at a constant speed to the end of a track, turns and sprints back to the start at the same speed.

   C A racing car travels away from the starting line at a steady speed.

7. Describe what happens at each section on the following graphs:

   (i) [Graph with points A, B, C, D, E, F — Distance from a point (m) vs Time (s)]

   (ii) [Graph with points O, A, B, C, D, E, F — Distance from a point (m) vs Time (s)]

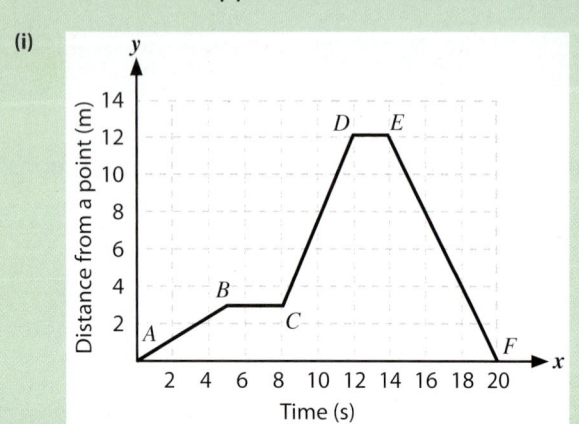

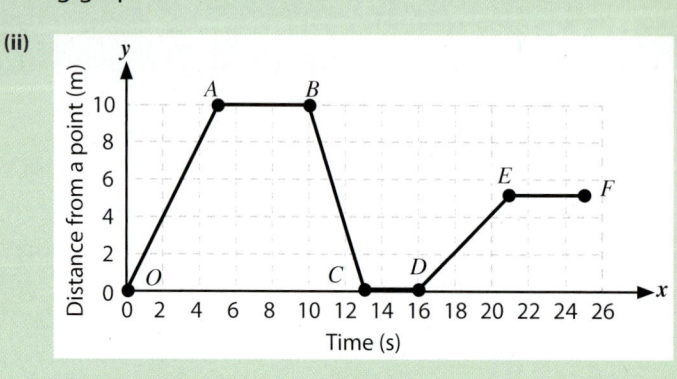

8. Match the following distance/time graphs with their description:

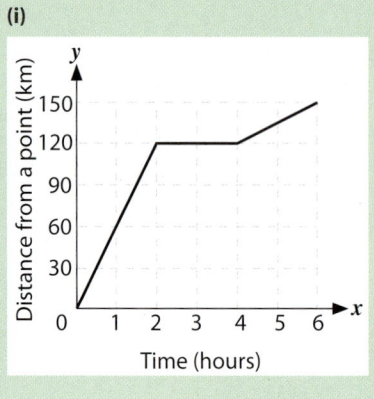

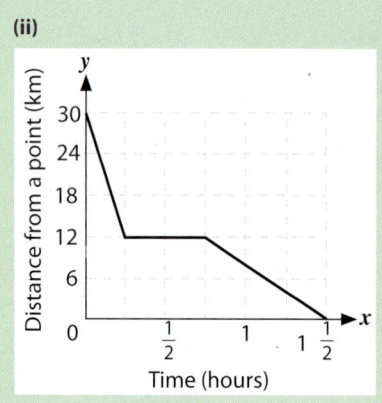

   (i) [Graph — Distance from a point (km) vs Time (hours), y-axis 0–150]

   (ii) [Graph — Distance from a point (km) vs Time (hours), y-axis 0–30]

   (iii) [Graph — Distance from a point (km) vs Time (min), y-axis 0–10]

   (iv) [Graph — Distance from a point (km) vs Time (min), y-axis 0–60]

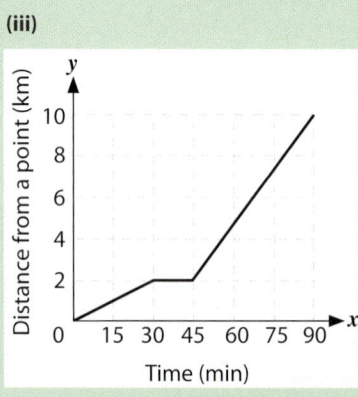

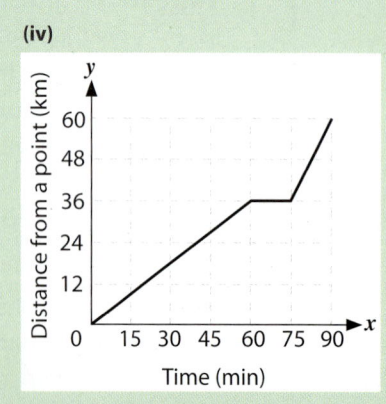

   A A cyclist cycles downhill towards home for 15 minutes. At the bottom of the hill she stops for a coffee. She then continues uphill towards home for the remaining 12 km.

   B A motorbike rider rides for 36 km at a steady speed. She stops to read the map for 15 minutes then rides for the remaining 24 km at 96 km/h.

   C A man travels at 60 km/h for 2 hours. He stops to have lunch for 2 hours, then travels in heavy traffic at 15 km/h for 30 km.

   D Tony walked slowly along the road, stopped to chat to a neighbour and looked at his watch, realised he was late, and then started running.

9. Match the containers shown to the graph representing the change in depth over time as it is filled. Explain why you chose each graph.

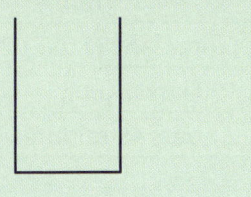

   (i)   (ii) 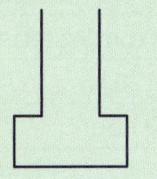   (iii)

   A 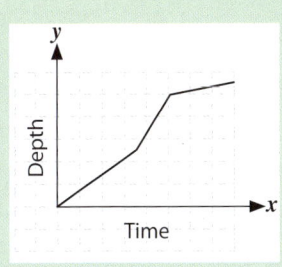   B 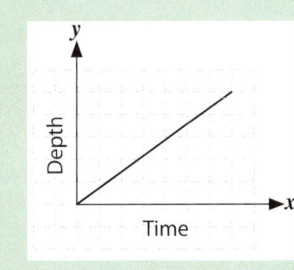   C

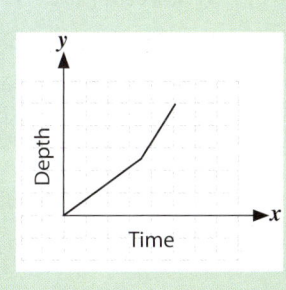

10. Draw a distance/time graph to represent the following situation.

    A driver gets into his car. He drives out of the car park, covering 25 metres in 5 seconds. Now on the main road, he travels 240 metres in 8 seconds. As the driver approaches traffic lights, he slows down over 3 seconds, covering 35 metres. He comes to a complete stop. He waits at the traffic lights for 4 seconds.

11. The container shown is filled with water at a steady rate of flow.
    Sketch a depth/time graph to represent the change in depth over time as the container is filled.

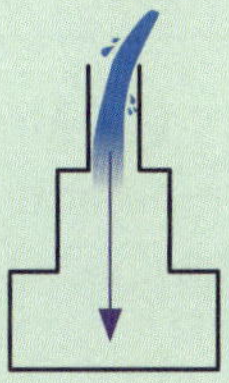

12. Katie walks from her house to her friend's house which is 3 km away. This takes her 25 minutes. When she gets there, she must wait for 15 minutes for her friend to get ready. Then they walk to school which is a further 1 km from her friend's house. This takes them 10 minutes.
    Draw a distance/time graph for this journey.

13. Denis is carrying out an experiment which involves liquid being added to and removed from a test tube. The graph shown represents the change in depth of the liquid over time. Match the different sections of the graph to the statements given.

    (i)   Some liquid is poured out quickly
    (ii) The test tube is emptied
    (iii) Liquid is added slowly
    (iv) The level of the liquid stays constant
    (v)   Liquid is added quickly

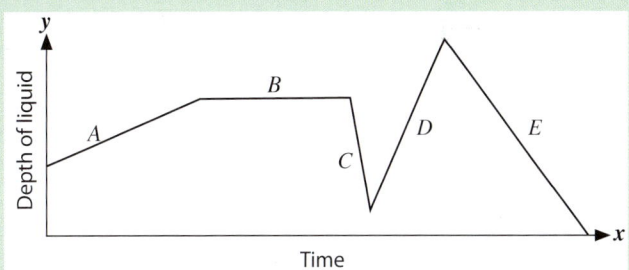

Revision questions

14A Core skills

1. Convert the following lengths of time into the units shown in brackets in each case.

   (i) 513 minutes (hours and minutes)
   (ii) 2 hours and 12 minutes (minutes)
   (iii) 1 week (hours)
   (iv) 90 minutes (seconds)

2. Use the table to work out the answers to the following questions:

	Train A	Train B	Train C
Journey	From Cork to Dublin	From Waterford to Dublin	From Galway to Dublin
Distance	220 km	170 km	190 km
Time taken	2·5 hours	2 hours	2 hours 45 minutes

   (i) Which train has the highest average speed?

   (ii) If train B continued at the same speed, how far would it travel in 4 hours?

   (iii) If train A continued at the same speed, how long would it take to travel another 120 km?

   (iv) What does the speed tell us about an object? Use the words 'time' and 'distance' in your answer.

3. The table shows the winning times for different races.

Athlete	Race	Time (s)	Speed (m/s)
A	1 000 m	250	
B	400 m	70	
C	100 m	13	
D	200 m	25	
E	800 m	150	

   Copy and complete the table by calculating the average speed, correct to one decimal place, for each athlete.

4. Peter travels 1 080 km in an airplane. For half of the distance the airplane flies at a speed of 920 km/h, and for the remainder of the distance it flies at a speed of 880 km/h.
   How long, in hours and minutes, does the trip take?

5. Jake and Billy leave their home at the same time. Jake has 60 km to travel and drives at 40 km/h. Billy has 80 km to travel and also drives at 40 km/h.

   (i) How long does Jake's journey take, in hours and minutes?

   (ii) How much longer does Billy spend driving than Jake?

6. The graph shown represents the change in depth over time as two different containers are filled.
   Which line, A or B, represents each of the following containers? Justify your answer.

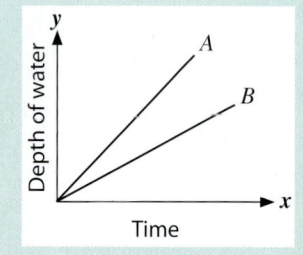

   (i)   (ii)

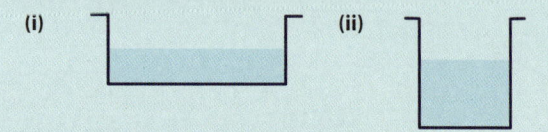

7. The graph shows how Tom's distance from home varies with time, when he visits Ian and returns home.

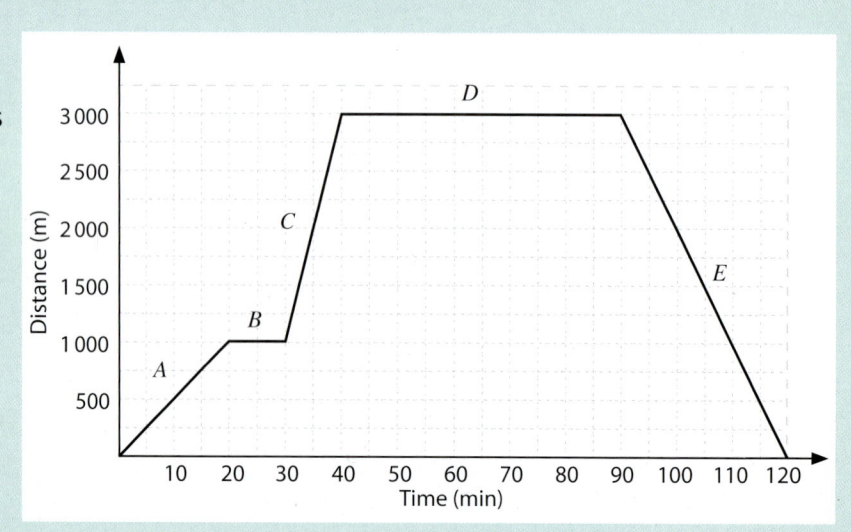

   (i) For how long does Tom stop on the way to Ian's?

   (ii) How far is it from Tom's home to Ian's?

   (iii) How long does Tom spend at Ian's?

   (iv) On which part of the journey does Tom travel the fastest? Justify your answer.

228 Linking Thinking 1

8. The distance/time graph shown is for a 3 000 m cross-country race, run by Rachel and James.

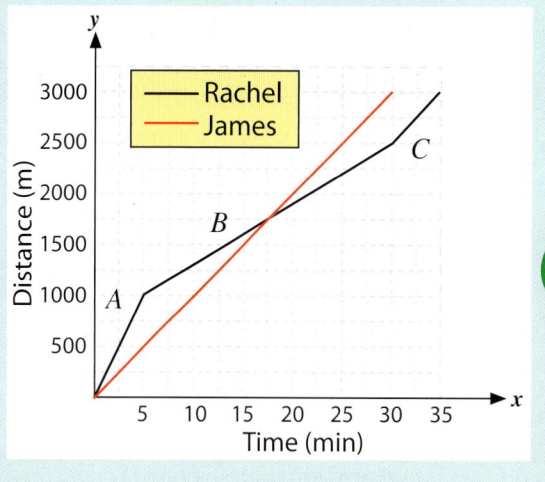

   (i) Describe how James runs the race.
   (ii) Describe how Rachel runs the race.
   (iii) When, and how far from the start, does James catch up with Rachel?
   (iv) Calculate the average speed at which James runs.
   (v) Calculate the average speeds at which Rachel runs in sections A, B, and C.
   (vi) Who wins the race?

9. The graph shown represents the changes in depth of water over time while Audrey takes a bath. Using the statements below, match the correct number to the correct letter, to tell the story of the graph.

   (i) Audrey gets into the bath
   (ii) Audrey turns off the cold tap
   (iii) Audrey relaxes in the bath
   (iv) Audrey pulls the bath plug
   (v) Audrey turns on the hot and cold taps
   (vi) Audrey turns off the hot tap and gets undressed
   (vii) Audrey gets out of the bath

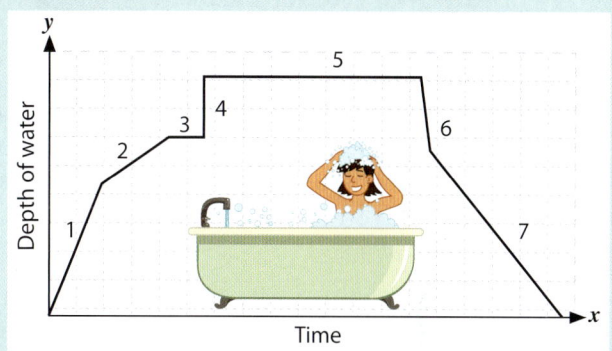

10. Joelle drives from home to her sister's house, which is 100 km away. This takes her 1 hour. She stays with her sister for half an hour.
    She then leaves and goes to her brother's apartment, which is a further 50 km away. This takes her 45 minutes. She spends 45 minutes with her brother and then returns home in an hour and a half.

    (i) Draw a distance/time graph to show this journey.
    (ii) On which part of the journey is Joelle's speed the slowest? Justify your answer.

14B Taking it FURTHER

1. A minibus drives 30 km with a constant speed of 120 km/h and a further 56 km with a constant speed of 48 km/h. 
   How much time, in hours and minutes, in total does it take the minibus to travel these distances?

2. Tadgh is travelling in his mother's car at 100 km/h to make it to school on time. He must be in school in 15 minutes or he will be late. He has 16 km to travel.
   Will he make it to school on time? Justify your answer.

3. Bob's airplane trip took 1 hour 24 minutes. For one-third of that time, the airplane flew at a speed of 600 km/h, and for the rest of the time, it flew at a speed of 792 km/h.
   What distance did Bob travel?

4. Some of the statements below are true and some are false. Decide which ones are true and which ones are false. Justify your answers.

   A Jason runs 5 km in 30 minutes. Donna runs 9 km in 60 minutes. They have the same average speed.

   B Rachel is driving in an area where the speed limit is 50 km/h. She travels 10 km in 10 minutes. She has broken the speed limit.

   C James runs one lap of the athletics track in 4 minutes. Paula runs one lap of the same track in 3 minutes. James is going faster than Paula.

   D A car that travels 60 km in 45 minutes is going faster than a car that travels 400 m in 12 s.

   E A train travels at an average speed of 150 km/h. It could have travelled faster than 150 km/h for part of the time.

5. Ger drove from Dublin to Cork. It took him 2 hours and 45 minutes at an average speed of 110 km/h. Lyn also drove from Dublin to Cork. She took 3 hours and 15 minutes.
   Assuming that Lyn drove along the same roads as Ger and did not take a break:
   (i) Work out Lyn's average speed, to the nearest km/h, from Dublin to Cork.
   (ii) If Lyn did not drive along the same roads as Ger, explain how this could affect your answer to part (i).

6. (i) At 9 am, Brandon left home on his bicycle. From 9 am to 9:36 am, he cycled at an average speed of 15 km/h. From 9:36 am to 10:45 am, he cycled a further 8 km. 
   Calculate his average speed for the entire journey above. Give your answer to one decimal place.
   (ii) From 10:45 am to 11 am, Brandon cycled at an average speed of 18 km/h.
   Find the distance Brandon cycled from 10:45 am to 11 am.

7. A train travels for 0·4 hours with a constant speed of 81 km/h and then for another 40 minutes with a constant speed of 36 km/h. 
   What is its average speed for the total trip? Give your answer correct to one decimal place.

8. Laura drives for 3 hours at 44 km/h. Clare drives 144 km in 4 hours. 
   (i) Who travels the greater distance?
   (ii) Who travels at a lower average speed?
   (iii) How far would Laura travel if she drove for 3 hours at the same speed as Clare?

9. The distance/time graph below shows a 1000-metre race.

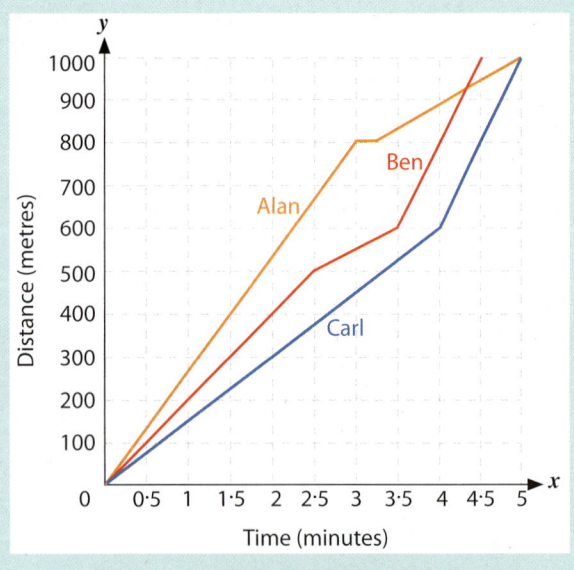

   (i) Who won the race? Justify your answer.
   (ii) Tell the story of the race. Make sure to include as much detail as possible and to refer to each of the runners.
   Use evidence from the graph to justify all statements made.

10. A conical vase is filled with water. The image below shows the shape of the vase and the depth/time graph representing the changes in depth as it is filled.

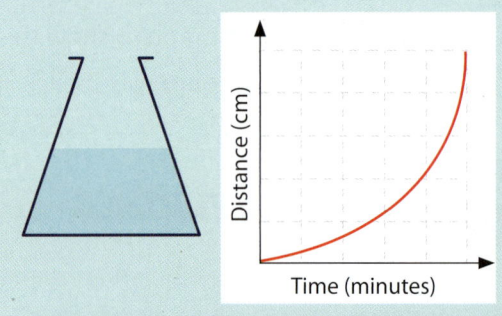

    (i) Explain why the graph is not a straight line by referring to the width of the vase and the effect this will have on the rate of change (slope).
    (ii) Draw a depth/time graph to represent the change in depth over time as the vase shown on the right is filled.

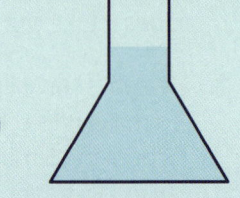

Now that you have completed the unit, revisit the

Something to think about ...

question posed at the start of this unit.

Now try questions 1 and 6 on pages 403–5

Unit 15

Polygons

Topics covered within this unit:
- 15·1 Introduction
- 15·2 Introduction to triangles
- 15·3 Constructing triangles using angles and sides
- 15·4 Types of triangles and area of triangles
- 15·5 Right-angled triangles
- 15·6 Interior and exterior angles in triangles

The Learning Outcomes covered in this unit are contained in the following sections:
GT.1 | GT.2a | GT.2c | GT.3a | GT.3b

Key words
Polygon
Quadrilateral
Triangle
Isosceles triangle
Scalene triangle
Equilateral triangle
Included angle
Included side
Right-angled triangle
Hypotenuse
Exterior angle
Interior angle

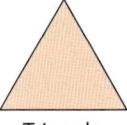

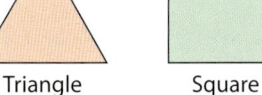

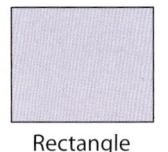

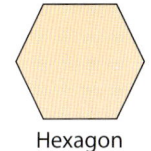

Something to think about ...

KEY SKILLS

A right angle is equal to 90°.

It has been suggested that the technique for the construction of a 'right angle by stretched rope', may have been used by the ancient Egyptians to survey their fields.

This technique involved a rope knotted at regular intervals, so that there are 12 equal segments.

Using this 'rope', sketch a 2D shape with:
- four sides and with two pairs of sides with different lengths
- four sides and four equal sides
- three sides which are all equal in length
- three sides where only two sides are equal in length
- three sides where no two sides are equal in length
- three sides and with one 90° internal angle

15·1 Introduction

By the end of this section you should:
- understand the terms: polygon, quadrilateral, rectangle and square
- understand the principle of area and the principle of perimeter
- be able to construct a rectangle

Polygons

A **polygon** is any two-dimensional shape formed with straight lines.

Polygons are many-sided figures, with sides that are line segments. Polygons are named according to the number of sides and angles they have. We have already met some polygons, but now we will examine them in more detail.

Side: any line segment which makes up the polygon.

Vertex: the end points where two sides meet (plural is **vertices**).

Adjacent sides: sides that meet.

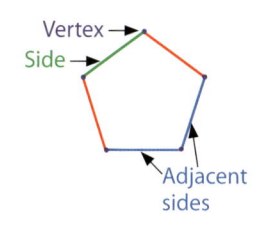

Triangle Square Rectangle Hexagon

Vertex
Side
Adjacent sides

Section B **Moving forward**   231

Quadrilaterals

> **A quadrilateral has four sides.** It is two-dimensional (a flat shape), closed (the lines join up), and has straight sides.

Examples of quadrilaterals include:

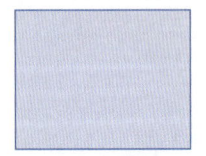

Perimeter is the distance around a two-dimensional shape.

It helps to imagine starting at a vertex and finding the distance to walk around the outside of the 2D shape.

Units: centimetres (cm) and metres (m)

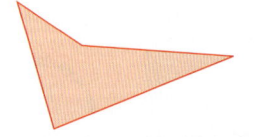

Area is the size of a surface.

It helps to imagine how much paint would cover the shape.

Units: centimetres squared (cm^2) and metres squared (m^2)

Square
Four sides are equal
Opposite sides are parallel
All angles are right angles (90°)

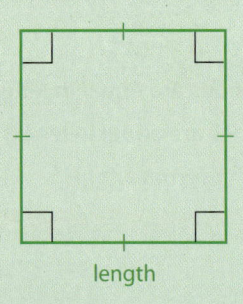

length

Perimeter = length + length + length + length
= 4(length)

Area = length × length

Has **four axes of symmetry**

Rectangle
Opposite sides (red sides, blue sides) are equal
Opposite sides are parallel
All angles are right angles (90°)

width
length

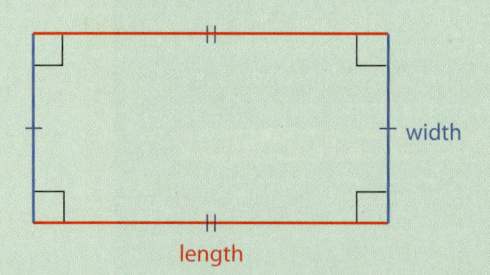

Perimeter = length + width + length + width
= 2(length) + 2(width)

Area = length × width

Has two **axes of symmetry**

Labelling a rectangle using the vertices

When labeling a rectangle, e.g. $ABCD$, the letters must follow around the outside of the figure, in order. You can go clockwise or anti-clockwise, and you may start at any vertex point.

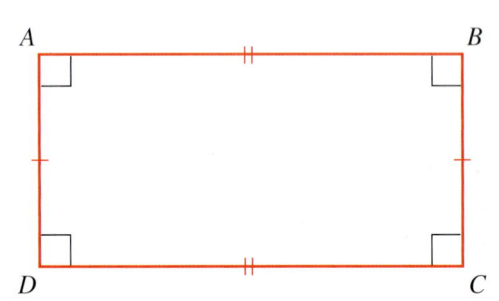

The length of the line between A and B is shown as $|AB|$

The length of the line between B and C is shown as $|BC|$

Construct a rectangle given the side lengths

Construct rectangle $ABCD$, $|AB|$ = 10 cm, $|BC|$ = 5 cm.

1 Always draw a rough sketch for construction of any 2D shape.

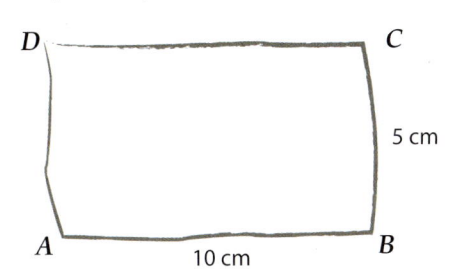

2 Draw line segment $[AB]$ of length 10 cm.

3 Draw a ray at A, perpendicular to the line segment $[AB]$.

4 With the point of the compass on A and compass width equal to 5 cm, draw an arc on the ray drawn in step 2. Label this point D.

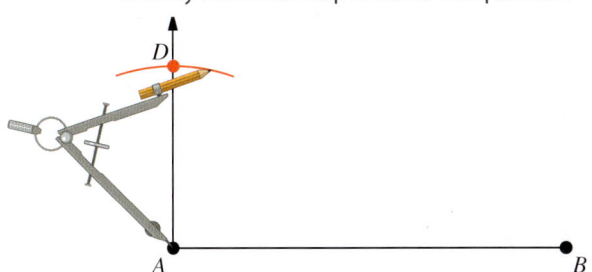

5 Repeat steps 3 and 4 at B and mark the point C.

6 Join C to D to produce the required rectangle.

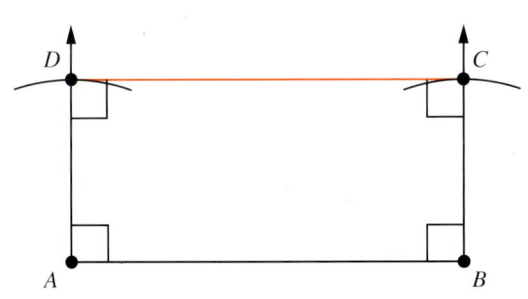

Mark in the right angles using the symbol ☐ or ∟

Worked example 1

Find (i) the perimeter and (ii) the area of the square on the right with side length $|AB|$ = 6 cm

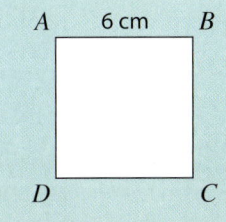

Solution

(i) Perimeter = length + length + length + length
Perimeter = 6 cm + 6 cm + 6 cm + 6 cm
= 4 × 6 cm
= 24 cm

(ii) Area = length × length
Area = (6 cm)(6 cm)
= 36 cm²

Worked example 2

Find (i) the perimeter and (ii) the area of the rectangle $WXYZ$, shown with side length $|WX| = 12$ cm and side length $|XY| = 8$ cm

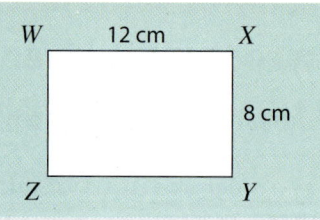

Solution

(i) Perimeter = length + width + length + width
Perimeter = 12 + 8 + 12 + 8
= 40 cm

(ii) Area = length × width
Area = 8 × 12
= 96 cm²

Practice questions 15·1

1. On the right is a sketch of a polygon. 
   (i) How many sides does the polygon have?
   (ii) Name the blue, green and red coloured parts of the polygon.

2. State if the following 2D shapes are polygons, quadrilaterals, both or neither.
   (i)   (ii)   (iii)
   (iv) (v)   (vi)

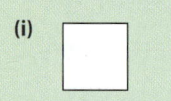

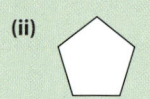

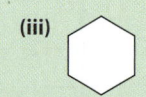

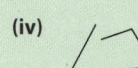

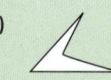

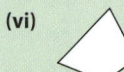

3. Construct rectangle $ABCD$, which has the length and width shown in the rough sketch below.
   (7 cm by 11 cm)

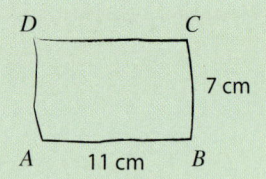

4. A bedroom is 3 m by 3 m. How many square metres of carpet is needed to cover the floor of the room?

5. A bedroom is 2·6 m by 2·8 m. How many square metres of carpet is needed to cover the floor of the room?

6. Construct rectangle $ABCD$, where $|AB| = 12$ cm, $|BC| = 6$ cm

7. Construct rectangle $MNOP$, where $|MN| = 10·5$ cm, $|NO| = 7·5$ cm

8. (i) Construct rectangle $XYWZ$, where $|XY| = 125$ mm, $|YW| = 80$ mm
   (ii) Find the perimeter of this rectangle.

9. (i) Construct rectangle $ABCD$, where $|AB| = 10$ cm, $|BC| = 5$ cm
   (ii) Find the perimeter of this rectangle.
   (iii) Find the area of this rectangle.

10. For each of the following, find (a) the area (b) the perimeter and (c) the type of quadrilateral.
    (i) 8 cm by 3 cm
    (ii) 3 cm by 3 cm
    (iii) 30 cm by 10 cm
    (iv) 8 cm by 4 cm
    (v) 25 cm by 1 cm
    (vi) 1 cm by 1 cm

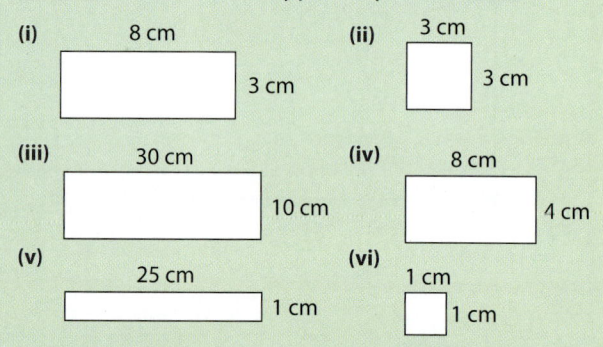

11. A rectangular field is 124 m by 110 m. What is the area of the field in square metres?

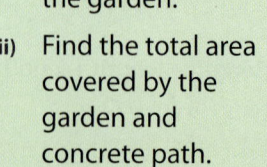

12. A concrete path 2 m wide surrounds a garden which is 40 m by 55 m as shown in the diagram below.
    (i) Find the area covered by the garden.
    (ii) Find the total area covered by the garden and concrete path. 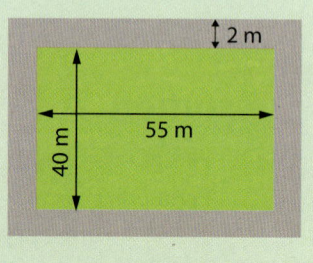
    (iii) Find the area covered by the concrete path.
    (iv) Using an appropriate scale, draw a scale diagram of this concrete path and garden.

Linking Thinking 1

13. A kitchen floor is covered in tiles; there is no space between the tiles. Each rectangular tile is 20 cm in width and 30 cm in length. Using the diagram below to count the tiles, find the area of floor covered by the tiles.

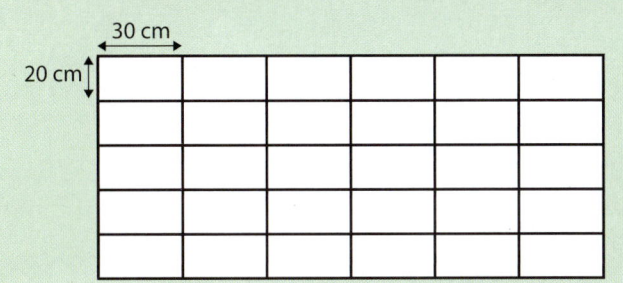

Taking it FURTHER

14. A rectangle has a perimeter of 320 m and its length is three times its width. Find the measure of:

(i) the length and width of the rectangle
(ii) the area of the rectangle.

15·2 Introduction to triangles

By the end of this section you should be able to:
- identify the parts of a triangle
- construct a triangle given the lengths of the three sides

A **triangle** is a polygon that has three sides and three angles.

Construct a triangle, given the lengths of the three sides

1 Draw a rough sketch of the triangle to be constructed. Include all given information in your sketch.

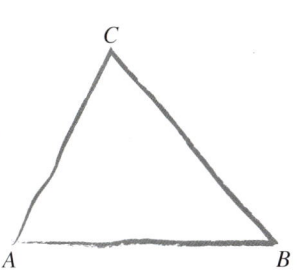

2 Draw a line segment [AB] which has a length equal to the longest length given.

3 With compass point on A and compass width equal to one of the other lengths given, draw an arc as shown.

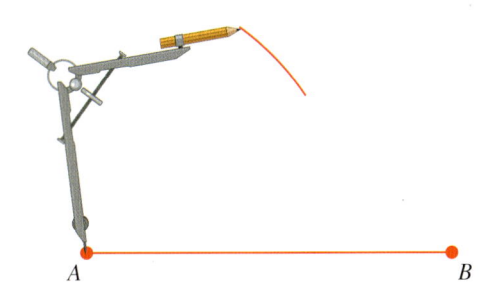

4 With compass point on B and compass width equal to the third length given, draw another arc that intersects the arc from step 3. Label the intersection point C.

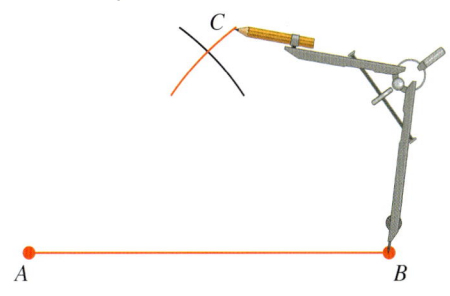

5 Using a ruler or straight edge, join A to C and B to C to produce the required triangle.

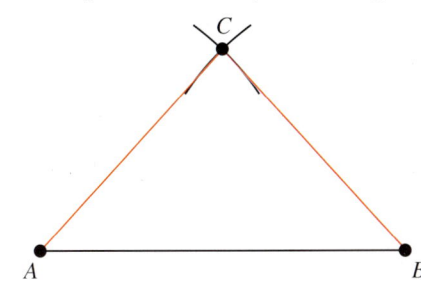

Section B Moving forward

Discuss and discover

Investigate the relationship between the three interior angles in a triangle.

(i) Work with a classmate to draw any triangle.

(ii) Using a protractor, find the measure of each of the three interior angles. Find the sum of these angles.

(iii) Tear the three corners off the triangle and place them together. What is the measure of the angle they form?

(iv) Repeat this activity for two more triangles.

What have you discovered about the three interior angles?

Labelling a triangle

The **sides** are labelled using **lower case letters**.

The points where two sides of a triangle meet is called a vertex of the triangle and are labelled using capital letters.

The **angles** are labelled **using capital letters**.

A triangle can be named by listing the vertices in the order that you meet them, as you go around the shape. You can start at any vertex and go clockwise or anti-clockwise, e.g. the triangle here could be named using the three vertices △**ABC**.

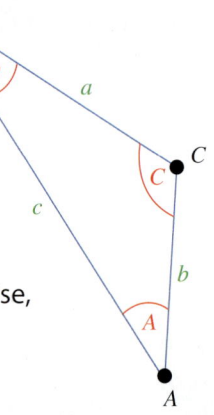

Theorem (4) The angles in any triangle add to 180 degrees

$|\angle A| + |\angle B| + |\angle C| = 180°$

Proof of Theorem 4

The angles in any triangle add to 180 degrees.

Remember: Junior Cycle Mathematics students should display an understanding of the proofs of theorems (full formal proofs are **not** examinable).

1 Take a triangle ABC

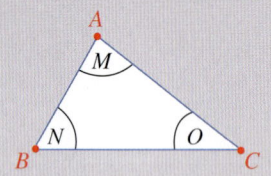

2 Draw line DE through A, parallel to BC

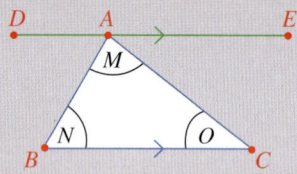

3 Then AB is a transversal of DE and BC
$|\angle P| = |\angle N|$ (alternate angles)

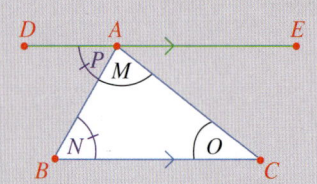

4 Similarly, AC is a transversal of DE and BC,
$|\angle Q| = |\angle O|$ (alternate angles)

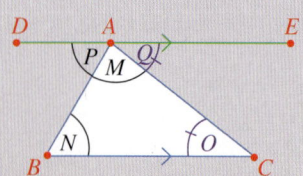

5 $|\angle P| + |\angle Q| + |\angle M| = 180°$ (straight line)
$|\angle N| = |\angle P|$ (from step 3)
$|\angle O| = |\angle Q|$ (from step 4)
$|\angle N| + |\angle O| + |\angle M| = |\angle P| + |\angle Q| + |\angle M|$
$|\angle N| + |\angle O| + |\angle M| = 180°$

Remember: If two lines are parallel, then any transversal will make equal alternate angles.

Linking Thinking 1

Worked example

Find the size of the angles marked with a letter in these triangles.
Write down the axiom or theorem used in each case.

(i) Triangle with angles 47°, 37°, and A

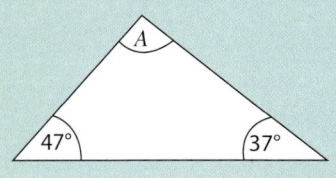

(ii) Triangle with angles 27°, 122°, and B

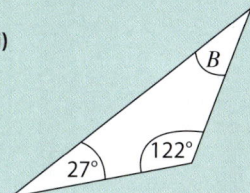

Solution

(i) $47° + 37° + |\angle A| = 180°$ **Theorem 4:** The angles in any triangle add to 180 degrees
       $84° + |\angle A| = 180°$
             $|\angle A| = 180° - 84°$ (subtracting 84° from both sides)
             $|\angle A| = 96°$

(ii) $27° + 122° + |\angle B| = 180°$ **Theorem 4:** The angles in any triangle add to 180 degrees
       $149° + |\angle B| = 180°$
             $|\angle B| = 180° - 149°$ (subtracting 149° from both sides)
             $|\angle B| = 31°$

Practice questions 15·2

1. Find the size of the angles marked with a letter in the following triangles. Write down the axiom or theorem used in each case.

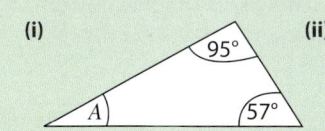

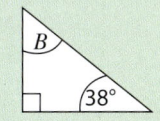

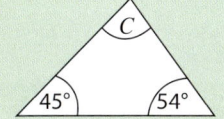

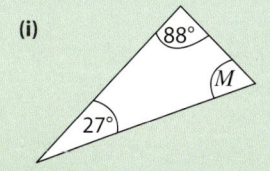

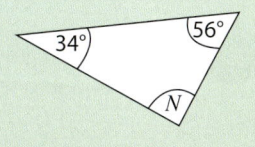

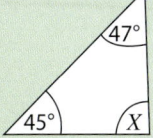

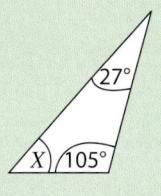

(i) Triangle with angles 95°, 57°, A
(ii) Triangle B with right angle and 38°
(iii) Triangle C with angles 45°, 54°
(iv) Triangle D with angles 47°, 47°

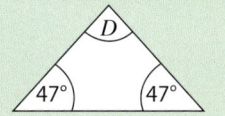

2. Find the size of the angles marked with a letter in the following triangles. Write down the axiom or theorem used.

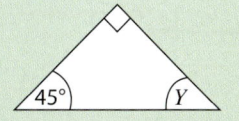

(i) Triangle M with angles 88°, 27°
(ii) Triangle N with angles 34°, 56°
(iii) Triangle X with angles 47°, 45°
(iv) Triangle Y with right angle and 45°
(v) Triangle X with angles 27°, 105°
(vi) Triangle Y with angles 87°, 45°

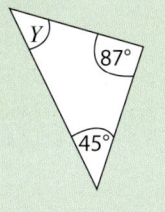

3. Migrating birds often form a triangle shape when flying, as shown. Find the measure of the ∠A.

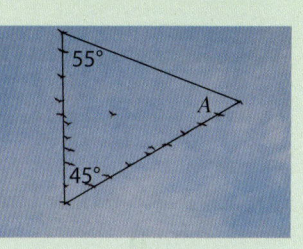

(Triangle with angles 55°, 45°, A)

4. Construct the following triangles using the rough sketches below.

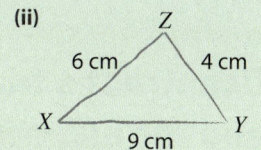

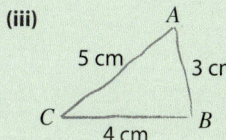

(i) Triangle ABC: AC = 3 cm, CB = 6 cm, AB = 7 cm
(ii) Triangle XYZ: XZ = 6 cm, ZY = 4 cm, XY = 9 cm
(iii) Triangle ABC: CA = 5 cm, AB = 3 cm, CB = 4 cm
(iv) Triangle ABC: AC = 7 cm, CB = 4 cm, AB = 9 cm

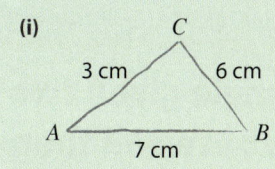

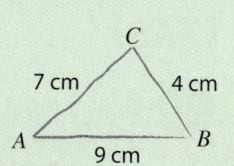

5. Construct the triangle ABC where $|AB| = 6$ cm, $|BC| = 5$ cm and $|AC| = 4$ cm

6. Construct the triangle PQR where $|PQ| = 7.5$ cm, $|QR| = 5$ cm and $|PR| = 4.5$ cm

7. Construct the triangle MNO where $|MN| = 5.5$ cm, $|NO| = 4.5$ cm and $|MO| = 3.5$ cm

8. Construct the triangle ABC where $|AB| = 50$ mm, $|BC| = 4.7$ cm and $|AC| = 68$ mm

Section B Moving forward   237

9. Find the size of angles X, Y and Z in the diagram.

10. A diagram of the Bermuda Triangle is shown. Using an appropriate scale, draw a scale diagram of the Bermuda Triangle.

11. Opposite is a diagram used as part of the proof for the theorem that states that the angles in any triangle sum to 180°.

Why does $|\angle ACB| = |\angle CAE|$?

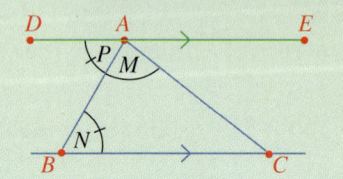

15·3 Constructing triangles using angles and sides

By the end of this section you should:
- understand what an included side and included angle are
- be able to construct a triangle given two sides and an included side
- be able to construct a triangle given two angles and a side
- be able to identify and find the measure of interior and exterior angles in a triangle

> An **included angle** is the angle between two given sides.

In this triangle, $\angle A$ is the **included angle** between sides b and c.

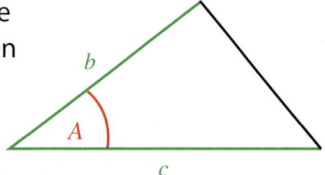

Construct a triangle given two sides and the angle in between them (SAS)

'Side, angle, side' is often shown using the letters 'SAS'.

11

① Draw a rough sketch of the triangle to be constructed. Include the given information in your sketch.

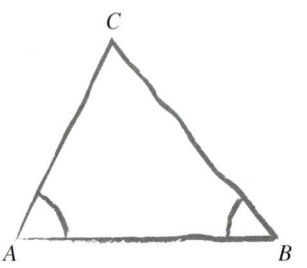

② Draw a line segment [AB], which has a length equal to the longest length given.

③ With the centre of your protractor on the point A and in line with [AB], measure the required angle. Mark the point X as shown. Draw a ray from A through X.

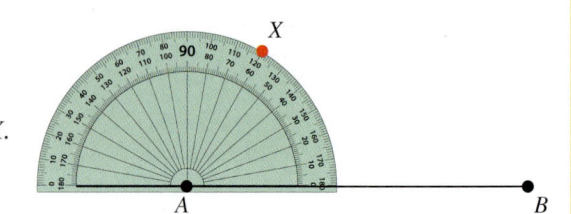

238 Linking Thinking 1

4 With compass point on A and compass width equal to the second length given, draw an arc on the ray [AX, as shown. Label the point of intersection of the arc C.

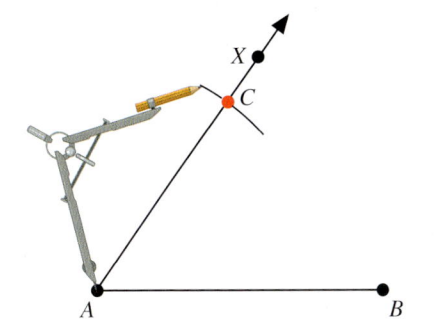

5 Using a ruler or straight edge, join B to C to produce the required triangle.

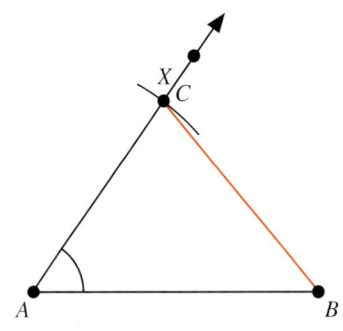

Included side is the side between two given angles.

In this triangle, the side c is the **included side** between $\angle A$ and $\angle B$.

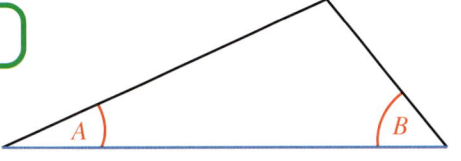

Construct a triangle, given two angles and the side in between them (ASA) — 12

1 Draw a rough sketch of the triangle to be constructed. Include the given information in your sketch.

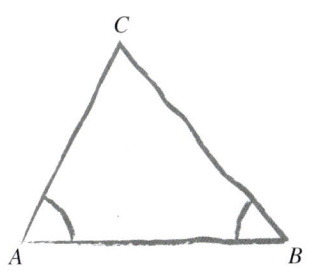

2 Draw a line segment, [AB], which has a length equal to the length given.

3 With the centre of your protractor on the point A and in line with AB, measure one of the given angles.
Mark the point X as shown.
Draw a ray from A through X.

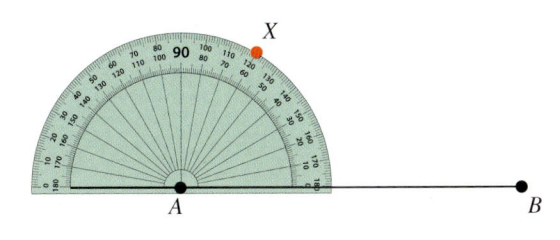

4 With the centre of the protractor on the point B and in line with AB, measure the other given angle.
Mark the point Y as shown.
Draw a ray from B through Y.

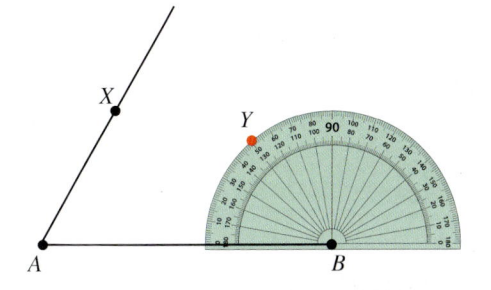

5 Label the intersection of the rays [AX and [BY that you constructed in steps 3 and 4 as C to produce the required triangle.

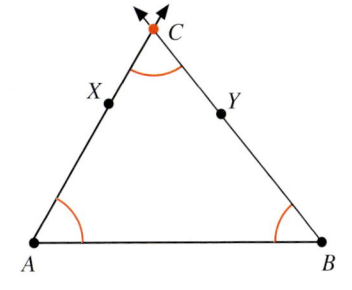

Section B Moving forward

Practice questions 15·3

1. Construct the triangles using the following rough sketches.

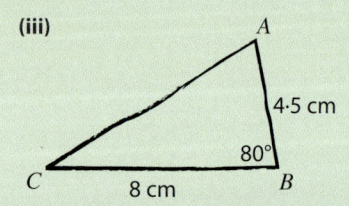

   (i) Triangle with $|AC| = 4$ cm, $|\angle A| = 50°$, $|AB| = 6$ cm.

   (ii) Triangle with $|XZ| = 7$ cm, $|\angle X| = 60°$, $|XY| = 8$ cm.

   (iii) Triangle with $|AB| = 4.5$ cm, $|\angle B| = 80°$, $|CB| = 8$ cm.

   (iv) Triangle with $|CB| = 7$ cm, $|\angle B| = 47°$, $|AB| = 7.5$ cm.

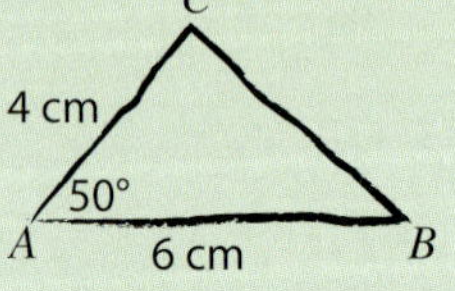

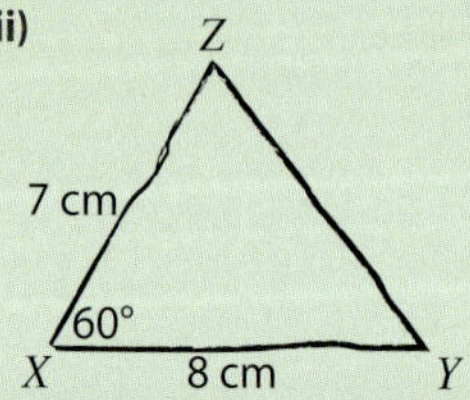

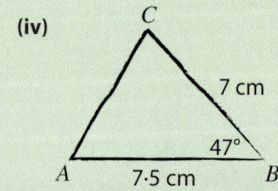

2. Construct the triangle ABC where:

   (i) $|AB| = 5$ cm, $|\angle BAC| = 50°$, $|AC| = 7$ cm

   (ii) $|AC| = 5$ cm, $|AB| = 3$ cm, $|\angle BAC| = 30°$

   (iii) $|AB| = 3.5$ cm, $|\angle BAC| = 140°$, $|AC| = 3.5$ cm

   (iv) $|AB| = 7$ cm, $|\angle CAB| = 95°$, $|AC| = 3$ cm

3. Construct the triangles using the following rough sketches.

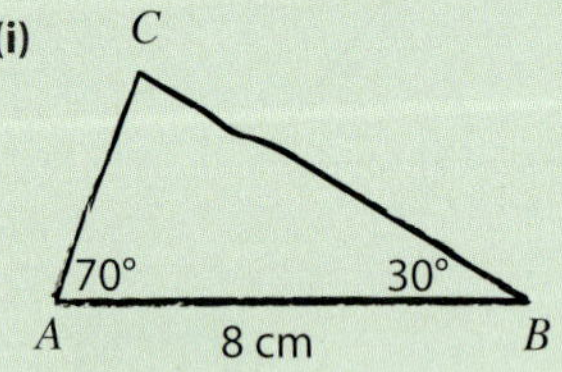

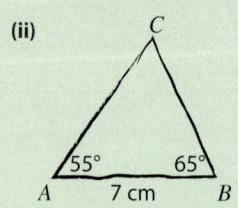

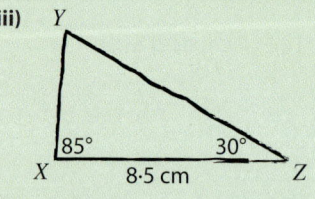

   (i) Triangle with $|\angle A| = 70°$, $|AB| = 8$ cm, $|\angle B| = 30°$.

   (ii) Triangle with $|\angle A| = 55°$, $|AB| = 7$ cm, $|\angle B| = 65°$.

   (iii) Triangle with $|\angle X| = 85°$, $|XZ| = 8.5$ cm, $|\angle Z| = 30°$.

   (iv) Triangle with $|\angle B| = 35°$, $|BC| = 9$ cm, $|\angle C| = 50°$.

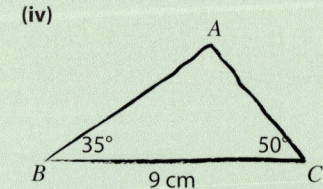

4. Construct the triangles when given the following information.

   (i) $|\angle QPR| = 60°$, $|PQ| = 7.5$ cm and $|\angle PQR| = 70°$

   (ii) $|\angle BAC| = 20°$, $|AB| = 6$ cm and $|\angle ABC| = 140°$

   (iii) $|\angle YXZ| = 60°$, $|YX| = 9$ cm and $|\angle XYZ| = 60°$

   (iv) $|\angle BAC| = 72°$, $|AB| = 8$ cm and $|\angle ABC| = 63°$

15·4 Types of triangles and area of triangles

By the end of this section you should:
- understand different types of triangles: isosceles, equilateral and scalene
- be able to calculate the area and perimeter of a triangle

Types of triangle

Equilateral triangles

Discuss and discover

KEY SKILLS

Investigate a triangle with three equal sides.

Work with a classmate to draw a triangle where the three sides of the triangle are all 7 cm.

(i) Using a protractor, find the measure of each of the three interior angles.

(ii) Repeat this activity for two more triangles, where all three sides are equal in length.

(iii) What have you discovered about the angles in a triangle of equal sides?

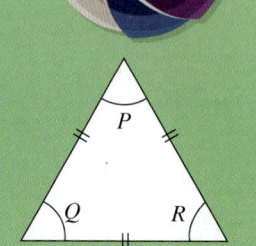

> An **equilateral triangle** has three equal sides and three equal angles, each measuring 60°.

Examples of **equilateral triangles** (diagrams not to scale):

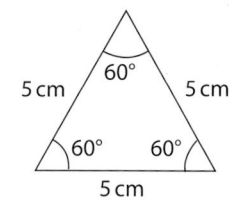

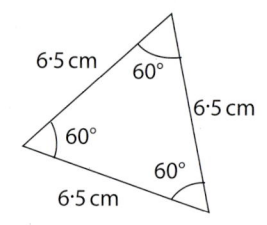

Triangle with sides 5 cm, 5 cm, 5 cm and angles 60°, 60°, 60°.

Triangle with sides 6.5 cm, 6.5 cm, 6.5 cm and angles 60°, 60°, 60°.

240 Linking Thinking 1

If we break up the word 'equilateral', it becomes equal-lateral ('lateral' means 'side'), so it's easy to remember equilateral triangles have all equal sides.

Matching dashes through two or more sides or angles shows that they are equal.

Isosceles triangles

Discuss and discover

Investigate a triangle with two equal sides.

Work with a classmate to draw a triangle where the two sides of the triangle are both 7 cm and the third side is 6 cm.

(i) Using a protractor, find the measure of each of the interior angles.
(ii) Repeat this activity for two more triangles, where only two sides are equal in length.
(iii) What have you discovered about the angles opposite the equal sides?

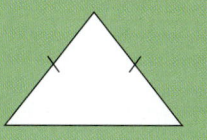

An **isosceles** triangle has two equal sides and two equal angles.

The word *isosceles* is Greek for 'equal legs'. We have two legs, so it's easy to remember isosceles triangles have two equal sides and two equal angles.

Examples of **isosceles triangles** (diagrams not to scale):

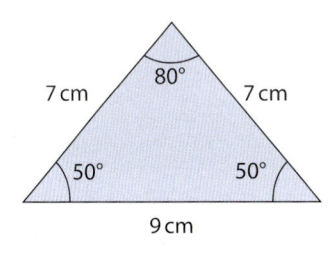

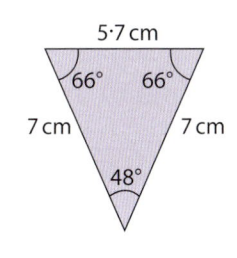

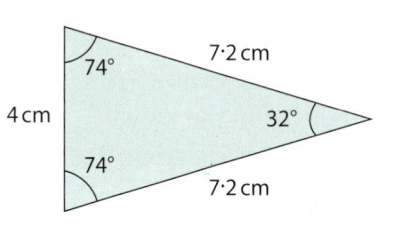

Scalene triangles

Discuss and discover

Investigate a triangle with no equal sides.

Work with a classmate to draw a triangle where the sides of the triangle are 8 cm, 7 cm and 6 cm.

(i) Using a protractor, find the measure of each of three interior angles.
(ii) Repeat this activity for two more triangles, where none of the sides of the sides are equal in length.
(iii) What have you discovered about the angles?

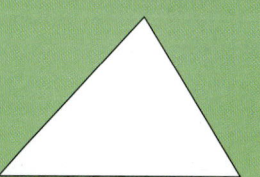

Section B Moving forward 241

A **scalene triangle** doesn't have any equal sides or equal angles.

Examples of **scalene** triangles (diagrams not to scale):

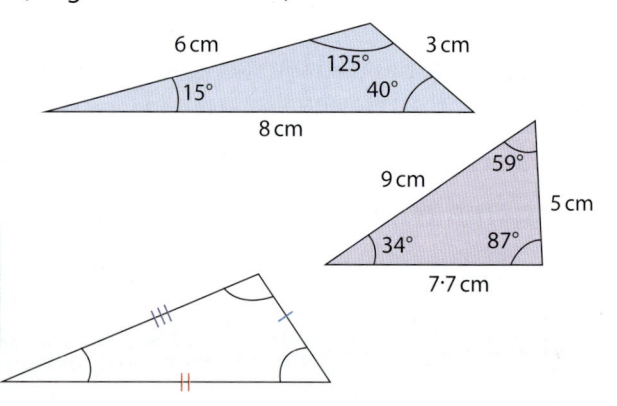

Scalene means 'uneven' or 'odd' in ancient Greek. Scalene triangles are 'uneven' as they have no equal sides.

One, two and three dashes on the sides and on the angles are used in scalene triangles to indicate no sides and no angles are of equal size.

Area and perimeter of a triangle

Discuss and discover

Investigate the area of a triangle.

Work with a classmate to draw a triangle where one side of the triangle is 7 cm, a second side is 5 cm and the third side is 9 cm.

(i) Draw a rectangle that fits perfectly over the triangle.
(ii) Find the area of this rectangle.
(iii) Using scissors, cut out the rectangle, and from the rectangle cut out triangles A and B.
(iv) Similar to a jigsaw puzzle, place triangles A and B onto the original triangle so that they cover it perfectly.
(v) Have you discovered a method to find the area of a triangle from this task?

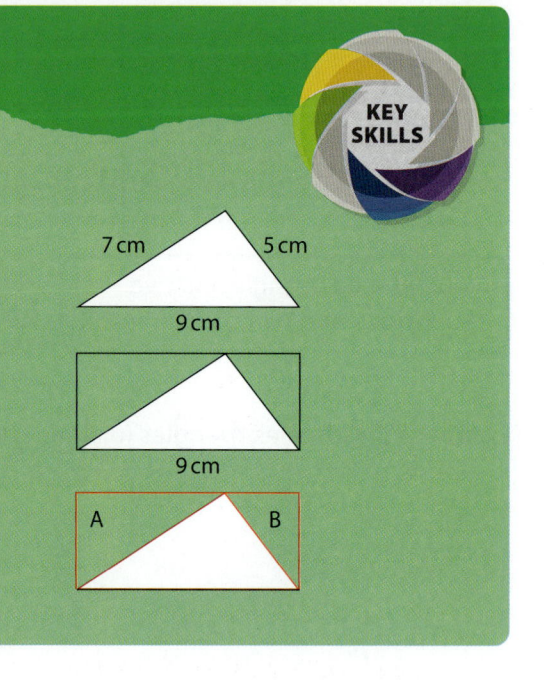

KEY SKILLS

The height of a triangle is the maximum **perpendicular height** from one of the sides (which is usually given the name **base**) to the apex.

The **perpendicular height** from one side to the vertex opposite that side is also called the **altitude**.

An **apex** (Latin for 'peak') is the vertex which is the 'highest' in the triangle.

The perimeter of a triangle is the sum of the three sides.

The perimeter of a triangle can be written as:

Perimeter = |XY| + |YZ| + |XZ|

Below is a sketch of $\triangle XYZ$

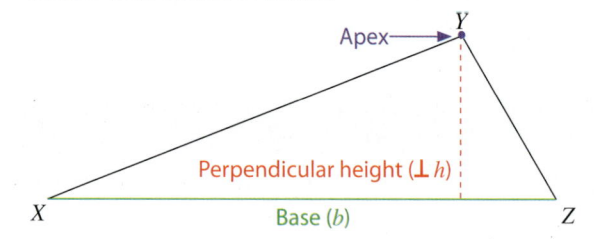

The area of the triangle is equal to half of the **base** (b) multiplied by the **perpendicular height or altitude** (h).

The area of a triangle can be written as:

Area of $\triangle = \frac{1}{2}[b \times \perp h]$

This formula appears in the *formulae and tables* booklet.

Remember: The symbol $\perp$ means perpendicular.

Linking Thinking 1

Worked example 1

Find the size of the angles marked with a letter in the following triangles.
Write down the axiom or theorem used in each case.

(i) [triangle with 40° at top, angle A at bottom right, two equal sides marked with double dash, base with single dash]

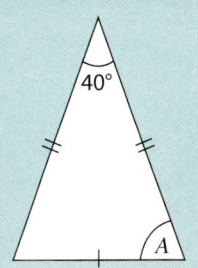

(ii) [triangle with 85° at top, 46° at bottom left, X at bottom right; sides marked with double dash, single dash, triple dash]

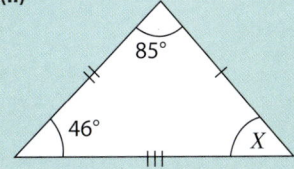

(iii) [triangle with angle Q at bottom left; all three sides marked with single dash]

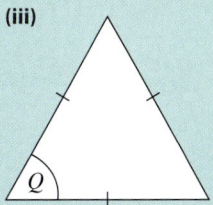

Solution

(i) This is an isosceles triangle because two sides have the same 'double dash', meaning they are equal. The side with one dash is not equal to any other side. The angles opposite the equal sides are also equal in size, so the unmarked angle and ∠A are equal.

$|\angle A| + |\angle A| + 40° = 180°$ (three angles in a triangle add to 180°)
$|\angle A| + |\angle A| = 180° - 40°$ (subtracting 40° from both sides)
$|\angle A| + |\angle A| = 140°$
$2|\angle A| = 140°$ (adding angle A to angle A)
$\frac{2|\angle A|}{2} = \frac{140°}{2}$ (dividing both sides by 2)
$|\angle A| = 70°$

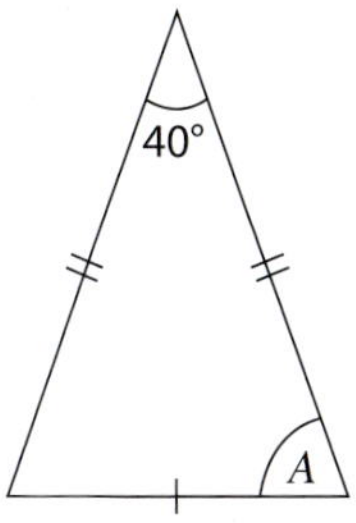

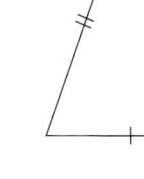

(ii) This is a scalene triangle because no two sides have the same number of dashes.

$|\angle X| + 46° + 85° = 180°$ (three angles in a triangle add to 180°)
$|\angle X| + 131° = 180°$
$|\angle X| = 180° - 131°$ (subtracting 131° from both sides)
$|\angle X| = 49°$

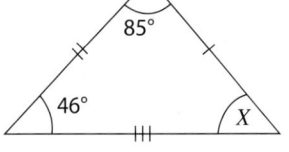

(iii) This is an equilateral triangle because the three sides of the triangle are marked with the same single dash.

All three angles in the triangle are also equal. Therefore all angles are equal to $|\angle Q|$. As it is a triangle, they all add up to 180°.

$|\angle Q| + |\angle Q| + |\angle Q| = 180°$
$3|\angle Q| = 180°$
$\frac{3|\angle Q|}{3} = \frac{180°}{3}$ (dividing both sides by 3)
$|\angle Q| = 60°$ (which is always the measure of each angle in an equilateral triangle)

Section B Moving forward 243

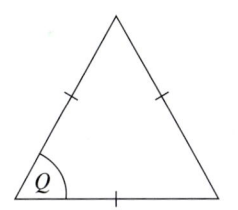

Worked example 2

Find the area and the perimeter of each of the triangles below.

(i) Triangle with sides 9 cm, 7 cm, 5 cm and perpendicular height 3 cm.

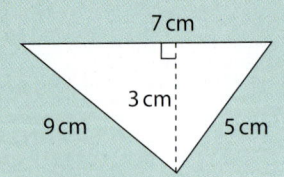

(ii) Triangle with sides 44 cm, 57 cm, 61 cm and perpendicular height 55 cm.

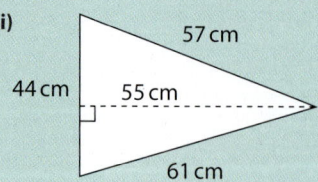

Solution

(i) Area of $\Delta = \frac{1}{2}[b \times \perp h]$

We identify which side is the base by checking which side we know the perpendicular height from.

Area of $\Delta = \frac{1}{2}[7 \text{ cm} \times 3 \text{ cm}]$

Area of $\Delta = \frac{1}{2}[21 \text{ cm}^2]$

Area of $\Delta = 10.5 \text{ cm}^2$

Perimeter = 7 cm + 9 cm + 5 cm

Perimeter = 21 cm

(ii) Area of $\Delta = \frac{1}{2}[b \times \perp h]$

We identify which side is the base by checking which side we know the perpendicular height from.

Area of $\Delta = \frac{1}{2}[44 \text{ cm} \times 55 \text{ cm}]$

Area of $\Delta = \frac{1}{2}[2\,420 \text{ cm}^2]$

Area of $\Delta = 1\,210 \text{ cm}^2$

Perimeter = 44 cm + 57 cm + 61 cm

Perimeter = 162 cm

Practice questions 15·4

1. Identify each type of triangle below, and give reasons for your answers.

   (i) (ii) 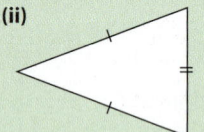 (iii) 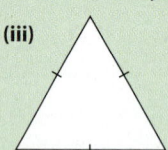 (iv) 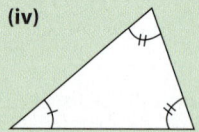 (v)

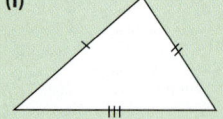

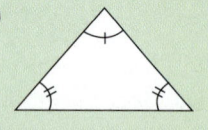

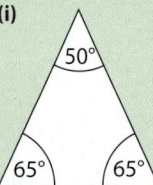

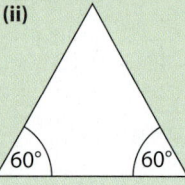

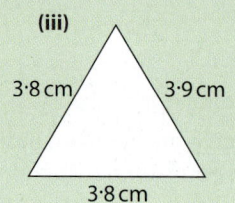

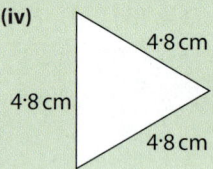

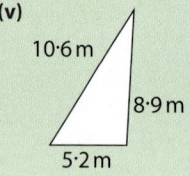

2. Identify each type of triangle below, and give reasons for your answers.

   (i) Triangle with angles 50°, 65°, 65°.

   (ii) Triangle with angles 60°, 60°.

   (iii) Triangle with sides 3·8 cm, 3·9 cm, 3·8 cm.

   (iv) Triangle with sides 4·8 cm, 4·8 cm, 4·8 cm.

   (v) Triangle with sides 10·6 m, 8·9 m, 5·2 m.

3. Find the size of the angles marked with a letter. Write down the axiom or theorem used in each case.

   (i) Triangle with sides 8 cm, 8 cm, 8 cm and angle C at top.

   (ii) Triangle with sides 5 cm, 5 cm, angle 45° and angle Y.

   (iii) Triangle with sides 7 cm, 7 cm, 9 cm, top angle 80° and angle X.

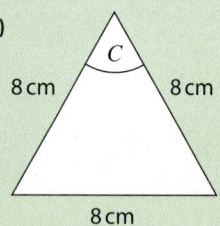

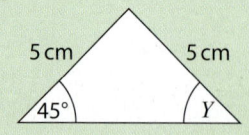

244 Linking Thinking 1

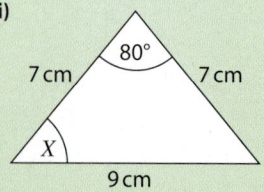

4. Find the area of each of the following triangles.

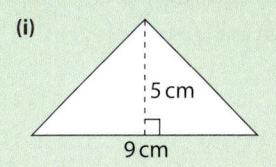

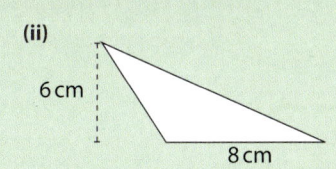

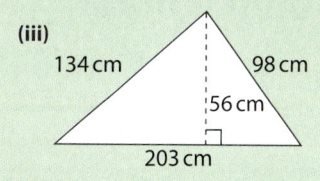

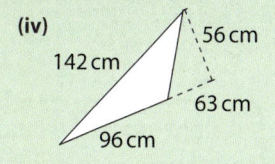

(i) 5 cm, 9 cm

(ii) 6 cm, 8 cm

(iii) 134 cm, 98 cm, 56 cm, 203 cm

(iv) 56 cm, 142 cm, 63 cm, 96 cm

5. What type of triangles are shown in these pictures?

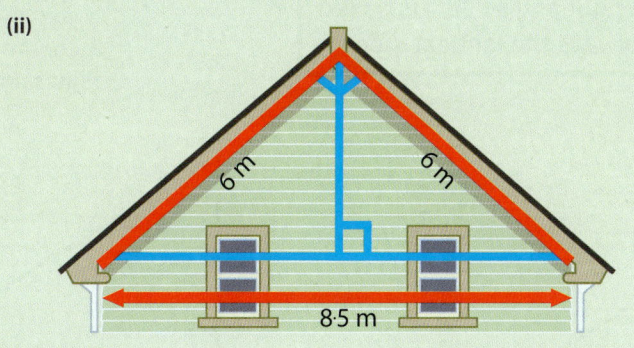

(i) GÉILL SLÍ sign

(ii) 6 m, 6 m, 8·5 m

6. Find the perimeter of each triangle.

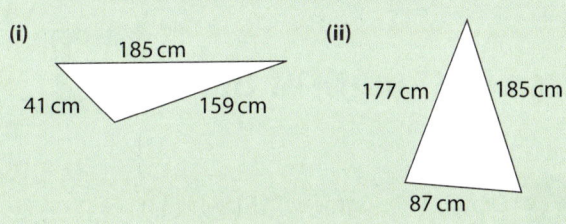

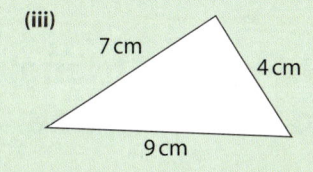

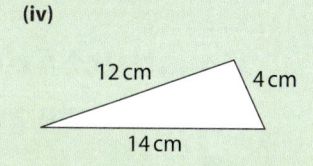

(i) 185 cm, 41 cm, 159 cm

(ii) 177 cm, 185 cm, 87 cm

(iii) 7 cm, 4 cm, 9 cm

(iv) 12 cm, 4 cm, 14 cm

7. A swan flies straight from Galway to Birr, from Birr straight to Limerick, and from Limerick straight to Galway.

The distance travelled by the swan from Galway to Birr was 90 km. The distance travelled by the bird from Birr to Limerick was 70 km. The total distance travelled by the swan was 250 km.

(i) Find the distance travelled by the swan between Limerick and Galway.

(ii) What type of triangle is traced out by the path of the swan?

(iii) Using an appropriate scale, draw a scale diagram of the triangle from part (ii).

8. A section of wallpaper is made out of triangles as shown. Find the total area covered by this section of wallpaper.

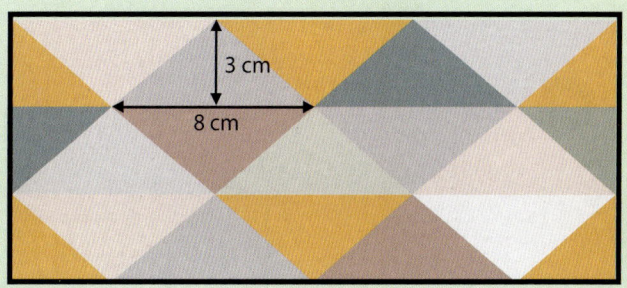

3 cm, 8 cm

Section B Moving forward 245

15·5 Right-angled triangles

By the end of this section you should be able to:
- identify and construct right angled triangles

A **right-angled triangle** (also called a right triangle) is a triangle with a right angle (90°) as one of its angles.

The side opposite the right angle (90°) is called the **hypotenuse**. It is always the longest side

Sometimes a triangle can have two names to describe it, e.g. it can be a right-angled triangle and also isosceles.

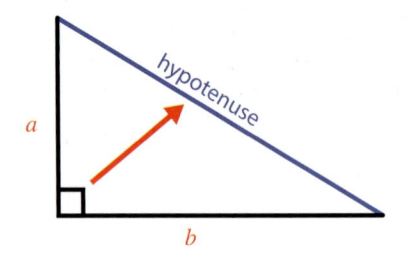

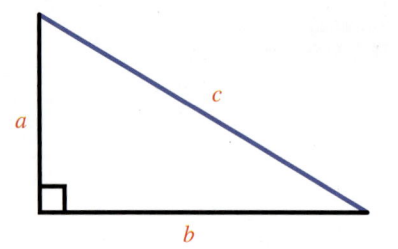

Construct a right-angled triangle, given the length of the hypotenuse and one other side

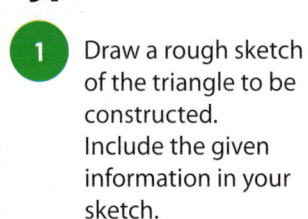

13

1 Draw a rough sketch of the triangle to be constructed. Include the given information in your sketch.

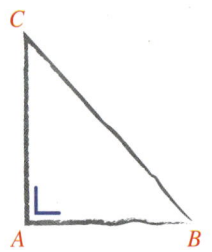

2 Draw a line segment [AB], which has a length equal to the side given that is not the hypotenuse.

3 With the centre of the protractor on the point A and in line with [AB], measure an angle of 90°. Mark the point X as shown. Draw a ray from A through X.

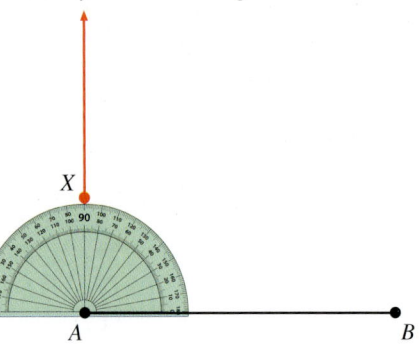

4 With the compass point on B and compass width equal to the length of the given hypotenuse, draw an arc on the ray [AX. Label the intersection of the arc C.

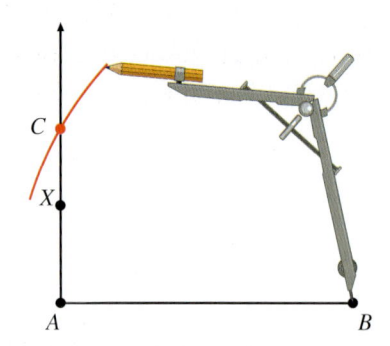

5 Join B to C to produce the required triangle.

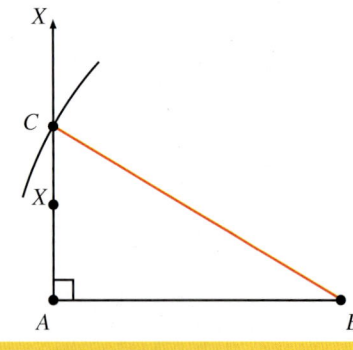

246 Linking Thinking 1

Construct a right-angled triangle, given one side and one of the acute angles

1 Draw a rough sketch of the triangle to be constructed. Include the given information in your sketch.

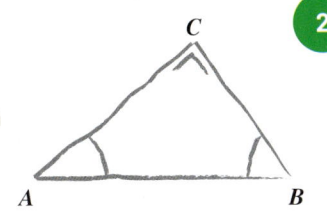

2 Draw a line segment [AB], which has a length equal to the given hypotenuse.

3 Using a protractor, construct the acute angle given at A. Mark the point X, as shown. Draw a ray from A through X.

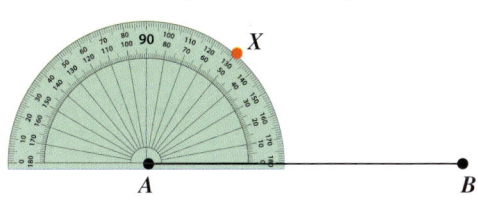

4 Work out the other acute angle (remember, the three angles in a triangle add up to 180°). Using a protractor, construct this acute angle at B. Mark the point Y as shown. Draw a ray from B through Y.

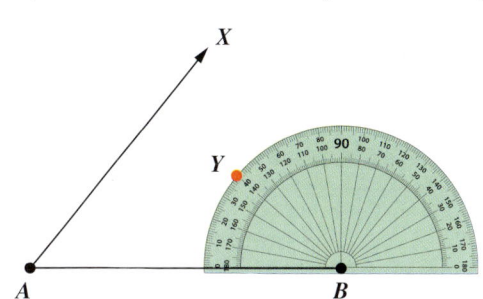

5 Mark the point where the rays [AX and [BY intersect as C. This is the required triangle.

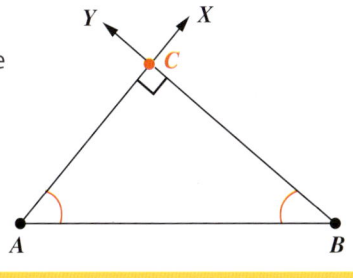

Discuss and discover

KEY SKILLS

Working with a classmate, draw three different right-angled triangles.

(i) Measure each of the angles.
(ii) Measure each of the sides.
(iii) What have you discovered about the relationship between the size of each angle and its opposite side?

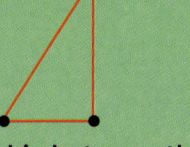

Practice questions 15·5

1. Construct the triangles using the rough sketches below:

(i) Triangle ABC: AB with 90° at B, BC = 5 cm, AC = 8 cm.

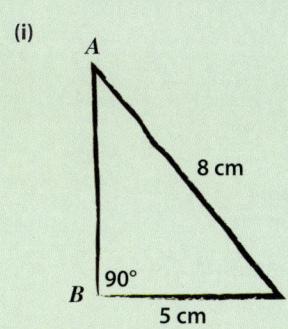

(ii) Triangle ABC: 90° at B, BC = 4 cm, AC = 9 cm.

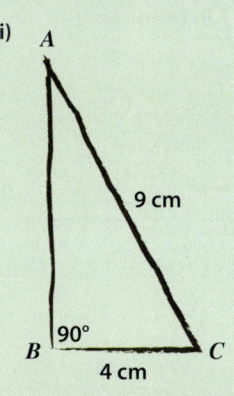

(iii) Triangle XYZ: 90° at Z, ZC = 3 cm, XC = 9 cm.

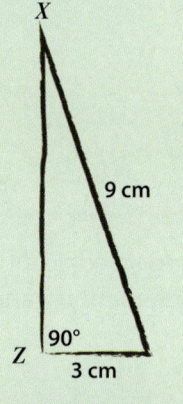

(iv) Triangle NOM: 90° at M, NM = 5 cm, ON = 8 cm.

Section B Moving forward 247

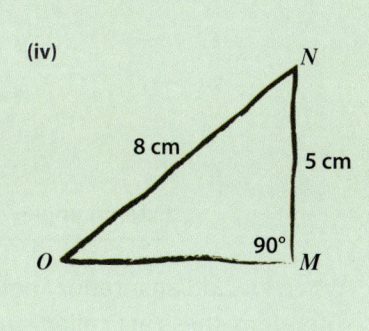

2. Construct a right-angled triangle ABC with |AB| as the hypotenuse when:
   (i) |AB| = 6 cm and |BC| = 4 cm
   (ii) |AB| = 5·5 cm and |BC| = 4·5 cm
   (iii) |AB| = 10 cm and |BC| = 6·5 cm

3. Construct triangles using the rough sketches below:

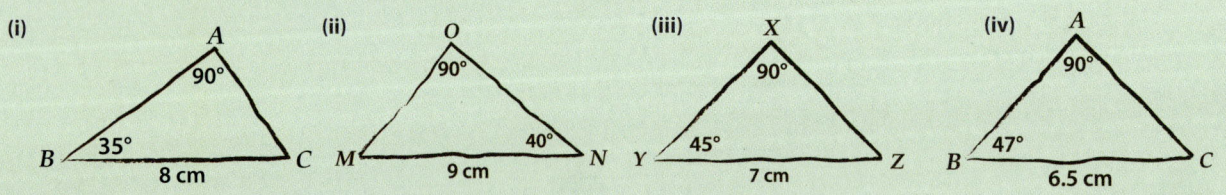

   (i) Triangle with A at top (90°), B at bottom left (35°), C at bottom right, |BC| = 8 cm
   (ii) Triangle with O at top (90°), M at bottom left, N at bottom right (40°), |MN| = 9 cm
   (iii) Triangle with X at top (90°), Y at bottom left (45°), Z at bottom right, |YZ| = 7 cm
   (iv) Triangle with A at top (90°), B at bottom left, C at bottom right (47°), |BC| = 6·5 cm

4. Construct a right-angled triangle ABC with |AB| as the hypotenuse when:
   (i) |AB| = 9·5 cm and |∠CAB| = 47°
   (ii) |AB| = 8·5 cm and |∠BAC| = 38°
   (iii) |AB| = 7·5 cm and |∠CAB| = 56°

5. Copy the table below and put a tick (✓) in the correct box in each row to show whether each statement is always true, sometimes true, or never true, for any triangle.

Statement		Tick **one** box only for each statement		
		Always true	Sometimes true	Never true
(i)	It is possible to construct a triangle with two 90° angles.			
(ii)	It is possible for a triangle to be both a right-angled triangle and isosceles.			
(iii)	It is possible for a triangle to be both a right-angled triangle and equilateral.			
(iv)	If a triangle is right-angled, the other two angles add up to less than 90°.			

15·6 Interior and exterior angles in triangles

By the end of this section you should be able to:
- identify the interior and exterior angles in a triangle
- find the measure of exterior angles in a triangle

An **exterior angle** is the angle between any side of a shape, and a line extended from the adjacent side.

An **interior angle** is an angle inside a shape.

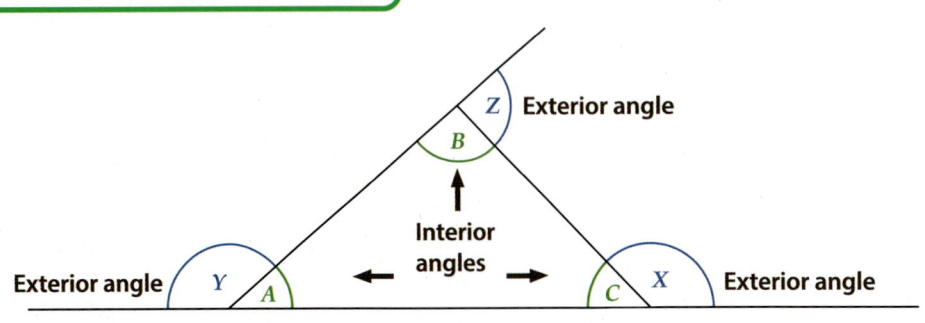

When we add an interior angle to an adjacent exterior angle, we get a straight line measuring 180°. Therefore, these are called **supplementary angles**.

248 Linking Thinking 1

Discuss and discover

KEY SKILLS

Investigate the relationship between the exterior angle and two interior opposite angles.

(i) Working with a classmate, draw any triangle with an exterior angle marked on a sheet of paper.

(ii) Using a protractor, find the measure of the exterior angle and the two interior opposite angles (to this exterior angle).

(iii) Tear the two opposite corners off the triangle and place them together into the exterior angle.

(iv) Repeat this activity for two more triangles.

(v) What have you discovered about the relationship between the exterior angle and the two interior opposite angles in a triangle?

Theorem 6: Each exterior angle of a triangle is equal to the sum of the interior opposite angles

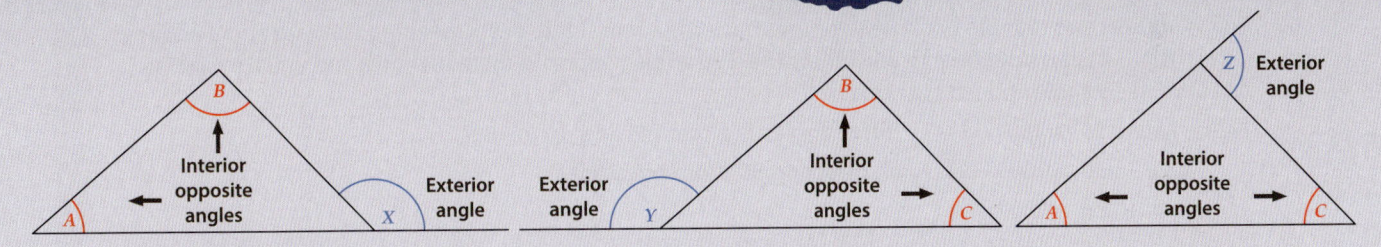

$|\angle X| = |\angle A| + |\angle B|$

$|\angle Y| = |\angle B| + |\angle C|$

$|\angle Z| = |\angle A| + |\angle C|$

$\angle X$ is the exterior angle
$\angle A$ and $\angle B$ are called (corresponding) interior opposite angles.

Proof of Theorem 6

Each exterior angle of a triangle is equal to the sum of the interior opposite angles.

Remember: Junior Cycle Mathematics students should display an understanding of the proofs of theorems (full formal proofs are **not** examinable).

1 In the triangle $\triangle ABC$, let M be an exterior angle at A.

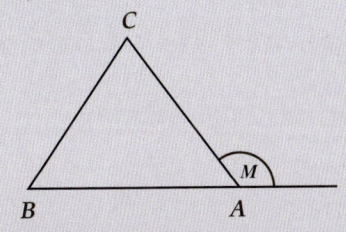

2 Mark angle N
$|\angle M| + |\angle N| = 180°$ (supplementary angles)

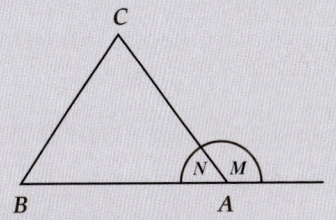

3 Mark in angles O and P
$|\angle N| + |\angle O| + |\angle P| = 180°$
(sum of three angles in triangle)

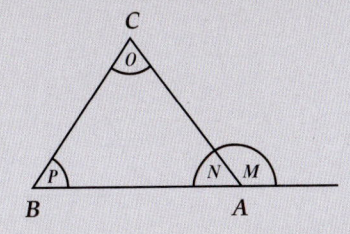

4 $|\angle N| + |\angle O| + |\angle P| = 180°$ (from step 3)
$|\angle M| + |\angle N| = 180°$ (from step 2)

Since $180° = 180°$
$|\angle N| + |\angle O| + |\angle P| = |\angle M| + |\angle N|$
Subtracting $|\angle N|$ from both sides gives:
$|\angle O| + |\angle P| = |\angle M|$

In this proof, we have used a single letter to name the angles.

Section B Moving forward

Worked example

Find the size of the angles marked with a letter in the following triangles. Write down the axiom or theorem used in each case.

(i) (ii) 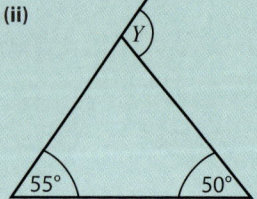 (iii) 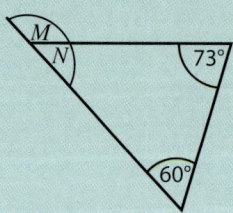 (iv)

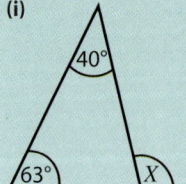

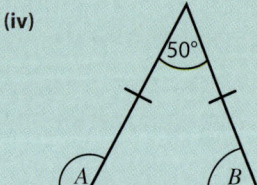

Solution

(i) $|\angle X| = 40° + 63°$ (exterior angle is equal to the sum of the interior opposite angles)
      $|\angle X| = 103°$

(ii) $|\angle Y| = 55° + 50°$ (exterior angle is equal to the sum of the interior opposite angles)
      $|\angle Y| = 105°$

(iii) $|\angle M| = 73° + 60°$ (exterior angle is equal to the sum of the interior opposite angles)
      $|\angle M| = 133°$
      $|\angle M| + |\angle N| = 180°$ (a straight angle = 180° (axiom))
      $133° + |\angle N| = 180°$
             $|\angle N| = 180° - 133°$ (subtracting 133° from both sides)
             $|\angle N| = 47°$

(iv) This is an isosceles triangle because two sides have the same single dash, meaning they are equal and the side with no dash is not equal to any other side. The angles opposite the equal sides are equal in size, so the unmarked angle and ∠B are equal.

   $|\angle B| + |\angle B| + 50° = 180°$ (three angles in a triangle add up to 180°)
   $|\angle B| + |\angle B| = 180° - 50°$ (subtracting 50° from both sides)
   $|\angle B| + |\angle B| = 130°$
        $2|\angle B| = 130°$ (adding angle B to angle B)
        $\dfrac{2|\angle B|}{2} = \dfrac{130°}{2}$ (dividing both sides by 2)
        $|\angle B| = 65°$

$|\angle A| = 50° + 65°$ (exterior angle is equal to the sum of the interior opposite angles)
$|\angle A| = 115°$

Practice questions 15·6

1. Find the size of the angles marked with a letter in the following triangles. Write down the axiom or theorem used in each case.

(i) (ii)  (iii) 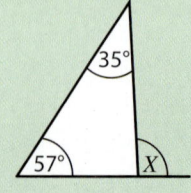 (iv)

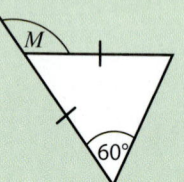

2. Find the size of the angles marked with a letter in the following triangles. Write down the axiom or theorem used in each case.

(i) (ii)  (iii) 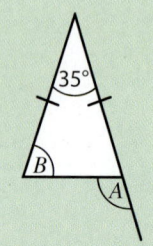 (iv)

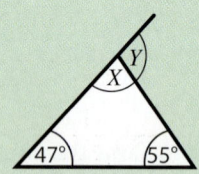

Linking Thinking 1

3. Triangle pose, or *trikonasana*, is a yoga pose.

   Find the size of the angles marked with a letter on the triangle pose shown. Write down the axiom or theorem used in each case.

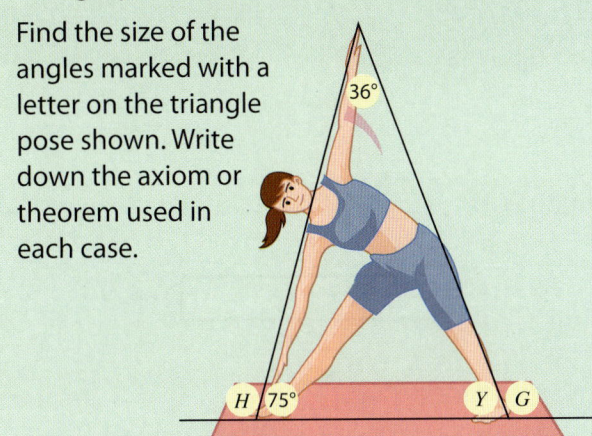

   (36°, H 75°, Y, G)

4. The diagram below is of a triangular house.

   |∠BAC| = 32° and |AB| = |AC|

   Find the following angles and the type of triangle.

   (i) |∠ACB| (iii) |∠DBA|
   (ii) |∠CBA| (iv) What type of triangle is △ABC?

5. The following is a sketch of a type of roof called a fink. Some angles are marked in the diagram.

   Note also that |AD| = |AE|

   Find the following angles.

   (i) |∠BDC| (iii) |∠ABD| (v) |∠DAE|
   (ii) |∠ADC| (iv) |∠CBD|

   (Angles shown: 45°, 45°, 50°, 50°, 60°)

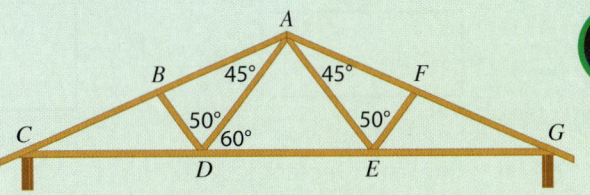

6. A triangular field has the shape of an equilateral triangle. The real-life size of one of the sides of the equilateral triangle is 1·5 km. Using an appropriate scale, draw a scale diagram of this field.

7. The diagram below is used as part of the proof of the theorem which states that each exterior angle of a triangle is equal to the sum of the interior opposite angles.

   (i) What is the total value for the sum of the angles |∠M| and |∠N|? Give a reason for your answer.
   (ii) What is the total value for the sum of angles |∠P|, |∠O| and |∠N|? Give a reason for your answer.

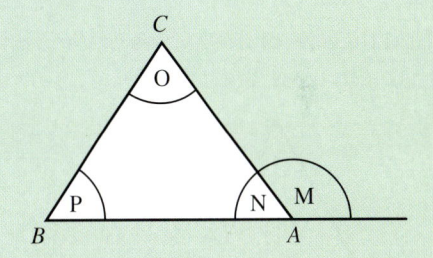

8. Copy the table below and put a tick (✓) in the correct box in each row to show whether each statement is always true, sometimes true, or never true, for any triangle.

	Statement	Tick **one** box only for each statement		
		Always true	Sometimes true	Never true
(i)	Each exterior angle in a triangle is equal to the sum of the two opposite interior angles.			
(ii)	The included side is the side between two angles in a triangle.			
(iii)	It is possible to construct a triangle when we only know one angle and one side.			
(iv)	The sum of three angles in a triangle is equal to 180°.			
(v)	A triangle can contain two 90° angles.			

15 Polygons

Section B Moving forward

Revision questions

15A Core skills

1. Find (i) the area and (ii) the perimeter of the following shapes.

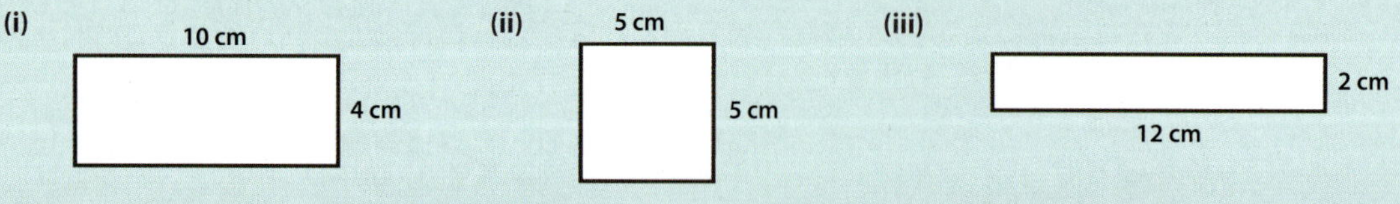

   (i) 10 cm × 4 cm rectangle

   (ii) 5 cm × 5 cm square

   (iii) 12 cm × 2 cm rectangle

2. (i) Construct rectangle $XYWZ$, $|XY| = 110$ mm, $|YW| = 80$ mm. (Hint: draw a rough sketch first.)

   (ii) Find the perimeter of this rectangle. (iii) Find the area of this rectangle.

3. Identify the types of triangle shown here. Give a reason for your answer. Note: in some cases, triangles can be two different types at the same time.

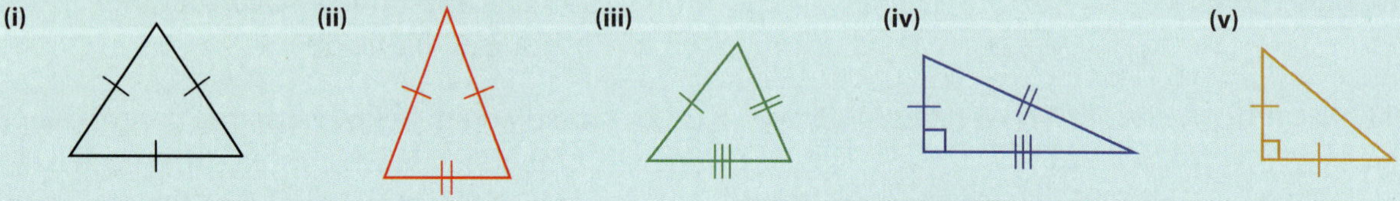

   (i) (ii) (iii) (iv) (v)

4. Construct the triangle ABC where $|AB| = 7$ cm, $|BC| = 5$ cm and $|AC| = 6$ cm.

5. Construct the triangle ABC where $|AB| = 6$ cm, $|\angle BAC| = 60°$ and $|AC| = 8$ cm.

6. Construct the triangle PQR where: $|\angle QPR| = 60°$, $|PQ| = 7.5$ cm and $|\angle PQR| = 70°$.

7. Construct the right-angled triangle ABC where $|AB|$ is the hypotenuse, $|AB| = 7$ cm and $|BC| = 5$ cm.

8. Construct the right-angled triangle ABC where $|AB|$ is the hypotenuse, $|AB| = 9.5$ cm and $|\angle CAB| = 47°$.

9. Find the size of the angles marked with a letter in the following triangles. Write down the axiom or theorem used in each case.

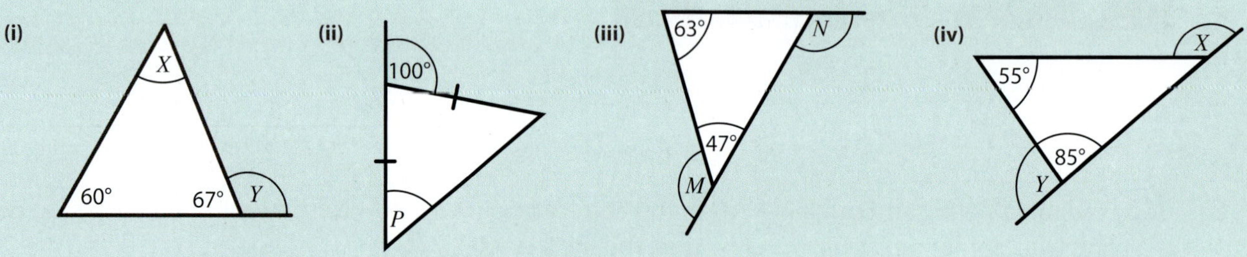

   (i) triangle with angles 60°, 67°, X, Y

   (ii) triangle with 100° angle, P

   (iii) triangle with angles 63°, 47°, N, M

   (iv) triangle with angles 55°, 85°, X, Y

10. Find the area of the shaded region in the following diagrams.

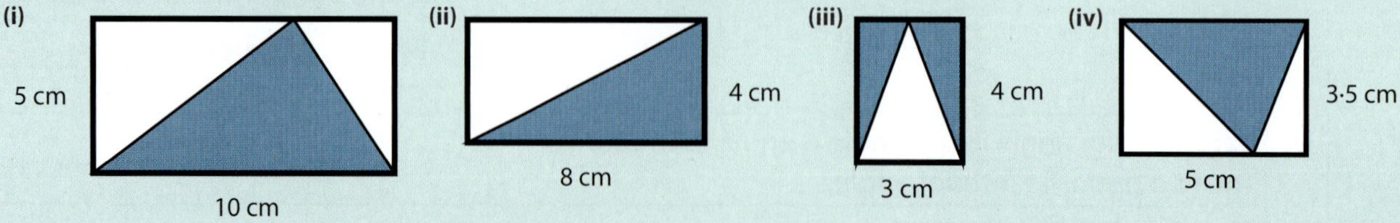

    (i) 5 cm × 10 cm rectangle with shaded triangle

    (ii) rectangle 8 cm wide with shaded triangle

    (iii) 4 cm × 3 cm with unshaded triangle

    (iv) 5 cm × 3.5 cm with shaded triangles

252 Linking Thinking 1

15B Taking it FURTHER

1. (i) What is the area of a rectangular gym wall that is 30 m wide by 1·5 m high?
   (ii) How much paint is needed for two coatings of the wall (a litre of paint will cover 15 m² on average)?
   (iii) If the paint comes in 5 litre buckets which cost €23·30, what is the cost of painting the gym wall?

2. The builder wants to put a 2 m wide concrete path around the outside of a 12 m square building. What is the area of the path? (Hint: draw a sketch.)

3. Two pitches next to each other are shown on the right.
   (i) Find the total area of the fields in metres squared (m²).
   (ii) If a person started at point A and walked around the very outside of the entire playing area and back to point A, what distance will they have travelled in metres?

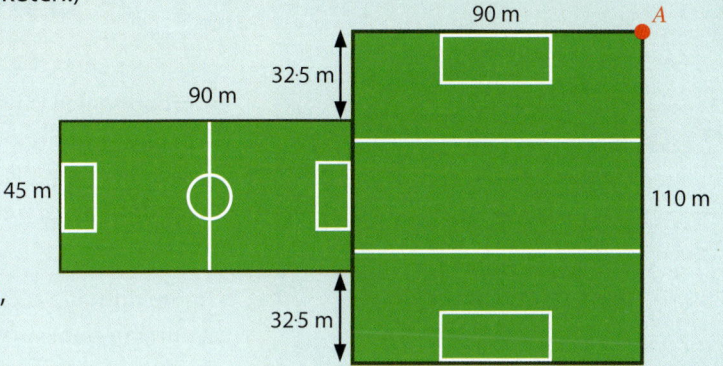

4. Seamus is making repairs to his house. He has leaned a piece of plywood against the wall of his sitting room. The plywood, floor and wall form a right triangle. The plywood and the wall form a 20° angle. What are the measures of the other two angles of the triangle? (Hint: draw a sketch.)

5. To the right is a sketch of a baseball field, a popular sight in the USA.
   In the diagram $|AB| = |AC|$ and $|\angle BAC| = 90°$
   Find:
   (i) $|\angle ABC|$
   (ii) $|\angle ACB|$
   (iii) What type of triangle is $\triangle ABC$?

6. A stone shed has a gable end as shown in the diagram.
   (i) Find the area of this gable end of the shed.
   (ii) The owner wants to plaster this end wall of the shed. The plaster comes in tubs, each of which will cover 3 m² of the wall. Given that the window occupies 1·5 m² of the gable end, how many **full** tubs of plaster will the owner need?
   (iii) Each tub of plaster cost €75 plus 21% VAT. The plasterer charges €400 plus 13% VAT to do the entire job. Find the total cost to the owner, of plastering the wall.

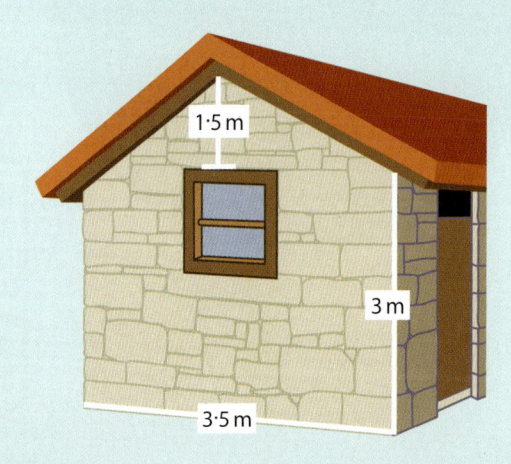

Now that you have completed the unit, revisit the

Something to think about ...

question posed at the start of this unit.

Unit 16

Circles 1

Topics covered within this chapter:
- 16·1 Introduction to circle terms
- 16·2 Area and perimeter of a disc
- 16·3 Compound shapes involving circles

The Learning Outcomes covered in this chapter are contained in the following sections:
GT.2a GT.2c GT.3a GT.3b

Key words
- Circle
- Radius
- Chord
- Diameter
- Tangent
- Arc
- Sector
- Semicircle
- Circumference
- Disc

Something to think about ...

KEY SKILLS

International Pi Day is celebrated on 14 March (3rd month, 14th day) around the world. Pi (Greek letter π) is the symbol used in Mathematics to represent a constant — the ratio of the circumference of a circle to its diameter — which is approximately 3·14159.

On the right is a picture of a circular swimming pool surrounded by a circular concrete path. This path is then surrounded by a circular patch of grass.

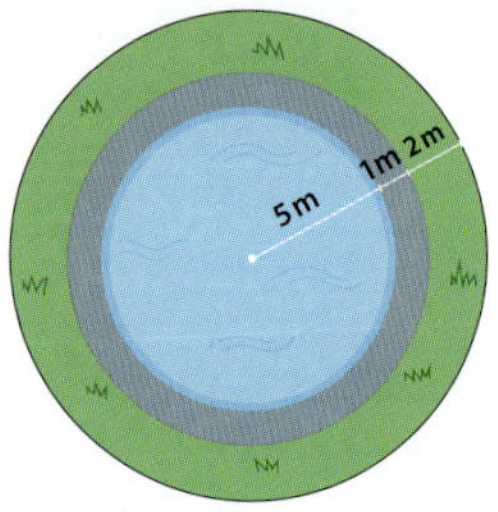

Can you the find the area covered by:

(i) the pool, given that it has a 5 metre radius?

(ii) the concrete path, given that it is 1 metre wide?

(iii) the grass, given that it is 2 metres wide?

16·1 Introduction to circle terms

By the end of this section you should be able to:
- understand the terms used to describe the parts of a circle
- understand what a sector of a circle is

A **circle** is a two-dimensional shape made by drawing a curve that is always the same distance from a centre point. It has infinite lines of symmetry.

The **radius** is the line segment joining the centre to a point on the circle. The plural of radius is **radii**.

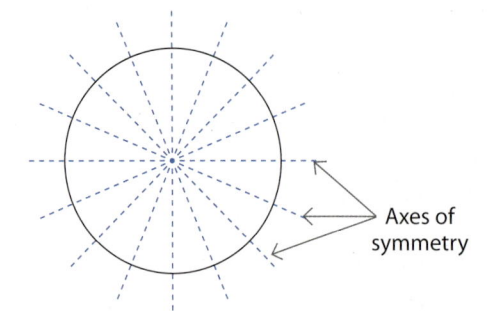

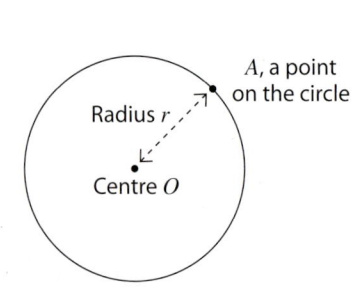

254 Linking Thinking 1

A **chord** is a line segment joining two points on the circle.

A **diameter** is a special chord that passes through the centre. A diameter is twice the length of the radius.

A **tangent** line (or simply **tangent**) to a curve is a straight line that 'just touches' the curve at a point without crossing the curve.

An **arc** is a part of the circumference.

A **sector** of a circle is two-dimensional shape enclosed by an arc and the two radii to its endpoints.

A **semicircle** is a sector whose arcs ends are the ends of a diameter.

The green part of the diagram is a semicircle

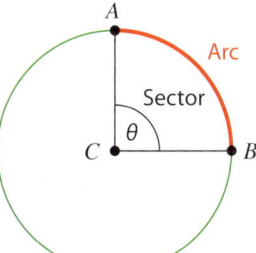

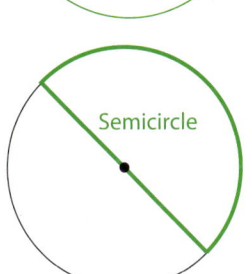

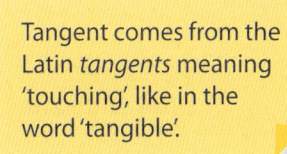

Tangent comes from the Latin *tangents* meaning 'touching', like in the word 'tangible'.

Parts of circles and their angles

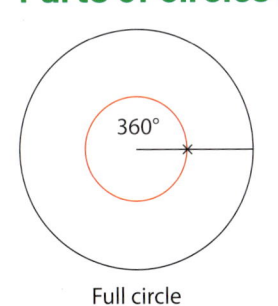

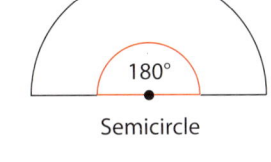

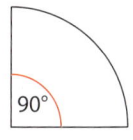

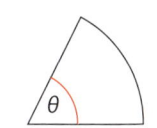

- 360° — Full circle
- 180° — Semicircle
- 90° — Quarter circle
- θ — Sector with acute angle

Practice questions 16·1

1. O is the centre of the circle on the right.

   Name each of the four different coloured parts of the circle.

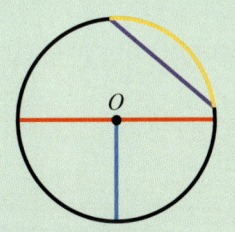

2. M is the centre each of the circles shown below. Name each of the outlines of the shaded regions in the circles as either a sector, semicircle, quarter circle or full circle.

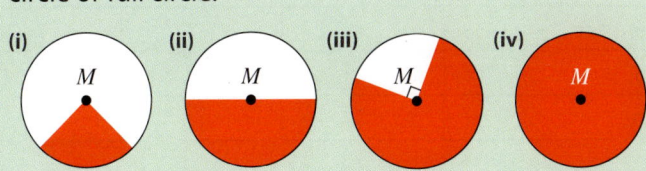

   (i) (ii) (iii) (iv)

3. Are the coloured outlines of the following shapes sectors, semicircles, quarter circles or circles?

   (i) (ii) (iii) (iv)

Section B **Moving forward** 255

4. State if the line segments AB, CD, EF, and GH shown in the pictures below represent a chord, a tangent, a diameter or a radius. (Assume C is the centre of each circle pictured.)

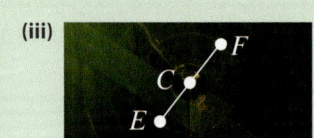

   (i)   (ii)   (iii)   (iv)

5. Using a compass, protractor and a ruler, draw the sectors shown in the sketches below.

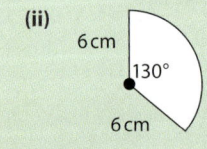

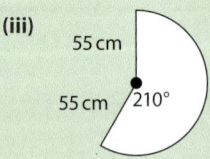

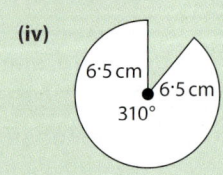

   (i) 4 cm, 60°, 4 cm   (ii) 6 cm, 130°, 6 cm   (iii) 55 cm, 55 cm, 210°   (iv) 6·5 cm, 6·5 cm, 310°

6. Using a compass, ruler and protractor draw:
   (i) a circle with radius of 5 cm
   (ii) a circle with diameter of 8 cm
   (iii) a sector with radius 5 cm and acute angle of 45°
   (iv) a sector with radius 6 cm and an acute angle of 60°
   (v) a sector with radius 4·5 cm and an acute angle of 75°

7. Find the measure of the unknown angles A to D below.

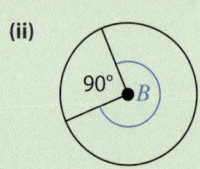

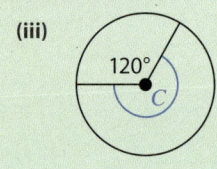

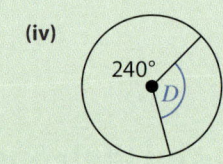

   (i) A   (ii) 90°, B   (iii) 120°, C   (iv) 240°, D

8. Find the measure of the unknown angles X to Z below.

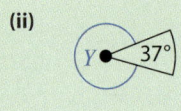

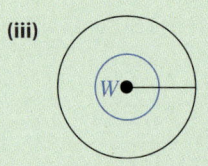

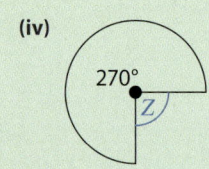

   (i) 137°, X   (ii) Y, 37°   (iii) W   (iv) 270°, Z

9. Using a compass and ruler and an appropriate scale, draw a scale diagram of each of the following.

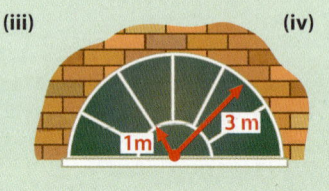

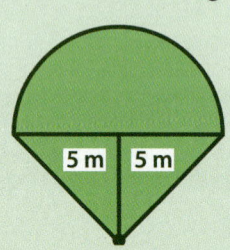

   (i) 90°, 55 m   (ii) 23 m   (iii) 1 m, 3 m   (iv) 5 m, 5 m

10. Copy the table below and put a tick (✓) in the correct box in each row to show whether each statement is always true, sometimes true, or never true.

	Statement	Always true	Sometimes true	Never true
(i)	The angle in a full circle is 360°.			
(ii)	The area of a semicircle is twice the area of the circle.			
(iii)	A line is both a chord and the diameter of the circle.			
(iv)	The diameter is longer than the circumference.			
(v)	A line can be both a tangent and a chord.			
(vi)	A circle has exactly two lines of symmetry.			

256   Linking Thinking 1

16·2 Area and perimeter of a disc

By the end of this section you should:
- understand how to find the circumference of a circle
- understand what a disc is
- understand how to find the area of a disc

Discuss and discover

While working with a partner, use a compass and ruler to draw circles with the measurements shown in the table below.

Using a piece of string and a ruler, measure the length of the circle (this is called the circumference).

Copy the table and fill in the missing values.

Radius	Diameter	Circumference	Circumference/Diameter
3 cm			
5 cm			
5·8 cm			
64 mm			

What have you discovered about the values in your last column?

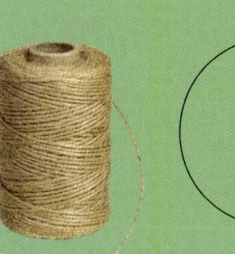

Length of a circle

The circumference is the length of the circle if it were opened up and straightened out to a line segment. This was the length of the string that fit exactly around each circle in the activity above.

> Circumference comes from the Latin *circumferens*, meaning 'carrying around'.

> The length of a whole circle is called its **circumference**.

From the activity above, you should have discovered that the values in the last column were approximately the same in each case. This value is a special number called pi, represented by the symbol π.

$$\pi = \frac{\text{circumference}}{\text{diameter}}$$

> π is a letter in the Greek alphabet called 'pi'.

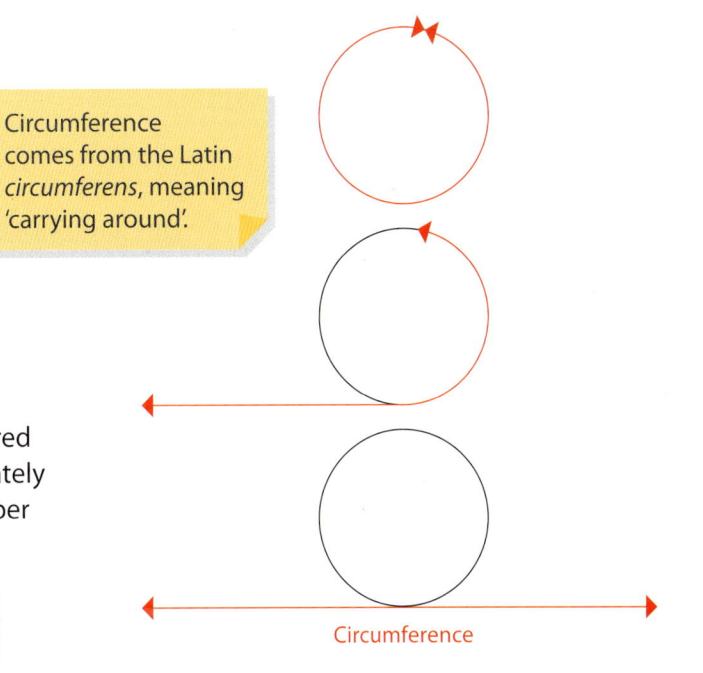

π is a constant value for all circles. The approximate values we use include 3·14 and $\frac{22}{7}$, or by using the π button on the calculator.

π is an **irrational number**, which is a real number that cannot be written as a simple fraction. This is why we use approximate values for π.

Section B Moving forward

Once we know the radius of a circle, we can calculate the length of the circle (circumference) and the area inside the circle (**disc**).

Circumference of a circle = 2 × π × radius
Circumference of a circle = 2πr

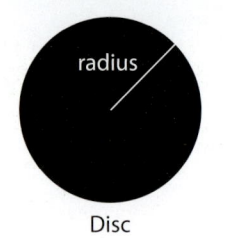

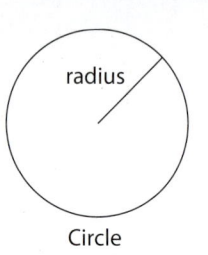

Disc

Circle

A **disc** is the region in a plane inside a circle.

Area of a disc = π × radius × radius
Area of a disc = πr^2

These formulae appear in the *formulae and tables* booklet.

Worked example 1

Taking π = 3·14, find (i) the circumference and (ii) the area of the disc shown on the right which has a radius of 4·5 cm. Give your answer correct to two decimal places.

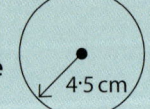

Solution

(i) Radius, r = 4·5 cm
Circumference of a circle = 2πr
Circumference of a circle = 2(3·14)(4·5)
Circumference of a circle = 28·26 cm

(ii) Area of a disc = πr^2
Area of a disc = (3·14)(4·5)^2
Area of a disc = (3·14)(20·25)
Area of a disc = 63·59 cm^2 (correct to two decimal places)

Worked example 2

Find the area the disc by (i) taking π = $\frac{22}{7}$ (ii) in terms of π, shown on the right which has a diameter of 12·6 cm.

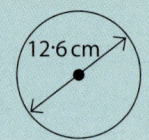

Solution

(i) Area of a disc = πr^2
Area of a disc = $\left(\frac{22}{7}\right)$(6·3)^2
Area of a disc = $\left(\frac{22}{7}\right)$(39·69)
Area of a disc = 124·74 cm^2

(ii) Area of a disc = πr^2
Area of a disc = (π)(6·3)^2
Area of a disc = (π)(39·69)
Area of a disc = 39·69π cm^2

If asked to leave answer 'in terms of π', then you can just leave the π in the answer. Do not substitute any approximation for π.

Worked example 3

The area of the circle on the right is 6 724π mm^2
Find (i) the radius and (ii) the circumference of the disc, correct to two decimal places.

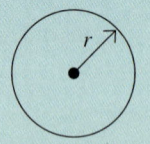

If no value for π is given in a question then use the π button on your calculator.

Solution

(i) Area of a disc = πr^2
6 724π = (π)r^2
6 724π = (π)r^2
$\frac{6\,724π}{π} = \frac{(π)r^2}{π}$ (divide both sides by π)
6 724 = r^2 (get the square root of both sides)
$\sqrt{6\,724} = \sqrt{r^2}$
82 mm = r

(ii) Circumference = 2πr
Circumference = 2(π)(82)
Circumference = 515·22 mm^2

Finding the **square root** is the reverse of squaring.

Discuss and discover

Investigate the area of a disc compared to a square.

(i) Working with a classmate, draw a square of side 10 cm. Then, using a compass, draw a circle which fits exactly inside this square (as shown).

(ii) What percentage of the area of the square is covered by the circle?

(iii) Repeat this activity with other circles drawn inside squares but change the size of the square used in each case.

What have you discovered about the percentage area taken up by a circle which fits exactly inside a square?

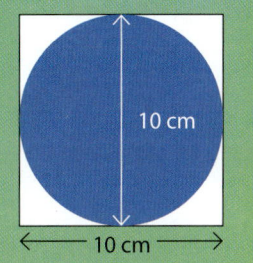

Practice questions 16·2

1. **(a)** Find the value of π for circles with the following measurements:
   (i) Diameter = 20 cm, circumference = 62·80 cm
   (ii) Radius = 4 cm, circumference = 25·12 cm
   (iii) Diameter = 180 cm, circumference = 5 652 mm

   (b) What do you notice about your answers to part (a)?

2. Write down the type of circle represented by each diagram below, i.e. circles, semicircles, discs or half discs.

   (i)   (ii)    (iii)    (iv)

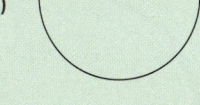

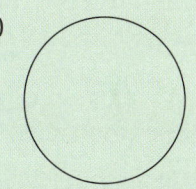

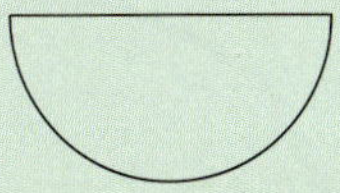

3. **(a)** Draw the following circles using a compass and a ruler.

   (i) 5 cm   (ii) 6 cm   (iii) 4·5 cm   (iv) 57 mm

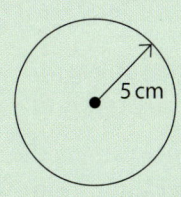

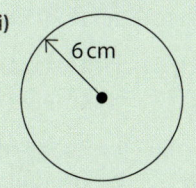

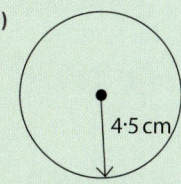

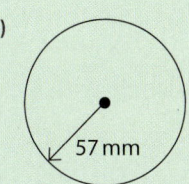

   (b) Taking $\pi = 3·14$, find the circumference of each of the circles in part (a), correct to two decimal places.

   (c) Taking $\pi = \frac{22}{7}$, find the circumference of each of the circles in part (a), correct to two decimal places.

   (d) Find, in terms of π, the circumference of each of the circles in part (a).

Section B Moving forward

4. (a) Draw the following discs using a compass and ruler.

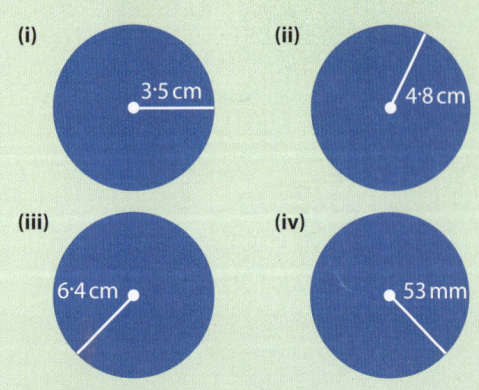

   (i) 3.5 cm
   (ii) 4.8 cm
   (iii) 6.4 cm
   (iv) 53 mm

   (b) Taking π = 3.14, find the area of each of the discs correct to two decimal places.
   (c) Taking π = $\frac{22}{7}$, find the area of each of the discs correct to two decimal places.
   (d) Find, in terms of π, the area of each of the discs.

5. Find the circumference of each of the following circles correct to two decimal places.
   (i) Radius of 12 cm
   (ii) Diameter of 14 cm
   (iii) Diameter of 16 cm
   (iv) Radius of 134 mm

6. Taking π = 3.14, find the area inside each of the following circles, correct to two decimal places.
   (i) Radius of 14 cm
   (ii) Diameter of 17 cm
   (iii) Diameter of 127 mm
   (iv) Radius of 148 mm

7. Find, in terms of π, the area of each of the following discs.
   (i) Radius of 55 cm
   (ii) Diameter of 23 cm
   (iii) Diameter of 248 mm
   (iv) Radius of 33 mm

8. Find the radius of each of the following.
   (i) A circle with a circumference of 48π cm
   (ii) A disc with an area of 81π cm²
   (iii) A circle with a circumference of 98π cm
   (iv) A half disc with an area of 32π mm²

9. A circular field is shown in the picture below.

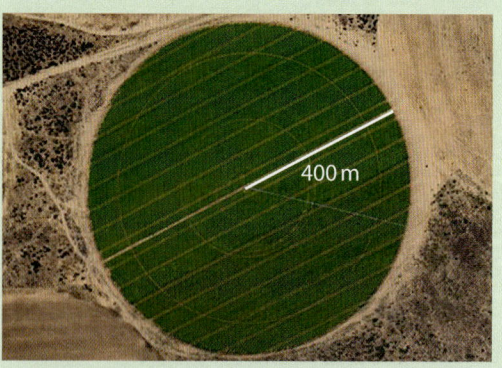

   A farmer would like to replace the fencing around this field. The field has a radius of 400 metres.
   (i) Find the length of the fence required.
   (ii) If posts to hold up the fence are placed 3 metres apart, what is the minimum number of posts the farmer should order for this fence?

10. Here is the centre circle on a GAA pitch. The diameter of the circle is 18·3 metres. 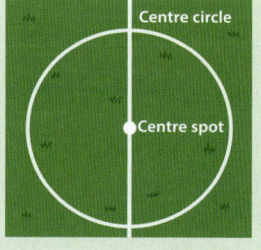
    (i) Taking π = $\frac{22}{7}$, find the circumference of the centre circle.
    (ii) Taking π = $\frac{22}{7}$, find the area enclosed by the centre circle.

11. Two rings (circles) are highlighted in a cross section of a tree trunk as shown here. The inner ring has a radius of 25 cm and the outer ring has a radius of 29 cm. 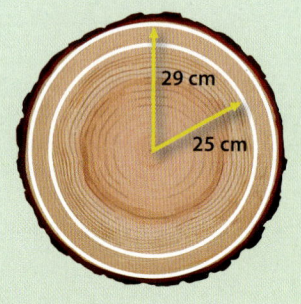
    (i) Find the circumference of the (a) smaller ring and (b) larger ring
    (ii) Find the total area enclosed by the (a) smaller ring and (b) larger ring
    (iii) Find the size of the area between the two rings.
    (iv) If another inner ring (not shown) has a circumference of 24π cm, find its radius.

16·3 Compound shapes involving circles

By the end of this section you should be able to:
- understand how to find the area of compound shapes involving circles, sectors and semicircles

Circle/disc
Area = πr^2

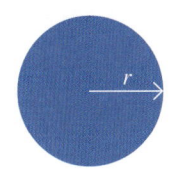

Circumference = $2\pi r$

Semicircle/half disc
Area = $\frac{1}{2}\pi r^2$

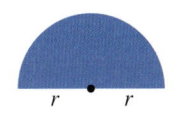

Perimeter = $\pi r + 2r$

Quarter circle/quarter disc
Area = $\frac{1}{4}\pi r^2$

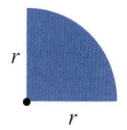

Perimeter = $\frac{1}{2}\pi r + 2r$

Worked example

Find the area of the coloured region in the diagrams on the right.

(i) 7·5 cm, 7·5 cm, 18 cm

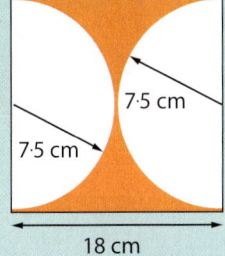

(ii) 8·9 cm, 8·9 cm

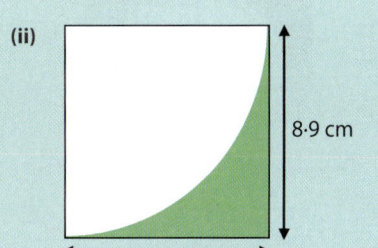

Solution

(i) The area of the outer rectangle:

Area = length × width

Area = 18 × 15

Area = 270

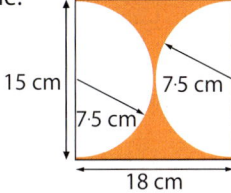

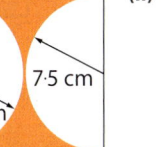

Area of half a disc = $\frac{1}{2}\pi r^2$

Area of half a disc = $\frac{1}{2}\pi (7·5)^2$

Area of half a disc = $\frac{1}{2}\pi (56·25)$

Area of half a disc = 88·36 cm²

Area of two half discs = 176·71 cm²

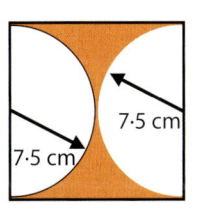

Area of shaded region = rectangle − two half discs

Area of shaded region = 270 − 176·71

Area of shaded region = 93·29 cm²

(ii) Area of the outer square:

Area = length × length

Area = 8·9 × 8·9

Area = 79·21

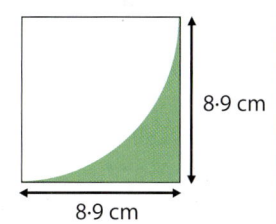

Area of quarter of a disc = $\frac{1}{4}\pi r^2$

Area of quarter of a disc = $\frac{1}{4}\pi (8·9)^2$

Area of quarter of a disc = $\frac{1}{4}\pi (79·21)$

Area of quarter of a disc = 62·21 cm²

Area of shaded region = square − quarter disc

Area of shaded region = 79·21 − 62·21

Area of shaded region = 17 cm²

Section B Moving forward

Practice questions 16·3

1. Find the area of the shaded region in each of the shapes below.

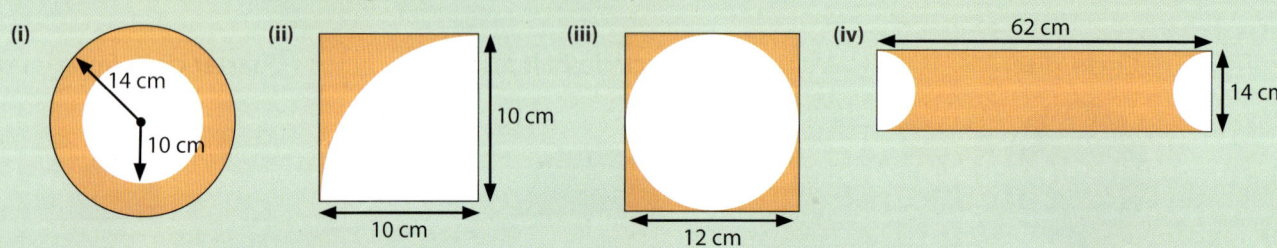

   (i) Circle with radius 14 cm (outer) and 10 cm (inner white circle)
   (ii) 10 cm × 10 cm square with a quarter circle removed
   (iii) Square of side 12 cm with an inscribed white circle
   (iv) Rectangle 62 cm × 14 cm with semicircles removed from each end

2. Find the perimeter of the following shapes.

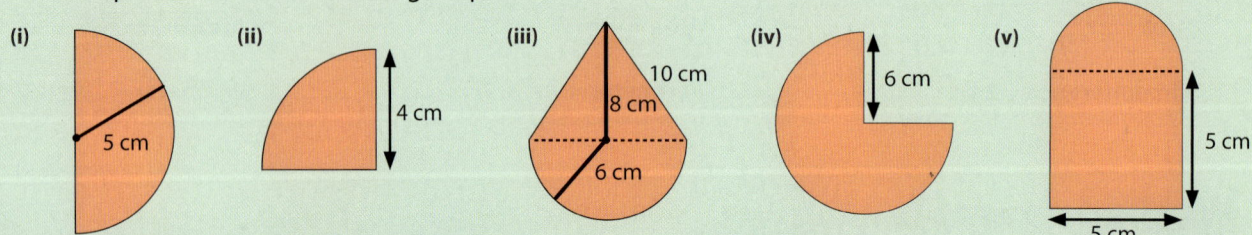

   (i) Semicircle with radius 5 cm
   (ii) Quarter circle with radius 4 cm
   (iii) Shape with 10 cm, 8 cm, and 6 cm measurements
   (iv) Three-quarter circle with radius 6 cm
   (v) Rectangle 5 cm wide and 5 cm tall topped by a semicircle

3. Find the surface area of the wall in the diagram on the right, excluding the glass section.
   (5·4 metres across top, 3 metres tall, 4·5 metres across bottom)

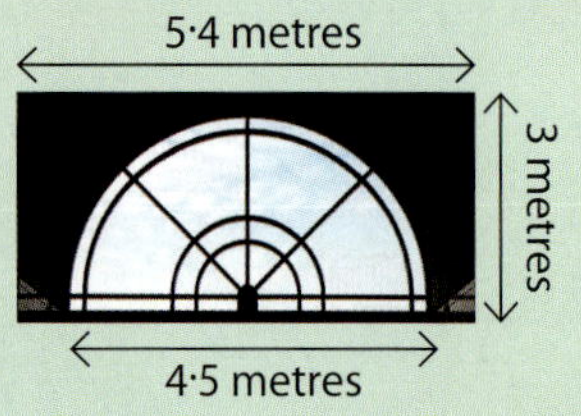

4. All of the circles in the diagram on the right have a diameter of 78 cm. Find the total length of all the circles combined.

5. The dart board shown on the right has a diameter of 45·2 cm. The dart board is fixed to a square cabinet. The width of the cabinet is 55 cm.
   (i) Find the area of wood that a player can see when throwing darts at this board. 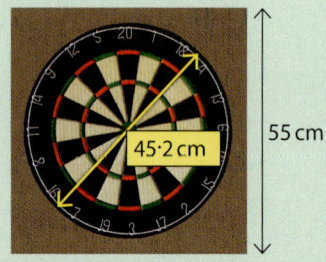
   (ii) Find the percentage of the cabinet covered by the dart board.
   (iii) If two half doors are to be placed on the front of this cabinet, find the area of one of these doors.

6. A bicycle wheel has a diameter of 53 cm.
   (i) Calculate the radius of the wheel.
   (ii) Find the distance moved by the bicycle if the wheel makes one full turn.
   (iii) How many turns will it take to travel 1 km?

   1 km = 1 000 m = 100 000 cm = 1 000 000 mm

7. An airplane tyre has a diameter of 1 400 mm. 
   (i) What would be the distance travelled down a runway if this tyre made 320 full rotations?
   (ii) How many full rotations of this tyre will it take to roll 2·5 km down a runway?

8. The end of a box of markers has 10 circular pens in it as shown below. Each of the markers has a diameter of 17 mm. 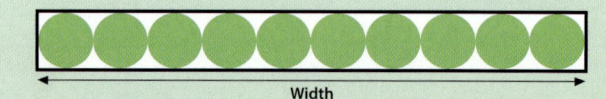
   (i) Find the width of the box.
   (ii) Find the area in white.

9. On the right is a diagram of a stained glass window with measurements shown. 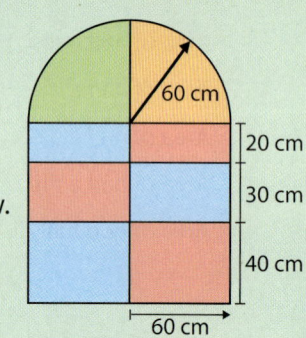
   (i) Find the area of the whole window.
   (ii) Find the area of the pink glass.
   (iii) Find the area of the blue glass.
   (iv) Find the area of the green glass.
   (v) If the orange glass costs 50 cents per 1 cm², find the cost of buying the orange glass.

   (60 cm radius arch top, 20 cm, 30 cm, 40 cm, 60 cm measurements)

262   Linking Thinking 1

Revision questions

16A Core skills

1. Match the parts of the circles from the list with the red part of the diagrams below them.

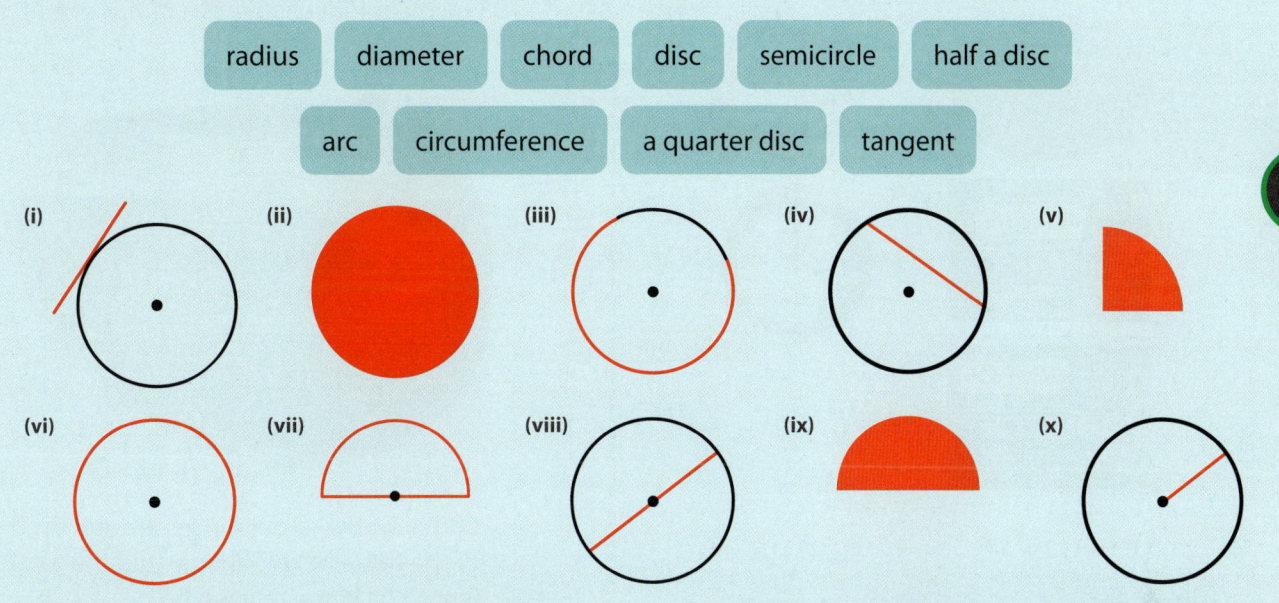

   radius   diameter   chord   disc   semicircle   half a disc

   arc   circumference   a quarter disc   tangent

   (i)   (ii)   (iii)   (iv)   (v)

   (vi)   (vii)   (viii)   (ix)   (x)

2. Taking π = 3·14, find the circumference of each of the following circles, correct to two decimal places.
   (i) Radius of 15 cm
   (ii) Diameter of 5·6 cm
   (iii) Diameter of 10·8 cm

3. Taking $\pi = \frac{22}{7}$, find the area of each of the following discs, correct to two decimal places.
   (i) Radius of 123 mm
   (ii) Diameter of 24·6 cm
   (iii) Diameter of 190 m

4. Find, in terms of π, the area of each of the following discs.
   (i) Radius of 22 cm
   (ii) Diameter of 18·8 cm
   (iii) Diameter of 404 mm

5. Find the circumference of each of the following circles, correct to two decimal places.
   (i) Radius of 73 cm
   (ii) Diameter of 60·8 m
   (iii) Diameter of 200·4 cm

6. Find the radius of each of the following circles.
   (i) Diameter of 40 cm
   (ii) Circumference of 26π cm
   (iii) Area of 36π cm^2
   (iv) Area of 121π cm^2

7. Copy the table below and put a tick (✓) in the correct box in each row to show whether each statement is always true, sometimes true, or never true.

	Statement	Tick **one** box only for each statement		
		Always true	Sometimes true	Never true
(i)	A circle has a maximum of 4 axes of symmetry.			
(ii)	A circle will fit into a square of sides equal to the diameter of the circle.			
(iii)	π is equal to exactly 3·14.			
(iv)	As the radius of a circle increases, the value of π increases.			

Section B Moving forward

16B Taking it FURTHER

1. Find the circumference and the area enclosed by the following circles to one decimal place.

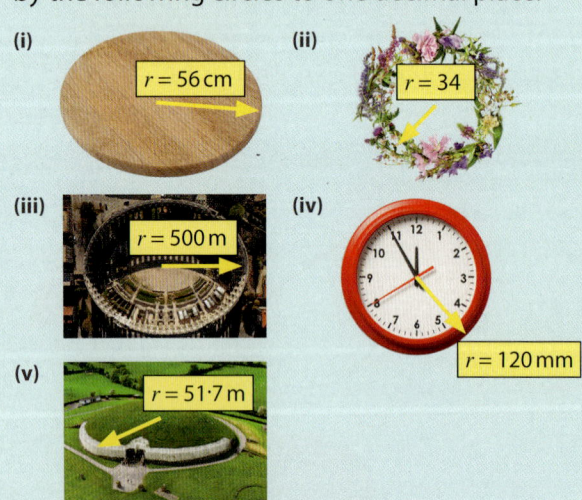

(i) $r = 56$ cm

(ii) $r = 34$

(iii) $r = 500$ m

(iv) $r = 120$ mm

(v) $r = 51.7$ m

2. Find the area of the shaded regions below:

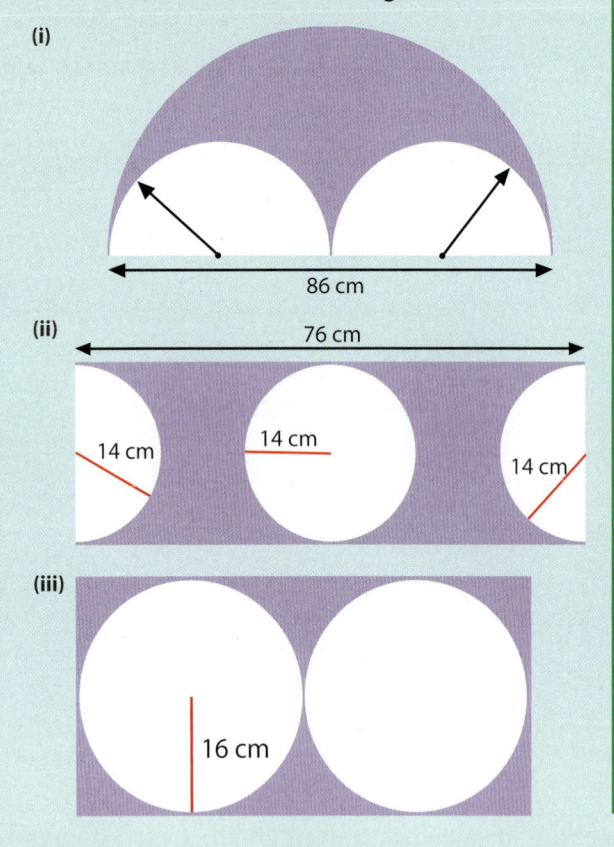

(i) 86 cm

(ii) 76 cm, 14 cm, 14 cm, 14 cm

(iii) 16 cm

3. Cathal owns three circular fields which are pictured below. The radius of the smallest field is 55 m, the middle field has a radius of 144 m and the largest field has a diameter of 720 m.

$r = 55$ m
$r = 144$ m
$d = 720$ m

(i) Cathal wants to put fences around each of the three fields. What would the total length of all the fencing be?

(ii) If posts are placed every 4 metres in each fence, what is the minimum number of posts Cathal should order to construct the three fences?

(iii) If the fencing costs €9 per 10 metres to construct, what will it cost Cathal to construct the fence?

(iv) Cathal wishes to spread fertiliser all over the three fields. What is the surface area he will have to cover with the fertiliser?

(v) Fertiliser is bought in bags which cover 200 m². How many bags should Cathal buy to spread fertiliser over all three fields?

(vi) If the fertiliser costs €27·50 per bag, how much money will Cathal require to purchase the fertiliser for all three fields?

(vii) If 1 hectare is equal to 10 000 m², how much land does Cathal have in hectares?

Now that you have completed the unit, revisit the

Something to think about ...

question posed at the start of this unit.

Unit 17

Area, volume and surface area

Topics covered within this unit:
17·1 Perimeter and area of shapes
17·2 Nets and surface area of rectangular solids
17·3 Volume of rectangular solids
17·4 Volume of a cylinder

The Learning Outcomes covered in this unit are contained in the following sections:

GT.2a GT.2b GT.2c GT.2d
AF.3a AF.3b N.1e

Key words
Net
Face
Edge
Vertex
Surface Area
Volume
Capacity
Cylinder

Something to think about ...

KEY SKILLS

A traditional 'square' bale of hay is actually in the shape of a rectangular solid.

Its dimensions are 40 cm by 56 cm by 112 cm.

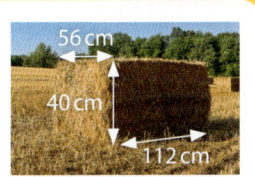

Round hay bales are in the shape of a cylinder. The dimensions are 1·5 metres high and a diameter of 1·8 m.

How many rectangular bales contain the same amount of hay as one large cylinder (round) bale?

17·1 Perimeter and area of shapes

By the end of this section you should be able to:
○ find the perimeter and area of basic shapes, such as squares, rectangles, triangles, circles
○ find the perimeter and area of a parallelogram

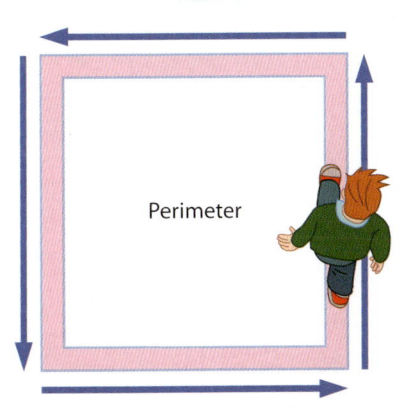

In Units 15 and 16, we learned about perimeter and area.

● **Perimeter** is the distance (total length) around a two-dimensional shape.

It helps to imagine starting at a vertex and finding the distance to walk around the outside of the 2D shape.

Units: millimetres (mm), centimetres (cm), metres (m), etc.

● **Area** is the size of a flat surface. It is the amount of space contained within the edges of a two-dimensional shape.

Units: millimetres squared (mm^2), centimetres squared (cm^2), metres squared (m^2), etc.

Sometimes a problem will give measurements in more than just one unit, for example: in millimetres and centimetres. Make sure you convert all measurements to the same unit before doing any calculations.

Section B Moving forward 265

The boxes below show the relationships between these units.

Units of length
1 kilometre (km) = 1000 metres (m)
1 metre (m) = 100 centimetres (cm)
1 centimetre (cm) = 10 millimetres (mm)

Units of area
1 km² = 1 km × 1 km = 1 000 m × 1 000 m = 10 000 m²
1 m² = 1 m × 1 m = 100 cm × 100 cm = 10 000 cm²
1 cm² = 1 cm × 1 cm = 10 mm × 10 mm = 100 mm²

Square

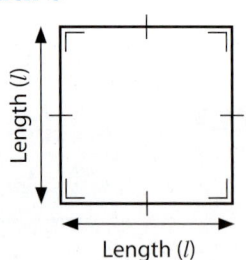

Length (l)

Perimeter = $l + l + l + l$
         = $4(l)$

Area = $l \times l = l^2$

Rectangle

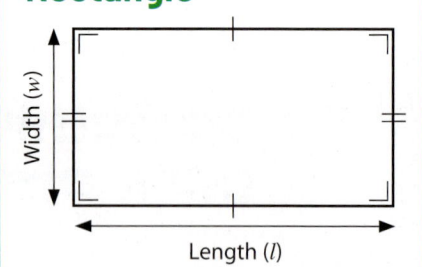

Width (w), Length (l)

Perimeter = $l + w + l + w$
         = $2(l) + 2(w)$

Area = $l \times w$

Triangle

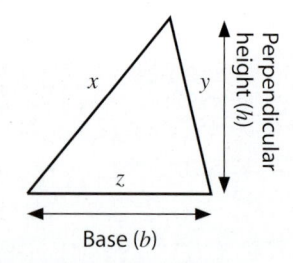

x, y, z, Base (b), Perpendicular height (h)

Perimeter = $x + y + z$

Area = $\frac{1}{2}$ base × perpendicular height

Area = $\frac{1}{2} b \times \perp h$

Circle

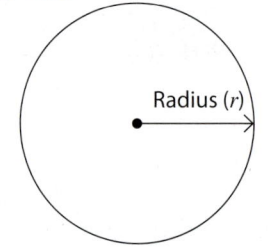

Radius (r)

Perimeter = $2 \times \pi \times$ radius
         = $2\pi r$

Area = $\pi \times r^2 = \pi r^2$

Perimeter of a circle is also known as its circumference.

Semicircle

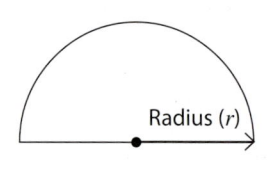

Radius (r)

Perimeter = $\pi \times r +$ diameter
         = $\pi r + d$

Area = $\frac{1}{2} \times \pi \times r^2$

Area = $\frac{1}{2} \pi r^2$

Sector

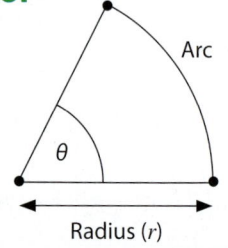

Arc, θ, Radius (r)

Length of arc = $\frac{\theta}{360} \times 2\pi \times r$

Total perimeter = arc + $2r$

Area of sector = $\frac{\theta}{360} \times \pi \times r^2$

Worked example 1

For the sector shown, find:

(i) the area, in terms of π
(ii) the arc length, in terms of π
(iii) the perimeter, to one decimal place.

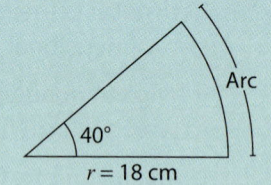

40°, $r = 18$ cm, Arc

Solution

(i) Area = $\frac{\theta}{360°} \times \pi r^2$

Area = $\frac{40°}{360°} \times \pi (18)^2$

Area = 36π cm²

(ii) Arc = $\frac{\theta}{360°} \times 2\pi r$

Arc = $\frac{40°}{360°} \times 2\pi(18)$

Arc = 4π cm

(iii) Perimeter = arc + 2(radius)

Perimeter = $4\pi + 2(18)$

Perimeter = $4\pi + 36$

Perimeter = 48·6 cm

Linking Thinking 1

Discuss and discover

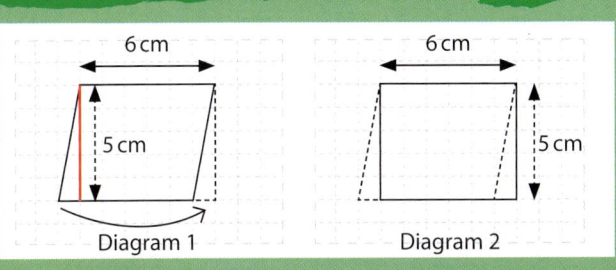

(i) Draw the parallelogram shown in Diagram 1 above, of width 6 cm and height 5 cm, on gridded paper and cut it out.

(ii) Draw a line from the top left vertex of the parallelogram straight down, forming a right-angled triangle (line marked in red on Diagram 1).

(iii) Cut along this line and move the triangle from the left side to the right, as shown in Diagram 2.

(iv) What new shape have you made? Can you find its area?

(v) What have you discovered about finding the area of a parallelogram?

Parallelogram

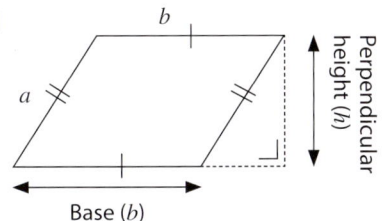

Perimeter $= a + b + a + b = 2(a) + 2(b)$

Area = base × perpendicular height

$A = b \times \perp h$

Worked example 2

Find (i) the area and (ii) the perimeter of the parallelogram shown.

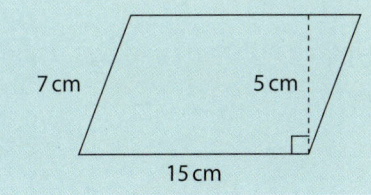

Solution

(i) Area = base × perpendicular height
Area = (15) × (5)
Area = 75 cm²

(ii) Perimeter = sum of outside edges
Perimeter = 15 + 7 + 15 + 7
Perimeter = 44 cm

Practice questions 17·1

1. Suggest an appropriate unit of length that should be used to measure the following.
   (i) The length of a pencil
   (ii) The height of a person
   (iii) The distance you walk to school
   (iv) The width of a human hair
   (v) The distance from Dublin to Donegal
   (vi) The length of a spider's leg

2. Estimate the length of the following, using the correct units, then check to see how close your answer was.
   (i) The height of your classroom's door
   (ii) The width of your desk
   (iii) The height of this Maths book
   (iv) The dimensions of your classroom
   (v) The width of your pencil case
   (vi) The thickness of a €2 coin

3. Sonia runs 9·2 km, while Michelle walks 4 500 metres. How much farther did Sonia run than Michelle walked?

4. A €1 coin is approximately 2·3 mm thick and a €50 note is approximately 0·15 mm thick. 
   (i) If you won €1 000 000 and received this sum in €50 notes, how tall would they be if you stacked each note horizontally on top of each other. Give your answer in metres.
   (ii) The Spire in Dublin is 121 metres tall. If you won €1 000 000 and received this sum in €1 coins, would the stack of coins be taller than the Spire? Justify your answer.

5. Find the area and perimeter of the following shapes. Give your answer to two decimal places where necessary.
   (i) Square, 5 cm × 5 cm
   (ii) Right triangle, 3 cm, 4 cm, 5 cm
   (iii) Circle, radius 7 cm
   (iv) Parallelogram, 8 m, 6·5 m, height 6·3 m

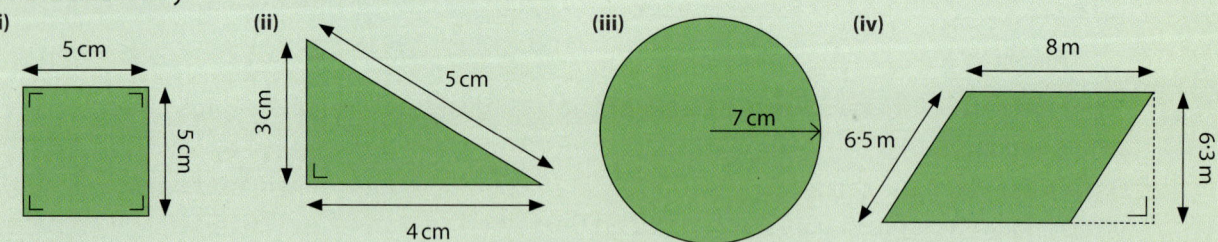

6. Find (a) the perimeter and (b) the area of each of the parallelograms below. Give your answer to one decimal place where necessary.
   (i) Parallelogram with side 3, slant 2·2, height 2
   (ii) Parallelogram with side 3, slant 2·2, base 2
   (iii) Parallelogram with side 5, slant 1·4, height 1

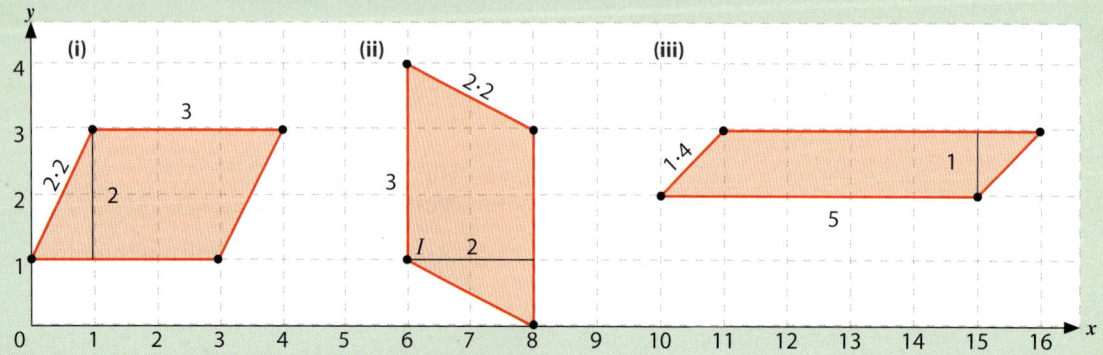

7. Find the area and perimeter of the following shapes, to two decimal places where necessary. Use the squares on the grid to help.
   (i) – (viii) [shapes on grids]
   (v) sector with a = 72°
   (vii) triangle with slant 5

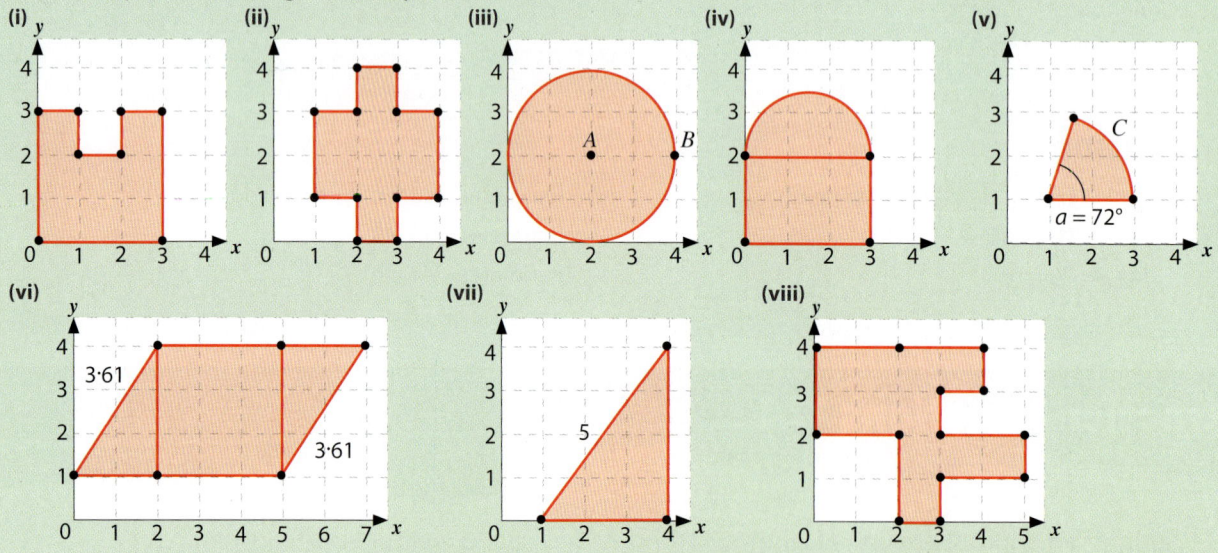

8. Find the area of the shaded sections in the diagrams provided. Give your answer to one decimal place where necessary.
   (i) Annulus, inner radius 1, outer radius 2
   (ii) Square 70 mm × 5 cm with triangle cut-out, base 3 cm
   (iii) Sector, radius (r) = 5 cm, a = 120°
   (iv) Circle with square inscribed, 350 cm, 5 m

268 Linking Thinking 1

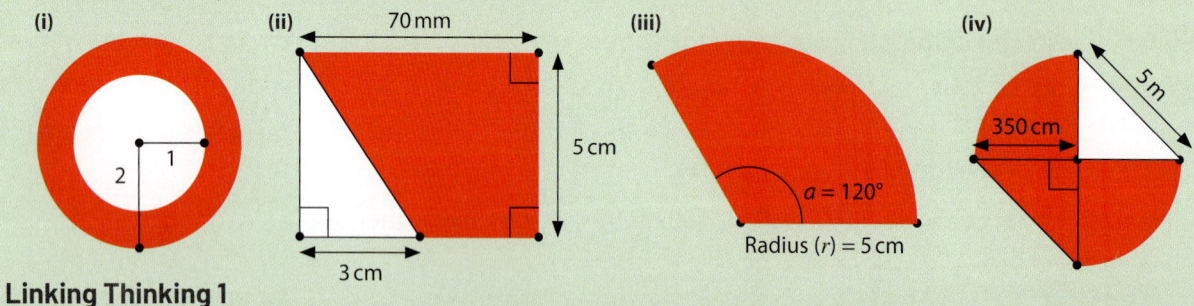

9. Stephen is making a display board for the Science department.

   The display board is 4·5 m by 620 cm. He wants to add a ribbon border around the entire display board.

   The ribbon costs €1·80 per metre, and you can only purchase it in lengths of 1 m (e.g. if you need 1·3 m you must purchase 2 m of ribbon).

   (i) How many metres of ribbon must Stephen buy?

   (ii) How much will it cost to purchase a ribbon to put around the Science display board?

Taking it FURTHER

10. Jodie saw a strange old bicycle at the museum. It had one very big wheel and one very small one. It was called a 'Penny Farthing'. Jodie looked it up on the internet and found that the big wheel has a diameter of 132 cm and the small wheel has a diameter of 46 cm.

    (i) What is the circumference of the big wheel? Give your answer to one decimal place.

    (ii) How many times must the cyclist turn the big wheel to travel 1 kilometre? Give your answer to one decimal place.

    (iii) How many times does the small wheel turn when the cyclist has travelled 1 kilometre?

    1 km = 100 000 cm

11. A rectangle has an area of 16 cm^2.

    (i) Draw and label three different rectangles that could have this area.

    (ii) In natural numbers, what is the smallest perimeter that this rectangle could have?

17·2 Nets and surface area of rectangular solids

By the end of this section you should:
- be able to match the net of a rectangular solid to the 3D solid
- understand how to draw the net of a rectangular solid
- be able to calculate the surface area of a rectangular solid

Most products are packaged in boxes or cans.
Think about how a box or can is made. How do you think the manufacturer chooses the shape and style of package?

Cardboard boxes used by companies such as pizza shops, are usually shipped flat, and then folded into the shape of the box.

This flattened version is known as the **net** of the solid.

> A **net** is a shape in 2D that you can cut and fold to make a solid 3D solid.

The diagram below shows a 2D net of a rectangular solid folded into a 3D rectangular solid.

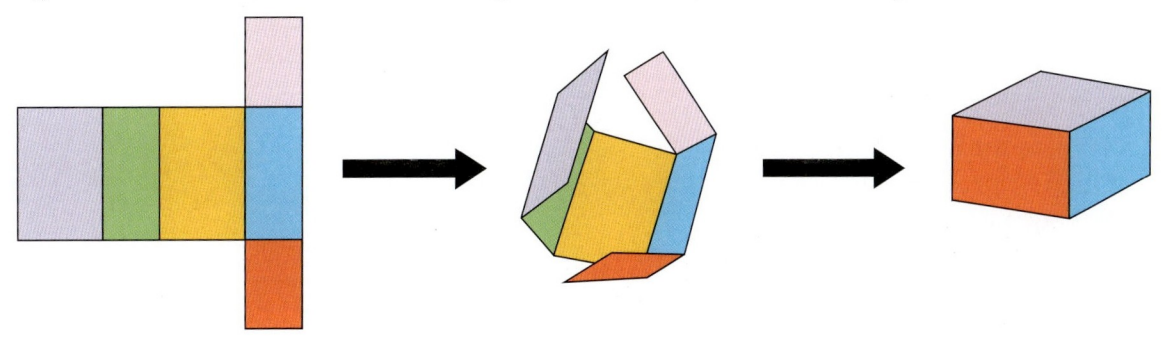

2D net of solid → Folding the net → 3D solid

Properties of a 3D solid

All 3D solids have certain properties in common. They will have several 'faces', 'edges' and 'vertices'.

This particular solid has 6 faces, 8 vertices and 12 edges.

- Each flat surface is called a **face**.
- The line where two flat surfaces meet is called an **edge**.
- The corner where three edges meet is called a **vertex** (plural = vertices).

Worked example 1

Which diagram below matches the net for this solid?

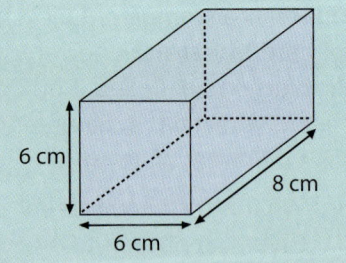

6 cm, 6 cm, 8 cm

Solution

Things to consider:
- The solid has 6 faces: 2 square and 4 rectangular.
- Opposite faces must have the same dimensions and area.
- When the net is folded back together, it must be the same size and have the same dimensions as the original 3D solid.

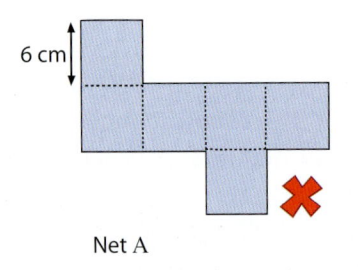

Net A — 6 cm
Net B — 8 cm, 6 cm
Net C — 8 cm, 6 cm

Net A has 6 square faces, so it is not the correct net.

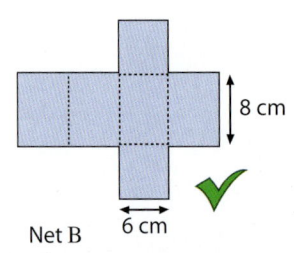

Net B has 2 square faces and 4 rectangular faces, so it is the correct net.

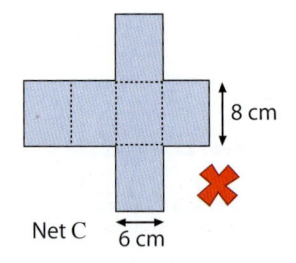

Net C has all rectangular faces, so it is not the correct net.

Discuss and discover

(i) Draw the following net on a piece of gridded card.

(ii) Using scissors, cut along the outside edges of the net you have drawn.

(iii) Fold the shape along the dotted lines to form a 3D solid. What is this solid called?

(iv) Calculate the total surface area of (a) the net and (b) the 3D solid. Are they the same? Why or why not?

(v) Can you explain how the net relates to its 3D solid?

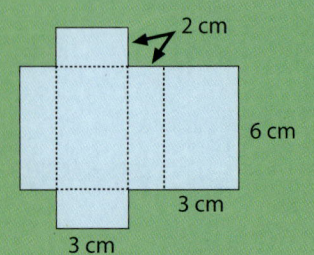

2 cm, 6 cm, 3 cm, 3 cm

270   Linking Thinking 1

Finding the surface area of a 3D solid

> The **surface area** of a 3D solid is the total area of all the faces on the solid.

There are two methods we can use to find the surface area of a 3D solid.

Worked example 2

Find the surface area of the rectangular cuboid.

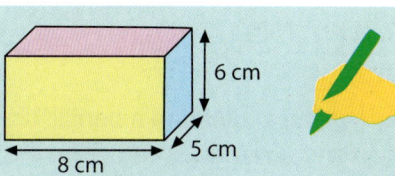

Solution

Method 1:

Step 1 Draw the net of the solid

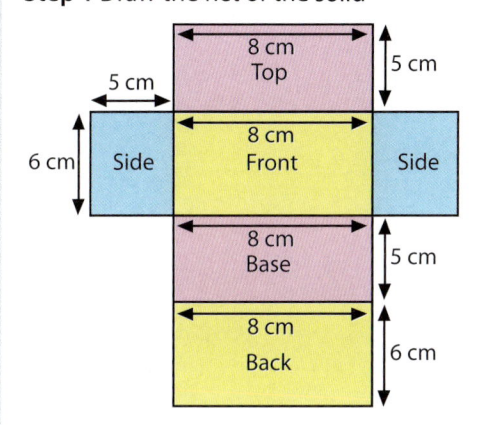

Step 2 Find the area of each face

Top = 8 × 5 = 40 units
Front = 8 × 6 = 48 units
Base = 8 × 5 = 40 units
Back = 8 × 6 = 48 units
Side = 6 × 5 = 30 units
Side = 6 × 5 = 30 units

Add up the area of each face

Total area = 236 units^2

Method 2:

We know the shape has 6 faces
We know:
Area of the front = area of the back
Area of the top = area of the base
Area of left side = area of right side

Area of front and back = (8 × 6)(2) = 96
Area of top and base = (8 × 5)(2) = 80
Area of sides = (5 × 6)(2) = 60

Add up the area of each face

Total area = 236 units^2

Practice questions 17·2

1. Copy these solids. For each solid, identify the following features.

   (i) A face   (ii) An edge   (iii) A vertex

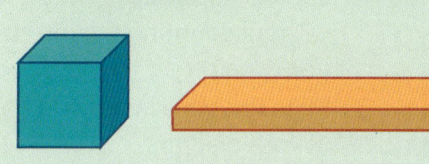

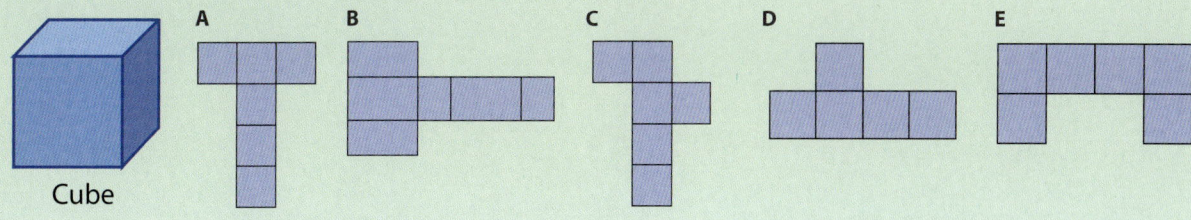

2. Which of the following diagrams could be the net of the cube given? Justify your answer.
   (Note: A solid can have more than one net. In fact, a cube has 11 unique nets.)

   Cube   A   B   C   D   E

Section B Moving forward

3. Which solid can be created using the net given? Justify your answer.

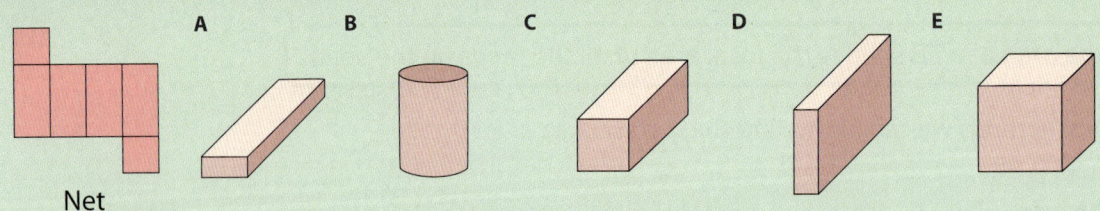

   A B C D E

   Net

4. Using a ruler and a pencil, draw the net of the solids below. On your diagram, be precise in your measurements, and write the lengths of all the lines you have drawn.

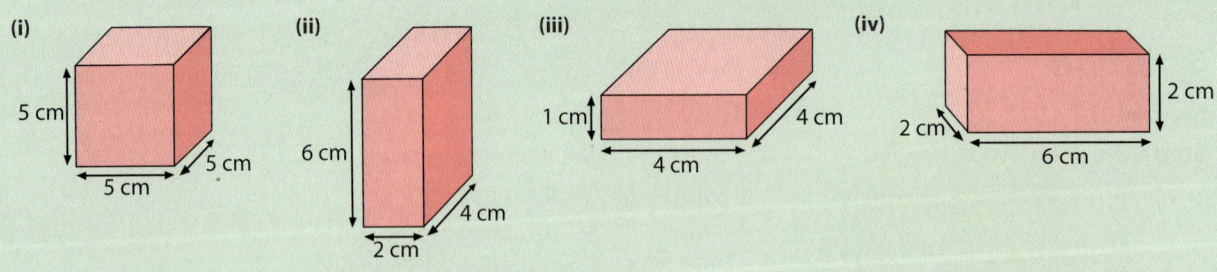

   (i) 5 cm × 5 cm × 5 cm
   (ii) 6 cm × 4 cm × 2 cm
   (iii) 1 cm × 4 cm × 4 cm
   (iv) 2 cm × 6 cm × 2 cm

5. Find the surface area of each of the rectangular cuboids given in question 4.

6. How many cm² of cardboard is needed to make the box shown? Assume there is no overlap in the cardboard.

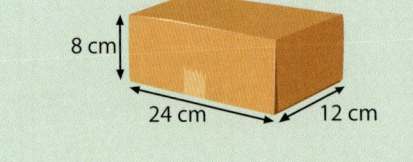

   8 cm, 24 cm, 12 cm

7. Find two rectangular solids in your classroom. Measure the faces. Calculate the surface area.
   (Hint: What shape is your desk, or this book?)

8. Wix Candle company would like to ship its candles in a new biodegradable wrapping with the dimensions shown. (4 cm × 4 cm × 15 cm)

   (i) If the wrapping fits exactly (no overlap), how many cm² of material do they need for each candle?

   (ii) If the wrapping costs €0·002 per cm², how much to the nearest euro will it cost to package 1 500 candles?

   (iii) If the company must pay VAT at 23%, what will their final bill be? Give your answer to the nearest euro.

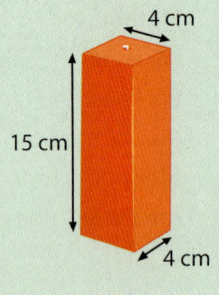

Taking it FURTHER

9. A pizza box has a square top, an edge length of 20 cm, and a height of 5 cm.

   (i) Draw and label a net of this pizza box using an appropriate scale. Treat the box as a 3D solid, without counting the interior flaps that a pizza box usually has.
   State the scale factor you have used at the end of your diagram.

   (ii) 1 inch = 2·4 cm. Mario orders a 7-inch pizza. Will his pizza fit in this box? Justify your answer.
   (Note: 7 inches is the diameter of the pizza)

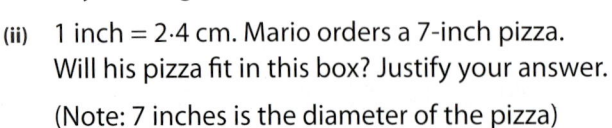

272 Linking Thinking 1

17.3 Volume of rectangular solids

By the end of this section you should:
- understand how to calculate the volume of a solid 3D shape
- be able to solve problems containing 3D shapes

> The **volume** of an object is how much space it takes up. Units are usually mm^3, cm^3 and m^3.

> **Capacity** is the amount of liquid a container can hold. Units are usually ml (millilitres) or l (litres).

In Mathematics, the total volume inside a solid equals its total capacity.
We can only find the volume or capacity of 3D solids.

Discuss and discover

A rectangular playing card has an area of 10 cm × 5 cm.
Imagine each card is 1 mm thick.
If you stacked 100 cards on top of each other like this, how could you work out the volume of the stack of cards?

To calculate the volume of rectangular solids or cubes, we use the following formula.

> **Volume = length × width × height**
> $V = l \times w \times h$

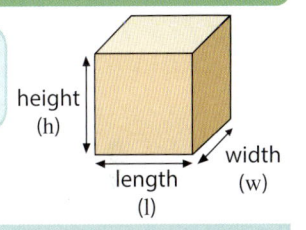

Worked example 1

Find the volume of the (i) cube and (ii) the rectangular solid below.

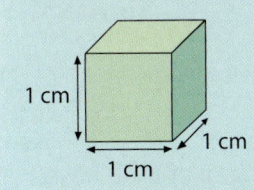

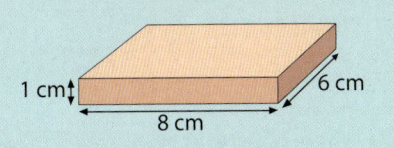

Units of volume to the power of 3 are always pronounced 'cubed', e.g. $5\ m^3$ would be read as 'five metres cubed'.

Solution

(i) Volume = length × width × height
$V = (1\ cm)(1\ cm)(1\ cm)$
Volume = $1\ cm^3$

(ii) Volume = length × width × height
$V = (8\ cm)(6\ cm)(1\ cm)$
Volume = $48\ cm^3$

Worked example 2

A goldfish tank has the dimensions shown.
(i) Calculate the volume of the goldfish tank.
(ii) If $1\ m^3$ equals 1 000 litres of water, how many litres of water are needed to fill the goldfish tank?

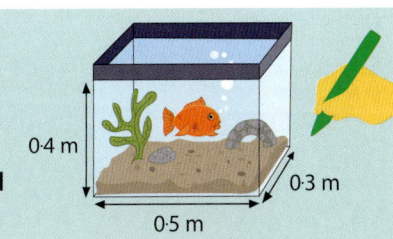

Solution

(i) $V = l \times w \times h$
$V = (0\cdot5)(0\cdot3)(0\cdot4)$
$V = 0\cdot06$
Volume = $0\cdot06\ m^3$

(ii) $1\ m^3 = 1\ 000$ litres
Therefore $0\cdot06\ m^3 = 0\cdot06 \times 1\ 000$
$0\cdot06\ m^3 = 60$ litres
It would take 60 litres of water to fill the goldfish tank

Section B Moving forward

Discuss and discover

(i) Find the volume of this rectangular solid.

(ii) What is the relationship between the area of the base multiplied by the height and the volume?

(iii) Verify this relationship for two more rectangular solids.

(iv) Explain why the volume formulas $V = l \times w \times h$ and $V = b \times h$ give the same results. (b represents the area of the base.)

Can you now explain two ways to find the volume of a rectangular solid?

Practice questions 17.3

1. The colourful solid is made from a number of cubes, of side length 1 cm. Calculate the volume of the solid.

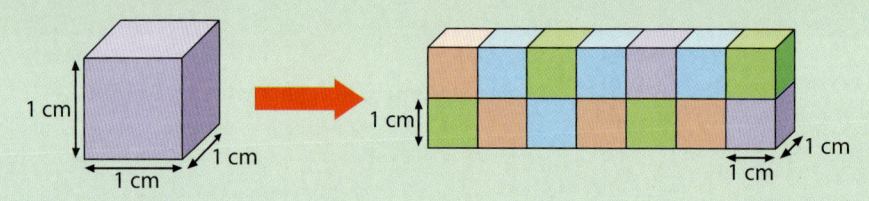

2. Find the volume of each of the following solids.

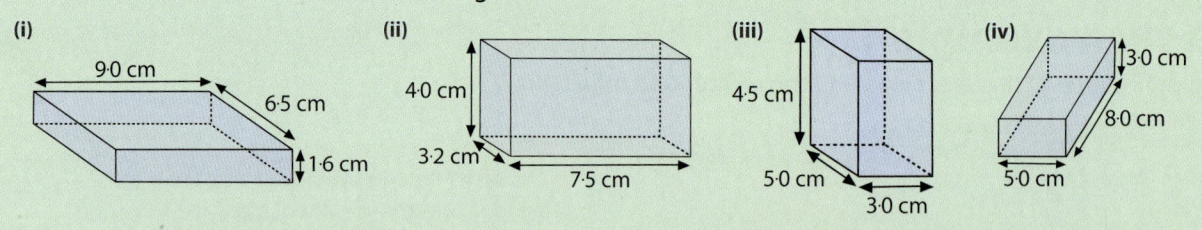

   (i)   (ii)   (iii)   (iv)

3. Find the volume of each of the following solids, given their height as shown and the area of their base.

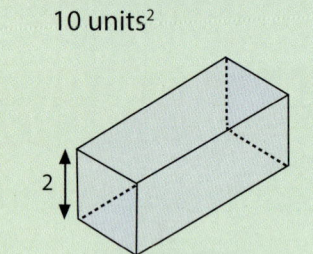

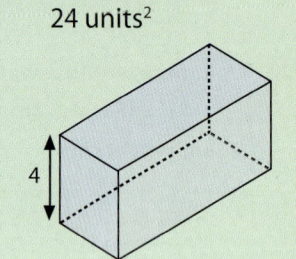

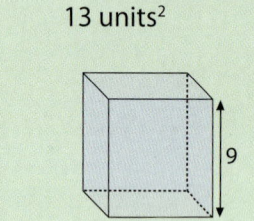

   (i) Area of base = 10 units²
   (ii) Area of base = 24 units²
   (iii) Area of base = 13 units²
   (iv) Area of base = 1.5 units²

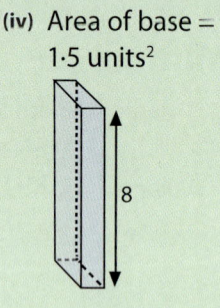

4. Find the volume of each of the rectangular buildings below.

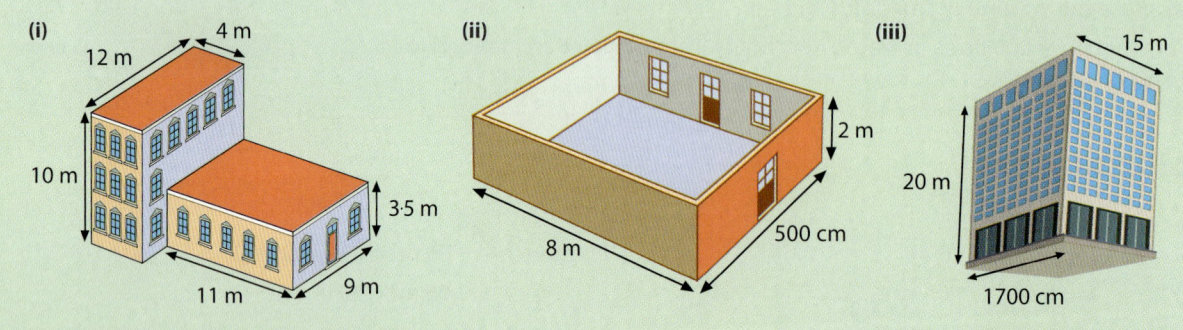

   (i)   (ii)   (iii)

274 Linking Thinking 1

5. Seán loves reading books. He has 10 fiction books, 15 comedy books and 8 true crime books.

   The dimensions of each type of book are provided in the table below.

   (i) Sketch a drawing of each book, showing the length, width and height.
   (ii) Find the total volume of all his books combined.

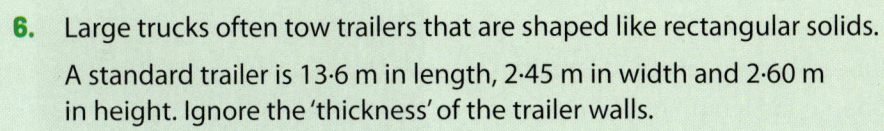

Dimensions	Length	Width	Height	Total volume of one book	Total volume of this genre
Fiction	23 cm	4 cm	18 cm		
Comedy	24 cm	3·4 cm	120 mm		
True crime	20 cm	300 mm	11·5 cm		
					Total volume = ?

6. Large trucks often tow trailers that are shaped like rectangular solids.

   A standard trailer is 13·6 m in length, 2·45 m in width and 2·60 m in height. Ignore the 'thickness' of the trailer walls. 

   (i) What is the greatest volume of cargo a standard trailer can hold? Give your answer to three decimal places.
   (ii) How many complete trailers would it take to transport 300 m³ of goods?
   (iii) Shane has a rectangular object with a length of 14·1 m, width of 2·3 m and height of 1·9 m. He thinks this volume is less than the volume of the truck trailer. Is he correct?
   (iv) The truck driver states that this cargo will not fit into his trailer. Do you agree? Justify your answer.

7. If a carton of milk has a square base 10 cm wide and 10 cm long.
   What is the minimum height the carton must be to hold 2 litres of milk?

8. Three rectangular solids are shown in the diagram.

   1 000 cm³ = 1 litre

   (i) Find the volume, in cm³, of each solid.
   (ii) What do you notice about the three volumes?
   (iii) Does the volume of a rectangular solid change if you place the solid on a different base? Justify your answer.

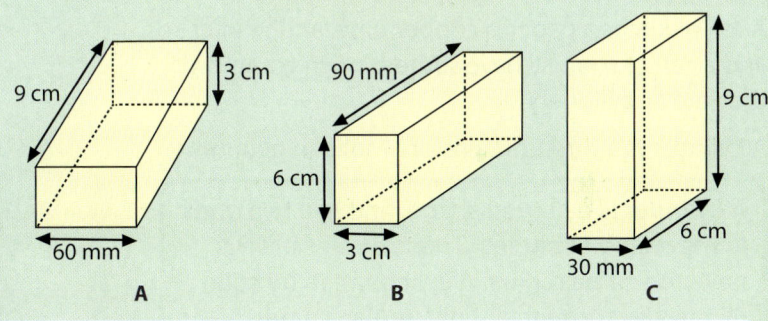

   A: 9 cm, 60 mm, 3 cm
   B: 90 mm, 3 cm, 6 cm
   C: 9 cm, 30 mm, 6 cm

Taking it FURTHER

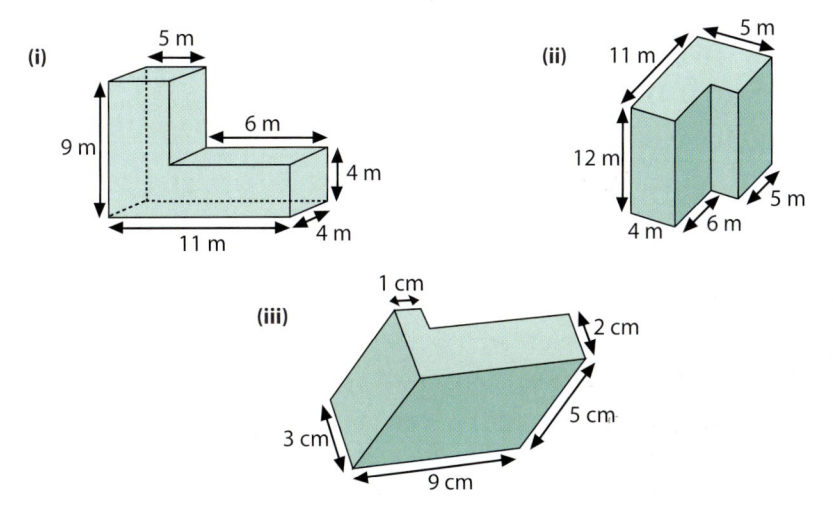

9. Calculate the volume of each of these solids.
   Hint: You can break each solid up into smaller rectangular solids.

   (i) 5 m, 9 m, 6 m, 4 m, 11 m, 4 m
   (ii) 5 m, 11 m, 12 m, 4 m, 5 m, 6 m
   (iii) 1 cm, 2 cm, 5 cm, 3 cm, 9 cm

Taking it FURTHER

10. Find the volume of each of the following solids.

    (i) Dimensions: $\frac{2}{3}$ m, $\frac{3}{4}$ m, $\frac{2}{5}$ cm

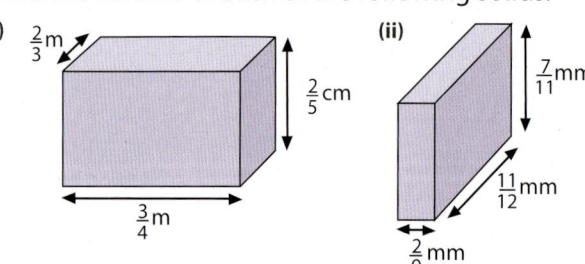

    (ii) Dimensions: $\frac{7}{11}$ mm, $\frac{11}{12}$ mm, $\frac{2}{9}$ mm

    (iii) Dimensions: 5 cm, 2 cm, $\frac{37}{6}$ cm, $10\frac{1}{2}$ cm, $\frac{13}{6}$ cm

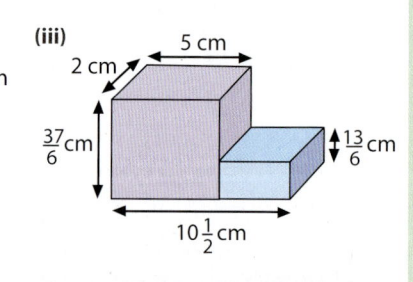

11. Mohammed needs to change the water in his goldfish tank. The dimensions of the tank are as follows: length = 0·8 m, width = 0·6 m and height = 0·5 m
    He uses a cube-shaped bucket to fill the tank. The bucket has a side length of 0·2 m. 
    (i) If 1 m³ = 1 000 litres of water, how many litres of water does
        (a) the goldfish tank hold?
        (b) the bucket hold?
    (ii) Calculate how many times Mohammed must fill the bucket to completely fill his goldfish tank.

17·4 Volume of a cylinder

By the end of this section you should:
- understand how to calculate the volume of a cylinder
- be able to solve problems involving volume of cylinders

A roll of kitchen paper, a copper pipe, a tube of crisps, and a can of soup all have something in common: they are all cylinders.

A cylinder is a three-dimensional solid in geometry.

> A **cylinder** is a curved shape, and has two ends in the shape of circles. These circles always have the same radius. A cylinder can be solid all the way through or hollow, like a pipe.

Some every day examples of cylinders include:

Discuss and discover

KEY SKILLS

When we analysed the volume of a rectangular solid, we discovered that the volume can be found by finding the area of its base and multiplying that by its height.

1. Use this method to find the volume of the cylinder shown.
2. Can you now write down a formula for finding the volume of a cylinder of radius r and height h?
3. Explain why the volume formulae $V = \pi r^2 h$ and $V = b \times h$ give the same results. (b represents the area of the base.)

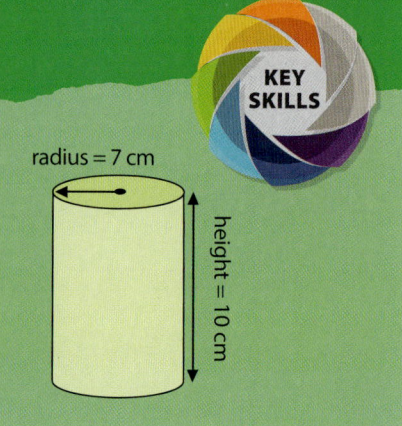

radius = 7 cm
height = 10 cm

276 Linking Thinking 1

Finding the volume of a cylinder

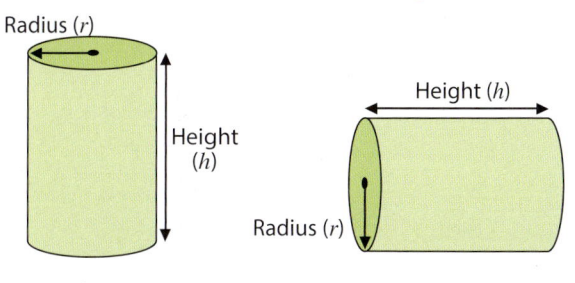

Volume of a cylinder = π × radius × radius × height
$$V = \pi r^2 h$$

This formula appears in the *formulae and tables* booklet.

When doing calculations involving π, use $\frac{22}{7}$ or 3·14 or leave answer in terms of π. Otherwise, use the π button on your calculator.

Worked example 1

Find the volume of the cylinder. Let π = 3·14

Solution

Volume = $\pi r^2 h$

$V = (3\cdot14)(4)^2(3)$

$V = 150\cdot72$ cm³

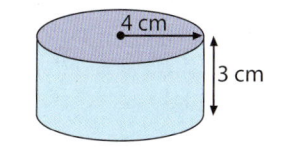

Worked example 2

Holly and Leo set up an inflatable cylindrical pool in their back garden. The diameter of the pool is 3 metres, and it is 0·4 metres high.

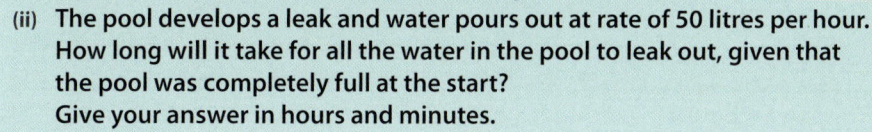

(i) What is the volume of the pool? (Let π = $\frac{22}{7}$)

(ii) The pool develops a leak and water pours out at rate of 50 litres per hour. How long will it take for all the water in the pool to leak out, given that the pool was completely full at the start?
Give your answer in hours and minutes.

Solution

(i) $V = \pi r^2 h$

$V = \frac{22}{7} \times (1\cdot5)^2 \times 0\cdot4$

$V = 2\cdot828$

$V = 2\cdot83$

Therefore, the volume of pool is 2·83 m³

(ii) 1 m³ = 1 000 litres of water

2·83 m³ = 1 000 × 2·83

2·83 m³ = 2 830 litres of water

Water is leaking at a rate of 50 litres per hour

$\frac{2830}{50} = 56\cdot6$ hours

Change 0·6 to minutes = 0·6 × 60 = 36 minutes

Total time = 56 hours and 36 minutes

Worked example 3

A cylinder has a radius of 5 cm and a volume of 150π cm³.
Find the height of the cylinder.

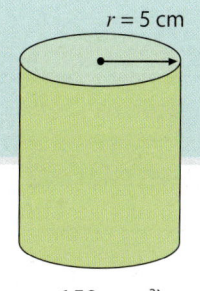

Solution

$V = \pi r^2 h$

$V = (\pi)(5)^2(h)$ (from the question, we know the volume = 150π cm³)

$150\pi = (25)(\pi)(h)$

$\frac{150\pi}{25\pi} = h$ (dividing both sides by 25π)

$6 = h$ Therefore, the height of the cylinder is 6 cm

Practice questions 17.4

1. Find the volume of the following cylinders. Give your answer to one decimal place where necessary. Let π = 3.14

   (i) 5 mm, 6 mm
   (ii) 3 m, 6 m
   (iii) 7 mm, 8 mm
   (iv) 5 cm, 12 cm
   (v) 1 m, 10 m

2. Find the volume of the following cylinders. Give your answer to the nearest whole number where necessary.

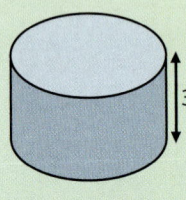

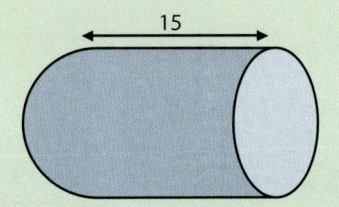

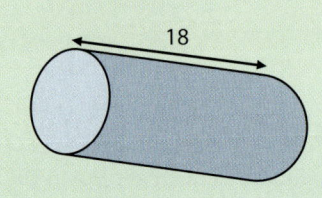

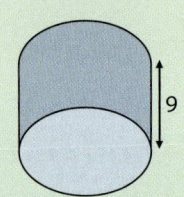

   (i) Area of base = 4 units², height 3
   (ii) Area of base = 16 units², length 15
   (iii) Area of base = 11 units², length 18
   (iv) Area of base = 8.5 units², height 9

3. Copy the table below and calculate the volume of each cylinder. Let $\pi = \frac{22}{7}$. Give answers to the nearest whole number.

Cylinder number	(i)	(ii)	(iii)	(iv)	(v)
Radius	5 m	8 mm	3 m	0.4 m	20 cm
Height	11 m	20 mm	40 cm	300 mm	0.6 m
Volume					

4. Copy the table below and calculate the volume of each cylinder. Give each answer in terms of π.

Cylinder number	(i)	(ii)	(iii)	(iv)	(v)
Diameter	12 cm	24 mm	5 m	1.2 m	16.4 cm
Height	6 cm	45 mm	7 000 mm	300 cm	700 mm
Volume					

5. An ice hockey puck is a solid piece of rubber with the dimensions shown. How much rubber is used to make a hockey puck? Give your answer in terms of π.

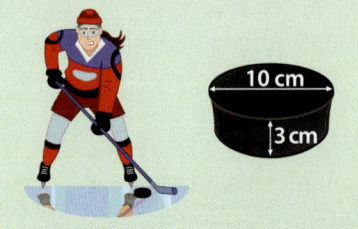

   (10 cm diameter, 3 cm height)

6. Copy the table provided. Calculate the height of each cylinder. Use the π button on your calculator.

Cylinder number	(i)	(ii)	(iii)	(iv)	(v)
Radius	6 cm	11 m	9 mm	11 cm	17 m
Height					
Volume	791.28 cm³	4 179.34 m³	3 052.08 mm³	1 061.32 cm³	9 074.6 m³

7. Enzar has 125 ml of water. He wants to pour it into one of four cylindrical bottles. Which bottle will hold all the water? How do you know?

   1 cm³ = 1 ml

   Bottle A: diameter = 7 cm, height = 3 cm
   Bottle B: radius = 2 cm, height = 6 cm
   Bottle C: radius = 3.5 cm, height = 7 cm
   Bottle D: diameter = 3 cm, height = 4 cm

8. Conan lives on a farm in Roscommon. He wants to drill his own private well. 
   Conan drills a cylindrical hole that is 4 metres deep and 2 metres wide. The soil from the well construction was removed and piled on the ground.
   (i) What is the volume of the soil in the pile on the ground? Give your answer to two decimal places.
   (ii) If 1 m³ of soil has a mass of 1 500 kg, what is the mass of the soil removed, to the nearest kilogram?

9. It is important to conserve water. Mr Jones has a leaking tap. In one hour, leaking water fills a cylinder of radius 5 cm and height 10 cm. 
   (i) How many litres of water is this? Give your answer to four decimal places.
   (ii) If the tap leaks overnight (12 hours), how many litres of water have been wasted?
   Give your answer to four decimal places.
   (iii) It takes Mr Jones 7 full days to get the tap repaired. How much water has been lost due to the leak? Assume one day = 24 hours. Give your answer to four decimal places.

   1 000 cm³ = 1 litre

10. A student measured the outside dimensions of a can of soup. The height was 10·5 cm and the diameter was 7·4 cm. The student calculated the volume to be 452 cm³, to the nearest whole number. 
    (i) Was the student correct? How do you know?
    (ii) The label on the can shows the actual volume of soup in the can is 400 ml. Why do you think the manufacturer would not fill the can with 452 ml of soup?

Taking it FURTHER

11. The steel barrel shown has developed a leak. 85·1 cm, 57·2 cm
    Liquid pours out of the barrel at a rate of 30 litres per hour.
    (i) Calculate the volume of the barrel. Give your answer to two decimal places.
    (ii) How many litres of liquid can the barrel hold? Give your answer to two decimal places. (1 litre = 1 000 cm³)
    (iii) How many cm has the height of the water dropped in 3 hours? Give your answer to the nearest whole number.
    (iv) How long, in hours and minutes, will it take for the barrel to be empty?

12. Orange juice is sold in cylindrical cans. A can has a height of 8 cm and a diameter of 7 cm.
    (i) What is the capacity (volume) of the can to two decimal places.
    (ii) What happens to the capacity of the can if the dimensions of the radius and height are swapped? Justify your answer.
    (iii) Why do you think this happens?

13. Four cubes of ice with an edge length of 4 cm each placed in a cylindrical glass of water with a radius of 6 cm.
    (i) What is the volume of one cube of ice?
    (ii) Calculate by how many cm the water will rise when all the ice cubes have melted. Give your answer to two decimal places.

14. Ann is making a candle by pouring melted wax into a mould in the shape of a cylinder. The diameter of the cylindrical mould is 6 cm and its height is 8 cm. To get the wax for the candles, Ann melts cubes of wax that are each 3 cm by 3 cm by 3 cm.
    How many full wax cubes will Ann need to make the candle?

Taking it FURTHER

15. A plastic garden greenhouse is shaped as a half cylinder with a diameter of 6 m and base length 20 m.
What is the volume of the greenhouse, correct to two decimal places?

16. 24 cans of soft drink are arranged in four rows, with six cans in each row, in a rectangular box.

The cans are packed tightly into the box with no extra space on the top, bottom, or sides.

A single can has a radius of 4 cm and a height of 15 cm.

(i) Calculate the volume of one can, to two decimal places.

(ii) Calculate the volume of 24 cans, to two decimal places.

(iii) Calculate the minimum dimensions of a box that could hold 24 cans in this arrangement.

(iv) Draw a sketch of this box, showing the dimensions.

(v) What is the volume of this box?

(vi) Is the volume of the box the same as the volume of the 24 cans? Explain why or why not.

(vii) What is the volume of empty space (space not taken up) when the box contains 24 cans? Give your answer to the nearest whole number.

Revision questions

17A Core skills

1. Identify which nets below will **not** form a cube. In each case, explain your decision.

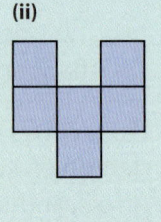

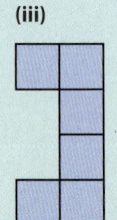

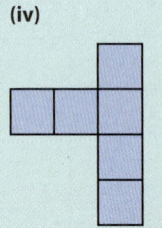

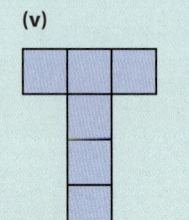

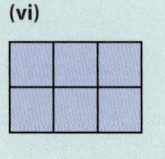

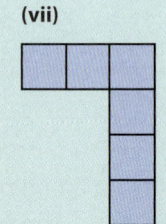

(i)   (ii)   (iii)   (iv)   (v)   (vi)   (vii)

2. The sum of the numbers on opposite faces of a die equals seven.

Copy each net onto graph paper. Label each face with a number from 1 to 6, so the net can fold to make a correct die.

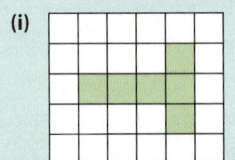

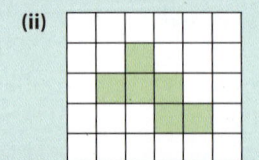

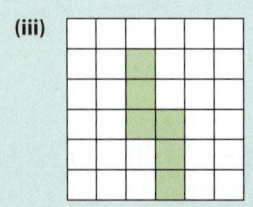

(i)   (ii)   (iii)

3. The diagram shows the end wall of Lynn's house.

It is made up of a triangle on top of a rectangle.

(i) What is the area of the triangle?

(ii) Calculate the total area of the end wall.

(iii) Lynn wants to paint this wall. A can of paint costs €19·99 and covers 10 m². How many cans of paint will she have to buy, and how much will it cost?

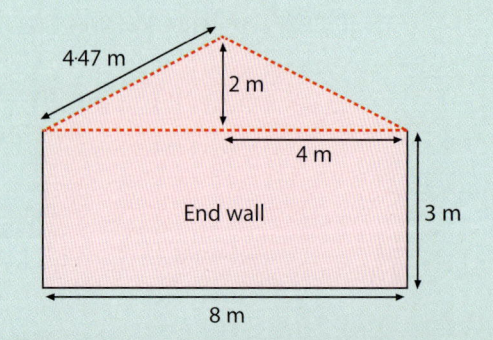

End wall: 4·47 m, 2 m, 4 m, 3 m, 8 m

280 Linking Thinking 1

4. Brona has a tablet. The dimensions are provided in the diagram to the right.

   (i) Calculate the total area of the front of tablet.

   (ii) Calculate the area of the screen.

   (iii) Brona states that the border of her tablet is only $\frac{1}{10}$ of the total area of the front.

   Is she correct? Justify your answer.

5. The volume of a cube is 64 cm³.

   (i) What is the length of one edge of the cube?

   (ii) What is the area of one face of the cube?

6. Sketch a net of this rectangular solid.

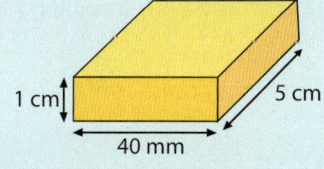

   (i) Calculate its surface area.

   (ii) Calculate its volume in cm³.

7. Find the volume of the following cylinders. Give your answer to two decimal places.

Cylinder	Radius	Height
A	5 cm	9 cm
B	11 cm	0·30 m
C	2·7 m	200 cm
D	$\frac{1}{1\,000}$ km	$\frac{3}{1\,000}$ km
E	0·2 mm	3 cm

8. How many square tiles measuring 20 cm by 20 cm are needed to cover the sides and base of a pool that is 10 m long, 6 m wide and 3 m deep?

9. The inside dimensions of a wooden sand pit for a local playground are 2 m by 3 m by 25 cm. The sandbox is a rectangular solid.

   (i) Calculate the internal surface area of the sand pit.

   (ii) Calculate the maximum volume of sand it will hold. Assume that the maximum volume of sand is level with the top of sand pit.

17B Taking it FURTHER

1. A window washing company is hired to wash the windows in an apartment block. The building is 60 m by 40 m by 200 m. Windows cover one-third of the building. What is the total surface area of the windows to be washed? Give your answer to the nearest whole m².

2. Out of the rectangular solids A, B and C shown below, which rectangular solid has …?

   (i) the greatest surface area

   (ii) the least surface area

   Justify your answer in each case.

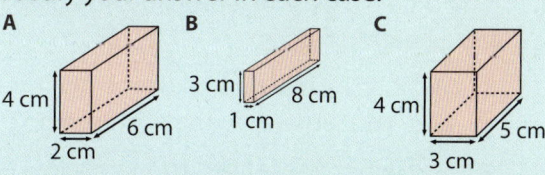

3. A rectangular solid has a square base with an area of 16 m². The total surface area of the shape is 48 m².
   What are the dimensions of the shape?

4. The diagram shows a wooden doorstop. The doorstop needs to be painted. The bottom rectangular face is covered with rubber and will not be painted. 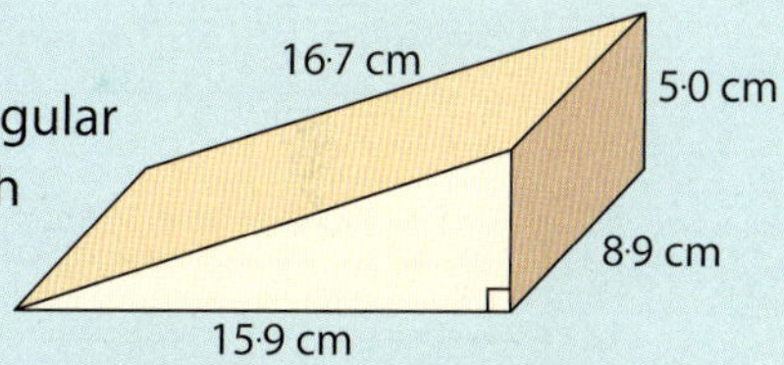
   Find the total surface area to be painted. Give your answer correct to one decimal place.

5. A rectangular swimming pool is to be filled with water. The pool has a uniform (constant) depth of 2 m and is surrounded by a wooden decking. The pool is 10 m wide and 25 m long.

   (a) How much water, in metres cubed, is needed for each of the following situations?

   (i) The pool is filled to the level of the decking.

   (ii) The pool is filled to 15 cm below the level of the decking. Give your answer to three decimal places.

   (b) How many litres of water are needed for the pool to be 50% full?

6. Students in Transition Year are filling shoeboxes with toys for children.
   A shoebox measures 30 cm by 18 cm by 16 cm.

   (i) Find the volume of a shoebox.

   (ii) The students fill 32 shoeboxes. Eight shoeboxes are packed into a larger box. What could the minimum dimensions of this larger box be?

   (iii) Do you think the larger box will have exactly the dimensions you have found? Justify your answer.

7. A farmer is buying a new water tank for her farm because she needs more water for her crops.
   Her current tank is a cylinder that is 5 metres high and 6 metres in diameter.

   At the shop, she is given a choice of two tanks that she could purchase:

   - The first one has twice the height of her current tank, but keeps the same width.
   - The second one has twice the width of her current tank, but keeps the same height.

   If both tanks cost the same amount of money, which one should she buy so she gets the highest capacity? Justify your answer.

8. John orders a glass of lemonade. The glass is a cylindrical shape with a radius of 4·5 cm and a height of 10 cm.

   (i) What is the maximum volume of lemonade that the glass could contain? Give your answer to the nearest whole number.

   (ii) The lemonade is filled to 1 cm below the top of the glass. Calculate the volume of lemonade in the glass. Give your answer to the nearest whole number.

   (iii) John likes 3 cubes of ice in his lemonade glass. Each ice cube has an edge length of 3 cm. If he places the ice in the glass, will the lemonade overflow and spill out? Justify your answer.

   (iv) What is the maximum height John's glass can be filled to, without overflowing, if he wants to have 3 cubes of ice. Give your answer to one decimal place.

9. Copy the table below and put a tick (✓) in the correct box in each row to show whether each statement is always true, sometimes true, or never true.

	Statement	Tick **one** box only for each statement		
		Always true	Sometimes true	Never true
(i)	If you change the perimeter of a rectangular shape, you change its area.			
(ii)	If the height of a cylinder stays the same, and the radius is doubled, the total volume will be doubled too.			
(iii)	If the diameter of a cylinder stays the same and the height is tripled, then the volume will triple too.			
(iv)	The surface area of a rectangular solid is the area of one face multiplied by six.			

Now that you have completed the unit, revisit the

Something to think about ...

question posed at the start of this unit.

Now try question 5 on pages 404–5

Unit 18

Collecting and representing data

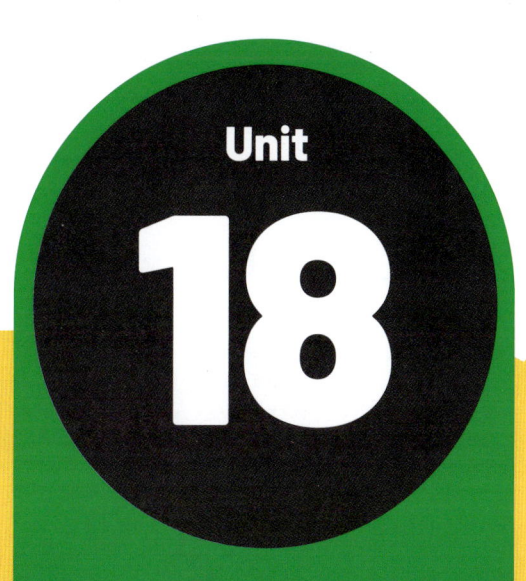

Topics covered within this unit:
- 18·1 Types of data
- 18·2 Gathering data
- 18·3 Representing data
- 18·4 Representing continuous data
- 18·5 Introduction to statistical investigations

The Learning Outcomes covered in this unit are contained in the following sections:

SP.3a SP.3b SP.3c SP.3d SP.3f

Key words
- Statistics
- Data
- Categorical data
- Numerical data
- Nominal data
- Ordinal data
- Discrete
- Continuous
- Population
- Census
- Sample
- Primary data
- Secondary data
- Bias
- Tally
- Frequency table
- Line plot
- Bar chart
- Histogram

Something to think about ...

Sara has read that schools in a different country are planning to stop giving students homework. She wants to conduct a survey to find out people's opinions on homework.

- She decides to survey five of her best friends. Is this a good sample? Justify your answer. Who else could she ask?

- One of the questions on her survey is: *'Homework is a waste of time; how many hours homework should we get?'* Is this a good question? How could you improve it?

- Sara wants to produce a report to give to the school principal. Design a questionnaire she could use to collect reliable data. Who should she ask other than students? Identify the types of data she will collect.

- What would be the best way to represent the data she collects in her report to the principal?

18·1 Types of data

By the end of this section you should:
- understand what statistics is and where it is used
- understand that there are different types of data
- be able to classify data

Statistics involves collecting **data** (information), analysing it (looking for patterns or trends, finding averages and spread), representing it (drawing tables and charts) and interpreting it (understanding what it means).

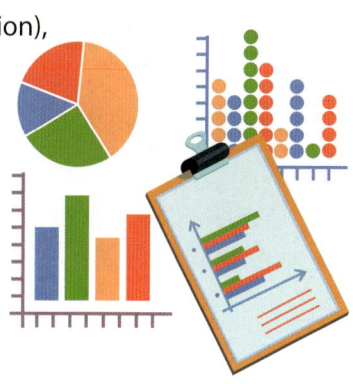

> **Statistics** is a branch of Mathematics that deals with the collection, analysis, representation and interpretation of data.

Section B Moving forward

Many government agencies, companies and organisations collect data to improve their services and products. Statistics can also be used to analyse the effects of certain changes that may have been made, or in predicting and planning for what might happen in the future.

Statistics are collected by carrying out questionnaires and surveys or by conducting experiments.

> **Data** is the actual information obtained from surveys, questionnaires or experiments.

Data types

Data can be either categorical or numerical.

> **Categorical data** can be put into groups or categories.

Examples of questions that generate categorical data:

What is your favourite colour? Where are you from? How often do you exercise?

This type of data is often in the form of words. Categorical data can be either nominal or ordinal.

> **Nominal data** is data that has no particular rank or order, e.g. eye colour or favourite sport.
>
> **Ordinal data** is data that can be categorised into groups in a particular order/rank, e.g. shirt sizes (S, M, L); always, sometimes, never.

> **Numerical data** involves quantities that are, usually, countable or measurable.

Examples of questions that generate numerical data:

What is your height? How many siblings do you have? How many hours of TV do you watch a week?

This type of data is usually in the form of numbers. Numerical data can be either discrete or continuous.

> **Discrete data** is data that can only take on certain values. It is data that can be counted, e.g. number of people.
>
> **Continuous data** is data that can take on any value within a range. It is data that can be measured e.g. height, time, etc.

These types of data can be summarised in the flowchart as shown:

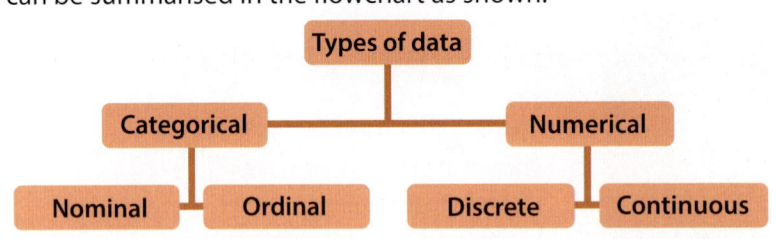

```
                    Types of data
                   /             \
            Categorical         Numerical
            /      \            /       \
        Nominal  Ordinal    Discrete  Continuous
```

Practice questions 18·1

1. Decide whether each of the following examples of data are categorical or numerical data. Justify your answers using your knowledge of data types.

   (i) Make of car
   (ii) Weekly wage
   (iii) Breed of dog
   (iv) Eye colour
   (v) Shoe size
   (vi) Favourite subject

2. Copy the table below and put a tick (✓) in the correct box in each row to show whether each of the following represent categorical or numerical data.

	Data recorded	Categorical nominal	Categorical ordinal	Numerical discrete	Numerical continuous
(i)	The heights, in centimetres, of a group of children				
(ii)	The numbers of visitors at a museum each day				
(iii)	The modes of transport that students in Second Year take to school				
(iv)	Countries of birth				
(v)	Time to complete 100 m sprint				
(vi)	Species of cat				
(vii)	Grades in a test				
(viii)	Percentages in a test				

3. An enrolment form for a school requests the following information:
    (i) Name
    (ii) Date of birth
    (iii) Gender
    (iv) Address
    (v) Number of siblings in the school
    (vi) Parents' phone numbers
    (vii) Subjects chosen
    (viii) Primary school attended

    For each of the pieces of information requested, decide whether the data collected is categorical or numerical data. Justify your answer in each case.

4. Read each of the questions below and decide whether the information collected is categorical nominal or ordinal; or numerical discrete or continuous. Justify your answers.
    (i) What countries have you visited?
    (ii) How long is your hair?
    (iii) What's your favourite sport?
    (iv) How many people are in your family?
    (v) How many languages can you speak?
    (vi) What type of music do you like?

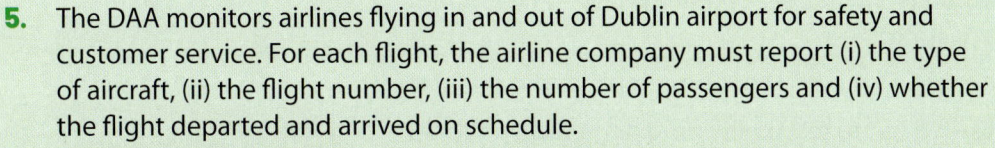

5. The DAA monitors airlines flying in and out of Dublin airport for safety and customer service. For each flight, the airline company must report (i) the type of aircraft, (ii) the flight number, (iii) the number of passengers and (iv) whether the flight departed and arrived on schedule. 
    Decide whether each piece of information gathered is categorical nominal or ordinal; or numerical discrete or continuous. Justify your answers.

6. Liz collects stamps from around the world. Decide whether each piece of information about each stamp in her collection is categorical nominal or ordinal; or numerical discrete or continuous. Justify your answers.
    (i) Length   (ii) Country of origin   (iii) Value   (iv) Colour

7. (i) Write three questions that could be used to collect categorical nominal data.
    (ii) Write three questions that could be used to collect categorical ordinal data.
    (iii) Write three questions that could be used to collect numerical discrete data.
    (iv) Write three questions that could be used to collect numerical continuous data.

8. Explain each of the following terms in your own words and give one example of each.
    (i) Categorical data
    (ii) Numerical data
    (iii) Nominal data
    (iv) Ordinal data
    (v) Discrete data
    (vi) Continuous data

18·2 Gathering data

By the end of this section you should:
- understand the various methods used to collect data
- be able to generate representative data
- be able to generate a statistical question
- understand bias

To carry out any form of statistical investigation, we must first collect some data. If we want to find out the favourite sport of the students in the school, for example, we could ask every student in the school.

> A **population** is the entire group being studied.
> Collection of data from a whole population is called a **census**.

It may not always be practical to question every single person in the population, however, as it could be very time consuming and expensive. Instead, we might decide to ask a group of students and use their results to predict the responses for the entire school.

> A **sample** is a group taken from within the population, a subset of the population.

Although any subset of a population can be considered as a sample, the purpose of the sample is to be representative of the population. Representative means the sample should be a small-scale replica of the population. In this way, any claims based on the sample can also confidently be made about the population.

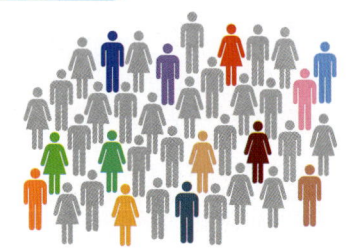

When choosing a sample from a population we must ensure the following:

- The sample must be large enough to ensure it is representative of the entire population.
- The sample must be random. This can be done by picking a name out of a hat, rolling a die or using a random number generator.
- All members of the population must have an equal chance of being selected.

Data collection methods

There are many ways to collect data. Some of these ways include:

- **Direct observations** e.g. standing at a set of traffic lights and counting the colours of the cars passing
- **Surveys and questionnaires** – by census or by a sample of the population
- **Experiments** – often carried out to test a new drug or medical treatment
- **Interviews** – face to face or over the phone
- **Databases** – looking up information that has been gathered by others e.g. an electoral register

Depending on how the data is collected, it may be considered primary or secondary data.

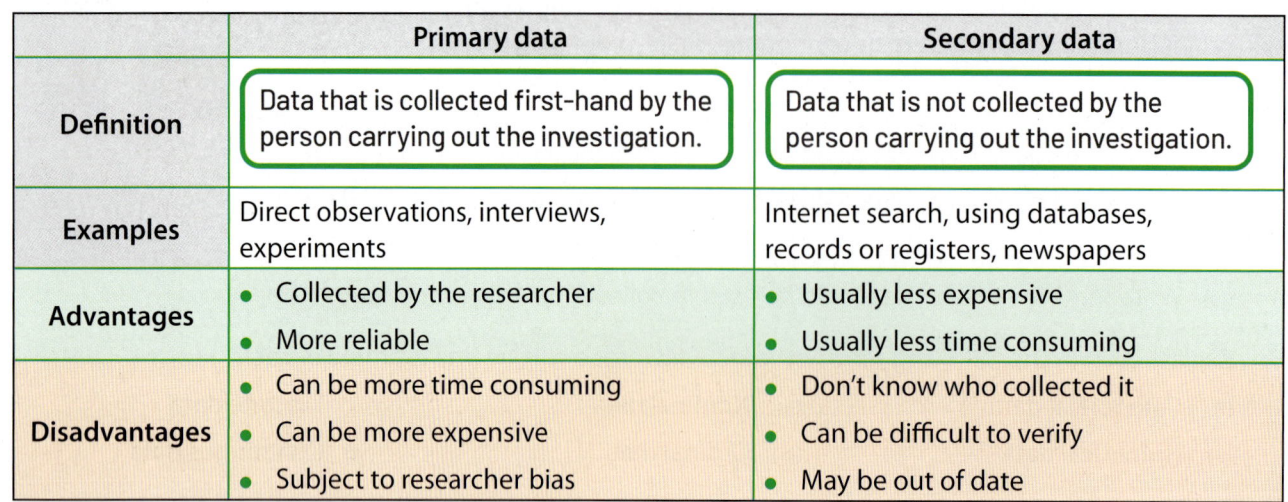

	Primary data	Secondary data
Definition	Data that is collected first-hand by the person carrying out the investigation.	Data that is not collected by the person carrying out the investigation.
Examples	Direct observations, interviews, experiments	Internet search, using databases, records or registers, newspapers
Advantages	• Collected by the researcher • More reliable	• Usually less expensive • Usually less time consuming
Disadvantages	• Can be more time consuming • Can be more expensive • Subject to researcher bias	• Don't know who collected it • Can be difficult to verify • May be out of date

Data collection methods have advantages and disadvantages, as shown below.

Method		Advantages	Disadvantages
Direct observations		• Inexpensive • Easy to do	• May include human error • Not suitable for all data collection
Surveys / questionnaires	(a) Phone	• Easily carried out • Questions can be explained • Many questions can be asked	• Response rate can be low • Limited to phone owners • Expensive
	(b) Internet	• Inexpensive and easily carried out • Anonymous • Done in participants own time	• Limited to people with internet access • Questions cannot be explained
Experiments		• Accurate data if carried out properly	• Expensive • Time consuming • Requires expertise • Focused on one task
Interviews		• Questions can be explained • High response rate • Many questions can be asked	• Expensive • Interviewers might influence answers • Respondents may not be totally honest
Databases		• Inexpensive • Fast • Easy to do	• Limited to databases available • May be out of date • Collection method unknown

Once the sample size and the method of collection have been decided, the questions to be asked must be designed. Writing good questions is very important to ensure the information gathered is useful.

Guidelines for writing good questions

Can you think of a better way to write the example questions?

1. **The question should be clear and easily understood by all people.**

   Imagine you want to find out how much TV people watch.

   You decide to ask: Do you watch a lot of TV?   Yes ☐   No ☐

   People may interpret 'a lot' differently.

2. **It should be possible for everyone to answer the question asked.**

   Imagine you want to find out people's favourite sport.

   You decide to ask: What is your favourite sport?   Football ☐   Hurling ☐

   Some people may prefer a different sport. Others may not like any sports.

   It can be useful to add options such as 'none of these' and 'other'.

3. **The question should be fair. It should not influence a person's answer. If it does, it is a *biased* question.**

   Imagine you want to find out people's opinions on how often students should have PE classes.

   You decide to ask: Studies have shown that daily physical activity for children is important. How often should secondary students have PE classes?'

   The question provides extra information that might lead a person to answer in a particular way.

> **Bias** is an in-built error that causes the data collected to be inaccurate. It can lead to misleading results.

Section B Moving forward

Bias can occur in statistics in many different ways. For example, bias exists where:
- the sample is not representative
- the sample size is too small
- all members of the population don't have an equal chance of being selected for a sample
- the question is leading or confusing, e.g. 'Don't you agree that …?'

Discuss and discover

Working with a classmate:
(i) Design a questionnaire to find out information about the students in your class.
(ii) What method will you use to collect the data?
(iii) Classify all data collected.
(iv) What conclusions can you draw from the data you collected?
(v) If you were to do this again, what could you improve? (Was your question fair or did it introduce bias? Was the data collected relevant?)

Practice questions 18·2

1. Each of the following questions can be improved. Write a more statistically correct question and explain why you think it is better.
   (i) Do you spend a lot of time doing homework?
   (ii) Do you usually walk to school or ride your bike?
   (iii) Do you prefer to watch mindless comedies or exciting dramas?
   (iv) Don't you think the price of a cinema ticket is too high?
   (v) Do you like fruits and vegetables?
   (vi) Do you agree that we need at least 8 hours sleep a night?
   (vii) Do you think students should be allowed to use spell check because it automatically improves spelling?
   (viii) What is the best football team in the Premier League?

2. For each question below, choose an appropriate method of data collection to investigate the question. Explain your choice.
   (i) What are the five largest (by population) cities in Ireland?
   (ii) What are the favourite bands of the students in your class?
   (iii) How many times does the average person blink per minute?
   (iv) How many red cars are in the car park?

3. The principal of a school visited each class in his school and asked for a show of hands to find out how many students had ever been bullied at school. Only two students raised their hands.
   (i) Do you think this is a good method to collect data? Justify your answer.
   (ii) What do you think the principal would conclude from his results? Do you think his conclusion would be accurate?
   (iii) Can you suggest a better way to find out how many students have been bullied?

4. The situations described below involve either a whole population or a sample. In each case, (a) decide whether the whole population or a sample should be used, and (b) explain why you think the whole population or a sample is best.
   (i) To determine the number of hours an AAA battery will last in a calculator.
   (ii) To determine the average number of siblings of your classmates.
   (iii) To determine the popularity of a new fruit-flavoured yogurt.

5. Give an example of a data collection method where the cost and time needed to complete the collection may lead to problems and justify your answer.

6. Common methods of surveying are by personal interviews, over the phone, or by email. Create a table where you explain the advantages and disadvantages of each of these methods of data collection.

7. For each of the following, identify a sample of people whose opinions would bias the survey results. Explain your choice.
   (i) Should fur from animals be used for coats?
   (ii) Should the legal voting age be reduced?
   (iii) Should households be fined for not recycling?
   (iv) Should people over 66 get free travel?

8. A TV talent show uses viewers' opinions to help determine the popularity of its contestants. At the end of each show, viewers cast votes for their favourite contestants by texting in at €1·15 per text. Do you think the opinions of the sample will reflect those of the population? Explain.

9. Siobhán wants to find out how often people go to the cinema. She stands outside the cinema and gives a questionnaire to all the women leaving.
   (i) Is Siobhán's sample biased? Give two reasons to support your answer.
   (ii) How could Siobhán improve her sample?

10. Copy the table and put a tick (✓) in the correct box in each row to show whether each statement is true or false. If the statement is false, explain why.

	Statement	True	False
(i)	A census is a survey completed by an entire population		
(ii)	Data is always numbers		
(iii)	The size of a sample doesn't matter		
(iv)	If all members of the population don't have an equal chance of being picked, the sample will be biased		
(v)	Secondary data is gathered first-hand by the researcher		

Taking it FURTHER

11. Every five years, the Central Statistics Office conducts a census of the population of Ireland.
    (i) Do they survey a sample or the whole population? Justify your answer.
    (ii) One question in the survey is used to determine the ages of the people in each household. Why would the government need to know people's ages?
    (iii) There is a legal obligation on people to complete the census. Why do you think this is the case?
    (iv) All the information that you give on the census form is confidential and can only be accessed by the CSO. Why do you think this is important?

18·3 Representing data

By the end of this section you should:
- understand the various methods used to represent data
- be able to select the most appropriate method to represent data
- be able to understand and read representations of data

Once we have collected data, we can use various methods to represent this data. Representing data in various different forms can make it easier to read and understand.

Some ways to represent data include frequency tables, line plots, bar charts, histograms, pie charts, and stem and leaf diagrams.

> Pie charts and stem and leaf diagrams will be covered in Section C, Unit 1: Analysing data.

Tallying and frequency tables

> A **tally** is a way of keeping count by drawing marks.

The following are the tally marks for 1 to 4:

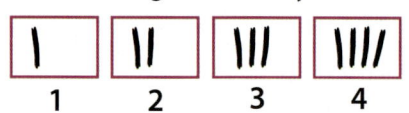

| 1 | 2 | 3 | 4 |

The fifth mark is made by drawing a line across the previous four: 𝍸𝍷 = 5

Then continue with single marks and gather **groups of 5**.

This tally 𝍸𝍷 𝍸𝍷 || represents 12: 2 groups of 5, plus 2 extra.

By counting the tally marks, we can work out how often a response occurs. This is known as the **frequency**.

> A **frequency table** is a table that lists items and shows the number of times they occur.

The table below represents the results of a survey of a group of people, to find their favourite colour:

Colour	Red	Green	Blue	Yellow	Purple
Tally	||||	𝍸𝍷 |	𝍸𝍷	|||	𝍸𝍷 ||||
Frequency	4	6	5	3	9

Worked example 1

The following are the results obtained when a group of students were asked how many siblings they have:
1, 2, 0, 3, 0, 4, 2, 1, 1, 0, 2, 2, 3, 4, 1, 2, 2, 3, 0, 1

(i) Use tally marks to draw a frequency table of these results.
(ii) How many students were questioned?

Solution

(i)

No. of siblings	0	1	2	3	4
Tally	||||	𝍸𝍷	𝍸𝍷 |	|||	||
Frequency	4	5	6	3	2

(ii) Number of students questioned
4 + 5 + 6 + 3 + 2 = 20 students

Line plots (dot plot)

> A **line plot** is a graph that displays data as dots or Xs above a number line.

The number line is divided into equal intervals and the number of dots (or Xs) above each interval represents the frequency of the data. Note that the size of dots (or Xs) must be the same, as must the vertical space between each dot.

The line plot on the right represents the following data:

Colour	Red	Black	Blue	Silver	Yellow	White
Frequency	6	8	2	9	0	4

6 cars in the car park are red, 8 are black, 2 are blue, etc.

Colours of cars in car park

Drawing a line plot

1. Draw a horizontal line and label it.
2. Place equally spaced marks along the line. Each mark represents a category of response.
3. Label each mark with the items or numbers given in the question.
4. Place an 'X' or dot above the relevant mark for each response.

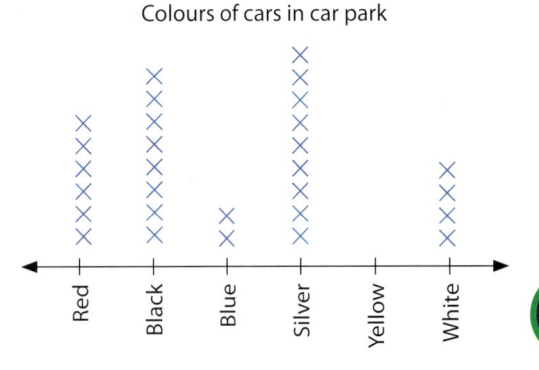

Worked example 2

The following are the ages of the students in Mr Whelan's First-Year Maths class:

11, 11, 13, 12, 12, 11, 13, 12, 12, 11, 12, 12, 11, 11, 13, 12, 12, 11, 12, 12, 12, 13, 11, 12

(i) Represent this data on a line plot.
(ii) What is the most common age?

Solution

(i) **Step 1** Draw the horizontal line and label it 'Age of students'

Step 2 Divide the line by placing 3 marks equally spaced apart because the students are aged 11, 12 or 13

Step 3 Label the marks 11, 12 and 13

Step 4 Place 8 dots above 11 as 8 students are 11 years old.
Place 12 dots above 12 as 12 students are 12 years old.
Place 4 dots above 13 as 4 students are 12 years old.
Make sure the size of the dots is the same and that the space between them is the same.

(ii) From the graph, 12 is the most common age because it has the highest frequency.

> The value that occurs most often is called the **mode**.

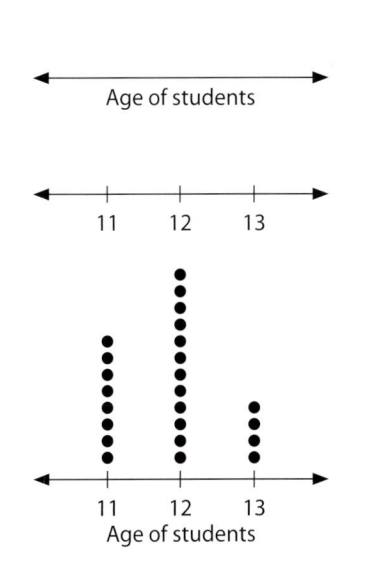

Section B Moving forward

Bar charts

A bar chart is a graph that displays data as rectangular bars of different heights (or lengths).

When drawing graphs, always remember **SALT**:

> **S**cale — Is the scale suitable?
> **A**xis — Are the intervals equal?
> **L**abel — Are the axes labelled? What are the units of measure?
> **T**itle — What is the purpose of the graph/chart?

Features of a bar chart

- It consists of rectangular bars of **equal** width.
- The space between the bars must be the **same**.
- Bars can be marked vertically or horizontally, but normally we use vertical bars.
- The height (or length) of the bar represents the frequency of the corresponding observation.
- A bar chart is used to display categorical and numerical discrete data.

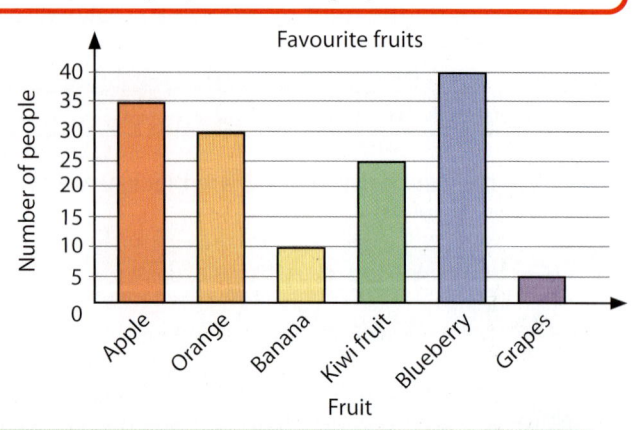

Drawing a bar chart

1. Draw a horizontal and a vertical axis and give your chart a title.
2. Label the axes.
3. Divide the axes into appropriate scales, making sure the spacing is even on each axis.
4. Use a ruler to draw each bar, making sure the width of the bars is equal and the gap between each bar is the same.

Worked example 3

Draw a bar chart to represent the data about the hair colours of a group of students shown in the frequency table below.

Hair colour	Brown	Blond	Black	Red
No. of students	16	8	12	10

In general, the top line of a frequency table is the horizontal axis, and the bottom line is the vertical axis.

Solution

Step 1 Draw a horizontal and a vertical axis and give your chart a title.

Step 2 Label the axes.

The horizontal axis is named in relation to the question, i.e. hair colour.

The vertical axis is named in relation to the responses, i.e. number (no.) of students.

Step 3 Divide axes into appropriate scales

The horizontal axis must be divided into 4 as there are 4 different hair colours.

The vertical axis has to go up to at least 16 as the this is the highest frequency.

Note that the spacing is even on each axis.

Step 4 Draw each bar, making sure all bars are the same width and equally spaced apart.

The height of the bars represents the number of students with that hair colour.

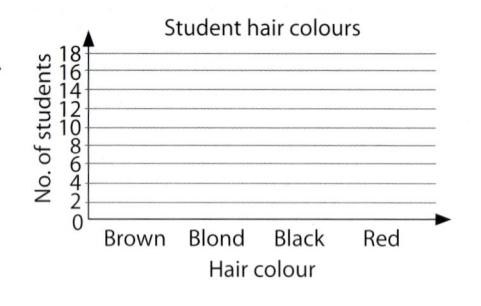

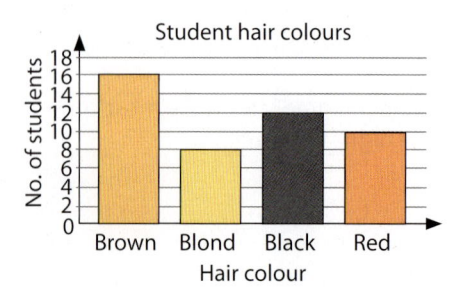

Practice questions 18·3

1. Complete the following frequency tables.

   (i)
Minutes of exercise	15	20	25	30
Tally	ЖЖ	//	ЖЖ //	/
Frequency				

   (iii)
Movies watched	2	4	6	8
Tally	ЖЖ ///	ЖЖ	////	////
Frequency				

   (ii)
Favourite pizza	Pepperoni	Hawaiian	Vegetarian	Margherita
Tally	ЖЖ /	ЖЖ //	ЖЖ ////	ЖЖ ЖЖ
Frequency				

2. Represent the data below in a frequency table using tally marks.

   (i)   1, 1, 1, 1, 1, 1, 1, 5, 5, 5, 5, 9, 9, 9
   (ii) 6, 6, 6, 4, 4, 4, 2, 2, 2, 2, 2
   (iii) 9, 9, 9, 9, 4, 4, 4, 4, 5, 5, 5, 1, 1, 1
   (iv) 3, 4, 7, 7, 8, 7, 8, 7, 3, 3, 4
   (v)   21, 25, 25, 25, 21, 22, 21, 21
   (vi) 48, 47, 47, 49, 49, 49, 49, 47

3. The line plot below shows the number of points scored by a team in 10 matches.

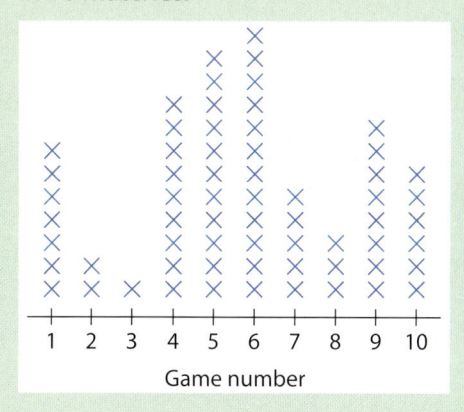

   (i)   What type of data is displayed on this line plot?
   (ii) How many points did the team score in the first game?
   (iii) Did the team score more points in game 4 or game 6?
   (iv) In how many games did the team score more than 12 points?
   (v)   What was the combined number of points scored in game 7 and game 9?
   (vi) Which game had the fewest points scored?

4. Match the tally to the bar chart.

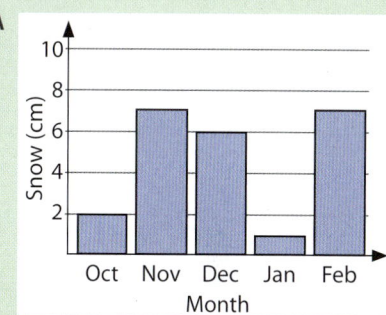

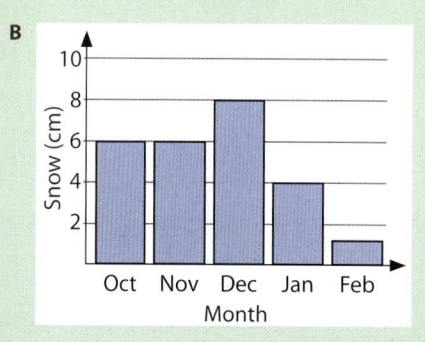

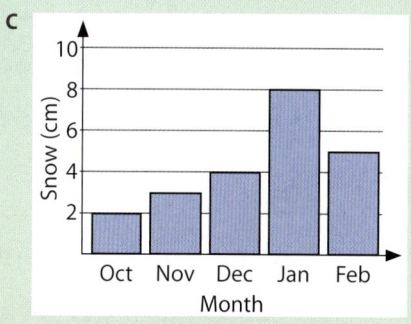

   (i)
Month	Snow (cm)
Oct	//
Nov	///
Dec	////
Jan	ЖЖ ///
Feb	ЖЖ

   (ii)
Month	Snow (cm)
Oct	//
Nov	ЖЖ //
Dec	ЖЖ /
Jan	/
Feb	ЖЖ //

   (iii)
Month	Snow (cm)
Oct	ЖЖ /
Nov	ЖЖ /
Dec	ЖЖ ///
Jan	////
Feb	/

5. The ages of a group of students in a dance class are given below.

   11, 5, 9, 13, 8, 9, 9, 11, 10, 8, 6, 7, 12, 11, 13, 12, 7, 6, 11, 12, 10, 8

   (i) How many students are in the class?
   (ii) Draw a line plot to represent this data.

Section B Moving forward   293

6. The bar chart shown represents data collected when a group of students were surveyed about how they travel to school.

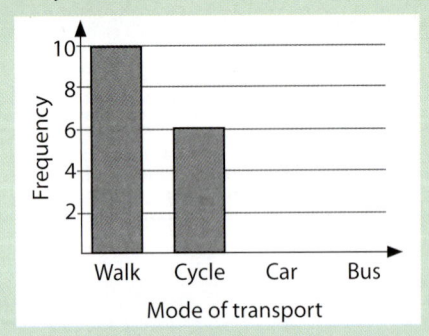

   (i) Copy the bar chart and complete it if 4 students travel by car and 7 students travel by bus.

   (ii) How many students cycle to school?

   (iii) What is the most popular way for the students to travel to school?

   (iv) How many students were surveyed?

   (v) If a student was chosen at random, what is the probability that they walked to school?

7. Draw a bar chart to represent the data shown in each frequency table below.

   (i)

No. of pets	0	1	2	3
No. of students	6	12	14	8

   (ii)

Hours spent online	1	2	3	4
No. of students	5	13	17	7

   (iii)

Holidays taken	0	1	2	3
No. of people	4	25	12	6

   (iv)

Matches won	0	2	4	6
No. of teams	14	16	9	3

8. Principal Grant recorded the number of students who arrived late to school on a given week. The results are shown in the table below.

Day	Monday	Tuesday	Wednesday	Thursday	Friday
No. of students	12	14	24	18	27

   (i) Draw a bar chart to represent this data.

   (ii) On what day were the most people late?

9. The table represents the number of different musical instruments sold in a certain music shop in a given month. Use the data to answer the questions below.

Guitar	Drums	Piano	Violin	Recorder
55	30	15	25	70

   (i) Identify the type of data collected.

   (ii) Draw a bar chart to represent this data.

   (iii) How many more guitars than drums were sold?

   (iv) What is the difference in sales between the most popular and least popular instrument? Give a possible reason for this sales difference.

   (v) How many instruments were sold altogether in this month?

   (vi) Would a line plot be a good way to represent this data? Give a reason for your answer.

Taking it FURTHER

10. Luigi's Pizzas took a survey about customers' favourite toppings and recorded the results in a bar graph. Use the bar graph below to answer the questions.

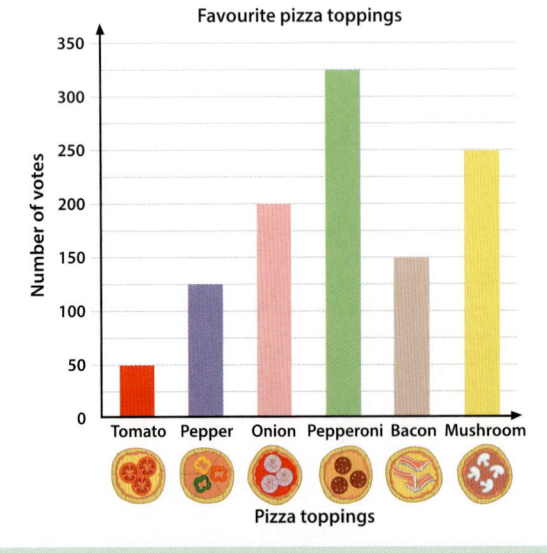

    (i) Which is the most popular topping?

    (ii) How many customers have chosen either tomato or pepper toppings?

    (iii) If 75 additional customers prefer bacon, which one will be more popular, bacon or onion?

    (iv) Which topping has 250 votes?

    (v) List the toppings in order from most popular to least popular.

    (vi) How many customers were surveyed?

18·4 Representing continuous data

By the end of this section you should:
- be able to understand and read representations of continuous data
- understand how to represent continuous data

Histograms

> A **histogram** is a graph that displays data as rectangular bars in which the area of each bar represents the frequency of the data.

A histogram looks very similar to a bar chart but there are **no gaps** between the bars. Histograms are used to represent **continuous data**, which is numerical data that can take on any value within a range (e.g. height, weight, time). There are no gaps because continuous data can take on any value within a range.

Consider the following data collected of the amount of money spent by each customer in a shop:

> €22·54, €12·35, €6·30, €9·99, €29·00, €22·25, €37·10, €17·42, €17·28, €28·58, €3·70, €5·97, €4·15, €28·89, €7·05, €23·18, €14·18, €10·00, €20·20, €33·68, €40·16, €2·29, €20·21, €41·65, €10·45, €43·75

Drawing a bar chart of this data would not be of much use, as no two people spent the same amount of money. It would be easier if we combined the amounts spent into certain groups (or intervals) such as €0–10, €10–20 etc. We can then form a frequency table which is called a **grouped frequency table.**

Step 1 To do this we would first arrange the numbers is ascending order as shown:

> €2·29, €3·70, €4·15, €5·97, €6·30, €7·05, €9·99, €10·00, €10·45, €12·35, €14·18, €17·28, €17·42, €20·20, €20·21, €22·25, €22·54, €23·18, €28·58, €28·89, €29·00, €37·10, €33·68, €40·16, €41·65, €43·75

All the numbers in red are 0 or more but less than 10, blue numbers are 10 or more but less than 20, etc.

Step 2 By counting the numbers in each group, we can complete the grouped frequency table of the data, which would look like this:

Amount spent (€)	0–10	10–20	20–30	30–40	40–50
No. of people	7	6	8	2	3

Note: 0 – 10 means 0 or more but less than 10

It is important that we include the note under the table to explain what our groups mean.

Step 3 We can then use a grouped frequency table to draw a histogram, as shown.

Money spent by customers in a shop

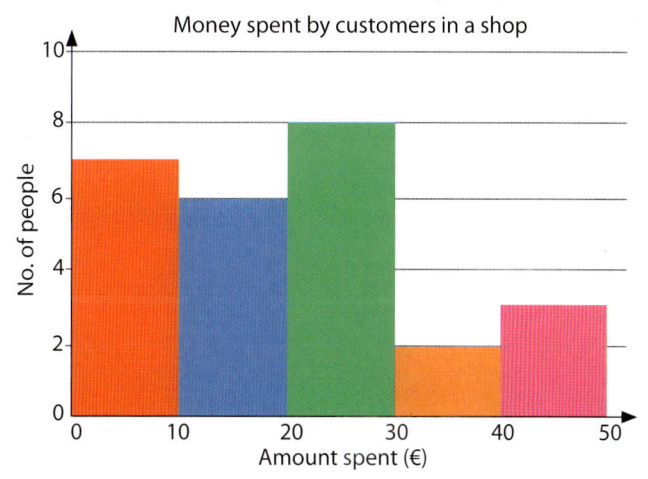

Features of a histogram

- It consists of rectangular bars that can vary in width. For our course we deal only with equal widths.
- There is no space between two consecutive bars.
- Bars can be drawn either vertically or horizontally, but we normally use vertical bars.
- The area of the bar represents the frequency of the corresponding observation.

Drawing a histogram

1. Draw a horizontal and a vertical axis and give your chart a title.
2. Label the axes.
3. Divide the axes into appropriate scales, making sure the spacing is even on each axis.
4. Use a ruler to draw each bar, making sure the width of the bars is equal and there is no gap between each bar.

Worked example

The list below shows the results (to the nearest percent) of a group of students in a Maths test:

84, 52, 9, 43, 70, 22, 64, 12, 58, 74, 90, 62, 38, 66, 18, 54, 44, 32, 63, 25, 62, 78, 15, 88, 49, 68, 73, 35, 41, 76, 85, 30, 46, 50, 75, 96, 29, 50, 27, 57, 61, 70, 74

(i) Copy and complete the grouped frequency table below.
(ii) Draw a histogram to represent this data.

Result	0–10	10–20	20–30	30–40	40–50	50–60	60–70	70–80	80–90	90–100
No. of students		3								

Note: 0–10 means 0 or more but less than 10%, and so on.

Solution

(i) **Step 1** Order the list given from smallest to biggest.

9, 12, 15, 18, 22, 25, 27, 29, 30, 32, 35, 38, 41, 43, 44, 46, 49, 50, 50, 52, 54, 57, 58, 61, 62, 62, 63, 64, 66, 68, 70, 70, 73, 74, 74, 75, 76, 78, 84, 85, 88, 90, 96

Step 2 Copy and complete the table.

Result	0–10	10–20	20–30	30–40	40–50	50–60	60–70	70–80	80–90	90–100
No. of students	1	3	4	4	5	6	7	8	3	2

(ii) **Step 1** Draw a horizontal and vertical axis and add the title 'Maths exam results'.

Step 2 Label the horizontal axis 'Results' and the vertical axis 'No. of students'.

Step 3 Divide the horizontal axis into 10 evenly spaced intervals.

Step 4 Divide the vertical axis, noting that the highest frequency is 8.

Step 5 Draw each bar, making sure they are equal widths and there are no gaps between them.

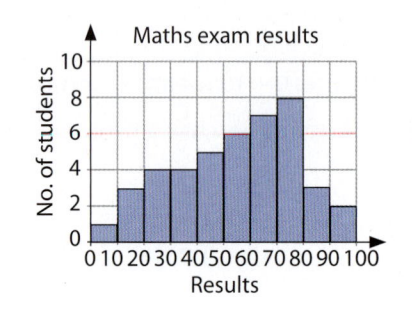

Practice questions 18.4

1. Use the histogram provided to answer the questions below.
   (i) What age group has the most people?
   (ii) What age group has the fewest people?
   (iii) How many people are aged 0–20?
   (iv) How many people are older than 10?
   (v) If a person is chosen at random, what is the probability they will be older than 30 years old?

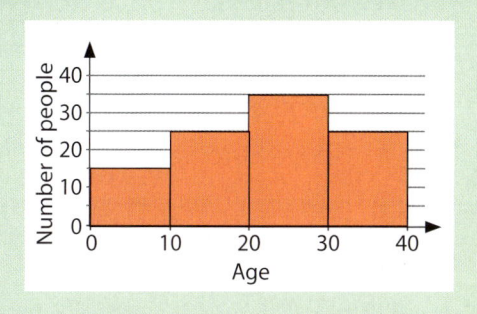

2. Draw a grouped frequency table to represent each of the following lists of data.
   (i) A scientist measures the weights (in g) of 20 apples in an experiment.
   121, 187, 143, 219, 191, 146, 203, 142, 172, 234, 163, 194, 241, 150, 125, 219, 162, 210, 120, 236
   (ii) A machine measures the length of a part in a car engine (in mm to the nearest 0·1 mm).
   11·1, 11·3, 10·7, 11·2, 11·6, 10·9, 10·6, 11·3, 11·2, 10·5, 10·4, 11·2, 11·1, 11·6, 10·6, 11·3, 10·9
   (iii) Pulse rate (per minute) of a group of people were recorded to the nearest minute.
   61, 75, 71, 72, 70, 65, 77, 72, 67, 80, 77, 62, 71, 74, 79, 67, 80, 77, 62, 74, 61, 70, 80, 72, 59, 78, 71

3. Draw a histogram to represent the data shown in the frequency tables below:

   (i)
Distance travelled (km)	0–20	20–40	40–60	60–80
No. of motorists	10	6	18	22

   (Note: 0–20 means 0 or more but less than 20, etc.)

   (ii)
Height (cm)	140–145	145–150	150–155	155–160
No. of students	12	24	36	16

   (Note: 140–145 means 140 or more but less than 145, etc.)

   (iii)
Weight (kg)	55–60	60–65	65–70	70–75
No. of people	10	34	46	52

   (Note: 55–60 means 55 or more but less than 60, etc.)

   (iv)
Rainfall (mm)	800–850	850–900	900–950	950–1000
No. of months	3	6	5	1

   (Note: 800–850 means 800 or more but less than 850, etc.)

4. The following are the distances (to the nearest km) a number of students travel to get to school.
   1, 18, 10, 4, 15, 2, 1, 3, 6, 15, 7, 4, 6, 12, 3, 17, 1, 13, 2, 6, 9, 5, 7, 14, 5, 4, 16, 5, 8, 5, 18, 5, 2, 9, 11
   (i) Represent this data on a grouped frequency table using the intervals 0–4, 4–8, etc.
   (ii) Draw a histogram to represent this data.

5. The following are the weights (to the nearest kg) of a selection of members in a given gym.
   63, 78, 85, 57, 61, 79, 81, 49, 58, 64, 77, 72, 66, 74, 68, 52, 48, 63, 72, 81, 69, 51, 79, 69, 71, 77, 56
   Using a grouped frequency table, draw a histogram to represent this data.

6. A Garda speed van was checking the speeds of cars passing a school. The table shows the speeds recorded.

Speed (km/h)	20–30	30–40	40–50	50–60
No. of vehicles	6	22	18	10

(Note: 20–30 means 20 or more but less than 30, etc.)

   (i) Describe the type of data collected.
   (ii) Draw a histogram to represent the data.
   (iii) How many vehicles were travelling at less than 50 km/h?

7. Explain the difference between a bar chart and a histogram. Refer to the type of data represented in your answer.

18.5 Introduction to statistical investigations

By the end of this section you should be able to:
- conduct a survey that will produce statistically accurate data
- present your data in the most appropriate way
- comment on your findings

Using the content we have covered so far in this unit, we will look at how to conduct a basic statistical investigation.

Carrying out a statistical investigation

1. **Design the questionnaire**

   When carrying out a survey, the first question to ask yourself is 'What do I hope to learn from asking the questions?' This helps to define the aim of your survey.

   Write down as many questions as you can think of, and then improve them. You can also ask the person about themselves, such as age group, so that you know the kind of people that you have been surveying. Think about how people will answer the questions and how you will present the data after it has been collected.

   Refer back to 18.2 when designing questions and forming samples.

2. **Decide who to ask**

   If you survey a small group, you can ask everybody; but if you want to survey a large group, you may not be able to ask everybody, so you should ask a sample of the population.

   When choosing a sample, remember that the sample must be random and representative of the population.

3. **Gather the data**

   Once you have decided who to ask you can give them your questionnaire. A useful way to combine all the data gathered is using a tally sheet. An example is shown on the right.

Information	Tally						
Own a pet	Yes			No			
Age	12	13	14	15	16	17	

4. **Represent the data**

   Choose the most appropriate form to represent the data you have gathered.

   Refer back to 18.3 when deciding how best to represent your data.

5. **Comment on your findings**

   Summarise the main things you learned from the survey, making sure to link back to your original question. Were there any patterns, e.g. did different age group or genders answer differently? What were the most common answers (mode)? Can you generalise your findings to a larger population? Discuss any bias present. How could your survey be improved?

Discuss and discover

Working with a classmate, perform a statistical investigation that you can carry out in your school.

(i) Design a questionnaire that has five questions, ensuring that at least two of your questions gather numerical data.

(ii) Decide who you are gathering data from.

(iii) Collect and represent your data.

(iv) Comment on your findings, linking back to your original question.

Practice questions 18·5

1. (a) Design a questionnaire for collecting data to answer each question below. Give at least four possible answers for your question each time.

    (i) What is the favourite food of Second-Year students?

    (ii) What is the favourite music of students in your class?

    (iii) What is the most popular brand of mobile phone in your school?

    (iv) How much sleep do Irish teenagers get a night?

   (b) For each of the questions in (a) above, answer the following.

    (i) Who should you ask?

    (ii) How could you pick a sample?

    (iii) How many people will you ask?

    (iv) What type of data will you collect?

2. The bar chart on the right shows the results of a questionnaire.

    (i) Complete the tally sheet that may have been used.

    (ii) Can you tell how many students were given the questionnaire? Explain.

    (iii) Write two things you know from this questionnaire.

    (iv) Could the results of this survey be generalised to the whole population? Justify your answer.

3. (a) Amira wanted to find out what the Second-Year students in her school wanted to be when they leave school. She wrote this question.

    What do you want to be when you leave school? Check one.
    Astronaut ☐   Designer ☐   Mechanic ☐   Nurse ☐

    (i) Is this a good question, in your opinion? Justify your answer.

    (ii) How would you ask this question?

   (b) Amira gave this question to the 66 students in Second-Year. Thirty-five people answered the question. Here are the results.

Occupation	Boys	Girls
Astronauts	||||	|||| |||
Designer	||||	||||	
Mechanic	///	/
Nurse	//	||||

   Amira concluded that most students will become astronauts or designers when they leave school.
   Is Amira's conclusion valid? Explain.

4. You want to find out if the students in your class are happy with the school uniform.

    (i) Design a questionnaire that could be used to answer this question.

    (ii) Decide who you will ask, how many will be asked and how you will pick them. Justify your reasoning.

    (iii) Collect your data and decide how best to represent it.

    (iv) Prepare a report on your findings that you could present to the student council on behalf of your class.

Revision questions

18A Core skills

1. Explain the following terms in your own words.
   - (i) Categorical data
   - (ii) Numerical data
   - (iii) Nominal data
   - (iv) Ordinal data
   - (v) Discrete data
   - (vi) Continuous data
   - (vii) Primary data
   - (viii) Secondary data
   - (ix) Census
   - (x) Population
   - (xi) Sample
   - (xii) Bias

2. Describe how bias can occur when carrying out a survey. List as many different ways as possible.

3. Form a frequency table to represent the following data:
   - (i) 2, 2, 2, 2, 2, 11, 11, 11, 2, 2, 2, 11, 11, 11, 11, 11, 11, 11, 2, 2, 2, 2
   - (ii) 1, 1, 1, 1, 1, 1, 1, 1, 1, 8, 8, 8, 8, 8, 8, 8, 8, 8, 8, 6, 6, 6, 6, 8, 8, 8, 8, 1, 1, 1, 1, 1, 1
   - (iii) 15, 15, 16, 15, 16, 15, 15, 16, 16, 17, 17, 15, 17, 15, 18, 18, 18, 15
   - (iv) 89, 86, 89, 86, 86, 86, 89, 91, 91, 86, 91, 91, 85, 85, 87, 87, 87

4. Draw a frequency table, a line plot and a bar chart to represent the set of data shown below.
   20, 20, 20, 30, 30, 30, 30, 40, 40, 60, 60, 70, 70, 70, 70, 80, 80

5. The table shows the distances travelled to school by a sample of students in a particular town.

Distance (km)	0–3	3–6	6–9	9–12	12–15
No. of students	4	20	16	10	4

   (Note: 20–30 means 20 or more but less than 30, etc.)
   - (i) Describe the type of data collected.
   - (ii) How many students were questioned?
   - (iii) Draw a histogram to represent this data.
   - (iv) What percentage of the students questioned lived 9 km or more from the school. Give your answer correct to two decimal places.

6. The student council want to carry out a survey about changes to the school canteen.
   - (i) Who should they question?
   - (ii) How could they pick the sample to be asked?
   - (iii) Write three questions that could be asked in the survey.
   - (iv) For each of your questions in (iii), identify the type of data being collected.
   - (v) Describe two different ways that the results of the survey could be represented.

7. For each of the following:
   - (i) Write a question whose responses could be represented by the data shown.
   - (ii) Determine the most common response in each case.

   (a)
No. goals	0	1	2	3	4
Frequency	7	13	10	6	4

   (b) Red, green, red, blue, yellow, red, blue, green, red, yellow, blue, green, red, blue, red

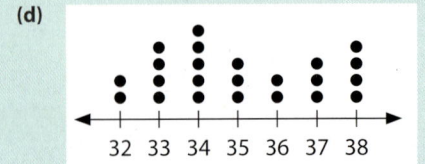

   (c) Visitors visit to a zoo (bar chart showing Number of visitors for April ≈ 400, May ≈ 350, June ≈ 450, July ≈ 600, August ≈ 550)

   (d) Line plot with dots above values 32 to 38.

300 Linking Thinking 1

18B Taking it FURTHER

1. The line plot on the right represents laptop sales for a certain shop in a given week.
   (i) How many laptops were sold on Monday?
   (ii) On which day did the shop sell the fewest laptops?
   (iii) Which was the most popular day for sales?
   (iv) How many laptops were sold over the weekend?
   (v) If a customer is picked at random, what is the probability that they bought a laptop on Friday?

2. (i) Find the most popular breakfast from the data shown in the bar chart on the right.
   (ii) If 70 more people vote for eggs, what would be the most popular breakfast?
   (iii) How many people voted for toast as their favourite breakfast?
   (iv) Find the difference between highest and lowest frequency?

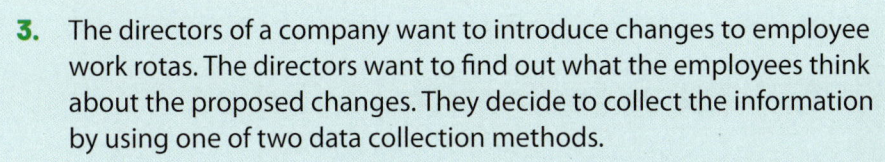

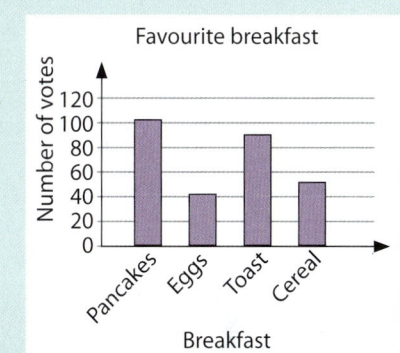

3. The directors of a company want to introduce changes to employee work rotas. The directors want to find out what the employees think about the proposed changes. They decide to collect the information by using one of two data collection methods.
   - Method 1: each employee will be interviewed by one of the directors.
   - Method 2: each employee will complete a questionnaire without filling in their name.

   There are 100 employees in the company.
   (i) List the advantages and disadvantages of each data collection method.
   (ii) Which method would you advise the directors to use? Justify your answer using the advantages and disadvantages of the data collection methods.

4. Mark wants to find out the types of film people like best.
   (i) Write a question that Mark could ask to find out this information.
   (ii) Design a suitable table for a data collection sheet he could use to collect this information.
   (iii) Mark collects his data by asking 10 students in his class at school. Is this a good data collection method? Give reasons for your answer.

5. Jim conducts a survey about eye colour and represents the data on a histogram.
   (i) Is this an appropriate way to represent this data? Justify your answer.
   (ii) What kind of chart could he have used? Justify your answer.

Now that you have completed the unit, revisit the Something to think about ... question posed at the start of this unit.

Now try question 12 on page 408

Unit 19

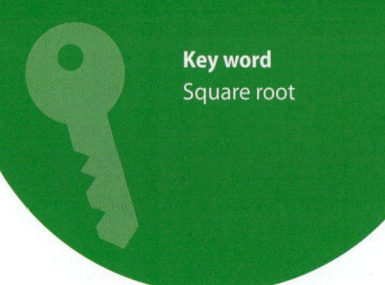

Indices

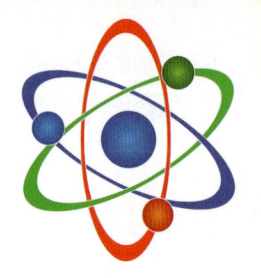

Topics covered within this unit:
- 19·1 Index (scientific) notation
- 19·2 Multiplying variables with powers
- 19·3 Dividing variables with powers
- 19·4 A power on a power
- 19·5 Square root of a number

The Learning Outcomes covered in this unit are contained in the following sections:

N.1c.I   N.1c.II   N.1f

Key word
Square root

A^n ← Power
Base

10^n ← Power
Base

Something to think about ...

Atoms are extremely small particles. The number of atoms of carbon in 12 grams of carbon is equal to 602 214 085 700 000 000 000 000

It's difficult to write this number when doing calculations. Can you write this number in another way?

KEY SKILLS

19·1 Index (scientific) notation

By the end of this section you should:
- be able to write numbers in index notation

Recall from Section A: The **exponent** (or index or power) of a number says how many times to use the number in a multiplication.

In Section A of this book, we were introduced to indices.

Recall,

5^3 means **5** × **5** × **5** = 125

It means: 5 is used **3** times in the multiplication

In words: 5^3 could be called '5 cubed' or '5 to the power 3'.

8^4 = 8 × 8 × 8 × 8 = 4 096

In words: 8^4 could be called '8 to the power 4'.

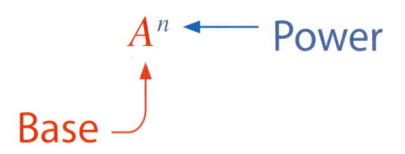

Powers of 10

'Powers of 10' is a very useful way of writing down large or small numbers.

Instead of having lots of zeros, you show how many powers of 10 will make that many zeros.

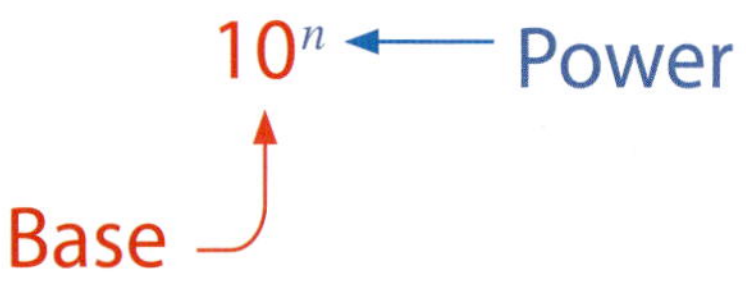

Example: 5 000 = 5 × 1 000 = 5 × 10 × 10 × 10 = 5 × 10^3

Scientists and engineers (who often use very big or very small numbers) like to write numbers this way.

It is commonly called **scientific notation**, or **index notation**.

302   Linking Thinking 1

For example, in scientific notation, we say that the Sun has a mass of $1{\cdot}988 \times 10^{30}$ kg, as it is easier to write than 1 988 000 000 000 000 000 000 000 000 000 kg.

A lightyear (the distance light travels in one year) is written as $9{\cdot}461 \times 10^{15}$ metres, rather than 9 461 000 000 000 000 metres.

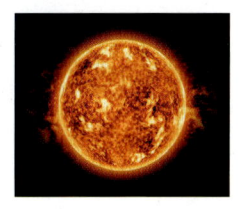

Writing numbers greater than or equal to 10 in index notation

1. Move the decimal place to the left until the number is equal to or greater than 1 and less than 10
2. Count the number of times you had to move the decimal place to the left in step 1
3. Write $\times 10^n$ after the new number, where n is the number of times you moved the decimal place to the left

> Index (or scientific) notation is when a number is written in the form $a \times 10^n$, where a is a number equal to or greater than 1 and less than 10 ($1 \le a < 10$) and $n \in \mathbb{N}$.

Worked example 1

Write the following numbers in scientific notation

(i) 8 000 (ii) 62 573·78

Solution

(i) Step 1

8000·

Step 2
Moved 3 places to the left

Step 3
$8{\cdot}000 \times 10^3$
8×10^3

(ii) Step 1

62573·78

Step 2
Moved 4 places to the left

Step 3
$6{\cdot}257378 \times 10^4$

Converting from index (scientific) notation to a regular number

When the power of 10 is a positive number, n, move the decimal place n times to the right to change a number from index form back to a regular number.

Worked example 2

The distance between Mars and the Sun is at least $2{\cdot}279 \times 10^8$ kilometres.
Write this distance as a regular number.

Solution

$2{\cdot}279 \times 10^8$

We move the decimal place 8 places to the right to change the number back to a regular number.

2·27900 000

$2{\cdot}279 \times 10^8$ is written as 227 900 000 as a regular number.

Section B Moving forward

Practice questions 19.1

1. Write the following numbers in index notation.
   - (i) 30 000 000 000
   - (ii) 679 000 000
   - (iii) 367 800 000 125
   - (iv) 367
   - (v) 6 890·87
   - (vi) 784·67

2. Write the following numbers in index notation.
   - (i) 45·6789
   - (ii) 77·899226
   - (iii) 8 945 677·92324
   - (iv) 1·56899
   - (v) 45·0000
   - (vi) 6382·29373

3. Write the numbers given in index notation as regular numbers.
   - (i) 6×10^4
   - (ii) 2×10^8
   - (iii) $2·678 \times 10^7$
   - (iv) $6·5678 \times 10^9$
   - (v) 1×10^2
   - (vi) $9·9888 \times 10^3$

4. Write the numbers given in scientific notation as regular numbers.
   - (i) $6·89536382 \times 10^3$
   - (ii) $7·89353728 \times 10^5$
   - (iii) $1·000005678 \times 10^8$
   - (iv) $6·45 \times 10$
   - (v) $5·463 \times 10^3$

5. The speed of sound depends on the type of medium and the temperature of the medium it is traveling through. The speed of sound in dry air at 15°C is about 1 227·93 kilometres per hour. Rewrite this number in the form $a \times 10^n$, where $1 \leq a < 10$, and $n \in \mathbb{N}$.

6. A human heart beats an average of 80 beats per minute. How many beats is this in an hour? Express your answer in the form $a \times 10^n$, where $1 \leq a < 10$, and $n \in \mathbb{N}$.

7. The average person blinks 17 times per minute. How many times does the average person blink in a three-hour period when awake? Express your answer in scientific notation.

8. The number of molecules in 1 gram of water is $3·34 \times 10^{22}$. Express this number as a regular number.

19.2 Multiplying variables with powers

By the end of this section you should be able to:
- multiply variables with powers

Discuss and discover

From 19.1, we know that indices (or exponents or powers) are numbers that tell us how often a number is to be multiplied by itself in a mathematical expression.

Working with a classmate, copy and complete the table below.

Expanded form		Index form
5×5	Written as a power of 5 =	5^2
$p \times p \times p$	Written as a power of p =	p^3
$4 \times 4 \times 4$	Written as a power of 4 =	
$6 \times 6 \times 6 \times 6$	Written as a power of 6 =	
$y \times y \times y$	Written as a power of y =	
$a^3 \times a$	Written as a power of a =	
$a^2 \times a^2$	Written as a power of a =	
$x^3 \times x^4$	Written as a power of x =	

Look carefully at the table to see if you can discover a rule (using powers) to find the missing answers.

What have you learned about multiplying terms and powers from completing this table?

Laws of indices

It is sometimes quicker and easier to work with numbers in index form, if we use laws of indices. There are three laws of indices that we will study in this course.

Law 1: Multiplying numbers in index form

Suppose we have a^3 and we want to multiply it by a^2

That is, $a^3 \times a^2 = a \times a \times a \times a \times a$

Altogether there are five a's multiplied together. This is the same as a^5.

This suggests our first law.

> **Law 1:** The first law of indices tells us that when multiplying two identical base numbers or letters together that have powers (e.g. $2^2 \times 2^3$), the answer will be the same base number to the power of both exponents added together.
> $$a^p \times a^q = a^{p+q}$$

This formula appears in the *formulae and tables* booklet.

Worked example

Simplify the following.

(i) $4^3 \times 4^5$ 　　(ii) $(x^4)(x^3)$ 　　(iii) $y \times y^2$

Solution

(i) $4^3 \times 4^5$
$= 4^{3+5}$
$= 4^8$
$= 65\ 536$

(ii) $(x^4)(x^3)$
$= x^{4+3}$
$= x^7$

(iii) $y \times y^2$
$= y^1 \times y^2$
$= y^{1+2}$
$= y^3$

> **Invisible Maths!**
> Every number has an index of 1, e.g. $y = y^1$

Practice questions 19.2

1. Simplify the following, leaving your answers in index form.
   (i) $(3^3)(3^5)$
   (ii) $8^2 \times 8^3$
   (iii) $(3)(3^8)$
   (iv) $y^2 \times y^5$
   (v) $(x^2)(x^9)$
   (vi) $b \times b^5$

2. Simplify the following, leaving your answers in index form.
   (i) $a^2 \times a^2$
   (ii) $(y)(y)$
   (iii) $m \times m^3$
   (iv) $(x^5)(x^6)$
   (v) $n^3 \times n^8$
   (vi) $(p^4)(p^8)$

3. Simplify the following, leaving your answers in index form.
   (i) $(x^8)(x^{10})$
   (ii) $(n^5)(n^9)$
   (iii) $p^{10} \times p^{34}$
   (iv) $x^2 \times x$
   (v) $y^0 \times y^8$
   (vi) $(y^4)(y^{10})$

   > **Invisible Maths!**
   > Anything to the power of 0 is equal to 1.

4. Express the following numbers in index form.
   (i) $27 = 3^{\square}$
   (ii) $32 = 2^{\square}$
   (iii) $100 = 10^{\square}$
   (iv) $64 = 2^{\square}$
   (v) $64 = 4^{\square}$
   (vi) $3125 = 5^{\square}$

   > This question uses trial and improvement.
   > How many times do you multiply a number by itself to get the result?
   > $3 \times 3 \times 3 = 27$. So, $27 = 3^3$

5. A stationery shop sold x^8 pens in one week. If each of the pens cost x euros, how much money in terms of x would they have made?

6. A delivery driver made exactly 32 stops each day. After 4 days, how many stops would he have made in total? Express your answer in the form 2^k.

7. A toy shop sold p^2 video games in one day. If each game cost p^2 euros, how much money, in terms of p, did they make?

19.3 Dividing variables with powers

By the end of this section you should be able to:
- divide variables with powers

Discuss and discover

Working with a classmate, copy and complete the table below.

$\frac{4}{4}$	Written as a power of 4 =	$4^0 = 1$
$\frac{2 \times 2}{2}$	Written as a power of 2 =	2
$\frac{6 \times 6 \times 6}{6}$	Written as a power of 6 =	6^2
$\frac{y \times y \times y}{y}$	Written as a power of y =	
$\frac{a^3}{a^2}$	Written as a power of a =	
$\frac{b^5}{b^2}$	Written as a power of b =	
$\frac{x^6}{x^3}$	Written as a power of x =	

Look carefully at the table to see if you can discover a rule (using powers) to find the missing answers.

What have you learned about dividing terms and powers from completing this table?

Law 2: Dividing numbers in index form

Consider dividing a^7 by a^3.

$$a^7 \div a^3 = \frac{a^7}{a^3} = \frac{a \times a \times a \times a \times a \times a \times a}{a \times a \times a}$$

Three of the as at the top and the three as at the bottom can be divided out:

$$= \frac{(\cancel{a \times a \times a})1 \times a \times a \times a \times a}{(\cancel{a \times a \times a})\,1}$$

So, we are now left with $\frac{a^4}{1}$, or simply a^4

The same answer is obtained by **subtracting the indices**, that is, $7 - 3 = 4$. This suggests our second law.

> **Law 2:** The second law of indices tells us that when dividing a number with an exponent by the same number with an exponent, we have to subtract the exponents (powers).
> $$\frac{a^p}{a^q} = a^{p-q}$$

The formula appears in the *formulae and tables* booklet.

Worked example

Simplify the following, leaving your answer in index form.

(i) $\frac{5^6}{5^4}$ (ii) $\frac{x^{10}}{x^7}$ (iii) $\frac{b^9}{b}$

Solution

(i) $\frac{5^6}{5^4}$
$= 5^{6-4}$
$= 5^2$

(ii) $\frac{x^{10}}{x^7}$
$= x^{10-7}$
$= x^3$

(iii) $\frac{b^9}{b^1}$
$= b^{9-1}$
$= b^8$

Practice questions 19.3

1. Simplify the following, leaving your answer in index form.
   (i) $\dfrac{4^5}{4^3}$ (ii) $\dfrac{2^6}{2^2}$ (iii) $\dfrac{10^6}{10}$ (iv) $\dfrac{x^8}{x^6}$ (v) $\dfrac{b^7}{b^2}$ (vi) $\dfrac{y^8}{y^3}$

2. Simplify the following, leaving your answer in index form.
   (i) $\dfrac{a^7}{a}$ (ii) $\dfrac{m^4}{m^2}$ (iii) $\dfrac{n^{12}}{n^4}$ (iv) $\dfrac{n}{n}$ (v) $\dfrac{n^3}{n^2}$ (vi) $\dfrac{x^2}{x}$

3. x^3 sweets were distributed equally among x^2 children. Find, in terms of x, how many sweets each child received.

4. n^5 grams of sweets were distributed among n^3 children. Find, in terms of n, the mass of sweets that was given to each child.

5. One steel plate has a mass of x^4 grams. If the mass of a number of steel plates is x^{10} grams, find, in terms of x, the number of plates.

6. There are y^4 rows with equal number of soldiers. If the total number of soldiers was y^{14}, find, in terms of y, how many soldiers are there in each row.

19.4 A power on a power

By the end of this section you should be able to:
- simplify variables with powers in a bracket with a power outside the bracket

Discuss and discover

Working with a classmate, copy and complete the table below.

(Bracket)^{Power}	Expanded bracket	Written as a power	
$(4)^1$	4^1	Written as a power of 4 =	4^1
$(3^2)^2$	$3^2 \times 3^2$	Written as a power of 3 =	3^4
$(5^2)^3$	$5^2 \times 5^2 \times 5^2$	Written as a power of 5 =	$5^\square$
$(x^3)^2$		Written as a power of x =	
$(y^4)^3$		Written as a power of y =	
$(n^4)^4$		Written as a power of n =	

Look carefully at the table to see if you can discover a rule (using powers).
What have you learned about powers from completing this table?

Law 3: Power on a power

Suppose we had a^4 and we want to raise it all to the power 3.

That is $(a^4)^3$. This means $a^4 \times a^4 \times a^4$

Our first rule tells us that we should add the indices together, which is 12.

But note also that 12 is 4×3.

This suggests that if we have a^p all raised to the power q the result is obtained **by multiplying the two powers** to get $a^{p \times q}$, or simply a^{pq}.

> **Law 3:** The third law tells us that when we have a number in index form and we want to raise it to a power, we multiply the two powers together to get the final answer in index form.
> $$(a^p)^q = a^{p \times q}$$

The formula appears in the *formulae and tables* booklet.

Worked example

Simplify the following leaving your answer in index form.

(i) $(4^3)^2$ (ii) $(x^5)^4$ (iii) $(y^9)^2$

Solution

(i) $(4^3)^2$
$= 4^{3 \times 2}$
$= 4^6$

(ii) $(x^5)^4$
$= x^{5 \times 4}$
$= x^{20}$

(iii) $(y^9)^2$
$= y^{9 \times 2}$
$= y^{18}$

Practice questions 19·4

1. Simplify the following, leaving your answers in index form.
   (i) $(2^3)^2$ (ii) $(5^4)^3$ (iii) $(6^3)^4$ (iv) $(x^2)^3$ (v) $(y^6)^5$ (vi) $(x^5)^2$

2. Simplify the following, leaving your answers in index form.
   (i) $(y^2)^8$ (ii) $(a)^5$ (iii) $(b^2)^2$ (iv) $(x^8)^4$ (v) $(b^2)^5$ (vi) $(a^9)^4$

3. Simplify the following, leaving your answers in index form.
   (i) $(u^7)^3$ (ii) $(p^6)^2$ (iii) $(n^7)^3$ (iv) $(n^{12})^2$ (v) $(u^1)^1$ (vi) $(u^2)^1$

4. Simplify the following, leaving your answers in index form.
   (i) $\dfrac{x^3 \times x^4}{x^2}$ (ii) $\dfrac{x^6 \times x^9}{x^5}$ (iii) $\dfrac{m^3 \times m}{m^2 \times m}$ (iv) $\dfrac{(x^3)^4}{x^2}$ (v) $\dfrac{(x^3)^4 \times x^2}{x^3}$ (vi) $\dfrac{(n^6)^2 \times n^2}{n^4}$

Taking it FURTHER

5. Write the following in the form 2^n.
   (i) $\dfrac{2^5}{8}$ (ii) $\dfrac{16}{4}$ (iii) $\dfrac{64}{2}$ (iv) 64×256 (v) 128×8 (vi) $(512)^4$

19.5 Square root of a number

By the end of this section you should be able to:
- find the square root (√) of a number

Discuss and discover

KEY SKILLS

Working with a classmate, copy and complete the table below.

Multiplication of two of the same number/variable	Answer	What number/variable squared would give the answer?
4 × 4	= 16	4
5 × 5	=	
	= 49	
		10
	= 1	
y × y		
p × p		

A square root of a number is a value that can be multiplied by itself to give the original number. Can you discover what the square root of each of the numbers/terms in the answer column is?

What have you learned about squaring or square rooting numbers by doing this exercise?

Many mathematical operations have an **inverse, or opposite, operation**. Subtraction is the opposite of addition, division is the inverse of multiplication, and so on.

Squaring, which we learned about previously, has an inverse too, called 'finding the square root'.

Remember, the square of a number is that number multiplied by itself.

The perfect squares are the squares of the natural numbers: 1, 4, 9, 16, 25, 36, 49, 64, 81, 100 …

> The **square root** of a number, n, written as $\sqrt{n}$ or $n^{\frac{1}{2}}$, is the number that gives n when multiplied by itself.

Here, we will only find the positive square roots of numbers.

> A square root can be converted into index form, as follows:
> $$\sqrt{x} = x^{\frac{1}{2}}$$

Worked example

Simplify the following.

(i) $\sqrt{100}$ (ii) $\sqrt{49}$ (iii) $289^{\frac{1}{2}}$

Solution

(i) $\sqrt{100}$
Using the √ symbol on your calculator
Answer = 10

(ii) $\sqrt{49}$
Using the √ symbol on your calculator
Answer = 7

(iii) $289^{\frac{1}{2}}$
$= \sqrt{289}$
Using the √ symbol on your calculator
Answer = 17

Section B Moving forward

Practice questions 19·5

1. Simplify the following.
   - (i) $\sqrt{36}$
   - (ii) $\sqrt{64}$
   - (iii) $\sqrt{81}$

2. Simplify the following.
   - (i) $\sqrt{4}$
   - (ii) $144^{\frac{1}{2}}$
   - (iii) $\sqrt{256}$

3. Simplify the following.
   - (i) $\sqrt{100}$
   - (ii) $\sqrt{676}$
   - (iii) $529^{\frac{1}{2}}$

4. Simplify the following.
   - (i) $\sqrt{784} \times \sqrt{100}$
   - (ii) $\sqrt{10\,000} \times \sqrt{16}$
   - (iii) $\sqrt{3\,969} \times \sqrt{64}$

5. Which of the following numbers is a perfect square? Justify your answer.
   - (a) 141
   - (b) 196
   - (c) 124
   - (d) 222

Taking it FURTHER

6. Which of the following numbers must be added to 6 072 to make it a perfect square? Justify your answer.
   - (a) 6
   - (b) 10
   - (c) 12
   - (d) 16

Revision questions

19A Core skills

1. Write the following numbers in index notation.
   - (i) 50·97689
   - (ii) 7 897·899226
   - (iii) 677 865 322·92324

2. Write the following numbers in scientific notation.
   - (i) 67 890·689
   - (ii) 9 000 000·456
   - (iii) 346 784·6547

3. Write the numbers given in index notation as regular numbers.
   - (i) 8.456×10^4
   - (ii) 2.5647×10^8
   - (iii) 8.678×10^2

4. Simplify the following, leaving your answers in index form.
   - (i) $(a^4)(a^2)$
   - (ii) $(y^6)(y)$
   - (iii) $64^{\frac{1}{2}}$

5. Simplify the following, leaving your answers in index form.
   - (i) $(b^7)(b^8)$
   - (ii) $(t^3)(t^2)$
   - (iii) $(n^4)(n^2)$

6. Simplify the following, leaving your answers in index form.
   - (i) $\dfrac{a^9}{a^5}$
   - (ii) $\dfrac{b^6}{b^2}$
   - (iii) $\dfrac{a^4}{a^0}$

Linking Thinking 1

7. Simplify the following, leaving your answers in index form.
   (i) $\dfrac{a^{12}}{a^7}$ (ii) $\dfrac{b^9}{b^8}$ (iii) $\dfrac{t^4}{t}$

8. Simplify the following, leaving your answers in index form.
   (i) $(x^3)^2$ (ii) $(b^4)^3$ (iii) $(t^3)^4$

9. Simplify the following, leaving your answers in index form.
   (i) $(u^4)^2$ (ii) $(y^8)^3$ (iii) $(b^9)^2$

10. Simplify the following, leaving your answers in index form.
    (i) $\dfrac{m^2 \times m^6}{m^4}$ (ii) $\dfrac{x^5 \times x^4}{x^4}$ (iii) $\dfrac{n^6 \times n}{n^3 \times n^2}$ (iv) $\dfrac{(p^4)^6}{p^3}$ (v) $\dfrac{(q^4)^4 \times q^4}{q^4}$ (vi) $\dfrac{(n^5)^2 \times n^2}{n^5}$

19B Taking it FURTHER

1. The average blue whale heart rate is 8 beats per minute. How many times would a blue whale's heart beat in 16·5 hours? Express your answer in the form $a \times 10^n$, where $1 \leq a < 10$, and $n \in \mathbb{N}$.

2. A hummingbird's wings flap 70 times per second. How many times would they flap in 24 hours of flight? Give your answer in index notation.

3. The speed of light is 186 000 miles per second, or about 671 000 000 miles per hour.
   (i) 1 mile is approximately equal to 1·61 kilometres. Find the speed of light in kilometres per second and kilometres per hour.
   (ii) Express these numbers in scientific notation.

4. Sarah had x^{12} shelves of DVDs. If each shelf had x^3 movies on it, find, in terms of x, how many movies she had in total.

5. p^{14} euros are distributed equally among p^2 people. How many euros, in terms of p, will each person get?

6. If c^{18} kg of wheat is packed in c^3 bags, what mass of wheat, in terms of c, will each bag contain?

7. A stadium can hold y^{24} seated spectators. If there are y rows of seats on the stadium, find in terms of y, how many seats are in each row.

8. Evaluate the following and give your answers in the form 5^n
   (i) $\dfrac{5^4}{25}$ (ii) $\dfrac{625}{125}$ (iii) $\dfrac{15\,625}{25}$ (iv) 25×125 (v) 625×125 (vi) $(125)^4$

Now that you have completed the unit, revisit the

? Something to think about ...

question posed at the start of this unit.

Unit 20

Working with expressions

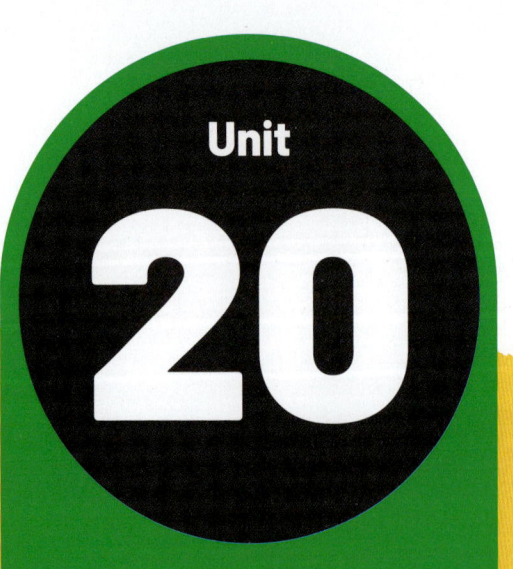

Topics covered within this unit:
- 20·1 Expressions
- 20·2 Evaluating expressions
- 20·3 Multiplying an expression by a term
- 20·4 Multiplying expressions
- 20·5 Factorising using a factor common to all terms in an expression
- 20·6 Factorising using common factors from groups of terms

The Learning Outcomes covered in this unit are contained in the following sections:

AF.3a.I AF.3a.II AF.3b AF.3c
AF.3d.I AF.3d.II AF.3d.III
AF.3d.IV

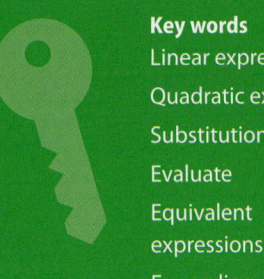

Key words
Linear expression
Quadratic expression
Substitution
Evaluate
Equivalent expressions
Expanding
Factorising expressions

Something to think about ...

KEY SKILLS

The algebraic expression for the momentum of a moving object is mass × velocity, or mv, where mass is in kg and velocity is in metres per second (m/s).

A balloon has a mass of 500 grams and a velocity of 2 m/s going in a particular direction.

A runner going in the same direction has a mass of 70 kg and a velocity of 4 m/s

Will the balloon or the runner have the greatest momentum?

20·1 Expressions

By the end of this section you should:
- understand what an expression is
- be able to write expressions from word problems

An expression is a mathematical sentence that can contain constants, variables (like x or y), and operators like +, −, ×, ÷

$$\underbrace{\underbrace{5x}_{\text{term}} \underbrace{-8}_{\text{term}} \underbrace{+5y}_{\text{term}}}_{\text{expression}}$$

A **numerical expression** contains only numbers and operations.

An **algebraic expression** may contain numbers, operations, and one or more variables.

312   Linking Thinking 1

Many **English phrases** translate directly into **algebraic expressions**, as shown in the table on the right.

A variable (x, for example) stands for 'an unknown number'.

Division is normally shown with a horizontal line.

English expression	Algebraic expression
A number plus eight	$x + 8$
Four less than a number	$x - 4$
A number divided by four	$\frac{x}{4}$
List four consecutive numbers	$x, x+1, x+2, x+3$
List four consecutive even numbers	$x, x+2, x+4, x+6$
Length multiplied by width	lw
Half the base multiplied by perpendicular height	$\frac{1}{2}b \times (\perp h)$

Worked example 1

Let x represent the total number of students in a Maths class. Write an algebraic expression for the number of students in the classroom on a given day if:

(i) 5 students were absent
(ii) 2 new students entered the room
(iii) y students from another class entered the room
(iv) the number of students in the room doubled
(v) one-third of the students left the room

Solution

(i) Total number of students less the 5 absent = $x - 5$
(ii) Total number of students + 2 new students = $x + 2$
(iii) Total number of students + y extra students = $x + y$
(iv) (Total number of students) $\times 2 = 2x$
(v) Total number of students − one third of the total = $x - \frac{1}{3}(x)$

Worked example 2

In a certain shop, the price of an apple is 50 cents, and the price of a banana is 35 cents. During a visit to the shop, John gives all his money to the shopkeeper while buying x apples and y bananas.

Mary gives the shopkeeper all her money, but gets twice as many bananas as John and also 4 apples.

(i) Write a mathematical expression for the money John gave to the to the shopkeeper.
(ii) Write a mathematical expression for the money Mary gave to the shopkeeper.
(iii) Write an expression for the total amount of money they had between them, going into the shop

Solution

(i) Money spent by John = $50x + 35y$
(ii) John bought y bananas therefore, Mary bought $2y$ bananas
Mary bought 4 apples, so $4 \times 50 = 200$ cents
Money spent by Mary = $200 + 35(2y)$
$= 200 + 70y$

(iii) Total amount of money = John + Mary
$= (50x + 35y) + (200 + 70y)$
$= 50x + 105y + 200$

Section B Moving forward

Types of algebraic expressions

> A **linear expression** is one in which the highest power of any variable is 1, e.g. $4x + 10$

> A **quadratic expression** is one in which the highest power of any variable is 2, e.g. $2x^2 + 4x + 3$

Adding and subtracting expressions

Where necessary, remove the brackets by multiplying each term inside the brackets by the term outside the brackets and then simplify.

Worked example 3

Simplify the following   (i) $(2x + 3y) - (5x - 27)$ (ii) $(m - 6n) - (6n - 5m) + 2(3m - 8)$

Solution

(i) $(2x + 3y) - (5x - 27)$

$1(2x + 3y) - 1(5x - 27)$

$2x + 3y - 5x + 27$ (simplifying like terms)

$-3x + 3y + 27$

> **Invisible Maths!**
> In part (i), each set of brackets has an invisible 1 in front of it.

(ii) $(m - 6n) - (6n - 5m) + 2(3m - 8)$

$1(m - 6n) - 1(6n - 5m) + 2(3m - 8)$

$m - 6n - 6n + 5m + 6m - 16$

$m + 5m + 6m - 6n - 6n - 16$

$12m - 12n - 16$

Worked example 4

Find the sum of these expressions: $\left(4x - \frac{3}{7}y\right) + \left(\frac{5}{2}y + 8x\right)$

Solution

$\left(4x - \frac{3}{7}y\right) + \left(\frac{5}{2}y + 8x\right)$

$4x - \frac{3}{7}y + \frac{5}{2}y + 8x$

$4x + 8x - \frac{3}{7}y + \frac{5}{2}y$

$4x + 8x - \left(\frac{3}{7}\right)\left(\frac{2}{2}\right)y + \left(\frac{5}{2}\right)\left(\frac{7}{7}\right)y$

$4x + 8x - \frac{6}{14}y + \frac{35}{14}y$

$12x + \frac{-6 + 35}{14}y$ (adding like terms)

Simplified: $12x + \frac{29}{14}y$

To simplify the fractions, they must have the same denominator. We do this by finding the LCM of the denominators and convert each fraction into an equivalent fraction with the LCM as the denominator.

> Adding and subtracting fractions was covered in Section A, Unit 5.

Practice questions 20·1

1. Write an expression for each of the following sentences.
   - (i) Five more than a number
   - (ii) Eight less than a number
   - (iii) A number multiplied by seven
   - (iv) Divide a number by three and subtract ten
   - (v) Subtract six from a number, then multiply by two
   - (vi) Divide a number by 2 then add 11
   - (vii) Double a number and add 5

2. Orla earns €7 per hour in her part time job.
   - (i) How much money will she earn in 4 hours?
   - (ii) How much money will she earn in 7·5 hours?
   - (iii) Write an expression you could use to find the amount of money earned in t hours.

3. Identify whether each of the following expressions are linear, quadratic or neither.
   - (i) $4x + 6$
   - (ii) $x^2 + 4x + 6$
   - (iii) $4a^2 + 6a + 5$
   - (iv) $4n^4 - 2n^2 + 3n$
   - (v) $-6 + x$
   - (vi) $10 - x^2$
   - (vii) $x^3 - 10x^2 + 4x + 3$
   - (viii) $10x^2$

4. Write each of the following expressions in words, calling the variable 'a number'.
   - (i) $x + 6$
   - (ii) $9y + 12$
   - (iii) $\frac{n}{2} + 2$
   - (iv) $4x - 3$
   - (v) $15x - 8$
   - (vi) $9 - 3b$

5. Find the sum of the following pairs of expressions.
   - (i) $(2 + 4x) + (5 + 6x)$
   - (ii) $(4x + 8) + 2(3 + 10x)$
   - (iii) $(3 + 6x) + (11x + 7)$
   - (iv) $(12m) - 5(3n + 14m)$
   - (v) $3(4p + 3q) + (5q - 6p)$
   - (vi) $(12a - 8y) - (14a - 10y)$

6. Find the sum of the following expressions.
   - (i) $(1 + x) + (1 + x)$
   - (ii) $(2q) - (-2)$
   - (iii) $(16a + 4) + (3 - 14a)$
   - (iv) $(2 + 2n) + (1 - n)$
   - (v) $(8 + 6x) - (3 + 2x) + (2x + 6)$

7. Find the sum of the following expressions.
   - (i) $(4x + 2) + (14x - 7) + (2x + 2)$
   - (ii) $(x + 5) - 3(4y + 13x) + (5x + 6y)$
   - (iii) $5(2 + x) + (2 + x) + 2(4x + 3)$
   - (iv) $(10t + s) - 6(9s + 4t) + (3t - 6)$
   - (v) $3(4x - 10) + \frac{5}{2} - 5(2x - 2)$

8. Give three examples of expressions whose sum is equal to $24x + 26y$.

9. Find the sum of the following expressions in terms of x and y.
   - (i) $(x - 9y) - 3(10y + 10x) - (5x - 6)$
   - (ii) $2(4x + 15y) + (10 + 3x) - (-4x)$
   - (iii) $(20x + 2) - (18 + 4x) - 5(-4x - 6)$
   - (iv) $4(-x - 10y) + 3(8x) + (-2x + 2y)$

10. Find the sum of the following expressions.
    - (i) $\left(\frac{3}{8}x + \frac{2}{5}n\right) - \left(\frac{1}{8}x + \frac{1}{5}n\right)$
    - (ii) $\left(\frac{3}{5}x + \frac{3}{8}y\right) - \left(\frac{3}{4}y - \frac{3}{10}x\right)$
    - (iii) $\left(\frac{3}{5}p - 5x\right) - \left(4p + \frac{2}{3}x\right)$
    - (iv) $\left(\frac{5}{12} + \frac{3}{8}m\right) + \left(\frac{5}{6} + \frac{3}{4}m\right)$
    - (v) $\left(x - \frac{1}{8}\right) + \left(10x + \frac{1}{9}y\right) - \left(\frac{1}{3}x - 19y\right)$

11. Let x represent the total number of students in a Maths class. Write an algebraic expression for the number of students in the classroom if:
    - (i) 3 students were absent
    - (ii) 5 new students entered the room
    - (iii) b students from another class entered the room
    - (iv) the number of students in the class tripled
    - (v) half of the students in the class left the room

12. Linda was selling tickets for the school play. She sold 10 more adult tickets than children's tickets, and she sold twice as many senior tickets as children's tickets.

    Let x represent the number of children's tickets sold.

    (i) Write an expression to represent the number of adult tickets sold.

    (ii) Write an expression to represent the number of senior tickets sold.

13. A cupboard contains x plates, y bowls, and z cups.

    Write algebraic expressions for each of the following.

    (i) The total number of plates, bowls and cups

    (ii) The total number of plates and bowls

    (iii) The number of cups in the cupboard after 3 cups are taken out

    (iv) The number of cups in the cupboard after 5 cups are added to it.

14. Let m represent the amount of money (€) in a money box on a particular day. Write an algebraic expression for the amount of money in the money box for each of the following (as separate events).

    (i) €1·50 is added to the box

    (ii) €5·25 is taken out of the box

    (iii) €b is added to the box

    (iv) €t is taken out of the box

    (v) The amount of money in the box is doubled

15. The sum of two expressions is equal to $7x + 12$. Find three possible pairs of expressions, where the sum of the pairs is equal to $7x + 12$.

Taking it FURTHER

16. Give an example of three expressions whose sum is equal to $-6x - 12y$

17. An airplane has economy and business-class seating.

    There are s seats in each row in economy.

    There are t seats in each row in business class.

    There are 9 rows in business class and 24 rows in economy.

    Write down an expression, in terms of s and t, for the number of seats on the airplane.

18. Find an expression for the perimeter of each of the following shapes.

    (i) Rectangle with length $11x + 7$ and width $5 + 6x$

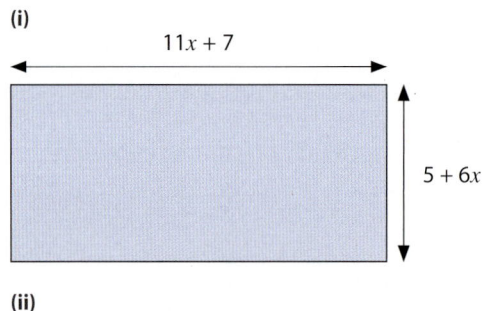

    (ii) Rectangle with length $4x - 1$ and width $2x + 1$

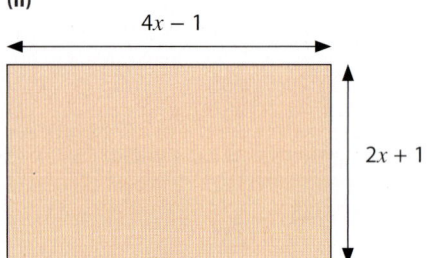

    (iii) Triangle with two sides $4m - 2$ and base $3 + 14m$

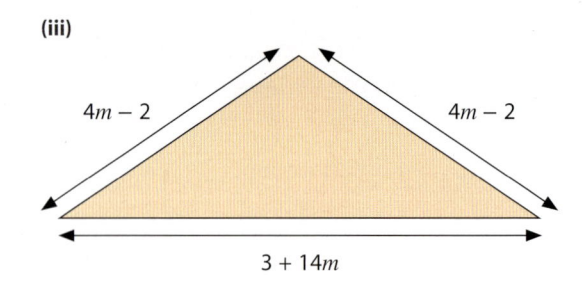

    (iv) Hexagon with sides $3a + 12$, $3a + 14$, $3a + 12$ (axis of symmetry)

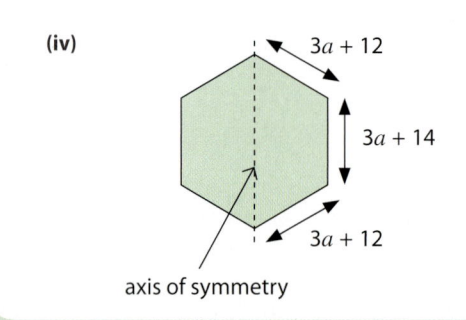

20.2 Evaluating expressions

By the end of this section you should:
- understand what it means to evaluate an expression
- be able to evaluate expressions given the value of the variables

To **evaluate** (find the value of) an algebraic expression, **substitute** a number for each variable. Then use the order of operations to find the value of the numerical expression.

> When using **substitution** in algebra, a variable (such as x or y) is replaced with a value/number.

> To **evaluate** means to find the value of an algebraic expression, when you substitute a number for each variable and perform the operations ($\times$, $\div$, $+$, $-$).

Worked example 1

$\frac{p}{3}$ means $p \div 3$

Evaluate the following.
(i) $6t$ when $t = -5$
(ii) $4n + 2m$ when $n = 5$ and $m = -6$
(iii) $20q - \frac{p}{3}$ when $p = -12$ and $q = 0.5$

Solution

(i) $6t$
   substitute -5 in for t
   $6(-5)$
   -30

(ii) $4n + 2m$
   substitute 5 in for n
   substitute -6 in for m
   $4(5) + 2(-6)$
   $20 - 12$
   8

(iii) $20q - \frac{p}{3}$
   $20(0.5) - \frac{(-12)}{3}$
   $10 - (-4)$
   $10 + 4$
   14

Worked example 2

The area A of a rectangle of length l and width w is given by the algebraic formula $A = lw$.
Find the area of the rectangle if length = 12.2 m and width = 4.6 m.

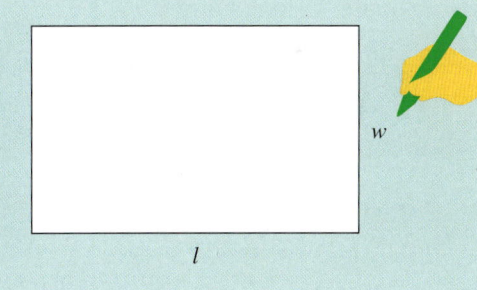

Solution

$A = lw$
$A = 12.2 \times 4.6$
$A = 56.12 \text{ m}^2$

Section B Moving forward

Worked example 3

The price of a mango is 50 cents and the price of an orange is 45 cents. Shelia plans to make a batch of smoothies and so she buys 12 mangos and 24 oranges on Tuesday morning. When she checks the oranges on Wednesday, she finds 4 of them are rotten. Sheila returns to the shop and the shopkeeper agrees to refund the price of the 4 rotten oranges.

(i) Write an expression in words for the total cost of any number of mangos and any number of oranges.
(ii) Write an algebraic expression for the cost (in cents) of any number of mangos and any number of oranges.
(iii) Write an algebraic expression for the cost (in euros) of any number of mangos and any number of oranges.
(iv) Find how much Sheila had to pay (in euros) for the mangos and oranges she bought on Tuesday.
(v) Find the value (in cents) of the mangos and oranges Sheila had at the end of Wednesday.

Solution

(i) (cost of mangos)(number of mangos) + (cost of oranges)(number of oranges)
(ii) $50a + 45b$ where a is the number of mangos and b is the number of oranges
(iii) $0 \cdot 50a + 0 \cdot 45b$

(iv) $0 \cdot 50a + 0 \cdot 45b$
 $0 \cdot 50(12) + 0 \cdot 45(24)$
 $6 + 10 \cdot 8$
 €16·80

(v) Oranges $24 - 4 = 20$
 $50a + 45b$
 $50(12) + 45(20)$
 $600 + 900$
 $1\,500$ cents

€1 = 100 cents

Practice questions 20·2

1. Evaluate the following if $b = 2$
 (i) $2b$
 (ii) $4b - b$
 (iii) $10b - 6b$
 (iv) $21b - 12b$
 (v) $0b$
 (vi) $-b - b$

2. Evaluate the following if $a = 3$, $b = -1$ and $c = 5$
 (i) $2a + 3b$
 (ii) $ac + b$
 (iii) $b + 2c - a$
 (iv) $\frac{3a - b}{c}$
 (v) $c(a - 3b)$
 (vi) c^a

3. Find the value of the following if $b = -4$
 (i) $\frac{2b}{2}$
 (ii) $8b - \frac{b}{2}$
 (iii) $b - \frac{6b}{8}$
 (iv) $\frac{b - 16b}{4}$
 (v) $\frac{-5b}{5} - 12$
 (vi) $\frac{-b}{4}$

4. Evaluate each of the following algebraic expressions when $x = 4$ and $y = 2$
 (i) $x + y$
 (ii) $x - y$
 (iii) $5x - 2y$
 (iv) $y - x$
 (v) $3x^2 - 5$
 (vi) $5y - 2y^2 + 10$

5. Evaluate the following expressions when $y = 6 \cdot 5$
 (i) $5y + 1$
 (ii) $30 - 26 \div y$
 (iii) $y^2 - 7$
 (iv) $1 \cdot 5 + y^2$

6. Mary is saving for a violin. Mary's aunt gives her €45 to start and Mary saves €3 each week.
 (i) Write an expression in words for the amount Mary would save in w weeks.
 (ii) Write an algebraic expression for the amount Mary would save in w weeks.
 (iii) Evaluate how much Mary will save in 14 weeks.
 (iv) Evaluate how much Mary will save in 20 weeks.

7. The area of a rectangle of length, l, and width, w, is given by the algebraic expression lw. Find the area of each of the following rectangles.
 (i) Length = 6 cm and width = 5 cm
 (ii) Length = 12·2 m and width = 4·6 m

Linking Thinking 1

8. The perimeter of a rectangle of length, l, and width, w, can be calculated using the algebraic expression $2l + 2w$.

    Calculate the perimeter of each of the following rectangles using the formula above.

    (i) Length = 5 cm and width = 2 cm

    (ii) Length = 16·5 cm and width = 9·7 cm

9. The area of a triangle, with base b, and perpendicular height h, is given by the expression $0·5bh$. Calculate the area of each of the following triangles.

    (i) Base of 6 mm and height of 2 mm

    (ii) Base of 8·2 cm and height of 5·8 cm

10. Harry earns $15n$ euros for mowing n lawns.

    (i) How much does Harry earn for mowing one lawn?

    (ii) How much does Harry earn for mowing seven lawns?

11. After t months, the length of a fingernail is $(10 + 3t)$ millimetres.

    (i) How long is the fingernail after eight months?

    (ii) How long is the fingernail after three years, assuming it wasn't cut or broken in that time?

12. The expression $20a + 13c$ is the cost in euros for a adults and c students to enter the Science Museum.

    (i) Find the total cost for 4 adults and 24 students.

    (ii) You find the cost for a group. The numbers of adults and students in the group both double. Does the cost double?

    Explain your answer using an example.

20.3 Multiplying an expression by a term

By the end of this section you should be able to:
- create equivalent expressions by expanding an expression and a term

Equivalent expressions

> **Equivalent expressions** are expressions that are the same or are equal to each other.

If you have two linear expressions that are equivalent to one another, and you substitute the same value for the variable in each of them, you will get the same result in each case.

The diagram shows two points A and B. The distance from A to B is divided into three equal sections.

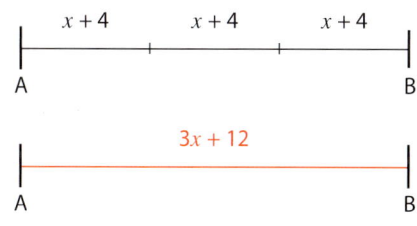

The distance between A and B could be described as

$= (x + 4) + (x + 4) + (x + 4)$

$= x + x + x + 4 + 4 + 4$

$= 3x + 12$ **OR** $3(x + 4)$

Thus $3x + 12$ and $3(x + 4)$ are **equivalent linear expressions.**

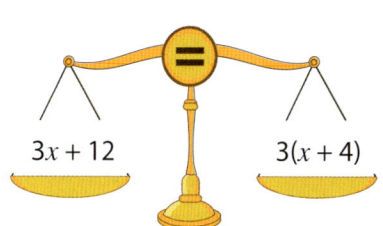

Examples of other equivalent expressions are:

18 is equivalent to $(3)(6)$

$(3x)(2)$ is equivalent to $6x$

$(4x - 6)$ is equivalent to $(2)(2x - 3)$

Expanding expressions

> **Expanding** means removing the brackets and multiplying out the expressions. It is also called distributing.

To **expand** brackets means to multiply each term in the brackets by the term or expression **outside** the brackets.

Equivalent expressions		
Given expression	=	Expanded expression
$(4)(6)$	=	24
$(3)(7x)$	=	$21x$
$(4x)(5x - 3)$	=	$20x^2 - 12x$

Two brackets side by side ( )( ) mean you multiply them together.

Whatever is inside the brackets needs to be treated as a package.

When multiplying: multiply the term on the outside by **everything** inside the brackets.

Multiplying an expression by a term: Term (expression)

Method 1: Multiply each inside term by the outside term

$$5x(2x^2 + 4x - 7)$$
Expanded $10x^3 + 20x^2 - 35x$

Method 2: Array method

1. Create a rectangle with the expressions on different sides of the rectangle.

2. Find the area of each of the rectangles by multiplying the sides of each of the smaller rectangles.

	$2x^2$	$+4x$	-7
$5x$	$10x^3$	$+20x^2$	$-35x$

Recall the **distributive property** of numbers from Section A, Unit 4.

3. Add the areas from Step 2: $10x^3 + 20x^2 - 35x$

Worked example

Expand the following and simplify if necessary.

(i) $4(2x + 4y + 3)$
(ii) $4q(7p - 6q)$
(iii) $-5x(7x^2 - 9x + 2)$

Solution

Method 1:

(i) $4(2x + 4y + 3)$
Expanded $8x + 16y + 12$

(ii) $4q(7p - 6q)$
Expanded $28pq - 24q^2$

(iii) $-5x(7x^2 - 9x + 2)$
Expanded $-35x^3 + 45x^2 - 10x$

Method 2:

Steps 1 and 2 Draw and fill an array diagram

	$2x$	$+4y$	$+3$
4	$8x$	$+16y$	$+12$

Step 3 Add the areas from Step 2
$8x + 16y + 12$

Steps 1 and 2 Draw and fill an array diagram

	$7p$	$-6q$
$4q$	$28pq$	$-24q^2$

Step 3 Add the areas from Step 2
$28pq - 24q^2$

Steps 1 and 2 Draw and fill an array diagram

	$7x^2$	$-9x$	$+2$
$-5x$	$-35x^3$	$+45x^2$	$-10x$

Step 3 Add the areas from Step 2
$-35x^3 + 45x^2 - 10x$

Linking Thinking 1

Practice questions 20.3

1. Expand the following and simplify if necessary.
   - (i) $6(8y + 1)$
   - (ii) $3(4z + 5)$
   - (iii) $4(4g - 5)$
   - (iv) $3(2n - 4)$

2. Expand the following and simplify if necessary.
   - (i) $y(3y + 2)$
   - (ii) $5b(3b - 2c)$
   - (iii) $2a(5a - 2)$
   - (iv) $-5(6b + 3u)$

3. Expand the following and simplify if necessary.
   - (i) $-7(a^2 - 4a + 2)$
   - (ii) $m(7m - 2)$
   - (iii) $t(2t^2 + 3t - 4)$
   - (iv) $-2d(3d - 4)$

4. Expand the following and simplify if necessary.
   - (i) $-3n(2n - 4)$
   - (ii) $3z(4z + 5x + 4)$
   - (iii) $6g(-4g + 5)$
   - (iv) $6u(3b - 4u)$

5. Expand the following and simplify if necessary.
   - (i) $-5w(3w - 2m)$
   - (ii) $-6c(2b + 2\cdot5c)$
   - (iii) $8t(0\cdot2x - 4y)$
   - (iv) $-2d(3\cdot5d - 4c)$

6. Expand the following and simplify if necessary.
   - (i) $2(x + 3) + 3x + 5$
   - (ii) $4(x - 3) + 2x - 1$
   - (iii) $3(a - 4) + 9a + 6$
   - (iv) $6(2b + 6) - 10b + 3$

7. Expand the following and simplify if necessary.
   - (i) $5(x - 2) - 3x - 10$
   - (ii) $2(5x - 2) + 5x + 4$
   - (iii) $4(y - 8) + 4y - 10$
   - (iv) $2y(3y + 1) + 8y^2$

8. The area of a rectangle is equal to the length l multiplied by the width w.
   Write an algebraic expression for the area of each of the following rectangles.

	Length l	Width w
(i)	$6x$	$(5x - 5)$
(ii)	$12m$	$(2n + 5)$
(iii)	$(4c)$	$(c - 7c)$
(iv)	$(n + 10)$	$(-5n)$

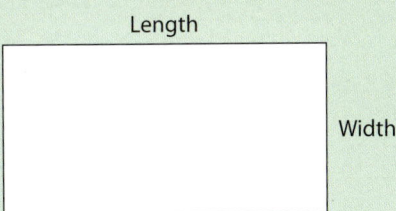

9. The area of a triangle is equal to half the base b, multiplied by the perpendicular height h.
   Write an algebraic expression for the area of the following triangles.

	Base (b)	Perpendicular height (h)
(i)	$12x$	$(4x - 2)$
(ii)	$22x$	$(4x + 5y)$
(iii)	$(2x)$	$(5x + 10)$
(iv)	$(2t + 8)$	$(-8t)$

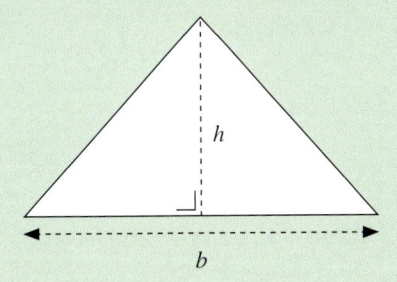

20.4 Multiplying expressions

By the end of this section you should be able to:
- create equivalent expressions by expanding two expressions

Expanding: Multiplying an expression by an expression

Method 1: Multiply each term of the first expression by each term of the second expression.

$$(5x + 4)(2x - 7)$$

$$5x(2x - 7) + 4(2x - 7)$$

Expanded $10x^2 - 35x + 8x - 28$

Simplified $10x^2 - 27x - 28$

Method 2: Array method

1. Create a rectangle with the each expression on different sides of the rectangle.

2. Find the area of each of the rectangles by multiplying the sides of each of the smaller rectangles.

	$5x$	$+4$
$2x$	$10x^2$	$8x$
-7	$-35x$	-28

3. Add the areas from Step 2.

$$10x^2 - 35x + 8x - 28$$
$$10x^2 - 27x - 28$$

Worked example 1

Expand the following and simplify if necessary.

(i) $(2x + 5)(x - 4)$ (ii) $(4x + 3)(x - 3)$ (iii) $(5x - 3)(5x - 8)$

Solution

Method 1:

(i) $(2x + 5)(x - 4)$
$2x(x - 4) + 5(x - 4)$
Expanded
$2x^2 - 8x + 5x - 20$
Simplified
$2x^2 - 3x - 20$

(ii) $(4x + 3)(x - 3)$
$4x(x - 3) + 3(x - 3)$
Expanded
$4x^2 - 12x + 3x - 9$
Simplified
$4x^2 - 9x - 9$

(iii) $(5x - 3)(5x - 8)$
$5x(5x - 8) - 3(5x - 8)$
Expanded
$25x^2 - 40x - 15x + 24$
Simplified
$25x^2 - 55x + 24$

Method 2:

Steps 1 and 2 Draw and fill an array diagram

	$2x$	$+5$
x	$2x^2$	$+5x$
-4	$-8x$	-20

Step 3 Add the areas from Step 2
$2x^2 - 8x + 5x - 20$
$2x^2 - 3x - 20$

Steps 1 and 2 Draw and fill an array diagram

	$4x$	$+3$
x	$4x^2$	$+3x$
-3	$-12x$	-9

Step 3 Add the areas from Step 2
$4x^2 - 12x + 3x - 9$
$4x^2 - 9x - 9$

Steps 1 and 2 Draw and fill an array diagram

	$5x$	-3
$5x$	$25x^2$	$-15x$
-8	$-40x$	$+24$

Step 3 Add the areas from Step 2
$25x^2 - 40x - 15x + 24$
$25x^2 - 55x + 24$

Worked example 2

Expand the following and simplify if necessary.

(i) $(x + y)(c - d)$ (ii) $(x - 8)(x + 8)$ (iii) $(m + 10)^2$

Solution

(i) Method 1:

$(x + y)(c - d)$
$x(c - d) + y(c - d)$
Expanded
$cx - dx + cy - dy$
Simplified
$cx - dx + cy - dy$

(ii) Method 1:

$(x - 8)(x + 8)$
$x(x + 8) - 8(x + 8)$
Expanded
$x^2 + 8x - 8x - 64$
Simplified
$x^2 - 64$

(iii) Method 1:

$(m + 10)^2$
$(m + 10)(m + 10)$
$m(m + 10) + 10(m + 10)$
Expanded
$m^2 + 10m + 10m + 100$
Simplified
$m^2 + 20m + 100$

Method 2:
Steps 1 and 2 Draw and fill an array diagram

	x	$+y$
c	cx	$+cy$
$-d$	$-dx$	$-dy$

Step 3 Add the areas from Step 2
$cx - dx + cy - dy$

Method 2:
Steps 1 and 2 Draw and fill an array diagram

	x	-8
x	x^2	$-8x$
$+8$	$+8x$	-64

Step 3 Add the areas from Step 2
$x^2 + 8x - 8x - 64$
$x^2 - 64$

Method 2:
Steps 1 and 2 Draw and fill an array diagram

	m	$+10$
m	m^2	$+10m$
$+10$	$+10m$	$+100$

Step 3 Add the areas from Step 2
$m^2 + 10m + 10m + 100$
$m^2 + 20m + 100$

In the examples above, the expressions given to be multiplied are **factors** of the expanded and simplified expression we get at the end.

For example,

$(2x + 5)(x - 4)$ are the **factors** of $2x^2 - 3x - 20$

$(x + 8)(x - 8)$ are the **factors** of $x^2 - 64$

Practice questions 20·4

1. Expand the following and simplify if necessary.

(i) $(x + 1)(x + 2)$ (iii) $(a + 2)(a + 1)$

(ii) $(n + 3)(n + 1)$ (iv) $(p + 1)(p + 4)$

2. Expand the following and simplify if necessary.

(i) $(p + 2)(p + 4)$ (iii) $(t + 1)^2$

(ii) $(b + 2)^2$ (iv) $(y + 3)^2$

3. Expand the following and simplify if necessary.

(i) $(2m + 1)(m + 1)$ (iii) $(2d + 1)(d + 2)$

(ii) $(x + 3)(x - 1)$ (iv) $(c + 4)(c - 1)$

4. Expand the following and simplify if necessary.

(i) $(m + 5)(m - 1)$ (iii) $(a + 2)(a - 3)$

(ii) $(p + 1)(p - 3)$ (iv) $(x + 2)(x + 3)$

5. Expand the following and simplify if necessary.

(i) $(r - 1)(r + 1)$ (iii) $(q - 2)(q + 2)$

(ii) $(f - 3)(f + 3)$ (iv) $(z - 5)^2$

6. Expand the following and simplify if necessary.

(i) $(2a + 3)(b - 1)$ (iii) $(3p + 1)(2q - 2)$

(ii) $(2m - 2n)(m + n)$ (iv) $(3x - y)(2x - 2y)$

7. The area of a rectangle is equal to the length l multiplied by the width w.
Write an expanded expression for the area of the following rectangles.

	Length l	Width w
(i)	$(6x - 5)$	$(x - 4)$
(ii)	$(12m - 6)$	$(2m + 5)$
(iii)	$(x - 5)$	$(x - 5)$
(iv)	$(n + 10)$	$(n - 10)$

8. The area of a triangle is equal to half the base b, multiplied by the perpendicular height h.
Write an expanded expression for the area of the following triangles.

	Base b	Perpendicular height h
(i)	$(12x - 5)$	$(5x - 3)$
(ii)	$(22x + y)$	$(4x + 5y)$
(iii)	$(2x - 3)$	$(5x + 10)$
(iv)	$(t + 8)$	$(t + 8)$

9. Darragh has to buy x footballs at €50 each and y sliotars at €5 each. Write an expression for the total value of the footballs and sliotars that Darragh needs to buy.

Taking it FURTHER

10. Emily has $4n + 6$ towels to place on each floor in her hotel. If there are $2m + 10$ floors in the hotel, write an expression for the total number of towels that Emily requires for all the floors in her hotel.

20.5 Factorising using a factor common to all terms in an expression

By the end of this section you should:
- be able to create equivalent expressions by factorising expressions using common factors
- recognise when to factorise using a common factor or grouping terms

Up to now we have expanded two factors to get an expression. Now we are going to do the reverse.

Factorising ←

Equivalent expressions

Factorised expression	=	Expanded expression
$(4)(6)$	=	24
$(3)(7x)$	=	$21x$
$(4x)(5x - 3)$	=	$20x^2 - 12x$

Expanding →

Factorising an original expression (or term), means dividing the expression (or term) into factors.

Factors are expressions (or terms) that multiply to give the original expression.

Recall **factorising numbers** from Section A, Unit 2: a pair of factors of 18 could be $(2)(9)$ or $(3)(6)$.

Factorising an expression using common factors

Type 1
Highest common factor – all terms

Type 2
Highest common factor – groups of terms

Linking Thinking 1

Type 1: Highest common factor – All terms

We can factorise by the method of factoring out the highest common factor, **when it is possible to divide every term** in an expression by a common factor.

To make it quicker, we will look for the largest common factor, known as the highest common factor (HCF). For example, in the expression $4x + 2$, the HCF is 2.

> You can verify your answer by expanding the factors and you will get the original expression.

Factorisation using the HCF

1. Find the HCF for all terms.
2. Write the HCF in a set of brackets.
3. Divide each term by the HCF and write the answers into a second set of brackets.

Worked example 1
Factorise $6 - 27x$

Solution
Step 1 Find the HCF for all terms. In this case, the HCF is 3

Step 2 Write HCF into a set of brackets

Step 3 Divide each term by the HCF and write each of the answers into a second set of brackets

$(3)\left(\frac{6}{3} - \frac{27x}{3}\right)$ (divide the numerator and the denominator by 3 in both fractions)

$(3)\left(\frac{2}{1} - \frac{9x}{1}\right)$

$(3)(2 - 9x)$ which is $6 - 27x$ factorised (verified by multiplying $(3)(2 - 9x)$)

Worked example 2
Factorise $5x^2 + 15x$

Solution
Step 1 Find the HCF for all terms. In this case, the HCF is $5x$ (as $5x$ divides into $5x^2$ and $15x$)

Step 2 Write HCF into a set of brackets

Step 3 Divide each term by the HCF and write each of the answers into a second set of brackets

$(5x)\left(\frac{5x^2}{5x} + \frac{15x}{5x}\right)$ (divide the numerator and the denominator by $5x$ in both fractions)

$(5x)\left(\frac{x}{1} + \frac{3}{1}\right)$

$(5x)(x + 3)$ (verified by multiplying $(5x)(x + 3)$)

which is $5x^2 + 15x$ factorised

Worked example 3
Factorise $4ab + 16ab^2$

Solution
Step 1 Find the HCF for all terms. In this case, the HCF is $4ab$

Step 2 Write the HCF into a set of brackets

Step 3 Divide each term by the HCF and write each of the answers into a second set of brackets

$(4ab)\left(\frac{4ab}{4ab} + \frac{16ab^2}{4ab}\right)$

$(4ab)\left(1 + \frac{(4)(b)}{(1)(1)}\right)$

$(4ab)(1 + 4b)$ (verified by multiplying $(4ab)(1 + 4b)$)

which is $4ab + 16ab^2$ factorised

Worked example 4

Factorise $10x^2y + 5xy - 20y$

Solution

Step 1 Find the HCF for all terms. In this case, the HCF is $5y$

Step 2 Write the HCF into a set of brackets $\quad (5y)\left(\dfrac{10x^2y}{5y} + \dfrac{5xy}{5y} - \dfrac{20y}{5y}\right)$

Step 3 Divide each term by the HCF and write each of the answers into a second set of brackets $\quad (5y)\left(\dfrac{(2)(x^2)(1)}{(1)(1)} + \dfrac{(1)(x)(1)}{(1)(1)} - \dfrac{(4)(1)}{(1)(1)}\right)$

$(5y)(2x^2 + x - 4)$ (verified by multiplying $(5y)(2x^2 + x - 4)$)

which is $10x^2y + 5xy - 20y$ factorised

Practice questions 20·5

1. Find an expression that has the following factor pairs.
   - (i) $(x)(4x + 6)$
   - (ii) $(4)(a + b)$
   - (iii) $(4)(a + 1)$
   - (iv) $(7x)(2x + 2y)$

2. Find the highest common factor of each of the following pairs of terms.
   - (i) $-4b$ and $8ab$
   - (ii) $6p$ and $-14pq$
   - (iii) $5mn$ and $15no$
   - (iv) $-3ay$ and $-9y$
   - (v) $-3m$ and 18
   - (vi) $-12ef$ and $-27fg$

3. Factorise fully the following expressions.
   - (i) $3x + 15$
   - (ii) $5x + 20$
   - (iii) $4 + 4a$
   - (iv) $10u - 10v$

4. Factorise fully the following expressions.
   - (i) $9v - 3w$
   - (ii) $9p + 45q$
   - (iii) $4x + 48y$
   - (iv) $10x - 100y$

5. Factorise fully the following expressions.
   - (i) $3z - 12xz$
   - (ii) $23a - ab$
   - (iii) $10pq - 14p$
   - (iv) $18p - 36pa$
   - (v) $6m^2 - 2m$
   - (vi) $-32ab - 8a^2$

6. Verify your answers in questions 4 and 5 by expanding the factors.

7. Find a pair of factors that form the expression $18x - 36$

8. Find two expressions, one for the length and one for the width, if the total area of a rectangle is described by the expression $3x - 9xy$

9. Factorise fully the following expressions
   - (i) $12x - xyp$
   - (ii) $wxy - 10xy$
   - (iii) $4ab + 14a^2b$
   - (iv) $6xy + 8x^2y$

10. Factorise the following expressions
    - (i) $4x^2 + 8xy + 12x$
    - (ii) $18pq - 3pq^2 + 9q^2$
    - (iii) $-28xy + 7x^2 + 14x$
    - (iv) $2a^2 + 10ab + 6a$
    - (v) $5x - 15x^2 + 10xy$
    - (vi) $3ab - a + 9ac$

Taking it FURTHER

11. Find three different pairs of factors that form the expression $40a - 80b$

12. If $10x - 4$ is a factor, find the other factor if the product of the two factors is $100x^2 - 40x$

13. Find two expressions, one for the length and one for the width, if the total area of a rectangle is represented by the expression $5b^2 - 25ab$

20.6 Factorising using common factors from groups of terms

By the end of this section you should:
- be able to create equivalent expressions by factorising expressions using common factors
- recognise when to factorise using a common factor to all terms or to group terms first

Type 2: Highest common factor – Groups of terms

Consider the expression $2xy + 2xc + 6mn + 4mq$

We cannot divide all terms in this expression by a common factor, but each pair of terms has a HCF.

We look at pairs (or groups) of terms in which we can divide by a common factor.

In this case, we can divide $2xy + 2xc$ by $2x$ (1st group) and we can divide $6mn + 4mq$ by $2m$ (2nd group)

Factorising by grouping within an expression

1. Group terms that have a common factor together in pairs (rearrange order if necessary)

2. Factorise each pair of terms separately (using the HCF method as before) such that the two 2nd brackets are identical.

3. Place the common factor (2nd brackets) in a new 1st set of brackets and the uncommon terms (1st brackets) in a new 2nd set of brackets.

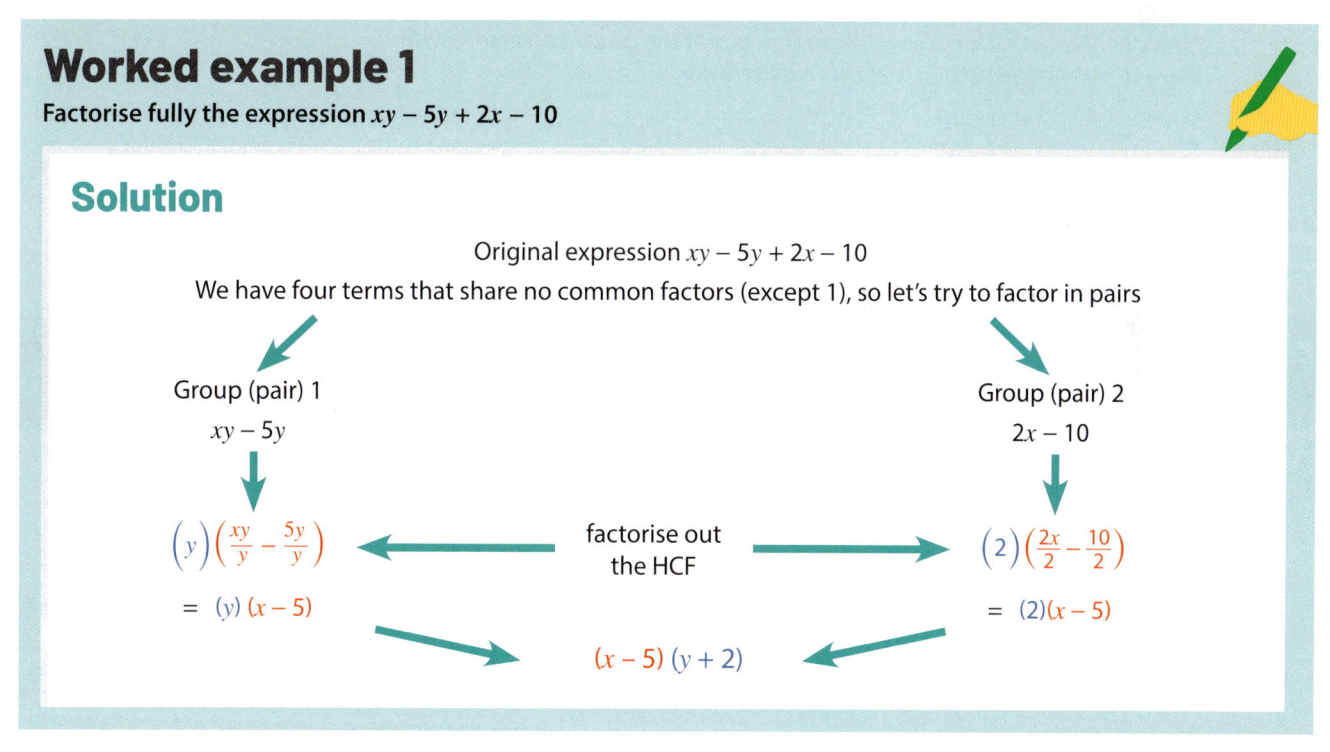

Worked example 1

Factorise fully the expression $xy - 5y + 2x - 10$

Solution

Original expression $xy - 5y + 2x - 10$

We have four terms that share no common factors (except 1), so let's try to factor in pairs

Group (pair) 1
$xy - 5y$

Group (pair) 2
$2x - 10$

factorise out the HCF

$(y)\left(\frac{xy}{y} - \frac{5y}{y}\right)$

$(2)\left(\frac{2x}{2} - \frac{10}{2}\right)$

$= (y)(x - 5)$

$= (2)(x - 5)$

$(x - 5)(y + 2)$

Grouping: two interesting cases

Case 1: If the pairs of terms do not have a common factor, other than 1, you may have to **rearrange the order of the terms**.

For example, the expression $ab + 2 + a + 2b$ needs to be rearranged before we can factorise by grouping.

We can try pairing the terms without 2s, and pairing the two other terms with 2s: $ab + a + 2b + 2$

Now a is the HCF of the 1st pair and 2 is the HCF of the 2nd pair: $a(b + 1) + 2(b + 1)$

Finally, take out the common factor $(b + 1)$: $(b + 1)(a + 2)$

Section B Moving forward

Case 2: Ensure the **common factor (bracket) in each pair is identical** by altering the signs.

For example, let's looks at how to factorise.
$$ak - at - 5k + 5t$$
↑   ↑
1st pair   2nd pair

If +5 is used as the HCF for the 2nd pair, then
$$(a)(k - t) + (5)(-k + t)$$

> $(k - t)$ is not equal to $(-k + t)$

Note that the 2nd bracket in each pair is not identical.

However, if −5 is used as the HCF for the 2nd pair, then we get the same second bracket in each pair:
$$(a)(k - t) + (-5)(k - t)$$

To complete the factorisation, we take out the common factor: $(k - t)(a - 5)$

Worked example 2

Factorise fully the expression $x^2 + 3y - 3x - xy$

Solution

Original expression: $x^2 + 3y - 3x - xy$

Rearranged expression: $x^2 - xy + 3y - 3x$ (rearrange the order so that each pair has common terms)

Step 1 Group pairs which have a common factor.
$(x^2 - xy) + (3y - 3x)$

Step 2 Factorise each pair of terms separately (using the HCF method as before).
Note: we have to factorise a negative sign out of the second pair along with the 3 to ensure the second brackets are identical.
$(x)(x - y) + (-3)(-y + x)$

> $(x - y) = (-y + x)$

Step 3 Place the common factor (2nd brackets) in a new 1st bracket and the uncommon factors (1st brackets) in a new 2nd bracket.
$(x - y)(x - 3)$

Practice questions 20·6

1. Factorise the following expressions fully.
   - (i) $p(x + a) + q(x + a)$
   - (ii) $m(x - y) + n(x - y)$
   - (iii) $ax + bx + ay + by$
   - (iv) $mx + nx + my + ny$

2. Factorise the following expressions fully.
   - (i) $5x + 5y + ax + ay$
   - (ii) $am + an + 4m + 4n$
   - (iii) $ac + bc + ad + bd$
   - (iv) $pq + pr + xq + xr$

3. (a) Factorise the following expressions fully.
   - (i) $xy + xz - y - z$
   - (ii) $2x - x^2 + 2y - xy$
   - (iii) $ax + 4p - 4a - px$

   (b) Verify your factors for part (a).

4. (a) Factorise the following expressions fully.
   - (i) $nq + nr + 4q + 4r$
   - (ii) $6my + 2ny + 3am + an$
   - (iii) $ax + bx + a + b$

   (b) Verify your factors for part (a).

5. (a) Factorise the following expressions fully.
   - (i) $3n + yz + 3y + nz$
   - (ii) $an - 5a - 5b + bn$
   - (iii) $a^2 + 2a - ab - 2b$

   (b) Verify your factors for part (a).

6. Factorise the following expressions fully.
   - (i) $xy - 5y - 2x + 10$
   - (ii) $x + 3y + x^2 + 3xy$
   - (iii) $ab + a + 2b + 2$

7. (a) Factorise the following expressions fully.
    (i) $10ab + 15b + 4a + 6$
    (ii) $6x^2 + 9xy - 14x - 21y$
    (iii) $5xy - 8x - 10y + 16$
   (b) Verify your factors for part (a)

8. Factorise the following expressions fully.
    (i) $12ab - 14a - 6b + 7$
    (ii) $6x^2 - 15x + 2xy - 5y$
    (iii) $4a - 21b^2 + 6ab - 14b$

9. Factorise the following expressions fully.
    (i) $8xy - 12y + 15 - 10x$
    (ii) $7 + y - 3xy - 21x$
    (iii) $32uv - 20u + 24v - 15$

10. Find two expressions, one for the length and one for the width of a rectangle which has a total area represented by the following expression.
    $$px + rs - pr - sx$$

11. Find two expressions, one for the length and one for the width of a rectangle which has a total area represented by the following expression.
    $$12wx + 4wy + 6zx + 2zy$$

12. The area of a rectangular field is given by the following expression:
    $$10xy + 30 + 25x + 12y$$
    Find an expression for the length and an expression for the width.

13. The number of chocolates Mary gives to Peter is described by one expression. The number of chocolates she gives to Judith is described by another expression. When Mary multiplies the two expressions the result is: 
    $$56ab + 14 - 49a - 16b$$
    Find an expression for the number of chocolates Mary gave to Peter and an expression for the number of chocolates she gave Judith.

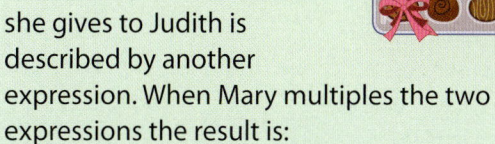

14. When Dougal multiplies the expression that describes the amount of money that he gave Ted by the amount of money he gave Jack, the expression he gets is: 
    $$5mn + 2m - 25n - 10$$
    Find an expression for the amount of money Dougal gave to Ted and an expression for the amount of money he gave Jack.

15. When the manager multiplies an expression that describes the number of rooms in her hotel by an expression that describes the number of chairs in her hotel, she gets: 
    $$3mn - 8m + 15n - 40$$
    Find an expression for the numbers of rooms and an expression for the number of chairs in the hotel.

Revision questions

20A Core skills

1. Write expressions for each of the following.
   (i) The sum of x and y
   (ii) Add a and 7
   (iii) Twice b plus 10
   (iv) The difference between m and n
   (v) The product of a and g
   (vi) b cubed
   (vii) Triple x and add five times the value of p
   (viii) Square x and subtract double x then add 7
   (ix) The product of m and the square of c
   (x) 6 times m added to 2·5 times m

2. The express bus from Galway to Belfast takes x minutes. The standard bus takes 29 minutes longer. Write an expression for the time the standard bus takes.

3. (a) Expand and simplify, if necessary, each of the following:
- (i) $2(x+5)$
- (ii) $6(2y-4)$
- (iii) $4(z+3)$
- (iv) $9(3z-5)$
- (v) $5(y+3)$
- (vi) $4(2x-1)$

(b) Evaluate each of parts (i)–(vi) above when $x=2$, $y=-1$ and $z=5$

4. Expand and simplify, if necessary, each of the following.
- (i) $a(4a+3)$
- (ii) $-p(2+3p)$
- (iii) $-5x(2x-3)$
- (iv) $7x(3x-2y)$
- (v) $6d(2d+3)$
- (vi) $-4y(2y-4x)$

5. (a) Expand and simplify each of the following.
- (i) $(x+4)(x-1)$
- (ii) $(x+1)(x-1)$
- (iii) $(x+2)(x-1)$
- (iv) $(x+2)(x-2)$
- (v) $(2x-1)(x+1)$
- (vi) $(3x-1)(2x-1)$

(b) Evaluate each of parts (i)–(vi) above when $x=-4$

6. Factorise each of the following.
- (i) $3x+15$
- (ii) $15c+3$
- (iii) $2a+8$
- (iv) $18d+9$
- (v) $6b+12$
- (vi) $12e+6$
- (vii) $3f-9$
- (viii) $5h-15$

7. Factorise each of the following.
- (i) $12r^2-15r$
- (ii) $-5b-20$
- (iii) $18x^2-12x$
- (iv) $-2d-10$
- (v) $12xy^2-18y^2$
- (vi) $-3c+6$
- (vii) $-6x^2+12x$
- (viii) $-6f^2+24f$

8. Factorise each of the following.
- (i) $14v^2+10v-7vy-5y$
- (ii) $7xy-49x+5y-35$
- (iii) $16xy-56x+2y-7$
- (iv) $15ab-6a+5b^2-2b$
- (v) $42r^2-49r+18rs-21s$
- (vi) $40r^3-8r^2-25r+5$

9. Apples cost one cent each. Bananas cost b cents each. Write down an expression for the total cost of 4 apples and 6 bananas.

10. Cathal is x years old. Jason is 3 years younger than Cathal. David is twice as old as Jason.
- (i) Write an expression for Jason's age.
- (ii) Write an expression for David's age.
- (iii) Write an expression for the sum of the three ages.

20B Taking it FURTHER

1. The area of a rectangle is found by multiplying the length by the width. For each of the following rectangles, find a simplified expression for the area.

	Length	Width
(i)	$6mn$	$(12 - 3m)$
(ii)	$(4x - 6)$	$(3x + 3)$
(iii)	(4)	$(4x^2 - 3x + 14)$
(iv)	$(2x)$	$(2x^2 + 6x - 7)$
(v)	$(4y)$	$(2x - 3y - 9)$

2. The perimeter of a rectangle $= (2l + 2w)$. For each of the following rectangles, find a simplified expression for the perimeter.

	Length (l)	Width (w)
(i)	$(3x - 10)$	$(2x + 6)$
(ii)	$(4x^2)$	$(4x^2 - 3x + 14)$
(iii)	$(2n + m^2)$	$(7m^2 + 9m - 10)$
(iv)	$(4y + 6x + 2z)$	$(10x - 45y - 7z)$

3. In one week, Martina spent x minutes on the internet. Seán spent 15 minutes less than Martina. Neil spent three times as long as Martina on the internet.

   (i) Write an expression for how long Seán spent on the internet.

   (ii) Write an expression for how long Neil spent on the internet.

   (iii) Write an expression for total time the three people spent on the internet.

4. Michael has a bag of marbles containing two sizes of marbles; one type of marble weighs 50 grams and the other type of marble weights 90 grams. In the bag, there are x of the 50-gram marbles and y of the 90-gram marbles.

   (i) Write an expression to describe the mass (all grams added together) in one bag of marbles.

   (ii) Michael plays marbles in a youth club. There are $4y$ groups in Michael's club on a particular day. Write an expression for the total mass of marbles required, if each group receives one bag of marbles.

   (iii) If $x = 28$ and $y = 6$, find the total mass of marbles used by the club on that particular day.

5. After n months, the length of a growing fingernail is $9 + 3n$ millimetres.

   Find an expression for each of the following. Give your answer in terms of n.

   (i) How long is the fingernail after eight months?

   (ii) How long is the fingernail after four years?

6. Find three pairs of factors that form the expression $200a - 50b$

7. Find two expressions, one describing the length and one describing the width, for a given rectangle, if the total area of that rectangle is $34a^2 - 27ab$

8. When Niles multiplies the expression that describes the amount of money that he gave Sarah by the amount of money he gave Gareth, the expression he gets is $28p^3 + 21p^2 + 20p + 15$

   Find an expression for the amount of money Niles gave to Sarah and an expression for the amount of money he gave Gareth.

Now that you have completed the unit, revisit the **Something to think about ...** question posed at the start of this unit.

Now try question 11 on pages 407–8

Unit 21

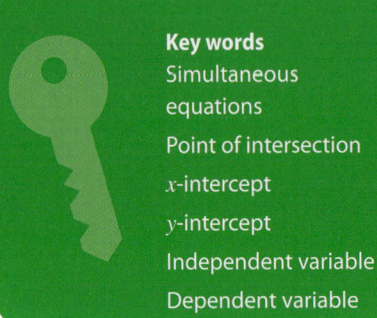

Linear relationships

Something to think about ...

In 1873, Wilhelm Jordan, a German mathematician, published a book in which he discussed Gauss's method of elimination to solve a given system of linear equations. We will discuss a version of this method in this unit.

Try this nuts and bolts of a question!

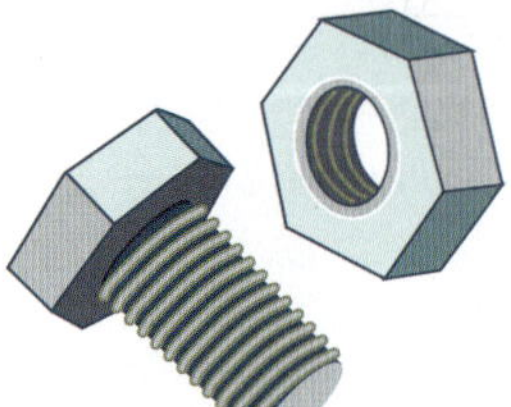

4 nuts and 2 bolts weigh 20 grams

3 nuts and 5 bolts weigh 29 grams

What do the following weigh?

(i) 2 nuts and 1 bolt   (iii) 1 nut and 1 bolt
(ii) 7 nuts and 7 bolts (iv) 1 bolt   (v) 1 nut

Topics covered within this unit:

21·1 Solving linear equations

21·2 Solving linear equations with two unknowns by graphing

21·3 Solving linear equations with two unknowns by trial and improvement and by elimination

21·4 Creating and solving simultaneous equations

21·5 Graphing linear functions

The Learning Outcomes covered in this unit are contained in the following sections:

AF.2c AF.4c N.3a N.3b AF.7a
AF.7c AF.1b AF.7b

Key words

Simultaneous equations
Point of intersection
x-intercept
y-intercept
Independent variable
Dependent variable

21·1 Solving linear equations

By the end of this section you should be able to:
- solve linear equations

Discuss and discover

Working with a classmate:

(i) Substitute the following numbers for x {−2, −1, 0, 1, 2} into the equation $y = 2x$ to find the values for y.

(ii) Pair up each x value with its corresponding y value, to make a point, e.g. (2, 4).

(iii) Plot these points on the coordinate plane and join them up.

(iv) Does the overall shape appear as a straight line or a curve?

(v) Repeat steps (i)–(iii) for the following equations. Use the same x values {−2, −1, 0, 1, 2}

(a) $y = x^2$ (b) $y = x^3$ (c) $y = 3x$

(vi) Which of the above equations were straight lines or curves when on the coordinate plane?

(vii) Can you tell by looking at the power on the variable of each equation which are lines and which are curves?

Revision of terms

Mathematical notation	Description
3, 0·5, −4·7 …	**Constants** have a fixed value
$x, y, a, b, \alpha, \beta$…..	**Variables** are numbers that you don't know. They are often represented by x or y, but any letter will do
$4x$	x is the variable and 4 is the **coefficient**. $4x$ means $4 \times x$
x	x is the variable and 1 is the coefficient
xy	Variable x multiplied by variable y
$\frac{a}{b}$	Variable a divided by variable b
$4x^2$ and $-3x^2$ $2ab$ and $6ab$	These are known as '**like terms**' because they have the exactly the same variables to the exactly the same power
$4x^2 - 3x^2 = x^2$ $2ab + 6ab = 8ab$ $4n^2 + 3n = 4n^2 + 3n$	It is possible to group together like terms It is impossible to group together unlike terms
$x^1 \times x^1 = x^{1+1} = x^2$ $x^2 \times x^1 = x^{2+1} = x^3$	When multiplying variables of the same base, we keep the base and add the powers
$12a \div 4a^2 = \frac{(12a)}{(4a^2)} = \frac{3}{a}$	Within any fraction, you can divide the numerator and denominator by the same number or variable to simplify the fraction

Comparing mathematical expressions and equations

	Expression	Equation
Meaning	An expression is a mathematical phrase that combines numbers, variables and operators to show the value of something.	An equation is a mathematical statement to show two expressions are set equal to each other.
What is it?	Stands for a single numerical value	Shows equality between two expressions
Result	Simplification	Solution
Relation symbol	None	Equal sign (=)
Sides	One-sided	Two-sided (left and right)
Example	$8x - 2(4x + 14)$	$7x - 5 = 19$

Simplifying an algebraic expression involves grouping and adding/subtracting like terms.

Solving an equation is finding the value(s) of the variable(s) that make the equation a true statement.

Variable(s) in linear equations

Variables in a linear equation cannot have exponents (or powers) other than 1.
That is, a linear equation will **not** contain any of the following:

x^2 or x^3 or 'x' times 'y' or xy; 'x' divided by 'y' or $\frac{x}{y}$ or $\sqrt{x}$

Section B **Moving forward**

Discuss and discover

KEY SKILLS

(i) Working with a classmate, discuss what you already understand about balance.

(ii) Next, balance a ruler on a pencil, as shown. Place a small item (e.g. a paper clip) at one end of the ruler. What do you observe?

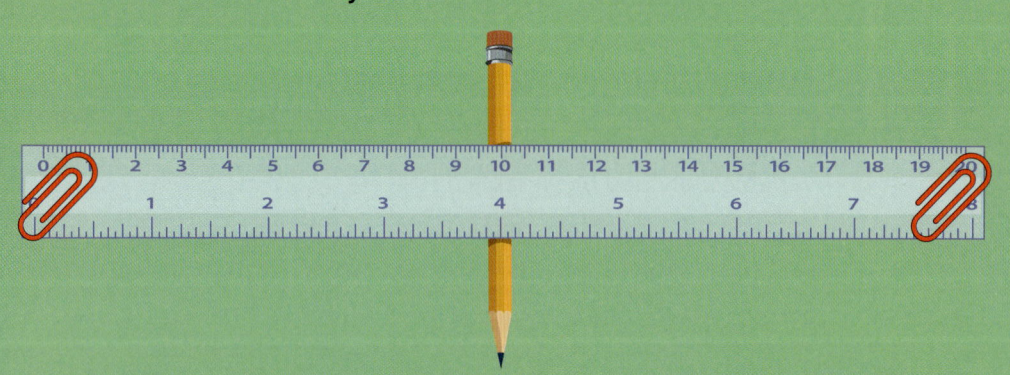

(iii) What would you need to place on the other end of the ruler to balance it again?

(iv) Try your solution.

(v) Repeat this with identical pairs of small items.

(vi) Place two different items at both ends of the ruler, e.g. a paper clip and a push pin at one end, and a push pin and a paper clip at the other end. Now remove a paper clip from one end. What would you need to do to the other end to restore balance?

(vii) Repeat this with different items, adding and taking away items from the ruler before restoring balance each time.

(viii) Can you come up with a general rule for how to make the ruler balanced again, if items are added or removed from either end?

Solving for unknown values in an equation

The **equals sign in a mathematical equation** indicates that the left-hand side (LHS) is equal to the right-hand side (RHS).

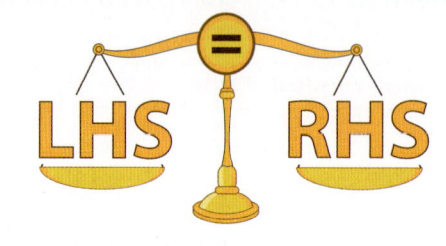

A fundamental rule

Whatever operation you do to one side of an equation (add subtract, divide, square, etc.) you must also do to the other side. This means the left-hand side and the right-hand side remain equal.

We use this rule to find the value for solutions to linear equations.

Worked example 1

Solve the following equations and verify your answers.

(i) $36k - 13 = 167$ (ii) $3(p + 4) - 5(p - 1) = 9p + 28$

> It is good practice to verify your answer after solving an equation.

Solution

(i) $36k - 13 = 167$

$36k = 167 + 13$ (add 13 to both sides)

$36k = 180$

$\dfrac{36k}{36} = \dfrac{180}{36}$ (divide both sides by 36)

$k = 5$

Verify answer:

$36k - 13 = 167$

$36(5) - 13 = 167$

$167 = 167$ ✓

(ii) $3(p + 4) - 5(p - 1) = 9p + 28$

Apply BIMDAS:

$3p + 12 - 5p + 5 = 9p + 28$

Simplify both sides:

$17 - 2p = 9p + 28$

$17 = 9p + 2p + 28$ (add $2p$ to both sides)

$17 - 28 = 11p$ (subtract 28 from both sides)

$\dfrac{-11}{11} = \dfrac{11p}{11}$ (divide both sides by 11)

$-1 = p$

Verify answer:

$3(p + 4) - 5(p - 1) = 9p + 28$

$3((-1) + 4) - 5((-1) - 1) = 9(-1) + 28$

$3(3) - 5(-2) = -9 + 28$

$9 + 10 = 19$

$19 = 19$ ✓

Worked example 2

If the perimeter of a rectangle is 10 metres, and the length is one metre longer than the width, how long are the sides?

Solution

Let the length be x. Then the width is $x + 1$.

Then the perimeter may be expressed as

$x + x + (x + 1) + (x + 1) = 10$

Solving: $4x + 2 = 10$

$4x = 8$ (subtract 2 from both sides)

$x = 2$ (divide both sides by 4)

So $x = 2$ m and $(x + 1) = 2 + 1 = 3$ m

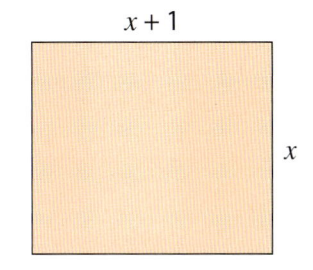

Worked example 3

Find a number such that 5 more than one-half of the number is equal to three times the number.

Solution

Let n be the unknown number.

Translating into Maths: $5 + \dfrac{n}{2} = 3n$

> $\dfrac{n}{2} = \dfrac{1}{2}n$

Solving: $5 + \dfrac{n}{2} = 3n$

$10 + n = 6n$ (multiplying all terms by 2 first to remove the fraction)

$10 = 5n$ (subtracting n from both sides)

$\dfrac{10}{5} = \dfrac{5n}{5}$ (dividing both sides by 5)

$2 = n$

Section B Moving forward

Worked example 4

The cost of two tables and three chairs is €705. If the table costs €40 more than the chair, find (i) the cost of one chair and (ii) the cost of one table.

Solution

(i) Let the cost of the chair be x.

Then the cost of the table = €$40 + x$

The cost of 3 chairs = $3 \times x = 3x$ and the cost of 2 tables = $2(40 + x)$

Total cost of 2 tables and 3 chairs = €705

Therefore, $2(40 + x) + 3x = 705$

$80 + 2x + 3x = 705$

$80 + 5x = 705$

$5x = 705 - 80$

$\dfrac{5x}{5} = \dfrac{625}{5}$

$x = 125$

Therefore, the cost of each chair is €125

(ii) $40 + x = 40 + 125 = 165$

Therefore, the cost of each table is €165.

Practice questions 21·1

1. State if each of the following is an expression or an equation, and give a reason for your answer in each case.

    (i) $3x + 4$

    (ii) $5x - 3 = 0$

    (iii) $5x - 3y = 7$

    (iv) $4x = 7 - 10y$

    (v) $2n + 3n + 4 - 2n$

    (vi) $4 = 2(2)$

    (vii) $4q + 6 = p$

    (viii) $2n - n = 8$

    (ix) $6x + 6 - 2$

    (x) $4m + 4 + 6w$

2. Simplify the following expressions.

    (i) $35n - 1 + 46$

    (ii) $-33v - 49v$

    (iii) $-10v + 6v$

    (iv) $-9r + 10r$

    (v) $1 - 3v + 10$

    (vi) $9 + 5r - 9r$

3. Simplify the following expressions.

    (i) $30n + 8n$

    (ii) $7x + 31x$

    (iii) $10x + 36 - 38x - 47$

    (iv) $-2(7 - n) + 4$

    (v) $-8(-5b + 7) + 5b$

    (vi) $-4p - (1 - 6p)$

4. Simplify the following expressions.

    (i) $4 - 5(-4n + 3m)$

    (ii) $1 + 7(a - 3b)$

    (iii) $-7(k - 8p) + 2k$

    (iv) $3n - 8(7m - 5n)$

    (v) $7p - 6pc + 3c - 2$

    (vi) $4(10x + 6) - 10$

5. Simplify the following expressions.

    (i) $3(1 + 2v) - 3(1 + 4v)$

    (ii) $4(x - 10) - 6(x - 4)$

    (iii) $7(1 + 10p) + 8(1 + 6p)$

    (iv) $10(3 + 8k) + 9(k + 3)$

    (v) $10(9 + 8n) - 6(7n + 9)$

    (vi) $6xy - 3x(2y - 3x)$

    (vii) $-8s(-2r - 2s) - 6r$

6. State if the following equations are linear or non-linear.
   (i) $4x + 3y = 10$
   (ii) $x^2 = 4$
   (iii) $x = 5$
   (iv) $3x = \sqrt{4}$
   (v) $3x^2 + 4y = 12$

7. Solve the following linear equations.
   (i) $2x + 6 = 0$
   (ii) $3x + 9 = -3$
   (iii) $4p + 10 = 2p - 20$
   (iv) $6n + 4 = 22$

8. Solve the following linear equations.
   (i) $2(x + 3) = 0$
   (ii) $4(x + 8) = -4$
   (iii) $2(10x - 1) = 28 + 5x$
   (iv) $3(m + 10) = 2m + 30$
   (v) $2(w - 40) = 4w - 20$
   (vi) $6(n + 3) = 2(12)n$

The value of a variable can equal 0

9. (i) Check whether $x = 1$ is a solution for $2x = 5$
   (ii) Check whether $x = -3$ is the solution to $2x + 3 = -3$
   (iii) Check whether $x = -12$ is the solution to $-x - 12 = 0$

10. Solve the following equations.
   (i) $5 + 4x - 7 = 4x - 2 - x$
   (ii) $0 \cdot 2x + 0 \cdot 9 = 0 \cdot 3 - 0 \cdot 1x$
   (iii) $\frac{1}{4}x + 1 = \frac{1}{6}x + \frac{1}{2}$
   (iv) $6x - (3x + 8) = 16$
   (v) $7(5x - 2) = 6(6x - 1)$

11. The sum of two numbers is 25. One number is 9 greater than the other. Find the numbers.

12. The difference between two numbers is 48. The ratio of the two numbers is 7 : 3, which means that we can let the first number be $7x$ and the second number be $3x$. What are the two numbers?

13. Solve the following equations.
   (i) $3(x - 2) = 6$
   (ii) $13 - (2x + 2) = 2(x + 2) + 3x$
   (iii) $2[3x + 4(3 - x)] = 3(5 - 4x) - 11$
   (iv) $3[x - 2(3x - 4)] + 15 = 5 - [2x - (3 + x)] - 11$

14. Oisín goes into a shop to buy apples. Each half-dozen apples costs €2·35.
   (i) Write an equation to represent the total money spent if he buys x apples.
   (ii) If the total amount he spends is €14·10, how many apples did Oisín buy?

A dozen = 12
A half-dozen = 6

15. The length of a rectangle is twice its width. If the perimeter is 72 metres, find the length and width of the rectangle.

16. Tom is currently 5 years younger than John. Four years from now, John will be twice as old as Tom. Find their current ages.

17. A number is divided into two parts such that one part is 10 more than the other. If the two parts are in the ratio 5 : 3, find the number and the two parts.

18. Paul's father is currently 4 times as old as Paul. In 5 years, his father will be three times as old as Paul will be. Find their current ages.

Taking it FURTHER

Supplementary angles sum to 180°.

19. The sum of two consecutive multiples of 5 is 55. Find these multiples.

20. The difference in the measures of two supplementary angles is 12°. Find the measure of the angles.

21. If $\frac{3}{5}$ of a number is 4 more than $\frac{1}{2}$ the number, what is the number?

22. Copy the table and put a tick (✓) in the correct box in each row to show whether each statement is always true, sometimes true, or never true.

Statement		Tick **one** box only for each statement		
		Always true	Sometimes true	Never true
(i)	All linear equations can be solved.			
(ii)	Linear equations have two variables.			
(iii)	$(-)(+) = +$			
(iv)	An expression has an equals sign.			
(v)	An equation has an equals sign.			

21·2 Solving linear equations with two unknowns by graphing

By the end of this section you should understand:
- what is meant by 'simultaneous equations'
- what it means to solve simultaneous equations
- how to graph a pair of simultaneous linear equations on the same axes and scales
- how to solve simultaneous equations graphically

Equations with two unknowns

Until now we have solved equations with one unknown, for example $2x - 3 = 10$ or $5y + 6 = 16$

Linear equations with one unknown like these have one solution, that is one value for x that makes the equation true.

If there is only one unknown in a problem, then you require only one equation to solve it.

Equations that have more than one unknown can have an infinite number of solutions when $x \in \mathbb{R}$.

For example, $2x + y = 10$ could be solved (satisfied) by:

$x = 1$ and $y = 8$ or $x = 2$ and $y = 6$

Sometimes we will need to find a solution to a given equation that also satisfies a second equation. It is possible to find the only pair of values that satisfy both equations by solving them together, or at the same time. This method is known as solving **simultaneous equations.**

> If the point (x, y) is on a line, when we substitute x and y into the equation the left hand side will **equal** the right hand side.

A pair of **simultaneous linear equations** are two linear equations in two variables for which there is one pair of values that can satisfy both the equations at the same time. An example of this is $3x + y = 11$ and $2x + y = 8$ can both be satisfied by the values $x = 3$ and $y = 2$.

> If you want to solve for **two unknowns** then you require **two equations**.

The unknowns of x and y have the same value in both equations. This fact can help us solve the two equations simultaneously (at the same time), finding the values of both x and y.

We will look at three methods of solving simultaneous equations:

1. Graphing
2. Trial and improvement
3. Elimination

Method 1: Solving simultaneous linear equations by graphing

This method involves graphing both linear equations on the same axes and scales and finding the point of intersection.

> The **point of intersection** is the point (x, y) on the Cartesian plane where two lines cross.

The x-**coordinate** will be the solution for one of the variables and the y-**coordinate** will be the solution for the other variable.

In the example on the right, two linear equations are graphed.

The value for x that satisfies both equations at the same time is 3, and the value for y that satisfies both equations at the same time is 2.

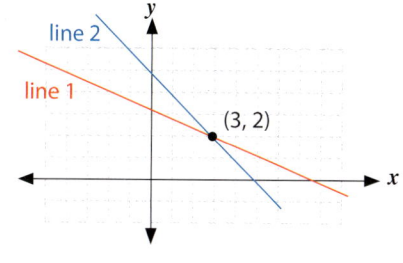

Two points are required to draw a line. The following method shows how to find two points on a line, namely the x-intercept and the y-intercept.

> The x-**intercept** is the x-coordinate of a point where a line intersects (crosses) the x-axis. To find the x-intercept of a linear equation, let $y = 0$ and solve.

> The y-**intercept** is the y-coordinate of a point where a line, intersects (crosses) the y-axis. To find the y-intercept of a linear equation, let $x = 0$ and solve.

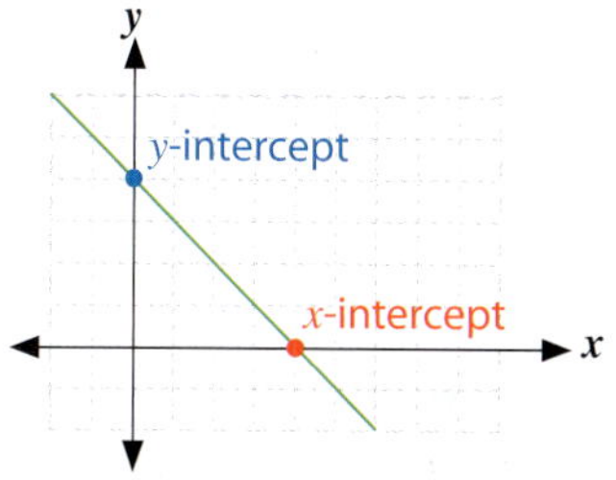

Solving two simultaneous linear equations by graphing

1. Write and label the two equations, e.g. equation A and equation B.

2. In the first equation, let $x = 0$. Replace x with 0, and solve the equation to find y. This will give you the value of the y-intercept.

3. Then, in the same equation, let $y = 0$ and solve the equation. This will give you the value of x-intercept.

4. Draw a coordinate plane. Mark the two intercepts from steps 2 and 3. Draw a line through these two points using a ruler, this line represents the first linear equation.

5. Repeats steps 1–4 for the second linear equation.

6. Look at the point where the two lines cross. This is the point of intersection. Write down its coordinates in the form (x, y).

We could choose any value for x and find the corresponding y value, but choosing 0 for the value of x simply makes it easier and quicker to find the corresponding value of y, which would be the y-intersect. The same applies to the value for y when finding the corresponding x value.

For a line that passes through the point (0, 0), chose another small whole number for x and for y (other than (0, 0)).

Worked example

Solve the following simultaneous equations graphically.

$$x + y - 3 = 0 \quad \text{and} \quad 4x + 2y - 8 = 0$$

Solution

Step 1

$x + y - 3 = 0$ (equation A) $\qquad$ $4x + 2y - 8 = 0$ (equation B)

Step 2 Find the y-intercept

$x + y - 3 = 0$ (equation A)
$(0) + y - 3 = 0$ (let $x = 0$)
$y - 3 = 0$
$y = 3$

Step 3 Find the x-intercept

$x + y - 3 = 0$ (equation A)
$x + (0) - 3 = 0$ (let $y = 0$)
$x - 3 = 0$
$x = 3$

Step 4

y-intercept $= 3$
x-intercept $= 3$

We can now draw our first line onto a coordinate plane:

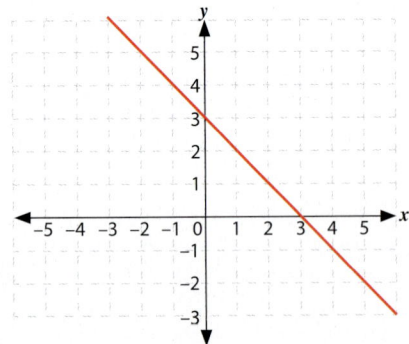

Step 5

$4x + 2 - 8 = 0$ (equation B)
$4(0) - 2y - 8 = 0$ (let $x = 0$)
$2y = 8$
$y = 4$

$4x + 2y - 8 = 0$ (equation B)
$4x + 2(0) - 8 = 0$ (let $y = 0$)
$4x - 8 = 0$
$4x = 8$
$x = 2$

y-intercept $= 4$
x-intercept $= 2$

We can now add our second line onto the plane:

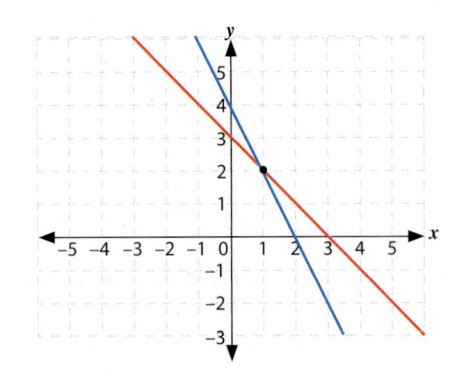

Step 6

From the graph, we can see that the solutions to both equations at the same time is when $x = 1$ and $y = 2$. This is the point where the lines intersect each other.

Verify answer by substituting values for x and y

$(1) + (2) - 3 = 0$ ✓ $\qquad$ $4(1) + 2(2) - 8 = 0$ ✓

Parallel lines do not intersect (cross), so they have no point of intersection.

There is no solution for those simultaneous equations represented by parallel lines. That means there is no set of values that will satisfy both equations simultaneously.

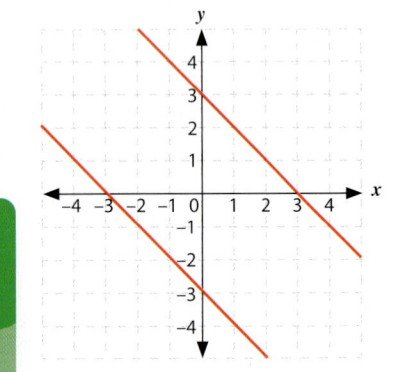

Discuss and discover

KEY SKILLS

Working with a classmate, investigate whether the lines represented by the following equations are parallel or not. Justify your answer.

$y + 2x = 2 \qquad 2y + 4x = -1$

340   Linking Thinking 1

Practice questions 21·2

1. Write down the coordinates of the x-intercept and y-intercept of the lines represented on each of the following graphs.

   (i) (ii) 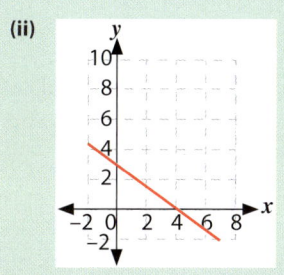 (iii) 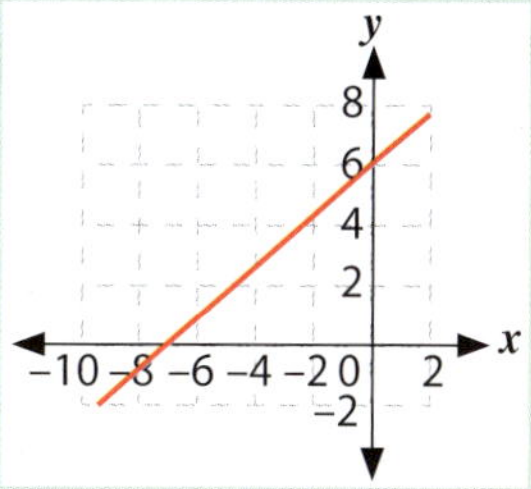 (iv)

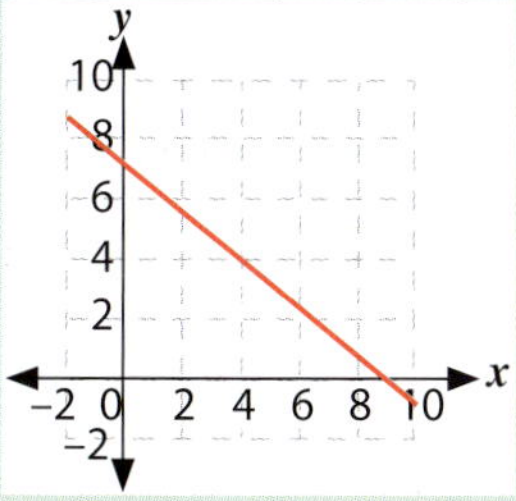

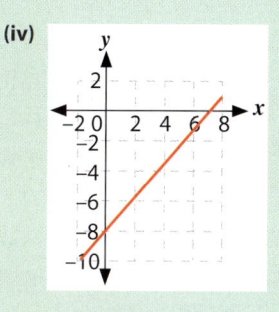

2. Write down the points of intersection of the following red and blue lines shown on the Cartesian plane.

   (i) (ii) 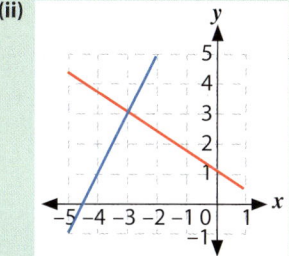 (iii)

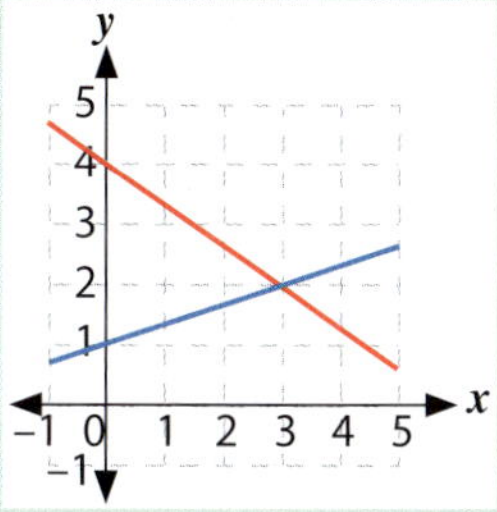

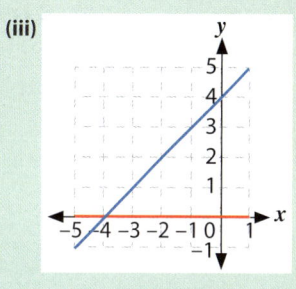

3. By finding the point of intersection in each case, find the value of x and the value of y that solve each pair of simultaneous equations (coloured red and blue).

   (i) (ii) 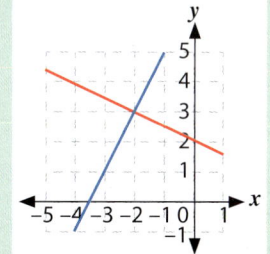 (iii)

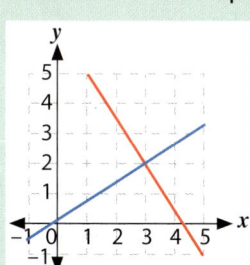

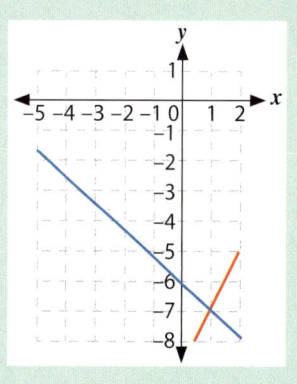

   (iv) 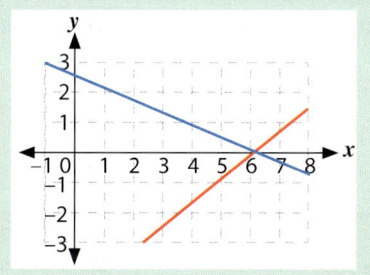 (v)

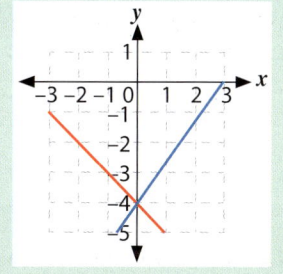

4. Find (a) the x-intercept and (b) the y-intercept of each of the following linear equations and hence graph each line.
   (i) $x + 2y = 6$
   (ii) $x - 2y = 10$
   (iii) $-x + 3y = 12$
   (iv) $5x + 90 = 3y$

5. Find (a) the x-intercept and (b) the y-intercept of each of the following linear equations and hence graph each line.
   (i) $x + y = 5$
   (ii) $3x + 2y = 12$
   (iii) $-5x - 2y = 10$
   (iv) $10y - 30 = 3x$

6. Solve the following simultaneous equations graphically.
   (i) $y - x = 1$ and $x + y = 3$
   (ii) $y - x = 1$ and $x + y = 5$
   (iii) $y = 6 - x$ and $y = x + 4$
   (iv) $x + y = 0$ and $2x - y = 9$

7. Solve the following simultaneous equations graphically and verify your answer in each equation.
   (i) $2x - 3y = 4$ and $3y - x = 4$
   (ii) $x + 3y = 4$ and $3x - y = 2$
   (iii) $5x - y = 2$ and $2x + y = 5$

8. Solve the following simultaneous equations graphically and verify your answer in each equation.
   (i) $x + y + 3 = 0$ and $x + 3y - 1 = 0$
   (ii) $x = y + 6$ and $y = 2x - 3$
   (iii) $x = y$ and $x = -y$
   (iv) $x + y = 4$ and $2x - y = 2$

9. The path of a beam of light is described using the equation $5x - 3y = 26$. The path of a second beam of light is described using the equation $2x + y = 17$. Find the point at which the two beams of light meet.

Taking it FURTHER

10. The path of a rocket is described using the equation $3x + 2y = 36$. A second rocket is fired to intercept the first. Its path is described using the equation $5x + 4y = 64$
    (i) Find the value for x and the value for y where these two rockets meet.
    (ii) Every one unit on the y-axis = 100 metres. Find the maximum height reached by both rockets.

11. Copy the table below and put a tick (✓) in the correct box in each row to show whether each statement is always true, sometimes true, or never true. Justify your answer in each case.

	Statement	Always true	Sometimes true	Never true
(i)	Graphs of linear equations cross the x-axis			
(ii)	Two lines on the Cartesian plane cross at some point			
(iii)	A graph of a linear equation can cross the x-axis more than once			

21·3 Solving linear equations with two unknowns by trial and improvement and by elimination

By the end of this section you should be able to:
- solve a pair of simultaneous equations using trial and improvement
- solve simultaneous equations by elimination

Method 2: Solving simultaneous equations using trial and improvement

Any equation can be solved by trial and improvement.

> **Solving simultaneous equations by trial and improvement**
>
> **1** Estimate a solution for the two variables.
>
> **2** Substitute these estimates into one of the equations to determine whether your estimate is too high or too low to allow the left-hand side equal the right-hand side.
>
> **3** Refine your estimate and repeat the process until you find two values such that the left-hand side equals the right-hand side.
>
> **4** Check the two variables that satisfy the 1st equation **also** satisfy the 2nd equation. If this is not the case, repeat the process until it is the case.

Worked example 1

Solve the simultaneous equations $3x + y = 11$ and $2x + y = 8$ using the trial and improvement method. Show all your workings.

Solution

Label both equations.

$3x + y = 11$ (equation A)
$2x + y = 8$ (equation B)

Choose two values to try, $x = 4$ and $y = 3$ in equation A

$3x + y = 11$
$3(4) + (3) = 11$
$12 + 3 = 11$
$15 \neq 11$ ✗

so letting $x = 4$ and $y = 3$ gave 15 on the LHS, which is **too high** as RHS = 11

The symbol ≠ means 'not equal to'

Try reducing the x value by one, so $x = 3$ and $y = 3$

$3x + y = 11$
$3(3) + (3) = 11$
$9 + 3 = 11$
$12 \neq 11$ ✗

so letting $x = 3$ and $y = 3$ gave 12 on the LHS, which is **too high** as RHS = 11

Try reducing the y value by one, so $x = 3$ and $y = 2$

$3x + y = 11$
$3(3) + (2) = 11$
$9 + 2 = 11$
$11 = 11$ ✓

so letting $x = 3$ and $y = 2$ gave 11 on the LHS which is **perfect** as RHS = 11

So by trial and improvement, it was found that $x = 3$ and $y = 2$ are a pair of solutions for equation A.
We now must check if this pair $x = 3$ and $y = 2$ also solves equation B.

$2x + y = 8$ (equation B)
$2(3) + 2 = 8$
$6 + 2 = 8$
$8 = 8$ true, as LHS = RHS

Because $x = 3$ and $y = 2$ satisfy (LHS = RHS) both equations they are the solutions to solving $3x + y = 11$ and $2x + y = 8$ simultaneously.

Trial and improvement can be very time consuming. Furthermore, if you work with equations where the unknown is not a whole number, it will take a lot of time to find the correct decimal. Therefore, it is not a method that we normally use.

Section B Moving forward

Method 3: Solving simultaneous equations by elimination

The elimination method involves subtracting or adding the equations to eliminate one of the unknowns.

The aim is to manipulate the two equations so that, when combined, either of the unknown terms (i.e. the x term or the y term) is eliminated. The resulting equation with just one unknown can then be solved.

Solving simultaneous equations using elimination

1. Put both equations in the form where the variables are on the LHS and any constants on the RHS (e.g. $ax + by = c$). Label both equations.

2. We need the coefficient (number in front) of one of the variables to be the same in each equation, but they must be opposite signs (e.g. one equation has $+3x$ and the other has $-3x$). If this is not the case, multiply one or both of the equations by a suitable number to make this be the case. Don't forget to multiply every term in the equation by this value.

3. Add the resulting equations to give an equation with one unknown.

4. Solve the equation with one unknown from step 3.

5. Substitute the solution from step 4 back into one of the original equations containing the two unknowns. This will reveal the second unknown.

Worked example 2

Solve the following pair of simultaneous equations using elimination.

$$2x + y = 22 \quad \text{and} \quad 4x + 9y = 30$$

Solution

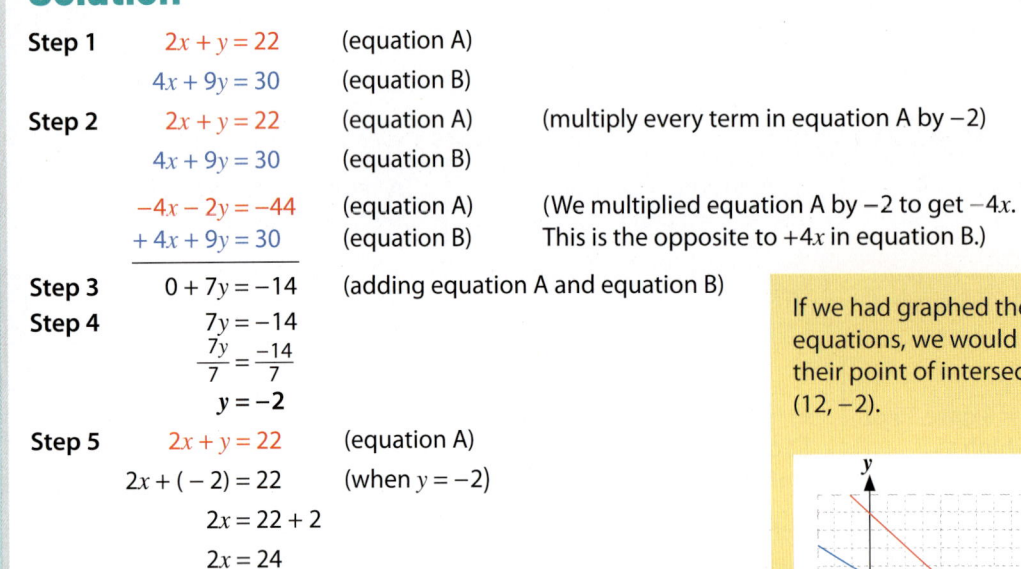

Step 1 $2x + y = 22$ (equation A)
          $4x + 9y = 30$ (equation B)

Step 2 $2x + y = 22$ (equation A)   (multiply every term in equation A by -2)
          $4x + 9y = 30$ (equation B)

          $-4x - 2y = -44$ (equation A)   (We multiplied equation A by -2 to get $-4x$.
          $+4x + 9y = 30$ (equation B)   This is the opposite to $+4x$ in equation B.)

Step 3 $0 + 7y = -14$ (adding equation A and equation B)

Step 4 $7y = -14$
          $\frac{7y}{7} = \frac{-14}{7}$
          $y = -2$

Step 5 $2x + y = 22$ (equation A)
          $2x + (-2) = 22$ (when $y = -2$)
          $2x = 22 + 2$
          $2x = 24$
          $\frac{2x}{2} = \frac{24}{2}$
          $x = 12$

When $x = 12$ and $y = -2$ both equations are satisfied simultaneously.
So the solution point is $(12, -2)$.

If we had graphed these two equations, we would have found their point of intersection to be at $(12, -2)$.

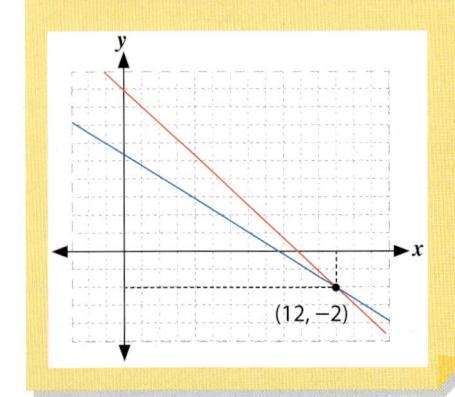

Worked example 3

Solve the following pair of simultaneous equations using elimination.

$$-2y = 6 - 5x \quad \text{and} \quad 2x = -3y + 10$$

Solution

Step 1
$5x - 2y = 6$ (equation A put in the form $ax + by = c$)
$2x + 3y = 10$ (equation B put in the form $ax + by = c$)

Step 2
$5x - 2y = 6$ (equation A) (multiply all terms in equation A by 3 to get $-6y$)
$2x + 3y = 10$ (equation B) (multiply all terms in equation B by 2 to get $+6y$)

$15x - 6y = 18$ (new version of equation A)
$+ 4x + 6y = 20$ (new version of equation B)

Step 3 $0 + 19x = 38$ (adding equation A and equation B)

Step 4 $19x = 38$
$\frac{19x}{19} = \frac{38}{19}$
$x = 2$

Step 5 $5x - 2y = 6$ (equation A)
$5(2) - 2y = 6$ (when $x = 2$)
$10 - 2y = 6$
$-2y = 6 - 10$
$\frac{-2y}{-2} = \frac{-4}{-2}$
$y = 2$

When $x = 2$ and $y = 2$ satisfy both equations simultaneously.
So the solution point is (2, 2)

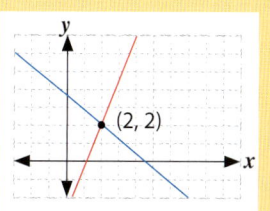

> If we had graphed these two equations, we would have found their point of intersection to be at (2, 2)

Practice questions 21·3

1. The following are two linear equations.
   $y = -2x$ and $y = x + 3$

   (i) Does the point (0, 4) make either equation true? Substitute it in and find out.

   (ii) Does the point (2, 5) make either equation true? Explain your answer.

   (iii) Does the point (–1, 2) make either equation true? Explain your answer.

   (iv) What point is the solution to both equations above at the same time?

   Plot both equations in the same axes and scales.

   (v) At what point do the two lines intersect? Compare this with your answer for part (iv). What do you notice?

2. Solve the following linear equations using trial and improvement method.

   (i) $y = 4x + 3$ and $y = -x - 2$

   (ii) $y - 2x = -4$ and $y = x - 2$

   (iii) $y = -x + 5$ and $y = x + 1$

3. Solve the following simultaneous equations using the elimination method.

   (i) $2x - y = 2$ and $x + y = 4$

   (ii) $2x + y = 2$ and $x - y = 4$

   (iii) $x + y = -2$ and $x - 2y = 10$

   (iv) $y = -x + 3$ and $y = x + 1$

4. Solve the following simultaneous equations algebraically.

   (i) $x - y = 2$ and $x + y = -6$

   (ii) $x + y = -2$ and $7x - 4y = 8$

   (iii) $x = 3 + 2y$ and $2x = y - 3$

   (iv) $5x + 3y = 19$ and $y = 1 + x$

   > To "solve algebraically" generally means to use the elimination method.

5. Solve the following simultaneous equations algebraically.

   (i) $7x + y = 25$ and $5x - y = 11$

   (ii) $8x + 9y = 3$ and $x + y = 0$

   (iii) $2x + 13y = 36$ and $13x + 2y = 69$

   (iv) $7x - y = 15$ and $3x - 2y = 19$

6. Solve the following pairs of equations algebraically.

(i) $2a = 4 + 3b$
$3b - a = 4$

(ii) $p = 4 - 3q$
$3p = 2 + q$

(iii) $5a = 3 + b$
$2a + b - 4 = 0$

7. Solve the following pairs of equations simultaneously.

(i) $x = 2y + 4$
$x = 3y - 1$

(ii) $a + 2\beta = 7$
$\beta + a = 4$

(iii) $3a - 2b - 7 = 0$
$2a + 5b - 11 = 0$

(iv) $b = 5a + 5$
$b = 6a + 5$

8. The path of a growing branch is described by the linear equation $2x + 3y = 15$. A second branch growing beside the first has a growth path described using the equation $4x - 3y = 3$. Find the point where the branches cross.

9. The direction of one sword pointed in the air is described as $6x - y = 59$ and the path of a second sword is described using the equation $x + 15y = 25$. Find the value for x and the value for y where the two swords cross.

21·4 Creating and solving simultaneous equations

By the end of this section you should be able to:
- form simultaneous linear equations
- use simultaneous equations to solve a problem

We have already learned the steps of forming linear equations from mathematical problems and different methods of solving simultaneous equations.

When we have a problem where we have to find the values of two unknown quantities, we assume the two unknown quantities as x, y or any two of other algebraic symbols.

Then we form equations **according to the given condition** or conditions and solve the two equations simultaneously to find the values of the two unknown quantities. Thus, we can work out the problem.

Solving word problems using simultaneous equations

Before starting, read all the information in the question carefully and organise it into two sets of information.

1 Let x equal one unknown and let y equal the other unknown. Split the information into two separate sentences, each of which include both include x and y. Form an equation for each sentence.

2 Solve the two equations simultaneously.

3 Answer the question that is asked in the original question.

Worked example 1

The sum of two numbers is 14 and their difference is 2. Find the numbers.

Solution

Step 1 Let the two numbers be x and y
$x + y = 14$ (equation A: the sum of two numbers is 14)
$x - y = 2$ (equation B: the difference between the two numbers is 2)

Step 2 $x + y = 14$
$\underline{x - y = 2}$ (add the equations)
$2x = 16$
$x = 8$

Substituting the value of x in equation A, we get
$8 + y = 14$
$y = 6$

Step 3 Therefore, $x = 8$ and $y = 6$
Hence, the two numbers are 6 and 8.

Verify answer:
$x + y = 14$ (equation A)
$8 + 6 = 14$
$14 = 14$ ✓

$x - y = 2$ (equation B)
$8 - 6 = 2$
$2 = 2$ ✓

Worked example 2

A total of 925 tickets were sold for €5 925. If adult tickets cost €7·50, and children's tickets cost €3·00, how many tickets of each kind were sold?

Solution

Step 1 Let x be the number of adult tickets. Let y be the number of children's tickets.

Here are the equations:

$x + y = 925$ (equation A – total number of adult tickets plus child tickets is equal to 925)

$7·5x + 3y = 5\,925$ (equation B – total money from all adult tickets at €7·50 and all children tickets at €3 is equal to €5 925)

In equation B, make the coefficients into whole numbers by multiplying every term in the equation by 10:

$x + y = 925$

$75x + 30y = 59\,250$ (new version of equation B)

Step 2 Multiply equation A by −30 to eliminate y

$-30x - 30y = -27\,750$ (new version of equation A)

$\underline{75x + 30y = 59\,250}$ (equation B)

$45x = 31\,500$ (add the equations)

$\dfrac{45x}{45} = \dfrac{31\,500}{45}$

$x = 700$

Substituting back into equation A

$700 + y = 925$ (equation A)

$y = 925 - 700$

$y = 225$

Step 3 $x = 700$ and $y = 225$

So 700 adult tickets were sold and 225 child tickets were sold.

Check/verify your answer

$x + y = 925$ (equation A)	$75x + 30y = 59\,250$ (equation B)
$700 + 225 = 925$	$75(700) + 30(225) = 59\,250$
$925 = 925$ ✓	$59\,250 = 59\,250$ ✓

Practice questions 21.4

1. If twice the age of a son is added to the age of his father, the sum is 56. If twice the age of the father is added to the age of the son, the sum is 82. Let the father's age be y and the son's age be x.

   (i) Write two equations in terms of x and y.

   (ii) Solve these equations simultaneously to find the ages of the father and son.

2. John thinks of two numbers. If he adds them together he gets 8. If he multiplies one of them by four and the other by two and then adds them, he gets 22. Let one number be x and the other number be y.

   (i) Write two equations in terms of x and y.

   (ii) Solve these equations algebraically to find two numbers.

3. Two pencils and one eraser cost 35 cents. Three pencils and four erasers cost 65 cents. Let the cost of a pencil be x and the cost of erasers be y.

   (i) Write two equations in terms of x and y.

   (ii) Solve these equations simultaneously to find the cost of a pencil and the cost of an eraser.

4. If 250 child tickets and 600 adult tickets are sold for a GAA game in Pearse Stadium Park, the takings will amount to €49 000.  
   However, if 500 child tickets are sold and 300 adult tickets are sold, the takings will amount to €39 500.
   Let the number of adult tickets be x and the number of child tickets be y.

   (i) Write two equations in terms of x and y.

   (ii) Use algebra to find how many adult tickets and how many child tickets were sold.

5. Conall has sheep and chickens on his farm. There are a total of 22 legs. There are eight heads, all looking at Conall. How many sheep and how many chickens does Conall have?

6. At Mary's Café, cakes cost four euros and sandwiches are two euros. Eight people go to Mary's Café and they all have either a cake or a sandwich. At the end of the day, Mary has made twenty-two euros.
   Let the number of cakes sold equal x and the number of sandwiches equal y. 

   (i) Write two equations in terms of x and y.

   (ii) Solve these equations simultaneously to find how many cakes and how many sandwiches Mary sold that day.

7. Frank routinely orders wheelbarrows for his shop. In June, he ordered 4 small wheelbarrows and 4 large wheelbarrows, which cost €776. In December, he ordered 1 small wheelbarrow and 5 large wheelbarrows, which cost a total of €726. 
   Let the cost of the small wheelbarrow be x and the and the cost of the large wheelbarrow be y.

   (i) Write two equations in terms of x and y.

   (ii) Use algebra to find how much the large wheelbarrow costs and how much the small wheelbarrow costs.

8. Patsy is building tables to sell at a furniture store. First, he built 6 small tables and 5 large tables, using a total of 463 nails. Later, he built 6 small tables and 2 large tables, using a total of 286 nails. 
   Let the number of nails for the small table be x and the number of nails required for the large table be y.

   (i) Write two equations in terms of x and y.

   (ii) Solve these equations simultaneously to find how many nails Patsy uses to build a small table and to build a large table.

9. Farrigan's High School sold tickets for a school musical. Seats in the auditorium cost €6 each and balcony seats cost €4. A total of 200 tickets were sold and €960 was collected. 
   Let the number of seats in the auditorium be x and the seats in the balcony be y.

   (i) Write two equations in terms of x and y.

   (ii) Using algebra, find how many tickets were sold for the auditorium and how many tickets were sold for the balcony.

10. The sum of four times a number and three times a second number is 15. The difference of three times the first number and twice the second number is 7. Find the numbers.

21·5 Graphing linear functions

By the end of this section you should:
- understand what a linear function is
- be able to graph a linear function

In Section A, Unit 9, we learned that a function is like a machine that has an input and an output. The output is related somehow to the input.

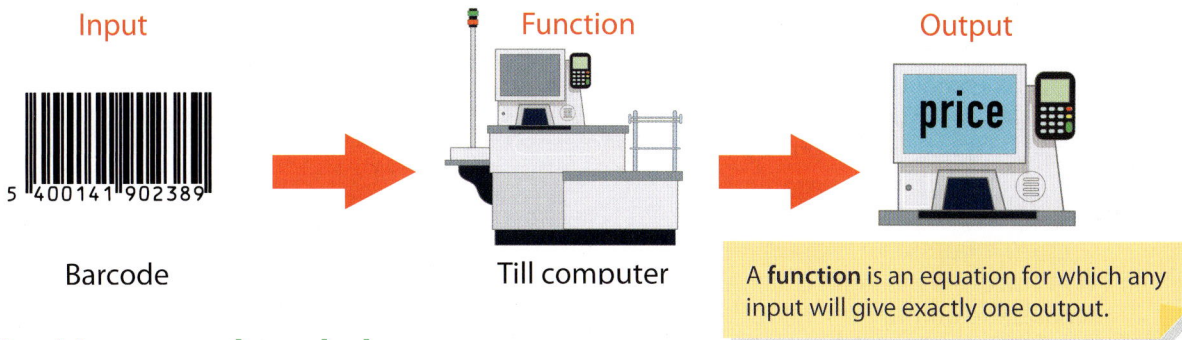

Input → Function → Output

Barcode → Till computer → price

A **function** is an equation for which any input will give exactly one output.

Important terms and symbols

Input	Output	Commonly used in
x	y	Coordinate geometry and linear equations
x	$f(x)$	Functions
domain	range $\in$ codomain	Functions
independent variable	dependent variable	Functions
n	T_n (term value)	Patterns

An **independent variable** is a variable (often denoted by x) whose value does not depend on that of another.

A **dependent variable** (often denoted by y) is a variable whose value depends upon independent variable x.

Linear functions

A linear function has the following form.

$$y = f(x) = a + bx$$

Linear functions are those whose graph is a straight line.

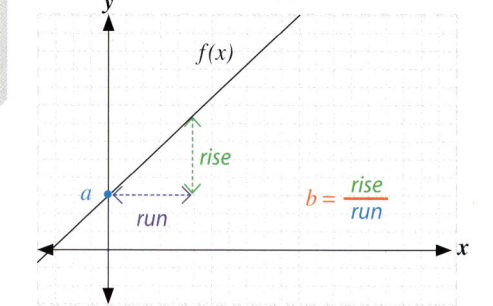

$b = \dfrac{\text{rise}}{\text{run}}$

A linear function has one independent variable (x) and one dependent variable (y).

a is the constant term or the y-intercept.

b is the coefficient of the independent variable. It is also known as the **slope** and gives the **rate of change** of the dependent variable.

- $f(a)$ means if the input (x) is a, what is the output (y)? (Where a is number or variable)
- $f(x) = a$ means if the output (y) is a, what is the input (x)? (Where a is some number or variable)

$f(x)$ is pronounced 'f of x'
It can also be written in the following three ways:
$f \to x$ OR $f:x$ OR y

Section B Moving forward

Worked example 1

A function is defined as $f(x) = 3x - 4$

Find:

(i) $f(5)$ (ii) $f(-1)$ (iii) $f(x) = 8$ (iv) $f(x) = 20$

Solution

(i) $f(5)$ means if the input (or x value) is 5, what is the output (y value)?

$f(5) = 3(5) - 4$
$f(5) = 15 - 4$
$f(5) = 11$

$f(5)$ is pronounced 'f of 5'

(ii) $f(-1)$ means if the input (x value) is -1, what is the output (or y value)?

$f(-1) = 3(-1) - 4$
$f(-1) = -3 - 4$
$f(-1) = -7$

(iii) $f(x) = 8$ means if the output (y value) is 8, what is the input (or x value)?

$8 = 3x - 4$
$8 + 4 = 3x$
$12 = 3x$
$4 = x$

$f(x) = 8$ is pronounced 'f of x is equal to 8'

(iv) $f(x) = 20$ means if the output (y value) is 20, what is the input (or x value)?

$20 = 3x - 4$
$20 + 4 = 3x$
$24 = 3x$
$8 = x$

Graphing a linear function

1 Find two points that satisfy the equation by creating a table. Choose any two values for x and find the corresponding y value. It is better to choose small whole numbers as they are easy to graph on the Cartesian plane.

Input (x value)	Function	Output (y value)	Point (x value, y value)

2 Plot the points on the Cartesian plane.

You need only two points to graph a linear function. Why is this?

3 Draw a straight line through both points.

Worked example 2

Graph the function $f(x) = 2 + 3x$

Solution

Step 1 Find two points that satisfy the equation by creating a table. Choose any two values for x and find the corresponding y value. It is best to choose small whole numbers as they are easy to graph on the Cartesian plane.

Input (x value)	Function $2 + 3x$	Output (y value)	Point (x value, y value)
1	$2 + 3(1) = 2 + 3$	5	$(1, 5)$
-1	$2 + 3(-1) = 2 - 3$	-1	$(-1, -1)$

Step 2 Plot the points on the Cartesian plane.

Step 3 Connect the points with a straight line.

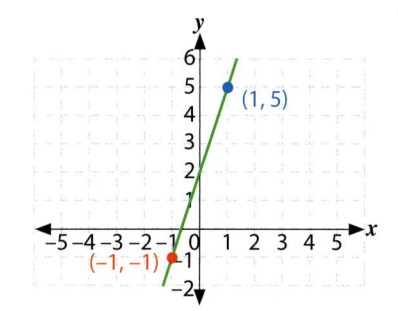

We can use the method of drawing linear functions to **find the point of intersection** of two linear functions graphed on the Cartesian plane.

Finding the intersection of two functions

1 Graph the first function.

2 Graph the second function using the same axes and scales as the first function.

3 Find the point of intersection on the Cartesian plane.

Worked example 3

Find the point of intersection of the function $g(x) = x + 3$ and the function $f(x) = 12 - 2x$

Solution

Step 1 Graph $g(x) = x + 3$

Input (x value)	Function $g(x) = x + 3$	Output (y value) $g(x)$	Point (x, y)
2	2 + 3	5	(2, 5)
−2	−2 + 3	1	(−2, 1)

Step 2 Graph $f(x) = 12 - 2x$

Input (x value)	Function $f(x) = 12 - 2x$	Output (y value) $f(x)$	Point (x, y)
4	12 − 2(4)	4	(4, 4)
7	12 − 2(7)	−2	(7, −2)

Step 3 Using the graph from step 2, the point of intersection of the two lines is (3, 6)

> As before, you can also use the x-intercept and the y-intercept to graph a linear function.

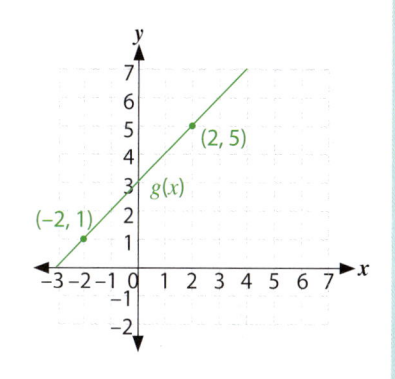

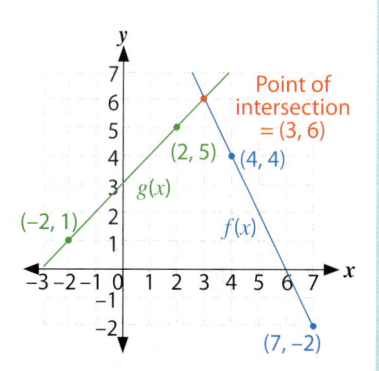

Practice questions 21·5

1. A function is defined as $f(x) = 2x + 1$
Find the following.
 (i) $f(1)$
 (ii) $f(5)$
 (iii) $f(x) = 9$
 (iv) $f(x) = 21$

2. A function is defined as $h(x) = 3x - 1$
Find the following.
 (i) $h(-1)$
 (ii) $h(4)$
 (iii) $h(x) = 17$
 (iv) $h(x) = 26$

3. A function is defined as $f(x) = -2x - 1$
Find the following.
 (i) $f(-5)$
 (ii) $f(-4)$
 (iii) $f(x) = 9$
 (iv) $f(x) = 15$

4. A function is defined as $f(x) = -6x - 12$
Find the following.
 (i) $f(-10)$
 (ii) $f(-12)$
 (iii) $f(x) = 60$
 (iv) $f(x) = 72$

5. Graph the following functions.
 (i) $f(x) = 4 - 8x$
 (ii) $f(x) = x - 9$
 (iii) $f(x) = x + 5$
 (iv) $f(x) = 2x + 4$

6. Graph the following functions.
 (i) $f(x) = -4 - x$
 (ii) $f(x) = 4x - 12$
 (iii) $f(x) = -x - 2$
 (iv) $f(x) = 2x$

7. Find the point of intersection for the following pairs of functions by graphing each function.
   (i) $f(x) = -x + 3$ and $g(x) = 2x - 6$
   (ii) $f(x) = -x + 3$ and $h(x) = x + 1$
   (iii) $g(x) = -2x + 10$ and $h(x) = 4 - x$
   (iv) $h(x) = x + 4$ and $g(x) = 2x + 7$

8. Find the point of intersection for the following pairs of functions by graphing each function.
   (i) $h(x) = 2x - 7$ and $g(x) = x - 4$
   (ii) $f(x) = -5x + 3$ and $g(x) = 5x - 7$
   (iii) $g(x) = -x - 2$ and $h(x) = x + 4$
   (iv) $h(x) = -2x - 3$ and $f(x) = x + 3$

9. (a) Find the point of intersection for the following pairs of functions by graphing each function first.
   (i) $y = x + 5$ and $y = 2x + 7$
   (ii) $y = -2x + 4$ and $y = 2x - 8$
   (iii) $y = -2x - 2$ and $y = 2x + 6$
   (iv) $y = -2x + 8$ and $y = x - 1$

   (b) Using algebra, find the point of intersection of the two functions in each of the pairs of functions in part (a).

10. The function $h(t) = 2t + 4$ describes the height h of a rocket off the ground at time t, where height is measured in metres and time is measured in seconds.
    (i) What is the height of the rocket from the ground at $t = 0$?
    (ii) What is the height of the rocket after 5 seconds?
    (iii) Graph the function on the coordinate plane.
    (iv) Find the height of the rocket after 100 seconds.
    (v) How many seconds does it take for the rocket to reach a height of 596 metres?
    (vi) How many seconds does it take for the rocket to reach a height of 1 004 metres?

Taking it FURTHER

11. Sandra is mowing lawns for a summer job. For every mowing job, she charges an initial fee of €10 plus a constant fee for each hour of work. Her fee for a 5-hour job, for example, is €35. Let $f(t)$ stand for Sandra's fee for a single job f (measured in euros) as a function of the number of hours t it took her to complete it.
    (i) What fee does Sandra charge per hour?
    (ii) Write the function's $f(t)$ formula.
    (iii) Graph the function.
    (iv) Using your graph, find how many hours Sandra would have to work for on one job to earn €42.

12. A phone company is offering its customers the following two 12-month phone plans.
    - Plan A: You can buy a new phone for €60 and pay a monthly flat rate of €40 per month for unlimited calls.
    - Plan B: You get a new phone for free and pay a monthly flat rate of €50 per month for unlimited calls.
    (i) Write a function to represent the amount charged on plan A.
    (ii) Write a function to represent the amount charged on plan B.
    (iii) Graph both functions on the same coordinate plane to show the cost up to 12 months.
    (vi) Using your graph, find when the cost will be equal with both plans.
    (v) If you were going to use the phone for four months, which plan would be the best value?
    (vi) If you were going to use the phone for two years, which phone would be the best value?

Revision questions

21A Core skills

1. Simplify the following expressions.
   (i) $20y + 3y - 4 - 2y$
   (ii) $17 - 5t - 7 - 2t + 7t$
   (iii) $2(6b - 4a) + 2(3a + 12b) - (3b + 2)$
   (iv) $-(4x - 5y) - 2(x - b) - (-5x - 2)$

2. Simplify the following expressions
   (i) $7e + 2e + 4ef + 2g + ef + 4$
   (ii) $6 + 3ac + 6cb + 4 + 2cb + 9ac$
   (iii) $3y^2 + 2w^2 + y^2 - w^2$
   (iv) $y^2 + y^2 + y^2$

3. (i) A five-sided polygon is shown. Find an expression of its perimeter. 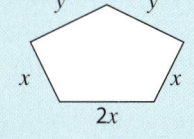
   (ii) An equilateral triangle is shown. Each side is $2x + y$. Find an expression for the perimeter of the triangle. 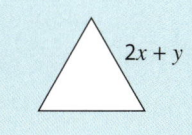
   (iii) Find an expression for the perimeter of this L shape.

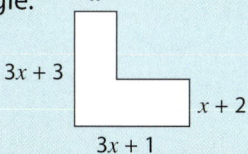

4. Solve the following linear equations.
   (i) $c + 8 = 9$
   (ii) $x - 4 = 6$
   (iii) $7 - y = 9$
   (iv) $5b + 8 = -27$
   (v) $6(x + 5) = 60$
   (vi) $9(y - 5) = 45$
   (vii) $2(3y + 5) = 76$
   (viii) $4(3z - 4) = 92$

5. Solve the following linear equations.
   (i) $8a + 9 = 3a + 19$
   (ii) $9z + 13 = 2z - 1$
   (iii) $10z - 21 = 3z + 21$
   (iv) $9z - 40 = 5z - 16$
   (v) $6a + 11 = 99 - 5a$
   (vi) $15 - 2a = 31 + 2a$

6. Solve the following linear equations.
   (i) $4x - 23 = 3(4x + 3)$
   (ii) $5(a + 3) = 3(a - 1)$
   (iii) $6(4a - 2) = 2(3a + 3)$
   (iv) $-7(y + 6) = -3(y + 10)$
   (v) $35 - 3a = 89 + 6a$
   (vi) $35 + 2b = 71 - 2b$

7. Solve the following simultaneous equations by graphing.
   (i) $y = x + 5$ and $y = 2x + 7$
   (ii) $y = -2x + 4$ and $y = 2x - 8$
   (iii) $y = -x + 1$ and $y = x + 3$
   (iv) $y = 2x - 1$ and $y = -2x - 5$

8. Solve the following simultaneous equations using the elimination method.
   (i) $5x + 3y = 41$
       $2x + 3y = 20$
   (ii) $2x + 4y = 26$
        $3x - y = 4$
   (iii) $3x + 2y = 16$
         $2x - 3y = 2$
   (iv) $3x + 5y = 1$
        $2x - 3y = 7$

9. (i) Given the function $g(x) = 6x + 4$, find the value of $g(5)$
   (ii) Given the function $f(x) = -3 - 5x$, find the value of $f(-6)$
   (iii) Given the function $h(x) = 10x + 2$, find the value of x when $h(x) = 22$
   (iv) Given the function $g(x) = -8x + 16$, find the value of x when $g(x) = 0$

10. Find the point of intersection for the following pairs of functions by graphing each function.
    (i) $f(x) = 2x - 1$ and $g(x) = -2x - 5$
    (ii) $g(x) = -x + 1$ and $h(x) = x + 3$
    (iii) $f(x) = 2x + 7$ and $h(x) = -3x + 17$
    (iv) $f(x) = -4$ and $g(x) = 5x - 19$

21B Taking it FURTHER

1. Sarah is x years old. Thomas is 3 years older than Sarah. David is twice as old as Sarah. The total of their ages is 51. 
   (i) Write an expression for Thomas's age in terms of x.
   (ii) Write an expression for David's age in terms of x.
   (iii) Form an equation in x and solve it to work out Sarah's age.

2. Jack has x cents. Hannah has 5 cents more than Jack. Liam has 2 cents less than Jack. The total amount of money they have is 75 cents. 
   (i) Use this information to write down an equation in x.
   (ii) Solve the equation to find out how much money Jack has.

3. The sum of two numbers is 25. One of the numbers exceeds the other by 9. Find the numbers.

4. The length of a rectangle is twice its width. If the perimeter is 72 metres, find the length and width of the rectangle.

5. Three angles make up a straight line as shown. 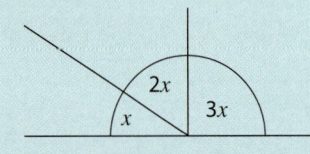
   (i) Form an equation in x.
   (ii) Solve the equation to find the value of x.
   (iii) Calculate the size of the middle angle.

6. A number is divided into two parts such that one part is 10 more than the other. If the two parts are in the ratio 5 : 3, find the number and the two parts.

7. Three bags and four pens together cost €257 whereas four bags and three pens together cost €324. Find the cost of a bag and 10 pens.

8. Paul collects Gaelic football cards and hurling cards. The number of Gaelic football cards is 10 more than twice the number of hurling cards. In total, Paul has 70 cards. How many of each type card does Paul have?

9. David buys 2 hats and 2 scarves in a shop and in total they cost €18. Saoirse buys 3 hats and 2 scarves in the same shop and they cost €22. Form two equations and solve to find the cost of each hat and each scarf.

10. Ever since Denise moved to her new home, she's been keeping track of the height of the tree outside her window. The function $H(t)$ models the height of the tree (in centimetres), t years since Denise moved in.
    $H(t) = 210 + 33t$
    (i) Graph this function on the coordinate plane.
    (ii) What will be the height of this tree 4 years after Denise moves in?

11. Emily took 1 hour to read 22 pages of a book. She has 132 pages left to read in order to finish the book. 
    (i) Write a function to represent the time it takes Emily to read any number of pages of the book.
    (ii) How much time should she expect to spend reading in order to finish the book?

12. A radar shows the paths of two ships out at sea. The path of one ship is described by the function $y = 8 - 3x$ and a second ship's path is described by the function $y = 3 + 2x$
    (i) By graphing the functions, find the point where the paths of the ships cross.
    (ii) Using algebra find the point at which the paths of the two ships cross.

Something to think about ...
Now that you have completed the unit, revisit the question posed at the start of this unit.

Now try questions 3, 7, 10, 14 and 16 on pages 403–10

Unit 22

Triangles

Something to think about ...

The Pythagorean theorem is named for the Greek philosopher Pythagoras, because he was the first person to record a proof for the theorem, around 540 BCE.

However, clay tablets from around 1700 BCE show that the Babylonians already knew how to calculate the length of the diagonal of a square.

It is also believed that the Egyptians may have used the same idea as Pythagoras to help design the pyramids around 2000 BCE.

In ancient Egypt, the River Nile overflowed every year and destroyed property boundaries. Because the land plots were rectangular, the Egyptians needed a way to mark a right angle.

The Egyptians tied 12 evenly spaced knots along a piece of rope and made a triangle.

Explain how this rope could have been used to mark a right angle.

Topics covered within this unit:
22·1 Theorem terms
22·2 Congruent triangles
22·3 Pythagoras's theorem

The Learning Outcomes covered in this unit are contained in the following sections:
GT.3b GT.3c GT.3d GT.3e

Key words
Implies
Corollary
Congruent triangles

22·1 Theorem terms

By the end of this section you should be able to:
- understand and use the terms axiom, theorem, proof, corollary, converse and implies

In geometry, there are a number of commonly used terms that we must be able to understand and use.

> An **axiom** is a statement that is taken to be true without the need for a proof.

Revise Section A, Units 3 and 11 and Section B, Unit 15.

Recall we encountered some of the axioms in Section A Unit 3. For example:

Axiom 1: Given any two points, you can draw exactly one straight line between them.

Section B Moving forward   355

> A **theorem** is a statement that can be proved from the axioms and other theorems by logical argument.

We have also encountered some theorems in Section A, Units 3 and 11, and Section B, Unit 15. For example:

Theorem 1: Vertically opposite angles are equal in measure.

> A **proof** is a step-by-step explanation that uses axioms and previously proven theorems to show another theorem is correct.

A proof is written as a series of statements accompanied by the reason why each statement is true.

If you use a piece of information that you have been told in the question as a statement, the reason is stated as 'given'.

For example, in Section A, Unit 3 you met the proof that vertically opposite angles are equal. We will look at it again here to show the structure of a proof.

To prove $|\angle 1| = |\angle 2|$

Statement	Reason
$|\angle 1| + |\angle 3| = 180°$	Straight line = 180° (supplementary angles)
$|\angle 2| + |\angle 3| = 180°$	Straight line = 180° (supplementary angles)
$|\angle 1| + |\angle 3| = |\angle 2| + |\angle 3|$	(subtract $|\angle 3|$ from both sides)
$|\angle 1| = |\angle 2|$	

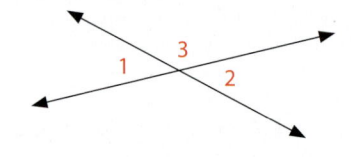

> A **corollary** is a statement that follows readily from a previous theorem.

> The **converse** of a theorem is the reverse of a theorem.

For example, if two lines are parallel then they never intersect. The converse is if two lines never intersect, then they are parallel.

> **Implies** is used in a proof when we can write a fact we have proven by our previous statements. The symbol for implies is $\Rightarrow$

The statement 'a implies b' means if a is true, then b must also be true.

For example, $x = 2$ implies $x + 1 = 3$

$x = 2 \quad \Rightarrow x + 1 = 3$

Practice questions 22·1

1. Explain each of the following terms.
   - (i) Axiom
   - (ii) Theorem
   - (iii) Proof
   - (iv) Implies
   - (v) Corollary
   - (vi) Converse

2. Given $|\angle 2| = |\angle 3|$
   Show that $|\angle 1| = |\angle 4|$
   Don't forget to give a reason for any statements made.

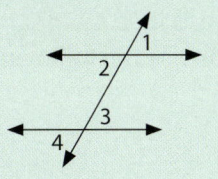

3. Make at least one true statement, including the reason it is true, for the diagrams shown.
   - (i) 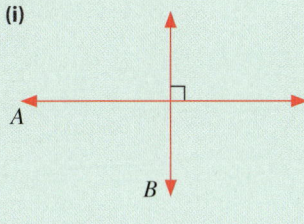
   - (ii)
   - (iii)

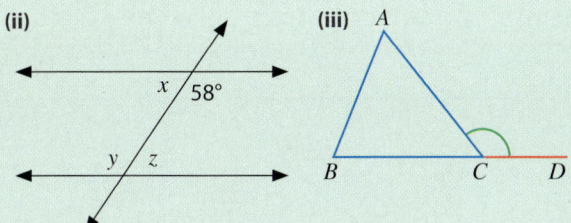

4. Write the converse of each of the following, and decide whether the converse statement is true or false.
   - (i) If an angle is 90°, then it is a right angle.
   - (ii) If $|\angle A| = 20°$, then $\angle A$ is acute.
   - (iii) If you are a guitar player, then you are a musician.
   - (iv) If you compete in the Olympics, then you are an athlete.
   - (v) If two angles are supplementary, then they add to 180°. 
   - (vi) If an angle measures less than 90°, then it is an acute angle.
   - (vii) If $3x + 10 = 16$, then $x = 2$.
   - (viii) If two lines are perpendicular, then they intersect to form right angles.
   - (ix) If it is bright outside, then it is 12 noon.

5. The triangle DEF shown has six angles labelled. A number of statements are listed below without reasons. Copy and complete the table by justifying each statement with a reason using evidence from the diagram.

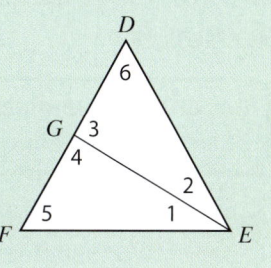

Statement	Reason
$|\angle 3| + |\angle 4| = 180°$	
$|\angle 4| = |\angle 2| + |\angle 6|$	
$|\angle 3| + |\angle 2| + |\angle 6| = 180°$	
If $|DE| = |FE|$ then $|\angle 5| = |\angle 6|$	

Taking it FURTHER

6. In the diagram below, [DE] is parallel to [BC]. The table contains some of the statements needed to prove the theorem that states the three angles of a triangle add up to 180°.

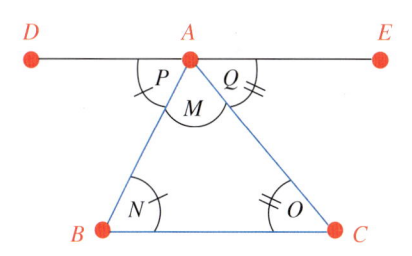

   (i) Copy and complete the table, justifying each statement with a reason using evidence from the diagram.

Statement	Reason
$|\angle P| + |\angle M| + |\angle Q| = 180°$	
$|\angle P| = |\angle N|$	
$|\angle Q| = |\angle O|$	

   (ii) Use the statements outlined in the table to show that the three angles of a triangle add up to 180°.

22·2 Congruent triangles

By the end of this section you should be able to:
- understand the term congruent
- prove that two triangles are congruent using SSS, SAS, ASA and RHS

Axiom 4

> **Congruent triangles** are identical triangles; that is, they have exactly the same shape and size. The symbol for congruence is ≡. This is read as 'is congruent to'.

Axiom 4 lists the conditions needed for triangles to be described as congruent. To prove two triangles are congruent, they must satisfy one of the folllowing conditions:

1. **Side-side-side (SSS)**
   When the three sides are the same, then the triangles are congruent.

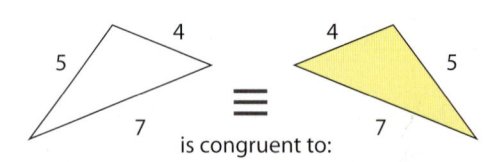

2. **Side-angle-side (SAS)**
   When two sides and the included angle (between them) are equal, then the triangles are congruent.

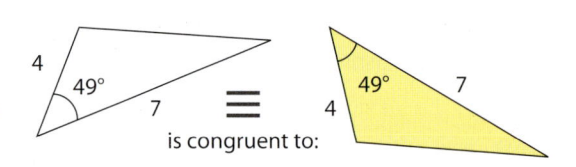

3. **Angle-side-angle (ASA)**
   When two angles and the included side are equal, then the triangles are congruent.

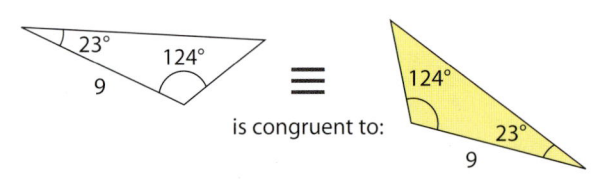

4. **Right angle-hypotenuse-any other side (RHS)**
   If two triangles are right-angled, have equal hypotenuses and another equal side, the triangles are congruent.

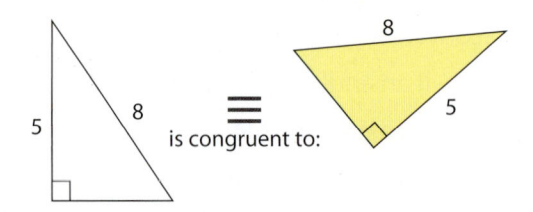

Discuss and discover

KEY SKILLS

Working with a classmate, complete the following.
(i) Construct the triangles given the conditions below.
   Triangle ABC: $[AB]$ = 4 cm, $[BC]$ = 7 cm and $[AC]$ = 6 cm
   Triangle XYZ: $[XY]$ = 4 cm, $|\angle XYZ|$ = 60° and $[YZ]$ = 7 cm
   Triangle PQR: $[QR]$ = 7 cm, $|\angle PQR|$ = 60° and $|\angle PRQ|$ = 35°
(ii) Measure all the sides and angles in each of the triangles you have constructed.
(iii) What do you notice?

Worked example

Show that the following pairs of triangles are congruent.

(i) [Triangle PQR with sides PQ = 6 cm, QR = 10 cm, PR = 8 cm; Triangle STU with sides US = 8 cm, ST = 10 cm, UT = 6 cm... actually ST = 10 cm, TU labeled]

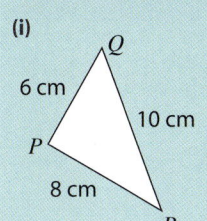

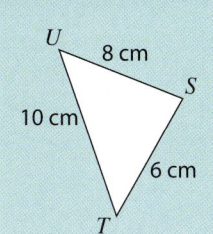

(ii) [Triangle ABC with ∠A = 70°, ∠C = 50°, CB = 10 cm; Triangle DEF with ∠E = 60°, ED = 10 cm, ∠F = 70°]

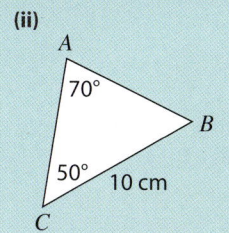

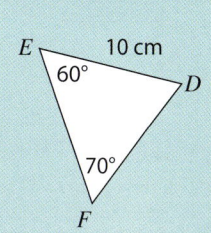

Solution

(i)

Statement	Reason
$\|PQ\| = \|ST\|$	Given (6 cm)
$\|PR\| = \|SU\|$	Given (8 cm)
$\|QR\| = \|TU\|$	Given (10 cm)
$\triangle PQR \equiv \triangle STU$	SSS

(ii)

Statement	Reason
$\|\angle CAB\| = \|\angle EFD\|$	Given (70°)
$\|\angle ABC\| = 180° - (70° + 50°)$ $= 60°$	3 angles of triangle add to 180°
$\|\angle ABC\| = \|\angle DEF\|$	Both 60°
$\|\angle EDF\| = 180° - (70° + 60°)$ $= 50°$	3 angles of triangle add to 180°
$\|\angle EDF\| = \|\angle ACB\|$	Both 50°
$\|BC\| = \|ED\|$	Given
$\triangle ABC \equiv \triangle DEF$	ASA

An application of congruent triangles

Congruency can be used to prove (mathematically show) some of the theorems in Junior Cycle Maths, including theorem 2, which is on the next page.

Discuss and discover

Work with a classmate to complete the following tasks.

(i) Draw the isosceles triangle on the right.
(ii) Using a protractor, find the measure the angles opposite the equal sides.
(iii) What do you notice about these angles?
(iv) Draw another two isosceles triangles and repeat steps (ii) and (iii) for each triangle. 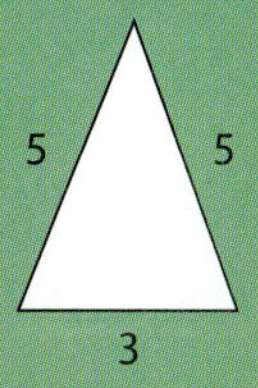
(v) What can you conclude about the angles opposite to the equal sides in an isosceles triangle?

22 Triangles

Section B Moving forward 359

Theorem 2: In an isosceles triangle the angles opposite the equal sides are equal.

Proof of theorem 2

In an isosceles triangle, the angles opposite the equal sides are equal.

> The full formal proofs are **not examinable** for Junior Cycle Mathematics, but you should be able to display understanding of the proofs.

1. Take a triangle ABC with $|AB| = |AC|$

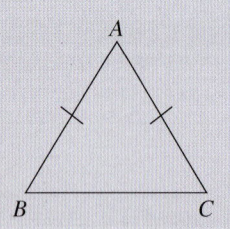

2. Join A to D so that $|BD| = |DC|$

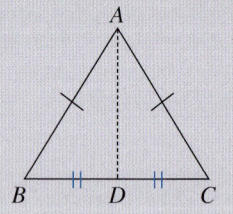

3. Consider triangles ABD and ACD
  $|AB| = |AC|$ Given
  $|BD| = |DC|$ Constructed
  $|AD| = |AD|$ Common
  $\Rightarrow \triangle ABD \equiv \triangle ADC$ SSS

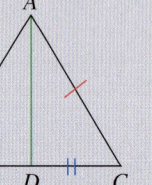

4. By congruency,
  $|\angle ABC| = |\angle ACB|$

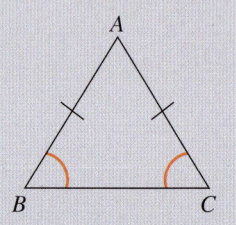

Converse of theorem 2: If two angles are equal, then the triangle is isosceles.

Practice questions 22·2

1. Show that the following pairs of triangles are congruent. In each case, state why they are congruent.

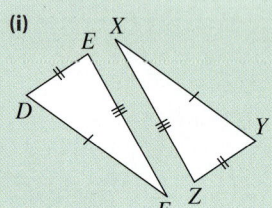

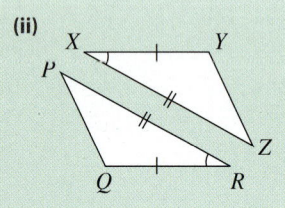

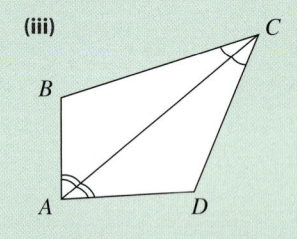

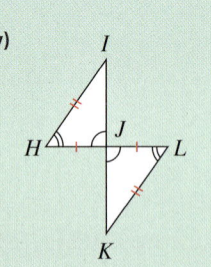

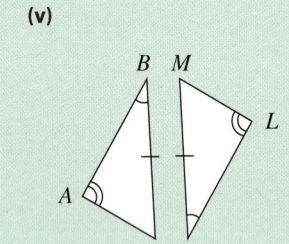

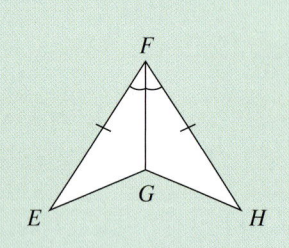

(i)

(ii)

(iii)

(iv)

(v)

(vi)

2. Which two of the triangles shown are congruent by ASA? Justify your answer.

3. In each case below, state what additional information is required in order to know that the triangles are congruent for the reason given.

(i) Reason: ASA

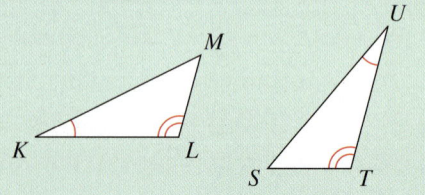

(ii) Reason: SAS

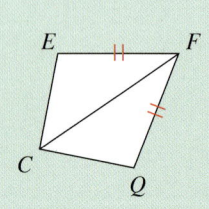

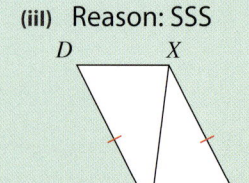

(iii) Reason: SSS

360   Linking Thinking 1

4. Ray built two triangular supports for a picnic table with the dimensions shown.

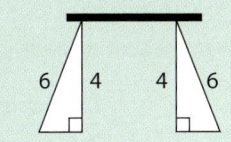

   Are the supports congruent? Explain your answer.

5. Name two pairs of congruent triangles in the shape shown below.

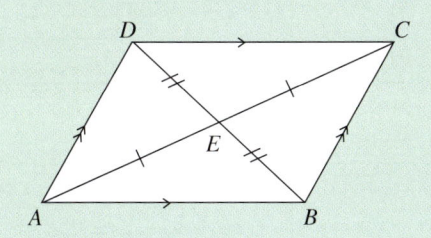

6. The image shown is a portion of a bridge.

   In the diagram, $[AX] \perp [BC]$.

   X is the midpoint of $[BC]$.

   Copy and complete the table below to show that $\triangle ABX \equiv \triangle ACX$.

Statement	Reason
	Common side
$\lvert \angle AXB \rvert = \lvert \angle AXC \rvert$	
	Given (midpoint)
$\Rightarrow \triangle ABX \equiv \triangle ACX$	

   > The midpoint is a point exactly halfway between the end points.

7. The diagram shows a rectangular gate $ABCD$.

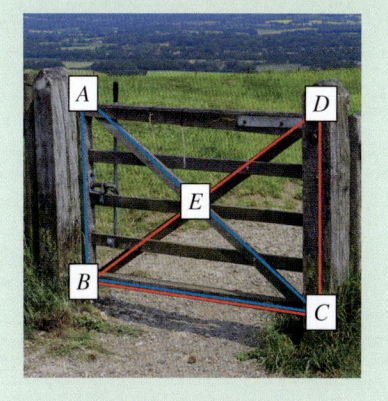

   (i) Copy and complete the table below to show that $\triangle ABC$ is congruent to $\triangle BCD$.

Statement	Reason
$\lvert BC \rvert = \lvert BC \rvert$	
	Both 90° (rectangle)
$\lvert AB \rvert = \lvert DC \rvert$	
$\Rightarrow \triangle ABC \equiv \triangle BCD$	

   (ii) Can you find any other pairs of congruent triangles? Justify your answer.

8. In each of the following isosceles triangles, equal sides are marked the same. Name the equal angles.

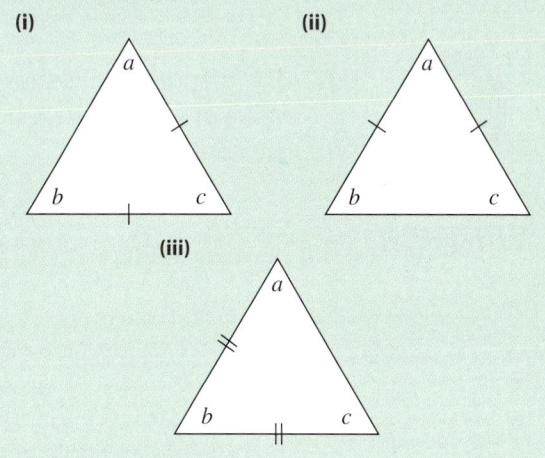

   (i)   (ii)

   (iii)

9. Calculate the value of x in each of the following.

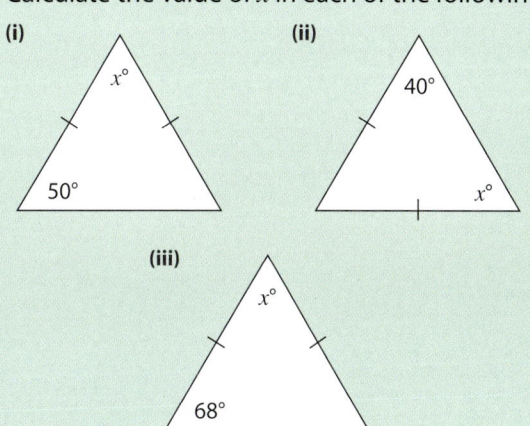

   (i)   (ii)

   (iii)

Section B Moving forward 361

10. Copy the table below and put a tick (✓) in the correct box in each row to show whether each statement is always true, sometimes true, or never true. Justify your answer in each case.

	Statement	Always true	Sometimes true	Never true
(i)	If two angles in a triangle are equal, the triangles are congruent.			
(ii)	If two triangles are congruent, then their corresponding sides are equal in length.			
(iii)	Angle-angle-angle (AAA) is a condition for congruency.			
(iv)	An isosceles triangle and a scalene triangle can be congruent to each other			
(v)	If two triangles are equilateral, then they are congruent to each other.			
(vi)	Right-angled triangles are congruent to each other.			

11. Given the isosceles triangle XYZ opposite, where $|XY| = |YZ|$ and W is the midpoint of $|XZ|$, show that $\triangle WXY$ is congrugent to $\triangle WZY$ by:

(i) side-side-side (SSS)

(ii) side-angle-side (SAS)

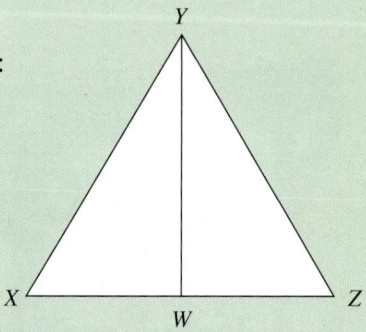

Taking it FURTHER

12. The triangle ABC is shown on the right. Find the value of x, given the traingles ACR and ABR are congruent.

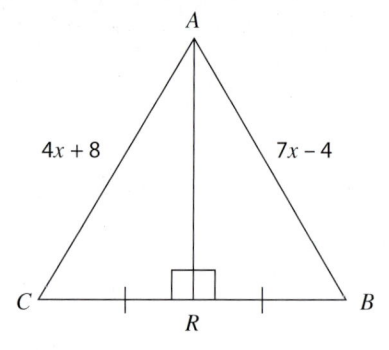

13. Mark constructs a triangle using an online geometry tool. He tells Alice that his triangle has an angle of 49° and sides of lengths 3·6 cm and 7·1 cm.

With only this information, will Alice be able to construct a triangle that is congruent to Mark's triangle?

22.3 Pythagoras's theorem

By the end of this section you should be able to:
- understand Pythagoras's theorem and its converse
- use Pythagoras's theorem to find unknown sides
- use Pythagoras's theorem to prove that a given triangle is right-angled

Discuss and discover

KEY SKILLS

Investigate the relationship between the sides of a right-angled triangle:

(i) Working with a classmate, draw the right-angled triangle on the right.
(ii) Square the value on each of the sides.
(iii) Add the squares of the two smaller sides.
(iv) Compare the sum of the squares to the square of the longest side. What do you notice?
(v) Draw another two right-angled triangles, measure the lengths of each of the sides and repeat steps (ii) to (iv) for each triangle.
(vi) What can you conclude about the sides of a right-angled triangle?

5 cm, 3 cm, 4 cm

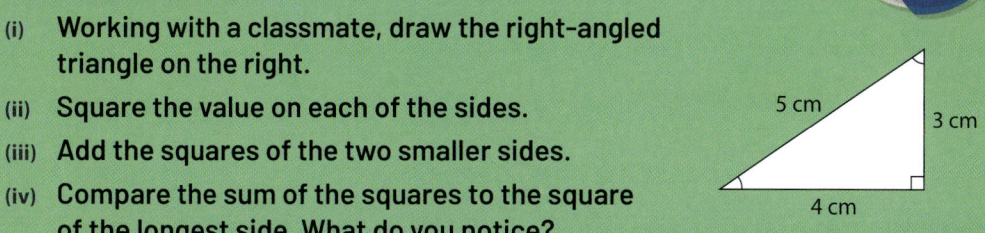

Theorem 14: In a right-angled triangle, the square of the hypotenuse is equal to the sum of the squares of the other two sides.

This theorem shows a relationship between the sides of a right-angled triangle. It states that if we were to form squares from each side of the triangle, then the biggest square has the exact same area as the other two squares added together.

This is called **Pythagoras's theorem** and it can be written in one short equation:

$$c^2 = a^2 + b^2$$

where c is the hypotenuse (the **longest side** of the triangle) and a and b are the other two sides.

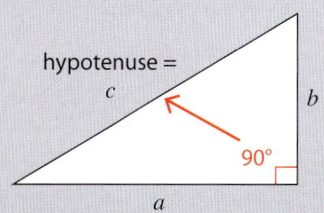

hypotenuse = c, b, 90°, a

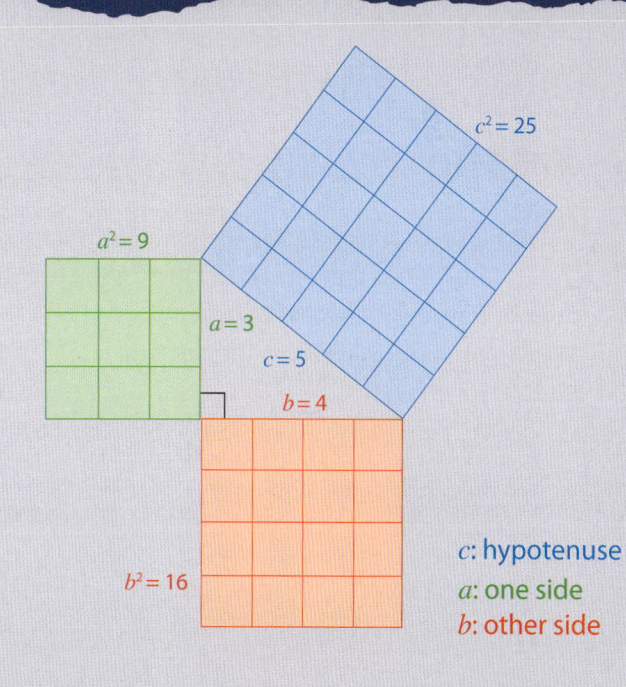

$a^2 = 9$, $a = 3$, $c = 5$, $b = 4$, $b^2 = 16$, $c^2 = 25$

c: hypotenuse
a: one side
b: other side

$c^2 = a^2 + b^2$
$(5)^2 = (3)^2 + (4)^2$
$25 = 9 + 16$

Pythagoras's theorem is in the *formulae and tables* booklet.
We will look at the proof of Pythagoras's theorem in Section C, Unit 34.

Finding the missing side of a right-angled triangle

1 Label the hypotenuse c and the other two sides a and b. It doesn't matter which you label a or b.

2 Write down the formula for Pythagoras's theorem.

3 Substitute the values for a, b, and c into the formula. $c^2 = a^2 + b^2$

4 Solve to find the unknown side.

> Remember, the hypotenuse is the longest side and is opposite the right angle.

Worked example 1

Find the length of the hypotenuse of this triangle.

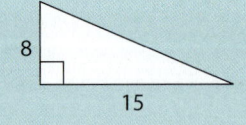

Solution

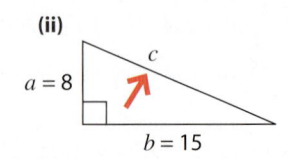

Step 1 Label the hypotenuse c. Label the other two sides a and b.
Step 2 Write down the formula $\qquad c^2 = a^2 + b^2$
Step 3 Fill in the formula $\qquad c^2 = 8^2 + 15^2$
Step 4 Solve to find the unknown side $\qquad c^2 = 64 + 225$
$\qquad c^2 = 289$
$\qquad c = \sqrt{289}$
$\qquad c = 17$

> To find c we do the opposite operation to 'squared', which is called 'getting the **square root**'.

Worked example 2

A 13 m ladder is placed against a wall and its base is 5 m from the wall, as shown. What height does the ladder reach on the wall?

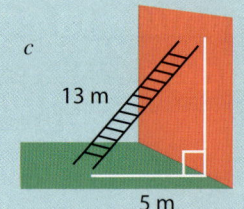

Solution

Step 1 In these types of real-life problems, we can assume that the wall and the ground are at right angles to each other.
This means that the ladder (13 m) is the hypotenuse. Label it c and the other two sides a and b.

Step 2 Write out Pythagoras's theorem $\qquad c^2 = a^2 + b^2$
Step 3 Insert the values from the diagram $\qquad 13^2 = a^2 + 5^2$
Step 4 Solve for a $\qquad 169 = a^2 + 25$
$\qquad 169 - 25 = a^2$
$\qquad 144 = a^2$
$\qquad \sqrt{144} = a$
$\qquad 12 = a$

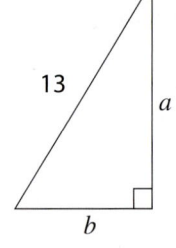

The height the ladder reaches on the wall is 12 m.

Theorem 15: Converse of Pythagoras's theorem –
If the square of one side of a triangle is the sum of the squares of the other two, then the angle opposite the first side is a right angle.

When the three sides of a triangle satisfy $c^2 = a^2 + b^2$, then the triangle is right-angled.

Investigating whether a triangle is right-angled

1. Label the sides of the triangle a, b and c. Remember c is the longest side.
2. Substitute the values of a, b and c in the Pythagoras formula.
3. Evaluate each side of the formula.
4. If the left-hand side (LHS) = the right-hand side (RHS) the triangle is right-angled.

Worked example 3

Investigate whether the following triangles are right-angled.

(i) Triangle LMN with $LM = 12$, $LN = 15$, $MN = 9$.

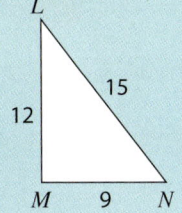

(ii) Triangle UVW with $UV = 7$, $UW = 11$, $VW = 6$.

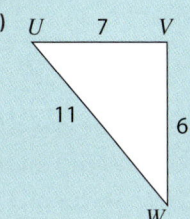

Solution

(i) **Step 1** $c = 15, a = 9, b = 12$
Step 2 $c^2 = a^2 + b^2$
$15^2 = 9^2 + 12^2$?
Step 3

LHS	RHS
225	81 + 144
225	225

Step 4 LHS = RHS, therefore the triangle is right-angled.

(ii) **Step 1** $c = 11, a = 7, b = 6$
Step 2 $c^2 = a^2 + b^2$
$11^2 = 7^2 + 6^2$?
Step 3

LHS	RHS
121	49 + 36
121	85

Step 4 LHS ≠ RHS, therefore the triangle is not right-angled.

Practice questions 22.3

1. Identify the hypotenuse in each of the following triangles. Justify your answer in each case.

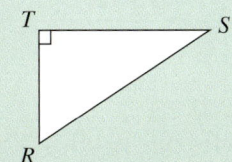

   (i) Triangle XYZ
   (ii) Triangle TRS
   (iii) Triangle SPQ

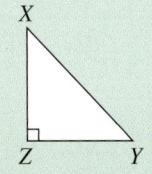

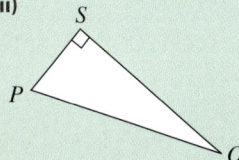

2. Find the length of the hypotenuse in each of the following right-angled triangles.

   (i) 4 cm, 3 cm
   (ii) 8 cm, 6 cm
   (iii) 8 m, 15 m
   (iv) 7 mm, 24 mm
   (v) 12 m, 35 m
   (vi) 63 mm, 16 mm

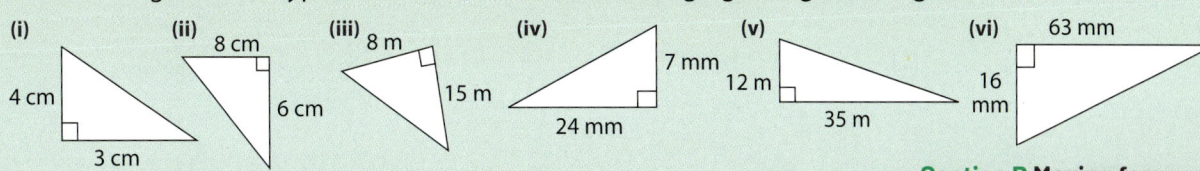

Section B Moving forward 365

3. Find the unknown side in each of the following right-angled triangles.

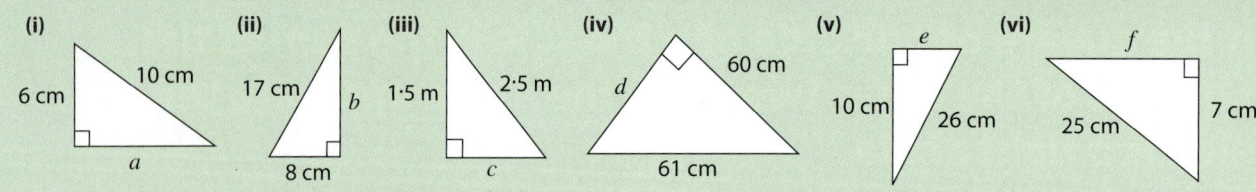

   (i) 6 cm, 10 cm, a
   (ii) 17 cm, 8 cm, b
   (iii) 1·5 m, 2·5 m, c
   (iv) 60 cm, 61 cm, d
   (v) 10 cm, 26 cm, e
   (vi) 25 cm, 7 cm, f

4. In each of the questions below you are given the lengths of the three sides of a triangle. Investigate whether each triangle is right-angled.

   (i) 9, 12, 15
   (ii) 4, 6, 8
   (iii) 10, 24, 26
   (iv) 7, 39, 40
   (v) 7, 24, 25
   (vi) 11, 12, 15

5. What is the length of the longest side of the sail of the boat shown on the right? (15 m, 20 m, ?)

6. Laptops, computers and televisions are often sold based on screen size. A 17-inch laptop means that the diagonal length of the screen is 17 inches, as shown. If the height of the screen is 8 inches, what is the width of the screen?

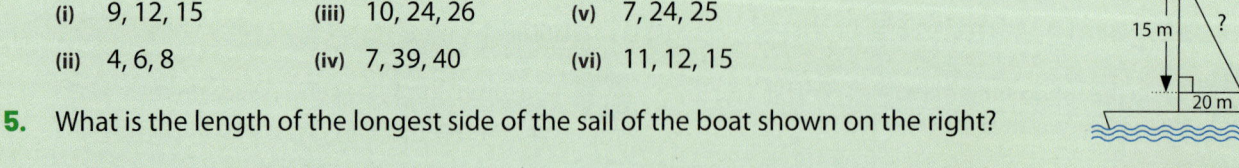

7. To perform the 'perfect dab', your extended arm should be at a right angle to your body. Calum performed a dab in which the measurements shown were recorded. He says it was a perfect dab.
   Do you agree with Calum? Justify your answer. (9, 40, 41)

Taking it FURTHER

8. For each of the parts below, draw a sketch of the situation and use it to help you find the answer to the question asked.

   (i) The bottom of a ladder must be placed 8 metres from a wall. The ladder is 17 metres long. How far above the ground does the ladder touch the wall?

   (ii) A training pitch is a rectangle 20 metres wide and 99 metres long. The coach asks players to run from one corner to the other corner diagonally across the pitch. What distance must the players run?

9. Copy the table below and put a tick (✓) in the correct box in each row to show whether each statement is always true, sometimes true, or never true. Justify your answer in each case.

	Statement	Always true	Sometimes true	Never true
(i)	The hypotenuse is opposite the right angle.			
(ii)	Pythagoras's theorem can be used to find an unknown side in a triangle.			
(iii)	The hypotenuse is the smallest side of a triangle.			
(iv)	If $c^2 = a^2 + b^2$, the triangle is a right-angled triangle, with c as the hypotenuse.			
(v)	The sides of an isosceles triangle satisfy Pythagoras's theorem.			

10. Two cyclists started at the same point. Cyclist A cycles due north at a constant speed of 20 km/h. Cyclist B cycles due east at a constant speed of 21 km/h. Calculate how far apart the cyclists are after 2 hours.

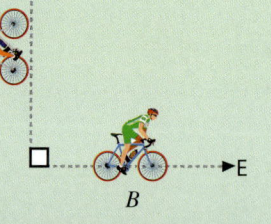

Revision questions

22A Core skills

1. Match the word on the left below with its definition on the right and rewrite them in your copybook.

Word	Definition
Theorem	Have the exact same shape and size
Converse	Statement that follows from a previous theorem
Axiom	Step-by-step explanation using axioms and theorems
Corollary	Used when a fact is proven by previous statements
Proof	A statement taken to be true without proof
Implies	Statement from axioms and theorems by logical argument
Congruent triangles	The reverse of a theorem

2. Show that the following pairs of triangles are congruent. Explain why they are congruent in each case.

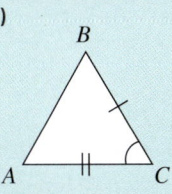

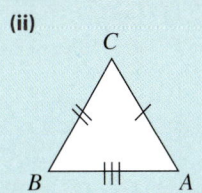

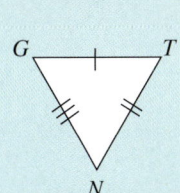

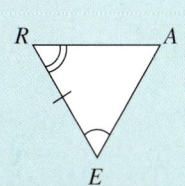

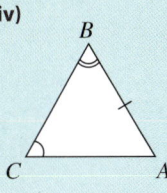

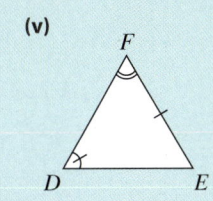

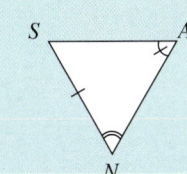

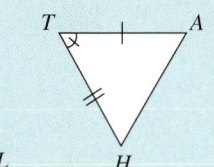

   (i) △ABC and △IWR

   (ii) △CBA and △GTN

   (iii) △JGH and △RAE

   (iv) △BCA and △STD

   (v) △FDE and △SAN

   (vi) △JKL and △TAH

3. Calculate the length of the missing side in each of the following right-angled triangles.

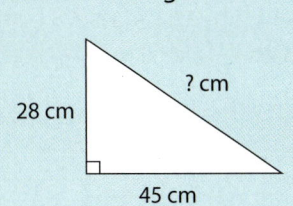

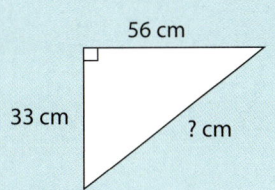

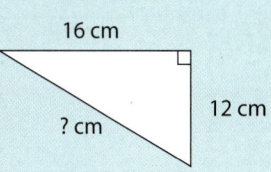

   (i) legs 28 cm and 45 cm, hypotenuse ? cm

   (ii) hypotenuse 56 cm, one leg 33 cm, other leg ? cm

   (iii) hypotenuse 16 cm, one leg 12 cm, other leg ? cm

4. Use Pythagoras's theorem to find the length of the unknown side in each of the following shapes.

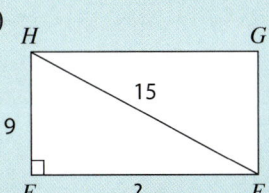

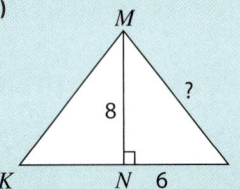

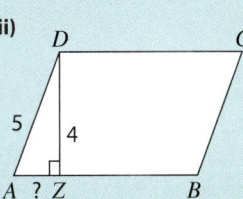

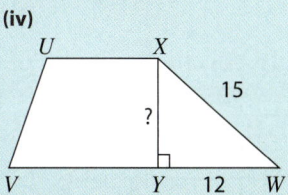

   (i) Rectangle EFGH, width 9, diagonal 15, length ?

   (ii) Triangle KML, MN = 8, NL = 6, ML = ?

   (iii) Parallelogram ABCD, DA = 5, AZ = 4, DZ = ?

   (iv) Trapezium UVWX, UX top, VY = 15, YW = 12, XY = ?

5. Investigate the following triangles to determine if they are right-angled or not.

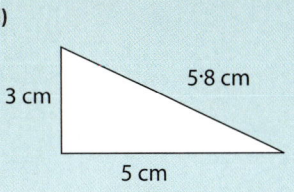

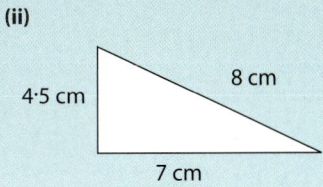

   (i) sides 3 cm, 5 cm, 5.8 cm

   (ii) sides 4.5 cm, 7 cm, 8 cm

6. Ethna makes a rectangular sandwich that is 12 cm long and 5 cm wide. If she cuts it in half diagonally, what is the length of the cut edge?

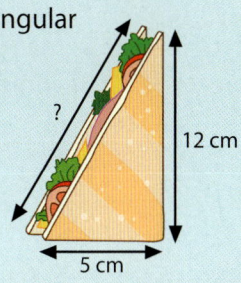

Section B Moving forward 367

7. Two boats started at the same point. After 2 hours, one boat had travelled 28 km due east. The other boat had travelled 45 km due north. How far apart are the boats at this time?

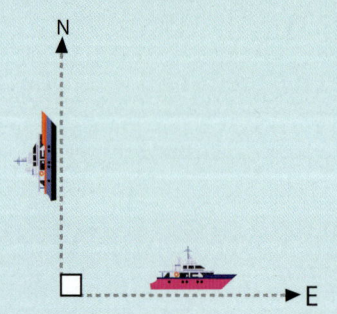

8. (i) Find $|BD|$
   (ii) Hence, find $|CD|$

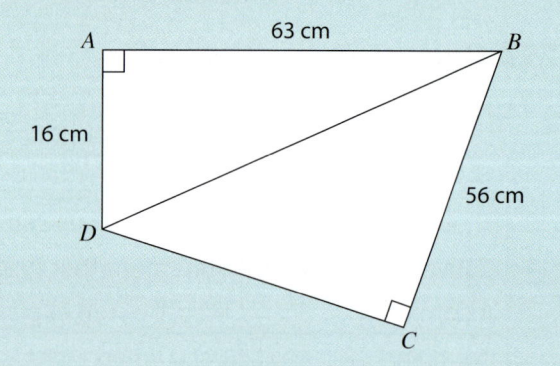

22B Taking it FURTHER

1. The triangle PQR is an isosceles triangle. PS is perpendicular to QR. Use congruent triangles to show that $|SQ| = |SR|$.

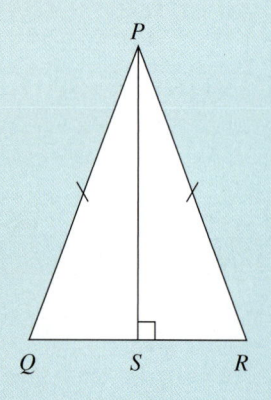

2. $PQRS$ is a rectangle.

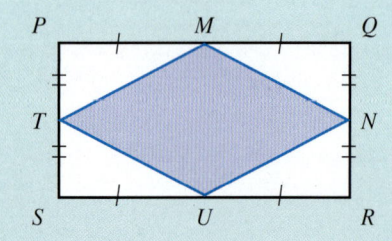

M is the midpoint of $[PQ]$, N is the midpoint of $[QR]$.
T is the midpoint of $[PS]$ and U is the midpoint of $[RS]$.

   (i) Show that the triangles PMT and RUN are congruent.
   (ii) Are the line segments $[TM]$ and $[UN]$ equal? Justify your answer.
   (iii) Is the triangle STU congruent to the triangle RNU? Justify your answer.

3. $ABCD$ is a kite.
$|AB| = |AD|$ and $|BC| = |CD|$
   (i) Show that triangles ABC and ADC are congruent. 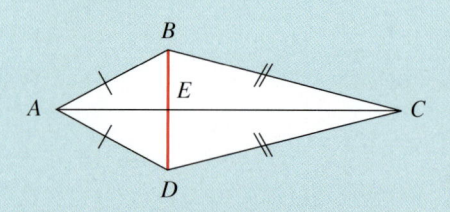
   (ii) The line joining B to D meets the diagonal AC at E and BD is perpendicular to AC. Explain why triangles ABE and ADE are congruent.

4. A town council wants to put a skateboard ramp into a local park.
   (i) If the ramp has the dimensions shown below, calculate the length, to the nearest metre, of the ramp along the ground.
   (ii) If Becky travels at an average speed of 4 m/s, how long will it take her to travel from the top to the bottom of the ramp?

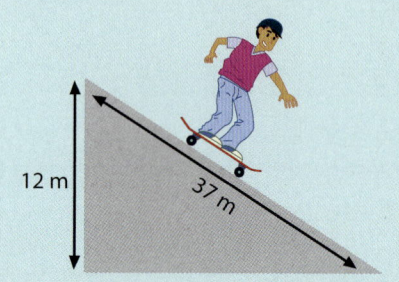

368   Linking Thinking 1

5. An airport radar spots a helicopter approaching the tower in a direct line. It is 17 km from the tower and 8 km ground distance away.

   What is the altitude (height) of the helicopter at this point?

6. A slide in a children's playground has dimensions as shown in the picture below.
   For health and safety reasons, the height of the slide cannot exceed 1·5 metres.
   Does the slide shown here meet health and safety requirements? Justify your answer.

   (2·31 m, 2 m)

7. The rectangle $PQRS$ represents the floor of a room.

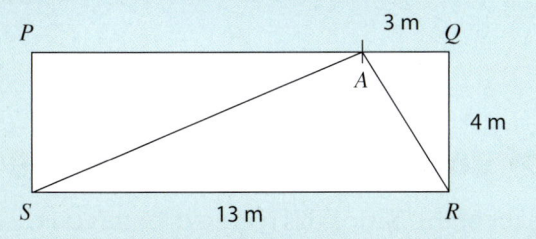

   (P, 3 m, Q, A, 4 m, S, 13 m, R)

   Ivor stands at point A. Calculate the distance between Ivor and:
   (i) the corner R of the room
   (ii) the corner S of the room.

8. Sharon went to a level field to fly a kite. She let out all 685 metres of the string and tied it to a stake. She then walked 684 m away from the stake until she was directly under the kite. The kite is flying high with its string tight.
   How high was the kite above the ground?
   Hint: Draw a sketch to represent the situation.

9. Draw a sketch to represent each of the following and use it to answer the question asked.

   (i) David leaves his house to walk to school. He walks 209 m west, and then turns and walks 120 m north. How far away, to the nearest metre, is he from his starting point?

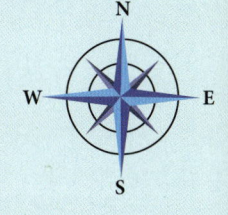

   (ii) The diagonal of a rectangle is 25 cm. The width is 15 cm. What is the length?

   (iii) How far from the base of the house do you need to place a 15-metre ladder so that it exactly reaches the top of a 12-metre-tall wall?

10. An electrical wire is attached at points A and B on two vertical poles standing on horizontal ground.

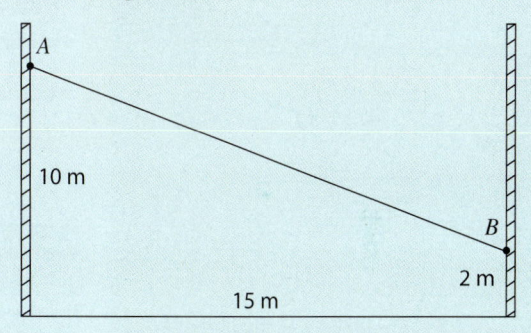

    Point A is 10 metres above the ground on one post.
    Point B is 2 metres above the ground on the other post.
    The horizontal distance between the two posts is 15 metres.
    Calculate the length of the electrical wire AB.

Something to think about ...

Now that you have completed the unit, revisit the question posed at the start of this unit.

Now try questions 4 and 15 on pages 404–10

Unit 23

Quadrilaterals and transformations

Topics covered within this unit:
- 23·1 Rectangles and squares
- 23·2 Compound shapes
- 23·3 Parallelograms: angles and sides
- 23·4 Parallelograms: diagonals bisecting
- 23·5 Transformations of objects

The Learning Outcomes covered in this unit are contained in the following sections:

GT.3c GT.3d GT.3b GT.6a GT.6b

Key words
Compound shape
Parallelogram
Rhombus
Equilateral
Regular polygon
Diagonal
Transformation
Object
Image
Translation
Axial symmetry
Central symmetry
Rotation

Something to think about ...

KEY SKILLS

A quadrilateral is a shape which has 4 straight sides. A quadrilateral can sometimes be called:

- a quadrangle ('four angles'), so it sounds like 'triangle'
- a tetragon ('four' + 'polygon'), so it sounds like 'pentagon, hexagon,' etc.

Consider a circle with twelve evenly-spaced dots around it, as in the diagram on the right.

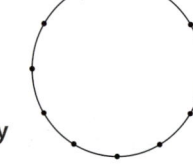

Redraw this circle.

How many different quadrilaterals can be made by joining the dots on the circle?

Name as many of the quadrilaterals you have drawn as you can.

23·1 Rectangles and squares

By the end of this section you should be able to:
- find the area and perimeter of a rectangle
- construct a rectangle

Revision of squares and rectangles

Unit 15 covered a lot of the basic skills required for this unit. Make sure you have a good understanding of Unit 15, as you will need those skills as you work through this unit.

Square

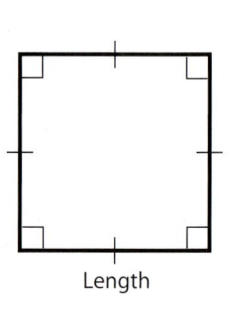

Four sides are equal in length

Opposite sides are parallel

All angles are right angles (90°)

Perimeter = length + length + length + length
        = 4(length) = $4l$

Area = length × length = l^2

Has four axes of symmetry

Length

Rectangle

Opposite sides (red sides, blue sides, below) are equal. Opposite sides are parallel

All angles are right angles (90°)

Perimeter = length + width + length + width
= 2(length) + 2(width)

Area = length × width

Has two axes of symmetry

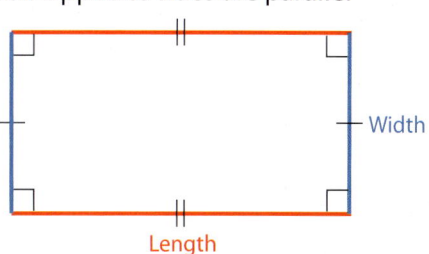

Worked example 1

Find the missing dimension of the rectangle shown, given an area of 275 cm².

Solution

Area of rectangle = $l \times w$

Let length = x cm and the width = 11 cm

$275 = x \times 11$

$\frac{275}{11} = \frac{11x}{11}$ (divide both sides by 11)

$25 = x$

25 cm = length

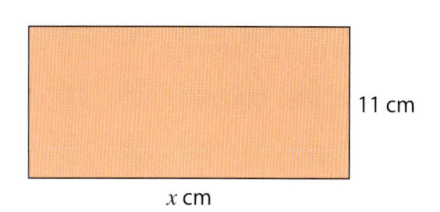

Worked example 2

The rectangle shown has perimeter of 140 cm. The width of the rectangle is 10 cm.
Find area of the rectangle.

Solution

First find the length then find the area.

Perimeter = 2(length) + 2(width)

Let length = x cm and the width = 10 cm

$140 = 2(x) + 2(10)$

$140 = 2x + 20$

$140 - 20 = 2x$ (subtract 20 from both sides)

$120 = 2x$

$\frac{120}{2} = \frac{2x}{2}$ (divide both sides by 12)

$60 = x$

Length = 60 cm

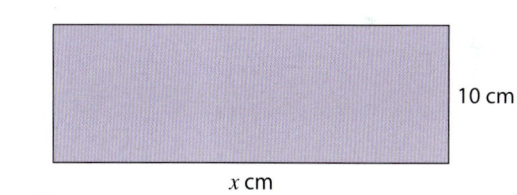

Area = length × width

Area = 10 × 60

Area = 600 cm²

Practice questions 23·1

1. Using the rough sketches below, construct the following rectangles and mark in the axis of symmetry in each of the constructions using a dashed line.

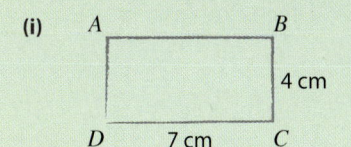

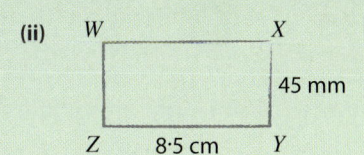

   (i) ABCD: AB = 7 cm, BC = 4 cm

   (ii) WXYZ: WX = 8.5 cm, XY = 45 mm

   Recall how to construct a rectangle from Unit 15.

2. (i) Construct rectangle MNOP, where $|MN| = 9.5$ cm and $|NO| = 6.5$ cm.
   (ii) Find the perimeter and the area of this rectangle.

3. (i) Construct rectangle PQRS, where $|PQ| = 100$ mm and $|QR| = 5$ cm.
   (ii) Find the perimeter and the area of this rectangle.

4. (i) Construct rectangle ABCD, where $|AB| = 11$ cm and $|BC| = 60$ mm.
   (ii) Find the perimeter and the area of this rectangle.

5. Find the perimeter and the area enclosed by each of the following quadrilaterals.
   (i) 5 cm, 3 cm
   (ii) 4 cm, 4 cm
   (iii) 6 cm, 1 cm
   (iv) 57 mm, 54 mm
   (v) 8·5 m, 435 cm
   (vi) 1 km, 1 000 m

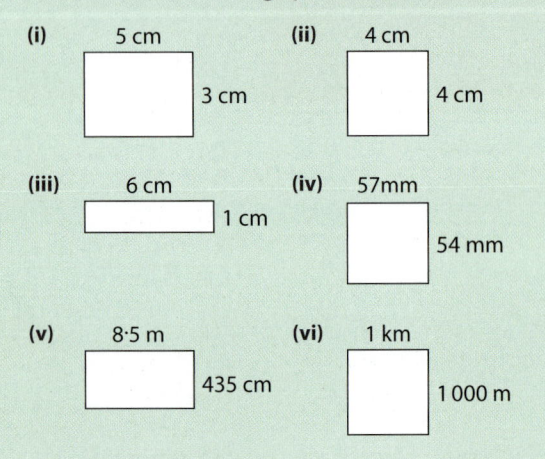

6. Find the missing dimension (x) of the rectangle shown, given an area of 231 cm². (11 mm, x cm)

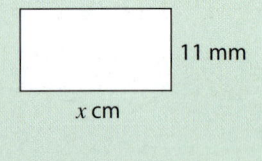

7. Find the missing dimension (x) of the rectangle shown, given an area of 480 cm². (20 cm, x cm)

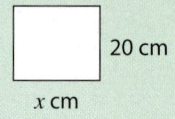

8. The rectangle on the right has an area of 65 cm². Find the value of y. (Area 65 cm², 5 cm, y)

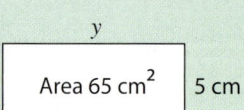

9. The rectangle shown has an area of 36 cm². This rectangle has length 9 cm and width 4 cm. Write down the length and width of two other rectangles with an area of 36 cm². (length 9 cm, 4 cm width)

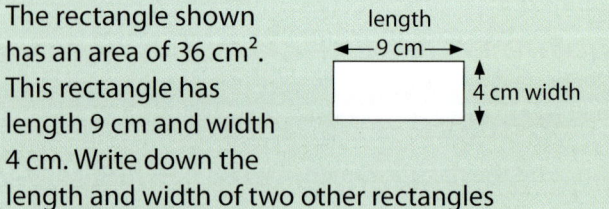

10. The diagram shows a square and a rectangle. The square and rectangle have the same area. Find y. (8 cm, 16 cm, y)

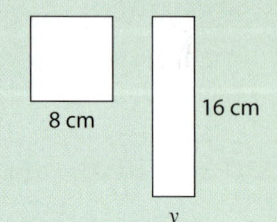

11. Find the length of the side of a square, given that its perimeter is 44 cm.

12. A square has a perimeter of 31·6 cm. Find the length of a side of the square.

13. A rectangle has a perimeter of 86 cm and a width of 14 cm. Find its length.

14. A rectangle has a perimeter of 100 cm and a length of 30 cm. Find its width.

23·2 Compound shapes

By the end of this section you should be able to:
- find the area and perimeter of a triangle
- find the area and perimeter of compound shapes

A **compound shape** is a shape that is made up from other simple shapes.

Finding the perimeter and area of a compound shape

1 Divide your shape into simple shapes (squares, rectangles, triangles). This can often be done in different ways.

2 Work out the missing lengths around the edge of the compound shape.

3 Add all exterior lengths to find the perimeter.

4 Work out the area of each simple shape.

5 Add the areas of the simple shapes together to give the total area of the compound shape.

Linking Thinking 1

Often a compound shape will involve a triangular part. Recall how to work with triangles.

The **area** of the triangle is half of base (b) times perpendicular height or altitude (h).

Which can be written

$$\text{Area of triangle} = \frac{1}{2}[b \times \perp h]$$

The symbol $\perp$ means perpendicular.

The **perimeter** of a triangle is the sum of the three sides.

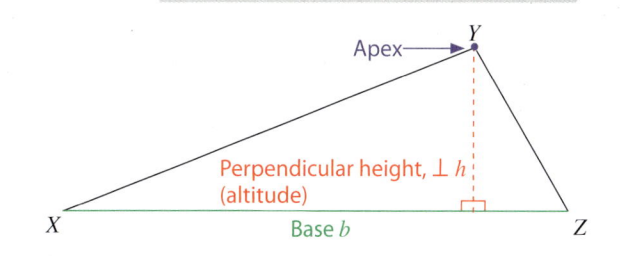

Worked example

Find the perimeter and area of the compound shape on the right.

Solution

Step 1 Find all missing lengths and change to same unit.

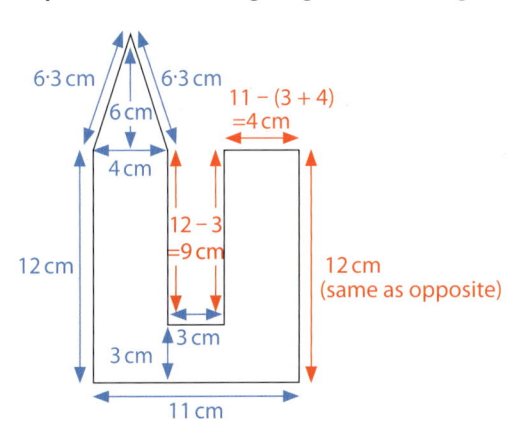

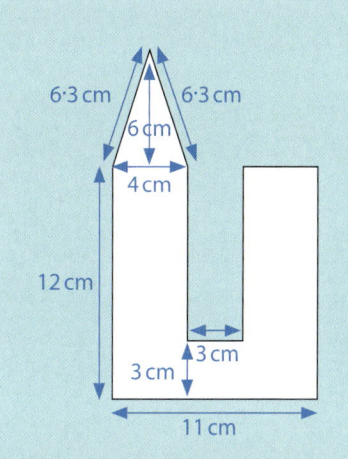

Make sure all dimensions are in the same units, in this case cm.

Step 2 Add up the lengths of all the sides to find the perimeter.
Perimeter of compound shape = 12 + 6·3 + 6·3 + 9 + 3 + 9 + 4 + 12 + 11
Perimeter of compound shape = 72·6 cm

Step 3 To find the area, split the compound shape into simple shapes.

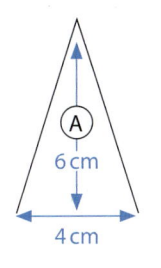

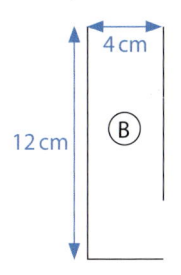

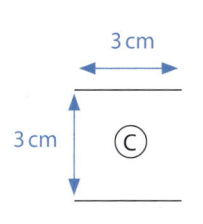

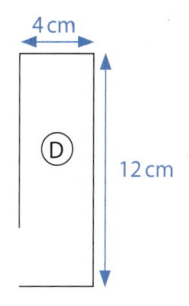

Step 4 Find the area of each simple shape.

Triangle A
Area of triangle = $\frac{1}{2} b \times \perp h$
Area of triangle = $\frac{1}{2}(4)(6)$
Area of triangle = $\frac{1}{2}(24)$
Area of triangle = 12 cm²

Rectangle B
Area of rectangle = $l \times w$
Area of rectangle = 4 × 12
Area of rectangle = 48 cm²

Square C
Area of square = $l \times l$
Area of square = 3 × 3
Area of square = 9 cm²

Rectangle D
Area of rectangle = $l \times w$
Area of rectangle = 4 × 12
Area of rectangle = 48 cm²

Step 5 Add the areas of the simple shapes together to give the total area of the compound shape.

Total area of compound shape = 12 + 48 + 9 + 48
Total area of compound shape = 117 cm²

It is important to give the answer in the correct units.

Section B Moving forward

Practice questions 23·2

1. A rectangle is 3 cm by 6 cm. Six of these rectangles are used to make a larger rectangle as shown on the right. Find the area of the larger rectangle.

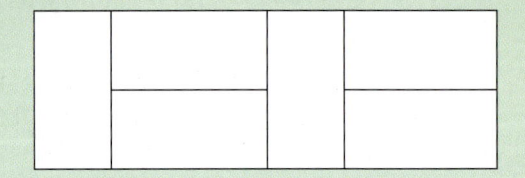

2. Find (a) the perimeter and (b) the area of the following compound shapes.

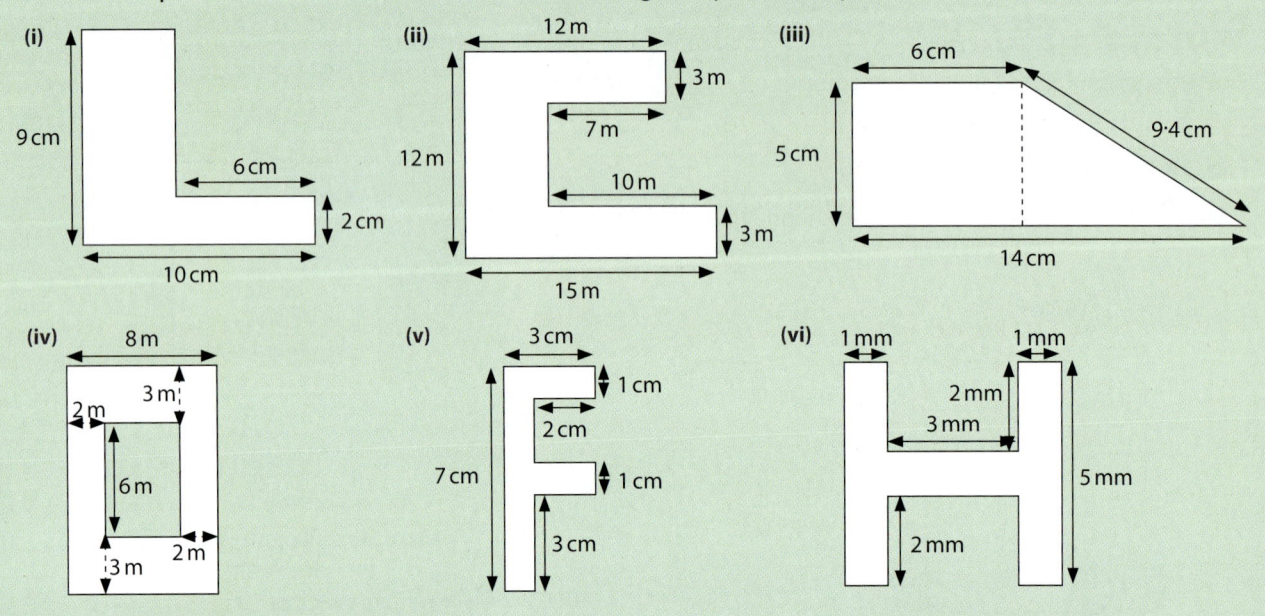

   (i) 9 cm, 6 cm, 2 cm, 10 cm

   (ii) 12 m, 3 m, 7 m, 12 m, 10 m, 3 m, 15 m

   (iii) 6 cm, 9·4 cm, 5 cm, 14 cm

   (iv) 8 m, 3 m, 2 m, 6 m, 2 m, 3 m

   (v) 3 cm, 1 cm, 2 cm, 7 cm, 1 cm, 3 cm

   (vi) 1 mm, 1 mm, 2 mm, 3 mm, 5 mm, 2 mm

3. Find (a) the perimeter and (b) the area of the shaded regions of the following compound shapes.

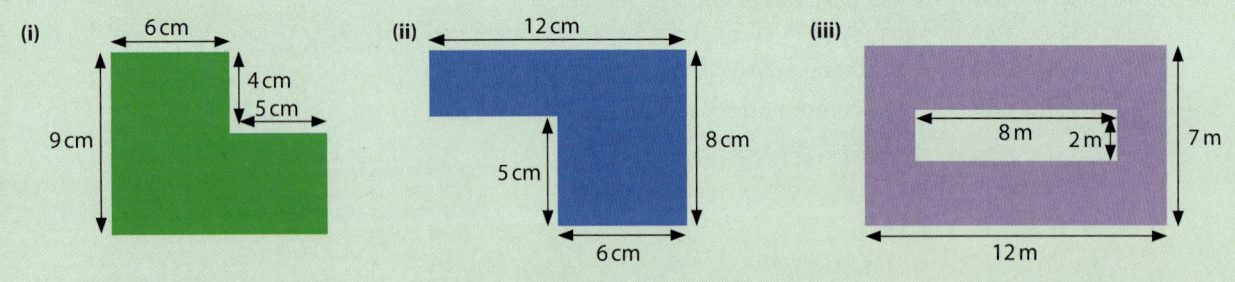

   (i) 6 cm, 4 cm, 5 cm, 9 cm

   (ii) 12 cm, 8 cm, 5 cm, 6 cm

   (iii) 8 m, 2 m, 7 m, 12 m

4. Find (a) the perimeter and (b) the area of the following compound shapes.

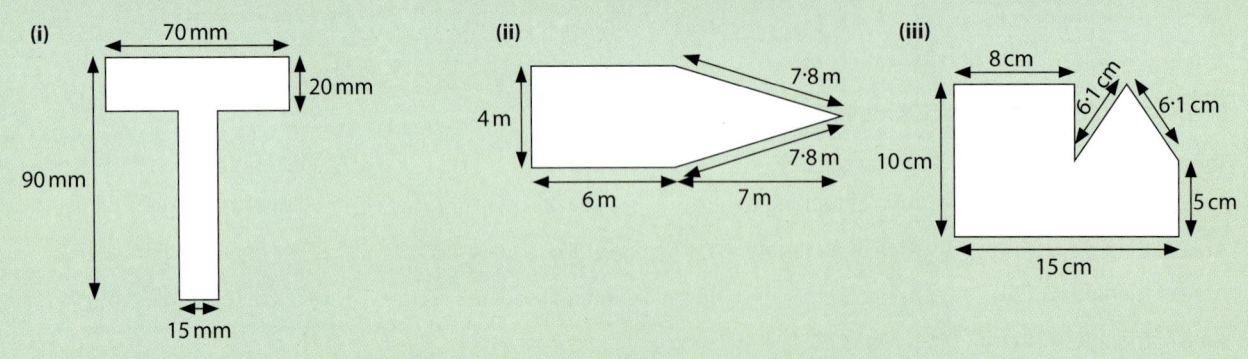

   (i) 70 mm, 20 mm, 90 mm, 15 mm

   (ii) 7·8 m, 4 m, 7·8 m, 6 m, 7 m

   (iii) 8 cm, 6·1 cm, 6·1 cm, 10 cm, 5 cm, 15 cm

5. Mrs Boyle is a chicken farmer. Her rectangular chicken pen is 18 m long and 8 m wide. Each chicken requires at least 3 m². What is the maximum number of chickens Mrs Boyle can keep?

23.3 Parallelograms: angles and sides

By the end of this section you should understand:
- what a rhombus and parallelogram are
- that opposite angles in a parallelogram are equal to each other

In Unit 15, we learned that a **quadrilateral** has four-sides. It is two-dimensional (a flat shape), closed (the lines join up), and has straight sides.

A **polygon** is a two-dimensional shape with three or more sides.

> A **parallelogram** is a quadrilateral for which both pairs of opposite sides are parallel (and therefore, opposite angles equal).

> A **rhombus** is a quadrilateral with four equal sides. It is sometimes called a diamond.

You can identify what kind of quadrilateral you have using the following flow chart.

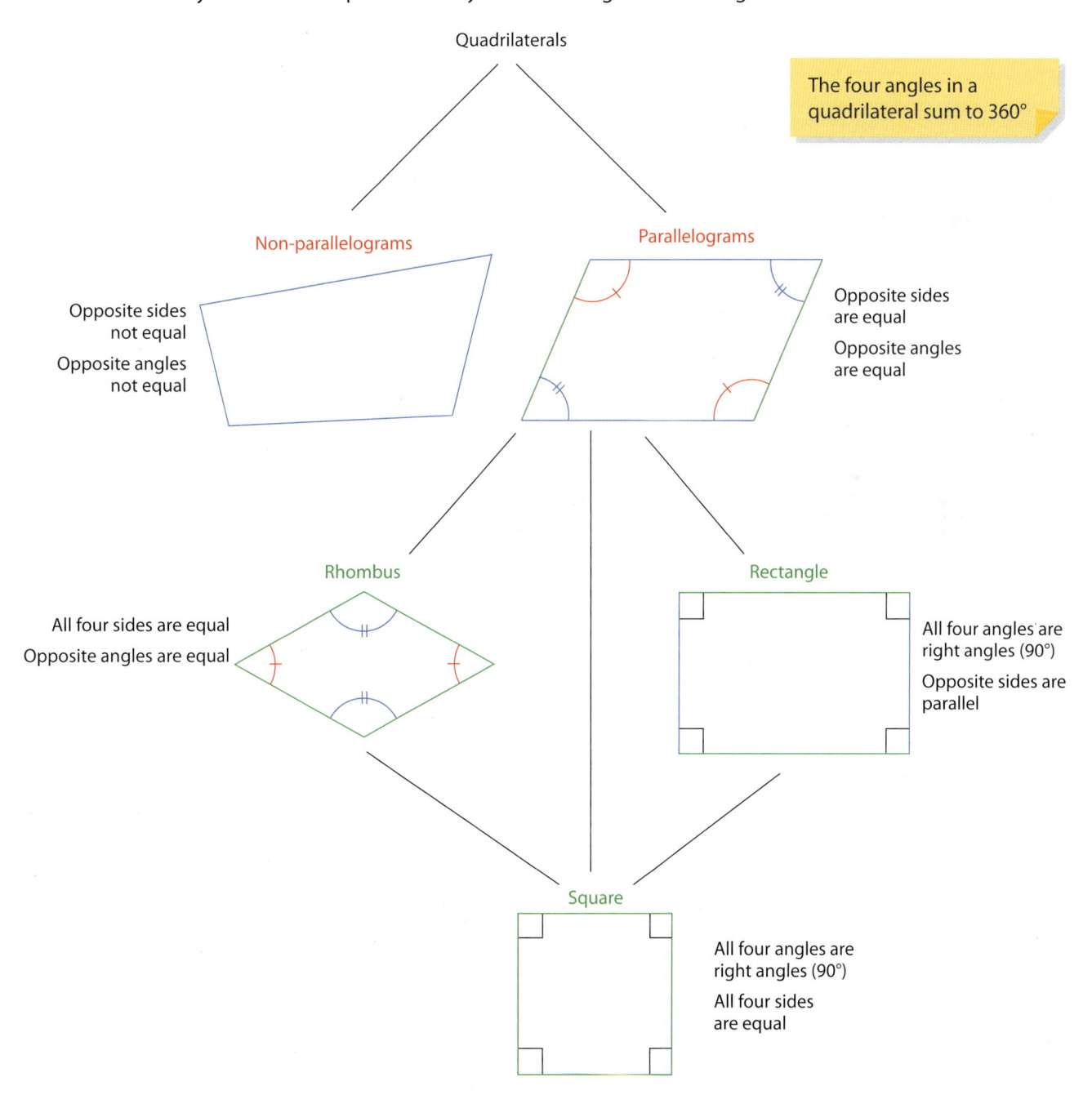

The four angles in a quadrilateral sum to 360°

Quadrilaterals

Non-parallelograms
- Opposite sides not equal
- Opposite angles not equal

Parallelograms
- Opposite sides are equal
- Opposite angles are equal

Rhombus
- All four sides are equal
- Opposite angles are equal

Rectangle
- All four angles are right angles (90°)
- Opposite sides are parallel

Square
- All four angles are right angles (90°)
- All four sides are equal

Section B Moving forward   375

The following Venn diagram shows how the different quadrilaterals relate to each other.

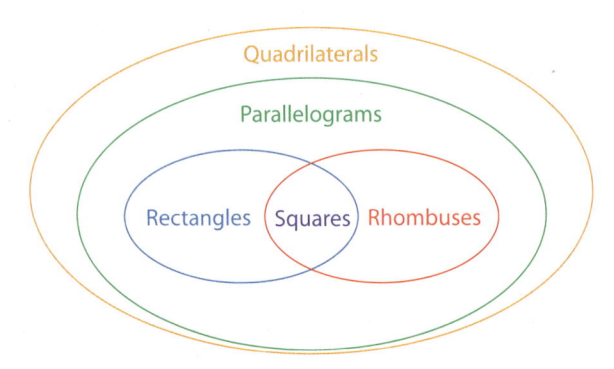

A square, rhombus and rectangle are also **parallelograms**.

A square also fits the definition of a **rectangle** (all angles are 90°) and a **rhombus** (all sides are equal length).

A polygon is **equilateral** if all its sides are equal. A square and a rhombus are equilateral polygons.

A **regular polygon** is a polygon where all sides are equal and all angles are equal, e.g. square, equilateral triangle.

Discuss and discover

Investigate the relationship between the opposite angles in a parallelogram.

(i) With a classmate, discuss what you already know about parallelograms.
(ii) Draw the parallelograms on the right.
(iii) Using a protractor, find the measure of each of the four interior angles. Find the sum of these angles.
(iv) What do you notice about opposite angles?
(v) What can you conclude about the opposite angles in a parallelogram?

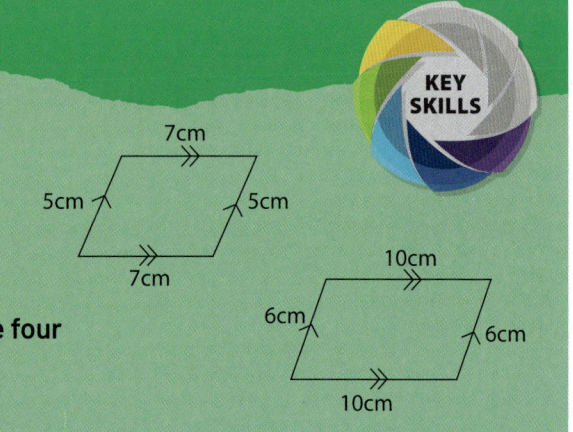

Theorem 9: In a parallelogram, opposite sides are equal and opposite angles are equal

In the diagram on the right:

$|AB| = |DC|$

$|AD| = |BC|$

and:

$|\angle BAD| = |\angle BCD|$

$|\angle ABC| = |\angle ADC|$

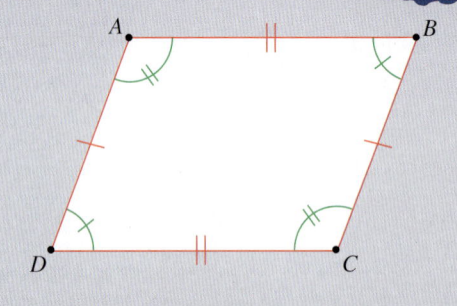

The full formal proofs are **not examinable** for Junior Cycle Mathematics, but you should be able to display understanding of the proofs.

Proof of Theorem 9

The proof uses the alternate angle theorem to show that a diagonal divides the parallelogram into two congruent (identical) triangles. This gives opposite sides and (one pair of) opposite angles equal.

Linking Thinking 1

1 Let $ABCD$ be a parallelogram, where $AB \parallel CD$ and $AD \parallel BC$

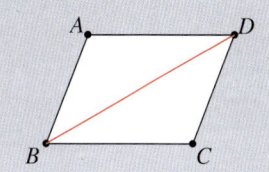

2 Draw a diagonal line from B to D.

> A **diagonal** is a line segment joining two vertices of a polygon, when those vertices are not on the same edge.

3 $AD \parallel BC$
Therefore BD is a transversal and
$|\angle ABD| = |\angle BDC|$ (alternate angles)
$|\angle ADB| = |\angle DBC|$ (alternate angles)

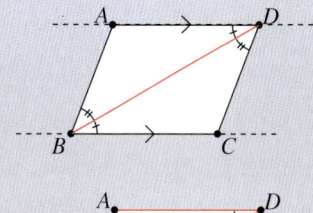

4 Look at triangle 1, $\triangle ABD$ and triangle 2 $\triangle BCD$
The diagonal drawn in step 2 is a common side to both triangles
$|\angle ABD| = |\angle BDC|$ and $|\angle ADB| = |\angle DBC|$ from step 3.

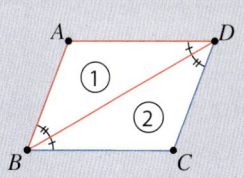

5 From step 4, we can say that the two triangles are congruent (identical) by angle-side-angle (ASA).
Therefore, in the parallelogram
$|AB| = |CD|$ (opposite sides are equal)
$|AD| = |BC|$ (opposite sides are equal)
$|\angle DAB| = |\angle BCD|$ (opposite angles are equal)

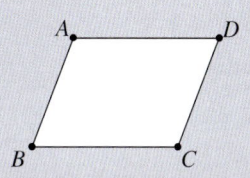

Converse 1 of Theorem 9: If the opposite angles of a quadrilateral are equal, then it is a parallelogram.

Converse 2 to Theorem 9: If the opposite sides of a quadrilateral are equal, then it is a parallelogram.

Worked example

Find the values of A and B and the length of the sides marked x and y in each if the following diagrams. Justify each of you answers using an axiom or theorem or corollary used to find the answer.

(i) [diagram: parallelogram with 14 cm, 120°, 60°, x, 12 cm, A, B, y]

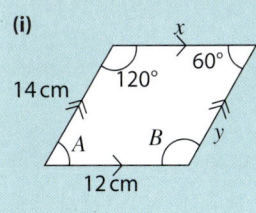

(ii) [diagram: parallelogram with y, 115°, A, 9 cm, x, B, 65°, 8 cm]

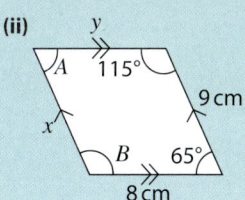

(iii) [diagram: parallelogram with x, 58°, 122°, y, 21 m, 4B+6, 6A+4, 8 m]

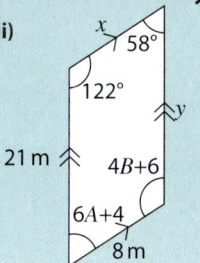

(iv) [diagram: photo with 75 m, x, B, 130°, A, y, 300 m]

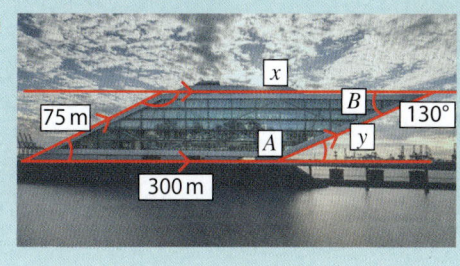

Solution

(i) $A = 60°$ (opposite angles in a parallelogram)
$B = 120°$ (opposite angles in a parallelogram)
$x = 12$ cm (opposite sides in a parallelogram)
$y = 14$ cm (opposite sides in a parallelogram)

(iii) $6A + 4 = 58°$ $4B + 6 = 122°$
$6A = 58 - 4$ $4B = 122 - 6$
$6A = 54$ $4B = 116$
$\frac{6A}{6} = \frac{54}{6}$ $\frac{4B}{4} = \frac{116}{4}$
$A = 9°$ $B = 29°$
$x = 8$ cm (opposite sides in a parallelogram)
$y = 21$ cm (opposite sides in a parallelogram)

(ii) $A = 65°$ (opposite angles in a parallelogram)
$B = 115°$ (opposite angles in a parallelogram)
$x = 9$ cm (opposite sides in a parallelogram)
$y = 8$ cm (opposite sides in a parallelogram)

(iv) $A = 130°$ (corresponding angles)
$B = 50°$ (supplementary angles)
$x = 300$ m (opposite sides in a parallelogram)
$y = 75$ cm (opposite sides in a parallelogram)

Practice questions 23·3

1. If a parallelogram is not a rectangle, how many right angles does it have?

2. Which one of the following statements is false?
   (a) A parallelogram can also be a rhombus.
   (b) A parallelogram can also be a rectangle.
   (c) A parallelogram can also be a square.
   (d) A parallelogram can also be a triangle.

3. ABCD is a parallelogram with two adjacent (beside each other) angles A and B equal to each other. Which of the following terms could be used to represent ABCD?
   (a) Rhombus
   (b) Triangle
   (c) Rectangle
   (d) None of these

4. For each of the following diagrams, write down if they represent a real parallelogram. Justify your answer in each case.

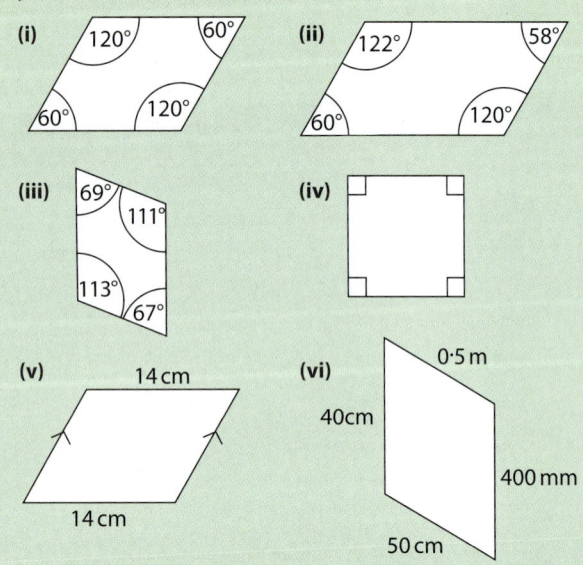

   (i) 120°, 60°, 60°, 120°
   (ii) 122°, 58°, 60°, 120°
   (iii) 69°, 111°, 113°, 67°
   (iv) [square with right angles]
   (v) 14 cm, 14 cm
   (vi) 0.5 m, 40 cm, 400 mm, 50 cm

5. For the parallelograms below, find the measure of the angles marked A and B. Justify your answer by stating the axiom, theorem, or corollary used.

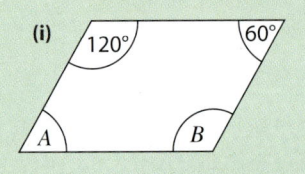

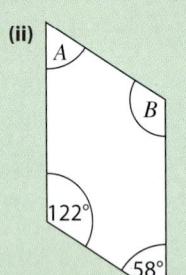

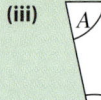

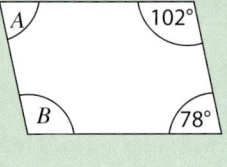

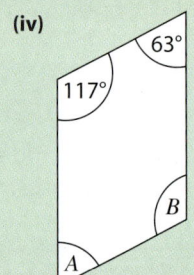

   (i) 120°, 60°, A, B
   (ii) A, B, 122°, 58°
   (iii) A, 102°, B, 78°
   (iv) 63°, 117°, B, A

6. Each square in the diagram shown has an area of 1 cm². How many ways can you find the area of the parallelogram in red without using a ruler or protractor? (Diagram not to scale)

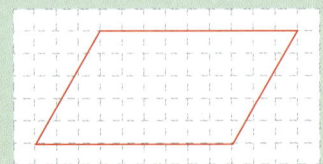

7. Find the value of x and the value of y in the following diagrams.

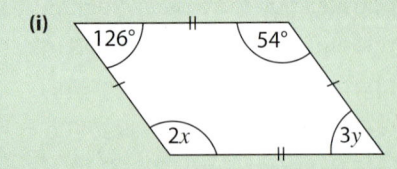

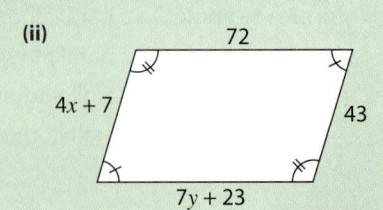

   (i) 126°, 54°, $2x$, $3y$
   (ii) 72, $4x + 7$, 43, $7y + 23$

8. The diagram on the right shows the treads of a tire that is made up of parallelogram shapes. Find the measure of the angles labelled A to D.

9. A parallelogram has side lengths in the ratio 3 : 4 and perimeter 280 cm. Determine the lengths of the sides.

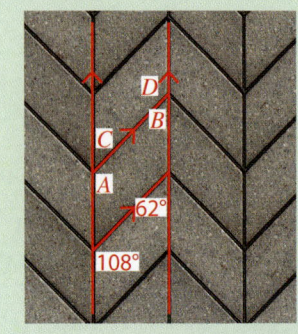

62°, 108°

10. Copy and complete the table below. Justify your answers by stating the theorem, axiom or corollary used in each case.

	Statement	True/False	Justify
(i)	The diagonals of a parallelogram are equal.		
(ii)	The diagonals of a rhombus are equal.		
(iii)	Every rectangle is a square.		
(iv)	Every square is a parallelogram.		
(v)	Every square is a rhombus.		
(vi)	Every rectangle is a parallelogram.		
(vii)	Every parallelogram is a rectangle.		
(viii)	Every rhombus is a parallelogram.		

11. Shown on the right is a diagram used as part of the proof for the theorem which states: In a parallelogram, opposite sides are equal and opposite angles are equal.

    Look at triangle 1, $\triangle ABD$ and triangle 2, $\triangle BCD$.

    Indicate the sides and angles that can be used to show triangle 1 and triangle 2 are congruent.

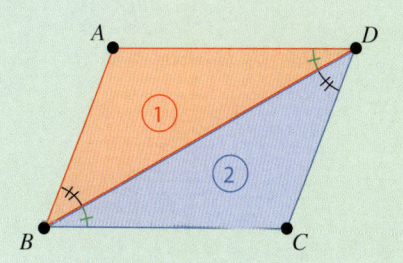

23.4 Parallelograms: diagonals bisecting

By the end of this section you should understand:
- that the diagonals of a parallelogram bisect one another

Discuss and discover

Investigate the diagonals in a parallelogram.

(i) Working with a classmate, discuss what you already know about parallelograms.

(ii) Draw a parallelogram.

(iii) Using a ruler, draw two diagonal lines as shown in red above.

(iv) Measure the length of one diagonal from one corner to where it crosses the other diagonal. Then measure the length on the same diagonal from the centre to the other corner.

(v) What do you notice about the length from the point where the diagonals cross to the corners on each diagonal?

(vi) Repeat this investigation by drawing two more parallelograms with diagonals drawn on them.

(vii) What have you learned about the diagonals of a parallelogram from this task?

Theorem 10: The diagonals of a parallelogram bisect one another

On the diagram to the right, AC bisects BD and BD bisects AC.
This means that:

$|AE| = |EC|$
$|BE| = |ED|$

> 'To bisect' means to divide into two equal parts.

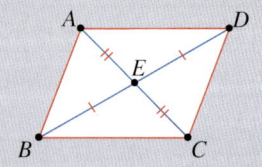

Proof of Theorem 10

The diagonals of a parallelogram bisect one another.

1 Let $ABCD$ be a parallelogram with $AB \parallel CD$ and $AD \parallel BC$

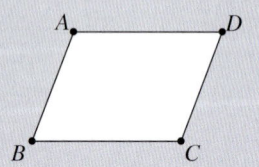

2 Draw a diagonal line from A to C and a diagonal line from B to D. Let AC intersect BD at E.

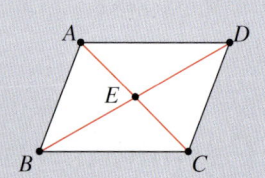

3 $|AD| = |BC|$ (opposite sides of a parallelogram)

$AD \parallel BC$
Therefore, AC is a transversal and
$|\angle EAD| = |\angle ECB|$ (alternate angles)

Therefore, DB is a transversal and
$|\angle EDA| = |\angle EBC|$ (alternate angles)

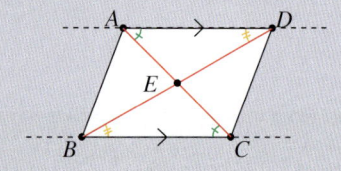

4 Look at triangle 1 $\triangle ADE$ and triangle 2 $\triangle BCE$.
From step 3: $|AD| = |BC|$
$|\angle EAD| = |\angle ECB|$
$|\angle EDA| = |\angle EBC|$

Therefore, triangle 1 $\triangle ADE$ and triangle 2 $\triangle BCE$ are identical (congruent) by angle-side-angle (ASA).

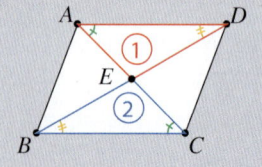

5 Since the triangles are congruent,
$|AE| = |EC|$ (corresponding sides are equal) AC bisected
$|BE| = |ED|$ (corresponding sides are equal) BD bisected
The diagonals of a parallelogram bisect each other.

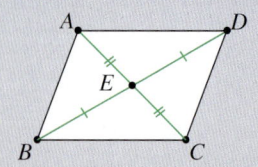

> The full formal proofs are not **examinable** for Junior Cycle Mathematics, but you should be able to display understanding of the proofs.

380   Linking Thinking 1

Worked example

Find the value of the unknown letters x and y in the following diagrams of parallelograms.

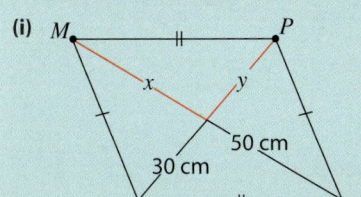

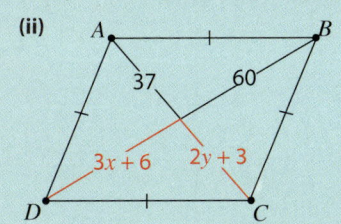

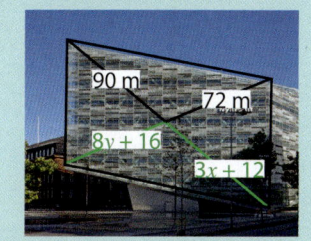

(i) Parallelogram MPON with diagonals, labelled x, y, 50 cm, 30 cm.

(ii) Parallelogram ABCD with diagonals labelled 37, 60, $3x+6$, $2y+3$.

(iii) Building diagram with 90 m, 72 m, $8y+16$, $3x+12$.

Solution

(i) $x = 50$ cm (half of a diagonal)
    $y = 30$ cm (half of a diagonal)

(ii) $3x + 6 = 60$ (half of a diagonal) $\qquad$ $2y + 3 = 37$ (half of a diagonal)
    $3x = 60 - 6$ (subtract 6 from both sides) $\qquad$ $2y = 37 - 3$ (subtract 3 from both sides)
    $3x = 54$ $\qquad\qquad$ $2y = 34$
    $\frac{3x}{3} = \frac{54}{3}$ (divide both sides by 3) $\qquad$ $\frac{2y}{2} = \frac{34}{2}$ (divide both sides by 2)
    $x = 18$ cm $\qquad\qquad$ $y = 17$ cm

(iii) $3x + 12 = 90$ (half of a diagonal) $\qquad$ $8y + 16 = 72$
    $3x = 90 - 12$ (subtract 12 from both sides) $\qquad$ $8y = 72 - 16$ (subtract 16 from both sides)
    $3x = 78$ $\qquad\qquad$ $8y = 56$
    $\frac{3x}{3} = \frac{78}{3}$ (divide both sides by 3) $\qquad$ $\frac{8y}{8} = \frac{56}{8}$ (divide both sides by 8)
    $x = 26$ $\qquad\qquad$ $y = 7$

Practice questions 23.4

1. For each of the following diagrams, write down if it is possible they represent a real parallelogram, justify for your answer in each case.

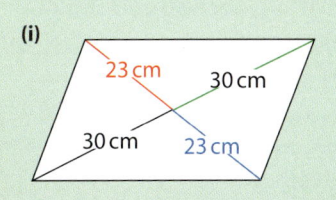

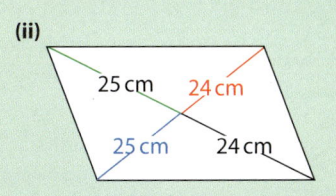

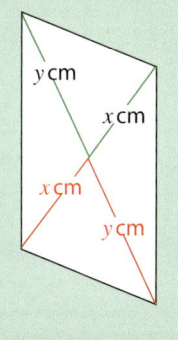

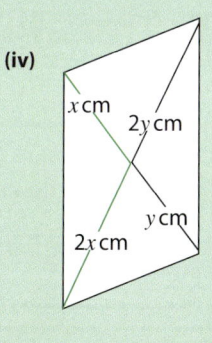

   (i) 23 cm, 30 cm, 30 cm, 23 cm

   (ii) 25 cm, 24 cm, 25 cm, 24 cm

   (iii) y cm, x cm, x cm, y cm

   (iv) x cm, $2y$ cm, $2x$ cm, y cm

2. Find the value of a and b in the following parallelograms. All units are in cm.

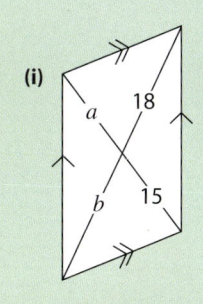

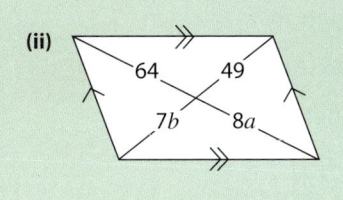

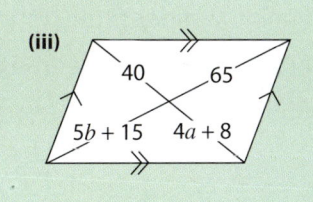

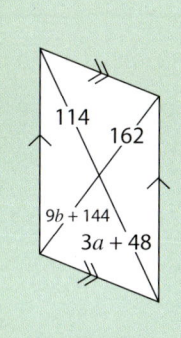

   (i) 18, a, b, 15

   (ii) 64, 49, $7b$, $8a$

   (iii) 40, 65, $5b + 15$, $4a + 8$

   (iv) 114, 162, $9b + 144$, $3a + 48$

3. By drawing and marking in the lines of symmetry, find the number of lines of symmetry in each of the parallelograms to the right.

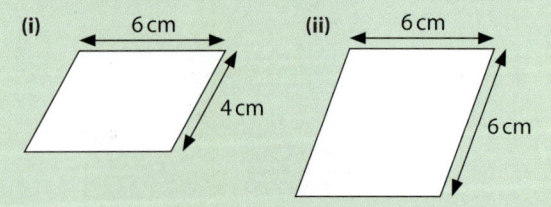

   (i) 6 cm, 4 cm

   (ii) 6 cm, 6 cm

4. Find the value of x and y in the following diagrams of parallelograms. All units are in metres.

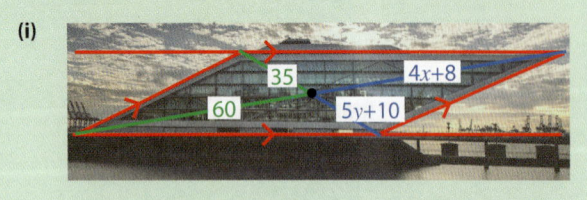

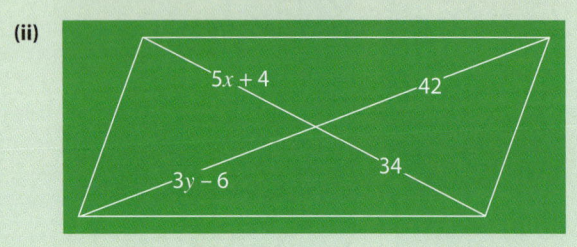

   (i) 35, 60, $4x+8$, $5y+10$

   (ii) $5x+4$, 42, $3y-6$, 34

5. Find the area of the shaded parallelograms in the diagrams below.

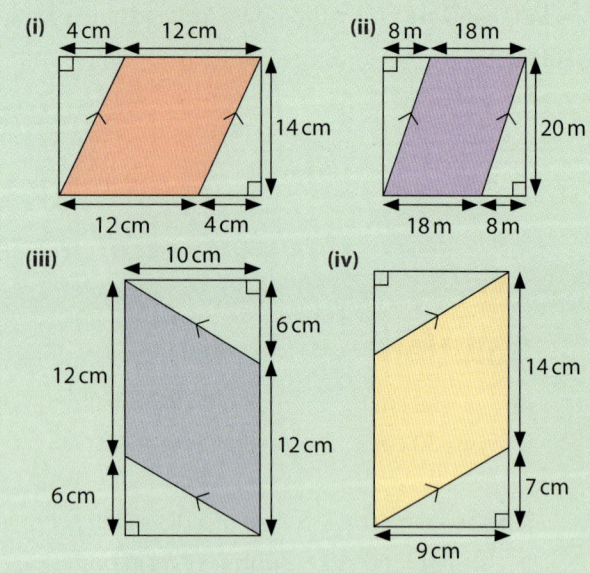

   (i) 4 cm, 12 cm, 14 cm, 12 cm, 4 cm

   (ii) 8 m, 18 m, 20 m, 18 m, 8 m

   (iii) 10 cm, 6 cm, 12 cm, 12 cm, 6 cm

   (iv) 14 cm, 7 cm, 9 cm

6. Shown below is a diagram used as part of the proof for the theorem which states:
   The diagonals of a parallelogram bisect one another.

   Look at triangle 1 $\triangle ADE$ and triangle 2 $\triangle BCE$.

   State why these triangles are congruent using angles and sides in your answer.

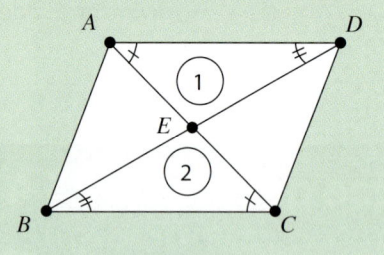

23.5 Transformations of objects

By the end of this section you should:
- understand the terms translation, central symmetry, axial symmetry and rotation
- be able to draw the image of objects under translation, central symmetry, axial symmetry and rotation

A **transformation** is a process which changes the position or the size and direction of a shape.

The **object** is the name given to the shape you start with.

The **image** is the name given to the shape after the transformation.

The point A' is the image of point A under some transformation.
The point B' is the image of point B under some transformation.
The point C' is the image of point C under some transformation.

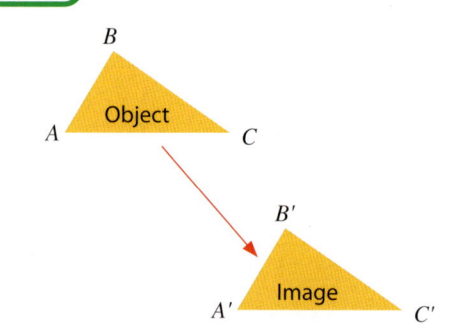

Types of transformation

1. Translation

Translation (also known as slide) moves a shape by sliding it up, down, sideways or diagonally, without turning it or making it bigger or smaller.

The F-shaped object below has three images shown. Images 1, 2, and 3 are all translations of the object.

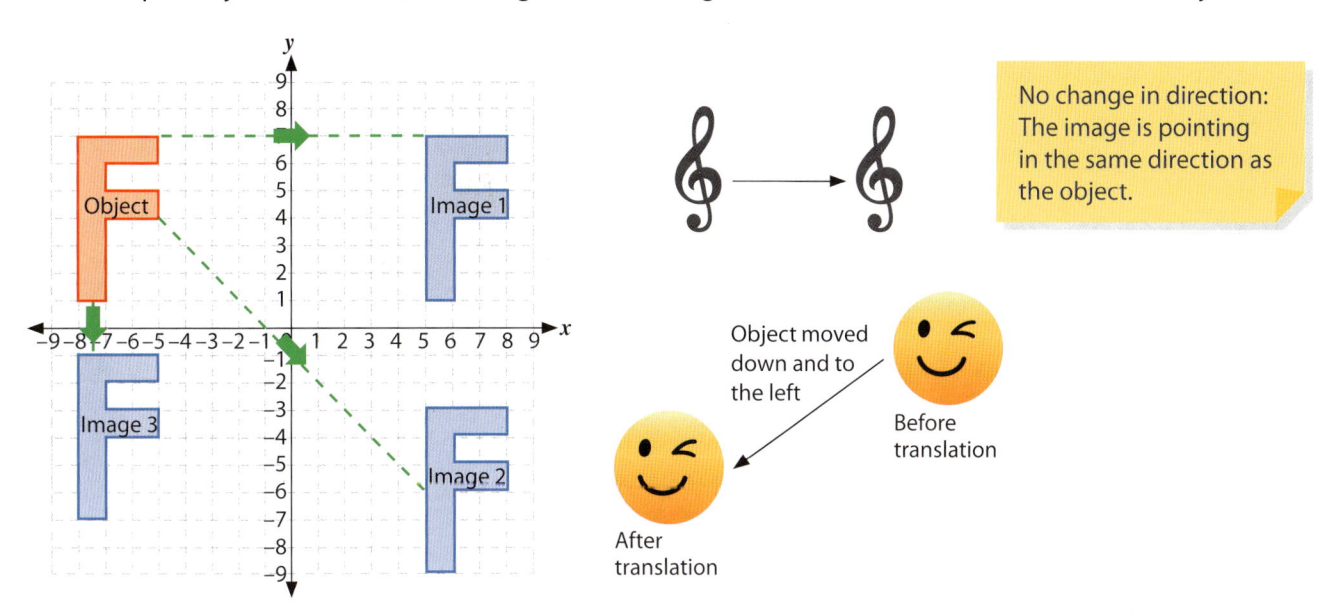

> No change in direction: The image is pointing in the same direction as the object.

Object moved down and to the left

Before translation

After translation

2. Axial symmetry

Axial symmetry (also known as flip) produces a mirror image (reflection) in which the corresponding points on the original shape and the mirror image are always the same distance from the mirror line (axis).

In the diagram below,

Image 1 is the object under axial symmetry in the *y*-axis (green line)

Image 2 is the object under axial symmetry in the *x*-axis (red line)

> Direction changed: The image is pointing in the opposite direction to the object.

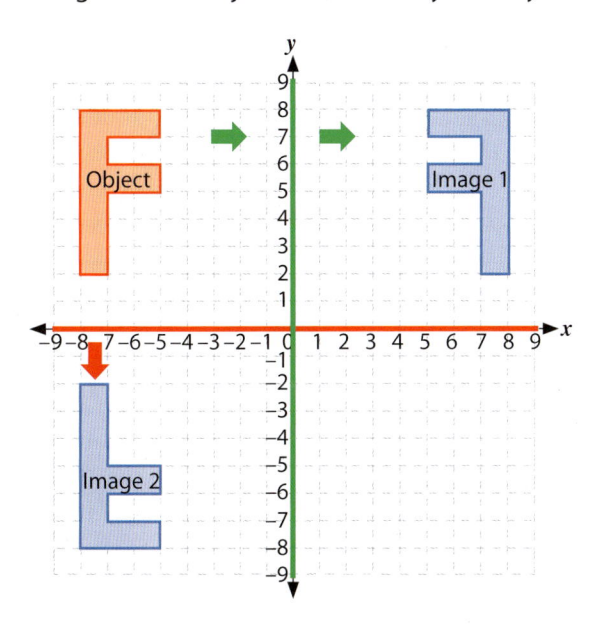

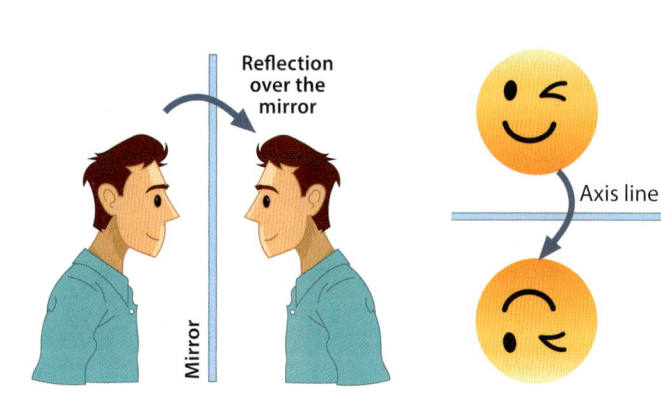

Reflection over the mirror

Axis line

3. Central symmetry

Central symmetry is when every part of the original object has a matching point on the image, and the image is the same distance from a fixed point but in the opposite direction.

The image looks the same as the object, just upside-down and back-to-front.

Image 1 on the right is the result of central symmetry of the object in the fixed point O, the origin $(0, 0)$.

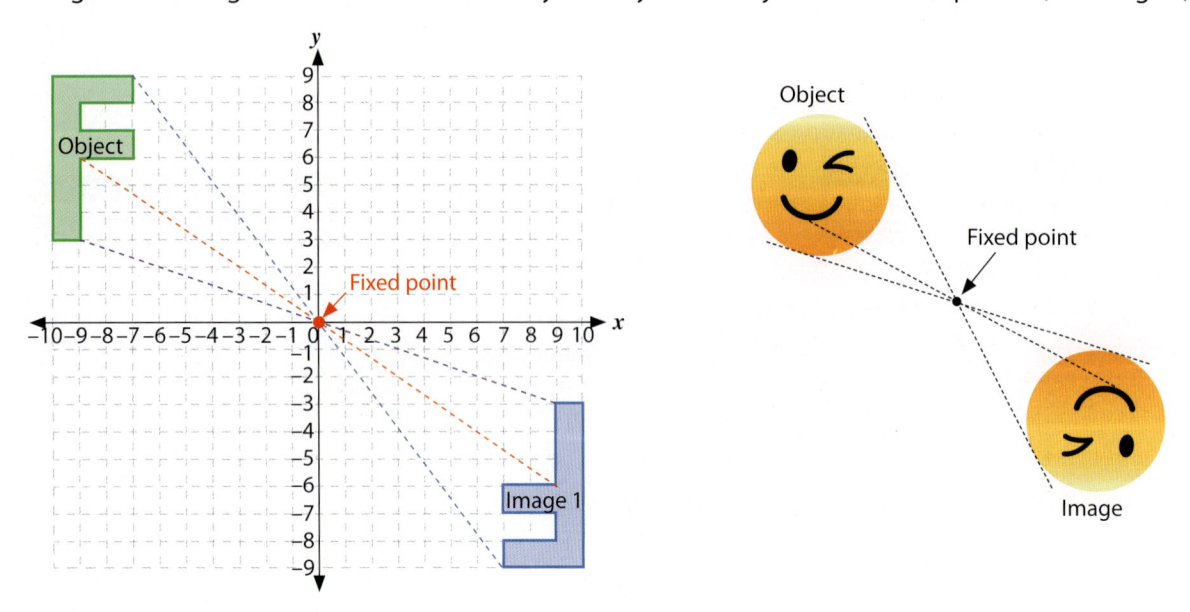

4. Rotation

> A **rotation** is the motion of a figure by holding one point fixed as the centre and turning the figure by a certain angle in a particular direction.

A rotation turns a shape through a clockwise or anti-clockwise angle about a fixed point known as the **centre of rotation**. The yellow, green and red images below are all different rotations of the purple object around the origin $(0, 0)$.

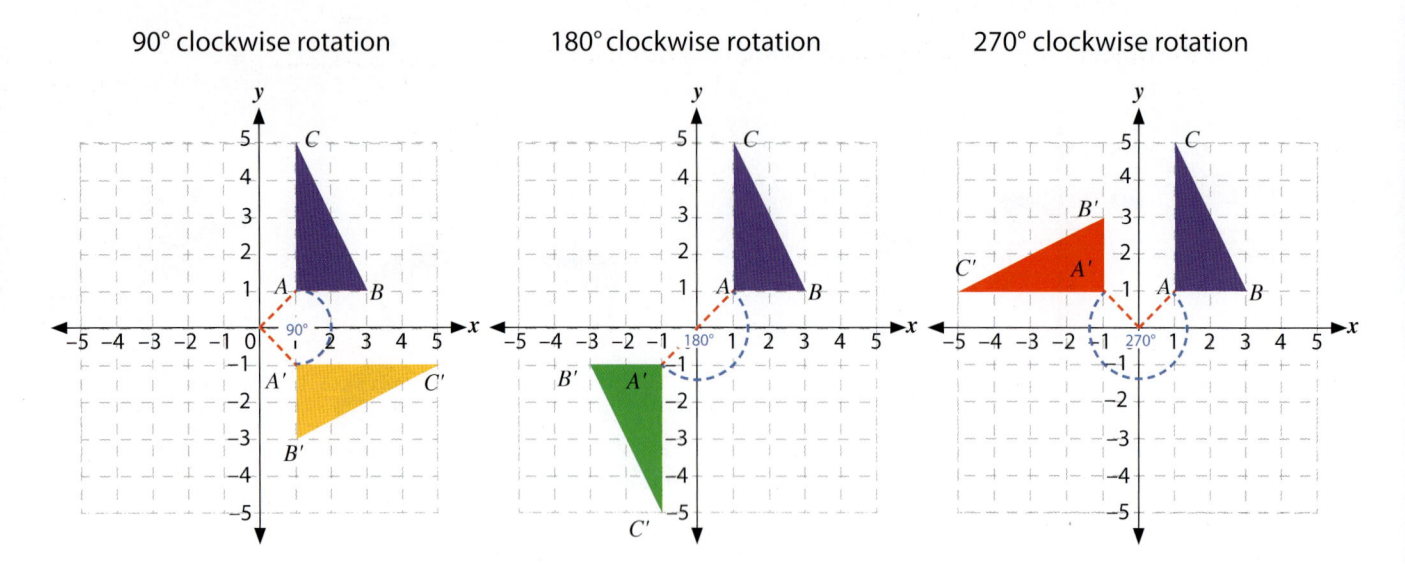

90° clockwise rotation

180° clockwise rotation

270° clockwise rotation

384 Linking Thinking 1

Worked example

State a possible transformation of the object shown, which would give

(i) image 1   (ii) image 2   (iii) image 3

Solution

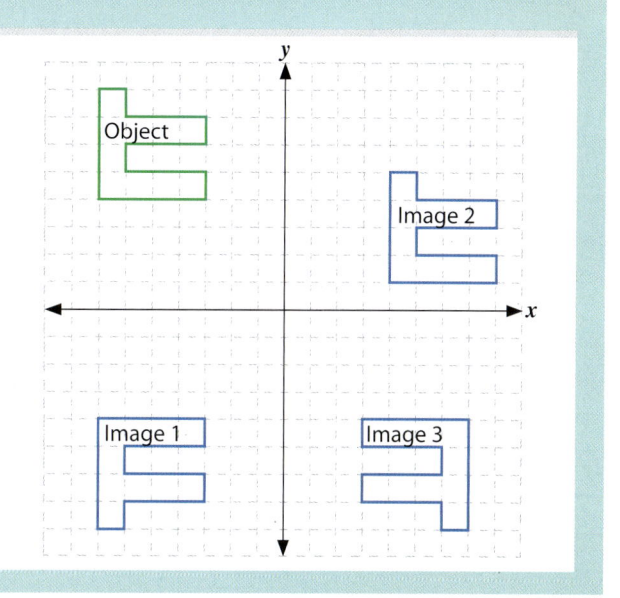

(i) Image 1 is due to axial symmetry in the x-axis, as every point on the image is the same distance as the object's points are on the other side of the x-axis.

(ii) The object could undergo a translation to produce image 2, as it has not changed direction, but just moved on the plane.

(iii) The object could undergo central symmetry to produce image 3. The fixed point for the central symmetry is the origin (0, 0). The image is the objected turned around and upside down. Image 3 could also be a 180° rotation around the origin (0, 0).

Practice questions 23.5

1. State whether each of the following is a translation, rotation, axial symmetry or central symmetry.

   (i)

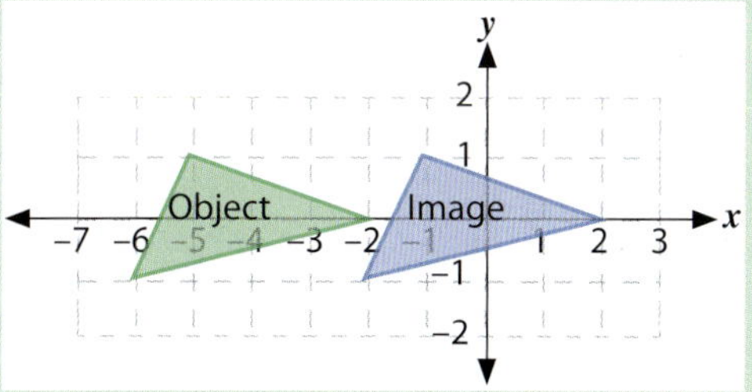

   (ii)

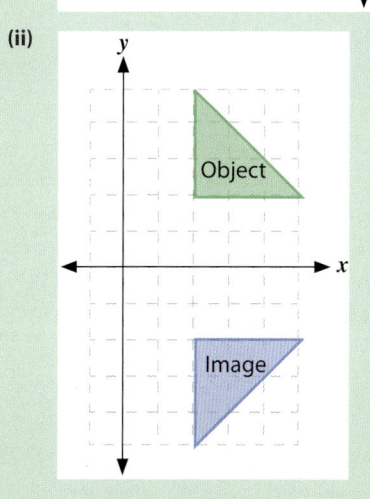

   (iii)

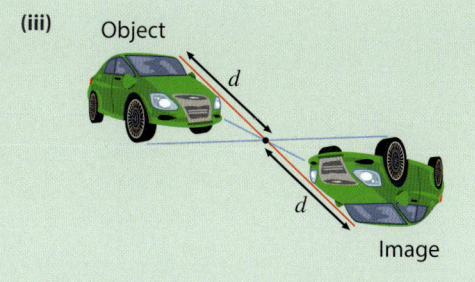

2. State whether each of the following is a translation, rotation, axial symmetry or central symmetry.

   (i)

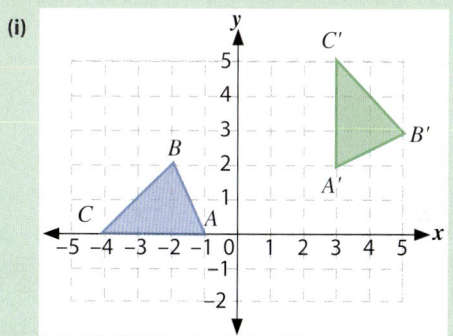

   (ii)

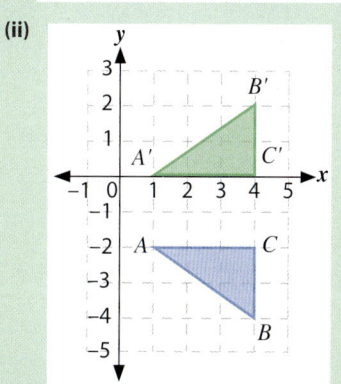

   (iii)

Section B Moving forward

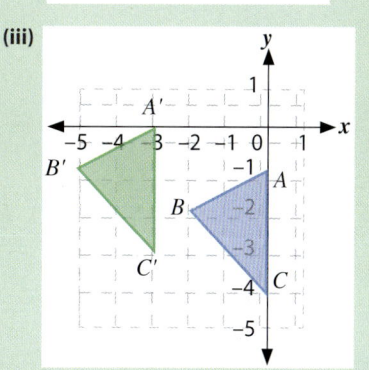

3. State a possible transformation of the object below which would give:

   (i) Image 1   (ii) Image 2

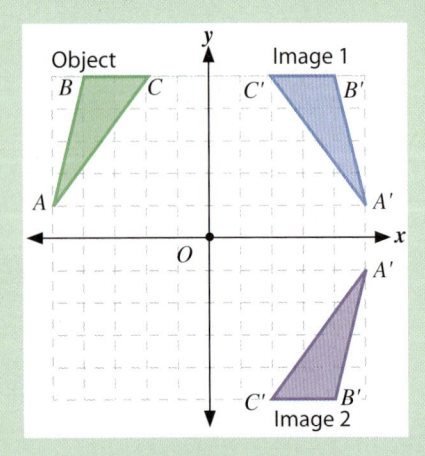

4. Redraw the diagram below (on graph paper) and insert the line for the axis that maps the object to its image.

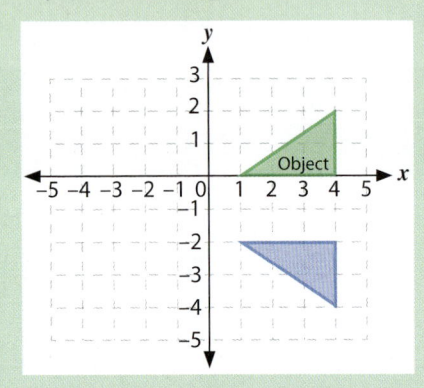

5. Redraw the diagram below (on graph paper) and show the image of the object under axial symmetry in the y-axis.

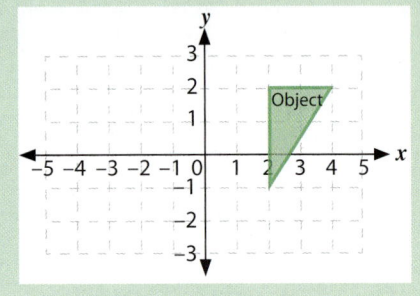

6. Redraw the diagram below (on graph paper) and show the image of the object under axial symmetry in the x-axis.

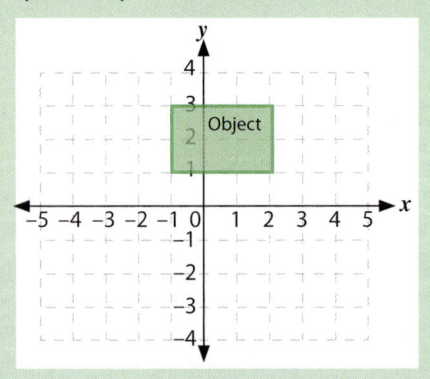

7. Redraw the box shown and translate it 4 squares to the right and 4 squares up.

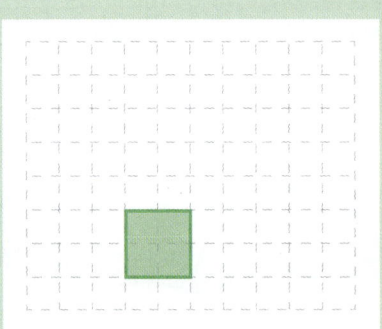

Revision questions

23A Core skills

1. Copy and complete the table showing properties of quadrilaterals, using **Y** for **yes** or **N** for **no**.

	Square	Rectangle	Parallelogram	Rhombus
Diagonals of equal length				
Four sides of equal length				
Four equal angles				
Exactly two pairs of parallel sides				
Two pairs of equal sides (but not all equal)				
Diagonals that bisect each other				
Two pairs of equal angles (but not all equal)				

2. (i) Construct a rectangle $PQRS$, where $|PQ| = 110$ mm, $|QR| = 5.5$ cm.
   (ii) Find the perimeter and the area of this rectangle.

   Remember: all dimensions should have the same units before area and perimeter are calculated.

3. A rectangle has a perimeter of 0·8 m and a width of 10 cm. Find its length.

4. A square has a perimeter of 12·4 cm. Find the length of a side of the square.

5. Find the perimeter and the area of each of the following shapes.

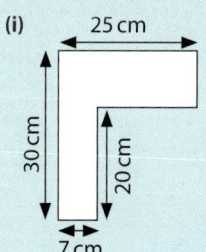

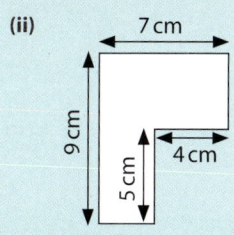

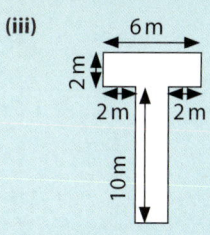

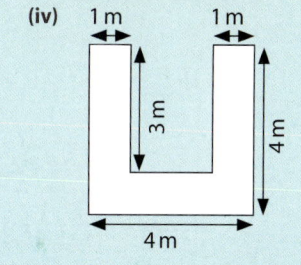

   (i) 25 cm, 30 cm, 20 cm, 7 cm
   (ii) 7 cm, 9 cm, 5 cm, 4 cm
   (iii) 6 m, 2 m, 2 m, 2 m, 10 m
   (iv) 1 m, 1 m, 3 m, 4 m, 4 m

6. Find the measure of angles labelled A to D and the sides m and n in the following diagrams. Justify your answer by giving the theorem or axiom used to find each answer.

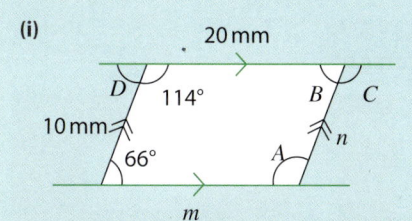

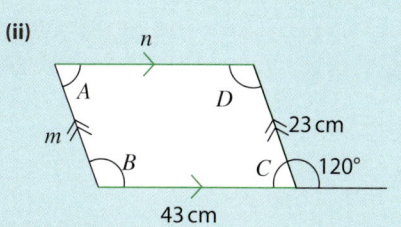

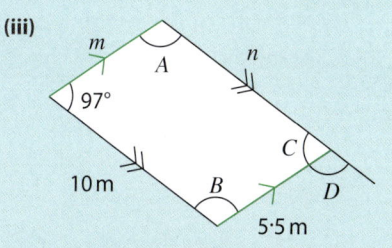

   (i) 20 mm, 10 mm, 114°, 66°, D, B, C, A, m, n
   (ii) 23 cm, 43 cm, 120°, A, B, C, D, m, n
   (iii) 10 m, 5·5 m, 97°, A, B, C, D, m, n

7. Find the value of x and y in each of the following diagrams. Justify your answer by giving the theorem or axiom used to find each answer.

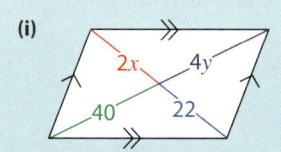

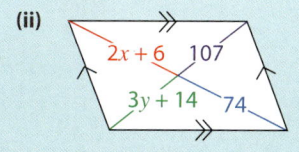

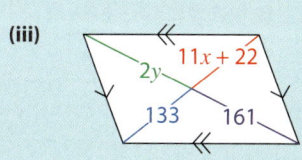

   (i) $2x$, $4y$, 40, 22
   (ii) $2x + 6$, 107, $3y + 14$, 74
   (iii) $11x + 22$, $2y$, 133, 161

8. Write down whether the object in each of the following has been transformed by reflection, rotation or translation. Justify your answer in each case.

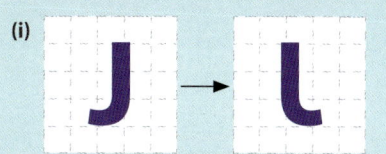

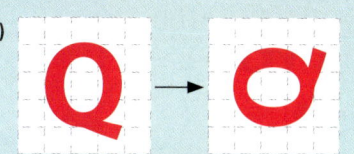

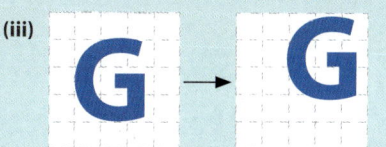

   (i) J → L
   (ii) Q → Q (red)
   (iii) G → G

Section B Moving forward 387

23B Taking it FURTHER

1. Study the images below and state which of the shapes are parallelograms. Justify your answer by stating the axiom, theorem or corollary used.

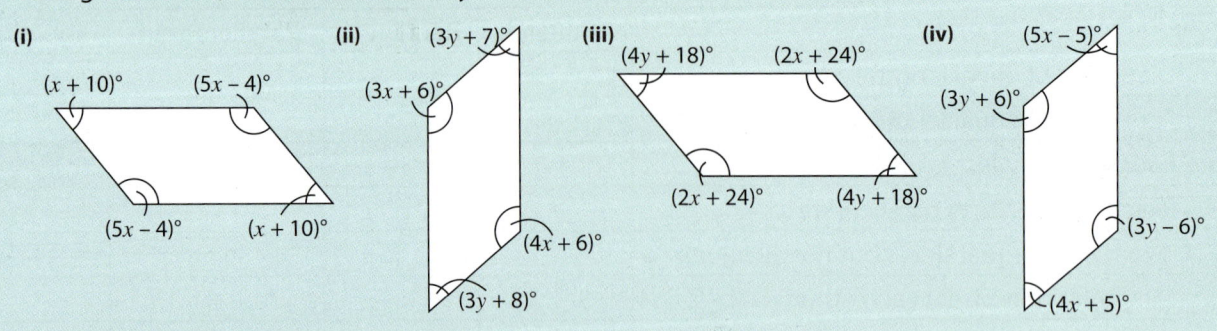

   (i) Angles: $(x+10)°$, $(5x-4)°$, $(5x-4)°$, $(x+10)°$

   (ii) Angles: $(3y+7)°$, $(3x+6)°$, $(4x+6)°$, $(3y+8)°$

   (iii) Angles: $(4y+18)°$, $(2x+24)°$, $(2x+24)°$, $(4y+18)°$

   (iv) Angles: $(5x-5)°$, $(3y+6)°$, $(3y-6)°$, $(4x+5)°$

2. Find the area and the perimeter of each of the following shapes.

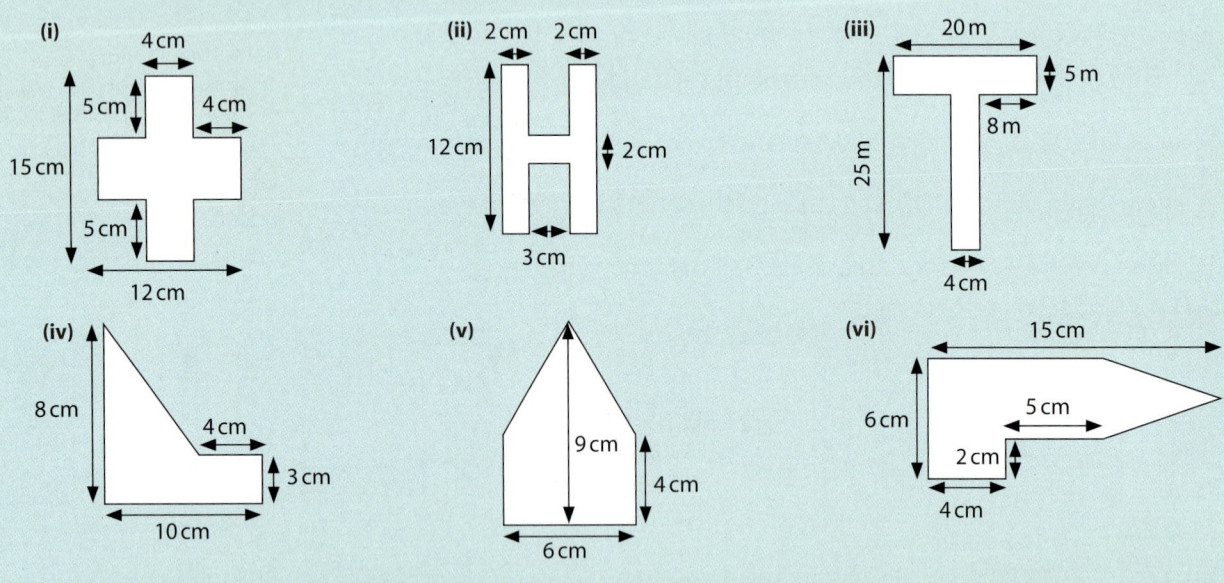

   (i) Cross shape: 4 cm, 5 cm, 4 cm, 15 cm, 5 cm, 12 cm

   (ii) H shape: 2 cm, 2 cm, 12 cm, 2 cm, 3 cm

   (iii) T shape: 20 m, 5 m, 8 m, 25 m, 4 m

   (iv) 8 cm, 4 cm, 3 cm, 10 cm

   (v) 9 cm, 4 cm, 6 cm

   (vi) 15 cm, 5 cm, 6 cm, 2 cm, 4 cm

3. Shown is a rectangle with length 20 cm and width 10 cm.

   The length of the rectangle is increased by 20%. The width of the rectangle is increased by 5%. Find the percentage increase in the area of the rectangle.

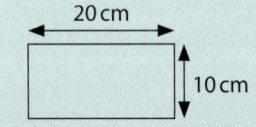

4. Declan is painting the front of his house as shown. His tin of paint can cover 16 m². Will he have enough paint? You must show your workings.

   Dimensions: 7 m × 3 m; door 0.9 m × 2 m; window 2 m × 1.3 m

5. The cross shape shown is made from five identical squares. The area of the shape is 180 cm². Find the length of side y.

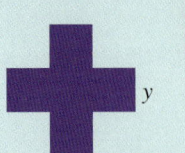

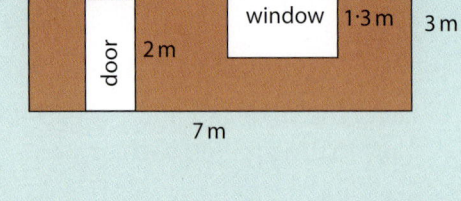

6. Write your name in block capitals on squared paper and find their images under axial symmetry in a horizontal line 3 cm from the base of your letters.

Now that you have completed the unit, revisit the **Something to think about ...** question posed at the start of this unit.

Now try question 2 on page 403

Unit 24

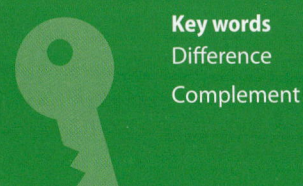

Further sets

? Something to think about ...

KEY SKILLS

In a certain town, 800 people are selected randomly. They are asked about how they travel to work.

280 go to work by car only, 220 go to work by bicycle only, and 140 use a mixture of both ways to travel, i.e. sometimes go with a car and sometimes with a bicycle.

If you chose a person at random, what would be the probability they travelled to work on a bicycle only?

Topics covered within this unit:
24·1 Revision of sets
24·2 Word problems involving two sets
24·3 Further operations used with set notation

The Learning Outcomes covered in this unit are contained in the following sections:
N.5a N.5b N.5c N.5d SP.2a SP.2b

Key words
Difference
Complement

24·1 Revision of sets

By the end of this section you should:
- have completed revision of basic sets

You have already studied some of the operations and notations used with sets in Section A, Unit 2 of this book. The basic symbols you have encountered so far are laid out in the table below.

Symbol	Symbol name	Meaning
{a, b, c}	set	A collection of well-defined elements; in this case a, b, c
$\in$	is an element of	An object contained within a set
$\notin$	is not an element of	Not an object contained within a set
#	cardinal number	The number of elements in a set
$\subset$	is a subset of	A set within a set
$\not\subset$	is not a subset of	Not a set within a set
$\emptyset$	null (empty set)	A set with no elements in it
$\cup$	union	A list of all elements in two (or more) sets combined
$\cap$	intersection	A list of elements common to two (or more) sets
$\mathbb{U}$	Universal set	The set of all possible elements

Section B Moving forward   389

You have also encountered the different regions of contained in a two-set Venn diagram.

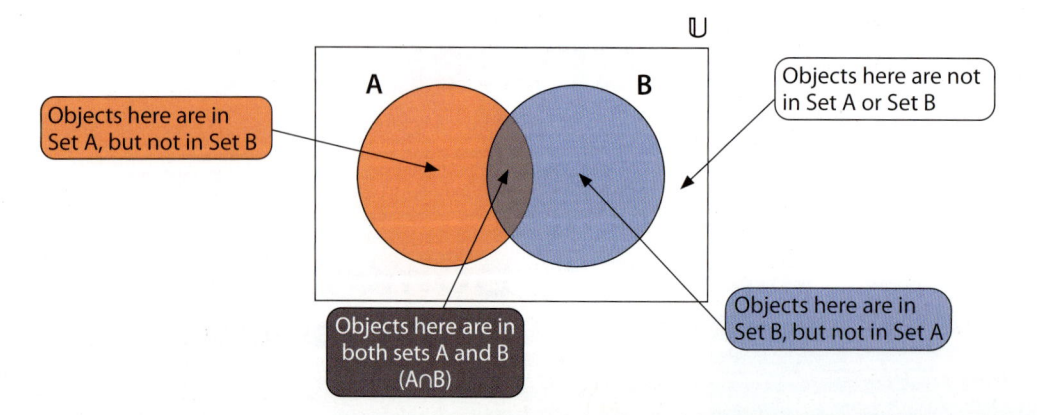

- Objects here are in Set A, but not in Set B
- Objects here are not in Set A or Set B
- Objects here are in both sets A and B (A∩B)
- Objects here are in Set B, but not in Set A

Practice questions 24.1

1. Copy the Venn diagram provided five times. Then shade in the following areas:

  (i)   X
  (ii) Y
  (iii) (X∩Y)
  (iv) (X∪Y)
  (v) $\mathbb{U}$

2. Using the Venn diagram provided, answer the following questions.

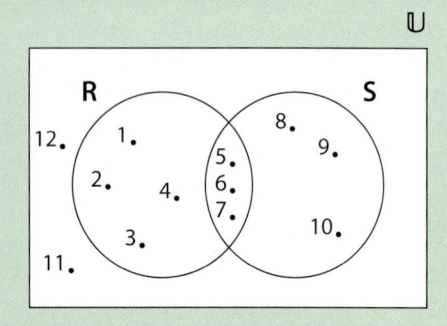

  (i)   List the elements of R.
  (ii)   List the elements of S.
  (iii) List the elements of $\mathbb{U}$.
  (iv)   List the elements of (R∩S).
  (v)   List the elements of (R∪S).
  (vi)   What is #$\mathbb{U}$?
  (vii) List two subsets of S.
  (viii) List two subsets of R.
  (ix)   If a number is choosen at random from the universal set, what is the probability it will be a prime number?

3. The Venn diagram below provides information regarding students' hobbies.

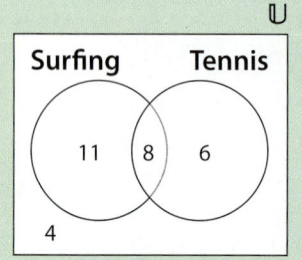

  (i)   How many students are represented in total?
  (ii)   How many students like tennis?
  (iii) How many students only like surfing?
  (iv)   How many students like both tennis and surfing?
  (v)   How many students like neither hobby?
  (vi)   How many students like surfing, but not tennis?
  (vii) If a student is picked at random, what is the probability they will only like tennis?

4. Write down all the possible subsets for each of the following sets.

  (i) $\{a, b\}$
  (ii) $\{7, 15, 24\}$
  (iii) $\{x, y, z\}$
  (iv) $\{d\}$
  (v)   ∅

390 Linking Thinking 1

5. Let A = {letters in the word kangaroo} and B = {letters in the word orangutan}
   - (i) Copy and complete the Venn diagram provided and fill in the missing information.
   - (ii) List the elements in A.
   - (iii) List the elements in B.
   - (iv) What is #(A∩B)?
   - (v) Write down a subset of A that has two elements and is also a subset of B.
   - (vi) Write down a subset of B that has two elements and is not a subset of A.

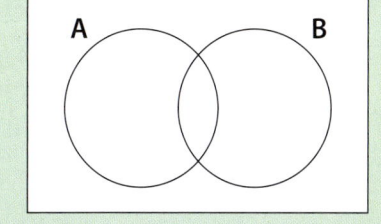

6. $\mathbb{U}$ = {natural numbers from 1 to 15 inclusive}
   P = {multiples of 3}
   Q = {prime numbers}
   - (i) Copy the Venn diagram and fill in the missing information.
   - (ii) State whether each of the following statements is true or false and justify your answer.
     - (a) (P∩Q) = ∅
     - (b) P ≠ Q
     - (c) (P∪Q) = $\mathbb{U}$
     - (d) {1}⊂Q
     - (e) {} ⊄ P
     - (f) {3} ∉ (P∩Q)

7. The statements below are about two non-empty sets A and B, and the universal set $\mathbb{U}$.

   Copy the table and put a tick (✓) in the correct box in each row to show whether each statement is always true, sometimes true, or never true. Justify your answer in each case.

Statement		Always true	Sometimes true	Never true	Give a reason for your answer
(i)	#(A∪B) = #A + #B				
(ii)	A∩B = B∩A				
(iii)	{ } ⊂ (A∪B)				
(iv)	#$\mathbb{U}$ less than # (A∩B)				

24.2 Word problems involving two sets

By the end of this section you should be able to:
- represent a word problem in a Venn diagram
- use Venn diagrams to solve word problems

Venn diagram word problems generally give you two different sets and and some information about each set. You then have to use the given information to draw a Venn diagram and figure out the remaining information.

Worked example 1:
when you know the value in the intersection

In a group of 40 students, 14 study German and 29 study Physics. There are five students who study both German and Physics.

(i) Draw a Venn diagram to represent this information.
(ii) How many students study neither subject?
(iii) How many students study only one subject?
(iv) How many students study German only?
(v) What is the probability that a randomly-chosen student from this group is only studying Physics?

Solution

(i) **Step 1** Draw a Venn diagram containing two sets, which represent German and Physics. Label each one with the number of elements they should contain.

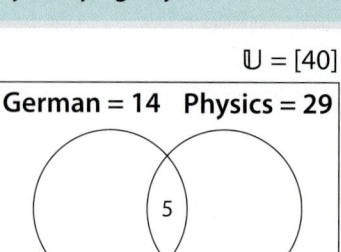

Step 2 We know 5 people study both subjects (intersection German∩Physics).

Place the number 5 in the intersection.

> Always fill in the intersection information first.

Step 3 We know the total number of students who study German = 14. We have already accounted for 5.

14 – 5 = 9, therefore we place the remaining 9 in the German set, as shown.

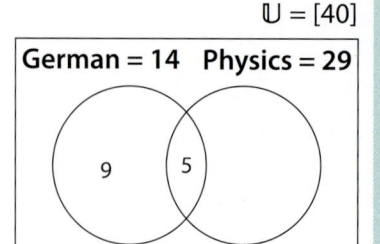

Step 4 Physics = 29, we already have 5.

29 – 5 = 24. We place this in the Physics set, as shown.

Finally, we add up all our numbers
9 + 5 + 24 = 38

There were 40 people in the group
40 – 38 = 2

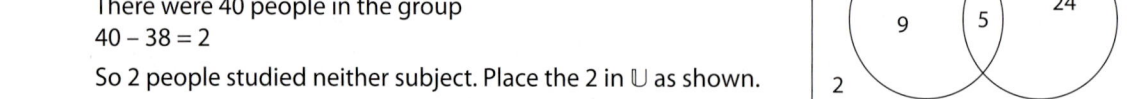

So 2 people studied neither subject. Place the 2 in $\mathbb{U}$ as shown.

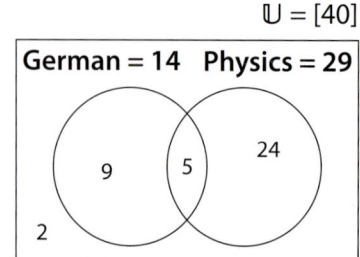

(ii) From the Venn diagram, we can see that 2 people study neither subject.

(iii) 9 students study German only. 24 students study physics only.

9 + 24 = 33

33 students study only one subject.

(iv) There are 40 students in the group. 24 students only study Physics.

P(only study Physics) = $\frac{24}{40} = \frac{3}{5}$

392 Linking Thinking 1

Worked example 2:
when you don't know the value in the intersection

A survey of 24 students was carried out to see which type of movies they like to watch.

16 students liked action movies, 12 students liked romantic comedies and 2 students liked neither.

(i) Draw a Venn diagram to show this information.

(ii) How many students liked both action movies and romantic comedies?

Solution

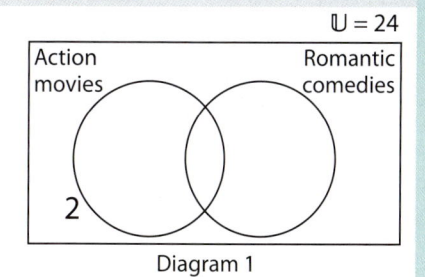

(i) **Step 1** There are a total of 24 students surveyed.

2 like neither type of movie.

Place the number 2 in the Universal set, outside of the circles. as shown in diagram 1.

Since 2 students don't like either type of movie, 24 − 2 = 22 like at least one type of movie.

Step 2 We know 16 students like action movies and 12 students like romantic comedies: 16 + 12 = 28

Since 28 is more than 22, some students must like both types of movie.

We must have an extra 6 people, since 28 − 22 = 6

Step 3 These 6 students must like both types of movie, therefore we place them in the centre (action movies ∩ romantic comedies) as shown in diagram 2.

Step 4 We can now fill in the rest of the information:

Students who like action movies only = 16 − 6 = 10

Students who like romantic comedies only = 12 − 6 = 6

Verify all elements within the set = 24
10 + 6 + 6 + 2 = 24

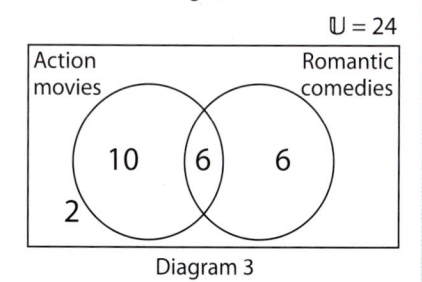

(ii) 6 students liked both types of movie

When you don't know the intersection, start from the outside.

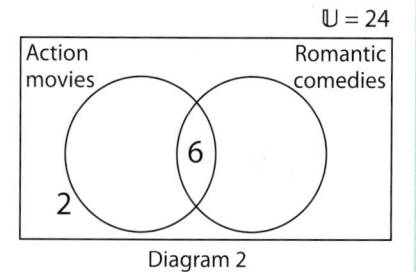

Practice questions 24·2

1. Twenty students in a group of 40 study Science. Eleven students study Art. Five students study both.
   (i) Draw a Venn diagram to represent this information.
   (ii) How many students study Science only?
   (iii) How many students study neither subject?
   (iv) Find the number of students who have chosen to study at least one of the two subjects.
   (v) If a student is choosen at random, what is the probability they don't study Science?

2. In a group of 24 friends, 11 play golf and 9 of them play basketball. Two play both sports.
   (i) Represent the data above in a Venn diagram.
   (ii) How many people play golf only?
   (iii) How many people, in total, do not play basketball?
   (iv) If a person was randomly selected from this group, what is the probability they would play neither sport? Give your answer as a percentage of the the total amount of people.

3. A class of 28 students were surveyed and asked if they ever had a dog or cat as a pet. 18 students said they had a dog. 16 students said they had a cat. 4 students said they had never had a dog or a cat.

    (i) Draw a Venn diagram to represent this information.
    (ii) How many students had both a cat and a dog?
    (iii) How many students had just one pet?
    (iv) What percentage of the students surveyed did not have a pet? Give your answer to the nearest whole number.

4. In a school of 320 students, 85 students have visited France, 200 have visited Spain and 60 students have visited both countries.

    (i) Draw a Venn diagram to represent this information.
    (ii) How many students have not visited either country?
    (iii) How many students have visited France only?
    (iv) What percentage of the students have visited Spain?
    (v) If a student was picked at random from this group, what is the probability they have visited France **or** Spain, but **not** both countries?

5. Of 100 people in a summer camp, 70 members said they play a sport and 25 members take music lessons. 5 members do neither of these.

    (i) Draw a Venn diagram to represent this information.
    (ii) How many members play a sport **or** take music lessons?
    (iii) If you were to pick a member at random, what is the probability they take music lessons **and** play sport?

6. A market researcher collecting data from a certain number of households found that 81% have a smart TV, 60% have high-speed broadband and 56% have both.

    (i) Draw a Venn diagram to represent this information.
    (ii) What percentage of households have a smart TV only?
    (iii) What percentage of people have neither a smart TV nor high-speed broadband?
    (iv) If 200 households were surveyed in total, how many households does your percentage in part (iii) represent?

24·3 Further operations used with set notation

By the end of this section you should understand:
- set difference and the complement of a set and be able to solve problems

The difference (subtraction) of two sets can be explained as follows. The set A less the set B consists of elements that **are** in A but **not** in B. Mathematically, we write A less B as A\B.

> The **difference** between two sets A and B is written as A\B.
> This is the set of elements which are contained in A but not in B.

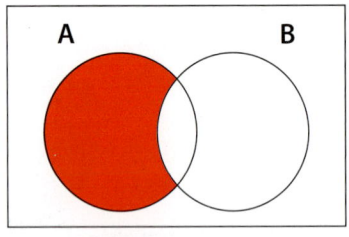

A\B is the **red** shaded area in the diagram.

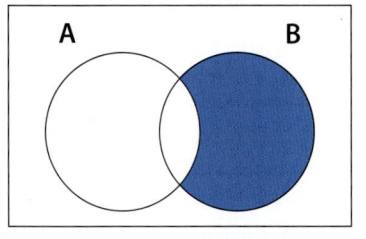

B\A is the **blue** shaded area in the diagram.

394 Linking Thinking 1

Worked example 1

If **A** = {1, 2, 3} and **B** = {3, 4, 5}, $\mathbb{U}$ = {1, 2, 3, 4, 5, 6, 7, 9}

(i) Find A\B   (ii) Find B\A

Solution

> Set difference is not commutative.
> A\B is not equal to B\A

(i) A\B
Draw a Venn diagram

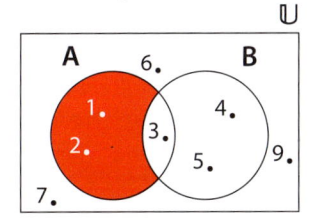

A\B = all the elements in A but not in B
(the **red** shaded area)
A\B = {1, 2}

(ii) B\A
Draw a Venn diagram

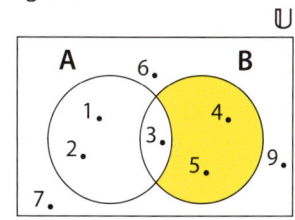

B\A = all the elements in B, but not in A
(the **yellow** shaded area)
B\A = {4, 5}

The complement of a set

The **complement** of a set A is the set of all elements in the universal set that are not in A. The symbol A′ (or sometimes A^c) is used to denote the complement of a set.

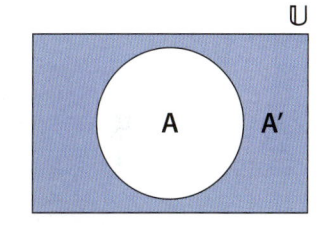

Worked example 2

At a farmers' market, 50 people were asked if they like strawberries or blueberries or both. 30 people like strawberries, 40 people like blueberries and 21 people like both.

(i) Draw a Venn diagram to represent this information.
(ii) Find the number of people who did not like blueberries.
(iii) Find the number of people who did not like strawberries.

Solution

(i) $\mathbb{U}$ = 50

Blueberries: 19, Strawberries: 9, Both: 21, Neither: 1

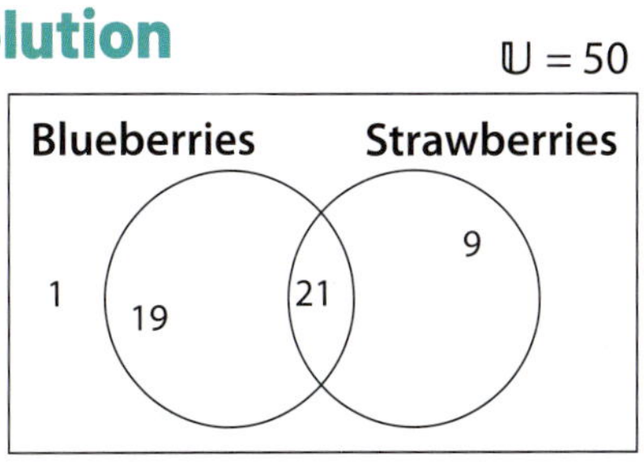

(ii) Number of people who did not like blueberries (this is B′), is shaded in the diagram below.

$\mathbb{U}$ = 50

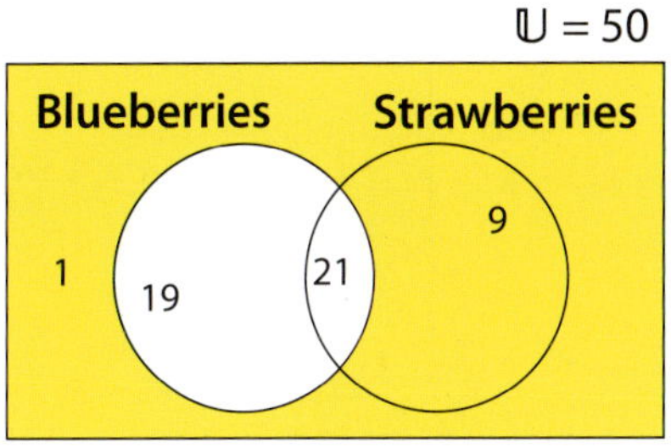

#B′ = 10

(iii) Number of people who did not like strawberries (this is S′), is shaded in the diagram below.

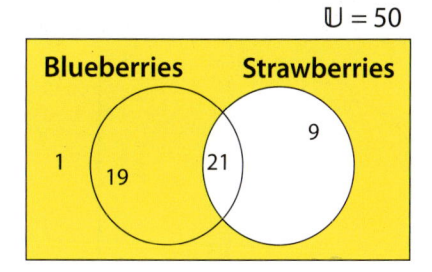

$\mathbb{U}$ = 50

#S′ = 20

24 Further sets

Section B Moving forward   395

Worked example 3

The universal set = {a, b, c, d, e, f, g, h, i, j, k, l}
Set X = {a, b, c, d, e, f, g}
Set Y = {e, f, g, h, i, j}

(i) Draw a Venn diagram to represent this information.
(ii) List the elements of (X\Y)
(iii) List the elements of Y\X
(iv) List the elements of X'
(v) List the elements of Y'
(vi) List the elements of (X∪Y)'
(vii) List the elements of (X∩Y)'

Solution

(i) Venn diagram showing X = {a, b, c, d, e, f, g} and Y = {e, f, g, h, i, j}, with k and l outside both sets.

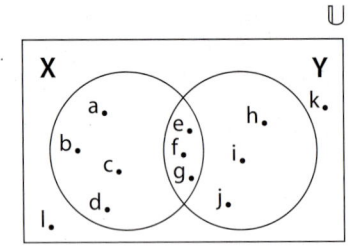

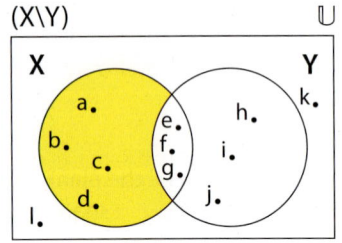

(ii) (X\Y) = {a, b, c, d}

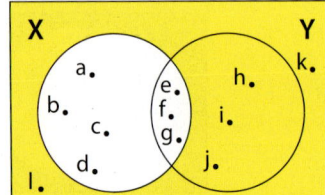

(iii) (Y\X) = {h, i, j}

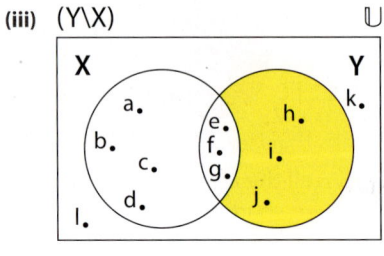

(iv) elements of X' — All elements except those in set X
X' = {h, i, j, k, l}

(v) elements of Y' — All elements except those in set Y
Y' = {a, b, c, d, k, l}

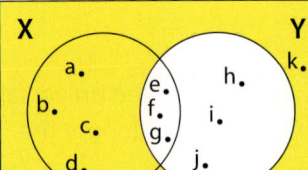

(vi) (X∪Y)' — All elements except those in set X and set Y
(X∪Y)' = {k, l}

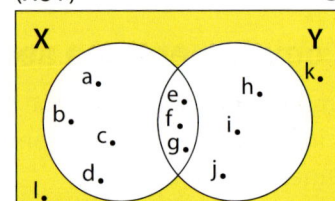

(vii) (X∩Y)' — All elements except those that X and Y have in common = (X∩Y)' = {a, b, c, d, h, i, j, k, l}

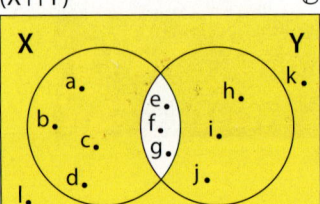

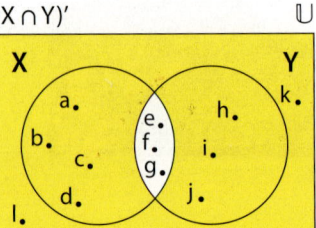

Practice questions 24.3

1. Copy the blank Venn diagram below for each question and shade in the required areas to show your answer.

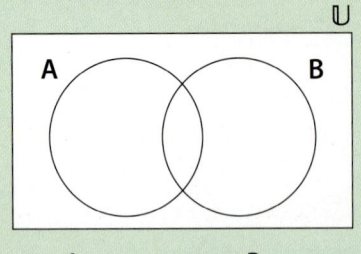

   (i) A
   (ii) B
   (iii) (A∪B)
   (iv) (A∩B)
   (v) 𝕌

2. Copy the blank Venn diagram below for each question, and shade in the required areas to show your answer.

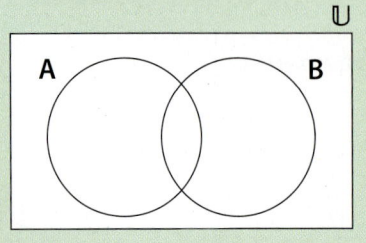

   (i) A'
   (ii) B'
   (iii) (A∪B)'
   (iv) (A∩B)'
   (v) (A\B)
   (vi) (B\A)
   (vii) (A\B)'
   (viii) (B\A)'
   (ix) A\B'
   (x) B\A'
   (xi) (B∪A)\A
   (xii) (B∪A)\(A∪B)

396 Linking Thinking 1

3. Use the Venn diagram provided to answer the following questions. List the elements of the following.

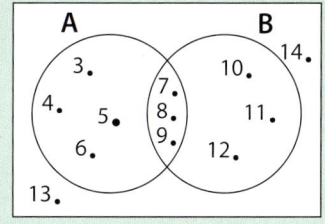

   (i) A
   (ii) B
   (iii) (A∪B)
   (iv) (A∩B)
   (v) A'
   (vi) B'
   (vii) (B\A)
   (viii) (A\B)
   (ix) 𝕌\(A∩B)
   (x) A'∩B'

4. $\mathbb{U} = \{x \mid 1 \leq x \leq 15, x \in \mathbb{N}\}$
   $A = \{x \mid x \text{ is a prime number that is less than } 15\}$
   $B = \{x \mid x \text{ is an even number less than } 15\}$

   List the elements of each of the following sets:

   Hint: Would it be useful to draw a Venn diagram?

   (i) A
   (ii) B
   (iii) A'
   (iv) B'
   (v) (A∪B)'
   (vi) (A\B)
   (vii) (B\A)'
   (viii) (A∪B)'

5. 𝕌 = {all the people who have a mobile phone}
   W = {people who use WhatsUp}
   S = {people who use ShareChat}

   Describe in words, the following sets.
   (i) (W∪S)
   (ii) (W\S)
   (iii) W'
   (iv) S'
   (v) 𝕌\(W∪S)
   (vi) (W∩S)'

6. The Venn diagram provides information on a number of people who like rugby (set R) and judo (set J).

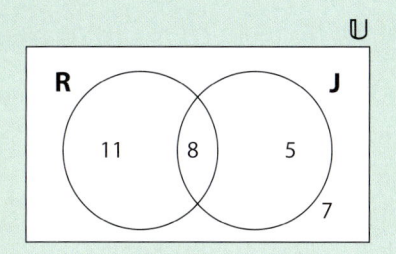

   (i) How many people are represented in the Venn diagram?
   (ii) How many people don't like rugby?
   (iii) How many people don't like judo?
   (iv) How many people like rugby but not judo?
   (v) If a person is selected at random, what is the probability they would like both sports?

7. In a group of 100 people, 70 people can speak English and 45 can speak French. All 100 can speak at least one of these languages.

   (i) Draw a Venn diagram to represent this information.
   (ii) How many can speak English only?
   (iii) How many can speak French only?
   (iv) How many can speak both English and French?

8. In a group of 80 Second-Year students, 9 students study French and German. 35 students only study French. 2 students do not study French or German.

   (i) Draw a Venn diagram to represent this information.
   (ii) How many students study both languages?
   (iii) How many students study only German?
   (iv) If a student was chosen at random, what is the probability they only study German? Give your answer as a percentage to the nearest whole number.

9. The universal set is the set of natural even numbers less than 30.
   Set A = {4, 8, 12, 16, 20, 24, 28}, and
   Set B = {6, 12, 18, 24, 28}

   (i) Draw a Venn diagram to represent this information.
   (ii) List the elements of A'
   (iii) List the elements of B'
   (iv) List the elements of (A\B)
   (v) List the elements of (A∪B)'
   (vi) If a number is chosen at random, what is the probability that the number is an element of the set A∩B?

10. 107 guests attended a wedding. The guests can have ice cream or custard or both with their dessert.
    71 guests had ice cream, 44 guests had custard and 13 guests did not have a dessert.

    (i) Draw a Venn diagram to represent this information
    (ii) How many people had custard only?
    (iii) How many people had both custard and ice cream?
    (iv) If a person was chosen at random, what is the probability they had **only** ice cream with their desert?

Section B Moving forward

11. There are 35 students in a group. 18 students play tennis, 12 students play tennis and badminton, 15 students play neither tennis nor badminton.
    (i) Draw a Venn diagram to represent this information.
    (ii) How many students play tennis only?
    (iii) If a student is chosen at random, calculate the probability they do **not** play badminton.

Taking it FURTHER

12. Match the set notation with the correct sentence, where A and B are two sets.

	Set notation		Sentence
A	#A = 20	(i)	The elements of A union B
B	B′	(ii)	The number of elements that are in both A and B
C	(A∪B)	(iii)	The number of elements in set A is 20
D	#(A∩B)	(iv)	A list of elements in the set B only
E	(B\A)	(v)	Everything in the set except the elements of B

Revision questions

24A Core skills

1. In a college, 200 students are randomly selected. 140 like tea, 120 like coffee and 80 like both tea and coffee.
   (i) Draw a Venn diagram to represent this information.
   (ii) How many students like only tea?
   (iii) How many students like only coffee?
   (iv) How many students like neither tea nor coffee?
   (v) What percentage of students like at least one of the beverages?
   (vi) Explain how you could collect a random sample from all of the students in the college.

2. There are 100 people living in an apartment building. Forty people have been to a football game. Thirty people have been to a live music concert, and twenty people have been to both.
   (i) Draw a Venn diagram to represent this information.
   (ii) How many people have been to a football game?
   (iii) How many people have been to a live music concert only?
   (iv) How many people have been to a football game or a live music concert or both?
   (v) If you were to choose a person at random, what is the probability they have been to neither of these events?

3. On Sarah's blog, there are 17 videos with cats in them, 15 videos with babies in them, and 2 of the videos have both cats and babies in them. How many videos are there on Sarah's blog?

Linking Thinking 1

4. Students were polled on whether or not they liked their Maths and English classes. The results are displayed in the Venn diagram.

(i) How many students were polled?

(ii) What is the probability that a student liked Maths only?

(iii) What is the probability that a student did not like English?

(iv) What is the probability that a student did not like either subject?

5. In a Jane Austen novel, a handsome but smug gentleman has recently moved to the village. At the Autumn Ball, there are 19 ladies who like the gentleman, 20 ladies who dislike him and 4 ladies who like but also dislike this mysterious newcomer. How many ladies at the dance expressed an opinion about the gentleman?

6. (i) Copy the Venn diagrams given below and use the table provided to put these people into the correct place in each Venn diagram.

	Shane	Fiona	Amber	Kyle	David	Rochelle
Boy/girl	boy	girl	girl	boy	boy	girl
Age	12	14	13	11	13	12
Height (cm)	120	136	139	118	125	135
Likes football	yes	no	yes	no	yes	no

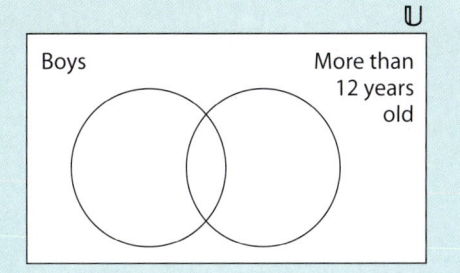

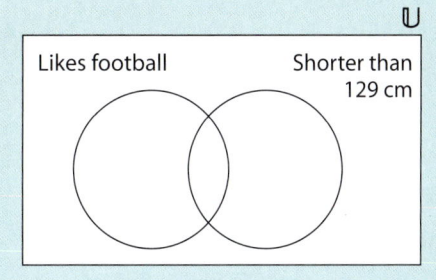

(ii) What is the probability that a person shorter than 129 cm likes football?

(iii) How many boys like football?

(iv) What percentage of girls are taller than 129 cm?

7. A marketing survey of 1 000 people found that 600 people listen to the news, 500 people listen to music, and 300 people listen to both. Let N = set of people who listen to news and M = set of people who listen to music.

(i) Draw a Venn diagram to represent this information.
(ii) List the elements of (N∩M).
(iii) List the elements of (N∪M).
(iv) What is #N'?
(v) Explain in words what #(N\M) means in the context of this set of information.

8. Copy the Venn diagram opposite six times, and in each case shade in the area that represents:

(i) A∩B (ii) A∪B (iii) A\B
(iv) A' (v) B' (vi) (A\B)'

9. Find two sets A and B such that (A∪B) = {1, 2, 3, 4, 5} and A∩B = ∅

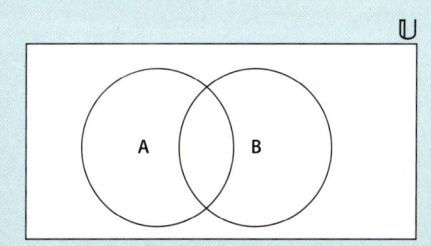

24B Taking it FURTHER

1. A survey was conducted with 100 students. The survey contained three questions.

   Technology Survey
   1. Do you own a smart watch? Yes / No
   2. Do you own a computer tablet? Yes / No
   3. Do you own a smart watch and a computer tablet? Yes / No

   The results of the survey are shown in the table below.

	Yes	No	Total
Smart watch	70	30	100
Computer tablet	50	50	100
Both	40	60	100

   (i) Using your knowledge from statistics, name the **type** of data that was collected in the survey.

   (ii) Draw a Venn diagram to represent this information.

   (iii) How many students own a computer tablet but do not own a smart watch?

   (iv) How many own a computer tablet or a smart watch?

   (v) How many own neither a computer tablet nor a smart watch?

   (vi) What is #(A\B)′, if A = watch and B = tablet?

2. Copy the Venn diagrams below and place the letters representing each shape in the correct place.

   A   B   C   D   E   F

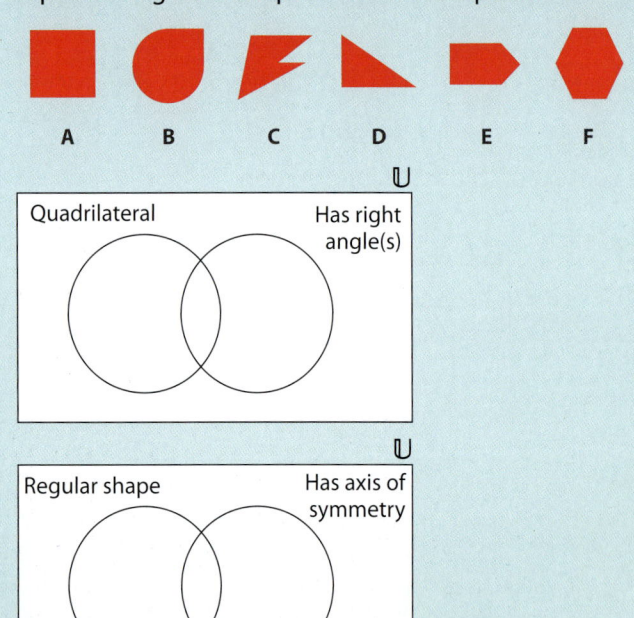

   Venn diagram: Quadrilateral / Has right angle(s)

   Venn diagram: Regular shape / Has axis of symmetry

3. Let $\mathbb{U}$ = {1, 2, 3, 4, 5, 6, 7, 8, 9}
   Set A = {1, 3, 5, 7, 9}, set B = {2, 4, 6, 8}, set C = {3, 5} and set D = {2, 4, 6, 8}

   (i) List the elements of:
   (a) (A∪B)   (b) (A∩B)
   (c) (A\B)   (d) #B′

   (ii) Copy and complete the Venn diagrams below.

   A B   C D
   A C   B D

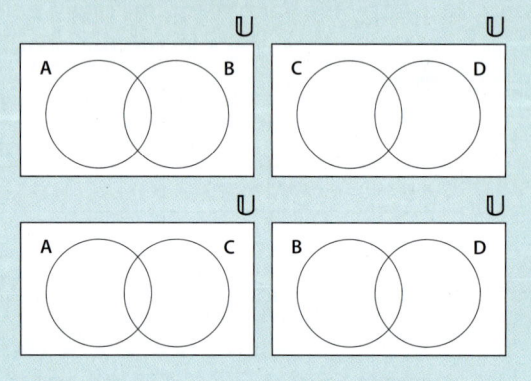

4. There are two sets displayed in the Venn diagram shown.
   There are 66 items in the universal set.

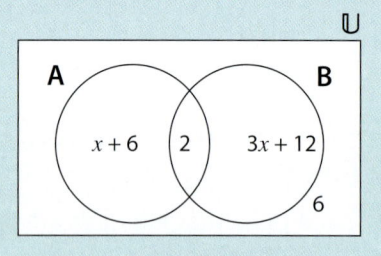

   A: $x+6$, 2 , B: $3x+12$, 6

   (i) Find the value of x.
   (ii) What is the value of #A?
   (iii) What is the value of #B?
   (iv) What is the value of #(A∪B)′?

5. Using the Venn diagram below, draw at least one quadrilateral shape that will satisfy the rules of each set represented. (Hint: place them into the diagram instead of A, B, C, and D.)

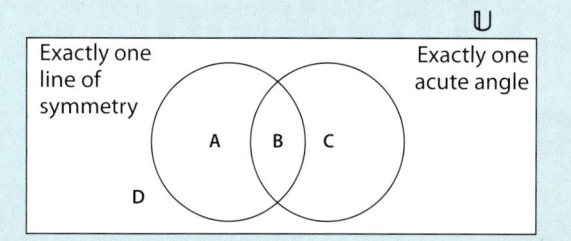

[Venn diagram: U; left circle "Exactly one line of symmetry"; right circle "Exactly one acute angle"; regions labelled A, B, C; outside D]

6. Using the Venn diagram below, think of a list containing four numbers that will satisfy the rules of each set represented. (Hint: place them into the diagram instead of A, B, C, and D.)

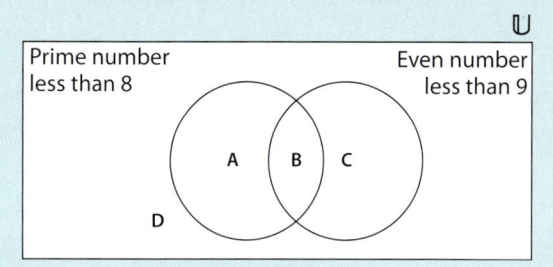

[Venn diagram: U; left circle "Prime number less than 8"; right circle "Even number less than 9"; regions A, B, C; outside D]

7. Using the Venn diagram below, write the dimensions of a rectangle, which will satisfy the rules of each set represented. Note: all dimensions used must be an $\in \mathbb{N}$.

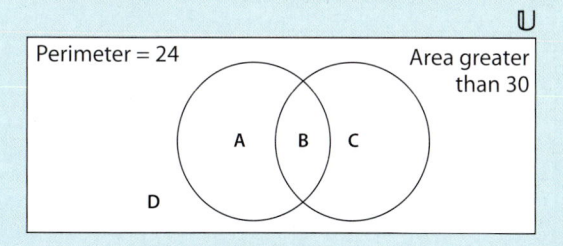

[Venn diagram: U; left circle "Perimeter = 24"; right circle "Area greater than 30"; regions A, B, C; outside D]

8. Using the Venn diagram below, write a decimal value that will satisfy the rules of each set represented.

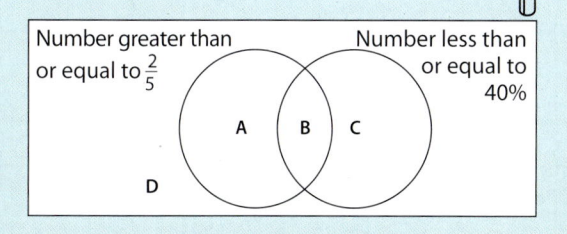

[Venn diagram: U; left circle "Number greater than or equal to $\frac{2}{5}$"; right circle "Number less than or equal to 40%"; regions A, B, C; outside D]

9. The universal set, $\mathbb{U} = \{$the set of natural numbers$\}$
$X = \{$multiples of 5$\}$ and $Y = \{$multiples of 3$\}$
Copy the Venn diagram and answer the questions below.

(i) Shade in the area that represents $X \cap Y'$

(ii) Write down three possible members of the set $X \cap Y'$

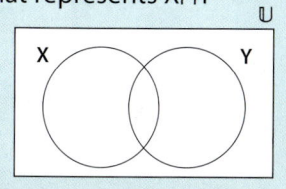

[Venn diagram: U, two overlapping circles X and Y]

10. Fifty students were asked in a survey whether they use texting or social media.

- 20 students said they only use texting.
- 8 students said they only use social media.
- 17 students said they use both texting and social media.

(i) Draw a Venn diagram to show this information.

(ii) How many of the students in the survey do not use texting or social media?

(iii) One of the students in the survey is chosen at random. What is the probability that this student uses texting?

11. Using the Venn diagram below, state whether each of the following statements is true or false. Justify your answers.

(i) $R = \{1, 2, 3\}$ (ii) $P \subset Q$

(iii) $P \cup Q = P$ (iv) $P \cap R = \emptyset$

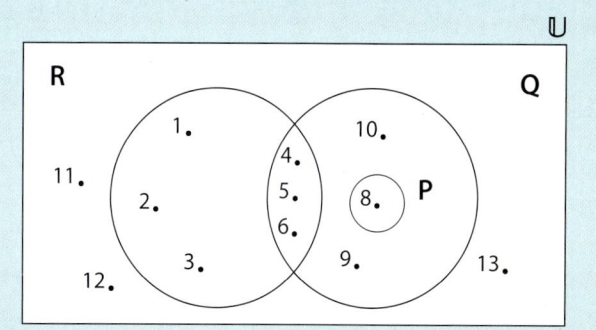

(v) $(Q \cup R)' = \{11, 12, 13\}$ (vi) $\#(Q \setminus R) = \#(R \setminus Q)$

[Venn diagram: U; R contains 1, 2, 11, 12; intersection of R and Q contains 4, 5, 6, 3; Q contains 10, 8, 9, 13; P is inside Q containing 8; outside 11, 12, 13]

Now that you have completed the unit, revisit the **Something to think about ...** question posed at the start of this unit.

Now try questions 8, 9 and 13 on pages 405–9

Unit 25
Linking Thinking revision material

By the end of this unit you should be able to:
- make connections between concepts and the real world
- work on problems individually or with others; compare approaches and adapt your own strategy
- break up a problem into manageable parts
- make sense of a given problem and use Maths to solve it
- represent a mathematical problem in a variety of different ways
- interpret and evaluate how reasonable your solution is, in the context of the original problem
- reflect on the strategy you used to solve a mathematical problem
- identify limitations and suggest improvements

Linking Thinking questions

Reference grid

		Money matters 1	Maths in motion	Polygons	Circles 1	Area, volume and surface area	Collecting and representing data	Indices	Working with expressions	Linear relationships	Triangles	Quadrilaterals and translations	Further sets
		B.13	B.14	B.15	B.16	B.17	B.18	B.19	B.20	B.21	B.22	B.23	B.24
Question number	1	✓	✓										
	2			✓		✓		✓		✓		✓	
	3	✓				✓				✓			
	4				✓						✓		
	5	✓		✓	✓	✓							
	6	✓	✓										
	7		✓						✓	✓			
	8			✓		✓		✓	✓		✓		✓
	9			✓			✓	✓					✓
	10	✓				✓	✓	✓		✓			
	11	✓		✓		✓			✓				
	12	✓	✓	✓		✓	✓						
	13		✓									✓	✓
	14	✓		✓	✓	✓			✓	✓			
	15			✓	✓						✓		
	16				✓	✓			✓	✓			

Questions

1. **(a)** Sharon is the manager of a hotel with 168 rooms. It has 128 standard rooms and 40 deluxe rooms. Each room is cleaned the day after it has been used.

Cleaning a room is 25 minutes' work for a standard room and 30 minutes' work for a deluxe room.

    (i) How many minutes will it take to clean all 128 of the standard rooms?

    (ii) How many minutes will it take to clean all 40 of the deluxe rooms?

    (iii) Each cleaner starts work at 8:30 am, finishes work at 2:00 pm and has two 20-minute breaks. How many minutes does each cleaner work in a day?

    (iv) On Tuesday night, all the rooms were occupied. How many cleaners are needed on Wednesday?

(b) Each day, the cleaners replace used milk cartons. Sharon estimates the cost of the milk cartons she needs next year using the following notes:

- 365 days in a year
- 75% of the 168 rooms will be used each day
- An average of 2·54 cartons per day for each room used

    (i) How many rooms does Sharon think will be in use each day?

    (ii) How many cartons of milk does Sharon think that she will need in a year?

    (iii) A box of 240 cartons costs €12·60. What is Sharon's estimate of the cost of the milk cartons?

2. **(a)** An area of land is a rectangle that is 10^4 m long and 10^3 m wide.

    (i) Using one of the laws of indices, find an expression for the area of the field and express your answer in the form 10^n, where $n \in \mathbb{N}$

    (ii) Write an expression for the perimeter of the field, then evaluate the expression and express your answer in the form $a \times 10^n$, where $1 \leq a < 10$ and $n \in \mathbb{N}$

    (iii) Explain why the laws of indices are helpful for solving area problems, but not for perimeter problems.

(b) Parts of the field are sold. The owner is left with a piece of land in the shape of a parallelogram, as shown.

    (i) What do you know about the opposite angles in a parallelogram?

    (ii) Find the value of x.   **(iii)** Hence, find the value of y.

Parallelogram angles: $(2x + 43)°$, $(5x - 20)°$, $(4y - 5x)°$

3. **(a)** A mobile phone company offers two different plans.

Plan A	Plan B
Monthly fee of €28	Monthly fee of €40
€0·45 per additional minute	€0·20 per minute

    (i) Write a formula for the cost of making x calls per month for each plan.

    (ii) Copy and complete the following table.

Minutes (x)	0	15	30	45	60	75	90	105
Plan A (€)								
Plan B (€)								

    (iii) Using the same axis and scale, draw a graph to represent the cost of the bill on plan A and plan B. Label each graph clearly.

    (iv) Using your graph, estimate the number of minutes for which the cost of plan A and plan B will be the same.

    (v) Use algebra to verify your answer to part **(iv)**.

    (vi) Which of the methods used in parts **(iv)** and **(v)** do you think is more accurate? Justify your answer.

(b) Abdul gets a new mobile phone and signs up to plan B, as described above. In a particular month, he makes 172 minutes of calls. Find:

    (i) the cost of Abdul's bill, before VAT is added

    (ii) the total cost of Abdul's bill, given that VAT is charged at a rate of 21%. Give your answer to the nearest euro.

(c) Jennifer did some research into the most common ways that teenagers access the internet. She surveyed 50 teenagers. The results are as follows.

Device	Phone	Tablet	Laptop	Home PC	Other
No. of students	22	9	12	4	3

    (i) Identify all the types of data Jennifer has collected.

    (ii) Represent this information by using an appropriate graphical method.

    (iii) What was the most popular method by which the students accessed the internet?

4. (a) The diagram shows a rectangle $ABCD$ drawn inside a circle, centre O. A, B, C and D are points on the circle.

The lengths of the rectangle are 8 cm and 6 cm, as shown.

    (i) What is the name given to the line segment $[AC]$?

    (ii) What is the name given to the line segment $[OC]$?

    (iii) What is the name given to the line segment $[AB]$?

    (iv) What is the name given to the piece of the **circle** joining A to D?

(b) (i) Find the length of the radius of the circle.

    (ii) Find the circumference of the circle. Give your answer correct to three significant figures.

    (iii) Find the area of the circle. Give your answer correct to one decimal place.

    (iv) What percentage (to the nearest whole number) of the area of the circle does the rectangle take up?

(c) What is the measure of $\angle ABC$?

Justify your answer, stating an axiom, theorem or corollary from your course.

5. The Maas Inn has a beautiful water feature in the centre of a paved courtyard. The water feature is surrounded by four identical triangular grass areas for visitors to picnic on, as shown.

Emily, the gardener, spreads fertiliser on the grass both in the spring and summer. The fertiliser costs €19·99 per bag, and each bag covers 400 m². She wishes to buy enough fertiliser for both the spring and the summer, as the shop currently has an offer of four bags for the price of three.

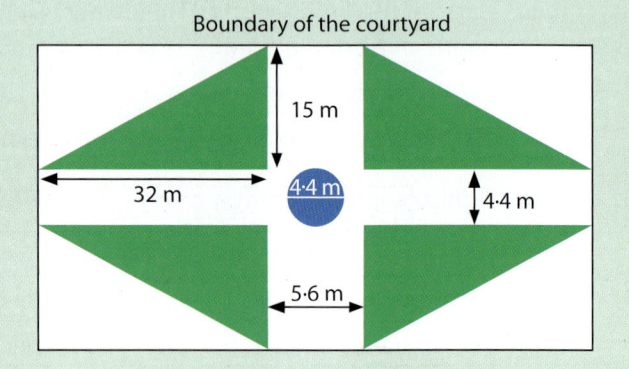

(a) (i) Find the area of the courtyard covered in grass.

    (ii) How much will it cost for the fertiliser Emily needs?

    (iii) If the circular water feature has a diameter of 4·4 metres, find its area and circumference. Give your answer to two decimal places.

    (iv) Find the area inside the courtyard not covered by grass or the water feature.

    (v) If the area found in part (iv) is to be paved with rectangular bricks that have a length of 20 cm and width of 10 cm, what is the minimum number of bricks required to cover this area?

    (vi) If each paving brick costs 75 cents, what is the total cost for all the bricks required? Give your answer to the nearest euro.

(b) Emily has a piece of fencing wire for the garden that is 240 m long. Emily cuts it into three pieces in the ratio 1 : 2 : 5

  (i) What is the length of the longest piece of wire?

  (ii) What is the length of the shortest piece of wire?

6. Below are the details of an airline return ticket from Dublin to Boston for two adults and one child.

Departure: All times are local		Return: All times are local	
From Dublin (DUB) to Boston (BOS)		From Boston (BOS) to Dublin (DUB)	
Thursday	Flight no. 137	Sunday	Flight no. 138
Depart Dublin(DUB)	10:00	Depart Boston (BOS)	06:20
Arrive Boston (BOS)		Arrive Dublin (DUB)	17:20

(a) (i) Local time in Boston is 5 hours behind local time in Dublin. The estimated flight time between these two cities is seven hours. Calculate the estimated time of arrival in Boston.

  (ii) The distance from Dublin to Boston is 4 806 km. Calculate the average speed of the plane, in km/hr, to the nearest whole number.

(b) The family has €2 500 spending money. Given an exchange rate of €1 = $US 1·14, convert the €2 500 to US dollars.

(c) The family spends $US 1 580 on accommodation and meals. Calculate the percentage (to the nearest whole number) of the family's spending money that this represents.

(d) The formula for converting temperature in Fahrenheit to Celsius is
$C = \frac{5(F - 32)}{9}$, where C = temperature in Celsius and F = temperature in Fahrenheit.

Given the temperature in Boston on the day the family arrived was 74 degrees Fahrenheit, convert this temperature to degrees Celsius. Give your answer to the nearest whole number.

7. Ann and Rachel are running in a road race. The map shows the route of the race.

The race consists of four laps of the route. Ann and Rachel run clockwise along the route at a constant speed.

(a) Using the map, work out the length of the entire race.

(b) Ann takes 3 minutes to run one kilometre.

  Rachel takes 6 minutes to run one kilometre.

  Copy and complete the table below.

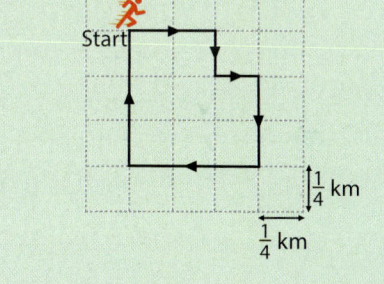

Time (min)	0	3	6	9	12	15	18	21	24	27	30	33	36
Ann's distance (km)													
Rachel's distance (km)													

(c) Using the same axis and scale, draw a graph to represent each runner's race.

(d) Calculate the speed of each runner in kilometres per minute.

(e) Find the slope of each graph. What do you notice about the slope of each graph and the speed of each person?

(f) Write an expression to represent the distance covered by each runner after t minutes.

(g) What distance will each runner have completed after 1·5 hours? Hint: Convert the time into minutes.

8. The diagram on the following page shows a computer screen with the dimensions written in terms of x cm.

   (a) The perimeter of the rectangle is 64 cm.

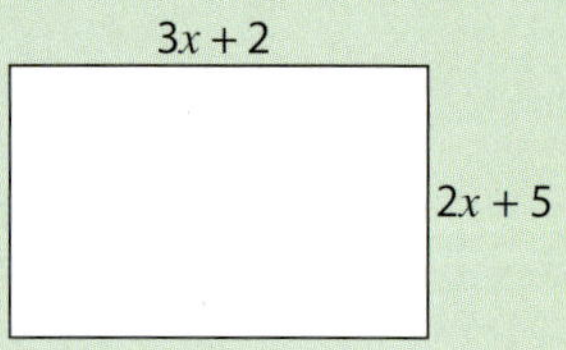

   $3x + 2$

   $2x + 5$

   (i) Form an equation for the perimeter in terms of x and hence solve it.

   (ii) Hence, find the length and width of the rectangle.

   (iii) Find the area of the screen.

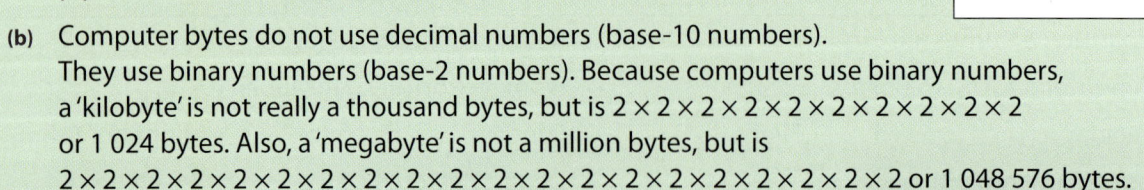

   (b) Computer bytes do not use decimal numbers (base-10 numbers). They use binary numbers (base-2 numbers). Because computers use binary numbers, a 'kilobyte' is not really a thousand bytes, but is $2 \times 2 \times 2 \times 2 \times 2 \times 2 \times 2 \times 2 \times 2 \times 2$ or 1 024 bytes. Also, a 'megabyte' is not a million bytes, but is $2 \times 2 \times 2 \times 2 \times 2 \times 2 \times 2 \times 2 \times 2 \times 2 \times 2 \times 2 \times 2 \times 2 \times 2 \times 2 \times 2 \times 2 \times 2 \times 2$ or 1 048 576 bytes.

   Write the value of a kilobyte:

   (i) in words

   (ii) using indices of base 2

   (iii) in the form $a \times 10^n$, where $1 \leq a < 10$ and $n \in \mathbb{N}$.

   Write the value of a megabyte:

   (iv) in words

   (v) using indices of base 2

   (vi) in the form $a \times 10^n$, where $1 \leq a < 10$ and $n \in \mathbb{N}$.

   (c) A cylindrical container with a radius of 10 cm and a volume of 1·571 litres is filled with computer cables so they can be stored.

   (i) Given that there are 1 000 cm³ in a litre, what is the volume of the container in cm³?

   (ii) Show that the height of the cylinder is 5 cm.

   (iii) If the total mass of the filled container is 2 kg and the mass of the empty container is 0·34 kg, what percentage of the filled container does the cables make up?

   (d) In a group of 60 people, 27 own computer tablets, 42 own laptops and each person owns at least one of the devices.

   (i) How many own both computer tablets and laptops?

   (ii) Draw a Venn diagram to represent this information.

9. (a) The length of a rectangular field is four times its width.

   (i) Write the length of the field, l, in terms of the width of the field, w.

   (ii) Which one of the following – A, B, C or D – represents the perimeter and area of the field, in terms of the width of the field?

A	Perimeter = 10 × width	Area = length × width
B	Perimeter = 5 × width	Area = 4 × (width)²
C	Perimeter = 10 × width	Area = 4 × (width)²
D	Perimeter = 5 × width	Area = (width)² ÷ 4

   (b) Assume there are 10 blades of grass per square centimetre in this field.

   (i) How many blades of grass would there be in one square metre? Write your answer in the form $a \times 10^n$ where $1 \leq a < 10$ and $n \in \mathbb{N}$.

   (ii) How many blades of grass would there be in one square kilometre? Write your answer in the form $a \times 10^n$, where $1 \leq a < 10$ and $n \in \mathbb{N}$.

(c) In a survey of 500 people, there are 125 people said they have an interest in farming, 257 people said they have an interest in mechanics and 52 people said they have an interest in both farming and mechanics.

    (i) Name all the different types of data collected by this survey.

    (ii) Create a Venn diagram to illustrate this information.

    (iii) How many people said they like farming only?

    (iv) How many people said they did not like either farming or mechanics?

(d) Soil contains many bacteria, which help release nutrients.
Every 20 minutes, the population of bacteria doubles. If there was 1 bacterium in a sample of soil, how many would there be after 2 hours?

10. (a) You are given the numbers 2^4 and $(-3)^3$ in index form.

    Answer the questions below for each number.

    (i) Identify the base number.

    (ii) Identify the index.

    (iii) Write the number in expanded form.

    (iv) Evaluate each of the numbers.

(b) Fiona's family just bought a cylindrical hot tub for their back garden.

    (i) The price of the hot tub is €246 excluding VAT at 21%.

    Calculate the total cost of the hot tub to the nearest euro.

    (ii) Given that the height of the hot tub is 73 cm and it has a diameter of 168 cm, show that its volume is 1·62 m^3, to two decimal places.

    (iii) Fiona wonders how long it will take to fill the hot tub. She knows the hose pumps 40 litres of water per minute. How many minutes will it take to completely fill the hot tub?

    Note, one cubic metre = 1 000 litres of water.

(c) An outdoor supplies shop is analysing their sales for the past year. Their results are as follows:

Item sold	Sauna	Hot tub (small)	Hot tub (large)	Gazebo	Log cabin
No. of sales	8	14	6	18	12

    (i) Represent this information by an appropriate graphical method.

    (ii) What was the least popular item they sold during that year?

11. (a) Patsy has been asked to design an aquatic area that will be part of a new leisure centre and will include a rectangular swimming pool. The space allocated within the leisure centre for the aquatic area measures 25 metres wide and 40 metres long. The swimming pool will take up exactly one-quarter of the total aquatic area.

    (i) Find the area of the swimming pool.

    (ii) The length of the pool is two-and-a-half times the width of the pool. If the width of the pool is W, find the length of the pool in terms of W.

    (iii) Form an equation, in terms of W, for the area of the pool.

    (iv) Hence, solve this equation to find the width and length of the pool.

(b) The full membership fee for the pool is €410 a year. Non-members must pay €4 per visit to use the pool.

Gerry is a non-member and he visits the pool twice a week for a year.

    (i) Calculate how much it costs Gerry to visit the pool twice a week for one year.

    (ii) Would Gerry save money if he became a member? If so, how much?

(c) The leisure centre was broken into and some tiles on the floor were damaged. Garda begin an investigation. Of the 22 290 tiles that were in the leisure centre, 234 of the tiles where damaged in the break in. Each tile is rectangular and has a width of 23 cm and a length of 42 cm.

  (i) What percentage of the total number tiles in the leisure centre were damaged in the break in? Give your answer to two decimal places.

  (ii) What was the area, in square metres, covered by one of the tiles?

  (iii) What was the total area covered by all of the tiles in the leisure centre?

  (vi) What was the total area of tiles damaged in the break in? Give your answer to one decimal place.

  (v) Fintan, the tiler, says that he can replace the tiles at a cost of €30 per square metre. Find the cost of replacing and repairing the tiles, to the nearest €10.

(d) The Garda's forensic scientists make use of a height-to-foot size ratio. If they know the size of someone's foot or footprint, they can use this ratio to estimate the height of the person that left it. Usually, the height-to-foot size ratio is 6·68 : 1, measured in centimetres. The Garda have found a footprint of 29·2 cm at the leisure centre which they believe was left by the vandal. They have three suspects with different heights: 2·00 metres, 1·67 metres and 2·17 metres.

  (i) What is the height of each suspect in centimetres?

  (ii) Which suspect is most likely to have left the footprint?

Suspect A 2·00 metres   Suspect B 1·67 metres   Suspect C 2·17 metres

12. In Tim's house, a rectangular swimming pool (blue) whose length is 30 metres and width 10 metres is surrounded by grass (green). The pool with the grassy area make a large rectangle whose length is 75 metres and width 20 metres.

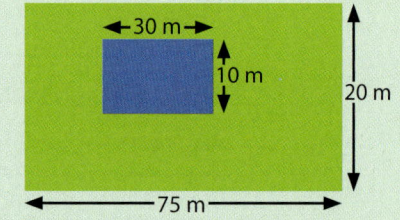

  (a) The swimming pool is filled at a rate of 2 500 litres per minute. If the total volume of the pool is 400 000 litres, how long will it take to fill the pool? Give your answer in hours and minutes.

  (b) (i) What area is occupied by the grass?

  (ii) If one bag of fertiliser covers 35m², how many bags of fertiliser does Tim require to cover his garden?

  (iii) The cost of the fertiliser is €12 per bag, including VAT. How much will it cost Tim to buy enough fertiliser for his garden?

  (iv) If the VAT was 20%, what would the total cost of the fertiliser be if Tim did not have to pay any VAT?

  (c) (i) Tim travels 490 m on his lawn mower in 14 minutes while mowing his lawn. What is his average speed?

  (ii) Tim plans on buying a different lawn mower, which is advertised to travel at 32 metres per minute. Is this faster or slower than Tim's current lawn mower?

  (d) (i) Tim examines his lawn and finds that 10% of the lawn is covered in moss, 20% in daisies, 5% in buttercups and the rest is grass. Draw a bar chart to represent this data.

  (ii) Tim throws a pen over his shoulder. What is the probability it will land on a daisy or a buttercup?

13. (a) When we describe the distance from Earth to objects in space, we use the measurement unit **light years**. A light year is the distance light travels in one Earth year. The speed of light is 3×10^8 metres per second.

  (i) How many seconds are in …?

   (a) one hour   (b) one day   (c) one year

  (Take 1 year = 365 days)

(ii) Using your answer from part (c) above, how far would a beam of light travel in one year?

Give your answer in (a) metres and (b) kilometres, in the form $a \times 10^n$ where $1 \leq a < 10$ and $n \in \mathbb{N}$.

(iii) One of the star constellations we can see at night is Orion. One particular star in this constellation is known as Bellatrix and is 243 light years away from Earth. Calculate the distance in kilometres between Earth and Bellatrix.

(iv) Using the image of Orion provided, identify a list of points which form a quadrilateral shape.

(b) The following are planets or dwarf plants in our solar system:
Mercury   Venus   Earth   Mars   Jupiter   Saturn
Uranus   Neptune   Pluto   Eris   Ceres

Eris, Ceres, and Pluto are dwarf planets.
Earth, Mars, Jupiter, Neptune, Pluto, Saturn, and Uranus each have at least one moon.

(i) Represent this information in the given Venn diagram, where D = set of dwarf planets and M = set of planets with at least one moon.

(ii) If you were to choose a planet at random, calculate the probability that it would be a dwarf planet with a moon.

14. (a) Martina is tiling her bathroom wall. The wall is 240 cm by 200 cm. The tiles are squares with a side length of 20 cm.

(i) Find the area of the bathroom wall.

(ii) Find the area of the tile.

(iii) How many tiles would Martina require for her wall?

(iv) Each box of tiles contains 15 tiles and costs €8·75 (excluding VAT). How much will it cost Martina for the tiles (excluding VAT)?

(v) If Martina must pay VAT of 20%, how much would it cost her to buy the tiles?

(vi) Using an appropriate scale, draw a scale diagram of Martina's bathroom wall.

(b) Martina has a wooden panel on her front door that needs to be replaced. The diagram on the right shows the panel, which is a rectangle with a circle cut out.

The rectangle is made out of wood and has length 20 cm and width 11 cm. The circle will hold a glass window and has a diameter of 8 cm.

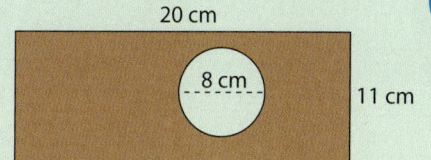

(i) Wood can only be purchased in rectangular shapes. What area of wood does Martina require for the panel on her door?

(ii) After Martina removes the circle from the wood to allow for the glass, what area of wood will be visible on one side of the door?

(iii) The glass is also sold only in rectangular shapes. Martina wants to purchase the glass for the panel, but with an extra 25% for wastage when cutting. What area of glass should Martina buy?

(c) Martina needs to work out the cost of the wooden panels and the glass sheets. Three panels and two sheets cost €95. Five panels and three sheets cost €151.
Let x represent the cost of a wooden panel and y represent the cost of a glass sheet.

(i) Form two equations in terms of x and y.

(ii) Solve these equations simultaneously to find the cost of a wooden panel and the cost of a glass sheet.

15. (a) Aoife practises her violin for at least 12 hours per week. She practises for three-quarters of an hour each session. Aoife has already practised 3 hours this week.

  (i) What proportion of her weekly practice goal has she reached?

  (ii) How many more sessions remain for her to meet her weekly practice goal?

(b) While practising her violin, Aoife started at point A and walked 3 m east to a point B. She then walked 4 m north to a point C and finally walked in a straight line back to point A.

  (i) Accurately represent her path travelled, in a scaled diagram.

  (ii) How far did she walk from point C to point A? Give answer to the nearest centimetre.

(c) Aoife needs a new table for organising her sheet music. She purchased a circular table top that is 230 cm in diameter. Aoife's front door is 105 cm wide and 208 cm tall. Explain one way that Aoife could get the table through the door. Justify your answer using calculations.

(d) Aoife bought a tablecloth with a design on it, which is shown opposite.

  $|\angle CBD| = 30°$ $|\angle BDC| = 90°$ $|CD| = 70$ cm

  $|\angle ABC| = 30°$ $|\angle BAC| = 90°$ $|AC| = 70$ cm

  $|BC| = 140$ cm

  (i) Find $|\angle ACB|$
  Justify your answer.

  (ii) Aoife thinks that $\triangle ABC$ is congruent to $\triangle BCD$.
  Is she correct? Justify your answer.

  (iii) Given the area of $\triangle ABC = 4243 \cdot 4$ cm, find the area of the blue region on this design. Give your answer to the nearest whole number.

16. (a) Sara and Adam play ice hockey. In a particular month, Sara played four more games than Adam. They played 12 games in total.

  (i) By letting x be the number of games Adam played, write an equation in terms of x to represent the total number of games played.

  (ii) Solve the equation formed in (i) to find out how many games Sara played.

(b) An ice hockey puck is cylindrical in shape and has the following dimensions:

  Diameter = 75 mm
  Height = 25 mm

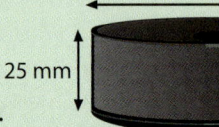

  (i) Draw the net of the puck. Include the dimensions on your diagram.

  (ii) Find the volume of rubber needed to make one puck. Give your answer to the nearest cm³.
  (1 cm = 10 mm)

(c) Sara purchased a pack of 50 ice hockey pucks that came in a rectangular box. The pucks were stacked in fives. Two stacks are placed side-by-side and five stacks are placed along the length of the box, as shown.

  (i) What is the minimum height of the box?

  (ii) What is the minimum width of the box?

  (iii) What is the minimum length of the box?

  (iv) Using the minimum dimensions above, find the volume of the box.

  (v) What percentage of the box is empty space? Give your answer to the nearest whole number.

(d) Adam decided to roll a puck on its side.

  (i) How far would it travel in one full revolution? Give your answer correct to two decimal places.

  (ii) How many revolutions would the puck complete if it rolled on its side for 5 km? Give your answer in the form $a \times 10^n$ where $1 \leq a < 10$ and $n \in \mathbb{N}$.

Linking Thinking 1

Mathematical investigations

Introduction to mathematical investigation

Maths can be used to investigate and solve problems in everyday life. In Junior Cycle Mathematics, you are required to carry out two classroom-based assessments (CBAs), which are investigations using your Maths skills.

In preparation for your CBAs, this section contains a list of investigations which you can do to practice and develop your skills as a mathematical investigator.

> Sometimes it's hard to come up with an idea. It can be helpful, throughout this process, to discuss with classmates how you could develop your investigation.

When carrying out an investigation, consider the following strategy:

1 **Define your problem** – Why did you pick this problem?
What are you trying to find out?
Can you predict what the outcome will be?

2 **Make assumptions where necessary** – Are these assumptions reasonable? (e.g. all prices are in euros)
Justify your assumptions.

3 **Break up the problem into manageable parts** – What are you going to do first?
What will you do after that? etc.

4 **Translate the problem into Maths** – Identify any variables.
Drawing a diagram is often very helpful.
Form an equation using mathematical notation, etc.

5 **Engage with the problem** – Research and record data where necessary.
Work out any calculations needed (show your work clearly).
Can you identify any patterns?
Use tables, graphs, formulas, etc.
Can you find more than one way to work out the problem?

6 **Present your solution** – Can you present it in different ways? (As a statement, a graph, a diagram, etc.)

7 **Interpret any findings** – Comment on your solution, linking it to the original problem.
Is it reasonable? Does it make sense?
Is it what you predicted?
Were your assumptions justified?

8 **Reflect on your investigation** – What were the strengths and weaknesses of your strategy?
If you were to investigate this problem again, what would you do differently?
What have you learned by carrying out this investigation?

9 **Extend and generalise your findings** – How could the results of your investigation apply to other problems?

Mathematical investigations

1. How many triangles is it possible to make using 24 matchsticks?

2. How many squares are there on a chessboard?

3. Investigate and compare different discount offers. For example, 'buy one, get one free', 'buy two, get second half price', '3 for the price of 2', etc.

4. How much water does a leaking tap waste in a year?

5. Can cylinders with the same surface area have different volumes?

6. Investigate the best phone plan, energy provider, etc.

7. Design a container to hold exactly 1 litre of liquid.

8. Investigate the relationship between:
   (a) the perimeter and the area of a square or rectangle
   (b) the length of time spent running and heart rate
   (c) the diameter and the circumference of a circle
   (d) the volume and the surface area of a cube or rectangular prism

9. Investigate the furthest distance you could get from your school with a budget of €1 000 and with a time limit of 36 hours.

10. Find the area of the school grounds.

11. To investigate the time, distance, cost and carbon footprint of a family trip within Ireland versus a family trip to Scotland.

12. A weekend street festival, including a parade with marching bands, is being planned. Such street festivals are devastated by wet weather. Undertake some research to recommend a weekend in the year that has the least chance of rain at your location.

13. An open-top box can be made from one large piece of cardboard material, which is cut and folded to form the box. Investigate how to make the biggest box from a fixed size of cardboard.

14. A cup of hot water will cool down over time. Investigate this cooling process mathematically.

15. Investigate the costing of:
    (a) designing your dream bedroom
    (b) planning a family holiday
    (c) attending an end-of-year formal ball (e.g. the Debs)
    (d) organising a party
    (e) owning a pet

16. Design and work out the costing of building:
    (a) a wooden bookcase
    (b) a monument for the school grounds
    (c) a garden shed
    (d) a fence for a given area

Section C
Applying our skills

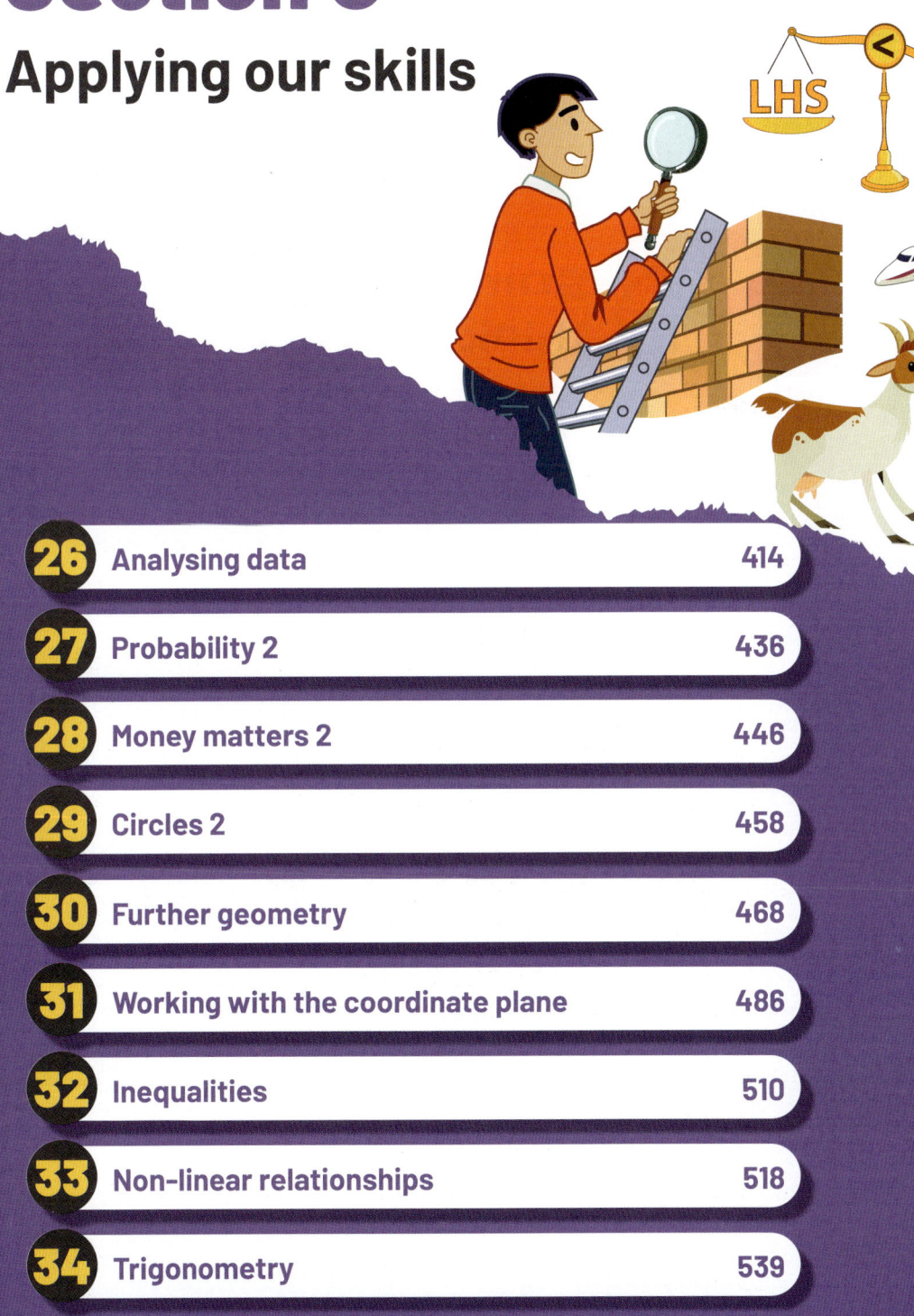

- **26** Analysing data — 414
- **27** Probability 2 — 436
- **28** Money matters 2 — 446
- **29** Circles 2 — 458
- **30** Further geometry — 468
- **31** Working with the coordinate plane — 486
- **32** Inequalities — 510
- **33** Non-linear relationships — 518
- **34** Trigonometry — 539
- **35** Linking Thinking revision material — 557

Unit 26

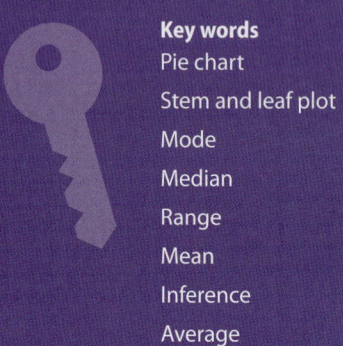

Analysing data

Topics covered within this unit:
- 26·1 Review of data collection
- 26·2 Representing data
- 26·3 Measures of central tendency and spread
- 26·4 Drawing conclusions and making inferences
- 26·5 Misuses of statistics

The Learning Outcomes covered in this unit are contained in the following sections:

SP.3a SP.3b SP.3c SP.3d SP.3e
SP.3f SP.3g SP.3h

Key words
Pie chart
Stem and leaf plot
Mode
Median
Range
Mean
Inference
Average

Something to think about ...

KEY SKILLS

You work for a company that has just produced a new energy drink. Your job is to develop an advertising campaign to prove that your drink is better than your competitor, Zoom energy drink.

Your advertisement should include graphs/charts and number statistics. The information you present must be truthful, but how it is represented is up to you.

My energy drink	
Nutrient	Typical value per 100 ml
Energy (kJ/kcal)	42/10
Protein (g)	Trace
Carbohydrate (g)	2
of which sugars (g)	1
Fat (g)	Nil
Salt (g)	Trace
	% RDA
Vitamin B6	0·073%
Vitamin B12	0·003%
Calcium	37·5%

Zoom energy drink	
Nutritional information typical values per 100 ml	
Energy	200 kJ
	47 kcal
Fat	0 g
of which saturates	0 g
Carbohydrates	12 g
of which sugars	11 g
Protein	0 g
Salt	0·19 g

26·1 Review of data collection

By the end of this section you should:
- recall material from Section B, Unit 18

In Section B, Unit 18, we were introduced to statistics. We covered how to form statistically valid and unbiased questions, types of data, sampling, different methods of collecting data and representing data using frequency tables, line plots, bar charts and histograms. Make sure you are familiar with this material before starting this unit. The following practice questions revise the material covered in Unit 18.

Practice questions 26·1

1. Which of the questions below are leading questions? Justify your answers.
   (i) Do you agree with the majority of people, that bankers earn too much?
   (ii) How has this class improved your Maths?
   (iii) Do you agree that giving your child a bottle is a really bad idea?
   (iv) How many TVs do you have in your house?
   (v) Do you agree that eating chocolate raises your IQ?
   (vi) Do you exercise?

2. A study into the eating habits of the adult population of Ireland is being conducted. Comment on any bias that might be introduced if a sample were taken from:
   (i) customers at a fruit and vegetable shop
   (ii) residents of a particular locality

3. Here are some open-ended questions that you might find on a survey. Create at least three possible answer options for each question.
   (i) Which type of film do you like watching?
   (ii) What sports should the new sport centre offer?
   (iii) What electronic gadgets do you use?

4. Identify which type of data collection method was used in each of the following situations.
   (i) Nick stood outside a movie theatre and asked the people leaving if the movie they saw was good.
   (ii) Jill searched the internet to find comments and reviews from people who owned the type of mobile phone she was thinking of buying.
   (iii) Yomi wants to find out which brand of microwave popcorn has the fewest un-popped kernels, so she tests different brands counting the un-popped kernels for each.
   (iv) Billie designs a questionnaire to find out her fellow students' opinions on the school uniform.

5. Describe the type of data in each of the following.
   (i) Nationalities of students in your school
   (ii) Ages of students in a Maths class
   (iii) Amount of fat (in grams) in 44 cookies
   (iv) The ratings of a movie, ranging from 'poor' to 'excellent'

6. Shauna asked all the students in her class how many siblings they had. The data she collected is shown below.
   1, 1, 4, 2, 4, 2, 0, 0, 2, 2, 1, 2, 0, 3, 3,
   4, 0, 1, 0, 3, 1, 2, 3, 1, 2, 4, 4, 2, 2, 1

   (i) Draw a line plot to represent Shauna's data.
   (ii) Copy and complete the frequency table below.

No. of siblings	0	1	2	3	4
Tally					
Frequency					

   (iii) Use the frequency table to draw a bar chart to represent Shauna's data.

7. Clark surveyed the students in his youth club to find out what age they were. The data he collected is shown below:
   17, 11, 15, 10, 12, 17, 12, 12, 10, 11, 14, 13, 17,
   12, 10, 17, 16, 11, 13, 11, 17, 17, 15, 17, 12

   (i) Copy and complete the grouped frequency table below.

Age	10–12	12–14	14–16	16–18
Tally				
Frequency				

   Note: 10–12 means 10 or more but less than 12, etc.

   (ii) Use the grouped frequency table to draw a histogram to represent Clark's data.
   (iii) What are the main differences between bar charts and histograms?

26·2 Representing data

By the end of this section you should be able to:
- draw and interpret pie charts
- draw and interpret stem and leaf plots
- decide the most appropriate graph to represent data

Pie charts

> A **pie chart** is a circular graph (360°) that shows the proportion that different categories contribute to an overall total.

Pie charts are particularly useful for representing categorical data. They cannot be used for continuous data.

In this pie chart, you can clearly see that romance was the most popular type of movie of the people questioned because it has the largest sector area. Drama was the least favourite type of movie because it has the smallest sector area.

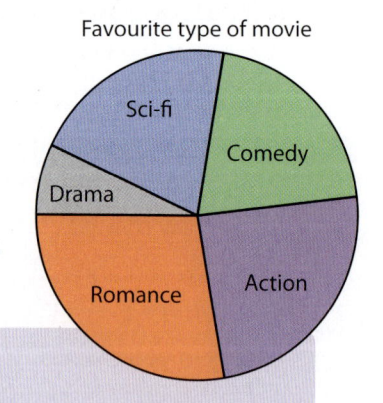

Drawing a pie chart

1. Find the total number surveyed.
2. Represent each category as a fraction of the total.
3. Work out the angle for each category by multiplying the fraction by 360°.
4. Mark a centre, use a compass to draw a circle and a start line from the centre to one side of the circle.
5. Use a protractor placed on the start line to begin measuring each of the angles around the circle. Each line drawn becomes the start line for the next angle.

The angle in a full circle is 360°.

Worked example 1

Represent the following data on a pie chart.

Favourite sport	Gaelic football	Hurling	Basketball	Rugby	Football
No. of students	4	5	6	1	4

Solution

Step 1 Find the total number of people surveyed: $4 + 5 + 6 + 1 + 4 = 20$

Step 2 Represent each category as a fraction of the total:

Gaelic football: $\frac{4}{20}$ Hurling: $\frac{5}{20}$ Basketball: $\frac{6}{20}$ Rugby: $\frac{1}{20}$ Football: $\frac{4}{20}$

Step 3 Since a full circle is 360° we multiply the fraction representing each category by 360° to work out the angle for each category:

Gaelic football: $\frac{4}{20} \times 360° = 72°$ Hurling: $\frac{5}{20} \times 360° = 90°$

Basketball: $\frac{6}{20} \times 360° = 108°$ Rugby: $\frac{1}{20} \times 360° = 18°$

Football: $\frac{4}{20} \times 360° = 72°$

Step 4 Draw a circle and use a protractor to measure each of the angles using the method shown below:
- Draw a radius from the centre and use it as the start line to measure the first angle.
- After you draw each angle, the arm of this angle becomes the start line for the next angle.
- When you're finished the pie chart should look something like this, (depending on where you draw your start line).

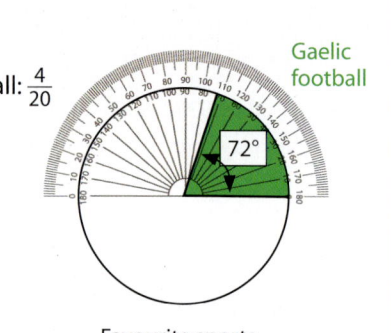

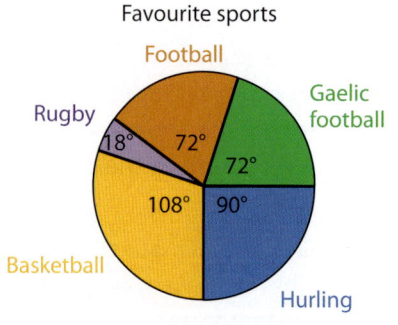

Stem and leaf plots

> A **stem and leaf plot** is a special table where each data value is split into a '**stem**' (the first digit or digits) and a '**leaf**' (usually the last digit).

```
Stem | Leaf
  0  | 6 7 8
  1  | 0 2 3 4 7 7 7 8 9
  2  | 1 3 4 4 5 7
  3  | 1 1 2 6 6 9
  4  | 1 5 5 6 9
  5  | 0
```

6 is recorded as 06

This is number 39

Key 2|5 = 25

The key shows us how to read the diagram

Stem and leaf plots are used to display numerical discrete and continuous data.

In a stem and leaf plot, the data is spread evenly along a branch in numerical order. Each data value is split into a **stem** and a **leaf**. The digit(s) in the largest place are referred to as the stem and the digit(s) in the smallest place are referred to as the leaf (leaves).

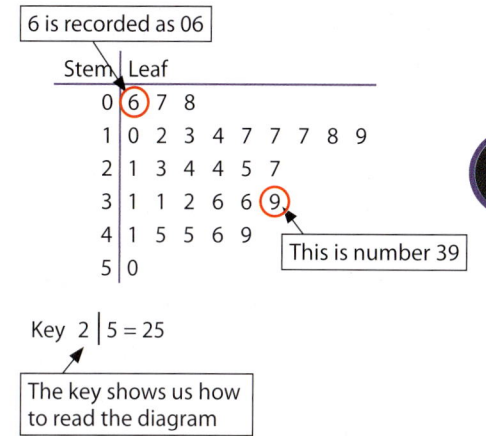

For example, in the number 32, 3 is the stem and 2 is the leaf. In the number 11·5, 11 is the stem and 5 is the leaf.

The stem is placed in a column and the leaves are placed in rows to the right of the column corresponding to their stems. Each value is seen, and data is sorted in ascending numerical order, from smallest to biggest.

Each stem and leaf plot must include a key to explain how to read the plot, and it is good practice to include units on the key, if appropriate.

Drawing a stem and leaf plot

1. Arrange the data in ascending numerical order.
2. Split the data into a stem and leaf and place the stems in the first column.
3. Place the leaves in rows that correspond to their stem, in ascending order.
4. A key must always be included.

Worked example 2

The following is a set of Maths test results:
73, 78, 57, 54, 42, 35, 32, 46, 89, 55, 46, 37, 56, 77, 37, 48, 68, 70, 69, 68, 33, 41

(i) Represent this data on a stem and leaf plot.
(ii) How many students sat the test?
(iii) What were the lowest and highest results?
(iv) Did any students receive the same result?

Solution

(i) To draw the stem and leaf plot, we complete the following steps:

Step 1 Arrange the data in ascending numerical order
32, 33, 35, 37, 37, 41, 42, 46, 46, 48, 54, 55, 56, 57, 68, 68, 69, 70, 73, 77, 78, 89

Step 2 Split the data into a stem and leaf and place the stems in a column

```
Stem
  3
  4
  5
  6
  7
  8
```

Step 3 Place the leaves in rows that correspond to their stem, in ascending order.

```
Stem | Leaf
  3  | 2 3 5 7 7
  4  | 1 2 6 6 8
  5  | 4 5 6 7
  6  | 8 8 9
  7  | 0 3 7 8
  8  | 9
```

Step 4 A key must always be included.
Key: 3|2 = 32 %

It is important that the leaves are placed directly under each other to maintain the correct shape of the plot.

If a number occurs more than once, it is repeated in the plot.

(ii) 22 students sat the test.
(iii) The lowest result was 32% and the highest result was 89%.
(iv) 2 students got 37%, 2 students got 46% and 2 students 68%.

Section C Applying our skills

Choosing the most appropriate graph

In Section B, Unit 18 – and in this unit – we have discussed different ways to represent data. The data representation methods we have worked with include frequency tables and grouped frequency tables, line plots, bar charts, histograms, pie charts and stem and leaf plots.

It is often possible to represent data in many different ways, but we should consider carefully which representations work best for the data we are trying to represent.

The table below summarises what types of data can be represented and the advantages and disadvantages of each type of data representation.

Type of representation	Data type best displayed	Advantages	Disadvantages
Frequency table	• Categorical • Numerical data	• Easy to read and understand • Easy to construct • Trends in data can be identified • Comparisons can be made between data	• Time consuming to complete
Grouped frequency table	• Numerical continuous data	• Reduces large amount of data	• Loss of original data in the grouping
Line plot	• Categorical • Numerical discrete data	• Easy to read • Easy to construct	• Difficult to plot large frequencies • Not suitable for a large number of categories
Bar chart	• Categorical • Numerical discrete data	• Easy to read • Easy to construct • Can compare two or three data sets	• Not easy to represent very large frequencies
Histogram	• Numerical continuous data	• Easy to see the distribution of the data	• Difficult to compare more than one data set
Pie chart	• Categorical data • Numerical discrete data	• Easy to compare data by the size of the sector • Easy to compare to the whole	• Can be confusing if too many categories • Difficult to compare more than one data set • Total unknown unless given
Stem and leaf	• Numerical data	• All data shown, making some analysis easier • Can be used to compare two data sets	• Can sometimes look messy and unappealing • Difficult to plot large frequencies

Discuss and discover

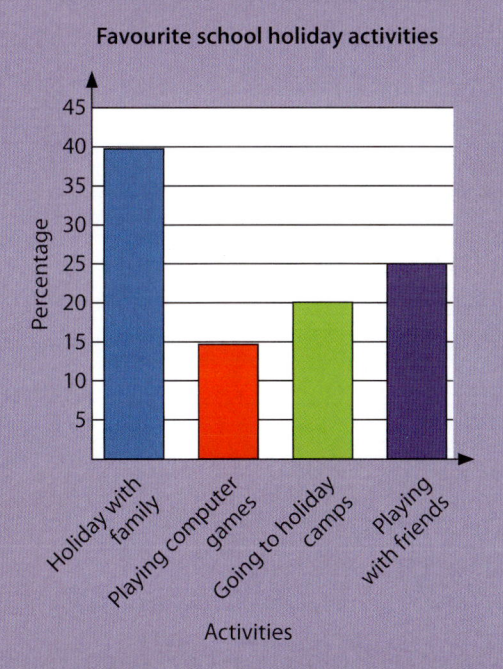

Working with a classmate, decide if each of the statements (i) to (v) are clearly shown on the bar chart, pie chart, both or neither.

Favourite school holiday activities (bar chart)
Favourite school holiday activities (pie chart)

- Holiday with family
- Playing computer games
- Going to holiday camps
- Playing with friends

(i) 40% said their favourite activity is going on holiday with family.
(ii) Going to holiday camps was a less popular choice than playing computer games.
(iii) A quarter of people said their favourite activity is playing with friends.
(iv) The most popular activity was going on holiday with family.
(v) Twice as many people picked going on holiday with their family than picked going to holiday camps.

Which chart do you think best represents the data? Justify your answer.

Practice questions 26.2

1. The table below shows the number of various types of fish caught in a lake one day

Type of fish	Trout	Pike	Bream	Carp	Salmon
Number in a lake	10	5	30	18	9

   (i) How many fish were caught in total that day?
   (ii) Represent each type of fish as a fraction of the total number of fish.
   (iii) Calculate the angle needed to represent each type of fish in a pie chart.

2. Work out the angles needed to draw a pie chart to represent the data in each of the following tables.

   (i)
Favourite music	Rock	Country	R&B	Jazz	Dance
Number of people	4	10	7	6	3

   (ii)
Favourite sandwich	Tuna	Ham	Cheese	Salad	Chicken
Number of students	20	25	24	15	6

3. Draw a pie chart to represent the following data in which the angles have been provided.

   (i)
Favourite football team	Manchester United	Arsenal	Liverpool	Chelsea	Aston Villa
Angle representing number of students	75°	35°	60°	84°	106°

   (ii)
Favourite colour	Red	Blue	Green	Yellow	Purple
Angle representing number of students	55°	98°	115°	32°	60°

4. Draw a pie chart to represent the data shown in the following tables.

   (i)
Car colour	Red	Blue	White	Black	Silver
Frequency	120	6	14	160	60

   (ii)
Subject of first class on Monday	Maths	Science	Art	French	Business
Number of students	8	10	5	3	4

5. A bag contains red, white and black marbles.
   The pie chart shows information about the marbles in the bag.

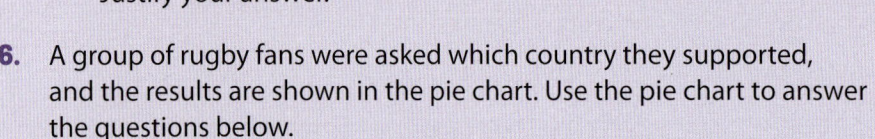

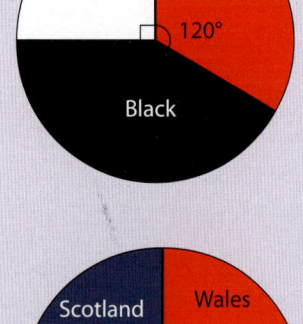

   (i) What percentage of the marbles are white?

   (ii) What fraction (in simplest form) of the marbles are red?

   (iii) Work out the angle that represents the black sector.

   (iv) If there are 24 marbles in the bag, how many of the marbles are black?

   (v) Identify the type of data represented in the pie chart. Justify your answer.

6. A group of rugby fans were asked which country they supported, and the results are shown in the pie chart. Use the pie chart to answer the questions below.

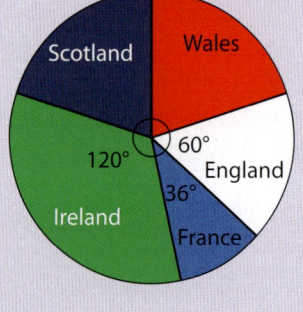

   (i) If the same number of people support Scotland and Wales, what angle represents each of these countries?

   (ii) If 150 people support England, how many people were questioned?

   (iii) What percentage of the total support France?

   (iv) If a fan was chosen at random, what is the probability that they support Wales?

7. The stem and leaf plot shown represents the numbers of cans of cola sold each day from a vending machine in a two-week period. Use the stem and leaf plot to answer the questions below.

   (i) What is the maximum number of cans sold in a day?

   (ii) How many days show sales of less than 60 cans?

   (iii) If a day was chosen at random, what is the probability that between 50 and 55 (inclusive) cans were sold on that day?

Stem	Leaf
5	0 2 8 9
6	0 3 3 5 9 9
7	2 5 7 8

   Key 5|0 = 50 cans

8. Identify the stem and the leaf in each of the following number sets.

   (i) 6, 37, 78, 9, 33, 49, 56, 19, 26

   (ii) 152, 547, 378, 743, 959

   (iii) 5·8, 1·4, 3·8, 7·5, 6·9, 8·4, 7·6, 6·4

9. List the data represented on the stem and leaf plots shown below.

(i)
Stem	Leaf
2	1 3 6 9
3	0 4 4
4	5 5 6
5	3

Key 2|1 = 2·1

(ii)
Stem	Leaf
0	2 6 8
1	3 4 5 8
2	1 2 4
3	0 5

Key 3|0 = 30

(iii)
Stem	Leaf
88	7
89	0 8 9
90	1 3 5 6 9
91	2 8

Key 90|1 = 901

10. Draw a stem and leaf plot and a histogram to represent each of the follow sets of data.

(i) 56, 22, 45, 24, 13, 39, 15, 34, 26, 45, 51, 18, 38, 26, 55

(ii) 293, 287, 309, 306, 295, 288, 285, 294, 306, 281

(iii) 6·6, 4·8, 3·7, 5·9, 4·6, 6·4, 5·8, 3·8, 5·4, 4·3

11. These graphs show the final grades for a Third-Year Maths class.

(i) Identify the types of graph shown in A and B.

(ii) Identify the type of data shown on these graphs.

(iii) List three things you know from graph A.

(iv) List three things you know from graph B.

(v) Which graph provides the simplest way to calculate the number of students who got a C grade? Justify your answer.

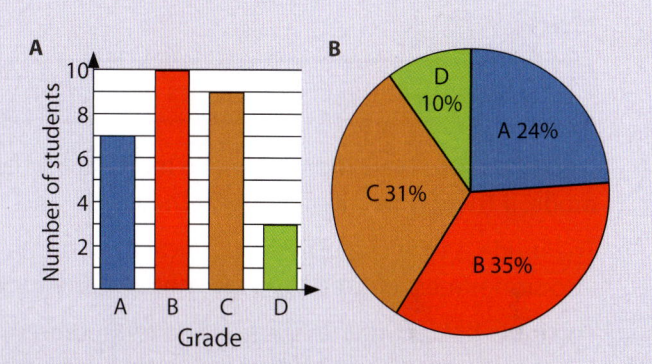

(vi) In your opinion, which graph is the most appropriate graph to represent this data? Justify your answer.

12. Choose the most appropriate graph to represent the following data sets. Justify your answer in each case.

(i) The time it takes students to get to school.

(ii) The hair colour of the students in your class.

(iii) The results obtained from rolling a die 20 times.

(iv) The number of homework questions given in Maths over a week.

13. One of the stem and leaf plots shown below is incorrect. Which one is it? Justify your answer.

A
Stem	Leaf
1	3 3 6 9
2	0 2 6
3	1 5 8
4	4

Key 2|0 = 20

B
Stem	Leaf
20	1 3 7 8
2	9
15	1 2 2 5
5	4 6 8
1	1

14. (a) Copy the table below and put a tick (✓) in the correct box in each row to show whether each statement is true or false. Justify your answer in each case.

	Statement	True	False
(i)	The angles in a pie chart add to 360°.		
(ii)	Tally marks should be in bundles of 10.		
(iii)	Stem and leaf plots are used for numerical data.		
(iv)	There should be spaces between the bars of a histogram.		

(b) Where the statement is false, write the correct statement.

26.3 Measures of central tendency and spread

By the end of this section you should:
- understand and calculate the measures of central tendency of a data set - mode, median and mean
- understand and calculate the spread of the data, range

After collecting data, we may also want to analyse the data we have collected.

One way to analyse data is to look at where the centre or middle of the data lies, as a representative of a 'typical' value of the data set.

This central or middle point is often called the **average**.

> The **average** is a measure of central tendency of a data set. The three most commonly used averages are the mode, median and mean.

Mode

> The **mode** is the value that occurs most often.

It is possible to have more than one mode (if there are two, it is called bimodal), and it is possible to have no mode. If there is no mode we write '**no mode**' and not zero, as zero itself could be the mode.

The mode is very useful for categorical (non-numerical) data when other averages won't work. The mode is also sometimes referred to as the **modal value** (or **class/group** in a histogram).

The table below outlines the method for finding the mode in various different situations.

Graph/representation of data	Method to find the mode
List of data	Pick the number or word that appears most often
Frequency table	Pick the category with highest frequency
Bar chart, histogram, or line plot	Pick the category that has the highest 'bar'
Pie chart	Pick the category that has the biggest sector
Stem and leaf plot	Pick the number that appears most often

Worked example 1

What is the mode of each of the following?

(i) 2, 3, 4, 2, 4, 2, 3, 2, 4, 3, 2

(ii)
Age	11	12	13
Frequency	9	18	10

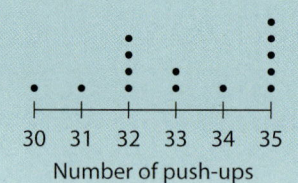

(iii) Number of push-ups (line plot from 30 to 35)

Solution

(i) 2 is the mode because it appears the greatest number of times (5) in the list.

(ii) 12 is the modal age because it has the highest frequency (18).

(iii) 35 is the mode because it is the number of push-ups completed by the greatest number of people (5). We can read this from the line plot, as it has the greatest number of dots.

Worked example 2

What is the mode of each of the following?

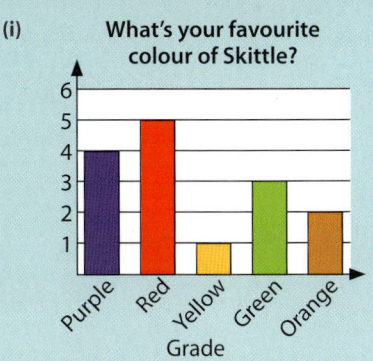

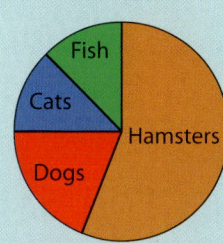

(i) What's your favourite colour of Skittle?

(ii) Favourite pets

(iii)
Stem	Leaf
4	1 2 2 5 7 8
5	2 7 8
6	5 6
7	0 5 8 8 8
8	0 0
9	5

Key 4|1 = 41

Solution

(i) Red is the mode, because the highest frequency of people (5) choose red as their favourite colour. We can read this from graph, as it has the highest bar.

(ii) Hamster is the mode, because the greatest number of people choose hamster. We can see this from the pie chart as it has the biggest sector.

(iii) 78 is the mode, as it appears the most times (3) in the stem and leaf plot.

Median

The median is the **middle** value when the data is arranged in ascending (from smallest value to largest value) numerical order.

Finding the median

1. From a set of data, list the data in ascending order

2. Pick the number at the middle position
e.g. 4, 9, **13**, 18, 27   median = 13

3. If there are two numbers in the middle, we find the number halfway between these two
e.g. 2, 6, **9, 13**, 19, 21 $\frac{9+13}{2} = \frac{22}{2} = 11$ median = 11

To find the position of the median (middle position) of a set of data, we can use the formula
$$\frac{n+1}{2}$$ **where n is the number of values in the set.**

For example, the middle position of 5 numbers is $\frac{5+1}{2} = 3$, so the value in the third position is the median.

The middle position of 10 numbers is $\frac{10+1}{2} = 5\cdot5$, so the median is found by adding the values in the fifth and sixth positions and dividing their sum by 2 (median = the value midway between the fifth and the sixth positions).

Section C Applying our skills

Worked example 3

The following is a list of the ages of people living in an apartment building.
21, 14, 30, 28, 17, 27, 10, 19, 17, 26, 29, 20
Find the median age of the people in the building.

Solution

To find the median, complete the following steps:

Step 1 Arrange the numbers in ascending order (if a number is there more than once, write it down as many times as it appears).
10, 14, 17, 17, 19, 20, 21, 26, 27, 28, 29, 30

Step 2 Find the middle position.
$n = 12$, therefore the middle position is $\frac{12+1}{2} = 6.5$,
Pick the value at the sixth and seventh position, add them and divide by 2

Median
↓
10, 14, 17, 17, 19, **20, 21**, 26, 27, 28, 29, 30

sixth position = 20   seventh position = 21
$\frac{20+21}{2} = 20.5$
Median = 20.5 years

> The median doesn't have to be an actual value within the data set.

Mean

The most commonly used average is the **mean**. To find the mean of a set of numbers we add up all the values and divide by the number of values.

$$\text{Mean} = \frac{\text{sum of the values}}{\text{number of values}}$$

Worked example 4

Find the mean of the following set of numbers.
34, 10, 9, 13, 34, 15, 18, 7, 35, 22

Solution

$\text{Mean} = \frac{\text{sum of the values}}{\text{number of values}}$

$\text{Mean} = \frac{34 + 10 + 9 + 13 + 34 + 15 + 18 + 7 + 35 + 22}{10}$

$= 19.7$

> The means doesn't have to be an actual value in the data set.

To find the mean of a frequency distribution table, we add up the frequency multiplied by the values and divide by the sum of the frequencies.

$$\text{Mean} = \frac{\text{sum of (frequency} \times \text{value)}}{\text{sum of frequency}}$$

> We encountered frequency distribution tables in Section B, Unit 18.

Worked example 5

The following data was gathered about the number of text messsages received by a group of students:

3, 3, 3, 3, 3, 5, 5, 5, 5, 8, 8, 8, 8, 8, 8, 8, 8, 8, 8, 8, 8, 8, 8, 8, 8, 8, 8, 10, 10, 10, 10, 10, 10, 10, 10, 10, 10, 10, 10, 10, 10, 10, 10, 10, 10, 10, 10, 12, 12, 12, 12, 12, 12, 12, 12, 12, 12, 12, 12

(i) Copy and complete the table below.

No. of messages	3	5	8	10	12
No. of students					

(ii) Find the mean of the data correct, to one decimal place.

Solution

(i)

No. of messages	3	5	8	10	12
No. of students	5	4	16	22	12

We could get the mean using the actual data values (or 'raw' data), however, using the table is more efficient.

(ii) Mean = $\frac{\text{total number of text messages received}}{\text{total number of students}}$

If 5 students each received 3 messages, then between them they received a total of 15 messages.

To find the total number of messages received we multiply the number of students by the number of messages that they received and add the results

$$\text{Mean} = \frac{(5 \times 3) + (4 \times 5) + (16 \times 8) + (22 \times 10) + (12 \times 12)}{5 + 4 + 16 + 22 + 12}$$

$$\text{Mean} = \frac{15 + 20 + 128 + 220 + 144}{59}$$

$$\text{Mean} = \frac{527}{59}$$

Mean = 8·9322033898

Mean = 8·9 texts

Range

Once the data has been arranged in ascending order it is very easy to calculate the range. The range is a measure of how **spread out** or variable the data is. In general, less spread out data is considered to be more reliable.

> The **range** is the difference between the highest value and the lowest value.

For example, in the data set 4, 7, 12, 16, 18, the highest value is 18 and the lowest value is 4. Therefore, it has a range of 18 − 4 = **14**.

> **Range = the highest value − the lowest value**

Discuss and discover

KEY SKILLS

Work with a classmate to answer the following questions.

(i) The following data was collected.

12 15 16 16 17 17 17 18 18 19 20 21

Find the (a) mode (b) median (c) range (d) mean

(ii) Now a much higher value (an 'extreme' value), for example 250, is added to the data.

12 15 16 16 17 17 17 18 18 19 20 21 250

Find the (a) mode (b) median (c) range (d) mean

(iii) What affect did the extreme value have on each of the results above?

(iv) Which value was least affected by adding the extreme value to the data set?

The table below summarises when each average is best used and the advantages and disadvantages of each.

Average	Best used	Advantages	Disadvantages
Mode	When asked to choose the most popular item.	• Extreme values (outliers) do not affect the mode	• Not necessarily unique – there may be more than one answer • When no values repeat in the data set, there is no mode • When there is more than one mode, it is difficult to interpret and/or compare
Median	To describe the middle of a set of data. It is useful when dealing with data that has extreme values (outliers).	• Extreme values (outliers) do not affect the median as strongly as they do the mean • Useful when comparing sets of data • It is unique – there is only one answer	• Not as popular or well understood as the mean
Mean	To describe the middle of a set of data that does not have an extreme value (outlier).	• Most popular measure in fields such as business, engineering and computer science • It is unique – there is only one answer • Useful when comparing sets of data	• Affected by extreme values (outliers)

Practice questions 26.3

1. Find the mode of each of the following lists of data. Justify your answers.
   (i) 6, 9, 4, 4, 2, 3, 3, 9, 3, 4, 9, 3, 6, 9, 6, 9
   (ii) 13, 6, 24, 18, 33, 5, 13, 48, 9, 11, 36, 28
   (iii) 5, 0, 2, 9, 0, 7, 5, 5, 0, 8, 10, 3, 0
   (iv) 82, 82, 68, 71, 68, 86, 67, 71, 75

2. Find the mode (or modes) of each of the following and justify your answer in each case.

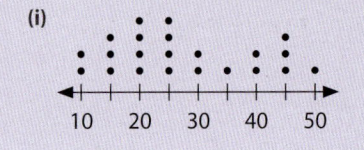

   (i) [dot plot with scale 10, 20, 30, 40, 50]

   (ii)
Time (min)	2	3	5	6	8	10
Number of students	1	2	6	8	3	1

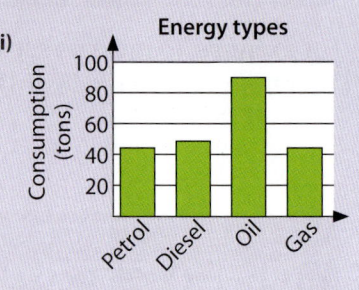

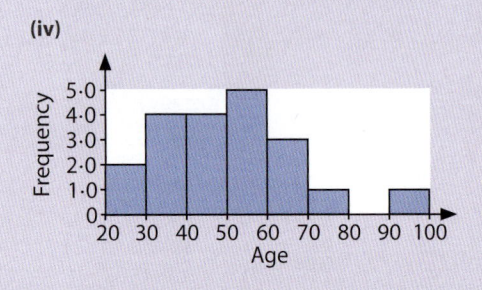

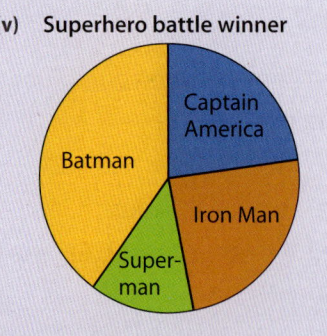

   (iii) Energy types [bar chart: Petrol, Diesel, Oil, Gas; Consumption (tons)]

   (iv) [histogram: Frequency vs Age, 20–100]

   (v) Superhero battle winner [pie chart: Captain America, Iron Man, Superman, Batman]

   (vi)
Stem	Leaf
0	5 7
1	1 2 2 2
2	0 4
3	
4	1 1 3

   Key 0|5 = 5

3. A data set has 6 numbers. Four of the numbers are 4, 3, 8 and 12. If the mode is 3, find at least three possibilities for the other two numbers.

4. Find **(a)** the median and **(b)** the range of the following data sets.

   (i) 92, 67, 82, 51, 50, 72, 53   (ii) 1, 9, 10, 42, 4, 50, 47, 21, 30   (iii) 14, 6, 4, 20, 7, 6, 11, 11, 2

5. Jason's French book has sixteen chapters. The number of pages in each chapter are given below.
   21, 29, 19, 16, 17, 18, 20, 19, 25, 28, 20, 24, 26, 15, 17, 26

   (i) Represent this data in a stem and leaf plot.
   (ii) Find the median number of pages per chapter.
   (iii) Find the range.

6. Find the mean of the following data sets. Give your answer correct to two decimal places where necessary.

   (i) 6, 9, 15, 10, 5
   (ii) 14, 8, 6, 16, 18, 17, 19
   (iii) 67, 29, 46, 29, 31, 92, 42
   (iv) 55, 84, 92, 75, 7, 58, 97, 21, 41
   (v) 0·3, 1·2, 1·5, 0·4, 0·6, 1·8
   (vi) −14, 3, 25, −14, −15, −12, 3, 26, 20

7. Find the mean of the following frequency distribution tables. Give your answer to two decimal places.

   (i)
Cups of coffee	0	1	2	3	4
Number of people	4	12	16	8	3

   (ii)
Days missed	0	1	2	3	4
Number of students	18	24	19	8	2

   (iii)
Age	11	12	13	14	15
Number of students	7	23	17	11	5

   (iv)
Text messages sent	0	1	2	3	4
Number of people	4	25	12	6	8

8. Find the mode, median, range and mean of each of the following lists of data.

   (i) 72, 80, 59, 3, 90, 72, 43, 30, 45   (ii) 94, 17, 92, 83, 96, 29, 6, 12

9. A health centre recorded the height (in cm) of a group of toddlers who came for vaccination. The heights are given below.

   64, 71, 70, 68, 71, 75, 66, 65, 71, 69, 72, 66, 65, 73

   (i) Represent this data on a stem and leaf plot.
   (ii) What is the modal height?
   (iii) Find the median height of the toddlers.
   (iv) What is the mean height?
   (v) What is the range of heights?

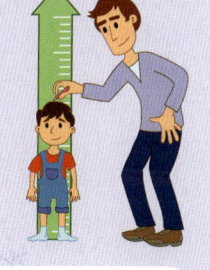

Taking it FURTHER

10. Find the mean of the first ten prime numbers.

11. A set of five numbers has a mode of 12, a median of 11 and a mean of 10. What could the five numbers be?

12. Copy the table below and put a tick (✓) in the correct box in each row to show whether each statement is always true, sometimes true, or never true. Justify your answer in each case.

	Statement	Tick **one** box only for each answer		
		Always true	Sometimes true	Never true
(i)	There is one mode.			
(ii)	The mean and median can be the same.			
(iii)	The mode is the middle number.			
(vi)	The mean is found by adding the numbers and dividing by the number of numbers.			
(v)	The mean is always a natural number.			
(vi)	The range is found by adding the first and last numbers.			

26.4 Drawing conclusions and making inferences

By the end of this section you should be able to:
- form conclusions based on data collected

Once we have collected and analysed our data, we can use our data to draw some conclusions. The conclusion stage is about answering the question posed at the beginning and giving reasons based on the analysis of the data collected.

A statistical conclusion links the evidence from the sample to a generalisation (inference) for the population.

> An **inference** is a generalisation about a population based on data from a sample.

It begins with what seems to be true about the sample, then it answers the question: 'How do you know this is true?'

Usually there are two sorts of evidence: **numerical values of statistics** (mean, mode, median and range) and a **description of graph(s)**.

The conclusion then sums up what is expected to be true for the population based on what is seen in the sample. However, we can never be 100% certain that the information from the sample is true for the entire population.

When making a conclusion we should consider the strategy below:

Making a conclusion

1. Answer the questions posed – a good beginning is, 'Based on the evidence from the data/bar chart/table, it seems …'
2. Quantify your answer – quote numerical values (with units) of measures of central tendency and spread, and describe graph features.
3. Generalise the answer (make an inference) to the entire population. One possible starter for the generalisation is 'I expect …'

" A list of suitable sentence starters for forming conclusions include:

- From this data …
- From this sample …
- It appears that …
- The sample data collected from …
- There is evidence to suggest …
- From the (type) graph …
- From this data, it is likely that the population may …
- The data tends to suggest…

- From this sample, the (average value) was … This suggests that …
- In general, the data suggests …
- Based on this data …
- I noticed that …
- Further investigation may assist …
- I wonder if …
- The data infers … "

Limitations of conclusions drawn from samples

Conclusions drawn from samples are only as good as the sample being analysed. It is important that the sample is large enough, random and representative of the population of interest.

Sometimes, when looking at statistics reported by others, we have no information about the sample used. In these cases, we must be wary of claims being made.

It is even possible that statistics can be manipulated so that they tell the story that the person using them wants to tell.

Because of these influencing factors, it is important to understand how to evaluate statistical information so that you can be a statistically aware citizen.

In an attempt to prevent companies from misleading customers, there are laws and standards that companies have to adhere to when advertising their products. You may have noticed that in certain advertisements, they will tell you how many people were surveyed.

Worked example

Linda attends a school of 400 students. She conducted a survey using a random sample of the junior students in her school. She drew the graphs below to represent the data she collected.
What conclusions could Linda make from the data shown?

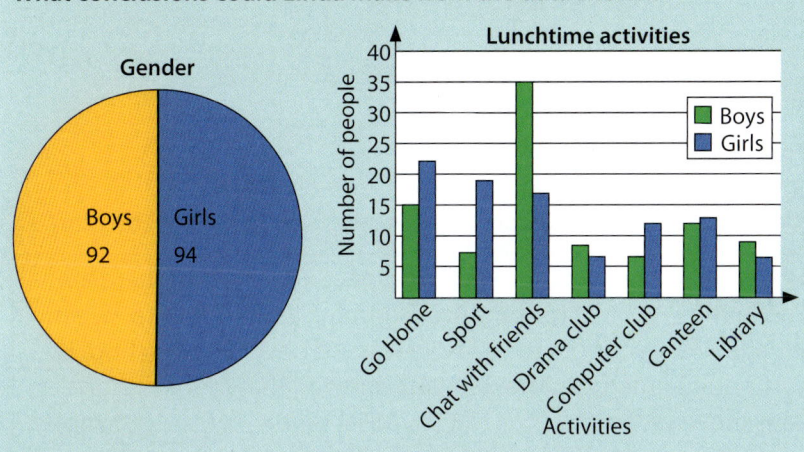

Gender: Boys 92, Girls 94

	Age
Mean	14·214
Median	13·5
Mode	14
Range	3

Solution

From this sample the **pie chart** suggests that there are approximately the same number of boys and girls in the sample. This tends to suggest that there are approximately the same number of boys and girls in the population. The fact that the pie chart contains the actual numbers allows us to work out the sample size. The sample size for this investigation was 186 students. This is a large sample size out of a population of 400, which means the data is likely to be reliable.

Based on the evidence of the **bar chart**, it seems the most popular lunchtime activity with boys was to chat with friends while the least popular activity for boys was computers. It appears that the most popular activities with girls are going home, followed by sport and the least popular activities were drama and going to the library.

The **table** shows that the average age, to the nearest year, of the students sampled was 14 with a mean age of 14·214, a median age of 13·5 and a mode of 14. The range of the age data is 3 which suggests that the spread of ages in the sample was relatively low.

Practice questions 26·4

1. Daniel owns a gym. He wants to investigate if lifting heavier weights affects how many reps a person can complete.
   The table below shows the results of an observational study he conducted.

Weight lifted (kg)	Number of reps
100	32
115	24
130	16
145	8

   (i) Can you identify any pattern/trend from this table?

   (ii) What conclusion could Daniel draw from this data?

   (iii) Can you think of any possible limitations to this conclusion?

   A rep means moving the weight up and down once.

2. Below is some of the data collected from a questionnaire.

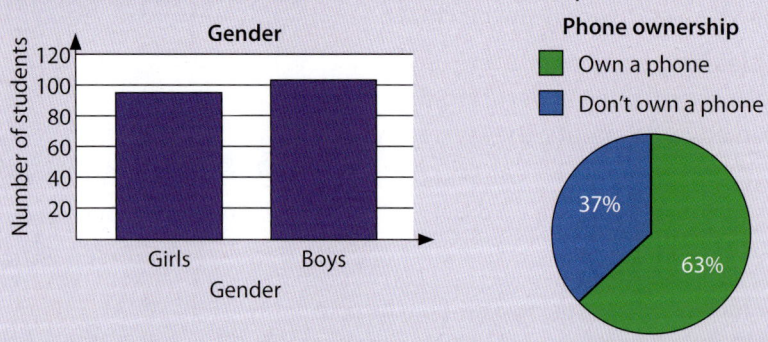

Gender (bar chart: Girls ~95, Boys ~105, Number of students)

Phone ownership (pie chart: Own a phone 63%, Don't own a phone 37%)

Average	Age
Mean	12·115
Median	12
Mode	12

How students travel to school

Age	Walk	Car	Bus	Train	Bicycle	Other
8–10	10	20	3	0	2	2
11–13	28	40	35	1	9	2
14–16	11	22	9	2	1	3

Copy the paragraph below and using the data provided and the suggested options in bold fill in the blanks.

> From this particular _____ (population/sample), the _____ (table/graph) suggests that there are _____ (slightly/a lot) less girls than boys in the _____ (population/sample). From this data, it can be seen that the _____ (mean/median) age of a student in the sample was 12. Travelling to school by _____ (car/train) appears to be the most popular method. The data also showed that mobile phone ownership is high for students with the data showing that _____ (37%/63%) of the _____ (sample/population) own a mobile phone. This _____ (proves/suggests) that more students own a mobile phone than don't own a mobile phone.

3. Sami recorded how many of various items his family recycled over a two-week period.

   The graph on the right represents the data he collected.

   Using evidence from the graph, write as many different conclusions as possible that Sami could come to using the data he collected.

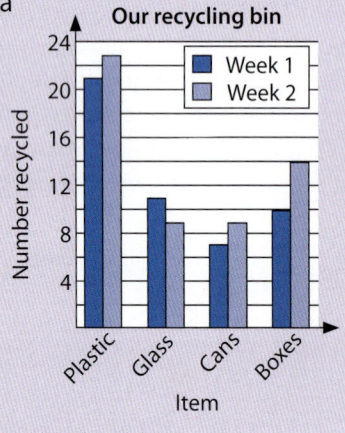

   Our recycling bin (bar chart: Plastic, Glass, Cans, Boxes; Week 1 and Week 2)

4. Evie wanted to investigate if older students spent more time online over the weekend. She asked 30 students of different ages how many hours they spent online last weekend. On the right is a graph of the results she obtained.

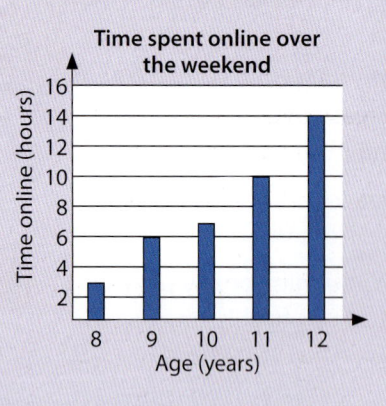

   Time spent online over the weekend (bar chart: ages 8–12, hours increasing)

   (i) Can you identify any pattern/trend from this bar chart?

   (ii) What conclusion can Evie draw from this data?

   (iii) Can you think of any possible limitations to this conclusion?

   (iv) Suggest improvements that Evie could make to ensure her conclusions are more reliable.

5. The bar chart on the right represents the number of visitors to an adventure centre over the course of a year.

   Visitors per month (bar chart Jan–Dec)

   (i) Describe the pattern in the number of visitors from April to November.

   (ii) Why do you think December doesn't seem to follow this pattern?

   (iii) Give one other conclusion you can draw from this bar chart.

6. A group of students are thinking about setting up a shop selling chocolate bars at lunchtime. They conducted a small survey among 30 people, asking the question:
   How many chocolate bars do you eat in a typical week?
   The raw data they found is shown below.

   > The responses gathered are known as the 'raw' data.

Male	Female	Male	Female	Male	Male	Male	Female	Male	Male
1 bar	4 bars	5 bars	1 bar	2 bars	25 bars	13 bars	0 bars	2 bars	9 bars
Male	Female	Female	Male	Male	Male	Female	Male	Male	Male
6 bars	16 bars	14 bars	10 bars	19 bars	11 bars	1 bar	0 bars	1 bar	3 bars
Female	Male	Female	Male	Female	Male	Male	Male	Male	Female
10 bars	25 bars	16 bars	13 bars	30 bars	8 bars	2 bars	0 bars	28 bars	0 bars

   (i) Choose the most appropriate tables, charts or graphs to represent the data clearly.

   (ii) Christine says:
   We have found that the total number of bars eaten by all the males is 183, and the total number eaten by all the females is 92. In general, this means that males eat more chocolate bars than females.
   Do you agree with Christine? Justify your answer.

   (iii) Write one conclusion (comparing males and females) that is supported by the data.

7. Jack wants to get to work as quickly and reliably as possible in the mornings.
   He tries three different transport methods and records his journey times:
   - cycle all the way
   - drive all the way
   - walk to the railway station, take the train, and walk from the station.

Bicycle	24	25	29	25	26	26	23	29	25	28
Car	19	21	32	57	31	27	21	24		
Walk-train-walk	21	24	31	26	24	30				

   (i) Use the data to make a case for why Jack should travel to work by bicycle.
   (ii) Use the data to make a case for why Jack should travel to work by car. (Hint: consider outliers)

8. Harry works in the zoo and is studying the difference in masses between males and females of a certain species. He plots the two graphs shown to represent his results.

   Using the graphs as evidence, write three separate statements comparing the differences and similarities between the masses for the males and the females.

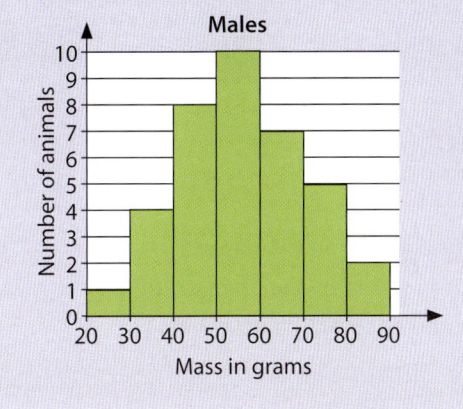

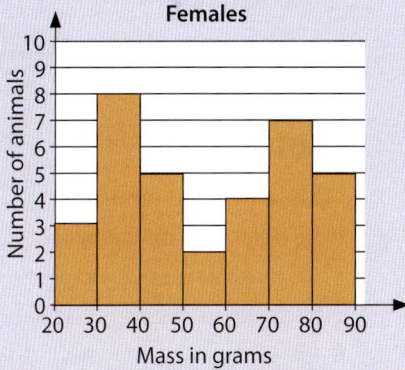

Taking it FURTHER

9. Adam and Paul's ice cream company launch a new advertisement in May. The sales of ice cream increase over the next three months. The advertisement company say the advertisement was successful.
   Do you agree or disagree with the advertisement company? Justify your answer.

10. In the 18th century, pirates roamed the seas and global warming was not an issue. In the 21st century, there are very few pirates roaming the seas and global warming is cause for concern.
    Therefore, we can say that pirates prevented global warming.
    Do you agree or disagree with this statement? Justify your answer.

26.5 Misuses of statistics

By the end of this section you should:
- understand that statistics can be misused
- be able to identify misleading statistics

Statistics are very important to allow us to identify patterns and relationships and allow us to make predictions based on existing data. Sometimes, however statistics can be misused.

Here are some ways in which this can happen.

- **Quoting statistics based on poor samples:** If a sample is too small or non-representative the statistics developed from it will not be reliable.
- **Choice of the average value for a sample:** Since the mean, mode and median are all averages, we can calculate all three and choose the one which is closest to the result we want, when a different average value might be more appropriate/accurate.
- **Using detached statistics:** Statements like 'one-third less' indicate that something is better than something else, but it doesn't mean much unless we know what it is in relation to.
- **Formatting graphs to mislead the eye:** The two bar charts opposite represent the exact same data.

  The first chart shows the scale starting from 0 whereas in the second the scale starts at 4. This emphasises the small differences in the heights of the bars. Changes to the scales of a graph can dramatically alter the look of the graph.

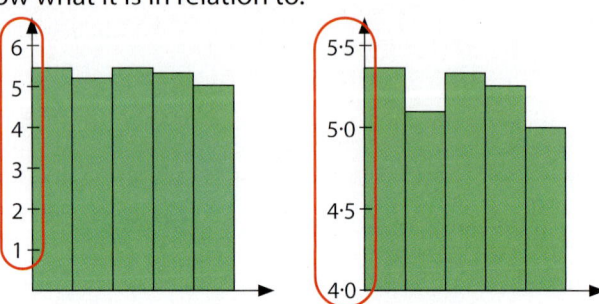

- **Designing questions to be used on a survey that will bias the results:** Survey questions can be designed to produce a more positive or negative response. These are called leading questions and should be avoided.

Worked example

Examine the data representation shown on the right and comment on whether you think it is misleading or not. Justify your answer.

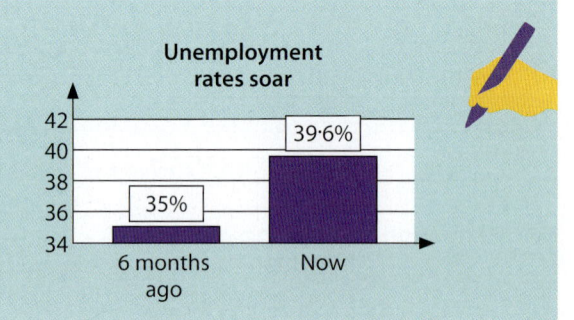

Solution

This bar chart is misleading.

The difference between 6 months ago and now is 39·6 – 35 = 4·6%

This is not a massive increase as suggested by the dramatic title of the graph.

The scale on this chart has been altered to only start at 34%.

Discuss and discover

(i) Using newspapers, magazines, or the internet, find a graph or statistic that creates a false impression.

(ii) Describe how the graph or statistic creates a false impression.

(iii) Why might the misleading graph or statistic be used?

(iv) How could the graph or statistic be changed to present the data accurately?

KEY SKILLS

Linking Thinking 1

Practice questions 26·5

1. A class wanted to raise money for their school trip. They are thinking about raising the money by selling raffle tickets. Before they decide to hold a raffle, they want to estimate how many students in the whole school would buy a ticket. They decide to do a survey to find out first.
   The school has 900 students in First to Sixth Year, with 150 students in each year.

   (i) How many students would you survey? How would you choose them? Explain your answers.

   (ii) Sarah got the names of all 900 students in the school and put them in a hat. Then she pulled out 90 names. What do you think of Sarah's sample selection? Explain your answer.

   (iii) Jack asked 15 children at after-school study. What do you think of Jack's sample selection? Explain your answer.

   (iv) Adam asked all of the 150 students in First Year. What do you think of Adam's sample selection? Explain your answer.

   (v) Ramon asked 90 of his friends. What do you think of Ramon's sample selection? Explain your answer.

   (vi) Caoimhe set up a stall outside the canteen. Anyone who wanted to stop and fill out a survey could. She stopped collecting surveys when she got 90 students to complete them.
   What do you think of Caoimhe's sample selection? Explain your answer.

2. The table below gives the height of rollercoasters at a theme park.

Rollercoaster	Height (m)
Viper	33
Monster	41
Red Dragon	35
Tornado	110
Riptide	38

   The park boasts that the average height of their rollercoasters is 50 metres. Explain how this is misleading.

3. In a certain company, the wages earned are as follows:
   Employee 1 earned €8 000
   Employee 4 earned €8 000
   Employee 2 earned €12 000
   The director of the company earned €175 000
   Employee 3 earned €8 000

   (i) Calculate the mean, mode and median of the wages.

   (ii) Is the mean a good reflection of the wages earned? Justify your answer.

   (iii) Which measure of central tendency would you choose to represent the average? Justify your answer.

4. Having collected data from her classmates about the sports they play, Gabi drew the two graphs shown opposite.

   (i) Write two statements comparing these two graphs on first impressions.

   (ii) What features of the graphs make it seem that the girls participate in sports more than the boys?

   (iii) How could the graphs be changed to present the data more accurately?

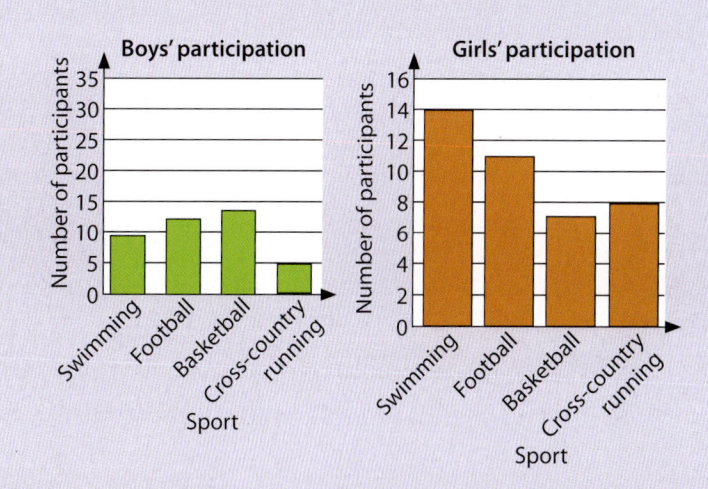

5. Why do some people represent data in a misleading way? Describe three ways a representation of data might be drawn to misrepresent data.

Taking it FURTHER

6. Draw a graph to show how the data in the table below can be displayed to get each of the following desired outcomes. Explain how you created each impression.

Board of Directors: Expenses	
Quarter	Expenses
1st	€95 000
2nd	€105 000
3rd	€120 000
4th	€155 000

(i) The directors want the expenses to look low.

(ii) The shareholders want to show the expenses are too high.

Revision questions

26A Core skills

1. (a) Draw a pie chart to represent the following sets of data and write the mode of each.

   (i)
Colour of car	Red	Blue	Green	Other
No. of people	20	10	3	7

   (ii)
Pet	Cat	Dog	Hamster	Fish	Other
No. of people	8	14	3	1	4

   (b) It is not possible to find the median and mean of the data shown in (i) and (ii) above. State why this is the case.

2. Draw a stem and leaf plot to represent the following data and calculate the median and mean (correct to two decimal places) of each.

   (i) 48, 45, 35, 26, 29, 49, 33, 25
   (ii) 5, 3, 9, 4, 10, 15, 13, 21, 22, 26, 19, 32, 35

3. Find the mean (correct to two decimal places), median, mode and range for each set of numbers.

   (i) 24, 31, 12, 38, 12, 15
   (ii) 5, 28, 16, 32, 5, 16, 48, 29, 5, 35
   (iii) 72, 43, 15, 66, 32, 72, 52, 19, 28, 81, 55
   (iv) 63, 40, 51, 70, 36, 21, 51, 28, 19

4. A Green Schools Committee collects plastic bottles for recycling. The number of bottles collected in two weeks are given below.

   84   97   77   31   84   63   58   72   47   84   69   94   43   68

   Find the mean (correct to two decimal places), mode, median and range of the number of bottles collected.

5. Four people in a group weigh 63 kg, 72 kg, 178 kg and 71 kg.

   (i) What is the mean weight of this group of people?
   (ii) What is the range of weights?

6. The daytime temperatures recorded over five consecutive days in October were: 15·1°C, 14·2°C, 13·6°C, 14·8°C, and 15·3°C.

   (i) What was the median temperature over the 5 days?
   (ii) What was the range of temperatures over the 5 days?

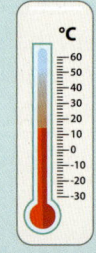

Linking Thinking 1

7. In a survey of 10 households, the number of children was found to be 4, 1, 5, 4, 3, 7, 2, 3, 4, 1
   (i) Draw a graph to represent this data and justify your reason for picking this type of graph.
   (ii) State the mode.
   (iii) Calculate the mean number of children per household.
   (iv) Calculate the median number of children per household.
   (v) The researcher says:
   The mode seems to be the best average to represent the data in this survey.
   Give at least one reason to support this statement.

26B Taking it FURTHER

1. The bar chart shows the amount of money spent by a family on their weekly shopping.
   (i) Calculate the mean weekly spend for the family.
   (ii) Calculate the median weekly spent.
   (iii) What is the range of this data?

2. A local shop recorded the amount of milk, in litres, sold per week, over a number of weeks. The results are shown below.
   34, 26, 12, 31, 18, 34, 28, 43, 28, 42, 34
   (i) Draw a stem and leaf plot to represent this data.
   (ii) Write down the modal amount of milk sold.
   (iii) Write down the median amount of milk sold.
   (iv) Work out the mean amount of milk sold.

3. Jessie thinks that the mean of the numbers 5, 12, 8, 3, 2, 4, 1 is equal to 7.
   (i) Do you agree or disagree? Justify your answer.
   (ii) How did Jessie get an answer of 7?

4. The pie charts below show the number of games won and lost by two soccer teams.

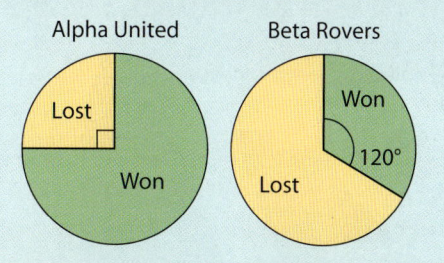

   (i) Based on these pie charts, which, do you think, is the better team? Justify your answer.
   (ii) The results for these pie charts are based on Alpha United playing 12 matches and Beta Rovers playing 57 matches. Does this additional information change your answer to part (i)?
   If so, how? Justify your answer.

5. Nick owns a bicycle shop. He wants to get a loan from the bank to expand his shop. He brings the graph shown below to the meeting with his bank manager.

   (i) Do you notice any problems with this graph?
   (ii) Why do you think Nick drew the graph in this way?
   (iii) Would any other type of graph be useful to display this data?
   (iv) Nick will also present figures for average monthly sales.
   Which average should he use? Justify with calculations.

Now that you have completed the unit, revisit the

Something to think about ...

question posed at the start of this unit.

Unit 27

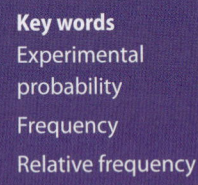

Probability 2

Topics covered within this unit:
- 27·1 Revision of basic probability and fundamental principle of counting
- 27·2 Experimental probability and relative frequency

The Learning Outcomes covered in this unit are contained in the following sections:
SP.2c

Key words
Experimental probability
Frequency
Relative frequency

Something to think about ...

KEY SKILLS

On a production line, light bulbs are tested to see how long they will last. After testing 1000 light bulbs, it is found that 980 will work for more than 1 600 hours.

Thomas purchases a light bulb.
What is the relative frequency that the light bulb will:

(a) work for more than 1 600 hours?

(b) not work for more than 1 600 hours?

27·1 Revision of basic probability and fundamental principle of counting

By the end of this section you should:
- recall and understand information from *Probability 1*

You have already studied basic probability in Section A, Unit 6. This is known as the **theoretical probability of an event** occurring.

For example, if you roll a die, the probability of obtaining the number 5 can be calculated in theory as:

$$P(E) = \frac{\text{number of outcomes favourable to that event}}{\text{number of possible outcomes}}$$

For a fair six-sided die:
- Number of possible outcomes = 6
- Number of outcomes favourable for throwing a five = 1
- P(throwing a five) = $\frac{1}{6}$

You have also studied the **fundamental principal of counting (FPoC)**:

When there are m ways to do one thing, and n ways to do another, then there are $m \times n$ ways of doing both.

Be sure you are familiar with the material covered in Section A, Unit 6 before attempting the following practice questions.

Linking Thinking 1

Practice questions 27.1

1. You have a six-sided die, containing the numbers 1, 2, 3, 4, 5, 6. If you were to roll the die one time, what is the probability that: 
   (i) it will land on a 1?
   (ii) it will **not** land on a 2?
   (iii) it will land on an even number?
   (iv) you will obtain a score of eight?

2. A bag contains six blue marbles, nine red marbles and five green marbles. 
   (i) How many marbles does the bag contain?
   (ii) Copy the probability scale given below and mark the following onto it.
      (a) The probability of choosing a green marble
      (b) The probability of choosing a blue marble
      (c) The probability of **not** choosing a red marble

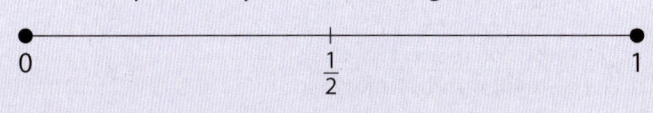

   0 — 1/2 — 1

3. The diagram opposite contains a number of different shapes.
   (i) How many shapes are there in total in the diagram? 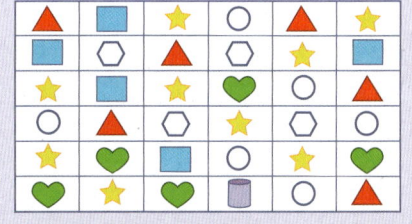
   (ii) If you were to select one shape at random from the diagram, what is the probability it will be a triangle?
   (iii) If you were to select one shape at random from the diagram, what shape do you have the greatest probability of selecting? Justify your answer.
   (iv) Which shape has a 25% chance of being selected? Justify your answer.

4. Bella visits a coffee shop that offers the following deal.
   (i) List all the possible combinations of a drink and treat that Bella could order.
   (ii) What is the probability that Bella would order a juice and a fruit pot?
   (iii) Bella's friend Ben joins her. What is the probability he will order juice and any treat?

   Any drink and a treat for €3
Drinks	Treats
Coffee	Muffin
Tea	Cookie
Juice	Fruit pot

5. Every time Ivan plays a chess match, the probability that he will win is 0.6 and the probability he will draw is 0.3.
   (i) What is the probability that he will lose a game?
   (ii) If Ivan plays two matches, copy the tree diagram provided and fill in all the missing information.

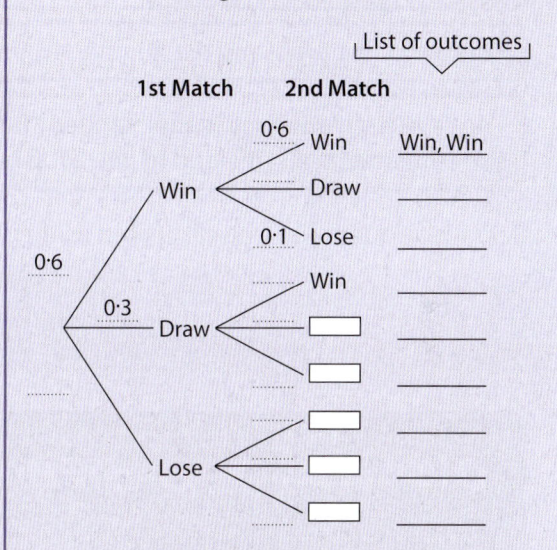

   1st Match — 2nd Match — List of outcomes
   Win (0.6) → Win (0.6): Win, Win
   Win → Draw
   Win → Lose (0.1)
   Draw (0.3) → Win
   Lose → ...

6. Lorraine visits a funfair and decides to play some games of 'Hook-a-Duck'. The probability that she wins at Hook-a-Duck is 0.4.
   (i) Find the probability that she will lose at Hook-a-Duck. 
   (ii) Draw a tree diagram to show all possible outcomes if Lorraine plays Hook-a-Duck three times.

7. A bag contains 5 yellow marbles and 4 red marbles. One marble is taken at random from the bag, the colour is recorded and then the marble is replaced. Then a second marble is taken from the bag and its colour recorded. Draw a tree diagram to represent all possible outcomes, showing the probabilities along each branch.

Section C **Applying our skills** 437

27·2 Experimental probability and relative frequency

Experimental probability

Imagine again that you have been asked to roll a number five on a standard six-sided die. There is only one number five on a standard six-sided die, and there are six numbers possible.

We can calculate the theoretical probability as $P(5) = \frac{1}{6}$

In real life, if we were to throw a fair die 12 times we would be unlikely to get *exactly* two number fives, as would be expected in theory. You can try it for yourself.

> The **experimental probability** that something will happen is based on how often the event occurs, after collecting a large amount of data or running a trial (an experiment). It is based specifically on direct observations.

> **Frequency** is how often (the number of times) an event occurs in a number of trials.

> The **relative frequency** is the number of times that the event occurs during experimental trials, divided by the total number of trials conducted.

Relative frequency can be calculated using the following formula.

$$\text{Relative frequency} = \frac{\text{number of successful trials}}{\text{the total number of trials}}$$

Discuss and discover

We already know how to calculate the probability of a simple event. For example if you toss a coin, the probability of heads is $\frac{1}{2}$ and the probability of a tail is $\frac{1}{2}$. However, does this mean if you flipped a coin 20 times, you would get exactly ten heads and ten tails?

(i) Work with a classmate (or on your own) and toss a coin 20 times. Record your results in a table. You may want to use tally marks |||| to help you keep count.

Outcome	Tally	Total
Number of heads		
Number of tails		

(ii) What percentage of heads and what percentage of tails did you get? Does this number agree with the predicted probability?

(iii) Combine the results from your whole class in a table like the one below.

Name	Number of heads	Number of tails	Total
Student 1			
Student 2			
...			
Last student			
	Total =	Total =	Total =

(iv) Now calculate the total percentage of heads that the whole class got, and calculate the percentage of tails that the whole class got. Are these values the same (or very close to) the predicted probability for a coin toss?

(v) How did the number of trials relate to the relative frequency of heads or tails on the coin?

Relative frequency can be expressed as a decimal, percentage or fraction.

It is important to note that when all the relative frequencies of a trial are added they must equal exactly 1. This is because the probability of any event **occurring** plus the **event not occurring** must **equal 1**.

Relative frequency can be referred to as **experimental probability**. It deals with results in the **long term**, after many trials have been conducted. Generally, **the more trials that are conducted, the more accurate the result**.

Relative frequency can help us decide if a game involving a die, spinner, coin etc, is fair or biased (not fair). If the relative frequency is very different from the theoretical probability, it generally indicates that the item under inspection is not fair.

> To determine if an object is fair or biased (not fair), you must complete many trials. For example, if you flip a coin 5 times and get 5 heads, it does not necessarily mean the coin is biased. However, if you flip a coin 1 000 times and get 900 heads, it is most likely biased.

If the trial is repeated multiple times, we can use the relative frequency to predict the expected number of times an outcome will occur.

> **The expected number of outcomes can be calculated by:**
> **Expected number of outcomes = (number of trials) (relative frequency)**
> OR
> **Expected number of outcomes = (number of trials) × P(event)**

Worked example 1

A bag containing 20 marbles of colours red, blue, green and grey. 20 people chose a marble out of the bag, recorded the colour and replaced the marble. The results are shown in the frequency table below.

Colour of marble	Red	Blue	Green	Grey	Total
Frequency	5	7	2	B	20
Relative frequency	0·25	A	0·1	0·3	C

(i) Find the values of A, B, and C in the frequency table above.

(ii) Based on the information above, which colour marble is there most of, in the bag?

(iii) If a marble was picked from the bag and replaced, as described above, 300 times, how many of the marbles picked would you expect to be green?

Solution

(i) Find A:

Relative frequency = $\frac{\text{number of successful trials}}{\text{the total number of trials}}$

Relative frequency (of A) = $\frac{7}{20}$ = 0·35

Find B:

There were 20 trials, so

$5 + 7 + 2 + B = 20$

$14 + B = 20$

$B = 20 - 14$

$B = 6$ (grey marbles)

Find C:

To find the value of C, we add up all the relative frequencies

$0·25 + 0·35 + 0·1 + 0·3 = C$

$1 = C$ (as expected)

(ii) Based on the table above, there are more blue marbles in the bag than any other colour. We can also see that blue has the highest relative frequency.

(iii) Expected number of outcomes = (number of trials) (relative frequency)

Expected number of outcomes = (300) (0·1)

Expected number of outcomes = 30 green marbles

Worked example 2

Aisling is at a carnival and sees a game which involves a spinner.

The spinner she will play is shown. The game seems fair, so Aisling decides to play.

(i) Looking at the spinner, what is the probability of Aisling
(a) winning (b) losing?

(ii) Do you think Aisling was right to assume this is a fair game?

(iii) Aisling plays the game five times and does not win at all. Aisling thinks the game is biased. Is she correct? Justify your answer.

(iv) Aisling doesn't play anymore games, but she watches 40 other people play the game and only 5 people win a prize. She is now convinced the game is biased. Is she correct? Justify your answer.

Solution

(i) Based on the spinner, the probability Aisling will (a) win is P(win) $\frac{4}{8} = \frac{1}{2}$ or (b) lose is P(lose) $\frac{4}{8} = \frac{1}{2}$

(ii) As the probability of winning or losing is the same, Aisling is correct to think this is a fair game.

(iii) Having only played five times, we do not have enough information to decide if this game is fair.

(iv) After 40 trials, the relative frequency of winning and losing are shown in the table below:

Result	Win	Lose	Total
Frequency	5	35	40
Relative frequency	$\frac{5}{40} = 0.125$	$\frac{35}{40} = 0.875$	1

Aisling is correct to think the game is biased as the relative frequency of winning should be $\frac{1}{2}$ or 0.5 and it is only $\frac{5}{40} = 0.125$

Relative frequency = $\frac{\text{number of successful trials}}{\text{the total number of trials}}$

Worked example 3

Each of the graphs provided show the results after a single six-sided die has been rolled a number of times.

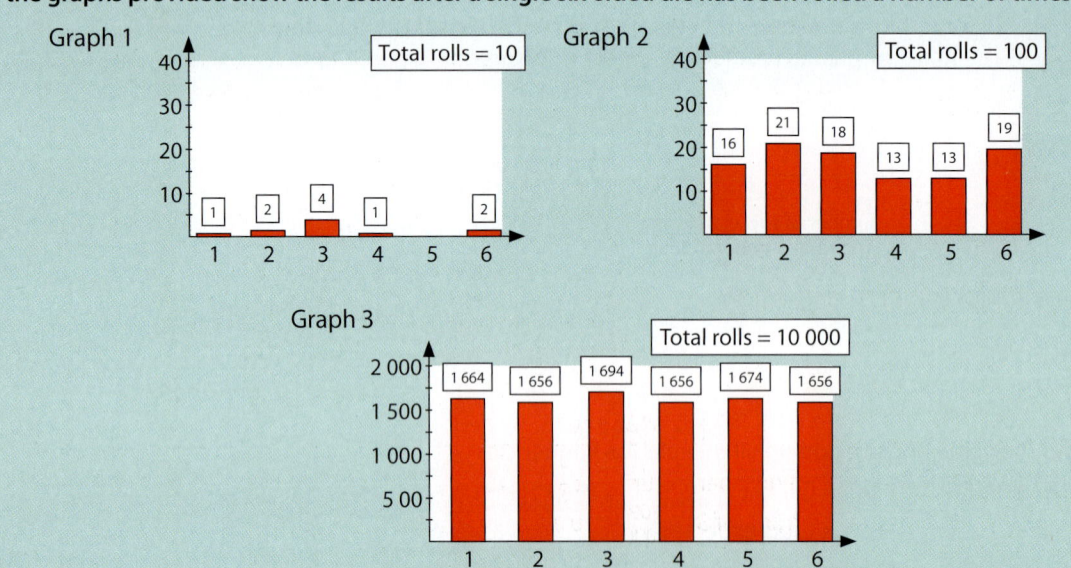

Graph 1 — Total rolls = 10
1: 1, 2: 2, 3: 4, 4: 1, 5: 0, 6: 2

Graph 2 — Total rolls = 100
1: 16, 2: 21, 3: 18, 4: 13, 5: 13, 6: 19

Graph 3 — Total rolls = 10 000
1: 1 664, 2: 1 656, 3: 1 694, 4: 1 656, 5: 1 674, 6: 1 656

For each graph:

(i) State the theoretical probability of any number between 1 and 6 being rolled.

(ii) Find the missing values A, B, and C in the frequency tables on the next page.

(iii) State if you think the die is fair, biased, or if there is not enough information to tell. Justify your answer.

(iv) State what you notice about the sum of all the relative frequencies.

Solution

Graph 1

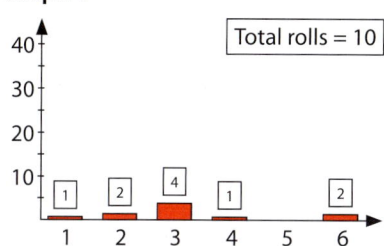

> Relative frequency = $\dfrac{\text{number of successful trials}}{\text{the total number of trials}}$

Total rolls = 10

Score	1	2	3	4	5	6	Total
Frequency	1	2	4	1	0	2	10
Relative frequency	0·1	0·2	A	0·1	0	B	C

(i) Theoretical probability of each number occuring is $\frac{1}{6} = 0\cdot 167$

(ii) **A** = Relative frequency of the number 3 = $\frac{4}{10}$ = 0·4, **A** = 0·4

  B = Relative frequency of the number 6 = $\frac{2}{10}$ = 0·2, **B** = 0·2

  C = Total sum of all the relative frequencies = 0·1 + 0·2 + 0·4 + 0·1 + 0 + 0·2, **C** = 1

(iii) Based on the data given, it would seem the die is biased, because the relative frequency of each number appearing does not match the predicted probability. More trials are needed for a definite answer.

(iv) The sum of all the relative frequencies = 1

Graph 2

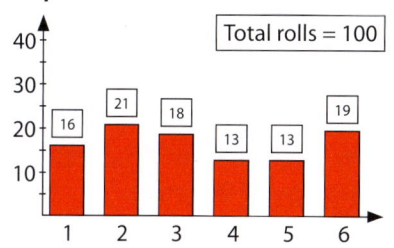

Total rolls = 100

Score	1	2	3	4	5	6	Total
Frequency	16	21	18	13	13	19	100
Relative frequency	0·16	0·21	A	0·13	0·13	B	C

(i) Theoretical probability of each number occuring is $\frac{1}{6} = 0\cdot 167$

(ii) **A** = Relative frequency of the number 3 = $\frac{18}{100}$ = 0·18, **A** = 0·18

  B = Relative frequency of the number 6 = $\frac{19}{100}$ = 0·19, **B** = 0·19

  C = Total sum of all the relative frequencies = 0·16 + 0·21 + 0·18 + 0·13 + 0·13 + 0·19, **C** = 1

(iii) Based on the data given, it would seem the die is biased, because the relative frequency of each number appearing does not match the predicted probability. More trials are needed for a definite answer.

(iv) The sum of all the relative frequencies = 1

Graph 3

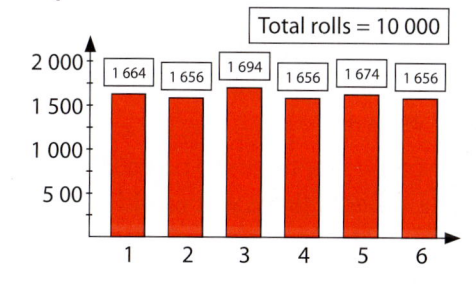

Total rolls = 10 000

Score	1	2	3	4	5	6	Total
Frequency	1 664	1 656	1 694	1 656	1 674	1 656	10 000
Relative frequency	0·166	0·166	A	0·167	0·167	B	C

(i) Theoretical probability of each number occuring is $\frac{1}{6} = 0\cdot 167$

(ii) **A** = Relative frequency of the number 3 = $\frac{1694}{10000}$ = 0·169, **A** = 0·169

  B = Relative frequency of the number 6 = $\frac{1656}{10000}$ = 0·166, **B** = 0·166

  C = Total sum of the relative frequencies = 0·166 + 0·166 + 0·169 + 0·167 + 0·167 + 0·166, **C** = 1

(iii) Based on the data given, the die is fair, because after 10,000 trials the predicted probability of $\frac{1}{6}$ or 0·167 is very close to the relative frequency of all of the numbers.

(iv) The sum of all the relative frequencies = 1 (to the nearest whole number)

Section C Applying our skills

Practice questions 27·2

1. There are 200 coins in a jar; 20 of these coins are €2 coins. What is the relative frequency of €2 coins in the jar?

2. David buys a box of toy blocks that contains 500 blocks.. If 120 of these blocks are blue, what is the relative frequency of blue blocks?

3. There is a general belief that if you drop a piece of toast on the floor, it always lands buttered side down. Jasmin decides to test this belief, and drops 50 slices of buttered toast. She records that 15 land buttered side down.

   (i) What is the relative frequency of a piece of toast **not** landing buttered side down?

   (ii) What conclusion could Jasmin make about the 'general belief' stated above?

4. To estimate the probability of a water bottle landing upright or on its side when flipped, Sarah flipped a water bottle 50 times and recorded her results in the frequency table, as shown.

Position	Vertical	Horizontal
Frequency	?	42

   (i) Calculate the number of times the bottle landed vertically on its base.

   (ii) If Sarah repeats the experiment 300 times, estimate the number of times the bottle will **not** land vertically on its base.

5. In a dog show, the number of each breed of dog that entered a competition is shown.

Breed of dog	Number	Relative frequency
Boxer	250	B
Collie	400	C
Bull terrier	200	0·1
Whippet	300	D
Bull dog	250	0·125
Golden retriever	A	E
Total	2 000	F

   (i) Copy and complete the frequency table to fill in the missing information.

   (ii) Jan says her dog has a probability of $\frac{1}{5}$ of winning the competition. What breed of dog does Jan have? Explain your answer.

6. A circular spinner has 4 equal sections, coloured blue, green, red and yellow. The spinner is spun 20 times and the results are listed below:
   B, B, Y, R, Y, G, R, B, Y, R, B, G, R, G, R, R, G, Y, Y, R

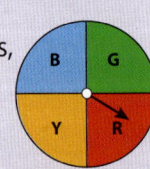

   (i) Copy and complete the frequency table provided. Show all your calculations.

Colour	Frequency	Relative frequency
Blue(B)	4	0·2
Green (G)		
Red (R)		
Yellow (Y)		0·25
Total		

   The table below shows the results after the spinner has been spun 100 times.

Colour	Frequency	Relative frequency
Blue (B)	20	
Green (G)	45	
Red (R)	?	
Yellow (Y)	20	
Total		

   (ii) Copy and complete the relative frequency table above. Show all calculations.

   (iii) Which of the two relative frequencies for the colour blue provides the best estimate for the spinner landing on blue? Justify your answer.

   (iv) The spinner continues to be spun. Estimate the number of times you would expect the colour red to appear after 5 000 spins.

7. A die is suspected of bias. Here are the results of 20 throws.
   1, 6, 3, 6, 1, 2, 3, 5, 4, 4, 1, 3, 5, 6, 2, 6, 5, 1, 6, 2

   (i) Copy and complete the relative frequency table shown below. Show all calculations.

Score	1	2	3	4	5	6	Total
Frequency							
Relative frequency							

442 Linking Thinking 1

(ii) Use the relative frequency you have found in part (i) to estimate the number of times you would expect to score a six in 60 throws of this dice.

(iii) Compare your answer in part (ii) with the expected number of sixes rolled in 60 trials.

(iv) Do you think this die is fair, biased, or if there is not enough information to decide? Justify your answer.

8. Two fair spinners are used for a game. The numbers from each spinner are are added together to give the final score.

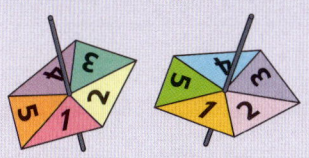

Number of spins	Number of times 8 scored (frequency)	Relative frequency
First 50	13	0·26
First 100	18	0·18
First 150	23	
First 200	35	
First 250	42	
First 500	80	

Conor played the game 500 times and recorded how many times he scored a value of 8 in the table shown.

(i) Copy and complete the relative frequency table shown. Show all calculations.

(ii) Which relative frequency result is the best estimate for scoring a total of 8? Justify your answer.

Revision questions

27A Core skills

1. Four teams – City, Rovers, County and United – play a competition to win a cup. Only one team can win the cup. The table below shows the relative frequency of each team winning the cup.

Team	City	Rovers	County	United
Relative freq.	0·1	0·5	0·25	x

Find the value of x.

2. A fruit pot contains pieces of the following types of fruit: strawberries, blueberries, grapes and kiwi.
The table shows the relative frequency of each piece of fruit.

Fruit	Strawberry	Blueberry	Grape	Kiwi
Relative Frequency	0·2	y	0·37	0·23

(i) Find the value of y.

(ii) If there were 20 pieces of fruit in the fruit pot, how many strawberries were there?

3. The probability that a biased die will land on a five is 0·25. Tony is going to roll the dice 500 times.

(i) What is the relative frequency the die will not land on the number five?

(ii) Work out an estimate for the number of times the die should land on a five.

4. Four surveys were conducted and the following results were obtained. Which result has the highest relative frequency? Justify your answer showing all work.

(a) Of 1 500 learner drivers, 75 had been involved in an accident.

(b) Of 1 200 phone chargers, 48 failed to work.

(c) Of 20 000 people attending a concert, 950 were attending their first concert.

(d) Of 50 cars inspected, 2 failed the NCT.

5. In a given week, 600 babies were born in Ireland. The day and number of children born are given below.

Day	M	T	W	T	F	S	S
No. of babies	100	150	150	100	?	30	20
Rel. freq.							

(i) How many babies were born on Friday?

(ii) Copy and complete the frequency table provided.

(iii) What is the probability a baby will be born on a Monday?

Section C Applying our skills

6. A GAA team plays 40 matches over a season and the results (wins, losses and draws) are shown below.
   L L L D W W D L W D L D L D
   W W L L L D W W D L L W W
   W L D L D D L W W W D D L 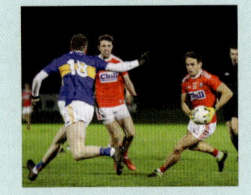

   (i) Put this information into a table showing the number of wins, losses and draws.

   (ii) Calculate the relative frequency of each result over a season.

27B Taking it FURTHER

1. Construct a relative frequency table for the following data.
   1, 4, 9, 6, 3, 3, 5, 7, 9, 2, 8, 2, 5, 8, 5, 8, 1, 10, 4, 2

2. A bag contains sweets that are yellow, orange and blue. You choose a sweet at random.

Colour	Yellow	Orange	Blue
Relative frequency	0·25	$3x$	$2x$

   (i) Calculate the value of x in the table.
   (ii) Copy and complete the table.
   (iii) What is the probability of **not** choosing a yellow sweet?
   (iv) If you choose a sweet at random from this bag, which colour would you have the highest probability of picking? Justify your answer.

3. A coin has been tossed 100 times with the result of 79 heads. 
   (i) Calculate the relative frequency of the coin landing heads.
   (ii) Do you think this coin is biased?
   (iii) The experiment is repeated 1 000 times. The result is 498 heads, and 502 tails. Calculate the relative frequency of getting (a) heads (b) tails.
   (iv) Why do you think the relative frequency has changed in part (i) and part (ii) of this question? Assume the same coin was used in both experiments.

4. Shamrock Limited manufactures parts for smart phones. The relative frequency (probability) that a part will be made with a fault is 0·05. Shamrock Limited manufacture 10 000 parts each day. Work out an estimate for the number of parts that will **not** contain a fault each day.

5. There are six colours of discs in a bag of 500 discs. 60 students each pick one disc from the bag, note the colour and return the disc to the bag.
   The results of the colours they picked are shown in the frequency table below.

Colour of disc	Number of times picked	Relative frequency
Red	9	
Blue	12	0·20
Green	9	
Orange	6	0·10
Yellow	21	
Brown	3	
Total	60	

   (i) Copy and complete the relative frequency table.
   (ii) Add up all the relative frequencies in the table. What do they equal?
   (iii) Based on the table above, if you were the first person to choose, what is the probability you would choose a red disc?
   (iv) Bobby thinks a person is more likely to choose a yellow disc from this bag, than any other colour. Based on the **data given** above, would you agree or disagree with Bobby? Justify your answer.

6. The Department of Education conducts a nationwide survey to see how many students choose Maths as their favourite subject. The results are listed below.

Sample size	Number of students choosing Maths	Relative frequency
5	1	0·2
10	2	
20	5	
30	6	
50	10	
100	20	
200	45	
500	120	
1 000	250	

   (i) Is the data collected categorical or numerical? Justify your answer.
   (ii) Copy the frequency table and fill in the missing relative frequencies.

Linking Thinking 1

(iii) Redraw the graph provided into your copybook, and draw the graph of relative frequency.

(iv) Why do you think the graph is not a straight line?

(v) If the sample size was 5 000 students, estimate how many students you think would choose Maths as their favourite subject. Justify your answer.

Relative frequency of Maths as favourite subject

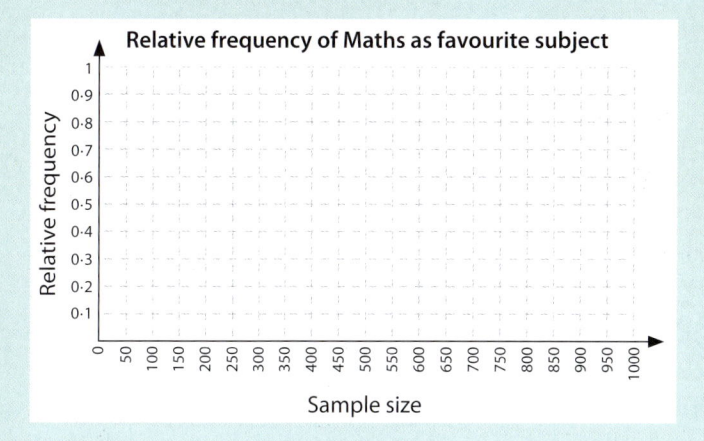

(graph: y-axis "Relative frequency" 0 to 1 in steps of 0·1; x-axis "Sample size" 0 to 1000 in steps of 50)

7. Finbar and Ben play a game involving a single six-sided die. If the number rolled is odd, Finbar wins, if the number rolled is even Ben wins. They roll the die 36 times.
The results are recorded below.

Score	1	2	3	4	5	6
Frequency	5	3	7	5	12	4

(i) Ben thinks this die might be biased, as the odd numbers appear more often than the even numbers.
Do you agree? Give a reason for your answer.

Finbar disagrees with Ben, and states *'If we roll this die many more times, you will see it is a fair die.'*

They play the game again and this time they roll the die 300 times. The results are recorded below.

Score	1	2	3	4	5	6
Frequency	48	52	53	47	49	51

(ii) Using the new data above, state if you think this die is biased? Justify your answer.

(iii) Why do you think the relative frequencies (probabilities) were different for each game?

8. Explain why the following statements are true.

(i) The sum of all relative frequencies will always equal exactly 1.

(ii) As the relative frequency of one event increases, the relative frequency of another event in the same experiment must decrease.

9. An examination was held to check whether Company ABC was producing faulty TV sets. 200 TVs were selected randomly and tested. After testing, it was observed that 25 out of 200 TVs were faulty.

(i) Calculate the relative frequency of defective TVs.

(ii) The following week, 1 000 TVs were tested, and 80 were found to be faulty. Calculate the relative frequency of faulty TVs.

(iii) Which sample above would give the best indication of the relative frequency of a TV being faulty? Justify your answer.

(iv) Using the information from part (ii) of this question, what is the probability that a TV will **not** have a fault?

Now that you have completed the unit, revisit the

Something to think about ...

question posed at the start of this unit.

Now try question 6 on pages 559–60

Unit 28

Money matters 2

Something to think about ...

Chris is very excited because he has a new job as an electrician and is going to get paid €35 000 a year.

Paula says: 'But you won't actually get that much money, because you have to pay income tax on every cent you earn.'

Chris finds out he has to pay gross tax on his wages at 21%, but he has something called a 'tax credit' worth €1 700.

What will his net wage be at the end of his first week of employment?

Topics covered within this unit:
- 28·1 Revision of *Money matters 1*
- 28·2 Percentage increase or decrease
- 28·3 Income tax and other deductions on earnings

The Learning Outcomes covered in this unit are contained in the following sections:

N.1e   N.2c   AF.1a

Key words
- Gross income
- Gross tax
- Tax credit
- Net tax
- Net income

28·1 Revision of *Money matters 1*

By the end of this section you should be able to:
- recall information from Section B, Unit 13 and solve revision problems

We have already learned about many different concepts (ideas) related to money. For example, we discovered a person has to pay VAT on many items purchased in shops. We discovered how to calculate profit (or loss) on the sale of items. We figured out how to convert money to different currencies, and how to choose the best rate. Finally, we explored the difference between simple interest and compound interest on savings and loans. Below are some of the key words we met in Section B, Unit 13.

- **VAT**: Value added tax (VAT) is a tax charged on the sale of most goods and services in Ireland
- **Profit** (or gain) = selling price − cost price
- **Loss** = selling price − cost price (loss will be a negative value)
- **Interest** is the sum of money that you pay for borrowing or that is paid to you for investing
- **Simple interest** is interest which is calculated on the initial principal
- **Compound interest** is interest that is calculated not only on the initial principal, but also the accumulated interest
- An **exchange rate** is the rate at which one currency may be converted into another

Be sure you are familiar with the formulae presented in Section B, Unit 13 before you complete the practice questions below.

Linking Thinking 1

Practice questions 28.1

1. Assuming a 40-hour week, convert the following annual salaries to (a) monthly (b) fortnightly (c) weekly and (d) hourly pay. Show all your calculations.

   (i) €45 000
   (ii) €52 800
   (iii) €74 850
   (iv) €23 200
   (v) €99 500

   > **Remember:** 1 year = 52 weeks
   > Monthly wage = $\frac{\text{annual wage}}{12}$
   > We cannot multiply weekly wage by 4 to find monthly wage, as some months may contain more than 4 weeks.

2. Paola has a part time job in a local clothing store. She works every Saturday and Sunday from 10 am to 5 pm.

   (i) How many hours does Paola work per week?
   (ii) Paola earns €161 per week. How much does she earn per hour?

3. Louis sells electrical goods for a living. He is paid a basic salary of €2 000 per month plus 4% commission on any sales he makes. In April, he sells goods worth €8 000. Calculate his total pay for the month of April.

4. The costs given for the following items do not include VAT.
   Copy and complete the table below, filling in the missing information to the nearest cent.

Item	Cost (excluding VAT)	Rate of VAT	VAT in euros	Final price (including VAT)
Camera	€450.00	23%		
Games console	€399.00	23%		
Haircut	€11.75	13.5%		
Coffee	€3.50	13.5%		
Holiday	€2 599	23%		

5. The cost of repairing a car is €466.17, which includes VAT at 23%.

   (i) How much VAT was paid?
   (ii) How much was the bill before VAT was added?

6. Cupcakes can be bought individually or in a box of twelve.
   The prices for the items are given inclusive and exclusive of VAT respectively. VAT is charged at 23% on both items. Calculate the cheapest way to buy 12 cupcakes and the amount saved.

   Box of 12 cupcakes €26 including VAT

   Single cupcake €2·00 excluding VAT

7. A TV was sold for €720. This price included VAT at 23%.

   (i) What was the cost price of the TV excluding VAT?
   (ii) If the VAT rate was reduced to 15%, what would the new selling price of the TV be?

8. Fiona is travelling from Dublin to Japan. She buys 100 000 Japanese yen in Dublin.

   (i) How much in euros did Fiona spend to buy the Japanese yen, given that €1 = 109·2 yen?

   (ii) When Fiona returned home, she had 15 000 Japanese yen, which she exchanged for euros. How much in euros did she receive, given that €1 = 118·6 yen at that time?

   (iii) If the exchange rate office charged a 3% commission on the exchange from yen to euros, how much (in euros) did she have to pay? Give your answer to the nearest cent.

9. Leo wants to convert złoty into euros.

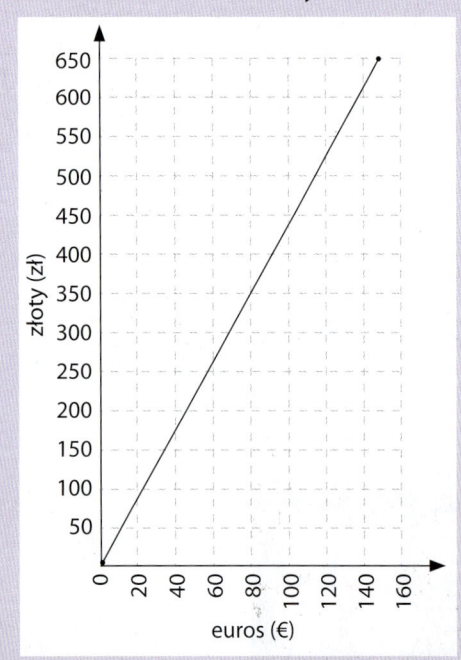

   The graph shows the relationship between euros and złoty.

   Using the graph provided, answer the following questions.

   (i) How many złoty can he get for €80?

   (ii) How may euros could he get for 450 złoty?

   (iii) Using the graph or otherwise, calculate the exchange rate for €1 to złoty.

   (iv) Verify your answers to part (i) and (ii) above using the exchange rate you have found in part (iii).

   (v) Is this a linear graph? Justify your answer.

10. A games console costs €299. This price includes VAT at 23%.

    (i) What is the price before VAT, to the nearest cent?

    (ii) The same console can be bought online from the USA. The total cost is $350 plus $35 postage. Which option is cheaper in euros, when €1 = $1·09 US dollars? Show all your calculations.

11. Calculate the percentage profit earned on the following items.

    (i) A smart watch bought for €119 and sold for €140

    (ii) A piece of art bought for €35 000 and sold for €81 000

    (iii) A car bought for €740 and sold for €1 050

12. A local bakery buys cakes for €2 each. They sell them for €2·80 each.

    (i) How much money do they make on each cake?

    (ii) What is the percentage profit they make on each cake?

    (iii) If the baker sold one dozen cakes:

    (a) How much profit would he make?

    (b) What would be his percentage profit?

13. Jason buys €300 worth of shares in a company. After one year, the share prices have risen by 40%.

    (i) How much are his shares worth now?

    (ii) If he were to sell his shares, how much profit would he make?

    (iii) Jason must pay an fee of 15% on the selling price of his shares. What is his final profit (in euros) after paying this fee?

14. (i) Calculate the difference in the amount of interest earned between:

    • €8 000 invested for three years with a simple interest rate of 5%

    • €8 000 invested for three years with a compound interest rate of 4·8%

    (ii) Why do you think that the lower interest rate generates a higher return?

15. You borrowed €29 000 for two years at 5·5%, which was compounded annually.

    (i) Calculate the total amount you will have to pay back.

    (ii) How much interest did you pay?

28·2 Percentage increase or decrease

By the end of this section you should be able to:
- calculate percentage increase or decrease

It is important to understand the difference between a percentage increase and a percentage decrease. Although the percentage might be the same, it is the actual amount of money or other items which needs to be considered.

$$\text{Percentage increase or decrease} = \frac{\text{change in value}}{\text{original value}} \times 100$$

Change in value is the difference between the original value and the final value.

A decrease in price or value of goods can also be known as **depreciation**.

Discuss and discover

Anita has a job in which she earns €100 per week. Her employer is very pleased with her work and gives her a 50% pay raise. A while later, the employer has to reduce everyone's pay and tells Anita he will have to reduce her wage by 50%. Anita thinks this is fine, and she will still earn €100 a week, as a 50% increase is the same as a 50% decrease. Is she correct?

What have you discovered about a percentage increases and decreases?

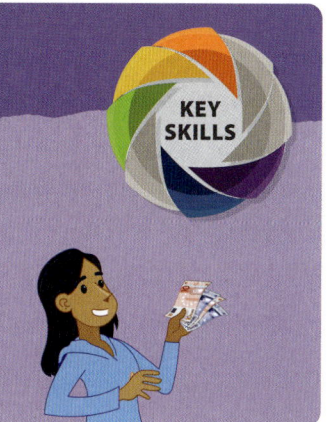

Worked example

A farmer bought a new tractor for €75 000, and seven years later he sold it for €30 000. What was the percentage decrease on the value of the tractor?

Solution

Decrease = cost price − selling price
Decrease = €75 000 − €30 000
Decrease = €45 000

A decrease in value of an item can also be called a **depreciation**.

Percentage decrease = $\frac{\text{decrease}}{\text{original price}} \times 100$

Percentage decrease = $\frac{45\,000}{75\,000} \times 100$

Percentage decrease = $0\cdot6 \times 100$

Percentage decrease = 60%

The tractor had decreased in value by 60%

Practice questions 28.2

1. Find the percentage increase or decrease that occurs in each of the following cases. Give your answer to two decimal places where necessary.
   (i) 80 kg increases to 100 kg
   (ii) 9 000 km decreases to 7 200 km
   (iii) €85 reduces to €82
   (iv) 100 cm³ increases to 350 cm³
   (v) 10 m reduces to 9·5 m
   (vi) €72 000 reduces to €48 000

2. Shaun has a flock of 64 sheep. He has lost eight of them. What percentage of the flock has he lost? Give your answer to one decimal place.

3. Last month Emma earned €150, but this month she earned €180. What percentage increase in pay did she receive?

4. Ciaran buys shares in a company for €82 000. He sells them for €104 000. What was the percentage increase of the shares? Give your answer to two decimal places.

5. Elvis bought a car for €3 400. He sold it two years later for €2 000. What was the percentage decrease of the car? Give your answer to one decimal place.

6. Mia bought a mobile home for €54 500. Eight years later, she sold it for €37 200. By what percentage had the price of the mobile home depreciated (decreased)? Give your answer to one decimal place.

7. Robin wants to trade in some old console games to buy a new headset. The shop offers to buy his games for 45% of their original value. Robin trades in four games. The original price he paid for each game is as follows.

Game	Original price
Pacey Man	€29·99
Speed Racer	€34·99
Wonder Falls	€19·99
Super Maria Cars	€24·99
Total (€)	?

   (i) The shop offer Robin €43·98 for all four games. Verify that this offer is not equal to 45% of their original value.
   (ii) Based on the value offered of €43·98, what percentage of the original price is the shop purchasing the games for? Give your answer to the nearest whole number.
   (iii) If you were Robin, how would you explain how to calculate the correct purchase price of the games to the shop assistant?

8. One hundred years ago, the average height of a female in Ireland was 154 cm, and the average height of a male was 166·4 cm. Today, the average height of a female is 165·1 cm and the average height of a male is 178·9 cm. Calculate the percentage increase in the height of (i) a female and (ii) a male over the past 100 years. Give your answers to two decimal places.

9. In 1970, the area of the Amazon rainforest was approximately 4·1 million km². In 2019, its area had decreased to 3·3 million km². Calculate the percentage decrease in the area of the Amazon rainforest. Give your answer to one decimal place.

Taking it FURTHER

10. By selling a table for €240, a carpenter loses 20%.
    (i) Calculate the cost price that the carpenter paid to make the table.
    (ii) What percentage would he gain or lose by selling it for €360?

11. The price of an item changed from €120 to €100. Then later the price decreased again from €100 to €80. Which of the two decreases was larger in percentage terms?

12. Between 2015 and 2020, the number of school age children in a town decreased by 23%. The number of children in this town in 2015 was 9 560.
    How many children were living in this town in 2020? Give your answer to the nearest whole number.

13. The number of pets in a shelter increases from 30 to 40 and then decreases from 40 to 30.
    (i) Find the percentage increase from 30 to 40 and the percentage decrease from 40 to 30.
    (ii) Are the percentages the same? Explain why or why not.

28.3 Income tax and other deductions on earnings

By the end of this section you should:
- understand how to calculate income tax and other deductions due from earnings

In Ireland, anyone who earns a wage (salary) may be required to pay a portion of this income to the state in the form of **income tax**, and other charges such as Universal Social Charge (USC) and Pay Related Social Insurance (PRSI). Taxes go towards funding for the environment, health, education and social services, among other areas.

The amount of income tax you pay is linked to how much you earn. In Ireland, there are two levels of income tax: a low level, usually around 20% and a higher level, usually around 40%.

How is income tax calculated?

James earns €25 000 per annum (year). This is known as his **gross income**.

> **Gross income** is the amount of salary or wages paid to the individual by an employer, before any deductions are made.

If James pays income tax on all of his earnings at 20%, the initial amount due will be:

$\frac{20}{100} \times €25\,000 = €5\,000$

This is known as the **gross tax**.

> **Gross tax** is the total amount of income tax due, before the tax credit is applied.

In Ireland, we don't have to pay tax on every single euro we earn. The Revenue Office (or the tax office) will give the majority of workers a 'tax credit'.

People are entitled to tax credits depending on their personal circumstances, e.g. married person or civil partner tax credit, home carer tax credit, employee (PAYE) tax credit, etc.

To find the tax you have to pay (tax payable), we calculate the gross tax and then subtract the tax credits.

> A **tax credit** is money that the government deducts from the amount of tax due. Tax credits reduce the final amount of tax you pay.

The following is called the income tax equation:

Net tax = gross tax – tax credits

> **Net tax (tax payable)** is the amount of tax due after the tax credit has been deducted.

If James has a tax credit of €1 500, his **net tax** (tax payable) will be: €5 000 – €1 500 = €3 500

Therefore, his final pay after deductions is €25 000 – €3 500 = €21 500

This is his **net income** (also known as **take home pay**).

Net income will always be less than or equal to gross income.

> **Net income** is the amount of salary or wages a person is paid after all deductions have been made.

Worked example 1

Lorraine earns a gross salary €32 000 per annum (per year). She must pay income tax of 21%, and she has a tax credit of €1 650.

(i) How much income tax must Lorraine pay?
(ii) Calculate Lorraine's net pay.

Solution

(i) 21% of €32 000 :

$\frac{21}{100} \times 32\,000 = 6\,720$

Lorraine's gross tax = €6 720

However, Lorraine has a tax credit of €1 650.

This must be subtracted from the amount she owes.

Therefore, Lorraine must pay

Net tax = gross tax – tax credit

Net tax = €6 720 – €1 650

Net tax = €5 070

(ii) Lorraine's net pay = gross pay – all deductions

net pay = €32 000 – income tax due

net pay = €32 000 – €5 070

net pay = €26 930

Worked example 2

Simon is a make-up artist. He earns €642·30 per week. He pays tax at 23%. He has a tax credit of €63·50 per week. Simon also has a car loan of €45 per week, and pays his local property tax at €9·50 per week. He gets both of these payments deducted from his gross wages at the end of each week.

(i) What is Simon's gross pay?
(ii) What is the gross tax due on Simon's wages each week?
(iii) How much tax does Simon actually pay each week?
(iv) After all deductions from Simon's wages are made each week, how much is his net pay?

Solution

(i) Simon's gross pay is €642·30 per week

(ii) Gross tax due = 23% of €642·30

Gross tax due = $\frac{23}{100} \times 642\cdot30$

Gross tax due = 147·729

Gross tax due = €147·73

(iii) Net tax due = €147·73 – €63·50 (tax credit)

Net tax due = €84·23

(iv) After **all** deductions

Net pay = gross pay – tax due – car loan – property tax

Net pay = €642·30 – €84·23 – €45 – €9·50

Net pay = €503·57

Simon's net pay is €503·57 per week

Practice questions 28·3

1. Mike earns €20 000 per year and must pay 18% income tax.
   (i) What is his gross pay per year?
   (ii) How much is Mike's gross tax per year?

2. Stephen earns €700 per week and must pay 21% income tax.
   (i) What is Stephen's gross salary per year?
   (ii) How much gross income tax must Stephen pay per year?

3. Sophie is a mechanic and earns €650 per week. She must pay 22% income tax on her gross earnings. She has a tax credit of €57·75 per week.
   (i) How much gross income tax must Sophie pay?
   (ii) How much net income tax must she pay?
   (iii) What is her net wage per week?

4. Jobs are usually advertised with a gross annual salary. If a person must pay tax at 23%, use the information below to work out what gross tax is due for each salary, and the net annual salary. Remember, money is generally calculated to two decimal places.

Employment	Gross pay (per year)	Gross tax due at 23%	Tax credit	Net tax due	Net pay (per year)
Private bus driver	€31 000		€1 650		
Restaurant server	€24 000		€1 700		
Delivery person	€19 000		€1 600		
Tour guide	€15 000		€1 450		
Dog walker	€12 000		€1 100		
Sales executive	€29 500		€1 750		

5. Harry earns €8 000 per year. He pays tax at a rate of 21%, and he has a tax credit of €1 700 per annum.
   (i) Calculate how much gross tax Harry will have to pay per year.
   (ii) How much tax does Harry actually have to pay? Justify your answer.

6. Sandy works in a local DIY store. She earns €9·50 per hour and works 38 hours per week.
   (i) How much does Sandy earn in:
       (a) a week? (b) a month? (c) a year?
   (ii) Sandy must pay tax at 22% on her gross salary. How much gross tax does Sandy pay in:
       (a) a week? (b) a month? (c) a year?
   (iii) Sandy has a tax credit of €67·50 per week. What is Sandy's take home pay each week?

7. Diane earns €35 600 per year. She pays tax at 21·5% and has a tax credit of €1 700. Diane also pays €1 100 for health insurance per year, and €170 for bin charges per year.
   (i) Calculate Diane's gross tax per year.
   (ii) Calculate her net tax per year.
   (iii) Calculate her net salary for a year after all deductions have been made.

8. Dillon is a fitness trainer. He earns €19 500 per annum, plus a yearly bonus of €3 500 for every 10 clients he signs up to the gym. Dillon pays tax on all income earned at a rate of 22%, and has a tax credit of €1 850 per year.
   Last year, Dillon signed 20 people up to join the gym.
   (i) What was Dillon's gross pay last year?
   (ii) What was Dillon's gross tax bill last year?
   (iii) How much was his net pay last year?

9. Charlie is an apprentice electrician. He earns €10·25 per hour and works 30 hours per week. He pays tax at a rate of 21% on his gross weekly salary and has a tax credit of €37·50 per week.

   (i) What is Charlie's gross pay per week?
   (ii) Calculate his gross tax per week.
   (iii) How much net tax per week does he have to pay?
   (iv) Charlie gets a tax-free sum of €27·50 per week towards the cost of his tools. Using all of the above information, calculate his net wages for one week.

Taking it FURTHER

10. Holly earns €32 500 per year. Last year, she was billed for gross tax amounting to €6 825, before tax credits were taken into account.

    (i) At what percentage rate does Holly have to pay tax?
    (ii) After her tax credit was taken into account, Holly paid €5 125 in income tax. How much is Holly's tax credit worth?

11. Marie earns €28 000 per year. She pays tax at 19% and has a tax credit of €1 700 per annum.

    (i) What is Marie's gross tax?
    (ii) What is her net tax?
    (iii) How much is her net pay?
    (iv) Marie gets an increase in her gross wages of 5%. What is her new gross wage?
    (v) If her tax rate and tax credits stay the same, has Marie's net wage also increased by 5%? Justify your answer.

Revision questions

28A Core skills

1. Find the resulting new increased or decreased quantities below. Give your answers to two decimal places, where appropriate.

   (i) 9% decrease in €450
   (ii) 5% increase in 25 km
   (iii) 12·5% increase in a speed of 600 km/h
   (iv) 20% decrease in a temperature of 30°C
   (v) 2·5% increase in a salary of €1 250

2. A German shepherd dog weighs 48 kg. After a diet and exercise program, he now weighs 41 kg. What is the percentage loss in weight? Give your answer to the nearest whole number.

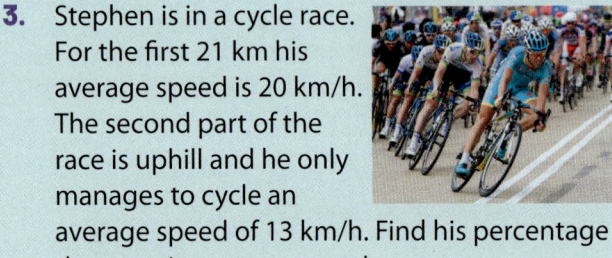

3. Stephen is in a cycle race. For the first 21 km his average speed is 20 km/h. The second part of the race is uphill and he only manages to cycle an average speed of 13 km/h. Find his percentage decrease in average speed.

4. The population of a town was 25 000 in the 2015 census. In the 2020 census, it was 30 000. By what percentage did the population increase?

5. A house was purchased in 2007 for €650 000. It is now valued at €552 000. By what percentage has the value of the house depreciated? Give your answer to the nearest whole number.

6. The length of a piece of copper wire is 7 cm. When heated, the length increases by 11%. Find the new length of the wire after it has been heated. Give your answer to one decimal place.

7. Find the net weekly take home pay after all deductions for each of the following.
   (i) Jim receives €711 a week and has €68 deducted in net tax.
   (ii) Betty receives a wage of €538 a week and has deductions of €87 in tax and €13·80 for property tax.
   (iii) Jack's wage is €827 a week and he has €157 deducted in tax, €27 deducted for health insurance and €10·30 deducted for union fees, each week.

8. Frank earns a salary of €57 655 per year.
   (i) What is his fortnightly salary?
   (ii) Each fortnight, his deductions are €421·19 in tax, €22·84 for health insurance, €9·15 for life insurance and €45·38 for car loan repayments. Calculate his net pay per fortnight.

9. Destiny earns a gross annual income of €32 500 as a crane operator. She pays tax at 23% and has a tax credit of €1 650 per annum. Calculate:
   (i) her gross tax due
   (ii) the amount of net tax due
   (iii) her net wage per annum

10. Kim earned €2 350 over a two-week period. Her gross tax bill is €352·50
    (i) What is the percentage rate of tax that Kim is required to pay?
    (ii) If Kim has a tax credit of €82·50 per fortnight, what will her net pay be after tax is deducted?

11. Taku earns €16·50 per hour as a nurse. He works 40 hours per week.
    (i) How much money does Taku earn per week?
    (ii) Taku's gross tax bill was €138·60. At what percentage did he have to pay income tax?
    (iii) If he has a tax credit of €68·31 per week, what is Taku's net wage per week?

12. Kate is making out her monthly budget. She has a gross monthly wage of €2 250 per month. She pays tax at a rate of 21·5% and has a tax credit of € 223·75
    (i) Calculate Kate's net pay.
    (ii) Kate makes a list of her spending each month, shown in the table below. Find the total amount Kate spends each month.

Item	Amount(per month) (€)
Rent	650
Car payment	250
Lunches	100
Socialising	400
Groceries	300
Total	?

    (iii) How much money does Kate have left at the end of each month after her expenses are taken into account?
    (iv) What would you suggest Kate should reduce her spending on if she wants to save €400 per month? Justify your answer.

13. Michael works as cabin crew on an airline. He pays tax at a rate of 22% and has a tax credit of €71·25 per week.

Weekly Pay Slip			
Employee Name	Michael Cleary	Date	21 June
Earnings		Deductions	
Basic wage	€350·50	Net tax	B
Overtime	€124·75	PRSI	€25·50
		USC	€4·75
		Property tax	€6·25
Gross pay	A	Total deductions	C
		Net pay due	D

    Copy the pay slip provided and fill in the missing information for A, B, C, and D.

28B Taking it FURTHER

1. Explain the following terms.
   (i) Gross tax
   (ii) Gross income
   (iii) Net tax
   (iv) Net income
   (v) Tax credit
   (vi) Percentage increase
   (vii) Percentage decrease

2. The price of stock in company ABC dropped from €26 per share to €14 per share.
   (i) What is the percentage decrease in the price of a share of stock in the company? Give your answer to two decimal places.
   (ii) Mary bought 150 shares in this company at €26 per share. How much money did she spend?
   (iii) She sold the 150 shares for €14 per share. What was her loss in euros?
   (iv) What percent of her original amount of money did Mary lose by investing in this stock? Give your answer to the nearest whole number.

3. When put under an increased amount of pressure, an aluminium can will be crushed.
   If a weight of 10 kg is applied to a can, it will be crushed to 30% of its original height.
   If a can is 18 cm tall and a 10 kg weight is placed on top of it, calculate the new height of the can in cm. Give your answer to one decimal place.

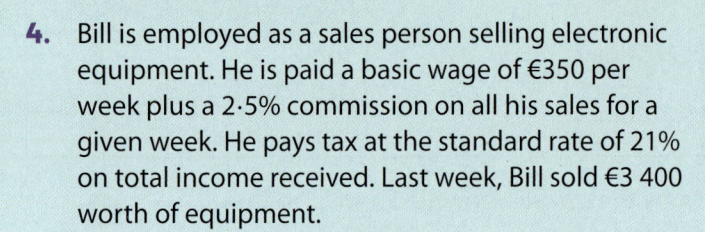

4. Bill is employed as a sales person selling electronic equipment. He is paid a basic wage of €350 per week plus a 2·5% commission on all his sales for a given week. He pays tax at the standard rate of 21% on total income received. Last week, Bill sold €3 400 worth of equipment.
   (i) What was Bill's gross wage for the week?
   (ii) If he has a tax credit worth €62·80 per week, what was his net wage?

5. Una works in a computer repair shop and earns €11·50 per hour. She works 38 hours per week.
   (i) Calculate Una's gross pay per week.
   (ii) Una must pay income tax at a rate of 23% on her gross pay. Calculate the gross income tax due.
   (iii) She has a tax credit of €61·50 per week. How much income tax must Una pay each week?
   (iv) What is Una's net wage per week, after tax has been deducted?
   (v) Una had saved €1 800 in a year, and received 3·5% interest on her savings. What is the total amount of money in her savings account now?
   (vi) Una wants to buy a moped with her savings. The moped costs €1 400 plus 23% VAT. Does Una have enough money saved to buy the moped? Justify your answer.

6. Provided is the Tax Credit Certificate for Hazel Nutte.

   (i) Copy the tax credit certificate provided and fill in the missing information.

   (ii) Based on the information, what is Hazel's net pay:

   (a) per month

   (b) per fortnight

   (c) per week?

   (iii) Copy the table below and place a tick (✓) in the correct box on each line to show the effect of each event on Hazel's net pay in a year.

Tax Credit Certificate for Hazel Nutte	
For the year January 2021 to December 2022	
Personal tax credit	€1 750
Travel tax credit	€700
Total tax credit	A
Gross income	€33 500
Amount of income taxable at 21%	B
Gross tax due	C
Net tax due	D
Net income for the year	E

	Weekly pay will increase	No effect on pay	Weekly pay will decrease
The rate of gross tax is changed from 21% to 23%			
The tax credit is changed from €1 750 to €1 650			
The travel allowance is changed from €700 to €785			
The tax rate increases for people who earn more than €40 000 per year			

7. A person has a gross income of €35 000 for the year. He pays tax on his gross pay at 20%.

   (i) What is the gross tax due on his salary each year?

   (ii) Copy and complete the table below.

Gross income earned (€)	0	5 000	10 000	15 000	20 000	25 000	30 000	35 000	40 000
Gross tax at 20% due (€)	0	1 000	2 000						

   (iii) Copy and complete the graph below to show the amount of gross income tax at 20% for every gross income up to €40 000 per year. Show all your workings out. The amount of income tax at 20% is shown for gross incomes up to €10 000.

   (iv) Callum earns a gross income of €27 500 per year.

   From the graph you have drawn, calculate the gross tax Callum must pay.

   (v) Using any valid mathematical method, calculate 20% of €27 500.

   (vi) Are your answers for part (iii) and part (iv) the same?

   (vii) Give a reason why they might be slightly different.

   (viii) Does the graph or the calculation give the most accurate answer? Justify your answer.

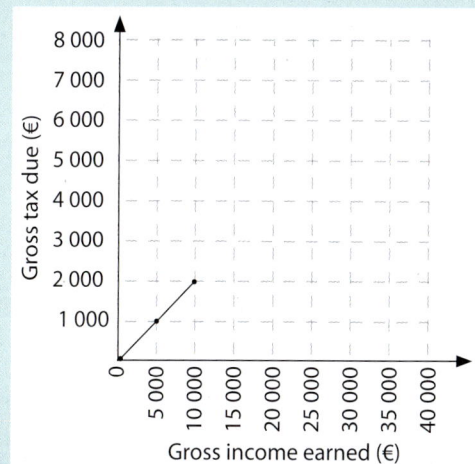

Now that you have completed the unit, revisit the Something to think about ... question posed at the start of this unit.

Now try questions 1 and 9 on pages 558–60

Unit 29

Circles 2

Topics covered within this unit:
29·1 Revision of *Circles 1*
29·2 Angles in a semicircle
29·3 Cyclic quadrilaterals

The Learning Outcomes covered in this unit are contained in the following sections:

GT.1 GT.2c GT.3c GT.3b GT.3d
GT.3e

Key words
Standing on the arc
Cyclic quadrilateral

Something to think about ...

The theorems of circle geometry are not obvious to us a lot of the time. In fact, most people are quite surprised by the results when they first see them. One such theorem is attributed to Thales of Miletus (c. 620–546 BCE) and involves angles in a circle.

A taco shell is in the shape of a semicircle.

Find the measure of $\angle EFG$, $\angle FEG$ and $\angle FGE$ in the taco shown without using a protractor, given that $|EF| = |FG|$.

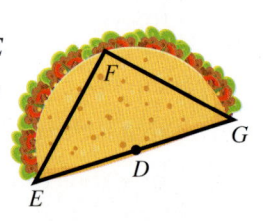

29·1 Revision of *Circles 1*

By the end of this section you should:
- be able to find the area and perimeter of shapes involving circles

We learned about circles in Section B, Unit 16.

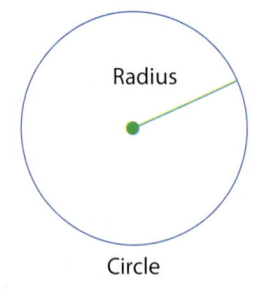

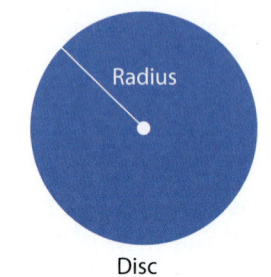

Circle

Disc

π is a constant value for all circles.

$$\pi = \frac{\text{circumference of a circle}}{\text{diameter of the circle}}$$

Area = πr^2
Circumference (length) = $2\pi r$

These formulae appear in the *formulae and tables* booklet.
π does not have an exact value, but when doing calculations, we can use the approximate values 3·14 or $\frac{22}{7}$ or use the π button on the calculator.

458 Linking Thinking 1

Worked example 1

A circle has a circumference equal to 6π cm.

Find (i) the diameter of the circle (ii) the area of the circle. Give your answer in terms of π.

Solution

(i) Circumference = $2\pi r$

$6\pi = 2\pi r$

$\dfrac{6\pi}{2\pi} = \dfrac{2\pi r}{2\pi}$ (dividing both sides by 2π)

$3 \text{ cm} = r$

Diameter = $2 \times r$

Diameter = 2×3

Diameter = 6 cm

(ii) Area = πr^2

Area = $\pi(3)^2$

Area = $\pi(9)$

Area = 9π cm^2

Worked example 2

A circle has an area of 81π cm^2.

Find (i) the radius of the circle (ii) the circumference of the circle, to two decimal places.

Solution

(i) Area = πr^2

$81\pi = \pi r^2$

$\dfrac{81\pi}{\pi} = \dfrac{\pi r^2}{\pi}$ (dividing both sides by π)

$81 = r^2$

$\sqrt{81} = r$ (square root both sides)

$9 \text{ cm} = r$

(ii) Circumference = $2\pi r$

Circumference = $2\pi(9)$

Circumference = 56·55 cm

When you are not given a value for π, use the π button on your calculator.

You should be familiar with Section B, Unit 16 before beginning the questions below.

Practice questions 29·1

1. Choosing from the following words, name the labelled parts of the circle shown: **circumference, centre, radius, diameter**

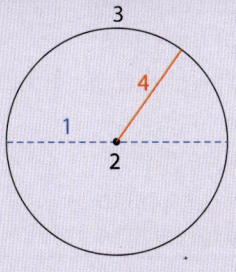

2. (i) Estimate the area of the circle on the right by counting the unit squares.

   (ii) Check your answer to part (i) by calculating the area using the formula.

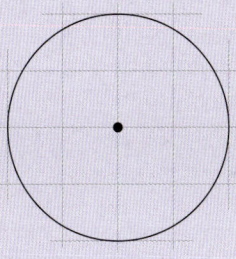

3. Find (i) the circumference and (ii) the area of the circle pictured on the right, rounding your answer to three significant figures. (94 cm)

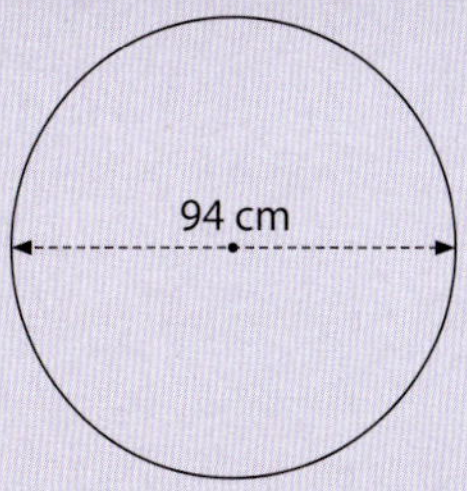

4. Find (i) the circumference and (ii) the area of the circle pictured on the right, rounding your answer to one decimal place. (6·4 cm)

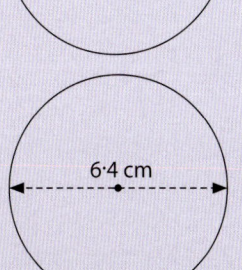

5. A circle has a radius of 2·8 cm. Taking $\pi = 3·14$, find (i) the circumference and (ii) the area of the circle, rounding your answers to two decimal places.

Section C Applying our skills

6. The diameter of a circle is 4 cm. Taking $\pi = \frac{22}{7}$, find the circumference of the circle, rounding your answer to nearest whole number.

7. Find the radius of a circle that has an area of 25π cm².

8. Find (i) the diameter and (ii) the area of a circle with a circumference of 25·12 cm (taking $\pi = 3·14$).

9. Find the diameter of a circle with a circumference of 37·28 cm (taking $\pi = 3·14$).

10. The area of a circle is 144π cm. Find the circumference of the circle, correct to one decimal place.

11. The area of a circle is 2·7 cm². Find the circumference of the circle, in terms of π.

12. Shown on the right is a semicircle. Find (i) the area and (ii) the perimeter of this shape.
    6 cm

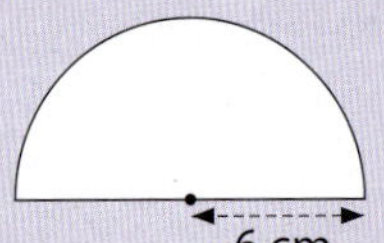

13. A mobile phone mast has a range of 4 km. Calculate the area of the region the mast signal can reach. Give your answer to two decimal places.
    4 km

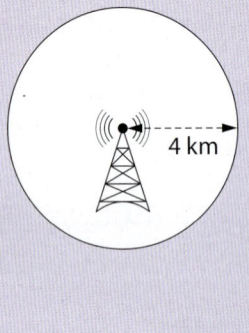

14. Shown is a compound shape made from a rectangle and semicircle. Calculate the area of the shape.
    11 cm
    4 cm

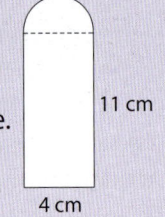

15. The side of a wooden shed is shown. The side wall is 12 m wide and 15 m high. There is a semi-circular glass window, 5 m wide. Liam wants to paint the shed wall. Each tin costs €1·99 and covers 5 m². Work out the total cost to paint the shed wall.
    15 m
    5 m
    12 m

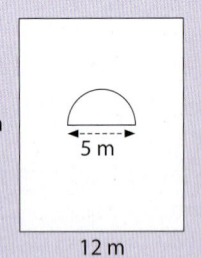

16. A circular floor has a radius of 40 metres. Draw a scale diagram of this floor using an appropriate scale and write down the scale you have used.

17. Shown in the diagram is a rectangular garden. Belle wants to re-seed the grass in her garden. The garden is 14 metres long and 9 metres wide. There is a vegetable patch that is 2·5 metres long and 2 metres wide. There is a circular pond that has radius 3 metres. The remainder of the garden is grass.

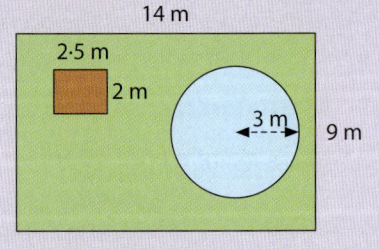

    14 m
    2·5 m
    2 m
    3 m
    9 m

    (i) Find the area covered in grass.

    (ii) Each bag of grass seed costs €4·60 and covers 10 m². Work out the total cost to re-seed the garden.

    (iii) Draw a scale diagram of the garden, including the vegetable patch and pond using and appropriate scale and write down the scale you have used.

18. If the actual diameter of a wheel is 4 metres, draw a scale diagram of the wheel, using an appropriate scale.

19. Copy the table below and put a tick (✓) in the correct box in each row to show whether each statement is always true, sometimes true, or never true. Justify your answer in each case.

Statement		Tick **one** box only for each statement		
		Always true	Sometimes true	Never true
(i)	An arc of a circle is shorter than the diameter of the circle			
(ii)	The chord of a circle is the diameter			
(iii)	π is equal to exactly 3·14			
(iv)	π is equal to the circumference divided by the diameter			

29.2 Angles in a semicircle

By the end of this section you should:
- understand how to find the angle in a semicircle

Circle terms revision

An **arc** is a part of the circumference.

A **semicircle** is a sector whose arc ends are the ends of a diameter.

A **chord** is a line segment joining two points on the circle.

A **diameter** is a special chord which passes through the centre.

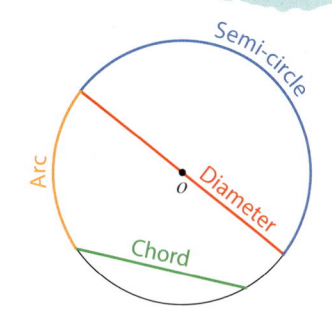

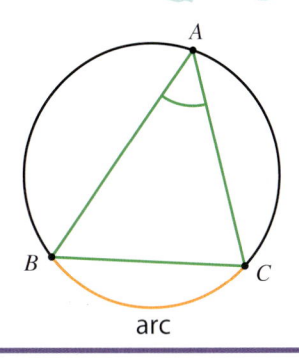

If B and C are the ends of an arc of a circle, and A is another point, not on the arc, then we say that the $\angle BAC$ is the angle at A **standing on the arc** BC. We also say that it stands on the chord $[BC]$.

Discuss and discover

Investigate the angle in a semicircle.

(i) Work with a classmate to draw the circles with the triangles inside them (inscribed), as shown. Ensure the longest side in the triangles is the diameter of the circle.

(ii) Using a protractor, find the measure of each of the three interior angles of the triangles. Find the sum of these angles.

(iii) Compare the angle opposite the diameter (angle marked A) in each of the triangles.

(iv) Repeat this activity for two more triangles inscribed in a circle, where one side of the triangle is the diameter.

(v) What do you notice? What is the measure of the angle opposite the diameter in each case?

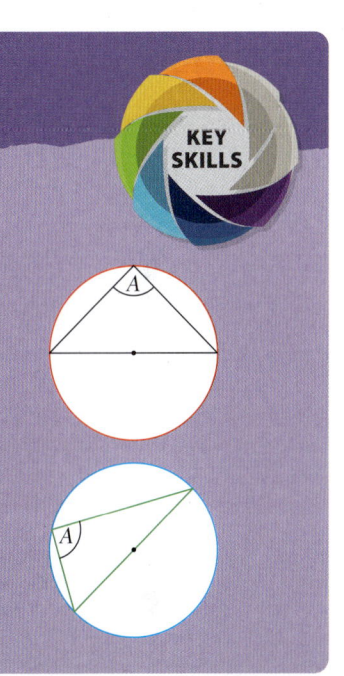

Corollary 3: Each angle in a semicircle is a right angle

Corollary 3 is sometimes called the 'angle in the semicircle theorem' or 'Thales's theorem'.

An angle inscribed in a semicircle is **always a right angle**.

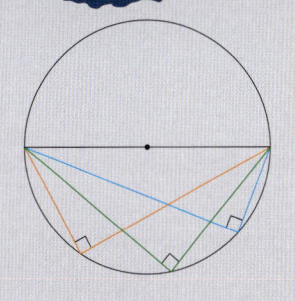

A **corollary** is a theorem that follows on from another theorem.

The end points are either end of a circle's diameter; the apex point can be anywhere on the circumference.

In symbols, if $[AC]$ is a diameter of a circle, and E is any other point of the circle, then $|\angle AEC| = 90°$.

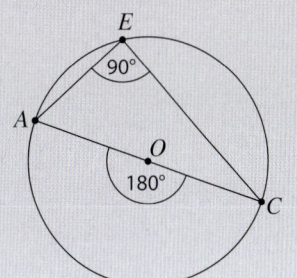

Section C Applying our skills

Worked example 1

Find the value of a in the diagram below (O is the centre of the circle).

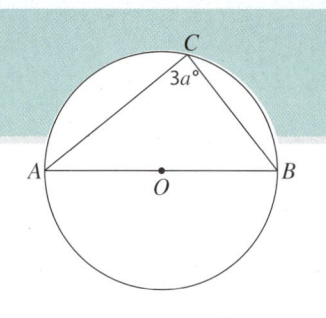

Solution

AB is the diameter as it passes through the centre O.
Therefore $|\angle ACB|$ is 90°

$3a° = 90°$ (angle in a semicircle)
$\dfrac{3a°}{3} = \dfrac{90°}{3}$ (divide both sides by 3)
$a° = 30°$

Worked example 2

Find the measure of $\angle CAE$ in the diagram shown (O is the centre of the circle).

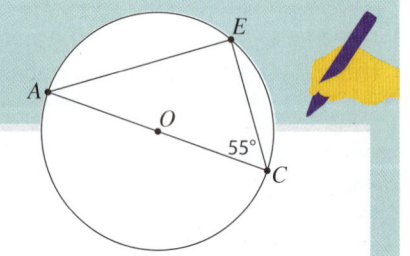

Solution

Corollary 3 tells us that $|\angle AEC| = 90°$
Knowing that the three angles of a triangle sum to 180°, we can find $|\angle CAE|$

$|\angle CAE| + 55° + 90° = 180°$
$\quad |\angle CAE| + 145° = 180°$
$\quad\quad |\angle CAE| = 180° - 145°$
$\quad\quad |\angle CAE| = 35°$

Worked example 3

Using the following diagrams find the length of the line segment BC in each case.
(O is the centre of each circle)

(i)

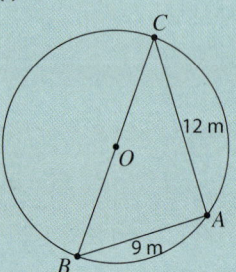

(ii)

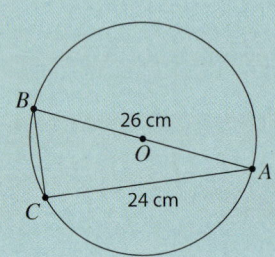

Solution

(i) Triangle ABC is a right-angle triangle (corollary 3)

$c^2 = a^2 + b^2$ (Pythagoras's theorem)
$|CB|^2 = (12)^2 + (9)^2$
$|CB|^2 = 144 + 81$
$|CB|^2 = 225$
$|CB| = \sqrt{225}$ ($\sqrt{}$ both sides)
$|CB| = 15$ m

(ii) Triangle ABC is a right-angle triangle (corollary 3)

$c^2 = a^2 + b^2$ (Pythagoras's theorem)
$26^2 = |BC|^2 + 24^2$
$676 = |BC|^2 + 576$
$676 - 576 = |BC|^2$ (subtract 576 from both sides)
$100 = |BC|^2$
$\sqrt{100} = |BC|$ ($\sqrt{}$ both sides)
10 cm $= |BC|$

Linking Thinking 1

Corollary 4: If the angle standing on a chord at some point of a circle is a right angle, then the chord is a diameter.

Worked example 4

State if the red line in each of the following is (a) a chord and a diameter or (b) just a chord. Justify your answer by stating the axiom, theorem or corollary used.

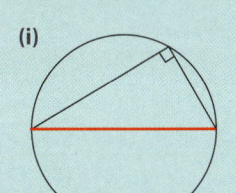

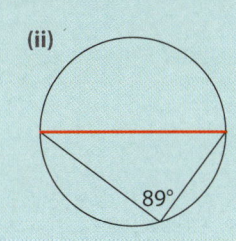

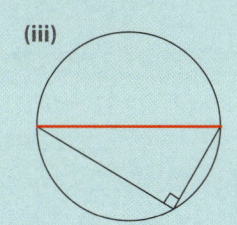

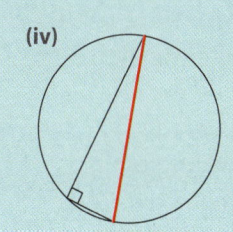

(i) (ii) 89° (iii) (iv)

Solution

(i) Red line is a chord and a diameter

Justification: The angle at the circle is 90° so it is standing on the diameter

(ii) Red line is a chord

Justification: The angle at the circle is not 90° so it is not standing on the diameter

(iii) Red line is a chord and a diameter

Justification: The angle at the circle is 90° so it is standing on the diameter

(iv) Red line is a chord and a diameter

Justification: The angle at the circle is 90° so it is standing on the diameter

Practice questions 29·2

1. Choosing from the following words, name the labelled parts of the circle shown: **segment, sector, chord, circumference, centre, radius, diameter, arc.**

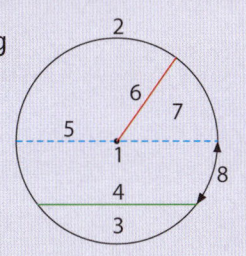

2. Name the angle that is standing on the arc AB in each of the following diagrams.
   (i)   (ii)

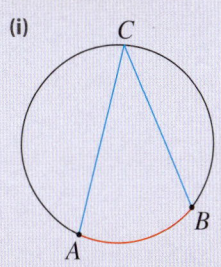

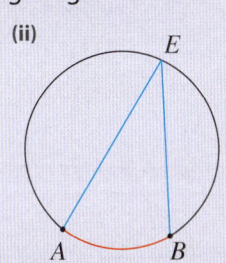

3. For each of the following diagrams, name the arc that $\angle MNO$ is standing on.
   (i)   (ii)

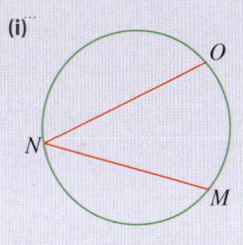

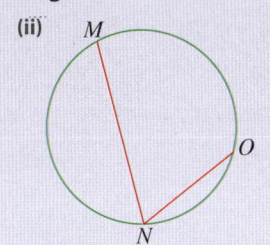

4. A circle with centre O has points A, B and C on the circumference. If $|\angle ABC| = 22°$, find the size of $|\angle BAC|$.

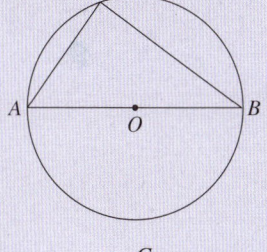

5. In the diagram shown, AB is a diameter of a circle, centre O. C is a point on the circumference of the circle, such that $|\angle CAB| = 28°$.
   What is the size of $\angle CBA$?

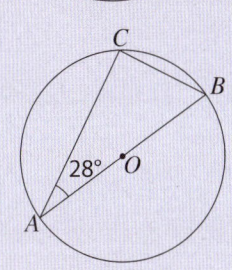

6. On the right is a circle with centre O. AC is a diameter of the circle and B is a point on the circumference. What is the size of angle CBA?

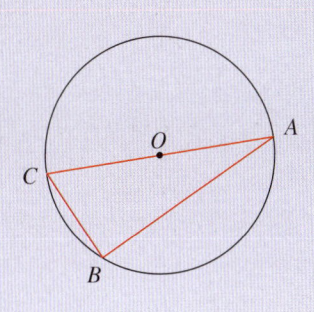

Section C Applying our skills 463

7. AB is the diameter of a circle, centre O. C is a point on the circumference of the circle, such that $|\angle CAB| = 2 \times |\angle CBA|$. What is the size of $\angle CBA$?

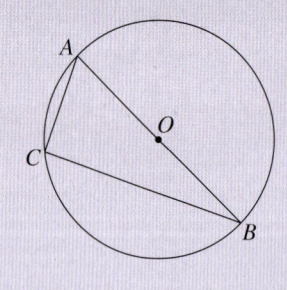

8. In the diagram on the right, $|\angle BAC| = 36°$. O is the centre of the circle. Find the measure of the following angles, giving reasons for your answers.
   (i) $\angle ABC$
   (ii) $\angle ACB$

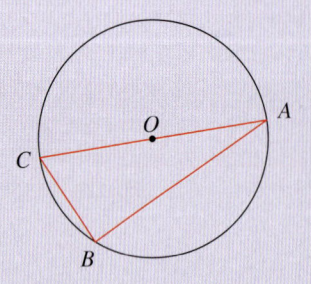

9. In the diagram, $|\angle BAC| = 38°$. O is the centre of the circle. Find the measure of the following angles, giving reasons for your answers.
   (i) $\angle ABC$
   (ii) $\angle ACB$

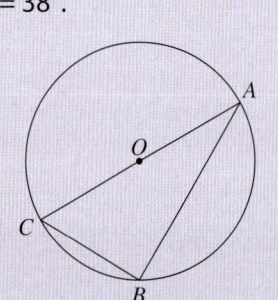

10. Find the value of x in each of the following diagrams (where O is the centre of each of the circles).
    (i)
    (ii)
    (iii)
    (iv)

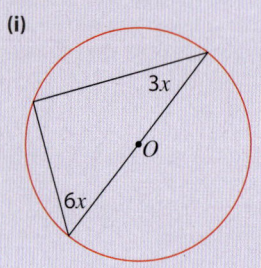

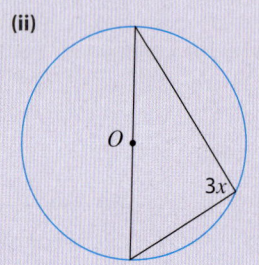

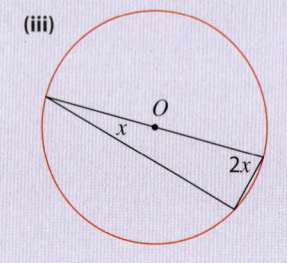

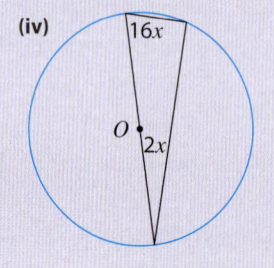

11. Find the length of the side of the triangle marked with the letter y in each of the following diagrams (where O is the centre of each of the circles).
    (i)
    (ii)
    (iii)
    (iv)

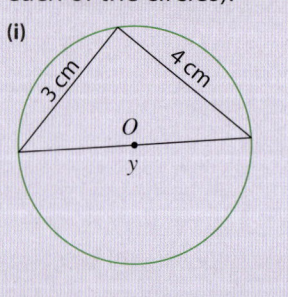

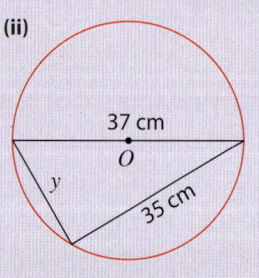

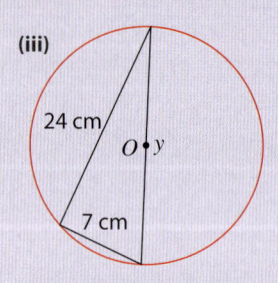

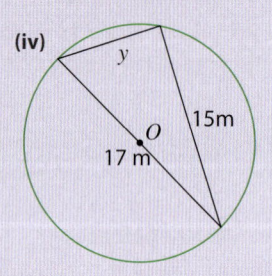

12. Rockall (point R) is a rocky outcrop off the coast of Donegal.
    Cathal would like to find the distance between Donegal (point D) and the most westerly part of Scotland (point S). Using the diagram, find the distance that Cathal wishes to find. O is the centre of the circle in the diagram.

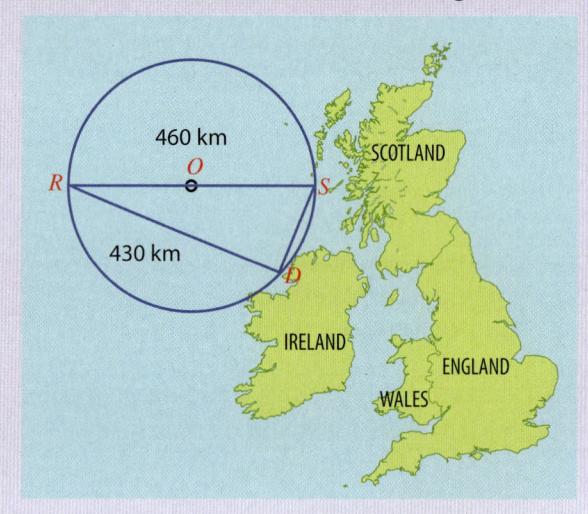

29.3 Cyclic quadrilaterals

By the end of this section you should:
- understand what a cyclic quadrilateral is

We learned in Section B, Unit 23 that a quadrilateral is a polygon with four sides and four vertices.

> A **cyclic quadrilateral** is one whose four vertices all lie on the same circle.

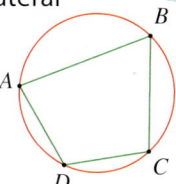

Worked example

A cyclic quadrilateral $ABCD$ is shown on the right. AC is the diameter of the circle.

Find:
(i) the circumference of the circle
(ii) the value of y
(iii) $|\angle BAC|$
(iv) $|BC|$

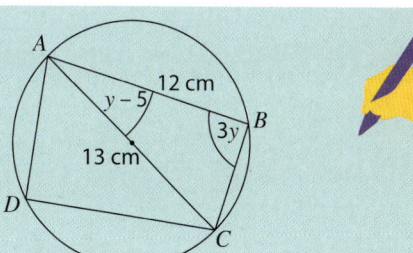

Solution

(i) Radius = $\frac{\text{diameter}}{2} = \frac{13}{2} = 6.5$ cm
Circumference = $2\pi(6.5)$
Circumference = 40.84 cm

(ii) $|\angle ABC| = 90°$ (angle in a semicircle)
$3y = 90°$
$y = 30°$

(iii) $|\angle BAC| = y - 5$
$|\angle BAC| = 30 - 5$
$|\angle BAC| = 25°$

(iv) Triangle ABC is a right-angled triangle (corollary 3)
$c^2 = a^2 + b^2$ (Pythagoras's theorem)
$13^2 = |BC|^2 + 12^2$
$169 = |BC|^2 + 144$
$169 - 144 = |BC|^2$ (subtract 144 from both sides)
$25 = |BC|^2$
$\sqrt{25} = |BC|$ ($\sqrt{}$ both sides)
5 cm $= |BC|$

Practice questions 29.3

1. For each of the following inscribed shapes, write down whether they are quadrilaterals, cyclic quadrilaterals, or neither.

(i) (ii) (iii) (iv) (v) (vi)

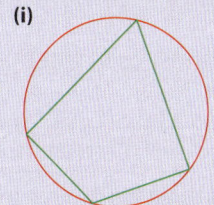

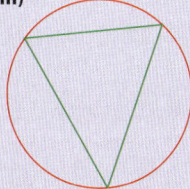

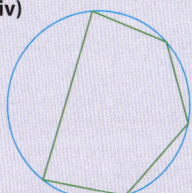

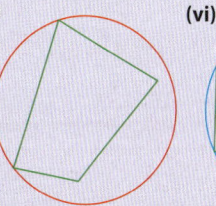

2. A cyclic quadrilateral is shown on the right.
Find:
(i) the length of the diameter
(ii) the measure of $\angle x$

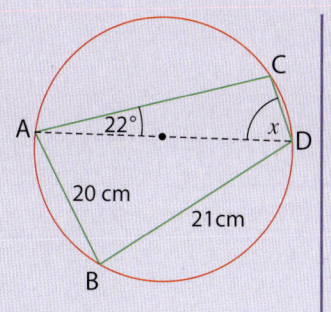

3. A cyclic quadrilateral is shown on the right.
Find:
(i) the length of the diameter
(ii) the measure of $\angle M$
(iii) the measure of $\angle N$

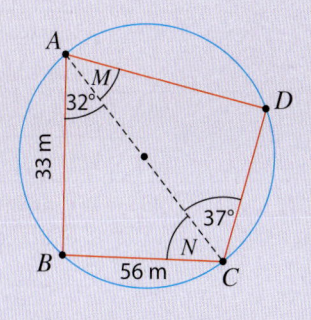

Section C Applying our skills

Revision questions

29A Core skills

1. In the diagram on the right, O is the centre of the circle and A, B and C are points on the circumference.
   Find the measure of the following angles.

   (i) $\angle ACB$

   (ii) $\angle ABC$

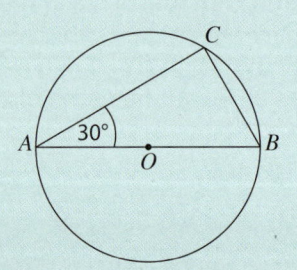

2. Find the measure of $\angle A$ in the following diagrams.

   (i) (ii) (iii) (iv) (v)

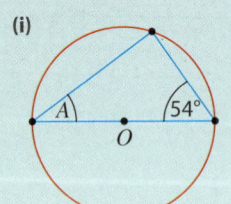

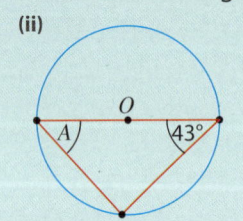

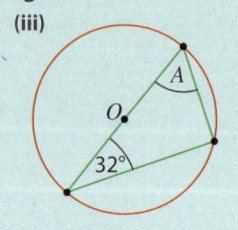

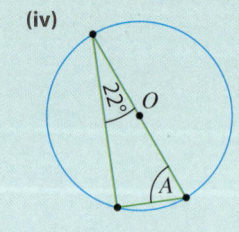

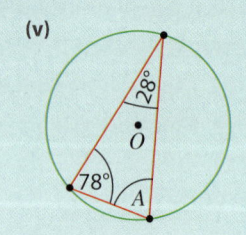

3. Find the value of the side of the triangle marked with the letter y in each of the following diagrams (where O is the centre of each of the circles).

   (i) (ii) (iii) (iv) (v)

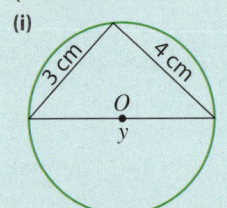

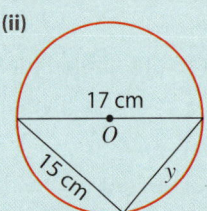

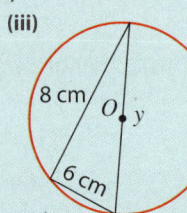

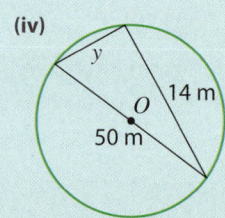

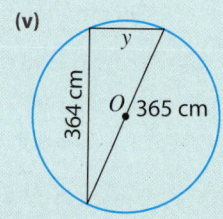

4. Write down whether each of the following inscribed shapes is a cyclic quadrilateral, a quadrilateral, or neither.

   (i) (ii) (iii) (iv) (v)

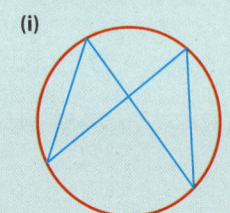

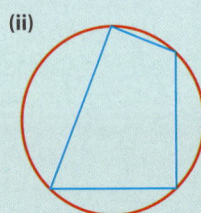

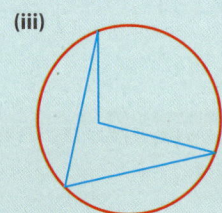

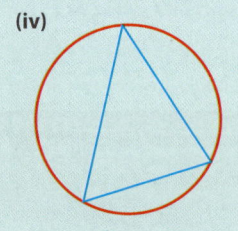

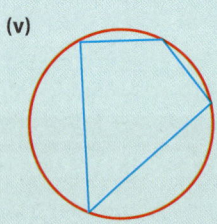

5. The area of a circle is 64π cm². Find the circumference of the circle, correct to one decimal place.

6. Find the diameter of a circle, where the circumference of the circle is 43·96 cm (taking $\pi = 3\cdot 14$).

7. Copy the table below and put a tick (✓) in the correct box in each row to show whether each statement is always true, sometimes true, or never true. Justify your answer in each case.

	Statement	Always true	Sometimes true	Never true
(i)	A quadrilateral has four sides.			
(ii)	A circle can be drawn through the four vertices (corners) of a quadrilateral.			
(iii)	A triangle inscribed in a circle has a right angle.			
(iv)	A triangle's angles sum to 180°.			
(v)	A diameter of a circle is a chord.			

Tick **one** box only for each statement

466 Linking Thinking 1

29B Taking it FURTHER

1. A goat is in a square field that has a side length of 14 m. The goat is tied to the middle of a 14 m fence on one side with a 5 m rope. Find the percentage of the field the goat can reach, to the nearest whole number.

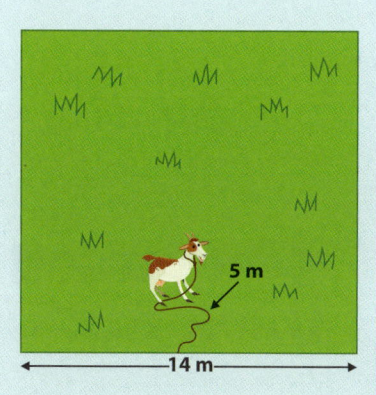

2. Shown on the right is a running track. The two end sections are semicircular. Calculate the area inside the running track, to nearest whole number.

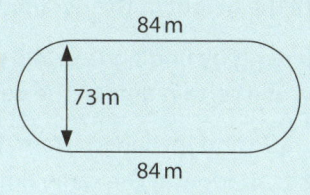

3. The semicircle and square shown on the right have the same area. Calculate the side length of the square.

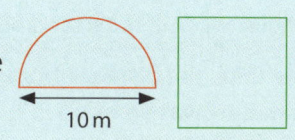

4. Shown is a circular photo frame. The photo part has a radius of 14 cm. The frame is shaded in the diagram, and has a width of 5 cm. Work out area of the frame. Leave your answer in terms of π.

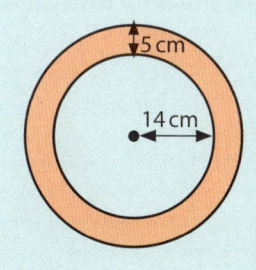

5. Find the measure of the angles marked with the letters on the dartboards below.

   (i) (ii) 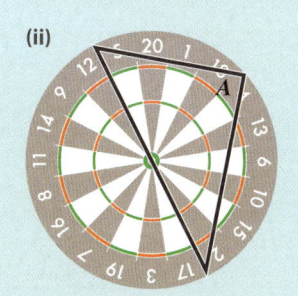 (iii) 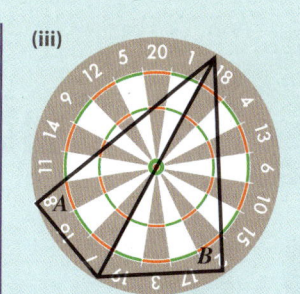 (iv)

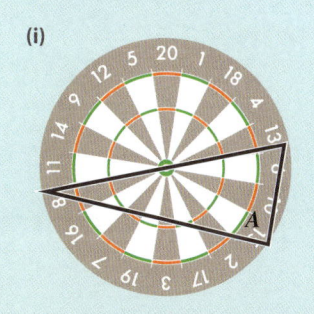

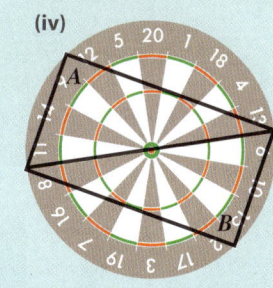

6. A circular building has a diameter of 50 metres. Draw a scale drawing of the base of building using the scale factor of 1 : 500.

7. A circular base for a building measures 500 m in radius.
   Using a compass, draw a scale diagram (using an appropriate scale) to represent the base of this building. Include the scale used in the diagram.

8. The diameter of the moon is 3.474×10^3 km. 
   (i) Write the diameter of the moon in decimal form (without scientific notation).
   (ii) Assuming the moon is perfectly circular, draw a scale diagram of the moon using an appropriate scale.

9. The radius of Earth is 6 371 km. 
   (i) Write the diameter of Earth in scientific notation.
   (ii) Assuming Earth is perfectly circular, draw a scale diagram of the Earth using an appropriate scale.
   (iii) How many times is the diameter of Earth bigger than that of the moon? Give your answer correct to two decimal places.

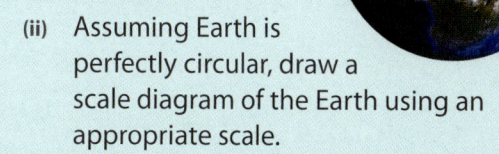

Now that you have completed the unit, revisit the

Something to think about ...

question posed at the start of this unit.

Unit 30

Further geometry

Topics covered within this unit:
30·1 Constructions revision
30·2 Further constructions
30·3 Theorems revision
30·4 Similar triangles

The Learning Outcomes covered in this unit are contained in the following sections:
GT.3a | GT.3b.II | GT.3c

Key words
Similar triangles

Something to think about ...

Thales, a Greek mathematician, is credited with finding an easy way to calculate the height of the pyramids of Egypt using shadows.

He worked it out by finding the ratio of his height to the length of his shadow at a certain time of the day.

Using this ratio and the length from the centre of the pyramid to the end of its shadow at the same time of the day, he calculated the height of the pyramid.

Imagine Thales was 1·8 m tall and his shadow was 1·2 m long.

At the same time, the distance from the centre of the pyramid to the end of its shadow was 98 m.

Use this information to calculate the height of the pyramid.

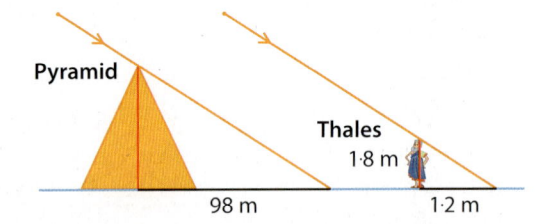

30·1 Constructions revision

By the end of this section you should:
- recall how to complete constructions 1, 2, 4, 5, 8, 9, 10, 11, 12, 13, 14 and 15

In this unit, we will revise all the constructions and theorems you have done so far and complete the remaining constructions and theorems for your course.

In Sections A and B of this textbook, you completed the following constructions.

Construction 1
Construct a bisector of a given angle.

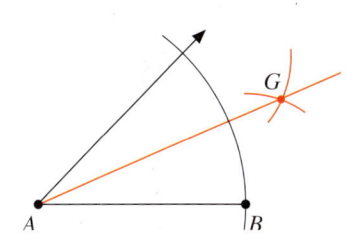

Construction 2
Construct the perpendicular bisector of a line segment.

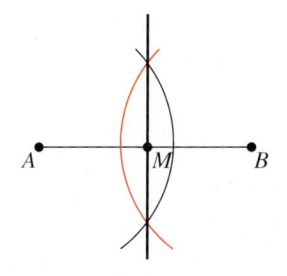

Construction 4
Construct a line perpendicular to a given line l passing through a point on the line.

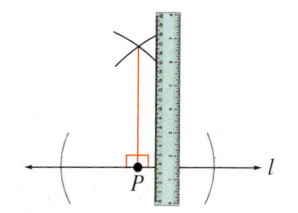

Construction 5
Construct a line parallel to a given line, using a set square and a straight edge.

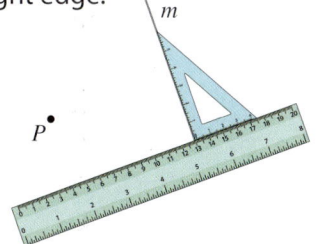

Construction 8
Construct a line segment of a given length.

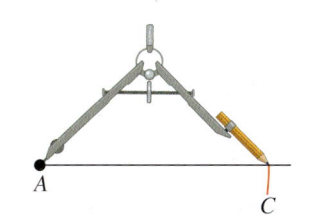

Construction 9
Construct an angle of given number of degrees with a given ray as one arm.

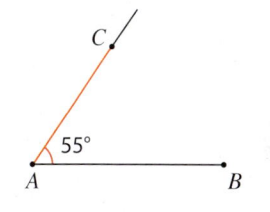

Construction 10
Construct a triangle, given the lengths of the three sides (SSS data).

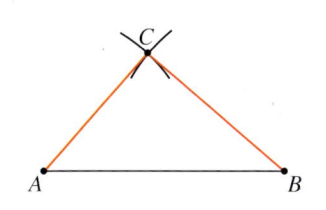

Construction 11
Construct a triangle, given two sides and the angle in between them (SAS data).

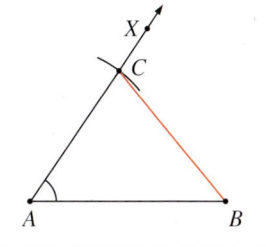

Construction 12
Construct a triangle, given two angles and the side between (ASA data).

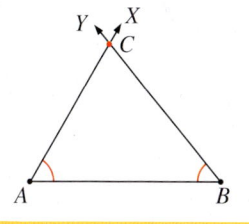

Construction 13
Construct a right-angled triangle, given the length of the hypotenuse and one other side.

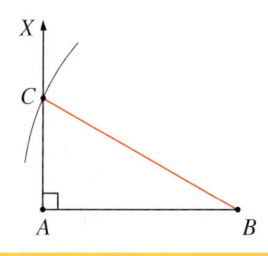

Construction 14
Construct a right-angled triangle, given one side and one of the acute angles.

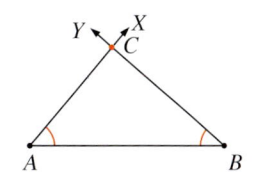

Construction 15
Construct a rectangle, given the sides of the rectangle.

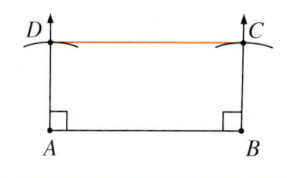

You should revise these constructions before you attempt the following practice questions.

Section C Applying our skills

Practice questions 30.1

1. Draw a line segment of any length in your copybook. Mark any point P on the line segment. Draw a line perpendicular to your line segment through the point P.

2. (i) Construct a line segment [AB] that is 8 cm in length.
   (ii) Construct the perpendicular bisector of [AB]. Mark the point of intersection of the bisector and [AB] as M.
   (iii) Confirm the perpendicular bisector divides the line segment [AB] in half by measuring |AM| and |BM|.

3. (i) Construct ∠XYZ of measure 60°.
   (ii) Construct the angle bisector of ∠XYZ.
   (iii) Confirm by measurement that ∠XYZ has been bisected.

4. Draw lines and points similar to the ones in the diagrams on the right and construct a line perpendicular to the given line, through the given point, P.

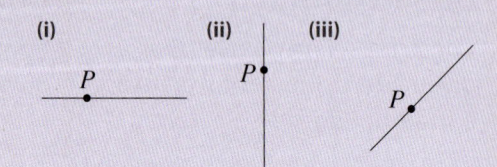

5. (i) Construct a rectangle of sides 6 cm and 8 cm.
   (ii) Verify by measuring that both diagonals are equal in length.

6. (i) Construct an equilateral triangle PQR of side length 5 cm.
   (ii) Measure the angles inside △PQR and use these measurements to confirm that △PQR is equilateral.

7. (a) Construct a triangle with sides measuring 5 cm, 6 cm and 8 cm.
   (b) Measure the three angles inside the triangle and investigate whether:
      (i) the smallest angle is opposite the smallest side
      (ii) the largest angle is opposite the largest side

Taking it FURTHER

8. (i) Construct a triangle DEF such that |DE| = 4 cm, |DF| = 6 cm and |∠EDF| = 40°.
   (ii) Construct the perpendicular bisectors of each of the line segments [DE], [DF] and [EF].
   (iii) The bisectors drawn above should intersect each other at a single point. With the point of intersection as the centre, draw a circle through D, E and F. This circle is called the **circumcircle**.

9. (i) Construct a triangle TUV where |TU| = 5 cm, |∠VTU| = 50° and |∠VUT| = 2|∠VTU|.
   (ii) Construct the bisectors of each of the angles VTU, VUT, TVU.
   (iii) The bisectors drawn above should intersect each other at a single point. With the point of intersection as the centre, draw a circle that fits inside the triangle TUV. This circle is called the **incircle**.

10. (i) Construct the triangle XYZ with |XY| = 4 cm, |∠XYZ| = 90° and |∠YXZ| = 37°.
    (ii) Measure the other sides and use Pythagoras's theorem to confirm that triangle XYZ is a right-angled triangle.

Linking Thinking 1

30·2 Further constructions

By the end of this section you should be able to:
- complete constructions 5 and 6

We have already looked at construction 5 in Section A, Unit 3. We will now look at an alternative method of carrying out this construction, using only a compass and a straight edge.

Construct a line parallel to a given line, using a compass and a straight edge **5**

1 Start by drawing a line m and a point P (not on m). Choose a point Q anywhere on the line m and draw QP.

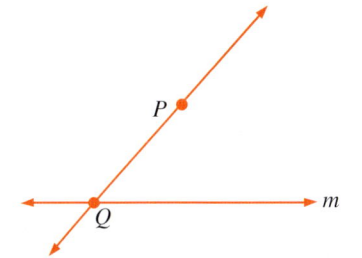

2 Place the compass point on Q and draw an arc that crosses QP and line m. Label the points of intersection A and B as shown.

Using the same compass setting, place the compass point on P and draw an arc on QP. Label point C, as shown.

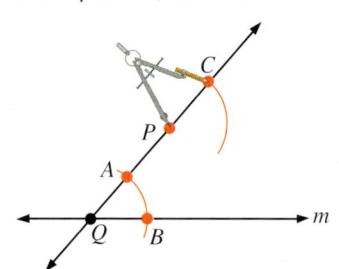

3 With a compass width $|PC|$, place the compass point on C and draw an arc such that it intersects the first arc, as shown.

Label the intersection of these arcs D.

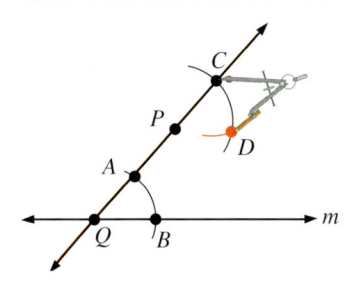

4 Draw PD. This line is parallel to line m.

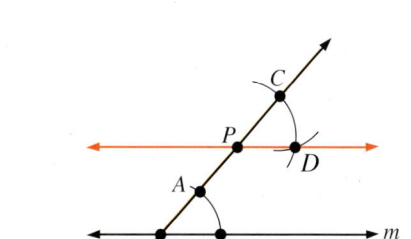

Section C Applying our skills

Division of a line segment into three equal segments, without measuring it

1 Draw a line AB of any length. Choose any point C not on AB. Draw the ray [AC].

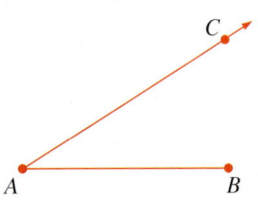

2 Place the point of a compass at A and make an arc of any radius intersecting AC. Label the point of intersection D.

Using the same compass setting, make two more arcs on AC, as shown.

Label the points of intersection E and F and note that |AD| = |DE| = |EF|.

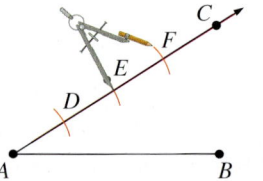

3 Join F to B.

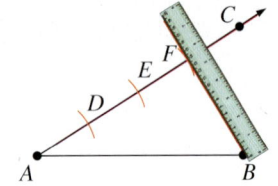

4 Using a set square and a ruler as shown, draw a line from E, parallel to FB, to a new point K on [AB].

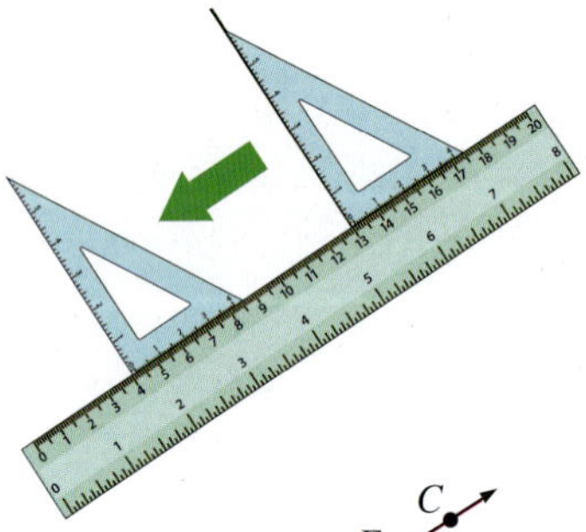

Using a set square and a ruler, draw a line from D, parallel to FB, to a new point J on [AB].

Lines DJ, EK, and FB are all parallel, and they divide AB equally so that |AJ| = |JK| = |KB|.

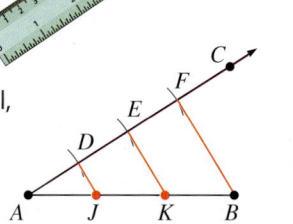

Practice questions 30·2

1. (i) Draw a line segment of any length in your copybook. Mark any point P not on the line segment.

(ii) Draw a parallel line through the point P, using a compass and a straight edge.

2. Copy each of the following diagrams and construct a line parallel to the given line, through the given point, using a compass and a straight edge.

(i)

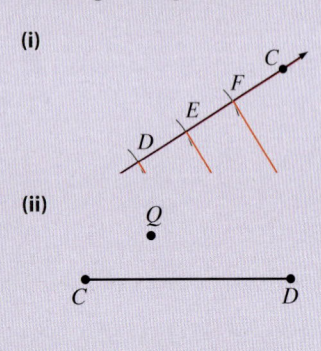

(ii)

(iii)

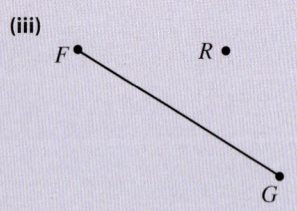

3. Copy the diagram shown into your copybook.

(i) Construct a line parallel to AB through C.

(ii) Construct a line parallel to AC through B.

(iii) What type of quadrilateral have you drawn? Explain how you know it is this type of quadrilateral.

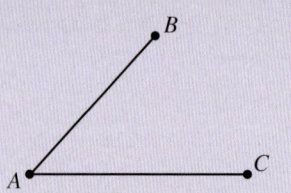

4. Construct a line segment PQ, 6 cm in length.

(i) Construct a line perpendicular to PQ through P. Mark a point R on this line.

(ii) Construct a line parallel to PQ through R. Mark a point S on this line, 6 cm from R.

(iii) Construct a line parallel to PR through S.

(iv) What type of quadrilateral have you drawn? Explain how you know it is this type of quadrilateral.

472 Linking Thinking 1

5. Draw a line segment 12 cm long. Using a compass and a straight edge, divide the line segment into three equal parts. Check your construction by measuring it with a ruler. Each part should be 4 cm long.

6. Draw a line segment of each of the given lengths. In each case, divide the line segment into three equal parts without measuring it.

    (i) 10·5 cm   (ii) 5·4 cm   (iii) 8·4 cm   (iv) 99 mm   (v) 54 mm   (vi) 75 mm

7. A local running club are planning a 5 km race along a straight track. The route will be divided into three equal sections by two water stations.

    (i) Draw a scale diagram of the route using the the scale 1 cm = 1 km.
    (ii) Use a construction on your scale diagram to identify the location of the water stations.

8. A straight section of motorway is 106 km long. The National Roads Authority wish to divide this stretch of motorway into three equal lengths, by building two service stations.

    (i) Draw a scale diagram of the motorway using the the scale 1 cm = 10 km.
    (ii) Use a construction on your scale diagram to identify the location of the service stations.

30·3 Theorems revision

By the end of this section you should:
- recall and be able to use theorems 1, 2, 3, 4, 5, 6, 9, 10, 14 and 15, and corollaries 3 and 4

In Sections A and B of this textbook, you studied the following theorems, converses and corollaries.

Theorem 1 Vertically opposite angles are equal in measure.

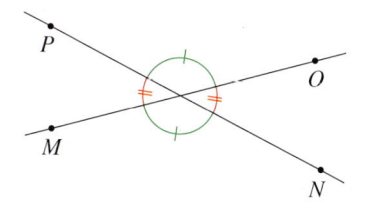

Theorem 2 In an isosceles triangle, the angles opposite the equal sides are equal.

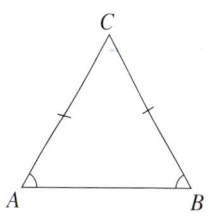

Theorem 3 If a transversal makes equal alternate angles on two lines, then the lines are parallel.

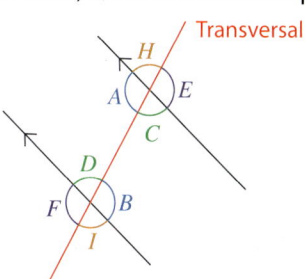

Theorem 4 The angles in any triangle add to 180 degrees.

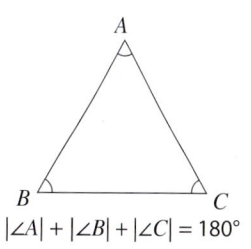

$|\angle A| + |\angle B| + |\angle C| = 180°$

Converse of Theorem 3 If two lines are parallel, then any transversal will make equal alternate angles with them.

Theorem 5 Two lines are parallel if and only if for any transversal, corresponding angles are equal.

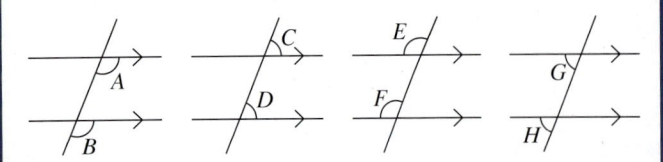

Theorem 6 Each exterior angle of a triangle is equal to the sum of the interior opposite angles.

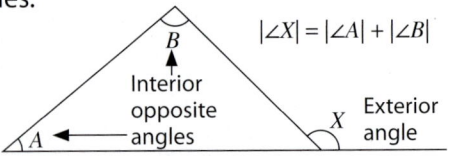

$$|\angle X| = |\angle A| + |\angle B|$$

Converse of Theorem 5 When the two lines being crossed by a transversal are parallel, the corresponding angles are equal.

Theorem 9 In a parallelogram, opposite sides are equal and opposite angles are equal.

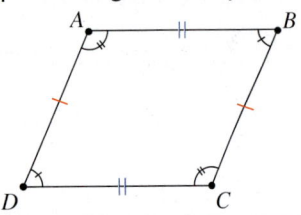

Theorem 10 The diagonals of a parallelogram bisect one another.

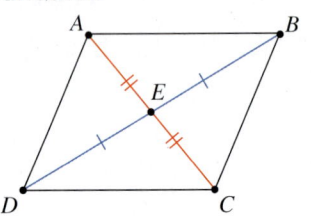

Converse 1 of Theorem 9 If the opposite angles of a quadrilateral are equal, then it is a parallelogram.

Converse 2 of Theorem 9 If the opposite sides of a quadrilateral are equal, then it is a parallelogram.

Theorem 14 (Pythagoras) In a right-angled triangle, the square of the hypotenuse is equal to the sum of the squares of the other two sides.

Theorem 15 (Converse of Pythagoras)
If the square of one side of a triangle is the sum of the squares of the other two, then the angle opposite the first side is a right angle.

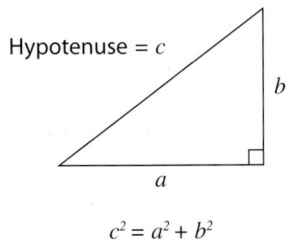

$$c^2 = a^2 + b^2$$

Corollary 3 Each angle in a semicircle is a right angle.

Corollary 4 If the angle standing on a chord at some point of a circle is a right angle, then the chord is a diameter.

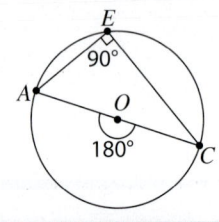

You should revise these theorems before you attempt the practice questions below.

Practice questions 30·3

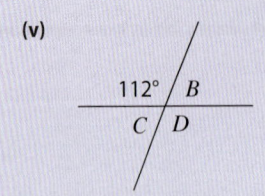

1. Calculate the missing angles in each of the following. Justify your answers in each case.

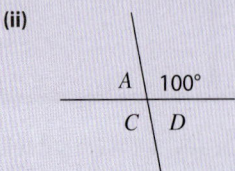

   (i) 124° at A
   (ii) 100° at A
   (iii) 149° at A
   (iv) 30° at A
   (v) 112° at B
   (vi) 144° at C

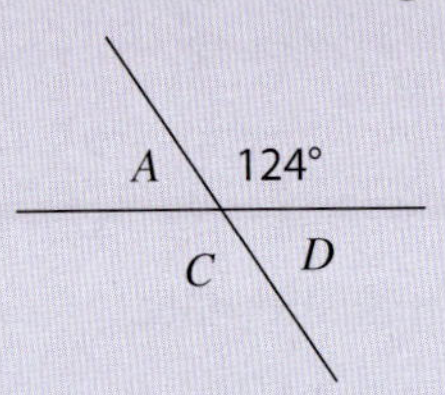

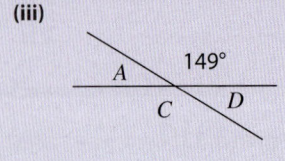

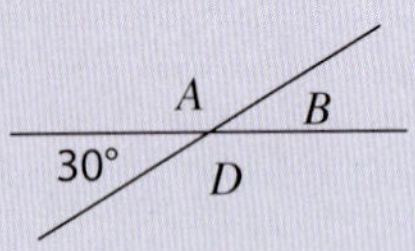

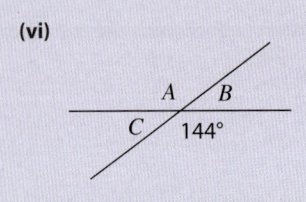

2. Calculate the missing angles in each of the following. Justify your answers in as many ways as possible, using the following terms: corresponding, vertically opposite, alternate, straight angle.

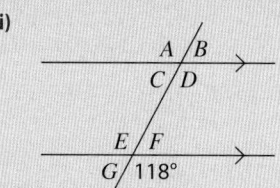

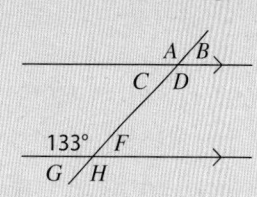

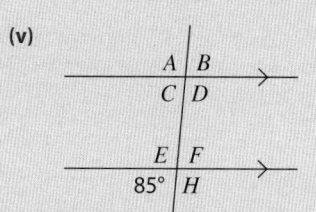

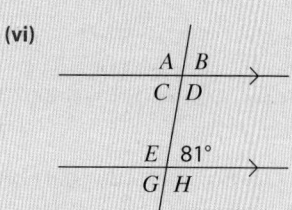

(i) 113° at A

(ii) 118° at G

(iii) 133° at E

(iv) 103° at A

(v) 85° at G

(vi) 81° at F

3. Calculate the value of x in each of the following. Justify the steps used in each case.

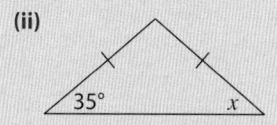

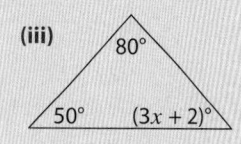

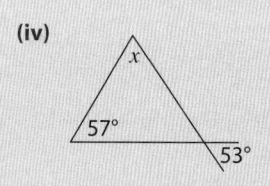

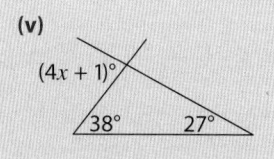

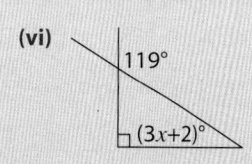

(i) Triangle with 115°, 31°, and x

(ii) Isosceles triangle with 35°, x (two equal sides marked)

(iii) Triangle with 80°, 50°, $(3x+2)°$

(iv) Triangle with exterior angle setup: x, 57°, 53°

(v) Triangle with $(4x+1)°$, 38°, 27°

(vi) Right triangle with 119°, $(3x+2)°$

4. Calculate the value of the unknown variables in each of the following. Justify the steps used in each case.

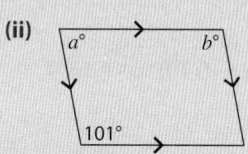

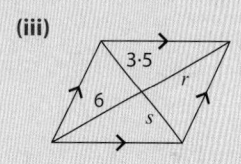

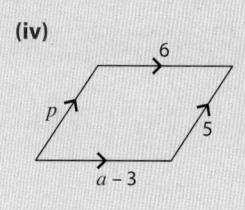

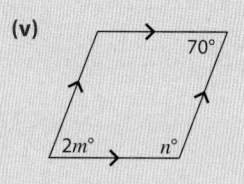

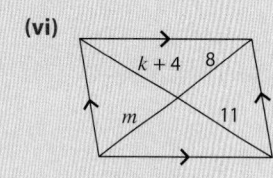

(i) Parallelogram with sides 14, 10, and x, y

(ii) Parallelogram with $a°$, $b°$, 101°

(iii) Parallelogram with diagonals 3.5, 6, r, s

(iv) Parallelogram with 6, 5, p, $a-3$

(v) Parallelogram with 70°, $2m°$, $n°$

(vi) Parallelogram with diagonals $k+4$, 8, m, 11

5. Find the value of x in the following circles. Justify your answer in each case.

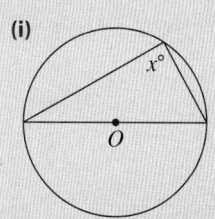

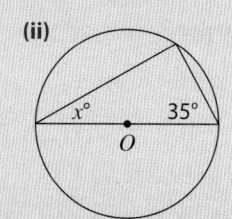

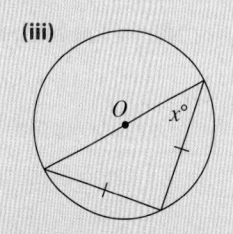

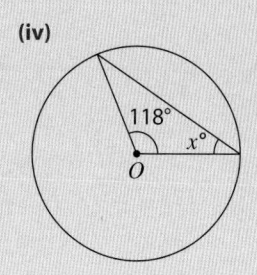

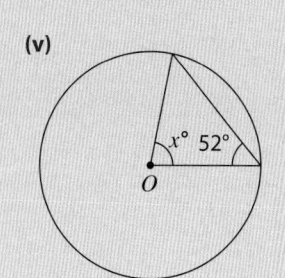

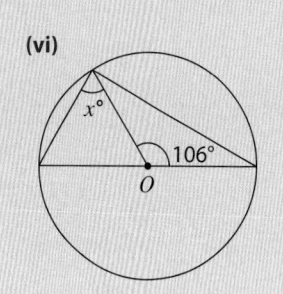

(i) Circle with centre O, $x°$ inscribed angle on diameter

(ii) Circle with centre O, $x°$ and 35°

(iii) Circle with centre O, $x°$ inscribed angle

(iv) Circle with centre O, 118° and $x°$

(v) Circle with centre O, $x°$ and 52°

(vi) Circle with centre O, $x°$ and 106°

Section C Applying our skills 475

6. In the diagram shown, PQR is a straight line.

$|PQ| = |QS| = |QR|$

$|\angle QPS| = 25°$

(i) What is the measure of angle w? Give a reason for your answer.

(ii) Calculate the measure of angle x.

(iii) Calculate the measure of angle y.

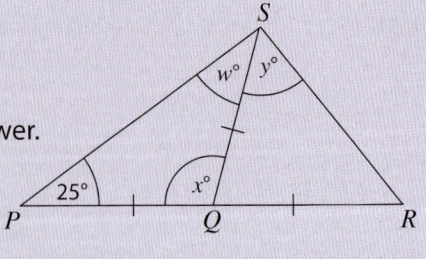

7. (i) Find the value of x as shown in the diagram. Justify your answer.

(ii) Find the value of y as shown in the diagram. Justify your answer.

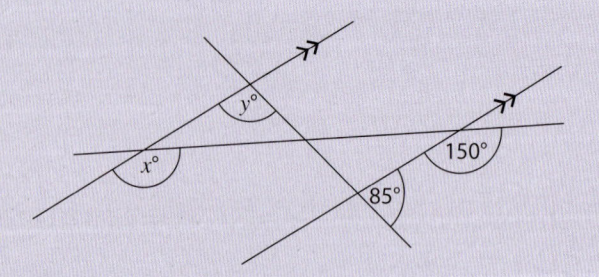

8. The shape $ABCD$ shown is a parallelogram.

Find the measure of the angle x shown in the diagram. Justify all steps used to find your answer.

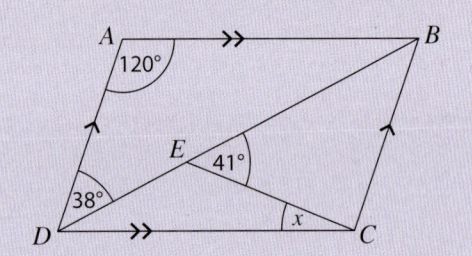

Taking it FURTHER

9. Calculate the value of x shown in the diagram. Justify all steps taken to find your answer.

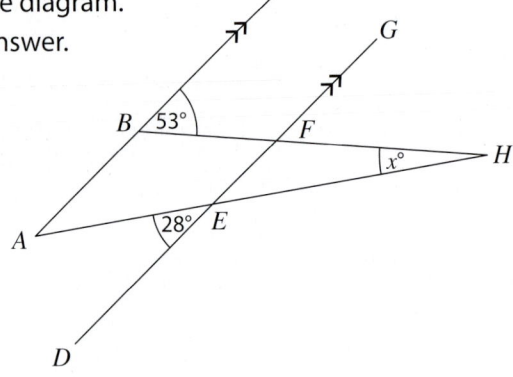

10. In the diagram shown, O is the centre of the circle.

(i) By what name is $[BC]$ better known?

(ii) Find the measure of $\angle OAC$.

(iii) Find the measure of $\angle AOB$.

Justify your answers in both (ii) and (iii).

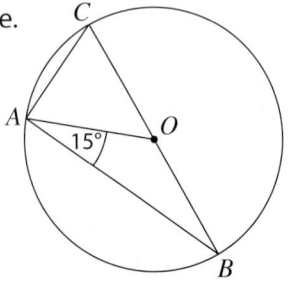

30·4 Similar triangles

By the end of this section you should:
- understand what similar triangles are
- be able to prove two triangles are similar
- be able to use the similar triangles theorem to find unknown sides

Discuss and discover

Work with the person beside you to complete the steps below.
(i) Construct a triangle ABC with side lengths $|AB| = 4$ cm, $|BC| = 6$ cm and $|AC| = 8$ cm.
(ii) Construct another triangle XYZ with side lengths $|XY| = 6$ cm, $|XZ| = 9$ cm and $|YZ| = 12$ cm.
(iii) Use a protractor to measure the angles in each of the triangles.
(iv) What do you notice?
(v) Are these triangles congruent (identical)?
Give a reason for your answer.

The word **similar** suggests a comparison between objects that are **alike but not the same**.
On the right, triangle ABC is similar to triangle DEF.
$|\angle A| = |\angle D|$ and $|\angle B| = |\angle E|$ (also $|\angle C| = |\angle F|$)

These triangles are not congruent (identical), as triangle DEF is smaller than triangle ABC. The symbol for similar is $|||$.

Therefore $\triangle DEF\ |||\ \triangle ABC$

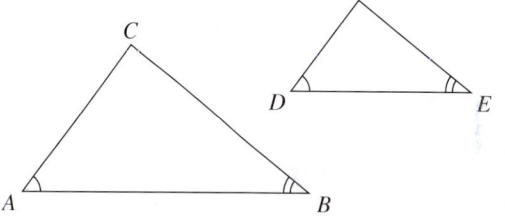

Given any triangle, we can make a triangle similar to it by shrinking it, enlarging it, rotating it, flipping it or getting the mirror image of it. In all of these cases, the angles in the new triangle remain the same.

$\triangle DEF\ |||\ \triangle ABC$ means that triangle DEF is similar to triangle ABC.

> **Similar triangles** have the same angles as each other.
> They are **equiangular**.

To prove that two triangles are similar, we must prove that at least **two of the angles** in the triangles are the **same**. If two angles in one triangle are the same as two angles in the other triangle, then the third angles in each triangle will be equal, by Theorem 4 (three angles in a triangle sum to 180 degrees).

We can mark equal angles using multiple arcs or dash lines, as shown.

$|\angle RST| = |\angle ABC|$ (single arc)
$|\angle SRT| = |\angle BAC|$ (double arc)
$|\angle RTS| = |\angle ACB|$ (double dashes)

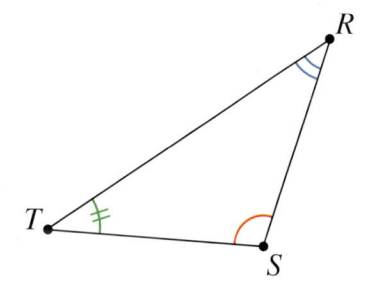

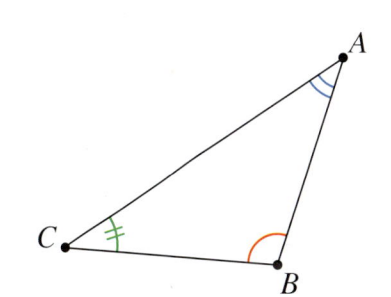

The angles that are equal are referred to as the **corresponding angles**.

Worked example 1

Explain how we can show that triangle ABC and triangle CDE are similar.

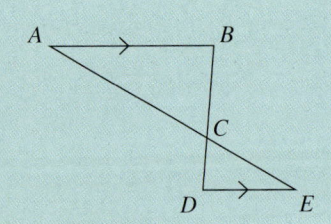

Solution

Note that $[AB]$ is parallel to $[DE]$ (indicated by the arrows on these line segments).

Statement	Reason
$|\angle ACB| = |\angle DCE|$ (single arc)	Vertically opposite angles
$|\angle BAC| = |\angle CED|$ (double arc)	Alternate angles

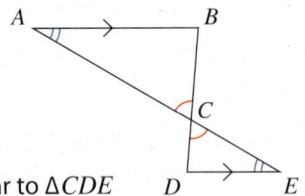

Since two of the angles are equal, we have now shown that $\triangle ABC$ is similar to $\triangle CDE$

Corresponding sides

The corresponding sides face the corresponding angles, as shown in the diagram on the right. For example, the sides that face the angles with two arcs are corresponding, and are shown in blue.

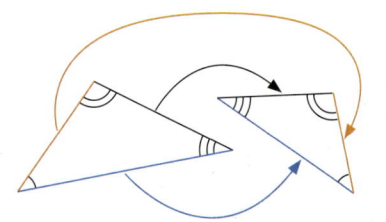

Worked example 2

Show that the triangles shown are similar and identify the corresponding sides.

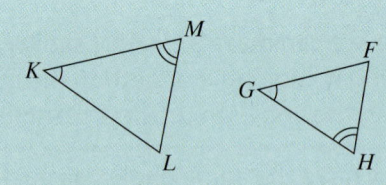

Solution

Statement	Reason
$|\angle LKM| = |\angle FGH|$ (single arc)	Given
$|\angle LMK| = |\angle FHG|$ (double arc)	Given

Two angles are equal $\Rightarrow \triangle KLM \;|||\; \triangle FGH$

Corresponding sides:

$[LM]$ corresponds to $[FH]$ (both facing single arc angle)

$[KL]$ corresponds to $[GF]$ (both facing double arc angle)

$[KM]$ corresponds to $[GH]$ (both facing the unlabelled angle).

Discuss and discover

KEY SKILLS

Work with a classmate to complete the steps below.

(i) Construct a triangle ABC with side lengths $|AB| = 6$ cm, $|BC| = 5$ cm and $|AC| = 4$ cm.

(ii) Construct another triangle XYZ with side lengths $|XY| = 12$ cm, $|XZ| = 10$ cm and $|YZ| = 8$ cm.

(iii) What is the relationship between the lengths of the sides of these two triangles?

(iv) Use a protractor to measure the angles in each of the triangles.

(v) What do you notice?

(vi) How would you describe these two triangles? Give a reason for your answer.

(vii) List the corresponding sides in these two triangles.

(viii) Investigate if $\dfrac{|AB|}{|XY|} = \dfrac{|AC|}{|YZ|} = \dfrac{|BC|}{|XZ|}$

Theorem 13: If two triangles are similar then their sides are proportional, in order

Converse of Theorem 13: If the corresponding sides of two triangles are proportional then the triangles are similar.

If $\triangle ABC$ is similar to $\triangle DEF$ then $\dfrac{|AB|}{|DE|} = \dfrac{|AC|}{|DF|} = \dfrac{|BC|}{|EF|}$

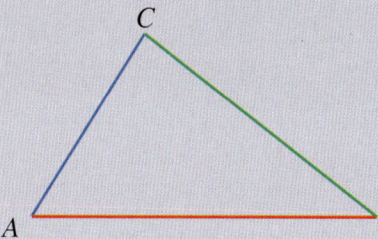

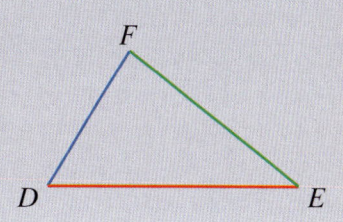

When using this theorem to find unknown sides, the following steps should be followed.

Using Theorem 13 to find unknown sides

1. Prove the triangles are similar, unless told in the question.
2. Identify the corresponding sides.
3. Write the ratio with the unknown side on the top left.
4. Fill in the relevant values.
5. Solve for the unknown.

This theorem will be used in Unit 34 to help prove Pythagoras's theorem.

Worked example 3

Find the value of x.

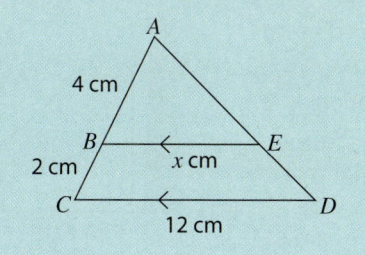

Solution

Step 1 The diagram shows two triangles, the large triangle $\triangle ACD$ and the small triangle $\triangle ABE$.

Statement	Reason
$|\angle CAD| = |\angle BAE|$	Same angle
$|\angle DCA| = |\angle EBA|$	Corresponding as $BE \parallel CD$
$|\angle CDA| = |\angle BEA|$	Corresponding

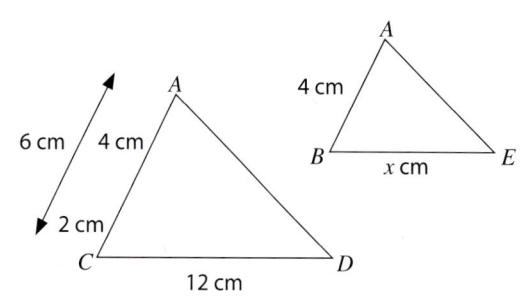

$\triangle CAD$ is equiangular to $\triangle BAE$ and therefore the triangles are similar.

Step 2 $|AC|$ corresponds to $|AB|$, $|CD|$ corresponds to $|BE|$ and $|AD|$ corresponds to $|AE|$.

Step 3 We are looking for $|BE|$ therefore the ratio is $\dfrac{|BE|}{|CD|} = \dfrac{|AB|}{|AC|}$

Step 4 $\dfrac{x}{12} = \dfrac{4}{6}$

Step 5 $12\left(\dfrac{x}{12}\right) = 12\left(\dfrac{4}{6}\right)$ (multiply both sides by 12)

$x = \dfrac{48}{6}$

$x = 8$ cm

Section C Applying our skills

Worked example 4

Investigate if the following pairs of triangles are similar.

(i)

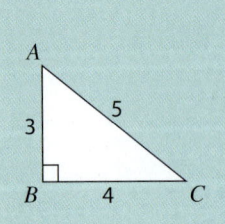

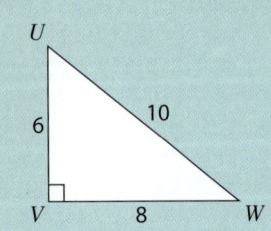

(ii)

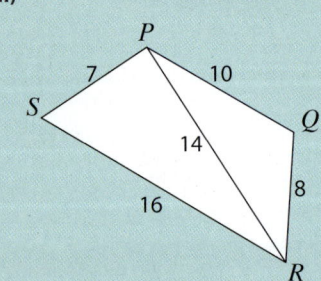

Solution

(i) If $\triangle ABC$ is similar to $\triangle UVW$ then

$$\frac{|AB|}{|UV|} = \frac{|AC|}{|UW|} = \frac{|BC|}{|VW|}$$

Is $\quad \frac{3}{6} = \frac{5}{10} = \frac{4}{8}$?

$$\frac{1}{2} = \frac{1}{2} = \frac{1}{2}$$

Therefore $\triangle ABC$ is similar to $\triangle UVW$

(ii) If $\triangle PQR$ is similar to $\triangle RPS$ then

$$\frac{|PQ|}{|RP|} = \frac{|PR|}{|RS|} = \frac{|QR|}{|PS|}$$

Is $\quad \frac{10}{14} = \frac{14}{16} = \frac{8}{7}$?

$$\frac{5}{7} \neq \frac{7}{8} \neq \frac{8}{7}$$

Therefore $\triangle PQR$ is not similar to $\triangle RPS$

Worked example 5

A tower casts a shadow of 40 metres, while a 4 metre street light nearby casts a shadow of 32 metres. How tall is the tower?

Solution

These types of real-life questions can be solved using similar triangles.

Step 1 Draw a sketch to represent the situation.

These triangles are similar, since we assume both the tower and the post are at right angles to the ground and as they are near each other the angle of the sun is the same.

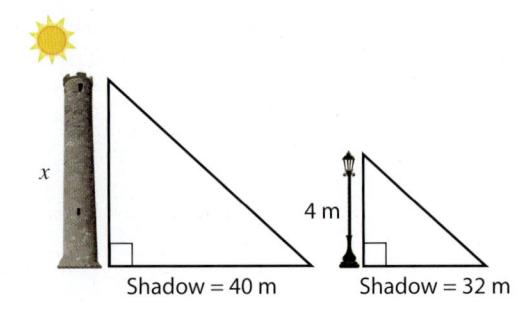

Step 2 Identify the corresponding sides.

Height of tower (x) corresponds to 4 m

Shadow of tower (40 m) corresponds to lamp post shadow (32 m)

Step 3 Write the ratio with the unknown side on the top left and solve for x.

$$\frac{x}{4} = \frac{40}{32}$$

$$4\left(\frac{x}{4}\right) = 4\left(\frac{40}{32}\right)$$

$$x = \frac{160}{32}$$

$$x = 5 \text{ metres}$$

Linking Thinking 1

Practice questions 30.4

1. Investigate if the following pairs of triangles are similar. Justify your answer in each case.
   (i) (ii) 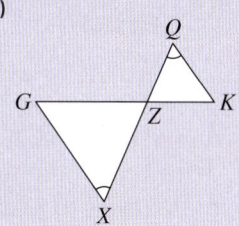 (iii)

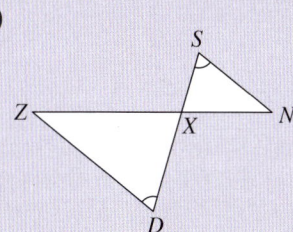

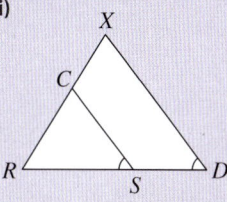

2. Investigate if the following pairs of triangles are similar, using Theorem 13.
   (i) (ii) 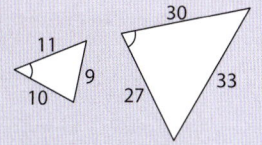 (iii) 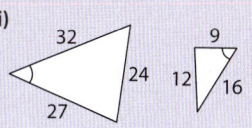
   (iv) 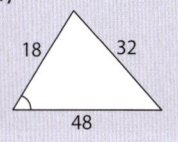 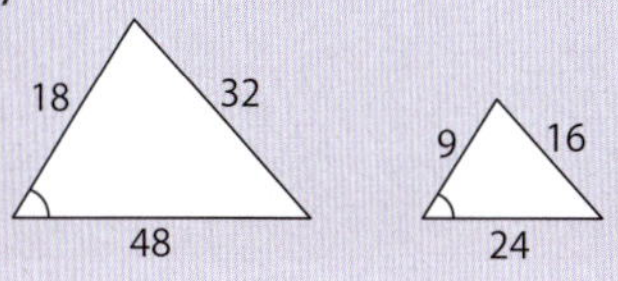 (v) 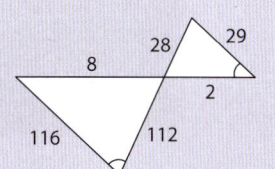 (vi)

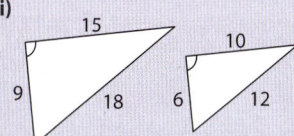

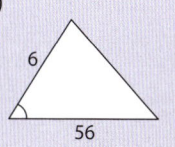

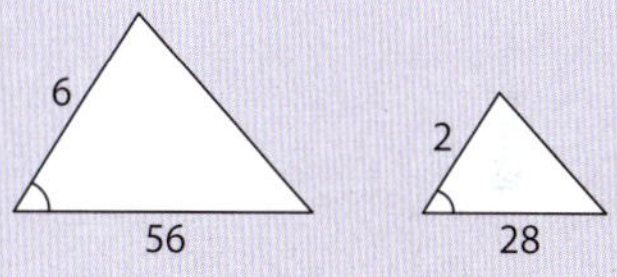

3. Find the length of the unknown sides in each of the following pairs of similar triangles.
   (i) (ii) 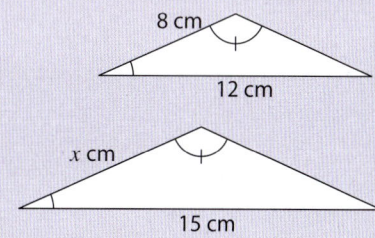 (iii) 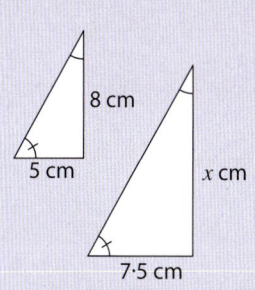 (iv)

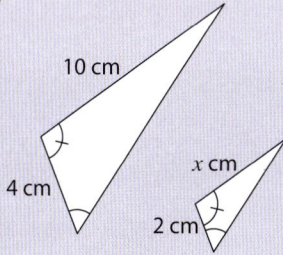

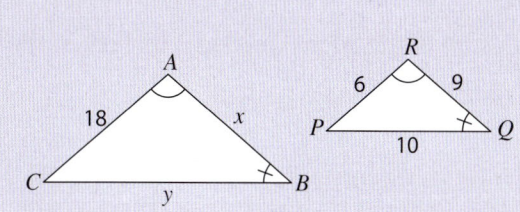

4. Study the diagram opposite.
   (i) Show that $\triangle PQR$ and $\triangle RTZ$ are similar. Justify all statements made.
   (ii) Find the value of x.
   (iii) Find the value of y.

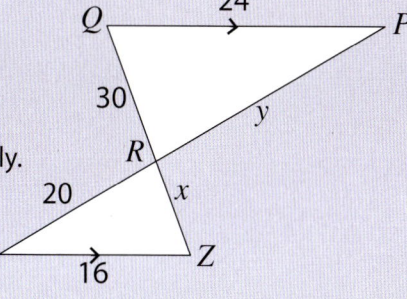

5. The length and width of a rectangular box are 10 cm and 8 cm, respectively. Another rectangular box has a length of 15 cm and a width of 12 cm.
   Are the length and width dimensions of the two rectangular boxes similar?

Section C Applying our skills

6. Two ladders are leaning against a vertical wall at the same angle.
   The 4·2 m ladder extends 2·4 m up the wall.
   How far up the wall will the 7 m ladder extend?

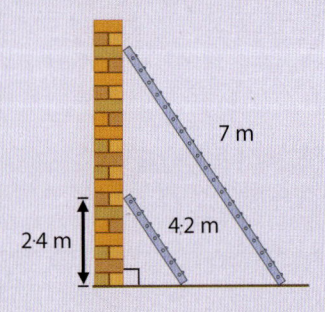

7. Erica is 1·60 m tall. Her shadow is 0·25 m long.
   Her shadow extends to the end of a tree's shadow when she stands 4·75 m from the tree.
   Calculate the height of the tree.

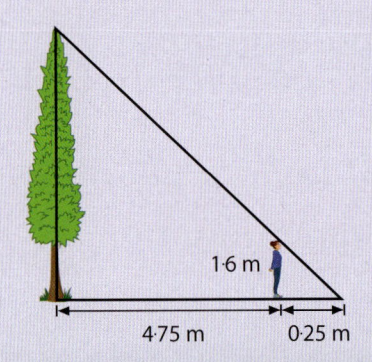

8. A tree with a height of 4·5 m casts a shadow 15 m long on the ground.
   Another tree beside it casts a shadow which is 20 m long at the same time of day.
   (i) Draw a sketch to represent both trees and their shadows.
   (ii) Find the height of the second tree.

9. A pool ball is hit at position A shown in the diagram. It is deflected off the side wall of the table at position B and then travels to position C.
   Calculate the distance travelled by the ball from A to C.
   Note: the angle the ball hits the wall and bounces back off it are the same.

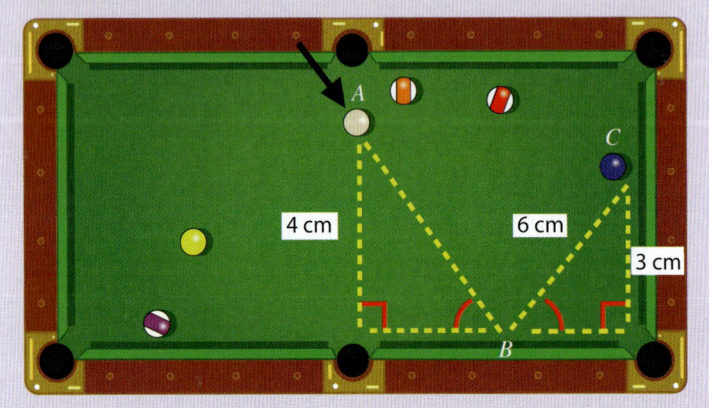

Revision questions

30A Core skills

1. Find the measure of the angle labelled A in each of the following. Justify your answer in each case.

   (i) 122°

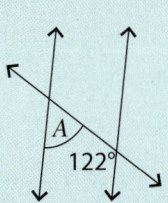

   (ii) 75°

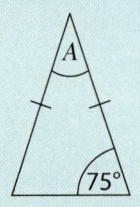

   (iii) 35°

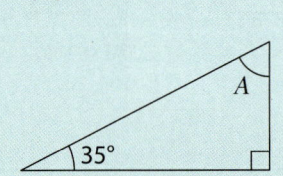

   (iv)

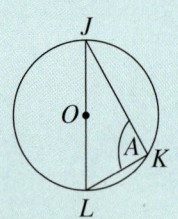

   (v) 114°, 35°

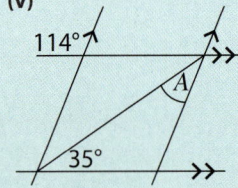

   (vi) 115°, 30°

482   Linking Thinking 1

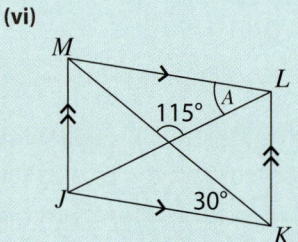

2. Find the values of x, y and z in the images below. Justify your answers in each case.

(i) Circle with centre O; points P, Q, R on circle. Angle at $P = 39°$, angle $x°$ at Q, angle $y°$ at R.

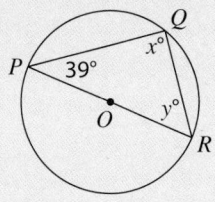

(ii) Two intersecting lines with angles $138°$, $x°$, $y°$, $z°$, and $73°$.

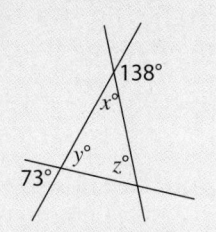

(iii) Triangle with parallel lines marked; angles $153°$, $x°$, $61°$, $y°$, $z°$.

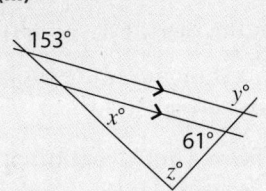

(iv) Two parallel lines cut by a transversal; angles $65°$, $z°$, $x°$, $y°$.

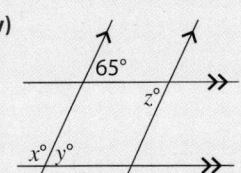

(v) Circle with diameter; angles $y°$, $x°$, $z°$, $106°$.

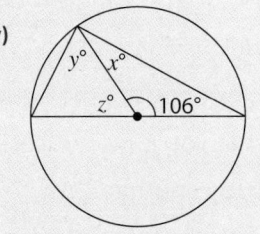

(vi) Triangle with angles $95°$, $x°$, $y°$, $80°$, $65°$, $z°$.

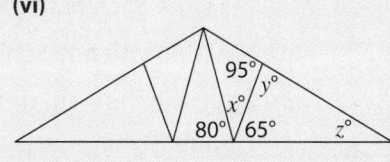

3. Copy the diagram shown into your copybook. On your diagram:
   (i) use the letter A to mark a pair of corresponding angles
   (ii) use the letter B to mark a pair of vertically opposite angles
   (iii) use the letter C to mark a pair of alternate angles
   (iv) use the letter D to mark any other pair of angles that are related to each other and describe the relationship between them.

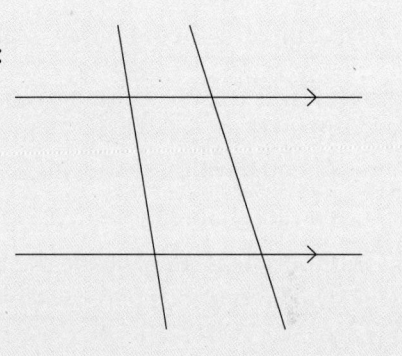

4. In the diagram below, AB and CD are parallel. PQ and PR are straight lines.
   (i) Find the value of x. Give a reason for your answer.
   (ii) Find the value of y. Give a reason for your answer.

(Diagram: AB horizontal with angles $62°$ and $71°$ at intersection points on AB; CD parallel below with angles $x°$ and $y°$ at point P.)

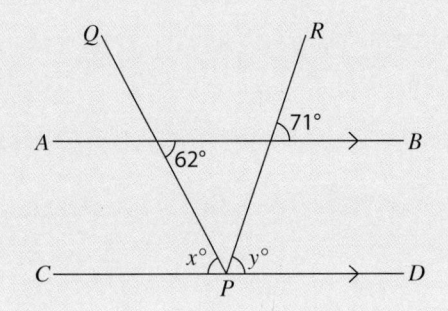

5. In the diagram below, AB and CD are parallel. PQ and PR are straight lines.
   (i) Find the value of x. Give a reason for your answer.
   (ii) Find the value of y. Give a reason for your answer.

(Diagram: triangle with P at top; AB through triangle with angle $y°$; $57°$ at A side; CD below with $x°$ at C and $109°$ at D; Q and R at bottom.)

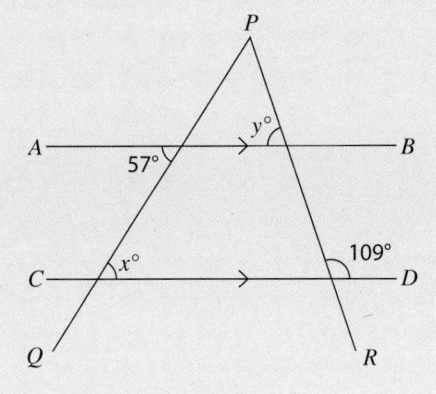

6. In the diagram, CE and BD are parallel. AC and AE are straight lines. Find the value of p. Give a reason for your answer.

(Diagram: CE top line, BD parallel below, meeting at A with angle $38°$; angle $p°$ at C.)

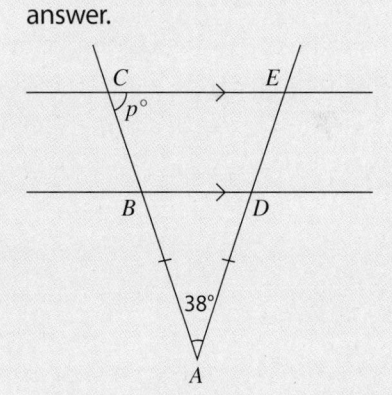

7. In the diagram, AD and BE are parallel. AC is a straight line.
   (i) Find the value of y. Give a reason for your answer.
   (ii) Find the value of z. Give a reason for your answer.

(Diagram: points A, B, C on line; D and E above; angle $28°$ at E, $36°$ at A, $y°$ at A, $z°$ at B.)

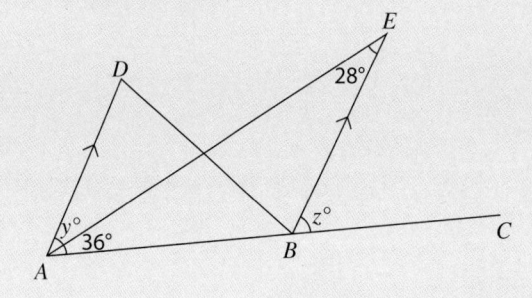

8. Two straight paths through a park intersect each other as shown in the diagram.

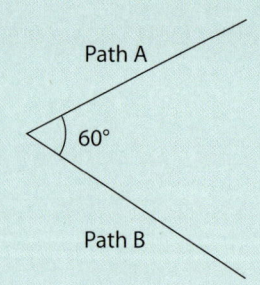

   (i) In your copybook, construct a diagram to represent these two paths.

   The local council want to build a fence exactly halfway between these two paths.

   (ii) Perform a construction on the diagram you have drawn to show the position of the fence.

9. Construct a triangle, ABC, with the base (AB) of the triangle = 6 cm, and AC and BC = 4 cm.

   (a) (i) Measure each of the angles in $\triangle ABC$.

   (ii) What do you notice about the angles opposite the equal sides?

   (iii) State the theorem that explains what you have noticed.

   (b) (i) Extend the line AB though point B, by another 3 cm, to point D and measure $\angle DBC$.

   (ii) What do you notice about $\angle DBC$ and the internal opposite angles of the triangle?

   (iii) State the theorem that explains what you have noticed.

10. Dermot wants to put a large glass patio door into his house. The width of the door will be 5·2 m. The door will consist of three separate panels of equal width, as shown.

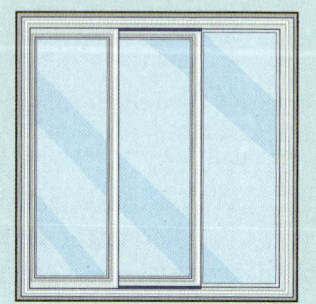

    (i) Construct a line segment, using a scale of 1 : 100, to represent the door.

    (ii) Without measuring, divide the line segment into three equal parts to shown where each panel will be positioned.

30B Taking it FURTHER

1. Find the value of x in each of the following and hence, calculate each of the angles shown. State the theorems used in each case.

   (i) Angles: $2x$, $x+23$, $3x-35$

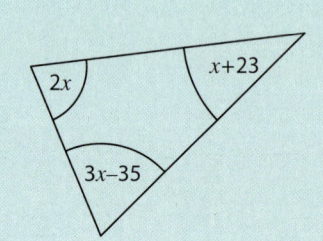

   (ii) Angles: $7x-35$, $x+55$, $3x+15$ (with points A, C, F, E, B, D)

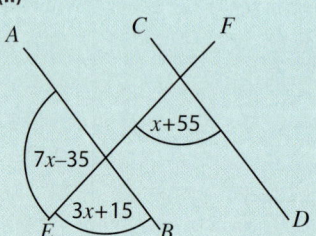

   (iii) Angles: $130°$, $2x+5y$, $4x-10$, $6x+10y$

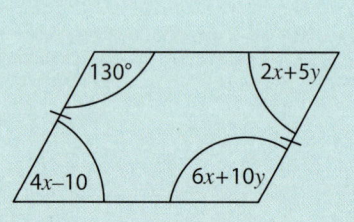

2. (i) Construct an isosceles triangle ABC such that $|AB| = 5$ cm and $|\angle ABC| = |\angle CAB| = 72°$

   (ii) Construct the bisector of the angle CAB and mark the point where the bisector intersects BC as D.

   (iii) Show that triangle ABC and triangle ABD are similar.

Linking Thinking 1

3. Given that the pairs of triangles shown are similar, find the value of x.

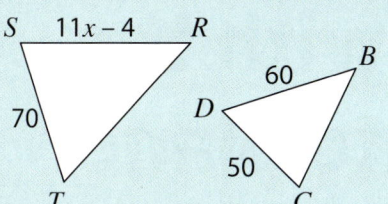

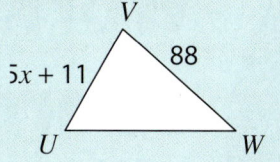

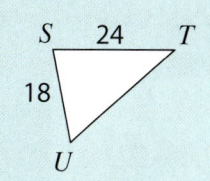

   (i) Triangle SRT with $SR = 11x - 4$, $ST = 70$; Triangle BDC with $DB = 60$, $DC = 50$.

   (ii) Triangle VUW with $VW = 88$, $UV = 5x + 11$; Triangle STU with $ST = 24$, $SU = 18$.

4. Consider the diagram shown.

   (i) Use Pythagoras's theorem to find the value of a.

   (ii) Show that the triangles ABE and ACD are similar.

   (iii) Use similar triangles to find the value of x.

   (iv) Find the value of b.

   (Diagram: right triangle ACD with $AB = 12$, $BC = 12$, $BE = 5$, $AE = a$, $ED = b$, $CD = x$.)

5. Mark is 1·75 m tall and his shadow measures 7 m.

   A mobile phone mast casts a shadow of 56 m.

   Calculate the height of the mobile phone mast.

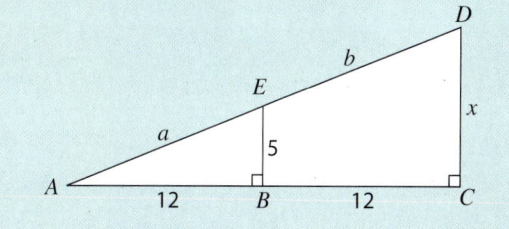

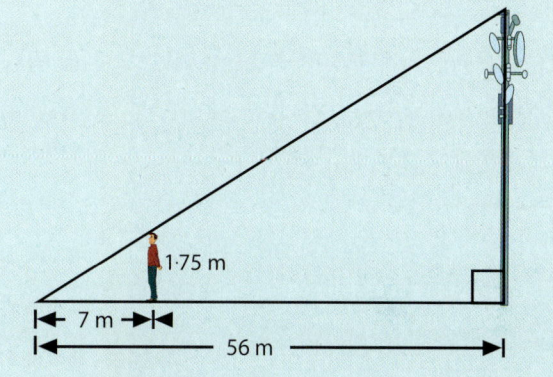

6. The diagram shown represents a player throwing a bounce pass, in which the angles formed by the basketball's path are the same, to his teammate.

   (i) Are the two triangles shown similar? Give reasons for your answer.

   (ii) Calculate the height of the ball when it is caught by the teammate.

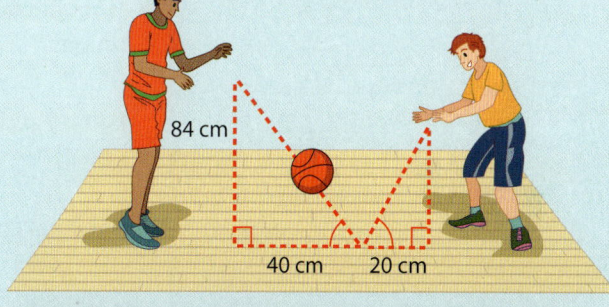

   (Diagram labels: 84 cm, 40 cm, 20 cm.)

7. The penalty spot on a Gaelic football pitch is located on the perpendicular bisector of the goal line.

   The width of the goal line is 6·5 m and the penalty spot is 11 m from the goal line.

   (i) Using a scale of 1 : 100, construct a line segment to represent the goal line.

   (ii) Construct the perpendicular bisector of your line segment and use it to show the position of the penalty spot.

Now that you have completed the unit, revisit the

Something to think about ...

question posed at the start of this unit.

Unit 31

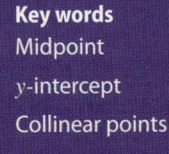

Working with the coordinate plane

Topics covered within this unit:

- 31·1 Midpoint of a line segment
- 31·2 Length of a line segment (distance between two points)
- 31·3 Slope of the line
- 31·4 Equation of a line
- 31·5 Working with the equation of a line
- 31·6 Graphing lines when given the equation of the line
- 31·7 Point of intersection of two lines (simultaneous equations)

The Learning Outcomes covered in this unit are contained in the following sections:

GT.5 | GT.6 | AF.4c | GT.3a | GT.3b

Key words
Midpoint
y-intercept
Collinear points

Something to think about …

KEY SKILLS

You are playing an online game in which you are navigating a battleship.

Your mission is to lay mines at the points where the enemy travel lanes intersect.

The enemy travel lanes are represented by the following equations.

Lane 1: $x - y = -4$

Lane 2: $5x - y = 8$

Lane 3: $x - 2y = -2$

At what three points should you lay your mines?

31·1 Midpoint of a line segment

By the end of this section you should:
- recall how to label and plot coordinates on a coordinate (Cartesian) plane
- recall the definition of a line segment
- understand and be able to calculate the coordinates of the midpoint of a line segment

In Section A, Unit 1, we introduced the Cartesian (coordinate) plane. We learned that it consists of an x-axis (horizontal line) and a y-axis (vertical line).

We learned that to label or plot a location on the coordinate plane, we use two coordinates (numbers) on the grid, which are written in the form (x, y). The x-coordinate represents the horizontal position and the y-coordinate represents the vertical position.

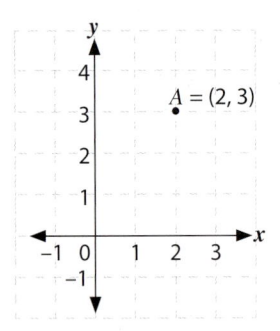

The point $(2, 3)$ shown has an x-coordinate of 2 and a y-coordinate of 3.

> x always comes first in coordinates.

486 Linking Thinking 1

Discuss and discover

KEY SKILLS

Work with a classmate to complete the following activity.

A and B are two points on a coordinate plane.

$A = (2, 1)$ and $B = (12, 7)$

The point M is halfway between A and B.

(i) Using a suitable strategy, find the point M that is exactly in the middle of $[AB]$ and note its coordinates.

(ii) Find the mean (average) of the x-values.

(iii) Find the mean (average) of the y-values.

(iv) How do these values relate to the coordinates of the middle point on the graph?

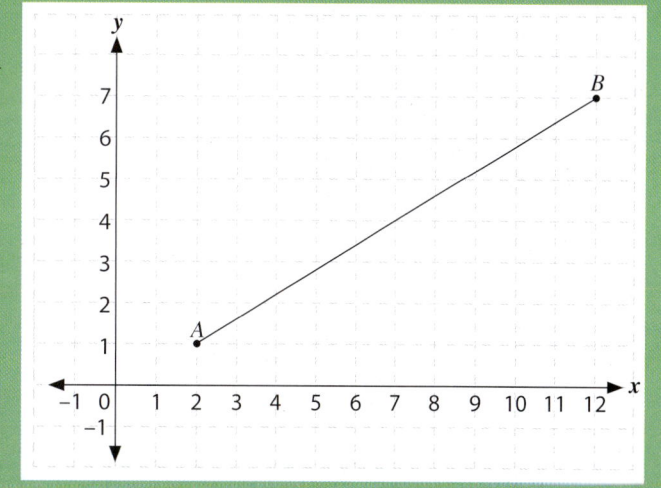

Taking it FURTHER

(v) If $A = (x_1, y_1)$ and $B = (x_2, y_2)$, using what you did above, can you find a mathematical formula to calculate the middle point of $[AB]$?

In Section A, Unit 3, we learned that a line segment is a part of a line that has two endpoints. We will now learn how to calculate the point that lies exactly in the middle of a line segment when given the coordinates of the endpoints of the line segment.

Middle point = mid point = midpoint

> The **midpoint** of a line segment is the point exactly halfway between the two endpoints.

In the diagram shown, M is the **midpoint** of the line segment $[AB]$, where (x_1, y_1) are the coordinates of the point A and (x_2, y_2) are the coordinates of the point B.

To find the midpoint of a line segment, we have to find the number in the middle (the average) of the x-coordinates and the number in the middle (the average) of the y-coordinates.

(x_1, y_1) are the coordinates of the first endpoint.

(x_2, y_2) are the coordinates of the second endpoint.

The formula to calculate the midpoint of a line segment is as follows:

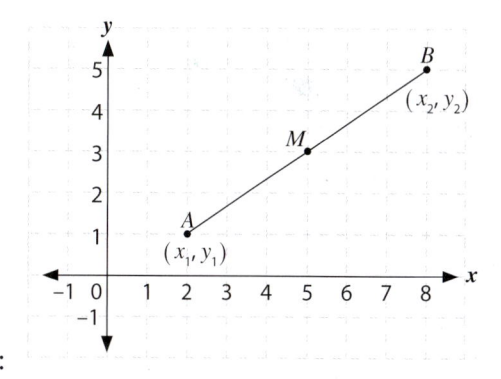

> **Midpoint of a line segment joining the points (x_1, y_1) and (x_2, y_2) is**
> $$\text{Midpoint} = \left(\frac{x_1 + x_2}{2}, \frac{y_1 + y_2}{2}\right)$$

The formula for the midpoint of a line segment appears in the *formulae and tables* booklet.

Finding the midpoint of a line segment

1. Label the coordinates of the first point (x_1, y_1) and the coordinates of the second point (x_2, y_2).
2. Write down the midpoint formula.
3. Substitute the values from the question into the formula.
4. Complete the calculations to find the x coordinate and y coordinate of the midpoint.

Worked example 1

Find the midpoint of the line segment joining the points $(-3, -1)$ and $(3, 5)$.

Solution

Step 1 $(-3, -1)$ and $(3, 5)$
$\quad\quad\quad\;\; (x_1, y_1) \quad\quad (x_2, y_2)$

Step 2 $\left(\dfrac{x_1 + x_2}{2}, \dfrac{y_1 + y_2}{2}\right)$

Step 3 $\left(\dfrac{-3 + 3}{2}, \dfrac{-1 + 5}{2}\right)$

Step 4 $\left(\dfrac{0}{2}, \dfrac{4}{2}\right)$
$\quad\quad\quad (0, 2)$

We can verify our solution visually by plotting the points on a coordinated graph, as shown.

We can see on the graph that the position of the midpoint is halfway between the points A and B.

The midpoint is a point on the coordinate plane, so the answer will be a point in the form (x, y).

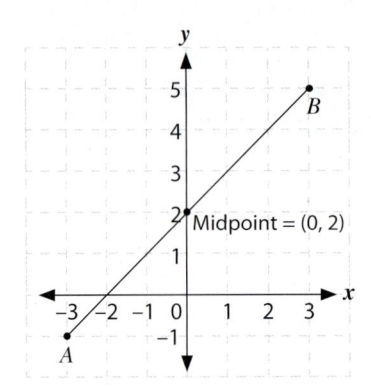

Midpoint = $(0, 2)$

Finding an unknown endpoint

Given one endpoint of a line segment and its midpoint and asked to find the other endpoint, remember that the midpoint is exactly halfway between each endpoint.

If M is the midpoint of $[PQ]$, then to get to Q from M we must move the exact same distance and direction we did to get from P to M. This is called a translation. We studied translations in Section B, Unit 23.

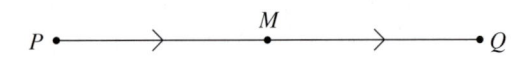

Translating a point

Consider the following situation, where C is the midpoint of $[AB]$ and we want to find the coordinates of B.

The coordinates of A are $(-4, 2)$ and the coordinates of C are $(1, -1)$.

Looking at the x-coordinates, we can see that to go from -4 to 1, we must add 5 to x-coordinate (move right 5 boxes).

Looking at the y-coordinates, we can see that to go from 2 to -1, we must subtract 3 from the y-coordinate (move down 3 boxes).

We now do the same to C to find the coordinates of B, which are $(6, -4)$.

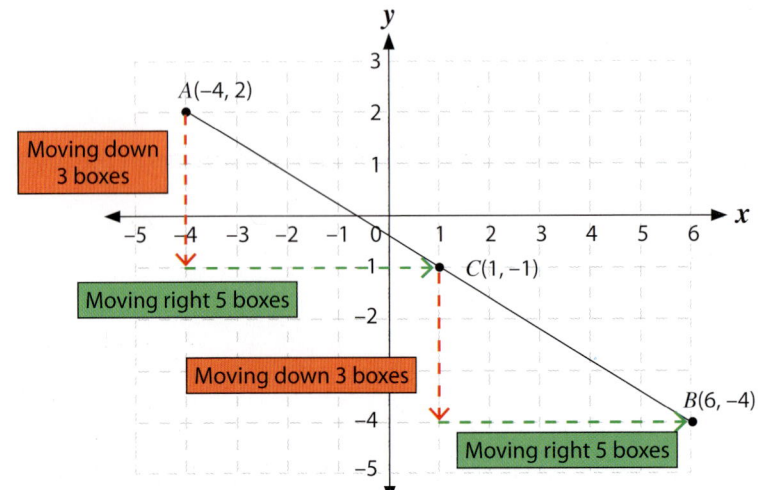

The following example shows how to find the endpoint without using the coordinate plane.

Worked example 2

R is the midpoint of $[PQ]$. The coordinates of P are (5, 3) and the coordinates of R are (3, −1). Find the coordinates of Q.

Solution

Method 1: Draw a diagram of the line segment

P (5, 3) •——→ R (3, −1) ——→• Q (?, ?)

The translation needed to go from P to R is:
- subtract 2 from the x coordinate
- subtract 4 from the y coordinate

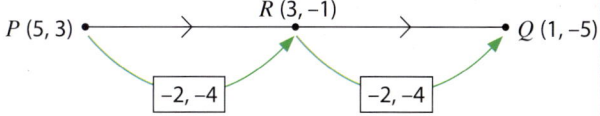

P (5, 3) •——→ R (3, −1) ——→• Q (1, −5)

−2, −4   −2, −4

Apply this same translation to the point R:

$R(3, -1) \Rightarrow (3-2, -1-4) \Rightarrow Q(1, -5)$

Method 2: Use the midpoint formula

$\frac{x_1 + x_2}{2} = 3$

$\frac{5 + x_2}{2} = 3$ (multiply both sides by 2)

$5 + x_2 = 6$ (subtract 5 from both sides)

$x_2 = 1$

$\frac{y_1 + y_2}{2} = -1$

$\frac{3 + y_2}{2} = -1$ (multiply both sides by 2)

$3 + y_2 = -2$ (subtract 3 from both sides)

$y_2 = -5$

$Q = (x_2, y_2)$ therefore $Q = (1, -5)$

Practice questions 31·1

1. **(a)** Identify the coordinates of each of the points shown on the Cartesian plane on the right.

   (b) State the quadrant (1, 2, 3 or 4) in which each of the following points are found.

   (i) E (ii) F (iii) P (iv) N

2. Draw a coordinate plane on graph paper and plot each of the points below on your plane.

   (i) $A(1, 1)$
   (ii) $B(-8, 3)$
   (iii) $C(1, -4)$
   (iv) $D(-5, -4)$
   (v) $E(2, 9)$
   (vi) $F(-5, -6)$
   (vii) $G(-3, 10)$
   (viii) $H(7, -2)$
   (ix) $I(9, 0)$
   (x) $J(0, 3)$

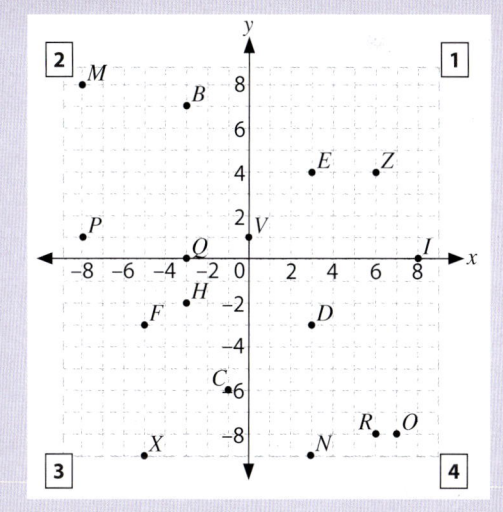

3. **(a)** Use the coordinate plane to find the midpoint of each of the following.

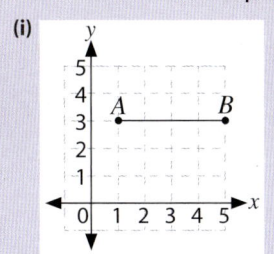

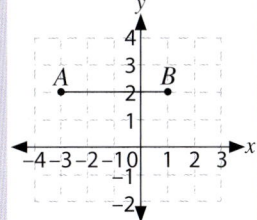

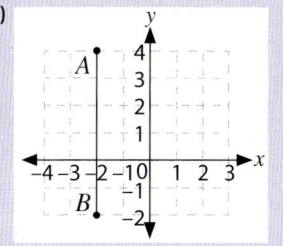

   (i), (ii), (iii)

   (b) Use the midpoint formula to verify your answers for part **(a)**.

Section C Applying our skills

4. Find the midpoint of the line segment joining these pairs of points.
   (i) (2, 4) and (6, 10)   (iv) (5, 10) and (−3, 6)
   (ii) (1, 4) and (9, 12)   (v) (−1, −6) and (3, 0)
   (iii) (0, 7) and (6, 1)   (vi) (−6, −10) and (−2, −8)

5. Find the midpoint of the line segment [AB] joining these pairs of points.
   (i) $A = (−4, 4)$ $B = (5, −1)$
   (ii) $A = (−1, −6)$ $B = (−6, 5)$
   (iii) $A = (2, −1)$ $B = (−6, 0)$
   (iv) $A = (5, 2)$ $B = (−4, −3)$
   (v) $A = (2, 4)$ $B = (1, −3)$
   (vi) $A = (−4, −1)$ $B = (−1, 4)$

6. Find the other endpoint of the line segment with the given endpoint and midpoint.
   (i)   Endpoint = (2, 5); midpoint = (5, 1)
   (ii) Endpoint = (6, 8); midpoint = (1, 2)
   (iii) Endpoint = (−2, 1); midpoint = (3, −2)
   (iv) Endpoint = (−4, 7); midpoint = (−5, 0)
   (v)   Endpoint = (−3, −6); midpoint = (1, −2)
   (vi) Endpoint = (9, 7); midpoint = (4, 12)

7. A jeweller needs to cut the gold chain shown exactly in half. At what point should he make the cut?

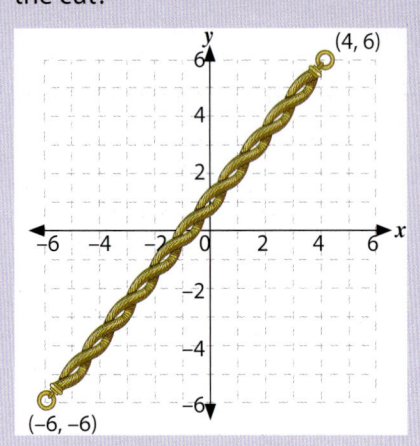

8. The coordinates of a diameter of a circle are (−2, 1) and (4, −3) as shown.
   Find C, the centre of the circle.
   Justify your answer.

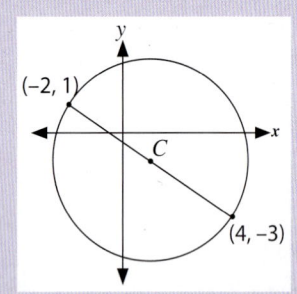

9. [DE] is the diameter of a circle whose centre is the point (4, 3).
   If the coordinates of D are (5, −2), find the coordinates of E.

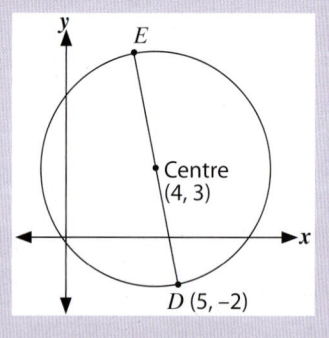

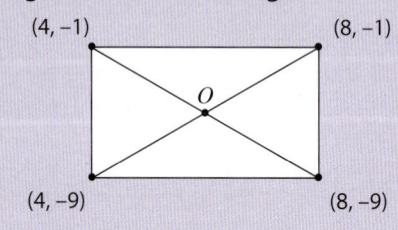

10. The image shown is a rectangle.
    (i) State the theorem that explains the relationship between the diagonals of a rectangle.
    (ii) Find the coordinates of the point O, the point of intersection of the diagonals of the rectangle shown.

Taking it FURTHER

11. A is the midpoint of the line segment PQ.
    B is the midpoint of the line segment PR.
    M is the midpoint of the line segment AB.
    Find the coordinates of the point M.

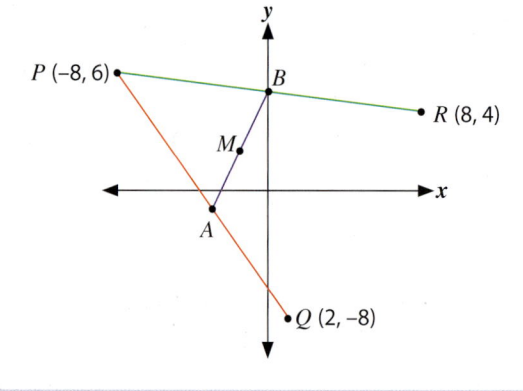

P (−8, 6)   R (8, 4)   Q (2, −8)

490 Linking Thinking 1

31.2 Length of a line segment (distance between two points)

By the end of this section you should be able to:
- calculate the length of a line segment

Discuss and discover

KEY SKILLS

Work with a classmate to complete this activity.

There are two points on a graph, $A = (2, 7)$ and $B = (10, 1)$, as shown in the diagram. Point C is vertically below point A.

(i) Identify the coordinates of point C.
(ii) Find $|AC|$ and $|BC|$.
(iii) Use Pythagoras's theorem to find $|AB|$.

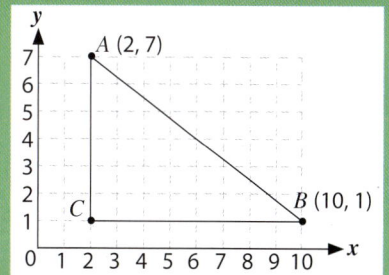

> $|AC|$ means the length of the line segment joining A to C.

↗ Taking it FURTHER

(iv) If $A = (x_1, y_1)$ and $B = (x_2, y_2)$, using what you did above, can you find a mathematical formula to calculate $|AB|$?

Consider point A with coordinates (x_1, y_1) and point B with coordinates (x_2, y_2).

The length of the line segment AC can be calculated by subtracting the x-coordinates.

Hence $|AC| = x_2 - x_1$ and likewise $|BC| = y_2 - y_1$

$|AB|$ can now be found using Pythagoras's theorem.

$|AB|^2 = |AC|^2 + |BC|^2$

$|AB|^2 = (x_2 - x_1)^2 + (y_2 - y_1)^2$

$|AB| = \sqrt{(x_2 - x_1)^2 + (y_2 - y_1)^2}$

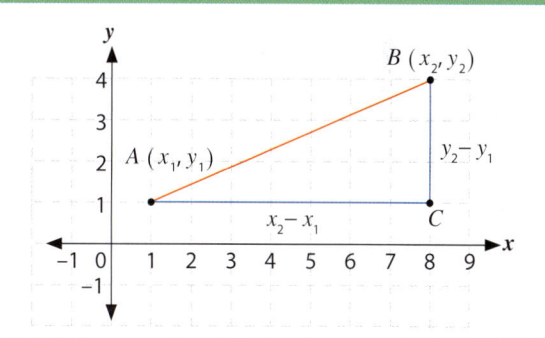

Distance between two points (x_1, y_1) and (x_2, y_2) is

$$D = \sqrt{(x_2 - x_1)^2 + (y_2 - y_1)^2}$$

This formula appears in the *formulae and tables* booklet.

Finding the length of a line segment

Method 1:
1. Label the coordinates of the first point (x_1, y_1) and the coordinates of the second point (x_2, y_2).
2. Write down the formula for length.
3. Substitute the values from the question into the formula.
4. Complete the calculations to find the length of the line segment.

Method 2:
1. Plot the points on a coordinate plane.
2. Form a right-angled triangle.
3. Use Pythagoras's theorem to find the length of the required line segment.

Section C Applying our skills

Worked example

Find the distance between the points (−2, 1) and (4, 9).

Solution

Method 1:

Step 1 (−2, 1)   (4, 9)
$\quad\quad\quad (x_1, y_1)\quad (x_2, y_2)$

Step 2 $D = \sqrt{(x_2 - x_1)^2 + (y_2 - y_1)^2}$

Step 3 $D = \sqrt{(4 - (-2))^2 + (9 - 1)^2}$

Step 4 $D = \sqrt{(6)^2 + (8)^2}$

$\quad\quad\quad D = \sqrt{36 + 64}$

$\quad\quad\quad D = \sqrt{100}$

$\quad\quad\quad D = 10$

Method 2:

Step 1 Plot the points (−2, 1) and (4, 9).

Step 2 Form a right-angled triangle, with the required line segment as the hypotenuse.

Step 3 Use Pythagoras's theorem:

$\quad\quad\quad D^2 = 6^2 + 8^2$

$\quad\quad\quad D^2 = 36 + 64$

$\quad\quad\quad D^2 = 100$

$\quad\quad\quad D = \sqrt{100}$

$\quad\quad\quad D = 10$

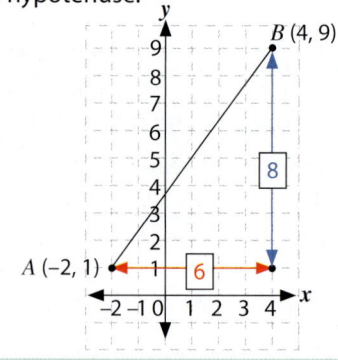

Practice questions 31·2

1. Calculate the distance between each of the following pairs of points. Give your answer correct to two decimal places where necessary.

   (i)   (1, 3) and (5, 7)
   (ii) (10, 6) and (1, −4)
   (iii) (3, 2) and (8, 2)
   (iv) (−8, −9) and (−4, −10)
   (v)   (9, −3) and (−1, 8)
   (vi) (−7, −2) and (6, 9)

2. Find the length of each of the following line segments. Give your answer correct to two significant figures where necessary.

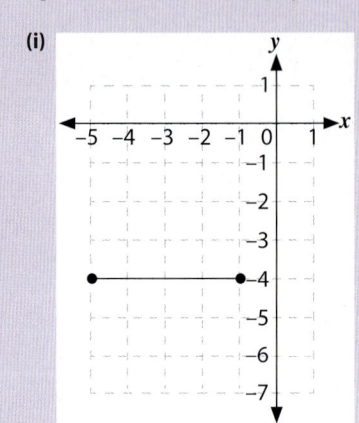

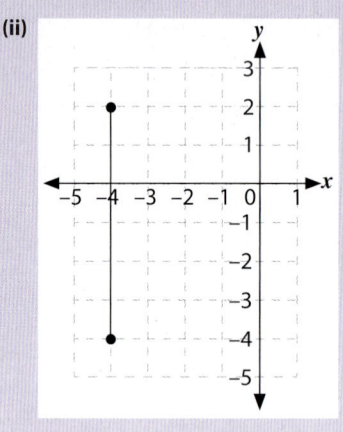

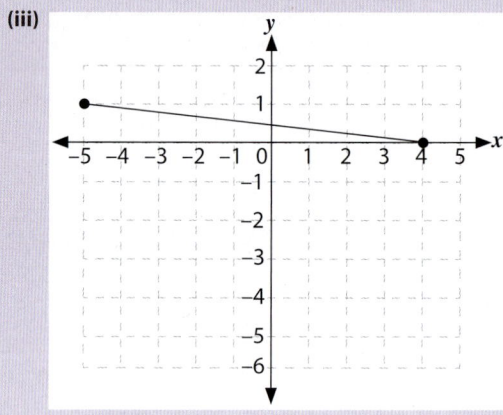

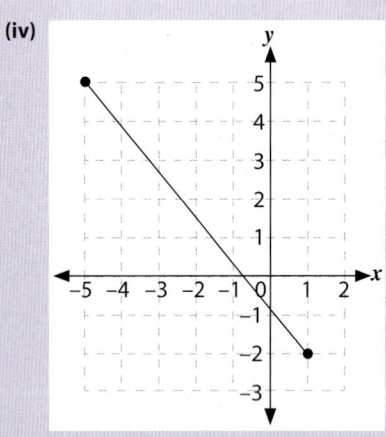

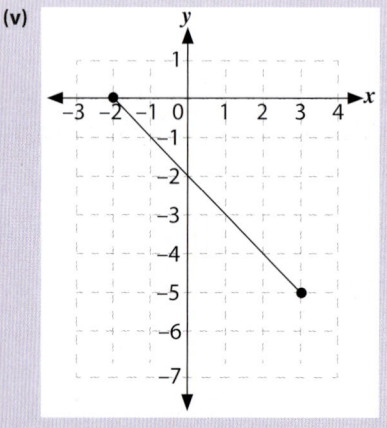

492 Linking Thinking 1

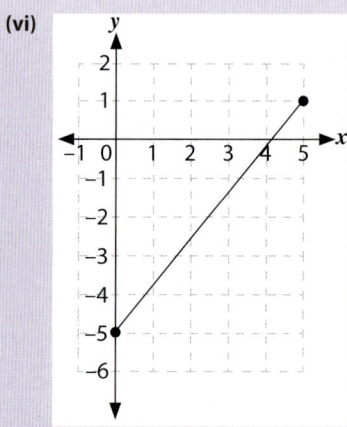

3. The point (−7, −3) lies on a circle. What is the length of the radius of this circle, to the nearest whole number, if the centre is located at (5, −6)?

4. Which point is closer to (3, 5); A (−2, 6) or B (5, 1)? Justify your answer.

5. The points (3, 2), (−2, −3) and (2, 3) form the vertices of a triangle. Determine whether the triangle is equilateral, isosceles or scalene. Justify your answer with mathematical calculations.

6. M is the midpoint of [AB]. If A = (−2, 10) and B = (2, 4):
   (i) Find the coordinates of M.
   (ii) Use the distance formula to verify that M is the midpoint of [AB].

7. The graph shows the positions of three players during a basketball game.
   Player A throws the ball in a straight line to Player B, who then throws the ball in a straight line to Player C.
   (i) How far did Player A throw the ball?
   (ii) How far did Player B throw the ball?
   (iii) How far would Player A have to throw the ball to throw it directly to Player C?
   Give your answers correct to one decimal place.

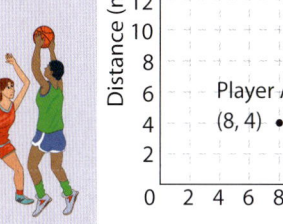

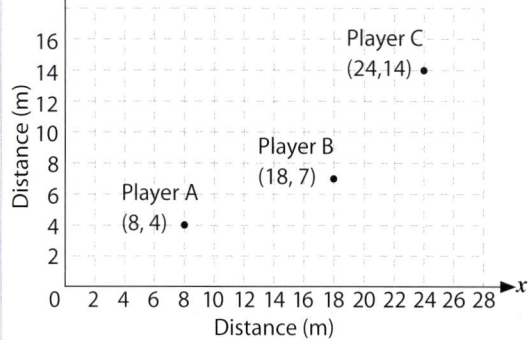

8. The points (−1, 5) and (7, −7) form the endpoints of the diameter of a circle.
   (i) Find the coordinates of C, the centre of the circle.
   (ii) Show that the diameter is twice the length of the radius.

9. A (−1, 5), B (2, 8), C (4, 4) and D (1, 1) are the vertices of a parallelogram, ABCD.
   (i) Show that ABCD is a parallelogram by showing that any pair of opposite sides are equal in length.
   (ii) Investigate if the diagonals are equal in length.

10. The coordinates for your house are given as (−3, 4). The coordinates of your school are given as (1, −6).
    (i) Plot the points representing your house and your school on a coordinate graph.
    (ii) Calculate the minimum distance from your house to the school, correct to two decimal places.
    (iii) Your friend's house is exactly halfway between your house and the school. Calculate the coordinates of your friend's house.

Taking it FURTHER

11. Steve is playing pool. He hits the cue ball and it travels along the path shown in red in the diagram, and stops.

    Calculate the total distance travelled by the cue ball, correct to two decimal places.

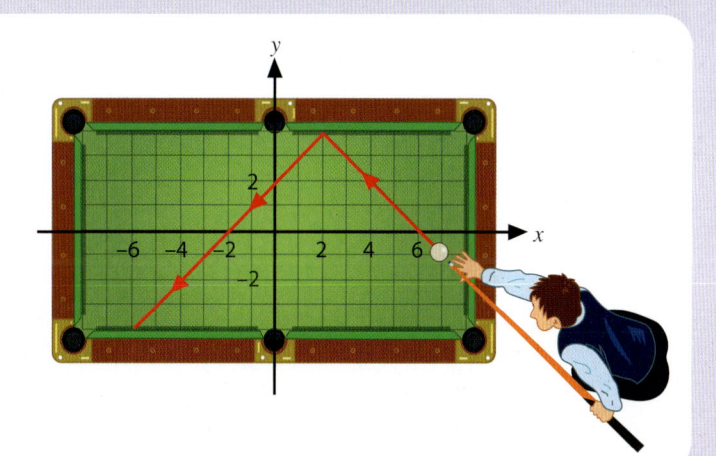

31.3 Slope of a line

By the end of this section you should:
- be able to calculate the slope of a line
- understand that parallel lines have the same slope

In Section A, Unit 7, we saw that the slope is the rate of change of a linear function. The steeper the line, the greater the slope and hence the greater the rate of change.

Slope can be calculated using the following formula:

$$\text{Slope } (m) = \frac{\text{rise}}{\text{run}}$$

Recall that if a line is going downwards, it will have a negative rise.

A lowercase m is used to represent slope.

The slope (rate of change) can be used to find the steepness of a line.

Discuss and discover

Work with a classmate to complete this activity.

The diagram shows a number of line segments.

Using $\frac{\text{rise}}{\text{run}}$, calculate the slope of each of the line segments.

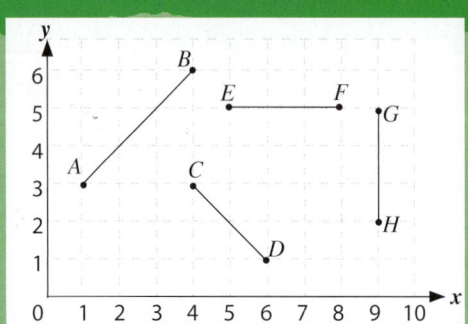

Positive and negative slopes

Graphs are read from left to right.

- When a line is increasing (going upwards), it has a positive slope.
- A horizontal line has a slope of zero.
- When a line is decreasing (going downwards), it has a negative slope.
- A vertical line has a slope which is undefined (cannot be calculated).

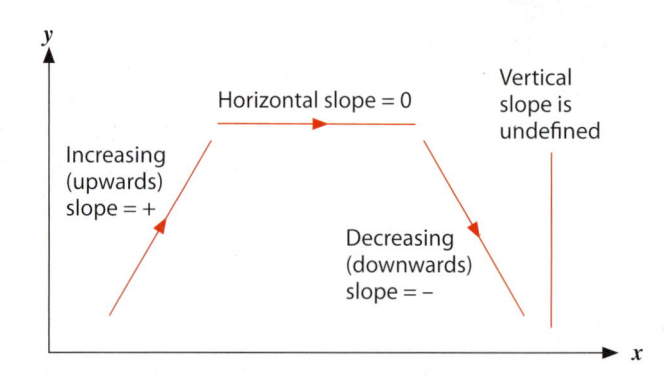

Discuss and discover

Work with a classmate to complete the following activity.

Given two points on a graph, $A = (3, 3)$ and $B = (7, 6)$ as shown in the diagram.

The point C is vertically below the point B.

(i) Identify the coordinates of the point C.
(ii) Find the run $|AC|$ and the rise $|BC|$.
(iii) Find the slope using the formula: **Slope** $(m) = \frac{\text{rise}}{\text{run}}$
(iv) The line segment $[PQ]$ is also shown on the graph. Find the slope of the line segment $[PQ]$.

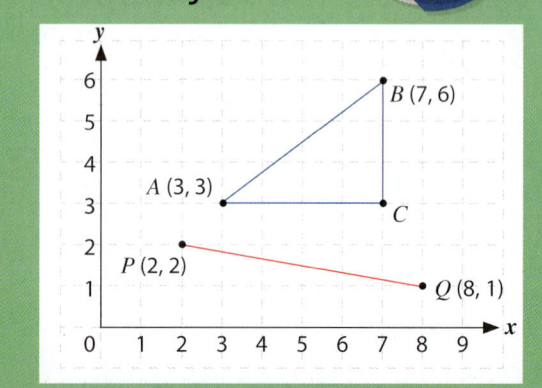

↗ Taking it FURTHER

(v) If $A = (x_1, y_1)$ and $B = (x_2, y_2)$, using what you did above, can you find a mathematical formula to calculate the slope of $[AB]$?

Linking Thinking 1

If we consider the points $A(x_1, y_1)$ and $B(x_2, y_2)$ as shown we can see that the rise is calculated as $y_2 - y_1$ and the run is calculated as $x_2 - x_1$.

This gives us the formula for calculating the slope,

Slope $(m) = \dfrac{y_2 - y_1}{x_2 - x_1}$

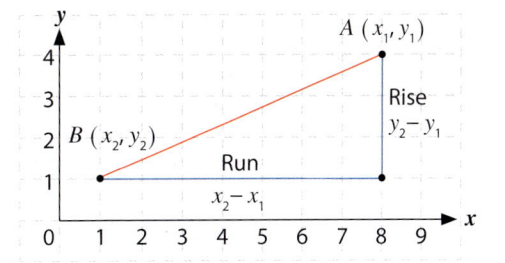

The formula for the slope of a line appears in the *formulae and tables* booklet.

Finding the slope of a line

Method 1:
1. Label the coordinates of the first point (x_1, y_1) and the coordinates of the second point (x_2, y_2).
2. Write down the slope formula.
3. Substitute the values from the question into the formula.
4. Complete the calculations to find the slope of the line.

Method 2:
1. Plot the points on the Cartesian plane.
2. Decide whether the slope is positive or negative.
3. Work out the rise and the run.
4. Substitute values from Step 3 into the formula: Slope $(m) = \dfrac{\text{rise}}{\text{run}}$

Worked example

The diagram shows a line AB.

(i) Use the formula slope $(m) = \dfrac{\text{rise}}{\text{run}}$ to calculate the slope of AB.

(ii) Use the formula slope $= \dfrac{y_2 - y_1}{x_2 - x_1}$ to calculate the slope of AB.

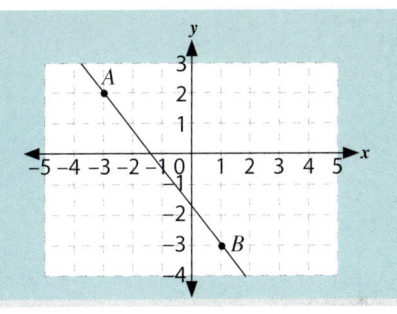

Solution

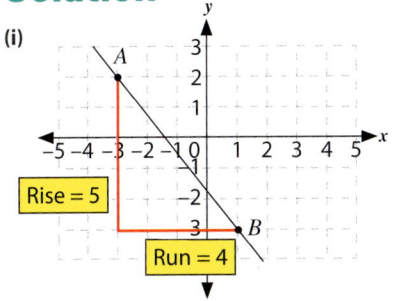

(i) Rise = 5, Run = 4

The slope is negative since the line is decreasing from left to right.

Slope $(m) = -\dfrac{\text{rise}}{\text{run}}$

$= -\dfrac{5}{4}$

(ii) **Step 1** $A = (-3, 2)$ $B = (1, -3)$
$(x_1, y_1)(x_2, y_2)$

Step 2 Slope $(m) = \dfrac{y_2 - y_1}{x_2 - x_1}$

Step 3 $= \dfrac{(-3) - 2}{1 - (-3)}$

Step 4 $= \dfrac{-5}{4}$

Slope $= -\dfrac{5}{4}$

The negative sign belongs to the whole fraction, i.e. $\dfrac{-5}{4} = \dfrac{5}{-4} = -\dfrac{5}{4}$

Parallel lines

If two lines are parallel, their slopes are equal.
If line 1 ∥ line 2, then slope of line 1 = slope of line 2.

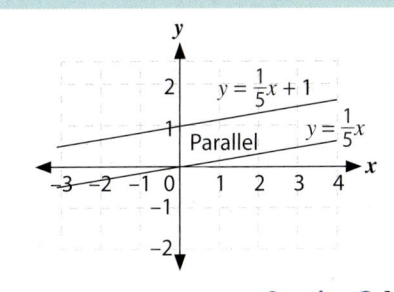

$y = \dfrac{1}{5}x + 1$

$y = \dfrac{1}{5}x$

Parallel

Section C Applying our skills

Practice questions 31·3

1. Identify the slope as positive, negative, zero or undefined from each graph.

   (i)   (ii) 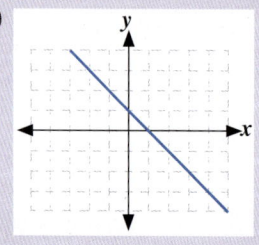   (iii)

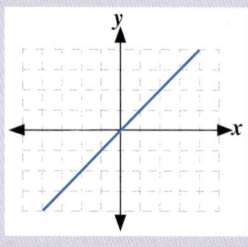

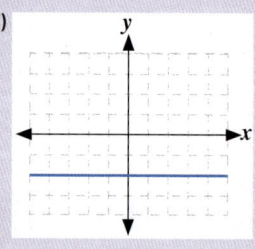

   (iv) 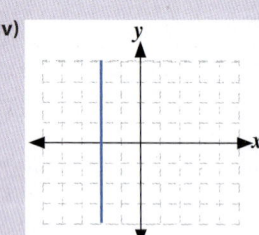   (v) 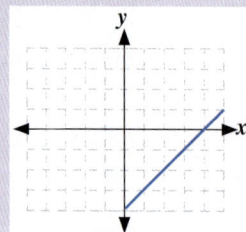   (vi)

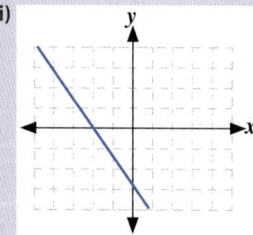

2. Use the formula slope $(m) = \frac{\text{rise}}{\text{run}}$ to calculate the slope of each of the blue lines.

   (i)   (ii) 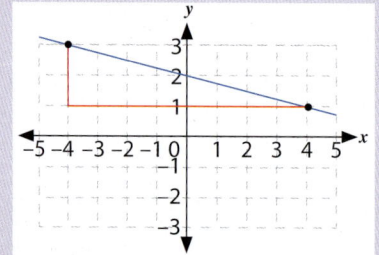   (iii)

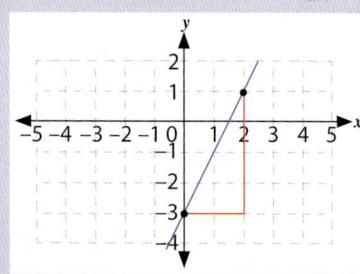

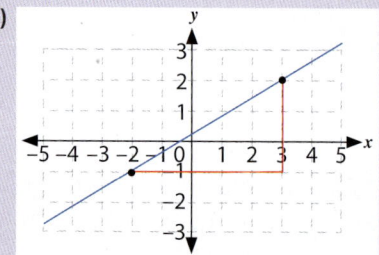

   (iv) 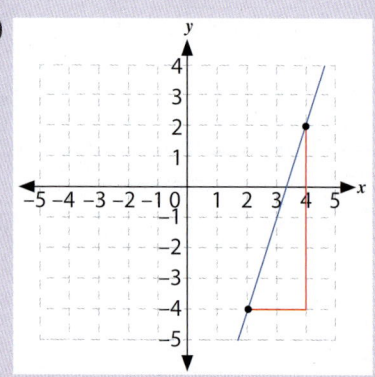   (v) 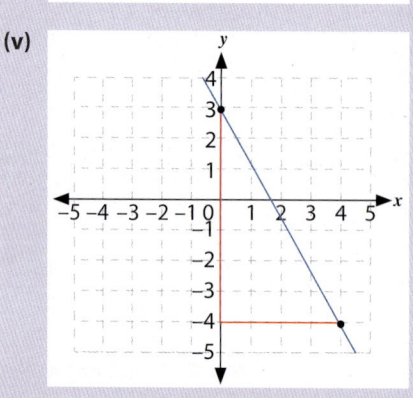   (vi)

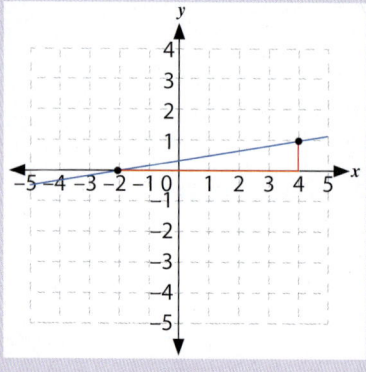

3. Calculate the slope of the line segments joining the following points.

   (i)   (7, 1) and (4, 8)   (iii)   (1, 4) and (7, −2)   (v)   (−8, 2) and (3, 5)

   (ii) (5, −3) and (−1, 6)   (iv)   (−6, 4) and (2, 9)   (vi) (−2, −3) and (−7, −1)

4. (i) Copy the table below and match the slope to the line. Give a reason for each answer.

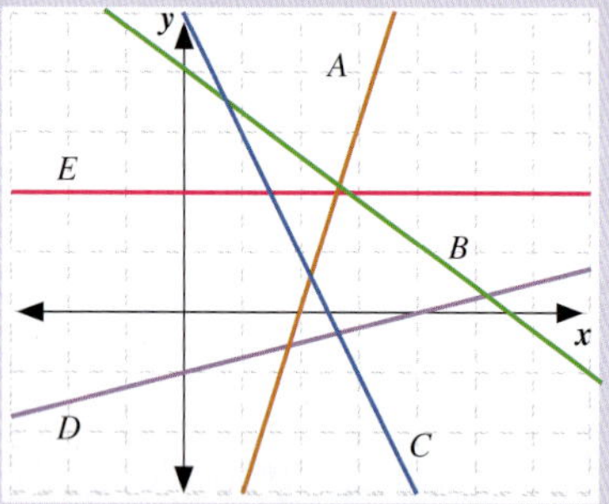

Slope	Line	Reason
$\frac{1}{4}$		
−2		
0		
3		
$-\frac{5}{7}$		

   (ii) Are any of these lines parallel? If so, state which ones and give a reason for your answer.

Linking Thinking 1

5. Investigate whether the lines PQ and RS are parallel when P, Q, R and S have the following coordinates.
   (i) $P(1, 0), Q(2, 0)$ and $R(5, -5), S(-10, -5)$
   (ii) $P(1, 2), Q(3, 1)$ and $R(0, -1), S(2, 0)$
   (iii) $P(0, 3), Q(3, 1)$ and $R(-1, 4), S(-7, -5)$
   (iv) $P(2, -1), Q(5, -7)$ and $R(0, 0), S(-1, 2)$

Taking it FURTHER

6. The diagram shows a ramp and a hill.
   Do you think it would be more difficult, considering the steepness of each, to walk up the ramp or the hill?
   Explain your answer using mathematical calculations.

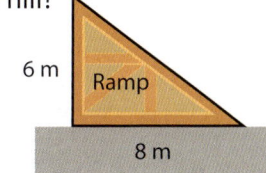

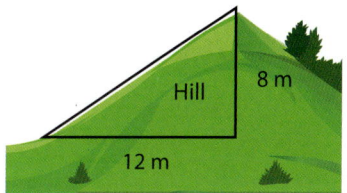

   Ramp: 6 m, 8 m
   Hill: 8 m, 12 m

7. Investigate whether each of the following quadrilaterals is a parallelogram. Justify your answer.
   (i) Quadrilateral $ABCD$
   (ii) Quadrilateral $KLMN$

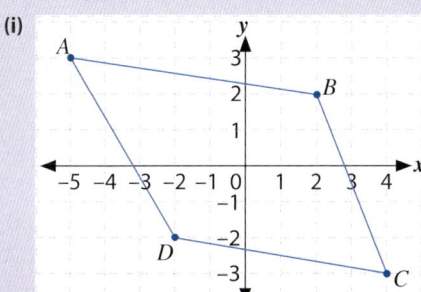

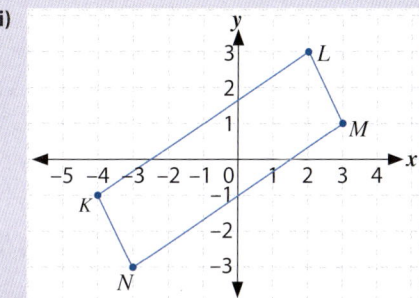

8. $A(6, -14)$ and $B(1, 7)$ are two points.
   (i) Plot the points A and B on a coordinate plane.
   (ii) Find the midpoint of $[AB]$.
   (iii) Find $|AB|$. Give your answer correct to one decimal place.
   (iv) Calculate the slope of the line AB.

31·4 Equation of a line

By the end of this section you should be able to:
- find the equation of a line in the form $y = mx + c$
- find the equation of a line in the form $y - y_1 = m(x - x_1)$

The equation of a line is a formula where every point on that particular line satisfies the formula.

This means that when we substitute the x-value and the y-value of the point, the left side of the formula will equal the right side.

We can use the equation to find where the line is located on the coordinate plane. You could **consider the equation to be the 'address' of the line**. No two lines will have the same location or equation.

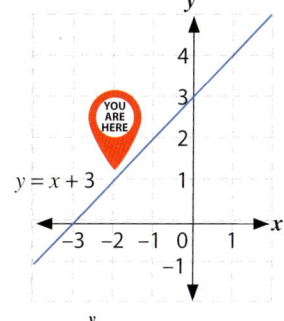

$y = x + 3$

Equation of a line in the form $y = mx + c$ (slope intercept form)

We have previously looked at linear functions and patterns in Section A, Units 7 and 9 and Section B, Unit 21. In these units, we learned that when a linear function is graphed it produces a straight line.

We learned to express the equation of this straight line as follows:

$$y = \text{starting value} + (\text{rate of change})\, x$$

Where the **starting value** is the point where the line crosses the y-axis.

For the given diagram, the line starts at 8 and rises by 4 for every one unit across, so the rate of change is 4.

Therefore, the equation of the line would be: $y = 8 + 4(x)$

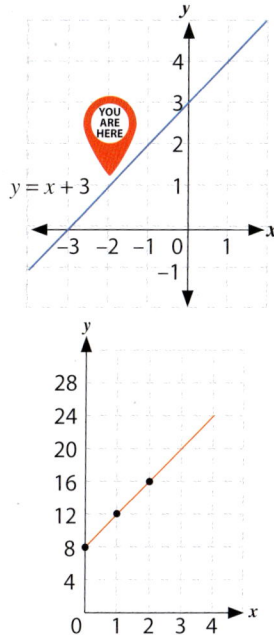

Section C Applying our skills

In general, any linear relationship can be expressed by an equation in the form:

$$y = c + mx \quad \text{or} \quad y = mx + c \text{ (as given in the tables)}$$
Where c = y-intercept
m = rate of change = slope of graph

The formula for the equation of a line appears in the *formulae and tables* booklet.

Worked example 1

Find the equation of each of following lines.

(i) Starts at 2 and increases by 4 for every 1 unit it goes across

(ii) y-intercept = 5, rate of change = −2

(iii) $c = -3$, $m = \frac{2}{3}$

Solution

(i) $c = 2 \quad m = 4$
$y = mx + c$
$y = 4x + 2$

(ii) $c = 5 \quad m = -2$
$y = mx + c$
$y = -2x + 5$

(iii) $c = -3 \quad m = \frac{2}{3}$
$y = mx + c$
$y = \frac{2}{3}x - 3$
$3y = 2x - 9$

It is good practice to remove the fraction, so we multiply both sides by 3.

Equation of a line in the form $y - y_1 = m(x - x_1)$ (point slope form)

Sometimes we are not given the y-intercept but another point (x_1, y_1) on the line.
In this case, we find the equation of the line using the following formula:

$$y - y_1 = m(x - x_1)$$

The formula for the equation of a line appears in the *formulae and tables* booklet.

To use this formula, we need to be given the slope (m) and a point (x_1, y_1) on the line. If we are not given the slope but have two points on the line, we can use the slope formula to calculate the slope first, then use it and one of the given points in the equation formula.

Worked example 2

Find the equation of each of following lines.

(i) Point on the line (−1, 5), slope = $-\frac{5}{4}$

(ii) Points on the line (4, −2) and (1, 4)

Solution

(i) $(-1, 5) \quad m = -\frac{5}{4}$
(x_1, y_1)

$y - y_1 = m(x - x_1)$
$y - 5 = -\frac{5}{4}(x - (-1))$
$y - 5 = -\frac{5}{4}(x + 1)$ (multiply by 4)
$4(y - 5) = -5(x + 1)$
$4y - 20 = -5x - 5$ (add 5x and 5 to both sides)
$5x + 5 + 4y - 20 = 0$
$5x + 4y - 15 = 0$

When using this formula, we substitute for m nd (x_1, y_1) only. Do not substitute for x and y.

(ii) $(4, -2) \quad (1, 4)$
$(x_1, y_1) \quad (x_2, y_2)$

$m = \frac{y_2 - y_1}{x_2 - x_1} = \frac{4 - (-2)}{1 - 4} = \frac{6}{-3} = -2$

$y - y_1 = m(x - x_1)$
$y - (-2) = -2(x - 4)$
$y + 2 = -2x + 8$
$2x - 8 + y + 2 = 0$
$2x + y - 6 = 0$

It is good practice to write the final equation in the form $ax + by + c = 0$.

Practice questions 31·4

1. Find the equation of each of the following lines, given the slope and the y-intercept.
   (i) Slope = –3; y-intercept = 4
   (ii) Slope = –1; y-intercept = 0
   (iii) Slope = 2; y-intercept = –1
   (iv) Slope = $\frac{1}{5}$; y-intercept = 5
   (v) Slope = $\frac{2}{3}$; y-intercept = –7
   (vi) Slope = $-\frac{3}{2}$; y-intercept = –3

2. Find the equation of each of the following lines, given the slope and a point on the line.
   (i) Slope = 5; point = (9, 2)
   (ii) Slope = –6; point = (–3, 6)
   (iii) Slope = 0; point = (–1, –2)
   (iv) Slope = $\frac{1}{2}$; point = (4, 2)
   (v) Slope = $-\frac{2}{3}$; point = (–5, 1)
   (vi) Slope = $-\frac{3}{4}$; point = (–2, –3)

3. Find the equation of each of the following lines, given two points on the line.
   (i) (12, 9) and (2, 7)
   (ii) (2, 5) and (–8, 4)
   (iii) (4, 7) and (–2, 6)
   (iv) (–10, 4) and (2, –5)
   (v) (7, 0) and (8, 0)
   (vi) (6, –7) and (1, 6)

4. Find the equation of each of the lines shown below.
   (i)
   (ii)
   (iii)

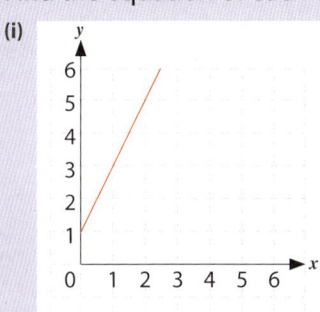

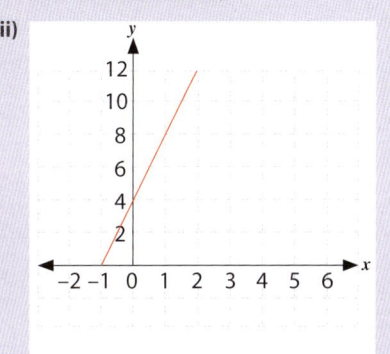

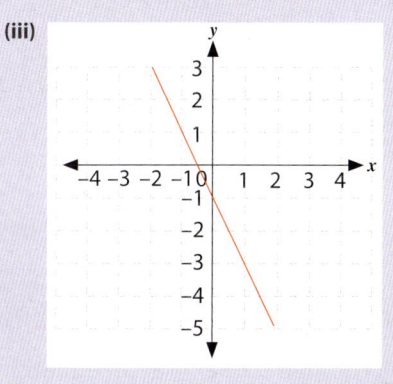

5. Write an equation of the line that has a y-intercept of 6 and is parallel to a line that has a slope of 9. Give your answer in the form $y = mx + c$.

6. Find an equation of the line that passes through the point (–3, 0) and is parallel to a line that has a slope of $-\frac{2}{3}$.

7. Write an equation of the line that is parallel to the line created by (2, 4) and (–4, 3) and passes through (10, –2).

8. The line L has a y-intercept of 4 and a slope of 3. The line M passes through (1, 0) and (0, –3).
   (i) Find the equation of the line L.
   (ii) Find the equation of the line M.
   (iii) Are the lines L and M parallel? Justify your answer.

31·5 Working with the equation of a line

By the end of this section you should be able to:
- find the slope and the y-intercept when given the equation of a line
- show a point is on a given line

Finding the slope and y-intercept when given the equation of a line

When an equation of a line is written in the form: $y = mx + c$ with the **y on its own** on the left-hand side, then:
slope = m = number in front of the x; and c = y-intercept = constant.

When an equation of a line is written in the form: $ax + by + c = 0$ with all terms on the left-hand side, then:

Slope = $-\frac{\text{coefficient of } x}{\text{coefficient of } y} = -\frac{a}{b}$

The coefficient of x is the number in front of x.

When an equation of a line is written in the form $ax + by + c = 0$ it is also possible to rearrange it into the form $y = mx + c$, where the slope is then the coefficient of the x and c is the y-intercept.

Section C Applying our skills

Worked example 1

Find the the slope and the y-intercept of the following lines.

(i) $5y = -2x - 10$ (ii) $3x - 2y + 6 = 0$

Solution

(i) $5y = -2x - 10$ ($\div$ by 5)

If we divide this equation by 5, it will be written in the form

$y = mx + c$

$y = -\frac{2}{5}x - 2$

Now, we can just pick the relevant numbers.

$m = -\frac{2}{5} \Rightarrow$ slope $= -\frac{2}{5}$

$c = -2$ is the y-intercept

The y intercept is the point where the line crosses the y-axis.

(ii) $3x - 2y + 6 = 0$

This equation is written in the form $ax + by + c = 0$, where $a = 3$ and $b = -2$

Slope $= -\frac{\text{coefficient of } x}{\text{coefficient of } y} = -\frac{a}{b}$

$= -\left(\frac{3}{-2}\right)$

$= -\left(-\frac{3}{2}\right)$ *$(-)(-) = +$*

$= \frac{3}{2}$

Coordinates of y-intercept $= (0, c)$ so fill in 0 for x to find c

$3(0) - 2c + 6 = 0$

$-2c + 6 = 0$ (subtract 6 from both sides)

$-2c = -6$ (divide both sides by -2)

$c = 3$

$\Rightarrow y$-intercept is 3

We could also rearrange the equation into the form $y = mx + c$.

To investigate if a point is on a line

We mentioned earlier that an equation of a line is a formula where every point on that particular line satisfies the formula.

Investigating if a point is on a line

1 Substitute the coordinates of the point in for x and y in the equation of the line.

2 If the equation is satisfied, it is balanced. That is, if the left-hand side (LHS) equals the right-hand side (RHS) then the point is on the line.

Collinear points are points that all lie on the same line.

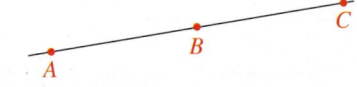

Points A, B and C are collinear.

Worked example 2

(i) Show that the line $2x + 3y + 4 = 0$ passes through the point $(-5, 2)$.

(ii) Investigate whether the point $(3, -4)$ is on the line $3x + y - 6 = 0$.

Solution

(i) We substitute -5 for x and 2 for y and see if it balances

$2x + 3y + 4 = 0$

Is $2(-5) + 3(2) + 4 = 0$?

Is $(-10) + 6 + 4 = 0$?

$0 = 0$

Since the LHS = the RHS, the equation balances, therefore showing that $(-5, 2)$ is on the line.

(ii) We substitute 3 for x and -4 for y and see if it balances

$3x + y - 6 = 0$

Is $3(3) + (-4) - 6 = 0$?

Is $9 - 4 - 6 = 0$?

$-1 \neq 0$

The point does not satisfy the equation.

Since the LHS $\neq$ the RHS the equation doesn't balance, so $(3, -4)$ is not on the line.

Practice questions 31·5

1. Find **(a)** the slope and **(b)** the y-intercept for each of the following equations

   (i) $y = 4x + 8$
   (ii) $y = -x + 5$
   (iii) $y = -3x - 1$
   (iv) $y = \frac{7}{3}x + 4$
   (v) $y = -\frac{4}{5}x - 7$
   (vi) $y = -\frac{1}{4}x - 3$

2. Rearrange the following equations into the form $y = mx + c$ and then find **(a)** the slope and **(b)** the y-intercept of each.

   (i) $6y = 5x + 24$
   (ii) $3x + y = -12$
   (iii) $x + 3y = 3$
   (iv) $5x - 2y = 10$
   (v) $4y - 8x = 9$
   (vi) $2x + 4y = 9$

3. Find **(a)** the slope and **(b)** the y-intercept for each of the following equations and **(c)** state whether the line is increasing or decreasing

   (i) $4x + y - 7 = 0$
   (ii) $3x - y + 5 = 0$
   (iii) $6x + 2y + 9 = 0$
   (iv) $x - 3y + 4 = 0$
   (v) $5y - 3x + 2 = 0$
   (vi) $2y - 3x + 6 = 0$

4. The table below gives the equations for each of the lines shown. Match the equation to its graph and justify your answer.

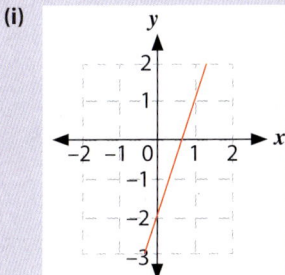

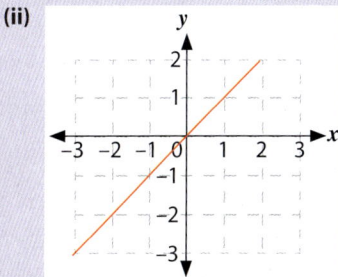

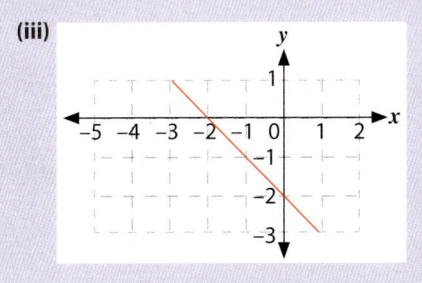

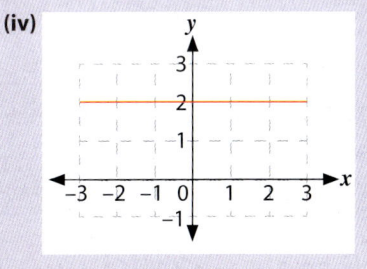

A	$y = x$
B	$y = -x - 2$
C	$2y = x - 2$
D	$y = 3x - 2$
E	$y = 2$

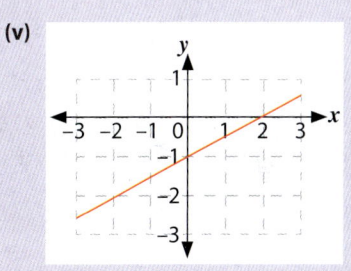

5. By finding the slope of each line, investigate whether or not p and q are parallel.

   (i) $p: y = 3x + 2$
   $q: y = 3x - 1$
   (ii) $p: y = 2x + 2$
   $q: 4y = 2x - 3$
   (iii) $p: 3y - 2x + 1 = 0$
   $q: 2x + 3y - 5 = 0$

6. Investigate if the given point is on the given line.

   (i) $(2, -3); y = 2x - 7$
   (ii) $(0, -3); 2y = 2x - 7$
   (iii) $(2, -1); 2x + 5y = 1$

7. Find the equation of the straight line passing through the points $(3, -4)$ and $(1, 2)$ and hence show that the three points $(3, -4)$, $(1, 2)$ and $(2, -1)$ are collinear.

8. The diagram shows the graph of a line. 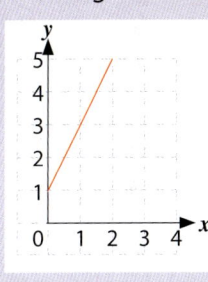
   (i) Find the equation of the line.
   (ii) This line is translated two units upwards on the y-axis. Find the equation of the new line.

9. For babysitting, Nicole charges a flat fee of €10, plus €8 per hour.
   (i) Write an equation for her earnings, y, after x hours of babysitting.
   (ii) What do you think the slope and the y-intercept represent?
   (iii) How much money will she make if she babysits for 5 hours?

Section C Applying our skills

31·6 Graphing lines when given the equation of the line

By the end of this section you should be able to:
- draw a graph of a line when given its equation

Method 1: Using the y-intercept and the slope

If we are given or can rearrange the equation of a line in the form $y = mx + c$, we can use the y-intercept and the slope of the line to draw a graph of line.

Recall from Section 31·4 that the y-intercept is the starting point (or the point where the graph crosses the y-axis) and the slope is the rate of change of the graph.

Consider the equation $y = 3x + 1$. The slope is 3 and the y-intercept of this graph is 1.

Recall that 3 can be written as $\frac{3}{1}$, so the rise is 3 and the run is 1. This means that for every 1 unit we go across, we go up 3 units.

Graphing this line

1. Plot the y-intercept (point (0, 1) for this line).

2. Using the slope of the line, find another point on the line. Move across 1 unit to the right, from this point and then move up 3 units from here. We get the point (1, 4).

3. Plot the point (1, 4), join it to (0, 1) and extend the line in both directions.

4. Shown is the graph of $y = 3x + 1$.

5. Label the line with its equation.

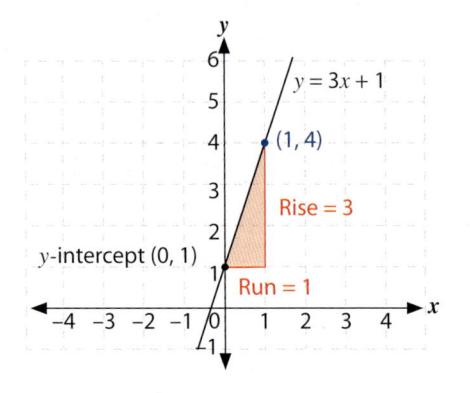

Worked example 1

Draw a graph of each of following lines.

(i) $y = -\frac{2}{3}x - 2$

(ii) $2x - y + 6 = 0$

Solution

(i) $y = -\frac{2}{3}x - 2$

The y-intercept of this graph is -2 and the slope is $-\frac{2}{3}$.
Remember that a negative slope means that the line is decreasing from left to right (going downwards).
In this case, for every 3 units we move across, we move down 2 units.
3 across and 2 down from (0, −2) gives us (3, −4).

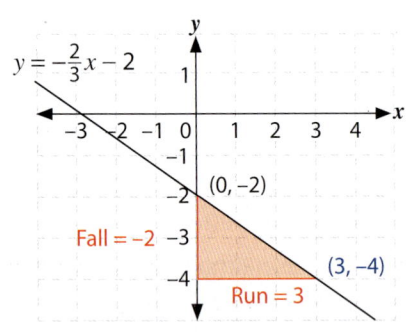

(ii) $2x - y + 6 = 0$

This equation needs to be rearranged to be in the form $y = mx + c$

$-y = -2x - 6$ (multiply both sides by −1)

$y = 2x + 6$

The y-intercept of this graph is 6 and the slope is 2.
In this case for every 1 unit we move across, we move up 2 units.
1 across and 2 up from (0, 6) gives (1, 8).

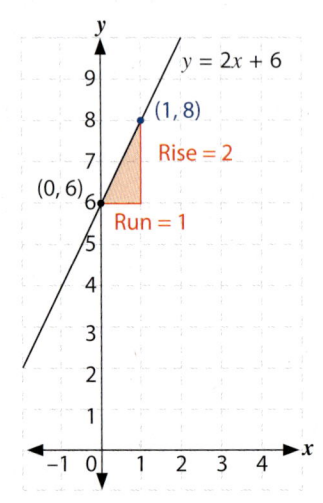

502 Linking Thinking 1

Method 2: Using points on the line

To draw a line, we need two points on the line. The easiest two points to find are the points where the line crosses the axes. These are known as the intercepts.

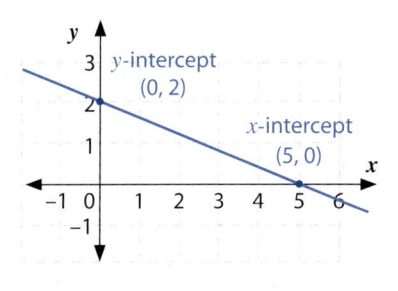

> ### Graphing a line using two points on the line
> 1. Find the y-intercept by letting $x = 0$ and finding y.
> 2. Find the x-intercept by letting $y = 0$ and finding x.
> 3. Plot these two points.
> 4. Draw a line which passes through these two points.

On the x-axis, $y = 0$
On the y-axis, $x = 0$

Worked example 2

Draw a graph of the line $3x - 2y - 12 = 0$

Solution

$3x - 2y - 12 = 0$

Let $x = 0$ to find the y-intercept	Let $y = 0$ to find the x-intercept
$3(0) - 2y - 12 = 0$	$3x - 2(0) - 12 = 0$
$-2y - 12 = 0$	$3x - 12 = 0$
$-2y = 12$	$3x = 12$
$y = -6$	$x = 4$
y-intercept $= (0, -6)$	x-intercept $= (4, 0)$

Plot the intercepts and draw a line passing through them both.

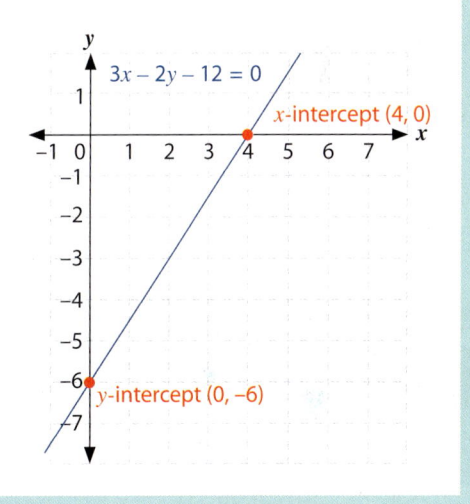

Two interesting cases

1. Lines through the origin

If the constant in the equation is equal to zero, so that the equation is in the form $ax + by = 0$, then the line passes through the origin $(0, 0)$, and so the intercept method will only give us one point to plot. In this case, we must find a different point which is on the line.

> ### Graphing a line through the origin
> 1. Let x equal the number in front of the y (or any suitable number). Solve for y.
> 2. Plot this point.
> 3. Draw a line that passes through the origin and this point.

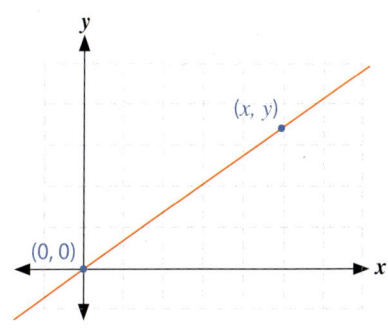

Section C Applying our skills

2. Lines parallel to the axes

Some lines are parallel to the x-axis (horizontal) and some lines are parallel to the y-axis (vertical).

The line $x = a$ is vertical and passes through the value a on the x-axis. Its slope is undefined.

The line $y = b$ is horizontal and passes through the value b on the y-axis. Its slope is zero.

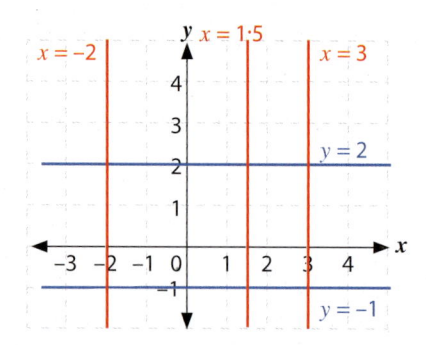

> $y = 0$ is the equation of the x-axis.
>
> $x = 0$ is the equation of the y-axis.

Worked example 3

Using the same axes and scales, draw a graph of each of following lines.

(i) $x - 2y = 0$ (ii) $y = 3$ (iii) $x = 2$

Solution

(i) Since the constant equals zero we know that the line passes through $(0, 0)$.

Let $x = -2$ to find y

$x - 2y = 0$
$-2 - 2y = 0$
$-2y = 2$
$y = -1$

Point $= (-2, -1)$

Plot $(0, 0)$ and $(-2, -1)$ and join to form $x - 2y = 0$

(ii) $y = 3$ is a horizontal line passing through 3 on the y-axis.

(iii) $x = 2$ is a vertical line passing through 2 on the x-axis.

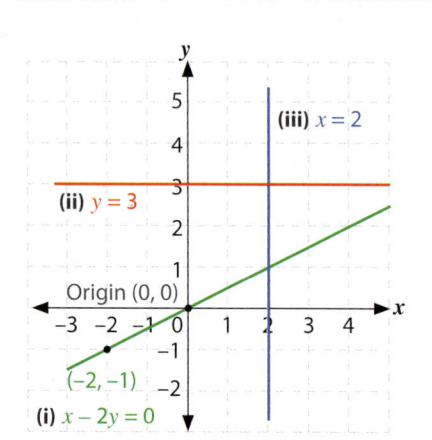

Practice questions 31.6

1. Draw a graph of each of the following lines.

    (i) $y = 2x + 4$
    (ii) $y = \frac{1}{2}x + 1$
    (iii) $y = -2x - 3$
    (iv) $y = 6 - 4x$
    (v) $x + y = 5$
    (vi) $2y = 5x + 2$

2. Draw a graph of each of the following lines.

    (i) $7x + y - 5 = 0$
    (ii) $3x + 5y + 5 = 0$
    (iii) $9x - 3y - 15 = 0$
    (iv) $x - 3y - 3 = 0$
    (v) $2x - 4y - 12 = 0$
    (vi) $3x - 4y + 16 = 0$

3. (a) Draw a graph of each of the following lines.

    (i) $x + y = 0$
    (ii) $x + 4y = 0$
    (iii) $7x - 2y = 0$
    (iv) $x - 8y = 0$
    (v) $2x - 3y = 0$
    (vi) $3x + 4y = 0$

   (b) What do you notice about all these graphs? Explain the reason for what you notice.

4. (a) Draw a graph of each of the following lines.

   (b) What do you notice about these graphs? Explain the reason for what you notice.

    (i) $x = 1$
    (ii) $y = 5$
    (iii) $x = -3$
    (iv) $y = -2$
    (v) $2y = -8$
    (vi) $2x - 4 = 0$

5. By finding the x- and y-intercepts, graph each of the following lines

    (i) $y = x + 2$
    (ii) $4x + 5y = 20$
    (iii) $2x - y - 4 = 0$

504 Linking Thinking 1

6. An oil tank holds 50 litres of oil. The owner of the tank notices a leak that is causing a loss of 5 litres of oil a day. 
   (i) Write an equation to represent this situation.
   (ii) Draw a graph to represent the situation.
   (iii) Use your graph to work out how many days it will take for the tank to become half full.

7. A hotel needs to arrange tables to seat 180 people for a function.
   Tables come in two sizes: small tables seat 4 people and large tables seat 6 people. 
   (i) By letting x be the number of tables that seat 4 people, and y be the number of tables that seat 6 people, write an equation to represent this situation.
   (ii) Find the x- and y-intercepts of the graph of the equation.
   (iii) Draw a graph of the equation.
   (iv) Give three possible combinations of tables seating 4 or 6 that can be used to seat all 180 people.

31·7 Point of intersection of two lines (simultaneous equations)

By the end of this section you should be able to:
- find the point of intersection of two lines both graphically and algebraically

The point of intersection of two lines is the point (x, y) at which the two lines cross.

To find the point of intersection graphically we draw both lines on the same axes and scales and write down the coordinates of the point where the two lines cross.

The point of intersection is the only point that will satisfy the equations of both lines at the same time (simultaneously).

In Section B, Unit 18, we learned how to find the point of intersection using graphing methods and by solving simultaneous equations in algebra.

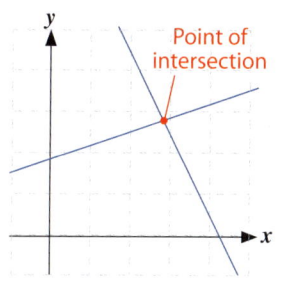

Worked example 1

(i) Using the same axes and scale, draw a graph of the following lines.
$$2x + y - 3 = 0 \qquad 3x - 4y - 10 = 0$$
(ii) Use the graph to find the point of intersection of these lines.

Solution

(i) Rearrange equations into $y = mx + c$ form

$2x + y - 3 = 0$

$y = -2x + 3$

y-intercept $= (0, 3)$, slope $= -2$

$3x - 4y - 10 = 0$

$-4y = -3x + 10$

$y = \frac{3}{4}x - 2\cdot5$

y-intercept $= (0, -2\cdot5)$, slope $= \frac{3}{4}$

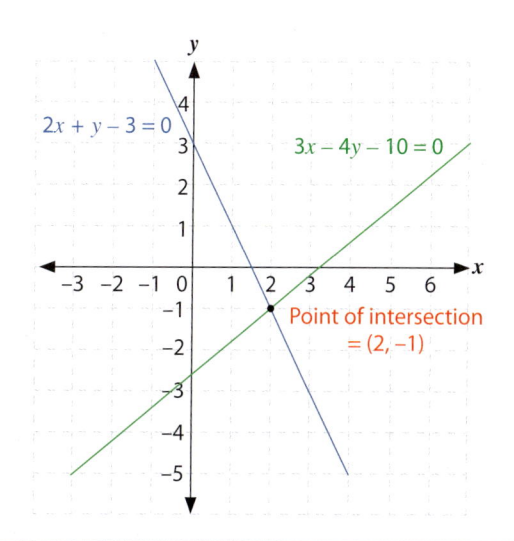

(ii) From the graph, you can see that the point where the two lines meet is $(2, -1)$

Point of intersection $= (2, -1)$

Worked example 2

(i) Use the graph shown to find the point of intersection P of the lines $3x + 4y = 23$ and $2x + y = 12$

(ii) Verify your answer to (i) by solving the equations simultaneously.

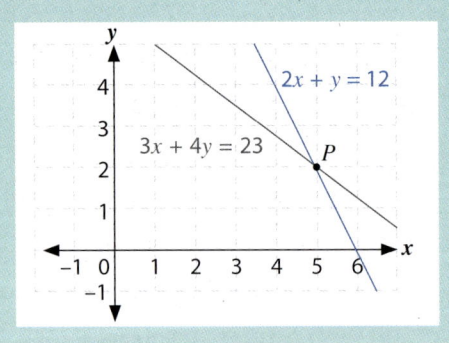

Solution

(i) The point of intersection is the point where the two lines cross.
From the graph, the point of intersection is (5, 2)

(ii) Using simultaneous equations

$3x + 4y = 23$ (equation a)
$2x + y = 12$ (equation b)

$3x + 4y = 23$
$-8x - 4y = -48$ (multiply equation b by –4)

$-5x = -25$
$x = 5$

$3x + 4y = 23$ (equation a)
$x = 5$ (substitute value for x)
$3(5) + 4y = 23$
$15 + 4y = 23$
$4y = 23 - 15$
$4y = 8$
$y = 2$

Point of intersection = (5, 2)

Practice questions 31·7

1. Find the point of intersection of each of the pairs of lines shown below.

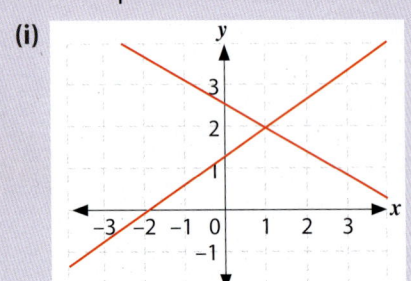

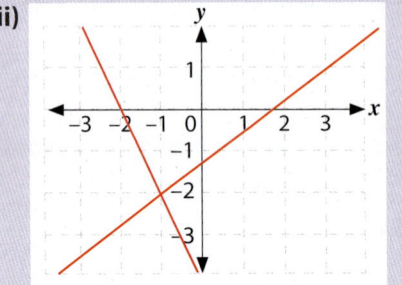

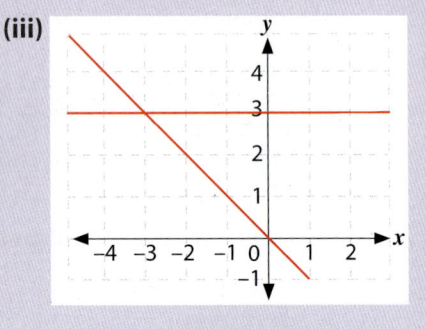

   (i), (ii), (iii) [graphs]

2. Find the point of intersection of each of the following pairs of lines by graphing each pair using the same axes and scales.

   (i) $x + y = 3$ and $2x + y = 5$
   (ii) $2x + y = 6$ and $2x + 3y = 10$
   (iii) $3x - 4y = 0$ and $2x - 3y = 0$
   (iv) $x + y = 5$ and $2x - y = 1$
   (v) $x - y = -3$ and $x + 2y = 9$
   (vi) $5x + 2y = 24$ and $3x - y = 10$

3. Use simultaneous equations to find the point of intersection of the following pairs of lines.

   (i) $x - 3y = 1$ and $4x + 3y = 34$
   (ii) $2y = -x + 4$ and $2x = y + 3$
   (iii) $3x + 2y = 7$ and $4x - y = 13$
   (iv) $6x - 5y = 29$ and $5x + 4y = 16$
   (v) $x + y - 2 = 0$ and $-y = -3x + 6$
   (vi) $2x = 3y + 13$ and $x - 4y - 9 = 0$

4. The diagram shows two straight lines intersecting at point A.
   The equations of the lines are:
   $y = 3x - 4$
   $y = 2x - 3$
   Work out the coordinates of A.

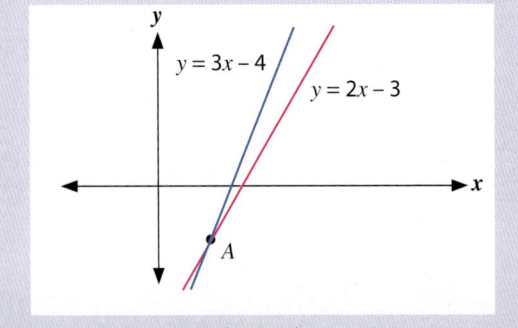

5. (i) Using the same axes and scales, draw a graph of the lines $x + y - 6 = 0$ and $2x - y = 6$
   (ii) Use your graph to find the coordinates of the point of intersection of the two lines.
   (iii) Verify the point of intersection using algebra?

6. Two straight sections of road are represented by the linear equations given on the diagram. These roads intersect each other at a point. Using the same axes and scales, graph the equations of the roads.

   $2x - y + 5 = 0$
   $x - 2y - 2 = 0$

   (i) Use your graph to find the point at which the roads intersect.
   (ii) Verify your answer to (ii) using simultaneous equations.
   (iii) Which method (graphing or algebra) do you think gives the most accurate answer for the point of intersection? Justify your answer.

7. One line has a slope of −2 and goes through the point (0, 3). Another line goes through the points (−2, 10) and (3, 5). What are the coordinates of their point of intersection?

8. The diagram shows information about the height of two hot air balloons over a period of time.

   Balloon 2 is 150 metres above the ground, descending at a rate of 20 metres per minute.

   Balloon 1 is 10 metres above the ground, rising at a rate of 15 metres per minute.

   (i) Use the information given in the diagram to form an equation to represent the height of each balloon at any given time.
   (ii) Using any method of your choosing, work out in how many minutes the balloons will be at the same height. Show all your work.

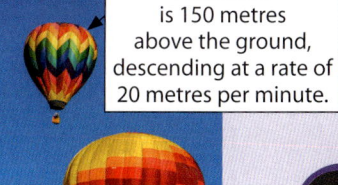

Revision questions

31A Core skills

1. Find the midpoint of each of the line segments joining each of the following pairs of points.
   (i) (0, 4) and (6, 2)
   (ii) (1, −3) and (3, 5)
   (iii) (−3, 4) and (1, −2)
   (iv) (3, −5) and (−5, 3)
   (v) (1, 6) and (−3, 2)
   (vi) (−5, −7) and (1, −1)

2. Find the distance between the following pairs of points. Give your answer to one decimal place.
   (i) (1, 2) and (3, 5)
   (ii) (−1, 3) and (2, −5)
   (iii) (−2, −1) and (3, 4)
   (iv) (1, −5) and (−2, −6)
   (v) (−3, 4) and (0, −3)
   (vi) (−3, 1) and (−2, −7)

3. Find (a) the slope and (b) the y-intercept of the following lines.
   (i) $y = 3x + 1$
   (ii) $2y = 6x - 1$
   (iii) $4y = x + 1$
   (iv) $2x + 4y - 9 = 0$
   (v) $4x + 2y - 3 = 0$
   (vi) $3x - y + 2 = 0$

4. Find (a) the slope and (b) the equation of the lines passing through the following pairs of points.
   (i) (2, 6) and (4, 12)
   (ii) (5, 1) and (6, 4)
   (iii) (1, 4) and (−2, 1)
   (iv) (2, −5) and (−1, 3)
   (v) (−1, 3) and (2, −4)
   (vi) (−1, −3) and (5, −1)

5. Graph the following lines on a coordinate plane.
   (i) $4x - 5y + 10 = 0$
   (ii) $x - 3y + 2 = 0$
   (iii) $2x + 6y - 12 = 0$
   (iv) $2y - 8x + 4 = 0$
   (v) $4y = 8 - 2x$
   (vi) $6y - 2x = 18$

6. Investigate whether each of the points are on the given lines.
   (a) $y = 3x + 5$
       (i) (2, 12)
       (ii) (0, 5)
       (iii) (3, 14)
       (iv) (4, 17)
   (b) $4x - y - 5 = 0$
       (i) (1, −1)
       (ii) (5, 15)
       (iii) (2, 13)
       (iv) (0, −5)

Section C Applying our skills 507

7. Investigate whether the following points are collinear.
   (i) (2, 4), (4, 6) and (6, 8)
   (ii) (0, 4), (1, 1) and (2, –1)
   (iii) (–2, 4), (4, 3) and (10, –2)

8. (a) Using the same axes and scales, graph the following lines.
      (i) $2x - y = 8$ $y = 3x$
      (ii) $y = x + 1$ $x + y = 3$
      (iii) $3x - y + 2 = 0$ $y + x = 6$
   (b) Use your graph to find the point of intersection of each pair of lines.
   (c) Verify your answers to (b) using simultaneous equations.

9. Copy the table below and put a tick (✓) in the correct box in each row to show whether each statement is always true, sometimes true, or never true. Justify your answer in each case.

	Statement	Always true	Sometimes true	Never true
(i)	The length of a line segment can be negative.			
(ii)	If C is a point on $[AB]$, then C is the midpoint of $[AB]$.			
(iii)	Parallel lines have the same slope.			
(iv)	There is only one point of intersection between two lines.			
(v)	If Z is on the line XY, then X, Y and Z are collinear.			

31B Taking it FURTHER

1. A is the point (–6, 7) and B is the point (8, 0).
   (i)   Find the midpoint of AB.
   (ii) Find $|AB|$, correct to one decimal place.
   (iii) Find the equation of the line AB.
   (iv) Find the equation of the line parallel to AB that passes through the point (1, 1).

2. (i)   Plot the points $P(2, 1)$ and $Q(6, 5)$ on a coordinate plane. Join the points to form the line segment $[PQ]$.
   (ii) Using your knowledge of constructions from Section A, Unit 3, construct the perpendicular bisector of the line PQ.
   (iii) From your graph, what are the coordinates of M, the midpoint of $[PQ]$?
   (iv) Use the midpoint formula to confirm your answer to (iii) above.
   (v)   Use the length of a line formula to verify that the line you constructed in (ii) bisects $[PQ]$.

3. (i)   Plot the points $X(4, 2)$, $Y(8, 0)$ and $Z(6, –4)$.
   (ii) Verify that the triangle XYZ is isosceles.
   (iii) Using Pythagoras's theorem, determine if this triangle is right-angled? Justify your answer using mathematical calculations.

4. (i)   Plot the points $H(2, 3)$, $I(–1, 5)$, $J(–2, 0)$ and $K(1, –2)$ on a coordinate plane.
   (ii) (a) Investigate if $|HK| = |IJ|$
         (b) Verify $|HI| = |JK|$
   (iii) Find the midpoint of $[HJ]$ and show that is also the midpoint of $[IK]$
   (iv) What type of shape is $HIJK$? Justify your answer.

5. Let the vertices of triangles ABC and PQR be defined by the following coordinates.
   $A(–2, 0)$, $B(0, 4)$ and $C(2, 0)$
   $P(–1, 1)$, $Q(0, 3)$ and $R(1, 1)$
   Show that the two triangles are similar.

6. The line l has the equation $y = 3x - 2$
   (i)   Find the slope of the line.
   (ii) Find the y-intercept of the line l.
   (iii) Determine whether the following points are on l.
         (a) (2, 4)
         (b) (–1, 5)
   (iv) The point $(–4, a)$ is on the line l. Find the value of a.
   (v)   Draw a graph of the line l, showing the answers to each of the parts above.
   (vi) The line k has the equation $y = –x + 6$. Find the point of intersection of l and k.

7. The graph shows the distance travelled by a cyclist over time.

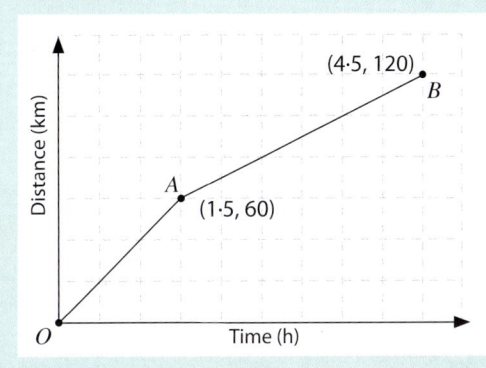

   (a) By looking at the graph, on which part of the journey does the cyclist travel fastest? Justify your answer.

   (b) Calculate the average speed of the cyclist:

   (i) from O to A

   (ii) from A to B

   (iii) for the whole trip

8. The objective of a particular computer game is to shoot missiles through escape hatches that randomly appear in an otherwise solid wall. The diagram represents a missile being fired from point A attempting to exit through escape hatch E.

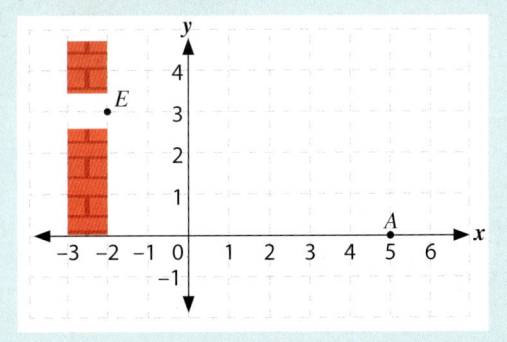

   (i) If the missile must travel in a straight line, find the equation of the line that represents a successful escape.

   (ii) Another missile is launched. The path of this missile is represented by the equation $3x + 13y = 33$. Investigate where the paths of the two missiles cross.

   (iii) Using your answer to (ii), or otherwise, determine whether the second missile can also exit through escape hatch E.

9. The table below gives some information about lines l, m, n and o.

Line	Slope	y-intercept	Equation
l	4	$(0, -3)$	
m		$(0, 5)$	$2y = x + 10$
n	-3		$y = -3x + 7$
o			$3x - y + 5 = 0$

   (i) Copy and complete the table.

   (ii) Which line is the steepest? Justify your answer.

   (iii) Is the point $(-1, 3)$ on o? Justify your answer.

10. The diagram shows the coordinates of the town where Saoirse lives.

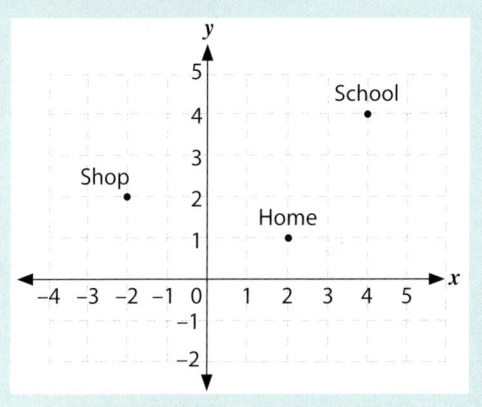

    (i) Write down the coordinates of Saoirse's home, the shop and the school.

    (ii) The swimming pool is halfway between Saoirse's home and the shop. Find the coordinates of the swimming pool.

    (iii) Yesterday, Saoirse cycled to school in the morning, to the shop after school and then home from the shop. If each unit on the diagram represents 1 km, calculate the distance Saoirse cycled yesterday. Give your answer correct to the nearest km.

Now that you have completed the unit, revisit the Something to think about ... question posed at the start of this unit.

Now try question 13 on page 562

Unit 32

Inequalities

Topics covered within this unit:
32·1 Graphing inequalities on the number line
32·2 Solving linear inequalities

The Learning Outcomes covered in this unit are contained in the following sections:
AF.4d

Key words
Natural numbers
Integers
Real numbers
Equality
Inequality

Something to think about ...

'Every mathematician loves an inequality' is part of the folklore of Mathematics. Euclid (who lived around 350 BCE) would express inequalities in words. He might say that one area was larger than another, using phrases such as 'is smaller than' or 'is bigger than'. It wasn't until the time of Isaac Newton (around 1650 CE) that mathematical notation was used to describe an inequality.

Try to solve this problem:
Rian and Aidan play in the same Gaelic team. Last Saturday Aidan scored 3 more goals than Rian, but together they scored fewer than 9 goals.

What are the possible number of goals Aidan scored?

32·1 Graphing inequalities on the number line

By the end of this section you should:
- understand the number systems $\mathbb{N}$, $\mathbb{Z}$, $\mathbb{R}$
- be able to graph solutions on a number line
- understand what inequality symbols mean in Maths

Revision of number systems on the number line

The **natural numbers**, $\mathbb{N}$, are all whole positive numbers above zero. The natural (or counting) numbers are {1, 2, 3, 4, 5 ...}

There are infinitely many natural numbers.

To graph certain natural numbers on the number line, place a shaded circle on each of the natural numbers you require. For example, the following graph shows the set of natural numbers {3, 4, 5, 6}

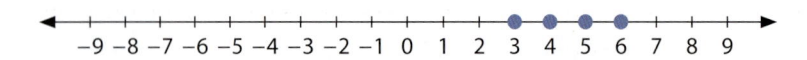

The **integers**, $\mathbb{Z}$, are the set of numbers consisting of all the whole positive numbers, whole negative numbers and zero {... –5, –4, –3, –2, –1, 0, 1, 2, 3, 4, 5, ...}

To graph certain **integers** on the number line, place a shaded circle on each of the integers you require.

For example, the following graph shows the set of integers {–2, –1, 0, 1, 2, 3}

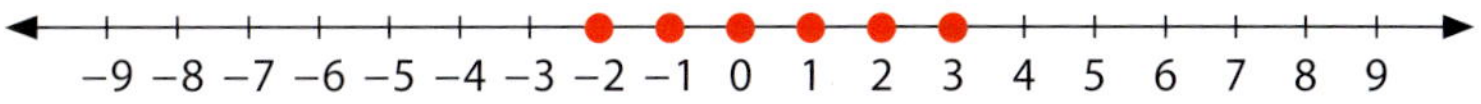

The **real numbers**, $\mathbb{R}$, are the set of all the numbers that can exist on the number line.

Real numbers include natural numbers, integers, all fractions and all decimals.

To graph certain real numbers which lie between two other real numbers on the number line, place a solid shaded line along the number line.

The graph here shows all the **real numbers** between –3 and +4, including –3 and **including** +4, on the number line:

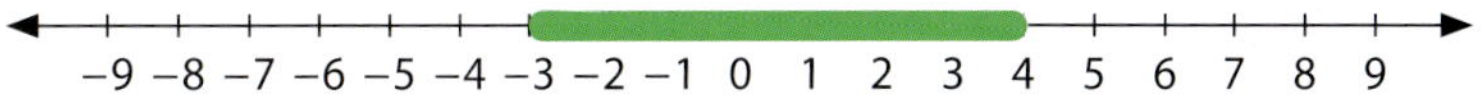

The following graph shows all the **real numbers** between –3 and +4, including –3 but **not including** +4, on the number line.

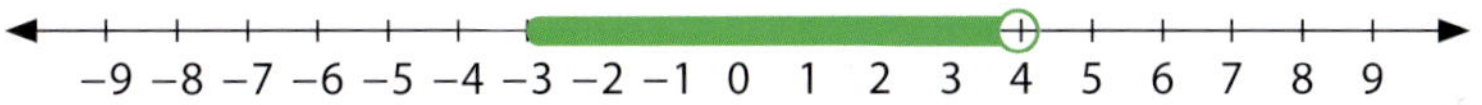

An unshaded (hollow) circle is placed on +4 to show that +4 **is not included** but the solid line goes right up to this unshaded circle to show that 3·999999999999999999999999 …, or 3·$\dot{9}$, **is included**.

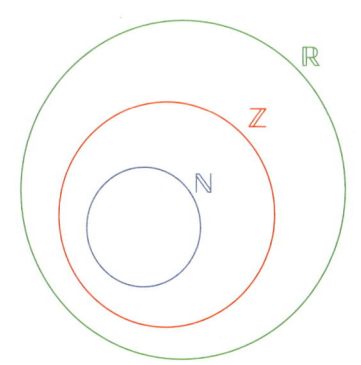

Natural numbers ($\mathbb{N}$) are a subset of the **integers** ($\mathbb{Z}$).

The **integers** ($\mathbb{Z}$) are a subset of the **real numbers** ($\mathbb{R}$).

Equalities and inequalities

Inequalities describe the relationships between two expressions which are not equal to one another.

An inequality tells us about the **relative size** of two values.

If Barry is taller than Andrew, then:

  Barry's height **is greater than** Andrew's height

   Barry's height > Andrew's height

We call this an **inequality** because they are not equal.

An **equality** is a mathematical statement that shows that one expression equals (=) another expression.

An **inequality** is a mathematical statement that shows that one expression is less than or more than (<, >, ≤, ≥) another expression.

Section C **Applying our skills**

Equality vs inequalities in Mathematics

	Equality	Inequality
Statement	Shows the equality of two variables	Shows the inequality of two variables
How the sides of an equation are related	LHS equals RHS 	LHS can be bigger, smaller or equal to RHS 
Symbol between sides	=	<, > We can also have inequalities that include 'equals', like ≤, ≥
Answers	An equation only has one answer	An inequality can have more than one answer

Symbols used in inequalites

LHS < RHS	LHS > RHS	LHS ≤ RHS	LHS ≥ RHS
Left hand side is **less than** the right hand side	Left hand side is **greater than** the right hand side	Left hand side is **less than or equal to** the right hand side	Left hand side is **greater than or equal to** the right hand side

Worked example 1

Place an inequality symbol between each of the following constants, to make each statement true.

(i) 4 ☐ 6   (ii) 50 ☐ –50   (iii) –3 ☐ –7   (iv) –1 250 ☐ –250

Remember: –10°C is colder than –2°C

Solution

(i) 4 is further to the left and less than 6 on the number line, so 4 < 6

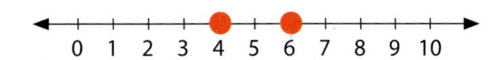

(ii) 50 is further to right and greater than –50 on the number line, so 50 > –50

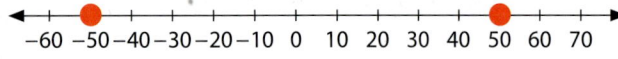

(iii) –3 is further to right and greater than –7 on the number line, so –3 > –7

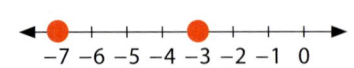

(iv) –1 250 is further to left and less than –250 on the number line, so –1 250 < –250

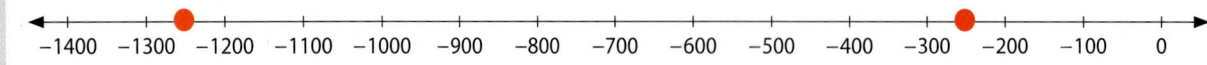

It may help you to draw a number line to answer these questions.

Worked example 2

Represent the following inequalities on a number line.

(i) $x < 6$, where $x \in \mathbb{N}$
(ii) $x \geq -6$, where $x \in \mathbb{R}$
(iii) $x > -4$, where $x \in \mathbb{N}$
(iv) $x < 8$, where $x \in \mathbb{R}$
(v) $x \leq 2$, where $x \in \mathbb{Z}$
(vi) List the first six elements of the solution set for part (v)

Solution

(i) $x < 6$, where $x \in \mathbb{N}$

$\mathbb{N}$ stands for the natural numbers (whole positive numbers not including zero)

< symbol means x is less than 6 but not equal to 6 and the natural numbers end at 1

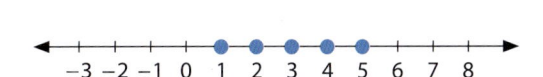

(ii) $x \geq -6$, where $x \in \mathbb{R}$

$\mathbb{R}$ stands for real numbers, and they are 'all the numbers' on the number line

≥ symbol means x is greater than or equal to -6

The arrow is placed at the end to show that x could be any real number above what is shown

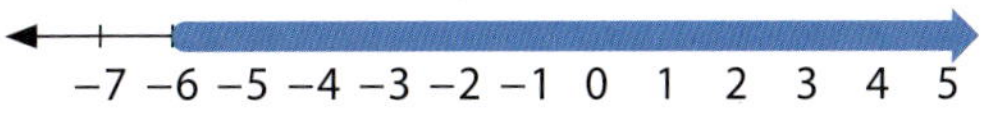

(iii) $x > -4$, where $x \in \mathbb{N}$

$\mathbb{N}$ stands for the natural numbers (whole positive numbers)

> symbol means x is greater than -4

But since x is a natural number, it must be greater than zero. So we start the dots on the number 1.

The arrow is placed at the end to show that x could be any natural number above what is shown

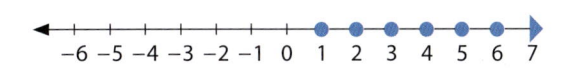

(iv) $x < 8$, where $x \in \mathbb{R}$

$\mathbb{R}$ stands for real numbers, and they are 'all the numbers' on the number line

< symbol means x is less than 8 but not equal to 8

The arrow is placed at the end to show that x could be any real number below what is shown

An unshaded circle is placed around 8 is to show that 8 is not included

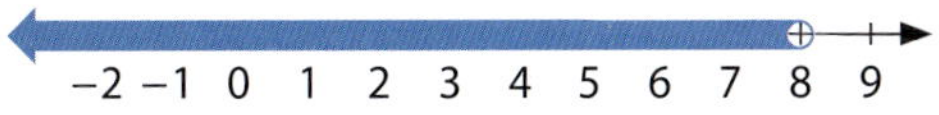

(v) $x \leq 2$, where $x \in \mathbb{Z}$

$\mathbb{Z}$ stands for the integers (whole positive and negative numbers and zero)

≤ symbol means x is less than or equal to 2

The arrow is placed at the end to show that x could be any integer below what is shown

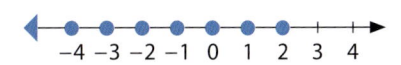

> Recall the { } brackets are used for listing elements of sets

(vi) $x = \{2, 1, 0, -1, -2, -3\}$

Practice questions 32.1

1. Using the inequality symbols, write an inequality to represent the following.
   (i) Tom is taller than Brian.
   (ii) A soccer field has a shorter length than a Gaelic football field.
   (iii) A tennis court is longer than a basketball court.
   (iv) Donegal airport's runway is shorter than Shannon airport's runway.

2. Insert the correct symbol, < or >, between the numbers below to make the statement true.
   (i) 42 ☐ 68
   (ii) −32 ☐ −68
   (iii) 32 ☐ −68
   (iv) −58 ☐ −720
   (v) 0 ☐ −98
   (vi) −3 ☐ −26

3. Copy and complete the table, stating whether each of the following mathematical statements is true or false.

Statement	True	False
(i) $3 \geq 8$		
(ii) $18 < 18$		
(iii) $-9 \leq -10$		
(iv) $-7 \leq -7$		

4. Copy the table below and write <, > or = in the middle box to make each of the mathematical statements true.

(i)	35		4×9
(ii)	73		7×10
(iii)	−40		5×8
(iv)	−35		7×5
(v)	3×6		$9 \times (-2)$
(vi)	$-2 \times (-6)$		-3×-4

5. Copy the table below and write <, > or = in the middle box to make each of the mathematical statements true.

(i)	900 cm		9·1 m
(ii)	500 g		0·5 kg
(iii)	4 000 cm³		3·98 litres
(iv)	5 km		20 × 50 m
(v)	200 cm		2·4 m
(vi)	300 g		0·28 kg
(vii)	3 000 ml		3 litres
(viii)	700 cm		6·7 m
(ix)	300 g		0·3 kg
(x)	5 000 ml		5·02 litres

6. Select the number line (a)–(d) that represents the inequality $x \geq 1$ where $x \in \mathbb{R}$. Explain your selection.

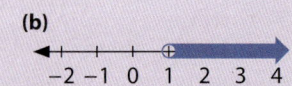

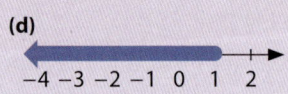

   (a) number line from −2 to 4, shaded from 1 rightwards with closed circle
   (b) number line from −2 to 4, shaded from 1 rightwards with open circle
   (c) number line from −4 to 2, shaded from 1 leftwards with open circle
   (d) number line from −4 to 2, shaded from 1 leftwards with closed circle

7. Write down an inequality which describes each of the number lines below, naming the number system in each case.

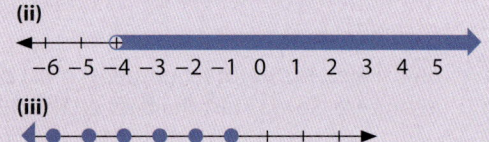

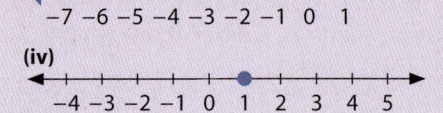

   (i) dots at 2, 3, 4, 5, 6, 7, 8, 9 on number line 0 to 9
   (ii) number line from −6 to 5, shaded from −3 rightwards with open circle
   (iii) dots at −7, −6, −5, −4, −3, −2 on number line −7 to 1
   (iv) number line from −4 to 5, closed circle at 1

8. Represent the following inequalities on a number line and list the first five elements of the solution set.
   (i) $x > 3$ where $x \in \mathbb{N}$
   (ii) $x < 7$ where $x \in \mathbb{N}$
   (iii) $x \leq 4$ where $x \in \mathbb{Z}$
   (iv) $-5 \leq x$ where $x \in \mathbb{Z}$

9. Represent the following inequalities on a number line.
   (i) $x \geq -2$ where $x \in \mathbb{N}$
   (ii) $x \leq 3$ where $x \in \mathbb{Z}$
   (iii) $x \leq 2$ where $x \in \mathbb{R}$
   (iv) $x \geq -2$ where $x \in \mathbb{R}$

10. Represent the following inequalities on a number line.
    (i) $x \geq -6$ where $x \in \mathbb{N}$
    (ii) $x < 3.5$ where $x \in \mathbb{Z}$
    (iii) $x < 8$ where $x \in \mathbb{R}$
    (iv) $x > -5$ where $x \in \mathbb{R}$

32.2 Solving linear inequalities

By the end of this section you should be able to:
- solve linear inequalities with one variable

Solving linear inequalities is very similar to solving linear equations.

That is we follow the rule, **whatever we do to one side of the inequality we do to the other**.

The aim of solving a linear inequality ($<$ $>$ $\leq$ $\geq$) with one variable is the same aim as for equations with equals signs: to **isolate the variable** on one side of the inequality.

> On our course we will only solve inequalities where $ax + b \leq k$, where $a \in \mathbb{N}$ and b and $k \in \mathbb{Z}$.

Worked example

Solve the following inequalities and show the solution on a number line.

(i) $5x - 2 < 18$ where $x \in \mathbb{N}$

(ii) $4a + 6 \geq 2$ where $a \in \mathbb{Z}$

Solution

(i) $5x - 2 < 18$
$5x < 18 + 2$
$\frac{5x}{5} < \frac{20}{5}$
$x < 4$ where $x \in \mathbb{N}$

(ii) $4a + 6 \geq 2$
$4a \geq 2 - 6$
$\frac{4a}{4} \geq \frac{-4}{4}$
$a \geq -1$ where $a \in \mathbb{Z}$

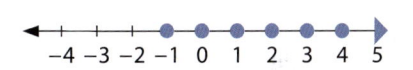

Practice questions 32.2

1. Solve the following inequalities and show the solution on a number line.
   (i) $3x - 8 > 16$ where $x \in \mathbb{R}$
   (ii) $2x - 1 < 9$ where $x \in \mathbb{N}$
   (iii) $3y - 4 > 17$ where $y \in \mathbb{Z}$
   (iv) $3b + 4 \leq 13$ where $b \in \mathbb{R}$

2. Solve the following inequalities and show the solution on a number line.
   (i) $x + 1 \geq 5$ where $x \in \mathbb{R}$
   (ii) $6y - 5 < 7$ where $y \in \mathbb{N}$
   (iii) $4x + 3 \geq -1$ where $x \in \mathbb{Z}$
   (iv) $y - 2 \geq 6$ where $y \in \mathbb{R}$

3. Solve the following inequalities and show the solution on a number line.
   (i) $6z + 7 \leq 1$ where $z \in \mathbb{R}$
   (ii) $y - 6 \leq 1$ where $y \in \mathbb{Z}$
   (iii) $3x + 29 < 83$ where $x \in \mathbb{Z}$
   (iv) $5y + 38 \geq 3$ where $y \in \mathbb{N}$

4. Solve the following inequalities and show the solution on a number line.
   (i) $4z + 7 \leq 27$ where $z \in \mathbb{Z}$
   (ii) $5z - 6 \geq -1$ where $z \in \mathbb{R}$
   (iii) $3x - 5 \geq -2$ where $x \in \mathbb{N}$
   (iv) $-7 + 2x \leq 1$ where $x \in \mathbb{N}$

5. Solve the following inequalities and show the solution on a number line.
   (i) $x + 3 > -6$ where $x \in \mathbb{N}$
   (ii) $5z + 8 > -7$ where $z \in \mathbb{N}$
   (iii) $3x + 16 \geq -20$ where $x \in \mathbb{Z}$
   (iv) $4x - 40 > -8$ where $x \in \mathbb{R}$

6. Write down the smallest three integer values of x that make this inequality true.

   $3x - 5 \geq 11$

Section C Applying our skills

7. Diarmuid has a €30 online gift voucher. He plans to buy as many books as he can. The cost of each book is €4. There is also a single shipping charge of €2.

    (i) Write an inequality to represent Diarmuid's situation.

    (ii) Use your answers from part **(i)** to find the maximum number of books Diarmuid can afford without spending more than his gift voucher amount.

Taking it FURTHER

8. Oisín is y years old. Michael is 9 years younger than Oisín. The sum of their ages is less than 41.

    (i) Write down in terms of y, an inequality to show this information.

    (ii) Work out the oldest age that Oisín can be. Give your answer as a whole number of years.

9. Ann, Mary and Angela go shopping. Ann spends m euros. Mary spends twice as much as Ann. Angela spends 5 euros more than Ann. The total amount of money spent, in euros, is more than €60.

    (i) Write down, in terms of m, an inequality to show this information.

    (ii) Each girl spends a whole number of euros. Work out the least each girl could have spent.

Revision questions

32A Core skills

1. Represent the following inequalities on a number line.

    (i) $x < 3$ where $x \in \mathbb{Z}$

    (ii) $x > -6$ where $x \in \mathbb{R}$

    (iii) $x > -5$ where $x \in \mathbb{N}$

    (iv) $x < 3$ where $x \in \mathbb{N}$

    (v) $x \leq 2$ where $x \in \mathbb{Z}$

    (vi) $x > -4$ where $x \in \mathbb{Z}$

2. Solve the following inequalities and show the solution on a number line.

    (i) $x + 5 > 12$ where $x \in \mathbb{N}$

    (ii) $3x - 7 < 5$ where $x \in \mathbb{R}$

    (iii) $3b + 2 > 8$ where $b \in \mathbb{R}$

3. Using the numbers in red below each inequality, decide which of the values for x satisfy each inequality ($x \in \mathbb{R}$).

    (i) $9(2 + 3x) < 72$
         1 3 −1 4

    (ii) $2(3x - 2) > -52$
         −10 −6 −8 −9

    (iii) $4(2x + 5) < -44$
         10 −8 −9 −10

4. Solve the following inequalities and show the solution on a number line.

    (i) $3(6x + 2) < 42$ where $x \in \mathbb{Z}$

    (ii) $8(1 + 2b) < 40$ where $b \in \mathbb{R}$

    (iii) $8x + 4 < 12$ where $x \in \mathbb{R}$

    (iv) $5y - 2 > 8$ where $y \in \mathbb{Z}$

5. Using the inequality $4 + x \leq 2$ where $x \in \mathbb{Z}$, find the answers to the following questions.
   (i) Find at least five numbers that make this inequality true.
   (ii) What is the largest number that makes this inequality true?
   (iii) On a number line, represent, all the numbers that make this inequality true.

6. Using the inequality $3x - 5 < 4$, find the answers to the following questions where $x \in \mathbb{Z}$.
   (i) Find at least five numbers that make this inequality true.
   (ii) How many solutions are there in total?
   (iii) What is the largest number that makes this true?

32B Taking it FURTHER

1. Write this mathematical sentence using algebra:
   6 is added to a number x. Then the result is multiplied by 9. The final answer is greater than 99.

2. Write this mathematical sentence using algebra:
   7 is subtracted from a number y. Then the result is multiplied by 3. The final answer is less than or equal to 12.

3. Write this mathematical sentence using algebra:
   A number z is multiplied by 4. Then 8 is subtracted from the result. The final answer is greater than or equal to 28.

4. A rectangular storage room fits at least 7 tables such that each have 1 square metre of surface area. The perimeter of the room is 16 m. What could the width and length of the room be?

5. Cillian has €500 in a savings account at the beginning of the summer. He wants to have at least €200 in the account by the end of the summer. He withdraws €25 each week for food, clothes and movie tickets.
   (i) Write an inequality that represents Cillian's situation.
   (ii) For how many weeks can Cillian withdraw money from his account? Justify your answer.

6. Glenties Taxi Service charges a €2·20 flat rate in addition to €0·65 per kilometre. Katie has no more than €10 to spend on a taxi fare.
   (i) Write an inequality that represents Katie's situation.
   (ii) How many kilometres can Katie travel without exceeding her budget? Justify your answer.

7. Gerry already has €50, but needs a total of at least €250 for his holiday. He gets paid €20 per day for delivering papers. What is the least number of days he must work to get enough money for his holiday?

Now that you have completed the unit, revisit the

Something to think about ...

question posed at the start of this unit.

Now try questions 2, 3 and 10 on pages 558–61

Unit 33

Non-linear relationships

Topics covered within this unit:

33·1 Non-linear patterns

33·2 Quadratic functions

33·3 Multiplying linear expressions revision

33·4 Factorising – Difference of two squares (quadratic expression)

33·5 Factorising – Quadratic trinomial expressions 1 (positive constant)

33·6 Factorising – Quadratic trinomial expressions 2 (negative constant)

33·7 Dividing expressions

33·8 Solving quadratic equations

The Learning Outcomes covered in this unit are contained in the following sections:

AF.3b | AF.3c | AF.3d.IV | AF.3d.V
AF.2c | AF.4b | AF.7a | AF.7b

Key words

Non-linear pattern
Second difference
Quadratic pattern
Minimum
Maximum
Quadratic function
Parabola
Quadratic expression
Double brackets
Quadratic trinomial
Two squares
Root

Something to think about ...

KEY SKILLS

The table shows the heights of a football at various times after a footballer kicks the ball to a teammate from a podium.

Time (seconds)	0	0·5	0·75	1	1·25	1·5	1·75	2	2·5
Height (metres)	6	22	27	30	31	30	27	22	6

If you were to graph the height of the ball against time, do you think this would be a linear graph?

If not, what shape do you think the graph will be?

Justify your answers.

33·1 Non-linear patterns

By the end of this section you should be able to:

○ identify a quadratic pattern

○ recognise a pattern as being linear or non-linear

In Section A, Unit 7 of this book, we learned that a pattern is linear when the first difference (the difference between the terms) is the same. When a linear pattern is graphed, it forms a straight line.

T_1 — T_2 — T_3 — T_4 — T_5

First difference | First difference | First difference | First difference

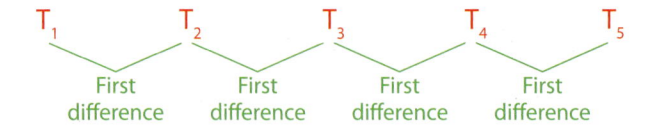

Example of a linear pattern: 5, 8, 11, 14, 17

The first difference in this linear pattern is +3

Consider the following pattern of numbers: 3, 6, 11, 18, 27

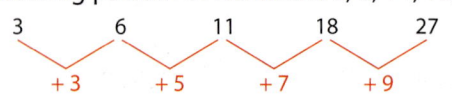

3 — 6 — 11 — 18 — 27
 +3   +5   +7   +9

The first difference between each term is not the same, so this pattern is **non-linear**.

A **non-linear pattern** is a pattern that does not form a straight line when graphed.

> On your course, you must be able to identify a pattern as being linear or non-linear.

Sometimes when we look at the difference of the first differences (**the second differences**) we may be able to see a pattern. In this case, each of the second differences is the same. They are all +2.

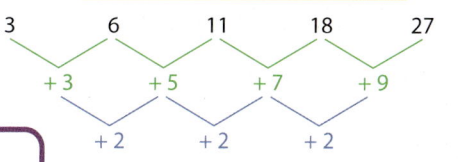

$$3 \quad 6 \quad 11 \quad 18 \quad 27$$
$$+3 \quad +5 \quad +7 \quad +9$$
$$+2 \quad +2 \quad +2$$

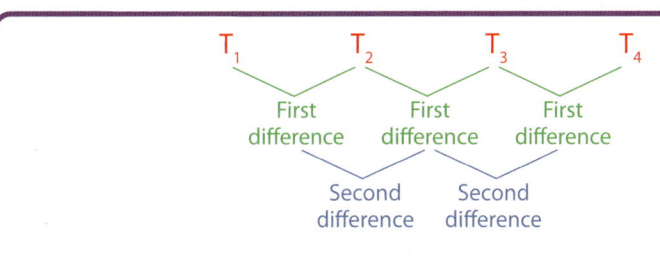

$T_1 \quad T_2 \quad T_3 \quad T_4$
First difference, First difference, First difference
Second difference, Second difference

The **second difference** is the difference between the first differences.

A sequence of numbers has a **quadratic pattern** when its second difference is constant (equal).

A quadratic pattern will be a curve and not a straight line when graphed. For this reason, quadratic patterns are non-linear patterns. Every quadratic pattern, when graphed, either:

decreases to a minimum before it starts to increase again (U-shaped or trough)

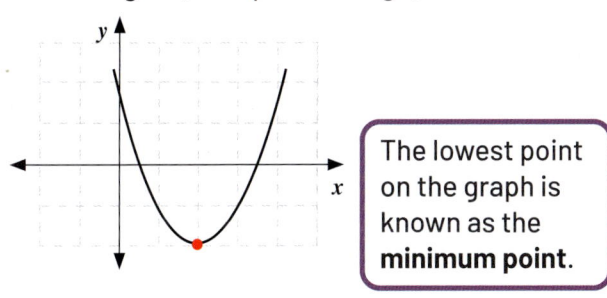

increases to a maximum before it starts to decrease again (∩-shaped or peaked).

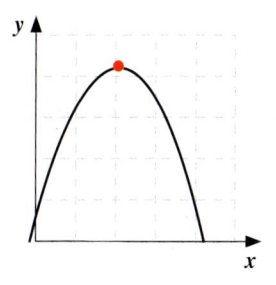

The lowest point on the graph is known as the **minimum point**.

The highest point on the graph is known as the **maximum point**.

Other non-linear patterns

Consider the following pattern of numbers: 2, 4, 8, 16, 32, 64, 128

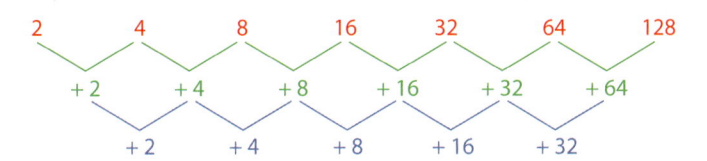

$$2 \quad 4 \quad 8 \quad 16 \quad 32 \quad 64 \quad 128$$
$$+2 \quad +4 \quad +8 \quad +16 \quad +32 \quad +64$$
$$+2 \quad +4 \quad +8 \quad +16 \quad +32$$

> Can you see a pattern or rule that describes the change from one term to the next?

The first or second **differences are not the same**, so this pattern is not linear and it is not quadratic. If you look at the values in the pattern, you will see that they are doubling every time.

Linear and non-linear graphs

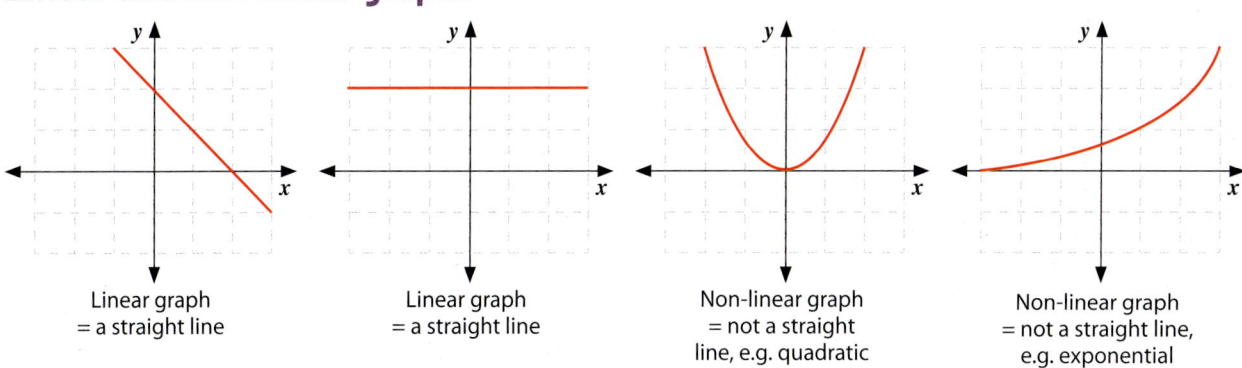

Linear graph = a straight line

Linear graph = a straight line

Non-linear graph = not a straight line, e.g. quadratic

Non-linear graph = not a straight line, e.g. exponential

Section C Applying our skills

Worked example

(a) State whether each of the following sequences of numbers are linear or non-linear give a reason for your answer.

(b) Draw a graph of each of the patterns putting the term position (e.g. term 1, term 2, etc.) on the x-axis.

(i) 11, 18, 29, 44, 63

(ii) 7, 14, 21, 28, 35

Solution

(i) (a) 11, 18 (+7), 29 (+11), 44 (+15), 63 (+19)

This is a non-linear pattern

Reason: the first differences are not the same

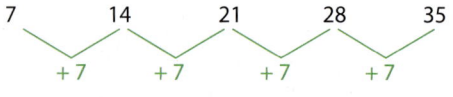

(b) [Graph showing points (1,11), (2,18), (3,29), (4,44), (5,63) with curved trend]

(ii) (a) 7, 14 (+7), 21 (+7), 28 (+7), 35 (+7)

This is a linear pattern

Reason: the first difference is the same.

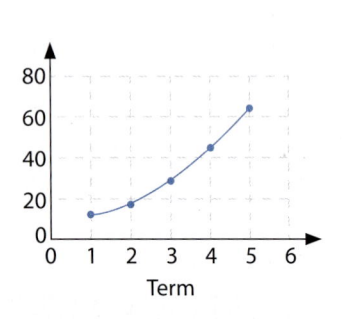

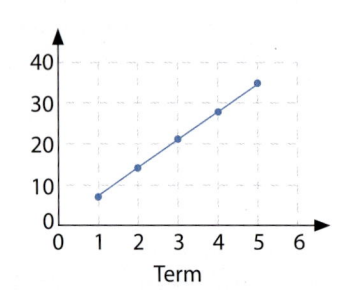

(b) [Graph showing points (1,7), (2,14), (3,21), (4,28), (5,35) in a straight line]

Practice questions 33·1

1. Determine whether each table or graph represents a linear or nonlinear function. Give a reason for your answer.

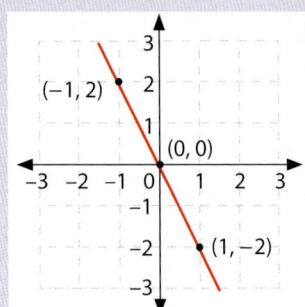

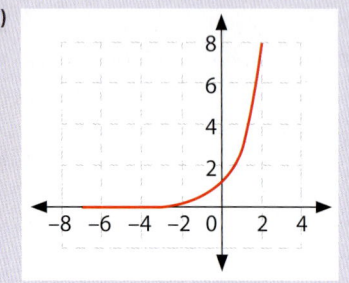

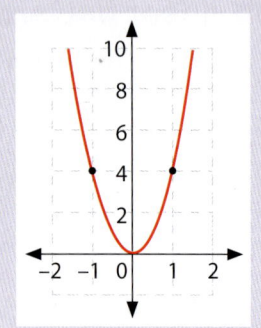

   (i) [Graph of a straight line passing through (−1, 2), (0, 0), (1, −2)]

   (iii) [Graph of an exponential-like curve]

   (v) [Graph of a parabola (U-shape)]

   (ii)
x	1	2	3	4
y	4	8	12	16

   (iv)
x	1	2	3	4
y	1	2	6	24

Linking Thinking 1

2. **(a)** State whether each of the following sequences of numbers are linear or non-linear. Give a reason for your answer.

   (i) 7, 12, 22, 37, … (ii) 6, 12, 18, … (iii) 1, 4, 9, 16, 25, …

   (b) Draw a graph of each of these sequences, putting the term position on the x-axis.

3. **(a)** State whether each of the following sequences of numbers are linear or non-linear. Give a reason for your answer.

   (i) 3, 6, 11, 18, 27, … (ii) 12, 24, 48, 96, … (iii) 7, 15, 23, 31, …

   (b) Draw a graph of each of these sequences, putting the term position on the x-axis.

4. **(a)** State whether each of the following sequences of numbers are linear or non-linear. Give a reason for your answer.

   (i) 6, 10, 14, 18, 27, … (ii) 61, 59, 55, 49, 41, … (iii) 4, 12, 36, 108, …

   (b) Draw a graph of each of these sequences, putting the term position on the x-axis.

5. **(i)** Draw the next pattern in the sequence.

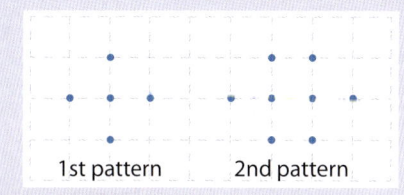

   1st pattern   2nd pattern

   (ii) The table below shows the number of dots used to make each pattern. Copy and complete the table.

Pattern number	1	2	3	4	5
Number of dots	5				

   (iii) Is the pattern of the number of dots linear or non-linear?

   Taking it FURTHER

6. Here is a sequence of patterns made from tiles.

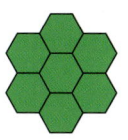

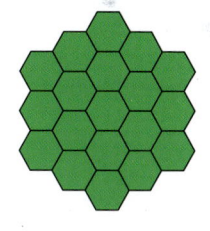

   Pattern 1   Pattern 2   Pattern 3

   (i) The table below shows the number of tiles used to make each pattern. Copy and complete the table.

Pattern number	1	2	3	4	5
Number of tiles	1				

   (ii) What type of pattern is formed by the number of tiles?

33.2 Quadratic functions

By the end of this section you should be able to:
- recognise a quadratic function
- graph a quadratic function

Recall that a function is a rule that changes an input into an output.

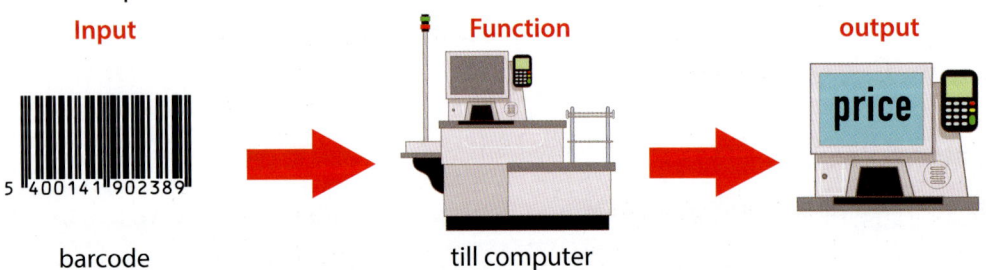

Input — barcode
Function — till computer
output — price

A **quadratic function** (in Latin, *quadratus* means 'squared') is a function in which the highest-power of the variable is 2, i.e. a function that looks like $f(x) = ax^2 + bx + c$, where a, b, and c are real numbers ($\mathbb{R}$) and where a is not equal to zero.

The graph of a quadratic function is a curve called a **parabola**.

A **parabola** is a curve that is symmetrical and is approximately U-shaped or ∩-shaped.

Parabolas may open **upward** or **downward** and vary in **width** or **steepness**, but they all have the same basic curved shape.

The diagram opposite shows three graphs (red, green and blue), all of which are parabolas.

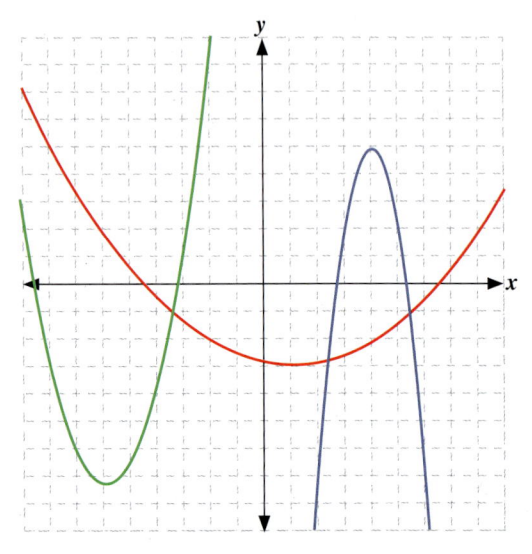

Graphing quadratic functions

1. Use an input-output table to find the points on the graph.

Input	Function	Output	Points
x	$ax^2 + bx + c$	y	(x, y)

2. The whole numbers from the lowest value to the highest value in the given domain will be used as the x-values for the points to be graphed. These numbers should be placed into the input or x-column in the table. For example, if the given domain is $-2 \leq x \leq 3$, then fill in the input x-column with $-2, -1, 0, 1, 2, 3$

3. Using the rows in the table, substitute in each of the x-values into the function to find the y-values of the points to be graphed.

4. Create the points to be graphed by pairing each of the x-values with its corresponding y-values in the rows in the table.

5. Draw an x- and y-axis, and plot the points from the table.

6. Join the points from step 4 in one continuous **smooth curve** (without using a ruler) to form the graph.

Worked example

Graph the function $f(x) = -x^2 + x + 1$ in the domain $-3 \leq x \leq 4$, where $x \in \mathbb{R}$.

Solution

Steps 1 and 2

The given domain is $-3 \leq x \leq 4$, so the whole numbers from -3 to 4 are $-3, -2, -1, 0, 1, 2, 3, 4$

These are placed in the input (x) column.

Input	Function	Output	Points
x	$-x^2 + x + 1$	y	(x, y)
-3	$-(-3)^2 + (-3) + 1$	-11	$(-3, -11)$
-2	$-(-2)^2 + (-2) + 1$	-5	$(-2, -5)$
-1	$-(-1)^2 + x(-1) + 1$	-1	$(-1, -1)$
0	$-(0)^2 + (0) + 1$	1	$(0, 1)$
1	$-(1)^2 + (1) + 1$	1	$(1, 1)$
2	$-(2)^2 + (2) + 1$	-1	$(2, -1)$
3	$-(3)^2 + (3) + 1$	-5	$(3, -5)$
4	$-(4)^2 + (4) + 1$	-11	$(4, -11)$

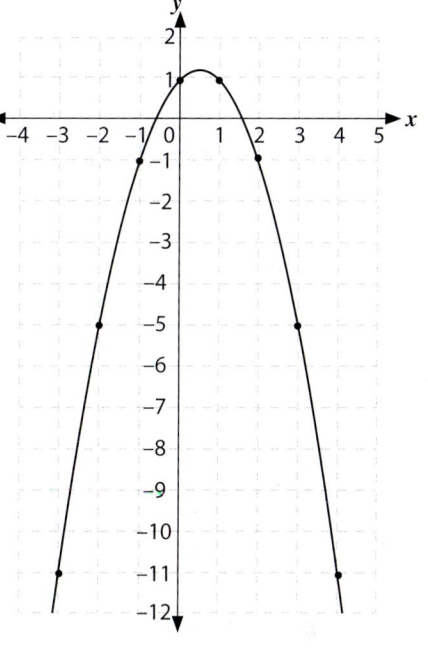

Step 3 ↑ (Input column)   Step 4 ↑ (Points column)

Steps 5 and 6

Discuss and discover

(i) Working with a classmate, graph each of the following graphs in the domain $-3 \leq x \leq 3$, where $x \in \mathbb{R}$, using the method in the example above.

Graph A: $y = x^2$

Graph B: $y = x^2 - 2x$

Graph C: $y = -x^2$

Graph D: $y = -x^2 - 2x$

(ii) What shape are graphs A and B?

(iii) What shape are graphs C and D?

(iv) What do you think is determining the shape of the graphs?

(v) Discuss anything you have learned about quadratic graphs from carrying out this task with a classmate.

Practice questions 33.2

1. (i) Complete the table for the equation $y = x^2$

x	−4	−3	−2	−1	0	1	2
y	16		4		0		4

   (ii) Draw $y = x^2$ on a coordinate plane.

   (iii) Describe the shape of your graph.

2. (i) Complete the table for the equation $y = x^2 + 2$

x	−3	−2	−1	0	1	2	3
y	11		3		3		11

   (ii) Draw $y = x^2 + 2$ on a coordinate plane.

   (iii) Describe the shape of your graph.

3. (i) Complete the table for the equation $y = x^2 − x$

x	−3	−2	−1	0	1	2
y	12		2		0	

   (ii) Draw $y = x^2 − x$ on a coordinate plane.

4. Graph the function $f(x) = x^2 + x$ in the domain $-2 \leq x \leq 3$, where $x \in \mathbb{R}$.

5. Draw the graph of $y = x^2 + x − 3$ in the domain $-5 \leq x \leq 4$, where $x \in \mathbb{R}$.

6. Draw the graph of $y = -x^2 − 2x − 3$ in the domain $-4 \leq x \leq 2$, where $x \in \mathbb{R}$.

7. Graph the function $f(x) = x^2 − 3x − 4$ in the domain $-2 \leq x \leq 5$, where $x \in \mathbb{R}$.

8. Draw the graph of $y = -x^2 − 3x − 4$ in the domain $-2 \leq x \leq 5$, where $x \in \mathbb{R}$.

9. Graph the function $g(x) = x^2 − 6x + 5$ in the domain $-1 \leq x \leq 7$, where $x \in \mathbb{R}$.

> A graph with a positive x^2 is U-shaped.
> A graph with a negative x^2 is ∩-shaped.

33.3 Multiplying linear expressions revision

By the end of this section you should be able to:
- multiply two linear expressions

A **linear expression** is one in which the highest power of each variable is 1.

In Section A, we learned how to multiply, or expand, a linear expression by a term. For example:

$$3(2x − 5) = 6x − 15$$

> A **quadratic expression** is an expression where the highest power is a squared term, e.g. $x^2 + 1$, $2a^2 + 4a + 6$ or a product term, e.g. $3xy − 2x + 1$

Now we will look at multiplying (expanding) two linear expressions. The resulting expression of this is called a quadratic expression.

Writing two brackets, with linear expressions in them, **next to each other**, means the expressions need to be multiplied together.

> **Double brackets** are two brackets next to each other.

For example, examine the double brackets below. There is a linear expression in each set of brackets.

$$(2a + b)(3x + 2y)$$

When expanding double brackets, every term in the first set of brackets has to be multiplied by every term in the second set of brackets. It is helpful to always multiply the terms in order, so none are forgotten.

Multiplying two expressions – Strategy 1

1. Split one of the expressions into its terms (normally the first expression or the expression with the fewest terms).
2. Multiply the second expression by each term identified in step 1.
3. Simplify the resulting expression if possible.

Worked example 1

Simplify $(x + 2)(x - 3)$

Solution

Step 1 Terms in the first expression are x and $+ 2$

Step 2 Multiply the second expression by each term identified in step 1

$$x(x - 3) + 2(x - 3)$$
$$x^2 - 3x + 2x - 6$$

> x multiplied by x equals x^2

Step 3 Simplify the resulting expression if possible.

$$x^2 - x - 6$$

A **quadratic trinomial** is a quadratic expression with three terms in the form $ax^2 + bx + c$ where a, b and c are real numbers but not zero.

Quadratic (highest power is two)

$$ax^2 + bx + c$$

Trinomial (three terms)

Worked example 2

Simplify
(i) $(3a - 2)(3a + 2)$
(ii) $(x - 2)^2$

Solution

(i) $(3a - 2)(3a + 2)$

Step 1 Terms in the first expression are $3a$ and -2

Step 2 $3a(3a + 2) - 2(3a + 2)$
$9a^2 + 6a - 6a - 4$

Step 3 $9a^2 - 4$

(ii) $(x - 2)^2 = (x - 2)(x - 2)$

Step 1 Terms in the first expression are x and -2

Step 2 $x(x - 2) - 2(x - 2)$
$x^2 - 2x - 2x + 4$

Step 3 $x^2 - 4x + 4$

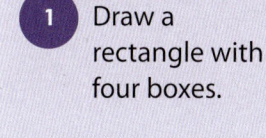

Multiplying two expressions – Strategy 2 (array method)

1. Draw a rectangle with four boxes.

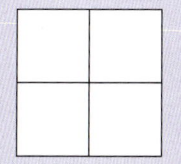

2. Place the terms on each side of the rectangle.

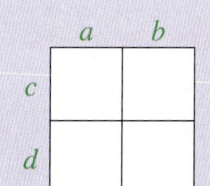

	a	b
c		
d		

3. Multiply the terms for the sides of each of the small rectangles by each other.

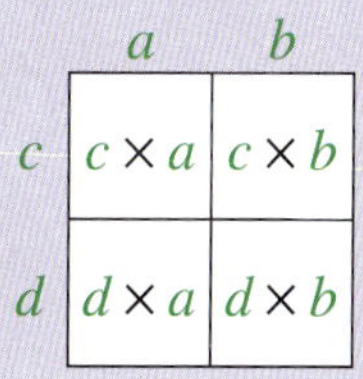

	a	b
c	c × a	c × b
d	d × a	d × b

4. Simplify, if possible, the four terms formed in step 3:
$ac + cb + ad + bd$

Section C Applying our skills

Worked example 3

Simplify $(x + 2)(x - 4)$

Solution

Step 1 Draw a rectangle with four boxes.

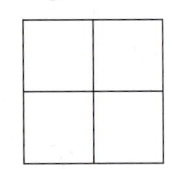

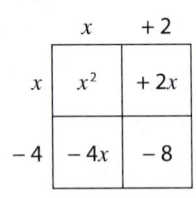

Step 2 Place the terms on each side of the rectangle.

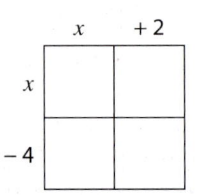

	x	$+2$
x		
-4		

Step 3 Multiply the terms for the sides of each of the small rectangles.

	x	$+2$
x	x^2	$+2x$
-4	$-4x$	-8

Step 4 Simplify the four terms formed in step 3.

$x^2 - 4x + 2x - 8$

$x^2 - 2x - 8$

Practice questions 33.3

1. Expand and simplify the following.
   - (i) $5(x + 4)$
   - (ii) $x(2 + x)$
   - (iii) $2y(3y - 3)$
   - (iv) $y(x + 1)$
   - (v) $4a(3b - a)$
   - (vi) $s(t - 2s)$

2. Expand and simplify the following.
   - (i) $(a + 3)(a + 4)$
   - (ii) $(3x + 1)(2 + x)$
   - (iii) $(y + 1)(2 + y)$
   - (iv) $(x + 1)(x + 1)$
   - (v) $(4x + 2)^2$
   - (vi) $(5 + 2m)^2$

3. Expand and simplify the following.
   - (i) $(2x - 5)(x + 2)$
   - (ii) $(2x - 3)(3x - 2)$
   - (iii) $(3x - 1)(2 - x)$
   - (iv) $(x + 1)(x - 1)$
   - (v) $(7x + 4)(7x - 4)$
   - (vi) $(x - 6)^2$

4. Expand and simplify the following.
   - (i) $(x + 5)(x - 1)$
   - (ii) $(a + 2)(a - 3)$
   - (iii) $(k + 1)(k - 3)$
   - (iv) $(x - 2)^2$
   - (v) $(3x + 1)(2x - 2)$
   - (vi) $(2b + 3)(b - 1)$

5. Expand and simplify the following.
   - (i) $(x + 2)(x - 1)$
   - (ii) $(x + 3)(x - 1)$
   - (iii) $(2c - 1)(5c + 2)$
   - (iv) $(x + 5)(x - 2)$
   - (v) $5(n - 1) - 2(n - 4)$
   - (vi) $-2(c + 2) - 2(c - 3)$

33.4 Factorising – Difference of two squares (quadratic expression)

By the end of this section you should be able to:
- factorise an expression, which is in the form of the difference of two squared terms

In Section 33.3, we were given the factors and we had to find the equivalent unfactored expression. Now we are given an unfactored expression and asked to find the factors, i.e. to 'factorise' the expression.

> A **two squares** quadratic expression is a quadratic expression where it is possible to write both terms as a perfect square, e.g. $9a^2 - 4$ can be written as $(3a)^2 - (2)^2$

A special case concerns what is known as the **difference of two squares**.

Area of square A is equal to $x \times x = x^2$
Area of square B is equal to $y \times y = y^2$

A square number is the product of a number multiplied by itself.

Subtraction (or the difference) of the area of **square B** away from area of **square A** is equal to $x^2 - y^2$

To factorise this, we need **a factor pair such** that the product of the pair of brackets is equal to $x^2 - y^2$

$(x - y)(x + y)$
$x(x + y) - y(x + y)$
$x^2 + xy - xy - y^2$
$x^2 - y^2$

We use this to factorise an expression that is the difference of two squares: **we do it in reverse.**

This method does not work for the sum of two squares, e.g. $x^2 + y^2$

Factorising the difference of two squares $x^2 - y^2$

1 Write both terms as perfect squares with brackets:

$$(x)^2 - (y)^2$$

1st square | 2nd square

Where x or y is normally a square number, such as 1, 4, 9, 16, 25, 36, 49, 64, 81, 100, 121, 144 …

2 Form two factors for the expression. The signs in the two brackets will always be opposite.

$$(x + y)(x - y)$$

One factor | Another factor

Worked example 1

Factorise fully the expression $x^2 - 144$

Solution

We must first identify that this is the difference of two squares; x^2 is a square and if we calculate $\sqrt{144}$ we find that it is whole number 12. Therefore, 144 is a square number.

$x^2 - 144$

Step 1 Write both terms as perfect squares with brackets.

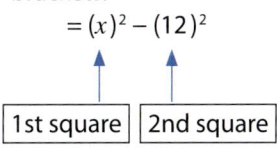

$= (x)^2 - (12)^2$

1st square | 2nd square

Step 2 Form two factors for the expression.

$(x - 12)(x + 12)$

*$\sqrt{144} = 12$
Likewise:
$\sqrt{x^2} = x$*

Section C Applying our skills

Worked example 2

Factorise fully the expression $1 - n^2$

Solution

We must first identify that this is the difference of two squares; n^2 is a square and if we calculate $\sqrt{1}$ we find that it is whole number 1. Therefore 1 is a square number.

$1 - n^2$ ← Two squares

Step 1 Write both terms as perfect squares with brackets
$= (1)^2 - (n)^2$
↑ 1st square ↑ 2nd square

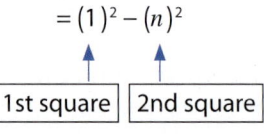

Step 2 Form two factors for the expression
$(1 - n)(1 + n)$

$\sqrt{1} = 1$
Likewise:
$\sqrt{n^2} = n$

Practice questions 33.4

1. Find the original expressions which have the following factor pairs.
   - (i) $(x - 4)(x + 4)$
   - (ii) $(x - 2)(x + 2)$
   - (iii) $(m + 2)(m - 2)$
   - (iv) $(x - 1)(x + 1)$

2. Fill in the expression missing from the following.
   - (i) $x^2 - 4 = (x + 2)(\quad)$
   - (ii) $(x^2 - 225) = (x - 15)(\quad)$
   - (iii) $(x^2 - 10\,000) = (x - 100)(\quad)$

3. Factorise the following quadratic expressions fully.
   - (i) $x^2 - 9$
   - (ii) $x^2 - 25$
   - (iii) $n^2 - 144$

4. Factorise the following quadratic expressions fully.
   - (i) $x^2 - 1$
   - (ii) $t^2 - 100$
   - (iii) $x^2 - 400$

5. Factorise the following quadratic expressions fully.
   - (i) $x^2 - 49$
   - (ii) $x^2 - 169$
   - (iii) $y^2 - 81$

6. If square A has side length of 4 units and square B has a side length x, find a term for the area of each square. Hence, write an expression for the difference in area of these two squares.

7. If square A has side length 2 and square B has a side length w, find a term for area of each square. Hence, write an expression for the difference in area of these two squares.

8. Factorise the following quadratic expressions fully.
   - (i) $y^2 - 196$
   - (ii) $121 - x^2$
   - (iii) $36 - p^2$
   - (iv) $a^2 - b^2$
   - (v) $w^2 - t^2$
   - (vi) $x^2 - y^2$

Taking it FURTHER

9. If the expression $9 - x^2$ describes the difference in area of two squares, write down a term for the perimeter of each of the two squares.

10. If the expression $a^2 - b^2$ describes the difference in area of two squares, write down a term for the perimeter of each of the two squares.

33.5 Factorising – Quadratic trinomial expressions 1 (positive constant)

By the end of this section you should be able to:
- factorise a quadratic trinomial expression, with a positive constant

We will look at two different methods to factorise quadratic trinomials.

Factorising quadratic trinomials – Strategy 1 (Cross method)

$x^2 + bx + c$

Left-hand side — Factors of x^2 term $(x)(x)$

Right-hand side — Factors of the constant, (c)

For our course, when factorising, all quadratic trinomials will begin with $1x^2$.

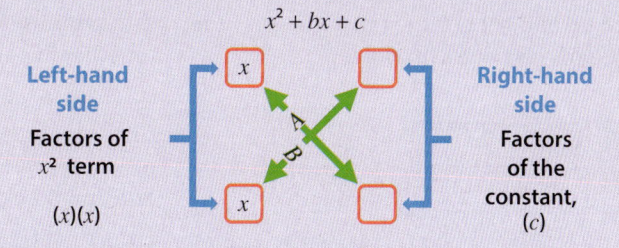

Be aware, if the middle term in the trinomial is negative, then the factors will both have a minus sign in the middle.

Multiply along diagonal A: (x)(bottom right box)
Multiply along diagonal B: $+ (x)$(top right box)
= the middle term (bx)

The factors are then read **left to right**: $(x + \text{top right})(x + \text{bottom right})$

Worked example 1

Factorise fully the expression $x^2 + 5x + 6$

Solution

$x^2 + 5x + 6$ Factors of $+6$: $(6)(1), (2)(3), (-6)(-1), (-2)(-3)$

The correct set of factors are found by the method of trial and improvement.

Attempt 1:

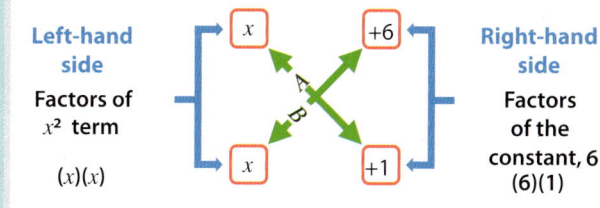

Left-hand side — Factors of x^2 term $(x)(x)$ — top: x, bottom: x

Right-hand side — Factors of the constant, 6 — top: $+6$, bottom: $+1$ — $(6)(1)$

$(x) \times (+1)$
$+ (x) \times (+6)$
$\overline{ 7x}$ ← this is **not** the required $5x$ term

Hence, we **reject** this option and try a different set of factors for the constant $+6$

Attempt 2:

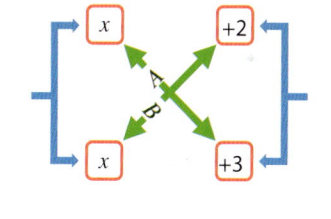

Left-hand side — Factors of x^2 term $(x)(x)$ — top: x, bottom: x

Right-hand side — Factors of the constant, 6 — top: $+2$, bottom: $+3$ — $(2)(3)$

$(x) \times (+3)$
$+ (x) \times (+2)$
$\overline{ 5x}$ ← this **is** the required $5x$ term

The factors are read left to right:
$(x + \text{top right})(x + \text{bottom right})$
$(x + 2)(x + 3)$

It doesn't matter in what order you put the factors (brackets).

Factorising quadratic trinomials – Strategy 2 (Guide number)

1. Find the 'guide number' by multiplying the coefficient of the x^2 term (the 'a' in ax^2) by the constant (c).
2. List the factor pairs of this guide number.
3. Chose a set of these factor pairs which add to give the x term (bx, the middle term).
4. Replace the x term (bx) with this factor pair.
5. Apply the factors by grouping method.

Worked example 2

Factorise $x^2 - 7x + 6$

Solution

This is the same example completed above. This time we will use the Guide number method.

Step 1 Find the guide number by multiplying the coefficient of the x^2 term by the constant (c)

$1 \times 6 = +6 =$ guide number

Step 2 List the factor pairs of +6 and choose the pair that add to give the coefficient of the middle term (–7).

Factors	Sum	Sum = +5
+1 × +6	+7	✗
–1 × –6	–7	✓
+2 × +3	+5	✗
–2 × –3	–5	✗

Step 3 Replace the x term (bx) with this factor pair.

$x^2 - 7x + 6$

$x^2 - 1x - 6x + 6$

Step 4 Apply the factors by grouping method (covered in Section B Unit 20).

$x^2 - 1x - 6x + 6$

(a) Group terms that have a common factor together in pairs.

$(x^2 - 1x) + (-6x + 6)$

(b) Factorise each pair of terms separately (using the HCF method) such that the two 2nd brackets are identical.

$x(x - 1) - 6(x - 1)$

(c) Place the common factor $(x - 1)$ in the front and the uncommon terms, x and –6, in a new 2nd bracket, as shown.

$(x - 1)(x - 6)$

Practice questions 33.5

1. Find the original equations that have the following factor pairs.
   (i) $(x + 4)(x + 6)$
   (ii) $(x + 2)(x + 10)$
   (iii) $(m - 5)(m - 3)$

2. Find an expression to represent the total area of a rectangular field if the length is represented by $(y + 10)$ and the width is represented by $(9 + y)$.

3. Complete the following equations.
   (i) $x^2 + 7x + 10 = (x + 2)(\quad)$
   (ii) $x^2 + 5x + 6 = (x + 3)(\quad)$

4. Factorise fully the following quadratic expressions.
   (i) $x^2 + 4x + 3$
   (ii) $x^2 + 3x + 2$
   (iii) $n^2 + 7n + 10$

5. Find two terms that will multiply to give the expression $x^2 - 7x + 12$

6. Factorise fully the following quadratic expressions.
   (i) $x^2 - 5x + 4$
   (ii) $x^2 - 8x + 12$
   (iii) $q^2 - 10q + 24$
   (iv) $x^2 - 13x + 12$

7. Factorise fully the following quadratic expressions.
   (i) $x^2 + 6x + 8$
   (ii) $x^2 + 14x + 45$
   (iii) $m^2 - 12m + 11$
   (iv) $w^2 + 7w + 10$

8. One side of a rectangle is represented by the expression $(x + 4)$ a second side by $(x + 10)$. Find an expression for the total area.

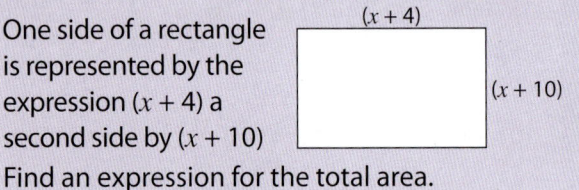

9. Factorise fully the following quadratic expressions.
   (i) $x^2 + 11x + 18$
   (ii) $p^2 - 11p + 10$
   (iii) $x^2 + 13x + 12$

10. For a moving object, distance travelled equals (speed)(time). If the total distance travelled by a car is $a^2 + 8a + 15$, find an expression to describe the speed and an expression to describe the time taken to travel the distance.

11. Factorise fully the following quadratic expressions.
    (i) $x^2 - 10x + 24$
    (ii) $x^2 + 14x + 45$
    (iii) $x^2 - 4x + 4$

12. Factorise fully and then verify your factors are correct by expanding them.

    (i) $x^2 + 6x + 9$
    (iii) $x^2 + 12x + 27$
    (ii) $x^2 + 19x + 48$

13. If the total area of a rectangular field is equal to $x^2 + 12x + 32$, find expressions for the length and width.

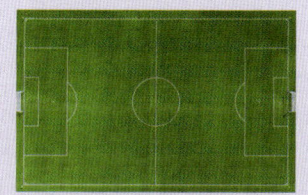

14. The fundamental principle of counting states if one event has m outcomes and another event has n outcomes, then the total number of possible outcomes from doing **both** events $= (m)(n)$

    An expression for the total number of possible outcomes from doing two events is $x^2 + 8x + 16$

    Find an expression, in terms of x, for the number of outcomes for each event.

33.6 Factorising – Quadratic trinomial expressions 2 (negative constant)

By the end of this section you should be able to:
○ factorise a quadratic trinomial expression with a negative constant

Quadratic (highest power is two)

$$ax^2 + bx - c$$

Trinomial (three terms)

For our course, $a = 1$ in all cases.

Here, the constant (c) is negative.

Strategy 1: Cross method, as covered in the previous section

This method is similar to the one outlined in the previous section, however the factors of the constant term will be of opposite sign.

Worked example 1

Factorise fully the expression $x^2 - 2x - 8$

Solution

$x^2 - 2x - 8$ Factors of -8: $(8)(-1), (2)(-4), (-8)(1), (-2)(4)$

Attempt 1:

Left-hand side
Factors of x^2 term
$(x)(x)$

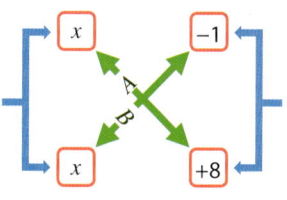

$x \quad -1$
$x \quad +8$

Right-hand side
Factors of the constant, -8
$(8)(-1)$

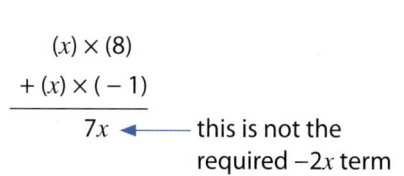

$(x) \times (8)$
$+ (x) \times (-1)$
———————
$7x$ ← this is not the required $-2x$ term

Hence, we reject this option and try another set of factors for the constant -8

Attempt 2:

Left-hand side
Factors of x^2 term
$(x)(x)$

$x \quad +2$
$x \quad -4$

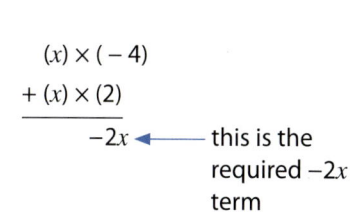

Right-hand side
Factors of the constant, -8
$(2)(-4)$

$(x) \times (-4)$
$+ (x) \times (2)$
———————
$-2x$ ← this is the required $-2x$ term

Hence the factors are read left to right
(top left + top right)(bottom left + bottom right)
$(x + 2)(x - 4)$

Strategy 2: Guide number, as covered in the previous section

Worked example 2

Factorise $x^2 - 9x - 22$

Solution

Step 1 Find the guide number by multiplying the coefficient of the x^2 term (1) by the constant (c).

$1 \times -22 = -22$ = guide number

Step 2 List the factor pairs of -22 and choose the pair that add to give the coefficient of the middle term (-9).

Factors	Sum	Sum = -9
-1×22	21	✗
2×-11	-9	✓

Step 3 Replace the x term (bx) with this factor pair.

$x^2 - 9x - 22$
$x^2 - 11x + 2x - 22$

Step 4 Apply the factors by grouping method (covered in Section B, Unit 20).

$x^2 - 11x + 2x - 22$

(a) Group terms that have a common factor together in pairs.

$(x^2 - 11x) + (2x - 22)$

(b) Factorise each pair of terms separately (using the HCF method) such that the two 2nd brackets are identical.

$x(x - 11) + 2(x - 11)$

(c) Place the common factor $(x - 11)$ in the front and the uncommon terms, x and $+2$, in a new 2nd bracket, as shown.

$(x - 11)(x + 2)$

Practice questions 33.6

1. Find the original equations which have the following factor pairs.
   - (i) $(x + 2)(x - 7)$
   - (ii) $(x - 3)(x + 8)$
   - (iii) $(m + 4)(m - 6)$

2. Find an expression to represent the total area of a rectangular field if the length is represented by $(y - 8)$ and the width is represented by $(y - 4)$.

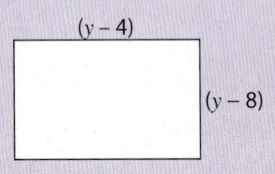

3. Complete the following equations.
   - (i) $x^2 + 7x - 18 = (x + 9)(\quad)$
   - (ii) $x^2 + x - 12 = (x - 3)(\quad)$

4. Find two expressions which multiply together to give the expression $x^2 - 4x - 12$

5. Factorise fully the following quadratic expressions.
   - (i) $x^2 + 5x - 6$
   - (ii) $x^2 - 2x - 3$
   - (iii) $m^2 - m - 12$
   - (iv) $w^2 - w - 6$

6. One side of a rectangle is represented by the expression $(x + 4)$ a second side is equal to $(x - 6)$. Find an expression for the total area.

7. Factorise fully the following quadratic expressions.
   - (i) $x^2 + 4x - 12$
   - (ii) $p^2 - p - 2$
   - (iii) $x^2 + x - 12$

8. For a moving object, distance travelled equals (speed)(time). If the total distance travelled by a car is $a^2 - 2a - 8$, find an expression to describe the speed and an expression to describe the time taken to travel the distance.

9. Factorise fully the following quadratic expressions.
   - (i) $x^2 - 5x - 24$
   - (ii) $x^2 - 2x - 24$
   - (iii) $x^2 + 3x - 40$

10. Factorise each of the following expressions. Verify your solutions by expanding the product of the factors.
    - (i) $x^2 + 8x - 20$
    - (ii) $x^2 - 28x - 60$
    - (iii) $x^2 + x - 2$
    - (iv) $x^2 - 2x - 8$

11. If the total area of a rectangular page is equal to $x^2 + 5x - 6$ find an expression for the length and an expression for the width.

12. Find two expressions that multiply together to give the resulting expression $x^2 - x - 42$

33.7 Dividing expressions

By the end of this section you should be able to:
○ divide a quadratic expression by a linear expression

Dividing a quadratic expression by a linear expression

In this section we will look at how to divide a quadratic expression by a linear expression.

(quadratic expression) ÷ (linear expression) is the same as $\frac{\text{quadratic expression}}{\text{linear expression}}$

Dividing a quadratic expression by a linear expression

1. Rewrite as a fraction (if not already a fraction).
2. Factorise the quadratic term.
3. Simplify by dividing the numerator and denominator by any common factors.
4. Write the simplified solution.

Worked example 1

Evaluate $\frac{x^2 - 3x - 10}{x + 2}$

Solution

Step 1 The question is already presented as a fraction, so we do not need to carry out step 1

$$\frac{x^2 - 3x - 10}{x + 2}$$

Step 2 Factorise the quadratic term using the guide number or the cross method

$$\frac{(x - 5)(x + 2)}{(x + 2)}$$

Step 3 Divide the numerator and the denominator by $(x + 2)$

$$\frac{(x - 5)\cancel{(x + 2)}\ (1)}{\cancel{(x + 2)}\ (1)}$$

Step 4 Write the simplified expression

$$x - 5$$

Worked example 2

Evaluate $x^2 - 4x - 21 \div x + 3$

Solution

Step 1 Rewrite the given problem as a fraction

$$\frac{x^2 - 4x - 21}{x + 3}$$

Step 2 Factorise the quadratic term using the guide number or the cross method

$$\frac{(x - 7)(x + 3)}{(x + 2)}$$

Step 3 Divide the numerator and the denominator by $(x + 3)$

$$\frac{(x - 7)\cancel{(x + 3)}\ (1)}{\cancel{(x + 3)}\ (1)}$$

Step 4 Write the simplified expression

$$x - 7$$

Section C Applying our skills

Practice questions 33·7

1. Evaluate the following expressions.
   (i) $(5a^2 + 6a) \div a$
   (ii) $(10x^2 - 4x) \div 2x$
   (iii) $(18y^2 + 6y) \div 6y$
   (iv) $(16y^2 - 32y) \div 16y$

2. Evaluate the following expressions.
   (i) $\dfrac{x^2 + 5x + 6}{x + 2}$
   (ii) $\dfrac{x^2 - 10x + 16}{x - 2}$
   (iii) $\dfrac{x^2 + x - 12}{x + 4}$

3. Evaluate the following expressions.
   (i) $\dfrac{x^2 + 3x + 2}{x + 1}$
   (ii) $\dfrac{x^2 + 7x + 12}{x + 3}$
   (iii) $\dfrac{x^2 - 11x + 24}{x - 8}$

4. Divide the quadratic expression $(x^2 + 2x - 15)$ by the linear expression $(x + 5)$

5. Divide $(x^2 - 9x - 10)$ by $(x + 1)$

6. Divide $(x^2 + 9x + 14)$ by $(x + 7)$

7. Divide $(x^2 - 3x - 10)$ by $(x - 5)$

8. The width of a rectangle is equal to (area) ÷ (length). The area of a rectangular football field is $t^2 + 17t - 18$ and its length is $t - 1$. Find the width of the football field, in terms of t.

9. The expression $x^2 + 9x + 14$ represents the number of people who go on a camping trip. Each tent can hold $x + 2$ people. Find an expression, in terms of x, for the number of tents the group need to bring.

10. Steve starts reading a new book. The book has $x^2 + 21x + 20$ pages and he reads $x + 1$ pages each night. Find an expression, in terms of x, for how many nights it will take Steve to finish the book.

11. $x^2 + 10x - 24$ children are waiting to get on a ride at an amusement park. Each carriage holds $x - 2$ people. Find an expression, in terms of x, for many carriages the children will fill.

33·8 Solving quadratic equations

By the end of this section you should be able to:
- solve quadratic expressions by factorising
- solve quadratic expressions by graphing

Solving quadratic equations by graphing

1 Graph the equation. This could be done by making a table of values as we did in section 33·2.

2 Identify the values for x where the graph crosses the x-axis. These are the solutions or roots of the function (i.e. the values of x where $y = 0$).

> A **root** is a point where the graph of an equation crosses the x-axis and is the value that, when substituted for the unknown variable in an equation, satisfies the equation.

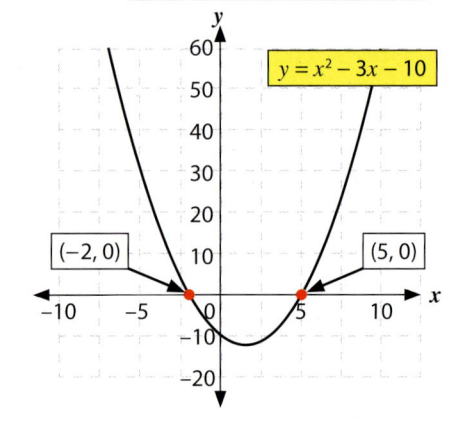

To solve the equation $x^2 - 3x - 10 = 0$ means to find the values of x for the function $y = x^2 - 3x - 10$, where $y = 0$. This occurs where the graph crosses the x-axis.

On the graph shown, the function $y = x^2 - 3x - 10$ crosses the x-axis at the points $(-2, 0)$ and $(5, 0)$.

The solutions of the equation $x^2 - 3x - 10 = 0$ are $x = -2$ and $x = 5$

These values are known as the **roots** of the function $y = x^2 - 3x - 10$.

534   Linking Thinking 1

Worked example 1

Solve the quadratic equation $-x^2 + 2x + 3 = 0$ using the graph of $y = -x^2 + 2x + 3$ shown.

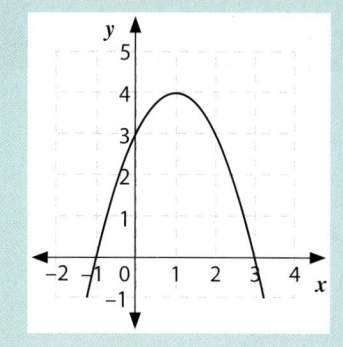

Solution

The solutions to the equation are the points at which the graph crosses the x-axis.
In this case, the solutions are $x = -1$ and $x = 3$, read from the graph.

Solving quadratic equations by factorising

1. Factorise the quadratic expression.

2. Let each factor equal zero, forming two new equations.

3. Solve each of the equations formed in step 2 to find the solutions for the original equation.

Worked example 2

Solve the equation $x^2 + 2x - 3 = 0$ by factorising.

Solution

$x^2 + 2x - 3 = 0$

Step 1 Factorise using the cross method or guide number method $\qquad (x - 1)(x + 3)$

Step 2 Let each factor $= 0$ $\qquad x - 1 = 0$ and $x + 3 = 0$

Step 3 Solve each of the resulting equations to find the solutions of the original equation $\qquad x = 1$ and $x = -3$ are the solutions (or the roots) of the original equation

Practice questions 33·8

1. (i) Solve the quadratic equation $x^2 - x - 2 = 0$ using the graph of $y = x^2 - x - 2$ shown.

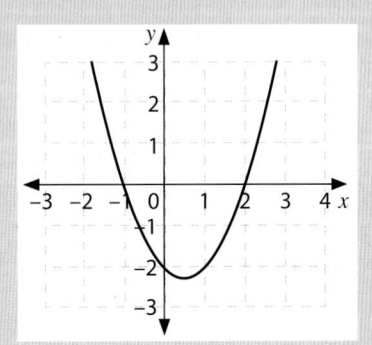

   (ii) Solve the quadratic equation $-x^2 - 3x - 2 = 0$ using the graph of $y = -x^2 - 3x - 2$ shown below.

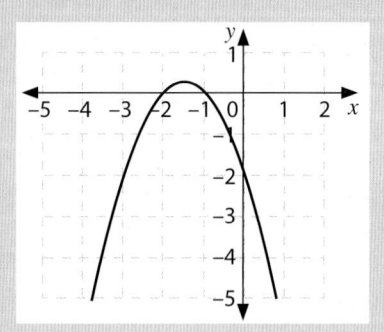

2. (i) Solve the quadratic equation $x^2 + 3x + 2 = 0$ using the graph of $y = x^2 + 3x + 2$ shown.

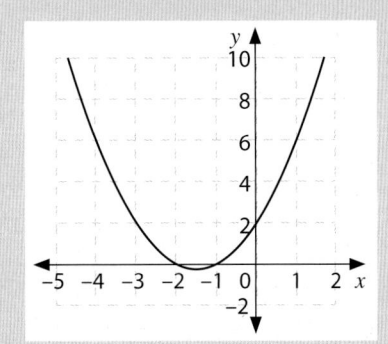

   (iii) Solve the quadratic equation $-x^2 - 2x + 3 = 0$ using the graph of $y = -x^2 - 2x + 3$ shown.

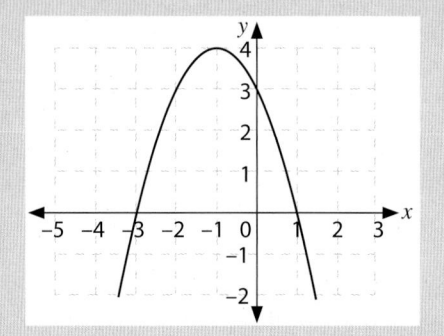

3. Solve the following quadratic equations using factorisation.
   (i) $y^2 + 3y + 2 = 0$
   (ii) $b^2 + 7b - 44 = 0$
   (iii) $b^2 - 7b - 60 = 0$
   (iv) $x^2 + 5x + 6 = 0$

4. Solve the following quadratic equations using factorisation.
   (i) $x^2 + 9x + 14 = 0$
   (ii) $x^2 + 21x + 20 = 0$
   (iii) $x^2 - 3x - 18 = 0$
   (iv) $x^2 - 49 = 0$

5. Solve the following quadratic equations using factorisation. Verify your answers by substituting the roots back into the quadratic equation.
   (i) $x^2 - 2x - 8 = 0$
   (ii) $x^2 + 10x - 24 = 0$
   (iii) $x^2 - 13x + 30 = 0$
   (iv) $y^2 + 4y - 12 = 0$

6. Solve the following quadratic equations using factorisation. Verify your answers by substituting the roots back into the quadratic equation.
   (i) $m^2 + 24m + 63 = 0$
   (ii) $m^2 - 16m + 64 = 0$
   (iii) $x^2 - 144 = 0$
   (iv) $n^2 - 64 = 0$

7. Solve the following quadratic equations using factorisation.
   (i) $y^2 - 6y = 27$
   (ii) $w^2 + 2w = 8$
   (iii) $x^2 = 8x - 15$
   (iv) $x^2 + 70 = 17x$

Linking Thinking 1

8. Solve the following quadratic equations using factorisation.
   (i) $y^2 + 9y + 2 = 8y + 58$ (ii) $x^2 - 100 = 0$ (iii) $x^2 - 225 = 0$

9. Seán is y years old. His brother Michael is four years older than Seán. The product of their ages is 780.
   (i) Set up an equation to represent this information.
   (ii) Solve your equation from (i) to find Seán's age.

Revision questions

33A Core skills

1. Simplify (by expanding) the following.
   (i) $(x)(x + 4)$
   (ii) $(x - 4)(x + 4)$
   (iii) $(m + n)(x + y)$
   (iv) $(x + 3)(x + 5)$

2. Divide the quadratic equation $x^2 - 13x - 30$ by the linear equation $x + 2$

3. Simplify (by expanding) the following.
   (i) $(x^2)(x + 4)$
   (ii) $(x - 2)(x + 10)$
   (iii) $(4 + w)(4 - w)$
   (iv) $(x - 4)^2$

4. (i) Draw the next stage of the pattern in the sequence.

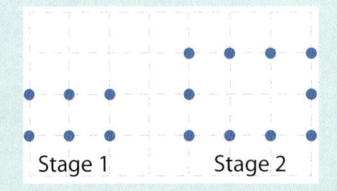

   Stage 1   Stage 2

   (ii) The table below shows the number of dots used to make each stage of the pattern. Copy and complete the table.

Stage number	1	2	3	4	5
Number of dots	6				

   (iii) Is the pattern formed by the number of dots linear or non-linear? Justify your answer.

5. Factorise fully the following quadratic expressions.
   (i) $x^2 + 8x + 15$
   (ii) $b^2 + 2b - 35$
   (iii) $y^2 - 121$
   (iv) $a^2 + 7a - 8$
   (v) $k^2 + 2k - 35$
   (vi) $a^2 - 169$

6. Graph the function $y = x^2 + 2x$ in the domain $-4 \leq x \leq 2$, where $x \in \mathbb{R}$.

7. Graph the function $y = x^2 - x - 2$ in the domain $-2 \leq x \leq 3$, where $x \in \mathbb{R}$.

8. Solve the quadratic equation $-x^2 + 14x - 48 = 0$ using the graph of $y = -x^2 + 14x - 48$ shown below. Verify your answers.

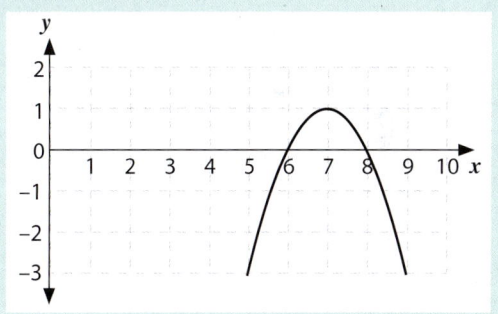

9. Solve the quadratic equation $x^2 - 8x + 15 = 0$

10. Solve the quadratic equation $n^2 + 3n - 12 = 6$

33B Taking it FURTHER

1. If there are $(x + 12)$ cats and $(x - 3)$ dogs in a kennel, write an expanded expression for the number of cats multiplied by the number of dogs in the kennel.

2. An artist wants to ship $y^2 + 4y - 12$ sculptures to an art gallery in another city. If he can fit $y + 6$ sculptures in each shipping crate, how many crates will the artist need to use?

3. If the total area of a rectangular room is equal to $x^2 - 13x + 30$, find expressions in terms of x for the length and the width.

4. Find two expressions, for two different trials, which have a total number of outcomes described by the expression $m^2 + 24m + 63$.

5. If the total area of a rectangular sheet is equal to $x^2 - 6x - 27$, find an expressions in terms of x for the length and for the width.

6. A rectangular field has a length described by the expression $m - 8$.
   The area of the field is $m^2 - 16m + 64$.
   Work out the perimeter of the field in terms of m.

7. Cathal threw an object upward from the ground. The height of the object, (measured in metres) t seconds after he threw it is given by $h = -16t^2 + 208t$.
   Find the time in seconds it took for the object to return to the ground.
   That is, when its height is zero again.

8. The distance a golf ball travels depends on the angle at which it is hit and on the speed of the golf ball. The table shows the distances a golf ball hit at an angle of 40° travels at various speeds.

   (i) Is the pattern of the distance linear? Justify your answer.

Speed (km/h)	80	85	90	95	100	105	110	115
Distance (metres)	194	220	247	275	304	334	365	397

   (ii) Draw a graph to show how the distance increases as the speed increases.

9. For a given wing area, the lift of an airplane (or a bird) is proportional to the square of its speed. The table shows the lifts for an aeroplane at various speeds.

Speed (km/h)	0	75	150	225	300	375	450	525	600
Lift (× 1 000 kg)	0	25	100	225	400	625	900	1 225	1 600

   (i) Is the pattern of the lifts linear? Explain your answer.

   (ii) Draw a graph to show how the lift increases as the speed increases.

Now that you have completed the unit, revisit the

Something to think about ...

question posed at the start of this unit.

Now try question 14 on page 562

Unit 34

Trigonometry

Topics covered within this unit:
- 34·1 Pythagoras revision
- 34·2 Trigonometric ratios
- 34·3 Using your calculator to work with trigonometric ratios
- 34·4 Finding missing sides and angles
- 34·5 Trigonometry in the real world

The Learning Outcomes covered in this unit are contained in the following sections:

GT.3b GT.4

Key words
- Trigonometric ratios
- Opposite
- Adjacent
- Angle of elevation
- Angle of depression
- Clinometer

Something to think about ...

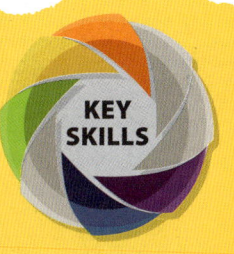

KEY SKILLS

For safety, windows can be fitted with window restrictors to prevent them from opening too far.

Standard window restrictors, extend the window to a maximum angle of 50° and allow the window to be opened no more than 100 mm.

Calculate the height of the window shown, given that the restrictor in the diagram is a standard restrictor.

34·1 Pythagoras revision

By the end of this section you should:
- recall how to use Pythagoras's theorem to find the lengths of the sides of right-angled triangles

We learned about **Pythagoras's theorem** in Section B, Unit 22. In that unit, we used the theorem to find the unknown third side of a right-angled triangle when we knew the other two sides. We also learned in Unit 31 that Pythagoras's theorem can be used to find the distance between two points.

Theorem 14 (Pythagoras's theorem): In a right-angled triangle, the square of the hypotenuse is equal to the sum of the squares of the other two sides.

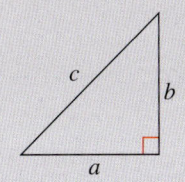

Pythagoras's theorem can be written in one short equation:

$$c^2 = a^2 + b^2$$

c is the hypotenuse, (longest side of the triangle) and a and b are the other two sides.

Section C **Applying our skills**

Proof of Pythagoras's theorem

1 Take △ABC with $|\angle ABC| = 90°$

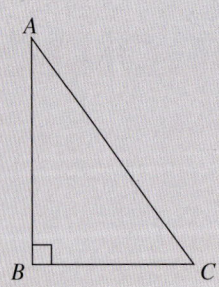

2 Draw the line BD from the vertex B to the hypotenuse AC so that it is perpendicular to AC

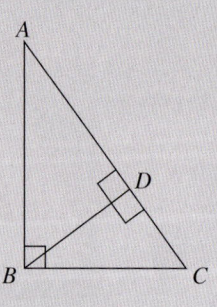

3 Looking at triangles △ABC and △ADB

$|\angle BAC| = |\angle BAD|$ Same angle
$|\angle ABC| = |\angle ADB|$ Both 90°
$\Rightarrow$ △ABC and △ADB are similar

> We learned about similar triangles in Unit 30.

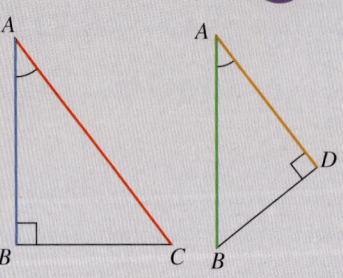

4 By similar triangles:

$$\frac{|AC|}{|AB|} = \frac{|AB|}{|AD|}$$

$$|AB|\left(\frac{|AC|}{|AB|}\right) = |AB|\left(\frac{|AB|}{|AD|}\right) \quad \text{Multiply by } |AB|$$

$$|AC| = \left(\frac{|AB|^2}{|AD|}\right)$$

$$|AD|(|AC|) = |AD|\left(\frac{|AB|^2}{|AD|}\right) \quad \text{Multiply by } |AD|$$

So, $|AD||AC| = |AB|^2$

5 Similarly, △ABC is similar to △BDC

$\Rightarrow \dfrac{|AC|}{|BC|} = \dfrac{|BC|}{|DC|}$

So, $|BC|^2 = |AC||DC|$

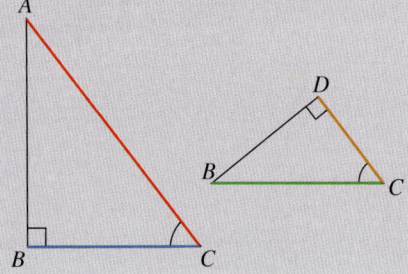

6 Adding the equations from Steps 4 and 5 gives

$|AB|^2 + |BC|^2 = |AD||AC| + |AC||DC|$

$|AB|^2 + |BC|^2 = |AC|(|AD| + |DC|)$ factorised

$|AB|^2 + |BC|^2 = |AC||AC|$ Since $|AC| = |AD| + |DC|$

$|AB|^2 + |BC|^2 = |AC|^2$

> Junior Cycle Mathematics students should display an understanding of the proofs of theorems (full formal proofs are **not** examinable).

Worked example

Find the lengths of the missing sides in the right-angled triangles below.

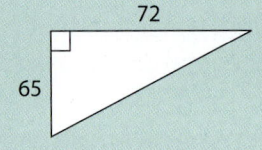

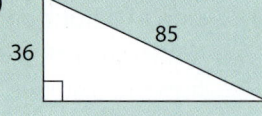

(i) 72, 65

(ii) 36, 85

Solution

(i) The unknown side is the hypotenuse, i.e. c
Let $a = 65$ and $b = 72$
$c^2 = a^2 + b^2$
$c^2 = 65^2 + 72^2$
$c^2 = 4\,225 + 5\,184$
$c^2 = 9\,409$
$c^2 = \sqrt{9\,409}$
$c = 97$

(ii) The unknown side is not the hypotenuse
Let $c = 85$ and $a = 36$
$c^2 = a^2 + b^2$
$85^2 = 36^2 + b^2$
$7\,225 = 1\,296 + b^2$
$7\,225 - 1\,296 = b^2$
$5\,929 = b^2$
$\sqrt{5\,929} = b$
$77 = b$

Practice questions 34.1

1. Find the length of the missing side in each of the right-angled triangles below.

   (i) sides 5 and 12

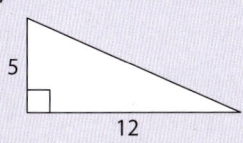

   (ii) sides 9 and 12 (hypotenuse)

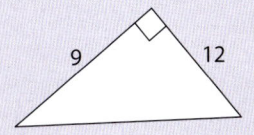

   (iii) sides 20 (hypotenuse) and 16

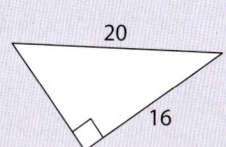

   (iv) sides 10 (hypotenuse) and 8

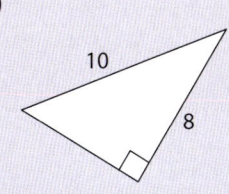

   (v) sides 20 (hypotenuse) and 15

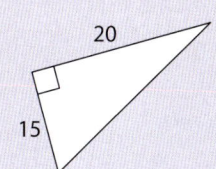

   (vi) sides 41 (hypotenuse) and 9

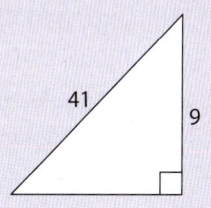

2. Find the length of the missing side in each of the right-angled triangles below.

   (i) sides 3 and 5 (hypotenuse)

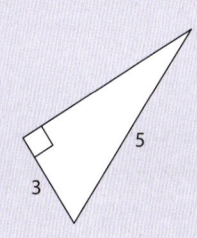

   (ii) sides 15 (hypotenuse) and 8

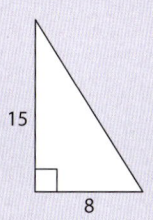

   (iii) sides 21 (hypotenuse) and 20

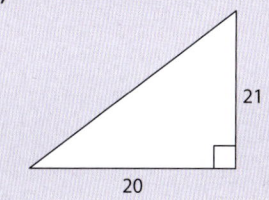

   (iv) sides 1·5 and 2·5 (hypotenuse)

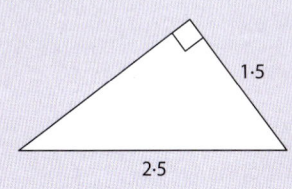

   (v) sides 12 and 37 (hypotenuse)

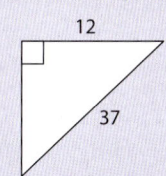

   (vi) sides 12·5 (hypotenuse) and 3·5

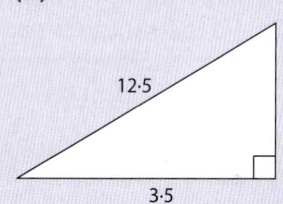

3. Using the diagram shown, find the length of QR.
   Hint: Can you find the base lengths of the two right-angled triangles within the shape?

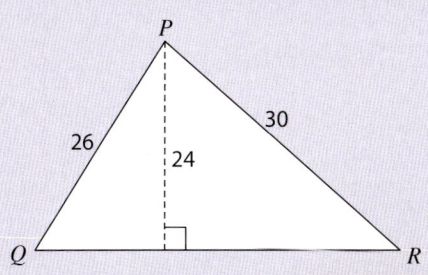

   (Triangle PQR with $PQ = 26$, $PR = 30$, and altitude from P of length 24 meeting QR at right angles.)

4. A triangle has sides of length 23·8 cm, 31·2 cm and 39·6 cm.
   Is this a right-angled triangle? Justify your answer.

   Remember: the hypotenuse is the longest side of a right-angled triangle.

5. A television has a length of 28 inches and the diagonal is 53 inches long.
   What is the width of the television?

6. A painter has to paint a wall that is 12·6 m high.
   In order to ensure the ladder won't slip, he has to put the base of the ladder 3·2 m away from the wall.
   What is the minimum length of ladder that the painter requires?

Section C **Applying our skills**   541

Taking it FURTHER

7. In the diagram of the two triangles shown on the right, calculate the value of x.

8. Amy cycles 12 km north, then 16 km west. What is the shortest distance back to her starting point? Hint: draw a sketch.

9. (i) Construct an isosceles triangle with base 6 cm and other two sides 5 cm, as shown.

   (ii) Draw a perpendicular line from A to the base $[BC]$ and mark the point of intersection D. Verify by measuring that $|AD| = 4$ cm.

   (iii) Using Pythagoras's theorem, calculate $|BD|$ and $|CD|$. What do you notice?

   (iv) Show that $\triangle ABD$ and $\triangle ACD$ are congruent.

   (v) Use your answer to (iv) to describe what drawing a line from the vertex of an isosceles triangle perpendicular to its base does to the base.

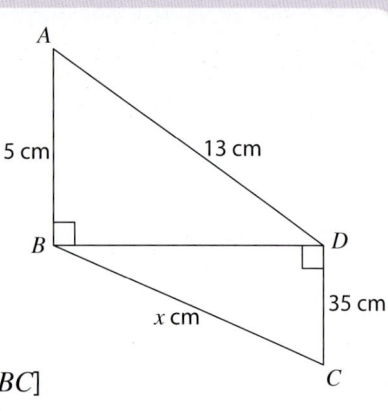

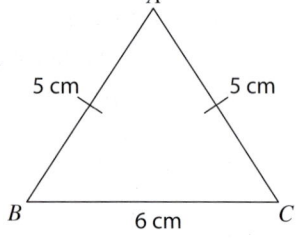

34·2 Trigonometric ratios

By the end of this section you should:
- understand what trigonometric ratios are
- be able to find the sine, cosine and tangent of an angle as a ratio
- be able to find all ratios if given the value of one of the ratios

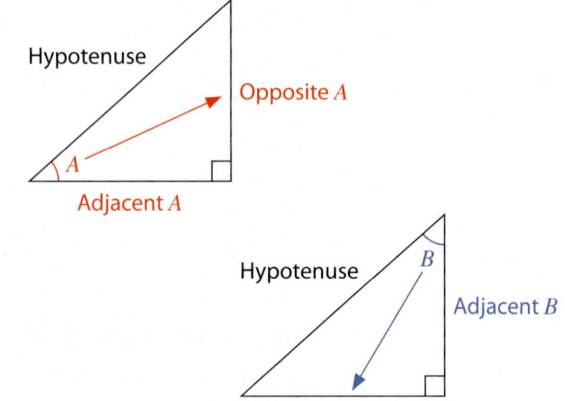

Trigonometric ratios relate the lengths of the sides of a right-angled triangle to its interior angles.

The trigonometric ratios are only used for right-angled triangles. They are found by taking one side of a right-angled triangle and dividing it by another side. Each ratio involves only two sides of the triangle.

In order to find these ratios we must be able label the sides of the triangle properly.

The names of the sides are:

- the **hypotenuse:** longest side of the triangle
- the **opposite:** side opposite the angle of interest
- the **adjacent:** side beside the angle of interest

Naming the sides of a right-angled triangle

1. Identify the right angle, go across from it and label the side as the hypotenuse.

2. Identify the angle of interest, go across from it and label the side as the opposite.

3. Label the last side as the adjacent. 'Adjacent' means 'beside', so it is the side beside the angle of interest.

Linking Thinking 1

Worked example 1

Identify the hypotenuse, opposite and adjacent in the following triangles.

(i)

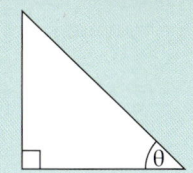

(ii)

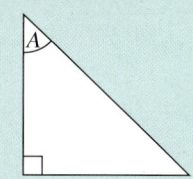

Solution

(i) The right angle is across from the hypotenuse.
The angle of interest is θ.
Across from it is the opposite.
The last side is the adjacent.
It is beside the angle of interest θ.

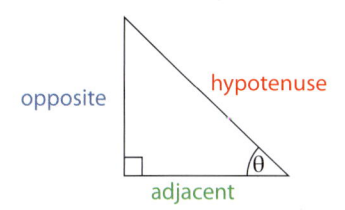

(ii) The right angle is across from the hypotenuse.
The angle of interest is A.
Across from it is the opposite.
The last side is the adjacent.
It is beside the angle of interest A.

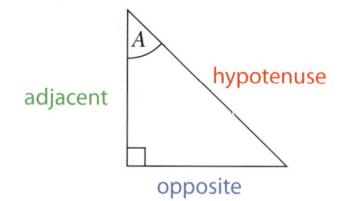

Discuss and discover

Work with a classmate to complete the following task.

(i) Construct three different right-angled triangles with an angle of 30°, as shown.
(ii) Measure the length of the hypotenuse and the other two sides.
(iii) Copy and complete the table below to find a relationship between each pair of sides.
(v) What do you notice?
(vi) Repeat (i), (ii) and (iii) for an angle of 60°.
(vii) Write a statement to apply your findings to all situations (generalise your findings).

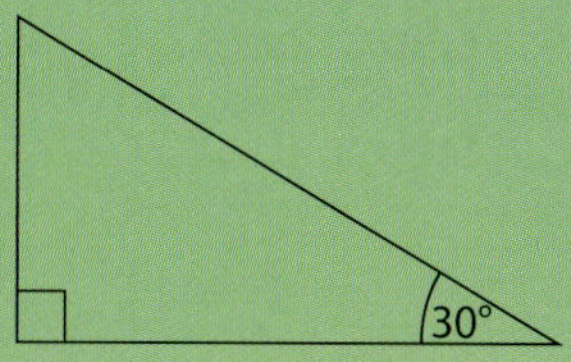

	Length of hypotenuse	Length of opposite	Length of adjacent	opp/hyp	adj/hyp	opp/adj
Triangle 1						
Triangle 2						
Triangle 3						

Express the answers as decimals correct to two places.

Having completed the activity above, we can see that each ratio is dependent purely on the angle – regardless of the size of the triangle. Therefore, the ratios of the sides remain the same.

The ratios of each pair of sides are named as follows:

Ratio	Abbreviation	Relationship to the sides of the triangle
sine	sin	$\sin A = \dfrac{\text{opposite}}{\text{hypotenuse}}$
cosine	cos	$\cos A = \dfrac{\text{adjacent}}{\text{hypotenuse}}$
tangent	tan	$\tan A = \dfrac{\text{opposite}}{\text{adjacent}}$

> To help us remember the sides for each ratio we can use the mnemonic **SOHCAHTOA**.

Finding the sin, cos or tan of an angle

1. Label the sides of the triangle hypotenuse, opposite and adjacent.
2. For sin, put the opposite side over the hypotenuse.
3. For cos, put the adjacent side over the hypotenuse.
4. For tan, put the opposite side over the adjacent side.

Worked example 2

Find the sin, cos and tan of the given angle in these triangles.

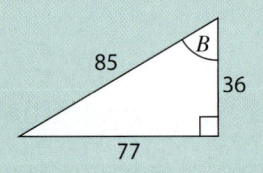

(i) Triangle with sides 21, 20, 29 and angle at A.

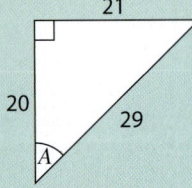

(ii) Triangle with sides 85, 36, 77 and angle at B.

Solution

(i) **Step 1** Hyp = 29
Opp = 21
Adj = 20

Step 2 $\sin A = \dfrac{\text{opp}}{\text{hyp}} \rightarrow \sin A = \dfrac{21}{29}$

Step 3 $\cos A = \dfrac{\text{adj}}{\text{hyp}} \rightarrow \cos A = \dfrac{20}{29}$

Step 4 $\tan A = \dfrac{\text{opp}}{\text{adj}} \rightarrow \tan A = \dfrac{21}{20}$

(ii) **Step 1** Hyp = 85
Opp = 77
Adj = 36

Step 2 $\sin B = \dfrac{\text{opp}}{\text{hyp}} \rightarrow \sin B = \dfrac{77}{85}$

Step 3 $\cos B = \dfrac{\text{adj}}{\text{hyp}} \rightarrow \cos B = \dfrac{36}{85}$

Step 4 $\tan B = \dfrac{\text{opp}}{\text{adj}} \rightarrow \tan B = \dfrac{77}{36}$

> Always write out the **SOHCAHTOA** formula and then put in the relevant numbers.

Practice questions 34.2

1. Copy the following triangles and label the hypotenuse, opposite and adjacent in each case.

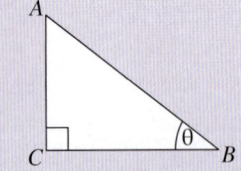

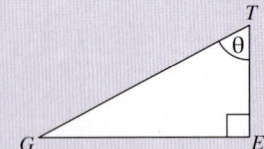

   (i) Triangle XYZ with right angle at Z, angle θ at X.
   (ii) Triangle LMN with right angle at M, angle θ at N.
   (iii) Triangle RST with right angle at T, angle θ at R.
   (iv) Triangle ABC with right angle at C, angle θ at B.
   (v) Triangle GET with right angle at E, angle θ at T.
   (vi) Triangle DEF with right angle at F, angle θ at E.

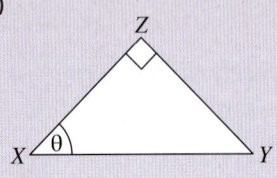

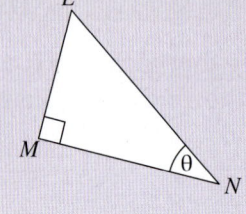

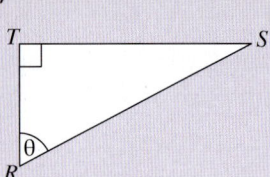

Linking Thinking 1

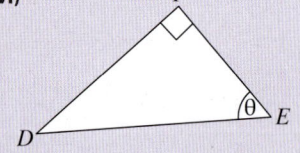

2. Find, as a fraction, the sin, cos and tan of the given angle in the following triangles.

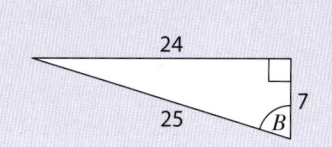

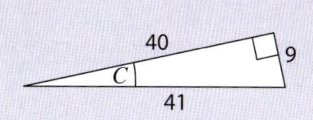

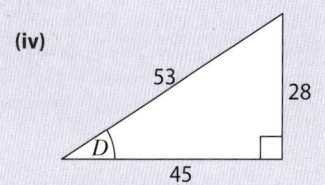

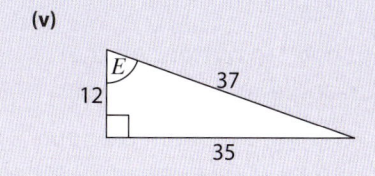

   (i) Triangle with sides 8, 17, 15, angle A.

   (ii) Triangle with sides 24, 25, 7, angle B.

   (iii) Triangle with sides 40, 41, 9, angle C.

   (iv) Triangle with sides 53, 28, 45, angle D.

   (v) Triangle with sides 12, 37, 35, angle E.

   (vi) Triangle with sides 65, 63, 16, angle F.

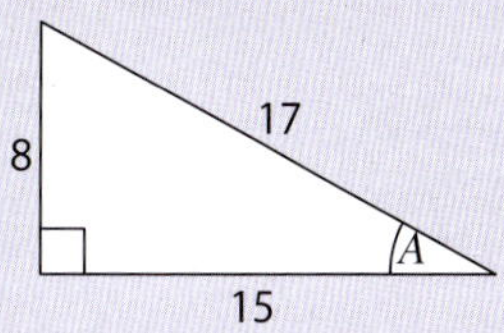

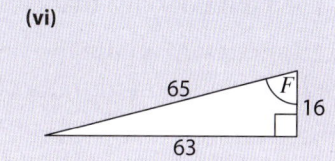

3. Find, as a fraction, the sin, cos and tan of the each of the given angles in the following triangles.

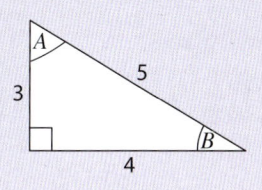

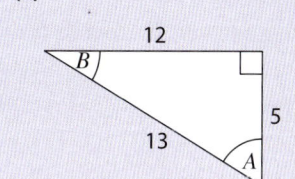

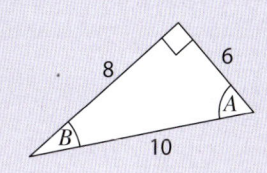

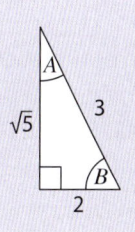

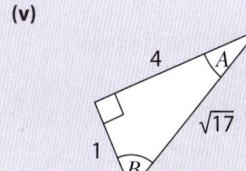

   (i) Triangle with sides 3, 5, 4, angles A and B.

   (ii) Triangle with sides 12, 13, 5, angles A and B.

   (iii) Triangle with sides 8, 10, 6, angles A and B.

   (iv) Triangle with sides $\sqrt{5}$, 3, 2, angles A and B.

   (v) Triangle with sides 4, $\sqrt{17}$, 1, angles A and B.

   (vi) Triangle with sides 2, 5, $\sqrt{21}$, angles A and B.

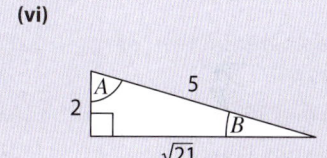

4. A five-metre ladder rests against the side of a wall. The bottom of the ladder is three metres from the base of the wall. The angle the ladder makes with the wall is called L.

   (i) Draw a sketch to represent the situation described.

   (ii) How high up the wall does the ladder reach?

   (iii) Write down the value of the sin, cos and tan of the angle L.

5. A wheelchair ramp is 10 m in length, up the incline. At the top, its height is 6 m. The angle where the ramp leaves the ground is labelled R.

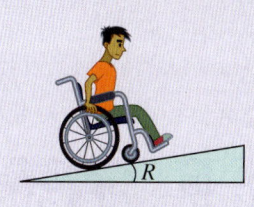

   (i) Draw a sketch to represent the situation described.

   (ii) What is the horizontal length of the ramp?

   (iii) Write down the value of the sin, cos and tan of the angle R.

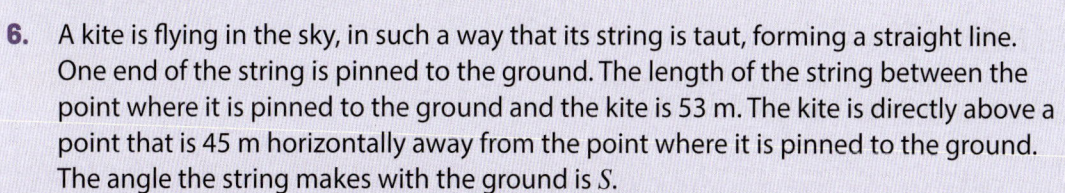

6. A kite is flying in the sky, in such a way that its string is taut, forming a straight line. One end of the string is pinned to the ground. The length of the string between the point where it is pinned to the ground and the kite is 53 m. The kite is directly above a point that is 45 m horizontally away from the point where it is pinned to the ground. The angle the string makes with the ground is S.

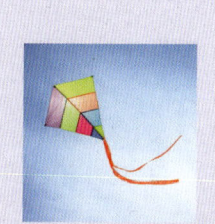

   (i) Draw a sketch to represent the situation described.

   (ii) How high is the kite?

   (iii) Write down the value of the sin, cos and tan of the angle S.

7. (i) Draw a sketch of a right-angled triangle and label one of the non-right angles X.

   (ii) If $\cos X = \frac{3}{5}$, write the dimensions of the known sides of the triangle on the sketch.

   (iii) Find the length of the third side of the triangle.

   (iv) Find the value of $\sin X$.

   (v) Find the value of $\tan X$.

34.3 Using your calculator to work with trigonometric ratios

By the end of this section you should be able to:
- use a calculator to find the sin, cos and tan of a given angle
- use the inverse ratio function on a calculator to find an angle when given its sin, cos or tan

In the previous section, we learned how to find sin, cos or tan as a fraction when given the sides of a triangle.

If we are given an angle, we can use the sin, cos and tan buttons on the calculator to find the trigonometric ratio of that angle, in decimal form.

When we use these buttons on the calculator it is very important that our calculator is in degree mode.

Worked example 1
Find the sin, cos and tan of the given angles. Give your answers correct to four decimal places.

(i) $\sin 35°$ (ii) $\cos 42°$ (iii) $\tan 56°$

Solution

(i) $\sin 35°$
Press the sin button then 35 and press =
$\sin 35° = 0.5735764364$
To four decimal places
$\sin 35° = 0.5736$

(ii) $\cos 42°$
Press the cos button then 42 and press =
$\cos 42° = 0.7431448255$
To four decimal places
$\cos 42° = 0.7431$

(iii) $\tan 56°$
Press the tan button then 56 and press =
$\tan 56° = 1.482560969$
To four decimal places
$\tan 56° = 1.4826$

Finding an angle when given the sin, cos or tan of the angle

If we are given the value of the sin, cos or tan of the angle we can use this to find the size of the angle. To do this we work backwards or perform the inverse operation.

> The inverse function is used when finding a missing angle.

On most calculators, the inverse sin function is above the sin button and is written as $\sin^{-1}$.
The inverse cos and tan are above the cos and tan buttons respectively.

Since $\sin^{-1}$ is above the sin button, we press the 'shift' first and then the 'sin' button. $\sin^{-1}$ should then appear on our screen.

Worked example 2
Find the angle whose sin, cos and tan values are given below.
Give your answer to the nearest whole number in each case.

(i) $\sin A = 0.9063$ (ii) $\cos B = \frac{3}{4}$ (iii) $\tan C = 0.8098$

Solution

(i) $\sin A = 0.9063$
Press shift, sin, 0.9063
$\sin^{-1}(0.9063) = 64.99894431$
To the nearest whole number
$A = 65°$

(ii) $\cos B = \frac{3}{4}$
Press shift, cos, $\frac{3}{4}$
$\cos^{-1}(\frac{3}{4}) = 41.4096221$
To the nearest whole number
$B = 41°$

(iii) $\tan C = 0.8098$
Press shift, tan, 0.8098
$\tan^{-1}(0.8098) = 39.00055251$
To the nearest whole number
$C = 39°$

Practice questions 34.3

1. Use your calculator to find the sin, cos or tan of the following angles. Give your answers correct to four decimal places where necessary.

   (i) sin 24° (iii) tan 88° (v) sin 43° (vii) sin 62° (ix) cos 60° (xi) cos 31°

   (ii) cos 45° (iv) tan 12° (vi) cos 79° (viii) sin 14° (x) tan 72° (xii) tan 25°

2. Find the measure of the angle in each of the following. Give your answer to the nearest degree.

   (i) $\sin X = 0.7547$ (iii) $\tan C = 0.1405$ (v) $\sin A = 0.4540$ (vii) $\cos W = 0.6157$

   (ii) $\cos Y = 0.5736$ (iv) $\cos B = 0.5000$ (vi) $\tan B = 0.6249$ (viii) $\tan Z = 19.0811$

Taking it FURTHER

3. (a) Use your calculator to find the value of:

   (i) sin 10° and cos 80°

   (ii) sin 20° and cos 70°

   (iii) sin 30° and cos 60°

   (b) Using the pattern shown in (a), or otherwise fill in the missing angle below.

   sin 40° and cos ☐

34.4 Finding missing sides and angles

By the end of this section you should be able to:
- use sin, cos and tan to find missing sides
- use sin, cos and tan to find missing angles

To find the length of a side

If we are given an angle and one side of the right-angled triangle, we can use sin, cos and tan to find the other sides.

Finding a missing side in a right-angled triangle

1. Label the sides of the triangle: hypotenuse opposite and adjacent.

2. Write down the measure of the angle we '**have**' (given in the question).

3. Write down the name of the side we '**have**' (given in the question).

4. Write down the name of the side we '**want**' (asked to find in the question).

5. Decide which ratio to use depending on the sides identified in steps 2–4.

6. Form an equation with the angle given and the sides identified in steps 2–4.

7. Solve the equation to find the unknown side.

Section C Applying our skills

Worked example 1

Find the length of the unknown side in each of the following. Give your answer to one decimal place.

(i) [Triangle with 40 m side, 14° angle, and unknown x]

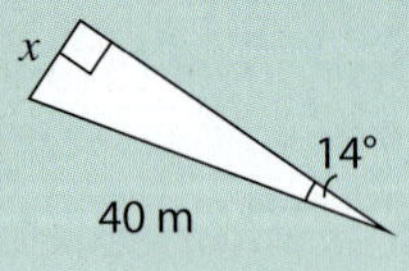

(ii) [Triangle with 5.6 cm side, 46° angle, and unknown y]

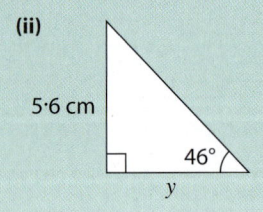

Strategy: 'We have … We have … We want …'

Solution

(i) 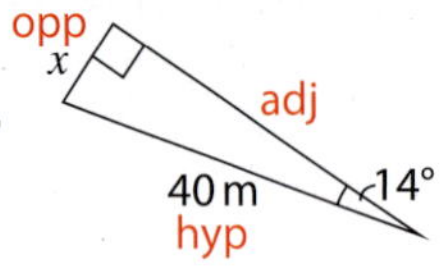
- **Step 1** Label the sides
- **Step 2** We have: angle = 14°
- **Step 3** We have: hyp = 40
- **Step 4** We want: opp = x
- **Step 5** We use: $\sin A = \dfrac{\text{opposite}}{\text{hypotenuse}}$
- **Step 6** $\sin 14° = \dfrac{x}{40}$
- **Step 7** $\sin 14° = \dfrac{x}{40}$ (multiply by 40)

$$40(\sin 14) = 40\left(\dfrac{x}{40}\right)$$
$$40(\sin 14) = x$$
$$9{\cdot}676875824 = x$$
$$9{\cdot}7 \text{ m} = x$$

(ii) 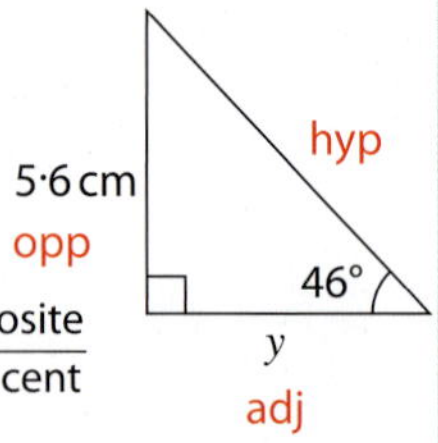
- **Step 1** Label the sides
- **Step 2** We have: angle = 46°
- **Step 3** We have: opp = 5·6
- **Step 4** We want: adj = y
- **Step 5** We use: $\tan A = \dfrac{\text{opposite}}{\text{adjacent}}$
- **Step 6** $\tan 46° = \dfrac{5{\cdot}6}{y}$
- **Step 7** $\tan 46° = \dfrac{5{\cdot}6}{y}$ (multiply by y)

$$y(\tan 46°) = 5{\cdot}6 \text{ (divide by } \tan 46°\text{)}$$
$$y = \dfrac{5{\cdot}6}{\tan 46°}$$
$$y = 5{\cdot}407857139$$
$$y = 5{\cdot}4 \text{ cm}$$

To find the measure of an angle

If we are given two sides of a right-angled triangle, we can use sin, cos and tan to find the angles.

Finding a missing angle in a right-angled triangle

1. Label the sides of the triangle: hypotenuse, opposite and adjacent.
2. Write down the names of the two sides we **'have'** (given in the question).
3. Write down the name of the angle we **'want'**.
4. Decide which ratio to use depending on the sides identified in step 2.
5. Form an equation with the angle required and the sides identified in step 2.
6. Solve the equation to find the unknown angle.

Worked example 2

Find the size of the angle k, in the given triangle. Give your answer to the nearest degree.

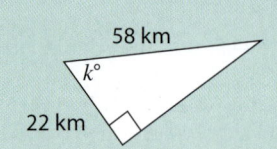

[Triangle with 58 km, 22 km and angle $k°$]

Strategy: 'We have … We have … We want …'

Solution

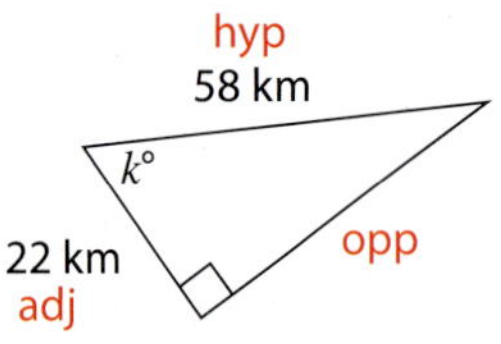

- **Step 1** Label the sides
- **Step 2** We have: hyp = 58
- **Step 3** We have: adj = 22
- **Step 4** We want: angle = k

We use: $\cos A = \dfrac{\text{adjacent}}{\text{hypotenuse}}$

- **Step 5** $\cos k° = \dfrac{22}{58}$
- **Step 6** $\cos k° = \dfrac{22}{58}$ find $(\cos^{-1})$

$$k° = \cos^{-1}\left(\dfrac{22}{58}\right)$$
$$k° = 67{\cdot}70902963$$
$$k° = 68°$$

Linking Thinking 1

Practice questions 34.4

1. Find the length of the labelled side in each of the following triangles. Give your answer correct to one decimal place.

   (i) Triangle with 11 m, 62°, side t, right angle.

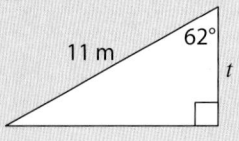

   (ii) Triangle with 61°, 105 mm, side x, right angle.

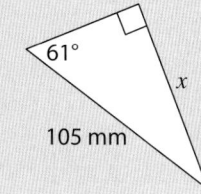

   (iii) Triangle with 55 mm, 5°, side w, right angle.

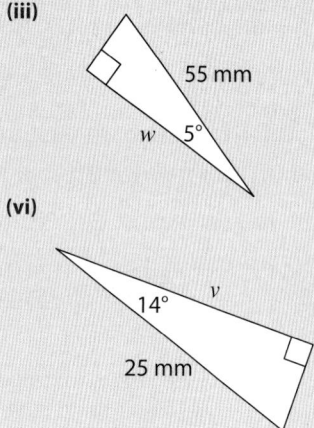

   (iv) Triangle with 16 cm, 28°, side z, right angle.

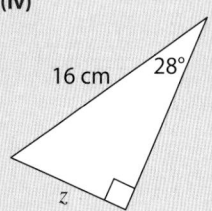

   (v) Triangle with 18°, 60 m, side x, right angle.

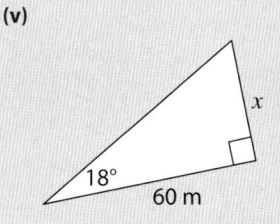

   (vi) Triangle with 14°, 25 mm, side v, right angle.

2. Find the length of the labelled side in each of the following triangles. Give your answer correct to one decimal place.

   (i) Triangle with side a, 64°, 10.8, right angle.

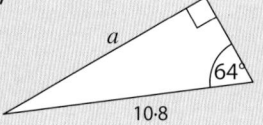

   (ii) Triangle with 3.5, 20°, side m, right angle.

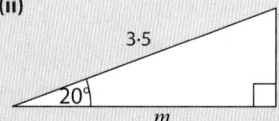

   (iii) Triangle with 40°, 17.3, side x, right angle.

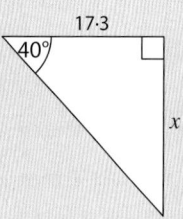

   (iv) Triangle with 60°, 4.1, side x, right angle.

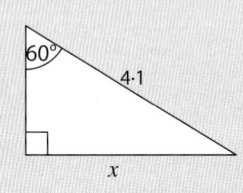

   (v) Triangle with 4.9, 46°, side x, right angle.

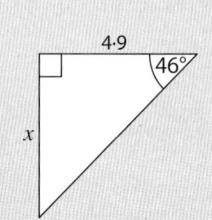

   (vi) Triangle with 40°, 2.43, side q, right angle.

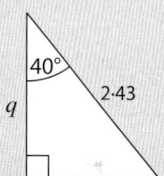

3. Find the length of the labelled side in each of the following triangles. Give your answer correct to one decimal place.

   (i) Triangle with side x, 38°, 7.8, right angle.

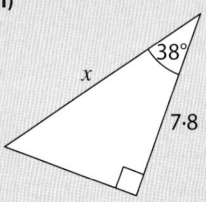

   (ii) Triangle with 35.8, 50°, side s, right angle.

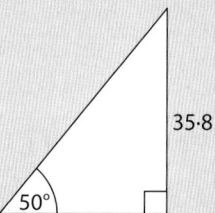

   (iii) Triangle with 35°, 8.4, side x, right angle.

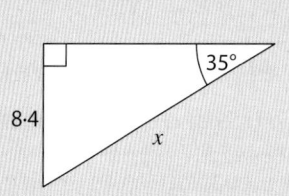

4. Find the measure of the labelled angles in each of the following triangles. Give your answer correct to the nearest degree.

   (i) Triangle with 9 cm, 4.8 cm, angle $x°$, right angle.

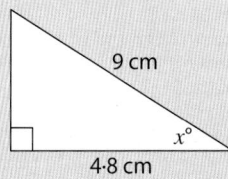

   (ii) Triangle with angle $a°$, 91 mm, 87 mm, right angle.

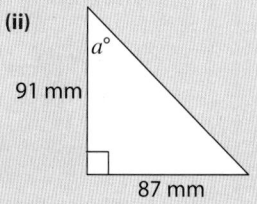

   (iii) Triangle with angle $m°$, 18.2 m, 15.1 m, right angle.

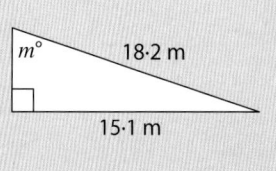

   (iv) Triangle with 13.7 m, angle $y°$, 5.6 m, right angle.

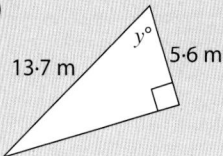

   (v) Triangle with 28 mm, angle $j°$, 60 mm, right angle.

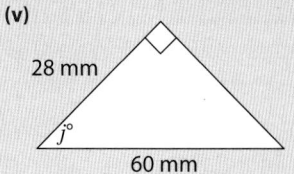

   (vi) Triangle with 8.6 cm, angle $a°$, 29.3 cm, right angle.

Section C Applying our skills   549

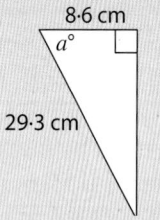

5. The diagram shows a right-angled triangle with unknown sides x and y.
   Find, to the nearest whole number, the length of:
   (i) the side labelled x (ii) the side labelled y

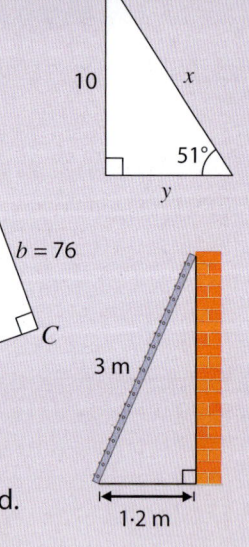

6. The diagram shows a right-angled triangle with unknown sides a and b.
   Find, to the nearest whole number, the values of:
   (i) the side labelled a (ii) the side labelled c

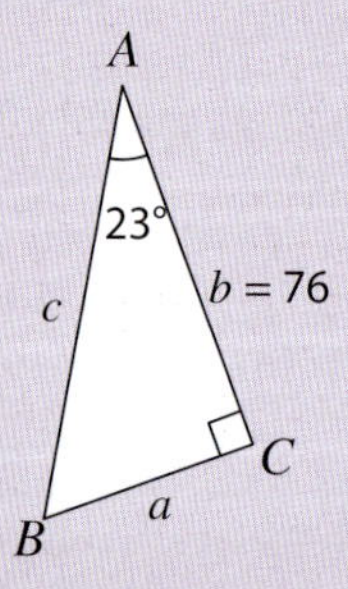

7. A 3 m long ladder is leaning against a vertical wall.
   Its foot is on horizontal ground 1·2 m away from the foot of the wall.
   (i) Calculate, to the nearest degree, the angle the ladder makes with the wall.
   (ii) Calculate, to the nearest degree, the angle the ladder makes with the ground.

Taking it FURTHER

8. Stephen is installing a flight of stairs in a new house. The height from the floor to the top of the stairs is 2·5 m. The length of the stairs is 3·9 m. 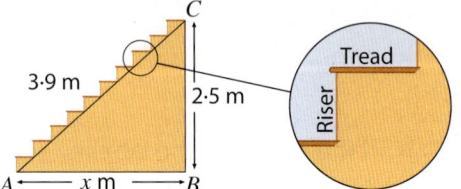
   (i) Find $|\angle CAB|$, the angle between the floor and the stairs, correct to the nearest degree.
   (ii) Find $|AB|$, distance from the foot of the stairs to the wall. Give your answer correct to the nearest metre.
   (iii) There are 10 steps on the stairs. Find the height of each riser, in metres.
   (iv) There are 10 steps on the stairs. Find the depth of each tread, in metres.

34·5 Trigonometry in the real world

By the end of this section you should:
- understand and be able to find angles of elevation and depression
- be able to use trigonometry to solve real world problems

Trigonometry is often used in real world situations to find missing angles or distances.

Angles of elevation and depression

Angles of elevation and depression are useful in helping to find unknown heights or distances.

An **angle of elevation** is the angle formed by a horizontal line and a line of sight to a point above the line.

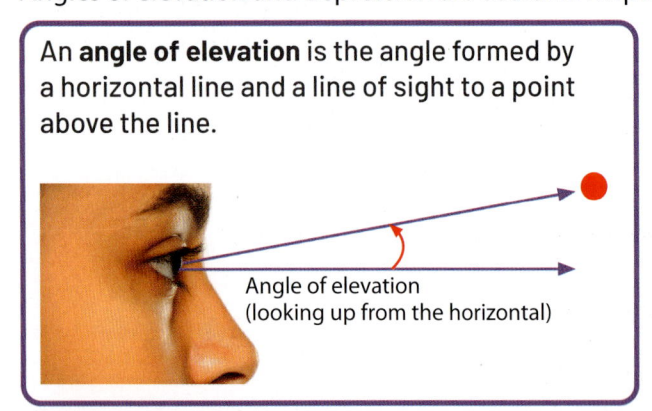

Angle of elevation (looking up from the horizontal)

An **angle of depression** is the angle formed by a horizontal line and a line of sight to a point below the line.

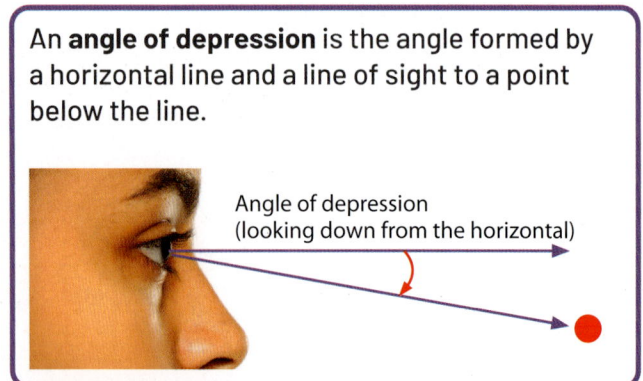

Angle of depression (looking down from the horizontal)

A **clinometer** is a device used to measure angles of elevation and/or angles of depression.

A clinometer might be used by motorway construction engineers, movie production engineers, forestry engineers and secondary school maths students in Ireland.

550 Linking Thinking 1

There are many different types of clinometer.

A very simple type is shown in the diagram on the right.

Answering 'real world' problems

1. If necessary, draw a sketch to represent the situation given.
2. Identify the angle given or required.
3. Label the sides of the triangle.
4. Use the '**we have, we have, we want**' strategy to form an equation.
5. Solve the equation to find the unknown angle or side.

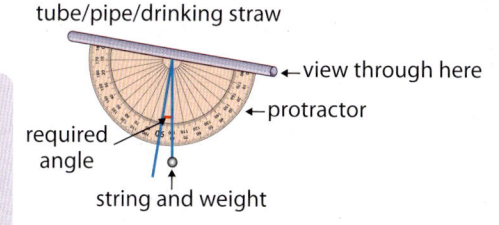

Discuss and discover

Work with a partner to make a clinometer and use it to measure the height of something in your school grounds.

KEY SKILLS

Worked example 1

A squirrel is sitting on the forest floor and looks up at an acorn at the top of a tree.
If he looks up at an angle of 26° and he is sitting 15 m from the base of the tree, how tall is the tree, to the nearest metre?

Solution

Steps 1, 2 and 3

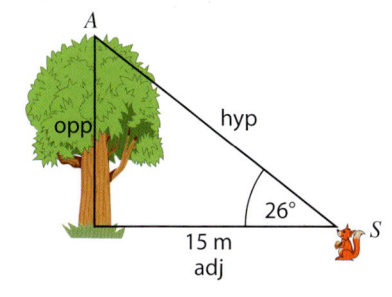

Steps 4 and 5

We have: angle = 26°
We have: adjacent = 15 m
We want: opposite = x
We use: $\tan A = \dfrac{\text{opposite}}{\text{adjacent}}$

$\tan 26° = \dfrac{x}{15}$

$15 (\tan 26°) = x$

$7·315988828 = x$

Height of tree = 7 metres

Worked example 2

A man standing on a cliff sees a boat at an angle of depression of 36°. If the cliff is 65 m tall, how far from the cliff is the boat? Give your answer correct to one decimal place.

Solution

Steps 1, 2 and 3

The angle of depression is **outside** the triangle. To find the angle inside, subtract it from 90°

Steps 4 and 5

We have: angle = 54°
We have: adjacent = 65 m
We want: opposite = x
We use: $\tan A = \dfrac{\text{opposite}}{\text{adjacent}}$

$\tan 54° = \dfrac{x}{65}$

$65 (\tan 54°) = x$

$89·46482483 = x$

Distance from the cliff = 89·5 metres

Section C Applying our skills

Practice questions 34.5

1. A builder wants to build a ramp [AC] to a step [AB] that is 1·5 m in height. The angle where the ramp meets the ground ∠ACB is 4°.
   Find the horizontal length of the ramp [BC], to the nearest metre.

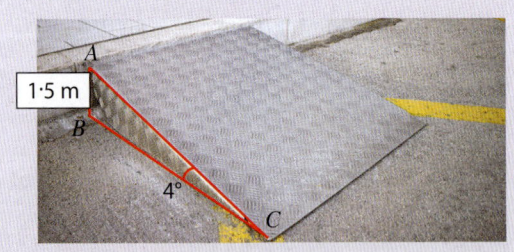

2. An electricity pole is 75 m high. A support wire is attached to the top of the pole for safety.
   If the support wire and the ground form an angle of 65°, how far is the support wire's anchor point from the base of the pole, to two decimal places?

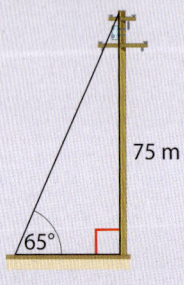

3. A 10-metre ladder is leaning against a building. The foot of the ladder is 8 metres from the building. Find the angle that the ladder makes with the building.
   Give your answer to the nearest whole number.

4. An airplane is approaching an airport to land. It needs to have an angle of elevation of between 12° and 16° from the runway to ensure it lands safely. Will the plane shown in the diagram be able to land safely?

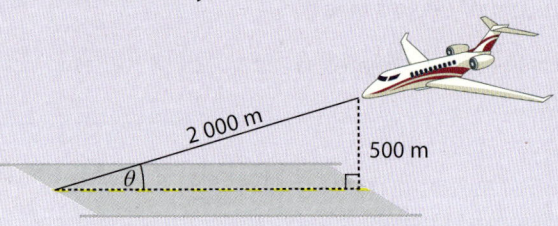

5. The beam of a see-saw is 3·6 m long. When one end is resting on the ground, the other end is 1·3 m above the ground.
   What angle, to the nearest degree, does the beam make with the ground?

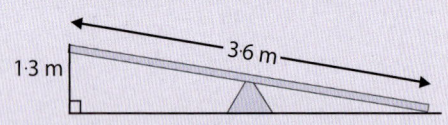

6. Amy decides to make a skateboard ramp with the dimensions shown in the diagram below. Calculate the angle, to the nearest degree, between the ramp and the ground.

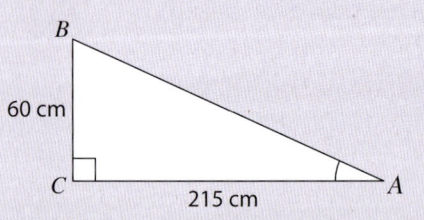

7. From a point on the ground 8 metres from the base of a flagpole, the angle of elevation of the top of the pole measures 43°.
   (i) Name an instrument that could be used to measure the angle of elevation. 
   (ii) How tall is the flagpole? Give your answer correct to two decimal places.

8. The angle of elevation from a point A at the base of hill to the point B at of the top of a hill is 53°, as shown. 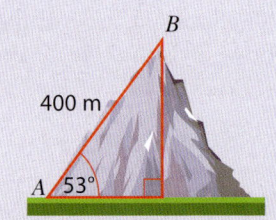
   If the distance between point A and point B is 400 m, find the vertical height of the hill at point B, to the nearest metre.

9. The pilot of a traffic helicopter sees an accident at an angle of depression of 16°. The height of the helicopter is 500 metres.
   What is the horizontal distance, to the nearest metre, from the helicopter to the accident?

10. A lighthouse built at sea level is 48 m high. A boat is situated 160 m away from the base of the lighthouse.
    Calculate the angle of elevation, to the nearest degree, from the boat to the top of the lighthouse.

552   Linking Thinking 1

11. A parasailer is attached to a boat with a rope that is 22 metres long.
    The angle of elevation from the boat to the parasailer is 38°.
    Calculate the parasailer's height above the sea, correct to one decimal place.

12. From the top of a tower 30 m high, a man is observing the base of a tree at an angle of depression measuring 30°. Find the distance, to the nearest metre, between the tree and the tower.

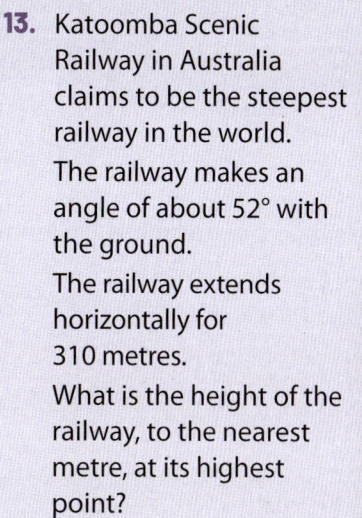

13. Katoomba Scenic Railway in Australia claims to be the steepest railway in the world.
    The railway makes an angle of about 52° with the ground.
    The railway extends horizontally for 310 metres.
    What is the height of the railway, to the nearest metre, at its highest point?

14. A balloon is connected to the ground, beside a meteorological station by a cable of length 220 m inclined at a 65° angle. Find the height, to the nearest metre, of the balloon from the ground.

15. A hill is inclined at 14° to the horizontal. It runs down to a beach with a constant slope so that its base is at sea level.
    (i) Paul walks 1·3 km up the hill. What is his height, to the nearest metre, above sea level?
    (ii) Jack is 600 m above sea level. How far up the hill, to the nearest metre, is Jack?

Taking it FURTHER

16. Copy the table below and put a tick (✓) in the correct box in each row to show whether each statement is true or false. Justify your answer in each case.

	Statement	True	False
(i)	The angle of elevation from your eye to the top of a tree increases as you walk towards the tree.		
(ii)	If you are on the fifth floor of a building, the angle of depression to the street is less than if you are on the fourth floor of the building.		
(iii)	As you watch a plane fly above you, the angle of elevation to the plane gets closer to 0° as the plane approaches directly overhead.		
(iv)	An angle of depression must be less than 90°.		

Revision questions

34A Core skills

1. Using Pythagoras's theorem, calculate the length of x in each of the following right-angled triangles.

   (i) x, 5 cm, 12 cm
   (ii) 65 m, 63 m, x
   (iii) 7 cm, 24 cm, x
   (iv) x, 85 mm, 36 mm

2. Use your calculator to find the value of each of the following. Give your answers correct to three decimal places.

   (i) tan 22°   (iii) tan 38°   (v) sin 42°   (vii) tan 31°   (ix) sin 45°   (xi) tan 65°
   (ii) cos 44° (iv) cos 60°   (vi) sin 80° (viii) cos 17° (x) cos 38°   (xii) sin 38°

3. Use your calculator to find the measure of angle X, to the nearest whole number, given the following.

   (i) sin X = 0·3456   (iii) tan X = 1·4552   (v) sin X = 0·5736   (vii) cos X = 0·682
   (ii) cos X = 0·4995 (iv) cos X = 0·9511   (vi) tan X = 0·404   (viii) tan X = 2·0503

4. For the given triangles, express the sin, cos and tan of angles A and B as fractions.

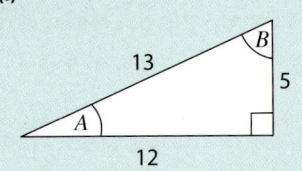

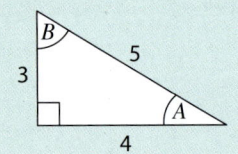

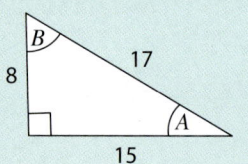

   (i) 13, 5, 12
   (ii) 3, 5, 4
   (iii) 8, 17, 15

5. Find the length of [AB], correct to two decimal places, in each of the following triangles.

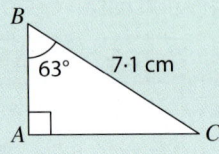

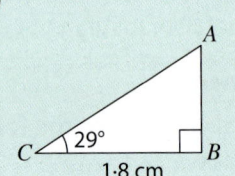

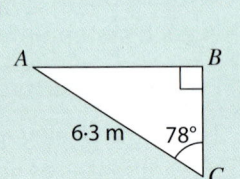

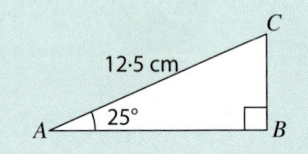

   (i) 63°, 7·1 cm
   (ii) 29°, 1·8 cm
   (iii) 6·3 m, 78°
   (iv) 12·5 cm, 25°

6. Find the measure of the angle marked x in each of the following right-angled triangles. Give your answer correct to the nearest degree.

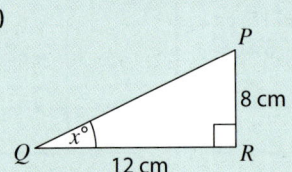

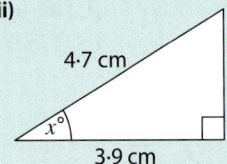

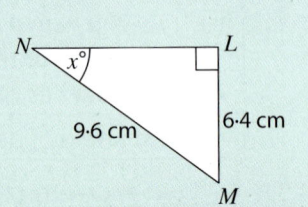

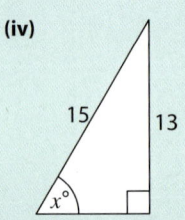

   (i) 8 cm, 12 cm
   (ii) 4·7 cm, 3·9 cm
   (iii) 9·6 cm, 6·4 cm
   (iv) 15, 13

7. A hot air balloon is tied to the ground by two straight ropes, as shown in the diagram.
   One rope is directly below the balloon and makes a right angle with the ground. The other rope makes an angle of 50° with the ground.

   (i) Calculate, to the nearest metre, the height of the balloon above the ground.
   (ii) Calculate, to the nearest metre, the distance between the two ropes.

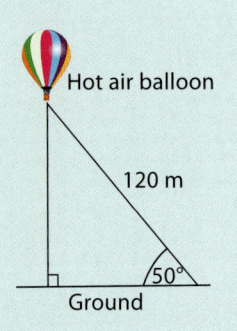

554 Linking Thinking 1

8. The diagram shows a suspension bridge across a river. Each of the triangular pieces of the bridge are identical.

   The base angle of each triangle is 34° and the perpendicular height of each triangle is 16m. Calculate the length of the bridge, correct to two decimal places.

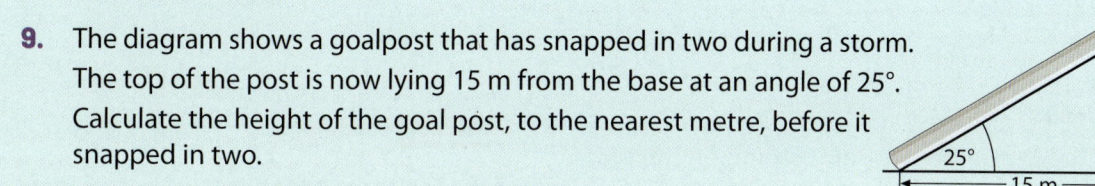

9. The diagram shows a goalpost that has snapped in two during a storm. The top of the post is now lying 15 m from the base at an angle of 25°. Calculate the height of the goal post, to the nearest metre, before it snapped in two.

10. An airplane climbs at an angle of 18° with the ground. Find the ground distance the plane has travelled when it has moved 2 500 m through the air. Give your answer to two significant figures.

↗ 34B Taking it FURTHER

1. Find the length of the side p and the measure of the angle m in the diagram shown.
   Give your answer to the nearest degree.

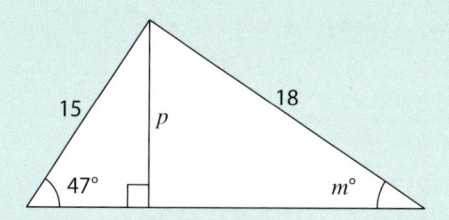

2. Find the value of the angle marked x in the diagram.

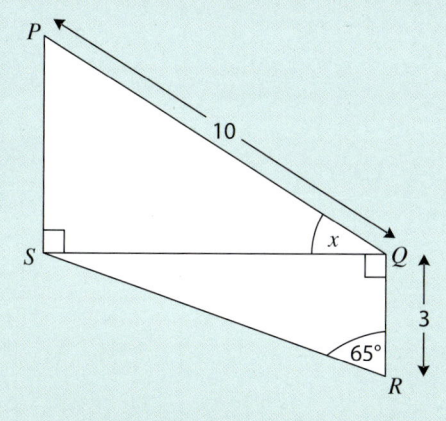

3. A passenger in a plane is told that the plane is flying at a height of 4 000 m and is 15 km from the airport. What is the angle of depression from the plane to the airport? Give your answer to the nearest degree.

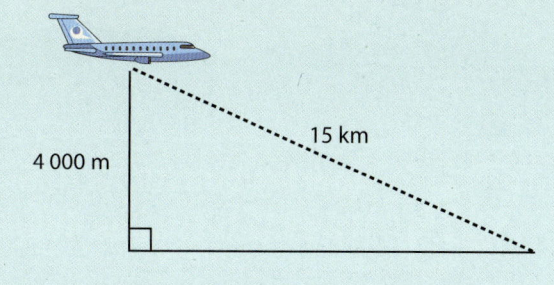

4. Sophie stands 5 m from a tree. From her eye level, the angle of depression of the base of the tree is 19° and the angle of elevation to the top of the tree is 64°.

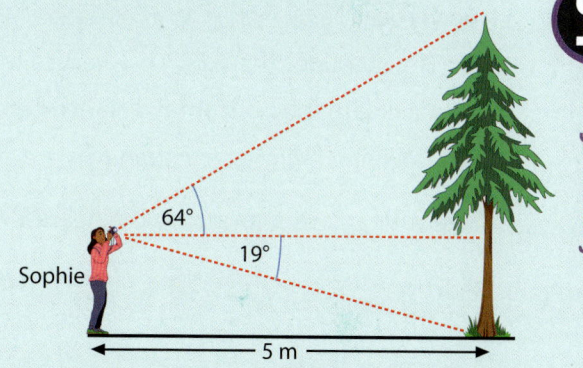

   (i) How tall is the tree? Give your answer to the nearest metre.

   (ii) Use the information to estimate Sophie's height, giving your answer to the nearest centimetre.

   (iii) What further information is needed to accurately calculate Sophie's height?

5. Tim and Sara are on the opposite sides on the outside of a building that is 180 metres in height. They measure the angle of elevation of the top of the tower as 42° and 58° respectively. Find the distance, to the nearest metre, between Tim and Sara.

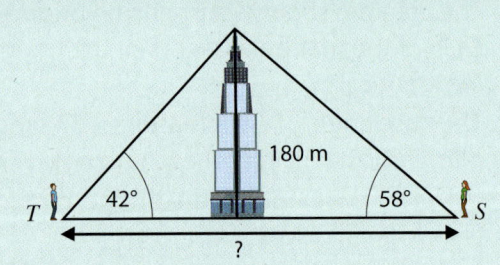

6. From a plane flying due west at 365 m above sea level, the angles of depression to two ships sailing on the sea below measure 34° and 24° respectively.
   How far apart are the ships, to the nearest metre?

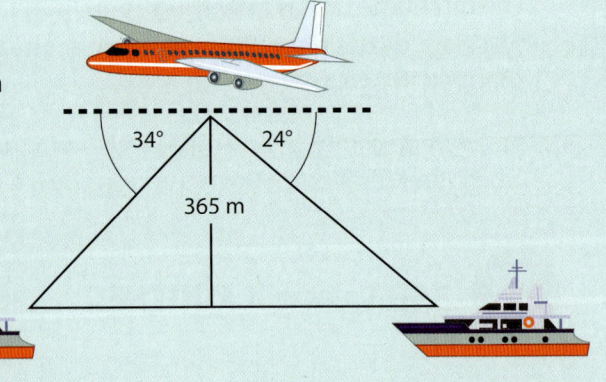

7. A ski lift connects B to T passing through M on its way. The lift travels 45 m from B to M at an angle of 54° off the vertical and a further 22 m from M to T at an angle of 72° off the vertical.
   (i) How far does the ski lift rise vertically going from B to M?
   (ii) Calculate the horizontal distance between M and T.
   (iii) How much higher is T than B?

   Give your answers correct to the nearest metre.

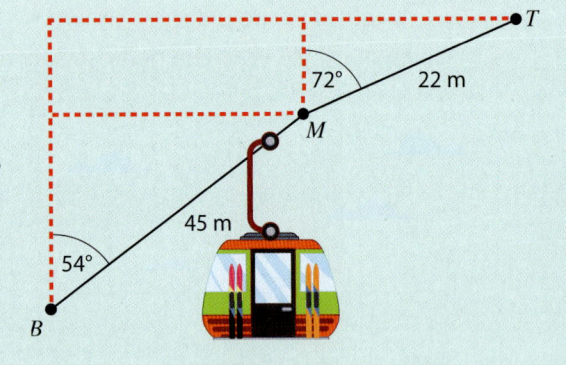

Now that you have completed the unit, revisit the

Something to think about ...

question posed at the start of this unit.

Now try questions 4, 5, 7, 11 and 12 on pages 559–61

Unit 35

Linking Thinking revision material

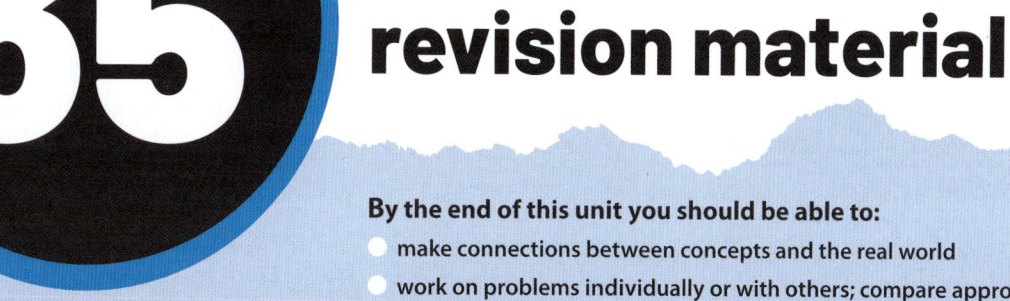

By the end of this unit you should be able to:

- make connections between concepts and the real world
- work on problems individually or with others; compare approaches and adapt your own strategy
- break up a problem into manageable parts
- make sense of a given problem and use Maths to solve it
- represent a mathematical problem in a variety of different ways
- interpret and evaluate how reasonable your solution is in the context of the original problem
- reflect on the strategy you used to solve a mathematical problem
- identify limitations and suggest improvements

Linking Thinking questions

Reference grid

	Analysing data	Probability 2	Money matters 2	Circles 2	Further geometry	Working with the coordinate plane	Inequalities	Non-linear relationships	Trigonometry
	C.26	C.27	C.28	C.29	C.30	C.31	C.32	C.33	C.34
1	✓	✓	✓						
2		✓					✓		
3	✓		✓				✓		
4					✓				✓
5						✓			✓
6	✓	✓							
7				✓	✓				✓
8					✓			✓	
9		✓	✓						
10		✓					✓		
11				✓	✓	✓			✓
12		✓							✓
13		✓					✓		
14	✓	✓	✓					✓	

Section C Applying our skills

Questions

1. (a) A survey of car sales is taken in a town during a given year. The results are shown in the table below.

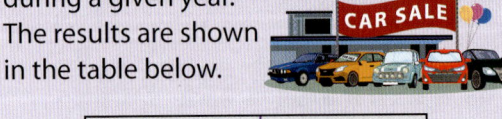

Make of car	Number of car sales
Volkswagen	750
Hyundai	400
Toyota	800
Skoda	350
Nissan	500

  (i) Identify the type of data collected in this survey.

  (ii) Draw any chart of your choice to represent this data. Justify your choice of chart.

  (iii) Calculate the mean and range of the numerical data above.

(b) The total sales of Volkswagen cars is €14 555 000. Calculate the average price paid for a Volkswagen car.

(c) (i) If a car is picked at random from the cars sold in this year, what is the probability that it will be a Hyundai?

  (ii) Hyundai cars are available for purchase in Ireland in a range of seven different models. Each model is available as a diesel, petrol or electric fuel type and in five different colour options. How many different versions of Hyundai cars are available for purchase in Ireland?

(d) Angie borrows €15 000 at the rate of 8% per annum compound interest to help her buy a car.

How much will Angie owe at the end of three years if she makes no repayments in the meantime?

2. A Maths test has 25 questions. Four points are given for each correct answer one point is deducted for each incorrect answer.
Keith answered all questions and scored 35. Keith answers x questions correctly and y incorrectly.

(a) (i) Write two equations to represent the above information.

  (ii) Using your answer from part (i) or otherwise, find how many questions Keith answered incorrectly.

(b) In Keith's class, 14 students are girls and 11 are boys. A student is selected at random from the class. What is the probability of picking a boy?

(c) Keith adds up the points from all the tests he has done in the term. Keith finds that he has a total of 167 points since the start of term. He wants to have at least 300 points by the end of the term. He estimates that he will score 35 points on each test for the rest of the term.

  (i) Write an inequality that represents Keith's situation.

  (ii) How many more tests will Keith have to do, assuming he scores 35 points per test, to achieve at least 300 points? Justify your answer.

3. (a) Tom invested €4 800 in the bank and the money earned 4% interest in the first year. He added €1 000 to the investment at the end of the first year and the whole investment earned 3% interest in the second year.

  (i) Find the amount of Tom's investment at the end of the second year.

  (ii) Tom buys a new car with the money at the end of the second year. The car costs €3 500. How much of the investment will Tom have left after buying the car?

  (iii) The car's cost of €3 500 includes VAT at 22%. Tom uses his car for work, so his company says they will pay for the VAT on the car. How much will the company give Tom to cover the cost of the VAT? Give your answer to the nearest euro.

(b) The table below shows the distance (km) travelled by Tom each day, for 28 days.

12·5	12·6	12·8	19·6	14·9	14·7	12·2
15·4	10·2	13·6	13·9	14·5	14·8	12·8
12·1	13·3	14·3	14·2	13·1	14·5	16·8
13·9	14·4	13·7	13·8	14·1	15·6	15·9

(i) Find the mean and the median of this data, to one decimal place where appropriate.

(ii) Represent the data in a stem and leaf plot.

(iii) Write down the range of the data.

(iv) Based on the mean, how many kilometres a year does Tom travel in his car, assuming he drives 5 days a week, 52 weeks of the year?

(c) Tom thinks about selling his car and renting a car, five days a week for work. The rate to rent a car is €30 per day, plus €0·50 per km. His company will pay €125 per week towards the cost, if Tom rents the car.
How much would it cost Tom to rent the car for the year based on the mean distance travelled in part **(b)**?

(d) Tom travels to Paris on holidays. A Parisian company rent Segways to tourists for a €20 flat fee, plus €35 per hour. Tom wants to rent a Segway, but he does not want to spend more than €150.

(i) Write an inequality to represent the situation. Be sure to explain the meaning of any letters you have used.

(ii) Solve the inequality to find how many full hours he afford to rent a Segway for.

4. (a) A Pythagorean triple is a set of three natural numbers which will satisfy the theorem of Pythagoras, for example, (3, 4, 5) and (5, 12, 13).

(i) Can you find two other Pythagorean triples?

(ii) Can you find one Pythagorean triple that contains three odd, natural numbers? Justify your answer.

(b) Using the Venn diagram below, sketch a triangle that will satisfy the rules of each set represented by letters A, B, C and D.

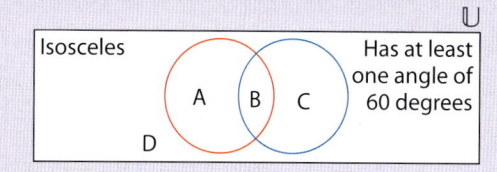

5. (a) (i) Plot the points $A(1, 1)$, $B(13, 6)$ and $C(13, 1)$ on a coordinate plane.

(ii) Find $|AB|$.

(iii) Use two different methods to find the slope of $[AB]$.

(b) (i) Prove that $\triangle ABC$ is a right-angled triangle.

(ii) Calculate, without measuring, $|\angle BAC|$. Give your answer to the nearest whole number.

(iii) State the theorem you could use to calculate $|\angle ABC|$. Hence, or otherwise find $|\angle ABC|$.

(c) (i) Draw $\triangle XYZ$ the image of $\triangle ABC$ under axial symmetry in the y-axis.

(ii) Calculate the area of the two triangles. What do you notice? Explain what you notice.

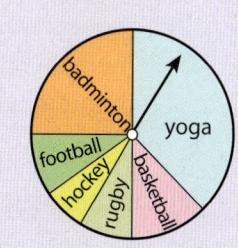

6. Ravi and Damien surveyed their friends and discovered that the six most popular extracurricular activities are football, basketball, badminton, rugby, hockey and yoga.
They want to randomly choose an activity for their classmates to do in PE, so they decide to make a spinner and a die showing each activity. The pictures above and right represent the spinner that Damien designed and the die that Ravi designed. The same six activities appear on the spinner and the cube.

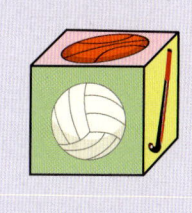

(a) Which of the following statements is true? Justify your answer in each case.

(i) Only the spinner can be used to select the activity fairly.

(ii) Only the cube can be used to select the activity fairly.

(iii) Neither the spinner nor the cube can be used to select the activity fairly.

(b) The table below shows the number of people who like each activity.

Activity	Number of people
Badminton	45
Yoga	60
Basketball	15
Football	15
Rugby	30
Hockey	15

  (i) How many people were surveyed?
  (ii) Draw a pie chart to represent this information.
  (iii) Could this data be represented by a histogram? Give a reason for your answer.

7. An artist designed this logo. It is a right triangle with a semicircle drawn on each side.

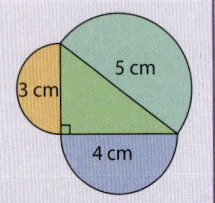

  (i) Calculate the area of each semicircle, in terms of π.
  (ii) Add the areas of the two smaller semicircles, and compare this sum to the area of the larger semicircle. What do you notice?
  (iii) One of the theorems you studied in geometry explains the relationship you found in part (ii). Name and state this theorem.

8. Mark has a design for a circular brick patio in the centre of his lawn.

  (i) Find, in terms of π, the area of the brick surface if the radius of the patio is 2 m.

Mark decides to investigate the effect of increasing the radius of the patio on the area of the brick surface. He produces the table below.

Radius patio (m)	Area of brick, in terms of π (m²)
0	
2	
4	
6	
8	
10	

  (ii) Copy and complete the table.
  (iii) Draw a graph to represent the data in the table. Put the radius of the patio on the x-axis and the area of brick surface on the y-axis.
  (iv) What type of relationship exists between the radius of the brick patio and the area of the brick surface? Justify your answer.
  (v) If the radius of the brick patio is 3 m, use your graph to estimate the area of brick.
  (vi) Is the pattern of the radius given in each case linear or non-linear? Justify your answer.
  (vii) Is the pattern of the area linear or non-linear? Justify your answer.

9. (a) David has only €5 notes and €10 notes in his wallet. He has five notes totalling €35.

  (i) How many of each does he have?
  (ii) If David selected a note at random, what is the probability it would be a €10 note?

(b) David has an annual salary of €28 000 and is entitled to a tax credit of €3 200. He is charged tax at a rate of 20%.

  (i) Calculate how much tax David will have to pay (net tax).
  (ii) Calculate David's net salary (salary after tax has been paid).

(c) David is playing a video game. The game is programmed to randomly put his character somewhere on the computer screen that has a rectangular lava pit on it. If you land in the lava pit, you lose points. The screen is 25 cm by 43 cm and the lava pit is 5 cm by 14 cm.

  (i) Find the area of the computer screen.
  (ii) Find the area of the lava pit.
  (iii) What is the probability that David will land in lava on this game?

10. (a) Jack and John call a taxi to take them to the train station. The taxi driver charges €1 when they get in the car. The charge is then €2 for each kilometre they travel.

   (i) They have budgeted €23 between them for the taxi. How far can they travel?

   (ii) They exit the taxi 3 km from the train station, so Jack and John walk the rest of the way to the train station. It takes them 40 minutes to walk the remaining 3 km. What is their average walking speed in km/hour?

   (iii) Jack and John get the train from Limerick to Waterford. The train travels at a speed of 108 km/hr and the journey takes 2 hours and 15 minutes. Find the distance travelled by the train.

(b) (i) Jack has p sweets. John has 13 fewer sweets than Jack. Write an expression that shows how many sweets John has.

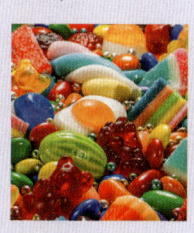

   (ii) If the total number of sweets is 47, find how many sweets Jack has and how may sweets John has.

(c) John won 40 teddy bears playing hoops at the Waterford fair. He gave two to every student in his Maths class. He has at least 7 teddy bears left.

   (i) Write an inequality to represent the situation. Be sure to explain the meaning of any letters you have used.

   (ii) Solve the inequality to find the maximum number of students in his class.

(d) In Jack's English class of 40 students, 18 are in the camogie club and 25 are in the Gaelic football club. Four students are not in either club.

   (i) Draw a Venn diagram to represent this information.

   (ii) If a student is selected at random, what is the probability that the selected student is in the camogie club only?

   (iii) If a student is selected at random, what is the probability that the student is in both clubs?

11. (a) Look at the grid. Without measuring, find another point that is the same distance from A as B is.

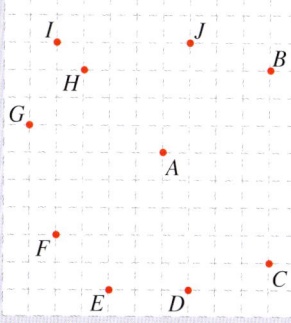

Describe and show a method to find this point, using skills from each of the following topics:

   (i) Geometry constructions

   (ii) Translations

   (iii) Coordinate geometry

   (iv) Trigonometry

(b) Did you find another way to find the required point? If so, explain how and show the method.

12. (a) A dart is thrown at a circular target board. The board has a white inner circle and a grey shaded outer ring, a shown.

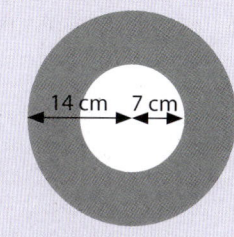

   (i) Find the area of the grey shaded region (let $\pi = 3.14$).

   (ii) A dart is thrown at random and hits the board. Find the probability that the dart will **not** land in the grey shaded region of the board.

(b) In front of the dart board is a ramp. The sloping face of this ramp is to be covered in carpet.

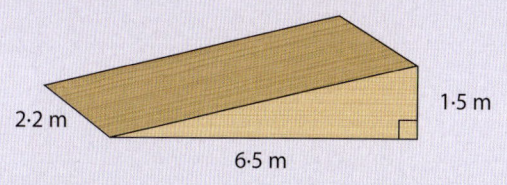

   (i) Calculate the length of the ramp, to the nearest tenth of a metre.

   (ii) Calculate the area of carpet needed.

   (iii) The carpet is available in rolls of 10 m², and costs €49·99 per roll. How many rolls will need to be purchased to fully carpet the ramp?

   (iv) Find the angle between the face of the ramp and the horizontal ground.

   (v) What (if any) percentage of the total carpet purchased is left over?

Section C **Applying our skills**

13. (a) The area of a picture frame is 99 cm².

    The length of the frame is x cm and the width of the frame is $(x - 2)$ cm.

    (i) Write an equation, in terms of x, for the area of the frame.

    (ii) By solving the equation from part (i), find the length and the width of the rectangular picture frame.

    (iii) Hence, find the perimeter of the frame.

(b) The picture frame from part (a) is being sold in a shop. Fourteen out of the last 224 customers who bought the frame damaged it while hanging it.

    (i) Based on previous experience, what is the probability that a customer does **not** damage the frame when hanging it up?

    (ii) The shop offers a service to hang the picture frame on a wall for a charge of 14% of the cost of the picture frame. If the picture frame costs €89·98, how much does the shop charge for hanging the picture frame?

(c) The diagonal lengths in cm, of the other frames in the shop are as follows.

    20   10   19   26   11   14   25   20   15

    For these diagonal lengths, find each of the following. Round your answers to three significant figures where necessary.

    (i) The mean
    (ii) The median
    (iii) The mode
    (iv) The range

(d) 80 customers enter the shop on a certain Tuesday. Nine customers buy a picture frame and glass. 35 customers only buy a frame.

    Two customers do not buy a frame or glass.

    (i) Represent this information on Venn diagram.

    (ii) What percentage of customers bought both a frame and glass?

    (iii) How many customers bought only glass?

14. (a) Archie sells gold for €52·20 per gram, before VAT. He has some 7 g weights and some 5 g weights.

    (i) Can he weigh exactly 38 grams of gold? Justify your answer.

    (ii) How much does 38 grams of gold cost, before VAT?

    (iii) If the total bill after VAT was added amounts to €2 439·83, find the rate at which VAT was charged.

    (iv) If the exchange rate is €1 = $1·12, how much would 1 kilogram of gold cost in dollars (excluding VAT)?

(b) A triangular garden has sides 56 m, 35 m and 35 m.

    (i) Using an appropriate scale, sketch a diagram of the triangle.

    (ii) What type of triangle have you drawn? Give a reason for your answer.

    (iii) Find the perpendicular height of the triangle and hence find the area of the triangle.

    (iv) The triangular garden contains a square vegetable patch. Given that the vegetable patch covers $\frac{2}{7}$ of the triangular garden, find the area of the vegetable patch.

    (v) If fencing panels cost €15 per metre, how much will it cost to place a fence around the perimeter of the vegetable patch?

Mathematical and statistical investigations

Introduction to mathematical and statistical investigations

Maths can be used to investigate and solve problems in everyday life. In Junior Cycle Mathematics, you are required to carry out two classroom-based assessments (CBAs), which are investigations using your Maths skills.

In the previous Linking Thinking units, we looked at how to perform a mathematical investigation. Now that we have completed the Statistics section of the course, we will look at how to perform a statistical investigation.

> Sometimes it is hard to come up with an idea. It can be helpful, throughout this process, to discuss how to develop your investigation with some classmates.

When carrying out a Statistical Investigation, consider the following strategy:

1. **Formulate a question** – Why did you pick this question?
   What are you trying to find out?
   Is your question statistically valid?
   Is your question ethically valid?

2. **Plan and collect data** – How will you collect your data? Primary or secondary?
   How will you select a representative sample?
   How will you make sure your data is unbiased?

3. **Organise and manage the data** – How are you going to record your data?
   Will you use pen and paper/ICT/a folder, etc.?

4. **Explore the data** – What type of data have you collected?
   What is the most appropriate way to represent your data?
   Have you noticed any unusual values in the data you have collected?

5. **Represent and analyse the data** – Use tables, graphs, formulas, etc.
   Look at central tendencies (Show your work clearly)
   What is the most appropriate average to use? Why?
   Look at spread; what is the range?
   Can you identify any patterns or trends?

6. **Answer the original question** – What did you discover?
   Comment on your analysis, linking it to the original question.
   Is it reasonable? Does it make sense? Justify your answer.

7. **Reflect on your investigation** – What were the strengths and weaknesses of your strategy?
   If you were to investigate this question again, what would you do differently?
   What have you learned by carrying out this investigation?

8. **Extend and generalise your findings** – Can you extend your findings to the general population? If not, why?

Statistical investigations

1. Investigate what the opinion of sports is in your school.

2. Investigate unemployment statistics over the last 24-month period. Comment on how the numbers change at different times in the year.

3. Investigate the number of passengers travelling through your nearest airport over a 12-month period. Comment on how the numbers change at different times in the year.

4. Investigate the average number of people in cars, passing your school gate over a period of time.

5. Investigate favourite pizza toppings/ice cream flavours/types of fruit, etc. of the students in your class.

6. Investigate modes of transport to school.

7. Investigate the average number of children per family.

8. Investigate the relationship between the average distance from school and time taken to get to school.

9. Investigate the percentage of students absent in your year group daily, over a period of time.

10. Investigate school bags of the students in your school – the average weight/colour/number of pockets/number of zips, etc.

11. Investigate how students spend their time. For example, on exercise, homework, watching TV, social media, video games, helping at home, a part-time job.

12. Investigate the sugar content of the most popular brands of breakfast cereal.

13. Investigate the carbon footprint of various energy sources including coal, gas, oil, wood.

14. Investigate the benefit of installing solar panels on your house. Include the cost of installation versus long-term savings.

15. Investigate the most popular foods sold by the school canteen.

Mathematical investigations

1. Investigate loans options. Include the cost difference in taking out a short-term loan versus a long-term loan.

2. Calculate the height of the tallest point in the school without using a ladder.

3. Investigate savings accounts in various financial institutions.

4. You are setting up a bus route in your area. Investigate how best to design the route in order to maximise your profit.

5. How many toothpicks can be made from a tree?

6. Is there a relationship between the area of the square that fits exactly outside a circle and the one that exactly inside the same circle?

7. Investigate the difference in income tax paid by single people and married people.

8. Investigate the cost of buying a car and applying for a five-year loan for the amount required.

9. Investigate patterns in the world around you.

10. Investigate if a corner in a room makes a 90° angle. Use multiple approaches.

KEY Answer key

Section A

Unit 1 Number, coordinate plane and symmetry

Practice questions 1·1

1. (i) 5, (ii) 0, (iii) –2, (iv) –2, (v) 2, (vi) –1, (vii) –6, (viii) –1, (ix) 4, (x) –6
2. (i) 5, (ii) 9, (iii) 4, (iv) 4, (v) –1, (vi) 3, (vii) –3, (viii) –4, (ix) –5, (x) –5, (xi) 8, (xii) –4
3. (i) Any three valid integers, e.g. –6, –5, –4
   (ii) Any three valid integers, e.g. 0, –1, –2
4. A natural number is a whole positive number, which does not include zero, and continues to infinity. Examples include: number of chairs in a room, number of books in your bag, number of students in your school (or any other valid examples)
5. An integer is a whole positive or negative number, including zero. Examples include: floors in a building – underground floors are negative, upper floors are positive; golf scores are listed as whole positive or negative numbers; temperatures, when expressed as whole numbers, can be classified as positive or negative integers (or any other valid examples)
6. Five flights of stairs
7. –4°C
8. Second floor/Floor 2
9. 3-cent increase
10. –11
11. (i) Always true
    (ii) Sometimes true
    (iii) Always true
    (iv) Never true
    (v) Sometimes true
    (vi) Never true

Practice questions 1·2·1

1. (i) Flower = (3, 2)
   (ii) Bee = (10, 5)
   (iii) Car = (4, 11)
   (iv) Duck = (1, 3)
   (v) Rabbit = (2, 8)
   (vi) Spider = (1, 10)
   (vii) Tree = (5, 7)
   (viii) Emoji = (7, 3)
   (ix) Dog = (11, 1)
   (x) Turtle = (8, 9)

3. (a) (ii) Rectangle
   (b) (ii) Triangle
   (c) (ii) Parallelogram
       (iii) Join point A to point D to make triangle ADC, or join point B to C to make triangle BCD

Practice questions 1·2·2

1. (i) Flower = (–5, –3)
   (ii) Bee = (4, 6)
   (iii) Car = (8, –2)
   (iv) Spider = (–8, 6)
   (v) Tree = (2, –7)
   (vi) Emoji = (–3, 2)
   (vii) Mouse = (–8, –7)
   (viii) Dog = (–3, –7)
   (ix) Rabbit = (–8, 3)
   (x) Turtle = (6, 2)

Practice questions 1·3·1

1. A: perimeter = 20 units; area = 25 units^2
   B: perimeter = 12 units; area = 9 units^2
   C: perimeter = 20 units; area = 16 units^2
   D: perimeter = 10 units; area = 6 units^2
   E: perimeter = 14 units; area = 6 units^2
   F: perimeter = 12 units; area = 9 units^2
   G: perimeter = 18 units; area = 10 units^2
   H: perimeter = 24 units; area = 19 units^2
2. (i) Area = 8 units^2; perimeter = 12 units
   (ii) Area = 24 units^2; perimeter = 20 units
   (iii) Area = 12 units^2; perimeter = 16 units
   (iv) Area = 24 units^2; perimeter = 20 units
   (v) Area = 10 units^2; perimeter = 14 units
   (vi) Area = 20 units^2; perimeter = 18 units

Practice questions 1·3·2

1. (i) (a) Area = 24 cm^2
       (b) Perimeter = 20 cm
   (ii) (a) Area = 22 mm^2
        (b) Perimeter = 26 mm
   (iii) (a) Area = 180 cm^2
         (b) Perimeter = 56 cm
   (iv) (a) Area = 56 mm^2
        (b) Perimeter = 30 mm
   (v) (a) Area = 25 km^2
       (b) Perimeter = 20 km
   (vi) (a) Area = 7 cm^2
        (b) Perimeter = 16 cm
2. 15 m^2
3. (i) Area = 16 m^2
   (ii) Perimeter = 16 m
4. (i) Area of Steve = 36 units^2
   (ii) Perimeter of Steve = 42 units
5. Wastage = 0·6 m^2

Practice questions 1·4

1. (i) 4 lines of symmetry
   (ii) 0 lines of symmetry
   (iii) 2 lines of symmetry
   (iv) Infinite lines of symmetry. Any line that passes through the centre of a circle is a line of symmetry.
   (v) 4 lines of symmetry
   (vi) Zero lines of symmetry
3. (d) (i) 2 lines of symmetry
       (ii) 1 line of symmetry
       (iii) 4 lines of symmetry
       (iv) 1 lines of symmetry
       (v) 4 lines of symmetry

Practice questions 1·5

5. (ii) (7, 4), (8, 6), (6, 8)
6. (i) Numerous correct answers
   (ii) The line of symmetry divides each figure into two mirror halves

Revision questions

1A Core skills

1. (i) 9, (ii) 7, (iii) 12, (iv) 8, (v) 5, (vi) 11, (vii) 6, (viii) 7
2. (i) 5, (ii) –2, (iii) –5, (iv) –4, (v) –1, (vi) –4, (vii) –4, (viii) 0
4. A (i) Area = 14 units^2
     (ii) Perimeter = 20 units
   B (i) Area = 12 units^2
     (ii) Perimeter = 26 units
   C (i) Area = 66 units^2
     (ii) Perimeter = 58 units
5. (i) 2 lines of symmetry
   (ii) 6 lines of symmetry
   (iii) 1 line of symmetry
   (iv) 1 line of symmetry
   (v) 1 line of symmetry
   (vi) 1 line of symmetry

1B Taking it further

1. (i) 23, **28**, 33, 38, 43, **48**, **53**
      Pattern is increasing by 5 each time
   (ii) 3, **11**, **19**, 27, 35, 43, **51**
        Pattern is increasing by 8 each time
2. (iii) No, the line $|AD|$ is not a line of symmetry, because it does not divide the figure into two mirror image halves.
5. (iii) The diagonals of a square are lines of symmetry, however the diagonals of a rectangle are not lines of symmetry.
6. (i) (a) Square, (b) Triangle, (c) Pentagon, (d) Rectangle
7. (i) Always true
   (ii) Sometimes true
   (iii) Never true
   (iv) Never true
   (v) Sometimes true

8. (i) 16 units^2
   (ii) 16 units
   (iii) Yes. Numerous valid answers, e.g. a rectangle with length of 2 and width of 8. Area = 16 units^2, perimeter = 20 units. If it had a length of 1 and a width of 16, area would be 16 units^2 but perimeter would be 34 units. Area is the same, but perimeters are not.
   (iv) 8 units × 2 units = 16 units^2
        16 units × 1 unit = 16 units^2
   (v) (a) Largest perimeter = 34 units
       (b) Smallest perimeter = 16 units
   (vi) False. It is possible to keep the same area and change the perimeter of a rectangle (see part (v) above).

Unit 2 Sets, number and chance

Practice questions 2·1

1. (i) {a, b, c, d, e}
   (ii) {red, orange, yellow, green, blue, indigo, violet}
   (iii) {a, p, l, e}
   (iv) {O, A}
   (v) {1, 2, 3, 4, 5, 6, 7, 8, 9, 10}
   (vi) {September, October, November, December}
2. (i) Months of the year starting with 'A'
   (ii) Fingers on a hand
   (iii) Days of the week starting with 'T'
   (iv) First four planets of the solar system
3. 1 = C; 2 = A; 3 = B; 4 = E; 5 = D
4. (i) $2 \in \mathbb{Q}$
   (ii) May $\notin$ {days of the week}
   (iii) #D = 8
   (iv) {1, 2} $\subset$ S
   (v) J = ∅
   (vi) $2 \notin$ {letters of the alphabet}
5. (i) A = B, the elements of A and B are the same
   (ii) A ≠ B, the elements of A and B are not the same
   (iii) A ≠ B, the elements of A and B are not the same
   (iv) A ≠ B, the elements of A and B are not the same
6. All are sets except (ii) Justification: (i), (iii) and (iv) are a well-defined collection of objects with something in common but (ii) is not well-defined.
7. (i) B $\not\subset$ A, (ii) C $\subset$ A, (iii) B $\not\subset$ C, (iv) C $\subset$ C, (v) ∅ $\subset$ B, (vi) C $\subset$ B
8. (i) {1, 2, 3, 4, 5}; $X = \{x \mid x$ is one of the first 5 counting numbers$\}$
   (ii) {M, A, T, H, E, I, C, S}; $X = \{x \mid x$ is a letter in the word MATHEMATICS$\}$
   (iii) {2, 3, 4, 5, 6, 7}; set of numbers between 2 and 7 inclusive
9. (i) Always true
   (ii) Sometimes true
   (iii) Always true
   (iv) Never true
10. (i) True: 13 ∈ P, 9 ∈ P but 22 $\notin$ P
    (ii) True: 5 ∈ P, 7 ∈ P and 12 ∈ Q
    (iii) False: 3 ∈ P, 13 ∈ P but 10 ∉ Q
    (iv) True: 7 ∉ Q, 9 ∉ Q but 16 ∈ Q

Practice questions 2·2·1

1. (i) {1, 2, 3, 6}
   (ii) {1, 3, 5, 15}
   (iii) {1, 3, 9, 27}
   (iv) {1, 2, 4, 5, 8, 10, 20, 40}
   (v) {1, 2, 4, 8, 16, 32, 64}
2. (i) {2, 4, 6, 8, 10 …}
   (ii) {3, 6, 9, 12, 15 …}
   (iii) {5, 10, 15, 20, 25 …}
   (iv) {6, 12, 18, 24, 30 …}
   (v) {8, 16, 24, 32, 40 …}
3. (i) {2, 3, 5, 7}
   (ii) {17, 19, 23}
   (iii) {101, 103, 107, 109}
4. (i) 2 × 3 × 3
   (ii) 2 × 2 × 2 × 2 × 2
   (iii) 2 × 2 × 2 × 5
   (iv) 3 × 3 × 5
   (v) 2 × 2 × 2 × 3 × 3
   (vi) 2 × 2 × 2 × 2 × 3 × 3
5. (i) 2, (ii) 9, (iii) 6, (iv) 4, (v) 6, (vi) 4, (vii) 15, (viii) 2
6. (i) 20, (ii) 24, (iii) 18, (iv) 30, (v) 24, (vi) 12, (vii) 30, (viii) 24
7. (a) (i) 60: 2 × 2 × 3 × 5
       (ii) 96: 2 × 2 × 2 × 2 × 2 × 3
   (b) 12
   (c) 480
8. 8 metres
9. 60th day
10. 3 pieces
11. (i) Even, e.g. LCM of 10 and 15 = 30
    (ii) HCF is smaller number; LCM is larger number, e.g. 3 and 6: HCF = 3; LCM = 6
    (iii) HCF = 1; LCM = product of the two numbers, e.g. 3 and 5: HCF = 1; LCM = 15

Practice questions 2·2·2

1. (i) False, e.g. $-3 \notin \mathbb{N}$, not positive
   (ii) True, e.g. $3 \in \mathbb{Q}$, can be written as $\frac{3}{1}$
   (iii) False, e.g. $-\frac{1}{2} \notin \mathbb{Z}$, not a whole number
   (iv) True, e.g. $-3 \in \mathbb{Q}$, can be written as $-\frac{3}{1}$
   (v) True, e.g. $5 \in \mathbb{Z}, \mathbb{N} \subset \mathbb{Z}$
   (vi) False, e.g. $-\frac{3}{4} \notin \mathbb{N}$, negative and not a whole number
   (vii) False, e.g. $\{\frac{1}{2}, \frac{1}{3} …\} \not\subset \mathbb{Z}$, not whole numbers
   (viii) True, e.g. {1, 2, 3…} $\subset \mathbb{Z}$, positive whole numbers
2. (i) {1, 2, 3, 4, 5}
   (ii) {11, 13, 17, 19}
   (iii) {−9, −7, −5, −3, −1, 1, 3, 5}
   (iv) {26, 28, 30, 32, 34}
   (v) {3, 6, 9, 12, 15, 18, 21, 24, 27}
   (vi) {1, 2, 4, 8, 16, 32}
3. (a) (i) Positive whole numbers
       (ii) $\mathbb{N}$
   (b) (i) Whole numbers, positive and negative
       (ii) $\mathbb{Z}$
   (c) (i) Numbers that can be written as fractions
       (ii) $\mathbb{Q}$
4. (i) $\frac{1}{3}$, (ii) $\frac{1}{2}$, (iii) $\frac{1}{4}$, (iv) $\frac{1}{5}$
5. (i) Sometimes true
   (ii) Sometimes true
   (iii) Always true
   (iv) Never true
   (v) Always true

Practice questions 2·3

2. (i) A = {1, 2, 3, 5, 6, 9}
   (ii) B = {2, 3, 4, 5, 7, 8, 10}
   (iii) A∩B = {2, 3, 5}
   (iv) A∪B = {1, 2, 3, 4, 5, 6, 7, 8, 9, 10}
   (v) 𝕌 = {1, 2, 3, 4, 5, 6, 7, 8, 9, 10, 11, 12}
3. (a) (i) A = {a, b, e, h, q, t}
       (ii) B = {a, d, f, g, h, j}
       (iii) 𝕌 = {a, b, d, e, f, g, h, i, j, p, q, y, t}
   (b) (i) 10
       (ii) 2
7. (i) 12 people play both basketball and football
   (ii) 52 people play basketball only
   (iii) 63 people play football only
   (iv) 8 people play neither basketball or football
   (v) 115
   (vi) 135
8. (i) 25, (ii) 7, (iii) 22, (iv) 47
9. (i) A: {1, 2, 3, 4, 6, 8, 12, 16, 24, 48}
       B: {1, 2, 4, 5, 10, 20}
   (iii) The factors of both 48 and 20
   (iv) 4
10. (i) (a) 𝕌
        (b) All of the elements
    (ii) (a) H∪N
         (b) All of the elements in both H and N
    (iii) (a) H∩N
          (b) Elements in common between H and N
11. (a) (i) P = {1, 3, 5, 7, 9, 11, 13, 15, 17, 19}
        (ii) Q = {3, 6, 9, 12, 15, 18}
        (iii) P∪Q = {1, 3, 5, 6, 7, 9, 11, 12, 13, 15, 17, 18, 19}
        (iv) P∩Q = {3, 9, 15}
    (b) (i) 10
        (ii) 6
        (iii) 13
        (iv) 3
12. (i) A = {2, 3, 5, 7}, (ii) B = {2, 4, 6, 8}, (iv) A∪B = {2, 3, 4, 5, 6, 7, 8}, (v) 1, (vi) Yes, 2 ∈ A

Practice questions 2·4

1. (i) $\frac{1}{2}$; 0·5; 50%
   (ii) $\frac{1}{4}$; 0·25; 25%
   (iii) $\frac{1}{4}$; 0·25; 25%
   (iv) $\frac{3}{4}$; 0·75; 75%
   (v) $\frac{1}{6}$; 0·1̇6; $16\frac{2}{3}$

2. (i) $\frac{1}{2}$; 0.5; 50%
   (ii) $\frac{1}{2}$; 0.5; 50%
   (iii) $\frac{2}{5}$; 0.4; 40%
   (iv) $\frac{4}{5}$; 0.8; 80%
   (v) $\frac{3}{10}$; 0.3; 30%
   (vi) $\frac{3}{10}$; 0.3; 30%
3. (i) $\frac{2}{5}$; 0.4; 40%
   (ii) $\frac{3}{10}$; 0.3; 30%
   (iii) $\frac{2}{5}$; 0.4; 40%
   (iv) $\frac{1}{10}$; 0.1; 10%
   (v) $\frac{1}{10}$; 0.1; 10%
   (vi) $\frac{1}{2}$; 0.5; 50%
4. (b) (i) $\frac{1}{2}$; 0.5; 50%
   (ii) $\frac{1}{2}$; 0.5; 50%
   (iii) $\frac{1}{20}$; 0.05; 5%
   (iv) $\frac{7}{20}$; 0.35; 35%
   (v) $\frac{1}{5}$; 0.2; 20%
   (vi) $\frac{3}{10}$; 0.3; 30%
5. (b) (i) $\frac{4}{11}$
   (ii) $\frac{7}{11}$
   (iii) $\frac{5}{11}$
   (iv) $\frac{5}{11}$

Revision questions
2A Core skills
1. (i) A number that will divide evenly into another number with no remainder
   (ii) A number multiplied by another whole number
   (iii) A positive whole number that has exactly two different whole number factors, which are 1 and the number itself
   (iv) A positive whole number
   (v) A whole number, which can be either positive or negative, including zero
   (vi) A number that can be written as a fraction
2. (i) 9, 13 or 27, (ii) 8, 10 or 48, (iii) 13, (iv) 8 or 48, (v) 13
   (vi) 10 + 9 = 19
        27 + 10 = 37
        13 + 10 = 23
        13 + 48 = 61
        9 + 8 = 17
3. (i) 2 × 3 × 5
   (ii) 2 × 2 × 2 × 7
   (iii) 3 × 3 × 3 × 3
4. (i) (a) 4
       (b) 120
   (ii) (a) 18
        (b) 270
5. (i) {1, 2, 3, 4, 5, 7, 8}, (ii) {2, 5}, (iii) 7
7. (i) {f, g, h, i, j, k, m, n}
   (ii) {f, g, h, i, j}
   (iii) {i, j, k}
   (iv) {f, g, h, i, j, k}
   (v) {i, j}
8. (b) (i) 8, (ii) 2, (iii) 5, (iv) 5

9. (a) 50
   (b) (i) $\frac{1}{10}$; 0.1; 10%
       (ii) $\frac{3}{10}$; 0.3; 30%
       (iii) $\frac{19}{50}$; 0.38; 38%

2B Taking it further
1. (a) (i) P = {2, 4, 6, 8, 10, 12, 14, 16, 18}
           Q = {4, 8, 12, 16}
       (ii) {2, 4, 6, 8, 10, 12, 14, 16, 18}
       (iii) {4, 8, 12, 16}
   (c) No, all the elements of P are not in Q
   (d) True
   (e) $\frac{2}{5}$; 0.4; 40%
2. (i) Always true
   (ii) Sometimes true
   (iii) Always true
   (iv) Sometimes true
3. (i) ∅; {m, p}; {m}; {p}
   (ii) 8 subsets; ∅; {k}; {j}; {n}; {k, j}; {k, n}; {j, n}, {k, j, n}
4. (i) Sometimes true
   (ii) Sometimes true
   (iii) Never true
   (iv) Always true
5. (b) (i) $\frac{3}{10}$, (ii) $\frac{7}{10}$, (iii) 1
6. 264 seconds
7. €9
8. 6 and 12
9. 72 and 144

Unit 3 Points, lines and angles
Practice questions 3·1
1. Two points are necessary to draw a straight line
2. A = line; B = ray; C = ray; D = line segment; E = none of these; F = point
3. (i) Line
   (ii) Line segment
   (iii) Ray
   (iv) A point is an exact location in a space or a plane
4. Rays
5. (i) A, B, C, D, E, F
   (ii) [AB], [AC], [AD], [AE], [AF], [BC], [BD], [BE], [BF], [CD], [CE], [CF], [DE], [DF], [EF]
12. (c) A ray, because it has a start and continues to infinity in one direction.

Practice questions 3·2
1. (i) Parallel: same distance apart and will never meet
   (ii) Perpendicular: two lines are perpendicular if they intersect like a perfect T or cross. This is known as a right angle.
   (iii) Neither parallel nor perpendicular
   (iv) Neither parallel nor perpendicular
2. (iii) By measuring the perpendicular distance between the lines; they are always the same distance – 5 cm – apart

3. (iii) By measuring the perpendicular distance between the lines; they are always the same distance – 70 mm – apart.
4. (iii) Check using a set square: check the two smaller angles around Q are 90°
5. (iii) Check using a set square: check the two smaller angles around N are 90°
6. (iii) By measuring: they are always the same distance – 4·7 cm – apart
7. (iii) Check using a set square: check the angle between the two lines is 90°. Using a ruler, check the distance between the perpendicular bisector and the two end points of line segment [PQ] is 4·5 cm.
8. (iii) Check using a set square: the angle between the two lines is 90°. Using a ruler, check the distance between the perpendicular bisector and the two end points of line segment [MN] is 5 cm.
9. (iii) Check using a set square: the angle between the two lines is 90°. Using a ruler, check the distance between the perpendicular bisector and the two end points of line segment [AB] is 5·5 cm.
10. Yes, the lines are perpendicular
11. (i) W. 26th St, W. 25th St, etc.
    (ii) W. 21st St, 5th Ave, etc.
    (iii) W. 23rd St, Broadway, etc.
12. (i) Parallel
    (ii) Parallel
13. (i) Perpendicular
    (ii) Parallel
14. (i) Parallel
    (ii) Perpendicular
15. (i) 65 m
    (ii) Perpendicular
    (iii) 2 × 65 = 130 m
16. (i) Perpendicular
    (ii) Train tracks, sides of roads, opposite sides of a football pitch or tennis court, etc.
    (iii) Tops and sides of a door, the floor and walls of a room; the side and end lines of a pitch, etc.

Practice questions 3·3
1. (i) 145°, (ii) 65°
2. (iii) Acute angle
3. (iii) Right angle
4. (iii) Obtuse angle
5. (ii) Straight angle
6. (ii) Reflex angle
7. (ii) Reflex angle
8. (i) |∠ABC| or |∠CBA|
   (ii) |∠FED| or |∠DEF|
   (iii) |∠HIJ| or |∠JIH|
   (iv) |∠MLK| or |∠KLM|
   (v) |∠PNO| or |∠ONP|
   (vi) |∠ABC| or |∠CBA|
   (vii) |∠DEF| or |∠FED|
9. (iii) |∠CAB| or |∠BAC|
10. (iii) |∠ZXY| or |∠YXZ|
15. (i) Best estimate
    (ii) Best estimate
    (iii) Best estimate

16. $|\angle ABC| = 115°$
17. $|\angle DEF| = 69°$
18. (i) $|\angle ABC| = 90°$
    (ii) $|\angle BCA| = 60°$
    (iii) $|\angle BAC| = 30°$
19. (i) 150°, (ii) Acute angle,
    (iii) Obtuse angle, (iv) Straight angle

Revision questions

3A Core skills

1. (i) Line
   (ii) Line segment
   (iii) Ray
   (iv) A point is an exact location in a space or a plane
3. (iii) By measuring the distance between the lines: they are always the same distance – 65 mm – apart
4. (iii) Using a set square, check that the angle between the two lines is 90°
6. (i) Obtuse, (ii) Reflex, (iii) Straight, (iv) Reflex, (v) Full, (vi) Acute
9. (i) Supplementary, as angles add up to 180°
   (ii) Not supplementary, as angles do not add up to 180°
   (iii) Supplementary, as angles add up to 180°
   (iv) Not supplementary, as angles do not add up to 180°

3B Taking it further

1. (i) 36°, (ii) 108°, (iii) 180°
2. (i) $|\angle BCT| = 30°$
   (ii) $|\angle CTB| = 90°$
   (iii) $|\angle TBC| = 60°$
4. (i) Parallel
   (ii) Perpendicular
   (iii) Parallel
   (iv) Perpendicular
   (v) Parallel

Unit 4 Working with numbers

Practice questions 4·1

1. (i) 12, (ii) 12, (iii) −16, (iv) −10, (v) −12, (vi) 6
2. (i) 450, (ii) 1 440, (iii) 754, (iv) 60, (v) 6, (vi) 4
3. (i) 437, (ii) 432, (iii) 5 070, (iv) 2 352, (v) 2 240, (vi) 3 735
4. (i) (+)126, (ii) (+)4, (iii) (+)56, (iv) −4, (v) (+)120, (vi) −216
5. (i) −27, (ii) −9, (iii) 0, (iv) 3, (v) 30, (vi) −24
6. (i) −4, (ii) −20, (iii) −2, (iv) −5, (v) −4, (vi) −4
7. (i) −6, (ii) 15, (iii) 12, (iv) −14, (v) 36, (vi) −7
8. (i) Always true
   (ii) Never true
   (iii) Never true
   (iv) Sometimes true
   (v) Always true

Practice questions 4·2

1. (i) 31, (ii) 12, (iii) 35, (iv) 13, (v) 10, (vi) 5
2. (i) 20, (ii) 24, (iii) 4, (iv) −4, (v) 16, (vi) 5
3. (i) 57, (ii) 14, (iii) 18, (iv) 25
4. (i) $2 + 3 + 4$
   (ii) $(2 × 3) + 4$
   (iii) $2 × (3 + 4)$
   (iv) $(2 + 3) × 4$
   (v) $(4 ÷ 2) × 3$
5. $10 + (20 − 12) ÷ 2 × 3 = 22$
   $10 + 20 − (12 ÷ 2) × 3 = 12$
   $10 + 20 − 12 ÷ (2 × 3) = 28$
6. $2 × (7 + 8) = 30$
   $(3 × 7) + 2 + 8 = 31$
   $(7 − 3) × 8 = 32$
   $(8 + 7) × 2 + 3 = 33$
   $2 × (7 + 8 + 2) = 34$
   $(2 + 3) × 7 = 35$
   $(7 + 8 + 3) × 2 = 36$
   $(8 × 2) + (7 × 3) = 37$
   $(7 × 2) + (3 × 8) = 38$
   $(7 + 8 − 2) × 3 = 39$
   $(2 + 3) × 8 = 40$
7. (i) $36 ÷ (4 × 3) = 3$
   (ii) $20 ÷ (5 × 2) + 3 = 5$
   (iii) $10 − 4 ÷ (2 − 1) = 6$
   (iv) $6 × (2 + 8) ÷ 4 = 15$
8. (i) Jane adds 3 and 8 first and then multiplies by 6.
      Mark multiplies 3 by 6 first and then adds 8.
   (ii) Mark, because multiplication comes before addition.
9. $(2 × 275) + (3 × 275) + (2 × 275) = 1\,925$
10. (i) Brian = 35; Lucy = 35 − 15; Cara = (35 − 15) ÷ 2
    (ii) 10
11. $(8 + 4) × (6 ÷ 3) = 24$
    $(8 + 4) × 6 ÷ 3 = 24$
    $(8 ÷ 4 + 6) × 3 = 24$
    $(8 + 4) ÷ 3 × 6 = 24$
    $(8 − 6) × (4 × 3) = 24$
    $(8 − 6) × 4 × 3 = 24$
    $(8 − 6) × 3 × 4 = 24$
    $(3 × 4) × (8 − 6) = 24$
    $(3 × 4 − 8) × 6 = 24$
    $3 × (8 ÷ 4 + 6) = 24$

Practice questions 4·3

1. (i) $6 × 2 × 5 = 60$; $2 × 6 × 5 = 60$; $6 × 5 × 2 = 60$
   (ii) $3 × 1 × 8 = 24$; $1 × 3 × 8 = 24$; $8 × 1 × 3 = 24$
   (iii) $7 × 9 × 4 = 252$; $9 × 7 × 4 = 252$; $4 × 9 × 7 = 252$
   (iv) $2 × 10 × 5 = 100$; $10 × 5 × 2 = 100$; $5 × 10 × 2 = 100$
   (v) $6 × 3 × 7 = 126$; $7 × 3 × 6 = 126$; $3 × 6 × 7 = 126$
   (vi) $2 × 9 × 8 = 144$; $8 × 9 × 2 = 144$; $9 × 2 × 8 = 144$
2. (i) $6 + 4 + 2 = 12$; $4 + 2 + 6 = 12$; $2 + 4 + 6 = 12$
   (ii) $9 + 2 − 7 = 4$; $2 + 9 − 7 = 4$; $−7 + 2 + 9 = 4$
   (iii) $12 + 4 + 3 = 19$; $3 + 4 + 12 = 19$; $4 + 3 + 12 = 19$
   (iv) $7 + 6 + 8 = 21$; $6 + 7 + 8 = 21$; $8 + 7 + 6 = 21$
   (v) $−3 + 9 + 11 = 17$; $11 + 9 − 3 = 17$; $9 + 11 − 3 = 17$
   (vi) $5 − 4 + 7 = 8$; $5 + 7 − 4 = 8$; $7 + 5 − 4 = 8$
3. (i) $3 + (2 − 4) = 1$; $(3 + 2) − 4 = 1$
   (ii) $5 + (10 + 8) = 23$; $(5 + 10) + 8 = 23$
   (iii) $(9 − 4) + 7 = 12$; $9 + (−4 + 7) = 12$
   (iv) $(7 + 6) + 2 = 15$; $7 + (6 + 2) = 15$
   (v) $(3 + 12) − 9 = 6$; $3 + (12 − 9) = 6$
   (vi) $(8 + 6) + 8 = 22$; $8 + (6 + 8) = 22$
4. (i) $(4 × 3) × 2 = 24$; $4 × (3 × 2) = 24$
   (ii) $2 × (3 × 5) = 30$; $(2 × 3) × 5 = 30$
   (iii) $8 × (3 × 1) = 24$; $(8 × 3) × 1 = 24$
   (iv) $6 × (7 × 5) = 210$; $(6 × 7) × 5 = 210$
   (v) $(10 × 3) × 2 = 60$; $10 × (3 × 2) = 60$
   (vi) $(9 × 5) × 2 = 90$; $9 × (5 × 2)$
5. (i) 40, (ii) 6, (iii) 48, (iv) −4, (v) −16, (vi) 60, (vii) 45, (viii) 12, (ix) −6
6. (i) Commutative, (ii) Associative, (iii) Distributive, (iv) Associative, (v) Associative
7. (i) Commutative, (ii) Distributive, (iii) Associative, (iv) Commutative, (v) Distributive, (vi) Associative
8. (i) $(4 + 6) + 9 = 19$ and $4 + (6 + 9) = 19$
   (ii) $9 × 12 = 108$ and $12 × 9 = 108$
   (iii) $10 × (7 × 5) = 350$ and $(10 × 7) × 5 = 350$
   (iv) $2 × (3 + 5) = 16$ and $2 × 3 + 2 × 5 = 16$
9. (i) Use the same number because $3 × 8$ is the same as $8 × 3$
   (ii) Area is the same because $4 × 10$ is the same as $4 × 5 + 4 × 5$
   (iii) All sell same number because $42 + 59 + 78 = 59 + 78 + 42 = 78 + 59 + 42$
10. (i) False
    (ii) True
    (iii) False
    (iv) True
    (v) True

Practice questions 4·4

1. (i) Base = 2, index = 5
   (ii) Base = 3, index = 6
   (iii) Base = 6, index = 8
   (iv) Base = 9, index = 7
   (v) Base = 4, index = 3
   (vi) Base = 5, index = 4
2. (i) 4^6, (ii) 22^5, (iii) 9^4, (iv) 17^3, (v) 10^6, (vi) 8^{10}
3. (i) $5 × 5 × 5 × 5 × 5 × 5 × 5 = 78\,125$
   (ii) $2 × 2 × 2 × 2 × 2 × 2 = 64$
   (iii) $1 × 1 × 1 × 1 × 1 × 1 × 1 × 1 = 1$
   (iv) $8 × 8 × 8 × 8 × 8 × 8 × 8 × 8 = 134\,217\,728$
   (v) $7 × 7 = 49$
   (vi) $4 × 4 × 4 = 64$
4. (i) 16, (ii) 64, (iii) 12, (iv) 81, (v) 27, (vi) 1
5. (i) 12^2; 12 squared
   (ii) $2 × 2 × 2$; 2^3; 8
   (iii) $1 × 1 × 1 × 1 × 1 × 1$; 1 to the power of 6; 1
   (iv) $5 × 5$; 5^2; 5 squared
   (v) $0 × 0 × 0 × 0 × 0 × 0$; 0^6; 0
6. (i) 17, (ii) 20, (iii) 15, (iv) 47
7. (i) $5^2 × 6^2$, (ii) $3^2 × 5^2$, (iii) $4^3 × 7^4$, (iv) $3^2 × 9^3$, (v) $2^3 × 5^2 × 6^3$, (vi) $4 × 5^2 × 8^4$
8. (i) (i) $2 × 2 × 2 × 2 × 2$
       (ii) $2 × 2 × 2$
       (iii) $2 × 2 × 2 × 2 × 2 × 2 × 2 × 2$
       (iv) 2^8
       (v) $2^5 × 2^3 = 2^8$
       Add the powers $5 + 3 = 8$

9. (i) $3 \times 3 \times 3 \times 3 \times 3 \times 3 \times 3$
   (ii) $3 \times 3 \times 3 \times 3$
   (iii) $3 \times 3 \times 3 \times 3 \times 3 \times 3 \times 3 \times 3 \times 3 \times 3 \times 3$
   (iv) 3^{11}
   (v) $3^7 \times 3^4 = 3^{11}$
   Add the powers $7 + 4 = 11$

Revision questions

4A Core skills

1. (i) 180, (ii) 312, (iii) 1 470, (iv) 2 666, (v) 4 212, (vi) 2 156
2. (i) −12, (ii) −36, (iii) −18, (iv) −6, (v) 16, (vi) −10
3. (i) 33, (ii) 180, (iii) 1, (iv) −8, (v) 176, (vi) 2
4. (i) $2^2 + 3 \times 5 = 19$
   (ii) $5 + 5 \times 6 − 3 = 32$
   (iii) $(3 + 5) \times 8 = 64$
   (iv) $12 + (40 \div 8)^2 − 7 = 30$
5. (i) Associative, groups have changed
   (ii) Commutative, order of numbers have changed
   (iii) Associative, groups have changed
   (iv) Distributive, multiplication is spread across two parts
   (v) Commutative, order of numbers has changed
   (vi) Distributive, multiplication is spread across two parts
6. (i) 2^7, (ii) 10^6, (iii) 3^6, (iv) 4^4, (v) 6^8, (vi) 8^5
7. (i) $12 \times 12 \times 12 \times 12 \times 12 \times 12 \times 12$
   (ii) $3 \times 3 \times 3 \times 3 \times 3 \times 3$
   (iii) $10 \times 10 \times 10 \times 10 \times 10$
   (iv) $2 \times 2 \times 2 \times 2 \times 2 \times 2 \times 2$
   (v) $4 \times 4 \times 4 \times 4 \times 4$
   (vi) $7 \times 7 \times 7 \times 7$
8. (i) $3^4 \times 7^3$, (ii) $2^2 \times 19^4$, (iii) $4^4 \times 13^2$, (iv) $2^2 \times 4^4$, (v) $3^3 \times 5^4$, (vi) $2^3 \times 6^2 \times 8^2$

4B Taking it further

1. Largest: $(5 \times 6) + 3 = 33$
   Smallest: $3 − (5 \times 6)$
2. $1 \div (5 \times 432)$
3. Possibilities include:
   $2 + 2 + 2 + 2 + 2 + 2 + 2 + (2 \div 2)$
   $(2 \times 2 \times 2) + (2 \times 2 \times 2) − (2 \div 2)$
   $(22 \div 2) + 2 + 2$
   $(22 \div 2) + 2^2$
   $(22 \div 2) + [(2 + 2 + 2) \div 2]$
4. $(1\,000 − 500) \div 5 − 60$
   €40 left
5. $(10 \times 20) + (10 \times 30)$
   Combined area $= 500 \text{ m}^2$
6. All volumes are the same because the commutative property says that the order you multiply numbers doesn't matter.
   $12 \times 8 \times 5 = 8 \times 12 \times 5 = 5 \times 8 \times 12$

Unit 5 Fractions, decimals and percentages

Practice questions 5·1

1. (i) $\frac{3}{4}$, (ii) $\frac{5}{6}$, (iii) $\frac{2}{5}$, (iv) $\frac{6}{7}$, (v) $\frac{2}{9}$, (vi) $\frac{2}{3}$
2. (i) Improper fraction: numerator greater than denominator
   (ii) Proper fraction: numerator less than denominator
   (iii) Mixed fraction: whole number and a fraction
   (iv) Proper fraction: numerator less than denominator
   (v) Mixed fraction: whole number and a fraction
   (vi) Improper fraction: numerator greater than denominator
3. (i) $3\frac{1}{2}$, (ii) $2\frac{4}{5}$, (iii) $3\frac{4}{7}$, (iv) $6\frac{2}{3}$, (v) $4\frac{3}{4}$, (vi) $4\frac{1}{8}$
4. (i) $\frac{17}{5}$, (ii) $\frac{25}{6}$, (iii) $\frac{14}{9}$, (iv) $\frac{19}{8}$, (v) $\frac{17}{3}$, (vi) $\frac{19}{2}$
5. (i) Yes. $\frac{3}{6} = \frac{1}{2}, \frac{2}{4} = \frac{1}{2}$
   (ii) No. $\frac{1}{3} \ne \frac{1}{2}$
   (iii) Yes. $\frac{2}{12} = \frac{1}{6}$
   (iv) Yes. $\frac{4}{6} = \frac{2}{3}, \frac{10}{15} = \frac{2}{3}$
   (v) No. $\frac{3}{7} \ne \frac{2}{5}$
   (vi) Yes. $\frac{2}{5} = \frac{4}{10}$
6. (i) $\frac{2}{5} = \frac{4}{10} = \frac{12}{30} = \frac{16}{40}$
   (ii) $\frac{3}{4} = \frac{12}{16} = \frac{18}{24} = \frac{33}{44}$
   (iii) $\frac{5}{3} = \frac{25}{15} = \frac{30}{18} = \frac{60}{36}$
   (iv) $\frac{80}{100} = \frac{40}{50} = \frac{20}{25} = \frac{4}{5}$
   (v) $\frac{3}{8} = \frac{9}{24} = \frac{15}{40} = \frac{21}{56}$
   (vi) $\frac{8}{40} = \frac{4}{20} = \frac{2}{10} = \frac{1}{5}$
7. (i) $\frac{2}{5}$, (ii) $\frac{1}{4}$, (iii) $\frac{7}{20}$
8. (i) $\frac{2}{5}$, (ii) $\frac{7}{10}$, (iii) $\frac{1}{5}$, (iv) $\frac{1}{10}$, (v) $\frac{2}{5}$

Practice questions 5·2·1

1. (i) $1\frac{3}{6} = 1\frac{1}{2}$, (ii) $1\frac{1}{14}$, (iii) $\frac{4}{12} = \frac{1}{3}$, (iv) $\frac{5}{18}$
2. (i) $\frac{5}{4} = 1\frac{1}{4}$, (ii) $\frac{29}{35}$, (iii) $\frac{11}{20}$, (iv) $\frac{67}{72}$, (v) $\frac{59}{30} = 1\frac{29}{30}$, (vi) $\frac{43}{18} = 2\frac{7}{18}$
3. (i) $\frac{3}{20}$, (ii) $\frac{3}{14}$, (iii) $\frac{1}{10}$, (iv) $\frac{7}{45}$, (v) $\frac{29}{24} = 1\frac{5}{24}$, (vi) $\frac{97}{20} = 4\frac{17}{20}$
4. (i) $4\frac{7}{8}$, (ii) $\frac{276}{35} = 7\frac{31}{35}$, (iii) $\frac{22}{15} = 1\frac{7}{15}$, (iv) $\frac{85}{24} = 3\frac{13}{24}$, (v) $\frac{124}{10} = 12\frac{2}{5}$, (vi) $\frac{31}{18} = 1\frac{13}{18}$
5. (i) Adam $= \frac{1}{8}$; Brother $= \frac{1}{4}$; Mother $= \frac{3}{8}$,
   (ii) $\frac{3}{4}$, (iii) $\frac{1}{4}$
6. Yes $1\frac{7}{24} < 2$
7. No $\frac{9}{12} > \frac{8}{12}$, so she will need $\frac{1}{12}$ of a cup more
8. $5\frac{5}{8}$
9. $30\frac{3}{10}$ metres
10. $10\frac{4}{45}$ km

Practice questions 5·2·2

1. (i) $\frac{1}{8}$, (ii) $\frac{1}{6}$, (iii) $\frac{2}{15}$, (iv) $\frac{6}{12} = \frac{1}{2}$, (v) $\frac{6}{15} = \frac{2}{5}$, (vi) $\frac{15}{24} = \frac{5}{8}$
2. (i) $\frac{8}{5} = 1\frac{3}{5}$, (ii) $\frac{12}{5} = 2\frac{2}{5}$, (iii) $\frac{2}{5}$, (iv) $\frac{6}{5} = 1\frac{1}{5}$, (v) $\frac{1}{5}$, (vi) $\frac{3}{5}$
3. (i) $\frac{3}{32}$, (ii) $\frac{8}{35}$, (iii) $\frac{5}{27}$, (iv) $\frac{21}{5} = 4\frac{1}{5}$, (v) $\frac{75}{8} = 9\frac{3}{8}$, (vi) $\frac{649}{36} = 18\frac{1}{36}$
4. (i) $\frac{1}{40}$, (ii) $\frac{4}{63}$, (iii) $\frac{2}{15}$
5. $\frac{8}{63}$
6. $\frac{9}{16}$
7. (i) $\frac{5}{32}$, (ii) $\frac{15}{32}$
8. $\frac{1}{4}$
9. $\frac{6}{35}$
10. $\frac{437}{48} = 9\frac{5}{48}$ metres
11. (i) $\frac{3}{10}$, (ii) 9

Practice questions 5·2·3

1. (i) 15, (ii) 3, (iii) 18, (iv) 4, (v) 2, (vi) 6
2. (i) $\frac{5}{3} = 1\frac{2}{3}$, (ii) $\frac{5}{6}$, (iii) $\frac{15}{32}$, (iv) 2, (v) $\frac{2}{3}$, (vi) $\frac{77}{150}$
3. $\frac{3}{20}$
4. 18
5. 2
6. (i) $\frac{11}{3} = 3\frac{2}{3}$, (ii) $\frac{11}{4} = 2\frac{3}{4}$, (iii) $\frac{11}{2} = 5\frac{1}{2}$
7. (i) $\frac{11}{32}$ hrs. We assume it took the same amount of time to mow each lawn
   (ii) $3\frac{2}{3}$ hrs
8. (i) Always true
   (ii) Sometimes true
   (iii) Sometimes true
   (iv) Always true
   (v) Sometimes true
   (vi) Never true
9. (i) $\frac{513}{160} = 3\frac{33}{160}$, (ii) $\frac{31}{72}$, (iii) $\frac{203}{9} = 22\frac{5}{9}$
10. (i) (a) $\frac{11}{2} = 5\frac{1}{2}$, (b) $\frac{5}{6}$
    (ii) (a) $\frac{10}{3} = 3\frac{1}{3}$, (b) $-\frac{10}{3}$
    (iii) (a) 6, (b) $\frac{1}{6}$
    (iv) (a) 6, (b) $\frac{1}{6}$

Practice questions 5·3

1. (i) Recurring: the 7 is repeated forever
   (ii) Terminating: stops after 4
   (iii) Neither: continues without repeating forever
   (iv) Terminating: stops after 6
   (v) Recurring: 312 repeats forever
   (vi) Neither: continues without repeating forever
2. (i) (a) 12·42, (b) 12·4, (c) 12
   (ii) (a) 84·35, (b) 84·4, (c) 84
   (iii) (a) 0·77, (b) 0·8, (c) 1
   (iv) (a) 104·94, (b) 104·9, (c) 105
   (v) (a) 8·44, (b) 8·4, (c) 8
3. (i) (a) 218, (b) 220, (c) 200
   (ii) (a) 3·09, (b) 3·1, (c) 3
   (iii) (a) 73·3, (b) 73, (c) 70
   (iv) (a) 0·608, (b) 0·61, (c) 0·6
   (v) (a) 0·00383, (b) 0·0038, (c) 0·004
4. (i) 0·5; 0·5, (ii) 0·25; 0·3, (iii) 0·35; 0·4, (iv) 0·$\dot{6}$ = ; 0·7, (v) 0·125; 0·1, (vi) 0·75; 0·8
5. (i) $\frac{7}{10}$, (ii) $\frac{13}{100}$, (iii) $\frac{11}{20}$, (iv) $\frac{1}{40}$, (v) $\frac{2}{25}$, (vi) $\frac{3}{5}$, (vii) $\frac{61}{200}$, (viii) $\frac{5}{8}$, (ix) $\frac{9}{25}$, (x) $\frac{1}{200}$
6. (i) $\frac{3}{5}$; 0·45, (ii) 0·75, 0·45
7. (i) Sometimes true
   (ii) Sometimes true
   (iii) Sometimes true
   (iv) Sometimes true
   (v) Always true

Practice questions 5·4

1. (i) 0·75; 75%, (ii) 0·6; 60%, (iii) 0·35; 35%, (iv) 0·05; 5%, (v) 0·32; 32%, (vi) 0·125; 12·5%

2. (i) $\frac{2}{5}$; 40%, (ii) $\frac{17}{100}$; 17%, (iii) $\frac{37}{50}$; 74%,
   (iv) $\frac{1}{20}$; 5%, (v) $\frac{3}{8}$; 37.5%, (vi) $\frac{9}{40}$; 22.5%
3. (i) 0.36; $\frac{9}{25}$, (ii) 0.55; $\frac{11}{20}$, (iii) 0.08; $\frac{2}{25}$,
   (iv) 0.03; $\frac{3}{100}$, (v) 0.245; $\frac{49}{200}$,
   (vi) 0.685; $\frac{137}{200}$
4. (i) $\frac{4}{5}$; 80%, (ii) $\frac{6}{25}$; 0.24, (iii) 0.875; 87.5%,
   (iv) $\frac{9}{20}$; 0.45, (v) $\frac{7}{50}$; 14%, (vi) $\frac{1}{20}$; 0.05,
   (vii) 0.4; 40%, (viii) $\frac{1}{50}$; 2%, (ix) $\frac{3}{5}$; 0.6,
   (x) 0.25; 25%
5. (i) 297, (ii) 3, (iii) 104, (iv) 132.5, (v) 6.64,
   (vi) 32.56
6. (i) 60%, (ii) 20%, (iii) 8.33%, (iv) 30%,
   (v) 25%, (vi) 80%
7. (i) 12%, (ii) 16.67%, (iii) 5%, (iv) 4%,
   (v) 100%, (vi) 6.67%
8. (i) $\frac{3}{4}$ of 80 cent = 60 cent > 10% of €4 = 40 cent
   (ii) 28% of 5 pizzas = 1.4 > $\frac{3}{5}$ of 2 pizzas
   (iii) Either, they both give you 9 sweets

Practice questions 5·5

1. Protein: 5%; Fat: 7.5%; Carbohydrate: 87.5%
2. 14 cm
3. 15
4. €18.75
5. (i) 14.29% profit, (ii) 6% loss, (iii) 25% profit, (iv) 8.75% loss, (v) 8% loss, (vi) 12.5% profit
6. (i) €11.87, (ii) €99.76
7. (i) €21.85, (ii) €116.85, (iii) €10.80, (iv) €90.80, (v) €207.65
8. Maths: 65%; English: 67.5%. She did better in English
9. The second decrease is larger
10. 15% profit

Revision questions

5A Core skills

1. (i) $\frac{1}{4}$ = 25%
   (iii) 0.4
   (iii) 5% = 0.05
2. 0.45, 42%, $\frac{3}{8}$, $\frac{1}{5}$, 12%, 0.0123
3. 0.04, 30%, $\frac{1}{3}$, 0.35, $\frac{3}{7}$, 45%
4. (i) 17.2%, (ii) 92.5%, (iii) 21.6%,
   (iv) 52.8%, (v) 37.5%, (vi) 21.9%
5. (i) 70% of 93, (ii) 10% of 649, (iii) 34% of 712
6. (i) $\frac{11}{20}$, (ii) $1\frac{3}{8}$, (iii) $1\frac{1}{5}$, (iv) $3\frac{7}{100}$
7. 12
8. (i) Never true
   (ii) Never true
   (iii) Always true
   (iv) Never true
   (v) Sometimes true
   (vi) Always true
   (vii) Sometimes true

5B Taking it further

1. $\frac{8}{27}$
2. Aytown
3. (i) €300
   (ii) 20%
4. 2.25% loss

5. 39% loss
6. €31.50
7. Yes. Assuming the VAT rate stays the same as cost increases, the VAT will increase
8. (i) 22 500 000 (22.5 million)
   (ii) 5 400 000 (5.4 million)

Unit 6 Probability 1

Practice questions 6·1

1. (i) 1
   (ii) 0.5 or $\frac{1}{2}$
   (iii) 0
   (iv) Numerous valid answers: open to discussion
   (v) 0
   (vi) Numerous valid answers: open to discussion
2. (iii) $\frac{2}{3}$, (vi) 72.4%, (vii) 0.001, (x) 0.999124
3. (i) A, (ii) C, (iii) F, (iv) E, (v) B, (vi) D
4. (i) 0, impossible, the sun rises in the east
   (ii) 1, certain, St Patrick's Day is always 17th March
   (iii) $\frac{1}{2}$
   (iv) 0, impossible, a standard die contains numbers 1 to 6
   (v) $\frac{1}{2}$, half of all natural numbers must be even
   (vi) 0, impossible as 32nd of June does not exist
5. Any relevant example, including:
   (i) Tossing a coin;
   (ii) Being born on a day beginning with 'T';
   (iii) Choosing a red marble from a box of 10, of which 7 are red and 3 are white;
   (iv) Rolling a value greater than 1 on a standard die

Practice questions 6·2

1. (i) Green tile, yellow tile, blue tile
   (ii) (a) $\frac{3}{6} = \frac{1}{2}$, (b) $\frac{2}{6} = \frac{1}{3}$, (c) $\frac{1}{6}$, (d) 0
2. (i) 1, 2, 3, 4, 5, 6
   (ii) (a) $\frac{1}{6}$, (b) $\frac{3}{6} = \frac{1}{2}$, (c) $\frac{3}{6} = \frac{1}{2}$, (d) $\frac{4}{6} = \frac{2}{3}$,
   (e) $\frac{6}{6} = 1$
3. (i) Black marble, red marble, orange marble, green marble
   (ii) (a) $\frac{13}{70}$, (b) $\frac{9}{70}$, (c) 0, (d) $\frac{48}{70} = \frac{24}{35}$
4. (i) $\frac{3}{32}$, (ii) $\frac{8}{32} = \frac{1}{4}$, (iii) $\frac{29}{32}$
5. (i) $\frac{2}{5}$, (ii) $\frac{3}{5}$, (iii) $\frac{3}{5}$, (iv) $\frac{3}{5}$
6. (i) $\frac{1}{250}$, (ii) $\frac{10}{250} = \frac{1}{25}$, (iii) $\frac{225}{250} = \frac{9}{10}$
7. (i) 0.6, (ii) 0.85 = 85%
8. (i) $\frac{8}{40} = \frac{1}{5}$, (ii) $\frac{12}{40} = \frac{3}{10}$, (iii) $\frac{20}{40} = \frac{1}{2}$

Practice questions 6·3

1. (i) 6
   (ii) Red t-shirt, jeans
       Red t-shirt, tracksuit bottoms
       Blue t-shirt, jeans
       Blue t-shirt, tracksuit bottoms
       White t-shirt, jeans
       White t-shirt, tracksuit bottoms

2. (i) 10, (iii) $\frac{1}{10}$
3. (i) 9
4. (i) 60
5. (i) 15
6. (ii) Blue, blue
       Blue, green
       Green, blue
       Green, green
   (iii) $\frac{1}{4}$
   (iv) $\frac{1}{2}$
7. (ii) $\frac{1}{2}$
   (iii) $\frac{1}{2}$
8. 90
9. 120
10. Three pairs of runners

Revision questions

6A Core skills

1. (i) 0.5, (ii) almost 0, (iii) almost 1, (iv) Numerous valid answers
2. (i) Picking a whole number less than four from the numbers 1 to 10 inclusive (or any other valid answer)
   (ii) Getting a tails when tossing a coin (or any other valid answer)
   (iii) Picking a number less than 10, from the numbers 1 to 10 inclusive (or any other valid answer)
   (iv) The sun will rise tomorrow (or any other valid answer)
   (v) The sun will not rise tomorrow (or any other valid answer)
3. (i) $\frac{1}{10}$, (ii) $\frac{4}{10} = \frac{2}{5}$, (iii) $\frac{3}{10}$, (iv) $\frac{5}{10} = \frac{1}{2}$, (v) 0
4. (i) 70%
   (ii) Yes or no acceptable, as long as it is based on justification (must mention 'unlikely to rain')
5. (i) $\frac{1}{9}$, (ii) $\frac{2}{9}$, (iii) $\frac{4}{9}$, (iv) $\frac{5}{9}$, (v) $\frac{7}{9}$, (vi) 0, (vii) 0
6. Box B: box B has a higher fraction of red so there is a higher probability of choosing red from box B
7. 600
8. 1 920
9. (ii) $\frac{1}{6}$
10. Five types of meat
11. (ii) (a) $\frac{7}{15}$, (b) $\frac{6}{15} = \frac{2}{5}$, (c) $\frac{3}{15} = \frac{1}{5}$, (d) $\frac{7}{15}$

6B Taking it further

1. (i) $\frac{15}{30} = \frac{1}{2}$, (ii) $\frac{3}{30} = \frac{1}{10}$, (iii) $\frac{14}{30} = \frac{7}{15}$
2. (ii) 48, (iii) $\frac{6}{48} = \frac{1}{8}$, (iv) $\frac{24}{48} = \frac{1}{2}$,
   (v) $\frac{16}{48} = \frac{1}{3}$, (vi) $\frac{29}{48}$
3. (i) $\frac{1}{4}$, (ii) $\frac{1}{2}$
4. (ii) $\frac{1}{8}$, (iii) $\frac{3}{8}$, (iv) $\frac{1}{8}$
5. Any valid mathematical explanation.
6. (i) 60, (ii) 15
7. Yes. There is a total of 54 possible outcomes, therefore there are 54 different outfits he could wear.
8. (i) 102
   (ii) (a) $\frac{15}{102} = \frac{5}{34}$, (b) $\frac{9}{102} = \frac{3}{34}$,
   (c) $\frac{58}{102} = \frac{29}{51}$, (d) $\frac{52}{102} = \frac{26}{51}$, (e) $\frac{41}{102}$

9. (i) (a) Actual number = 195 × 99 × 89 × 105 × 74 = 13 349 986 650
   (b) 13 300 000 000
   (c) Thirteen billion, three hundred and forty-nine million, nine hundred and eighty-six thousand, six hundred and fifty
   (ii) Yes he is, because it can produce over 13 billion faces

Unit 7 Patterns

Practice questions 7·1
1. Owl, lion
2. Yellow, green, red
5. (i) 13, 15, 17, (ii) 8, 11, 14, (iii) 29, 35, 41, (iv) −18, −23, −28, (v) 110, 121, 132
6. (i) 8, 12, 16, (ii) 21, 42, (iii) 90, 78, (iv) 0, −9, (v) −10, 0, (vi) $\frac{1}{2}$, 4, 16
7. Nine green smarties
8. 32 points
9. (i) 22 rides, (ii) 56 rides
10. (i) 40 minutes, (ii) 5th day, (iii) There will be no day when the viewing time = 0 mins because half of any time allowed will not = 0
11. (i) N, C, I
    (ii) N

Practice questions 7·2
1. (iii) Variables = number of days, amount saved
2. (iii) Variables = number of days, height (cm)
3. (i) −4°
   (iii) Variables = temperature of ice cube (°C), time (minutes)
4. (i) 14 cakes
   (iii) Variables = number of cakes, number of plates
5. (iii) 66 complete gingerbread men
6. (i) 7 seconds
   (iii) Variables = number of seconds passed, height of ball (h)
7. (i) 6 stops
   (iii) 4th stop
8. (iv) Week 5
9. (iv) Yes, at 5 minutes

Practice questions 7·3
1. (i) 1, (ii) $3\frac{2}{3}$, (iii) $\frac{1}{2}$, (iv) Slope = $-\frac{1}{3}$, (v) −5, (vi) $-\frac{1}{3}$
2. (iii) Slope = 2·5
   (iv) The slope of graph equals the daily rate at which plant is growing (slope = rate of change in height of plant per day)
   (v) No, because the plant could run out of food/killed by frost/be damaged, etc. Any valid answer
3. (iii) Slope = 8
   (iv) The slope of the graph and the rate of change for fuel being used compared to distance travelled is the same
   (v) 6 litres of fuel
4. (ii) Joe starts by lifting 24 kg and then he lifts an extra 4 kg for each week that passes
   (iii) 25 weeks
   (iv) No, because Joe is a human and eventually weights will become too heavy for him to lift

Practice questions 7·4
1. (i) Linear, first difference is constant
   (ii) Not linear, first difference is not constant
   (iii) Linear, first difference is constant
   (iv) Not linear, first difference is not constant
   (v) Linear, first difference is constant
   (vi) Linear, first difference is constant,
   (vii) Not linear, first difference is not constant
   (viii) Not linear, first difference is not constant
2. (iii) Linear pattern, first difference is constant, +3
3. (iii) Slope = 2
   (iv) Linear pattern, first difference is constant, +2
   (v) Slope = first difference, therefore rate of change is the same
4. (ii) Linear pattern, first difference is constant and equals +2
   (iv) Slope = 2
   (v) The rate of change, slope, and the first difference are equal
5. (i) Linear pattern, first difference is constant, $\frac{2}{6}$ or $\frac{1}{3}$
   (ii) Linear pattern, first difference is constant, 0·4
   (iii) Linear pattern, first difference is constant, $-\frac{1}{2}$
   (iv) Not linear pattern, first difference is not constant
6. (iv) Graph not linear
   (a) Not linear, not straight line graph
   (b) First difference is not constant

Revision questions
7A Core skills
1. (i) 15, 18, 21, (ii) 35, 42, 49, (iii) −16, −20, −24, (iv) 0, 2, 4, (v) 110, 121, 132, (vi) −1, −4, −7, (vii) −1, −9, −17, (viii) $\frac{1}{32}$, $\frac{1}{64}$, $\frac{1}{128}$
2. (i) Linear, (ii) Linear, (iii) Not linear, (iv) Not linear, (v) Not linear, (vi) Linear, (vii) Linear, (viii) Linear
3. (ii) 6 blocks need to make step 6
   (iii) Linear, first difference is constant
   (iv) Variables = step number, number of blocks
4. (i) 258th stage = N
   (ii) 1 000th stage = H
5. (iii) 9 hours
   (iv) Linear pattern, same common difference of €9·50
   (v) Variables = hours worked, money earned
6. (iii) Variables = kilometres travelled, cost of trip
   (iv) Slope = 2
   (v) It is a linear pattern, as it forms a straight line and has a constant first difference of +2
   (vi) Slope (rate of change) and first difference are the same value
   (vii) €20
   (viii) 7 km

7B Taking it further
1. (iii) Slope = 20
   (iv) Linear pattern as graph is straight line, and has constant first difference of 20
   (v) The slope and the first difference are the same, so the rate of change is the same
2. (iii) Slope = −125
   The slope of the graph and rate of change at which the snowman is melting are the same.
   (iv) It is a linear pattern, as the graph forms a straight line. It has a constant first difference of −125
3. (ii) Big Claw will win
4. (i) Rory = 187·5 seconds, Marie = 225 seconds
   (ii) At 150 seconds Rory and Marie have the same amount of liquid in their cup
5. (iv) Slope = 2
   (v) The slope of the graph and the rate at which the triangles are increasing are the same. Slope = rate of change
   (vi) Yes, linear pattern, first difference is constant and equals +2
   (vii) The slope and the first difference are the same value
6. (iv) Slope = 4
   (v) The slope of the graph and the rate at which the number of chairs are increasing are the same (i.e. +4)

Unit 8 Working with variables

Practice questions 8·1
1. Like terms, power of x; Unlike terms, 3 has no a; Unlike terms, different powers; Like terms, powers are the same; Unlike terms, different powers on the variables a and b
2. (i) Coefficient 4, variable x, constant 6
   (ii) Coefficient −4, variable y, constant 10
   (iii) Coefficient 1, variable x, constant 12
   (iv) Coefficient 0·5, variable a, constant −5
   (v) Coefficient $\frac{3}{4}$, variable x, constant −0·0006
   (vi) Coefficient 1, variable a, constant 0·78
3. (i) $1x^1$, (ii) $2x^1$, (iii) $5x^1 - 1y^1$
4. (i) $6a$, (ii) $3x + 2y$, (iii) $10x + 12y$
5. (i) $10x + 7$, (ii) $4x + 21$, (iii) $17x + 10$, (iv) $26m + 3n$, (v) $-2p + 8q$, (vi) $6a - 18y$, (vii) $4x - 2$, (viii) $4b + 5$
6. (i) $12a + 14b$, (ii) $-19\alpha + 23\beta$, (iii) $51m - 28n$
7. (i) $2x^2 + 2y$, (ii) $22x^2 + 11y$, (iii) $39ab + 25bc$
8. (i) $18dc - 15db$, (ii) $4m^2 - 23m^3 + 23n^2$, (iii) $19m^2 - 68n^2$
9. (i) $12x - \frac{11}{12}y$, (ii) $4x - \frac{3}{5}y$, (iii) $\frac{3}{2}x - 17\frac{1}{3}y$, (iv) $8p - 5x + 2xb - 6$, (v) $12\frac{5}{6} + 9\frac{3}{4}m$

Answer key 571

10. (i) $8x + 10y$, (ii) $31c + 9b$, (iii) $27\frac{1}{6}d$
11. $10x + 17y$
12. $14m + 68n + 23$
13. Length $6d$; width $7c$

Practice questions 8·2

1. (i) x^3, (ii) ab^2, (iii) a^6, (iv) $6p^3$,
   (v) $-15m^6$, (vi) $8a^2b^4$
2. (i) $10a$, (ii) $14x$, (iii) $21a$, (iv) $28n$,
   (v) $18y$, (vi) $24m$
3. (i) $12ab$, (ii) $10bc$, (iii) $4wx$, (iv) $-24dt$,
   (v) $-14sy$, (vi) $-7gk$
4. (i) $12g^2$, (ii) $27h^2$, (iii) $-12t^2$, (iv) $-35d^2$,
   (v) $-30eh$, (vi) $-27np$
5. (i) $2w$, (ii) $3d$, (iii) $-5x$, (iv) $-\frac{1}{6}y^2$,
   (v) $-\frac{1}{3}m^3$, (vi) $-\frac{1}{5}m^3$
6. (i) $12a^2b$, (ii) $-12p^3$, (iii) $16s^3$,
   (iv) $-15m^3n^2$, (v) $-20a^2b^3$, (vi) $-\frac{1}{3}x^3y$
7. (i) $-20x^3y$, (ii) $-10p^3q^3$, (iii) $-x^3y^3$,
   (iv) $-4mn^2$
8. (i) $8x^4y^2$, (ii) $-5x^4y^4$, (iii) $-a^3b^4$,
   (iv) $-4mn^2$
9. (i) $12a^2$, (ii) $48a^2b^2$, (iii) $120a^2b^2$
10. (i) $8a^2$, (ii) $27·6a^2b^3$, (iii) $\frac{1}{2}a^2b$
11. $42xy$

Practice questions 8·3

1. (i) $2a$, (ii) $-2e$, (iii) $3y$, (iv) $-2n$, (v) $-3c$,
   (vi) $2m$
2. (i) $3m$, (ii) $-4p$, (iii) $5d$, (iv) $\frac{-3b}{2}$, (v) $\frac{-t}{3}$,
   (vi) $\frac{9d}{2}$
3. (i) 2, (ii) 2, (iii) -5, (iv) -3, (v) -4, (vi) -2
4. (i) $-3y$, (ii) $4w$, (iii) $2x$, (iv) $-3b$, (v) -2,
   (vi) -2
5. (i) $3y$, (ii) $\frac{-9g}{2}$, (iii) $-2d$, (iv) $\frac{-w}{4}$, (v) -3,
   (vi) $\frac{-2}{3b}$
6. (i) $-16a$, (ii) 32, (iii) $-3c^2d$, (iv) $-3xy^2$,
   (v) $-3b$, (vi) 2
7. $8x$
8. $6y$
9. x^2
10. $6b$
11. $70xy$
12. $10x$
13. (i) $2x$, (ii) $5a$, (iii) $-2p^2$, (iv) $5x^2$,
    (v) $3a^2b^4$, (vi) $4x^2y$

Revision questions

8A Core skills

1. (i) $7x + 6$, (ii) $4x + 7$, (iii) $10x + 3$,
   (iv) $9a^2 + 2$, (v) $7a + 8$, (vi) $3a + 4b$,
   (vii) $4a + 8b$, (viii) $5x^2 + 10$
2. (i) $5x^2 - 3y$, (ii) $23ab - bc$, (iii) $-9x^2 + 10y^2 + 2y$, (iv) $18ab + 15bc$
3. (i) $16s^2$, (ii) $-15m^3n^2$, (iii) $40x^4$,
   (iv) $-28p^3n^2$, (v) $6de^3$, (vi) $-24a^3b^2$,
   (vii) $30a^4by$, (viii) $20m^3n^3$
4. (i) $4x$, (ii) $7x$, (iii) $2d$, (iv) $2x^2$, (v) $7x^4$,
   (vi) $2x$, (vii) -5, (viii) $2x$, (ix) $-8b$, (x) $\frac{24}{c^3d}$
5. (i) $\frac{1}{3}w$, (ii) $\frac{-2}{21}x^2$, (iii) $\frac{-3}{5}m^3$, (iv) $\frac{3}{13}ad$,
   (v) $-\frac{1}{4}xy$, (vi) $\frac{-2}{11}m^2n$

8B Taking it further

1. (i) $16yx$, (ii) $80x^2y$, (iii) $30m^2n^2$
2. (i) $12a$, (ii) $12m + 8m^2$, (iii) $28xy$
3. $12x$

4. $10xy$
5. $6x$
6. $6xy$, $18xy^2$, $108x^2y^3$
7. 113 rows
8. (i) $224ab$, (ii) $896b$

Unit 9 Solving linear equations

Practice questions 9·1

1. (i) a, c; 5, (ii) t, b; 5, (iii) f, m, d; none,
   (iv) x, y; -7, (v) k, g; 2, (vi) t, p; -4,
   (vii) θ, e; -24, (viii) r, x; -7, (ix) β, y; -12,
   (x) d, n; -6
2. (i) Total value $= 4 + 6a$
   (ii) Total value $= 2 + 9v$
   (iii) Total value $= 7 - 3t$
   (iv) Total value $= -10 + 2d$
   (v) Total value $= -50 - 8n$
   (vi) Total value $= -21 + 4s$
   (vii) Total value $= 117 - 34r$
   (viii) Total value $= 1\,024 - 64t$
   (ix) Total value $= -99 + 24k$
   (x) Total value $= 0 - 59x$
3. (i) 7; 24; y, (ii) -4; 13; s, (iii) 31; -76; n,
   (iv) -17; -3; q, (v) 10; 2; x
4. (i) Height =
       $2 + 1$(number of months)
   (ii) Number of cakes =
       $5 + 3$(number of hours)
   (iii) Number of pages =
       $50 + 8$(number of hours)
   (iv) Number of blocks =
       $100 - 8$(layer number)
5. (i) €12·80
   (ii) €52
   (iii) €91·20
   (iv) €375·30
6. (i) Fare = $4 + 1·10$
       (number of kilometres travelled)
   (ii) €14
   (iii) You could travel 21 kilometres
7. (ii) Stage 2: 2, 8, 10; Stage 3: 2, 12,
       14; Stage 4: 2, 16, 18; Stage 5: 2,
       20, 22; Stage 6: 2, 24, 26
   (iii) Variables = number of blue
       blocks, total number of blocks
   (iv) Total number of blocks =
       $2 + 4$ (stage number)
   (v) $T = 2 + 4s$, where T = total
       number of blocks and s = stage
       number
   (vii) (a) 402
       (b) 2 red blocks
       (c) 400 blue blocks
8. (ii) Stage 2: 1, 8, 9; Stage 3: 1, 12, 13;
       Stage 4: 1, 16, 17; Stage 5: 1, 20,
       21; Stage 6: 1, 24, 25
   (iii) Variables are T and s
   (iv) Total number of dots =
       $1 + 4$(stage number)
   (v) $T = 1 + 4s$ where T = total
       number of dots and s = stage
       number (or any valid variation
       of this)
   (vi) (a) Total = 229 dots
       (b) Green dots = 1
       (c) Black dots = 228
   (vii) 19th stage

Practice questions 9·2

1. (i) 3, (ii) 12, (iii) 13, (iv) 53, (v) 20, (vi) 8,
   (vii) 3, (viii) 14·5, (ix) 3·5, (x) $1\frac{1}{3}$, (xi) -6,
   (xii) -4
2. (i) 23, (ii) 20, (iii) 33, (iv) 26
3. (i) 4, (ii) -25, (iii) 12, (iv) 3
4. (i) 11, (ii) 18, (iii) 13, (iv) 16, (v) 12, (vi) 21
5. (i) 5, (ii) 4, (iii) 6, (iv) 4, (v) 6, (vi) 2,
   (vii) 11, (viii) 10
6. (i) 11, (ii) 7, (iii) 1, (iv) 9
7. (i) $\alpha = 4$
   (ii) $x = 4$
   (iii) $w = 10$
   (iv) $k = 5$
   (v) $z = 10$
   (vi) $\beta = 8$
   (vii) $h = 11$

Practice questions 9·3

1. (i) 2, (ii) -2, (iii) 6, (iv) 8, (v) -2, (vi) -1,
   (vii) 5 (viii) 12
2. (i) 4, (ii) -4, (iii) 2, (iv) 3, (v) -3, (vi) 15,
   (vii) -1 (viii) 13
3. (i) 2, (ii) 4, (iii) 2, (iv) -2, (v) -1, (vi) 4,
   (vii) 3, (viii) 10
4. (i) 1, (ii) 2, (iii) 5, (iv) 1, (v) -14, (vi) 1,
   (vii) 14, (viii) -17
5. (i) 35, (ii) 16, (iii) 77, (iv) 126, (v) 183,
   (vi) -81, (vii) 357, (viii) -13, (ix) 4, (x) 4
6. (i) 5, (ii) 8, (iii) 10, (iv) 6, (v) 16, (vi) 31,
   (vii) 143, (viii) 150, (ix) -386, (x) 351

Practice questions 9·4

1. €6
2. Pedro is 16 years old, José is 20 years old
3. Jan potted 26 plants
4. Henry solved 16 problems and Frank
   solved 64 problems
5. Bicycle costs €1 200 and car costs
   €14 400
6. Width = 18 cm, length = 36 cm
7. Present ages: Simon = 14 and his
   mother = 42
8. (i) Games won = 21, (ii) Games lost = 25
9. Length of field = 60 m
10. Width = 15 m, length = 45 m
11. Person with fewest votes = 6 689,
    person with most votes = 7 000
12. (i) $8x + 4$
    (ii) 9 metres
13. (i) $x + 3x + (3x + 30) = 180$
    (ii) Smallest angle $x = 30°$
    (iii) Largest angle = 90°

Practice questions 9·5

1. (i) $4(2)$, 8; $4(4)$, 16; $4(6)$, 24; $4(8)$, 32;
       $4(10)$, 40
   (ii) $2(7) + 3$, 17; $2(9) + 3$, 21; $2(11) + 3$, 25; $2(13) + 3$, 29; $2(15) + 3$, 33
   (iii) $5(4) - 8$, 12; $5(8) - 8$, 32; $5(12) - 8$, 52; $5(16) - 8$, 72; $5(20) - 8$, 112
   (iv) $14 - 6(1)$, 8; $14 - 6(2)$, 2; $14 - 6(3)$, -4; $14 - 6(4)$, -10; $14 - 6(5)$, -16
   (v) $\frac{1}{2}(10) + 6$, 11; $\frac{1}{2}(20) + 6$, 16; $\frac{1}{2}(30) + 6$, 21; $\frac{1}{2}(40) + 6$, 26; $\frac{1}{2}(50) + 6$, 31
   (vi) $\frac{1}{3}(27) - 2$, 7; $\frac{1}{3}(30) - 2$, 8; $\frac{1}{3}(33) - 2$, 9; $\frac{1}{3}(36) - 2$, 10; $\frac{1}{3}(39) - 2$, 11
2. (i) $x + 7$, (ii) $2x$, (iii) $2x + 2$, (iv) $3x - 20$,
   (v) $\frac{1}{2}x + 10$, (vi) $-2x - 4$

3. **(i)** This is a function, because input has only one output
   (ii) This is a function, because input has only one output
   (iii) This is not a function, because some inputs have more than one output
   (iv) This is not a function, because some inputs have more than one output
   (v) This is a function, because input has only one output
4. **(i)** {1, 2, 3, 4}; {5, 10, 15, 20}; {5, 10, 15, 20}; (1, 5), (2, 10), (3, 15), (4, 20)
   (ii) {4, 5, 6}; {9, 11, 13}; {9, 11, 13, 25}; (4, 9), (5, 11), (6, 13)
   (iii) {10, 20, 30}; {31, 91}; {31, 61, 91, 25}; (10, 31), (30, 91)
   (iv) {6, 12}; {−7, 13}; {−7, −13, −19, −25}; (6, −7), (12, −13)
   (v) {cat, dog, cow}; {kitten, calf, puppy}; {kitten, calf, puppy, chick}; (cat, kitten), (dog, puppy), (cow, calf)
5. **(b)** **(i)** {1, 2, 3, 4}; {5, 10, 15, 20}; (1, 5), (2, 10), (3, 15), (4, 20)
   (ii) {1, 2, 3, 4}; {6, 11, 16, 21}; (1, 6), (2, 11), (3, 16), (4, 21)
   (iii) {3, 6, 9, 12}; {10, 22, 34, 46}; (3, 10), (6, 22), (9, 34), (12, 46)
   (iv) {9, 11, 13, 15}; {−11, −15, −19, −23}; (9, −11), (11, −15), (13, −19), (15, −23)
   (v) {18, 24, 30, 36}; {3, 6, 9, 12}; (18, 3), (24, 6), (30, 9), (36, 12)
6. **(i)** $2x + 1$, **(ii)** $4x − 2$, **(iii)** $7x − 102$, **(iv)** $4x + 1$, **(v)** $−3x − 5$

Practice questions 9·6
1. **(i)** $H = 5 + 2t$ or any valid variation of this
   (ii) 13 cm
   (iii) 6 minutes
   (v) Yes graph is linear, as first difference is constant, it equals 2
2. **(i)** $R = 3 + 2w$ or any valid variation of this
   (ii) 15 kg of paper
   (iii) 6 weeks
   (v) Yes graph is linear, as first difference is constant, it is 2
3. **(i)** $W = 0·5 + 1m$ or any valid variation of this, e.g. $W = 500 + 1\,000m$ if given in grams
   (ii) $W = 7·5$ kg
   (iv) After 3·5 months Snowball will weigh 4 kg
   (v) Graph is linear, as first difference is constant, in this case 0·5
4. **(i)** Cost = start amount plus €3 per kilometre travelled, $C = 2 + 3k$ or any valid variation
   (ii) €29
   (iii) 5 km
   (iv) 10 km
   (vi) Linear, as the first difference is constant, +3
5. **(i)** $W = 1\,000 − 150m$ or any valid variation
   (ii) 600 ml
   (iv) Linear, as first difference is constant (−150)

   (v) 6·6 minutes
   (vi) 5 minutes

Practice questions 9·7
1. Package B
2. 195 logs
3. 38 stones
4. **(i)** €50
   (ii) No, as she only has €50
5. 130 students
6. 78 chimes
7. **(i)** 13 rows
   (ii) 9 cans left over
8. **(i)** 10 red tiles
   (ii) **(a)** 22 red tiles **(b)** 202 red tiles **(c)** 2 598 red tiles
   (iii) **(a)** 33 blue tiles **(b)** 69 blue tiles **(c)** 951 blue tiles
   (iv) 15 blue tiles
   (v) Stage 5 = 10 red tiles and 33 blue tiles
   (vi) 10 red tiles
   (vii) Stage 3
   (viii) **(b)** 44 tiles and **(c)** 45 tiles cannot be used to create a complete pattern

Revision questions
9A Core skills
1. **(i)** $x = 5$, **(ii)** $a = 15$, **(iii)** $p = −3$, **(iv)** $z = 2$, **(v)** $t = 5$, **(vi)** $v = 100$, **(vii)** $h = 6$, **(viii)** $f = 9$
2. **(i)** $d = 9$, **(ii)** $r = 1$, **(iii)** $a = 3$, **(iv)** $w = −2$, **(v)** $x = −2$, **(vi)** $k = 1$, **(vii)** $\alpha = 2$, **(viii)** $\beta = −1$
3. **(i)** $d = 3$, **(ii)** $p = 5$, **(iii)** $x = 2$, **(iv)** $n = 2$, **(v)** $f = −4$, **(vi)** $t = −3$, **(vii)** $x = −3$, **(viii)** $\alpha = −5$
4. **(b)** **(i)** Domain = {3, 5, 7, 9, 11}; Range = {5, 9, 13, 17, 21}; Couples = {(3, 5), (5, 9), (7, 13), (9, 17), (11, 21)}
   (ii) Domain = {14, 19, 24, 29, 34}; Range = {−45, −60, −75, −90, −105}; Couples = {(14, −45), (19, −60), (24, −75), (29, −90), (34, −105)}
   (iii) Domain = {−2, −4, −6, −8, −10}; Range = {−0·5, 0·5, 1·5, 2·5, 3·5}; Couples = {(−2, −0·5), (−4, 0·5), (−6, 1·5), (−8, 2·5), (−10, 3·5)}
5. **(a)** **(i)** Rule = $2x + 4$
   (ii) Rule = $0·5x + 0·5$ or any other valid explanation
   (iii) Rule = $4x − 4$
6. **(i)** If Gia's age = x, Gia's mother = $4x$, Gia's brother = $x − 6$
   (ii) $x + 4x + x − 6 = 48$ or $6x − 6 = 48$
   (iii) Gia's age = 9 years
   (iv) 27 years old
7. **(i)** Perimeter = $4x + 10$ or any other valid equation
   (ii) Length = 18 cm
8. **(i)** $x = 9$ metres
   (ii) Perimeter = 68 metres
9. **(i)** Function
   (ii) Not a function
   (iii) Function
   (iv) Function

10. **(i)** Domain = {1, 2, 3, 4}; range = {3, 5, 7, 9}; codomain = {1, 2, 3, 4, 5, 6, 7, 8, 9, 10}
   (ii) {(1, 3), (2, 5), (3, 7), (4, 9)}
11. 72 deer

9B Taking it further
1. **(i)** $5r + 9$
   (ii) $r = 8$ cm
2. **(i)** $C = 50 + 10x$ or any other valid answer
   (ii) 45 people
3. **(i)** Fan oven is 27 minutes faster
   (ii) Normal oven is 35·5 minutes slower
   (iii) $W = 34$ kg
4. Mike = 11 years old, Mike's grandfather = 66 years old
5. **(i)** **(a)** $f(x) = x^2$; Pattern is not linear, as first difference is not constant.
   (ii) **(b)** $f(x) = 6x − 4$; Pattern is linear, as first difference is constant.
   (iii) **(c)** $f(x) = 4x$; Pattern is linear, as first difference is constant
6. **(i)** Charge = $4·1 + 1·03k$ or any valid variation
   (ii) €9·25
   (iii) No, Bruno does not have enough money
   (v) Linear graph, first difference constant, = 1·03
   (vi) Cost = €8·74
   (vii) It is cheaper to use Emma's new pricing policy for distances less than 12 km, but it is cheaper to use the old pricing policy for distances over 12 km. Many valid solutions available to show this

Unit 10 Ratio, proportion and scaling
Practice questions 10·1
1. **(i)** 4 : 3, **(ii)** 3 : 4, **(iii)** 5 : 3, **(iv)** 2 : 6, **(v)** 6 : 5, **(vi)** 2 : 7
2. **(i)** 2 : 1, **(ii)** 9 : 5, **(iii)** 4 : 9, **(iv)** 7 : 4, **(v)** 1 : 5, **(vi)** 4 : 5
3. **(i)** €20 : €30
   (ii) 45 km : 36 km
   (iii) 99 g : 22 g
   (iv) 56 hr : 49 hr
   (v) 104 cm : 65 cm
   (vi) 12 c : 16 c
4. 1 : 4
5. **(i)** 15 boys, **(ii)** 9 girls
6. **(i)** 3 : 2, **(ii)** Spending €60, **(iii)** Saving €40
7. Total votes = 1 920
8. Flour = 21 g
9. White cars = 24
10. 16 sheep
11. €54
12. €83
13. First glass = $\frac{2}{5}$ orange juice; Second glass = $\frac{1}{3}$ orange juice. $\frac{2}{5} > \frac{1}{3}$ so first glass is more concentrated.

Practice questions 10·2

1. (i) 300 cm, (ii) 4 cm, (iii) 200 000 cm, (iv) 350 000 cm, (v) 1 000 cm, (vi) 50 cm, (vii) 125 000 cm
2. (ii) 48 cm, (iii) 1 : 6, (iv) 0·6 m, (v) 60 mm, (vi) 1 : 30 000, (vii) 12, (viii) 1 : 1 500
3. (c) A scale
4. 1 620 m
5. (i) 1 cm : 5 000 cm
   (ii) 225 m or 0·225 km
6. 105 km
7. 44 km
8. 2·8 cm : 14 km
9. 15 m by 19·5 m
10. 1 : 20
11. 400 cm
12. 20 : 40 000. The model will be 20 cm high
13. 360 m
14. 5 cm × 2·5 cm rectangle
15. 10 000 cm or 100 m
16. 500 : 1
17. 500 : 1
18. A scaled diagram on a scale of 1 cm : 100 cm

Revision questions

10A Core skills

1. (i) €49 : €21, (ii) 24·75 m : 41·25 m, (iii) 36 kg : 108 kg, (iv) 65 hr : 13 hr, (v) 208 cm : 32 cm, (vi) 175 c : 50 c
2. €18
3. 9 m
4. 31 cm
5. 400 : 1
6. 500 : 1
7. 700 : 1
8. 40 000 cm or 400 m
9. 440 g of plain flour, 100 g of lard, 100 g of butter, 960 g of mincemeat

10B Taking it further

1. 64
2. 1 : 60 000
3. 8 cm
4. 400 000 : 1
5. 2 km
6. Appropriate scale would be 1cm = 1 km, so a scale of 1 : 1 000 000 cm. Draw a square of side length 10 cm
7. 12 : 13
8. 1 : 27

Unit 11 Angles

Practice questions 11·1

1. (i) $|\angle A| = 80°$ vertically opposite angles are equal
   (ii) $|\angle B| = 35°$ vertically opposite angles are equal
   (iii) $|\angle D| = 110°$ vertically opposite angles are equal
        $|\angle E| = 70°$ vertically opposite angles are equal
   (iv) $|\angle B| = 35°$ straight angle is equal to 180°
        $|\angle D| = 145°$ vertically opposite angles are equal
2. (i) $|\angle Z| = 60°$ straight angle
   (ii) $|\angle X| = 120°$ vertically opposite angles
   (iii) $|\angle Y| = 60°$ vertically opposite angles
3. (i) $|\angle B| = 150°$, (ii) $|\angle C| = 80°$, (iii) $|\angle B| = 170°$, (iv) $|\angle D| = 170°$
4. (iii) Vertically opposite angles are equal
   (iv) Sum of the four angles = 360°
   (v) Repeats will give the same result in (iii) and (iv)
5. (i) Always true, (ii) Never true, (iii) Always true, (iv) Never true

Practice questions 11·2

2. (i) $|\angle A| = 85°$ alternate angles
   (ii) $|\angle B| = 95°$ straight angle
   (iii) $|\angle C| = 85°$ vertically opposite angles are equal
   (iv) $|\angle D| = 95°$ straight angle
   (v) $|\angle E| = 95°$ vertically opposite angles are equal
   (vi) $|\angle F| = 85°$ vertically opposite angles
3. (i) $|\angle A| = 115°$ straight angle and alternate angles
   (ii) $|\angle B| = 115°$ alternate angle
   (iii) $|\angle C| = 115°$ vertically opposite angles
   (iv) $|\angle D| = 115°$ straight angle
   (v) $|\angle E| = 65°$ straight angle
   (vi) $|\angle F| = 65°$ alternate angle
4. (i) $|\angle UTV| = 58°$ straight angle
   (ii) $|\angle TVW| = 58°$ alternate angles
   (iii) $|\angle STV| = 122°$ vertically opposite angles
   (iv) $|\angle WVY| = 122°$ alternate angles
   (v) $|\angle XVY| = 58°$ vertically opposite angles
5. (i) Yes, this pair of lines are parallel, as the transversal makes equal alternate angles
   (ii) No, this pair of lines are not parallel, as the transversal makes unequal alternate angles
6. (i) $|\angle FCD| = 78°$ alternate angles
   (ii) $|\angle GFH| = 78°$ vertically opposite angles
   (iii) $|\angle ACF| = 102°$ straight angle
   (iv) $|\angle ACB| = 78°$ vertically opposite angles
   (v) $|\angle BCD| = 102°$ vertically opposite angles
7. (i) $|\angle A| = 66°$ straight angle
   (ii) $|\angle E| = 114°$ alternate angles
   (iii) $|\angle C| = 38°$ alternate angles
   (iv) $|\angle B| = 66°$ alternate angles
   (v) $|\angle G| = 142°$ straight angle
   (vi) $|\angle F| = 142°$ vertically opposite angles
   (vii) $|\angle D| = 142°$ vertically opposite angles
8. (i) $|\angle A| = 67°$ alternate angles
   (ii) $|\angle B| = 113°$ straight angle
   (iii) $|\angle C| = 113°$ straight angle or using alternate angles
9. (i) $|\angle E| = 68°$ alternate angles
   (ii) $|\angle B| = 68°$ vertically opposite angles
   (iii) $|\angle A| = 68°$ alternate angles
   (iv) $|\angle D| = 112°$ straight line

Practice questions 11·3

1. (iv) Corresponding angles are equal
   (v) Part (iv) will be true for every repeat
2. (i) $|\angle A| = 134°$ corresponding angles
   (ii) $|\angle B| = 46°$ straight angle
   (iii) $|\angle C| = 46°$ corresponding angles
   (iv) $|\angle D| = 134°$ vertically opposite angles
   (v) $|\angle E| = 46°$ alternate angles
   (vi) $|\angle F| = 134°$ alternate angles
   (vii) $|\angle G| = 46°$ vertically opposite angles
3. (i) $|\angle M| = 58°$ corresponding angles
   (ii) $|\angle N| = 122°$ straight angle
   (iii) $|\angle O| = 58°$ vertically opposite angles
   (iv) $|\angle P| = 58°$ vertically opposite angles
   (v) $|\angle Q| = 122°$ straight angle
   (vi) $|\angle R| = 22°$ vertically opposite angles
   (vii) $|\angle S| = 22°$ corresponding angles
4. (i) Yes, lines are parallel because the corresponding angles are equal
   (ii) No, lines are not parallel because the corresponding angles are not equal
   (iii) Yes, lines are parallel because the corresponding angles are equal
   (iv) Yes, lines are parallel because the corresponding angles are equal
5. (i) $|\angle A| = 95°$ corresponding angles
   (ii) $|\angle B| = 85°$ straight angle
   (iii) $|\angle C| = 85°$ straight angle
6. (i) $|\angle A| = 78°$ corresponding angles
   (ii) $|\angle B| = 102°$ straight angle
   (iii) $|\angle C| = 102°$ corresponding angles
   (iv) $|\angle D| = 102°$ vertically opposite angles
   (v) $|\angle E| = 78°$ vertically opposite angles
7. (i) $|\angle A| = 64°$ corresponding angles
   (ii) $|\angle B| = 64°$ alternate angles
   (iii) $|\angle C| = 116°$ corresponding angles

Revision questions

11A Core skills

1. (iii) Alternate angles are equal
2. (i) $\angle D$, (ii) $\angle H$, (iii) $\angle F$, (iv) $\angle C$, (v) $\angle B$, (vi) $\angle B$, (vii) $\angle E$, (viii) Many possible answers, e.g. $\angle E$ and $\angle F$
3. (i) Corresponding angles
   (ii) Vertically opposite angles
   (iii) Alternate angles
   (iv) Alternate angles
4. (i) $|\angle Y| = 122°$ vertically opposite angles
      $|\angle X| = 122°$ corresponding angles
   (ii) $|\angle Y| = 133°$ straight angle
      $|\angle X| = 133°$ corresponding angles and vertically opposite angles
   (iii) $|\angle Y| = 131°$ vertically opposite angles or corresponding angles
      $|\angle X| = 131°$ alternate angles

574 Linking Thinking 1

5. (i) |∠A| = 66° corresponding angles
   |∠B| = 114° straight angle
   |∠C| = 114° vertically opposite angles
   |∠D| = 66° alternate angles
   |∠F| = 114° vertically opposite angles
   |∠G| = 66° vertically opposite angles
   (ii) |∠J| = 63° vertically opposite
   |∠H| = 63° corresponding angles
   |∠I| = 63° vertically opposite angles
   |∠K| = 117° straight angle
   |∠L| = 117° straight angle
   |∠M| = 117° vertically opposite
   |∠N| = 117° vertically opposite
   (iii) |∠O| = 47° straight angle
   |∠P| = 47° straight angle
   |∠Q| = 47° vertically opposite angles
   |∠R| = 133° straight angle
   |∠S| = 47° straight angle
   |∠T| = 133° corresponding angles
   |∠U| = 133° vertically opposite angles
6. (i) Sometimes true, (ii) Sometimes true, (iii) Always true, (iv) Sometimes true, (v) Never true

11B Taking it further

1. (i) |∠A| = 75° corresponding angles
   (ii) |∠B| = 105° straight and alternate angles
   (iii) |∠C| = 105° vertically opposite and corresponding angles
   (iv) |∠D| = 105° corresponding angles
   (v) |∠E| = 75° corresponding angles
   (vi) |∠F| = 105° straight angle or corresponding angles
   (vii) |∠G| = 105° corresponding angles
   (viii) |∠H| = 75° corresponding angles
   (ix) |∠I| = 75° corresponding angles
   (x) |∠J| = 75° alternate angles
2. (i) |∠A| = 103° straight angle
   (ii) |∠X| = 77° alternate angles
   (iii) |∠Y| = 103° alternate angles
3. (i) |∠A| = 56° corresponding angles
   (ii) |∠B| = 124° straight angle
   (iii) |∠C| = 124° vertically opposite angles
   (iv) |∠D| = 56° vertically opposite angles
   (v) |∠E| = 124° alternate angles
   (vi) |∠F| = 124° vertically opposite angles
   (vii) |∠G| = 56° vertically opposite angles
4. (i) |∠A| = 66° straight and corresponding angles
   (ii) |∠B| = 114° corresponding angles
   (iii) |∠C| = 114° vertically opposite angles
   (iv) |∠D| = 66° vertically opposite angles
   (v) |∠E| = 114° vertically opposite angles or corresponding angles
5. (i) |∠M| = 78° alternate angles
   (ii) |∠O| = 102° straight angle
   (iii) |∠P| = 102° alternate angles

Unit 12 Linking Thinking revision material
Questions
1. (a) (i) 2, 1, 3, 6, 9; whole, positive numbers
   (ii) 2, 0, 1, 3, −5, 6, −7, 9; whole numbers, both negative and positive
   (iii) 2, $\frac{1}{2}$, 0, 1, 3, $\frac{2}{7}$, −5, 6, −7, 9; numbers that can be written as fractions
   (b) (i) {1, 2, 3, 6}
   (ii) Any of {1, 2}, {1, 3}, {1, 6}, {2, 3}, {2, 6}, {3, 6}
   (iii) 2
   (c) (i) 0, (ii) $\frac{1}{2}$, (iii) $\frac{2}{7}$
   (d) (i) (1 + 2) + 3 = 1 + (2 + 3)
   (ii) 2 × 3 = 3 × 2
   (iii) 2 × (1 + 6) = (2 × 1) + (2 × 6)
2. (a) (i) 12 minutes
   (ii) 194 mins/3 hours 14 mins
   (b) (i) 5·15%, (ii) 15·46%, (iii) 74·22%
   (c) €350, €210, €140
3. (a) (i) Jakob: −4; Larissa: −3; Jakob is the winner.
   (ii) Linear: same first difference
   (b) The Eiffel Tower: (i) 243 m (ii) 182·25 m (iii) 5 bounces
   The Statue of Liberty: (i) 69·75 m (ii) 52·3125 m (iii) 5 bounces
   The Burj Khalifa: (i) 621 m (ii) 465·75 m (iii) 5 bounces
   (c) (i) (a) $\frac{3}{14}$ (b) 0·21 (c) 21·43%
   (ii) (a) $\frac{7}{14} = \frac{1}{2}$ (b) 0·5 (c) 50%
   (iii) (a) $\frac{1}{14}$ (b) 0·07 (c) 7·14%
   (iv) (a) $\frac{12}{14} = \frac{6}{7}$ (b) 0·86 (c) 85·71%
4. (a) (i) A = 270°, B = 90°, C = 150°, D = 210°, E = 60°, F = 300°, G = 90°, H = 270°
   (ii) A = reflex; B = right-angled; C = obtuse; D = reflex; E = acute; F = reflex; G = right-angled; H = reflex
   (b) (i) A = {2, 4, 6, 8, 10, 12}; B = {1, 3, 5, 7, 9, 11}
   (iii) (a) {1, 2, 3, 4, 5, 6, 7, 8, 9, 10, 11, 12}; (b) { }; (c) 6
5. (b) Stones A. 8 bags of small Stones A €1 118 and 10 bags of Stones B cost €1 285
   (c) (i) 202·5 m², (ii) 69%
6. (a) (i) 3 : 2, (ii) 10 litres
   (b) (i) 6 litres
   (ii) White: 3·6 litres; black: 2·4 litres
   (c) (i) Variable = number of hours worked; constants = €100 and €50
   (ii) Cost = €50(number of hours) + €100
   (iii) 150; 200; 250; 300; 350; 400; 450; 500
   (v) 50
   (vi) €375
   (vii) 3·5 hours
7. (a) (i) D, (ii) B, (iii) E and C, (iv) A and C, (v) C: it is cheaper and weighs more
   (b) (i) 405 calories and 540 calories
   (ii) 649 calories; 24%
   (c) (i) €1·92
   (ii) 390 g of oats, 42 g of nuts, 168 g of the mix
   (d) (i) 600 g
   (ii) 4 : 1
   (iii) 480 g
8. (a) (i) 72 cm, (ii) 20, (iii) 120 bricks
   (b) €91·94
   (c) 90
   (d) 105 kg

Section B

Unit 13 Money matters 1
Practice questions 13·1
1. (i) (a) Monthly = €3 041·67
   (b) Fortnightly = €1 403·85
   (c) Weekly = €701·92
   (d) Hourly = €17·55
   (ii) (a) Monthly = €4 058·33
   (b) Fortnightly = €1 873·07
   (c) Weekly = €936·54
   (d) Hourly = €23·41
   (iii) (a) Monthly = €1 645·83
   (b) Fortnightly = €759·62
   (c) Weekly = €379·81
   (d) Hourly = €9·50
   (iv) (a) Monthly = €5 499·58
   (b) Fortnightly = €2 538·27
   (c) Weekly = €1 269·13
   (d) Hourly = €31·73
   (v) (a) Monthly = €8 750·00
   (b) Fortnightly = €4 038·46
   (c) Weekly = €2 019·23
   (d) Hourly = €50·48
2. (i) (a) Fortnightly = €1 615·38
   (b) Weekly = €807·69
   (c) Hourly = €20·19
   (ii) (a) Fortnightly = €2 065·38
   (b) Weekly = €1 032·69
   (c) Hourly = €25·82
   (iii) (a) Fortnightly = €2 774·77
   (b) Weekly = €1 387·38
   (c) Hourly = €34·68
   (iv) (a) Fortnightly = €2 515·38
   (b) Weekly = €1 257·69
   (c) Hourly = €31·44
   (v) (a) Fortnightly = €1 231·15
   (b) Weekly = €615·58
   (c) Hourly = €15·39
3. (i) Jane has a higher weekly wage
   (ii) She earns €30·60 more per week than Simon
4. Jill worked 32 hours
5. (i) 12 hours
   (ii) €8·75 per hour
6. (i) Yes, Bobby has been underpaid [show supporting work for justification]
   (ii) €399·50
7. €276·00
8. €3 856·00
9. €10 670·00

Practice questions 13·2
1. Cost before VAT = €569·11
2. €193·50
3. (i) €48·56, (ii) €259·71, (iii) €14·85, (iv) €124·85, (v) €384·56
4. (i) €148·37, (ii) €34·13
5. €26 562·50
6. (i) Ireland = €306·27; France (online) = €274·99
   (ii) Any valid justification, e.g. I would choose the France option as it is cheaper OR I would choose Ireland option as I don't want to wait for delivery, etc.
7. (i) €399·00
   (ii) 23%
8. €6·08; €51·08; 35%; €114·75; €43·70; €233·69; 13·5%; €1·19; €42·50; €5·74

Practice questions 13·3
1. (i) 775 units
   (ii) €116·25
2. €8·55
3. (A) = 638 units; (B) = €80·71; (C) = €17·48; (D) = €98·19; (E) = €13·26; (F) = €111·45
4. (i) 1 200, 97·20, 107·70, 14·54, 122·24
   (ii) 560, 27·44, 35·80, 4·83, 40·63
   (iii) 268, 16·94, 22·44, 3·03, 25·47
   (iv) 630, 35·28, 38·64, 5·22, 43·86
   (v) 301, 33·71, 41·20, 5·56, 46·76
5. (i) €371·41
   (ii) €421·55
6. €79·80
7. (i) He should choose the Pay as You go package, as it is cheaper
   (ii) She should choose the Red 15 package, as it is cheaper
   (iii) If you are going to use more than 748 minutes per month, then the Red 15 is cheaper

Practice questions 13·4
1. (i) 30·25%, (ii) 41·92%, (iii) 41·89%
2. (ii) €178, 43·8% profit
   (iii) €700, 72% loss
   (iv) €3 174, 21·1% loss
   (v) €7 200, 16·7% profit
   (vi) €6 432, 5·4% loss
   (vii) €7 600, 44·8% profit
   (viii) €98 700, 1·5% loss
   (ix) €966 999, 3·3% loss
3. Sale price = €42·50
4. 40% profit
5. (i) €750, (ii) €1 114, (iii) €225, (iv) €450
6. (i) €918·75, (ii) €637·50, (iii) €420, (iv) €54, (v) €911, (vi) €8 250
7. €60
8. 8% profit
9. €10
10. (i) €17, (ii) €16·32
11. He made a loss of €1 000

Practice questions 13·5
1. (i) F = variable, P = variable, 1 = constant, i = variable, t = variable
   (ii) F = Final amount, P = Principal, i = interest rate, t = time
2. (i) €10 600, (ii) €10 609
3. (i) €105, €5
   (ii) €721, €21
   (iii) €2 625, €125
   (iv) €5133, €783
   (v) €10302·25, €302·25
   (vi) €341·21, €42·21
   (vii) €261 250, €11 250
   (viii) €261 419·59, €11 419·59
   (ix) €28 731, €5 181
   (x) €3 045 225·38, €45 225·38
4. (i) €540·90, (ii) €45·90
5. (i) €2 060, (ii) €2 121·80, (iii) €2 185·45
6. Loan A interest = €2 100, Loan B interest = €2 079·50, so loan B offers the lower interest rate
7. Difference = €12·15
8. Final amount due = €29 160
9. €13 860
10. €1 502·50
11. (i) €288, (ii) 1·44%

Practice questions 13·6
1. €47·06
2. (i) £46, (ii) €97·83
3. €43·47
4. (i) 1144·50 Turkish lira, (ii) €15
5. No William does not have enough money, he is $6·40 short, so he needs another €5·16
6. Total bill = €34·38
7. (i) UK company offering cheaper flight
   (ii) €6·81
8. New Zealand = €6·72; London = €5·11; USA = €4·85; Turkey = €3·00; Switzerland = €5·59; Poland = €4·56
9. (i) (a) $348·00 (b) $5·22
   (ii) (a) €199·50 (b) €1
   (iii) (a) 1 188 Swiss francs (b) €430 (c) €6·45
   (iv) (a) €1 200 (b) €18 (c) 294·48 złoty (d) €1·08 (e) Commission = €19·08

Revision questions
13A Core skills
1. €645·80
2. €2 193·75
3. (i) Per month = €666 666·67
   (ii) Per week = €153 846·15
   (iii) Per day = €21 917·81
   (iv) Per hour = €913·24
4. Bank A is better, as you receive more US dollars, even after commission is taken into account
5. Yes, the percentage difference is 20·72%
6. (A) 402 units (B) €44·22 (C) €76·79 (D) €10·37 (E) €87·16
7. 30%; €43; €22·50; €67; 60%; 133·33%; €15
8. €1 630·79
9. (i) €162 180
   (ii) €167 045·40
   (iii) €218 545·40

13B Taking it further
1. (i) €1 168·20, (ii) €1 475
2. €10·88 per kg
3. (i) €20 720·46, (ii) €4 720·46, (iii) €1 710·86
4. Live Style has the cheapest jersey at €58·33, so you would buy it there
5. (i) Beta Bank offers the best rate
   (ii) Beta Bank requires one year
   (iii) If only for one year choose Beta Bank, if a minimum of two years, choose Awe Bank
6. (i) €20·62, (ii) 23%
7. (i) Shop A = €396, shop B = €352, shop C = €460
   (ii) Shop B, because it offers the best value
8. (i) Clear Power: 114·70; 124·17; 16·76; 140·93
   Power One: 0; 142·50; 142·50; 19·24; 161·74
   (ii) Difference = €20·81
   (iii) Price with 7% discount = €150·42
   (iv) Mia should get her electricity from Clear Power, as it is the cheapest

Unit 14 Maths in motion
Practice questions 14·1
1. (i) Kilometres
   (ii) Millimetres or centimetres
   (iii) Metres
   (iv) Minutes
   (v) Hours
   (vi) Seconds
2. Millimetres, centimetres, metres, kilometres
3. (i) 10 000 m, (ii) 5 000 mm, (iii) 1 800 s, (iv) 1 hr, (v) 1·2 m, (vi) 1 440 min
4. (i) 1·67 hr, (ii) 3·17 hr, (iii) 2·3 hr, (iv) 2·38 hr
5. (i) 03:15, (ii) 20:25, (iii) 00:00, (iv) 14:55, (v) 01:27, (vi) 12:00
6. (i) 7:40 am, (ii) 6:27 pm, (iii) 12:01 am, (iv) 10:35 am, (v) 7:54 pm, (vi) 5:56 am
7. (i) 53 minutes, (ii) 08:56
8. (i) 30 minutes, (ii) 35 minutes, (iii) 1 hour 53 minutes, (iv) No
9. (i) 10:55 because the next one arrives too late
   (ii) 07:00
   (iii) 1 hour 20 minutes
   (iv) 17:55
   (v) 9 minutes
10. (i) 09:50; arrives at 11:10
    (ii) 1 hour 20 minutes
    (iii) 08:05

Practice questions 14·2
1. (i) Every hour he travels 60 km, (ii) 30 km, (iii) 12 minutes
2. 10·44 m/s
3. 390 m
4. 75 s
5. 56 km/h
6. (i) 250 km, (ii) 16·5 km, (iii) 45 km, (iv) 67·5 km
7. (i) 4 hr, (ii) 1·5 hr, (iii) 12 hr, (iv) 5·5 hr
8. (i) 71 km, (ii) 498 km, (iii) 371 km, (iv) 36 km
9. (i) 7·5 m/s, (ii) 32 km/hr, (iii) 16·67 m/s, (iv) 48 km/hr, (v) 800 m/min, (vi) 104 km/hr
10. (i) 1 hr 24 mins, (ii) 9 000 m, (iii) 108 km/hr, (iv) 169 km, (v) 3·81 m/s, (vi) 6·4 s
11. 28·09 km/hr
12. (i) 1·04 m/s, (ii) 0·74 m/s
13. 12:35 pm
14. Vehicles B and C are speeding

Practice questions 14·3

1. (i) Rate of change describes how one quantity changes in relation to another.
   (ii) Linear pattern is a pattern where the rate of change (increase or decrease) remains constant
   (iii) Directly proportional is a relationship between two variables beginning at 0 where, as one increases the other also increases
   (iv) The slope of a line represents the rate of change of the line. It is the steepness of the line
2. (a) (i) 60 km, (ii) 105 km
   (b) (i) 3 hr, (ii) 1·5 hr
3. (i) 6 km/hr, (ii) 10 km/hr, (iii) 30 m/s, (iv) 0 m/s
4. C, A, B. Line C is the steepest line so the fastest speed, then line A. Line B is the least steep line so is the slowest
5. (i) B. The slope is 0, so the speed is 0 km/hr, i.e. the car has stopped
   (ii) A. The line is steeper therefore, the speed is faster
6. (i) B, (ii) C, (iii) A
7. (i) $[AB]$: slow steady speed (1 m/s) for 5 seconds
      $[BC]$: stopped for 3 seconds
      $[CD]$: faster speed (1·75 m/s) for 4 seconds
      $[DE]$: stopped for 2 seconds
      $[EF]$: fast return (2 m/s) to the original starting point
   (ii) $[OA]$: fast speed (2 m/s) for 5 seconds
       $[AB]$: stopped for 5 seconds
       $[BC]$: return to starting point at faster speed (3·3 m/s)
       $[CD]$: stopped for 3 seconds
       $[DE]$: slower steady speed (1 m/s) for 5 seconds halfway back to where they were
       $[EF]$: stopped for 4 seconds
8. (i) C, (ii) A, (iii) D, (iv) B
9. (i) B, container has same width throughout so a constant rate of change (increase in depth)
   (ii) C, the bottom is wider than the top so will fill up slowly (line less steep) then faster (line more steep)
   (iii) A, the container has three widths and the graph has three sections; the bottom is wider than the middle so will fill up slowly (line less steep); the middle is narrowest so will fill fastest (steepest line); the top is the widest so will fill the slowest (least steep line)
13. (i) C, (ii) E, (iii) A, (iv) B, (v) D

Revision questions

14A Core skills
1. (i) 8 hr 33 min, (ii) 132 mins, (iii) 168 hr, (iv) 5 400 sec
2. (i) Train A, (ii) 340 km, (iii) 1·36 hrs, (iv) The distance it travels in a certain amount of time
3. A = 4 m/s; B = 5·7 m/s; C = 7·7 m/s; D = 8 m/s; E = 5·3 m/s
4. 1 hr 12 min
5. (i) 1 hr 30 min, (ii) 30 min
6. (i) B, it is wider so fills up slower and therefore, is represented by the less steep slope
   (ii) A, it is narrower so fills up faster and is represented by the steeper slope
7. (i) 10 mins, (ii) 3 km, (iii) 50 mins, (iv) C. This part has the steepest slope
8. (i) James runs the race at a constant speed.
   (ii) Rachel runs faster at the start and the end but slower in the middle section of the race.
   (iii) 17·5 mins, 1 750 m
   (iv) 100 m/min
   (v) Section A: 200 m/min; Section B: 60 m/min; Section C: 100 m/min
   (vi) James
9. (i) 4 (ii) 2 (iii) 5 (iv) 7 (v) 1 (vi) 3 (vii) 6
10. (ii) Between her sister's and brother's homes, because it is 66·7 km/hr but is 100 km/hr on the other parts

14B Taking it further
1. 1 hr 25 min
2. Yes. The journey will take 9·6 minutes and he has 15 minutes to get there
3. 1 019 km
4. A = false. Jason travels at 10 km/hr and Donna travels at 9 km/hr
   B = true. She travels 10 km in 10 minutes so 60 km in 60 minutes or 60 km/hr which is above the speed limit
   C = false. Paula is faster because she covers the same distance in a shorter time
   D = false. The first car is travelling at 22·2 m/s and the second at 33·3 m/s
   E = true. The train could have travelled faster and slower than the average speed
5. (i) 93 km/hr
   (ii) If they drove on different roads the distance could be different.
6. (i) 9·7 km/hr, (ii) 4·5 km
7. 52·7 km/hr
8. (i) Clare, (ii) Clare, (iii) 108 km
9. (i) Ben. He reached the end in 4·5 mins while Alan and Carl took 5 mins.
   (ii) Alan starts the race in the lead, steepest line. He falls/stops at 3 mins (horizontal line) and continues at a slower pace (less steep line) to the finish line. Ben starts the race at a steady pace then slows down after 2·5 minutes (less steep line). He runs faster after 3·5 minutes (steeper line). He overtakes Alan after around 4·2 minutes. Carl starts the race at the slowest pace (least steep line). He increases his speed after 4 minutes (steeper line) and reaches the finish line at the same time as Alan.
10. (i) The width of the vase is decreasing so the speed (rate of change) will increase. Since the rate of change is not constant, the graph is not a straight line

Unit 15   Polygons

Practice questions 15·1
1. (i) 6 sides, (ii) Blue = side, green = vertex/point, red = adjacent sides
2. (i) Both, (ii) Polygon, (iii) Polygon, (iv) Neither, (v) Both, (vi) Both
4. 9 m^2
5. 7·28 m^2
8. (ii) 410 mm
9. (ii) 30 cm, (iii) 50 cm^2
10. (i) (a) 24 cm^2 (b) 22 cm (c) Rectangle
    (ii) (a) 9 cm^2 (b) 12 cm (c) Square
    (iii) (a) 300 cm^2 (b) 80 cm (c) Rectangle
    (iv) (a) 32 m^2 (b) 24 m (c) Rectangle
    (v) (a) 25 cm^2 (b) 52 cm (c) Rectangle
    (vi) (a) 1 cm^2 (b) 4 cm (c) Square
11. 13 640 m^2
12. (i) 2 200 m^2, (ii) 2 596 m^2, (iii) 396 m^2, (iv) Scale 1 cm = 10 metres
13. 18 000 cm^2
14. (i) Width = 40 m, length = 120 m
    (ii) 4 800 m^2

Practice questions 15·2
1. (i) 28°, the three angles in any triangle add to 180°
   (ii) 52°, the three angles in any triangle add to 180°
   (iii) 81°, the three angles in any triangle add to 180°
   (iv) 86°, the three angles in any triangle add to 180°
2. (i) 65°, the three angles in any triangle add to 180°
   (ii) 90°, the three angles in any triangle add to 180°
   (iii) 88°, the three angles in any triangle add to 180°
   (iv) 45°, angles opposite the equals sides in an isosceles triangle are equal
   (v) 48°, the three angles in any triangle add to 180°
   (vi) 48°, the three angles in any triangle add to 180°
3. 80°
9. $Z = 40°, Y = 60°; X = 50°$
10. Scale 1 cm = 200 km
11. If two lines are parallel, then any transversal will make equal alternate angles

Practice questions 15·4
1. (i) Scalene: all sides are different
   (ii) Isosceles: two equal sides
   (iii) Equilateral: three equal sides
   (iv) Isosceles: two equal angles
   (v) Isosceles: two equal angles
2. (i) Isosceles: two equal angles of 65°
   (ii) Equilateral: three equal sides of 60°
   (iii) Isosceles: two equal sides of 3·8 cm
   (iv) Equilateral: three equal sides of 4·8 cm

Answer key   577

(v) Scalene: all three sides are different
3. (i) 60°, (ii) 45°, (iii) 50°
4. (i) 22·5 cm², (ii) 24 cm², (iii) 5 684 cm², (iv) 2 688 cm²
5. (i) Equilateral: all sides are equal in length
   (ii) Isosceles: two sides are equal in length
6. (i) 385 cm, (ii) 449 cm, (iii) 20 cm, (iv) 30 cm
7. (i) 90 km
   (ii) Isosceles triangle (2 sides, 90 km)
   (iii) 1 cm = 10 km
8. 216 cm²

Practice questions 15·5

5. (i) Never true, (ii) Sometimes true, (iii) Never true, (iv) Never true

Practice questions 15·6

1. (i) 145°, exterior angle in a triangle equals the sum of the interior opposite angles
   (ii) 110°, exterior angle in a triangle equals the sum of the interior opposite angles
   (iii) 92°, exterior angle in a triangle equals the sum of the interior opposite angles
   (iv) 120°, angles opposite the equal sides in an isosceles triangle are equal. Exterior angle in a triangle equals the sum of the interior opposite angles
2. (i) $|\angle X| = 78°$, the angles in any triangle add to 180°
   $|\angle Y| = 102°$, each exterior angle of a triangle is equal to the sum of the interior opposite angles.
   (ii) $|\angle A| = 107·5°$ $|\angle B| = 62°$
   (iii) $|\angle A| = 107·5°$
   $|\angle B| = 72·5°$
   Each exterior angle of a triangle is equal to the sum of the interior opposite angles
   (iv) $|\angle X| = 60°$ $|\angle Y| = 120°$
   Equilateral triangle, all angles are equal
3. $|\angle H| = 105°$ Straight angle is equal to 180°
   $|\angle Y| = 69°$ Three angles in a triangle sum to 180°
   $|\angle G| = 111°$ Straight angle is equal to 180°
4. (i) 74°, (ii) 74°, (iii) 106°, (iv) Triangle ABC is isosceles as |AB| is equal to |AC|
5. (i) 70°, (ii) 120°, (iii) 85°, (iv) 95°, (v) 60°
7. (i) 180°: Straight angle is equal to 180°
   (ii) 180°: Three angles in a triangle sum to 180°
8. (i) Always true, (ii) Always true, (iii) Sometimes true, (iv) Always true, (v) Never true

Revision questions

15A Core skills

1. (i) Area = 40 cm², perimeter = 28 cm
   (ii) Area = 25 cm², perimeter = 20 cm
   (iii) Area = 24 cm², perimeter = 28 cm

2. (ii) 380 mm
   (iii) 8 800 mm²
3. (i) Equilateral (3 sides equal in length)
   (ii) Isosceles (2 sides equal in length)
   (iii) Scalene (all sides different of different length)
   (iv) Right-angled /scalene (triangle has right angle and 3 sides of different length)
   (v) Right-angled /isosceles (triangle has right angle and 2 sides of equal length)
9. (i) $|\angle X| = 53°$
   $|\angle Y| = 113°$
   (ii) $|\angle P| = 50°$
   (iii) $|\angle N| = 110°$
   $|\angle M| = 133°$
   (iv) $|\angle X| = 140°$
   $|\angle Y| = 95°$
10. (i) 25 m², (ii) 16 cm², (iii) 6 cm², (iv) 8·75 cm²

15B Taking it further

1. (i) 45 m², (ii) 6 litres, (iii) €46·60
2. 112 m²
3. (i) 13 950 m², (ii) 580 m
4. 90° and 70°
5. (i) 45°, (ii) 45°, (iii) Isosceles and right-angled
6. (i) 13·125 m², (ii) 4 full tubs, (iii) €815

Unit 16 Circles 1

Practice questions 16·1

1. Red = diameter; blue = radius; purple = chord; yellow = arc
2. (i) Sector, (ii) Semicircle, (iii) Sector, (iv) Full circle
3. (i) Semicircle, (ii) Full circle, (iii) Sector, (iv) Quarter circle
4. (i) Tangent, (ii) Radius, (iii) Diameter, (iv) Chord
7. (i) 180°, (ii) 270°, (iii) 240°, (iv) 120°
8. (i) 223°, (ii) 323°, (iii) 360°, (iv) 90°
10. (i) Always true
    (ii) Never true
    (iii) Sometimes true
    (iv) Never true
    (v) Never true
    (vi) Never true

Practice questions 16·2

1. (a) (i) $\pi = 3·14$, (ii) $\pi = 3·14$, (iii) $\pi = 3·14$
   (b) Value for π is constant
2. (i) Semi-circle, (ii) Disc, (iii) Half disc, (iv) Circle
3. (b) (i) 31·4 cm, (ii) 37·68 cm, (iii) 28·26 cm, (iv) 357·96 mm
   (c) (i) 31·43 cm, (ii) 37·71 cm, (iii) 28·29 cm, (iv) 358·29 mm
   (d) (i) 10π cm, (ii) 12π cm, (iii) 9π cm, (iv) 114π mm
4. (b) (i) 38·465 cm², (ii) 72·35 cm², (iii) 128·61 cm², (iv) 8 820·26mm²,
   (c) (i) 38·5 cm², (ii) 72·41cm², (iii) 128·73cm², (iv) 8 828·29mm²
   (d) (i) 12·25π cm², (ii) 23·04π cm², (iii) 40·96π cm², (iv) 2 809π mm²
5. (i) 75·4 cm, (ii) 43·98 cm, (iii) 50·27 cm, (iv) 841·94 mm

6. (i) 615·44 cm², (ii) 226·87 cm², (iii) 12 661·27 mm², (iv) 68 778·56 mm²
7. (i) 3 025π cm², (ii) 132·25π cm², (iii) 15 376π mm², (iv) 1 089π mm²
8. (i) 24 cm, (ii) 9 cm, (iii) 49 cm, (iv) 8 mm
9. (i) 2 513·27 m, (ii) 838 posts
10. (i) 57·51m, (ii) 263·13m²
11. (i) (a) 157·08 cm (b) 182·21 cm
    (ii) (a) 1 963·5 cm² (b) 2642·08 cm²
    (iii) 678·58 cm²
    (iv) 12

Practice questions 16·3

1. (i) 301·59 cm², (ii) 21·46 cm², (iii) 30·9 cm², (iv) 714·06 cm²
2. (i) 25·71 cm, (ii) 14·28 cm, (iii) 38·85 cm, (iv) 40·27 cm, (v) 22·85 cm
3. 8·25 m²
4. 1 225·22 cm
5. (i) 1 420·4 cm², (ii) 53·04%, (iii) 1 512·5 cm²
6. (i) 26·5 cm, (ii) 166·50 cm, (iii) 600·58 turns
7. (i) 1·4 km, (ii) 569 rotations
8. (i) 170 mm, (ii) 620·2 mm²
9. (i) 16 454·87 cm², (ii) 5 400 cm², (iii) 5 400 cm², (iv) 2 827·43 cm², (v) €1 413·72

Revision questions

16A Core skills

1. (i) Tangent, (ii) Disc, (iii) Arc, (iv) Chord, (v) Quarter disc, (vi) Circumference, (vii) Semicircle, (viii) Diameter, (ix) Half a disc, (x) Radius
2. (i) 94·2 cm, (ii) 17·58 cm, (iii) 33·91 cm
3. (i) 47 548·29 mm², (ii) 475·48 cm², (iii) 28 364·29 m²
4. (i) 484π cm², (ii) 88·36 cm², (iii) 40 804π mm²
5. (i) 458·67 cm, (ii) 191·01 m, (iii) 629·58 mm
6. (i) 20 cm, (ii) 13 cm, (iii) 6 cm, (iv) 11 cm
7. (i) Never true, (ii) Always true, (iii) Never true, (iv) Never true

16B Taking it further

1. (i) Circumference 351·9 cm, area = 9 852 cm²
   (ii) Circumference 213·6 units, area = 3 631·7 units²
   (iii) Circumference 3 141·6 units, area = 785 398·2 units²
   (iv) Circumference 754 mm, area, = 45 238·9 mm²
   (v) Circumference 324·8 m, area = 8 397·1 m²
2. (i) 1 452·2 cm², (ii) 896·5 cm², (iii) 439·5 cm²
3. (i) 3 512·30, (ii) 879 posts, (iii) €3 161·07, (iv) 481 797·79 m², (v) 2 409 bags, (vi) €66 247·50, (vii) 48·16 hectares
4. (iii) A = 4 084π mm²

Unit 17 Area, volume and surface area

Practice questions 17·1

1. (i) Centimetres (cm), (ii) Metres (m), (iii) Kilometres (km), (iv) Millimetres (mm), (v) Kilometres (km), (vi) Millimetres (mm)

3. Sonia ran 4 700 m (4·7 km) farther than Michelle walked
4. (i) €50 notes = 3 metres tall
   (ii) €1 coins = 2 300m, therefore much higher than the Spire
5. (i) Area = 25cm², perimeter = 20 cm
   (ii) Area = 6 cm², perimeter = 12 cm
   (iii) Area = 153·94 cm², perimeter = 43·98 m
   (iv) Area = 50·4 m², perimeter = 29 m
6. (i) (a) Perimeter = 10·4 units
      (b) Area = 6 units²
   (ii) (a) Perimeter = 10·4 units
       (b) Area = 5 units²
   (iii) (a) Perimeter = 12·8 units
        (b) Area = 6 units²
7. (i) Area = 8 units², perimeter = 14 units
   (ii) Area = 8 units², perimeter = 14 units
   (iii) Area = 12·57 units², perimeter = 12·57 units
   (iv) Area = 9·53 units², perimeter = 11·71 units
   (v) Area = 2·51 units², perimeter = 5·26 units
   (vi) Area = 15 units², perimeter = 17·22 units
   (vii) Area = 6 units², perimeter = 12 units
   (viii) Area = 11 units², perimeter = 20 units
8. (i) Shaded area = 9·43 units²
   (ii) Shaded area = 27·5 cm²
   (iii) Shaded area = 26·18cm²
   (iv) Shaded area = 25·4 m²
9. (i) Must buy 22 metres of ribbon
   (ii) €39·60
10. (i) 414·7 cm
    (ii) 241·1 times
    (iii) 692 times
11. (i) Possible answers 8 × 2, 4 × 4, 16 × 1
    (ii) 16 cm

Practice questions 17·2

2. A and C
3. C
5. (i) 150 cm², (ii) 88 cm², (iii) 48 cm², (iv) 56 cm²
6. 1 152 cm²
8. (i) 272 cm², (ii) €816, (iii) €1 004
9. (ii) Yes, because the box has enough room

Practice questions 17·3

1. 14 cm³
2. (i) 93·6 cm³, (ii) 96 cm³, (iii) 67·5 cm³, (iv) 120 cm³
3. (i) 20 units³, (ii) 96 units³, (iii) 117 units³, (iv) 12 units³
4. (i) 826·5 m³, (ii) 80 m³, (iii) 5 100 m³
5. (ii) 86 448 cm³
6. (i) Greatest volume = 86·632 m³
   (ii) 4 trailers
   (iii) Shane's volume = 61·617 m³, Shane is correct
   (iv) Agree with the truck driver, as cargo is too long to fit into trailer.
7. 20 cm

8. (i) A = 162 cm³, B = 162 cm³, C = 162 cm³
   (ii) The three volumes are the equal (the same)
   (iii) No. Changing the orientation of a solid does not change its volume (or any other valid mathematical answer)
9. (i) 276 m³, (ii) 588 m³, (iii) 95 cm³
10. (i) $\frac{1}{5}$ m³, (ii) $\frac{7}{54}$ mm² (or 0·13 mm²)
    (iii) $\frac{171}{2}$ cm³ (or 85·5 cm³)
11. (i) (a) 240 litres (b) 8 litres
    (ii) 30 times

Practice questions 17·4

1. (i) 471 mm³, (ii) 169·6 m³, (iii) 1 230·9 mm³, (iv) 942 cm³, (v) 31·4 m³
2. (i) 12 units³, (ii) 240 units³, (iii) 198 units³, (iv) 77 units³
3. (i) 864 m³
   (ii) 4 023 mm³
   (iii) 11 m³ or 11 314 286 cm³
   (iv) 0·15 m³ or 150 857 143 mm³
   (v) 7·5 m³ or 75 429 cm³
4. (i) 216π cm³
   (ii) 6 480π mm³
   (iii) 43·75π m³
   (iv) 1 080 000π cm³
   (v) 4 706 800π mm³
5. 75π cm³
6. (i) 7 m, (ii) 11 m, (iii) 12 mm, (iv) 3 cm, (v) 10 m
7. Bottle C, it has a volume of 269 cm³
8. (i) 12·57 m³, (ii) 18 855 kg
9. (i) 0·7854 litres
   (ii) 9·4248 litres
   (iii) 131·9469 litres
10. (i) Yes the student was correct
    (ii) Any valid answer, e.g. If the can was frozen, the soup would expand and burst the can; if the can was completely full, it might spill when opened, etc.
11. (i) 218 681·23 cm³
    (ii) 218·68 litres
    (iii) Water will have dropped by 35 cm
    (iv) 7 hours and 17 minutes
12. (i) 307·88 cm³
    (ii) The capacity of the can of orange juice will increase
    (iii) Because the radius is squared, changing it by a small amount has a greater influence on the volume of a cylinder than the height
13. (i) 64 cm³
    (ii) Water will rise, h = 2·26 cm
14. 9
15. 282·74 m³
16. (i) 753·98 cm³
    (ii) 18 095·52 cm³
    (iii) Many valid answers, e.g. if cans are stacked in rows of 6 and columns of 4, then, minimum values are: length = 48 cm, width = 32 cm, height = 15 cm
    (v) 23 040 cm³
    (vi) No, due to empty space between cans
    (vii) 4 945 cm³

Revision questions

17A Core skills

1. (ii), (iii), (iv), (vi) and (vii)
3. (i) 8 m², (ii) 32 m², (iii) 4 cans of paint needed, cost = €79·96
4. (i) 180 cm², (ii) 117 cm², (iii) Brona is not correct, border is 35% of the screen
5. (i) 4 cm, (ii) Area = 16 cm²
6. (i) 58 cm², (ii) Volume = 20cm³
7. A = 706·86 cm³,
   B = 11 403 cm³ or 0·01m³,
   C = 4 580 442·09 cm³ or 4·58 m³,
   D = 9 420 000 cm³ or 9·42 m³,
   E = 37·70 cm³
8. 3 900 tiles
9. (i) Total internal surface area = 8·5 m²
   (ii) Maximum volume = 1·5 m³

17B Taking it further

1. 13 333 m²; there are no windows on the roof or underneath the apartment block
2. (i) C, (ii) B; show calculations to justify answer
3. Dimensions – 4 × 4 × 2
4. 272·6 cm³
5. (a) (i) Volume of water = 500 m³
       (ii) 462·5 m³
   (b) 250 000 litres
6. (i) Volume = 8 640 cm³
   (ii) Minimum volume must be 69 120 cm³
   (iii) No, there would have to be some space between the boxes
7. She should buy second tank as it has a larger volume (first tank volume = 282·74 m², second tank volume = 565·49 m²)
8. (i) 636 cm³, (ii) 573 cm³,
   (iii) Yes, volume of ice = 81cm³ and the volume of space in the glass is only 63 cm³ (iv) 8·7 cm
9. (i) Sometimes true, (ii) Never true, (iii) Always true, (iv) Sometimes true

Unit 18 Collecting and representing data

Practice questions 18·1

1. (i) Categorical, can be put into groups
   (ii) Numerical, measurable
   (iii) Categorical, can be put into groups
   (iv) Categorical, can be put into groups
   (v) Numerical, measurable
   (vi) Categorical, can be put into groups
2. (i) Numerical continuous
   (ii) Numerical discrete
   (iii) Categorical nominal
   (iv) Categorical nominal
   (v) Numerical continuous
   (vi) Categorical nominal
   (vii) Categorical ordinal
   (viii) Numerical discrete
3. (i) Categorical, can be grouped
   (ii) Numerical, measurable, countable

- (iii) Categorical, can be grouped
- (iv) Categorical, can be grouped
- (v) Numerical, measurable, countable
- (vi) Numerical, measurable, countable
- (vii) Categorical, can be grouped
- (viii) Categorical, can be grouped

4. (i) Categorical nominal, can be grouped but has no order
   (ii) Numerical continuous, measurable and can take on any value within a range
   (iii) Categorical nominal, can be grouped but has no order
   (iv) Numerical discrete, measurable but can only take on certain values
   (v) Numerical discrete, measurable but can only take on certain values
   (vi) Categorical nominal, can be grouped but has no order

5. (i) Categorical nominal, can be grouped but has no order
   (ii) Numerical discrete, measurable but can only take on certain values
   (iii) Numerical discrete, measurable but can only take on certain values
   (iv) Categorical nominal, can be grouped but has no order

6. (i) Numerical continuous, measurable and can take on any value within a range
   (ii) Categorical nominal, can be grouped but has no order
   (iii) Numerical discrete, measurable but can only take on certain values
   (iv) Categorical nominal, can be grouped but has no order

7. There are many possible answers here. Some suitable answers are:
   (i) What colour are your eyes? (ii) What grade did you get in the test? (iii) What is your shoe size? (iv) What height are you?

8. (i) Data that can be put into groups, e.g. eye colour
   (ii) Data that can be counted or measured, e.g. age
   (iii) Data that has no order, e.g. hair colour
   (iv) Data that can be ranked or ordered, e.g. clothing sizes (S, M, L)
   (v) Data that can only take on certain values, e.g. age in years
   (vi) Data that can take on any value within a range, e.g. temperature

Practice questions 18·2

1. (i) People may interpret 'a lot' differently. How long do you spend doing your homework?
   (ii) Not everyone walks or cycles. How do you travel to school?
   (iii) 'Mindless' and 'exciting' are leading, all options not covered. What is your favourite movie genre?
   (iv) Question is biased as it is leading. What is a fair price for a cinema ticket?
   (v) Some people may never eat fruits and vegetables. How often do you eat fruits and vegetables?
   (vi) Question is biased as it is leading. How many hours sleep do you think we need each night?
   (vii) Question is biased as it is leading. Do you think students should be allowed to use spellcheck?
   (viii) 'Best' can be interpreted differently. Who is the best soccer team in the Premier League, in your opinion?

2. (i) Database, e.g. CSO census data, easy to do
   (ii) Questionnaire, easy to do
   (iii) Experiment, accurate data can be obtained
   (iv) Direct observation, easy to do

3. (i) No. Students may be uncomfortable answering in front of the class
   (ii) Very few students are being bullied. May not be accurate as students may not have answered honestly
   (iii) Anonymous student survey

4. (i) (a) Sample (b) Very expensive to test every battery
   (ii) (a) Whole population (b) Easy to survey everyone
   (iii) (a) Sample (b) Difficult and time consuming to ask everyone

5. Interviews could be time consuming and expensive

6. Phone interviews: Advantages – easily carried out; questions can be explained; many questions can be asked; Disadvantages – response rate can be low; limited to phone owners; expensive; interviewer may influence response
   Email interviews: Advantages – inexpensive and easily carried out; anonymous; done in participants' own time; Disadvantages – limited to people with internet access; questions cannot be explained

7. (i) Animal rights organisations; against beliefs
   (ii) People under current voting age; may feel unheard
   (iii) Regular recyclers or people who never recycle; may be strongly for or against
   (iv) People over 66; may be strongly in favour

8. No, people mainly text when they have strong opinions, could lead to bias

9. (i) Yes: she is outside the cinema; she is only asking women
   (ii) Ask a random sample of males and females in the town centre

10. (i) True, (ii) False, (iii) False, (iv) True, (v) False

11. (i) Whole population; census is sent to every household
    (ii) Estimate tax revenues, plan for health services, schools, etc.
    (iii) Make the data as accurate as possible by making sure everyone replies
    (iv) No fear of data being made public or used by others, may encourage more honest responses

Practice questions 18·3

1. (i) 5, 2, 7, 1, (ii) 6, 7, 9, 10, (iii) 8, 5, 4, 4
3. (i) Numerical discrete, (ii) 7, (iii) Game 6, (iv) 0, (v) 13, (vi) Game 3
4. (i) → C, (ii) → A, (iii) → B
5. (i) 22
6. (ii) 6, (iii) Walk, (iv) 27, (v) $\frac{10}{27}$
8. (ii) Friday
9. (i) Categorical nominal, (iii) 25, (iv) 55; pianos are big and expensive, recorders are small and less expensive, (v) 195, (vi) No, the frequencies are quite high so would be difficult to draw
10. (i) Pepperoni, (ii) 175, (iii) Bacon, (iv) Mushroom, (v) Pepperoni, mushroom, onion, bacon, pepper, tomato, (vi) 1 100

Practice questions 18·4

1. (i) 20–30, (ii) 0–10, (iii) 40, (iv) 85, (v) $\frac{1}{4}$
6. (i) Numerical continuous, (ii) 46
7. A bar chart is used to display numerical discrete data, has gaps between bars; a histogram is used to display numerical continuous data, has no gaps

Practice questions 18·5

1. (i) (a) What is your favourite food? a. Pasta b. Burgers and chips c. Roast dinner d. Stir fry e. Other – please specify
   (b) (i) All Second Years (if possible)
       (ii) Pick 10 students from each class out of a hat
       (iii) 50
       (iv) Categorical nominal

1. (ii) (a) What is your favourite type of music? a. Pop b. Rock c. Hip-hop d. Indie e. Dance f. Other – please specify
   (b) (i) Whole class (ii) Not needed as population is small (iii) All class members (iv) Categorical nominal

1. (iii) (a) What brand of phone do you have? a. Samsung b. iPhone c. Huawei d. Sony e. Other brand – please state
   (b) (i) Students from each year in the school (ii) All students' names in a hat and randomly pick out names (iii) 100 (iv) Categorical nominal

1. (iv) (a) How many hours of sleep do you get per night on average? a. 6 b. 7 c. 8 d. 9 e. Other – please state
   (b) (i) Irish teenagers (ii) Send an email to the Maths teachers in 50 randomly chosen schools and ask them to get 2 students from each year to answer the question (iii) 600 (iv) Numerical discrete

2. (ii) Yes, by adding up the numbers on the chart we get 45 students; or No, maybe some students were given the questionnaire but did not answer
   (iii) 5 of the students asked didn't have a computer. The most popular location for a computer is the family room
   (iv) No, sample size is too small
3. (a) (i) No, only 4 options given.
       (ii) Let students write whatever they want.
   (b) No, only 35 answered and options were very limited
4. (i) 1. Do you like the colour of our school uniform? Yes ___ No ___
       2. What one part of the school uniform do you like? Leave blank if none.
       3. If any, what one part of the uniform do you not like?
       4. Are there any changes you would make to the school uniform?
   (ii) All the students in the class – easy to do and gives most accurate results

Revision questions

18A Core skills

1. (i) Categorical data, can be put into groups or categories
   (ii) Numerical data, involves quantities that are usually countable or measurable
   (iii) Nominal data, has no particular rank or order
   (iv) Ordinal data, has a rank or order
   (v) Discrete data, can only take on certain values
   (vi) Continuous data, can take on any value in a range
   (vii) Primary data, collected first-hand by the person carrying out the investigation
   (viii) Secondary data, not collected first-hand by the person carrying out the investigation
   (ix) Census, data collected from the whole population
   (x) Population, the entire group being studied
   (xi) Sample, group taken from the population
   (xii) Bias, an in-built error causing data collected to be inaccurate
2. Choosing a sample that is not representative; Sample size too small; All members of the population don't have an equal chance of being chosen; Questions phrased in a way that would influence answers
5. (i) Numerical continuous, (ii) 54, (iv) 25·93%
6. (i) A random sample of students from each year
   (ii) Put students in each year in alphabetical order, pick every tenth student

(iii) 1. Do you use the canteen?
      2. Are you happy with the menu?
      3. What would you like added to the menu?
(iv) 1. Categorical nominal,
     2. Categorical nominal,
     3. Categorical nominal
(v) Bar chart or pie chart
7. (a) (i) How many goals were scored by a team over 40 games?
       (ii) 1 goal
   (b) (i) What is your favourite colour?
       (ii) Red
   (c) (i) What was the most popular month to visit the zoo?
       (ii) July
   (d) (i) What are the ages of people in a snooker club?
       (ii) 34

18B Taking it further

1. (i) 12, (ii) Friday, (iii) Sunday, (iv) 40, (v) $\frac{2}{27}$
2. (i) Pancakes, (ii) Eggs, (iii) 90, (iv) 60
3. (i) Method 1: Advantages – Every employee included, questions can be explained; Disadvantages – May not answer truthfully, very time consuming
       Method 2: Advantages – Every employee included, time efficient, more likely to be honest; Disadvantages – Questions can't be explained
   (ii) Method 2, less time consuming and more accurate data
4. What is your favourite film genre? a. Horror b. Thriller c. Comedy d. Action e. Romance f. Other – please specify
   (iii) No, sample size is very small
5. (i) No, histograms are used to represent numerical continuous data, eye colour is categorical nominal data
   (ii) Bar chart or pie chart, can be used to represent categorical nominal data

Unit 19 Indices

Practice questions 19·1

1. (i) 3×10^{10}, (ii) $6·79 \times 10^8$, (iii) $3·67800000125 \times 10^{11}$, (iv) $3·67 \times 10^2$, (v) $6·89087 \times 10^3$, (vi) $7·8467 \times 10^2$
2. (i) $4·56789 \times 10^1$, (ii) $7·7899226 \times 10^1$, (iii) $8·94567792324 \times 10^6$, (iv) $1·56899 \times 10^0$, (v) $4·5 \times 10^1$, (vi) $6·38229373 \times 10^3$
3. (i) 60 000, (ii) 200 000 000, (iii) 26 780 000, (iv) 6 567 800 000, (v) 100, (vi) 9 988·8
4. (i) 6 895·36382, (ii) 789 353·728, (iii) 100 000 567·8, (iv) 64·5, (v) 5 463
5. $1·22793 \times 10^3$ km/hr
6. $4·8 \times 10^3$ beats/hr
7. $3·06 \times 10^3$ blinks/3 hrs
8. 33 400 000 000 000 000 000 000

Practice questions 19·2

1. (i) 3^8, (ii) 8^5, (iii) 3^9, (iv) y^7, (v) x^{11}, (vi) b^6
2. (i) a^4, (ii) y^2, (iii) m^4, (iv) x^{11}, (v) n^{11}, (vi) p^{12}
3. (i) x^{18}, (ii) n^{14}, (iii) p^{44}, (iv) x^3, (v) y^8, (vi) y^{14}
4. (i) 3^3, (ii) 2^5, (iii) 10^2, (iv) 2^6, (v) 4^3, (vi) 5^5
5. x^9
6. 2^7
7. p^4

Practice questions 19·3

1. (i) 4^2, (ii) 2^4, (iii) 10^5, (iv) x^2, (v) b^5, (vi) y^5
2. (i) a^6, (ii) m^2, (iii) n^8, (iv) 1, (v) n, (vi) x
3. x
4. n^2
5. x^6
6. y^{10}

Practice questions 19·4

1. (i) 2^6, (ii) 5^{12}, (iii) 6^{12}, (iv) x^6, (v) y^{30}, (vi) x^{10}
2. (i) y^{16}, (ii) a^5, (iii) b^4, (iv) x^{32}, (v) b^{10}, (vi) a^{36}
3. (i) u^{21}, (ii) p^{12}, (iii) n^{21}, (iv) n^{24}, (v) u^1, (vi) u^2
4. (i) x^5, (ii) x^{10}, (iii) m, (iv) x^{10}, (v) x^{11}, (vi) n^{10}
5. (i) 2^2, (ii) 2^2, (iii) 2^5, (iv) 2^{14}, (v) 2^{10}, (vi) 2^{36}

Practice questions 19·5

1. (i) 6, (ii) 8, (iii) 9
2. (i) 2, (ii) 12, (iii) 16
3. (i) 10, (ii) 26, (iii) 23
4. (i) 280, (ii) 400, (iii) 504
5. (i) 196 is a perfect square because $\sqrt{196} = 14$
6. (c) 12

Revision questions

19A Core skills

1. (i) $5·097689 \times 10^1$
   (ii) $7·897899226 \times 10^3$
   (iii) $6·7786532292324 \times 10^8$
2. (i) $6·7890689 \times 10^4$
   (ii) $9·000000456 \times 10^6$
   (iii) $3·467846547 \times 10^5$
3. (i) 84 560, (ii) 256 470 000, (iii) 867·8
4. (i) a^6, (ii) y^7, (iii) 8
5. (i) b^{15}, (ii) t^5, (iii) n^6
6. (i) a^4, (ii) b^4, (iii) a^4
7. (i) a^5, (ii) b, (iii) t^3
8. (i) x^6, (ii) b^{12}, (iii) t^{12}
9. (i) u^8, (ii) y^{24}, (iii) b^{18}
10. (i) m^4, (ii) x^5, (iii) n^2, (iv) p^{21}, (v) q^{16}, (vi) n^7

19B Taking it further

1. $7·920 \times 10^3$
2. $6·048 \times 10^6$
3. (i) 299 460 km/sec
       1 080 310 000 km/hr
   (ii) $2·9946 \times 10^5$
        $1·08031 \times 10^9$
4. x^{15}
5. p^{12}
6. c^{15}
7. y^{23}
8. (i) 5^2, (ii) 5, (iii) 5^4, (iv) 5^5, (v) 5^7, (vi) 5^{12}

Unit 20 Working with expressions

Practice questions 20·1

1. (i) $x + 5$, (ii) $x - 8$, (iii) $7x$, (iv) $\frac{x}{3} - 10$, (v) $2(x - 6)$, (vi) $\frac{x}{2} + 11$, (vii) $2x + 5$
2. (i) €28, (ii) €52·50, (iii) $7t$
3. (i) Linear, (ii) Quadratic, (iii) Quadratic, (iv) Neither, (v) Linear, (vi) Quadratic, (vii) Neither, (viii) Quadratic
4. (i) Six more than a number
   (ii) Multiply a number by nine then add twelve
   (iii) Divide a number by two the add two
   (iv) Three less than four times a number
   (v) A number multiplied by fifteen then subtract eight
   (vi) Three times a number subtracted from nine
5. (i) $7 + 10x$, (ii) $24x + 14$, (iii) $17x + 10$, (iv) $-58m - 15n$, (v) $6p + 14q$, (vi) $-2a + 2y$
6. (i) $2x + 2$, (ii) $2q + 2$, (iii) $2a + 7$, (iv) $n + 3$, (v) $6x + 11$
7. (i) $20x - 3$, (ii) $-33x - 6y + 5$, (iii) $14x + 18$, (iv) $-11t - 53s - 6$, (v) $2x - 17\frac{1}{2}$
8. $2(12x + 13y)$, $12x + 13y + 12x + 13y$, $1(8x + 25y) + 1(16x + y)$, $14x + 5y + 10y + 21y$, etc.
9. (i) $-34x - 39y + 6$
   (ii) $15x + 30y + 10$
   (iii) $36x + 14$
   (iv) $18x - 38y$
10. (i) $\frac{1}{4}x + \frac{1}{5}n$, (ii) $\frac{9}{10}x - \frac{3}{8}y$, (iii) $-3\frac{2}{5}p - 5\frac{2}{3}x$, (iv) $\frac{5}{4} + \frac{9}{8}m$, (v) $10\frac{2}{3}x + 19\frac{1}{9}y - \frac{1}{8}$
11. (i) $x - 3$, (ii) $x + 5$, (iii) $x + b$, (iv) $3x$, (v) $x - \frac{1}{2}x$
12. (i) $x + 10$, (ii) $2x$
13. (i) $x + y + z$, (ii) $x + y$, (iii) $z - 3$, (iv) $z + 5$
14. (i) $m + 1·50$, (ii) $m - 5·25$, (iii) $m + b$, (iv) $m - t$, (v) $2m$
15. $(3x + 4) + (4x + 8)$, $(5x + 1) + (2x + 11)$, $(9x + 16) - (2x + 4)$, etc.
16. $(x - 11y) + (-5x + y) + (-2x - 2y)$
17. $9t + 24s$
18. (i) $34x + 24$, (ii) $12x$, (iii) $22m - 1$, (iv) $18a + 76$

Practice questions 20·2

1. (i) 4, (ii) 6, (iii) 8, (iv) 18, (v) 0, (vi) −4
2. (i) 3, (ii) 14, (iii) 6, (iv) 2, (v) 30, (vi) 125
3. (i) −4, (ii) −30, (iii) −1, (iv) 15, (v) −8, (vi) 1
4. (i) 6, (ii) 2, (iii) 16, (iv) −2, (v) 43, (vi) 12
5. (i) 33·5, (ii) 26, (iii) 35·25, (iv) 43·75
6. (i) Forty-five plus three multiplied by the number weeks
   (ii) $45 + 3w$
   (iii) €87
   (iv) €105
7. (i) 30 cm², (ii) 56·12 m²
8. (i) 14 cm, (ii) 50·4 cm
9. (i) 6 mm², (ii) 23·78 cm²
10. (i) $15n^2$, (ii) $105n$
11. (i) 34 mm, (ii) 118 mm
12. (i) 392

Practice questions 20·3

1. (i) $48y + 6$, (ii) $12z + 15$, (iii) $16g - 20$, (iv) $6n - 12$
2. (i) $3y^2 + 2y$, (ii) $15b^2 - 10bc$, (iii) $10a^2 - 4a$, (iv) $-30b - 15u$
3. (i) $-7a^2 + 28a - 14$, (ii) $7m^2 - 2m$, (iii) $2t^3 + 2t^2 - 4t$, (iv) $-6d^2 + 8d$
4. (i) $-6n^2 + 12n$, (ii) $12z^2 + 15xz + 12z$, (iii) $-24g^2 + 30g$, (iv) $18bu - 24u^2$
5. (i) $-15w^2 + 10wm$, (ii) $-12bc - 15c^2$, (iii) $1·6tx - 32ty$, (iv) $-7d^2 + 8cd$
6. (i) $5x + 11$, (ii) $6x - 13$, (iii) $12a - 6$, (iv) $2b + 39$
7. (i) $2x - 20$, (ii) $15x$, (iii) $8y - 42$, (iv) $14y^2 + 2y$
8. (i) $30x^2 - 30x$, (ii) $24mn + 60m$, (iii) $-24c^2$, (iv) $-5n^2 - 50n$
9. (i) $24x^2 - 12x$, (ii) $44x^2 - 55xy$, (iii) $5x^2 + 10x$, (iv) $-8t^2 - 32t$

Practice questions 20·4

1. (i) $x^2 + 3x + 2$, (ii) $n^2 + 4n + 3$, (iii) $a^2 + 3a + 2$, (iv) $p^2 + 5p + 4$
2. (i) $p^2 + 6p + 8$, (ii) $b^2 + 4b + 4$, (iii) $t^2 + 2t + 1$, (iv) $y^2 + 6y + 9$
3. (i) $2m^2 + 3m + 1$, (ii) $x^2 + 2x - 3$, (iii) $2d^2 + 5d + 2$, (iv) $c^2 + 3c - 4$
4. (i) $m^2 + 4m - 5$, (ii) $p^2 - 2p - 3$, (iii) $a^2 - a - 6$, (iv) $x^2 + 5x + 6$
5. (i) $r^2 - 1$, (ii) $f^2 - 9$, (iii) $q^2 - 4$, (iv) $z^2 - 10z + 25$
6. (i) $2ab - 2a + 3b - 3$, (ii) $2m^2 - 2n^2$, (iii) $6pq - 6p + 2q - 2$, (iv) $6x^2 - 8xy + 2y^2$
7. (i) $24m^2 - 48m - 30$, (ii) $24mn + 60m - 12n - 30$, (iii) $x^2 - 10x + 25$, (iv) $n^2 - 100$
8. (i) $30x^2 + 30\frac{1}{2}x + 7\frac{1}{2}$, (ii) $44x^2 + 57xy + 2\frac{1}{2}y^2$, (iii) $5x^2 + 2·5x - 15$, (iv) $\frac{1}{2}t^2 + 8t + 32$
9. $50x + 5y$
10. $8mn + 40n + 12m + 60$

Practice questions 20·5

1. (i) $4x^2 + 6x$, (ii) $4a + 4b$, (iii) $4a + 4$, (iv) $14x^2 + 14xy$
2. (i) $4b$, (ii) $2p$, (iii) $5n$, (iv) $3y$, (v) 3, (vi) $3f$
3. (i) $3(x + 5)$, (ii) $5(x + 4)$, (iii) $4(1 + a)$, (iv) $10(u - v)$
4. (i) $3(3v - w)$, (ii) $9(p - 5q)$, (iii) $4(x + 12y)$, (iv) $10(x - 10y)$
5. (i) $3z(1 - 4x)$, (ii) $a(23 - b)$, (iii) $2p(5q - 7)$, (iv) $18p(1 - 2a)$, (v) $2m(3m - 1)$, (vi) $8a(-a - 4b)$
6. $2(9x - 18)$, $3(6x - 12)$, etc.
7. $3(x - 3xy)$, $x(3 - 9y)$
8. (i) $x(12 - yp)$, (ii) $xy(w - 10)$, (iii) $2ab(2 + 7a)$, (iv) $2xy(3 + 4x)$
9. (i) $4x(x + 2y + 3)$, (ii) $3q(6p - p^2 + 3q)$, (iii) $7x(-4y + x + 2)$, (iv) $2a(a + 5b + 3)$, (v) $5x(1 - 3x + 2y)$, (vi) $a(3b - 1 + 9c)$
10. $2(20a - 40b)$, $4(10a - 20b)$, $8(5a - 10b)$, etc.
11. $10x$
12. $5b(b - 5a)$, etc.

Practice questions 20·6

1. (i) $(p + q)(x + a)$, (ii) $(m + n)(x - y)$, (iii) $(x + y)(a + b)$, (iv) $(x + y)(m + n)$
2. (i) $(5 + a)(x + y)$, (ii) $(a + 4)(m + n)$, (iii) $(c + d)(a + b)$, (iv) $(p + x)(q + r)$
3. (i) $(x - 1)(y + z)$, (ii) $(x + y)(2 - x)$, (iii) $(a - p)(x - 4)$
4. (i) $(n + 4)(q + r)$, (ii) $(2y + a)(3m + n)$, (iii) $(x + 1)(a + b)$
5. (i) $(3 + z)(n + y)$, (ii) $(a + b)(n - 5)$, (iii) $(a - b)(a + 2)$
6. (i) $(y - 2)(x - 5)$, (ii) $(1 + x)(x + 3y)$, (iii) $(a + 2)(b + 1)$
7. (i) $(5b + 2)(2a + 3)$, (ii) $(3x - 7)(2x + 3y)$, (iii) $(x - 2)(5y - 8)$
8. (i) $(2a - 1)(6b - 7)$, (ii) $(3x + y)(2x - 5)$, (iii) $(2a - 7b)(2 + 3b)$
9. (i) $(4y - 5)(2x - 3)$, (ii) $(1 - 3x)(7 + y)$, (iii) $(4u + 3)(8v - 5)$
10. Length $(p - s)$, width $(x - r)$
11. Length/width $(4w + 2z)$; length/width $(3x + y)$
12. Length/width $(2y + 5)$; length/width $(5x + 6)$
13. Peter $(7a - 2)$; Judith $(8b - 7)$
14. Ted $(m - 5)$; Jack $(5n + 2)$
15. Rooms $(m + 5)$; average cost $(3n - 8)$

Revision questions

20A Core skills

1. (i) $x + y$, (ii) $a + 7$, (iii) $2b + 10$, (iv) $m - n$, (v) ag, (vi) b^3, (vii) $3x + 5p$, (viii) $x^2 - 2x + 7$, (ix) c^2m, (x) $6m + 2·5m$
2. $x + 29$
3. (a) (i) $2x + 10$, (ii) $12y - 24$, (iii) $4z + 12$, (iv) $27z - 45$, (v) $5y + 15$, (vi) $8x - 4$
   (b) (i) 14, (ii) −36, (iii) 32, (iv) 90, (v) 10, (vi) 12
4. (i) $4a^2 + 3a$
   (ii) $-2p - 3p^2$
   (iii) $-10x^2 + 15x$
   (iv) $21x^2 - 14xy$
   (v) $12d^2 + 18d$
   (vi) $-8y^2 + 16xy$
5. (a) (i) $x^2 + 3x - 4$, (ii) $x^2 - 1$, (iii) $x^2 + x - 2$, (iv) $x^2 - 4$, (v) $2x^2 + x - 1$, (vi) $6x^2 - 5x + 1$
   (b) (i) 0, (ii) 15, (iii) 10, (iv) 12, (v) 27, (vi) 117
6. (i) $3(x + 5)$
   (ii) $3(5c + 1)$
   (iii) $2(a + 4)$
   (iv) $9(2d + 1)$
   (v) $6(b + 2)$
   (vi) $6(2e + 1)$
   (vii) $3(f - 3)$
   (viii) $5(h - 3)$
7. (i) $3r(4r - 5)$
   (ii) $5(-b - 4)$ or $-5(b + 4)$
   (iii) $6x(3x - 2)$
   (iv) $2(-d - 5)$ or $-2(d + 5)$
   (v) $6y^2(2x - 3)$
   (vi) $3(-c + 2)$ or $-3(c - 2)$
   (vii) $6x(-x + 2)$ or $6x(x - 2)$
   (viii) $6f(-f + 4)$ or $-6f(f - 4)$
8. (i) $(2v - y)(7v + 5)$
   (ii) $(7x + 5)(y - 7)$
   (iii) $(8x + 1)(2y - 7)$
   (iv) $(3a + b)(5b - 2)$
   (v) $(7r + 3s)(6r - 7)$
   (vi) $(5r - 1)(8r^2 - 5)$
9. $4 + 6b$
10. (i) $x - 3$
    (ii) $2x - 6$
    (iii) $4x - 9$

20B Taking it further

1. (i) $72mn - 18m^2n$
   (ii) $12x^2 - 6x - 18$
   (iii) $16x^2 - 12x + 56$
   (iv) $4x^3 + 12x^2 - 14x$
   (v) $8xy - 12y^2 - 36y$
2. (i) $10x - 8$
   (ii) $16x^2 - 6x + 28$
   (iii) $16m^2 + 18m + 4n - 20$
   (iv) $32x - 82y - 10z$
3. (i) $x - 15$
   (ii) $3x$
   (iii) $5x - 15$
4. (i) $50x + 90y$
   (ii) $200xy + 360y^2$
   (iii) 46 560 grams
5. (i) $72 + 24n$
   (ii) $432 + 144n$
6. $50(4a - b)$, $25(8a - 2b)$, $10(20a - 5b)$, etc.
7. Length/width $a/34a - 27b$
8. $(7p^2 + 5)(4p + 3)$

Unit 21 Linear relationships

Practice questions 21.1

1. (i) Expression
   (ii) Equation
   (iii) Equation
   (iv) Equation
   (v) Expression
   (vi) Equation
   (vii) Equation
   (viii) Equation
   (ix) Expression
   (x) Expression
2. (i) $35n + 45$, (ii) $-82v$, (iii) $-4v$, (iv) r, (v) $-3v + 11$, (vi) $9 - 4r$
3. (i) $38n$, (ii) $38x$, (iii) $-28x - 11$, (iv) $-10 + 2n$, (v) $45b - 56$, (vi) $2p - 1$
4. (i) $4 + 20n - 15m$
   (ii) $1 + 7a - 21b$
   (iii) $-5k + 56p$
   (iv) $43n - 56m$
   (v) $7p - 6pc + 3c - 2$
   (vi) $40x + 14$
5. (i) $-6v$, (ii) $-2x - 16$, (iii) $118p + 15$, (iv) $89k + 57$, (v) $38n + 36$, (vi) $9x^2$, (vii) $16sr + 16s^2 - 6r$
6. (i) Linear, (ii) Non-linear, (iii) Linear, (iv) Linear, (v) Non-linear
7. (i) $x = -3$, (ii) $x = -4$, (iii) $p = -15$, (iv) $n = 3$
8. (i) $x = -3$, (ii) $x = -9$, (iii) $x = 2$, (iv) $m = 0$, (v) $w = -300$, (vi) $n = 1$
9. (i) Not a solution, (ii) Is a solution, (iii) Is a solution
10. (i) $x = 0$, (ii) $x = -2$, (iii) $x = -6$, (iv) $x = 8$, (v) $x = -8$
11. 8, 17
12. 84 and 36
13. (i) $x = 4$
    (ii) $x = 1$
    (iii) $x = -2$
    (iv) $x = 3$
14. (i) $x_n = \frac{2 \cdot 35x}{6}$
    (ii) 36 apples
15. Width = 12 m, length = 24 m
16. Tom's age = 1, John's age = 6
17. Number = 40, parts = 15 and 25
18. Paul's age = 10 years, Paul's father's age = 40 years
19. 25 and 30
20. 84° and 96°
21. 40
22. (i) Sometimes true
    (ii) Sometimes true
    (iii) Never true
    (iv) Never true
    (v) Always true

Practice questions 21.2

1. (i) (9, 0) (0, 7)
   (ii) (4, 0)(0, 3)
   (iii) (−7, 0) (0, 6)
   (iv) (7, 0) (0, −8)
2. (i) (3, 2)
   (ii) (−3, 3)
   (iii) (−4, 0)
3. (i) (3, 2)
   (ii) (−2, 3)
   (iii) (1, −7)
   (iv) (6, 0)
   (v) (0, −4)
4. (i) (a) (6, 0) (b) (0, 3)
   (ii) (a) (10, 0) (b) (0, −5)
   (iii) (a) (−12, 0) (b) (0, 4)
   (iv) (a) (−18, 0) (b) (0, 30)
5. (i) (a) (5, 0) (b) (0, 5)
   (ii) (a) (4, 0) (b) (0, 6)
   (iii) (a) (−2, 0) (b) (0, −5)
   (iv) (a) (−10, 0) (b) (0, 3)
6. (i) $x = 1, y = 2$
   (ii) $x = 2, y = 3$
   (iii) $x = 1, y = 5$
   (iv) $x = 3, y = -3$
7. (i) $x = 8, y = 4$
   (ii) $x = 1, y = 1$
   (iii) $x = 1, y = 3$
8. (i) $x = -5, y = 2$
   (ii) $x = -3, y = -9$
   (iii) $x = 0, y = 0$
   (iv) $x = 2, y = 2$
9. $x = 7, y = 3$
10. (i) $x = 8, y = 6$
    (ii) 600 m
11. (i) Sometimes true
    (ii) Sometimes true
    (iii) Never true

Practice questions 21.3

1. (i) No
   (ii) (2, 5) makes $y = x + 3$ true
   (iii) (−1, 2) makes both equations true
   (iv) (−1, 2)
   (v) (−1, 2)
2. (i) $x = -1, y = -1$
   (ii) $x = 2, y = 0$
   (iii) $x = 2, y = 3$
3. (i) $x = 2, y = 2$
   (ii) $x = 2, y = -2$
   (iii) $x = 2, y = -4$
   (iv) $x = 1, y = 2$
4. (i) $x = -2, y = -4$
   (ii) $x = 0, y = -2$
   (iii) $x = -3, y = -3$
   (iv) $x = 2, y = 3$
5. (i) $x = 3, y = 4$
   (ii) $x = -3, y = 3$
   (iii) $x = 5, y = 2$
   (iv) $x = 1, y = -8$
6. (i) $a = 8, b = 4$
   (ii) $p = 1, q = 1$
   (iii) $a = 1, b = 2$
7. (i) $x = 14, y = 5$
   (ii) $\alpha = 1, \beta = 3$
   (iii) $a = 3, b = 1$
   (iv) $a = 0, b = 5$
8. $x = 3, y = 3$
9. $x = 10, y = 1$

Practice questions 21.4

1. (i) $2x + y = 56$ and $x + 2y = 82$
   (ii) Son's age = 10, father's age = 36
2. (i) $x + y = 8$, $4x + 2y = 22$
   (ii) $x = 3, y = 5$
3. (i) $2x + y = 35$, $3x + 4y = 65$
   (ii) Pencil = 15 cents, eraser = 5 cents
4. (i) $600x + 250y = 49\,000$
       $300x + 500y = 39\,500$
   (ii) Adult tickets = 65, child tickets = 40
5. Sheep = 3, chickens = 5
6. (i) $4x + 2y = 22$ and $x + y = 8$
   (ii) Cakes = 3, sandwiches = 5
7. (i) $4x + 4y = 776$, $x + 5y = 726$
   (ii) Small = €61, large = €133
8. (i) $6x + 5y = 463$, $6x + 2y = 286$
   (ii) Small table nails = 28, large table nails = 59
9. (i) $6x + 4y = 960$, $x + y = 200$
   (ii) Auditorium = 80, balcony = 120
10. First number = 3, second number = 1

Practice questions 21.5

1. (i) 3, (ii) 11, (iii) $x = 4$, (iv) $x = 10$
2. (i) −4, (ii) 11, (iii) $x = 6$, (iv) $x = 9$
3. (i) 9, (ii) 7, (iii) −5, (iv) −8
4. (i) 48, (ii) −84, (iii) $x = -12$, (iv) $x = -14$
7. (i) (3, 0), (ii) (1, 2), (iii) (6, −2), (iv) (−3, 1)
8. (i) (3, −1), (ii) (1, −2), (iii) (−3, 1), (iv) (−2, 1)
9. (a) (i) (−2, 3)
       (ii) (3, −2)
       (iii) (−2, 2)
       (iv) (3, 2)
   (b) (i) (−2, 3)
       (ii) (3, −2)
       (iii) (−2, 2)
       (iv) (3, 2)
10. (i) 4, (ii) 14, (iv) 204 metres, (v) 296 seconds, (vi) 500 seconds
11. (i) €7 per hour
    (ii) $F(t) = 7t + 10$
    (iv) 4·57 hr
12. (i) $f(x) = 60 + 40x$ (x = no. of months)
    (ii) $g(x) = 50x$ (x = no. of months)
    (iv) After 6 months
    (v) Plan A = €220, Plan B = €200
    (vi) Plan A = €1 020, Plan B = €1 200

Revision questions

21A Core skills

1. (i) $21y - 4$, (ii) 10, (iii) $33b - 2a - 2$, (iv) $-x + 5y + 2b + 2$
2. (i) $9e + 5ef + 2g + 4$, (ii) $12ac + 8cb + 10$, (iii) $4y^2 + w^2$, (iv) $3y^2$
3. (i) $2y + 4x$, (ii) $6x + 3y$, (iii) $12x + 8$

4. (i) $c = 1$, (ii) $x = 10$, (iii) $y = -2$,
   (iv) $b = -7$, (v) $x = 5$, (vi) $y = 10$,
   (vii) $y = 11$, (viii) $z = 9$
5. (i) $a = 2$, (ii) $z = -2$, (iii) $z = 6$, (iv) $z = 6$,
   (v) $a = 8$, (vi) $a = -4$
6. (i) $x = -4$, (ii) $a = -9$, (iii) $a = 1$,
   (iv) $y = -3$, (v) $a = -6$, (vi) $b = 9$
7. (i) $(-2, 3)$, (ii) $(3, -2)$, (iii) $(-1, 2)$,
   (iv) $(-1, -3)$
8. (i) $x = 7$, $y = 2$, (ii) $x = 3$, $y = 5$,
   (iii) $x = 4$, $y = 2$, (iv) $x = 2$, $y = -1$
9. (i) 34, (ii) 27, (iii) $x = 2$, (iv) $x = 2$
10. (i) $(-1, -3)$, (ii) $(-1, 2)$, (iii) $(2, 11)$,
    (iv) $(3, -4)$

21B Taking it further

1. (i) $x + 3$
   (ii) $2x$
   (iii) 12
2. (i) $x + (x + 5) + (x - 2) = 75$
   (ii) 24
3. 17 and 8
4. Length = 24 m, width = 12 m
5. (i) $x + 2x + 3x = 180$
   (ii) $x = 30°$
   (iii) 60°
6. Two parts, 25 and 15
7. Total price = €155
8. Football cards = 50, hurling cards = 20
9. Hat = €4, scarf = €5
10. (ii) 342 cm
11. (i) Number of hours = $\frac{\text{number of pages}}{22}$
    (ii) 6 hrs
12. (ii) (1, 5)

Unit 22 Triangles

Practice questions 22·1

1. (i) Axiom: A statement that is taken to be true without the need for a proof
   (ii) Theorem: A statement that can be proved from the axioms and other theorems by logical argument
   (iii) Proof: Step-by-step explanation that uses axioms and previously proven theorems to show another theorem is correct
   (iv) Implies: Used in a proof when we can write a fact we have proven by our previous statements
   (v) Corollary: A statement that follows readily from a previous theorem
   (vi) Converse: The reverse of a theorem
2. $|\angle 2| = |\angle 3|$, given
   $|\angle 2| = |\angle 1|$, vertically opposite angles
   $|\angle 2| = |\angle 4|$, corresponding angles
   $\Rightarrow |\angle 1| = |\angle 4|$, both are equal to $|\angle 2|$
3. (i) Line A is perpendicular to line B: there is a 90° angle between them
   (ii) $x = 122°$, $180° - 58° = x$ (supplementary angles)
   $x = z$, alternate angles
   $y + z = 180°$, straight line = 180°
   (iii) $|\angle ACB| + |\angle ACD| = 180°$, straight line
   $|\angle ACD| = |\angle ABC| + |\angle CAB|$, exterior angle = the sum of the two interior opposite angles
4. (i) True, (ii) False, (iii) False, (iv) False, (v) True, (vi) True, (vii) True, (viii) True, (ix) True
5. Straight line = 180°; Exterior angle in a triangle = sum of interior opposite angles; Angles in a triangle sum to 180°; Opposite angles in an isosceles triangle are equal in measure
6. (i) Straight line = 180°; Alternate angles; Alternate angles
   (ii) $|\angle P| + |\angle M| + |\angle Q| = 180°$
   $|\angle P| = |\angle N|$
   $|\angle Q| = |\angle O|$
   $\Rightarrow |\angle N| + |\angle M| + |\angle O| = 180°$

Practice questions 22·2

1. (i) $|DE| = |ZY|$, given
   $|DF| = |XY|$, given
   $|EF| = |XZ|$, given
   $\Rightarrow \triangle DEF \equiv \triangle XYZ$, SSS
   (ii) $|XY| = |QR|$, given
   $|\angle YXZ| = |\angle PRQ|$, given
   $|XZ| = |PR|$, given
   $\Rightarrow \triangle XYZ \equiv \triangle PQR$, SAS
   (iii) $|\angle BAC| = |\angle DAC|$, given
   $|AC| = |AC|$, common side
   $|\angle BCA| = |\angle ACD|$, given
   $\Rightarrow \triangle ABC \equiv \triangle ACD$, ASA
   (iv) $|\angle IHJ| = |\angle JLK|$, given
   $|\angle HJI| = |\angle LJK|$, vertically opposite
   $|HJ| = |JL|$, given
   $\Rightarrow \triangle IHJ \equiv \triangle JLK$, ASA
   (v) $|\angle ACB| = |\angle LMN|$, given 2 equal angles so third also equal (sum to 180°)
   $|BC| = |MN|$, given
   $|\angle ABC| = |\angle LNM|$, given
   $\Rightarrow \triangle ABC \equiv \triangle LMN$, ASA
   (vi) $|EF| = |FH|$, given
   $|\angle EFG| = |\angle HFG|$, given
   $|FG| = |FG|$, common side
   $\Rightarrow \triangle EFG \equiv \triangle FGH$, SAS
2. $|\angle BAC| = |\angle KJL|$, given
   $|AB| = |KJ|$, given
   $|\angle ABC| = |\angle JKL|$, given
   $\Rightarrow \triangle ABC \equiv \triangle JKL$, ASA
3. (i) We need to know the length of side KL is equal to side UT
   (ii) We need to know the angles EFC and QFC are equal
   (iii) We need to know $|DX|$ is equal to $|ZY|$
4. Yes, they are congruent by the condition RHS
5. $\triangle AED \equiv \triangle BEC$ (SAS)
   $\triangle DEC \equiv \triangle AEB$ (SAS)
6. $|AX| = |AX|$, common side
   $|\angle AXB| = |\angle AXC|$, both 90°
   $|BX| = |CX|$, given (midpoint)
   $\Rightarrow \triangle ABX \equiv \triangle ACX$, SAS
7. (i) $|BC| = |BC|$, common side
   $|\angle ABC| = |\angle DCB|$, both 90° (rectangle)
   $|AB| = |DC|$, opposite sides in a rectangle
   $\Rightarrow \triangle ABC \equiv \triangle BCD$, SAS
   (ii) $\triangle AEB \equiv \triangle DEC$ (SAS); $\triangle ADE \equiv \triangle BCE$ (SAS); $\triangle ABD \equiv \triangle DCA$ (SAS)
8. (i) $|\angle a| = |\angle b|$
   (ii) $|\angle b| = |\angle c|$
   (iii) $|\angle a| = |\angle c|$

9. (i) $x = 80°$
   (ii) $x = 40°$
   (iii) $x = 44°$
10. (i) Sometimes true
    (ii) Always true
    (iii) Never true
    (iv) Never true
    (v) Sometimes true
    (vi) Sometimes true
11. (i) $|XY| = |ZY|$, given
    $|WY| = |WY|$, common side
    $|XW| = |WZ|$, given (midpoint)
    $\Rightarrow \triangle WXY \equiv \triangle WZY$, SSS
    (ii) $|XW| = |WZ|$, given (midpoint)
    $|\angle YXW| = |\angle YZW|$, angles opposite equal sides in isosceles triangle are equal
    $|XY| = |YZ|$, given
    $\Rightarrow \triangle WXY \equiv \triangle WZY$, SAS
12. $x = 4$
13. Yes, if she places the given angle between the two given sides, her triangle will be congruent by SAS

Practice questions 22·3

1. (i) $|XY|$, it is opposite the right angle
   (ii) $|RS|$, it is opposite the right angle
   (iii) $|PQ|$, it is opposite the right angle
2. (i) 5 cm, (ii) 10 cm, (iii) 17 m, (iv) 25 mm, (v) 37 m, (vi) 65 mm
3. (i) 8 cm, (ii) 15 cm, (iii) 2 m, (iv) 11 cm, (v) 24 cm, (vi) 24 cm
4. (i) Right-angled, (ii) Not right-angled, (iii) Right-angled, (iv) Not right-angled, (v) Right-angled, (vi) Not right-angled
5. 25 m
6. 15
7. Yes, $41^2 = 40^2 + 9^2$
8. (i) 15 m
   (ii) 101 m
9. (i) Always true, (ii) Sometimes true, (iii) Never true, (iv) Always true, (v) Sometimes true
10. 58 km

Revision questions

22A Core skills

1. Theorem: Statement from axioms and theorems by logical argument
   Converse: The reverse of a theorem
   Axiom: A statement taken to be true without proof
   Corollary: Statement that follows from a previous theorem
   Proof: Step by step explanation using axioms and theorems
   Implies: Used when a fact is proven by previous statements
   Congruent triangle: Have the exact same shape and size
2. (i) SAS, (ii) SSS, (iii) ASA, (iv) ASA, (v) ASA, (vi) SAS
3. (i) 53 cm, (ii) 65 cm, (iii) 20 cm
4. (i) 12, (ii) 10, (iii) 3, (iv) 9
5. (i) Not right-angled
   (ii) Not right-angled
6. 13 cm
7. 53 km
8. (i) 65 cm
   (ii) 33 cm

22B Taking it further

1. $\triangle PQS \equiv \triangle PSR$ by SAS, therefore $|SQ| = |SR|$
2. (i) $|PT| = |RN|$, given
   $|\angle TPM| = |\angle NRU|$, both 90°
   (corners of rectangle)
   $|PM| = |RU|$, given
   $\Rightarrow \triangle PMT \equiv \triangle RUN$, SAS
   (ii) Yes, because $\triangle PMT$ and $\triangle RUN$ are congruent
   (iii) Yes, by SAS similar to (i)
3. (i) $|AB| = |AD|$, given
   $|BC| = |CD|$, given
   $|AC| = |AC|$, common side
   $\Rightarrow \triangle ABC \equiv \triangle ADC$, SSS
   (ii) $|AB| = |AD|$, given
   $|\angle BEA| = |\angle DEA|$, both 90° ($BD \perp AC$)
   $|AE| = |AE|$, common side
   $\Rightarrow \triangle ABE \equiv \triangle ADE$, SAS
4. (i) 35 m
   (ii) 9·25 seconds
5. 15 km
6. Yes, 1·16 m < 1·5 m
7. (i) 5 m
   (ii) 12 m
8. 37 m
9. (i) 241 m
   (ii) 20 cm
   (iii) 9 m
10. 17 m

Unit 23 Quadrilaterals and transformations

Practice questions 23·1

2. (ii) Perimeter = 32 cm, area = 61·75 cm²
3. (ii) Perimeter = 30 cm, area = 50 cm²
4. (ii) Perimeter = 34 cm, area = 66 cm²
5. (i) Perimeter = 16 cm, area = 15 cm²
   (ii) Perimeter = 16 cm, area = 16 cm²
   (iii) Perimeter = 14 cm, area = 6 cm²
   (iv) Perimeter = 222 mm, area = 3 078 mm²
   (v) Perimeter = 2 570 cm, area = 369 750 cm²
   (vi) Perimeter = 4 km, area = 1 km²
6. $x = 21$ cm
7. $x = 24$ cm
8. $y = 13$ cm
9. 18 cm × 2 cm
   6 cm × 6 cm
10. 4 cm
11. 11 cm
12. 7·9 cm
13. 29 cm
14. 20 cm

Practice questions 23·2

1. (i) 108 cm²
2. (a) (i) 38 cm, (ii) 68 m, (iii) 34·4 cm, (iv) 40 cm, (v) 24 cm, (vi) 28mm
   (b) (i) 48 cm², (ii) 99 m², (iii) 50 cm², (iv) 72 cm², (v) 11 cm², (vi) 13 mm²
3. (a) (i) 40, (ii) 40, (iii) 38
   (b) (i) 79 cm², (ii) 66 cm², (iii) 58 cm²
4. (a) (i) 320 mm, (ii) 31·6 m, (iii) 55·2 cm
   (b) (i) 2 450 mm², (ii) 38 m², (iii) 132·5 cm²
5. 48

Practice questions 23·3

1. (i) It has no right angles
2. (i) D: A parallelogram can also be a triangle
3. (i) A: Rectangle
4. (i) Yes, (ii) No, (iii) No, (iv) Yes, (v) Yes, (vi) Yes
5. (i) $A = 60°, B = 120°$
   (ii) $A = 58°, B = 122°$
   (iii) $A = 78°, B = 102°$
   (iv) $A = 63°, B = 117°$
6. (i) 45 cm²
7. (i) $x = 27°, y = 42°$
   (ii) $x = 9, y = 7$
8. $A = 108°, B = 62°, C = 62°, D = 108°$
9. 20 cm
10. (i) True, (ii) True, (iii) False, (iv) True, (v) True, (vi) True, (vii) False, (viii) True

Practice questions 23·4

1. (i) Real parallelogram
   (ii) False parallelogram
   (iii) Real parallelogram
   (iv) False parallelogram
2. (i) $a = 15$ cm, $b = 18$ cm
   (ii) $a = 8$ cm, $b = 7$ cm
   (iii) $a = 8$ cm, $b = 10$ cm
   (iv) $a = 22$ cm, $b = 2$ cm
3. (i) No lines of symmetry
   (ii) 2 lines of symmetry
4. (i) $x = 13$ m, $y = 5$ m
   (ii) $x = 6$ m, $y = 16$ m
5. (i) 168 cm², (ii) 360 cm², (iii) 120 cm², (iv) 126 cm²

Practice questions 23·5

1. (i) Translation
   (ii) Axial symmetry
   (iii) Central symmetry
2. (i) Rotation
   (ii) Axial symmetry
   (iii) Translation
3. (i) Image 1: axial symmetry in the y-axis
   (ii) Image 3: central symmetry in origin

Revision questions

23A Core skills

2. (ii) Perimeter = 33 cm, area = 60·5 cm²
3. (i) 30 cm
4. (i) 3·1 cm
5. (i) Perimeter = 110 cm, area = 390 cm²
   (ii) Perimeter = 32 cm, area = 43 cm²
   (iii) Perimeter = 36 m, area = 32 m²
   (iv) Perimeter = 22 m, area = 10 m²
6. (i) $A = 114°, B = 66°$ (opposite angles of a parallelogram are equal)
   $C = 114°, D = 66°$ (straight angle = 180°)
   (ii) $m = 23$ cm, $n = 43$ cm (opposite angles of a parallelogram are equal), $C = 60°$ (straight angle = 180°), $A = 60°$ (opposite angle), $B = 120°$ (corresponding angle to 120°), $D = 120°$ (opposite angle)
   (iii) $m = 5·5$ m, $n = 10$ m (opposite sides of a parallelogram are equal), $C = 97°$ (opposite angles of a parallelogram are equal), $D = 83°$ (straight angle = 180°), $B = 83°$ (corresponding angle to $D = 83°$), $A = 83°$ (opposite angles of a parallelogram are equal)
7. (i) $x = 11, y = 10$, theorem 10
   (ii) $x = 34, y = 31$, theorem 10
   (iii) $x = 10\frac{1}{11}, y = 80·5$, theorem 10
8. (i) Axial symmetry (mirror image)
   (ii) Central symmetry or rotation (upside down and back to front)
   (iii) Translation (moving shape by sliding it up or down)

23B Taking it further

1. (i) and (iii) are parallelograms as the opposite angles are equal
   (ii) and (iv) are not parallelograms as the opposite angles are not equal
2. (i) Perimeter = 54 cm, area = 100 cm²
   (ii) Perimeter = 58 cm, area = 54 cm²
   (iii) Perimeter = 90 m, area = 180 m²
   (iv) Perimeter = 32·81 cm, area = 45 cm²
   (v) Perimeter = 25·66 cm, area = 39 cm²
   (vi) Perimeter = 38·65 cm, area = 56 cm²
3. 26%
4. He will not have enough paint, as he needs 16·6 m²
5. $y = 6$ cm²

Unit 24 Further sets

Practice questions 24·1

2. (i) R = {1, 2, 3, 4, 5, 6, 7}
   (ii) S = {5, 6, 7, 8, 9, 10}
   (iii) $\mathbb{U}$ = {1, 2, 3, 4, 5, 6, 7, 8, 9, 10, 11, 12}
   (iv) {5, 6, 7}
   (v) {1, 2, 3, 4, 5, 6, 7, 8, 9, 10}
   (vi) 12
   (vii) Any two valid subsets, e.g. {5, 6}, {8, 9, 10}
   (viii) Any two valid subsets, e.g. {4, 5}, {1, 2, 3}
   (ix) $\frac{5}{12}$
3. (i) 29, (ii) 14, (iii) 11, (iv) 8, (v) 4, (vi) 11, (vii) $\frac{6}{29}$
4. (i) {a}, {b}, {a, b}, ∅
   (ii) {7}, {15}, {24}, {7, 15}, {7, 24}, {15, 24}, {7, 15, 24}, ∅
   (iii) {x}, {y}, {z}, {x, y}, {x, z}, {y, z}, {x, y, z}, ∅
   (iv) {d}, ∅
   (v) ∅
5. (ii) A = {k, a, n, g, r, o}
   (iii) B = {o, r, a, n, g, u, t}
   (iv) 5
   (v) Any valid subset, e.g. {r, n}
   (vi) {u, t}
6. (ii) (a) False (b) True (c) False (d) False (e) True (f) False
7. (i) Sometimes true, some elements may be in the intersection
   (ii) Always true, they are commutitive

(iii) Always true, the null set is always a subset
(iv) Never true, all elements are in universal set

Practice questions 24·2
1. (ii) 15, (iii) 14, (iv) 26, (v) $\frac{20}{40} = \frac{1}{2}$
2. (ii) 9, (iii) 15, (iv) $\frac{6}{24} = 25\%$
3. (ii) 10, (iii) 14, (iv) 25%
4. (ii) 95, (iii) 25, (iv) 62·5%, (v) $\frac{165}{320} = \frac{33}{64}$
5. (ii) 95, (iii) $\frac{0}{100} = 0$
6. (ii) 25%, (iii) 15%, (iv) 30 people

Practice questions 24·3
3. (i) {3, 4, 5, 6, 7, 8, 9}
   (ii) {7, 8, 9, 10, 11, 12}
   (iii) {3, 4, 5, 6, 7, 8, 9, 10, 11, 12}
   (iv) {7, 8, 9}
   (v) {10, 11, 12, 13, 14}
   (vi) {3, 4, 5, 6, 13, 14}
   (vii) {10, 11, 12}
   (viii) {3, 4, 5, 6}
   (ix) {3, 4, 5, 6, 10, 11, 12, 13, 14}
   (x) ∅
4. (i) {2, 3, 4, 5, 7, 11}
   (ii) {2, 4, 6, 8, 10, 12, 14}
   (iii) {1, 4, 6, 8, 9, 10, 12, 14, 15}
   (iv) {1, 2, 3, 5, 7, 9, 11, 13, 15}
   (v) {1, 15}
   (vi) {3, 5, 7, 11, 13}
   (vii) {1, 2, 3, 5, 7, 9, 11, 13, 15}
   (viii) {1, 9, 15}
5. (i) People use WhatsUp or ShareChat
   (ii) People who use WhatsUp but not ShareChat
   (iii) People who have a mobile phone and do not use WhatsUp
   (iv) People who have a mobile phone and do not use ShareChat
   (v) People who have a mobile phone and do not use ShareChat or WhatsUp
   (vi) People who have a mobile phone and do not use ShareChat and WhatsUp
6. (i) 31, (ii) 12, (iii) 18, (iv) 11, (v) $\frac{8}{31}$
7. (ii) 55, (iii) 30, (iv) 15
8. (ii) 9, (iii) 34, (iv) $\frac{35}{80} = 44\%$
9. (ii) {2, 6, 10, 14, 18, 22}
   (iii) {4, 8, 16, 20, 2, 10, 14, 22}
   (iv) {4, 8, 16, 20}
   (v) {2, 10, 14, 22}
   (vi) $\frac{3}{29}$
10. (ii) 23, (iii) 21, (iv) $\frac{50}{107}$
11. (ii) 6, (iii) $\frac{21}{35}$
12. A(iii), B5(v), C(i), D(ii), E(iv)

Revision questions
24A Core skills
1. (ii) 60
   (iii) 40
   (iv) 20
   (v) 90%
   (vi) Any valid mathematical answer, e.g. give each student in the college a number and randomly select the numbers to be surveyed

2. (ii) 40, (iii) 10, (iv) 50, (v) $\frac{50}{100} = \frac{1}{2}$
3. 30 videos
4. (i) 50, (ii) $\frac{24}{50} = \frac{12}{25}$, (iii) $\frac{14}{25}$, (iv) $\frac{2}{25}$
5. 35
6. (i) $\frac{2}{6} = \frac{1}{3}$, (ii) $\frac{2}{3}$, (iii) 2, (iv) 100%
7. (ii) 300
   (iii) 800
   (iv) 600
   (v) The number of people who listen to the news but don't listen to music
9. Set A = {1,2,3} and set B = {4, 5}

24B Taking it further
1. (i) Categorical data, (iii) 10, (iv) 80, (v) 20, (vi) 30
3. (i) (a) {1, 2, 3, 4, 5, 6, 7, 8, 9}
       (b) Null set
       (c) {1, 3, 5, 7, 9}
       (d) #=5
4. (i) x = 10, (ii) 18, (iii) 44, (iv) 6
5. Numerous valid answers
6. Numerous valid answers, e.g. A = 3, B = 2, C = 8, D = 10
7. Numerous valid answers, e.g. A = length 9, width 3; B = length 8, width 4; C = length 9, width 5; D = length 3, width 4
8. Numerous valid answers, e.g. A = 0·45, B = 0·4, C = 0·35, D = 0·15
9. (ii) Numerous valid answers, e.g. {30, 45, 60}
10. (ii) 5
    (iii) $\frac{37}{50}$
11. (i) False, (ii) True, (iii) False, (iv) True, (v) True, (vi) False (any valid mathematical justification for questions accepted)

Unit 25 Linking Thinking revision material
Questions
1. (a) (i) 3 200 min
       (ii) 1200 min
       (iii) 290 min
       (iv) 16
   (b) (i) 126
       (ii) 116 815
       (iii) €6 136·20
2. (a) (i) 10^7 m^2
       (ii) $2·2 \times 10^4$ m
       (iii) The rules can be applied to the product of two values, but cannot be applied to the sum of two values
   (b) (i) Opposite angles in a parallelogram are equal in measure
       (ii) 21°
       (iii) 50°
3. (a) (i) (a) Cost = 28 + 0·45x
           (b) Cost = 40 + 0·20x
       (ii) Plan A: 28, 34·75, 41·5, 48·25, 55, 61·75, 68·5, 75·25
            Plan B: 40, 43, 46, 49, 52, 55, 58, 61
       (iv) 49 min
       (v) 48 min
       (vi) Algebraic method

   (b) (i) €74·40
       (ii) €90·02
   (c) (i) Categorical nominal; numerical discrete
       (iii) Phone
4. (a) (i) Diameter
       (ii) Radius
       (iii) Chord
       (iv) Arc
   (b) (i) 5 cm
       (ii) 31·4 cm
       (iii) 78·5 cm^2
       (iv) 61%
   (c) 90°; an angle standing on a diameter of a circle is 90°
5. (a) (i) 960 m^2
       (ii) €79·96
       (iii) 13·82 m; 15·21 m^2
       (iv) 1 419·03 m^2
       (v) 70 952
       (vi) €53 214
   (b) (i) 150 m
       (ii) 30 m
6. (a) (i) 12:00
       (ii) 687 km/hr
   (b) $2 850
   (c) 55%
   (d) 23°
7. (a) 12 km
   (b) Ann's distance (km): 0, 1, 2, 3, 4, 5, 6, 7, 8, 9, 10, 11, 12
       Rachel's distance (km): 0, 0·5, 1, 1·5, 2, 2·5, 3, 3·5, 4, 4·5, 5, 5·5, 6
   (d) Ann: $\frac{1}{3}$ km/min; Rachel: $\frac{1}{6}$ km/min
   (e) $\frac{1}{3}, \frac{1}{6}$; the slopes are equal to the speeds
   (f) Ann: $\frac{t}{3}$ km; Rachel: $\frac{t}{6}$ km
   (g) Ann: 30 km; Rachel: 15 km
8. (a) (i) $2(3x + 2) + 2(2x + 5) = 64$; 5
       (ii) 17 cm, 15 cm
       (iii) 255 cm^2
   (b) (i) One thousand and twenty-four
       (ii) 2^{10}
       (iii) $1·024 \times 10^3$
       (iv) One million, forty-eight thousand, five hundred and seventy-six
       (v) 2^{20}
       (vi) $1·05 \times 10^6$
   (c) (i) 1 571 cm^3
       (iii) 83%
   (d) (i) 9
9. (a) (i) $l = 4w$
       (ii) C
   (b) (i) 1×10^5
       (ii) 1×10^{11}
   (c) (i) Numerical discrete and categorical nominal
       (iii) 73
       (iv) 170
   (d) 64
10. (a) (i) 2, −3
        (ii) 4, 3
        (iii) $2 \times 2 \times 2 \times 2$; $−3 \times −3 \times −3$
        (iv) 16, −27
    (b) (i) €298
        (iii) 40·5 min
    (c) (ii) Hot tub (large)
11. (a) (i) 250 m^2
        (ii) $2·5W$
        (iii) $W = 10$ m, $L = 25$ m

(b) (i) €416
    (ii) Yes, €6 saving
(c) (i) 1·05%
    (ii) 0·0966 m^2
    (iii) 2 153·214 m^2
    (iv) 22·6 m^2
    (v) €680
(d) (i) A = 200 cm, B = 167 cm, C = 217 cm
    (ii) Height = 195·06 cm, Suspect A

12. (a) 2 hr 40 mins
(b) (i) 1 200 m^2
    (ii) 35 bags
    (iii) €420
    (iv) €350
(c) (i) 35 m/min
    (ii) Slower
(d) (ii) $\frac{1}{4}$

13. (a) (i) (a) 3 600 (b) 86 400 (c) 31 536 000
    (ii) 9·46 × 10^{15} m; 9·46 × 10^{12} km
    (iii) 2·3 × 10^{15} km
    (iv) DEFG
(b) (i) $\frac{1}{11}$

14. (a) (i) 48 000 cm^2
    (ii) 400 cm^2
    (iii) 120
    (iv) €70
    (v) €84
(b) (i) 220 cm^2
    (ii) 169·73 cm^2
    (iii) 80 cm^2
(c) (i) $3x + 2y = 95$; $5x + 3y = 151$
    (ii) €17, €22

15. (a) (i) $\frac{1}{4}$
    (ii) 12
(b) (ii) 500 cm
(c) Use the diagonal length of the door
(d) (i) 60°
    (ii) Yes
    (iii) 6 907 cm^3

16. (a) (i) $x + (x + 4) = 12$
    (ii) 8 games
(b) (ii) 110·45 cm^3
(c) (i) 12·5 cm
    (ii) 15 cm
    (iii) 37·5 cm
    (iv) 7031·25 cm^3
    (v) 21%
(d) (i) 23·56 cm
    (ii) 2·1 × 10^4

Section C

Unit 26 Analysing data

Practice questions 26·1

1. (i), (iii) and (v) use 'do you agree', which indicates how you would like the person to respond; (ii) assumes improvement
2. (i) Fruit and vegetables are healthy options, so people here may eat more healthily
    (ii) Particular area may be biased by age, gender, socio-economic background, availability of shops, takeaways, etc.
3. (i) Comedy, romance, action, horror, drama, other (please specify)
    (ii) Soccer, GAA, tennis, basketball, badminton, handball, other (please specify)
    (iii) Smart phone, tablet, games console, fitness tracker, wireless headphones, other (please specify)
4. (i) Interview
    (ii) Direct observation/research
    (iii) Experiment
    (iv) Questionnaire/survey
5. (i) Categorical (nominal)
    (ii) Numerical (discrete)
    (iii) Numerical (continuous)
    (iv) Categorical (ordinal)
6. (ii) Frequency: 5, 7, 9, 4, 5
7. (i) Frequency: 7, 7, 3, 8
    (iii) No gaps between bars in histogram, gaps between each bar in a bar chart; Histograms represent continuous data

Practice questions 26·2

1. (i) 72
    (ii) $\frac{5}{36}, \frac{5}{72}, \frac{5}{12}, \frac{1}{4}, \frac{1}{8}$
    (iii) 50°; 25°; 150°; 90°; 45°
2. (i) 48°; 120°; 84°; 72°; 36°
    (ii) 80°; 100°; 96°; 60°; 24°
4. (i) 120°; 6°; 14°; 160°; 60°
    (ii) 96°; 120°; 60°; 36°; 48°
5. (i) 25%
    (ii) $\frac{1}{3}$
    (iii) 150°
    (iv) 10
    (v) Categorical, colours are categories not numbers
6. (i) 72°, (ii) 900, (iii) 10%, (iv) $\frac{1}{5}$
7. (i) 78 cans
    (ii) 4 days
    (iii) $\frac{1}{7}$
8. (i) Stem: 0, 3, 7, 0, 3, 4, 5, 1, 2
        Leaf: 6, 7, 8, 9, 3, 9, 6, 9, 6
    (ii) Stem: 15, 54, 37, 74, 95
        Leaf: 2, 7, 8, 3, 9
    (iii) Stem: 5, 1, 3, 7, 6, 8, 7, 6
        Leaf: 8, 4, 8, 5, 9, 4, 6, 4
9. (i) 2·1, 2·3, 2·6, 2·9, 3·0, 3·4, 3·4, 4·5, 4·5, 4·6, 5·3
    (ii) 2, 6, 8, 13, 14, 15, 18, 21, 22, 24, 30, 35
    (iii) 887, 890, 898, 899, 901, 903, 905, 906, 909, 912, 918
11. (i) A = bar chart; B = pie chart
    (ii) Categorical
    (iii) 7 got A, 10 got B, 9 got C, 3 got D; 29 in the class
    (iv) 24% got A, 35% got B, 31% got C, 10% got D
    (v) Graph A, because you can see the number and graph B only shows the percentage
    (vi) Graph A, easier to know the number of students
12. (i) Histogram as it is numerical data that may have a wide range
    (ii) Line plot, bar chart or pie chart as it is categorical data
    (iii) Line plot, bar chart or pie chart as there are only 6 answer options
    (iv) Bar chart as frequency may be large
13. B; the data is not in order and there is no key
14. (i) True
    (ii) False, should be in groups of 5
    (iii) True
    (iv) False, should be no space between the bars in a histogram

Practice questions 26·3

1. (i) 9: it appears the most times (5)
    (ii) 13: it appears the most times (2)
    (iii) 0: it appears the most times (4)
    (iv) 82, 71, 68: all appear twice
2. (i) 20, 25: have the highest number of dots (4)
    (ii) 6 minutes: it has the highest frequency (8)
    (iii) Oil: it has the highest bar
    (iv) 50–60: it has the highest bar
    (v) Batman: it has the largest section of the pie chart
    (vi) 12: it appears most, 3 times in the stem and leaf plot
3. Many possible answers e.g. 4, 3, 8, 12, 3, 3 or 4, 3, 8, 12, 3, 1 or 4, 3, 8, 12, 3, 2, 3 must appear more than once and no other number more than it.
4. (i) Median = 67, range = 42
    (ii) Median = 21, range = 49
    (iii) Median = 7, range = 18
5. (ii) Median = 20
    (iii) 14
6. (i) 9, (ii) 14, (iii) 48, (iv) 58·89, (v) 0·97, (vi) 2·44
7. (i) 1·86, (ii) 1·32, (iii) 12·75, (iv) 1·80
8. (i) Mode = 72, median = 59, range = 87, mean = 54·8
    (ii) No mode, median = 56, range = 90, mean = 53·625
9. (ii) 71 cm
    (iii) 69·5 cm
    (iv) 69 cm
    (v) 11 cm
10. 12·9
11. Numerous valid answers, e.g. 5, 10, 11, 12, 12; 6, 9, 11, 12, 12; 7, 8, 11, 12, 12
12. (i) Sometimes true
    (ii) Sometimes true
    (iii) Sometimes true
    (iv) Always true
    (v) Sometimes true
    (vi) Never true

Practice questions 26·4

1. (i) As weight increases (by 15 kg) the number of reps decreases (by 8)
    (ii) The heavier the weight lifted, the fewer reps can be done
    (iii) Sample size may be too small, only people in the gym surveyed
2. Sample, graph, slightly, sample, median car, 63%, sample, suggests
3. Evidence to suggest that plastic is the most recycled material in both weeks; Notice an increase in the numbers of all materials recycled, except glass in week 2; Appears cardboard boxes are the second highest material recycled over the two weeks

4. (i) As the age of the students increases, the length of time online increases
   (ii) Based on this data, time spent online increases with age
   (iii) Sample size is small, may not be random so may not be representative, don't know how many of each age group were asked
   (iv) Ask more students, make sure sample is representative, ask the same number of each age group
5. (i) Visitors increase from April to August and then decrease from August to November
   (ii) People would be on Christmas holidays so might want to visit
   (iii) The data suggests the centre may have been closed in February and March (no visitors)
6. (i) A tally and frequency table, a bar chart or pie chart to compare males to females
   (ii) No: the data suggests this but more males (20) were questioned than females (10)
   (iii) Mean number of bars eaten by males and females suggests males and females eat a similar amount of chocolate bars
7. (i) Bicycle took less than 30 minutes every day: mean = 26, median = 25·5, mode = 25 and range = 6
   (ii) Removing the extreme time (57 minutes), mean = 25, median = 24 and mode = 21, all lower than bicycle averages
8. Most of the males weigh 50–60 kg (modal weight), this is the weight with the lowest frequency for females
   Females weights vary more and are more unevenly spread than males weights which lies mainly between 40–70 kg
   Females weights are mainly either very low or high
9. Disagree: the most popular time for ice creams is June–August (summer) so there is not enough evidence to suggest the advertisement worked
10. Disagree: many factors affect global warming there is no evidence to suggest a connection between pirates and global warming; the observation is coincidental

Practice questions 26·5

1. (i) 150 students, 25 from each year, randomly selected from the roll
   (ii) Students chosen could all be from the same year; All students have equal chance of being picked
   (iii) Sample size is very small; not all students have an equal chance of being picked
   (iv) Not all students have an equal chance of being picked; only First Years chosen so sample is not representative
   (v) Not all students have an equal chance of being picked; friends so may be biased
   (vi) Sample may not be representative
2. Only 1 rollercoaster is above 50 metres, and most are a lot smaller; The mean is 50 metres due to the extreme value of 110 metres; The median of 38 metres would be a more accurate average
3. (i) Mean = €42 200; mode = €8 000; median = €8 000
   (ii) No: only one employee earns more than the mean and most earn a lot less; the mean is affected by the one extreme wage of €175 000
   (iii) The median, as it is not affected by extreme values
4. (i) Girls participate more in all sports; a lot fewer boys participate in cross country than girls
   (ii) The boys scale goes up in 5s, the girls in 2s; The width of the bars in the girls' graph is bigger than in the boys' graph; The gap between the bars on the girls' graph is narrower than on the boys' graph
   (iii) Have both scales going up by the same amount, make the widths of the bars the same and make the gap between the bars the same
5. To produce the desired response to the data; Starting the scales at different points, altering the width of the bars or the gap between the bars, use of 3D effects, shading, colour, etc.

Revision questions

26A Core skills

1. (a) (i) Mode = red
       (ii) Mode = dog
   (b) Data is categorical
2. (i) Median = 34, mean = 36·25
   (ii) Median = 15, mean = 16·46
3. (i) Mean = 22, median = 19·5, mode = 12, range = 26
   (ii) Mean = 21·9, median = 22, mode = 5, range = 43
   (iii) Mean = 48·64, median = 52, mode = 72, range = 66
   (iv) Mean = 42·11, median = 40, mode = 51, range = 51
4. Mean = 69·36, median = 70·5, mode = 84, range = 66
5. (i) 96 kg, (ii) 115 kg
6. (i) 14·8°C, (ii) 1·7°C
7. (i) Line plot, because it is easy to draw and the data set is small
   (ii) 4 children
   (iii) 3·4
   (iv) 3·5
   (v) 4 is a whole and you can't have fractions of children

26B Taking it further

1. (i) €46, (ii) €40, (iii) €70
2. (ii) 34 litres
   (iii) 31 litres
   (iv) 30 litres
3. (i) Disagree, the mean is 5
   (ii) She may have just counted the numbers and called that the mean
4. (i) Alpha United, they won $\frac{3}{4}$ of their matches
   (ii) No, Alpha United won $\frac{3}{4}$ of their matches but Beta Rovers only won $\frac{1}{3}$;
   OR Yes, Alpha United only won 9 matches and Beta Rovers won 19 matches
5. (i) This scale starts at 25 instead of 0
   (ii) To make his sales look bigger
   (iii) Pie chart
   (iv) The mode is the highest average so this would be best to show the highest sales: mean = 37·5, median = 36·5 and mode = 44

Unit 27 Probability 2

Practice questions 27·1

1. (i) $\frac{1}{6}$, (ii) $\frac{5}{6}$, (iii) $\frac{1}{2}$, (iv) 0
2. (i) 20
   (ii) Numbers should appear as (a) P(Green) = $\frac{1}{4}$; (b) P(Blue) = $\frac{3}{10}$; (c) P(not red) = $\frac{11}{20}$
3. (i) 36
   (ii) $\frac{1}{6}$
   (iii) Star; any valid justification, e.g. there are more stars than any other shape
   (iv) Star, as its probability = $\frac{9}{36}$ = 25%
4. (i) Coffee + muffin; tea + muffin; juice + muffin; coffee + cookie; tea + cookie; juice + cookie; coffee + fruit pot; tea + fruit pot; juice + fruit pot
   (ii) $\frac{1}{9}$
   (iii) $\frac{1}{3}$
5. 0·1
6. (i) P(lose) = 0·6
7. Possible outcomes = (Y, Y), (Y, R), (R, R), (R, Y)

Practice questions 27·2

1. 0·1
2. 0·24
3. (i) 0·7
   (ii) Any mathematical justification, e.g. the general belief is incorrect, or more trials needed
4. (i) 8
   (ii) 252
5. (i) A = 600, B = 0·125, C = 0·2, D = 0·15, E = 0·3, F = 1
   (ii) Collie
6. (i) G = 4, 0·2; R = 7, 0·35; Y = 5, 0·25
   (ii) The second table provides the best estimate, as sample size is much larger
   (iii) 750
7. (i) Frequency: 4, 3, 3, 2, 3, 5
   Relative frequency: 0·2, 0·15, 0·15, 0·1, 0·15, 0·25
   (ii) 15 times
   (iii) Expected 6 in fair die = 10, number of 6 with this die = 15
   (iv) Die may be biased, more trials needed to confirm

8. (i) 0·1533, 0·175, 0·168, 0·16
   (ii) 0·16 is the best estimate, as it has the largest number of trials

Revision questions
27A Core skills
1. $x = 0.15$
2. (i) $y = 0.2$
   (ii) 4
3. (i) 0·75
   (ii) 125
4. (a), learner drivers involved in an accident
5. (i) 50
   (ii) 0·166, 0·25, 0·25, 0·166, 0·083, 0·05, 0·033
   (iii) 0·166
6. (i) Win = 13, lose = 15, draw = 12
   (ii) 0·325, 0·375, 0·3, 1

27B Taking it further
2. (ii) $x = 0.15$
   (ii) 0·45, 0·3
   (iii) 0·75
   (iv) Orange, as it has highest relative frequency
3. (i) 0·79
   (ii) Yes, for 100 trials, it appears to be biased
   (iii) Heads = 0·498, tails = 0·502
   (iv) The relative frequency has changed as the number of trails has been increased, which gives a more reliable result
4. 9 500
5. (i) 0·15, 0·15, 0·35, 0·05
   (ii) 1
   (iii) 0·15 or $\frac{3}{20}$
   (iv) Agree with Bobby, as yellow has the highest relative frequency
6. (i) Numerical data
   (ii) 0·2, 0·25, 0·2, 0·2, 0·2, 0·225, 0·24, 0·25
   (iv) The responses changed as the sample size increased
   (v) Estimate = 1 250; this number was found by noticing that for 1 000 students the relative frequency was 0·25, or any other valid mathematical justification
7. (i) It appears to be biased, but the sample is very small, as the die has only been rolled 36 times (or any other valid mathematical answer)
   (ii) I think the die is fair, as the relative frequency for each number is very similar (or any other valid mathematical answer)
   (iii) Because the number of trials increased, the more trials completed, the greater the accuracy of the relative frequency (or any other valid mathematical answer)

8. (i) Each relative frequency is the probability value in decimal form, so the sum of all relative frequencies must equal 1, as 1 is certain to happen in an event for probability (or any other valid mathematical answer)
   (ii) True, as the sum of relative frequency in the same experiment must equal 1
9. (i) 0·125
   (ii) 0·08
   (iii) The second test is more reliable as the sample size is 1 000
   (iv) 0·92

Unit 28 Money matters 2
Practice questions 28·1
1. (i) (a) €3 750 (b) €1 730·77 (c) €865·38 (d) €21·63
   (ii) (a) €4 400 (b) €2 030·77 (c) €1 015·38 (d) €25·38
   (iii) (a) €6 237·50 (b) €2 878·85 (c) €1 439·42 (d) €35·99
   (iv) (a) €1 933·33 (b) €892·31 (c) €446·15 (d) €11·15
   (v) (a) €8 291·67 (b) €3 826·92 (c) €1 913·46 (d) €47·84
2. (i) 14 hours
   (ii) €11·50 per hour
3. Total pay = €2 320
4. €103·50, €553·50; €91·77, €490·77; €1·59, €13·34; €0·47, €3·97; €597·77, €3 196·77
5. (i) €87·17
   (ii) €379
6. Cheaper to buy a box of 12 cupcakes, amount saved = €3·52
7. (i) €585·37
   (ii) €673·18
8. (i) €915·75, (ii) €126·48, (iii) €3·80
9. (i) 350 zloty
   (ii) €100 to €102 (approx)
   (iii) €1 = 4·375 zloty
   (iv) Any valid mathematical justification accepted
   (v) Yes it is linear, as it has a common first difference **or** accept constant slope
10. (i) €243·01
    (ii) The first option is cheaper
11. (i) 17·65%, (ii) 131·43%, (iii) 41·89%
12. (i) 80 cent
    (ii) 40%
    (iii) (a) €9·60 (b) 40%
13. (i) €420, (ii) €120, (iii) €63
14. (i) €8·18
    (ii) Compound interest is based on the value of the investment for each individual year
15. (i) €32 277·73
    (ii) €3 277·73

Practice questions 28·2
1. (i) 25% increase
   (ii) 20% decrease
   (iii) 3·53% decrease
   (iv) 250% increase
   (v) 5% decrease
   (vi) 33% decrease

2. 12·5%
3. 20%
4. 26·83%
5. 41·2%
6. 31·8%
7. (i) No, they should offer €49·48
   (ii) 40%
   (iii) Any valid mathematical explanation accepted
8. (i) 7·21%
   (ii) 7·51%
9. 19·5%
10. (i) €300
    (ii) Gain 20%
11. The second decrease was larger in terms of percentage
12. 7 361
13. (i) 33% and 25%
    (ii) No, percentage increase and decrease are based on the whole value that the increase or decrease is being applied to

Practice questions 28·3
1. (i) €20 000
   (ii) €3 600
2. (i) €36 400
   (ii) €7 644
3. €143
   €85·25
   €564·75
4. Gross tax due at 23%: €7 130, €5 520, €4 370, €3 450, €2 760, €6 785
   Net tax due: €5 480, €3 820, €2 770, €2 000, €1 660, €5 035
   Net pay (per year): €25 520, €20 180, €16 230, €13 000, €10 340, €24 465
5. (i) €1 680
   (ii) Harry does not pay any tax, as his tax credits are greater than the gross tax due
6. (i) (a) €361 (b) €1 564·33 (c) 18 722
   (ii) (a) €79·42 (b) €344·15 (c) €4 129·84
   (iii) €349·08
7. (i) €7 654, (ii) €5 954, (iii) €28 376
8. (i) €26 500, (ii) €5 830, (iii) €22 520
9. (i) €307·50, (ii) €64·58, (iii) €27·08, (iv) €307·92
10. (i) 21%, (ii) €1 700
11. (i) €5 320
    (ii) €3 620
    (iii) €24 380
    (iv) €29 400
    (v) No, her net wage only increased by 4·65%

Revision questions
28A Core skills
1. (i) €409·50
   (ii) 26·25 km
   (iii) 675 km/h
   (iv) 24°C
   (v) €1 281·25
2. 15%
3. 35%
4. 20%
5. 15%
6. 7·8 cm
7. (i) €643, (ii) €437·20, (iii) €632·70
8. (i) €2 217·50, (ii) €1 718·94

9. (i) €7 475, (ii) €5 825, (iii) €26 675
10. (i) 15%, (ii) €2 080
11. (i) €660, (ii) 21%, (iii) €589·71
12. (i) €1 990
    (ii) €1 700
    (iii) €290
    (iv) Any valid mathematical answer, e.g. reduce amount spent on socialising
13. (A) = €475·25 (B) = €33·31 (C) = €69·81 (D) = €405·44

28B Taking it further

1. (a)–(e) Any valid mathematical explanations accepted
2. (i) 46·15%
   (ii) €3 900
   (iii) €1 800
   (iv) 46%
3. New height = 12·6 cm
4. (i) €435, (ii) €406·45
5. (i) €437, (ii) €100·51, (iii) €39·01, (iv) €397·99, (v) €1 863, (vi) Yes, as the motorbike costs €1 722
6. (i) (A) = €2 450 (B) = €33 500 (C) = €7 035 (D) = €4 585 (E) = €28 915
   (ii) (a) €2 409·58 (b) €1 112·12 (c) €556·06
   (iii) Decrease, decrease, increase, no effect
7. (i) €7 000
   (ii) 3 000; 4 000; 5 000; 6 000; 7 000; 8 000
   (iv) €5 500 (or valid answer based on graph drawn)
   (v) €5 500
   (vi) Valid answer based on answers to (iii) and (iv)
   (vii) Answers may be slightly different due to small errors in graph
   (viii) The mathematical calculation is more accurate than the graph, as there may be small errors when reading or drawing the graph (or any valid mathematical justification)

Unit 29 Circles 2

Practice questions 29·1

1. (i) 1 = diameter; 2 = centre; 3 = circumference; 4 = radius
2. (i) 14 square units
   (ii) Area = 12·566 units
3. (i) Circumference = 295 cm
   (ii) Area = 6 940 cm^2
4. (i) Circumference = 20·1 cm
   (ii) Area = 32·2 cm^2
5. (i) Circumference = 17·59 cm
   (ii) Area = 26·63 cm^2
6. Circumference = 13 cm
7. Radius = 5 cm
8. (i) Diameter = 8 cm
   (ii) Area = 50·24 cm^2
9. Diameter = 11·87
10. Circumference = 75·4 cm^2
11. Circumference = 1·85π cm
12. (i) Area = 56·55 cm^2
    (ii) Perimeter = 30·85 cm
13. Area = 50·27 km^2
14. Area = 50·283 cm^2
15. €67·66
17. (i) 92·726 m^2
    (ii) €46
19. (i) Sometimes true
    (ii) Sometimes true
    (iii) Never true
    (iv) Always true

Practice questions 29·2

1. (i) 1 = centre; 2 = circumference; 3 = segment; 4 = chord; 5 = diameter; 6 = radius; 7 = sector; 8 = arc
2. (i) ∠ACB or ∠BCA
   (ii) ∠AEB or ∠BEA
3. (i) Arc OM
   (ii) Arc OM
4. 68°
5. 62°
6. 90°
7. 30°
8. (i) 90°, (ii) 50·24°
9. (i) 90°, (ii) 52°
10. (i) 10°, (ii) 30°, (iii) 30°, (iv) 5
11. (i) Y = 5 cm, (ii) Y = 12 cm, (iii) Y = 25 cm, (iv) Y = 8 cm
12. 163·40 km

Practice questions 29·3

1. (i) Cyclic quadrilateral
   (ii) Quadrilateral
   (iii) Neither
   (iv) Neither
   (v) Quadrilateral
   (vi) Cyclic quadrilateral
2. (i) Diameter = 29 cm
   (ii) 68°
3. (i) 65 m, (ii) 53°, (iii) 58°

Revision questions

29A Core skills

1. (i) 90°, (ii) 60°
2. (i) 36°, (ii) 47°, (iii) 58°, (iv) 68°, (v) 74°
3. (i) Y = 5 cm, (ii) Y = 8 cm, (iii) Y = 10 cm, (iv) Y = 48 m, (v) Y = 27 cm
4. (i) Neither
   (ii) Cyclic quadrilateral
   (iii) Quadrilateral
   (iv) Neither
   (v) Cyclic quadrilateral
5. 50·3
6. 14
7. (i) Always true
   (ii) Sometimes true
   (iii) Sometimes true
   (iv) Always true
   (v) Always true

29B Taking it further

1. 20%
2. 10 317 m^2
3. 6·26π m
4. 165π cm^2
5. (i) A = 90°
   (ii) A = 90°
   (iii) A = 90°
   (iv) A = 90°, B = 90°
8. (i) 3 474 km
9. (i) Diameter = 1·2742 × 10^4
   (iii) 3·67

Unit 30 Further geometry

Practice questions 30·2

3. (iii) Parallelogram, opposite sides are parallel
4. (iv) Rectangle opposite sides are equal and parallel, PR⊥PQ and QS⊥PQ

Practice questions 30·3

1. (i) A = 56°, straight angle; C = 124°, vertically opposite; D = 56°, vertically opposite
   (ii) A = 80°, straight angle; C = 100°, vertically opposite; D = 80°, vertically opposite
   (iii) A = 31°, straight angle; C = 149°, vertically opposite; D = 31°, vertically opposite
   (iv) A = 150°, straight angle; B = 30°, vertically opposite; D = 150°, vertically opposite
   (v) B = 68°, straight angle; C = 68°, vertically opposite; D = 112°, vertically opposite
   (vi) A = 144°, vertically opposite; B = 36°, straight angle; C = 36°, vertically opposite
2. (i) A = 67°; B = 113°; D = 67°; E = 67°; F = 113°; G = 113°; H = 67°
   (ii) A = 118°; B = 62°; C = 62°; E = 118°; F = 62°; G = 62°
   (iii) A = 133°; B = 47°; C = 47°; D = 133°; F = 47°; G = 47°; H = 133°
   (iv) A = 77°; C = 103°; D = 77°; E = 77°; F = 103°; G = 103°; H = 77°
   (v) A = 95°; B = 85°; C = 85°; D = 95°; E = 95°; F = 85°; H = 95°
   (vi) A = 99°; B = 81°; C = 81°; D = 99°; E = 99°; G = 81°; H = 99°
3. (i) 34°, (ii) 35°, (iii) 16°, (iv) 70°, (v) 16°, (vi) 9°
4. (i) x = 14, y = 10; opposite sides of a parallelogram are equal
   (ii) b = 101°, opposite angles in a parallelogram are equal; a = 79°
   (iii) r = 6, s = 3·5; the diagonals of a parallelogram bisect each other
   (iv) p = 5, a = 9
   (v) m = 35°, n = 110°; opposite angles of a parallelogram are equal
   (vi) m = 8, k = 7; the diagonals of a parallelogram bisect each other
5. (i) 90°, (ii) 55°, (iii) 45°, (iv) 31°, (v) 76°, (vi) 53°
6. (i) 25°, the angles opposite the equal sides in an isosceles triangle are equal
   (ii) 130°
   (iii) 65°
7. (i) 150°, corresponding
   (ii) 95°, straight angle, corresponding
8. 19°
9. 25°
10. (i) Diameter
    (ii) 75°
    (iii) 150°

Practice questions 30·4

1. (i) Similar, (ii) Similar, (iii) Similar
2. (i) Similar, (ii) Similar, (iii) Not similar, (iv) Similar, (v) Similar, (vi) Not similar
3. (i) 5, (ii) 10, (iii) 12, (iv) $x = 27, y = 30$
4. (i) $|\angle QRP| = |\angle TRZ|$ vertically opposite; $|\angle QPR| = |\angle RTZ|$ alternate, (ii) 20, (iii) 30
5. Yes
6. 4 m
7. 32 m
8. 6 m
9. 14 cm

Revision questions

30A Core skills

1. (i) 58°, corresponding and straight angle
   (ii) 30°, angles opposite equal sides in an isosceles triangle are equal
   (iii) 55°, angles in a triangle sum to 180°
   (iv) 90°, angle in a semi-circle is 90°
   (v) 31°, vertically opposite, opposite angles in a parallelogram and 3 angles in a triangle
   (vi) 35°, alternate angles and 3 angles in a triangle
2. (i) $x = 90°$, angle in a semi-circle; $y = 51°$, angles in a triangle
   (ii) $x = 42°$, straight angle ; $y = 73°$, vertically opposite; $z = 65°$, angles in a triangle
   (iii) $x = 27°$, straight angle and corresponding; $y = 119°$, straight angle and corresponding; $z = 92°$, angles in a triangle
   (iv) $x = 115°$, straight angle and corresponding; $y = 65°$, corresponding; $z = 65°$, opposite angles in a parallelogram
   (v) $x = 37°$, isosceles triangle; $y = 53°$, angle in a semi-circle; $z = 74°$, straight angle
   (vi) $x = 35°$, straight angle; $y = 85°$, straight angle; $z = 30°$, angles in a triangle
3. (i) $x = 62°$, alternate angle
   (ii) $y = 71°$, corresponding angle
4. (i) $x = 57°$, alternate angle
   (ii) $y = 71°$, straight angle and corresponding
5. $p = 71°$, isosceles, angles in a triangle and corresponding
6. (i) $y = 28°$, alternate
   (ii) $z = 64°$, angles in a triangle, straight angle
7. (a) (ii) They are equal
       (iii) In an isosceles triangle the angles opposite the equal sides are equal
   (b) (iii) The sum of the internal angles is equal to $|\angle DBC|$
   (iii) The exterior angle of a triangle is equal to the sum of the interior opposite angles

30B Taking it further

1. (i) $x = 32°$; $2x = 64°$; $x + 23 = 55°$; $3x - 35 = 61°$; 3 angles in a triangle add up to 180°
   (ii) $x = 20°$; $7x - 35 = 105°$; $3x + 15 = 75°$; $x + 55 = 75°$; angles in a straight line add up to 180°
   (iii) $x = 15°$; $y = 4°$; $4x - 10 = 50°$; $2x + 5y = 50°$; $6x + 10y = 130°$; opposite angles in a parallelogram are equal
2. (i) $x = 8$
   (ii) $x = 11$
3. (i) $a = 13$
      $|\angle DAC| = |\angle DAC|$ same angle
      $|\angle DCA| = |\angle EBA|$ right angles
   (ii) $|\angle DAC| = |\angle EAB|$ (common)
   (iii) $x = 10$
   (iv) $b = 13$
4. 14 m
5. (i) Yes, all the angles in one triangle are equal to the corresponding angles in the other triangle
   (ii) 42 cm

Unit 31 Working with the coordinate plane

Practice questions 31·1

1. (a) $B = (-3, 7); C = (-1, -6); D = (3, -3); E = (3, 4); F = (-5, -3); H = (-3, -2); I = (8, 0); M = (-8, 8); N = (3, -9); O = (7, -8); P = (-8, 1); Q = (-3, 0); R = (6, -8); V = (0,1); X = (-5, -9); Z = (6, 4)$
   (b) (i) First quadrant
       (ii) Third quadrant
       (iii) Second quadrant
       (iv) Fourth quadrant
3. (a) (i) (3, 3)
       (ii) (-1, 2)
       (iii) (-2, 1)
4. (i) (4, 7), (ii) (5, 8), (iii) (3, 4), (iv) (1, 8), (v) (1, -3), (vi) (-4, -9)
5. (i) $\left(\frac{1}{2}, \frac{3}{2}\right)$, (ii) $\left(-\frac{7}{2}, -\frac{1}{2}\right)$, (iii) $\left(-2, -\frac{1}{2}\right)$, (iv) $\left(\frac{1}{2}, -\frac{1}{2}\right)$, (v) $\left(\frac{3}{2}, \frac{1}{2}\right)$, (vi) $\left(-\frac{5}{2}, \frac{3}{2}\right)$
6. (i) (8, -3), (ii) (-4, -4), (iii) (8, -5), (iv) (-6, -7), (v) (5, 2), (vi) (-1, 17)
7. (-1, 0)
8. (1, -1)
9. (3, 8)
10. (i) The diagonals of a parallelogram bisect each other
    (ii) (6, -5)
11. $\left(-\frac{3}{2}, 2\right)$

Practice questions 31·2

1. (i) 5·66
   (ii) 13·45
   (iii) 5
   (iv) 4·12
   (v) 14·87
   (vi) 17·03
2. (i) 4
   (ii) 6
   (iii) 9·1
   (iv) 9·2
   (v) 7·1
   (vi) 7·8
3. 12
4. Point B
5. Scalene: all sides are different lengths
6. (i) (0, 7)
7. (i) 10·4
   (ii) 9·2
   (iii) 18·9
8. (i) (3, -1)
   (ii) $D = 14.42, r = 7.21$, therefore $D = 2r$
9. (ii) Not equal
10. (ii) 10·77
    (iii) (-1, -1)
11. 18·38

Practice questions 31·3

1. (i) Positive
   (ii) Negative
   (iii) Zero
   (iv) Undefined
   (v) Positive
   (vi) Negative
2. (i) 2, (ii) $-\frac{1}{4}$, (iii) $\frac{3}{5}$, (iv) 3, (v) $-\frac{7}{4}$, (vi) $\frac{1}{6}$
3. (i) $-\frac{7}{3}$, (ii) $-\frac{3}{2}$, (iii) −1, (iv) $\frac{5}{8}$, (v) $\frac{3}{11}$, (vi) $-\frac{2}{5}$
4. (i) 3, A, goes up 3 (rise) for every 1 across (run); $-\frac{5}{7}$, B, goes down (negative rise) 5 for every 7 across; −2, C, goes down 2 (negative rise) for every 1 across (run); $\frac{1}{4}$, D, goes up 1(rise) for every 4 across (run); 0, E, doesn't rise or fall
   (ii) No, no two lines have the same slope
5. (i) Parallel
   (ii) Not parallel
   (iii) Not parallel
   (iv) Parallel
6. The ramp, as it has a higher slope (0·75) than the hill (0·6)
7. (i) Not a parallelogram, slope of $AD \neq$ slope of BC
   (ii) Parallelogram, slope of $KN =$ slope of LM
8. (ii) $\left(\frac{7}{2}, -\frac{7}{2}\right)$
   (iii) 21·6
   (iv) $-\frac{21}{5}$

Practice questions 31·4

1. (i) $y = -3x + 4$
   (ii) $y = -x$
   (iii) $y = 2x - 1$
   (iv) $5y = x + 25$
   (v) $3y = 2x - 21$
   (vi) $2y = -3x - 6$
2. (i) $5x - y - 43 = 0$
   (ii) $6x + y + 12 = 0$
   (iii) $y = -2$
   (iv) $x - 2y = 0$
   (v) $2x + 3y + 7 = 0$
   (vi) $3x + 4y + 18 = 0$
3. (i) $x - 5y + 33 = 0$
   (ii) $x - 10y + 48 = 0$
   (iii) $x - 6y + 38 = 0$
   (iv) $3x + 4y + 14 = 0$
   (v) $y = 0$
   (vi) $13x + 5y - 43 = 0$
4. (i) $2x - y + 1 = 0$
   (ii) $4x - y + 4 = 0$
   (iii) $2x + y + 1 = 0$

5. $y = 9x + 6$
6. $2x + 3y + 6 = 0$
7. $x - 6y - 22 = 0$
8. (i) $y = 3x + 4$
   (ii) $y = 3x - 3$
   (iii) Yes, they both have the same slope (3)

Practice questions 31·5

1. (i) (a) 4 (b) 8
   (ii) (a) −1 (b) 5
   (iii) (a) −3 (b) −1
   (iv) (a) $\frac{7}{3}$ (b) 4
   (v) (a) $-\frac{4}{5}$ (b) −7
   (vi) (a) $-\frac{1}{4}$ (b) −3
2. (i) (a) $\frac{5}{6}$ (b) 4
   (ii) (a) −3 (b) −12
   (iii) (a) $-\frac{1}{3}$ (b) 1
   (iv) (a) $\frac{5}{2}$ (b) −5
   (v) (a) 2 (b) $\frac{9}{4}$
   (vi) (a) $-\frac{1}{2}$ (b) $\frac{9}{4}$
3. (i) (a) −4 (b) 7 (c) decreasing
   (ii) (a) 3 (b) 5 (c) increasing
   (iii) (a) −3 (b) $-\frac{9}{2}$ (c) decreasing
   (iv) (a) $\frac{1}{3}$ (b) $\frac{4}{3}$ (c) increasing
   (v) (a) $\frac{3}{5}$ (b) $-\frac{2}{5}$ (c) increasing
   (vi) (a) $\frac{3}{2}$ (b) −3 (c) increasing
4. (i) D; slope = 3, y-intercept = −2
   (ii) A; slope = 1, y-intercept = 0
   (iii) B; slope = −1, y-intercept = −2
   (iv) E; slope = 0, y-intercept = 2
   (v) C; slope = $\frac{1}{2}$, y-intercept = −1
5. (i) Parallel
   (ii) Not parallel
   (iii) Not parallel
6. (i) Is on the line
   (ii) Is not on the line
   (iii) Is not on the line
7. $3x + y - 5 = 0$
8. (i) $y = 2x + 1$
   (ii) $y = 2x + 3$
9. (i) $y = 8x + 10$
   (ii) Slope = rate per hour; y-intercept = flat fee
   (iii) €50

Practice questions 31·6

3. (b) All graphs go through (0, 0)
4. (b) Lines are horizontal, parallel to x-axis, slope = 0; or vertical, parallel to y-axis, slope is undefined
6. (i) $y = -5x + 50$
   (iii) 5 days
7. (i) $2x + 3y = 90$
   (ii) y-intercept = (0, 30); x-intercept = (45, 0)
   (iv) 30 4-seaters and 10 6-seaters; 15 4-seaters and 20 6-seaters; 0 4-seaters and 30 6-seaters

Practice questions 31·7

1. (i) (1, 2)
   (ii) (−1, −2)
   (iii) (−3, 3)
2. (i) (2, 1)
   (ii) (2, 2)
   (iii) (0, 0)
   (iv) (2, 3)
   (v) (1, 4)
   (vi) (4, 2)
3. (i) (7, 2)
   (ii) (2, 1)
   (iii) (3, −1)
   (iv) (4, −1)
   (v) (2, 0)
   (vi) (5, −1)
4. (1, −1)
5. (ii) (4, 2)
6. (ii) (−4, −3)
   (iii) Algebra; graphs can be slightly inaccurate
7. (−5, 13)
8. (i) Balloon 1: $y = 15x + 10$; Balloon 2: $y = -20x + 150$
   (ii) 4 minutes

Revision questions

31A Core skills

1. (i) (3, 3), (ii) (2, 1), (iii) (−1, 1), (iv) (−1, −1), (v) (−1, 4), (vi) (−2, −4)
2. (i) 3·6, (ii) 8·5, (iii) 7·1, (iv) 3·2, (v) 7·6, (vi) 8·1
3. (i) Slope = 3; y-intercept = 1
   (ii) Slope = 3; y-intercept = $-\frac{1}{2}$
   (iii) Slope = $\frac{1}{4}$; y-intercept = $\frac{1}{4}$
   (iv) Slope = $-\frac{1}{2}$; y-intercept = $\frac{9}{4}$
   (v) Slope = −2; y-intercept = $\frac{3}{2}$
   (vi) Slope = 3; y-intercept = 2
4. (i) Slope = 3; equation = $3x - y = 0$
   (ii) Slope = 3; equation = $3x - y - 14 = 0$
   (iii) Slope = 1; equation = $x - y + 3 = 0$
   (iv) Slope = $-\frac{8}{3}$; equation = $8x + 3y - 1 = 0$
   (v) Slope = $-\frac{7}{3}$; equation = $7x + 3y - 2 = 0$
   (vi) Slope = $\frac{1}{3}$; equation = $x - 3y - 8 = 0$
6. (a) (i) Not on the line
       (ii) On the line
       (iii) On the line
       (iv) On the line
   (b) (i) On the line
       (ii) On the line
       (iii) Not on the line
       (iv) On the line
7. (i) Collinear
   (ii) Not collinear
   (iii) Not collinear
8. (i) (−8, −24)
   (ii) (1, 2)
   (iii) (1, 5)
9. (i) Never true
   (ii) Sometimes true
   (iii) Always true
   (iv) Always true
   (v) Always true

31B Taking it further

1. (i) $\left(1, \frac{7}{2}\right)$
   (ii) 15·7
   (iii) $x + 2y - 8 = 0$
   (iv) $x + 2y - 3 = 0$
2. (iii) (4, 3)
3. (ii) $|XY| = |YZ|$, therefore the triangle is isosceles
   (iii) right angled; $|XZ|^2 = |XY|^2 + |YZ|^2$
4. (ii) $|HK| = |IJ|$, $|HI| = |JK|$
   (iii) $\left(0, \frac{3}{2}\right)$
   (iv) Rectangle: opposite sides are equal, and the diagonals bisect each other
6. (i) 3
   (ii) y-intercept = (0, −2)
   (iii) (a) on the line; (b) not on the line
   (iv) −14
   (v) (2, 4)
7. (a) The first part as the line is steepest there
   (b) (i) 40 km/h
       (ii) 20 km/h
       (iii) 26·6 m/h
8. (i) $3x + 7y - 15 = 0$
   (ii) (−2, 3)
   (iii) Yes, because (−2, 3) is on the line $3x + 13y = 33$
9. (i) $y = 4x - 3$, $\frac{1}{2}$, (0, 7), 3, (0, 5)
   (ii) L because it has the highest slope
   (iii) Not on O
10. (i) Home = (2, 1); Shop = (−2, 2); School = (4, 4)
    (ii) $\left(0, \frac{3}{2}\right)$
    (iii) 14 km

Unit 32 Inequalities

Practice questions 32·1

1. (i) Tom > Brian
   (ii) Length of soccer field < length of Gaelic football field
   (iii) Length of tennis court > length of basketball court
   (iv) Donegal airport runway < Shannon airport runway
2. (i) 42 < 68
   (ii) −32 > −68
   (iii) 32 > −68
   (iv) −58 > −720
   (v) 0 > −98
   (vi) −3 > −26
3. (i) False
   (ii) False
   (iii) False
   (iv) True
4. (i) 35 < 4 × 9
   (ii) 73 > 7 × 10
   (iii) −40 < 5 × 8
   (iv) −35 < 7 × 5
   (v) 3 × 6 > 9 × −2
   (vi) −2 × −6 = −3 × −4
5. (i) 900 cm < 9·1 m
   (ii) 500 g = 0·5 kg
   (iii) 4 000 cm³ > 3·98 L
   (iv) 5 km > 20 × 50 m
   (v) 200 cm < 2·4 m
   (vi) 300 g > 0·28 kg

(vii) 3 000 ml = 3 L
(viii) 700 cm < 6·7 m
(ix) 300 g = 0·3 kg
(x) 5 000 ml < 5·02 L
6. (a) The number 1 is included and the number line is a thick shaded line, which means $x \in \mathbb{R}$
7. (i) $x > 2, x \in \mathbb{N}$
   (ii) $x > -4, x \in \mathbb{R}$
   (iii) $x \leq -2, x \in \mathbb{Z}$
   (iv) $0 < x < 2, x \in \mathbb{N}$
8. (i) $x = \{4, 5, 6, 7, 8\}$
   (ii) $x = \{6, 5, 4, 3, 2\}$
   (iii) $x = \{4, 3, 2, 1, 0\}$
   (iv) $x = \{-5, -4, -3, -2, -1\}$

Practice questions 32·2

1. (i) $x > 8$, (ii) $x < 5$, (iii) $y > 7$, (iv) $b \leq 3$
2. (i) $x \geq 4$, (ii) $y < 2$, (iii) $x \geq -1$, (iv) $y \geq 4$
3. (i) $z \leq -1$, (ii) $y \leq 7$, (iii) $x < 18$, (iv) $x \leq 7$, (vi) -7
4. (i) $z \leq 5$, (ii) $z \geq 1$, (iii) $x \geq 1$, (iv) $x \leq 4$
5. (i) $x > -9$, (ii) $z > -3$, (iii) $x \geq -12$, (iv) $x > 8$
6. $x = \{6, 7, 8\}$
7. (i) $4x + 2 \leq 30$
   (ii) $x = 7$, he can buy 7 books
8. (i) $2y - 9 < 41$
   (ii) 24
9. (i) $4m + 5 > 60$
   (ii) Ann = €14, Mary = €28, Angela = €19

Revision questions

32A Core skills

2. (i) $x > 7$, (ii) $x < 4$, (iii) $b > 2$
3. (i) $x < 2 \therefore 1$ and -1, (ii) $-8 < x \therefore -6$, (iii) $x < -8 \therefore -10$ and -9
4. (i) $x < 2$, (ii) $b < 2$, (iii) $x < 1$, (iv) $y > 2$
5. (i) $\{-2, -3, -4, -5, -6\}$
   (ii) -2 is the largest
6. (i) $\{2, 1, 0, -1, -2\}$
   (ii) Infinite number of solutions
   (iii) 2 is the largest

32B Taking it further

1. $9x + 54 > 99$
2. $3(y - 7) \leq 12$
3. $4z - 8 \geq 28$
4. Length = 5 m, width = 3 m
5. (i) $500 - 25w \geq 200$
   (ii) 12 weeks
6. (i) $2·20 + 0·65k \leq 10$
   (ii) 12 km
7. 10 days

Unit 33 Non-linear relationships

Practice questions 33·1

1. (i) Linear, first difference is constant
   (ii) Linear, first difference is constant
   (iii) Non-linear, the first difference is not constant
   (iv) Non-linear, first difference is not the constant
   (v) Non-linear, first difference is not constant
2. (a) (i) Non-linear, first difference is not constant
   (ii) Linear, first difference is constant
   (iii) Non-linear, first difference is not constant
3. (a) (i) Non-linear, first difference is not constant
   (ii) Non-linear, the first difference is not constant
   (iii) Linear, first difference is constant
4. (a) (i) Linear, first difference is constant
   (ii) Non-linear – the first difference is not constant
   (iii) Non-linear – the first difference is not constant
5. (ii) 5; 8; 11; 14; 17
   (iii) Linear, first difference is constant
6. (i) 1; 7; 19; 37; 61
   (ii) Non-linear, first difference is not constant

Practice questions 33·2

1. (i) 16; 9; 4; 1; 0; 1; 4
   (iii) This is U-shaped graph. It has a positive x^2 coefficient
2. (i) 11; 6; 3; 2; 3; 6; 11
   (iii) This is U-shaped graph. It has a positive x^2 coefficient
3. (i) 12; 6; 2; 0; 0; 2

Practice questions 33·3

1. (i) $5x + 20$, (ii) $2x + x^2$, (iii) $6y^2 - 6y$, (iv) $yx + y$, (v) $12ab - 4a^2$, (vi) $st - 2s^2$
2. (i) $a^2 + 7a + 12$, (ii) $3x^2 + 7x + 2$, (iii) $y^2 + 3y + 2$, (iv) $x2 + 2x + 1$ (v) $16x^2 + 16x + 4$, (vi) $4m^2 + 20m + 25$
3. (i) $2x^2 - x - 10$, (ii) $6x^2 - 13x + 6$, (iii) $-3x^2 + 7x - 2$, (iv) $x^2 - 1$, (v) $49x^2 - 16$, (vi) $x^2 - 12x + 36$
4. (i) $x^2 + 4x - 5$, (ii) $a^2 - a - 6$, (iii) $k^2 - 2k - 3$, (iv) $x^2 - 4x + 4$, (v) $6x^2 - 4x - 2$, (vi) $2b^2 + b - 3$
5. (i) $x^2 + x - 2$, (ii) $x^2 + 2x - 3$, (iii) $10c^2 - c - 2$, (iv) $x^2 + 3x - 10$, (v) $3n + 3$, (vi) $-4c + 2$

Practice questions 33·4

1. (i) $x^2 - 16$, (ii) $x^2 - 4$, (iii) $m^2 - 4$, (iv) $x^2 - 1$
2. (i) $(x - 2)$, (ii) $(x + 15)$, (iii) $(x + 100)$
3. (i) $(x - 3)(x + 3)$, (ii) $(x - 5)(x + 5)$, (iii) $(n - 12)(n + 12)$
4. (i) $(x + 1)(x - 1)$, (ii) $(x - 20)(x + 20)$, (iii) $(t - 10)(t + 10)$
5. (i) $(x + 7)(x - 7)$, (ii) $(x - 13)(x + 13)$, (iii) $(y - 9)(y + 9)$
6. $16 - x^2$
7. $4 - w^2$
8. (i) $(y - 14)(y + 14)$, (ii) $(11 - x)(11 + x)$, (iii) $(6 - p)(6 + p)$, (iv) $(a - b)(a + b)$, (v) $(w - t)(w + t)$, (vi) $(x - y)(x + y)$
9. Perimeter = 12
   Perimeter = $4x$
10. Perimeter = $4a$
    Perimeter = $4b$

Practice questions 33·5

1. (i) $x^2 + 10x + 24$
   (ii) $x^2 + 12x + 20$
   (iii) $m^2 - 8m + 15$
2. $y^2 + 19y + 90$
3. (i) $(x + 2)(x + 5)$
   (ii) $(x + 3)(x + 2)$
4. (i) $(x + 3)(x + 1)$
   (ii) $(x + 1)(x + 2)$
   (iii) $(n + 2)(n + 5)$
5. $(x - 4)(x - 3)$
6. (i) $(x - 4)(x - 1)$
   (ii) $(x - 6)(x - 2)$
   (iii) $(q - 6)(q - 4)$
   (iv) $(x - 12)(x - 1)$
7. (i) $(x + 4)(x + 2)$
   (ii) $(x + 9)(x + 5)$
   (iii) $(x - 11)(x - 1)$
   (iv) $(w + 5)(w + 2)$
8. $x^2 + 14x + 40$
9. (i) $(x + 9)(x + 2)$
   (ii) $(p - 10)(p - 1)$
   (iii) $(x + 12)(x + 1)$
10. $(a + 5)(a + 3)$
11. (i) $(x - 6)(x - 4)$
    (ii) $(x + 9)(x + 5)$
    (iii) $(x - 2)(x - 2)$
12. (i) $(x + 3)(x + 3)$
    (ii) $(x + 16)(x + 3)$
    (iii) $(x + 9)(x + 3)$
13. Length $(x + 8)$, width $(x + 4)$
14. $(x + 4)(x + 4)$

Practice questions 33·6

1. (i) $x^2 - 5x - 14$
   (ii) $x^2 + 5x - 24$
   (iii) $m^2 - 2m - 24$
2. $y^2 - 12y + 32$
3. (i) $(x + 9)(x - 2)$
   (ii) $(x - 3)(x + 4)$
4. $(x - 6)(x + 2)$
5. (i) $(x + 6)(x - 1)$
   (ii) $(x - 3)(x + 1)$
   (iii) $(m - 4)(m + 3)$
   (iv) $(w - 3)(w + 2)$
6. $x^2 - 2x - 24$
7. (i) $(x + 6)(x - 2)$
   (ii) $(p - 2)(p + 1)$
   (iii) $(x + 4)(x - 3)$
8. $(a - 4)(a + 2)$
9. (i) $(x - 8)(x + 3)$
   (ii) $(x - 6)(x + 4)$
   (iii) $(x - 5)(x + 8)$
10. (i) $(x + 10)(x - 2)$
    (ii) $(x - 30)(x + 2)$
    (iii) $(x + 2)(x - 1)$
    (iv) $(x + 2)(x - 4)$
11. $(x + 6)(x - 1)$
12. $(x - 7)(x + 6)$

Practice questions 33·7

1. (i) $5a + 6$, (ii) $5x - 2$, (iii) $3y + 1$, (iv) $y - 2$
2. (i) $(x + 3)$, (ii) $(x - 8)$, (iii) $(x - 3)$
3. (i) $(x + 2)$, (ii) $(x + 4)$, (iii) $(x - 3)$
4. $x - 3$
5. $x - 10$
6. $x + 2$
7. $x + 2$
8. $t + 18$
9. $x + 7$
10. $x + 20$
11. $x + 12$

Practice questions 33·8

1. (i) $x = -1, x = 2$
   (ii) $x = -1, x = -2$
2. (i) $x = -1, x = -2$
   (ii) $x = -3, x = 1$
3. (i) $y = -2, y = -1$
   (ii) $b = -11, b = 4$
   (iii) $b = 12, b = -5$
   (iv) $x = -3, x = -2$
4. (i) $x = -7, x = -2$
   (ii) $x = -1, x = -20$
   (iii) $x = 6, x = -3$
   (iv) $x = 7, x = -7$
5. (i) $x = 4, x = -2$
   (ii) $x = -12, x = 2$
   (iii) $x = 3, x = -10$
   (iv) $y = -6, y = 2$
6. (i) $m = -21, m = -3$
   (ii) $m = 8, m = 8$
   (iii) $x = 12, x = -12$
   (iv) $n = -8, n = 8$
7. (i) $y = 9, y = -3$
   (ii) $w = -4, w = 2$
   (iii) $x = 3, x = 5$
   (iv) $x = 7, x = 10$
8. (i) $y = -8, y = 7$
   (ii) $x = 10, x = -10$
   (iii) $x = -15, x = 15$
9. (i) $y(y + 4) = 780$
   (ii) Seán is 26

Revision questions

33A Core skills

1. (i) $x^2 + 4x$
   (ii) $x^2 - 16$
   (iii) $mx + my + nx + ny$
   (iv) $x^2 + 8x + 15$
2. $x - 15$
3. (i) $x^3 + 4x^2$
   (ii) $x^2 + 8x - 20$
   (iii) $16 - w^2$
   (iv) $x^2 - 8x + 16$
4. (ii) 6, 10, 14, 18, 22
   (iii) Linear, first difference is constant
5. (i) $(x + 5)(x + 3)$
   (ii) $(b + 7)(b - 5)$
   (iii) $(y - 11)(y + 11)$
   (iv) $(a + 8)(a - 1)$
   (v) $(k + 7)(k - 5)$
   (vi) $(a - 13)(a + 13)$
8. $x = 6, x = 8$
9. $x = 5, x = 3$
10. $n = -6, n = 3$

33B Taking it further

1. $x^2 + 9x - 36$
2. $y - 2$
3. $(x - 3)(x - 10)$
4. $(m + 21)(m + 3)$
5. $(x - 9)(x + 3)$
6. $4m - 32$
7. $t = 13$
8. (i) Non-linear: first difference is not constant
9. (i) Non-linear: first difference is not constant

Unit 34 Trigonometry

Practice questions 34·1

1. (i) 13, (ii) 15, (iii) 12, (iv) 6, (v) 25, (vi) 40
2. (i) 4, (ii) 17, (iii) 29, (iv) 2, (v) 35, (vi) 12
3. 28
4. No, because $(39·6)^2 \neq (31·2)^2 + (23·8)^2$
5. 45 inches
6. 13 m
7. 37 cm
8. 20 km
9. (iii) $|BD| = 3; |CD| = 3$
   (v) Drawing a line from the vertex of an isosceles triangle perpendicular to its base bisects the base

Practice questions 34·2

1. (i) Hypotenuse = [XY]; opposite = [YZ]; adjacent = [XZ]
   (ii) Hypotenuse = [LN]; opposite = [LM]; adjacent = [MN]
   (iii) Hypotenuse = [RS]; opposite = [ST]; adjacent = [RT]
   (iv) Hypotenuse = [AB]; opposite = [AC]; adjacent = [BC]
   (v) Hypotenuse = [GT]; opposite = [EG]; adjacent = [ET]
   (vi) Hypotenuse = [DE]; opposite = [DF]; adjacent = [EF]
2. (i) $\sin = \frac{8}{17}; \cos = \frac{15}{17}; \tan = \frac{8}{15}$
   (ii) $\sin = \frac{24}{25}; \cos = \frac{7}{25}; \tan = \frac{24}{7}$
   (iii) $\sin = \frac{9}{41}; \cos = \frac{40}{41}; \tan = \frac{9}{40}$
   (iv) $\sin = \frac{28}{53}; \cos = \frac{45}{53}; \tan = \frac{28}{45}$
   (v) $\sin = \frac{35}{37}; \cos = \frac{12}{37}; \tan = \frac{35}{12}$
   (vi) $\sin = \frac{63}{65}; \cos = \frac{16}{65}; \tan = \frac{63}{16}$
3. (i) $\sin A = \frac{4}{5}; \cos A = \frac{3}{5}; \tan A = \frac{4}{3};$
       $\sin B = \frac{3}{5}; \cos B = \frac{4}{5}; \tan B = \frac{3}{4}$
   (ii) $\sin A = \frac{12}{13}; \cos A = \frac{5}{13}; \tan A = \frac{12}{5};$
        $\sin B = \frac{5}{13}; \cos B = \frac{12}{13}; \tan B = \frac{5}{12}$
   (iii) $\sin A = \frac{8}{10}; \cos A = \frac{6}{10}; \tan A = \frac{8}{6};$
         $\sin B = \frac{6}{10}; \cos B = \frac{8}{10}; \tan B = \frac{6}{8}$
   (iv) $\sin A = \frac{2}{3}; \cos A = \frac{\sqrt{5}}{3}; \tan A = \frac{2}{\sqrt{5}};$
        $\sin B = \frac{\sqrt{5}}{3}; \cos B = \frac{2}{3}; \tan B = \frac{\sqrt{5}}{2}$
   (v) $\sin A = \frac{1}{\sqrt{17}}; \cos A = \frac{4}{\sqrt{17}}; \tan A = \frac{1}{4};$
       $\sin B = \frac{4}{\sqrt{17}}; \cos B = \frac{1}{\sqrt{17}}; \tan B = \frac{4}{1}$
   (vi) $\sin A = \frac{\sqrt{21}}{5}; \cos A = \frac{2}{5}; \tan A = \frac{\sqrt{21}}{2};$
        $\sin B = \frac{2}{5}; \cos B = \frac{\sqrt{21}}{5}; \tan B = \frac{2}{\sqrt{21}}$
4. (ii) 4 m
   (iii) $\sin L = \frac{3}{5}; \cos L = \frac{4}{5}; \tan L = \frac{3}{4}$
5. (ii) 8 m
   (iii) $\sin R = \frac{6}{10}; \cos R = \frac{8}{10}; \tan R = \frac{6}{8}$
6. (ii) 28 m
   (iii) $\sin S = \frac{28}{53}; \cos S = \frac{45}{53}; \tan S = \frac{28}{45}$
7. (iii) 4
   (iv) $\sin X = \frac{4}{5}$
   (v) $\tan X = \frac{4}{3}$

Practice questions 34·3

1. (i) 0·4067, (ii) 0·7071, (iii) 28·6363, (iv) 0·2126, (v) 0·6820, (vi) 0·1908, (vii) 0·8829, (viii) 0·2419, (ix) 0·5000, (x) 3·0777, (xi) 0·8572, (xii) 0·4663
2. (i) 49°, (ii) 55°, (iii) 8°, (iv) 60°, (v) 27°, (vi) 32°, (vii) 52°, (viii) 87°
3. (a)(i) $\sin 10° = 0·1736$; $\cos 80° = 0·1736$
       (ii) $\sin 20° = 0·3420$; $\cos 70° = 0·3420$
       (iii) $\sin 30° = 0·5$; $\cos 60° = 0·5$
   (b) $\sin 40°$ and $\cos 50°$

Practice questions 34·4

1. (i) 5·2 m, (ii) 91·8 mm, (iii) 54·8 mm, (iv) 7·5 cm, (v) 19·5 m, (vi) 24·3 mm
2. (i) 9·7, (ii) 3·3, (iii) 14·5, (iv) 3·6, (v) 5·1, (vi) 1·9
3. (i) 9·9, (ii) 30, (iii) 14·6
4. (i) 58°, (ii) 44°, (iii) 56°, (iv) 66°, (v) 62°, (vi) 73°
5. (i) 13, (ii) 8
6. (i) 32, (ii) 83
7. (i) 24°, (ii) 66°
8. (i) 40°, (ii) 3 m, (iii) 0·25 m, (iv) 0·3 m

Practice questions 34·5

1. 21 m
2. 34·97 m
3. 37°
4. Yes
5. 21°
6. 16°
7. (i) A clinometer
   (ii) 7·46 m
8. 319 m
9. 1 744 m
10. 17°
11. 13·5 m
12. 52 m
13. 397 m
14. 199 m
15. (i) 314 m
    (ii) 2 480 m
16. (i) True
    (ii) False
    (iii) False
    (iv) True

Revision questions

34A Core skills

1. (i) 13 cm, (ii) 16 m, (iii) 25 cm, (iv) 77 mm
2. (i) 0·404, (ii) 0·719, (iii) 0·781, (iv) 0·5, (v) 0·669, (vi) 0·985, (vii) 0·601, (viii) 0·956, (ix) 0·707, (x) 0·788, (xi) 2·145, (xii) 0·616
3. (i) 20°, (ii) 60°, (iii) 56°, (iv) 18°, (v) 35°, (vi) 22°, (vii) 47°, (viii) 64°
4. (i) $\sin A = \frac{5}{13}; \cos A = \frac{12}{13}; \tan A = \frac{5}{12};$
       $\sin B = \frac{12}{13}; \cos B = \frac{5}{13}; \tan B = \frac{12}{5}$
   (ii) $\sin A = \frac{3}{5}; \cos A = \frac{4}{5}; \tan A = \frac{3}{4};$
        $\sin B = \frac{4}{5}; \cos B = \frac{3}{5}; \tan B = \frac{4}{3}$
   (iii) $\sin A = \frac{8}{17}; \cos A = \frac{15}{17}; \tan A = \frac{8}{15};$
         $\sin B = \frac{15}{17}; \cos B = \frac{8}{17}; \tan B = \frac{15}{8}$
5. (i) 3·22 cm, (ii) 1 cm, (iii) 6·16 cm, (iv) 11·33 cm
6. (i) 34°, (ii) 34°, (iii) 42°, (iv) 60°

7. (i) 92 m, (ii) 77 m
8. 142·33 m
9. 24 m
10. 2 400 m

34B Taking it further
1. 38°
2. 50°
3. 15°
4. (i) 12 m
   (ii) 172 cm
   (iii) The distance from her eye level to the top of her head
5. 312 m
6. 1 361 m
7. (i) 26 m, (ii) 21 m, (iii) 33 m

Unit 35 Linking Thinking revision material

Questions
1. (a) (i) Make of car: categorical nominal; number of sale: numerical discrete
   (iii) Mean = 560, range = 450
   (b) €19 406·67
   (c) (i) $\frac{1}{7}$
       (ii) 105
   (d) €18 895·68
2. (a) (i) $x + y = 25, 4x - y = 35$
       (ii) 13
   (b) P(boy) = $\frac{11}{25}$
   (c) (i) $167 + 35x \geq 300$
       (ii) 4 tests
3. (a) (i) €6 171·76
       (ii) €2 671·76
       (iii) €631
   (b) (i) Mean = 14·1, median = 14
       (iii) 9·4
       (iv) 3 666 km
   (c) €3 133
   (d) (i) $20 + 35h < 150$, h = number of hours
       (ii) 3 hours
4. (a) (i) 6, 8, 10 and 9, 40, 41 (or any other acceptable answer)
       (ii) No
5. (a) (ii) 13, (iii) $\frac{5}{12}$
   (b) (ii) 23°, (iii) Three angles in a triangle sum to 180°; 67°
   (c) (ii) 30 square units: equal area as they are the image of each other
6. (a) (i) False, (ii) True, (iii) False
   (b) (i) 180
       (iii) No, it is not continuous data
7. (i) Small = $\frac{9}{8}\pi$ cm², medium = 2π cm², large = $\frac{25}{8}\pi$ cm²
   (ii) They are equal
   (iii) Pythagoras's theorem

8. (i) 4π m²
   (ii) 0; 4π; 16π; 36π; 64π; 100π
   (iv) Non-linear (quadratic)
   (v) 28 m²
   (vi) Linear
   (vii) Non-linear
9. (a) (i) Two €10 and three €5
       (ii) $\frac{2}{5}$
   (b) (i) €2 400, (ii) €25 600
   (c) (i) 1 075 cm², (ii) 70 cm², (iii) $\frac{14}{215}$
10. (a) (i) 11 km, (ii) 4·5 km/hr, (iii) 243 km
    (b) (i) $P - 13$, (ii) Jack = 30, John = 17
    (c) (i) $40 - 2x \geq 7$, (ii) 17 (16 plus John himself) (d) (ii) $\frac{11}{40}$ (iii) $\frac{7}{40}$
11. (i) F (a) Draw a circle centre A and radius $[AB]$
    (b) Translate from B to A and then out the far side.
    (c) Use distance formula to find another point the same distance from A as point B
    (d) Use Pythagoras's theorem to find another point the same distance from A as point B
    (ii) Counting boxes to find a point the same distance away
12. (a) (i) 461·58 cm², (ii) $\frac{1}{4}$
    (b) (i) 6·7 m, (ii) 14·74 m², (iii) 2, (iv) 13°, (v) 26·3%
13. (a) (i) $x(x - 2) = 99$
        (ii) $L = 11$ cm, $W = 9$ cm
        (iii) 40 cm
    (b) (i) $\frac{15}{16}$
        (ii) €12·60
    (c) (i) 17·8 cm, (ii) 19 cm, (iii) 20 cm, (iv) 16 cm
    (d) (ii) 11·25%, (iii) 34
14. (a) (i) Four 7 g and two 5 g
        (ii) €1 983·60
        (iii) 23%
        (vi) $58 464
    (b) (ii) Isosceles
        (iii) 588 m²
        (iv) 168 m²
        (v) €780